REF. HC15 .O94 2003
v.2

The Oxford encyclopedia
of economic history /
2003.

2003 12 17

W9-ACA-439

Centennial College
P.O. Box 631, Station A,
Scarborough, Ont.
M1K 5E9

THE OXFORD ENCYCLOPEDIA OF

ECONOMIC HISTORY

EDITORIAL BOARD

EDITOR IN CHIEF

Joel Mokyr

Northwestern University

ASSISTANT EDITOR

Maristella Botticini

Boston University

EDITORS

Maxine Berg

University of Warwick, Coventry, England

Loren Brandt

University of Toronto

Erik Buyst

Katholieke Universiteit Leuven, Belgium

Louis P. Cain

Loyola University, Chicago

Jan de Vries

University of California, Berkeley

Paul E. Lovejoy

York University, Toronto

John H. Munro

University of Toronto

ADVISERS

Michael D. Bordo	Michael R. Haines
Bruce M. S. Campbell	Eric L. Jones
K. N. Chaudhuri	Naomi R. Lamoreaux
François Crouzet	Deirdre McCloskey
Stanley S. Engerman	Osamu Saito
Charles Feinstein	Alice Teichova
Steven Haber	Gabriel Tortella

THE OXFORD ENCYCLOPEDIA

OF

ECONOMIC

HISTORY

Joel Mokyr

Editor in Chief

150302

VOLUME 2

Cooperative Agriculture and Farmer Cooperatives
—
Hughes, Jonathan

OXFORD

UNIVERSITY PRESS

2003

Centennial College
Resource Centre

OXFORD
UNIVERSITY PRESS

Oxford New York
Auckland   Bangkok   Buenos Aires   Cape Town   Chennai
Dar es Salaam   Delhi   Hong Kong   Istanbul   Karachi   Kolkata
Kuala Lumpur   Madrid   Melbourne   Mexico City   Mumbai   Nairobi
São Paulo   Shanghai   Taipei   Tokyo   Toronto

Copyright © 2003 by Oxford University Press, Inc.

Published by Oxford University Press, Inc.
198 Madison Avenue, New York, New York 10016
www. oup.com

Oxford is a registered trademark of Oxford University Press

All rights reserved. No part of this publication may be reproduced,
stored in a retrieval system, or transmitted, in any form or by any means,
electronic, mechanical, photocopying, recording, or otherwise,
without the prior written permission of Oxford University Press.

Library of Congress Cataloging-in-Publication Data

The Oxford encyclopedia of economic history / Joel Mokyr, editor in chief.
p. cm.
Includes bibliographical references and index.
ISBN 0-19-510507-9 (set)
ISBN 0-19-517090-3 (v. 1: alk. paper)
ISBN 0-19-517091-1 (v. 2: alk. paper)
ISBN 0-19-517092-X (v. 3: alk. paper)
ISBN 0-19-517093-8 (v. 4: alk. paper)
ISBN 0-19-517094-6 (v. 5: alk. paper)
1. Economic history–Encyclopedias. I. Title: Encyclopedia of
economic history. II. Mokyr, Joel. III. Oxford University Press.
HC15 .O94 2003
330'.03–dc21

2003008992

1 3 5 7 9 8 6 4 2
Printed in the United States of America
on acid-free paper

Common Abbreviations Used in This Work

AD	*anno Domini*, in the year of the Lord	n.	note
ASEAN	Association of Southeast Asian Nations	NAFTA	North American Free Trade Association
b.	born	NBER	National Bureau of Economic Research
BCE	before the common era (= BC)	n.d.	no date
c.	*circa*, about, approximately	NGO	nongovernmental organization
CE	common era (= AD)	no.	number
CEO	chief executive officer	n.p.	no place
cf.	*confer*, compare	n.s.	new series
d.	died; penny (pl., pence)	OECD	Organization for Economic Cooperation and Development
diss.	dissertation		
EC	European Community	OEEC	Organization for European Economic Cooperation
ed.	editor (pl., eds), edition		
EEC	European Economic Community	OPEC	Organization of Petroleum Exporting Countries
EU	European Union		
f.	and following (pl., ff.)	p.	page (pl., pp.)
FAO	Food and Agriculture Organization	pt.	part
FDI	foreign direct investment	r.	reigned
fl.	*floruit*, flourished	R&D	research and development
FTA	free trade area	rev.	revised
GATT	General Agreement on Tariffs and Trade	s.	shilling
GDP	gross domestic product	SEC	Securities and Exchange Commission (United States)
GNP	gross national product		
G-10	Group of Ten industrialized countries	ser.	series
IMF	International Monetary Fund	supp.	supplement
ISI	import-substitution industrialization	UNESCO	United Nations Educational, Scientific, and Cultural Organization
l.	line (pl., ll.)	UNRRA	United Nations Relief and Rehabilitation Administration
LDC	less developed country (pl., LDCs)		
MDC	more developed country (pl., MDCs)	USD	U.S. dollar(s)
MFN	most-favored nation	USSR	Union of Soviet Socialist Republics
MITI	Ministry of International Trade and Industry (Japan)	vol.	volume (pl., vols.)
		WHO	World Health Organization
MNC	multinational company (pl., MNCs)	WIPO	World Intellectual Property Organization

THE OXFORD ENCYCLOPEDIA OF

ECONOMIC HISTORY

C

(CONTINUED)

COOPERATIVE AGRICULTURE AND FARMER COOPERATIVES. The application of cooperative (or collective) methods of organization to agricultural production and marketing can be traced to antiquity, for cooperation is as old as organized society. Archaeologists have found evidence of cooperation in ancient societies. In China, complex financial cooperatives existed before the Common Era; in Babylonia, people farmed cooperatively; and in Egypt, Greece, and Rome, craft and burial societies flourished. Cooperation waned during the Dark Ages, when it was practiced primarily in monasteries. Medieval guilds and associations made formal arrangements for collective production and selling, but hostile competitors bedeviled these efforts. Cooperation had its own rebirth with the Renaissance in Europe. The Industrial Revolution, world exploration and colonization, and the rapid increase in technology in nearly all areas of commerce transformed markets, societies, and nations. To protect investments and reduce liability, the wealthy formed joint stock companies, a kind of cooperative designed specifically for business transactions.

The advent of corporately organized economic activities carried significant implications for farmers and agriculture. The transformation of work, from individual or small-group artisanry to factory production, changed the way people lived and their relationship to the land. Joint stock companies and corporations altered the nature of ownership in capitalist market systems. Cooperatives gained powerful advocates during the eighteenth and nineteenth centuries, as such radicals as Karl Marx (1818–1883), Frederick Engels (1820–1895), Robert Owen (1771–1858), Charles Fourier (1772–1837), and Louis Blanc (1811–1882) advocated various cooperative approaches to replace unbridled individualism in markets defined by private rights and private property. The intellectual, social, and political upheaval in nineteenth-century Europe imbued cooperation with multiple meanings and made the practice of cooperative enterprise highly variable. The blossoming of cooperation as an instrument of social reform and economic change contributed greatly to the modern form of farmer cooperatives. The modern form of agricultural cooperation was shaped by both the socialist critique of capitalism and the legal innovation and experimentation that accompanied industrialization.

Cooperation and Utopian Socialism. Nineteenth-century experiments in communal living used cooperative ideas and practices to organize work and social arrangements. Robert Owen, a British industrialist and philanthropist, believed that whole societies could be built on the foundation of cooperative principles. The Owenite community at New Harmony, Indiana, eliminated individual profit and competition, treating its inhabitants as equal in every regard. This noble purpose was undermined by the disillusionment that followed when everyone received the same reward regardless of contribution. Yet the Owenist principles of voluntary membership, democratic control, and nonprofit service to members became the benchmark of modern cooperation.

French social philosopher François Marie Charles Fourier followed a similar path. He aimed not to eliminate individual talents and differences but to safeguard producers' and workers' rights. The Fourierist colony in Brook Farm, Massachusetts, initially thrived with an infusion of intellectual capital from the likes of George Ripley (1802–1880), Margaret Fuller (1810–1850), Ralph Waldo Emerson (1803–1852), and Nathaniel Hawthorne (1804–1864), but it collapsed after four years. The Fourierist Wisconsin Phalanx colony fared a little better, but it too foundered on the contradiction between individual incentive and radical equality.

These movements associated cooperation with withering critiques on individualism and capitalism. Consequently, from the late eighteenth century through the mid-nineteenth century, defenders of private market relations derided and discredited experiments in economic cooperation. Attacks on private property and the market were part of a larger political critique that led to revolution and war in Europe. Nevertheless, experimentation with cooperative buying and selling continued among craftspersons, artisans, farmers, and other small-scale producers during this time. The aim of these collective enterprises was not to achieve social reform but to give individuals access to markets and enable them to increase their incomes. Cooperatives became powerful vehicles for self-help.

Nineteenth-Century Buying and Selling Cooperatives. The purpose, nature, and form of cooperative enterprise varied greatly with time, place, and political system.

1

In Europe, patron-owned cooperatives pursued solutions that worked within existing market structures. In colonial America, protective unions arose among workers clustered in cities. Consumer societies were popular in England; credit unions flourished in Germany; and French workers, influenced by revolutionary ideology, formed collectives to bargain for wages. Certain types of businesses, such as insurance, credit, consumer purchasing, and, of course, agricultural marketing, seemed particularly amenable to organization and operation along cooperative lines. It was not until mid-century, however, that these lines of experimentation converged and produced a unified theory of cooperative organization and practice.

A group of flannel weavers in Rochdale, England, transformed the basic idea of cooperation by devising both a broad philosophical foundation for cooperation and a specific organizational framework for it. After repeated strikes failed to bring improvements in wages and living conditions, twenty-eight weavers established a cooperative store in 1844. The Rochdale plan emphasized participation according to contribution of goods or patronage rather than investment of capital. Of the twelve original Rochdale principles, four emerged repeatedly in subsequent practice. They included business or services performed at cost, on a cash basis, with net returns paid to members in proportion to business transacted; democratic control—one person, one vote; limited dividends on invested capital; and ownership limited to patrons—those who patronized the store or who belonged to the occupation the cooperative was established to serve. As Eliot Mears and Mathew Tobriner noted (*Principles and Practices of Cooperative Marketing*, Boston, 1926), the weavers' store wisely refrained from undercutting the prices of neighborhood stores, survived what otherwise might have been ruinous competition, and became an international success story.

The Rochdale principles crossed the Atlantic just prior to the Civil War. In 1859, *New York Tribune* editor Horace Greeley (1811–1872), a supporter of communitarian alternatives to industrial society, published English historian George Jacob Holyoake's (1817–1906) book on the Rochdale pioneers, *Self-Help by the People*. In lionizing the Rochdale experiment, Greeley assumed that the model would work for all kinds of collective enterprise. Farmers could particularly benefit, he believed, from applying Rochdale to the problem of reaching distant regional and national markets. In Denmark, farmers had organized along commodity lines to form efficient, competitive cooperatives for marketing their crops. These farmers reinforced cooperation's move away from Owen's original plan and toward the idea of self-help within a capitalist framework. Yet in the United States, the Rochdale emphasis on limited capital stock led to serious miscalculations. The capital-intensive nature of processing, storing, transport-

ing, and retailing sounded a death knell for cooperatives attempting at once to market agricultural commodities and coordinate consumer and producer purchasing. During the 1870s, the cooperatives formed by the Granger movement promptly collapsed, due to lack of capital and their failure to specialize. Twenty years later, Populist cooperatives fared little better. Like the Grangers, they failed to focus on exclusive service to members or to address specific marketing problems.

During the industrial transition, three features of the market made it essential for farmers to achieve some measure of self-empowerment. First, markets broadened in scope from regional to national. Second, processing, packing, transportation, and distribution came under monopoly control. Third, futures trading made farm prices subject to speculation. These developments left farmers scrambling to recover their production costs. With their limited capital, Rochdale associations could not contend with monopolies and price speculation, and as long as membership remained voluntary, cooperatives faced the persistent threat of collapse due to member disloyalty. Farmer cooperatives constituted agriculture's response to industrial conflict that consisted of both the ruinous competition from nonproducers and the cutthroat conditions of individual selling that forced farmers to compete against each other.

Solving the Free-Rider Problem. The preeminent practical and theoretical problem of cooperation in agriculture is free riding, in which outsiders to the association reap the benefits of united action without bearing their fair share of the risks and burdens. Mancur Olson (*The Logic of Collective Action*, Cambridge, 1965) argued that organizations pursuing public goods on behalf of individuals cannot rely on voluntary participation and support; rather, for group-oriented action to succeed, organizations must require participation while supplying sufficient incentives for individuals to remain loyal to the group. Like labor unions and other private associations, cooperatives pursue benefits that help all individuals similarly situated. In practice, the attempt often fails, marking free riders as the enemy of the community. Historically, the problem of free riding was further compounded by the antitrust liability that attached to collective action impacting price.

After 1890, the American cooperative marketing movement employed law in novel and innovative ways to solve the free-rider problem while avoiding antitrust prosecution. Legal change greatly assisted the conversion of cooperatives from informal voluntary associations into economically potent organizations that resembled corporations in nearly everything but name. Farmers refined and adapted aspects of the business corporation to market their crops. The most fertile garden of legal innovation grew in California, where growers of raisins, citrus, walnuts, and almonds formed cooperatives that combined the specialized approach of Danish cooperatives with the trustlike features of the American corporation.

The California Model. Whether organized through a combination of local associations (the federated cooperative) or by a single industrywide association (the centralized cooperative), the California horticultural associations that formed between 1885 and 1912 all emphasized monopoly control of their crops and vertical integration into processing and packing. They developed brand names to associate their commodities with their organizations, hired trained managers, and invested large sums in advertising. These organizations had an advantage that the nation's field crop and livestock farmers did not: horticultural production tended to concentrate in delimited geographic areas, making it easier to organize and maintain the loyalty of member growers. The raisin growers even agreed to a membership contract that ran with the land, meaning that whoever owned the vineyard was bound to sell to the cooperative, no matter how many times the land changed hands.

During the Progressive era, the legal status of these new organizations was hardly secure. Routinely accused of anticompetitive behavior, cooperatives enjoyed practical immunity under most state antitrust laws. Federal law was less clear. Though farmers' organizations were exempted from federal antitrust penalties under the Clayton Antitrust Act (1914), the exemption pertained only to those cooperatives that operated without capital stock. Capital-stock organizations, such as the California cooperatives, were more vulnerable to attack from competing processors and distributors, who argued that cooperative monopolies over the growers deprived them of the right to buy and sell. The issue of whether a cooperative that looked and acted like a regular corporation could still enjoy Clayton Act immunity came to a head in 1920, when a federal prosecution of the California Associated Raisin Company threatened the legal assumptions of the California model of cooperation. The lawsuit prompted Congress to enact the Capper-Volstead Act (1922), which extended the Clayton Act to all cooperatives regardless of their capital stock holdings. Dubbed agriculture's Magna Carta by economists and lawyers, the law imposed one significant restraint: if cooperatives unduly enhanced prices, then they would be subject to prosecution. Subsequent judicial decisions made it clear that a cooperative could also lose its immunity if it conducted too much business with nonmembers.

The California model is often associated with Aaron Sapiro (1884–1959), a lawyer who promoted this style of cooperation in the United States and Canada during the 1920s by advocating that farmers use iron-clad contracts and corporate trusts to market their crops. Sapiro wrote a uniform state cooperative marketing law that was adopted in thirty-eight states by 1928. Many agricultural leaders disapproved of Sapiro's top-down style of organizing, believing it repudiated traditional cooperative democracy. Edwin G. Nourse (1883–1974), an agricultural economist, led a contrasting school of thought. He believed that cooperatives should not monopolize but instead compete efficiently with other businesses. Today, most cooperatives belong to one of these two denominations.

Federal and State Policy on Cooperatives. Despite divisions among agricultural leaders, federal policy has continued to grant agricultural cooperatives substantial legal privileges and promote the growth of cooperative enterprise in significant ways. In 1926, Congress exempted cooperatives from federal income taxes and created a federal agency to support and encourage farmer cooperatives. In 1929, the Federal Farm Board was established and given power to grant loans to cooperatives. The New Deal's agricultural relief program, which imposed production controls in many commodities, coordinated marketing plans with cooperatives. State marketing plans relied even more heavily on cooperatives, and farmers participated directly in drafting laws and running the programs at the state level.

The economic significance of farmer cooperatives lies not in their role as agents of social change but in their unique form of organization. The amount of agricultural business conducted cooperatively in the United States has grown from $1 billion in 1922 to $93.8 billion in 1995. Statistical evidence supports the argument that cooperatives have raised farm income and improved the quality of rural life generally over the past one hundred years. Cooperatives have proven no less subject to the vagaries of the business cycle than other forms of enterprise, and cooperatives and their members have decreased in number since 1960. Yet because of the lasting political influence of farmers, cooperatives retain their distinctive legal and economic character to this day.

[*See also* Collective Agriculture and Collectivization.]

BIBLIOGRAPHY

Barron, Hal. *Mixed Harvest: The Second Great Transformation in the Rural North, 1870–1930*. Chapel Hill, N.C., 1997. Imaginative analysis of changes in rural society, including organizational and institutional shifts.

Cobia, David, ed. *Cooperatives in Agriculture*. Englewood Cliffs, N.J., 1989. Invaluable textbook covering theory and principles, forms of organization, history, and legal status.

Guarneri, Carl J. *The Utopian Alternative: Fourierism in Nineteenth-Century America*. Ithaca, N.Y., 1991. Sophisticated analysis of utopian socialism.

Heflebower, Richard B. *Cooperatives and Mutuals in the Market System*. Madison, Wis., 1980. Economic treatment of cooperatives as a form of industrial organization, focusing particularly on vertical integration.

Knapp, Joseph G. *The Rise of American Cooperative Enterprise, 1620–1900*. Danville, Ill., 1969. Encyclopedic history of cooperation in the United States from colonial times to the mid-twentieth century.

Knapp, Joseph G. *The Advance of American Cooperative Enterprise, 1920–1945.* Danville, Ill., 1973.

Lauck, Jon. *American Agriculture and the Problem of Monopoly: The Political Economy of Grain Belt Farming, 1953–1980.* Lincoln, Nebr., 2000. Valuable survey of political activity of farm organizations in the post–World War II era.

Mueller, Willard F., Peter G. Helmberger, and Thomas W. Patterson. *The Sunkist Case: A Study in Legal-Economic Analysis.* Lexington, Mass, 1987. Discussion of 1977 Federal Trade Commission allegation of monopoly by Sunkist.

Nourse, Edwin G. *The Legal Status of Agricultural Co-operation.* New York, 1927. Thorough, insightful legal analysis of contemporary legal developments; essential overview of cooperative development in the United States.

Nourse, Edwin G. "The Revolution in Farming." *Yale Review* 9 (1918–1919), 90–105. Influential essay on the commercial transformation of American agriculture through World War I.

Steen, Herman. *Cooperative Marketing: The Golden Rule in Agriculture.* New York, 1923. Published by the American Farm Bureau Federation to support cooperative marketing laws at federal and state levels.

Taylor, Henry C., and Anne Dewees Taylor. *The Story of Agricultural Economics in the United States, 1840–1932.* Ames, Iowa, 1952. Treats cooperative marketing programs in states, agricultural extension programs, and state and federal law; analyzes cooperatives' needs by industry.

Woeste, Victoria Saker. *The Farmer's Benevolent Trust: Law and Agricultural Cooperation in Industrial America, 1865–1945.* Chapel Hill, N.C., 1998. Uses California Associated Raisin Growers (Sun-Maid) as case study in the status of cooperatives under federal and state corporation and antitrust laws.

VICTORIA SAKER WOESTE

CORN LAWS. The Corn Laws generally refer to a variety of restrictions placed on the import and export of corn, wheat, and other agricultural products. The laws were enacted by the British Parliament in the early 1800s, first in 1804 and then were modified or revised every few years until 1815. These laws also hearkened back to the system first introduced in 1773, prior to the Napoleonic War, which prohibited exports of wheat when the price rose above a certain level and imposed a bounty below that price; and limited imports by imposing duties on a sliding scale that declined as the price of wheat rose. Corresponding duties and restrictions on corn, rye, barley, oats, and so on were also imposed. These laws had been passed to protect the interests of landowning farmers who had benefited greatly from lack of trade with continental Europe throughout the Napoleonic War. Interestingly enough, Adam Smith seemed to be believe that such restrictions were inevitable, however desirable worldwide free trade might be in theory, and was primarily critical of the bounties on exports more than the duties on imports (Smith, 1776). His main objection was to the other restrictions on imports of other products, which went back to the early eighteenth century that he believed were derived from the mercantile interests of various sectors of industry and agriculture.

However, the shifting economic interests in a nation that had rapidly been transformed into an urban rather than a rural one at the end of the eighteenth century, and which had begun to shift her production and trade to manufacturing rather than agriculture, led to modification of the Corn Laws after 1815.

The Corn Laws became a special focus of attention in the 1830s and 1840s thanks to an ideological interest in freer trade and the formation of the Anti-Corn Law League headed by such statesmen as Richard Cobden—who would later go on to negotiate the Anglo-French Treaty of Commerce in 1860—with the express purpose of repealing the Corn Laws.

The 1832 Reform Act, which gave the vote to a larger share of industrial workers, contributed to the growing strength of the urban and industrial interests. Robert Peel's conviction that manufacturing was the future of Great Britain led him to promote the repeal of the Corn Laws in the 1840s. The onset of the Irish Potato Famine in 1845, combined with a growing interest in lowering the price of items consumed by industrial workers, gave Peel the opportunity to repeal the Corn Laws totally in 1846. This is generally cited as the beginning of British free trade since the repeal of the Corn Laws was followed by a reduction in or removal of restrictions on many other goods. However, a few important tariffs on coffee, tobacco, sugar, tea, and wine and spirits remained at extremely high levels until the 1860s, partly for the purpose of deriving revenue and partly because the interests in favor of the tariff were not offset by local groups clamoring for their repeal as had been the case with the Corn Laws.

The relative prosperity of British agriculture even after repeal of the Corn Laws led to the belief by numerous contemporaries and some modern historians that repeal had no real economic impact. But this view is clearly falsified by the substantial increase in British imports of agriculture rising from less than 10 percent of consumption in the 1830s to about half of all consumption by the last quarter of the 1800s. However, although the producers of agriculture had clearly benefited from this favorable transfer in the form of protection, it was not so important to British welfare as to make a substantial impact on the overall economy upon repeal. Undoubtedly, the political importance of repeal was greater than its subsequent impact on the nation as a whole. In terms of measurable loss of social surplus, it is likely that the tariffs on wine, sugar, coffee, tea, and tobacco, which persisted through the 1840s and 1850s, had a more substantial deleterious impact on British welfare. Reform in these areas did not come until the Anglo-French Treaty of 1860. Nonetheless, it is still the case that the repeal of the Corn Laws in the 1840s is associated in most people's minds with the beginning of British, and some would say, European free trade.

[*See also* Commercial Policy *and* Free Trade.]

BIBLIOGRAPHY

Dakhlia, Sami, and John V. C. Nye. "Tax Britannica: Nineteenth Century Tariffs and British National Income." Washington University working paper, 2001.

Hilton, Boyd. *Corn, Cash, and Commerce: The Economic Policies of the Tory Governments, 1815–1830.* Oxford, 1977.

Howe, Anthony. *Free Trade and Liberal England, 1846–1946.* Oxford, 1997.

Smith, Adam. *The Wealth of Nations.* 2 vols. Reprinted Indianapolis, 1981.

Williamson, Jeffrey G. "The Impact of the Corn Laws Just Prior to Repeal." *Explorations in Economic History* 27 (1990), 123–156.

JOHN V. C. NYE

CORPORATE FINANCE. All models of economic growth stress the importance of capital investment for long-run growth. Whether the emphasis is on the quantity or the quality of capital, there is consensus among the economics profession that the economy that best sustains its investment is the economy that will best prosper. Investment in capital, however, requires finance. If one can intrinsically understand the importance of investment at the macroeconomic level, then how does one explain the mechanics whereby, at the micro level, firms raise the necessary monies to finance investment?

Financing the Firm. How does the firm raise monies to both establish itself and to finance growth? Most small-scale enterprises in most parts of the world throughout history were financed largely through the largesse (and risk taking) of the firm's owner and his or her friends, family, and business acquaintances. This indeed continued to be the model most commonly applied during industrialization in most parts of the world. Working capital—the monies required to support the ongoing day-to-day activities of the firm—and investment capital—those monies required to finance long-term development—tended to be "personal." Friends and family provided the monies to establish the firm, and retained profits were used to finance working capital and future investment.

Matters became more complex with the growth in scale and scope of the firm. Investment in larger-scale plants and associated technology required funds beyond the remit of the personal network. Increasingly access to alternative sources had to be sought. The solution came with use of monies from the financial markets, largely banks, for working capital requirements and through the stock exchange for long-run investment purposes. With industrialization, firms increasingly raised money from the financial markets through equity capital and bonds. In the primary market, firms were able to raise capital through the sale of bonds, equities, or other securities (the secondary market refers to the trading in existing securities by investors). The process meant a closer—and sometimes fraught—ongoing relationship between industry and the financial markets.

For the first half of the twentieth century firms on both sides of the Atlantic sought (and did not always obtain) working capital from merchant and clearing banks; new money was raised via bonds and equities and other securities. Not all firms, however, were able to raise working capital with ease. This becomes a matter of importance in explaining the "relative decline of the United Kingdom." To what extent was the United Kingdom's failure to develop the industries of the second Industrial Revolution (electrical engineering, chemicals, and motor vehicles) a reflection of the failure of merchant and clearing banks to loan necessary monies? Some observers regard the problem as a demand side issue—banks would have lent money had firms required it. The fact that there was limited demand for such monies was a reflection of an absence of entrepreneurial zeal in industry rather than a supply side problem in the financial markets. Others, however, see the reluctance of banking support as a signal of a "supply side problem" that, in the more extreme version, becomes part of the argument that sees British economic misfortunes in the twentieth century as founded in the aversion of the "city" to assist "industry" (Hutton, 1995).

The question of risk is important, and this applies to all firms in industrialized capitalist economies. The evidence suggests that the financial market has been, is, and was willing and able to supply monies to established firms with good credit history and the potential for growth (Capie and Collins, 1992). From the banks' perspective, this would appear to reflect rational economic judgment. The problem arises if risk aversion deters entrepreneurial drive and constrains the dynamic growth that underpins long-run economic success. This does appear to have been a problem in the United Kingdom, where small and medium firms have experienced difficulties in raising capital from the financial markets throughout the twentieth century. The problem then was not one of supporting existent firms but one of support of those who wished to begin and those who wished to develop from initial beginnings to sustained growth—the engines, so-called, of long-run dynamic change and growth. It is easy to support the successful, less so to take risk in supporting the unproven.

Bonds and Equities in Mature Industrialization. By the beginning of the twenty-first century the size of the world bond market was $31 trillion (this compares with the $36 trillion value for world equities). The United States has become the world's largest bond market; its nearest rivals are (in descending order) Japan, Germany, Italy, and France. Historically the main issuers of bonds have been governments. By 2000 government bonds accounted for 53 percent of U.S. bonds and 72 percent of Japanese bonds. Globally the trend is for most countries to have larger equity than bond markets. There are, however, important exceptions, namely Japan, Germany, and Italy, where the bond market is larger than the equity market. At the other extreme in the United Kingdom the bond market is only a third of the size of its equity market. Why? The relative importance of the two markets largely reflects macroeconomic policy and in particular the size of the public sector. Countries with larger public sectors and more nationalized industries tend to have larger bond markets. On a micro level, those countries with bank-based financial systems placed more emphasis on debt than equity finance, which in turn encouraged the growth of larger corporate bond markets. Examples of this include Germany, Japan, and Italy (Dimson, Marsh, and Staunton, 2002, see in particular chapter 2).

Firms also raised finance through the equity and hence stock markets. It is notable that stock exchanges have a long history. The earliest founding dates of stock markets are 1611 in the Netherlands, 1685 in Germany, and 1698 in the United Kingdom. By the end of the eighteenth century they had been established in France, Austria, and the United States (1724, 1771, and 1792 respectively). By the beginning of the twenty-first century 111 different countries had stock markets, and the combined value of shares traded on those markets exceeded $36 trillion (Dimson et al., 2002, Table 2.3, pp. 11, 20).

Mature industrial capitalism on both sides of the Atlantic witnessed the growth of limited liability companies and the resort of firms to capital through the issue of equity. By the end of the nineteenth century, 783 companies traded their shares on the London Stock Exchange. Initially in both the United States and the United Kingdom railroads dominated, but by the mid-twentieth century chemicals, brewing, tobacco, and retailing had all grown in importance. Chemicals and retailing continued their strong profile throughout the rest of the century (Dimson et al., 2002, chapter 2).

The Implications of Trends in Equity Financing for the Firm. This article is concerned with the implications of the above trends for the firm and concentrates on the ramifications of equity capital. The fact that ownership of the firm was shared among owners of the equity of the company meant that ownership became divorced from management. The manager of the firm was no longer the owner of the firm; ownership became the province of shareholders. The owners of those shares were largely private individuals who sought a return on their investment in the form of dividends but who rarely interfered in the business of the firm. In the second half of the twentieth century equity finance became dominated by the financial institutions in the United States, the United Kingdom, France, Germany, and Japan, to name but five leading economies where this applied (Charkham, 1994).

The implications of this form of corporate finance becomes intertwined with the issue of corporate governance and provides a running theme in explanations of why Germany and Japan performed well in the second half of the twentieth century and the United Kingdom less so (Dimsdale and Prevezer, 1994). Whereas the first half of the twentieth century witnessed a transition from the owner-managed firm to limited liability and ownership in the hands of individual private shareholders, the second half witnessed a switch in equity holdings from the private to the institutional investor made possible by the growth of the pension and insurance industries. The rise of the institutional investor was premised on the assumption of a steady stream of dividend income.

The divorce of ownership from control, which dated from the emergence of the publicly quoted firm in the nineteenth century, was characterised by the mid-1960s in the United Kingdom by a highly skewed share distribution, whereby the equity in any one company was shared among thousands of shareholders. The diffusion of ownership among thousands of shareholders in any one company led to a dilution of ownership responsibility. Where there is no clear owner, there is no clear obligation on any one individual or institution to assume those duties. Dispersed ownership creates free rider constraints on any one shareholder incurring the costs of intervention on behalf of all other shareholders; shareholders perceive the cost of communication with other shareholders and companies as higher than that of constant trading.

Why is this a problem? In Germany and in Japan it is seen as being a positive advantage. There is, however, a subtle difference in the distribution of shareholding between those countries and the United Kingdom. Although the distribution of shares did change from small holdings by numerous private individuals to large block holdings by the financial institutions, shareholding in the United Kingdom and the United States is characterized now, and was still more so prior to the 1980s, by small widely dispersed shareholdings and unitary boards. In Germany and Japan large block holdings (especially by banks) together with two-tier board systems mean large shareholders exist with sufficient equity holdings to influence the company (Charkham, 1994; Dimsdale and Prevezer, 1994).

Theoretical Approaches to Understanding Interplay between Corporate Finance and Corporate Governance. This difference in the raising of financial capital and the implications for corporate governance has raised concerns on both sides of the Atlantic. Dispersed ownership among financial institutions, so it is claimed, has led to a pressure on industrial companies to prioritize dividends at the expense of plowed-back profits for reinvestment. There are four theoretical approaches to understanding the interplay between corporate finance and corporate governance in this respect. All build on the dilution of ownership resulting from the diffusion of ownership among thousands of shareholders. The difference lies in their predictions as to how (and why) shareholders behave. Ownership, according to the residual rights hypothesis, becomes the right to accrue income, both from dividend returns and from trading in shares on the stock market (Grossman and Hart, 1983). The property rights hypothesis stresses transferable rights, where ownership may be transferred to the highest bidder in the marketplace (Mayer, 1994). This interpretation stresses the tendency of shareholders to treat equity ownership as conferring property rights that may be transferred at any time to the highest bidder. The property rights hypothesis treats ownership as a transferable commodity that may be traded on the stock exchange. Managerial failure is corrected through support for mergers and takeovers. The third theoretical approach is the bipartite hypothesis, which predicts loyalty and communication from larger shareholders (Charkham, 1994). The first type concentrates its portfolio on fewer stocks, has larger stakes in individual companies, develops close communication with the companies in which such investments are made, demonstrates a high loyalty factor to those companies, engages in few dealings in those shares, has less freedom to deal with the whole stakes because of the effect on the market, and has a general interest in corporate governance matters in general. Large insurance companies and pension houses, it is argued, fall into this type. The argument is that, given their stakes in a limited number of companies, these institutions have a disproportionate effect on the market. Selling by these institutions would be picked up by the market and could trigger wider selling. These institutions, given their stakes, could suffer a decline in their own asset values. Signals sent by the major institutional holders were assigned greater weight than that of smaller holders such that they could not sell without turning the market against them. The second group of shareholders includes private individuals, small insurance companies and pension houses, unit trusts, and nominee companies, all of which have widely diversified portfolios with small numbers of shares in a large number of companies and have only superficial communication with them. They are characterized as being mainly interested in short-term influences on prices and feel no loyalty to any one company. As a result they are likely to engage in frequent dealing and have no interest in corporate governance issues. Signals sent by this group have little weight in the markets, and they have freedom to trade at will.

Finally, the public policy hypothesis notes the influence of government policy on behavioral patterns (Roe, 1994). Roe's work largely focuses on the United States, but he finds support for his thesis in other mature economies. Roe predicts inertia from existent shareholders in anticipation of public ownership. This approach stresses that most analyses of city-industry relations have operated in a political vacuum, despite the self-evident truism that the political climate in which institutions operate will have ramifications for governance mechanisms. Recent research has suggested that systems of regulation as well as perceptions of government regulation and intervention did determine the options available to city institutions, their equity holdings of underperforming companies, and how they perceived their ownership responsibilities. This is especially the case in the United Kingdom, where legal regulation of the external and internal mechanisms of corporate governance are weak. Roe has argued that corporate governance in this country has always been determined by perceptions of public policy with respect to public ownership, while recent research has shown that, where public ownership is perceived to be a real policy option, shareholders may feel they are relieved of ownership responsibilities. If a third party offers the promise of a transfer of ownership, namely in circumstances where public policy favors greater government intervention through regulation or even public ownership, this may deter owners from pursuing their own ownership responsibilities (Bowden, 2000). The public policy hypothesis predicts an abrogation of ownership responsibilities by shareholders but would trace this to prevailing policy regimes.

The interplay between corporate governance and corporate finance is critical to an understanding of investment behavior and long-run economic performance. Growth theories, be they neoclassical or new growth, stress the importance of capital investment in explaining growth. Yet the manner in which financial capital is raised in the United Kingdom and the United States has created a situation whereby, it is claimed, short-run financial returns are prioritized at the expense of long-run investment and firms are at the mercy of their shareholders (largely financial institutions) who seek to maximize their asset (share) values and income (dividend return) streams. Dividends remain the crucial barometer of performance, and less than acceptable returns may leave the firm exposed to takeover. Finances are raised by the firm but at the price of a prioritization of short-run emphasis on dividend returns. The firm has been able to raise monies via equity finance only to find itself a victim of the need of the financial markets to protect their own income streams and asset values. The results have been an ongoing pressure on management to protect market values at the cost of allocating resources to long-term investment and a vacuum of responsibility if and when the company is underperforming. Finance has been raised, but at a price.

BIBLIOGRAPHY

Bowden, Sue. "Corporate Governance in a Political Climate: The Impact of Public Policy Regimes on Corporate Governance in the U.K." In *The Political Economy of the Company*, edited by John Parkinson, Gavin Kelly, and Andrew Gamble, chap. 8, pp. 175–194. Oxford, 2000.

Capie, F., and M. Collins. *Have Banks Failed British Industry? An Historical Survey of Bank/Industry Relations in Britain, 1870–1990.* London, 1992.

Charkham, Jonathon. *Keeping Good Company: A Study of Corporate Governance in Five Countries.* Oxford, 1994.

Dimsdale, Nicholas, and Martha Prevezer, eds. *Capital Markets and Corporate Governance.* Oxford, 1994.

Dimson, Elroy, Paul Marsh, and Mike Staunton. *Triumph of the Optimists: 101 Years of Global Investment Returns.* Princeton, 2002.

Grossman, S. J., and O. D. Hart. "An Analysis of the Principal Agent Problem." *Econometrica* 51 (1983), 7–45.

Hutton, Will. *The State We're In.* London, 1995.

Mayer, Colin. "Stock-Markets, Financial Institutions, and Corporate Performance." In *Capital Markets and Corporate Governance*, edited by Nicholas Dimsdale and Martha Prevezer, pp. 179–194. Oxford, 1994.

Roe, Mark J. *Strong Managers, Weak Owners: The Political Roots of American Corporate Finance.* Princeton, 1994.

SUE BOWDEN

CORPORATION. *See* Firm.

CORPORATISM. Corporatism or, as it is sometimes labeled after World War II, corporativism, is a set of political doctrines and institutions aimed at governing the economy and organizing civil society on the basis of professional and occupational representation. The goal is to resolve class or interest groups' conflicts through the harmonizing and coercive role of the state. The result is often an expansion of state's control over the economy and the society.

There are four historical periods during which corporatism played a significant role in politics and in the economy. The first example of corporatism occurred during the Roman Republic and Empire, ending with the economic reforms of the emperor Diocletian (r. 284–305). Toward the end of the Middle Ages, many European city-states featured a corporatist organization of their economy and government before the rise of the absolutist state ended these forms of government. A third period occurred in the early twentieth century, mainly in Italy during the Fascist period (1922–1943) and in some South American countries, such as Brazil. Modern corporatism arises after World War II in many social democracies of the Western world, such as the Scandinavian countries, Germany, the United Kingdom between 1965 and 1979, and Australia and New Zealand until the late 1980s (Pekkarinen, Pohjola and Rowthorn, 1992) and still exists in various forms with different degrees of success. While the pre–World War II forms of corporatism have been studied mainly from an economic history viewpoint (Bini, 2000; Halevi, 1990; Mancini, Parillo, and Zagari 1982), modern versions of corporatism are the subject of theoretical and empirical analyses of their effects on economic performance and income distribution (Alesina and Perotti, 1997; Calmfors and Driffil, 1988; Gal-li and Padovano, 2001; Olson, 1982; Pekkarinen, Pohjola, and Rowthorn, 1992; Siaroff, 1999). In what follows, we summarize the conclusions about these two separate strands of literature.

Corporatism in Ancient Rome. In Roman law, *corpora* or *collegia* were the voluntary associations of individuals who shared the same professions or functions in society. The earliest of such associations to be known are the *collegia* of priests. In the late Republic, under Lucius Cornelius Silla (138–78 BCE), the *collegia* of craftsmen, with goals of mutual assistance, were quite important and comprehensive. The success of these *collegia* in furthering the members' businesses led to the creation of profit-oriented societies (*funeraticii*). The best known of these societies are the *collegia publicanorum*, which gathered the owners of monopoly rights to collect state revenues, manage state land and properties, and so on (Marcus Licinius Crassus [114–53 BCE] was an outstanding member).

The frequent abuses led, under the emperor Augustus (r. 27 BCE – AD 14), to the promulgation of a *lex Iulia corporaria*, around the year 18 BCE. This law regulated the formation of *corpora* and *collegia* and subjected them to the adherence to a set of guidelines in order to receive state approval. Each association had to publish a statute (*statuta*, *capitula*), indicate their leaders (*defensores*, *priores*), possess a common treasury (*arca*), and administer justice according to the statute to the affiliates. This law greatly reduced the transaction costs for private individuals to create a professional association. The ensuing large demand for licenses to create professional associations allowed the empire to effectively extend its control over the economy and the organization of labor (Perelli, 1994). The result was the first corporatist organization of the economy and society. It was a corporatist reform "from above."

This system became more radical and effectively ended under the emperor Diocletian. Because of the economic hardships of the time, Diocletian reformed the corporatist organization of the economy into an effectively coercive system. Belonging to a corporation became a compulsory as well as a hereditary requisite in order to exercise one's profession. This reform further stifled economic activity and was in fact repealed soon after Diocletian's death. A century later, the turmoil of the barbarian invasions swept the corporations away.

Corporatism in the Middle Ages. At the beginning of the twelfth century, the move toward independence from the feudalist system led to the almost simultaneous creation of the *Comune* in political life and of new corporations in economic life. Corporations cropped up throughout Europe. In Italy, the first to appear were the corporations of merchants (*mercadantia*); of professionals, like the *collegia notariorum*; and of craftsmen, the *artes*. In France, these associations were called *confréries*;

in England, Sweden and Holland they were *guilds*; Germany saw the birth of such sworn associations as the *Innungen*, the *Gilden*, or *Zünfte*. Similar to the latter were the *gremios* of Spain and Sardinia.

With respect to their Roman ancestors, the most significant innovation of the medieval corporations was the development of the judicial concept of *juridica persona* (legal personhood). The establishment of corporations as *juridicae personae* allowed them to represent their members within political institutions. The corporations entered into and often replaced the government bureaucracies, as was the case in Genoa, Rouen, and Bruges. In other cases, such as in Milan and Florence, the corporations became represented in the collective representative and decision-making bodies of the *Comune* (Najemy, 1982). This process gave birth to a corporatist system "from below," which became evident especially in the Italian *Comuni* of the thirteenth and fourteen centuries. Leaders of corporations became important political leaders, as in the case of the Medici family in Florence, formerly representatives of the corporations of bankers and traders. Moreover, the corporation administered justice in economic matters through the *tribunale de classe*. This tribunal evolved into the special tribunal for commercial matters within the chambers of commerce.

The close connection between economic and political roles of the corporation is one of the likely causes of the political instability of the Italian *Comuni* of the fourteenth century. As a result, corporatist representation of interests collapsed as the political system of these cities evolved into the autocratic *Signoria* (Tullock, 1987). Similarly, the birth of the absolute state meant the end of corporatist representation in the main European countries.

Corporatism in the Early Twentieth Century. The early twentieth century's corporatism has its ideological roots mainly in nineteenth-century French and Italian Catholic social thought, as well as in German romanticism and idealism. The basic idea is that class conflict is not inherent in the capitalist system of production and ownership relations, provided that civil society is organized on the basis of professional and occupational representation (Halevi, 1990).

Corporatist ideas were espoused by eminent European thinkers. In his *Philosophy of Right*, Hegel thought of a corporate structure in which the estates constituted the link between civil society and the state (Hegel, 1821). Durkheim's view of corporatism specifically related to the division of labor engendered by modern industry. He maintained that the task of the corporations is to diversify at the level of each industry the general principles of industrial legislation formulated by the political assemblies (Durkheim, 1893). The Catholic strand is best summarized in the encyclical letter *Rerum Novarum* (1891). In that letter, Pope Leo XIII (1810–1903) rejected the notion that

"class is naturally hostile to class, and that the wealthy and the working men are intended by nature to live in mutual conflict." Quite significantly, while the *Rerum Novarum* recognized the legitimacy of independent workers' unions, it gave preference to the creation of a single organization embracing both employers and employees. The strength of the Socialist unions, however, coupled with the refusal of the industrialists to organize a single corporation that embraced the workers' representatives left this proposal without application.

The Italian Fascist regime provided the first realization of a "corporatist" system to carry the name. This system was the brainchild of the idealist jurist Alfredo Rocco (1875–1935). He viewed corporatism as an instrument for fostering the productive power of the nation and considered the corporations as organs of the state. When he became Mussolini's Minister of Justice in 1926, Rocco outlawed all unions that were not fascist. In 1927, he institutionalized the Italian corporate state by promulgating a labor charter (*Carta del Lavoro*). In 1934, a law established twenty-two corporations, whose delegates formed the *Camera del Fasci e delle Corporazioni*, which replaced the Chamber of Deputies in 1939. It must be stressed that Italy's corporative state did not coordinate economic activity; rather, it enabled the government to control labor relations by establishing tutelage over the newly created labor unions.

The Italian corporatist system became a reference for populist movements in South America. One important example is the *Estado Novo* established in Brazil under President Getúlio Vargas (1883–1954) between 1937 and 1946. As in Italy, a labor charter was first issued; in 1939, a set of laws exercised by the Ministry of Labor legalized government prerogatives over labor unions. Unlike Italy, however, Brazilian corporatism allowed the emergence of strong reformist demands. Although labor relations were governed by norms that prevented the formation of alliances between different groups of workers, the process leading to the corporative state also marked the appearance of formal unionism. Hence in Brazil during the liberal phase (1946–1964), populist forces were capable of using institutions designed to control the working class for the purpose of giving political power to labor leaders (Erickson, 1977). Yet the strengthening of corporatism came from the conservative forces themselves, which after the coup d'état of 1964 tightened the controls over labor organizations.

Contemporary Corporatism. Today, the word *corporatism* is most often used to refer to tendencies in politics for legislators and administrations to be influenced or dominated by the interests of corporations rather than citizens. Instead of an institutionalized response to class conflict, as it was described in the early twentieth century, modern corporatism can be rationalized as an attempt to solve the inability of the "one man, one vote principle" of electoral democracy to account for different intensities of voters' preferences (Buchanan and Tullock, 1962). The more the government intervenes in the economy and the more it is involved in wealth redistribution, the more its decisions face preferences that vary not only in direction but also in intensity. Special interest groups thus arise informally to push policymakers to enact favorable policies (or revoke unfavorable ones). Corporatism is a way to institutionalize this form of representation of interests (Olson, 1970, 1982). It is no accident that corporatist governance aims to address and reconcile the interests of the two most encompassing types of organizations that further economic interests: labor unions and confederations of employers.

Olson (1982) provides the first coherent "general equilibrium" theory of the economic effects of corporatism. He argues that the formation of distributional coalitions or interest groups, such as trade unions and employer associations, leads to an increase of market power that induces wasteful rent-seeking behavior and hampers the efficient allocation of resources. These inefficiencies are lowest when the scope of the interests of the single union/association of employers is at the extremes. In decentralized systems, where wage claims are settled at the firm level, attempts by single unions to raise real wages cause the firm involved to lose market shares and shed jobs. The high elasticity of labor demand forces unions to mitigate their claims. When, instead, their interests are all encompassing, unions and employers' association internalize the social effects of their activities by adopting centralized systems of governance. The participation of government in these negotiations reflects the broad scope of their subject matter, which generalizes from wage negotiations to any type of economic reform, and guarantees that whatever agreement is reached will be transferred into legislation (Ciampi, 1996). Yet Olson argues that corporatism is a second-best solution with respect to the decentralized system. Corporatism involves higher transaction costs and free-riding problems within the interest groups that are absent when governance is decentralized. Starting from an approach of labor economics, Calmfors and Driffill (1988) provide a similar analysis, though they do not foresee a difference in transaction costs between decentralized and corporatist governance, which should be equally efficient.

Political scientists have investigated how ideological differences in governments engaged in corporatist governance affect economic performance. Alvarez, Garrett, and Lange (1991) formulate a "conditional influence hypotheses," which holds that corporatist governance has positive effects on economic growth (and negative effects on the inflation and unemployment rate) provided that the degree of union density in the labor force is high and government is controlled by left-wing parties. If, instead, the labor force is scarcely unionized and right-wing parties are the majority, a decentralized system is the efficient solution. Mixed combinations (low union density with left-wing parties and high unionization with right-wing governments) produce the least efficient results, regardless the governance system. The idea is that leftist governments find it easier to reach agreements with powerful unions through centralized negotiations. The lack of social conflicts increases the stability of the economic system and stimulates capital accumulation. Conversely, right-wing governments need to encounter little resistance from labor movements to successfully enact their growth-maximizing policies. Otherwise, too much social conflict between rightist governments and strong unions hinders productive efficiency. Similarly, policies of a leftist government lacking the support of unions as a transmission mechanism receive little credit from investors.

Alesina and Perotti (1997) use a similar theoretical structure to analyze the fiscal implications of corporatism. They set up a world with three classes of agents (interests): firms, unions (workers' agents), and "pensioners/unemployed"—a group of individuals who do not work and live off income redistribution. In this setup, an increase in labor taxation, used to finance income redistribution to pensioners and/or unemployed workers, pushes labor unions to increase wage pressure, which in turns induces higher labor costs and a loss of competitiveness (measured as the ratio of domestic to foreign total unit labor costs). Moreover, the distortions caused by fiscal policy depend on the institutional features of the labor market. Distortions are low when labor markets are close to being perfectly competitive and increase with the average size of the unions. However, at very high levels of centralization of the labor market, when wage negotiations take place at the national level, the mechanism by which labor taxation is transmitted to labor costs changes. In economywide bargaining, the unions are able to internalize the positive link between higher taxation and welfare benefits, especially if the government too is involved in the negotiations. This induces the union to moderate its wage claims.

The theoretical debate has generated a large body of empirical literature on the economic effects of corporatism (Siaroff, 1999). Interest in these studies is also motivated by the seemingly contradictory reforms that, in the 1990s, several countries introduced to corporatist institutions for essentially the same reason: to increase the productive efficiency of the economy. Examples of corporatism long believed to be highly successful, such as Sweden and Australia, collapsed for allegedly having hampered productivity growth (OECD, 1997). At the same time, countries that built their postwar development on decentralized bargaining, such as Italy, resorted to corporatism to tackle the loss of efficiency of the economy induced by distorting wage indexation, generous pension systems, and so on (Ciampi, 1996). If a conclusion may be reached from these varied empirical analyses, it seems that more decentralized systems of governance increase the productive efficiency of the economy and its long-run growth. After controlling for government political orientation, there is mild evidence that corporatism has positive effects on growth when unionism is pervasive, irrespective of government ideology. Corporatism thus seems to coopt union leadership into the formal structure of government, thereby reducing the antigrowth effects of union activities. When, instead, union influence is low, decentralized decision making appears the first-best governance system. These results are consistent with Olson (1982), and partly with political science models, such as Alvarez, Garrett, and Lange (1991), which place greater emphasis on the effects of government ideology. Galli and Padovano (2001) find evidence that corporatist governance tends to worsen economic performance *indirectly* by imposing constraints on the policy decision-making process that typically yields growth-retarding policy decisions. Corporatist and decentralized countries are systematically different with respect to the policies they adopt, since they appear to have a higher growth of government consumption (which is actually decreasing in decentralized countries); a slightly lower rate of physical capital accumulation; a lower variability of inflation; and a much higher percentage of nonagricultural labor force unionized and deteriorating terms of trade (which are instead improving in decentralized countries). With the exception of a lower variability of inflation, all these variables tend to be negatively correlated with improvements in economic performance.

[*See also* Craft Guilds *and* Merchant Guilds.]

BIBLIOGRAPHY

Alesina, A. and Perotti, R. "The Welfare State and Competitiveness." *American Economic Review*, 87 (1997), 921–939.

Alvarez, R., G. Garrett, and P. Lange. "Government Partisanship, Labor Organization, and Macroeconomic Performance." *American Political Science Review* 85 (1991), 539–556

Bini, P. "The Making of Economic Policy in Italy in the Inter-War Years (1922–1940)." *Soria del Pensiero Economico* 40 (2000), 5–40.

Buchanan, J. M., and G. Tullock. *The Calculus of Consent: The Logical Foundations of Constitutional Democracy*. Ann Arbor, 1962.

Calmfors, L., and Driffill, J. "Bargaining Structure, Corporatism, and Economic Performance." *Economic Policy* 3 (1988), 13–61.

Ciampi, C. A. *Un metodo per governare*. Bologna, Italy, 1996.

Durkheim, E. *The Division of Labour in Society*. London, 1893. Reprinted (1933. reprint).

Erickson, K. *The Brazilian Corporate State and Working Class Politics*. Berkeley, 1977.

Galli, E., and F. Padovano. "Direct and Indirect Effects of Corporatism on Economic Growth." *Rivista di Politica Economica* 91.6 (2001), 5–32

Halevi, J. *Corporatism*, In *The New Palgrave: Problems of the Planned Economy*, edited by J. Eatwell, M. Milgate, and P. Newman. pp. 77–79. New York, 1990.

Hegel, G. F. *The Philosophy of Right*. London and New York, 1821. Reprinted 1967.

Leo XIII. *Rerum Novarum*. (The Condition of Labor: The Encyclical Letter of His Holiness, Pope Leo XIII.) Mount Loretto, Staten Island, N.Y., 1891.

Mancini, O., F. Parillo, and E. Zagari. *La teoria economica del corporativismo*. Naples, Italy, 1982.

Najemy, J. M. *Corporatism and Consensus in Florentine Electoral Politics, 1280–1400*, Chapel Hill, N.C., 1982.

Olson, M. *The Logic of Collective Action*. Cambridge, Mass., 1970.

Olson, M. *The Rise and Decline of Nations*, New Haven, 1982.

Organization for Economic Cooperation and Development. *Employment Outlook*. Paris, 1997.

Pekkarinen, J., M. Pohjola, and B. Rowthorn, eds. *Social Corporatism: A Superior Economic System?* Oxford, 1992.

Perelli, L. *La corruzione politica nell'antica Roma*. Milano, Italy, 1994.

Siaroff, A. "Corporatism in Twenty-Four Industrial Democracies: Meaning and Measurement." *European Journal of Political Research*, 36 (1999), 175–205.

Tullock, G. *Autocracy*. Dordrecht, Netherlands, 1987.

FABIO PADOVANO

CORT, HENRY (1740–1800) English inventor.

Henry Cort developed methods for purifying and pressing iron efficiently that were widely used in the Industrial Revolution. His two major inventions, puddling and rolling, created scale economies and labor savings in the production of wrought iron.

Pig iron, the output of a blast furnace, has 2.5 percent or more carbon content and is therefore brittle. The conversion of pig iron into more malleable wrought iron had required hours of heating and hammering to burn the carbon away, giving a final product with less than 1 percent carbon suitable for nails, wire, bolts and other hardware, ship plating, gates, fencing, and guns. Cort's puddling process, patented in 1784, converted pig iron to wrought iron with less labor and cheaper fuel than the older method, by employing a reverberatory furnace, in which a low wall separated the pig iron from the fuel. In Cort's design the fuel did not physically contact the iron; so mineral coal, which was more impure and burned hotter than charcoal, could be used. Cooking the pig iron in this way, an activity later called puddling, would raise the temperature high enough to separate the iron, with its high melting point, from other materials, which would melt or burn. A worker, the puddler, inserted tools through ports in the furnace to stir and eventually to collect the iron into a ball and separate it from the remaining liquid slag. A skilled puddler could produce a ton of wrought iron in a day, ten times as much as previously made.

The rolling method took hot, soft, wrought iron, possibly straight from a furnace, and pressed it between attached grooved rolls, thus squeezing out impurities, which fell away. Cort incorporated rolling into the wrought iron production process, mechanizing a labor-intensive process. Both the reverberatory furnace and rolling were preexisting technologies, which were subsequently improved enormously and extended to other purposes, notably steel manufacture. Cort was perhaps the first to use them successfully in the mass manufacture of wrought iron. Partly because of his inventions, British production of wrought iron tripled from 1788 to 1805.

Cort's life has been used as an example of the British way of improving technology, as he was a tinkerer without a technical education. Cort experienced personal catastrophe, however. Fallout from a backer's questionable financial practices, along with delays and denials of revenues from licenses, led to the loss of Cort's assets, including his patents. He was bankrupt from 1790 through the rest of his life and lived for years on poor relief and later a small special pension allocated by Parliament.

Cort's processes were used and improved for the next century and a half, in iron and steel manufacture. Essential improvements were made around 1790 at Cyfartha, and in 1830 by Joseph Hall's replacement of the sand hearth by cast iron and firebrick and the addition of iron oxide in the furnace. Thus "wet" puddling gradually succeeded Cort's original "dry" puddling. Continuing efforts to mechanize puddling further were mostly unsuccessful, and in the 1800s puddlers developed into a highly paid and somewhat recalcitrant class, outlasting other craftsmen in an industrial age.

BIBLIOGRAPHY

Burn, Duncan. *The Economic History of Steelmaking, 1867–1939: A Study in Competition*. Cambridge, 1940.

Gordon, J. E. *The Science of Structures and Materials*. New York, 1988.

Hyde, Charles K. *Technological Change and the British Iron Industry, 1700–1870*. Princeton, 1977.

Landes, David. *The Unbound Prometheus*. Cambridge, 1969.

Misa, Thomas J. *A Nation of Steel: The Making of Modern America, 1865–1925*. Baltimore, 1995.

Mott, Reginald A. In *Henry Cort: The Great Finer*, edited by Peter Singer. London, 1983.

Mokyr, Joel. *Lever of Riches: Technological Creativity and Economic Progress*. Oxford, 1990.

Rosenberg, Nathan. *Inside the Black Box*. Cambridge, 1993.

Swank, James M. "Statistics of the Iron and Steel Production of the United States." In vol. 2 of the U.S. Census. Washington, D.C., 1883.

PETER B. MEYER

COSMETICS INDUSTRY. Though the wearing of cosmetics goes as far back as ancient Egypt, the economic history of its business practices can be traced to the late eighteenth-century consumer revolution. In both England and France, the middle classes entered the market as consumers of luxury goods for the first time due to the availability of affordable imitations. Among these new purchases, cosmetics were an essential means of representing social position and wealth, especially mimicking the white face paint and rouge worn at court. Aristocratic courtiers, both men and women, traditionally bought their makeup from reputable master artisans. In France, the guild of perfumers controlled the production of perfumes and creams, regulating new innovations and outlawing any means of publicity.

By the 1770s, however, independent sellers benefited from the new customer base, marketing their products through newspaper advertisements, money-back guarantees, and instructional pamphlets. Many cosmetic sellers were innovative entrepreneurs who profited from the toppling of traditional hierarchies and the expansion of consumer markets promoted by the Enlightenment and fully realized by the French Revolution of 1789. A number of prominent eighteenth-century beauty businesses survived the Revolution unscathed. Some, such as Maille (founded in 1747, maker of vinegar rouges) and Dissey & Piver (1774), are still around today.

As cosmetics developed public visibility, so did concern over the ingredients they contained. Doctors warned that the addition of lead, hydroxide, arsenic, and other minerals to face paints could be deadly. Horror stories of death and disfigurement were common fare in England. In France, the Academy of Medicine attempted to control the sale of dangerous products by instituting a system of scientific examination for all cosmetic patent requests.

Medical concerns were matched by growing criticisms against the application of visible makeup. By the end of the century, a new ethos of beauty had triumphed that emphasized hygiene, health, and naturalness. Men were no longer to pamper themselves and women were to do so with the goal of emphasizing their inherent traits rather than applying layers of paint. Water was the best cosmetic, and the roses of youth the best makeup. This shift forced cosmetic sellers to reevaluate their selling strategies. New products, such as creams for face whitening, hair loss potions, and toilette soaps, became popular. Old products were renamed and relabeled. For instance, rouge became "vegetable rouge" and was marketed as being able to mimic the first blush of youth without any visible artifice. This transformation of meanings and products allowed cosmetics sellers to survive in a period that emphasized unadulterated beauty.

The majority of cosmetic manufacturers in the early nineteenth centuries were small family businesses. It was not until the 1830s that these artisanal workshops expanded into industrial enterprises. The development of distillation through vapor, the use of volatile solvents, and the manufacture of industrial glass allowed perfumers to sell their goods more widely and cheaply. Guerlain, established in 1828, had a bustling factory by the 1850s and a range of highly original flowery scents.

As the historical base for flower growing, the city of Grasse in the south of France became the center of industrial production, boasting sixty-five perfumeries by 1866. Select French perfumers provided the courts of Europe with scents, while cosmetic manufacturers sent their wares as far as the Americas. Advertisers evoked the dominance of the national industry to represent French industrial and commercial progress. During the European quest for colonies in the nineteenth century, cosmetics became symbols of national pride, a process that often implied the transformation of exotic ingredients into European commodities. British imperialists may have learned to appreciate bathing from their Indian subjects, but the very English toilette soap was marketed as the ultimate tool for civilizing the natives.

Europeans, specifically the French, dominated innovation and industrial production of cosmetics during the nineteenth century. In the United States, only a handful of companies had industrial capabilities. Most cosmetic products were fabricated in small batches and sold by itinerant hawkers. Women were central to the development of recognizable brand names. They opened beauty parlors, invented new products, and marketed their goods across America. Many of these women came from poor backgrounds, finding in the beauty trade the possibility of stable female employment.

Women, however, faced discrimination in a business world that privileged the professional skills of male chemists and perfumers. African-American women had an even harder time finding shelf space for their products in white drugstores, often preferring door-to-door and catalog sales. Trained African-American beauticians, working for a specific brand, such as Annie Turnbo's *Poro* hair system, were at the vanguard of franchise and pyramid schemes.

These small businesses focused on hair care, face creams, and bath products, few venturing into the disrespectable world of makeup or the sensual world of perfume. Rouge and face paint were associated with actresses and prostitutes, and many of these products still contained zinc oxide. Perfumes made with real animal or vegetable scents were seen as sexual enticements or extreme luxury products for the elite. Developments in chemistry and pharmaceutical research, however, made the compositions of cosmetics more reliable as well as cheaper by the end of the century.

The discovery that organic matter could be synthesized in the 1860s led to the first synthetic scent in 1868 by Houbigant. Synthetic scents were much cheaper than organic ones, allowing for greater production and distribution. In 1906, the United States and France both passed laws to control cosmetic manufacture, prohibiting the use of lead and other harmful ingredients. Increasingly, leading cosmetics firms hired chemists to help develop new products and by 1933 adopted animal testing to guarantee safety.

Developments in science may have made cosmetics safer and cheaper, but a radical change in women's roles was necessary before they garnered mass-market appeal. The late nineteenth century saw the development of department stores, national magazine advertisements, and photography, all focusing attention on the feminine quest for beauty. Advertising campaigns promoted the use of toilette soap, toothpaste, and shampoo.

By the turn of the century, the high price of personal hygiene was an accepted aspect of consumerism. After World War I, even the use of makeup gained mass-market appeal as a result of radio and newspaper advertising campaigns. The New Woman, the flapper, and the screen star offered new models of femininity that represented liberation from past fetters, public display, and self-sufficiency. Makeup could ensure self-confidence and sex appeal while also functioning as a political statement: in a 1912 rally in New York City, suffragettes consciously adopted red lipstick as a sign of rebellion.

As the image of the made-up woman became acceptable, many female-run businesses declined because of competition from larger corporations that could afford mass advertising, industrial production, and cheaper prices. The association of beauty treatments with African-American dignity and self-advancement promoted by Annie Turnbo's *Poro* line was replaced with advertisements that associated cosmetics with sexuality and whiteness.

In addition to being unable to match the ploys of big business, many female entrepreneurs, both white and African American, did not survive the difficult years of the Great Depression. A few women who started small did thrive in this new competition, deploying their feminine identities as a key marketing ploy. Helena Rubinstein (1870–1965), a Polish immigrant to Australia, opened her first beauty salon in 1900 and by World War I had developed an international empire of luxurious beauty care. Elizabeth Arden (1884–1966), a Canadian who immigrated to New York City in 1908, built up a multinational company by the 1940s. Both women were from modest backgrounds, and focused on creating an exclusive, high-fashion image, while extending their brand as widely as possible to all women who could afford the high pricetag.

Other successful companies targeted the larger market of middle- and working-class women. Working in Holly-

COSMETICS INDUSTRY. "Little daubs of powder, little daubs of paint; make a very pretty thing, of a thing that aint." Woman seated at mirror using cosmetics, circa 1909. (Prints and Photographs Division, Library of Congress)

wood from 1908, the Russian immigrant Max Factor invented shades of makeup that looked natural under the camera lights. In great demand as the makeup artist to the stars, Max Factor's reputation allowed his family to build up an empire of mass-market products distributed through supermarkets and drugstores. His pancake makeup and lipsticks advertised by the stars promised to turn everyday women into Joan Crawford or Bette Davis.

Founded in 1886 as the California Perfume Company, Avon developed a national network of door-to-door saleswomen who gave it a firm hold on rural America. One of the few companies able to grow and prosper during the Great Depression, by the mid-1950s Avon had expanded into Latin America, and by 2000 it boasted selling networks in 140 countries. Avon promoted itself as a women's company with global concerns, aiming to empower local women through direct selling, create personal bonds be-

tween representatives and clients, and emphasize the role of beauty aids in building self-esteem.

Europe and America were not the only places to develop international brands. In Japan, Shiseido, first established in 1872 as a Western-style pharmacy, proposed an alternative to the traditional chalk-white face and red lips. Its founder, Yushin Fukuhara, marketed Western-style compacts filled with skin-toned powders or colorful pastel shades. These powders were popular not only among aristocratic, westernized women but also among more traditional, middle-class women as well. Fukuhara's son Shinzo developed the brand, copying European-style packaging and promoting a liberated female figure. Today, Shiseido has become one of the world's most profitable cosmetics companies, rivaling L'Oréal and Revlon with its distinct hold on the Asian market.

World War II brought with it shortages and belt-tightening. Governments debated the utility of cosmetic spending, while efficiency experts argued that makeup would enhance women's productivity in their new role as workers. For a small price, cosmetics fulfilled desires for scarce luxuries, thereby boosting morale for both men and women. After the war, the cosmetics industry continued to grow, with sales increasing from 1.2 billion to 2.9 billion dollars from 1955 to 1965 in the United States. Much of this increase was a result of an almost total acceptance of makeup as essential to proper femininity.

Women were told that without makeup they would not be able to get or even keep a man. Lipsticks with evocative names and available in a dazzling array of shades were worn by 80 to 90 percent of American women by 1948. New product lines appeared to take advantage of the increased consumer affluence. While Estée Lauder (founded in 1946) sold high-end products in department stores, Revlon (1932) sold sex and fantasy in women's magazines and Cover Girl (1960) targeted the growing teenage market. Though aimed at different demographics of American women, none of these brands took into consideration African-American skin tone or beauty needs.

By the 1960s, young politicized African Americans condemned face whiteners and hair straightners, adopting "black is beautiful" as a political cry for action. The white feminist movement also denounced lipstick and bras, burning these latter symbols of female oppression in a 1968 protest of the Miss America beauty pageant. The cosmetics industry was blamed for reinforcing the patriarchal capitalist economy and limiting women's role to that of an object.

By the late 1970s, animal rights groups also began to target cosmetic companies for their use of vivisection, further turning the production of beauty into a political affair. The growing concern with natural, cruelty-free, politically correct products led to the creation of The Body Shop by

Anita Roddick in 1976. Mass-market firms revised the tone of their advertisements, created new ethnic lines, and promoted female emancipation in an attempt to woo back customers. By the 1980s, makeup and cosmetics had regained their hold over women's wallets. Increasingly, women's-rights activists stressed the personal empowerment of self-fashioning, best represented by power-suited businesswomen on Wall Street and "lipstick lesbians" in the counterculture.

In the 1990s, scientific promises helped sell new products, such as the fast-growing lines of fake-tanning lotions, anti-aging formulas, and cellulite creams. New ingredients, such as ceramides, alpha-hydroxy acids, and liposomes, not to mention botox treatments, intensified the quest for youth. Multinational cosmetic firms continued to grow by buying out smaller local cosmetics businesses, specifically targeting ethnic markets. Such companies as L'Oréal, Avon, and Revlon have also expanded rapidly into Latin America, Asia, and eastern Europe. With L'Oréal as the unquestioned leader, the top ten companies controlled 55 percent of worldwide cosmetics sales. With increasingly trendy packaging designs, celebrity endorsements, sophisticated advertising campaigns, and almost total social acceptance in the Western-influenced world, cosmetics seem to be an invincible economic force.

[*See also* Fashion Industry *and* Personal Services.]

BIBLIOGRAPHY

Chahine, Nathalie, ed. *Beauty: The 20th Century*. New York, 2001. Collection of essays focusing on different aspects of the beauty cult.

Corson, Richard. *Fashions in Makeup, from Ancient to Modern Times*. London, 1972. Detailed overview of the history of beauty and makeup.

Martin, Morag. "Consuming Beauty: The Commerce of Cosmetics in France, 1750–1800." Ph.D. diss., University of California, Irvine, 1999. A history of changing cosmetic fashions and their implication for business practices.

Piess, Kathy. *Hope in a Jar: The Making of America's Beauty Culture*. New York, 1998. The development of a late-nineteenth-century cosmetics market led by women entrepreneurs and the social acceptance of makeup on a mass scale in the twentieth century.

Plitt, Jane R. *Martha Matilda Harper and the American Dream: How One Woman Changed the Face of Modern Business*. Syracuse, N.Y., 2000. Business history of Rochester entrepreneur and developer of modern chain stores.

Richards, Thomas. *The Commodity Culture of Victorian England: Advertising and Spectacle, 1851–1914*. Stanford, Calif., 1990. Incisive analysis of the marketing of British toilet products under Imperialism.

Scranton, Philip, ed. *Beauty and Business: Commerce, Gender, and Culture in Modern America*. Scranton, Pa., 2001. Collection of essays addressing the commodification of beauty.

Vinikas, Vincent. *Soft Soap, Hard Sell: American Hygiene in an Age of Advertisement*. Ames, Iowa, 1992. The importance of advertising in the development of a mass-market cosmetics industry.

Williams, Neville. *Powder and Paint: A History of the English Woman's Toilet*. London, 1957. Very complete anecdotal history of cosmetics from the seventeenth to nineteenth centuries.

MORAG MARTIN

COSTA RICA. *See* Central American Countries.

CÔTE D'IVOIRE AND GHANA. The republics of Ghana and Côte d'Ivoire date from their political independence from colonial rule, in 1957 (from Britain) and 1960 (from France), respectively. For economic historians they represent an intriguing comparison because these neighbors combine similar natural environments and (at least by the time censuses began to be conducted, in the early twentieth century) population densities with often contrasting institutional and policy histories. In both cases the north and much of the center of the country is savanna, separated from the coast by a forest zone. Ghana, however, has much greater mineral resources.

Before Colonial Times. Before the emergence of the Atlantic trade the local economies appear to have been linked to each other, and beyond, by trade networks. For what is now Côte d'Ivoire and probably until about 1800 for much of what is now Ghana, the major commercial connections across and beyond state boundaries were in the hands of Muslim Dioula traders, one of the major trading diasporas of precolonial Africa. A major feature of the political economy in approximately the fifteenth to the eighteenth centuries was the interaction of state formation and extrasubsistence economic activity, with some polities being founded by entrepreneur-warriors who obtained war materials through trade. When the Portuguese established the first European presence, at Elmina on the coast of Ghana (the "Gold Coast") in 1482, their aim was to bypass the Saharan routes by which gold had been traded to Europe. The gold came largely from Akan-speaking polities in the forest zone of Ghana and eastern Côte d'Ivoire.

By the eighteenth century gold was surpassed, and to a large extent superseded, by slaves as the object of European trade. The Gold Coast became a major center of the Atlantic slave trade, with chartered companies from rival European states establishing forts along the coast. Côte d'Ivoire was also involved, though less intensively. Over 700,000 slaves were shipped from the Gold Coast between 1640 and 1810, including captives from eastern Côte d'Ivoire. Also smaller numbers of slaves (apparently tens of thousands) were exported both before 1640 and after British abolition in 1807, and some captives from western Côte d'Ivoire must be included in totals for Sierra Leone (see P. Lovejoy, *Transformations in Slavery*, Cambridge,

1983; P. Richardson, "Slave Exports from West and West-Central Africa, 1700–1810," *Journal of African History* 30 (1989), 1–22). Most of the captives seem to have been taken in wars or raids in the interior, reaching the sea via middlemen—rulers or large merchants. There has been controversy over how much the prices offered by Europeans for slaves contributed to the high incidence of organized violence in this period.

The eighteenth century saw the emergence of a large territorial state, the kingdom of Asante, with its capital at Kumasi, which at its peak controlled much of what is now Ghana, partly directly and partly through tributary states. This actively centralizing monarchy represented a qualitative break from the smaller polities that had characterized much of the area and, outside Asante control, continued to do so. Also in the eighteenth century, a group of Dioula traders founded the kingdom of Kong, a savanna state based in northern Côte d'Ivoire and encompassing much of what is now southern Mali.

With the closing of the Atlantic slave market, primarily between 1807 and 1840, the economies previously engaged in the trade had to restructure to varying degrees. The coastal societies exported palm oil and, in the late nineteenth century, wild rubber. Asante revived its sales of gold in the maritime trade while exporting increasing quantities of kola nuts to the expanding market of the central Sudan, based on the Sokoto Caliphate, a jihadist state founded in the early nineteenth century in what is now northern Nigeria. With the decline in external demand for slaves, African economies that expanded in the period between 1807 and the European colonial annexations (such as Asante, much more than western Côte d'Ivoire) did so in part by increasing the use of slaves in production. Most new slaves were strangers in the polity in which they were held—imported notably by forest states, directly or indirectly, from politically decentralized societies in the savanna. Many were incorporated into the households of relatively small producers and/or traders, whose share of market output seems to have risen in this period.

Colonial Times. The European partition of this area, between France, Britain, and Germany (whose colony of Togo included much of what is now Ghana east of the Volta River, until the colony was conquered by Britain and France in 1914) took place in the late nineteenth century. Its motivation was partly exogenous to the economic history of the area, but it was also a response to increasing demands from European merchants on their own governments to use force to facilitate their commercial penetration of the local economies.

Throughout the twentieth century, assisted by the introduction of rail and motor transport, the major economic opportunity for both countries lay in the exploitation of the relatively lightly populated forest zone to grow cocoa and, in Côte d'Ivoire, coffee for the overseas markets. In the early colonial period European planters attempted this. In the Gold Coast they received no state help and failed in competition with African farmers, whose efforts were largely responsible for the veritable take-off of cocoa farming from the 1890s. Gold Coast cocoa exports increased from zero in 1890 to nearly 40,000 tons in 1910–1911, thereby overtaking Brazil as the world's largest exporter, before passing the 200,000-ton mark in 1923. By contrast, in Côte d'Ivoire European planters benefited from state intervention, notably the provision of forced labor. Among African responses to this imposition was a seasonal exodus of young men from savanna villages to the Gold Coast to hire out their labor to European mine-owners and, mainly, to African cocoa farmers. On both sides of the border African cocoa farmers organized themselves effectively for collective action. In the Gold Coast, farmers' associations, crucially with the support of African produce brokers and chiefs, held a series of "hold-ups," culminating in a season-long protest in 1937–1938, to oppose the establishment of price-fixing cartels by the European produce-buyers. In Côte d'Ivoire, Félix Houphouët-Boigny began his political career as an African cash-crop farmers' leader. Elected to the postwar French Constituent Assembly, he returned in triumph having helped to secure the formal abolition of forced labor in 1946. Only with the removal of that basic institutional constraint on African enterprise did the Ivoirian cocoa economy emulate, and ultimately overtake, the Ghanaian one.

Post-Colonial Era. For over twenty years after independence the two countries followed contrasting economic strategies. Both relied for food production, and for the bulk of export earnings, very largely on private farms (and timber contractors, timber having become a major export). Both had broadly "patrimonial" regimes; but Côte d'Ivoire, under Houphouët-Boigny, followed an orthodox (to critics, "neo-colonial") policy, remaining within the franc zone and exploiting the country's existing comparative advantage in export agriculture. In contrast, by 1966, when Ghana's first president, Kwame Nkrumah, fell to a military coup, economic policy was based firmly on the substitution of administrative for price mechanisms. State-led import-substituting industrialization was envisaged. Ghana had a new cocoa-planting boom from the later 1950s, taking output to a new world record of over half a million tons in 1965; but later output dwindled and then shrank, to a low of 180,000 tons in 1982–1983. Conversely, Ivoirian output continued to rise, overtaking Ghana's in the late 1970s and proceeding to expand further. The difference cannot be attributed to the often-lamented existence of a government export monopoly in Ghana because

Côte d'Ivoire also had one (in both cases inherited from the late colonial period); but, unlike Côte d'Ivoire, from 1964–1965 onward Ghana maintained a basically non-convertible currency, whose official exchange rate became increasingly overvalued. This served as an increasingly penal form of implicit taxation on export producers, thus eliminating incentives to replant or maintain cocoa farms. An influential explanation of the policy difference relates it to the greater political influence of cash-crop farming interests in Côte d'Ivoire, epitomized in the person of the president (cf. Robert H. Bates, *Markets and States in Tropical Africa*, Berkeley, 1981). In Ghana cocoa farmers were no longer an organized, autonomous lobby after the mid-1950s, when they split between Nkrumah's party and an Asante-based party that unsuccessfully demanded a federal constitution (which would have enabled cocoa-producing regions to retain most of the cocoa income).

Ghanaian gross domestic product (GDP) per head declined in the 1960s, and by 1974 was little higher than it had been in 1950. It then fell almost 40 percent by 1983 (D. Rimmer, *Staying Poor: Ghana's Political Economy 1950–1990*, Oxford, 1992; J. Styker, E. Dumeau, and J. Wohl, *Trade, Exchange Rate, and Agricultural Pricing Policies in Ghana*, Washington, D.C., 1990). Then the government of J. J. Rawlings, contrary to its initial inclinations, embarked on structural adjustment: economic liberalization with IMF support. Rawlings' coup of 31 December 1981 was his second and Ghana's fifth within sixteen years. By the time the Ivoirian economic "miracle" ended in 1978, precipitated by collapsing cocoa and coffee prices, it had comprised nearly two decades of GDP growth averaging 7 percent a year. Côte d'Ivoire had not only surpassed Ghana in income per head, but also in manufacturing output and in reducing the historic neglect of the northern savanna, primarily through a sustained postcolonial expansion of cotton production by peasants.

The era of structural adjustment coincided with generally low world prices for beverage crops. The Ghanaian economy, beginning in 1983 well within its production possibility frontier, was able to start a substantial economic recovery, based on restoration of the price mechanism as the official major means of resource allocation and boosted by an inflow of loans from the IMF and the World Bank. Côte d'Ivoire, with much less room for "catch-up" growth and facing high costs in servicing the debts to foreign commercial banks that its previous credit-worthiness had allowed it to incur during the boom, now faced a struggle to maintain per capita expansion. Côte d'Ivoire's own program of IMF–World Bank assistance, begun in 1980, took place in a very different context from the Ghanaian one. These changing economic trajectories were, in part, reflected in shifts in political stability. In

Ghana the 1981 coup proved to be the last of the century. The Rawlings regime, having presided over an average of 5 percent annual GDP growth since 1983, was able to make a transition to constitutional democracy in 1992, by holding and winning democratic elections. Conversely, the Ivoirian leadership faced increasing opposition even before Houphouët-Boigny's death in 1993. An increasingly sensitive political issue has been the status of adopted Ivoirians, perhaps one-third of the population, who entered the country (primarily from what is now Burkina Faso) to participate in, and contribute to, the economic expansion of earlier decades. The country's first coup took place in 1999.

The biggest achievements of postcolonial policy in both states have been in making education much more broadly available and in improving public health. The present level of income per head in the two countries are similar. As of 1997, for example, in purchasing power parity terms Côte d'Ivoire's gross national product (GNP) per head was estimated at U.S. $1,640 and Ghana's at U.S. $1,790, with populations of nearly fifteen and nearly eighteen million, respectively (World Bank figures). In the twenty-first century, in the context of population densities that have risen greatly since 1945, both face the long-term prospect of having to find a satisfactory alternative to land-extensive growth.

BIBLIOGRAPHY

WORKS ON CÔTE D'IVOIRE

Note that the literature on Ivory Coast is mostly in French.

Amin, Samir. *Le développement du capitalisme en Côte d'Ivoire*. Paris, 1967. Still the major statement of the dependency-theory perspective. Not a translation or a full English-language substitute, but see his *Neo-Colonialism in West Africa*, Harmondsworth, 1973.

Bassett, Thomas J. *The Peasant Cotton Revolution in West Africa: Côte d'Ivoire, 1880–1995*. Cambridge, 2001. The most important single study for either country of the economic history of the northern savanna.

Chauveau, Jean-Pierre, and Eric, Léonard. "Côte d'Ivoire's Pioneer Fronts: Historical and Political Determinants of the Spread of Cocoa Cultivation." In *Cocoa Pioneer Fronts since 1800*, edited by W. G. Clarence-Smith, pp. 176–194. London, 1996.

Terray, Emmanuel. "Long-Distance Exchange and the Formation of the State: the Case of the Abron Kingdom of Gyaman." *Economy and Society* 3 (1974), 314–345. An influential article by a leading contributor to the precolonial historiography. Provoked controversy, for which see Dumett, Raymond E., "Traditional Slavery in the Akan Region in the Nineteenth Century: Sources, Issues, and Interpretations," in *West African Economic and Social History: Studies in Memory of Marion Johnson*, edited by David Henige and T. C. McCaskie, pp. 7–22, Madison, Wis., 1990.

WORKS ON GHANA

Arhin, Kwame. "Rank and Class Among the Asante and Fante in the Nineteenth Century." *Africa* 53 (1983), 2–22. Succinct introduction to the variations of social and political structure even within the Akan-speaking region of Ghana, and to the work of a major social and economic historian of Ghana.

Hill, Polly. *The Migrant Cocoa-Farmers of Southern Ghana: A Study in Rural Capitalism.* 2d ed. Hamburg and Oxford, 1997. The second edition of this classic 1963 study of indigenous enterprise has a new introduction (by G. Austin) that relates it to the considerable volume of more recent research on the history of Ghanaian cocoa production.

Kay, G. B. *The Political Economy of Colonialism in Ghana: A Collection of Documents and Statistics, 1900–1960.* Cambridge, 1972. Useful distillation of colonial published sources with a thought-provoking introductory essay.

Wilks, Ivor. *Forests of Gold: Essays on the Akan and the Kingdom of Asante.* Athens, Ohio, 1993. Stimulating exploration of the interactions among gold production, trade, food farming, and the social and political organization of the forest zone in the fifteenth through the seventeenth centuries, followed by a discussion of the political economy of the Asante state in the eighteenth and nineteenth centuries.

Rimmer's book, cited in the text, provides a careful, broadly neoclassical, account of economic policy from Nkrumah to Rawlings.

COMPARATIVE WORK

Boone, Catherine. "Rural Interests and the Making of Modern African States." *African Economic History* 23 (1995), 1–36. Focused on Ghana, Ivory Coast, and Senegal.

GARETH AUSTIN

COTTON, the seed-hair fiber from a variety of plants of the genus *Gossypium*. The plant produces seedpods, known as cotton bolls. Seed hairs, or fibers, grow from the skin of the seedpod, which bursts open when it is ripe. The plant grows up to 6 meters (18 to 20 feet) high, although usually it is closer to 1 to 2 meters (3 to 6 feet) in height.

Each growing region produces cotton fibers of a different staple length (the average length of the fibers). The longest, most lustrous fibers are grown in the Nile Delta of Egypt, in Brazil, on the Sea Islands off South Carolina's coast, and in Texas. These long-staple cottons are relatively limited in production and are used for fine-quality fabrics. The medium-staple cottons are the most common, and they include the cottons of the American Uplands (the South), which are used for good-quality fabrics. Short-staple cottons are mainly grown in India (denoted as Surats and Bengals), and they are used for coarse-quality goods (India also makes cottons of the sheerest and finest quality, as well as utility-grade fabrics).

Cotton is harvested when the bolls open. Until the mid-twentieth century, cotton bolls were hand picked. Cotton-harvesting machines have gradually supplanted the hand picking. This conversion has had significant effect on the agricultural labor force of the American South and of other cotton-growing regions. Separating the cottonseed by hand from the bolls was a laborious process prior to the invention of the cotton gin; the hand process retarded the expansion of cotton production. In the early years of the United States of America, Eli Whitney's 1793 invention of the cotton gin made the process economical, and cotton production then increased rapidly. The harvested cotton—of several hues, from white to tan, green, and brown—is compressed into bales that weigh up to 200 kilos (500 pounds). The cotton must be cleaned of debris and carded (combed), before it is spun into yarn.

History. Cotton cultivation began in prehistoric India. In 333 BCE, Alexander the Great's soldiers, while campaigning in India, brought news of a plant that produced "vegetable wool," which was convertible into cloth. In the words of Thomas Ellison (1886:1–2):

> [Cotton] fabrics as fine as any that can be turned out at the present day . . . were produced by the nimble fingers of Hindoo spinners, and the primitive looms of Hindoo weavers . . . at a period when the inhabitants of the British Isles were attired in the skins of wild animals.

In Ellison's praise for these early spinners, he included the observation that they were working with the "much despised Surats, and still more despised Bengals." Overland traders brought cotton fabrics to Europe from India for hundreds of years. In addition, the Moors began cultivating cotton in Spain as early as 712 CE, having conquered the Iberian Peninsula in 711. During the Italian Renaissance, the city-states of Venice and Genoa sought to monopolize the overland trade in cotton, with Venice gaining dominance. The other European states, chafing under that monopolization, sought alternative ways to get Indian cotton. When the Portuguese sea captain Vasco da Gama discovered the Atlantic to Indian Ocean route around Africa in 1497, a new era began; Spain, France, Holland, and England competed for the burgeoning trade. The increased supply of cotton textiles in Europe soon reduced their prices. (Yet the great importance of da Gama's voyage was its spur to the European age of discovery, which led to the discovery and colonization of the Western Hemisphere and, ultimately, to European U.S. hegemony worldwide.)

Because, in 1328, King Edward III of England had induced Flemish weavers to relocate to Manchester, England had a thriving wool industry. By the 1700s, when English warships supplanted Spanish, French, and Dutch navies as the dominant force on the seas, British traders went to the Indian subcontinent to deal with textile producers there. In addition, such British colonies as Georgia and South Carolina in North America proved to be fertile grounds for cotton cultivation. The British East India Company and dominance of the world's sea lanes soon placed Great Britain in an enviable position in the cotton textile market. British industrial inventions—John Kay's fly-shuttle (1733), James Hargreaves's spinning jenny (1764), Richard Arkwright's water-frame (1769), Samuel

COTTON. Mangbetu workers removing seeds from cotton pods, Mongomasi, Zaire (present-day Democratic Republic of the Congo), 1972. (Eliot Elisofon/Eliot Elisofon Photographic Archives/National Museum of African Art, Smithsonian Institution, Washington, D.C.)

Crompton's mule (1774), Edmund Cartwright's power loom (1787), and James Watt's steam engines (1769)—transformed the conversion of cotton into yarns and cloth. Soon, cotton textiles were produced by machinery tended by workers in factories and factory towns in Britain and the new United States; by the mid-to-late 1800s, such machinery was common throughout Europe, the Middle East, and India.

With increased productivity in the manufacturing of textiles, a better supply of raw cotton was needed. Then, with the spread of cotton gins after 1793, U.S. production of raw cotton increased rapidly. The cotton gin and the increased acreage devoted to cotton helped maintain slavery on cotton plantations in the American South. South Carolina and Georgia were the initial regions of cotton production, with planters also on the islands off South Carolina who specialized in the finest long-staple Sea Island cotton. American cotton growers moved westward, into Alabama, Mississippi, and Texas; just before the American Civil War (1861–1865), Mississippi was the largest producer of U.S. raw cotton. Throughout the nine-

teenth century, U.S. medium-staple cotton was considered superior to the cottons from India.

By the mid-1800s, growers in the American South supplied about 80 percent of the Western world's cotton; their growing domination of the world supply of raw cotton and their importance to the American economy was reflected in U.S. export figures—cotton typically comprised the country's largest export (in terms of value) until the Civil War (the War between the States, the War of Secession). As that war became imminent, British leaders worried about their industry's dependence on American-grown raw cotton; attempts to improve cotton production and quality in India had failed. From 1850 to 1860, the Western world's demand for raw cotton grew at a per annum rate of 5 to 6 percent. That strong market for raw cotton finally spurred Indian growers to increase their 1860–1861 exports to Europe. The American Civil War disrupted the world market for raw cotton. Between the Confederate States of America's informal embargo on the export of their raw cotton and the Union navy's blockade of Southern ports, exports of Southern-grown raw cotton dwindled to about 10 percent of the prewar volume. The real price of raw cotton, already strong before the war, then tripled in Great Britain and Europe and quadrupled in the United States. Even with these dislocations, the Confederacy's hopes for "King Cotton," as an economic or political lever to induce European intervention or alliance, were disappointed.

Some historians have attributed the failure of King Cotton diplomacy to a glut of cotton and cotton textiles; economic historians have debated the direction of world demand for raw cotton. One thesis holds that the American Civil War upheavals masked an underlying weakness in the market. Such upheavals make interpreting the data difficult, and the evidence also supports the view that, in the absence of the upheavals, the world demand for raw cotton would have continued to grow at a healthy rate. The war did spur Egypt to encourage its nascent Nile Delta cotton-growing industry. After a lag of about a year, cotton producers in Egypt, Brazil, and India had increased their acreage and shipments to Europe—yet all these growers were only able to replace about half of the shortfall of American-grown cotton. In addition, Indian cotton comprised much of the increased shipments, but it was of inferior quality.

After the war, which preserved the Union, these producers largely receded in importance; the Southern United States regained much of their dominance in the world market. Nevertheless, the Civil War and its aftermath disrupted labor practices in the South. Slavery was abolished by President Abraham Lincoln's Emancipation Proclamation of 1863. Southern growers had to convert to hired labor, sharecroppers, and other forms of quasi-independent or seasonal labor. By 1875, Southern growers were producing about the same amount as they had in 1860. Cotton production in the Southern states continued to increase throughout the rest of the nineteenth century, and California, Arizona, and New Mexico used irrigation to open up vast new lands for cotton production. By 1910, American growers were producing almost three times as much cotton as before the Civil War.

American dominance began to wane as a boll weevil infestation started in Texas in 1892, then spread to the north and east. India, China, Russia (the Soviet Union after the Revolution of 1917), and Brazil expanded their production. The U.S. cotton belt stagnated throughout the 1920s and into the Great Depression (1929–1941). Cotton acreage and production in the United States fell throughout the mid-twentieth century. The federal farm programs of the 1930s failed to restore the eastern cotton-growing regions to their former profitability. Eventually, the use of mechanized harvesting and shrinking cotton acreage forced sharecroppers off the land, which was soon owned and operated as agribusiness. The United States remained the leading producer of cotton, but its market share had fallen to below 20 percent by 1971. The post–World War II development and aggressive marketing of synthetic fibers reduced the demand for raw cotton, further damaging the industry. With growing ecological concerns and the OPEC oil price manipulations of the 1970s, cotton has once again become a favored natural fiber. Since petrochemicals (made from petroleum byproducts) are the source of synthetic fibers, as well as many dyes and fertilizers, the 1973 OPEC oil embargo caused concerned, eco-conscious Western consumers to seek natural, organic substances. By the 1980s, a new cotton industry provided the fabrics that such consumers sought, for everything from underware and sleepware to upholstery, bedding, and floor coverings. Labels indicate pure cotton, organic cotton, and natural undyed cotton by symbols devised by the cotton marketing board.

[*See also* Cotton Industry *and* Textiles.]

BIBLIOGRAPHY

Ellison, Thomas. *The Cotton Trade of Great Britain*. London, 1886 and 1968.

Farnie, D. A. *The English Cotton Industry and the World Market, 1815–1896*. Oxford, 1979. Provides a good description of the growth of the British cotton textile industry, as do Ellison (1886) and Scherer (1916).

Fogel, Robert W. *Without Consent or Contract: The Rise and Fall of American Slavery*. New York, 1989. Surveys the literature concerning the economics of slavery and cotton.

Harnetty, Peter. *Imperialism and Free Trade: Lancashire and India in Mid-Nineteenth Century*. Vancouver, 1972. Examines the efforts of Lancashire producers to encourage greater cotton production in India.

Heywood, Colin. *The Cotton Industry in France, 1750–1850*. Loughborough, U.K., 1977.

Scherer, James. *Cotton as a World Power*. New York, 1916 and 1969.

Surdam, David G. *Northern Naval Superiority and the Economics of the American Civil War*. Columbia, S.C., 2001. Describes the state of the world market for raw cotton and cotton textiles just before the American Civil War and argues that, in the absence of the war-related upheavals, the demand for raw cotton would have remained strong.

Watkins, James L. *King Cotton: A Historical and Statistical Review, 1790 to 1908*. New York, 1908 and 1969. Provides a statistical overview and history of cotton production in the United States.

Woodman, Harold D. *King Cotton and His Retainers: Financing and Marketing the Cotton Crop of the South, 1800–1925*. Lexington, Ky., 1968 and 1990. Provides a thorough examination of the structure of the market for raw cotton.

Wright, Gavin. *The Political Economy of the Cotton South*. New York, 1978. Provides the strongest defense of the argument that the world demand for raw cotton on the eve of the American Civil War was destined for a prolonged slump.

DAVID G. SURDAM

COTTON INDUSTRY *[This entry contains three subentries, a historical overview and discussions of technological change and industrial organization, markets, and trade.]*

Historical Overview

The cotton industry became the first industry to manufacture textiles by means of power-driven machinery housed within factories. It became the first international industry of the modern world. It served as a prime mover in the economic expansion of Great Britain and Japan and in the process of global economic development. As the most widely studied of all manufacturing industries, it has generated an unending series of debates.

The industry originated in India, where spinning and dyeing developed to the highest degree possible to manual labor. Indian textiles were exported throughout Asia and, from the seventeenth century, to Europe, where the calico-printing industry developed, in order to compete with India in the supply of material for dresses. The growing demand for printed calico was reinforced by that for fustian and for cotton hosiery. An unanticipated revolution in supply was then created by means of mechanization, to which cotton lent itself more readily than any other fiber. Cotton proved superior to wool and flax in its tensile strength, which enabled it to withstand rough handling by machines, by chemicals, and by washerwomen. It proved highly amenable to bleaching and dyeing as well as to printing.

Great Britain. The process of spinning was transformed by the "Great Inventions," which comprised the jenny (1764), the roller spinning frame (1769) and the mule (1779). Power was supplied first by the water wheel and then by the steam engine. The first factories built from 1771 were spinning mills, which supplied yarn to an expanding army of hand-loom weavers. Productivity increased at an unprecedented rate and diffused its benefits throughout the economy. Nicholas Crafts estimated in 1985 that the industry generated some 60 percent of the increase in total factor productivity (1788–1856). Weaving was mechanized more slowly and by means of the "steam loom" developed from 1803 onward. The preparatory and finishing processes were both transformed in technology through the successive invention of the carding machine in 1775, the rotary printing press in 1785, bleaching powder in 1799, and coal-tar dyestuffs in 1856.

The rapid expansion of the cotton industry remains one of the most astonishing episodes in history. Its growth unleashed a positive avalanche of productive power and detonated a demographic explosion as population multiplied in direct proportion to the increased consumption of raw cotton (Table 1). It also stimulated urbanization, the development of transportation facilities, and the growth of a complex of ancillary industries. The expansion of trade proved to be as significant as the expansion of the manufacturing industry. During the years from 1784 to 1788,

TABLE 1. *The Consumption of Raw Cotton in the United Kingdom, 1770–1840 (in thousands of pounds)*

1770	3,246
1780	6,553
1790	30,604
1800	52,000
1810	124,000
1820	120,300
1830	247,600
1840	458,900

SOURCE. Mitchell, Brain R. *British Historical Statistics*, pp. 330–332. Cambridge, 1988.

Great Britain experienced a threefold revolution in economic standing. From 1784 it became the largest producer of cotton goods in Europe. From 1787 its foreign trade became the largest in the world. From 1788 it became a net exporter of cotton manufactures, remaining such for 172 years until 1960. Thus, Lancashire accomplished a notable feat of import substitution and reversed the balance of textile trade with Asia. India was surpassed by Great Britain as an exporter of cotton goods, probably in the 1790s, and by the United States from 1821 as an exporter of raw cotton. Cotton manufactures replaced woolens as the principal export of the United Kingdom and retained that primacy for nearly 140 years (1803–1942), even during the great hiatus of the Cotton Famine (1861–1865). Both Liverpool and Manchester rose to preeminence as great merchant cities. From the 1820s, Manchester acquired an expanding colony of foreign merchants, who provided the indispensable link to world markets.

From 1962, historians challenged the traditional view of the role of the cotton industry in the transformation of the British economy during the period from 1760 to 1860. By the use of quantitative analysis, they established that the industry was less important in enlarging national income than in expanding foreign trade. Between 1800 and 1860, the industry's contribution to the trebling in the value of exports amounted to 43.4 percent, but the value added to the material processed by the industry contributed only an estimated 8.4 percent of the threefold increase in national income. That revisionist thesis failed, however, to set the industry in its full international context. The contribution made by the industry to national income was in fact larger in Great Britain than in any other country, apart from Japan, while the value added to its raw material formed a much higher proportion of national income than in any other state. The external functions fulfilled by the industry became more significant than its domestic functions and remain incapable of measurement by a purely national system of accounting. Thus the industry served for almost a century as the supreme model of machine production

Centennial College Resource Centre

and factory organization, as the pattern of a market economy, and as a stimulus to emulation abroad. As an exporter first of yarn and cloth and then of machines, steam engines, engineers, mill plans, and mill supplies, the dynamic influence of Lancashire extended almost to the confines of the inhabited globe.

Continental Europe. In continental Europe, the cotton industry had been established in Italy since the twelfth century and in Germany since the fourteenth century. From the seventeenth century, the printing of "indiennes" was added to the manufacture of fustians. Machine spinning was adopted during the era of the Continental Blockade (1806–1812). A cotton industry developed in nine regions, centered around Ghent, Rouen, Barcelona, Mulhouse, Zürich, Chemnitz, Lodz, Ivanova, and Milan. None of those regional capitals developed the quasi metropolitan functions of Manchester. Further development proved to be slow for two reasons. First, such a development would have proved most disadvantageous. It would have entailed higher costs than those borne in Lancashire. It would have necessitated dependence upon Lancashire for textile machinery. It would have supplied no stimulus to domestic agriculture. Above all, it would have damaged all of the established textile industries in societies dedicated to the protection of producers rather than to the service of consumers. It would also have reduced the profits made in the export of Lancashire goods by the foreign merchants domiciled in Manchester. Second, such a development would have offered few advantages. It would have created a product low in value, with limited market potential and restricted export opportunities. It would have supplied no suitable material to the established clothing industries of Europe, which were much more important than those of Great Britain. Switzerland became the first state in the world to recognize that the cotton industry offered entrepreneurs no royal road to wealth or to social status. From 1872 onward, it therefore reduced manufacturing capacity and became more prosperous than ever before by diverting resources into more productive fields. The average share in gross domestic product (GDP) contributed by the cotton industries of some eleven states in 1887 was only 2 percent, or one-quarter of the corresponding British share. On the basis of such comparative analysis, the revisionist thesis set forth in 1962 seems to be much more applicable to continental Europe or to America and much less applicable to Great Britain.

United States. The U.S. cotton industry was established during the wartime mill-building boom from 1812 to 1814. Its career differed markedly from that of Great Britain, especially in its prolonged use of water power, in its adoption of the business corporation, and in its acquisition of tariff protection. Its pace of expansion after 1820 became even faster than that of Lancashire, sustained by the largest market in the world. Per capita consumption of cotton goods became from the 1840s the highest in the world, as per capita income rose to the highest level in the world. The homogeneity of the American market permitted the manufacture of staple goods to be standardized and production to undertake long continuous runs, so generating all the economies of large-scale production. The process of manufacture integrated power-loom weaving with spinning, creating rising levels of labor productivity and falling costs of production. Technology became capital intensive and labor saving, in the form of the ring spinning frame (1828–1844) and the automatic weft-changing loom (1895).

The United States surpassed the United Kingdom in the volume of its production from 1897 and in its value from 1919, so as to acquire the largest industry in the world. That industry, however, provided only a limited contribution to economic development, supplying 6.5 percent of GDP in 1860: in terms of value added, its contribution was only one-quarter of the corresponding British proportion. The industry increased the value of its gross product more slowly (1810–1913) than either gross national product (GNP) or the value of the farm crop of raw cotton. Throughout the nineteenth century, it remained dwarfed by the immense size of the expanding cotton-growing industry of the American South. Only in 1919 did the cotton manufacturing industry generate a product more valuable than the cotton crop. The new cotton mills of the South built after 1880 failed conspicuously to unleash an industrial revolution within their rural and agricultural world. The real achievements of the industry were made within the social field rather than in the economic sphere. Thus it generated none of the "Great American Fortunes" investigated in 1907 by Gustavus Myers but served to diffuse wealth widely throughout the nation. In particular, it offered employment to successive cadres of unskilled workfolk within a trade where union density remained low. One product of the "industrial Utopia" of Lowell, Massachusetts, remained unique in the annals of world literature, *The Lowell Offering* (1840–1850), a monthly magazine written by mill girls working twelve hours a day.

Japan. In Japan, the cotton industry played an even more important role in economic development than it did in Great Britain. It developed along distinctively Japanese lines and expanded (1855–1919) at double the pace of Lancashire from 1760 to 1812. Its entrepreneurs made the industry into a seedbed of innovation in technology, management, and, above all, marketing. They established the most powerful trade association in the world and used statistical analyses in order to enhance both productivity and market share. The Japanese spinning industry became the cheapest producer in the world during the 1890s and a secondary pole of financial capitalism, distinct from the pole of the zaibatsu. In 1919, the industry generated its peak share, 13.4 percent, of GNP. The number of its production units, both factory and nonfactory, rose in 1919 to a maximum of 566,779, compared with the 1968 separate units in contemporary Lancashire. The industry became more important than its British rival in the proportion of the population employed, in its wide geographical diffusion, and in the high imperial purposes that it served. It supplied the pattern for the modernization of the whole industrial structure of Japan, where the cotton mill became a national icon such as it never was in Great Britain. From 1911, Japan's spinning companies undertook the large-scale establishment of cotton mills in China and for a generation made those mills into the most efficient in the world. Japan became the first state to compete successfully with Lancashire. It surpassed Great Britain in 1933 as the principal supplier of the world market, retaining that position for twenty-seven years (1933–1941 and 1951–1968) and remaining a net exporter for eighty-nine years (1898–1987).

The industry reached its climacteric during the years 1926–1930. Global mill employment peaked at 3.8 million in 1926 and world spindleage at 165 million in 1930, as productivity continued to increase. During the sustained boom of 1950–1973, the textile trade of the world was transformed by the expansion in production of manmade fiber, by the decline of the share of raw cotton in world fiber production, by the reconstruction of textile firms into multifiber, multiprocess concerns, and by the homogenization of global patterns of clothing, as the influence of fashion came to prevail over that of tradition. Leading firms geared their operations to the supply of fashionable women's wear as world trade in clothing expanded at a faster pace than world trade in textiles.

China. During the past three centuries, the world market for cotton manufactures has been revolutionized three times by the irruption of new low-cost producers in the form of Lancashire in the 1780s, Japan in the 1930s, and China in the 1980s, driving prices down to a permanently lower level. The meteoric rise of Japan stimulated emulation by the "tiger economies" of East Asia, first by Hong Kong from 1948 and then by Taiwan and South Korea from the 1960s. Those three states made textiles and clothing into spearhead export industries and their key to economic development, so stimulating a further wave of emulation throughout the Asian world. China began to establish cotton spinning mills from 1890, but preserved its ancient and widespread rural hand-loom industry, until the 1950s. Its emergence as a textile superpower checked from 1988 any further expansion by the "little tigers." From 1969, China became the world's largest producer of cotton yarn and cloth in succession to the United

States as well as the world's largest exporter of cotton cloth in succession to Japan. It acquired the largest loomage from 1970 and the largest spindleage from 1971. It became the world's largest producer of raw cotton from 1981–1982, the world's largest exporter of clothing from 1988, and the largest exporter of textiles from 1991. That resurgent "dragon economy" became the core of a new world system. Asia reclaimed the textile industry for itself and developed a large-scale export trade to the West. The world's leading importers of cotton piece goods, which had been India (1840–1938) and Indonesia (1939–1957) became the United Kingdom (1958–1965) and, from 1966, the United States. In the West, a protectionist reaction was led by the United States, where the cotton industry was first recognized in 1961 as vital to national security. That reaction became effective from 1962 and achieved its greatest triumph in the Multi-Fiber Arrangement of 1974.

[*See also* Clothing Trades; Cotton; *and* Textiles.]

BIBLIOGRAPHY

Chapman, Stanley D. *The Textile Industries.* 4 vols. London, 1997. Part of the Tauris Industrial Histories, Third Series, which reprints seventy-nine articles including thirty-three on the cotton industry.

Chaudhuri, Kirti N. *The Trading World of Asia and the English East India Company, 1660–1760.* Cambridge, 1978.

Farnie, Douglas A. *The English Cotton Industry and the World Market, 1815–1896.* Oxford, 1979.

Farnie, Douglas A. "The Era of the Great Inventions in the English Cotton Industry, 1764–1834." *Mitteilungen des Chemnitzer Geschichtsvereins* 69 (1999), 38–55.

Farnie, Douglas A. "Four Revolutions in the Textile Trade of Asia, 1814–1994: The Impact of Bombay, Osaka, the Little Tigers, and China." In *Asia Pacific Dynamism, 1550–2000,* edited by A. J. H. Latham and Heita Kawakatsu, pp. 49–69. London, 2000.

Farnie, Douglas A., Tetsuro Nakaoka, David J. Jeremy, John F. Wilson, and Takeshi Abe, eds. *Region and Strategy in Britain and Japan: Business in Lancashire and Kansai, 1890–1990.* London, 2000. Includes a forty-three-page chapter on "Japan, Lancashire, and the Asian Market for Cotton Manufactures, 1890–1990," by Douglas A. Farnie and Takeshi Abe.

Farnie, Douglas A. "Cotton (1780–1914)." In *The Cambridge History of Western Textiles,* edited by David T. Jenkins. Cambridge, 2003.

Howe, Anthony. *The Cotton Masters, 1830–1860.* Oxford, 1984.

Jeremy, David J. *Transatlantic Industrial Revolution, 1790–1830s.* Oxford, 1981.

Lazonick, Willam. *Organisation and Technology in Capitalist Development.* Aldershot, U.K., 1992.

Mazzaoui, Maureen F. *The Italian Cotton Industry in the Later Middle Ages, 1100–1600.* Cambridge, 1981.

Rose, Mary, B, ed. *International Competition and Strategic Response in the Textile Industries since 1870.* London, 1991.

Rose, Mary, B, ed. *The Lancashire Cotton Industry: A History since 1700.* Preston, 1996.

Singleton, John S. *The World Textile Industry.* London, 1997.

Toms, J. Steven. "Growth, Profits and Technological Change: The Case of the Lancashire Cotton Textile Industry." *Journal of Industrial History* 1.1 (1998), 35–55.

Wadsworth, Alfred P., and Julia Mann. *The Cotton Trade and Industrial Lancashire, 1600–1780.* Manchester, 1931.

Wright, G avin. *Old South, New South: Revolutions in the Southern Economy since the Civil War.* New York, 1986.

Wyke, Terry, and Nigel Rudyard, eds. *Cotton: A Select Bibliography on Cotton in North West England, Bibliography of North West England,* 17. Manchester, U.K., 1997.

DOUGLAS A. FARNIE

Technological Change

Prior to the Industrial Revolution, cotton was processed in homes, with relatively simple machinery, using human power and manual dexterity. Afterward, cotton was processed in factories, using much more complex machinery, in which neither human power nor manual dexterity was the key to production. With the notable and celebrated exception of Eli Whitney's gin, the story of technological change in the cotton industry is essentially a British Industrial Revolution story, and, within Britain, a story largely confined to one small corner, the county of Lancashire. Most economic historians see the move from a preindustrial to an industrial world as relatively slow and gradual. However, although Britain, the first industrial nation, is no longer regarded as having been suddenly overrun by "a wave of gadgets," the notion of rapid change is more accurate for the cotton industry than for other industries. Its history is a story of heroes, independent inventors who transformed every stage of production. Productivity soared, prices fell, and output expanded dramatically, leaving an industry very different from what had existed.

There are two analytically and historically distinct phases in the technological-productivity revolution. The first replaces the dexterity of human fingers with sometimes complex machines; the second applies nonhuman power to those machines. Each stage in the process of transforming raw cotton into clothing is essentially self-contained; so it is possible for one stage to be transformed by technology without affecting the production methods of any other stage. This essay looks at both the invention of new machinery, and, briefly, the international diffusion of such inventions. Clearly, machinery must be invented if it is to be diffused; but its mere invention was not always sufficient to ensure its diffusion, especially in the early years of the Industrial Revolution.

Before the Industrial Revolution. The idea of transforming vegetable and animal fibers, such as flax, cotton, and wool, into clothing goes back many millennia to the beginnings of technological civilization. Cotton has advantages in production and use: softer than flax, it is easier to work with; unlike wool, it is naturally straight, and so less prone to tangling while being worked. It is easier to bleach and to dye than either material, and washes well. These advantages meant that as early as the end of the Middle Ages cotton had overtaken leather, linen, and wool to become the most common raw material used for clothing in areas where it could readily be grown, such as southern Europe and the Middle East.

Before the great wave of textile inventions, cotton goods were manufactured by hand. Before the cotton left the field, seeds were pulled from the fibers by hand; and once it was in the home, the first stage was to make the cotton fibers parallel, an essential prerequisite for successful spinning. This process, carding, was performed by women and children, who placed a small amount of raw cotton between two wooden blocks covered in short metal spikes. The two blocks were moved up and down by hand until the fibers were aligned.

The next stage, spinning, is an amalgam of three separate jobs. The first is to draw out the carded, parallel cotton fibers so that they are only the width of a piece of thread; the second is to twist those fibers together to give the yarn strength; and the third is to wind the yarn into a convenient package. Although these jobs are separate, they cannot be separated: drawing out without spinning would result in an intermediate product too weak to survive, whereas spinning without winding would result in a tangled web of yarn. Simple spinning wheels used human dexterity to allow all three jobs to be done simultaneously. The yarn spun was not especially strong, and could not withstand the pressures of being held in place as warp yarn in the loom. As a result, weavers used linen for warp and cotton for weft, the resulting cloth being called fustian.

Of all the stages of production, weaving was best developed on the eve of the Industrial Revolution. Although made of wood rather than metal, preindustrial looms were recognizably the same as postindustrial examples. The warp threads were held parallel in a large frame, and the weft thread passed back and forth across the warp to make cloth. Originally the process was very labor-intensive, as the weft was passed from side to side by hand, requiring an operative on either side of the loom. The most significant invention in weaving, which occurred immediately before the Industrial Revolution, was John Kay's invention of the flying shuttle—a wheeled torpedo-shaped wooden box containing a cop of weft yarn—patented in 1733 and widely adopted from 1750 on. To use it, the weaver pulled a cord that moved a slide that literally struck the shuttle, propelling it smoothly to the other side of the loom. The next pull on the cord moved it back again, and so on. This procedure was much faster than passing the weft across the loom by hand, and required only one operative, rather than two. The resulting cloth was also of higher quality. The flying shuttle was effective in replacing human dexterity with a simple mechanical device, but deserves to be seen as a preindustrial machine: it was designed to be hand-powered and for use in the home.

Although unbleached cloth could be made into clothing directly, it was common for the cloth first to be bleached and printed. Before the Industrial Revolution, bleaching was a very slow process. The cloth was soaked in an alkaline solution made from plant ashes and then spread out in the open for weeks, with the process repeated a number of times. Then the cloth was soaked in sour buttermilk and again left out in the open, with the process again repeated many times. The mid-eighteenth-century discovery that sour buttermilk could be replaced by sulfuric acid halved the time taken to bleach cloth from eight to four months, but those four months were still fairly labor-intensive.

Printing too was a labor-intensive task. The first step was to make a block, about one foot square, generally out of wood, with a pattern raised in profile on it. Next the block was lightly inked, placed on the fabric, and struck with an iron mallet to ensure that the ink was transferred from block to fabric. Then the block was removed, reinked, and placed on the fabric next to the piece already printed. If the block was not inked or struck the same way each time, the amount of dye left on the cloth would vary. The process was time-consuming and did not always yield high-quality results.

The Industrial Revolution. Although not responsible for the idea of making clothing out of cotton, the Industrial Revolution revolutionized the means by which each stage of production was undertaken. Of the many stages, spinning—with its three jobs—was the hardest sector in which to replace human dexterity with machinery. If spinners were to tend many spindles, inventors had to produce a machine that would handle all three jobs successfully. Mechanizing only two of the processes would still require the spinner's presence for the third, implying little, if any, productivity gain. It was this challenge, rather than the application of power to the resulting spinning machine, that proved difficult. The first "near miss" came in China in the Middle Ages. The Chinese machine was conceptually similar to the later British spinning jenny, but did not have the jenny's device for drawing out the raw cotton for spinning. Although that device seems both simple and obvious to anyone who has seen it, its invention apparently eluded the Chinese, whose machine allowed one person to spin at most four spindles and was not sufficiently advantageous to be widely adopted. The first serious British attempt was Richard Haines and Richard Dereham's spinning machine, patented in 1678, which did not prove commercially viable. Lewis Paul and John Wyatt's roller spinner of 1738 was good enough to be installed in a number of premises, but not so good as to be widely adopted. Concerned about growing labor shortages in the 1740s and 1750s, the Royal Society of Arts resorted to offering a prize to anyone who could invent a spinning machine that allowed one person to spin six threads at once. Although there were a number of entries, none was successful; but the potential commercial returns were great, and inventors continued to work

on the problem. Two of them finally proved successful, the first being James Hargreaves, whose spinning jenny was invented in 1764 and patented in 1770. The first models had 16 spindles, but later versions contained up to 130. The jenny was a hand-powered intermittent spinner, first drawing out, then spinning, and then winding the yarn onto the spindle; but it did all three jobs successfully. Like the earlier spinning wheels, the jenny produced relatively weak yarn suited only to weft.

The second breakthrough was Richard Arkwright's 1769 improved version of Paul and Wyatt's roller spinner, known as a throstle, or water-frame, after its source of power. It produced coarse, strong yarn more suited to warp than weft, and thus was complementary to, rather than a rival of, the jenny. This meant that all-cotton cloth could be produced for the first time. Doing this was in fact illegal, but Arkwright persuaded Parliament to repeal the relevant act in 1774.

Ten years later, both machines were surpassed by Samuel Crompton's mule spindle, so called because it combined elements of both the jenny and the water-frame. Like the jenny it was an intermittent spinner, but it used the water-frame's system of rollers to draw out the fibers. Early versions were hand-powered, and required considerable skill and strength for their operation; so the number of spindles was limited to 144 per operative. By 1790, William Kelly, a Scot, had produced a power-assisted mule that more than doubled the number of spindles that could be tended, as well as increasing the speed at which each spindle turned. Improvements culminated in Richard Roberts's automatic, "self-acting" mule of 1825–1830. All important aspects of the machine were powered, and greater automation allowed the spinner to tend over six hundred spindles.

These developments in spinning were matched by the successful mechanization of both of the prespinning stages of production, ginning and carding. Ginning, which removes the seeds from the cotton fibers, originally was done by hand; but in 1793 Yale-educated Eli Whitney realized that the fibers could be separated from the seeds if wire hooks, mounted on a revolving drum, pulled the fibers through a wooden grid whose slits were too narrow to allow the seeds to pass through. Easy to manufacture and power, the machine also was easy to understand and copy.

Carding requires that the fibers be held between two parallel surfaces that move relative to the other in only one direction. In hand carding, that is achieved by moving two flat pieces of wood up and down in opposite directions. Lewis Paul realized that the same effect could be achieved by moving only one piece, while holding the other still. The moving piece could be cylindrical, provided that the stationary piece was curved to fit around it. The cylinder could be powered to revolve constantly. Richard Arkwright's 1775

COTTON PRODUCTION. African American workers using a cotton gin, wood engraving by William L. Sheppard. *Harper's Weekly*, 18 December 1869. (Prints and Photographs Division, Library of Congress)

model improved on Paul's earlier design, and was commercially successful. These cylinder-based machines also meant that raw cotton fed into one side of the cylinder emerged carded at the other side, where it could be combed off in an easy-to-store form. The invention of roller carding transformed carding from batch production to continuous-flow production.

The productivity effects of replacing hands with machinery, and hand power with water and steam power, were remarkable. For example, a hand-operated gin raised productivity tenfold, whereas a horse-powered gin did the work of fifty people. Before the Industrial Revolution, a spinner took over five hundred hours—almost ten weeks—to produce one pound weight of cotton on a spinning wheel. Crompton's first mules, equipped with forty-eight spindles, reduced the time to twenty hours. Hand mules steadily improved, so that by 1785 this process took ten hours. The application of power reduced the figure to three

hours in 1795 and to about an hour and twenty minutes in 1825. The self-acting mule reduced the time to less than an hour upon its invention, and to under twenty minutes by 1914. Combined with the shift from home to factory work, this, truly, was an industrial revolution.

These inventions in spinning represented a product revolution as well as a productivity revolution. Although previous generations of machinery, including the jenny and the water-frame, were better suited to coarse yarns, the mule could spin fine yarns, too. Productivity rises caused the price of coarse yarn (18-count) to fall by 40 percent between 1780 and 1800, the price of medium yarn (40-count) to fall by two-thirds, and the price of fine yarn (100-count) to fall by more than 90 percent. The greater falls in the price of finer yarns made relatively high-quality cotton goods available to a much wider market. These falls in price caused a massive expansion in production: the total output rose ninefold in these two decades.

Invention of the gin and the mule meant that by 1800 weaving technology lagged behind the other production stages. Since the yarn still had to be woven, the number of handloom weavers expanded dramatically, from 75,000 in 1795 to 225,000 by 1811. Power is harder to apply to intermittent, nonrotary actions such as weaving than to continuous rotary motions such as ginning, carding, and spinning. The incentive to produce a power loom was great, but neither Robert and Thomas Barber's 1770s power loom nor Edmund Cartwright's 1787 power loom proved successful. William Horrocks's 1802 machine was installed by a number of manufacturers, but not adopted widely. Further incremental improvements meant that by 1815 power looms were reliable for coarse cloths, and by the 1830s were increasingly used for cloth made from finer yarns. At this point, the number of hand-loom weavers began to decline, and 200,000 would lose their jobs in the following twenty years. The power loom was further improved in 1841, when William Kenworthy and James Bullough made a machine capable of stopping when the weft thread broke, which allowed manufacturers to raise the number of machines tended per worker beyond the two previously possible. This development was taken to its logical conclusion in 1894 when George Draper, a U.S. firm, invented an automatic machine that not only stopped the loom when the weft shuttle was empty, but inserted new yarn so that it could continue without the operative's intervention.

The Industrial Revolution also saw revolutions in both parts of the finishing process, with bleaching showing perhaps the more dramatic improvement. In 1799 the previous method of bleaching was entirely superseded by a process using a bleaching powder that combined chlorine and slaked lime. This combination was much easier to handle than other chlorine-based products, and the process allowed cloth to be bleached in little more than a day. With no need to take the cloth into and out of the fields, the new process was easy to mechanize and power. The printing process was transformed by the same intuition as had transformed carding, that cylindrical rollers can replace square blocks, which can be powered to make a continuous high-throughput process. Roller printing, using engraved copper rollers, was invented by Joseph Bell in 1783, and, when perfected by the 1830s, raised productivity a hundredfold compared with earlier block-printing methods.

After the Industrial Revolution. By the 1830s, all stages in the manufacture of cotton cloth had been transformed. Cotton was now ginned mechanically, carded mechanically, spun on a mule or—less frequently—a water-frame, woven increasingly often on a power loom, whitened with bleaching powder, and roller-printed. There were both improvements to existing machinery designs and new machinery, but once mechanization had occurred and power had been applied, the subsequent rounds of innovation did not have the same dramatic effects as earlier ones. However, the cumulative productivity effects were not small. Improvements in the self-acting mule, for example, allowed each spinner to tend four times as many spindles in 1913 as in 1830. Similarly, the ring spindle, invented by John Thorp in 1828, and essentially a U.S. refinement of the water-frame, steadily improved and was an effective competitor to the mule in the last quarter of the nineteenth century and beyond. It used continuous rather than intermittent motion, simultaneously spinning the yarn and winding it onto bobbins. Compared with the mule, the ring had higher output per spindle per hour, and could be operated by unskilled workers, making it suited to industries using migrant labor, as in Japan, or immigrant labor, as in the United States.

If technological change in cloth production after 1830 was essentially a series of refinements, a breakthrough did occur in one area: sewing. By the end of the Industrial Revolution, the technology used to transform cloth into clothing had barely changed despite much work. By 1846, seventeen different machines had been produced in Britain, the United States, and continental Europe; all claimed to be able to sew mechanically and all were beset by technical problems. The year 1846 saw the patenting of the necessary breakthrough: not a machine, but a new stitch design. Instead of trying to mimic hand stitching, whereby the needle passes through the fabric, Elias Howe's lock stitch used two threads, one above the cloth and one below. The fabric is sewn by pushing the upper thread through the cloth, and intertwining it with the lower thread, a process far easier to mechanize than the traditional method. Although Howe built a successful sewing machine, Isaac Merritt Singer, founder of the eponymous sewing machine company, produced the first commercially successful machine. It had the advantage of being treadle (foot) powered, allowing the operative to use both hands to guide the cloth accurately. The earliest sewing machine raised productivity fivefold. Annual production of sewing machines rose from twenty-two hundred in 1853 to half a million in 1870; and, quite remarkably, the basic design remains unaltered to this day. Unlike most other inventions in cotton processing, the sewing machine did not require more power than the operative could readily supply; so it did not lead to factory production but was used in homes. Such an outcome should not be romanticized: home-based sweatshops offered conditions every bit as bad as those of early factories.

Technological Diffusion. After machinery has been invented, it must be accepted and diffused if it is to transform production. Historically there have been three major constraints on the adoption of technology. First, early inventor-manufacturers were not always happy to allow others access to their technology. Second, workers, fearful that new machinery would lead to work intensification for the few and unemployment for the many, might oppose new inventions. In some circumstances, governments have supported workers and hindered or banned new technologies. An opposing constraint is that a state might object to having other nations learn about its secrets, and might support diffusion within, but not beyond, the country.

Inventors' opposition to diffusion had limited effects in the eighteenth century, partly because the patent system was relatively weak. Kay was bankrupted by patent litigation, and both Hargreaves and Arkwright had their patents declared void in the courts. In any case, the patents of both Kay and Hargreaves would have been difficult to enforce because the flying shuttle and the jenny were used in homes, where they were difficult to observe. British inventors' problems were not unique: Whitney's patent was signed by George Washington, but wars over the patent even led to his arrest. Later on, governments recognized that inventors needed greater protection. Besides gradually improving the patent system, the British Parliament gave special grants to Crompton, who never patented the mule, and Cartwright, who lost his power-loom patent to a creditor; and the South Carolina legislature voted to pay Whitney fifty thousand dollars, an immense sum in his day.

The massive rise in output and employment in Lancashire meant that opposition from workers, although present, was never universal. Hargreaves's early jennies were smashed, and he moved from Lancashire to Nottingham, the home of the hosiery industry. Antimachinery feeling generally came to the fore during downturns. During the trade depression of 1779, machinery was attacked systematically, with rioters targeting the machinery they believed more suited to factory than home production. The army was used to suppress the riots. In 1780, spinners petitioned Parliament to ban mechanical spinning machines; but their petition, like all similar textile petitions, was denied. The downturn of 1826, which led to short-time working and cuts in piece rates, caused serious rioting, with over one thousand power looms destroyed in East Lancashire. The attitude of the state again proved uncompromising. Not only were forty-three individuals imprisoned or transported, but local communities were held collectively responsible and required to pay a special levy to fund the replacement of the looms. Thereafter, although there were many strikes about wages and conditions, including manning levels, steady gains in productivity makes it is hard to see the (often female-dominated) textile industry as a bastion of worker militancy against new machinery.

The British state unfailingly supported entrepreneurs. Laws against cloth made solely from cotton were rescinded after Arkwright's water-frame made such cloth technically possible; and, on occasion, grants were paid to textile machinery inventors by a grateful nation. In 1769, the willful destruction of machinery became punishable by death, and machinery breakers were dealt with severely. The state also took a role in protecting domestic industry, by trying to enforce laws against the migration of people and machinery. Emigration from Britain was severely restricted until 1824, and the export of machinery had a restrictive licensing system until 1843. These laws were reinforced by several factors: because Britain is an island, it was relatively easy to enforce such laws; Britain was at war with France and her allies for twenty-four years between 1780 and 1815; and there were tense times between Britain and the United States, culminating in war from 1812 to 1814. These events dramatically reduced the flow of emigrants. Finally, until the invention of interchangeable parts, machinery was harder to reproduce than it is now, not least because two halves of separate machines could not be made into a single machine. Similarly, early machinery was not easy to run; so a single emigrant able to operate a machine in Lancashire would find it hard to operate and still harder to repair or build such a machine elsewhere.

As news of Lancashire's success spread, many foreigners were keen to acquire British secrets. In time, both European and U.S. entrepreneurs were able to evade British laws aimed at preventing them from establishing their own textile industries. The two most celebrated information carriers were Samuel Slater and Francis Cabot Lowell. Drawn by a bounty, Slater evaded British emigration rules and became the first person to introduce Arkwright-style water-frames to the United States. Instead of trying to attract a knowledgeable emigrant, Francis Lowell visited Lancashire in 1810–1811; and his industrial espionage allowed him to have a power loom built on his return to the United States. As the separation between machinery makers and cotton processors became established around 1830, the machinery makers realized that their interests were best served by openness, in order to persuade both domestic and foreign firms that their newest machines really were improvements. Nations that developed after 1850, such as Russia, India, and Japan, were able to purchase the latest Lancashire machinery on equal terms, as firms in Lancashire and in these countries developed textile industries based on off-the-peg imported machinery, and often on imported technical personnel. These three countries used British machinery makers extensively, but Japan also imported ring spindles from the United States at the end of the nineteenth century, and, with the formation of the Toyoda loom works (the forerunner of today's Toyota car company), began to develop its own machinery-building sector.

BIBLIOGRAPHY

Copeland, Melvin Thomas. *The Cotton Manufacturing Industry of the United States.* Cambridge, Mass., 1923.

Chapman, S. D. *The Cotton Industry in the Industrial Revolution.* 2d ed. London, 1987.

Dublin, Thomas. *Lowell: The Story of an Industrial City*. Official National Park Handbook 140. Washington, D.C., 1992.

Jeremy, David J., "Lancashire and the International Diffusion of Technology." In *The Lancashire Cotton Industry: A History since 1700*, edited by Mary B. Rose, pp. 29–62. Preston, U.K., 1996.

Harley, C. Knick. "Cotton Textile Prices and the Industrial Revolution." *Economic History Review* 51.1 (1998), 49–83.

Hughes, Jonathan. *The Vital Few: The Entrepreneur and American Economic Progress*. Expanded ed. New York and Oxford, 1986.

Mokyr, Joel. *The Lever of Riches: Technological Creativity and Economic Progress*. New York, 1990.

Timmins, Geoffrey. "Technological Change." In *The Lancashire Cotton Industry: A History since 1700*, edited by Mary B. Rose, pp. 29–62. Preston, U.K., 1996.

TIMOTHY LEUNIG

Industrial Organization, Markets, and Trade

The expansion of cotton textile production has often been associated with industrialization and modernization, but cotton manufacture had a long history before the technological and organizational changes of the eighteenth and nineteenth centuries. "India," Thomas Ellison, an early historian of the British cotton textile industry, wrote, "is undoubtedly the birthplace of cotton manufacture. It is known from the sacred books of the country that the industry must have been in existence there, in a high state of perfection, three thousand years ago." Cotton manufacture could easily be transplanted from one region to another because the raw material was easily transported and because labor was the most important factor of production. Wages, during the heyday of industrialization, comprised about two-thirds of the conversion costs of turning raw cotton into yarn and cloth. However, low wages did not necessarily translate into industrial success on an international scale, and an effective industrial organization could offset high wages. With regard to demand, the production of yarn and woven goods was highly sensitive to price and income. Exploiting these changes in demand and supply, the industry has seen continuous migration—an unbroken thread in its history—and from very early on, regional industries faced global competition. "The Indian cotton tree," Ellison continued, "spread to Southern Europe and Northern Africa." By the middle of the sixteenth century, Germany and the Netherlands had established industries. Later in the century, Walloon and Dutch immigrants to Norwich and other towns introduced in Great Britain the manufacture of fustian, a mixture of linen and cotton, the latter being imported from the Middle East.

The Early Industry. Before the Industrial Revolution, India was the center of cotton textile production. The spinning wheel came to India with the Muslims and it raised productivity some sixfold in comparison with the handspindle. The numbers of weavers increased proportionally. Spinning was generally done by women in their homes and they sold their goods to weavers who were generally located in workshops. The industry had well-developed internal markets for raw cotton and overseas markets for finished products, consisting of a range of coarse and luxury goods. In Bengal, which specialized in very fine muslins, the bulk of the cotton used was imported from areas as distant as Gujarat. Mughal India was the largest supplier of cotton goods to the world, but exploiting the industry's long established networks, the Dutch and English came to control shipping and marketing, first to Europe and then elsewhere.

The Growth of British Industry. At the outset, the industry in Britain exploited rudimentary technologies, and productivity surpassed Indian levels only late in the eighteenth century. The early industry gravitated around London, the hub of the import and export trade as well the financial center. London manufacturers also mastered Indian techniques for printing fustians with bright-colored designs. Many of these fustians were woven in Lancashire where production, organized on a putting-out or domestic system, soon displaced the woolen industry. Under the domestic system, an entrepreneur or merchant, commonly a resident in Manchester, distributed raw materials, cotton and linen, to spinners and weavers in the countryside who owned their own equipment and who combined wage work with agricultural tasks. A sexual division of labor developed early, with women and children responsible for spinning and men for weaving. The system had its advantages: it gave entrepreneurs flexibility in production, starting or shutting down operations with variations in demand and fashion or the availability of raw materials. For workers, it enabled families to raise their earnings and break the traditional dependence of age of marriage and family size on the size and availability of agricultural land. At the outset, labor supply was cheap in the countryside, especially in comparison to the corporate controls of urban guilds.

An embryonic network of Lancashire-based commercial and financial resources was soon established around Manchester and Liverpool (the latter climbing in stature in maritime traffic from fifth to third place, after London and Newcastle, in the course of the eighteenth century). Over the following one hundred and fifty years, this network developed into an extremely sophisticated system of markets that facilitated and promoted contracts and exchanges outside firms and permitted small and specialized firms to survive, if not prosper, in the major branches of operation, spinning, weaving, and finishing. Exempted from the Calico Acts (1721), which prohibited the importation of printed fabrics from the East, and drawing on its pool of qualified domestic workers and commercial and financial networks, Lancashire entrepreneurs met the challenge of increased demand that resulted from the growing popularity of women's cotton dresses and plain cloths for men's wear in the mid- to late eighteenth century. These were imitations of Oriental imports from India. Such was the expansion of the domestic market in Great Britain that it consumed at least two-thirds of the industry's output at this time. exports were directed to Africa, Europe, and the West Indies. By 1800, Great Britain had replaced India as the largest supplier of cotton goods to the world.

It was the transition from the countryside to the factory that made Lancashire's development exceptional. Forced to cut prices in order to conserve and obtain further market share, Lancashire entrepreneurs were under constant pressure to reduce costs. The domestic system had its limitations: entrepreneurs could not easily monitor activities, and there was much waste of raw materials, in addition to the problem of embezzlement. It was easier to monitor activities and ensure steady production flows in a centralized unit of operation. Centralization did away with the middleman. Moreover, beginning in the 1770s, factory production took advantage of the lower costs of exploiting central power sources. There is much debate about whether the industry's move to the factory was technologically (tying new machinery to the central power source) or socially (employer's desire to control production and get a larger share of the profits by doing away with middlemen) determined, but the three major spinning innovations of the period between the 1760s and 1780s, Hargreaves's jenny, Arkrwright's water-frame, and Crompton's mule could all be hand operated. In fact, the jenny was operated only in hand workshops. The indeterminate relationship between technological change and changes in the organization of production was to be a recurrent feature of the Lancashire as well as the global industry.

Industrial Organization in Lancashire. Spinning was the first process to be housed in factories. The early factories, without past models to follow, were confronted with many organizational problems, particularly the recruiting of stable and disciplined workforces. How Lancashire resolved the labor problem impacted on the industry's organization. In the countryside, some mills recruited entire families and parish apprentices, mainly from the south of England. Urban mills relied more heavily on local sources. Alongside men, women initially operated spinning machinery, as they had done in the countryside, and children assisted in operations, such as mending or piecing broken threads. But after the French Wars, men began to dominate spinning operations, while women were relegated to such preliminary operations as cleaning cotton, or they became weavers outside the factory. The origins of the new sexual division of labor have been debated. One view is that women did not have the physical strength to push the carriage on the new and longer spinning mules. Others have argued that male spinners, who were not averse to using threats and punishments, were better supervisors of junior workers than women were. Still others have asserted that the early trade unions were able to block the entry of women into the profession. Whatever its origins, the new sexual division of labor was invented on the strong belief—as opposed to fact—that women did not have the set of skills required to spin.

To get work out, employers delegated authority on the mill floor to their spinners. There was a general lack of supervision in the new factories. To eliminate monitoring problems and to motivate workers, employers paid by the piece. Spinners, in turn, were responsible for paying their young assistants and piecers; they generally hired them as well. Spinners were also responsible for the maintenance of equipment and changing speeds of operation. This system of work organization was functioning well before 1850, and it became formalized after midcentury with the development of complicated regional pay or wage lists that stipulated earnings for spinning different counts (fineness) of yarn on mules of various sizes, operating at different speeds. These pay lists were the basis of negotiation between workers and employers, and, together with the system of work organization, became a cornerstone of the industry for more than one hundred years.

Throughout its history, the organization of the Lancashire industry was highly varied. Before 1850, there were rural mills, like the Gregs, mostly powered by water, that integrated spinning coarse yarn and weaving; there were large mills powered by steam in Manchester, like M'Connel and Kennedy, employing more than a thousand workers who spun very fine yarns; and there were smaller enterprises, employing at times between as few as fifty to as many as one hundred workers, in Oldham, spinning coarse yarn exclusively and sharing factory space and power sources. Technical change was much slower in weaving, and spinners would continue to put out their yarns to be woven. This gave textile production continued flexibility, and hand-loom weavers absorbed the brunt of most crises. When the transition to mechanical weaving was completed about 1850, the industrial map of Lancashire exhibited a high degree of specialization: weaving factories were mainly localized in northern and western regions, with the south and southeast remaining predominately spinning areas. Regional specialization complemented vertical specialization (or disintegration). Within the spinning region around Manchester, Oldham was known for its coarse yarns and Bolton for its fine counts. Even Lancashire's union structure, which matured after 1870, was noted for its regionalism and sectionalism.

The development of cotton and yarn markets in Liverpool and Manchester paralleled the growing trend to specialization. By midcentury there were nearly one hundred brokers in Liverpool, and the competitive nature of the cotton market approximated the economist's definition of a perfect market. Cotton (in order of importance) came from the United States, India, Egypt, and Brazil. While large spinning firms had their own agents in Great Britain and abroad, smaller spinners could rely upon yarn merchants or brokers to market their products. A regional transportation system moved coal, raw cotton, yarn, and finished goods by water and rail. With the establishment of a warehouse system, Manchester replaced London as the commercial and financial center of the industry. Every Tuesday, manufacturers and merchants met to transact business at the Royal Exchange, which one contemporary referred to as the "parliament house of the lords of cotton"; and with the completion of an intercontinental network of cables between 1870 and 1872, the city became the center of the world market. Alongside these networks, an engineering industry took root, whose leading manufacturer, Platt Brothers of Oldham, came to specialize in the production of self-acting mules for the home and foreign market, as well as ring-spinning machines, mainly for export. The network of industries drew the attention of Alfred Marshall, who in 1891 attributed the growth of the industry and the steady flow of innovations to the presence of external economies. These same economies meant that the average Lancashire firm remained small and specialized, a trend that probably quickened after 1850 or so. Family firms dominated, and it was only the Oldham (coarse spinning) region that erected new mills, using the principles of limited liability as set out in the Joint Stock Acts of 1855 and 1862. But despite these new sources of capital, even large Oldham firms remained vertically specialized.

The heyday of British industry was about 1870, although it continued to expand thereafter. At this juncture, the number employed in the industry, about 450,000, represented about 20 percent of Lancashire's population (but only about 4 percent of the U.K. labor force). Its factories housed roughly 55 percent of world spindleage (the actual peak was in 1877). Its export trade was diversified. About half of its exports in value terms were taken by four markets (21 percent by India, 9 percent by the United States, and about 7 percent by Turkey and by China separately). Indeed, the export market was expanding at midcentury. Exports as a percentage of total U.K. cotton consumption reached about 70 percent in 1870 (the actual summit was 80.5 percent in 1885), and the industry's share of world exports reached its peak of 80 percent in 1882.

Lancashire and India. Lancashire's expansion had repercussions for Indian industry, although whether the subcontinent "deindustrialized" remains a source of contention. On the eve of the colonial period, the Indian handicraft sector was large and modern factories employed a small share of the workforce into the 1920s. British firms took over the raw cotton trade to Europe and the Far East.

The loss of the export trade for finished goods was offset to some extent by the growth in domestic demand. That said, in the thirty-year period after 1850, around four million spinning and weaving jobs were lost in the subcontinent. Lancashire's imports and market organization drove down the price of Indian cloth, and pushed the handicraft sector into the low-quality end of the market. But the fear of Indian competition haunted British cotton manufacturers who pressured London to abolish the Indian tariff in 1882. In the face of these changes, a factory industry was established, centered in Bombay and Ahmedabad, based on available supply of cheap labor and run by local capitalists. Expansion was uneven. The Bombay industry was known for its labor troubles, disruptive work practices, and low levels of productivity, measured by low worker-to-spindle and worker-to-loom ratios. Like the British, Indian industry did not switch to rings—of more later—and in the interwar years could not match Japanese competition in their home market and abroad. On the eve of World War II, self-imposed rationalization, the fate of the British, was the only recourse for Indian industry.

Lancashire's Decline. Beginning in the 1880s, Lancashire faced competition from France and Germany in its continental markets (fine yarns) and from India and Japan (coarser fabrics) in Asia. It was competition from the cheap labor countries that posed the most serious threat to the British industry; but despite its high wage labor force, especially in spinning operations, Lancashire remained the industry leader into the interwar years. Notwithstanding its remarkable longevity as world leader, the industry's decline has been the subject of heated debate. The debate has focused most on causes as opposed to timing. An earlier generation of economic historians ascribed Lancashire's decline to entrepreneurial failure. Its enterprises remained too small, too specialized, too closely attached to traditional technologies, such as mule spinning and the Lancashire loom, and too dependent on recalcitrant trade unions. Entrepreneurs failed to adopt new technologies (ring spinning and the Northrop or automatic loom) or organizational models (large vertically integrated organizations) found elsewhere. Indeed, Lancashire was exceptional in its fierce attachment to specialized spinning and weaving operations.

Subsequent generations of economic historians have revisited these arguments. Lars Sandberg argued that British firms were rational in their choice of technique in comparison with those in the United States. Ring spinning, for a given count of yarn, required longer, more expensive raw cotton than did mules; however, for the same count, labor costs of ring and mule spinning were similar in both the United States and Great Britain. But as Great Britain had a greater supply of skilled spinners and since labor costs rose with count spun, it was appropriate that British firms

INDIAN COTTON INDUSTRY. Workers in a textile mill, Bombay (Mumbai), circa 1941. During World War II, 35 percent of India's annual cotton textile production, amounting to about 5,000,000,000 yards, went to into creating war materials for India and the United Nations. (Prints and Photographs Division, Library of Congress)

stuck with mules above a certain threshold, generally taken to be medium counts. This line of argument posed as many questions at it resolved. For counts below the threshold, why did Lancashire firms still show a preference for mule spinning? Were there any advantages lost from not integrating operations? And why did Lancashire fail to specialize to a greater degree in fine yarns—markets less exposed to foreign competition from cheap labor countries?

William Lazonick sought an explanation of the persistence of the mule, even for low counts of yarn, in the interaction between the system of industrial relations and the organization of cotton and yarn markets in Lancashire. The mule was less likely than rings to break thread spun from inferior grades of cotton, and it was precisely this type of cotton that manufacturers could purchase cheaply and on short notice on the Liverpool exchange. The system of industrial relations in place was compatible with spinning poor grades of cotton. Managers motivated spinners to get more effort out. Despite more yarn breakages, spinners desired to maintain their level of earnings. Spinners, in turn, could coax more effort from their assistants, who generally were paid by the day or week. With regard to industrial organization, Lazonick attributed the perseverance of specialized mule-spinning operations to the fact that ring yarn had to be transported to the loom on heavy wooden bobbins and then returned. These distances were

not insubstantial as a result of the industry's history of regional specialization and because these divisions were reinforced by the wage lists. Thus regional specialization implied that Lancashire could not take advantage of the technical complementarities of operating rings and automatic looms under one roof.

Lazonick's insights have helped to establish the current research agenda for a new generation of economic historians. Lazonick's research was based on industrywide studies; new work such as that of J. S. Toms, on the histories of individual firms, has found that specialized mule-spinning firms were as profitable, if not more so, than vertically integrated ring-spinning outfits. Still other studies, for example by Timothy Leunig, have tried to measure the actual distances between spinning and weaving operations; this research has shown that distance was not a constraint on vertical integration. Technical complementarities that existed between the ring spindle and the automatic loom were not sufficient to demand coordinated introduction of both machines in the same unit of operation. In all, technical choice was independent of industrial organization.

The decline in the interwar period was dramatic. In 1938, output and employment levels were about half that of those in 1913, while Lancashire's share of international trade in cotton cloth declined to about 25 percent. There was agreement that Lancashire's dependence on a restricted number of poor countries for exports was a source of its problems. India alone absorbed about 80 percent of British exports in 1913. When India was granted tariff autonomy in 1919, the decline in exports and profits was rapid. The responses of workers, firms, and government authorities have all been questioned. The sectional nature and interests of trade unions made a common response by organized labor difficult to obtain. Employers in the Yarn Association formed in the late 1920s tried to maintain prices by fixing production quotas, but as John Maynard Keynes and others noted, this only encouraged inefficient firms to survive. Many other firms opted out. As for central authorities, when the Bank of England formed the Lancashire Cotton Corporation in 1928, it did so to save the Lancashire banking system rather than rationalize the industrial structure. It became apparent that a central organization was necessary to *sauve qui peut*, but a joint committee of employers, merchants, and trade unionists had limited powers. It took years for the industry to agree on proposals that were eventually set out in the Cotton Spinning Industry Act of 1936 (a scheme to buy obsolete spinning equipment) and the Cotton Industry Reorganization Act of 1939, which set up schemes to fix prices and set quotas. But it was too little and too late. In the end, it was Lancashire's hubris—the fierce independence of workers and firms, the very source of its initial success—which led to its demise.

The Cotton Textile Industry around the World. In comparing the British cotton industry with developments elsewhere, differences would appear to outweigh similarities. There was no fixed relationship between technology and industrial organization (specialized or integrated units of operation), and no necessary relationship between technology and the number and type of labor inputs and their effort levels. This line of study is most closely associated with the work of Gary Saxonhouse and Gavin Wright.

The origins of the U.S. industry are traced to Samuel Slater, a former overseer in an English mill, who in the late eighteenth century re-created from memory—the export of technology and skilled artisans was banned in Great Britain until 1843—Arkwright's spinning machine. From the outset, the New England industry was protected, and there is little evidence that the U.S. industry could compete abroad. Even as late as 1910, only a little more than 5 percent of U.S. cotton cloth was exported. Still, the growth of the U.S. industry was impressive. By 1900, the U.S. industry consumed more cotton than the British, although the latter had twice as many spindles.

The early mills, such as at Waltham founded in 1814 by Francis Cabot Lowell, were large and vertically integrated, and, unlike the British example, used power looms. These types of mills specialized in highly standardized coarse yarn and cloth, and because throstles, the predecessor to ring spinning, were used in preference to mules, production was continuous. Again, unlike the British model, the labor supply in the Waltham-Lowell system was composed of young women who lived in company houses or dormitories. By midcentury, a family-based approach to labor recruitment (the Rhode Island system) had become widespread in mill towns in Connecticut and southern Massachusetts, such as Fall River. Many of the immigrants to these towns were skilled spinners from Great Britain who found work due to the rapid expansion of mule-spinning capacity after the Civil War. But unlike the British model, American management retained complete control of the work organization, the functions of the American spinner more closely resembling the senior piecer in Lancashire. New England manufacturers survived, despite the alternative of cheap labor locales in the south, because they continuously broadened the scope of labor recruitment. U.S. manufacturers were always integrated (thus they had no transportation costs of moving yarn), and given the availability of high-quality raw cotton, they quickly took advantage of technical improvements in ring frames, specifically the development of the high-speed Sawyer-Rabbeth spindle. Moreover, American mule spinners, renowned for their mobility, were relatively scarce. New mule machinery was rarely installed during the merger movement at the turn of the century.

The expansion of textile mills in the southern states from the 1870s was based on a labor supply composed of families. Because the labor force was unskilled and manufactured low-count yarns in integrated mills, mules were very rare in the southern branch of the U.S. industry. Ring-frame spinners were predominately female, but in an attempt to raise the experience levels of its workers and hence productivity, older men were used in many of the other semiskilled machine-tending jobs in cotton preparation, weaving, and dyeing. Thus an entirely different sexual division of labor was fashioned in the South as compared with Britain and New England.

The Japanese industry, a latecomer in comparison with the United States and Great Britain, provides a third model of development. Its rate of growth was rapid. By the interwar years, it was Lancashire's main rival. The turning point was 1933, when it became the world leader in exports of cotton goods. Japan's success was based on imitation and innovation. Mules imported from Lancashire were well fitted to the initial organization of the industry in the 1870s and 1880s. Japan grew short-stapled, poor-quality cotton suitable for coarse spinning on mules and, as in Lancashire, weavers were geographically dispersed. But when Japan began to import slightly higher-quality Chinese and Indian cottons, manufacturers moved over to ring frames. By 1890 or so, the use of rings was nearly universal. The Japanese industry was unique in its almost complete reliance on young women workers (more than 80 percent in certain establishments) who were recruited from farms to live in dormitories and to work for short periods prior to marriage. Labor was a partial substitute for capital. Inexperienced workers operated fewer ring spindles than elsewhere, although they were run at very fast speeds.

The organization of the industry was oligopolistic and there was a wave of mergers at the turn of the century. Vertical integration was less common than in the United States, because large firms were dependent on agents both to purchase raw material and to market their yarn. Still other firms set up in weaving districts to reduce costs of transporting wooden bobbins. Cloth was marketed by giant trading companies that secured large orders and long runs of export output; by 1900, the China market was captured from India. Large Japanese firms built up centralized organizations, and many Osaka spinning companies employed university-educated engineers. There was an emphasis on research and development in the blending of raw cottons, the standardization of yarn, and in marketing. Personnel decisions were also centralized. This penchant for research and development was also manifested in the development of an indigenous textile technology, following the prior examples both of Great Britain and the United States. In Japan, the key innovations came from the enterprises of Sakichi Toyoda, who pioneered the development of an inexpensive but productive power loom that small weaving firms could use instead of either the hand loom or the expensive power loom imported from Platt Brothers of Oldham. Spinning companies, trading companies, and engineering firms all shared in the costs of research in perfecting the power loom. As a result, the Japanese cotton industry, unlike its U.S. and British rivals, remained competitive with lower wage industries in Asia into the 1980s.

Concluding Observations. The evidence from the cotton industry gives credence to the view that there is more than one way to industrialize. Technological choice was not determined by industrial organization, or vice versa. Across time, there was no tendency for one type of organization to dominate. Across space, different types of workers performed the same functions. Cheap labor was not a guarantee of success. India, despite its tradition of textile production and the fact that its wages in the interwar years were roughly 25 percent of those in Great Britain and 75 percent of those in Japan, failed to compete on a international scale. The upshot is that Great Britain and Japan maintained their superiority over long periods of time because they combined different types of industrial and work organizations to offset the disadvantages of high wages and low-quality raw cottons.

BIBLIOGRAPHY

Chapman, Stanley D. "Financial Restraints on the Growth of Firms in the Cotton Industry, 1790–1850." *Economic History Review* 32.1 (1979), 50–69.

Clark, Greg. "Why Isn't the Whole World Developed? Lessons from the Cotton Mills." *Journal of Economic History* 54.1 (1987), 134–167. Shows that manning levels varied with wage levels across countries.

Copeland, Melvin Thomas. *The Cotton Industry of the United States.* Cambridge, Mass., 1912.

Ellison, Thomas. *The Cotton Trade of Great Britain.* London, 1886; reprinted 1968. A good contemporary study of the strengths and weakness of British industry.

Farnie, Douglas A. *The English Cotton Industry and the World Market, 1815–1896.* Clarendon Press, 1979. The best work in the field, especially on industrial organization and markets.

Farnie, Douglas A., and Shin'ichi Yonekawa. "The Emergence of the Large Firm in the Cotton Spinning Industries of the World, 1883–1938." *Textiles History* 19.2 (1988), 171–210.

Huberman, Michael. *Escape from the Market: Negotiating Work in Lancashire.* Cambridge and New York, 1996. A study of labor recruitment, wage incentives, and industrial organization during the key years of industrialization.

Lazonick, William. *Competitive Advantage on the Shop Floor.* Cambridge, Mass., 1990. A synthesis of the author's studies of the interaction between industrial relations, industrial organization, and technical choice in the British and U.S. industries, with emphasis on the former.

Lazonick, William. "The Cotton Industry." In *The Decline of the British Economy,* edited by Bernard Elbaum and William Lazonick, pp.18–51. Oxford, 1986.

Leunig, Timothy. "New Answers to Old Questions: Explaining the Slow Adoption of Ring Spinning in Lancashire, 1880–1913." *Journal of Economic History* 61.2 (2001), 439–466.

Mass, William, and William Lazonick. "The British Cotton Industry and International Competitive Advantage: The State of the Debates." *Business History* 32.4 (1990), 9–65.

Metha, M. J. *The Ahmedabad Cotton Textile Industry: Genesis and Growth.* Ahmedabad, 1982.

Patel, Sujatha. *The Making of Industrial Relations: The Ahmedabad Textile Industry, 1918–1939.* Delhi, 1987.

Rose, Mary B., ed. *The Lancashire Cotton Industry: A History since 1700.* Preston, U.K., 1996. A collection of articles on all aspects of Lancashire's rise and decline, especially strong on origins and foreign competition, but weaker on labor aspects and working conditions.

Rose, Mary B. *Firms, Networks and Business Values: The British and American Cotton Industries since 1750.* Cambridge and New York, 2000.

Rose, Sonya O. *Limited Livelihoods: Gender and Class in Nineteenth-Century England.* Berkeley, 1992.

Sandberg, Lars G. *Lancashire in Decline: A Study in Entrepreneurship, Technology, and International Trade.* Columbus, Ohio, 1974.

Saxonhouse, Gary R., and Gavin Wright. "New Evidence on the Stubborn English Mule and the Cotton Industry, 1878–1920." *Economic History Review* 37.4 (1984), 507–519.

Saxonhouse, Gary R., and Gavin Wright. "Two Forms of Cheap Labor in Textile History." In *Technique, Spirit, and Form in Making of the Modern Economies: Essays in Honor of William N. Parker. Research in Economic History.* Supplement 3 (1984), 3–31.

Toms, J. S. "Growth, Profits, and Technological Change: The Case of the Lancashire Cotton Textile Industry." *Journal of Industrial History* 1.1 (1998), 35–55.

Twomey, Michael J. "Employment in Nineteenth Century Indian Textiles." *Explorations in Economic History* 20.1 (1983), 37–57.

Wright, Gavin. *Old South, New South.* New York, 1986.

MICHAEL HUBERMAN

COURTAULD FAMILY, English textile entrepreneurs. Samuel Courtauld (1793–1881) established the firm that became Samuel Courtauld & Co. in 1816. By 1850, it was the foremost British producer of black mourning crepe, a type of silk cloth that had become fashionable for middle- and upper-class Englishwomen to wear after the death of a relative. The firm's success in its production was the result of both innovation and good fortune: booming demand; the rural Essex location of the mills, which provided the firm with a cheap, abundant labor supply; development of a proprietary technology involving machinery specifically adapted to the needs of crepe production; and a sharp fall in raw silk prices after the late 1860s.

After Samuel's death in 1881, Courtaulds fell into a brief but sharp period of decline. In response, the directors in 1893 hired Henry G. Tetley (1851–1921), an outsider who was charged with reorganizing the manufacturing side of the business. Tetley, in turn, brought with him a new sales manager, Thomas Latham (1855–1931). Initially, the two moved the firm away from its strict focus on black crepe, broadening the product line to include more fashionable colored-silk fabrics. Although these changes put the firm out of its immediate danger, it soon became clear that they were not enough to completely revive its fortunes.

Thus, in 1904, Tetley and Latham convinced a majority of the Courtaulds board to purchase the British patent rights to the new viscose process for making "artificial silk," or rayon, a fiber produced by chemically treating and spinning wood pulp. This move transformed the firm into an industrial giant. Courtaulds became the largest rayon producer, responsible for 40 percent of world output by 1918. Success in the commercialization of rayon can be attributed to the fact that Courtaulds was the only competitor with any experience in textiles. The firm was able to exploit know-how in textile production to develop the only type of mass-producible rayon yarn suitable for cloth weaving and hosiery knitting, while leveraging its expertise in textile marketing to sell the new product to a potentially vast market of cloth manufacturers. Another factor was the patent, which allowed Latham to charge monopoly prices in Great Britain, and later in the United States, after the American patent rights were acquired in 1909.

Samuel Courtauld (1876–1947), a nephew of the firm's patriarch, assumed control of the firm in 1921 upon the retirement of Tetley. He presided over a period of stagnation in the firm's fortunes, punctuated by the forced sale of the highly profitable American subsidiary in 1941. Unlike his predecessors, his managerial style was cautious; he preferred cooperation and conciliation to aggressive competition, but his policies lacked dynamism. Although (or perhaps because) the firm was still profitable, not until the late 1930s did Samuel realize how far it had fallen behind in research and development, the extent to which middle ranks of management were understaffed, or the degree of obsolescence and inefficiency of shop-floor organization. He failed to appreciate quickly enough the changes that were needed to overcome the limits to growth of what was still, essentially, a family-run enterprise. As a result, Courtaulds was slower than its competitors to improve existing production processes or to commercialize new products, such as cellophane.

After the mid-1950s, when profitability finally began to suffer so much that continued survival was in question, the firm diversified into paint manufacture and packaging; acquired rival firms, including its main domestic competitor, British Celanese; and developed the "Courtelle" acrylic fiber. During the 1960s, a new managerial regime took control of the company and implemented a strategy of vertical integration through acquisition of textile manufacturing and distribution companies. In the 1990s, the firm spun off its textile businesses into a new enterprise, Courtaulds Textiles, and subsequently the Dutch firm Akzo Nobel acquired the chemicals and other nontextile businesses. Thus, at the dawn of the twenty-first century the firm had returned to its nineteenth-century roots in textiles.

BIBLIOGRAPHY

Chandler, Alfred D., Jr. *Scale and Scope: The Dynamics of Industrial Capitalism.* Cambridge, Mass., 1990.

Coleman, D. C. *Courtaulds: An Economic and Social History.* 3 vols. Oxford, 1969, 1980.

Knight, Arthur. *Private Enterprise and Public Intervention: The Courtaulds Experience.* London, 1974.

THOMAS GERAGHTY

CRAFT GUILDS. Although there is no direct evidence for the existence of associations of trader-craftsmen distinguished by occupation in ancient Mesopotamia and Egypt and in pre-Hellenistic Greece, they are well documented in the urban economies of medieval and early-modern China, Japan, India, Islamic countries, and Europe. Most drew on de facto or fictive bonds of kinship based on clan, caste, or religious belief, identified with specific towns or regions rather than occupations, and operated under strong political supervision. Although guilds outside Europe are poorly documented, their purpose appears to have been mainly social and religious rather than economic. The same applies to the ancient Greek and Roman guilds or clubs (*collegia, sodalitates*), attested during the Hellenistic and late Republican eras (third to first centuries BCE). Placed under state control during the early imperial era (first century BCE to first century CE), these guilds had turned a century later into closed, hereditary institutions, and had disappeared from the western empire by the late fourth century CE; but they survived in Byzantine Constantinople and persisted as Christian institutions under state supervision in the western part of the Ottoman Empire.

Guilds of manual craftsmen based in family-owned workshops reappeared around 1100 CE in the most urbanized regions of Italy, the Rhineland, and the Low Countries and spread quickly across western Europe. Medieval and early modern (premodern) European craft guilds differed profoundly from their Asian, Islamic, and classical namesakes, and were in many ways unique. Bonds of association were individualistic and voluntary, guild membership was optional rather than prescriptive, craft guilds from different cities were not allowed to amalgamate, and the majority of craft guilds were self-governed and politically independent. They were "bottom-up," autonomous associations that negotiated with the state for public recognition but never became mere tools of public authority. Crafts were associations of employers rather than of workers. Active membership was restricted to the shop-owning masters, but apprentices and salaried journeymen were subject to craft discipline and compelled to swear loyalty to the craft constitution.

Medieval European crafts emerged in response to resurgent trade and manufactures, and to growing demand for skilled workers within an increasingly receptive legal and political context. Improved access to public-law courts reduced the costs of contracting and hastened the growth of free labor markets in which employment could be rescinded at will; fragmented and competitive feudal power proved ideally suited to the development of free, individual associations based on a hybrid of Roman law and Germanic custom. Faced with medieval rulers' inability to assert full authority, craft guilds produced an independent corpus of legal thought to underpin claims to be quasi-autonomous, corporate bodies. They were most successful where public authority was more contested, as in northern Italy, German-speaking Europe, the Low Countries, and southern France; whereas they developed more slowly and tentatively in more politically centralized regions such as the Iberian Peninsula and southern Italy (which forbade craft guilds by law before the fifteenth century), Scandinavia, and England.

The historiography on guilds is divided into two phases. Nineteenth- and early-twentieth-century historians followed the eighteenth-century French Physiocrat Turgot and the Scottish political economist Adam Smith in portraying premodern crafts as archaic institutions that imposed irrational or self-serving fetters on competitive markets. This early hostility was reinforced with the adoption by the German National Socialist and Italian Fascist regimes of guild-inspired corporatist policies in the 1920s and 1930s. Whereas historians of this period relied on normative and prescriptive sources and emphasized the reasons for the guilds' decline, the social historians who rediscovered the guilds in the 1980s focused instead on the reasons for the craft guilds' extraordinary longevity, and

challenged the effectiveness of craft regulations by examining day-to-day practice. Similarly, economic historians now emphasize the craft guilds' competitive success rather than their weaknesses, although they generally persist in viewing the crafts as self-contained "firms" and pay less attention than social historians to the political, legal, and market context of craft actions.

Recent interpretations suggest that crafts responded to information asymmetries in thin markets with high transaction costs. Craft guilds mediated between members with market power and negotiated with powerful merchants; they supplied members with financial support and cheap credit; they enforced quality standards and fixed prices to reduce information asymmetries, particularly in foreign markets; and they protected members from exploitation by opportunistic urban elites. However, these explanations face two difficulties. First, they fail to consider that craft guilds did not offer the only or the most efficient solution to such problems. Price comparison was achieved by clustering craft shops; quality control was supervised by town authorities and merchant exporters; income volatility was reduced through a combination of religious associations, kinship networks, urban provisioning structures, and state "poor laws"; and credit was widely available through similar formal and informal sources. These and other benefits of membership also fail to explain why crafts enforced compulsory membership.

The second difficulty with these explanations is that none of the preceding features was present universally among premodern craft guilds. The only such feature that was both unique and universal was apprenticeship, whose main purpose was to transmit artisan skills and activities. Enforcement of apprenticeship rules explains most of the known features of craft guilds. Contracts were enforced to impede masters or apprentices from cheating (defaulting). Compulsory craft membership stopped nonmembers from free riding by sharing the benefits of skilled labor without incurring the training costs. Membership fees and fines for misbehavior (except for poaching of apprentices) were kept low, indicating that crafts were concerned with keeping members in rather than out. Quality enforcement, credit provision, welfare support, and other benefits were ways to attract membership and raise the opportunity costs of defection. This was necessary because opportunities for free riding were considerable (most guilds, particularly in larger cities, lacked the administrative and legal resources to police themselves effectively), and because guild jurisdiction did not extend over many church and feudal "freedoms" within the city walls and in the suburbs outside them.

The crafts' role as political and economic cartels is among their most controversial but least researched features. Guild political activities are hard to evaluate

CRAFT GUILD. Sign of the shoemakers' guild of Nuremberg, Germany, 1600. Restored in 1786. (Germanisches Nationalmuseum, Nuremberg, Germany/Scala/Art Resource, NY)

because they were affected by a variety of factors, including the status of independent guild members, the weight of the craft within a town, the competing pressures of merchants and rival guilds, and the balance of power between local and territorial authorities. Nonetheless, the more extreme criticisms appear overstated, for craft privileges were revocable, and few crafts achieved significant and lasting power. Before the eighteenth century, the correlation between craft density and industrial retardation is poor. Urban manufacture was underdeveloped in Castile and southern Italy, where craft guilds were weakest, and was most successful in northern Italy, central Europe, and the Low Countries, where crafts were most numerous and institutionally entrenched.

Similar doubts apply to craft monopolies in product markets. Evidence here is largely restricted to guilds producing for local markets in the twelfth and thirteenth centuries when "official" prices were posted. However, these postings were probably a solution to high price volatility caused by thin markets with few and irregular transactions, and disappeared during the later Middle Ages when product markets became better integrated. Craft monopsonies are also more likely to have been exerted over local rather than imported inputs, which were normally controlled by large-scale merchants, and by supply trades (especially of foodstuffs) rather than by manufacturing ones; but once more there is little hard evidence of such practices. From the fourteenth century on, urban governments became increasingly hostile toward forms of price collusion that might penalize consumers; and after 1500 most public comment on the matter died away, indicating that it was no longer viewed as a significant political issue. Cartel-like actions were in greater evidence in reducing capacity during trade recessions than during prosperity, but restrictions were generally ineffective in the more export-led and dynamic industries.

Evidence that guilds deliberately and systematically stifled innovation is equally ambiguous. The craft master was at the same time an employer, foreman, and skilled workman, a buyer of raw materials and intermediate goods, and a seller of finished products; he thus faced competition across different markets toward which no consistent strategy applied. Masters were limited in the number of apprentices they could employ, but these restrictions were often flaunted, and limits to the number of waged journeymen were far looser than limits on apprentices; such flexibility produced significant differences in firm size and artisan wealth. Craft regulations enforced by official "searches" were aimed at upholding quality standards by forbidding night work and the use of inferior materials, and left the production process unregulated. The existence of guilds—masons, stonecutters, goldsmiths, woodcutters, and painters—in Renaissance Italy, Germany, and the Low Countries suggests that the guild system did not stifle individual initiative or have a leveling effect on originality.

It is often unclear whether craft opposition to technological innovation was motivated by rent seeking or by a rational assessment of the innovation's value. Late-thirteenth-century cloth makers refused to adopt fulling mills because the early machines damaged better-quality fabrics, but opposition melted away once the mills were improved. As Reinhold Reith has demonstrated, other oft-cited evidence of craft Luddism in early modern central Europe is based on a misreading of the sources. In principle, crafts opposed capital-intensive innovations that devalued investments in current skills and reduced incentives to invest in new ones; in practice, technical choices were dictated as much by political as by economic criteria. Craft guilds generally lacked the authority to stop innovations completely, in part because members pursued conflicting agendas. Opposition to labor-saving innovations was greater among poorer craftsmen than among wealthier artisans, who stood to gain from capital-intensive change. Innovation thus depended on the balance of forces between these groups and on support from the political authorities; although the latter normally sided with the wealthier and more innovative masters, they backed the smaller craftsmen when labor-saving innovations coincided with a major economic downturn. From the seventeenth century on, however, continental European states increasingly allied themselves with merchant exporters, who tended to be technologically conservative in order to protect established foreign markets. In England, by contrast, political support for craft guilds and craft-based production waned after the Civil War (1640–1648), making restrictive legislation more difficult to enforce.

The overall technological contribution of craft guilds appears to have been largely positive. One kind of innovation came from the clustering of artisan shops in towns and "industrial districts," which produced positive organizational and technological externalities. Another came from technological cross-fertilization caused by temporary and permanent migration. Increasingly, after the Protestant Reformation, military and economic competition between states fostered technological diffusion. Artisans from the most technologically advanced cities were attracted by financial and legal inducements, and, if necessary, protection from guild obstruction, although most migrants found themselves in guilds where they could impart their techniques to other skilled workers. Traveling journeymen also were important carriers of technical innovation although they were less likely to cross major linguistic and cultural boundaries than emigrant artisans. The third and least analyzed source of innovation was the protection (equivalent to a patent) that crafts offered members who invented a technical "secret," in the expectation that other masters would sooner or later pick up any significant breakthroughs.

Craft guilds remained the main manufacturing organization in premodern Europe up to the eighteenth century. They were never seriously challenged by rival industrial organizations such as rural putting-out and centralized factories, and they influenced informal craft associations such as the French *confrèries* and the Iberian *hermandades* profoundly. The crafts' final demise occurred by political decrees, in France (1791, after a failed attempt in 1768), Rome (1807), England (1835), Spain (1840), Austria (1859), Italy (1864) and Germany (1869). Whereas legal abolition in England occurred long after the craft guilds' de facto decline, abolition in continental Europe was part of a wider attack by national states on jurisdictional particularism. Couched by reformers as a struggle between modern economic efficiency and premodern communitarian justice, the process established the terms of historical debate up to this day. The question of whether industrial capitalism would have brought about the craft guilds' natural demise or abolition was a politically motivated attack against premodern corporatist separatism has still to be answered satisfactorily; but the fact that the most central element of the premodern craft guild, apprenticeship, has remained an important feature of most modern European societies suggests that the crafts did not die simply of functional obsolescence.

[*See also* Apprenticeship; Corporatism; Journeymen; *and* Merchant Guilds.]

BIBLIOGRAPHY

Black, Antony. *Guilds and Civil Society in European Political Thought from the Twelfth Century to the Present*. London,1984. An important study of the relationship between guild and corporate values and political thought and the state, which shows the Enlightenment origins of modern theories of craft guilds.

Bossenga, Gail. "Protecting Merchants: Guilds and Commercial Capitalism in Eighteenth-Century France." *French Historical Studies* 15 (1989), 693–703. Discussion of how the eighteenth-century French state allied with the merchants to bring autonomous export-led crafts to heel.

Cracco-Ruggini, L. "Le associazioni professionali nel mondo romano-bizantino." In *Artigianato e tecnica nella società dell'Alto medioevo occidentale*, pp. 215–245. Spoleto, 1971. An overview of craft associations in the Roman and Byzantine empires that stresses their lack of economic aims.

Epstein, Steven. *Wage Labor and Guilds in Medieval Europe*. Chapel Hill and London, 1991. An informative survey of medieval craft guilds focused on southern Europe.

Epstein, S. R. "Craft Guilds, Apprenticeship, and Technological Change in Preindustrial Europe." *Journal of Economic History* 53.4

(1998), 684–718. An interpretation of craft guilds in the light of their contribution to skills training and technological progress.

Farr, James R. *Artisans in Europe, 1300–1914.* Cambridge, 2000. A textbook survey mainly of north-central Europe after 1500, with extensive bibliographies.

Gustafsson, Bo. "The Rise and Economic Behaviour of Medieval Craft Guilds." In *Power and Economic Institutions*, edited by Bo Gustafsson, pp. 69–106. Aldershot, U.K., 1991. A discussion of the enforcement of quality standards.

Hickson, C. R., and E. A. Thompson. "A New Theory of Guilds and European Economic Development." *Explorations in Economic History* 28.1 (1991), 127–168. A wide-ranging discussion of the political context of craft activities, which argues that they protected members from excessive taxation by urban elites but fails to consider why crafts required compulsory membership to do so.

Howell, Martha C. "Achieving the Guild Effect without Guilds: Crafts and Craftsmen in Late Medieval Douai." In *Les métiers au Moyen Âge*, edited by P. Lambrechts and J.-P. Sosson, pp. 109–128. Louvain-la-Neuve, 1994. A discussion of a city exporting high-quality cloth that lacked formal craft guilds to enforce standards.

Jain, B. *Guild Organization in Northern India (from Earliest Times to 1200 AD).* Delhi, 1990. A survey of northern Indian craft associations that also applies to southern India.

Kaplan, Steven. "Les corporations, les 'faux ouvriers' et le faubourg Saint-Antoine au XVIIIe siècle." *Annales: Economies, Sociétés, Civilisations* 43.2 (1988), 353–378. A seminal study of how craftsmen living in Parisian jurisdictional "freedoms" evaded control by the guilds but benefited from their activities.

Mickwitz, G. *Die Kartellfunktionen der Zünfte und ihre Bedeutung bei der Entstehung des Zunftwesens.* Helsinki, 1936. A much-cited analysis of the cartel-like functions of medieval craft guilds.

Raymond, A. "Şinf." In *Encyclopedia of Islam*, vol. 9, 2d ed., edited by C. E. Bosworth, E. van Donzel, W. P. Heinrichs, and G. Le Comte, pp. 644–646. Leiden, 1997. An article that emphasizes the absence in Islamic law of corporate bodies analogous to European guilds.

Reith, Reinhold. "Technische Innovationen im Handwerk der frühen Neuzeit? Traditionen, Probleme und Perspektiven der Forschung." In *Stadt und Handwerk in Mittelalter und früher Neuzeit*, edited by K. H. Kaufhold and W. Reininghaus, pp. 21–60. Cologne, 2000. An important survey of the German literature on early modern crafts and technological innovation.

Sonenscher, Michael. *Work and Wages: Natural Law, Politics and the Eighteenth-Century French Trades.* Cambridge, 1989. The first modern study to use court and individual records to examine guild activities in practice.

Thrupp, Sylvia L. "The Gilds." In *Cambridge Economic History of Europe*, vol. 3, *Economic Organization and Policies in the Middle Ages*, edited by M. M. Postan, E. E. Rich, and E. Miller, pp. 230–280. Cambridge, 1963. Still the best survey of medieval European guilds. Deeply sceptical of traditional criticisms of the craft guilds, it is much cited but little read.

S. R. EPSTEIN

CREDIT COOPERATIVES. Credit cooperatives (or cooperative banks) are mutual organizations that provide banking services to their members and others. First formed in the mid-nineteenth century in Europe, cooperatives have spread to most of the world. In some countries very large cooperatives comprise important parts of the financial system. This article pays particular attention to the origins and development of cooperative credit in Germany because the modern movement arose there, and most of the main issues in cooperative organization are evident in the German system.

Most modern credit cooperatives owe their inspiration to two Germans, Hermann Schulze-Delitzsch (1808–1883) and Friedrich Wilhelm Raiffeisen (1818–1888). In Germany, as elsewhere, credit cooperatives were part of a larger cooperative movement that included consumer cooperatives and purchasing and marketing cooperatives. Schulze-Delitzsch's cooperatives were primarily urban and focused on artisans, handworkers, and small shopkeepers. Raiffeisen's cooperatives were primarily rural and included farmers, farm laborers, and others who lived in small towns and villages. Schulze-Delitzsch saw his movement as serving to develop a middle class, whereas Raiffeisen stressed assistance to the poor; and the membership of their cooperatives reflects this difference. Schulze-Delitzsch and Raiffeisen differed on many details of organizational design such as liability structure, payment of staff, and size of the institution. Over time these organizational differences became less pronounced, and the national organizations merged in the early twentieth century.

Credit cooperatives typically have a structure that allows democratic control over major policy decisions and the selection of leadership. Some cooperatives adhere to a strict policy of one member, one vote; others allow those who have made a greater capital contribution a larger voice. Beyond this basic definition, however, organizational details of cooperatives differ considerably across time and place. Some have restricted their loans to members, but today many do not. Most fund their loans both with shares purchased by members and with deposits from members and nonmembers, but the source of capital varies across institutions. In some places credit cooperatives stress service to particular occupations (such as farmers); in others they strive to serve entire communities. In some countries cooperatives are taxed; others, such as those in the United States, do not pay taxes but in return are limited in their membership and activities.

Reasons for Credit Cooperatives. Credit cooperatives have thrived in many economic and social contexts, including some (such as nineteenth-century Germany) that have had highly developed formal banking systems. Just how small institutions such as credit cooperatives can compete with large banks is the implicit question underlying much recent research, on credit markets generally and on credit cooperatives in particular. Most scholars argue that cooperatives are not competing with banks, but are serving a market that for-profit financial intermediaries either ignore or serve only partially. Recent research on the economics of information and contracts in credit markets has shown why cooperatives can thrive while lending to people who are not profitable bank customers. Successful lending requires a great deal of information on potential borrowers and the projects they seek to fund, as well as low-cost ways to enforce repayment of loans. Information on poor people often is expensive for a formal lender to acquire because of social or geographic distance, lack of formal record-keeping, and so on. Similarly, the costs of recourse to the legal system to compel repayment of very small loans can be high relative to loan size. Thus it is too costly for many for-profit financial intermediaries to lend to some groups of people. The cooperative succeeds because the information required for it to lend successfully is available to it at a low cost or even for free. The cooperative's members and depositors live in the same community as the potential borrowers, often for their entire lifetimes, and so know the borrowers well. The cooperatives draw on local information and ties through what is often called peer monitoring. Enforcement in this context can rely on low-cost sanctions, both economic and extra-economic.

This understanding of credit markets and the rationale for cooperative credit is implicit in the writings of both Schulze-Delitzsch and Raiffeisen. They saw poor people turning to moneylenders and others whose interest rates were very high and whose methods could lead to the loss of cattle, tools, or other valuable equipment necessary to generate income. Both thought that a small, local institution could succeed where others lenders failed. In Raiffeisen's rural cooperatives, especially, this idea was put into practice in full force. Members (who were also neighbors in small villages) knew each other well and could use this knowledge to make decisions on credit applications. The ability to harness the information and ties implicit in settled rural social life accounts for the striking success of the German credit cooperatives.

The movement grew rapidly throughout the nineteenth century. More important, the cooperatives were able to lend to poor people on very unusual terms and at interest rates only slightly higher than those charged to the best customers of banks. Especially noteworthy were the long-term loans (ten and even twenty years) offered by rural credit cooperatives at a time when most bank credit was for three or six months. Short-term loans were a device banks used to keep borrowers on a short leash, and the cooperatives' ability to dispense with this lending tool demonstrates their knowledge of and control over their borrowers. Schulze-Delitzsch cooperatives operated in larger cities than the Raiffeisen cooperatives, where members knew each other less well, and adopted methods that were somewhat more like those of commercial banks.

Most loans were used for productive activities, including raw materials and inventory, livestock, repair of buildings, and so on. Cooperatives at first avoided requiring collateral security for loans, but by the early twentieth century many rural cooperatives made mortgage loans. In the rare cases of borrower default, cooperatives could and did resort to legal proceedings. Cooperatives also used other sanctions (such as ejection from the institution) and more frequently tried to work out repayment plans that avoided the need for default.

Regional Cooperative Organizations. By the 1870s both branches of the German credit cooperative group had recognized one weakness of their institutions' design. Being small and local enabled each cooperative to take advantage of social ties among members in the way described, but it also left them open to serious problems. A shock to the local economy (such as a crop failure or the decline of an important local industry) could lead to the withdrawal of deposits and the inability to repay loans. Rural cooperatives especially faced seasonal imbalances in the supply of deposits and the need for credit. To deal with this problem, and after some experimentation, German cooperatives developed a series of centrals or regional banks that served credit cooperatives and other cooperatives. The centrals could lend funds among cooperatives and acted as conduits to the larger capital market. Most European countries developed a similar system.

Another general theme appears in Germany during the nineteenth century. Schulze-Delitzsch feared any political involvement in the cooperative movement, and consistently rejected state assistance. Raiffeisen was less worried on this score. When the Prussian Cooperative Central Bank (usually called the Preussenkasse) was chartered in 1895, it acted as a sort of central for centrals and as a conduit for state aid to credit cooperatives. The operations of the Preussenkasse itself were subsidized by the Prussian government, and it could make low-cost agricultural loans via credit cooperatives. The Preussenkasse came along after the German cooperatives were well established in most of the country; so state aid cannot be seen there as the reason for cooperative success. The same cannot be said elsewhere. In many instances, including France in the nineteenth century, cooperative banking groups were cotrolled by the state, and much of their loan capital consisted of money provided by the state. The same is true of cooperative credit in many countries outside of Europe.

Spread within Europe. Germany's credit cooperatives quickly spread to Italy, Belgium, the Netherlands, and elsewhere in the nineteenth century. In many countries, such as Denmark and Russia, the credit cooperatives competed with other institutions that served similar ends. In some countries, such as France, the introduction of German-style cooperatives provided the impetus for creating stronger, more influential alternative credit institutions. France's Banques Populaires were introduced in the nineteenth century in imitation of Germany's Schulze-Delitzsch cooperatives, and Crédit Mutuel traces its ancestry to Raiffeisen's ideas. Crédit Agricole was created by the French government in the 1890s, partly in reaction to the success of these other two institutions. Credit cooperatives were a favorite tool of agricultural reformers, who in some cases (such as Ireland) introduced cooperatives that did not succeed, either because they were not needed or because some feature of local conditions undermined their ability to function.

European cooperatives also were influential outside of Europe. The Desjardins movement in Quebec, as well as credit cooperatives in East Africa, South Asia, and East Asia, all trace their intellectual and often organizational roots to European, usually German, origins. In Europe itself credit cooperatives experienced all the vicissitudes of their countries' economies during the twentieth century; but at century's end, many comprised major sectors of the banking system. In France the mutual Crédit Agricole vies for the role of the world's largest bank; in Germany the cooperative banking system includes very large institutions such as the DG Bank, and in 1995 it collectively held about one-fourth of all nonbank deposits in that country. Cooperative banks are important in virtually all western European countries with the exceptions of Britain and Ireland. Elsewhere cooperative banking groups also play central roles in their national banking system. In some developing countries, credit cooperatives have been revitalized by interest in their use as a tool of development policy; in others, such as the Republic of Korea, the cooperatives play a strong role by virtue of their ties to the rural economy.

Credit cooperatives never have been major financial institutions in the United States although credit unions (which trace their origins to German credit cooperatives via Quebec's Desjardins group) provide banking services to millions of households. The U.S. credit unions must restrict themselves to a "field of membership," defined as the employees of a firm or a set of firms, members of a nonprofit group, and so on. This restriction amounts to an indirect limit on size and diversification. (The rules governing credit unions and their operations are, at this writing, under revision as part of an overall deregulation of the U.S. financial services industry.) Credit unions whose members are mostly employed by a single firm face a diversification problem similar to that of the small rural German cooperatives in the nineteenth century; trouble in that firm means that the credit union loses deposits and faces an increased demand for credit. In return for these restrictions, however, U.S. credit unions are not taxed and are not subject to some restrictions imposed on other banking institutions.

Related Institutions. Other lending institutions, including present-day ones have resembled credit cooperatives. In the nineteenth century loan funds appeared in several places, where poor people could borrow money at low interest. In some instances, such as in Ireland, these loans were financed by deposits, and the funds operated as small banking institutions. In others, the loans amounted to gifts, and the loan funds were essentially charities. Cooperatives leaders often condemned the loan funds as confusing charity with self-help. Starting in the 1970s a different form of institution arose, the micro-lender. Favored as a tool of development policy, institutions such as Bangladesh's Grameen Bank use distinctive lending methods to make small, low-cost loans to poor people in developing countries. The Grameen Bank has a commercial bank charter; it is not a cooperative. However, its lending policies aim to harness the local information and ties at the heart of the peer-monitoring approach to credit cooperatives; and the economic logic of credit cooperatives and Grameen-like institutions share some common features. Grameen imitators have spread across the globe and even appear in poor regions of some wealthy countries.

One issue facing both the older credit-cooperative movements and the newer lenders such as the Grameen Bank is the effect of economic and social change on the institutions' rationale and sustainability. German credit cooperatives at the turn of the twenty-first century are, for example, nearly indistinguishable from commercial banks; the poverty and the isolation that sustained the pioneers has been eradicated by Germany's economic development. Similarly, some of the methods used by Grameen and other lenders work only for very poor people in underdeveloped economies. To the extent that credit cooperatives and related institutions promote economic development, they make their clientele better customers of for-profit banks. As they succeed, credit cooperatives must transform themselves into more conventional financial intermediaries or cease operations.

BIBLIOGRAPHY

A'Hearn, Brian. "Could Southern Italians Cooperate? Banche Popolari in the Mezzogiorno." *Journal of Economic History* 60.1 (2000), 67–93.

Baker, Anita B. "Community and Growth: Muddling Through with Russian Credit Cooperatives." *Journal of Economic History* 37.1 (1977), 139–160.

Banerjee, Abhijit, Timothy Besley, and Timothy W. Guinnane. "Thy Neighbor's Keeper: The Design of Credit Cooperative, with Theory and a Test." *Quarterly Journal of Economics* 109.2 (1994), 491–515.

Galassi, Francesco L., "Measuring Social Capital: Culture as an Explanation of Italy's Dualism." *European Review of Economic History* (Jan. 2001), 29–59.

Ghatak, Maitreesh, and Timothy W. Guinnane. "The Economics of Lending with Joint Liability: Theory and Practice." *Journal of Development Economics* 60 (1999), 195–228.

Gueslin, André. *Les origines du crédit agricole (1840–1914)*. Nancy, France, 1978.

Guinnane, Timothy W. "A Failed Institutional Transplant: Raiffeisen's Credit Cooperatives in Ireland, 1894–1914." *Explorations in Economic History* 31.1 (1994), 38–61.

Guinnane, Timothy W. "Cooperatives as Information Machines: German Rural Credit Cooperatives, 1883–1914." *Journal of Economic History* 61.2 (2001), 366–389.

Herrick, Myron T., and R. Ingalls, *Rural Credits: Land and Cooperative.* New York, 1914.

Hollis, Aidan, and Arthur Sweetman. "Microcredit in Prefamine Ireland." *Explorations in Economic History* 35.4 (1998), 347–380.

Hulme, David, and Paul Mosley. *Finance against Poverty.* 2 vols. New York, 1996.

Morduch, Jonathan. "The Microfinance Promise." *Journal of Economic Literature* 37.4 (1999), 1569–1614.

U.S. Congress. Senate. *Agricultural Cooperation and Rural Credit in Europe.* 63rd Cong., 1st sess. Doc. 214.

TIMOTHY W. GUINNANE

CREDIT MARKETS. *See* Agricultural Credit; Banking; Consumer Credit; Informal Credit; Pawnbroking and Personal Loan Markets; *and* Usury.

CROATIA. *See* Balkans.

CROFTERS. In Scotland prior to 1886 and the introduction of a precise legal definition, the term *crofter* was used loosely to denote an agrarian tenant holding a small area of land, usually on a year-to-year basis (i.e., without a formal written lease). In the nineteenth century the term became particularly associated in common usage with the Highlands of Scotland, but in earlier periods it was used in the Lowlands as well. More specifically, prior to about 1815, during the early part of the process of agrarian transformation known as the Highland clearances, landed proprietors broke up traditional communal townships, used the land for commercial sheep farming, and relocated the population to crofting townships that they had prepared. The most thorough of these clearances took place in Sutherland, but they were evident throughout the north. In these new environments, crofters had insufficient land for agricultural subsistence and were impelled to work in industries, such as the harvesting of seaweed for the production of alkali, designed to yield further profit to the proprietor.

The economics of the structure were unstable, especially with the collapse of the kelp industry after the end of the Napoleonic Wars, and crofting communities were able to subsist only with resort to the intensive cultivation of potatoes, upon which they became dependant. This economic vulnerability was compounded in the years from 1846 to 1855 with the repeated failure of the potato crop, due to blight leading to a famine in the western and island areas, which depended most heavily on the potato. A new round of clearances ensued; this time the objective of proprietors was to break up crofting communities and encourage emigration. In the 1860s and 1870s surviving crofting communities often were placed under great pressure by landlords, and their economic survival depended upon earnings gained from nonagricultural activities such as temporary migration to Lowland Scotland in search of wage labor.

In the early 1880s, after a return of severe economic depression, a series of protests over the issue of land rights took place in the West Highlands and the Hebrides. The Liberal government appointed a Royal Commission that investigated the grievances of the crofters and, ultimately, after the election of a number of Crofter members of Parliament for northern constituencies, the Crofters' Holdings (Scotland) Act was passed in 1886. Modeled on the Irish land act of 1881, it gave a precise legal definition to the term crofter (a year-to-year tenant paying less than £30 per annum in rent) and defined the areas of northern Scotland (most parishes in the counties of Shetland, Orkney, Caithness, Sutherland, Ross and Cromarty, Inverness, and Argyll) to which it was applicable. The legal definition has remained in place, with only minor modifications, down to the time of this writing. In economic terms, some of the original conditions remain relevant; in particular, most crofts are part-time agricultural units, and most crofters gain their primary income from other activities.

BIBLIOGRAPHY

Cameron, Ewen A. *Land for the People? The British Government and the Scottish Highlands, c. 1880–1925.* East Linton, 1996.

Devine, Thomas M. *From Clanship to Crofters' War: The Social Transformation of the Scottish Highlands.* Manchester, 1994.

Devine, Thomas M. *The Great Highland Famine: Hunger, Emigration and the Scottish Highlands in the Nineteenth Century.* Edinburgh, 1988.

Hunter, James. *The Making of the Crofting Community.* 2d ed., Edinburgh, 2000.

MacPhail, I. M. M. *The Crofters' War.* Stornoway, 1989.

EWEN A. CAMERON

CROP AND PLANT DISEASES. The economic and social consequences of pests and diseases in crops have been extensive. In 1870 Ceylon (Sri Lanka) was one of the leading coffee producers in the world, with about 400,000 acres planted with the crop. Twenty years later the coffee plantations had all but gone, victims to the depredations of the coffee rust fungus. The rust was spreading throughout southeast Asia, and soon the coffee plantations would disappear from other countries in this region. As a consequence, the center of coffee production moved to South America and Africa. Ceylon's economy was rebuilt with tea as its foundation, the British becoming a nation of tea drinkers in the process. In other parts of southeast Asia, new crops, including rubber, replaced coffee.

Potato blight in Ireland in 1845–1846 resulted in the population of that country being cut by a third with the immigration of the Irish to the United States sufficient to form a significant proportion of the U.S. population; and it brought a change in British government policy as the Corn

Laws were repealed to allow free trade in agricultural produce. The same blight in Germany in 1916, destroying many of the stocks of potatoes, most likely weakened German ability and resolve to defeat the Allies in World War I. The phylloxera epidemic in France in the late nineteenth century seriously undermined that country's wine trade. That opened the way for whiskey to capture a large part of the market in Britain and the United States, and it would take the better part of a century for French wine to be reestablished in those countries.

The effects of fungal and bacterial diseases and the depredations of pests have been extensive throughout the world and in all ages. The full extent of the losses is hard to measure, but losses of 20 percent or more over wide areas have been common. To take one example, an outbreak of barley yellow dwarf in 1959 in South Dakota reduced the crops of oats by 50 percent, wheat by 30 percent, and barley by 20 percent. The potato blight of 1846 resulted in losses of 75 percent in provinces of the Netherlands.

Understanding Plant Diseases. Pests and diseases have been a constant feature of agriculture. By its very nature, with large areas given over to similar species of plants, settled agriculture creates the conditions in which pests can thrive. The adoption of more intensive farming practices could increase the production not merely of crops but of insects and diseases also. In England the adoption of the four-course rotation in the eighteenth and nineteenth centuries and the introduction of artificial fertilizers introduced the problems of turnip fly and finger-and-toe disease (andury) in turnips. The development of hybrid varieties could intensify susceptibility to pests and diseases by narrowing the genetic base compared with the heterogeneous land races. By encouraging monoculture, these varieties also made it easier for some diseases to spread. This was the experience in the United States in 1970 when 15 percent of the corn crop was lost to corn leaf blight.

Many of the afflictions of crops have been known since ancient times. Rusts, weevils, locusts, mildew, and ergot all have been identified in prehistoric finds. The famine in Egypt during biblical times was almost certainly the result of rust attacks in wheat. The locust, probably the most widespread and certainly most feared pest of the ancient and classical world, is mentioned regularly by classical writers and in the Bible, with Exodus, Chapter 10, giving a very clear account of a locust attack. Some diseases have not made their presence felt until more recent times. Panama wilt in bananas was not really known until the 1920s, for example. Diseases and pests have also created international problems for centuries. Fungi and insects have not been respecters of boundaries, and as farmers have taken crops, even varieties of crops, around the world, they often have taken pests and diseases as well. Improvements in

transport and more concerted efforts, in agriculture and horticulture, to seek out new varieties worsened the problem of pests and diseases crossing boundaries during the nineteenth century. At the same time, advances in science made it more likely that the source of infection might be identified, and governments began to introduce measures of control. Phylloxera and downy mildew in grapes came to Europe with American vines imported for crossing with European types. The American varieties had built up an immunity that the European ones, never having been exposed to these diseases, had not. The introduction of the new varieties was followed by devastating outbreaks of phylloxera and downy mildew in France in the 1860s and 1870s. The boll weevil spread from its native South America to Texas in 1892 and from there across the entire cotton belt of the United States by 1921.

Although pests and diseases had been part of agriculture since cultivation began, an understanding of their true nature did not come until relatively recent times. The identification, in the late seventeenth century, of ergot in rye as a fungal attack was one of the first great developments. In the late eighteenth and early nineteenth centuries, progress was made in identifying many of the fungal diseases. The British naturalist Sir Joseph Banks published positive identification of the fungus causing mildew in wheat in a booklet issued in 1805, having been inspired by some previously ignored work of the Italian Felice Fontana. In the 1750s, Mathieu Tillet of France showed that smut was a fungal disease. Other work by scientists in Germany and France, including Anton de Bary and Julius Kuhn, had established the nature of the rusts and mildews in grain crops. Even so, the scientific study of the afflictions of plants was still in its infancy in 1850, and many older theories still had a strong following. The great epidemic of potato blight in the 1840s produced a lively debate as to whether the fungal growths were a cause or a symptom of the disease. A number of detailed reports attributed the disease to atmospheric conditions or to aphids. Not until the 1860s was it generally accepted that fungi caused this blight. Bacterial diseases remained to be identified in the late nineteenth and twentieth centuries. American Thomas Burrill was the first investigator to link Pasteur's discovery of bacteria to plant disease. Among the viruses to be identified early on were those causing fire blight in fruit trees and potato leaf roll.

Control Measures. The relatively recent advancement of knowledge about pests and diseases has meant that most of the means of combating them are likewise of recent development. Throughout most of history, the farmer has had to accept losses to vermin and disease as a way of life. The war against pests and diseases was conducted with a minimum of technology. Scaring birds, shaking caterpillars from plants, hunting, and trapping are all time-honored tactics. At times these have been communal activities, whether through farmers' societies promoting the trapping of vermin or through public bodies. In classical times, laws were passed in the city of Cyrene requiring all citizens to crush both the eggs and adult locusts. Several American states paid bounties for the eradication of gray squirrels in the eighteenth century. Many countries followed similar practices even into the mid-twentieth century. In Saskatchewan and Alberta in the 1920s and 1930s, a campaign against flickertail gophers was boosted by bounties paid for the animals' tails.

Eradication of contaminated plants to prevent disease spreading has been another attempt at control. The connection between barberry and rust in wheat was observed long before its precise nature was scientifically proved. As early as 1660, a law was passed in France for the eradication of barberry, with some effect, and some American states passed similar laws in the eighteenth century. As scientific knowledge of pests and diseases grew, and governments assumed greater responsibility for their control, quarantine measures were introduced. Germany introduced quarantine in 1875 to prevent entry of the Colorado beetle. The United States followed with regulations to control gall louse in 1881 and citrus canker in the 1910s and 1920s. Since then, quarantine, along with rigorous eradication of diseased plants, has been a common means of controlling a variety of pests and diseases.

Advances in scientific knowledge of pests and diseases from the eighteenth century onward caused chemical and biological technologies to assume greater importance as means of control.

Chemical and Biological Treatment and Biotechnology. The earliest uses of chemical treatments were as barriers against pest attack. Mixtures of soda and lees of olive oil were spread over stored grain to ward off locusts in the ancient world. In the seventeenth and eighteenth centuries, there were similar practices, such as spreading soot on fields of cereals to kill snails and using soft soap mixtures to keep slugs off.

Steeping seed in chemical solutions to clean it became common as a preventive measure in the early-modern period, and continues to be used as a means of preventing a number of infections. In the seventeenth century, soaking rye seed in brine proved reasonably effective against ergot. A potassium solution was later found to be a better steeping medium, and with that the fungal attacks on rye and the deadly ergotism afflicting people eating infected rye declined. The practice of steeping wheat seeds was also used to prevent attacks of bunt or smut, among the most damaging of cereal fungi. Various steeping solutions were used, including brine, alum, urine, and potash. There was similar variety in solutions used in steeping turnip seed against attack by turnip fly; the solutions were made either of soot or train oil (boiled whale or fish oil) or various mixtures of soot, camphor, and tobacco. How effective these treatments were is open to question. Abbé Prévost of France discovered in 1807 that copper sulfate was the most effective additive to the steeping solution, but his view gained slow acceptance. In the mid-nineteenth century, Europe's farmers were still getting indifferent results with brine, alum, and other steeping solutions.

Effective fungicides and pesticides were introduced during the second half of the nineteenth century. Solutions of arsenic, such as Paris Green (originally used to deter people from stealing grapes in France), were increasingly used as insecticides. They were joined by solutions of copper sulfate, most notably Bordeaux mixture, a compound of water, copper sulfate, and lime. Introduced in 1885 as a treatment for downy mildew of grapes, a few years later it was found to be effective against potato blight and subsequently against most major fungal diseases. By the end of the century, Bordeaux mixture and its successor formaldehyde had become general treatments, and it remains one of the farmer's principal weapons. Solutions of arsenic, copper, and nicotine, the last used mainly in horticulture, were the principal chemical pesticides in use until World War I. Washes derived from coal tar were introduced in the Netherlands in 1921 as antidotes to aphids and moths, and were used especially in orchards. During World War II, organo-phosphate pesticides were developed, which laid the foundations for the rapid growth in their use in the late twentieth century. The first of these, DDT and benzene hexachloride (BHC), had been formulated some time earlier (BHC by Faraday as long ago as 1825), but their insecticidal properties were established only during the 1940s. Their successful use was followed by the development of systemic and selective pesticides, a large number of new products being introduced during subsequent decades. These new insecticides opened the way for much greater control over pests, several of which, such as the boll weevil, had proved almost impossible to counter. Increases in agricultural production, especially in Western economies, owed much to these chemicals.

Biological controls, such as the use of predator insects, have been known at least since the eighteenth century, with Linnaeus and Reaumur among the scientists who advocated their use, such as the breeding of ladybirds for control of aphids. Since the 1970s there has been increased interest in biological control, whether by the use of predator insects or by a more mixed planting regime, in reaction to what many see as excessive use of chemical pesticides. However, this has remained a minority interest, as the agrochemical industry has continued to grow.

Finding disease-resistant crops and varieties has been one of the main antidotes since ancient times. With the development of scientific breeding from the nineteenth century onward, a major part of the breeder's work has gone into disease-resistant strains. This became a global effort in the twentieth century as plant breeders searched the world for the land races that might form the basis for new strains of crops. Blight-resistant potatoes, cereals resistant to mildew and rust, and bananas resistant to wilt were among the products of the plant breeders during the twentieth century. Since the 1970s, the rise of biotechnology has led to research into genes resistant to disease. Early efforts included work on genes resistant to corn blight.

One of the main economic effects of the efforts to control and eradicate pests and disease has been the creation of the agricultural chemical industry. Firms selling sprays and seed dressings of copper sulfate and arsenic began to grow during the mid-nineteenth century, and the 1860s to the 1880s saw the development of spraying equipment. Reactions to the major outbreaks of blight and phylloxera and the successful use of Bordeaux mixture increased the demand for chemical sprays, and a large number of firms appeared in Europe and America. There was dramatic expansion of the agricultural chemical industry after 1945. Growth in demand adjusted for inflation was at 1 percent or more per annum throughout the 1980s and 1990s, with most of the demand coming from North America and Europe, followed by Australasia. Consolidation created an industry dominated by multinational businesses, with the leading ten accounting for 86 percent of world sales in 1995.

Although the great increases in agricultural production following the introduction of organo-phosphate pesticides and disease-resistant strains of crops seemed to imply victory in the war against pests and diseases in the late twentieth century, this was an illusion. Many diseases have resisted eradication, among them some of farmers' oldest enemies, such as smut and rust. New chemicals and disease-resistant varieties of wheat have been followed very shortly by the appearance of new strains of both of these diseases. Devastating epidemics have continued to appear from time to time. Concern about the environmental effect of the chemicals have arisen, leading to the banning of DDT in the 1970s; but that concern has not stopped the growth in the use of chemicals. Chemical technologies not withstanding, governments have continued also to resort to traditional methods, including eradication programs, such as a program against the boll weevil launched in the late 1970s. As chemicals have seemed to have their limitations, some have argued that the future lies in biological controls and biotechnology. The fight against pests and diseases goes on.

[*See also* Animal and Livestock Diseases; Crop Failures; Famines; *and* Irish Famine.]

BIBLIOGRAPHY

Carefoot, G. L., and E. R. Sprott. *Famine on the Wind: Plant Diseases and Human History*. London, 1969.

Jones, E. L. "Creative Disruption in American Agriculture, 1620–1820." *Agricultural History* 48 (1974), 510–528.

Isern, Thomas D. "Gopher Tales: A Study in Western Canadian Pest Control." *Agricultural History Review* (1988), 188–198.

Kloppenburg, J. R. *First the Seed: The Political Economy of Plant Biotechnology, 1492–2000*. Cambridge, 1988.

Ordish, George. *The Constant Pest*. London, 1976.

Smith, Allen E., and Diane M. Secoy. "Organic Materials used in European Crop Protection before 1850." *Chemistry and Industry* (1977), 863–869.

JONATHAN BROWN

CROP FAILURES. In the biblical allegory, Joseph's forecast of seven years of plenty followed by seven years of drought serves as a metaphor for the vagaries of nature and the possibility that crop failure may be so severe and extended as to induce famine. Likewise, Joseph's policy advice, to tax production (at 20 percent) during abundant times as "a store . . . against the seven years of famine" (Genesis 41:36) is a metaphor for the prudence of government intervention. Economic history affords an opportunity to examine this view. Crop failure is usually associated with unseasonable weather, pests, and disease, but also may be caused or exacerbated by inappropriate government policy. Whether the consequences of crop failure are moderate or severe depends not only on the extent and duration of damages but also on government policy. The examples that follow illustrate the diversity of causes and consequences of crop failure and the role of public policy in both.

The crop failures contributing to the great famine in Europe (1315–1317) were caused by cooler climates. Low temperatures and unseasonable rainfall impeded both planting and harvesting. Peasants survived the low harvests of 1315 by consuming their food reserves. Without reserves and with forest edibles depleted, peasant families slaughtered draft animals and consumed their seed grain following the continuation of abnormally low yields in 1316. When normal weather returned in 1317, farmers were unable to cultivate their entire farms, and low harvests and famine continued, gradually abating from 1318 to 1325. Since villages were largely independent, assistance from higher levels of government was unavailable in Europe during this period. Particularly low harvests returned from 1345 to 1348, and the ensuing malnutrition contributed to low resistance to bubonic plague, resulting in the Black Death (1346–1351). This example illustrates, in accordance with the dismal economics of Thomas Malthus (1766–1834), that famine, disease, and death are more likely to result from crop failure under conditions of overpopulation. Even before the Black Death, population in Europe had already risen to the point where good harvests were necessary to its maintenance.

Crop failure can also be induced or exacerbated by political factors. Russia's scorched-earth policy in 1812 is a rather direct example, having the consequences not only of depriving Napoleon's armies but also of starving crop-dependent Russian people. The notorious 1840s potato famine in Ireland illustrates how crop failure, population pressure, and government neglect can jointly bring disaster. By 1845, Ireland's population had swelled to more than 9 million, and England's penal laws and land reform had succeeded in extracting all economic surplus from the Catholic peasantry, who were reduced to poverty in the best of times. Land fragmentation was extreme. Peasant families produced cash crops (mainly oats, barley, and corn), and later pigs, in order to pay their rents to English landlords, and subsisted almost entirely on potatoes. Because of this extreme dependence, the potato blight wiped out 2 million in Ireland and drove 2 million more to emigrate, principally to the New World.

The recurrent episodes of wind erosion in the Great Plains region of the United States from 1931 through 1940 provide an interesting example of crop failure predisposed by unsustainable economic policies. While severe drought and high winds in the 1930s was the proximate cause of the ensuing Dust Bowl and the out migration of 3.5 million people, inappropriate distribution of land played a critical role in aggravating the extent of wind erosion. The Homestead Act of 1862 restricted the size of new homesteads to 160 acres, inappropriately small for the semiarid Great Plains, requiring farmers to intensively cultivate virtually all of their land in order to keep the farm financially sustainable. In addition, the high fixed cost of such crucial soil conservation techniques as strip cropping, wide spacing of crops, contour plowing, and diversification into livestock were financially infeasible for the homesteads, more so during the Great Depression. The region's exposed topsoil, robbed of the anchoring, water-retaining roots of its native grasses, was carried off by heavy spring winds. The Resettlement Administration attempted to reverse the small farm bias of the Homestead Act and encouraged the consolidation of small farms into more viable units (although this in turn was partially offset by small farm subsidies in the Agricultural Adjustment Act (Worster, 1979). Thus, government policies had contradictory effects, both exacerbating and mitigating the consequences of crop failure.

The famine in China that lasted from 1959 to 1961 exemplifies a case wherein government policies contributed both to crop failure and the disastrous consequences thereof. The official estimate of the 1958 grain harvest was 375 million tons, even though later figures showed that the real output was approximately 200 million tons. Local party officials apparently exaggerated their statistical reports out of ideological enthusiasm and fears of being labeled counterrevolutionary that resulted from the Great Leap Forward (1958–1961). The corresponding illusion of superabundance led economic planners to reduce acreage planted in wheat and rice (replacing grain production with cash crops) and to divert agricultural laborers into industry, further increasing the demand for grain. As a result of these errors, production was suppressed and grain reserves negligible when floods in the South, coupled with drought in the North, struck in 1959. Natural disasters continued to affect a large percentage of planted hectarage (still low) in 1960 and 1961. Large, politically motivated grain exports to the Soviet Union in these years exacerbated the problem. Because of its previous dependence on the Soviet Union, and to the Soviets' severing relations in June of 1960, China was unable to avail itself of significant international assistance. The famine that took place in the aftermath of the Great Leap Forward undoubtedly was one of the worst of human record. The loss in population due to the resulting famine is estimated at eighteen and one-half additional deaths and almost 31 million lost births (Yao, 1999).

Even a country with adequate foreign relations, however, may suffer serious consequences from crop failure. A successive number of droughts from 1981 to 1985 led to a catastrophic collapse of Ethiopia's food output, grain reserves, and purchasing power. When international aid was mobilized late in 1984 (largely in response to the Live Aid concert), logistical difficulties prevented effective famine relief. Ethiopia had inadequate port facilities, a shortage of trucks, and an absence of spare parts and maintenance capabilities, and the road networks were poor or nonexistent. The resulting excess mortality was estimated to be more than 3 percent of Ethiopia's population.

To put the various causes of crop failure in perspective as precursors of famine, it is useful to consider that famine may occur without widespread crop failure. High international prices, low foreign-exchange reserves, low grain stores (due to government decisions not to set aside reserves from the preceding bumper crop), and severe flooding all fueled speculation and spiraling grain prices in Bangladesh in the summer of 1974. The price of rice during the famine months was 250 percent higher than during the same period in 1973. When the actual winter harvest came in, prices plummeted, but many could not afford the high prices during the interim. Excess mortality is estimated at 1.5 million (Ravallion, 1985).

In summary, crop failure results both from natural events and public policy. Adverse consequences of crop failure, especially famine, are more likely to occur when crop failures are sequential, such that coping mechanisms are exhausted, or when market and/or public institutions are prevented from smoothing consumption relative to fluctuating production. Crop failure does not inevitably result in severe adverse consequences; yet famine can occur without crop failure.

[*See also* Crop and Plant Diseases; Crop Yields; *and* Famines.]

BIBLIOGRAPHY

Alamgir, Mohiuddin. *Famine in South Asia: Political Economy of Mass Starvation*. Cambridge, 1980.
Howell, Philippa. "Crop Failure in Dalocha, Ethiopia: A Participatory Emergency Response." *Disasters* 22.1 (1998), 57–76.
Kumar, B. G. "Ethiopian Famines 1973–1985: A Case-Study." In *Political Economy of Hunger*, edited by Jean Dreze and Amartya Sen, pp. 173–216. Oxford, 1990.
Libecap, Gary D., and Zeynep K. Hansen. "United States Land Policy, Property Rights, and the Dust Bowl of the 1930s." Working paper, 2001.
Nikiforuk, Andrew. *The Fourth Horseman*. New York, 1991.
Ravallion, Martin. "The Performance of Rice Markets in Bangladesh during the 1974 Famine." *Economic Journal* 95 (1985), 15–19.
Sen, Amartya. *Poverty and Famines*. Oxford, 1981.
Williams, Jeffrey C., and Brian D. Wright. *Storage and Commodity Markets*. New York, 1991.
Worster, Donald. *Dustbowl: The Southern Plains in the 1930s*. Oxford, 1979.
Yao, Shujie. "A Note on the Causal Factors of China's Famine in 1959–1961." *Journal of Political Economy* 107.6 (1999), 1365–1369.

JAMES ROUMASSET

CROP ROTATION. Crop rotation is a management technique used in arable agriculture (the production of crops). Suppose that the farmer has four fields and cultivates a different crop in each of them—say, wheat (field 1), turnips (field 2), barley (field 3), and clover (field 4). The following year, the same crops are cultivated, but the farmer plants each of them in a different field—say, clover (field 1), wheat (field 2), turnips (field 3), and barley (field 4). In our simple example, the farmer has a four-year cycle. That is, a different crop is grown in each field for each of four years; then, in the fifth year, wheat will once again come to be grown in field 1. In this sense, the crops are "rotated" around the farm on a regular cycle.

Historically, crop rotation was used predominantly (though not exclusively) in western Europe and came to be adopted in other parts of the world following European settlement. Crop rotations have always varied greatly from place to place, in terms of the crops used in the rotation and the frequency with which they were repeated in the cycle. Hence, any introductory discussion can hope only to sketch the most important facets of crop rotation history.

European agriculture in the early medieval period (1000 to 1300 CE) was strongly associated with the two-field system. That is, the arable land was divided into two fields of roughly equal size; one of the fields was sown with grains,

and the other was left fallow. (Fallowing is the practice of leaving the field for a year with no crop at all; we discuss the motivation for this below.) Each year, grain cultivation was switched from one field to the other, so that each field produced a crop every second year (it being fallow for a year in between grain crops). After 1300, this practice was superseded by the three-field system: for example, one field of wheat, one field of legumes (peas or beans), and one field of fallow. This meant that the total amount of land on the farm producing a crop in any given year rose from 50 percent to 66 percent, thus increasing total output. This was a response to population pressures that increased the demand for food and required a more intensive use of land.

In general, the medieval system did not use land resources very intensively—in any given year, one-third to one-half of the land produced no crops at all. Thus, until 1850, the major focus of technological improvement in European agriculture was the discovery of new crops that were suitable for replacing fallow in the rotation. This goal was initially realized in England in the 1700s, when the Norfolk four-course rotation came into general use; this replaced fallow with turnips and clover and resulted in the system described in the first paragraph (see Overton, 1996). This rotation was then refined and adapted to other European countries. For example, in the late 1800s, German farmers adopted a similar four-course rotation but replaced turnips with sugar beet (another root vegetable).

Crop rotation has been used much less widely in Europe since World War II. Farmers in other parts of the world have never used crop rotation, for example, in the Nile Delta of Egypt and the rice paddy fields of Asia. How can we explain these variations across space and time? Let us begin by thinking about the reasons why a farmer would want to use crop rotation as a management technique.

Why would a farmer bother to rotate crops? This apparently simple question must be broken into two parts. First, why would the farmer bother to grow more than one crop? Surely the farmer would simply cultivate the most profitable crop on all the fields of the farm. Second, even if the farmer wanted to cultivate several crops on the farm, it is not obvious why he would want to move them around every year. Surely some fields would be better suited to one particular crop, and so it would be best to grow that particular crop in the same field every year. Let us consider each of these questions in turn.

There are four factors that encourage the farmer to cultivate several different crops on the farm in the same season.

First, cultivating a variety of crops enables the farmer to use his inputs more effectively. For example, harvesting a crop of wheat takes a large amount of labor—so much labor that farmers used to hire any extra able-bodied workers that they could find (including factory workers who temporarily went out to work in the countryside). If the farmer chooses several crops that have slightly different production cycles, then he can spread his demand for harvest labor over a longer period—say, clover can be harvested in April and July before wheat is harvested in August. This argument holds for capital equipment as well as labor, notably horses and wagons. In England in the eighteenth century (which saw important advances in crop rotation techniques), this desire to spread labor demand is cited as a primary motive for innovation (see Timmer, 1968).

Second, cultivating several different crops enables the farmer to use his outputs more effectively. Before the advent of chemical fertilizers, farmers had to rely on organic fertilizers, of which the primary source was animal dung. Therefore, it was normal to keep large numbers of animals on the farm and produce both arable outputs (crops) and pastoral outputs (meat, dairy, and hides). This system is known as mixed farming. To keep these animals, the farm had to produce fodder for them such as clover and turnips. (We therefore distinguish between intermediate outputs such as clover and turnips—these were fed to animals to produce meat and dairy—and final outputs such as wheat and barley, which were sold onto the market for human consumption.) Of course, it would not make any sense to produce only wheat this year and only clover next year because the animals have to eat every year, so the farm has to produce all the crops every year.

Third, farming is a risky activity because it is highly dependent on the weather, which can vary greatly from one year to the next. This was even more true historically than today because farmers were less able to offset any adverse weather effects through the use of capital equipment. For example, large-scale movable irrigation systems to counteract drought conditions did not come into general use until the twentieth century. But ideal weather conditions vary from one crop to another. For example, a wet April would be disastrous for the wheat harvest in England but would probably produce a good crop of clover. So the farmer can partially insure himself against the weather by cultivating several different crops on the farm—it is unlikely that all the crops will be adversely affected by the weather in any particular year. This type of motivation has been proposed by McCloskey (1978) to explain the decision of medieval farmers to scatter their crops in geographically dispersed units in the open fields of the village (so-called strip scattering).

Fourth, crops will grow successfully only when the soil has a good balance of nutrients. Notably, grain crops such as wheat withdraw large amounts of nitrogen from the soil (much of which is physically removed from the farm when the grain is sent to the cities for human consumption). This nitrogen must be replaced by cultivating other crops in the rotation, such as legumes (peas, beans, and clover) that draw nitrogen directly from the air and deposit it in the soil. Even fallowing (i.e., growing no crop at all) raises the nitrogen content of the soil by promoting the decomposition of organic matter in the earth. That is why medieval farmers used fallow in their crop rotation. Notice also that legumes give a very low yield per acre if they are grown year after year because plant diseases become entrenched in the soil. For example, continuous cultivation of clover results in the land becoming "clover sick" and giving very low yields; hence, the yield of legumes will be higher if grain crops are included in the rotation. So cultivating a variety of crops will raise the yield of all the crops in the rotation. This benefit of biodiversity was emphasized by Charles Darwin, who noted that the total volume of plant life per unit of land area was higher when a variety of plants were grown.

We have now seen four reasons why a farmer would want to grow several crops in each season. The fourth of those reasons—soil fertility—also holds the key to our second question. Why would the farmer want to cultivate any particular crop (say, wheat) in a different field every year? He would do so because the nitrogen deposited in the soil by legumes can be used subsequently by a crop of wheat only if it is grown on that particular plot of land. The nitrogen cannot easily be transferred to another field, so the farmer must rotate all of his crops so that nutrients can be exchanged between them.

We can now understand why crop rotation has become less important since World War II. Nowadays it is possible to control plant diseases and pests (insects) by the use of herbicides and pesticides; also, the farmer can add nitrogen to the soil by using chemical fertilizers. So it is no longer necessary to maintain soil fertility by using crop rotation, and the farmer can simply plant a single crop that maximizes profits. (This is not quite true. Crop rotation still has some benefits on soil structure, and it is used to a limited extent. But crop rotation has become much less common.) We can also understand why crop rotation was never used in the Nile Delta. Every year the Nile floods and fresh soil is deposited in the delta by the floodwaters washed down from the rich lands upstream. This natural mechanism for replenishing soil fertility makes crop rotation unnecessary, and instead local farmers cultivate the crops that are most profitable.

Finally, why were crop rotations of the sort described above less important outside Europe? The purpose of crop rotation is to increase the intensity of land use without exhausting the soil. Such rotations were not needed in regions where land was abundant. In the Americas, for example, low population densities allowed indigenous peoples to adopt slash-and-burn agriculture. This involved clearing fields (often by burning the forest or jungle) and cultivating a crop (typically maize) for several years. When the soil showed signs of exhaustion, the cultivators abandoned the fields to nature and moved on to repeat the process in another area. After a generation or more, the cultivators might return to the abandoned fields, now overgrown with forests and brush. This might be seen as a particularly extended form of crop rotation.

At the other extreme are agricultural zones, most common in Asia, where a single crop (typically rice) is grown annually, or even twice annually, on the same fields. Such continuous, single-crop agriculture required large applications of labor (weeding and manuring) and capital (irrigation facilities) to compensate for the natural loss of soil fertility. In this context, the crop rotations characteristic of European agriculture hold an intermediate position with respect to population density and land productivity. With strong links to the mixed farming system, crop rotations sought to maximize yields subject to the availability of land and the application of capital and labor.

[*See also* Mixed Farming *and* Open-Field System.]

BIBLIOGRAPHY

Allen, R. C. "Agriculture and the Origins of the State in Ancient Egypt." *Explorations in Economic History* 34 (1997), 135–154.

Hallam, H. E., ed. *The Agrarian History of England and Wales*, vol. 2. Cambridge, 1988.

McCloskey, D. N. "The Open Fields as Behaviour towards Risk." *Research in Economic History* 1 (1976), 124–170.

Miller, E., ed. *The Agrarian History of England and Wales*, vol. 3. Cambridge, 1991.

Overton, M. *The Agricultural Revolution.* Cambridge, 1996.

Timmer, P. "The Turnip, the New Husbandry and the English Agricultural Revolution." *Quarterly Journal of Economics* (1968), 375–395.

LIAM BRUNT

CROP YIELDS are the basis for how well a farm is doing. Yields are absolute figures—so many tons or bushels per acre or per hectare—and they can also be used comparatively, to gauge whether farmers are doing better or worse than in previous years. To economic historians, crop yields are important as measures of how a nation's farm fares. In the history of the first industrial nation, Britain, the wheat yield is the most important, since the Northern European diet is a wheat-bread diet; therefore, wheat production is often the measure of national output. In other parts of the world, either maize or rice is the most important crop.

Grain Yields and the British "Agricultural Revolution." Economic historians are interested in agricultural yields (of crops and/or animals) because of an ongoing debate about the relationship between agricultural surpluses and the rise of industrialization. Although agriculture provided the raw materials for early industrialization, the trend in its yields should indicate the long-term surplus needed—that which is in excess of subsistence for a given population. Agriculture is thereby linked to demographics and the Industrial Revolution. Within the debate, the big question is: Did an agricultural revolution precede the European demographic and industrial revolutions of the eighteenth century and the nineteenth?

Medieval England is well researched, and its wheat yields varied between 11 and 15 bushels per acre. By the early eighteenth century, England's wheat yields were closer to 20 bushels per acre. The advances from medieval times were impressive, and they initially support the idea that an agricultural revolution may have occured. Still, no supporting evidence suggests that this resulted from anything but the process of gradual improvement. By the 1750s, England's yields had improved modestly, to 22 or 23 bushels per acre, but by the 1790s they were as low as 19 bushels per acre. The real test for British agriculture was yet to come. From 1800 to 1850, the population of England and Wales doubled. How was this achieved when the long-term increase in imports did not equal the same rate of growth as the population? The challenge was met by an increase in land productivity. In the 1850s, wheat yields increased to 27.5 bushels per acre—with the greatest growth after about 1820. The British barley crop had a yield of 30 bushels per acre from the 1720s to the 1770s. Then, similar to British wheat, there was a brief decline before yields of 35 bushels of barley per acre in the 1850s. The yield of British oats rose from 25 bushels per acre in the 1720s to 30 in the 1750s, from 37 in the 1790s to almost 50 in the 1840s.

There is and will be continuing speculation about the reasons for this seeming revolution in land productivity. One interpretation is that British farmers underperformed for centuries until they were encouraged to do better, as the rise of the maket place took effect. Yet the market is only one of the contributing institutions. Another is the organization of farming, especially through the imposition of the Enclosure laws. The one material gain was the more efficient use of seed, which resulted in the demonstrable rise in per acre yields; there was also a decline in the number of seeds sown (the sowing or seeding rate) and hence a rise in the yield rates or ratios (bushels harvested per bushel of seed sown)—as was particularly so for barley and oats. The better yield rate of barley and oats, hence the saving on barley and oats seeds, coupled with changing dietary habits toward more wheat bread, can all be translated as an increase in the land available to wheat production. The area for wheat in England increased to a high in the early 1840s. The wheat-yield ratio rose dramatically to 16 or 17 in the 1840s and 1850s from 6 in the 1720s and 8 in 1800. The yield rate for barley fluctuated more widely, but increased in England from 4 in the 1720s to 5.5 in the 1790s to almost 13 in the 1840s; oats went from almost 4 in the 1720s to almost 6 in the 1790s to about 8 from the 1820s onward. The equivalent yield-to-seed ratios in late medieval England had been under 4 for wheat and barley, under 3 for oats, thus emphasizing the achievements since 1700 and particularly since 1800. In the wider European economy, especially in the Netherlands, there were individually reported yield ratios that equaled those of England. More generally (the Netherlands apart), the rise in yield ratios for the seventeenth century and the eighteenth centuries was most impressive in England.

The revolution in British agriculture was not only from better organization or the better use of seed but also from soil fertilization—increasing the supply of plant nutrients (nitrogen, phosphorous, and potassium). Then there were some improved methods in countering the competition for nutrients from weeds, as well as the replacement of broadcast sowing of seed by the use of the hand dibble or the mechanical seed drill. The greatest advance from medieval times to the nineteenth century was the rotation of nitrogen-fixing plants (legumes—such as peas and clover—and sainfoin and other grasses) into nitrogen-robbing crops. There was also the result of an increase in fodder crops, such as turnips. Together, the nitrogen-rich grasses and the root vegetables, increased the nitrogen in nature's manure, animal dung. From 1770 to 1880, the nitrogen in the soil was increased by 60 to 70 percent, with similar yield response. From about 1820, nonagriculturally based nutrient additives were applied to the soil—nitrates, potassium, and phosphoric acid—from home industrial byproducts, overseas mineral imports, and bird dung (guano). The effect of such external supplies has probably been exaggerated, not least because the application of science to agriculture was much discussed but little understood until about 1945. In addition, now it is known that there is an upper limit on the improvement possible through raising the organic content of the tilth bed—plants can have too much nitrogen.

The World's Major Cereals: Wheat, Maize, and Rice. There was the long, gradual increase in yields from late medieval times to the eighteenth century, then a steep growth in yields during the nineteenth century, from which it was difficult to extend yields. Seemingly, this limit to growth was not confined to England and to western Europe. Estimated world wheat yields grew modestly from 13 bushels per acre in the 1880s to 15 bushels per acre by 1914; they fell to 14 bushels per acre in the 1930s with the U.S. drought and dustbowl conditions in the Midwest and the failure of the Soviet Union's wheat fields. Although the wheat-producing countries operated at different absolute productivity levels, they nonetheless exhibited a similar plateau profile.

The pattern of maize and rice yields from medieval times is impossible to construct for anything but very local

examples. The consensus seems to be that maize yields in North America (the continent of origin of the crop) may have doubled from about 1500 to 1750 (from 10 to 20 bushels per acre), then was increased by another 50 percent by World War II. Rice yields in Asia in that same period increased from 2 tons per hectare in 1500 to 3 tons by 1900. As with wheat, this was a gradual change rather than a revolutionary change. Then, as the twentieth century progressed, revolutionary changes in these three crop yields occurred. Estimates of their yields are also more accurate because of agencies created by first the International Institute of Agriculture in 1905, then the Food Agricultural Organization (FAO) of the United Nations, which offer figures for comparisons (these are summarized in Table 1). World food output doubled from 1970 to 2000, but the land base from which it came has remained more or less stable. In short, there has been a remarkable revolution in land productivity, and crop yields, called the Green Revolution. That local or regional food shortages occur, verging on or descending into famines, has nothing to do with the capacity of the world agricultural system to produce enough food. They have everything to do with politics, distribution systems, and the property rights of the victims.

Wheat Yields. The more or less flat trend in international wheat yields that began in the 1800s continued until about 1950. There then was at first a gradual, then a sudden, rise in yields, especially in Europe; elsewhere, wheat production rose but not by so great a degree and perhaps a decade or so later. The equivalent rises in maize and rice yields also date from that era. The increases are attributed to the scientific revolution in agriculture that involved vast applications of artificial, laboratory-based chemical additives (euphemistically called fertilizers), improved pest control through similar scientific methods, and improved plant-breeding methods—hybridization in plants and the genetic modification of plants. Plant-breeding methods especially reduce some of the historically worst effects of external factors, such as the weather (by shortening the growing season). The sum effect of the changes has been high-yielding seeds.

The resulting chronological profile of crop yields overshadows previous achievements: wheat yields in Britain have increased by 140 percent and barley yields by 150 percent since 1970, and more widely, world cereal yields have increased by similar proportions since 1950. A noticeable international feature of the trend in wheat yields—more so than for other crops, since at some level wheat is grown worldwide—is the way countries have dealt with resource constraints. Western Europe boasts the highest yields historically, especially in those countries where few areas of virgin territory might extend agriculture. That is also the case in Japan and New Zealand,

TABLE 1. *World Trends in Wheat, Maize, and Rice Yields (100 kilograms/hectare)*

WHEAT	1930[a]	1940	1950	1960	1970	1980	1990	2000
World	9.5	10.2	10.8	12.4	14.6	18.6	26.4	28.4
Europe	12.6	11.9	14.5	19.3	24.4	37.9	48.0	48.8
N/C America	10.3	11.0	11.2	13.8	20.6	21.3	25.7	27.3
S America	8.9	11.3	10.5	11.3	12.5	13.1	17.3	23.9
Asia	7.8	8.9	8.8	10.5	11.1	16.1	23.8	27.8
Africa	10.4	6.3	7.3	7.1	8.7	11.0	16.0	16.3
Oceania	7.5	8.4	10.8	11.3	12.4	9.8	16.5	19.6
USSR	7.5	—	—	11.0	14.3	15.1	21.1	16.6
MAIZE	1930[a]	1940	1950	1960	1970	1980	1990	2000
World	13.8	14.8	15.7	20.5	23.2	31.4	38.0	43.1
Europe	12.6	14.9	12.3	22.2	32.5	44.8	44.0	52.3
N/C America	14.9	16.5	21.0	27.4	36.1	48.3	60.5	68.2
S America	17.0	17.0	13.0	13.4	16.4	18.6	20.4	31.0
Asia	10.9	10.6	10.1	9.5	17.0	23.3	33.1	35.5
Africa	9.3	7.7	8.9	9.5	11.4	15.6	14.9	17.4
Oceania	17.5	12.6	18.6	24.0	28.2	40.9	52.6	68.0
USSR	8.9[b]	—	—	13.8	28.1	31.8	34.8	27.0
RICE	1930[a]	1940	1950	1960	1970	1980	1990	2000
World	15.6	14.7	16.0	19.6	25.8	30.1	39.4	42.4
Europe	47.6	50.8	45.5	45.1	45.0	50.2	53.5	61.8
N/C America	19.0	20.8	21.9	27.1	37.5	43.3	50.9	56.0
S America	16.1	17.6	17.2	18.4	17.5	19.0	24.3	35.5
Asia	15.5	14.4	15.9	19.5	24.0	27.9	36.2	39.2
Africa	13.9	13.0	12.5	14.9	18.2	17.4	20.4	22.6
Oceania	34.2	35.4	35.9	40.0	52.4	49.9	81.3	91.8
USSR	16.6	—	—	22.1	34.0	38.9	35.3	23.6

[a]1930, in fact the average of 1926–1930.   [b]USSR maize, 1926–1930, in fact 1932.
The FAO database allows the user to reconstruct the former USSR and other territories that have undergone revolutionary political change. The table is, therefore, more or less a representation of a constant geography in c.1950.
SOURCES: FAO, *Yearbook of Food and Agricultural Statistics*, later renamed *Production Yearbook*. Rome, annual. International Institute of Agriculture, *International Yearbook of Agricultural Statistics*. Rome, annual.

where high yields are achieved but where topographical constraints limit farm land, Egypt also achieves high yields. Not only do these countries achieve high wheat yields but also some of the world's highest maize and rice yields (Japan and Egypt for all crops; high maize, rice, and wheat yields in several of the European countries). In contrast, countries like Canada and the United States may boast high production, but they do so with relatively poor yields; in both, the 1990s wheat yield was less than one third of that achieved in much of western Europe—a case of extensification versus intensification. Worldwide wheat yields are, however, beginning to achieve their plateau levels. In terms of yields, the limits to growth may have been reached, although not yet for maize and rice.

Maize and Rice Yields. In some ways, the trend of maize yields since 1930 is not unlike that of wheat, but the continent that more than others really depends on maize—Africa—shows a general inability to grow much beyond the yield level reached in 1930. The highest yielding maize areas are North America and Europe, but exceptionally high

yields are also achieved in the small maize crops of the Middle East and in Oceania. The trend in rice yields mirrors the other crop yields, although it has a much greater international dispersion. Some of the southern European countries had a tradition of greater rice yields by 1930 than did oriental producers, and they continued to do so into the 1990s (Greece, Spain, and Portugal), as did North America. The former Soviet Union had a significant dip in all crop yields in the years after the 1991 breakup of its constituent republics into autonomous countries. In contrast, China continued to perform very well in rice crop yields; since 1960, general grain yields have increased in China by more than 260 percent. With the notable exception of Egypt, Africa remains the continent that lags in all measures of yields.

[*See also* Crop Failures; Famines; *and* Total Factor Productivity.]

BIBLIOGRAPHY
Chorley, G. Patrick H. "The Agricultural Revolution in Northern Europe, 1750–1880: Nitrogen, Legumes, and Crop Productivity." *Economic History Review* 34.1 (1981), 71–93.

Food Agricultural Organization of the United Nations (FAO). *Yearbook of Food and Agricultural Statistics*; renamed *Production Yearbook*. Rome.

Grigg, David. *The Transformation of Agriculture in the West.* Oxford, 1992.

Johnson, D. Gale, and Robert L. Gustafson. *Grain Yields and the American Food Supply.* Chicago, 1962.

Malenbaum, Wilfred. *The World Wheat Economy.* Cambridge, Mass, 1953.

Perkins, Dwight. *Agricultural Development in China, 1368–1968.* Chicago, 1969.

Shiel, Robert S., "Improving Soil Productivity in the Pre-Fertiliser Era." In *Land, Labour and Livestock: Historical Studies in European Agricultural Productivity*, edited by B. M. S. Campbell and M. Overton, pp. 51–77. Manchester, 1991.

Simon, Julian, L., ed. *The State of Humanity.* Oxford, 1995.

Slicher van Bath, B. H. "Yield Ratios, 1810–1820." *A.A.G. Bijdragen* 10 (1963).

Turner, M. E., J. V. Beckett, and B. Afton. *Farm Production in England, 1700–1914.* Oxford, 2001.

MICHAEL TURNER

CUBA. With an area of more than 44,000 square miles (114,400 square kilometers), Cuba is the largest of the Caribbean islands. The political jurisdiction encompasses hundreds of neighboring islands, the largest of which is the Isla de la Juventud (Isle of Youth, formerly called Isle of Pines) to the southwest of the main island. Cuba is mostly flat or gently rolling, with three pronounced elevations—the Guaniguanico range in the west, the Sierra de Trinidad in the center, and the Sierra Maestra, the most prominent, in the east. Hundreds of small, short rivers, flowing mostly southward, drain the plains. The longest, the Rio Cauto, with its tributary, the Rio Salado, meanders for 230 miles before entering Manzanillo Bay. The tropical location of the island produces consistently moderate temperatures with little seasonal variation except for alternating wet and dry seasons. Occasional hurricanes between June and November often result in extensive physical destruction and great human suffering.

Population. The earliest inhabitants, called Tainos, migrated from South America. At the time of the first Spanish settlements in 1511, the indigenous population amounted to slightly more than 100,000. Within a few years after their arrival, the Spaniards decimated the indigenous population and only a few scattered individuals remained in the eastern part of the island. Cuba remained a Spanish colony until 1898, by which time it had become the most prosperous Spanish colony.

For more than five centuries after its colonization, Cuba received an ethnically diverse immigrant stream not only of Spaniards and Africans but also Chinese, Jews, Germans, Anglo-Saxons, and Maya from the neighboring Yucatan peninsula. Between 1518 and 1850, Cuban slave owners imported more than 760,000 Africans mainly to work in agriculture, especially the sugar cane fields that expanded after 1763. Those Africans were a variegated group that included Yoruba and Bantu peoples, who originated from a vast area between the Senegal River and the Guinea Coast in Africa. Between 1853 and 1874, Cuban landholders imported more than 125,000 indentured Chinese laborers, mainly from Canton, to facilitate the transition from slavery to wage labor. The Spanish abolished slavery in 1886. During the third sugar boom between 1915 and the late 1920s, Cuba permitted the entrance of more than 30,000 Cantonese, small groups of Japanese, as well as more than 200,000 Antillean contract workers, mainly from Jamaica and Haiti. Although whites have invariably constituted a majority, the nonwhite component of the population has been substantial.

Although the country is nominally Roman Catholic in keeping with its Spanish colonial tradition, other religious sects have flourished in Cuba including Santería (an eclectic cult devoted to certain African deities formally identified with Catholic saints), Jewish, and Protestant groups. During the first years of the Cuban revolution led by Fidel Castro, the hostility between the revolutionary government and religious groups resulted in the departure of more than 70 percent of all priests, 90 percent of all nuns, all rabbis, and a significant proportion of the Protestant clergy. The 1976 constitution declared the state to be nonsectarian but guaranteed individual religious tolerance. Gradually a modus vivendi developed and the pope made a successful visit to the island in 1998.

Productivity. Agriculture is the mainstay of the Cuban economy, and the island is potentially self-sufficient in basic nutritional categories—a rarity in the Caribbean. Sugar cane cultivation is the principal agricultural activity, although yields vary considerably and sugar prices on the world market have been discouragingly low. Other important products include tobacco, rice, citrus fruits, bananas, coffee, cocoa, pineapples, sweet potatoes, potatoes, corn, manioc, and beans. Cattle and small stock breeding and farming have not been impressive, given their potential. Industrial production centers on food processing, petroleum production, nickel, copper, chrome, and pyrite exploitation, along with other precious minerals such as manganese, magnetite, limestone, kaolin, and marble. Tourism has rapidly assumed an important economic role in the past years, and in 2000 was second only to family remissions from abroad as a contributor to the gross domestic product. Cuba maintains a very large, modern fishing fleet.

History. Cuban history falls into three periods: the Spanish colony from 1511 to 1898, the period of North American hegemony between 1898 and 1958, and the Castro revolution after 1959.

Christopher Columbus claimed Cuba for the monarchs of Castile on 27 October 1492. Diego Velázquez started

A SUGAR ESTATE.

A SUGAR ESTATE. Illustration from *Harper's New Monthly Magazine*, vol. 6, 1852. (Prints and Photographs Division, Library of Congress)

permanent settlement in 1511, founding Baracoa and a number of small towns. By 1515 Cuba had several municipal divisions, including Havana, Remedios, Trinidad, Sancti-Spíritus, Puerto Príncipe, Bayamo, Santiago de Cuba, and Baracoa. Each had a *cabildo*, or town council, that regulated legal, commercial, and administrative affairs and defended local interests such as slave trading and the *encomienda* (a system of labor distribution) before the royal council. But before the late eighteenth century, Cuba was a struggling colony with a relatively small population that depended heavily on irregular subsidies from New Spain, and whose international importance derived mainly from the strategic location of the harbor at Havana. The sugar revolutions after 1763 and the slave trade transformed both the society and the economy. By 1860 the population had grown to more than 1.3 million, with slaves accounting for the most dramatic increase—from some 39,000 in 1773 to more than 400,000 in the 1840s. Despite the drastic curtailing of the international transatlantic slave trade, Cuba imported more than 600,000 Africans during the nineteenth century and supplemented the labor force with free recruits from elsewhere. During the nineteenth century, the Cuban sugar industry became the most technologically advanced in the world, utilizing narrow-gauged railroads, steam-driven mills, and centrifuges to produce approximately one-third of the world's

sugar. The sugar economy produced a new, wealthy, cosmopolitan class of slave owners and integrated Cuba fully into the international transatlantic capitalist system.

Along with the economic and social transformations of the nineteenth century came also profound political ferment, aggravated to some extent by the inconsistency of internal Spanish domestic politics. Economic and political forces led to the Ten Years' War between 1868 and 1878, which ended in stalemate. In 1895, as the political and economic crisis deepened, a new war for independence broke out. By that time investment from the United States exceeded $50 million, and annual trade $100 million. The brilliant poet, writer, and propagandist José Martí, who died during his first engagement with Spanish forces, skillfully coordinated Cuban political organizations both on the island and abroad. Spain deployed more than 200,000 troops and in three years of devastating war brought all commercial activity to a halt. Excited by the "yellow press" and a mysterious explosion aboard the USS *Maine*, its battleship visiting Havana's harbor, the United States declared war on Spain on 25 April 1898. By August Spain signed a peace protocol ending hostilities. The Treaty of Paris signed on 10 December 1898, granted Cuban independence under the auspices of the United States.

The United States military occupation restored normalcy and created a quasi-independent political system.

Beginning in 1902 Cubans exercised a limited franchise to elect their own officials, although the Platt Amendment (1901) to their constitution gave the United States the right to oversee international agreements, the domestic economy, and internal affairs as well as the right to establish naval stations on the island in perpetuity. Although both countries abrogated the amendment in 1934, the United States continued to maintain a naval base at Guantánamo Bay.

Incessant political discontent culminated in the revolution of Fidel Castro, who overthrew the government of Fulgencio Batista in 1959. Castro dismantled the capitalist state and created a socialist state that allied itself closely with the Soviet Union, especially after 1970. The nationalization of hundreds of millions of dollars of foreign property in the first years of the revolution attracted the unmitigated hostility of the United States. It broke diplomatic relations with Cuba, initiated a trade embargo that lasted for decades, and secretly supported an unsuccessful invasion by Cuban exiles at the Bay of Pigs in April 1961, as well as numerous schemes to assassinate Castro. In October 1962 the world faced nuclear war over some missiles that the Soviet Union installed in Cuba. Apart from a difference of political philosophy, Cuban military and civilian assistance to countries in Africa, Latin America, and the Caribbean created continuous friction with the United States. Over the period of the revolution, hundreds of thousands of Cubans left their fatherland, mostly for the United States. In 1977 Cuba and the United States opened interests sections in Washington and Havana. The two countries signed an agreement in 1987 allowing for the emigration of up to twenty thousand Cubans annually to the United States. The collapse of the Soviet Union in 1991 dramatically dislocated the Cuban economy and society for several years, forcing Castro to declare a "special period in peacetime" of severe food rationing, drastic energy conservation, and steep reduction in public services. By the late 1990s a significantly modified system created a curious hybrid of socialist and capitalist measures that helped restore the collapsed economy and reoriented commerce to a global market. In 2001 Castro had outlasted nine U.S. administrations, and the Cuba of the twenty-first century looked a lot different from the socialist nirvana that its leaders had predicted in the early 1960s.

[*See also* Caribbean Region *and* Spain, *subentry on* Spanish Empire.]

BIBLIOGRAPHY

Dye, Alan. *Cuban Sugar in the Age of Mass Production: Technology and the Economics of the Sugar Central, 1899–1929.* Stanford, 1998.

Domínguez, Jorge I. *Cuba: Order and Revolution.* Cambridge, Mass., 1978.

Feinsilver, Julie. *Healing the Masses: Cuban Health Politics at Home and Abroad.* Berkeley, 1993.

Helg, Aline. *Our Rightful Share: The Afro-Cubans Struggle for Equality, 1886–1912.* Chapel Hill, 1995.

Knight, Franklin W. *Slave Society in Cuba during the Nineteenth Century.* Madison, Wisc., 1970.

Moreno-Fraginals, Manuel. *The Sugar Mill.* New York, 1976.

Pérez, Jr., Louis A. *Cuba: Between Reform and Revolution.* New York, 1988.

Pérez-Sarduy, Pedro, and Jean Stubbs, eds. *Afro-Cuban Voices: On Race and Identity in Contemporary Cuba.* Gainesville, Fla., 2000.

Pérez-Stable, Marifelí. *The Cuban Revolution: Origins, Course, and Legacy.* New York, 1999.

Zanetti, Oscar, and Alejandro García. *Sugar and Railroads: A Cuban History, 1837–1959.* Chapel Hill, 1998.

FRANKLIN W. KNIGHT

CUSTOM. The term *custom*, or *social custom*, refers to the set of habits, attitudes, and convictions prevailing in a society, as inherited from the past. Used in another sense, custom refers to the forces that shape those habits, attitudes, and convictions. Thus it may be said that the forces of custom mold the prevailing conventions, mores, usages, manners, and habits as well as the prevailing preferences, behavioral inclinations, moral attitudes, and social norms. Phrased differently, the term *custom* refers to the tacit elements of culture, that is, to those parts that are not formalized or institutionalized but emerge and form spontaneously, and to the forces that govern these regularities. The formalized and institutionalized parts of culture—formalized law, religious organization, and other cultural conventions, institutions, and artifacts—rely on elements of custom, and are often shaped by the same behavioral tendencies that give rise to custom.

Social and economic structures and processes are thoroughly permeated by elements of custom—customary ways of behaving, of thinking, and of evaluating all kinds of actions and events. The economic and social institutions in any given society rely in a fundamental way on prevailing customs. Yet custom cannot be taken as a given for purposes of long-term analysis because it is molded, bent, and shaped by the very social and economic processes that build on it.

Custom as a System. The amalgam of habits, attitudes, and convictions to which we refer as "custom" forms an interlocking complex, where each element stabilizes the others. Consider customary attitudes that link social status to skin color. These prejudices will give rise to various rationalizations, reconfirming and stabilizing discriminatory attitudes and habits. As a result, the discriminatory habits, values, preferences, and cognitions mutually reinforce each other. In addition, customs are mutually dependent upon each other. The custom of greeting by raising one's hat cannot be maintained without the custom of wearing a hat, for example, and has vanished more recently along with the custom of wearing hats. Typically, each custom depends on many others. The system of habits, behavioral inclinations, and associated convictions must be conceived as a system—not in any mechanical sense, but rather as a very comprehensive net of mostly weak and vague interdependencies.

Custom as an Agent of Production. The importance of the impact that custom has had on economic performance, both its constraining and enabling effects, have been stressed. Many economists emphasize that custom often presents an impediment to economic change and social development. The economist Alfred Marshall (1842–1924) spoke of the "yoke of custom" as "hindering the method of production and the character of producers from developing themselves freely," and the economist John Stuart Mill (1806–1873) saw competition and custom as two alternative mechanisms of economic coordination, with progress dependent upon the forces of competition, and held that the sphere of competition would expand while the sphere of custom would shrink over time, in the course of economic and social modernization.

On the other hand, custom is an important agent of production, easing or even enabling production and social coordination in many important ways. Alfred Marshall emphasized this positive aspect of custom as well. He observed that businesses, as organizational forms, rely on specific elements of business morality without which they would not be feasible. Contracting—a prerequisite of all kinds of economic coordination—has a largely relational nature and is not usefully enforceable in court. Instead it relies on the presence and mutual acceptance of business practices. In former times, a businessman's handshake was worth more than a written contract, and cognate practices survive in modern specialized markets. This is of obvious advantage for easing economic transactions.

Furthermore, custom and competition are not mutually exclusive, as Mill thought, but often mutually complementary. Business morality is a case in point. As another example, consider gratuities. A custom of giving, say, 10 or 15 percent as a normal gratuity for certain services may enhance economic performance. The customer may give less if dissatisfied and give more if fully satisfied. In this way, an effective incentive for maintaining the quality of the service is established that would be absent without the custom.

Inadequacy of Functionalistic and Individualistic Explanations. This is not to say that customs, such as tipping, form "optimally" in the sense of establishing themselves such that economic efficiency is optimized for the relevant transactions. Empirically, tipping practices in similar countries such as the United States and Australia differ significantly. Given the similarity of these societies, we would expect roughly similar standards from an efficiency point of view, but actual practices diverge. Further,

other customs—ownership of human beings in slave societies, or caste systems, to name just two—seem not to foster economic or other types of efficiency. Their possible positive side effects in terms of efficiency—if there are any—can usually be taken care of by alternative and preferable arrangements. The functionalist position that custom forms "optimally" seems problematic. Custom is neither fully "optimal" nor entirely detrimental. In some ways it is an impediment, in others an important productive asset. In both senses, it is an important agent of production.

The example of tipping—relating to a widely observed custom in modern economies, which contributes significantly to income in some occupations—also illustrates the other point that custom cannot be explained in terms of self-interest, often identified with methodological individualism. This approach falls short of accounting for the common practice of offering gratuities in nonrepeated exchanges. Even if the individuals are assumed to prefer conforming to the social norm of leaving gratuities, or to fear social sanctions by not conforming, each individual will find that there is scope for conforming with the custom in a self-seeking way; for instance, by rounding downward rather than upward in cases of doubt. This would drive average gratuities down over time and would thereby extinguish the custom.

Reciprocity. Such customs as giving gratuities seem to rely on reciprocity, that is on a desire of the individuals to reciprocate gifts with countergifts, and to retaliate offenses with counter-offenses. Consider a market where gratuities are not customary. The customers may pay, however, more than the stated price if satisfied, simply by leaving $5.00 to cover a bill of $4.73, but they cannot pay less, even if dissatisfied. Customers who are reciprocators will behave this way. As a consequence, tipping may occur occasionally, gradually making it acceptable and customary. There will emerge an average positive level of gratuities in the market. Customers, motivated by reciprocity, will start giving some gratuities even for average service and will deviate in the one or the other direction, according to the quality of the service provided.

Many aspects of economic interaction can be understood in this manner. For example, relational contracting, the reliance on tacit mutual obligations in contract interpretation and execution, relates to this class of phenomena. Other economically important instances are provided by the widespread practice, found in so many firms, of paying wages in excess of what would be required to attract workers, and the workers' willingness to work more than "strictly by the rules." Firms can thrive with these behavioral propensities by creating a strong corporate culture. Furthermore, keeping promises and engaging in the faithful execution of contractual obligations—fundamental to economic performance—may be understood in terms of reciprocity.

Reciprocity builds on certain standards of entitlement and obligation, as reciprocation is prompted by deviations from what is considered the norm. The norm itself is a matter of custom, in that normality itself generates the norm. In this sense, reciprocity builds on custom. The desire to reciprocate itself can be traced to a desire of humans to establish regular patterns of behavior and to balance deviations from those patterns by appropriate counter deviations.

Conventions. Conventions are important elements of custom. Typical conventions relate to greeting, expressing agreement, holding market days, or using certain commodities rather than others as means of exchange. The essential aspect of a convention is that it is reasonable for everybody to follow it if the others comply. (In terms of game theory, a convention is a Nash equilibrium.) An obvious example is provided by the convention of driving on the right-hand side of the road in some countries, and driving on the left-hand side in others. Given that everybody drives on the right-hand side in the former, it is imperative that everyone should do the same.

Many approaches to problems of social interaction seek to understand all kinds of social regularities, including institutions, as conventions. The prototype argument has been developed by the Austrian economist Carl Menger (1840–1921) with regard to the evolution of money. In an exchange economy, individuals will accept certain commodities for payment even if they have no use for the commodity, as long as they can expect to find others who will willingly accept it in exchange for something they need. If a commodity is widely used for exchange purposes, everybody will accept it, and it will turn into money. (Some primitive moneys provide counterexamples to this logic, however.)

Generalization. Consider the convention of driving on the right-hand side of the road. If a traveler, arriving in a foreign country, observes that people drive on the right-hand side of Harbor Street and Broadway, he will conclude that this is the prevailing custom. This inference is, logically speaking, not defensible because there is no evidence that the rule applies to other roads. Yet the custom is grasped by this kind of quick and superficial induction. Many customs that are not formally transmitted rely on such spontaneous generalization, which is a precondition for tacit transmission.

Generalization is not only important for the transmission of a custom; it entails behavioral generalization, too. The custom of driving on the right-hand side of the street, for instance, usually encompasses walking on the right-hand side of sidewalks and stairs. The custom to discriminate according to skin color in business transactions leads to discrimination in other spheres of social life. The converse is also true. If market forces bring about a racial integration of the workforce in a discriminatory society, this will weaken discriminatory attitudes and practices in other spheres of life: Equality and equal treatment at work weaken the belief that the groups differ in any fundamental way. The theories that seek to depict all customs as conventions neglect this important motivational force arising from generalization.

Private Customs and Social Conventions. The custom-as-convention view also neglects some other behavioral tendencies beyond generalization. This is readily seen if we consider private habits and customs. The term *private custom* refers to the amalgam of habits, convictions, attitudes, and preferences entertained by individuals not facing social interaction. Arguments relating to social interaction are inappropriate here, because there is no interaction. Still, we find that individuals develop behavioral habits, emotional and cognitive attitudes ("habits of the mind"), and preferences in a given setting and do carry these over to new situations. These regularities seem often related to "ownership effects" and "commitment effects," a class of phenomena studied by psychologists. Custom seems to rely as much on these psychological regularities as it relies on the logic of conventions—a point very clearly stated by David Hume (1711–1776) in his thoughts about the customary origins of property.

Custom as Inertia. Custom is sometimes portrayed as a force of inertia, maintaining everything as it is as long as no other forces come into action. (Alfred Marshall expressed this view, for instance, and evolutionary economics with its emphasis on "routines" governing economic interaction suggests a similar stance.) The "inertia view" is misleading because customs may grow and spread, change over time, or erode. The forces governing the growth and decay of customs are, in this sense, active forces and not merely forces of inertia. As an example, consider the arguments about the emergence of gratuities from reciprocity in conjunction with the argument about generalization. Taken together, they may explain the spreading of the custom of giving gratuities in markets where quality can be observed on the spot. We may even speculate that new technologies, such as the Internet, render new modes of transaction dominant, bringing about supporting customs. These new customs and etiquettes may then spread to traditional modes of transactions. It is misleading to depict such processes of growth and generalization as instances of inertia.

Custom as Friction. A related view, also developed by Alfred Marshall, is that custom amounts to friction in the sense of slowing down all processes that would otherwise run faster. Eventually, however, custom will adapt to new exigencies. If it is expedient to honor promises, honesty will spread; if it is profitable to cheat, honesty will be eroded. In the long term, custom would be molded entirely by economic and other incentives. As an upshot of this argument, custom would not matter in the long term and could be entirely disregarded for purposes of analysis. It would amount to friction, but could not provide an active force generating some kind of structure and development. Although such an argument points to important phenomena that render custom adaptive in many ways, this view entirely neglects the active elements of custom. Because of its active elements, custom exerts an important influence on its own, and the adaptive view of custom is often inadequate.

Custom as Preference. Custom may also be understood as a force that molds the preferences of the individuals in a given society, making them prefer customary ways of behavior. The customary part of their preferences is, however, not idiosyncratic but rather shared by many individuals in society. In this, it relates directly to social norms. These customary preferences can be taken as relatively stable givens to be fixed under a *ceteris paribus* clause for purposes of short-run analysis. In the long term, however, the adaptive and active aspects of custom formation interact with economic processes, and it is misleading to fix customs or social norms hypothetically, under a *ceteris paribus* clause when dealing with issues of long-term historical change.

Custom as a Constraint. Given that people foster certain customs and associated preferences, habits, and convictions, these givens can be considered as constraints for each individual's action. Everybody faces the reactions of the other members of society, as molded by custom. In this sense, custom can be viewed as a constraint for purposes of partial analysis.

Custom as a Situational Force. It is customary to analyze economic action by assuming that individuals act according to their preferences, subject to certain constraints. As custom may be viewed as affecting both preferences and constraints, all behavioral effects of custom could be couched in these terms, yet this may be misleading. While it is true that all action can be framed as determined by tastes and constraints, this is a theoretical perspective that complicates matters unduly, and thereby hinders rather than helps in understanding. A direct approach of viewing customary action as prompted by the interpretation and perception of the situation, and by a desire of the individuals to live up to what "the situation demands," is often preferable.

Custom usually requires certain actions that are prompted by certain situations. The behavior elicited in this way may not be brought about by fear of formal or informal sanction; it may not be prompted either by a preference for the required action as such. A customer may resent having to leave a gratuity on the restaurant table upon departure because doing so would leave him without the fare for going home by bus. He thinks, however, that the waiter deserves a tip because he has served him well. If he does not give the gratuity, he will feel uneasy, even if he personally condemns and dislikes the custom. The choice between giving the gratuity and going home by bus differs from his earlier choice between fish and meat because it involves an obligation that is prompted by the situation and by the custom that prescribes that type of behavior in this situation. In this sense, behavior does not reflect a simple preference, even if it can be theoretically rephrased in such terms.

The Pervasiveness of Custom. Custom is a pervasive element in social and economic organization. The example of gratuities provides a very clear instance of an economically relevant custom that can be theoretically detached from the underlying transaction. Customs that cannot be theoretically isolated as nicely from the "purely economic" aspects are much more common and much more important. When customary features are tightly integrated with economic incentives, institutions, and laws, custom is particularly important and remains, at the same time, almost invisible. Comparing economies across time and space may render these customary influences visible, and help explain how some customs have supported certain developments and frustrated others, and how the ensuing developments have molded those customs in turn.

[*See also* Gifts and Gift Giving *and* Inheritance Systems.]

BIBLIOGRAPHY

Akerlof, George. "A Theory of Social Custom, of Which Unemployment. May be One Consequence." *Quarterly Journal of Economics* 94.4 (1980), 749–775. Rationalizes the persistence of individually costly customs by the desire to maintain a socially accepted reputation.

Akerlof, George, and Rachel E. Kranton. "Economics and Identity." *Quarterly Journal of Economics* 105.3 (2000), 715–753. Rationalizes conforming to custom by the individual's desire to maintain his or her identity as defined by custom.

Camic, Charles. "The Matter of Habit." *American Journal of Sociology* 91 (1985), 139–187. A broad investigation of the concept of habit in sociology.

Harris, Marvin. *Cows, Pigs, Wars, and Witches: The Riddles of Culture.* New York, 1974. Gives a functionalist interpretation of many customs.

Hume, David. *On Human Nature.* Oxford, 1888. Book 3 contains Hume's theory of property, which can be seen as a model for the theory of custom.

Jones, Eric L. "Culture and Its Relationship to Economic Change." *Journal of Institutional and Theoretical Economics* 151 (1995), 269–285. Discusses stickiness and malleability of culture from a historian's perspective.

Kreps, D. M. "Corporate Culture and Economic Theory." In *Perspectives on Positive Political Economy,* edited by J. E. Alt and K. A. Shepsle, pp. 90–143. New York and Melbourne, 1990. Proposes to view corporate culture as a set of conventions.

Lewis, David K. *Convention: A Philosophical Study.* Cambridge, Mass., 1969. Develops the theory of conventions.

Marshall, Alfred. *Principles of Economics.* 8th ed. London, 1920. This classic treatise contains many important but dispersed comments on the economic influence and significance of custom.

Menger, Carl. "On the Origins of Money." *Economic Journal* 2 (1892). 239–255. A classic interpretation of money as a convention.

Mill, John Stuart. *Principles of Political Economy.* London, 1848. Book 2, chapter 4 of this classic treatise juxtaposes custom and competition as two alternative mechanisms of coordination.

Nelson, Richard. R., and Sidney G. Winter. *An Evolutionary Theory of Economic Change.* Cambrige, Mass., 1982. Places great emphasis on "routines" as governing economic interaction.

North, Douglass. *Institutions, Institutional Change, and Economic Performance.* Cambridge, 1990. Emphasises the role of informal constraints for economic performance.

Schelling, Thomas. *The Strategy of Conflict.* Cambridge, Mass., 1960. A classic treatise of conventions.

Schlicht, Ekkehart. *On Custom in the Economy.* Oxford, 1998. Gives this author's theory of custom, building on fundamental psychological mechanisms. It relies on David Hume's theory of property.

Schlicht, Ekkehart. "Aestheticism in the Theory of Custom." *Journal des Économistes et des Études Humaines* 10.1 (2000), 33–51. Offers an evolutionary argument for this author's view of custom.

Schotter, Andrew. *The Economic Theory of Economic Institutions.* Cambridge, 1981. Depicts institutions as conventions.

Sugden, R. *The Economics of Rights, Co-operation, and Welfare.* Oxford, 1986. Develops the idea of conventions from a game-theoretic point of view.

Ullmann-Margalit, Edna. *The Emergence of Norms.* Oxford, 1977. Discusses the formation of social norms in a game-theoretic framework.

Weber, Max. *Economy and Society, an Outline of Interpretive Sociology.* Edited by Guenther Roth and Claus Wittich. New York, 1968. Volume 1 contains on pages 67–70 and 319–325 some relevant conceptual distinctions. Weber combines the "customs-as-conventions" view with the "customs-as-preference" view.

EKKEHART SCHLICHT

CUSTOMS UNIONS. *See* Commercial Policy, *subentry on* Customs Unions.

CZECHOSLOVAKIA AND THE CZECH AND SLOVAK REPUBLICS.

The end of World War I brought the Czechs and Slovaks an independent democratic state. The First Czechoslovak Republic (ČSR), which comprised the Czech Lands (Bohemia, Moravia, and Silesia), Slovakia, and from 1919 sub-Carpathian Ruthenia, was established on 28 October 1918 as one of the successor states of Austria-Hungary. In 1921, the state's multinational population amounted to 13.6 million, and the republic covered an area of 140,519 square kilometers. While only encompassing a fifth of the total area and a quarter of the inhabitants of the former Austria-Hungary, it contained more than half of its industrial potential and just under half of the workers employed in its industry.

The Slav peoples represented 70 percent of the inhabitants, with the Czechs as the dominant nationality, followed by Slovaks, Ruthenians (Ukrainians), and a small minority of Poles. The German speakers, representing a fifth of the population, inhabited mainly the border areas of the Czech Lands. Magyars numbered less than 5 percent and lived largely in southern Slovakia, while the majority of Poles lived in the Těšín-Ostrava region. Minorities enjoyed greater democratic freedoms than other minority groups in the neighboring states. Nevertheless, economic and social life took on nationalistic overtones, whereby the difficulties minorities suffered were exploited, above all, by National Socialist Germany and semi-Fascist Hungary. After the end of World War II, owing to the tragic fate of the Jewish population, the cession of sub-Carpathian Ruthenia to the Soviet Union, the transfer of Germans, and the return of emigrated Czechoslovak citizens, the percentage of Czechs and Slovaks rose to 95 percent in 1948 and did not undergo any changes until the end of 1992, when Czechoslovkia divided into the Czech Republic and the Slovak Republic. From 1947 to 1992, its population increased from 12.2 to 15.6 million.

Interwar Years. During the interwar years, the increase in industrial production in the ČSR's economy was greater than in the majority of European countries, resulting from the growth of capital investment and increasingly efficient industrial capacity in the 1920s. If one hundred is taken as the average of the years 1925 to 1929, Czechoslovak industrial production increased by 71.8 percent in comparison with 1913. Average growth in Europe, excluding the USSR, was 36.9 percent. The distribution of employment underlined the west-east gradient of development. While the Czech Lands' agriculture was intensive (25.6 percent of the active population was employed in agriculture and forestry in 1930) and 92 percent of the country's industrial potential and resources of energy were concentrated there, Slovakia maintained its agrarian character until the mid-twentieth century (58.5 percent of the active population was employed in agriculture and forestry in 1930 and still 53.5 percent in 1950). As part of the ČSR, Slovakia benefited from the democratic political system and from its progressive social and cultural policy, but in the economic sphere, competition from Czech industry caused serious problems.

The currency reform in 1919 stabilized the Czechoslovak crown (Kč), while all neighboring states experienced hyperinflations. Concurrently, land reform legislation relating to 29 percent of all land was introduced. Although 57 percent of the land earmarked for redistribution, especially forests, was returned to the original owners, a large number of small and medium holdings as well as new, relatively large agricultural estates (one hundred hectares each) were created. Agricultural capital was concentrated in the centralized federative organs of agricultural cooperatives, which came to control credit, trade with agricultural products, and the agricultural industry. By means of investments in the large joint-stock companies of the chemical and armaments industry, the cooperatives became powerful partners of industrialists and bankers, and through their control of the Agrarian Party, their leading politicians held important government posts.

The process of concentration of production and capital as well as cartelization came to encompass all branches of industry, and the economic strength of the large banks, with their dependent industrial concerns, grew. Direct foreign capital investment amounting to 27 percent of total Czechoslovak share capital from leading financial groups in Britain, France, Belgium, and Holland was concentrated mainly in mining and metallurgy, chemicals, engineering, banking, and insurance. Czechoslovak capital was exported mostly to central and southeast Europe, led by the Škoda Works, the largest central European engineering concern, and Bat'a, the interwar world's largest shoe manufacturer.

In late 1929, the rising trend in economic growth was interrupted by the world economic crisis. Of all European countries, Czechoslovakia suffered the most severe drop in its vital exports, 71 percent, and industrial production, 40 percent, and it was the slowest to recover. Although the armament industry was revived in 1936–1937 as a reaction to the threat from National Socialist Germany, the Czechoslovak economy failed to reach the level of 1929 before the dismemberment of the republic in 1938.

Following the Munich Agreement of 29–30 September 1938, which sealed the fate of the First Czechoslovak Republic, extensive border regions were annexed to Germany, Poland, and Hungary. The Second Republic of Czecho-Slovakia survived only until 15 March 1939, when the German army occupied the Czech Lands, which, as the Protectorate of Bohemia and Moravia, received colonial status. Slovakia had seceded and declared its independence on 14 March 1939 to become a vassal state of the Third Reich.

Post–World War II. Following the total defeat of National Socialist Germany, the Czechoslovak state was recreated within its pre-Munich borders except for sub-Carpathian Ruthenia, which was ceded to the Soviet Union. War damage and losses amounted approximately to the total gross national product of Czechoslovakia between 1932 and 1937. Further, 360,000 victims of National Socialist terror and warfare lost their lives, and 947,000 persons returned from Germany and Austria, mainly ex-prisoners of concentration camps and forced laborers, whose health was broken. Czechoslovakia received little in reparations. Valuable immediate aid during postwar restoration was provided by the United Nations Relief and Rehabilitation Administration (UNRRA) but was not continued with loans for reconstruction.

Economic policy in the renewed Czechoslovakia was directed to postwar reconstruction, the conversion of a war economy into a peace economy, the reintegration of the parts of the state dismembered in 1938–1939, currency reform, and solving the problems connected with the repatriation of refugees and displaced persons and the transfer of Germans. At the same time, the nationalization of properties of enemies, traitors, collaborators, and war profiteers and land reforms were decreed. After the first wave of the widely supported first Nationalization Decree of October 1945, banks, insurance firms, and large companies were nationalized. Nationalized and confiscated industrial companies employed about 86 percent of all workers. The Two-Year Plan of the Renewal of the National Economy, introduced in 1947 with the aim to restore the 1937 level of the Czechoslovak economy, reached its targets in terms of national income per head by 1948. Of all central and southeast European countries, only Czechoslovakia succeeded in regaining the prewar standard of living within three years. During this period, the Czechoslovak government gave way to Soviet pressure and rejected the Marshall Plan. Political conflict intensified as the Communist Party of Czechoslovakia (KSČ) demanded further land reforms and nationalization, and in February 1948 that party gained control over the reins of power.

Whereas the two-year plan permitted market signals to play a role in economic processes, under the Communist regime the market mechanism was eliminated in the course of the first five-year plan (1949–1953) and was replaced by central administrative economic planning in imitation of the Soviet system. With the beginning of the Cold War and the founding of the Council for Mutual Economic Assistance (CMEA), Czechoslovakia become the armament workshop of Eastern Europe, its foreign trade was redirected from west to east, and high pressure industrial production strained the economy to the breaking point. The economic policy of continuous increase in gross capital investment and the output of producer goods with the aim of catching up with the West resulted in unbalanced growth characterized by neglect of the agricultural and consumer goods sectors, transport, communications, and housing. Simultaneously, the collectivization of agriculture was implemented forcibly, leaving the tertiary sector to stagnate. Inflation began to soar, and on 1 June 1953 a radical currency reform was imposed that dramatically curtailed the purchasing power of the population. Because of imbalances, the economy developed into a state-controlled sellers' market. Until the demise of Communism in 1989, altogether eight five-year plans were introduced. Most dramatically the third five-year plan (1961–1965) ran into a severe economic crisis and had to be abandoned after the first year as it became apparent that the centrally administered planned economy was not capable of coordinating economic life. An economic reform movement, based on the interaction of plan and market, gathered strength and turned into political momentum from 1965 to 1968. Major efforts of the reform movement to align economics and politics with the aim of "socialism with a human face" were suppressed in the invasion of Czechoslovakia by the Warsaw Pact troops on 21 August 1968. The only aim of the reform movement actually fulfilled was the federalization of the two parts of Czechoslovakia on 1 January 1969 into two symmetric autonomous states, the Czech Socialist Republic and the Slovak Socialist Republic.

During the 1970s and 1980s, Czechoslovakia succeeded in equalizing the economic levels in both federal parts such a degree that, when the common state fell apart on 1 January 1993, economic differences were less than at any previous time of the common existence of the state. Surveying the whole period from 1948 to 1989, Czechoslovakia attained a relatively respectable economic growth. However, this positive result was diminished by relatively high material and energy consumption in industry and by lagging behind the technical levels of economically highly developed states.

BIBLIOGRAPHY

Kaser, Michael C., and Edward A. Radice, eds. *The Economic History of Eastern Europe, 1919–1975*. 3 vols. Oxford, 1985–1986.

Kvaček, Robert. "The Rise and Fall of a Democracy." In *Bohemia in History*, edited by M. Teich, pp. 244–266. Cambridge, 1998.

Mamatey, Victor S., and Radomír Luža, eds. *A History of the Czechoslovak Republic, 1918–1948*. Princeton, 1973.

Myant, Martin. *Socialism and Democracy in Czechoslovakia, 1945–1948*. Cambridge, 1981.

Pátek, Jaroslav. "Economic, Social, and Political Aspects of Multinational Interwar Czechoslovakia." In *Economic Change and the National Question in Twentieth-Century Europe*, edited by A. Teichova, H. Matis, and J. Pátek. Cambridge, 2000.

Průcha, Václav. "Economic Development and Relations, 1918–1989." In *The End of Czechoslovakia*, edited by J. Musil, pp. 40–76. Budapest, London, and New York, 1995.

Průcha, Václav. "Continuity and Discontinuity in the Economic Development of Czechoslovakia, 1918–1991." In *Central Europe in the Twentieth Century: An Economic History Perspective*, edited by A. Teichova, pp. 23–41. Aldershot, U.K., Brookfield, Vt., Singapore, Sydney, 1997.

Průcha, Václav. "The Labour Market in Interwar Czechoslovakia." In *The Market in Interwar Central Europe*, edited by A. Teichova, A. Mosser, and J. Pátek, pp. 213–228. Prague, 1997.

Průcha, Václav. "The Economy and the Rise and Fall of a Small Multinational State: Czechoslovakia, 1918–1992." In *Nation, State, and the Economy in History*, edited by A. Teichova and Herbert Matis. Cambridge, 2003.

Šik, Ota. *Czechoslovakia: The Bureaucratic Economy*. Vienna, Munich, Zurich, 1969, reprint White Plains, N.Y., 1972.

Teichova, Alice. *An Economic Background to Munich: International Business and Czechoslovakia, 1918–1938*. Cambridge, 1974.

Teichova, Alice. *The Czechoslovak Economy, 1918–1980*. London and New York, 1988.

Teichova, Alice. "The Protectorate of Bohemia and Moravia, 1939–1945: The Economic Dimension." In *Bohemia in History*, edited by M. Teich, pp. 267–305. Cambridge, 1998.

Wallace, William W. *Czechoslovakia*. London, 1977.

ALICE TEICHOVA

D

DAIMLER, GOTTLIEB (1834–1900), a founder of the motor industry.

Daimler developed one of the first commercially viable four-stroke, gasoline-fueled, internal-combustion engines. Outside his native Germany, licensees and subsidiaries making cars with his engine were quickly established in France, the United States, Britain, and Austria-Hungary.

Daimler demonstrated that his engine was an effective power source not only for road vehicles and workshops or small factories but also for water and air transport. Self-employed, he moved to Canstatt in Württemberg (where he had studied) at the beginning of 1882. Daimler and his close collaborator Wilhelm Maybach (1846–1929) began experimental work in the back garden of Daimler's house. His basic patent of 1883 was for an incandescent tube that provided self-ignition, thereby avoiding the need for a battery; he patented a valve activator the same year. In 1885 he made a water-cooled, enclosed flywheel engine that operated at seven hundred to nine hundred revolutions a minute. The following year he tested his engine on a motorboat, and in 1888 a two-cylinder model powered a balloon. Daimler's two-seater carriage attracted little attention at the 1889 Paris exhibition, but his two-horsepower engine, powering thirty electric lights, created something of a stir.

Daimler's designed his first ten-horsepower, four-cylinder car in 1890, when Daimler-Motoren-Gesellschaft was established. Two years later his Phoenix two-cylinder engine with Maybach's spray carburetor was completed. Most of the earliest successful cars in the 1894 and 1895 French road trials, in particular those of Panhard and Levassor and Peugeot, were powered by Daimler's two-cylinder engine. Panhard and Levassor, licensed to build Daimler engines for ships and commercial purposes in France, constructed their first motorcar in 1890. The same year Peugeot also began producing a motorcar that used Daimler engines. In the United States, the National Machine Company built the first Daimler under license at Hartford, Connecticut, in 1891. Frederick R. Simms and the British Motor Syndicate bought the Daimler patents for Britain. In the Austro-Hungarian Empire, a Daimler subsidiary (Bierenz, Fischer and Co.) was founded in 1899.

The now most prestigious model based on Daimler engines, Mercedes, originated with the eccentric Austro-Hungarian consul in Nice, Emil Jellinek, who began to sell Daimlers in 1897. Jellinek persuaded Daimler's company to make a low-center-of-gravity, high-power, front-engined, four-cylinder model, which won the Nice races decisively in 1901. Named after Jellinek's daughter, the Mercedes dominated motor racing for some years afterward, and set a trend in car design.

Broad experience and education had prepared Daimler well for these achievements. Born in Scharndorf in the Rems valley, the son of a baker and wine bar keeper, Gottlieb Daimler was apprenticed to a gun maker in Württemberg. On completion of his apprenticeship, he enrolled at the School for Advanced Training in the Industrial Arts at Stuttgart. Daimler received a travel grant in 1853 to work in an engineering firm near Strasbourg (F. Rollé and Schwilqué), where regular courses of theoretical instruction were provided. When the Grafenstaden firm began manufacturing locomotives, Daimler was appointed foreman at the age of twenty-two. After one year he received a scholarship to study engine design and related subjects, including English, at Stuttgart Polytechnic. Shortly after he returned to Strasbourg in 1859, Daimler's interest in finding a new type of engine led him to resign and travel to Paris, where the Lenoir gas engine had been patented the previous year. From there he went to work in engineering companies in Leeds (Smith, Peacock and Tannet), Manchester (Roberts), and Coventry (Whitworths). He met his future colleague, Wilhelm Maybach, while serving as managing director of Bruderhaus Engineering Works (1863–1869). From Bruderhaus, Daimler moved to Karlsruhe as director of a large engineering firm, ensuring that Maybach followed him. In 1872 the two joined Gasmotoren-Fabrik Deutz in Cologne, the first internal-combustion-engine firm.

Daimler's success can be explained not merely by his talents but also by his technologically precocious environment, a corridor of western Germany stretching from Cologne to Munich. Many well-trained engineers were experimenting to improve upon the fuel efficiency of Lenoir's 1860 noncompression (piped) gas engine and to find a more convenient power source than the steam engine. At Deutz, Daimler was attempting to improve the Otto atmospheric engine, when the owner, Nikolaus August Otto, invented the first viable four-stroke engine in 1876. Daimler's contemporary, Karl Benz, whom he never met, road-tested his own motor car in Mannheim in 1886, the same year as did Daimler, but employing electric ignition. Also in 1886, Robert Bosch began manufacturing in Stuttgart, Daimler's hometown. In due course, he converted Daimler to magneto ignition. Using a different combustion principle, Rudolf Diesel's engine was patented in 1892 and developed in Augsburg. In 1927 his engine was given an enormous boost by Bosch's fuel-injection system.

Daimler and his wife, Emma (Kurz), had three sons and two daughters. Two of his sons, Paul and Adolf, followed their father in his company.

BIBLIOGRAPHY

Barker, Theo C., ed. *The Economic and Social Effects of the Spread of Motor Vehicles.* Basingstoke, U.K., 1987.

Cummins, C. Lyle, Jr. *Internal Fire.* Lake Oswego, Oreg., 1976.

Diesel, Eugen, Gustav Goldbeck, and Friedrich Schildenberger. *From Engines to Autos: Five Pioneers in Engine Development and Their Contributions to the Automotive Industry.* Chicago, 1960.

Laux, James M. *The European Automobile Industry.* New York, 1992.

Siebertz, Paul. *Gottlieb Daimler.* Stuttgart, 1950.

JAMES FOREMAN-PECK

DAIRY FARMING. The practice of dairying, dating from the prehistoric era, developed over time from a supplemental subsistence activity of autonomous producers to a specialized industry shaped by the global markets of modern agriculture. Ancient cultures endowed cows with honor and prestige, in part because their nutritional and caloric contribution to diets rendered them highly valuable. Populations across Europe, northern Africa, and parts of Asia relied mostly on cattle for milk and cheese, though ewes, goats, yaks, and buffalo also figured as key sources of raw milk. In India and northern Europe, cream was churned into butter, a staple ingredient of cooking and a garnish or spread prevalent in prosperous cuisines. With an increase in market demand for dairy products in the early modern period, Europeans became interested in maximizing the output of livestock and further systematizing the methods of dairy production. Changes in the organization of dairying in Europe and North America thus boosted production, fostering a growth in knowledge and technology that spread to other parts of the world. Yet, in many places, for varying reasons, dairying is still pursued as a small-scale activity, employing only the labor of family members, in particular, the work of women.

The Geography of Dairying. Dairying has always required a relatively temperate climate and land suitable to pasture. Small-scale production took place in areas inhospitable to arable farming, such as the upland regions found across Asia and Europe; but large-scale dairy industries evolved only where extensive land could be devoted to both pasture and feed crops. Established trade routes and culinary traditions also influenced the development of dairy production. As early as the thirteenth century, long-distance passage across Europe encouraged regional specialization. The Po Valley in Italy dominated the production of cheese for export by 1200, and by the thirteenth and fourteenth centuries, Norway and Sweden were sending butter to other parts of Europe. Commercial and colonial exchange made for unpredictable results: though trade regulations forbade it for example, transatlantic merchants sold Dutch cheeses in Spanish America as early as the sixteenth century. By the eighteenth century, Parisians could choose between high-quality butter from nearby regions and from Ireland. Evidence of fraud in the marketing of dairy products, apparent since medieval times, indicates that competitors sought to intrude upon regional monopolies by offering imitations of sought-after imports alongside a considerable quantity of adulterated commodities.

By the late nineteenth century, dairy products became part of the mass marketing of inexpensive foodstuffs, which thrust producers into the midst of worldwide competitive innovation and price reduction. With the growing importation of grain from North and South America after 1870, producers in Denmark, to use one example, transformed their role in a global economy into a leading specialization in dairying. Two factors enabled them to do so: technological and scientific expertise, possible at the end of the nineteenth century as a result of advances in chemistry and engineering; and an organizational trend toward cooperation and consolidation of large-scale enterprises. Cooperative creameries solved the dilemma of the small farmer: By enabling every dairy producer, large and small, to contribute to an up-to-date and high-quality mechanized facility, even the humble farmer was able to receive competitive sums for his or her output. While Denmark addressed its market difficulties in a remarkably rapid transition between 1880 and 1900, the problematic impact of such developments outside Europe cannot be overstated. By the beginning of the twentieth century, and particularly after 1945, underdeveloped nations confronted insuperable competition as they strove to market their own dairy products.

The dietary dependence of Europeans on dairy products, such as milk, cream, and butter, affected other parts of the world as early as the sixteenth century. From the time of Columbus, Europeans brought their cattle and dietary preferences across oceans, first to Santo Domingo and later to other parts of North America and Asia. In need of dairy products in order to feed colonial administrators and large armies, Britons introduced nonindigenous stock and new methods of dairying into Africa and Asia, with mixed success because of the spread of disease and the expense of processing equipment. Cheap imported products

CHEESE MAKING. Kneading and molding of cheese in Holland, nineteenth century. (Private Collection/Lauros-Giraudon/Art Resource, NY)

The perishability of some dairy products dictated that consumption needed to be close to sites of production. Thus, early demand for fresh milk required purchasing directly from the producer, who hauled milk in large cans, or, alternatively, led the animals to customers before milking, even in urban areas. The liquid milk trade in Europe was launched into a more modern phase of organization in the early nineteenth century, when "dairymen" retailers offered milk from fixed shops in London, and in the 1880s and 1890s, when joint-stock and limited dairy companies grew to control more than 40 percent of the marketing of milk in the metropolis. These larger operations were able to introduce expensive technological innovations, such as pasteurization (demonstrated by Louis Pasteur by 1862 and developed mechanically around 1895) and bottling equipment (with milk bottles developed in the 1880s), which raised the standards generally held for cleanliness and uniformity. Throughout this reorganization, which diminished the small vendor's share of the trade, door-to-door delivery remained central to the urban retailing of milk and, by implication, to the spread of its consumption to nearly universal proportions. The degree of demand for liquid milk also encouraged many cheesemakers in England to cease their production of cheese in favor of the less-labor-intensive trade in milk.

Twentieth-century innovations in processing techniques, as well as new forms of consumption, expanded still further the uses of milk. Gail Borden developed condensed milk in the United States in the 1850s, and the commodity found widespread use during the American Civil War. Evaporated milk, a similar product processed without sugar, became essential during both World Wars, when great quantities were shipped from America to Europe. Joining forces with sugar enabled milk to take the twentieth-century diet by storm. Malted milk, invented by William Horlick of Racine, Wisconsin, in 1883, quickly became part of a new pattern of purchasable shop treats in the early twentieth century. The process of making powdered milk, improved and patented from 1900, contributed greatly to the use of milk in chocolate, sweets, and ice cream. And though ice cream had enjoyed esteem as a luxury commodity since at least the seventeenth century, a new mass-produced variety appeared in America during the first decade of the twentieth century. Served atop sugar cones, which were launched at the Lewis and Clark Exposition of 1904, ice cream became spectacularly popular over the course of the following century, boosting the demand for milk to new levels.

Labor and Gender. Designs on pottery, jewelry, and coffins show that men milked cows and sheep in the ancient world, but other evidence suggests that handling animals was assigned to the lowest levels of the workforce, thus, in many cases, to women and slaves. According to

from the West had a similarly equivocal impact on underdeveloped economies in the twentieth century: by exporting liquid and dry milk and other dairy products worldwide, modernized economies sometimes undercut efforts to develop indigenous production in many parts of Africa and Asia. Yet a higher consumption of protein-rich dairy products improved the nutrition of poor countries, particularly in such nations as India, where a large percentage of the population followed vegetarian diets. With government sponsorship, many developing countries established modern milk-processing plants and other production sites, contributing to a wider distribution of inexpensive native dairy products in the twentieth century.

Changes in Demand and Distribution. Cheese with bread constituted an important part of the diet of many early modern peoples, particularly in areas of peasant farming, such as France and Switzerland. While this form of consumption remained relatively constant, the growth of urban populations and a pressing demand for cheap, transportable food opened the way for an expansion of cheese production, especially after 1700. Institutions, such as hospitals and standing armies demanded great supplies of such commodities. Similarly, urban consumption of ale and peas benefited from dollops of butter, and the popular taste for tea and coffee expanded the use of milk and cream, particularly within large cities, where public leisure in coffeehouses and pleasure gardens generated concentrated demand.

customs around the world, dairying was the province of women from the early medieval era. This sexual division of labor assigned the breeding of stock to men, while women assumed the careful management of milk-producing animals. The location of most dairies, attached to the kitchen of farming households, indicated the integral part played by women, as both mistresses and servants, in the production of butter and cheese. Folklore and proverbial knowledge confirm this general impression.

Governed largely by custom, dairying techniques long remained obscure, despite the efforts of advocates of agricultural improvement to demystify the methods of female practitioners in the eighteenth century. Determinations in the procedures of making cheese and butter depended on idiosyncratic judgment and taste, usually passed down from one generation of a household to the next. Since the qualities of the product also depended on environmental factors, which sometimes varied even according to neighborhood, production resisted predictability and uniformity. Not until the twentieth century were certain chemical processes fully understood. In spite of the demonstrated significance of female knowledge, skill, and even brute strength in the work of dairying, new constructions of authority in dairy science began to affect the role played by women from the middle of the nineteenth century. Deploying a self-consciously modern perspective, men led a widely communicated effort to develop the business and management of dairying. As technological innovations asserted the need for advanced training, sometimes including chemistry, new forms of knowledge displaced customary know-how. Educational institutions promoted the dissemination of modern techniques, but they also led to a more marked sexual and social division of labor. In the case of Sweden, training diverged into two streams, with women entering programs focusing on practical skills, while men were trained in theoretical aspects of dairying and management. Though an occasional woman could be found within higher levels of expertise, for the most part, the traditional art of women became the science and business of men.

Changes in the Technology of Dairying. The most pronounced alterations in dairying before the technological innovations of the nineteenth century came in the feeding and breeding of livestock. The introduction of red clover into England in 1645 was heralded as a landmark in the production of milk. Throughout the continents of Europe and America, experimentation in stock breeding produced strains of cattle capable of increased output of milk. By the late nineteenth century, breeding was carried on in an international context, producing strains of cattle capable of satisfying the demand for both milk and beef.

Judging from the many agricultural exhibitions of the second half of the nineteenth century, the production of dairy products tapped the ingenuity of unpretentious mechanics. Technological innovations before the late nineteenth century were often simple in design. Cheese curd breakers, which at first relied on a simple axle and crank, eliminated some of the labor of cutting the curds by the 1830s. At the Great Exhibition of 1851 in London, mechanized churns by French, English, and American designers came away with prizes, though patents for such inventions had been issued at least by the 1820s. Refrigerators originally used for cooling beer were applied to milk around 1870, an application that made possible long-distance transportation. Creamer separators were developed in Germany, Denmark, Sweden, and England between 1860 and 1880, relying on the principle of centrifugal force to achieve their ends. By the 1880s, machines built for small and large dairies offered the opportunity to "work" the butter without touching it, eliminating the need for the dairymaid with a cool hand. "Lactometers" and "creamometers," designed to measure the degree of creaminess of milk samples, appeared in affordable form around the same time. Thermometers were introduced into the processes of dairying in Denmark around 1870.

The most difficult process to replace mechanically was the work of the milker, the laborer in shortest supply on dairy farms. Though several patents appeared in England throughout the nineteenth century, and though America, Germany, Denmark, and Sweden pursued several early designs, no milking machine was without drawbacks at the turn of the century. Most mechanical inventions proved to be too expensive for the majority of dairy farmers, who continued to work on a small scale with mainly family labor. The modern milking machine, patented by a Scottish inventor in 1895, introduced pulsating vacuum pressure to extract milk; it has advanced greatly in sophistication since that time.

The development of cheese factories in America marked a departure from the characteristic household mode of production. Jesse Williams, a large dairy farmer of Oneida County, New York, combined the output of his large herd with that of his son, creating the need to produce cheese at a third location. From the 1870s, such factories were ubiquitous across areas of American and Canadian farmland; they appear in England after 1870. By this time, transportation allowed for large-scale export of factory-made commodities, which, despite their inferior quality when compared with high-grade cheeses, were more reliable than typical local products formerly available to markets.

A revolution in transportation worked the greatest change upon the organization of dairying. As early as the 1830s, dairying cooperatives appeared in Switzerland, and later, in America and England, allowing several farms to combine their milk and cream in order to produce butter and cheese more efficiently in bulk. These were not cooperatives of a socialist kind, but rather arrangements that enabled the small farmer to employ the equipment and labor of a cooperative "factory." Such early creameries produced inferior butter for the allegedly undiscriminating urban consumer until the 1880s, when factory cream separators introduced new levels of cleanliness and efficiency. Combined with further improvements in long-distance transportation at the end of the century, the competition of foreign butter forced changes upon large-scale production of butter everywhere.

BIBLIOGRAPHY

Atkins, P. J. "The Retail Milk Trade in London, c. 1790–1914." *Economic History Review* n.s., 33.4 (1980), 522–537. An empirical account of the delivery of milk within an evolving urban environment.

Bourke, Joanna. "Dairywomen and Affectionate Wives: Women in the Irish Dairy Industry, 1890–1914." *Agricultural History Review* 38.2 (1990), 149–164. An insightful analysis of gender in the modernization of dairy production.

Braudel, Fernand. *The Structures of Everyday Life*. Translated by Sian Reynolds. New York, 1981. An indispensable, definitive history of material life.

Fussell, G. E. *The English Dairy Farmer, 1500–1900*. London, 1966. An early treatment with more general application than its title indicates.

Dairying Throughout the World. Munich, 1966. Monographs on dairying in a number of countries throughout the world published on the occasion of the Seventeenth International Dairy Congress.

Khurody, D. N. *Dairying in India: A Review*. Mumbai (Bombay), India 1974. Informative account of colonial and modern practices.

McMurry, Sally. *Transforming Rural Life: Dairying Families and Agricultural Change, 1820–1885*. Baltimore, 1995. Superlative detailed study of the social dimensions of dairying.

Pirtle, T. R. *History of the Dairy Industry*. Chicago, 1926. Unrivaled comparative compilation, not yet superseded.

Sommestad, Lena. *Fran mejerska till Mejerist: En studie av mejeriyrkets maskuliniseringsprocess*. Lund, 1992. Cogent analysis of the impact of modernization on women's work in dairying. Includes brief summary in English.

Valenze, Deborah. *The First Industrial Woman*. New York, 1995. Includes chapter on the role of gender in the transformation of authority in English dairying.

Waters-Bayer, Ann. *Dairying by Settled Fulani Agropastoralists in Central Nigeria: The Role of Woman and Implications for Dairy Development*, vol. 4, *Farming Systems and Resource Economics in the Tropics*. Kiel, Germany, 1988. Highlights the interdependence of modes of production in the Third World and foreign imports.

DEBORAH VALENZE

DANUBE. The Danube is Europe's second-longest river (2,860 kilometers, or 1,773 miles), connecting ten countries of central and southeastern Europe (Germany, Austria, Slovakia, Hungary, Croatia, Serbia, Romania, Bulgaria, Ukraine, Moldavia). This is the only major European river that flows from west to east, from the Black Forest to the Black Sea. Beyond its connective functions, the Danube served as a borderline separating civilizations, empires, and political and economic systems.

The Danube was the fortified borderline of the Roman Empire and was used for military purposes. From the early Middle Ages on, the river's commercial importance increased as some continental and shipping routes reached the Near East along the Danube. The waterfalls in the central section, the peripheral situation of the Black Sea, and the fragmentation of feudal powers and city rights reduced the Danube's significance as a long-distance trade route. From the fifteenth century, the Turkish invasion and relocation of major trade routes to the North Atlantic led to a further decline of its economic role. It served as a military route for the Turkish Empire, which isolated the Balkan periphery until the late nineteenth century.

Between the sixteenth and mid-twentieth centuries, the Danubian countries exported agricultural products to western Europe. The major trade routes were first waterways, then railway lines. The first steam-powered vessels on the Danube, introduced by the First Austrian Danubian Steamship Company in 1830, offered passenger and freight transportation service from Regensburg to the Danube Delta. This company also had an important role in the development of the area's mining, railway building, and urban growth. Before World War I, it maintained the largest inland fleets in Europe and, even after 1918, remained the leading shipping enterprise on the Danube.

River control in the Iron Gate strait (1898) facilitated navigation along the entire river. The unified customs zone of Austria-Hungary created favorable conditions for industrialization and economic growth. Grain transportation on the Danube accelerated the industrial development of Budapest, turning the city into a metropolis of 1 million residents as well as the world's second-largest milling center, after Minneapolis, by 1900. The intensification of commerce contributed to the urban development of riverbank cities and several capitals of the Danubian countries: Vienna, Bratislava, Budapest, and Belgrade. The granting of free shipping rights was guaranteed by international agreements signed by the great powers and riparian states, providing preconditions for free navigation. The Paris (1856) and the Versailles Treaties (1919) declared the Danube an international waterway and established the Danube Commission for the management of navigation issues.

The growth of freight transport was hindered by the fact that the Danube flows eastward, going through underdeveloped rural areas of the Balkans, and its mouth is situated far away from the major international trade routes. With the exception of the lower Romanian part, which had an important role in grain export, freight volume was quite low. In 1911, the Rhine although two-thirds shorter, had fifty-eight million tons of freight traffic, while the Danube had only seven million.

After World War I, freight traffic decreased. The unified Austro-Hungarian customs zone disintegrated, and the successor states, striving for economic autarchy, introduced high customs tariffs in their seven new customs zones. The expansion period of the German Nazi state in southeastern Europe was the first peak of the Danube freight traffic (bewteen 1939 and 1942, the highest volume of imported military resources to Germany), but this brought free navigation to an end.

At the end of World War II, the Iron Curtain divided the Danube region, and with the exception of West Germany and Austria the riparian countries became part of the communist block. During the Cold War, Soviet bloc states initiated expansion of heavy industry and built up their plants along the Danube, which were supplied by Soviet resources. This significantly increased the freight traffic of the Danube during the second peak period (1960–1980). The 6 to 8 million tons of freight traffic before World War II increased to 26 million tons by 1960 and exceeded 90 million tons by 1980. The recession and industrial restructuring following the crisis and fall of the Communist regimes reduced traffic to one-fourth of its peak volume, which was a clear mark of the decreasing importance of the waterway. The 1992 opening of the Danube-Main-Rhine Canal connecting the North Sea with the Black Sea was a dramatic event, but the canal increased traffic only in the upper section. In the 1990s, traffic of the central and lower sections was hindered by political-military confrontation (Yugoslavian war) and the poor economic performance of the lower regions.

BIBLIOGRAPHY

East, Gordon. "The Danube Route-Way." In *An Historical Geography of Europe*. London, 1935.

Focas, G. Spiridon. *The Lower Danube River in the Southeastern European Political and Economic Complex from Antiquity to the Conference of Belgrade of 1948*. New York, 1987.

Jac, J. de. *The Rhine-Main-Danube Connection and Its Economical Implications for Europe*. Rotterdam, Netherlands, 1976.

Lessner, Erwin. *The Danube: The Dramatic History of the Great River and the People Touched by Its Flow*. Garden City, N.Y., 1961.

Murphy Lyons, Irene. *The Danube: A River Basin in Transition*. Dordrecht, Netherlands, 1997.

Ránki, György. *Economic and Foreign Policy: The Struggle of the Great Powers for the Hegemony in the Danube Valley, 1919–39*. New York, 1983.

Wagner, F. S., ed. *Toward a New Central Europe: A Symposium on the Problems of Danubian Nations*. Astor Park, Fla., 1970.

ZOLTÁN GÁL

DEBASEMENT. *See* Inflation Tax *and* Money and Coinage.

DEBS, EUGENE VICTOR, (1855–1926), labor leader and Socialist Party presidential candidate, was born in Terra Haute, Indiana.

EUGENE V. DEBS. (Prints and Photographs Division, Library of Congress)

Debs's life encompassed work as a union organizer, speaker, writer, and political candidate. He went to work on the railroad at age fourteen and helped organize a local of the Brotherhood of Locomotive Firemen five years later. Believing that it would increase the bargaining strength of railroad workers, he attempted to organize the separate brotherhoods into a single federation. When this effort failed, he organized the American Railway Union (ARU) in 1893. The ARU, one of the first industrial unions, attracted not only the craft workers of the individual brotherhoods but also many previously unorganized semiskilled and unskilled railroad workers. Under Debs's leadership the ARU led a successful strike against the Great Northern Railroad in 1894, but soon after it became embroiled in the Pullman boycott, which led to Debs's imprisonment for six months.

The government's intervention in support of Pullman and the defeat of the Populist (and Democratic) Party presidential candidate William Jennings Bryan (1896) weakened Debs's faith in reform efforts. Viewing more radical change as necessary to solve workers' problems, he joined in founding the Social Democratic Party (later the Socialist Party) and became its first presidential candidate in

1900. Debs ran as Socialist Party presidential candidate four more times, amassing 6 percent of the vote in 1912. He ran from jail in 1920 while serving a sentence for violation of the Espionage Act (a result of his speeches against U.S. entry into World War I). His sentence was commuted to time served by President Warren Harding in 1921, but Debs would later write a series of articles describing prison conditions and condemning the inequities of the penal system (*Walls and Bars*, Chicago, 1927). In addition to his Socialist Party activity, Debs lent his organizing efforts to the American Labor Union (founded in 1902) and the Industrial Workers of the World (founded in 1905).

Debs viewed industrial (as opposed to craft) unionism as a more powerful force in bargaining with the large-scale business organizations that had developed in the late nineteenth century, but saw socialism as the only means of solving the class conflict inherent in capitalist society. Debs's primary source of livelihood came from lecture tours espousing these views and from writing for publications such as the *Firemen's Magazine*, *Railway Times*, and *Appeal to Reason*. His long association with the Socialist Party would brand him as a "radical" and "undesirable citizen" to some, but he was a charismatic leader to many working men and women of his time and his legacy was as a champion of working-class interests. His demonstration of the potential strength of organizing across skill lines (with the ARU) and his continued support for industrial unionism would be revived with the creation of the Congress for Industrial Organizations (CIO) in the 1930s. Many of the labor issues he fought hard to resolve (though not the complete overturning of the capitalist system) would be addressed when New Deal policy established labor's right to organize (the Wagner Act of 1935), unemployment insurance, and minimum wages.

BIBLIOGRAPHY

Constantine, J. Robert, ed. *Letters of Eugene V. Debs*. 3 vols. Urbana, 1990. An annotated collection of correspondence providing insight into both the public and the private life of Debs.

Ginger, Ray. *The Bending Cross: A Biography of Eugene Victor Debs*. New Brunswick, N.J., 1949. A detailed, sympathetic biography of Debs's entire life.

Salvatore, Nick. *Eugene V. Debs: Citizen and Socialist*. Urbana, Ill., 1982. A "social" biography focusing on Debs's life within its cultural context.

LAURA J. OWEN

DEERE, JOHN (1804–1886), American entrepreneur.

Deere manufactured and marketed the most widely used plows in the United States during the mid-nineteenth century. He should be remembered not for his inventive genius—for he more often borrowed ideas from others than envisioned his own—but for his business instincts. He owed his success to determination, perceptiveness, hard work, and a willingness to take risks. An important example of the American ideal of the self-made person, Deere contributed to the growth of Midwestern manufacturing, and his legacy is the monolithic producer of farm and construction equipment bearing his name.

John Deere's start in this world was modest, to say the least. He was born in Rutland, Vermont, in 1804. His father died early in his childhood, and at age seventeen he was apprenticed to a Middlebury blacksmith. Thereafter, Deere found work as a journeyman and a blacksmith. Bad luck, miscalculations of his own, and a stagnant local economy left him destitute, however. Chased by creditors and lured by the prospect of a fresh start, Deere moved his family to Grand Detour, Illinois, in 1836.

On the frontier, Deere became a successful manufacturer and seller of farm implements and machinery. He opened a blacksmith shop in Grand Detour and immediately established a reputation for fine craftsmanship. He was also a tireless salesman who made a practice of visiting local farmers. Their most pressing need, he found out, was a plow that scoured of soil. The moist prairie soil adhered to the cast-iron moldboards of the plows in use. Deere proposed a solution, although it is unlikely his idea was original. He fashioned a plow whose share and moldboard were made out of polished steel. Deere quickly realized the steel plow's commercial potential and by 1839 was devoting most of his energy to its manufacture. He made improvements to the original design, mostly by trial and error, but also by borrowing the ideas of others. By 1843, Deere's firm employed ten persons, three forges, and a cupola for casting iron. Annual production was 400 plows, a fourfold increase over output just two years earlier.

Prospects for growth were even greater elsewhere, so in 1848 Deere moved his family and business to Moline, Illinois, on the Mississippi River. Here, Deere entered into a succession of partnerships that brought his young son, Charles, and his son-in-law, James Chapman, into the business. By 1849, John Deere—now the company name—sold 2,136 plows, mostly in the Midwest. The shop became increasingly mechanized with planing, boring, and cornering machines. Moreover, the company adopted many of the features of a modern business: a sales force, brand differentiation, and the extension of credit to merchants. In advertising his plows, Deere stressed their high-quality steel components, interchangeable parts, and affordability. Deere plows garnered endorsements and praise at agricultural fairs, where they won numerous competitions. By 1856, the John Deere company was manufacturing 14,000 plows annually, making it one of the six largest plow manufacturers in the United States.

As the company became increasingly complex, Deere yielded more and more of the day-to-day management responsibilities to his better-educated son, Charles Deere, and James Chapman. The economic downturn of 1857 almost bankrupted the company and resulted in handing control to the twenty-one-year-old Charles. Nonetheless, John Deere remained active, overseeing product development and keeping his title as company head until his death in 1886. During his son's tenure, the John Deere company was transformed into the world's largest manufacturer of plows.

BIBLIOGRAPHY

Broehl, Wayne G. *John Deere's Company: A History of Deere & Company and Its Times.* New York, 1984.

Danhof, Clarence. *Change in Agriculture: The Northern United States.* Cambridge, 1969.

Gates, Paul W. *The Farmer's Age: Agriculture, 1815–1860.* New York, 1960.

Meyer, David. "Midwestern Industrialization and the American Manufacturing Belt in the Nineteenth Century." *Journal of Economic History* 49.4 (1989), 921–937.

Rasmussen, Wayne D. "The Impact of Technological Change on American Agriculture, 1862–1962." *Journal of Economic History* 22.4 (1962), 578–591.

JAMES I. STEWART

DEMESNE. *See* Feudalism, *subentry on* Manorial System.

DEMOGRAPHIC METHODS. Demographic methods are primarily methods designed to assess the size and composition of a population and their change over time. Demographic methods can also be understood more broadly as methods that are designed to refine the study of a given phenomenon in a population by taking into consideration the particular size and composition of that population. Age and sex are central to these analyses; race, marital status, residential area, and socioeconomic status are also frequently considered. Demographic methods traditionally operate from individual-level data aggregated at the group level and trace out the consequences of individual behavior for aggregate processes. In turn, these methods often yield summary measures that can be interpreted as the typical experience of an individual member of the group.

Population Data. The traditional source of data on population size and composition is the population census, an investigation in which selected characteristics of each individual member of the population are recorded. Population data are also increasingly collected in surveys, by combining sampling procedures and statistical methods of inference from the sample to the population; these techniques are not described here but have become standard in demographic analysis. Population registers list all members of the population and continuously update a few selected individual characteristics. They are mostly main-tained in northern European countries and provide some of the most suitable data for demographic analysis. More frequently, only selected events are registered on a continuous basis. Family genealogies and parish registers are among the earliest such instances, providing records of births, deaths, and marriage over extended periods. In many countries, statistics on such events are now collected and centralized by governmental agencies, but even today, few of the events that affect population size and composition are continuously recorded.

The population size changes only with birth, death, and migration; these events have received special attention in demographic analysis. Population composition depends on additional events that mark transitions across categories (e.g., marriage), unless the compositional analysis is restricted to individual characteristics that can be treated as either invariant (such as sex) or fully determined by the passage of time (such as age). Most events affecting population size or composition can be related to the behavior of an individual present in the population prior to the event. Hence, taking into consideration the size of the population yields measures of the intensity of demographic events that are believed to be more meaningful than absolute counts of events, in particular in comparisons over time or across populations.

The basic measure of the intensity of a demographic event in a population is the crude period rate that relates a count of events during a period of reference to the amount of exposure to the "risk" of experiencing the event during the period in the population (known as occurrence/exposure in statistics). A simple approximation of the amount of exposure is the product of (1) the size of the population at the middle of the period and (2) the length of the period. When time is measured in years (annualized rate) and the period is equal to one year (annual rate), the length of the period is one and does not appear numerically. The Crude Birth Rate (CBR) and Crude Death Rate (CDR) in a given year are thus measured as the annual number of births and deaths respectively, divided by a mid-year estimate of population size. Even when the reference to time is implicit, period rates are measured in inverse of a time unit (akin to a frequency in physics). In historical population studies, demographers often found data on vital events (the numerators) that predate census data on population totals (the denominators). French demographers around Louis Henry developed the family reconstitution method to reconstitute a population over time through rigorous linkages of birth and death records. The entire French settlement in the Saint Lawrence Valley (Quebec, Canada) has thus been reconstructed from 1609 to 1800. Overall, the method is best applied when vital records were diligently maintained over a long period of time, illegitimate births were rare, family names were stable, and residential mobility was low.

An Egyptian Census. List of all *nomoi* (districts) of Egypt on the walls of the jubilee chapel of Pharaoh Sesostris I (1971–1928 BCE), Karnak, Egypt. The list includes the size of each district, the names of the capitals, and the number of heads of cattle in each district. (Erich Lessing/Art Resource, NY)

Age Composition. The above approximation of the amount of exposure in the period is exact when every member of the population is at risk of the event at any time, and when the size of the population changes linearly during the period. While the linear assumption is numerically inconsequential in most applications, the assumption of uniform risk is more problematic; demographic risks strongly vary across individuals. The interest in population composition largely originates in the recognition of this risk heterogeneity, and demographic analysis often begins with the identification of the categories within which the risk is less variable. Age composition has been privileged in demographic analysis for at least three reasons. First, most demographic events are strongly age patterned. The intensity of a demographic event in a population thus depends in part on the age composition of that population. Second, age compositions vary across human population. Third, the age composition is itself a demographic variable uniquely determined by the recent history of age-specific fertility, mortality, and migration rates. (An important correlate is that, in the long term, age distribution becomes independent of earlier age distributions: populations are thus said to "forget their past.") The study of the age composition of a population involves the same events as the study of its size. Finally, data on age are routinely collected. In most cultures, age is a salient individual characteristic well remembered. The relationship between age composition and age-specific fertility, mortality, and migration provides methods to assess the internal consistency of demographic data and, in particular, the quality of age reporting.

Hence, many demographic methods are centered on age-specific rates in which both the count of events and the amount of exposure are limited to a specific age group. The estimation of these age-specific rates requires both the age distribution of the population and the age distribution of the persons to whom events occur. The technique of age standardization consists of estimating a hypothetical all-age rate in the population, were the population age-specific rates to prevail and its age composition to match a selected standard age distribution. The effect of the actual age composition on the all-age rate is thus removed; age-standardized comparisons across populations then reveal differences in event intensity over the life course. In historical population studies, however, the age distribution of the persons to whom events occur might not be available. For example, distributions of birth by age of the mother were unavailable to Ansley Coale and colleagues in the Princeton European Fertility Project, a study of fertility change in Europe during the nineteenth century. In such situations, indirect standardization is used instead, comparing the total number of events to the number that would be obtained in the population with the prevailing age composition and a standard set of age-specific rates.

Age-specific rates can be defined for a reference period or a cohort, a group of people who experienced a reference event during a given period (the most common ones being birth cohorts). The Lexis diagram is a useful tool designed to assist in visualizing the events and amount of exposure of respective period and cohort age-specific rates. With age on the vertical axis and time on the horizontal axis, the diagram consists of vertical lines delineating periods, horizontal ones delineating age groups, and forty-five-degree diagonals delineating cohorts. Cohort analysis might be more pertinent when the individual behavior of interest depends more on past biographical events than on the current conditions of the period. If couples have a maximum number of children that they do not want to exceed, for instance, their fertility behavior will depend on their number of births to date (parity).

Borrowed from cohort analysis, the concept of a synthetic cohort is central to the analysis of the individual- and population-level implications of the demographic conditions of a period. A synthetic cohort is an imaginary group of people born during a period of reference and who, at every age throughout their life, experience events at the age-specific rate of that reference period. The total fertility rate and the net reproduction rate are widely used synthetic measures, but the best-known example of the synthetic cohort approach is carried out in the life table. This powerful device displays information about the gradual dying out of a real or synthetic birth cohort. At the individual level, the life table provides several indicators of the survival of an average individual under the mortality conditions of the period were he or she to remain unchanged throughout his or her life course (e.g., life expectancy at birth). At the population level, the life table also provides several characteristics of the stationary population corresponding to a given set of unchanging age-specific mortality rates. Life-table applications have become increasingly varied substantively and methodologically. Life-table analysis can readily be applied to the study of any group of individuals whose likelihood to leave the group changes with the duration of their group membership (decrement). Multiple-decrement tables follow the depletion of a group of susceptible individuals through different events (competing risks). Increment-decrement tables follow individuals between several states (also known as multistate life tables). Proportional hazard models merge the life-table framework and regression analysis by allowing the individual risk to be scaled up or down by multiplicative factors that depend on individual characteristics (event history analysis).

Model Life Tables. Past studies of demographic events have documented much empirical regularity across populations, allowing demographers to develop some empirical model of population processes. Foremost, empirical regularities in age variations as regards the risk of death led to the development of model life tables. Model life tables consist of full life tables ordered by an overall mortality level, typically life expectancy at birth. For instance, model life tables are key to the back projection method, developed by historians E. Anthony Wrigley and Roger Schofield to reconstruct the population of England between 1541 and 1871. The selection in each period of the model life table that best matches an age distribution at the end of the period and the total number of deaths during the period provides a full set of age-specific survival ratios (estimated proportions that would survive to the next age group). With these ratios, the age structure of the population is then reconstructed backward from a terminal age-and-sex distribution and time series of births and deaths. The difference between the initial size of a birth cohort and the number of deaths estimated over the life course is attributed to migration; and through iterations, consistent numbers of births, deaths, and migration are achieved for each birth cohort. The back projection method identifies only one of the internally consistent demographic scenarios, however, and is unfortunately not very robust, primarily because "populations forget their past." Two different initial age distributions would hence produce terminal distributions indistinguishable from each other. If estimates of population size are available in addition to the births and deaths series, Ronald Lee's method of inverse projection avoids this indetermination.

Formal and empirical relationships between demographic variables have also yielded methods to assess and improve data quality, or even to estimate missing data from data on other variables, the latter being referred to as indirect estimation. In contemporary developing countries, indirect methods of estimation are designed to assess demographic quantities, on which data are unavailable or unreliable, from simple questions on related demographic variables. William Brass established the children ever born/children surviving technique, for instance, deriving probabilities of children to survive from birth to different ages from the proportions of surviving children reported by mothers at different ages. Errors in dates of birth and death of children reported in retrospect by mothers have been shown to be error prone, and in situations where such errors are expected, the indirect approach is believed to be more reliable. With the increasing availability of data and with the incorporation of many statistical techniques, demographic methods have become increasingly varied, but this traditional concern with the quality of data before subjecting them to a sophisticated analytical apparatus remains one of the enduring characteristics of the demographic approach to data analysis.

[*See also* Fertility; Mortality; *and* Population.]

BIBLIOGRAPHY

Bogue, Donald J., Eduardo E. Arriaga, and Douglas L. Anderton. *Readings in Population Research Methodology*. Chicago, 1993.

Brass, William. *Methods for Estimating Fertility and Mortality from Limited and Defective Data: Based on Seminars Held 16–24 September 1971 at the Centro Latino Americo de Demografia (Celade), San Jose, Costa Rica*. Chapel Hill, N.C., 1975.

Coale, Ansley J. "The Decline of Fertility in Europe Since the Eighteenth Century as a Chapter in Demographic History." In *The Decline of Fertility in Europe: The Revised Proceedings of a Conference on the Princeton European Fertility Project*, edited by Ansley J. Coale and Susan C. Watkins, pp. 1–30. Princeton, 1986.

Coale, Ansley J., and Paul Demeny, with Barbara Vaughan. *Regional Model Life Tables and Stable Populations*. 2d ed. New York, 1983.

Fleury, Michel, and Louis Henry. *Nouveau manuel de dépouillement et d'exploitation de l'état civil ancien*. 2d ed. Paris, 1977.

Keyfitz, Nathan. *Applied Mathematical Demography*. 2d ed. New York, 1985.

Lee, Ronald D. "Estimating Series of Vital Rates and Age Structures from Baptisms and Burials: A New Technique." *Population Studies* 28.3 (1974), 495–512.

Legare, Jacques. "A Population Register for Canada under the French Regime: Context, Scope, Content and Applications." *Canadian Studies in Population* 15.1 (1988), 1–16.

Namboodiri, N. Krishnan. *Demographic Analysis: A Stochastic Approach*. San Diego, 1991.

Pressat, Roland. *Demographic Analysis: Methods, Results, Applications*. Chicago, 1972.

Preston, Samuel H., Patrick Heuveline, and Michel Guillot. *Demography: Measuring and Modeling Population Processes*. Oxford, 2001.

Shryock, Henry S., and Jacob S. Siegel. *The Methods and Materials of Demography*. 4th ed. Washington, D.C., 1980.

United Nations. *Manual IV: Methods for Estimating Basic Demographic Measures from Incomplete Data*. New York, 1967.

United Nations. *Manual X: Indirect Techniques for Demographic Estimation*. New York, 1983.

Wrigley, E. Anthony, and Roger S. Schofield. *The Population History of England, 1541–1871: A Reconstitution*. Cambridge, 1981.

PATRICK HEUVELINE

DEMOGRAPHIC TRANSITION. Demographic transition is the large decline in death and birth rates that is associated with a society's economic and social development or with its exposure to modern technologies and lifestyles. In an early stylized depiction, a high-mortality, high-fertility, low-population-growth equilibrium before the transition is transformed into a low-mortality, low-fertility, low-population-growth equilibrium. Although later research and observation have not supported the existence of either equilibrium as such, the broad generalization of a major transformation of demographic regime is well founded. Where, as typically happens, death rates decline before birth rates, the period of transition is one of rapid population growth.

The term *demographic transition* was first used by the American demographers Kingsley Davis and Frank Notestein in the 1940s (Davis, 1945, and Notestein, 1945). The French demographer Adolphe Landry, one of several precursors, had earlier described the phenomenon as a demographic revolution (Landry, 1934). The linking of demographic transition to urban industrialization, and of fertility decline to a prior mortality decline, was specified as a theory of transition: essentially, individuals and families were seen as responding to the pressures and opportunities created by the new social and economic circumstances by limiting their childbearing. Such formulations continue to be influential, although many later writers have criticized them as over-general and poorly matching the diversity of the historical record. (See Kirk, 1996, for an overview and Szreter, 1993, for an intellectual history.)

Components or related aspects of the demographic transition are often discussed as transitions in their own right: in particular, mortality and fertility transitions, but also an epidemiological transition (in cause-composition of mortality, from infectious to degenerative diseases [see Preston, 1976]), and a health transition (in the sociocultural and behavioral determinants of health and in the nature of healthcare systems [see Johansson, 1991]. There is claimed to be a transition in dominant types of migration and often a shift from net emigration to net immigration. (Another proposed transition—in family structure, from extended to nuclear—has not survived empirical scrutiny in many instances.) More generally, the development experience can itself be described as a parallel series of transitions—in savings behavior, production structure, urban proportions, and so on—with fertility and mortality decline seen as one structural shift among many. Such a depiction was set out in Hollis Chenery and Moises Syrquin's *Patterns of Development* (London, 1975).

Historical Experience. Pretransition demographic regimes were characterized by average annual death rates of 25 to 35 per 1,000 population, or even higher, with evidence of large year-to-year fluctuations and perhaps long-term swings as well. Infant mortality rates (deaths in the first year of life per 1,000 births) were typically 150 or higher; life expectancy, heavily influenced by the high early-age mortality, was below forty years, and often below thirty-five. Fertility levels needed to be high enough over the long run to balance this attrition but may also have shown long swings. Total fertility rates (average lifetime births per woman) were probably in the range of 4 to 6. Higher numbers are sometimes recorded but were probably not long-term averages: In most of Europe, fertility was at the lower end of the range, reflecting the unusually large proportions of women (by world standards) who never married, fertility rates for married women were therefore substantially higher. The population produced by these demographic conditions had a very youthful age structure.

A secular decline in mortality seems to have begun in the more advanced regions of Europe in the mid-to-late eighteenth century. A careful study of parish records for England and Wales shows a marked narrowing of fluctuations in annual death rates in this period (Wrigley and Schofield, 1981, Table 8.7). There is clearer evidence of a mortality decline spreading regionally across Europe from about the mid-nineteenth century: first Scandinavia, then England and Wales, then France, Belgium, and the Netherlands, then Germany and southern Europe, and, well into the twentieth century, eastern Europe (Chesnais, 1986). The data are most complete for infant mortality, but trends in this measure are a reasonable indicator of overall mortality trends. Parts of Asia and Latin America experienced some improvement in mortality after World War I (in Japan probably from the late nineteenth century), but for most of these regions and for Africa, the major declines came after World War II. A significant, though it is hoped temporary, reversal is occurring in countries with severe HIV epidemics.

The earliest sustained fertility declines were in France, beginning in the late eighteenth century, and in the United States, from the early nineteenth century. The fertility transition in most of western Europe and in Argentina, Australia, and New Zealand began in the last quarter of the nineteenth century, and in eastern and southern Europe, Canada, and Japan in the early twentieth century. Declines could be seen in a few parts of the nonindustrialized world in the 1930s, but they became widespread only in the 1960s or later. In many sub-Saharan African countries, fertility had shown little or no decline by the end of the twentieth century.

In years prior to the fertility decline, many countries experienced a rise in fertility, apparently caused by earlier and increased rates of marriage, shorter birth intervals resulting from curtailed breastfeeding, (breastfeeding tends to suppress ovulation), or lessened rates of sterility (Dyson, and Murphy, 1985). The very high total fertility rates (six to seven children per woman) recorded in many African and Asian demographic surveys in the post–World War II decades probably reflect such changes, disrupting earlier patterns of social regulation of fertility. Once underway, however, the fertility transition has appeared irreversible. Some transitions proceeded with great rapidity: Bulgaria experienced a halving of its total fertility rate from 1920 to 1940, Japan from 1945 to 1960, China from 1970 to 1980 (Chesnais, 1986).

Prior to the development of effective modern methods of contraception (intrauterine devices and hormonal methods), birth control appears to have been exercised mainly through the practice of coitus interruptus and abstinence and the use of crude barrier methods. Abortion also may have been widely practiced. Extending knowledge of such birth control methods, often against strong clerical and state opposition, was an early cause promoted by the women's movement. With a high level of motivation, low fertility could be and was achieved without modern contraception, albeit not reliably so at the individual level.

The demographic transition is conventionally viewed as completed when fertility has fallen to a two-child average per woman, which is "replacement-level" fertility under low-mortality conditions. This may occur well before the population growth rate reaches zero (i.e., before the birth-rate falls to the level of the death rate). Where the decline has been rapid, the transitional surge in population growth may persist for several more decades—until the age structure stabilizes in its mature form with few children and many elderly people. Paradoxically, the death rate (but not life expectancy) in the population at this stage is likely to be higher than it was earlier in the transition, since there are relatively more people in the high-mortality older age groups.

Estimated birth and death rates over the course of demographic transition for France, England and Wales, and Japan are graphed in Figure 1. France is distinctive in the early timing of the transition (though its exceptionality in this respect has been questioned—see Wrigley, 1985), and the absence of much population growth over its course.

Explanations of Demographic Transition. The theory of demographic transition came into favor and then into disfavor along with modernization theory, to which it has a close connection. In very brief summary, child mortality began to fall as economic conditions improved and early public health measures were adopted. The larger number of surviving children imposed economic pressures on families. At the same time, industrialization and urbanization brought wider cultural horizons and greater opportunities for mobility, both social and geographic. The transformed labor market and rising consumption and investment demands, when translated into effects on the utilities and costs of children (notably education costs), created conditions favoring smaller families. Parents responded by limiting the number of their children. The process was well described in F. W. Taussig's *Principles of Economics* (New York, 1911), the standard American economics textbook of the early twentieth century.

The contributing factors to the mortality decline, if not their weighting in particular cases, are clear enough: more reliable food supplies and better nutrition; improved knowledge and practice of hygiene; public health interventions—in particular, improvement in water supply and sewage disposal; vaccination and other medical advances; better housing; and improved public order. (See Preston, 1996 on the general relationship between mortality and economic development.) The determinants of the fertility decline are in greater dispute.

To the extent that fertility decline merely maintains the number of surviving children of earlier and higher-mortality times, fertility transition can be seen as an initially conservative response to changing circumstances. The stimulus

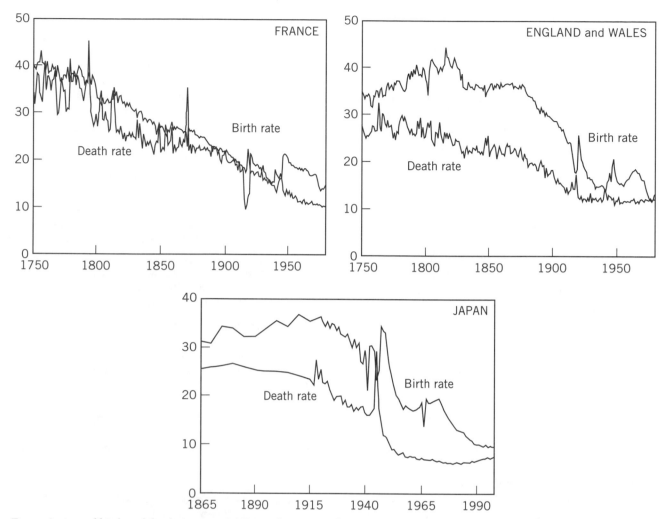

FIGURE 1. Annual birth and death rates per 1,000 population over the course of the demographic transition for France, England and Wales, and Japan. Pre-1920 estimates for Japan are 5-year averages. SOURCE: Chesnais (1986), Wrigley and Schofield (1981), and *United Nations Demographic Yearbook,* various issues.

would be larger numbers of children in the household and increased crowding in the job market (Montgomery and Cohen, 1998). Moreover, since the uncertainties about child survival at the family level are reduced as mortality falls, birth planning makes more sense. Confining responses to the single dimension of fertility change, however, is an arbitrary constraint. Families have migration options, especially in an industrializing economy, and they can make adjustments through changes in productivity and labor supply. A simple rule for demographic transition is not to be expected.

A nine-country empirical study of European transitions, the Princeton European Fertility Project, sought to test the fertility propositions of transition theory against historical experience, using province- or county-level data for the century or so up to 1960. The country monographs reporting on this enterprise, and the project's summary volume (Coale and Watkins, 1986), challenged several elements of the the-

ory. There was more variation in pretransition demographic conditions than had been supposed. There were no uniform socioeconomic thresholds, such as in levels of education or urbanization, marking the onset of the transition. On the other hand, there was often simultaneity of change within regions or language groups, suggesting a process of cultural diffusion of new ideas and behaviors. The fertility transition, in the view of many of the project's participants, was adoption of the innovation of birth control by married couples. The result was a shift from "natural fertility"—where individual-level intentional birth control is absent, even though fertility may be far below its biological maximum—to controlled fertility, where rational decision making by individuals has been extended to family size. Similar interpretations of post–World War II fertility transitions have been drawn from household survey data such as the World Fertility Survey (Cleland and Wilson, 1987).

The view of fertility transition as innovative behavior diffusing through a natural-fertility population has in turn been challenged. There is scattered evidence of deliberate birth control (and its near functional equivalent, infanticide) being practiced in many pretransitional societies, although the extent to which it influenced their overall levels of fertility is not agreed upon. However, the notion that parents in pretransitional societies simply accepted the number of children that came, with no reference to their economic (or maternal health) interests, has seemed inherently implausible to many researchers—even where there was effective social regulation of fertility. Such regulation existed at the level of parish or village in much of preindustrial western Europe and in Japan through the control of marriage or household formation.

Microeconomic theorists of fertility, such as Becker (1990), take for granted that an individualized economic calculus of decision making applies to reproductive behavior. Some social demographers, such as Caldwell (1982), similarly see fertility decisions in terms of a parental (though mainly paternal) benefit-cost framework. Those decisions are made with reference to price relativities, household budget and time constraints, and a complex array of preferences. Individual perceptions and idiosyncratic valuations of the factors entering fertility decisions introduce a subjective element, but this does not amount to ideational determination of the outcome.

Doubtless here, as with much other human behavior, the material and ideal are thoroughly confounded. Changing economic conditions and expectations were pushing families to shift from investing in social capital to investing in physical and human capital, encouraging curtailment of childbearing. At the same time new attitudes to reproduction and fuller knowledge of birth control were conveyed through social networks (see Bongaarts and Watkins, 1996).

The issues raised by this debate on the determinants of historical fertility transition have been important for the design of population policies in contemporary high-fertility countries. If innovation is the key, strategies to lower fertility should favor outreach activities to spread information and promote the new behavior: that is a principal rationale for family planning programs. If high fertility reflects family-level demand conditions in the society, strategies need to be concerned with a broader array of economic and institutional changes. Analysis of the widespread declines that have taken place in developing-country fertility since the 1960s, however, has not settled the matter.

Posttransition Demographic Regimes. The convergence of countries to a zero-growth-rate equilibrium after the demographic transition, which was once expected, has not occurred. In what some have called the second demographic transition (Van de Kaa, 1987), fertility has continued to fall, reaching levels well below a two-child aver-

age in much of Europe and in Japan. Even though longevity has continued to increase, growth rates (aside from migration) below zero are widely forecast—signaling a future of continued population aging and declines in population size. Forecasts for some developing countries, notably China, show similar trends a decade or two delayed. Survey responses may still indicate a desired family size of two children, but actual family size distributions show a majority of women having one child or none and very few having more than two. A notable prior episode of low fertility, in the United States and other western developed countries in the 1930s, was followed by a spontaneous recovery in the 1940s (and by a baby boom in the 1950s). Effective pronatalist policies that might be turned to should that not happen again have yet to be demonstrated.

BIBLIOGRAPHY

Becker, Gary S. *A Treatise on the Family*. Enlarged Cambridge, 1990.

Bongaarts, John, and Susan Cotts Watkins. "Social Interactions and Contemporary Fertility Transitions." *Population and Development Review* 22 (1996), 639–682.

Caldwell, John C. *Theory of Fertility Decline*. New York, 1982.

Chesnais, Jean-Claude. *La transition démographique: Étapes, formes, implications économiques*. Paris, 1986. Translated as *The Demographic Transition: Stages, Patterns, and Economic Implications*. Oxford, 1992.

Cleland, John, and Chris Wilson. "Demand Theories of the Fertility Decline: An Iconoclastic View." *Population Studies* 41 (1987), 5–30.

Coale, Ansley J., and Susan Cotts Watkins, eds. *The Decline of Fertility in Europe*. Princeton, 1986.

Davis, Kingsley. "The World Demographic Transition." *Annals of the American Academy of Political and Social Science* 273 (1945), 1–11.

Dyson, Tim, and Mike Murphy. "The Onset of Fertility Transition." *Population and Development Review* 11 (1985), 399–440.

Johansson, S. Ryan. "The Health Transition: The Cultural Inflation of Morbidity during the Decline of Mortality." *Health Transition Review* 1 (1991), 39–68.

Kirk, Dudley. "Demographic Transition Theory." *Population Studies* 50 (1996), 361–387.

Landry, Adolphe. *La révolution démographique: Études et essais sur les problèmes de la population*. Paris, 1934.

Montgomery, Mark R., and Barney Cohen, eds. *From Death to Birth: Mortality Decline and Reproductive Change*. Washington, 1998.

Notestein, Frank. "Population: The Long View." In *Food for the World*, edited by T. W. Schultz, pp. 36–57. Chicago, 1945.

Ohbuchi, Hiroshi. "Demographic Transition in the Process of Japanese Industrialization." In *Japanese Industrialization and Its Social Consequences*, edited by Hugh Patrick, pp. 329–361. Berkeley, 1976.

Preston, Samuel H. *Mortality Patterns in National Populations: With Special Reference to Recorded Causes of Death*. New York, 1976.

Szreter, Simon. "The Idea of Demographic Transition and the Study of Fertility Change: A Critical Intellectual History." *Population and Development Review* 19 (1993), 659–701.

Van de Kaa, Dirk J. "Europe's Second Demographic Transition." *Population Bulletin* (Population Reference Bureau) 42.1 (1987).

Wrigley, E. A. "The Fall of Marital Fertility in Nineteenth Century France: Exemplar or Exception?" *European Journal of Population* 1 (1985), 31–60, 141–177.

Wrigley, E. A. and R. S. Schofield. *The Population History of England 1541–1871: A Reconstruction*. London, 1981.

Geoffrey McNicoll

DENMARK. *See* Nordic Countries.

DEREGULATION. Governmental regulation of commercial and industrial activity has existed nearly as long as commerce has thrived. During the second half of the nineteenth century, however, new forms of industrial activity such as intercity and intraurban railways, gas illumination, electrical power, and telecommunications led to the belief that monopoly was a natural or an unavoidable form of organization for some industries. How the cost-saving benefits of large-scale operation were to be achieved while consumers were protected from monopolistic exploitation was widely debated. In Europe, the typical choice was to have a governmental entity operate important large-scale public service enterprises. In the United States, the founders of the American Economic Association questioned in 1885 whether government ownership emulating the German model or active governmental oversight of private enterprises was preferable. The public at large had an ideological bias toward private enterprise; so new regulatory institutions were created, beginning at the federal-government level in 1887 with the Interstate Commerce Commission.

Gradually, however, disillusion set in. That regulated entities often "captured" their regulators to favor the regulated firm over consumers was asserted *inter alia* by Edmund James in an early issue of the *Publications of the American Economic Association* (1886). Theoretical and empirical work by economists contributed to the realization that regulatory mechanisms were working badly. In the *American Economic Review* (December 1962), Harvey Averch and L. L. Johnson demonstrated mathematically that when prices are set to yield a "fair return" on the "fair value" of assets employed by a regulated firm, the firm often has an incentive to choose technologies that are inefficiently capital-intensive. In *Wealth of Nations* (1776), Adam Smith observed much earlier that "monopoly . . . is a great enemy to good management." John Meyer and others showed in *The Economics of Competition in the Transportation Industries* (Cambridge, 1959) that the rigid formulaic prices set by the Interstate Commerce Commission induced a substantial misallocation of resources among alternative transportation modes. That regulated airline prices were set in such a way as to encourage inefficiently frequent scheduling of half-empty aircraft was documented by George Douglas and James C. Miller in *Economic Regulation of Domestic Air Transport* (Washington, D.C., 1974). Governmental investigations revealed that the regulated telephone monopolies resisted technological changes such as facsimile and answering machines and attempted to impede the entry of competing communications media. These and other problems resulting from the system of public utility regulation in the United States and (with variants) other nations were laid out systematically in a magisterial book, *The Economics of Regulation* (New York, 1970), by Alfred Kahn.

As the intellectual seeds favoring less-regulatory approaches were being sown, the U.S. political climate simultaneously altered. Disappointing productivity growth and "stagflation" during the mid-1970s led Presidents Gerald Ford and Jimmy Carter and Congress to seek alternative solutions placing more emphasis on open competition and less on governmental regulation. Leaders of many, but not all, regulated enterprises welcomed change, in part because they wanted greater operational freedom and because—in a period of high interest rates—the inflexible "fair return on fair value" price-setting rules adversely affected stock market values. Alfred Kahn was installed as chairman of the Civil Aeronautics Board in 1977 with a mandate to begin removing and ultimately to eliminate most forms of airline price and entry regulation. Deregulation of the railroads and then competing common carrier trucklines began with the Railroad Revitalization and Regulatory Reform Act of 1976 and the appointment in 1979 of reform leadership to the Interstate Commerce Commission. Deregulation of communications took form gradually, at first (beginning in the late 1960s) through easing of interconnection and new entry restrictions by the Federal Communications Commission and then with the 1982 breakup of the American Telephone & Telegraph Co. into eight distinct parts in settlement of an antitrust action.

Total deregulation proved to be infeasible in some of the traditionally regulated industries. In airlines, for example, governmental agencies continued to coordinate the allocation of scarce takeoff and landing slots at airports and to monitor the airlines' safety efforts. In railroading, consumers of such bulk commodities as coal remained dependent upon a single transportation supplier. Regulatory price controls were continued for such exceptional cases. In telecommunications, at least with the technology as it existed during the 1980s and 1990s, competing telephone service providers had to feed many of their calls through central office switching facilities owned by the traditional local telephone service providers, and competing electric energy generators had to transmit their power over the local distribution lines owned by the entrenched local electric utilities. There were sharp differences of opinion among economists, communications executives, and regulators on how access to these natural monopoly facilities was to be priced so as to balance efficiency and equity goals.

The governments of industrialized nations in Europe, Asia, and Latin America recognized that the problems endemic to government regulation of private enterprises were mirrored or even aggravated when governmental entities provided so-called public utility goods and services, subject to oversight by central government staffs. Under the prime ministership (1979–1990) of Margaret Thatcher, the United Kingdom was the first to mount an aggressive privatization and deregulation effort for electricity supply, the railways, water provision, natural gas supply, and other previously government-owned industries, such as steel. With the advice of economists, the British privatization efforts attempted to achieve self-regulation by fragmenting previously monolithic public enterprises into a sufficient number of competing entities. This was not always possible when compelling economies of scale and scope required that a single entity own bottleneck facilities such as local distribution wires and pipelines. Governments implementing deregulation measures were often torn between maintaining monopoly structures within the privatized industries, which raised the price at which an industry's assets could be sold, and fragmenting the industries so as to achieve effective competition from which consumers were likely to benefit directly. Nevertheless, research such as the study of Mexico by Raphael La Porta and Florencio Lopez-de-Silanes (*Quarterly Journal of Economics*, November 1999) revealed that substantial efficiency gains could be realized through privatization and complementary deregulation measures.

BIBLIOGRAPHY

Bernstein, Marver. *Regulating Business by Independent Commission.* Princeton, 1955.

Crandall, Robert W., and Kenneth Flamm, eds. *Changing the Rules: Technological Changes, International Competition, and Regulation in Communications.* Washington, D.C., 1989.

Mueller, Juergen, and Ingo Vogelsang. *Staatliche Regulierung.* Baden-Baden, 1979.

Stigler, George J. "The Theory of Economic Regulation." *Bell Journal of Economics and Management Science* 2 (1971), 3–21.

Transportation Research Board, National Research Council. *Entry and Competition in the U.S. Airline Industry.* Special Report 255. Washington, D.C., 1999.

Vickers, John, and George Yarrow. *Privatization: An Economic Analysis.* Cambridge, Mass., 1988.

World Bank. *Bureaucrats in Business: The Economics and Politics of Government Ownership.* Oxford, 1995.

F. M. SCHERER

DIAMOND INDUSTRY *[This entry contains three subentries, a historical overview and discussions of technological change and industrial organization. The bibliography for this entry can be found at the end of the last subentry.]*

Historical Overview

The history of the diamond trade is usually divided into three main periods according to the gems' prevalent source. Until the mid-eighteenth century, most of the known diamonds came from the Indian subcontinent. The second phase began in 1730, when diamonds were found in Brazil, then a Portuguese possession. After that date, Brazilian stones dominated the world market for a century and a half. In 1866 the accidental discovery of a diamond in South Africa ushered in the third phase. In the following decades, African diamonds took over and retained the largest share of world production, even after major diamond fields were discovered in Siberia in the 1950s and in western Australia in the late 1970s.

Early History. Relatively little is known about Indian diamonds before the early modern period. They were probably mined in alluvial deposits located along the Mahanadi River, 200 miles south of Varanasi (also known as Benares). This area, centered on the town of Sambalpur, was the provenance of the diamonds known to the ancient western world. Pliny the Elder, the Roman naturalist, discussed the properties of diamonds in detail in the first century CE, while Ptolemy, the Greek astronomer, mentioned the Indian mines in the following century. Western traders came into closer contact with Indian diamonds in the thirteenth century. Marco Polo, for example, mentions them in his memoirs. Around this time, new diamond fields were opened to the south, especially around the fortress of Golconda. The diamond trade, however, was institutionalized only after the European expansion of the fifteenth century, first by the Portuguese from their commercial base in Goa, and then by the British and the Dutch, based in Madras. Throughout India, mining was carried out by the lower castes, while local rulers aimed to control production and trade. As late as the end of the nineteenth century, for example, local rulers around Panna, south of the Ganges River, confiscated all large diamonds, together with one-fourth of the value of all other stones.

The Second Phase, 1730–1866. Brazilian diamonds entered the international scene when the Indian fields began to show signs of depletion. In the late 1720s, many prospectors stumbled upon the precious stones in the mountain rivers of Minas Gerais, a province northwest of Rio de Janeiro. Like their Indian counterparts, Brazilian diamonds were alluvial and therefore easy to mine, but their average size tended to be smaller. After a few months of unregulated prospecting and mining, the Portuguese Crown imposed a system of heavy taxation, first on the prospectors and their black slaves, and then on the diamonds themselves. The borders of the diamond district, centered on Diamantina, were laid out to monitor the flow of goods and people in and out of the area. As early as 1733, the Crown established the office of intendant of mines to administer the diamond claims and collect taxes. But this did not prevent the extensive smuggling that ensued. In 1739 the government centralized the industry by granting a mining monopoly to the highest bidding company or individual. The Crown became the only legal buyer of the stones mined in Brazil. Around the same time, diamonds were also first used to back letters of credit and promissory notes.

In 1753 the Portuguese Crown discontinued the system of concessions by establishing a government monopoly on production as well as on selling. Royal agencies, called *caixas*, were founded both in Brazil and in Lisbon to receive, sort, and sell diamonds to private buyers. Lisbon soon became the leading diamond trading center in the world. Competing merchants bid for a monopoly contract on diamond selling in the Portuguese capital, and then they shipped the stones to northern Europe, especially to Amsterdam, Antwerp, and London. From 1771 to 1787, the legal trade in Brazilian diamonds remained in the hands of one Dutch merchant, Daniel Gildemeester, who fell into disfavor after being suspected of involvement in contraband. Smuggling, in fact, continued unabated. A remarkable and ever-growing portion of the Brazilian diamond production reached northern Europe directly through illegal channels. The Gildemeester era was followed by the close partnership between Joaquim Pedro Quintela, the chief contractor between 1791 and 1817, and another Dutch merchant and banker, John Hope, who acted as the main commercial agent in northern Europe. A parallel partnership between Hope and the British banker Alexander Baring was instrumental in granting the Portuguese Crown the extensive Anglo-Dutch Diamond Loan of 1802, whereby the government in Lisbon mortgaged the Brazilian diamonds to repay the debt contracted on account of the wars against France in 1795 and against Spain in 1801.

The Napoleonic campaigns disrupted the diamond trade worldwide, especially after French troops occupied Portugal from 1807 to 1808. The Portuguese court escaped to Brazil in 1807, carrying to Rio the larger part of the diamond stocks deposited in Lisbon. The French army confiscated and sent to France most of the stones left behind in Portugal. While in Rio, the Portuguese government tried to tighten its control over diamond production and trade even further, in the face of the miners' discontent and resistance. The new intendant of mines after 1807, Manoel Ferreira do Câmara, tried to modernize the industry by introducing a degree of mechanization and by promoting the creation of joint-stock companies. Production increased, but it fell short of the Crown's insatiable demand, even after the Anglo-Dutch Diamond Loan was repaid in 1817. Miners' resistance to over-regulation expressed itself in the form of illegal trade. According to one estimate, half of the Brazilian diamonds mined in the first half of the nineteenth century were smuggled to northern Europe and Portugal.

At the same time, British presence in Brazil was increasing steadily. London-based Samuel, Phillips & Company arrived in Rio in 1808 together with other British merchant banks. The company established profitable ties both with the ruling dynasty of the Braganças, who sold them diamonds, and with Nathan Rothschild, head of the powerful London bank. This partnership combined trade in diamonds with international banking and other commercial activities until 1855, when the British company pulled out of Brazil. This institutional arrangement weathered first the nationalization of the diamond industry in 1821 by the Portuguese Cortes and then the independence of Brazil from Lisbon in 1822. At first the independent Brazilian government claimed the Portuguese monopoly rights for itself, but in the course of the 1830s and 1840s a series of measures liberalized the industry to create a modus vivendi for the thousands of *garimpeiros* ("independent prospectors and miners") who searched for diamonds under Brazilian national authority. The contractual ambiguity of this arrangement and the gradual exhaustion of the fields led to a steep decline of Brazilian diamond production after 1850. Even though diamond mining has never been completely abandoned in Brazil, its share of world production is now less than 2 percent.

The Third Phase: 1866–Present. Again, another major source of diamonds emerged as the output of the Brazilian mines declined. In 1866 the first South African diamond was found on the banks of the Orange River by a Boer family. Another discovery of a large stone by an African shepherd in 1869 led to a massive prospecting rush along the Vaal River. By 1870 more than ten thousand miners—most of them Americans, Europeans, and Australians—crowded the region. In 1871 diamonds were found in the area that was to become the city of Kimberley. Unlike the early alluvial findings, diamonds in this area were embedded in a superficial layer of yellow soil over a much deeper "pipe" of blue ground. The digging began, carried out in four main mines (Kimberley proper, De Beers, Dutoitspan, and Bulfontein) with over 750 claim holders. The use of African labor was the norm from the beginning. A sort of "miners' democracy" characterized the early years of digging. At first only one claim per digger was permitted; then the quota was raised to ten.

Nonetheless, coordination problems soon developed in the Kimberley area mines and a gradual process of consolidation took place. The two main consolidators were Cecil Rhodes, a young British entrepreneur who became the main proprietor in the De Beers mine by 1880, and Barney Barnato, a Jewish actor and boxer from London, who achieved a similar position of leadership in the Kimberley mine. Rhodes's De Beers Company, founded in 1880, took

DIAMONDS. Worker checking the facets of a diamond, Botswana, 1993. (© Jason Laure/Woodfin Camp and Associates, New York)

over Barnato's firm in 1888. After that date, Rhodes remained the world's largest diamond magnate until his death in 1902. A more rapid process of consolidation took place in trading. In 1893 a group of London merchants founded the first Diamond Syndicate, establishing close ties with De Beers. In the first half of the twentieth century, under the leadership of Ernest Oppenheimer and his son Harry Oppenheimer, South African control over the international diamond trade increased steadily. After becoming chairman of De Beers, Ernest founded Diamond Corporation Ltd. in 1930 to coordinate production. Selling was centralized with the establishment of Diamond Trading Company in 1934. The famous commercial and financial holding, the Central Selling Organization, was established soon after World War II, which led to the creation of one of the most successful and powerful cartels in history.

[*See also* Jewelry Industry *and* Luxury Trades.]

DARIO GAGGIO

Technological Change

Diamonds are used for two widely different purposes: as gemstones and as boring or cutting material in a variety of industries, including mining, construction, and machine building. Industrial diamonds are also used to cut and polish gemstones, and both natural and synthetic diamonds are employed for industrial purposes. Although the earliest uses of diamonds were ornamental and religious, during the second half of the twentieth century demand for industrial diamonds—both natural and synthetic—increased steadily, outstripping the quantitative demand for gemstones.

The basic notions and techniques related to diamond cutting originated in India and reached Europe via Venice in the early fourteenth century. From Venice faceting techniques spread throughout the continent, even though diamond cutters soon realized the advantages of meeting in specialized centers such as Antwerp, Amsterdam, and—during the late eighteenth century—Lisbon. These cities were located at the end of the commercial routes of precious stones. Antwerp, for example, developed into a major diamond-cutting center in the second half of the sixteenth century, when Portuguese traders in precious stones and pearls converged in the city on the Schelde River. In 1618 there were 164 master diamond cutters in Antwerp. After a period of crisis in the early eighteenth century, also due to the competition of Amsterdam, the diamond industry of the Flemish city grew again after the discovery of the Brazilian diamond fields. Around the same time, the Portuguese Crown promoted a diamond-cutting industry in Lisbon, where 107 master cutters were active in 1790.

Not until of the twentieth century, did other major diamond-cutting centers challenge the leadership of Antwerp and Amsterdam. After World War I the South African government fostered the development of a local diamond-cutting industry. Starting in the 1930s, Jewish refugees from Europe, led by the renowned cutter Zvi Rosenberg, established the thriving Israeli diamond-cutting industry, centered in the town of Netanya. But not all diamonds were cut in these celebrated artisanal districts. Starting in the 1960s, for example, sweatshops were established in the Indian city of Surat, an industrial center north of Mumbai, where fifty thousand workers—many of whom were children—cut and polished very small stones for extremely low wages.

Diamond cuts have grown in complexity from the late Middle Ages on. The earliest cut, the point cut, consisted in the polishing of the eight triangle faces of the octahedron, the most common diamond crystal shape. In the fourteenth century, the point cut was superseded by the table cut, consisting in the removal of one or more points of the octahedron. Starting in the early fifteenth century, the rose cut, with a flat bottom rising to a dome covered with triangle facets, became increasingly popular. The more complex brilliant cut, with 58 facets, was perfected by Vincenzo Peruzzi in Venice at the end of the seventeenth century. This shape became the basis for the standard brilliant and emerald cuts, which are applied to the vast majority of gem-quality rough diamonds worldwide.

At least in the case of the most valuable stones, diamond cutting remains a largely manual task that requires extensive training. The basic cutting machinery, dating back to the fourteenth century, consists of a holding device (the dop), in which the stone is firmly embedded in special metal alloys, a device regulating the orientation of the stone (the tang), and a lapping wheel that polishes the diamond. The application of electricity, however, transformed parts of the production process in the early twentieth century. Electric motors, for example, made diamond sawing more common as well as faster and more accurate. Grinding and polishing wheels were also electrically operated. Laser technology has been widely applied to remove impurities and imperfections from gemstones.

Only approximately one-third of the natural diamonds mined worldwide are of gem quality. The rest of the production—often referred to as bort—is employed for industrial purposes. The early use of industrial diamonds dates back to the late nineteenth century. The introduction of the diamond grinding wheel in the 1930s and the needs of the armament industry during World War II turned industrial diamonds into a material of strategic importance. This explains the innovative drive toward the production of synthetic diamonds after the end of the conflict. After some early experiments in Scotland in the 1870s and in Paris in the 1900s, the first authenticated synthetic diamond was produced in 1953 by a Swedish company, Allmänna Svenska Elektriska Aktiebolaget (ASEA), which applied great pressure and electrically obtained high temperatures to a combination of graphite and metal. General Electric (GE) followed suit in 1955, and in 1958 it was De Beers's turn to enter this rapidly expanding industry. The first synthetic diamonds were extremely small and very expensive, but their costs have declined considerably in recent decades, as their obtainable size has increased.

Since the 1960s De Beers, the South African company that holds a monopoly position in the trade of natural diamonds, has exercised a high degree of control over synthetic diamonds as well. De Beers reached a patent agreement with General Electric, purchased ASEA, and then established a major factory in Shannon, Ireland. De Beers and GE's virtual duopoly over synthetic diamonds—a crucial defense material and an effective semiconductor—has spurred a great deal of controversy in recent years, also due to suspicions of collusion between the duopolists. In the 1980s the production of synthetic diamonds outstripped that of natural stones one to three, even though natural diamonds were at least ten times as valuable as synthetic ones. But because synthetic diamonds are virtually indistinguishable from natural ones, allegations have been made that the duopoly is part of De Beers's general strategy of keeping the price of gem diamonds at artificially high levels.

Dario Gaggio

Industrial Organization

Diamonds are mined by a variety of companies, both private and public, in many countries, notably several southern and western African nations, Russia, and Australia. The marketing of rough diamonds, however, is strictly controlled by one organization, which is also one of the world's most successful cartels. Every fifth Monday of the year, the Central Selling Organization summons a selection of the world's two hundred most important wholesale dealers to London for a "sight." Rough diamonds of diverse size and quality are handed out to the dealers in cardboard boxes, each dealer receiving his supply of stones for the next several months. Dealers can either accept or reject the offer, but they cannot haggle over the diamonds' price and quality. Very few dealers have ever refused. The history of the diamond industry's organization in the twentieth century largely coincides with the strategies adopted by De Beers, the South African leader of the cartel, to achieve and preserve control over the diamond trade in the face of repeated challenges to its monopolistic power.

Early History. The Portuguese, who exploited the Brazilian diamond fields in the eighteenth century, already sought to achieve control over the supply and trade of diamonds, to preserve—and possibly increase—their value. Despite Lisbon's monopolistic control over Brazilian mining, however, the Portuguese had to contend with a variety of legitimate and illegitimate traders based in England and in the Netherlands. These multiple commercial channels thwarted the Portuguese Crown's monopolistic ambitions. Nevertheless, diamonds' relative rarity seemed sufficient guarantee of their ongoing value.

The discovery of enormous deposits in South Africa in the 1860s and 1870s threatened to flood the market and radically reduce the value of diamonds. Nonetheless, for a few years it seemed that free trade would shape the destiny of the industry. Wildcat miners and improvised traders flocked to the African fields from all corners of the globe, seeking quick riches and easy profits. Rising coordination problems among the miners, as well as the international crisis of 1873, brought free trade to its rapid end. At this stage, Cecil Rhodes began to use his stronghold in the De Beers mine to amalgamate the diamond claims scattered around the city of Kimberley. Rhodes already envisaged the creation of one economic organization capable of co-ordinating production and marketing in a planned manner. With the support of the Rothschild financial empire, in the 1880s Rhodes managed to first challenge, and then co-opt, the company of Barney Barnato, his main rival and leading claim holder in the Kimberley mine. This event made possible the official foundation of De Beers Consolidated Mines in 1888, when the company already controlled 90 percent of South African diamonds.

The 1880s also saw the creation of a distinctive labor management system, which survived with minor variations until very recently. Forced to enter the monetary economy by the tax requirements of the British colonial government, thousands of African workers left their homes—often located hundreds of miles from Kimberley—to earn wages in the diamond mines. By 1891 there were already six thousand African laborers working underground. Hired on renewable three-month contracts, black laborers were confined to the mines and annexed facilities, the notorious "compounds," for the duration of their stay. There they were subjected to ruthless discipline, humiliating searches, and savage forms of punishment. The official rationale for the establishment of the compounds was the struggle against smuggling, known in the trade as Illegal Diamond Buying (IDB), which was estimated to consume half of all production in the 1870s. By the 1890s IBD had been reduced tenfold. Compounds, however, also guaranteed a stable supply of cheap and pliant labor. Around the same time, a law was passed that banned the possession of diamonds unless the buyer could prove to have purchased them through a licensed dealer. Consolidation of marketing channels paralleled the amalgamation of mining companies. In 1893 De Beers and the other major South African producers came to an agreement with the leading diamond traders. The result was the establishment of the London-based Diamond Syndicate, the first organization meant to regulate supply and prices by coordinating production and marketing worldwide. Barnato committed suicide in 1895, and Rhodes died in 1902, at the end of the Boer War. Not coincidentally, the future leader of the diamond industry did not emerge from the miners' ranks, but from the world of international traders. Ernest Oppenheimer came to Kimberley in 1902 as an executive of Dunkelsbuhlers & Company, one of the trading companies affiliated with the Diamond Syndicate. Oppenheimer soon realized that the pursuit of Rhodes's monopolistic project needed a firm—even ruthless—leadership, and he set out to follow in Rhodes's footsteps with new determination.

Twentieth Century. The 1900s and 1910s saw repeated challenges to the cartel's hegemony. In 1902 Percival Tracey and Thomas Cullinan discovered a rich diamond pipe at Elandsfontein, in the Transvaal, and founded the Premier Diamond Company to exploit it. This was the mine that in 1905 produced the largest diamond ever found, the Cullinan, which weighed 3,024 carats (1 carat equals 200 milligrams). Premier began to sell independently, triggering a phase of price instability that peaked in 1908–1909, when diamond value plummeted to half its level of 1904. It was only in 1911 that Barnato Brothers, now led by Barney's nephew Solly Joel, managed to take Premier over and bring the Elandsfontein mine into the cartel's sphere of influence. The mine was then sold to De Beers in 1917. But an even more dangerous threat now emerged from the German colony of South-West Africa (present-day Namibia), where rich alluvial deposits of diamonds were discovered in 1908. The German colonial government established a competing cartel based in Berlin and began to sell in the Antwerp market. Cautious negotiations were carried out between the Germans and the London syndicate, with Oppenheimer playing an increasingly important role. But the outbreak of World War I ended these negotiations.

Germany's defeat and the establishment of a South African mandate over Berlin's former colony brought South-West African diamonds under the syndicate's control. In the meantime, however, Oppenheimer sought U.S. capital to develop mining interests in the British colonies of southern Africa. The fruit of this venture was the foundation of Anglo-American Corporation in 1917, soon to become De Beers's main rival for market control. The support of J. P. Morgan, the powerful American magnate, helped Oppenheimer to establish the Consolidated Diamond Mine of South-West Africa (CDM) in 1919, which threatened to upset the unstable balance of power between the South African government and De Beers in the newly controlled territory. Barnato Brothers and Anglo-American also jointly began to extend their diamond-mining interests to other parts of Africa, especially Belgian Congo (present-day Democratic Republic of the Congo) and Portuguese West Africa (present-day Angola).

The rising tension between Oppenheimer and De Beers came to a head in the interwar years, an extremely volatile period for the diamond trade. Determined to use Anglo-American as a stepping stone toward the complete control over the diamond industry, Oppenheimer established a privileged commercial relationship with the southwestern African producers, who began to sell in Antwerp independently of the syndicate. Outraged, the syndicate expelled Anglo-American in 1925. These tensions, combined with new discoveries of diamond deposits in many parts of Africa, led to a sharp decline in prices in the late 1920s, which Oppenheimer deftly used to force De Beers into an alliance. Threatened with the potential collapse of the entire trade, De Beers gave in by appointing Oppenheimer as its chairman in 1930. In the following years, the old syndicate was reorganized into Diamond Corporation Ltd., which bought stones from mining companies and guaranteed them minimum purchases, and Diamond Trading Company, devoted to the selling and marketing of diamonds. These two companies, linked to De Beers and Anglo-American through interlocking partnerships, provided the backbone of the Central Selling Organization, founded after World War II. This complex institutional arrangement was capable of weathering both the Great Depression and the world conflict by reducing—or even stopping—production, and accumulating enormous stocks of diamonds to be released into the market in a planned manner. Rhodes's dream had finally come true.

Despite the cartel's power, Oppenheimer's empire had to face a variety of challenges in the post–World War II decades. In the early 1950s, for example, rich diamond deposits were found on the banks of the Vilyui River in Siberia, which led to a sharp decline of De Beers's shares and to new fears of an impending crisis. In a characteristic move, De Beers came to an informal agreement with the Soviet Union, whereby the South African company employed a complicated channel of intermediaries to pay the Soviet government higher prices than the market rate in exchange for its exclusive control over the sale of Siberian diamonds. Similar agreements were reached with the postcolonial governments of Tanzania, Ghana, and Sierra Leone, which—like the USSR—refused to deal directly with South African companies for political reasons. In west Africa, the main player was the Consolidated African Selection Trust (CAST), founded by the U.S. mining magnate Alfred Beatty in 1924, shortly after the discovery of extensive diamond fields in the Gold Coast (present-day Ghana). Until CAST's nationalization in 1972, however, Beatty and Oppenheimer's empires established a modus vivendi and even shared boardroom representation.

Ernest Oppenheimer died in 1957 and was succeeded by his son Harry. Under his leadership, De Beers and Anglo-American became important—if somewhat shady—actors in the economic and political lives of several African countries after the end of colonial rule. Worth mentioning are the cases of Tanzania, the recipient of an extensive loan in the early 1970s in exchange for exclusive rights on the Williamson mine, and Zaire (former Belgian Congo, the present-day Democratic Republic of the Congo, and the largest producer of industrial diamonds), where exclusive rights were exchanged for close financial ties with Mobutu's notoriously corrupt regime. Harder to control has been the extensive smuggling carried out by independent African miners, even though De Beers has been alleged to use both the carrot and the stick to bring the smugglers into line. In the case of democratic countries, the South African empire has employed a more open negotiating strategy. In the early 1980s, for example, De Beers managed to convince Australia's Labor government that there was no alternative to the Central Selling Organization, from whose activities both parties were bound to profit. Only a very particular and easily recognizable kind of stone mined at Lake Argyle, in western Australia, was sold independently of De Beers until 1996. After that date, the Australians began independent marketing operations in Antwerp and India.

No account of the organization of the diamond industry, however brief, would be complete without mentioning De Beers's advertising campaigns, widely regarded as among the most successful in history. In 1938 De Beers signed a contract with the American advertising company N. W. Ayer. Despite the fact that the Sherman Antitrust Act prevented De Beers from conducting business directly on U.S. soil, an aggressive advertisement campaign turned the United States into the world's largest market for gem diamonds. Virtually unknown in the 1930s, diamond engagement rings became increasingly common in the 1950s and grew into the object of a widespread collective ritual in the 1960s, when 80 percent of U.S. men presented their fiancées with the glittering stone. The slogan "Diamonds are forever," launched in 1948, and the Hollywood trope "Diamonds are a girl's best friend" turned De Beers into an American household name.

After conquering the United States, De Beers successfully penetrated the Japanese market, where diamonds were not part of traditional life. Despite allegations of unfair practices (the U.S. Justice Department has been investigating the diamond cartel at least since 1973), De Beers's monopolistic practices have indeed preserved the notion that diamonds are immensely valuable items. In this case, consumers are at least as invested in perpetuating this belief as the monopolists themselves, despite some observers' opinion that the high value of diamonds is one of the most deftly crafted economic and cultural constructions of the modern era.

BIBLIOGRAPHY

Bauer, Max. *Precious Stones*. New York, 1968.

Bernstein, Harry. *The Brazilian Diamond in Contracts, Contraband and Capital*. London, 1986.

Blakey, George. *The Diamond*. London, 1977.

Epstein, Edward. *The Rise and Fall of Diamonds: The Shattering of a Brilliant Illusion*. New York, 1982.

Evans, Joan. *A History of Jewellery, 1100–1870*. London, 1953.

Greenhalgh, P. A. L. *West African Diamonds, 1919–1983: An Economic History*. Manchester, 1985.

Gregory, T. E. *Ernest Oppenheimer and the Economic Development of South Africa*. Cape Town, 1962.

Harlow, George, ed., *The Nature of Diamonds*. Cambridge, 1998.

Lenzen, G. *The History of Diamond Production and the Diamond Trade*. London, 1970.

Newbury, Colin. *The Diamond Ring: Business, Politics, and Precious Stones in South Africa*. Oxford, 1989.

Tillander, H. *Diamond Cuts in Historic Jewellery, 1380–1910*. London, 1995.

Watermeyer, Basil. *Diamond Cutting: A Complete Guide to Diamond Processing*. Cape Town, 1980.

Wilks, J. W., and E. Wilks. *The Properties and Applications of Diamonds*. Stoneham, Mass., 1995.

Worger, William. *South Africa's City of Diamonds: Mine Workers and Monopoly Capitalism in Kimberley, 1867–1895*. New Haven, 1987.

DARIO GAGGIO

DIANDI is a Chinese term meaning "pawning (*dian*) land (*di*) for a loan." It is also called *dangdi*. A very ancient practice in China, *diandi* lasted until 1956 when Communists pressed ahead for collectivization following the Stalinist model.

There were four preconditions for *diandi*: first, a legally free peasantry in a non-feudal society who were engaged in business voluntarily in a predominantly private economy; second, wide-spread private property rights over land; third, an exchange economy where a factor (land) market developed; and fourth, personal debts (compatible with the private economy) because of economic hardships such as crop failure, personal misfortune (such as illness), or state tax burden.

Evidence suggests that all these conditions began to exist in China well before the Common Era. The first de facto private landownership was recorded in 685 BCE, when the Qi kingdom decided to tax peasants on land output capacities. In 359 BCE the Qin kingdom carried out a sweeping reform to promote a landholding peasantry. After that it was only a matter of time until land entered the market despite state restrictions on land transactions and speculations.

To pawn land for funds to bridge difficult times was a welcome solution given that the pawner kept the option to redeem the land later. As in the pawning of other commodities, the pawnee normally charged a monthly interest of 3 to 5 percent. However, compared with the 6 to 24 months' limit on redeeming movable assets, land had a much longer period for further redemption even after the pawner failed to redeem in the first incident (when the pawn period expired)—sometimes as long as 30 to 40 years. Here, customary residual property rights remained active after land changed hands, clearly reflecting the general attitude toward real estate in China.

Normally, the pawner continued farming the land during the term as a tenant, because pawnees often lacked the resources and knowledge (and desire) to farm. Also, it was in the interest of both parties for the pawner to keep farming to pay back the loan. Furthermore, from the pawner's point of view, to till the land was part of his customary property rights.

Land was pawned for many reasons, some of them ingenious moneymaking schemes. For example, land was pawned to improve liquidity for religious, communal, and clan ceremonies, business investment, and the like—not just to earn subsistence income. Normally, these were short-term deals and the pawner usually redeemed the property by repaying the loan. In the early twentieth century, it was common in parts of China (mainly the north and northeast where land supply was relatively abundant) for the pawnee household to farm the land. In this case, the user rights to the land acquired by the pawnee effectively served as interest. It also became a mechanism for land-poor households to acquire land for farming.

Meanwhile, there was another line of development also called *diandi* meaning "right conversion from freehold to leasehold." Such conversion involved the sale of the land deed on condition that the seller was granted permanent leasehold. This form of *diandi* originated in Ming times when land tax was increased for ordinary landowners but waived for the gentry. So the landowners saw the opportunity to avoid taxes by selling freehold rights to the gentry. As long as the rent for leasehold was less than land tax, there was a net gain for the landowner. For the gentry buyers, there was a net gain in rent income. So, in a twist, this conversion was Pareto optimal for both parties.

BIBLIOGRAPHY

Deng, Gang. *The Premodern Chinese Economy: Structural Equilibrium and Capitalist Sterility*. London and New York, 1999.

Myers, Ramon H. *The Chinese Peasant Economy: Agricultural Development in Hopei and Shangtung, 1890–1949*. Cambridge, Mass., 1970.

KENT G. DENG

DIESEL, RUDOLF (1858–1913), German engineer and inventor.

The son of an unsuccessful German shopkeeper, Diesel was born in Paris. When war broke out in 1870, the family moved to London, but Rudolf was soon sent alone to Germany to live with relatives. The boy did well at an industrial school in Augsburg, decided to be an engineer, and won a scholarship to the engineering school in Munich. Here, he established a brilliant record and developed a religious faith in science.

Diesel spent the next decade in the mechanical refrigeration business, with headquarters in Paris, later in Berlin. He also started a family, and in his spare time worked on his own inventions, usually aimed at improving the steam engine or finding a better kind of power for small workshops. Around 1890 he developed a new way of operating an internal-combustion engine. Instead of filling the cylinder with a mixture of fuel and air and then compressing the mixture and lighting it, as the ordinary engine does, he proposed drawing plain air into the cylinder, and then in the next stroke compressing the air and injecting fuel into the compressed air, which would then be so hot that no special ignition device would be necessary. For a time Diesel also thought that by controlling the combustion in such an engine, he could achieve what is known in thermodynamics as the Carnot cycle, so that the engine would have the highest thermal efficiency possible for a heat engine. He patented this theoretical engine in 1892 and wrote a book about it. It was a "rational" engine, he said, destined to replace the steam engine.

Critics disagreed on the feasibility of such an engine. It would have to use pressures far beyond the state of the art. But Diesel was able to persuade the Maschinenfabrik Augsburg to give him technical help and space in the middle of a large steam-engine factory to build a simplified version of his scientific engine. Four years later, he announced success and began to negotiate contracts to produce engines under his patent in a dozen countries. These contracts made him a rich man, but there were difficulties. One was that the patent was vulnerable. Another was that no licensee could make an engine that satisfied a customer. Diesel's own company had to take back every engine it made, and Diesel himself, always a neurotically hard worker, was overwhelmed and had to take time out for a rest cure in a sanatorium. He made no further major contributions to the design of his engine.

Back from his rest cure, Diesel built a luxurious house for his family in Munich, with room for a small staff to help with his rather visionary plans for the engine. He traveled widely in Europe and America, calling on industrial leaders and giving lectures. He also read widely in contemporary utopian literature, for he had always been interested in what he called the social question. In 1903 he published his own utopia, a blueprint for a rational society—with love and thrift for motive power—which he named Solidarity and offered as an alternative to socialism. His plans for both the rational engine and the rational society were now published, and he left notes for a book on a rational religion.

At a professional meeting in 1912, Diesel gave a paper on the origin of his engine that was attacked in the discussion period by two distinguished engineers who said that credit for the invention should go to the Maschinenfabrik Augsburg rather than to Diesel. This controversy continued in four books, one by Diesel and three by his critics. Diesel was deeply disturbed by these attacks on his integrity, and he was also financially ruined by unwise investments. In September 1913, he disappeared from a cross-channel steamer that was taking him to a directors' meeting in England.

The work of making the engine reliable and economical was done by a whole generation of practical engineers in several countries. They slowly learned how to cope with the very high pressures and temperatures required by the new process, and how to find the right fuel. The key problem was fuel injection: how to insert liquid fuel into very dense air, in carefully timed pulses, several pulses per second. These problems were solved in different ways for different purposes. Diesel-powered ships became common in the 1920s. Lighter and faster diesels took over American railroads in the 1950s; still lighter and faster ones were developed for trucks and buses. By the end of the century nearly all commercial transportation on land and at sea was powered by descendants of Diesel's original idea for an engine.

BIBLIOGRAPHY

Bryant, Lynwood. "The Development of the Diesel Engine." *Technology and Culture* 17 (1976), 432–446.

Diesel, Eugen. *Diesel: Der Mensch, das Werk, das Schiksal.* 9th ed. Stuttgart, 1948.

Diesel, Rudolf. *Theorie und Konstruktion eines rationellen Wärmemotors zum Ersatz der Dampfmaschinen und der heute bekannten Verbrennungsmotoren.* Berlin, 1893.

Diesel, Rudolf. *Solidarismus: Natürliche wirtschaftliche Erlösung des Menschen.* Munich, 1903.

Diesel, Rudolf. *Die Entstehung des Dieselmotors.* Berlin, 1913.

Sass, Friedrich. *Geschichte des deutschen Verbrennungsmotorenbaues von 1860 bis 1918.* Berlin, 1962.

LYNWOOD BRYANT

DISEASES *[This entry contains two subentries, on infectious diseases and deficiency and parasitic diseases.]*

Infectious Diseases

Among the vast numbers of microorganisms, a relative few are pathogens. Those that do cause illness do so either acutely, typically resulting in immunity or death, or chronically, resulting in persisting illness, many periods of infectivity, and often progressing disabilities. A few pathogens can infect yet lie dormant within hosts, only later to cause sudden exacerbation of the disease process. Some common viruses may eventually produce cancers or lead to rapid debilitation and death long after infection, but the historical role of such pathogens cannot be determined from available evidence. Thus by their effects on human bodies, the social and economic effects of infectious disease pathogens can be grouped by the time parameters of typical infection into acute and chronic. In the past, individuals often carried many infections simultaneously, making assessment of the historical effects of infectious diseases difficult.

After some general remarks about infectious disease experience in the past and about the reliability of historical evidence, this article provides a brief summary of the historical issues surrounding noted acute and chronic infectious diseases. A final section reviews principal changes in global infectious disease experience within the last century, including present concern with emerging infectious diseases and antibiotic resistance.

General Considerations. The overall health of a population is bracketed by a rich variety of common environmental exposures to ubiquitous microorganisms. The robust well-being of people in the developed world today relies upon minimizing exposure to pathogens. Simple routines such as hand washing significantly reduce risks of illness and death. Most pathogens enter human bodies through water, earth (e.g., food, soil), and air. Most are destroyed by fire. Broadly speaking, waterborne viruses, bacteria, and parasites take their greatest toll on the youngest members of a population. Airborne pathogens are typically most lethal to the oldest members of the group.

Infectious disease experience in the past. From Neolithic agricultural communities to the millions of people teeming around great urban centers today, good health for the whole population depends foremost upon a relatively unpolluted food and water supply. Survival rates of infants and young children are quickly compromised when the population group is under stress. Whether by war, food shortage, adverse weather, crowding, or forced migration, or even disproportionate, differential impoverishment within a population, young children are more likely exposed to alterations in water and food quality than older ones. The younger the child is, the higher the proportion of body surface area to body mass, which means that a gentle diarrhea response to a ubiquitous, nonvirulent pathogen (e.g., rotovirus, *E. coli*) becomes life-threatening because it leads to rapid dehydration. Maternal antibodies and nonspecific immune factors in breast milk offer a good measure of protection.

The elderly are more immediately threatened by circulatory collapse than by waterborne pathogens and acute dehydration. Compromised lung function, as with pneumonia (once called "the old man's friend" because it was believed to speed individuals to the grave), places stress on the aging heart. The immunity to many diseases acquired through long life decays rapidly with aging. Because in the past waterborne infections propagated most readily in warmer seasons, and airborne infections spread most easily when groups of people shared the same confined airspace in order to stay warm, young children were more likely to fall ill and die during the summer months, the elderly in the winter.

Despite these commonplaces, the greatest demographic costs to premodern populations came with pathogens that compromised older children and young adults. Before the invention of antibiotics in the twentieth century, organisms residing perennially on the skin and in the mouth were the most common source of death-dealing infections after the first few years of life. Staphylococcus, streptococcus, *Candida* (yeast) species, and the fusiform bacilli common in the mouth could become causes of severe illness and cause death quite capriciously, as when the skin was broken or when tooth decay proceeded to regional (neck, head) and finally systemic (bloodborne) infection. All premodern medical texts testify to the results of ordinary skin bacteria opportunistically invading a previously healthy body. Examples include such pathological conditions as osteomyelitis (infection of a bone), abscesses from a poorly healing wound site, damage to heart valves or other internal organs from bloodborne skin bacteria or the microbes causing tooth decay and gum disease, infection of the uterus after a healthy delivery, or tetanus (caused by soil bacilli entering the bloodstream from a cut, a puncture, or an abrasion). These generalizations presume an otherwise healthy adult or older child, and exclude the developmental process of puberty. Underlying chronic infectious disease and/or malnutrition compromised every aspect of the normal healing process. Thus the burden of chronic infections within a population undoubtedly moderated nonepidemic mortality and morbidity, though historians are unable to measure these costs with available records.

Available historical evidence. Civic registration of causes of death did not become routine in affluent nations until the late nineteenth century; registration of underlying or contributing causes of death is still not ubiquitous. Systematic collection of morbidity statistics began in the twentieth century. Even where mortality records existed, there are problems translating those recorded causes into modern disease categories. Medical and governmental changes in the classification, diagnosis, and recording of disease after the 1850s led to the collection of information about nonepidemic causes of disease and death, improving the statistical basis for the study of infectious diseases. Current systems of classifying causes of death and disease originated with William Farr and Alphonse Quetelet (1850s and 1860s) and Jacques Bertillon (1890s).

It is unfortunate that the significant changes in ideas and records related to infectious disease, including the formulation of the germ theory of disease with Louis Pasteur and Robert Koch, temporally coincided with sharply rising life expectancy among all but the poorest within industrial nations. The modern rise of population that began in Europe around 1700 followed steep declines in first adult and then childhood mortality. Because changes in classification and diagnosis of disease paralleled these changes in disease experience, historians cannot be certain how changes in nonepidemic infectious disease experience may have contributed to improvements in survival.

During the 1970s, two different historical hypotheses offered explanatory frameworks for the dramatic modern rise of population, both centering on arguments about the role of infectious diseases in history. Thomas McKeown argued that improvements in nutrition, and secondarily in public health and sanitation, rather than specific medical interventions or the mix of reigning infectious diseases, were responsible for the earliest gains in life expectancy. Purification of water, other beverages, and food was then, in the late nineteenth and early twentieth centuries, responsible for plummeting rates of infant mortality. Abdel Omran, in contrast, offered a model of epidemiological transition, focusing on the control of recurrent, multiple, and demographically costly epidemic infectious diseases as the leading cause of change. Omran drew attention to chronic and noninfectious diseases as a kind of residuum that became demographically important once the punishing acute infections of young and middle-aged adulthood receded. Changes internal to the evidence used to examine these hypotheses rigorously still confound investigators.

The assessment of trends in historical demography depends upon whether variations in mortality and morbidity were predictably determinants of population change. Debate about the extent to which lethal infectious diseases were autonomous or exogenous mediators of population change led many investigators to distinguish crisis mortality from normal mortality in the study of causes. Crisis mortality, defined as some multiple of the level of expected or typical mortality, was due to the unpredictable appearance of epidemic diseases or climate- and war-caused food shortages. Because premodern mortality was inherently unstable, demographers have focused on the economic and social mechanisms of stabilization, as well as the measurable impacts of diet, fertility, medical intervention, and migration, rather than on the causes of normal mortality. Some interest has remained in geographical variation in normal mortality, particularly as studies of urban, agricultural, pastoral, and non-European populations have revealed substantial differences in normal mortality experience.

Similarly, noncrisis morbidity and mortality provoked little attention in the past. In historical accounts, acute infections, and the acute episodes of chronic infectious disease, typically elicited eyewitness accounts when the effects on a society were unpredictable and costly. Coming to expect high mortality among the poor, for example, the governing elite often made little inquiry into extraordinarily high annual mortality that was not due to a feared plague or pestilence. People living in malarial zones adopted casual and dismissive models to explain high morbidity among recent immigrants or among the very young. Accepting high mortality among European soldiers and colonists sent to other regions, Europeans developed complicated race-based explanations to account for high mortality among indigenous peoples. Deaths of children were similarly expected, even when such losses were bitterly mourned. In sum, what is known directly from the remote past about infectious disease experience typically depends upon then-perceived differences in mortality that departed from the expected. Archaeological material can be useful,

but any acute cause of illness and death will not be reflected in bony remains.

Specific Infectious Diseases. Acute and chronic infectious diseases are considered here, with particular attention given to malaria, tuberculosis, leprosy, and sexually transmitted diseases.

Acute infectious disease. In the remote past, but likely after the end of the last Ice Age (12,000 BCE), humans throughout Eurasia and Africa domesticated several animal species. Animal pathogens capable of infecting human cells, the zoonoses, account for the origins of many historically important infectious diseases. In domesticating animals, humans had also created agricultural settlements, obviating the need for continual migration. A diet of grains and pulses improved survival among young children. Despite novel pathogens, population numbers soared. A substantial range of once uncommon infectious diseases over time became common childhood diseases that provided lifelong immunity to a second infection, once an individual had recovered. Wherever settlement and/or trade was dense, previously uninfected young children were the most susceptible group.

The emergence of such diseases had world-shaping consequences. Measles, rubella, chickenpox (varicella virus), mumps, diphtheria, pertussis (whooping cough), and even smallpox all descended from animal pathogens. Some of these diseases subsequently evolved to infect only human cells, smallpox and measles being the most dramatic examples in historical records. Yet leaving aside the effects of acute community infections on previously nonexposed "virgin soil" populations, the demographic consequences were minimal in groups larger than 250,000 to 300,000. Most of these diseases have significantly lower morbidity and mortality rates among prepubescent children than they do among those first infected as adults.

Until the last five centuries in human history, acute infectious disease morbidity and mortality were recorded only as a disease affected prominent individuals or in epidemics that took heavy tolls among adults. A few pathogens can cause high morbidity and mortality either by the sudden virulence of the pathogen or by the immunological status of the host or the host population. Diphtheria and influenza provide striking examples of the former category. Diphtheritic sore throat, long common in human populations, has appeared in intermittent epidemic waves since the sixteenth century. Frighteningly, young children who had successfully passed through the greater dangers of infancy would suddenly be unable to breathe, and would turn blue and die within the space of an hour. Research begun during World War I and completed and proved after World War II demonstrated that some strains of diphtheria were particularly virulent because of infection of the bacterium with a viruslike phage particle.

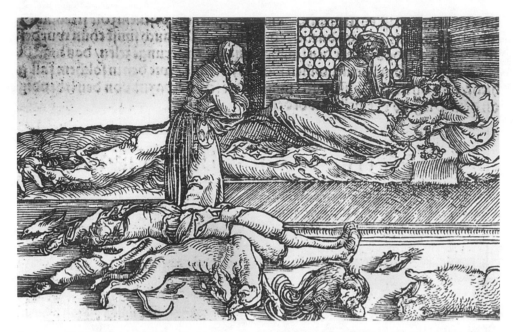

DISEASES. *Neither Man nor Animal is Immune to the Plague,* woodcut by Hans Weiditz. A man lies in bed with an open sore on his left. He is attended by a man and a woman. All three have their faces covered. Scattered around the room are the bodies of a man, a child, and various animals, all victims of the plague. Illustration from Francesco Petrarca's *De remediis utriusque fortunae* in a German version, *Von der Artzney bayder Glück, des guten vnd widerwertigen,* 1532. (Courtesy of the National Library of Medicine, Bethesda, Maryland)

The mutation of influenza virus during World War I caused the single most dramatic epidemic in recorded history, resulting in the deaths of an estimated 25 to 40 million people worldwide. The virus responsible for the 1918–1919 pandemic also caused demographically significant mortality among young adults rather than the very old or the very young, whom influenza affects more in its quiescent years. In this highly unusual historical instance, a recombination of animal and human influenza strains occurred. However, even in normal influenza epidemics, infection in individuals is accompanied by some temporary loss of cell-mediated immunity, and so population groups co-infected with tuberculosis or with other viral illnesses can experience far more severe consequences than populations without such burdens of ongoing illness. Other severe pandemic waves of influenza occurred in 1580 and 1781.

In these examples, influenza and diphtheria, pathogens became more virulent independently of any human actions. Similarly, streptococcus bacteria can develop virulence, as in the appearance of rheumatic fever in the eighteenth and nineteenth centuries, for example, or spiking death rates in maternal mortality called puerperal sepsis, related to more virulent strains of streptococci in the community. However, population dislocation, such as crowding in military settings, hospitals, or other institutions,

and increasing immiseration of many people, as in war or during early industrialization, increased mortality and morbidity from influenza. Herding children together in protective isolation or into orphanages or schools facilitated the spread of lethal streptococcal or diphtheria strains. Medical recognition of puerperal sepsis occurred when male physicians became involved in obstetrics, and when lying-in hospitals were created for poor urban women.

The most celebrated recurrent acute epidemic diseases in recorded history are usually described as exogenous events, those not caused by human actions. Bubonic plague, Asiatic cholera, and yellow fever were the three greatest historical actors. Plague is not a human disease, but rather a zoonotic infection adapted best to rodents. Moreover, plague is usually transmitted by a flea vector. Humans do not form long-lasting immunity, even upon recovery from infection with *Yersinia pestis*. Bubonic plague epidemics, evidenced by the appearance of acutely swollen lymph nodes in many victims, recurred in Europe and Mediterranean Africa and the Middle East from the mid-fourteenth through the early eighteenth centuries, causing frighteningly high mortality (up to 50 percent) in both rural and urban settings. The historical effects of recurrent plagues, however, seem best summarized by the kinds of public health strategies and institutions created in response: isolation and quarantine, death and disease surveillance, and institutionalized health monitoring. Most of the historical effects of discrete or recurrent plagues otherwise are localized to time and place.

Historical records give disproportionate attention (relative to the demographic costs) to dramatic, periodic epidemics of (viral, mosquito-borne) yellow fever and waterborne cholera. In the eighteenth and nineteenth centuries, both diseases were novel infections to Europeans; both evoked broad changes in international public health practices as well as reinvigoration of scientific discussion and investigation into the causes of infectious diseases. Although no specifically effective solutions to the threat of yellow fever or cholera emerged during these centuries, Europeans at home and abroad inaugurated sanitary programs and institutionalized, international disease surveillance that helped to create the global patterns of infectious disease experience operant today. By the beginning of the twentieth century, Western scientific medicine possessed the ideological tools to attack specific disease threats individually.

Historical demographers understandably view these capricious changes in an organism's virulence as autonomous and exogenous mediators of mortality. Molecular and evolutionary models of change in particular pathogens' virulence exist to offer some pattern and scientific prediction to these variations. In the 1950s, Frank Fenner and others illustrated, with a mosquito-borne tumor virus relatively avirulent for Brazilian rabbits, that a huge and unwieldy rabbit population in Australia could be reduced by nearly 75 percent when myxoma virus was introduced. Within three years, however, the rabbit host population began to stabilize. Fenner proved that less virulent strains of the virus survived because rabbits infected with the less lethal mutant survived longer and thus fed more mosquitoes. This general evolutionary approach to competing strains of acute viral and bacterial pathogens in human populations has been applied to the study of cholera, with the appearance, probably around 1900, of a milder strain, the El Tor, named after an East African quarantine station that interrupted the spread of the disease along Muslim pilgrimage routes to Mecca. The appearance of a less lethal strain of smallpox virus in East Africa during the late nineteenth century probably followed a similar selection path. In other words, public health and other measures to interrupt the spread of a lethal infectious pathogen tend to select for strains that cause diminished host morbidity and mortality. Yet virulence is only one property of microorganisms; the pathogen's replication rate, and its infectivity—how easily it can access and utilize host resources—respond to selection pressures as well.

Most variations in human morbidity and mortality from epidemic infections diseases, however, relate to variation in host immunities. In addition to the vulnerabilities of the very young and the elderly, particular population groups can be at enhanced risk simply because they were not exposed in childhood to acute community infections. Rural-to-urban migration, typically by young adults in search of greater economic opportunity or through military mobilization, carries risks of exposure to multiple pathogens. Such phenomena continued regularly into the twentieth century, as, for example, with the heavy mortality and morbidity of Australian and rural Canadian troops shipped to the European theaters of war. Young adults experience more difficulty recovering from some of the viral diseases than do young children, and thus have protracted courses of illness following these later infections. In children, mumps virus causes discomfort and swelling of the parotid glands (under the chin and mandible), but in adult men it causes a far more painful acute swelling in the testicles as well.

Variation in the immunity of human population groups to specific infectious diseases played a particularly important historical role among peoples living outside Eurasia and Africa. The enhanced vulnerability of young adults previously not exposed to pathogens common in the larger population may have played some role in shaping a society's "winners" and "losers." In the era of European overseas exploration and colonization, so-called virgin soil epidemics were explosive among native Americans and Pacific islanders. From the seventeenth century into the twentieth century, epidemics of smallpox, measles, and other lesser killers caused staggering losses because everyone was attacked at roughly the same time, and because the healthy young adults on whom the infants, children, and elderly all depended were unable to extend care, food, water, or other basic services to their dependents. Breakdown of normal care bonds quickly led to pollution of water and spoilage of food, if indeed both remained available.

Chronic infectious diseases. In history, and especially in the archaeological record, chronic infectious diseases have the greatest impact on group survival and well-being. As is also true of acute infectious diseases, the specific pathogenic mechanisms of different microbial species can vary considerably. In general, however, one can say that some infectious microorganisms continue to live and reproduce within the host, placing others at risk of infection; and some produce deficits and disabilities that steadily compromise the individual's social and economic well-being.

Among the hundreds of still-common pathogens in this category, a few have been globally dispersed since prehistory and have been only partly tamed during the twentieth century. Malaria parasites, mycobacteria (especially tuberculosis and leprosy), shistosomes, and treponemes (among them syphilis and yaws) occupy substantial places in the history of human infectious diseases. Recently, and under historical conditions keenly debated among virologists, the emergence of human immunodeficiency virus (HIV) has been added to this lugubrious list.

Malaria. Evidence for severe chronic anemia, such as malaria causes, can be found in human bones from Greco-Roman antiquity. The existence of anomalous human blood groups such as sickle cell and thalassemia genes further points to long-standing population-group exposure to the parasite that causes malaria. Thus independent of historical sources, diverse and abundant evidence of this pathogen's long association with humans asserts its importance. Sweeping historical changes or effects attributed to malarial environments have included the waning of Greek and perhaps Roman cultural dominance, the dominant strain of environmentalism in most premodern medical systems (since malaria is associated with regions more than with individuals), the dominance of northern over southern civilizations (in the Northern Hemisphere), the technological backwardness of some regions or even whole continents, and even the justification or the origins of robust biologically based racism, used to underpin projects of enslavement or colonization. Since the late nineteenth century, when British meteorologists in India first kept continuous weather records, malaria even has been demonstrated to take epidemic form, redoubling mortality and morbidity after famine-causing droughts ended with monsoon rains. Although often depicted as a tropical disease, malaria can exist worldwide, and has done so, even in far northern climes, because many anopheline species can spread the pathogen.

The conquest of malaria—usually a reference to its disappearance from temperate zones—proceeded through the nineteenth and twentieth centuries along two main paths. First, economic development distanced anopheline breeding sites from human habitation, or (as in the American Midwest) supplied alternative hosts for the mosquito (e.g., cattle). Simple inventions, such as screens and netting, offered protection when drainage and other building was not an option. Quinine, an early-nineteenth-century chemical derivative of cinchona tree bark infusions in use since the seventeenth century, possibly reduced mortality and morbidity among some particular groups at risk (e.g., Union soldiers in the American Civil War, European colonialists in Africa, and French and American laborers building the Panama Canal). The ecology of malaria transmission was understood by the early twentieth century, and chemicals were available to kill adult and larval mosquitoes. DDT spraying began in World War II and was used systematically in the postwar decade, until resistant mosquitoes emerged by the early 1960s.

Tuberculosis. The antiquity of tuberculosis (TB), dubbed "captain of all these men of death" by a seventeenth-century Englishman, can be documented with archaeological records. Clear medical descriptions of the slow "consumption" of TB victims by respiratory tuberculosis—with breathing difficulty, coughing up blood-tinged sputum, a face that resembles a bird, scapulae protruding like a bird's wings—can be found in Greco-Roman treatises. Tuberculosis typically involves an initial (or primary) infection with *Mycobacterium tuberculosis*, an organism that naturally infects only humans. Infants and young children with compromised immune systems may die from an overwhelming infection. Most survive the initial infection, however, only to succumb to secondary infection at a physiologically stressful point in the life course—puberty, pregnancy, adult infection with one of the immunizing diseases of childhood, or old age.

Tuberculosis has been globally distributed and on all inhabited continents except Australia since ancient times, but it has been seen as an epidemic disease associated with industrialization and modernization. It peaked as a health concern during the early nineteenth century in Europe and North America; both voluntary and forced isolation of its active sufferers as well as improving nutritional resources probably sped its decline. It seems to have become an epidemic elsewhere in the wake of European colonial expansion. Effective antibiotic treatment for tuberculosis appeared only during World War II, but each of three very different antibiotics developed then caused resistant strains to develop within a short time. By 1950, a triple therapy, using all three antibiotics simultaneously for nearly a year's duration, offered a strategy of control still in favor for it and many other chronic infections.

Leprosy. A close microbial cousin to tuberculosis, leprosy had a very different historical profile. In most ancient cultures that produced written medical treatises, leprosy was described as a strongly stigmatized affliction. The weight of evidence presently suggests that leprosy emerged only two to three thousand years ago, in both Europe and Asia. But the only known nonhuman carrier of its causative organism, *Mycobacterium leprae*, is a North American mammal, the armadillo.

In the West, the Judeo-Christian biblical image of the leper created a tradition of exclusion, radical isolation, and intermittent philanthropic assistance for those with the diagnosis. So strong was stigmatization of individuals labeled as lepers that in the twentieth century the disease was renamed Hansen's disease, after the physician who first described the microorganism in the nodular skin lesions of its victims. Leprosy was always believed to be highly contagious, though it is perhaps the most difficult disease to transmit through casual acquaintance. Its prominence in Judeo-Christian theology and ideology led to persistent and substantial missionary efforts in non-European settings, providing a counterpoint to other Western initiatives in the global control of disease.

Sexually transmitted diseases. There is some justification for considering all of the sexually transmitted diseases known through the twentieth century together as chronic infectious diseases, even though the microbiological and pathological mechanisms of the various agents differ considerably. Even the ubiquitous gonococcus, though causing an acute urinary tract infection far more noticeable to the male sufferer than the vaginal and peri-uterine infection that women acquire, can cause ongoing damage to the human host. Many women become infertile through pelvic inflammatory disease, a clinical category describing the effects of many different sexually transmitted bacteria upon reproductive organs. Several of the causative microorganisms—including chlamydiae, gonococci, and treponemes (causing syphilis)—also can produce infection of other mucous membranes, such as in the eye and the mouth. Damage to mucous membranes led to long-lasting consequences for infected individuals in preantibiotic times.

For medical, demographic, and economic historians, the stories of syphilis (a bacterial disease) and human immunodeficiency virus (HIV) have particular importance. HIV/AIDS is considered in the following section. As with AIDS (acquired immune deficiency syndrome), the distinctive history of syphilis focuses on blame and origins. Syphilis was not distinctively described and named until the sixteenth century, and its origins were assigned to the less-developed Western Hemisphere. Modern efforts to trace the distinctive effects of syphilis on the human skeleton, in order to determine whether this particular bacterium was unique to the Americas before Columbus, have not produced conclusive results. Its early victims were perhaps the first to be treated with chemical and herbal mixtures believed to target the disease—in this case mercurial preparations and guaiac bark, new to European *materia medica*e with discovery of the Western Hemisphere. The tradition of using heavy-metal preparations lasted until the antibiotic era. Even more important in syphilis history was the early-twentieth-century discovery of a way to test blood for probable exposure to the organism. The VDRL antibody test appeared almost simultaneously with the discovery of the organism and the elaboration of scientific theories of immunity. Within four years, the first "magic bullet"—Paul Ehrlich's arsenical preparation shown to cause the death of the organism in laboratory animals—appeared, in 1910. Thus syphilis history, like that of leprosy, tuberculosis, and malaria, illustrates core features of modern Western approaches to infectious disease control.

History of Infectious Disease in the Twentieth Century. Over the past century, the health and the longevity of most people improved substantially, through control of acute and chronic infectious diseases. Thus the emergence of novel infectious diseases became more noticeable. Poliovirus epidemics initially seem a clear example of such recent emergence because there are no recorded instances of polio epidemics before the late nineteenth century. Before the nineteenth-century sanitary revolution in privileged Western nations, most infants were exposed to the three main types of "wild" poliovirus. Early-life exposure produced a very mild diarrhea in the infant. The older the individual was at first exposure to the virus, however, the more likely was the virus to affect the central nervous system, causing high fever, temporary or permanent paralysis, and even death. Thus a waterborne virus that infected humans and chimpanzees since prehistory was seen to produce a new, emergent disease. Concern with acceleration of dangerous new microorganisms—whether antibiotic-resistant strains of long-familiar pathogens, mutations of animal pathogens spread by rapid global trade and travel, or even human-created bioterrors—in the early twenty-first century tends to undervalue the ecological message of poliovirus history.

The polio story is nonetheless linked to a dominant, optimistic version of twentieth-century history with infectious diseases. Americans Jonas Salk and Albert Sabin developed two different approaches to vaccine protection against poliovirus in the 1950s, following frightening increases in the number of victims of paralytic polio. After the 1960s, the gap between societies with the available vaccine and resources to administer it to infants and the societies without such advantages created a wake of paralyzed adults in the developing world. Vaccination against specific disease threats began in the eighteenth century, with the practice of inoculating individuals who had not previously experienced infection with small amounts of pus from a smallpox pustule. The concept was not European in origin, but was rapidly adopted, and then adapted (by Edward Jenner in 1796) with the use of a kindred infection, cowpox, to provide limited immunity. In the late nineteenth century, Louis Pasteur offered a complex, poorly explained remedy for human exposure to rabies virus, in the form of a series of injections of laboratory-cultured preparations. Neither Jenner nor Pasteur operated from a knowledge of the nature of viruses; neither had a scientifically defensible concept of immunity. The processes that led to Salk and Sabin instead proceeded from experimentation in the early germ theory era, up to 1920. Their successes against polio ushered in the modern emphasis on vaccination to control epidemic viral diseases. The World Health Organization inaugurated the first global eradication program targeting a human disease, smallpox, in the 1960s, inventing the strategy of containing discrete outbreaks rather than envisioning mass, repeated vaccination of all humanity. Smallpox has not occurred naturally since 1978. Both poliovirus and measles virus could be similarly eradicated, with sufficient political and economic will.

Despite vaccination's long history, antibiotic development and use had the greatest success and impact on infectious diseases of any measures taken over the twentieth century. Loudon (1992) has demonstrated that the age-old risk of sepsis following labor and delivery dramatically disappeared with the first use of antibiotics in the 1930s. Antibiotics discovered and used first during World War II—principally penicillin, the antituberculosis drugs, and the sulfa and sulphone compounds—had dramatic clinical results, widely and perhaps justly seen as miraculous. Building on the optimism of these early successes, substantial resources and postwar investment created an ever-expanding arsenal of antimicrobial agents to confront ancient bacterial enemies. The appearance of resistant strains of most common microorganisms was apparent within an impressively short time after each chemical invention, but was not widely recognized as a distinct scientific problem until late in the century. At the dawn of the twenty-first century, the difficult work of interrupting and modifying this particular approach to the management of infectious diseases, individually or in epidemics, is just beginning.

Parasitic diseases such as malaria have not responded well to either the vaccination or the antibiotic approaches. Instead environmental control, with chemical agents aimed at the insect vectors, has characterized industrialized nations' efforts. Development strategies pursued by the World Bank and other international business concerns tackle the issues surrounding infectious disease control differently from the World Health Organization, with its vaccination programs, or the affluent nations, with their preference for antibiotics.

HIV/AIDS was first noticed in North America and Europe in the early 1980s, with high mortality among recreational intravenous drug users and homosexual men. Massive investments in virology to understand the cause, transmission, and hopeful cure of the infection characterized the scientific response of affluent nations. Proportionately less was and is being spent in the developing nations, which are expected to have 95 percent of the new cases by 2010. The disease's high mortality among young adults, the inability to continue vaccination and antibiotic approaches to control other infections in the face of a disease that suppresses the human immune system, and the certainty of sustained global warming over the twenty-first century—which will alter the priorities and investments of affluent nations—lead to predictions of historical effects as profound as those of the era of recurrent plagues and overseas exportation of Old World infections to the Americas and Pacific islanders.

[*See also* Epidemics; Health; Health Industry; *and* Public Health.]

BIBLIOGRAPHY

Ewald, Paul. *Evolution of Infectious Diseases.* Oxford and New York, 1994.

Farmer, Paul. *Infections and Inequalities: The Modern Plagues.* Berkeley, 1998.

Fenner, Frank, and Bernardino Fantini. *Biological Control of Vertebrate Pests: The History of Myxomatosis, an Experiment in Evolution.* New York, 1999.

Fiennes, Richard. *Zoonoses and the Origins and Ecology of Human Disease.* London, 1978.

Flinn, Michael W. *The European Demographic System, 1500–1820.* Baltimore, 1981.

Grmek, Mirko. *Diseases in the Ancient Greek World.* Baltimore, 1989.

Hardy, Anne. *The Epidemic Streets: Infectious Diseases and the Rise of Preventive Medicine, 1856–1900.* Oxford and New York, 1993.

Harrison, Gordon. *Mosquitoes, Malaria and Man: A History of Hostilities since 1880.* New York, 1978.

Humphreys, Margaret. *Malaria: Poverty, Race and Public Health in the United States.* Baltimore, 2001.

Kiple, Kenneth, ed. *The Cambridge World History of Human Disease.* Cambridge, 1993.

Kunitz, Stephen J. *Disease and Social Diversity: The European Impact on the Health of Non-Europeans.* Oxford, 1994.

Loudon, Irvine. *Death in Childbirth: An International Study of Maternal Care and Maternal Mortality, 1800–1950.* Oxford and New York, 1992.

McKeown, Thomas. *The Origins of Human Disease.* Oxford and Cambridge, Mass., 1991.

Omran, Abdel R. "The Epidemiological Transition: A Theory of the Epidemiology of Population Change." *Milbank Memorial Fund Quarterly* 4 (1971), 509–538.

Riley, James C. *Rising Life Expectancy: A Global History.* Cambridge, 2001.

Rosenkrantz, Barbara. *From Consumption to Tuberculosis: A Documentary History.* New York, 1994.

Schofield, Roger, David S. Reher, and Alain Bideau, eds. *The Decline of Mortality in Europe.* Oxford and New York, 1991.

ANN G. CARMICHAEL

Deficiency and Parasitic Diseases

Nutritional and parasitic diseases primarily afflict agrarian and pastoral economies. Hunter-gatherer societies inclined toward a varied and nutritional diet, while agricultural communities, who depended on a few staple crops, were more prone to nutritional disorders. Nutritional diseases were mild prior to the Age of Exploration (approximately 1450–1650) and the early industrial period (1694–1930), when they became more severe and widespread.

The early industrial period began with the establishment of Bank of England and subsequent ease of capital flows to industry and ended with the Great Depression and increased controls on business due to government regulation. Concurrent with the rise of industry, commercial agriculture proliferated, leading to a reduction in the types and variety of crops produced. The new nutritionally anemic diet resulted in weakened and precarious health, an increased susceptibility to other disorders, and increased malnutrition.

Parasitic disease also favored nonmobile populations for contact and reinfestation. Irrigation and successful farming altered the ecological balance between host and parasite, creating opportunities for hyperinfestation with a resultant parasitic population explosion. The agricultures of past agrarian societies and modern developing nations are nearly identical and therefore produce the same parasitic infections and nutritional deficiencies.

As societies industrialized and matured, clean water sources, widespread systems of sanitation and quarantine, and insect control programs reduced parasitic disease. Nutritional deficiencies also are rare in developed nations that make a cornucopia of agricultural products available through extensive transportation and distribution networks and that establish governmental mandates on vitamin fortification of flour and salt.

Economic Measures. The economic impact of nutritional or parasitic disease is a result of reduced labor hours and labor intensity owing to impaired physical capacity. Both nutritional and parasitic diseases are especially detrimental to pregnant women and to young children, who carry the economic consequences into the future workforce. Young children may be stunted both mentally and physically, which is of consequence to later productivity. Communicable, infectious diseases tend to kill the nonproductive, for example, the very young or very old. Conversely, nutritional deficiencies and parasitic infections afflict and kill those in middle age, at their most productive.

Parasites and nutrient deficiencies almost invariably cause stunted growth and a low body mass index (BMI), which have been shown to be highly associated with reduced labor productivity. Economists generally use these measures and daily caloric intake estimates to examine the economic consequences of parasitic and nutritional diseases, since little historical data exists on prevalence rates, which is simply the number of individuals afflicted with a disorder divided by the entire population at a given point in time. Where feasible, economists use actual prevalence data to assess the economic impact of a disease or its eradication.

Public health officials and medical practitioners use years of life lost (YLL) or disability-adjusted life years (DALY) measures when estimating the impacts of both nutritional disorders and parasitic diseases on human populations. YLLs and DALYs are used to directly compare disease burdens on a country's national income and product accounts. Once the degree of impairment has been calculated, the economic value of a YLL or a DALY can be assigned based upon wage rates or average income measures.

Comparing specific disease YLLs or DALYs indicates the greatest relative economic losses and therefore the greatest potential for increasing agricultural productivity. Cur-

TABLE 1. *1996 Global Economic Burden of Common Parasitic Infections and Nutritional Disorders*

	YLL	DALY
Nutritional Disorders		
Protein Energy Malnutrition	11,080	20,957
Iodine	795	1,562
Vitamin A	3,722	3,838
Iron Deficiency	2,627	24,614
Total	18,224	50,971
Parasitic Infections		
Malaria	28,038	31,706
Trypanosomiasis	1,346	1,467
Chagas Disease	300	641
Schistosomiasis	156	1,519
Leishmaniasis	1,628	2,092
Lymphatic Filiariasis		3,997
Ascariasis	406	1,750
Trichuriasis	269	1,788
Necatoriasis	78	1,484
Total	2,221	6,444
Grand Total	50,445	97,415

Thousands of YLLs on DALYs. Adjustments are made for age standardization and for time discounting.
SOURCE: Murray and Lopez (1996), annex tables 7i, 9i, and 10i; pp. 501–504, 573, 609–612.

rently parasitic infections are far more damaging economically than the most common nutritional disorders. This pattern is most likely true historically. A debate between the relative economic damage from diet versus disease is ongoing in the economic literature with little expectation of a settlement in the near future. Conventional wisdom among economists maintains that nutritional disorders, including gross malnutrition, are far more economically damaging than parasitic diseases, while public health practitioners tend to hold the opposite view.

Nutritional Disorders. Nutrient deficiencies are widespread in developing countries and affect approximately 2.5 billion people. The most common deficiencies are protein-energy malnutrition (PEM), iron, vitamin A (xerophthalmia), and iodine (goiter and cretinism). Deficiencies of vitamin C (scurvy), vitamin D (rickets), niacin (pellagra), and thiamin (beriberi) were important historically but are no longer of great concern or economically damaging. Causing the greatest economic harm during the late nineteenth century and the early twentieth century, these nutritional diseases are now of concern only during severe crop failures or among displaced populations.

Specific Dietary Deficiencies. PEM, iron deficiency, and vitamin A deficiency are highly correlated and nearly always occur simultaneously. Protein and iron tend to be from the same food source, and vitamin A deficiency depletes iron stores. Drought, flooding, invasions, displaced populations, and coerced labor, as in slavery, contributed to historic instances of PEM and iron deficiency and resulted in reduced agricultural productivity. Chronic undernutrition produces physical and mental stunting and is a major cause of death in children in developing countries, where 20 percent of the children suffer from PEM. Iron anemia causes death in pregnant women and young children, and mild-to-moderate anemia reduces the labor productivity of adults by 10 to 15 percent. In developing nations approximately 50 to 60 percent of young children, 20 to 30 percent of nonpregnant women, and 50 to 60 percent of pregnant women are iron deficient. The World Bank (1998) recently estimated a return of U.S. $500 for every U.S. $1 spent on iron supplements for developing nations. Vitamin A deficiency, the most common deficiency syndrome in displaced populations, causes night blindness in early stages and permanent eye damage and blindness in later stages. Of about 3 million children are currently afflicted, 250,000 to 500,000 suffer blindness.

Iodine occurs naturally in various soils and in seafoods, so a deficiency is rare among seafaring or coastal populations. If a soil lacks iodine, agricultural output also lacks iodine, and without an external source, such an agrarian or pastoral society suffers. Effects range from mild retardation to severe retardation, known as cretinism. The most recognizable symptom in iodine-deficient populations is goiter, which was recorded by all the ancient civilizations. The oldest reference to goiter, from China in 2838 BCE, recommends seaweed as a cure. Another ancient reference to goiter is in the Ebers papyrus, dating to 1650 BCE which recommends surgery as treatment.

Historical Deficiency Diseases. Beriberi, common among populations for whom rice is a main staple, is marked by inflammatory or degenerative changes of the nerves, digestive system, and heart. It was known in China as early as 2600 BCE and was noted by Europeans in the mid-1600s among sailors of the Dutch East India Company. In the late 1800s approximately 40 percent of Japanese sailors suffered from beriberi. The prevalence and severity of beriberi dramatically increased during the late 1800s and the early 1900s as steam-driven mills popularized less-nutritious white rice.

Pellagra affects the skin, gastrointestinal-intestinal tract, and nervous system and is sometimes called the "3Ds," dermatitis, diarrhea, and dementia. Populations relying on corn as a primary food source are most vulnerable. This disease was not common among the Mesoamericans who domesticated corn since they treated the maize flour with lime, converting the niacin to a biologically available form. During the Age of Exploration, New World explorers introduced corn into southern Europe, where it spread widely and where pellagra was first recorded. Cases of pellagra were widespread in the American South at the beginning of the twentieth century, when the new flour mills stripped away much of the nutrition of the grain, unlike the previous grist mills that retained the nutrients.

Rickets adversely affects bone development, resulting in bowing of the legs and crippling in severe cases. A lack of exposure to sunlight causes this vitamin D deficiency disease, which has been known since ancient times. It was noted in large cities during the Middle Ages but became widespread in Europe from the late 1600s to the third decade of the 1900s. Rickets is associated with early industry, particularly the textile industry, which used children extensively. In Great Britain the disease appeared to be universal, and it became known throughout Europe as the "English disease." Rickets is still seen in the Middle East, where, purdah, the complete covering of women, is practiced, and in some Southeast Asian countries, where child labor is extensive.

Scurvy is characterized by spongy gums, loosening of the teeth, bleeding into the skin and mucous membranes, and death. Historically a dearth of fresh foods was common among sailors on long voyages, among farmers in the winter and spring months and during famines or droughts, and among displaced populations. Greek writings about the time of Julius Caesar (100–44 BCE) describe Roman armies suffering from scurvy. In Europe at the end of the thirteenth century, peasants, believing fruits were unwholesome, endured seasonal scurvy before summer, when vegetables were harvested.

As early as 1593, during a voyage to the South Pacific, Sir Richard Hawkins recommended that scurvy be treated with oranges and lemons. In 1636, John Woodall, the "father of naval hygiene," published *The Surgeon's Mate* claiming that scurvy could be prevented by consuming fresh vegetables, lemons, and oranges. Still, it was not until 1795 that the British Admiralty mandated lemon juice for all sailors.

Scurvy was also prevalent in infants during the late nineteenth century. In 1650, Francis Glisson reported the first case of infantile scurvy among infants suffering from rickets. The condition reappeared around 1900 among U.S. and British infants who were weaned off breast milk and fed a diet of heated cows' milk and foods lacking in vitamin C.

Parasitic Infections. According to the World Health Organization and the World Bank, parasitic diseases cause substantially more economic damage than nutritional disorders. In 1950 there were 2.5 billion cases of parasitic infection, not counting malaria, while the world population was 2.1 billion. Multiple infections are still common, and though progress has been made toward eradication, lack of resources and political instability severely hamper efforts. It is not unreasonable to conclude that, even with a world population of over 6 billion, the cases of parasitic infection outnumber people on this planet.

PREVENTIVE MEASURES. Malaria control program in Vietnam, circa 1960. (Courtesy of the National Library of Medicine, Bethesda, Maryland)

Specific Parasitic Diseases. Malaria, spread by mosquitoes and caused by a plasmodium parasite, is believed to have infected humans and prehumans for the past two million years. It originated in either Africa or Southeast Asia and spread to areas with the proper climatic conditions. In particular the rise and spread of slash-and-burn farming methods, irrigation, and pastorialism increased epidemic intensities. Malarial symptoms were well described in Hippocratic writings in classical Greece (480–300 BCE), and the disease was carried to Central and South America during the European voyages of discovery (1492–1650). It then spread to all regions harboring the anopheles mosquito, which is hardy and tends to replace native species and was probably already in the Americas. The malarial parasite has caused the greatest economic damage of all parasites.

Schistosomiasis, also known as bilharzia and referenced in the Ebers papyrus (1650 BCE), is a disease caused by parasitic worms that currently infects 200 million people. Infection occurs when skin comes in contact with freshwater contaminated with certain types of infected snails. Eggs lodge in the brain or spinal cord of the host and cause seizures, paralysis, or spinal cord inflammation. The parasite eventually damages the internal organs and causes death. In the early decades of the twentieth century, the Egyptian *fellaheen* suffered more than any other people with estimates of infection rates of 47 percent among the entire population and 80 percent in some areas.

African trypanosomiasis or sleeping sickness is contracted through the bite of an infected tsetse fly. Symptoms include fever, severe headaches, irritability, extreme fatigue, personality changes, slurred speech, seizures, difficulty in walking and talking, and death. In 1900 trypanosomiasis was one of the most severe public health problems in northern Africa, where it killed 4 million out of 6.5 million Ugandans. A resurgence currently afflicts an estimated 10 percent of the population of sub-Saharan Africa in large part because of political upheaval. Over 100,000 new cases are reported each year. Estimates by the World Bank on the economic benefits of eradicating Chagas disease, the American form of trypanosomiasis, are $3.5 trillion a year at an annual eradication cost of $19–35 million.

Hookworm, ascariasis, and necatoriasis are gastrointestinal helminths that inhabit the small intestine and are transmitted via fecal-oral contamination or through unprotected skin in contact with infected soils. They originated in Africa and spread to the other continents principally via the slave trade. The Ebers papyrus and the somewhat later Brugsch papyrus (c. 1400 BCE) refer to medical conditions recognized as hookworm that are still common in modern Egypt. Heavy infestations lead to disabling fatigue and physical and mental retardation caused by severe anemia. Infection is most common in tropical and subtropical areas, where sanitation and hygiene are poor. In the United States infection is rare but was common in the rural South after the Civil War (1861–1865). Approximately 40 percent of the decline in southern agricultural output in the aftermath of the Civil War has been attributed to an increase in hookworm prevalence.

Hookworm infection among southern soldiers was widespread during the War of Rebellion because of poor sanitation and diet and a lack of protective footwear. When the war ended, hookworm-infected soldiers returned home and unknowingly spread the parasite. It was not until the eradication and extensive sanitation education campaigns in the 1910s that hookworm sufferers were "cured." The region experienced a 30 percent increase in output from the hookworm eradication campaign of the 1910s. Numerous economic studies dating to that decade have demonstrated dramatic increases in agricultural productivity from reducing or eliminating hookworm.

Filariasis or elephantiasis is caused by microscopic, threadlike worms that live in and damage the lymph system. It affects over 120 million people in 73 countries throughout the tropics and subtropics. While the disease usually is not life-threatening, fluid collects and causes swelling in the arms, breasts, legs, and for men the genital area, so the skin hardens and thickens. People with the disease can suffer pain, disfigurement, and sexual disability. Lymphatic filariasis is a leading cause of long-term and permanent disability worldwide. World Bank cost estimates to eliminate filiariasis are estimated at U.S. $.05 to .10 per person per year over a five-year period with a total economic return of $4 trillion per year in increased agricultural output.

The Future. Efforts toward eliminating dietary deficiencies other than gross malnutrition are promising. Genetically altered staple crops designed to include all essential vitamins can make widespread specific dietary diseases a thing of the past. In addition, to alleviate gross malnutrition, large quantities of food have been stockpiled under United Nations auspices for distribution during times of need.

Vaccines and other types of eradication campaigns are planned to eliminate or reduce parasitic infections, such as malaria, or helminth infections, like schistosomiasis, filariasis, hookworm, and ascariasis. The United Nations has an active research program with goals to eliminate the most damaging parasitical infections by the year 2020. A vaccination program has been modeled upon the World Health Organization's successful smallpox eradication program.

BIBLIOGRAPHY

Brinkley, Garland L. "The Decline in Southern Agricultural Output, 1860–1880." *Journal of Economic History* 571 (March 1997), 116–138.
Bulletin of the World Health Organization, vol. 76, suppl. 2. Geneva, 1998.
Carpenter, Kenneth J. *The History of Scurvy and Vitamin C*. New York, 1986.
Cartwright, Frederick F. *Disease and History*. New York, 1972.
Ciba Foundation Symposium 127: Filariasis. Chichester, U.K., 1987.
Diamond, Jared. *Guns, Germs, and Steel*. New York, 1999.
Etheridge, Elizabeth. *The Butterfly Caste*. Westport, Conn., 1972.
Farley, John. *Bilharzia*. New York, 1991.
Fogel, Robert William, and Stanley L. Engerman. *Time on the Cross*. Boston, 1974.
Gomes, Melba. "Economic and Demographic Research on Malaria: A Review of the Evidence." *Social Science and Medicine* 17.9 (1993), 1093–1108.
Harris, Leslie. *Vitamins and Vitamin Deficiencies*, vol. 1. London, 1938.
Hetzel, Basil S. *The Story of Iodine Deficiency*. Oxford, 1989.
Jarrett, Richard J., ed. *Nutrition and Disease*. Baltimore, 1979.
Kiple, Kenneth, ed. *The Cambridge World History of Human Disease*. New York, 1993.
McNeill, William H. *Plagues and Peoples*. Garden City, N.Y., 1976.
Murray, Christopher, and Alan Lopez, eds. *The Global Burden of Disease: A Comprehensive Assessment of Mortality and Disability from Diseases, Injuries, and Risk Factors in 1990 and Projected to 2020*. Cambridge, Mass., 1996.
Nur, E. "The Impact of Malaria on Labour Use and Efficiency in the Sudan." *Social Science and Medicine* 17.9 (1993), 1115–1119.
Playfair, John, L., J. M. Blackwell, and H. R. P. Miller. "Parasitic Diseases." *Lancet* 335, 1263–1266.

GARLAND L. BRINKLEY

DISTILLERIES AND SPIRITS. From an international perspective, the repertoire of spirits is extensive. (Table 1 shows a selection.) This is not surprising because a wide range of raw materials is available to the distiller. Spirits can be made from two types of raw material: those containing natural sugars and those containing carbohydrates, which can be transformed into sugars by enzymes. The distillation process is also simple and involves heating a liquid containing ethyl alcohol (or ethanol). Because the boiling point of the alcohol (78.5°C) is lower than that of water (100°C), the alcohol vapors rise first when the fermented liquor boils; and they are recondensed to produce a liquid with a greater alcoholic strength than that of the first liquid. Successive redistillation of the distillate concentrates the spirit, raising its strength. The equipment required for producing spirits ranges from very small stills containing as little as twenty to forty gallons to the highly capital-intensive distillery producing several million gallons annually. Production within the household economy was, and is, compatible with factory production.

History. The early history of distilling is obscure and disputed, but discovery of distillation is generally credited to Arab scientists in the tenth to eleventh centuries. There is no reliable evidence that alcohol was discovered by the Arabs, though the word is of Arabic origin (*al-kohl*). The transmission of the Arab science to Europe is believed to have occurred during the Crusades. Benedictine monks in Salerno, Italy, are said to have been the first to distill alcohol from wine, sometime between 1050 and 1150. This late discovery of alcohol may have been due to the imperfect

TABLE 1. *Types of Spirits and Raw Materials*

NAME	AREA(S) OF PRODUCTION	RAW MATERIALS
Arrack	Indonesia, Malaysia, Sri Lanka, Thailand	Rice, palm juice, cane molasses, coconut
Bambuse	Indonesia	Bamboo seed
Bourbon	United States	Maize, wheat, wheat malt
Brandy	France, Spain, Portugal, South Africa, Australia	Grapes
Calvados	France (Normandy)	Apples
Geneva	Netherlands	Barley malt, wheat
Gin	England	Barley, molasses
Kan shi na	China	Sorghum
Kirschwasser	Germany, Switzerland	Cherries
Mao tai	China	Cracked rice, rice malt, sorghum
Marc	France	Grape skins and pips
Moutwijn	Netherlands	Barley malt
Ouzo	Greece	Dates
Rachin	Hungary	Prunes
Raki	Turkey	Raisins
Rum	Latin America, West Indies	Sugar cane, molasses
Sake	Japan	Rice
Schnapps	Germany	Potatoes, beet, wheat malt, barley
Slivovitz	Hungary, Czech Republic, Romania, Yugoslavia	Plums
Tequila	Mexico	Agave sap
Vodka	Russia, Poland	Barley, rye, potatoes
Whiskey	Ireland, Scotland, Canada, United States	Barley malt, barley, oats, rye, maize

apparatus used by the Arabs; cooling by means of air alone was inadequate for condensing a volatile substance such as alcohol. Arnold of Villanova (1235–1312) was the first person to apply to alcohol the name aqua vitae, or "water of life"; and spirits were at first used for medical purposes. Knowledge of the process was probably confined to religious institutions, and the timing of its external diffusion remains unclear. However, the following dates have been suggested for the first production of European types of spirits: French cognac, 1334; Russian vodka, 1448–1478; English gin, 1485; Scotch whiskey, 1494; German brauwein, 1520–1522. Outside vine-growing areas, diffusion depended on the earlier discovery, at some time in the fourteenth and fifteenth centuries, that alcohol could be made from cereals.

Because spirits had to compete with established preferences for beer and wine, mass consumption could develop only if the cost was lowered, the product refined, and there were either surpluses in the existing raw materials—grain and wine—or new materials emerged. These conditions were gradually fulfilled during the seventeenth century. Improvements in distilling apparatus increased the scale of production. Copper, an ideal material in terms of weight, strength, and heat conductivity, replaced glass and pottery in the traditional distilling vessel, the pot still. Larger, more efficient stills came into use in Europe and, later, in European colonies in the New World. A new cheap, imported, base material, sugar, and its by-product, molasses, were used to distil rum. Rum was distilled both in Europe—from syrup, a by-product of sugar refining—and in the Caribbean colonies. Reaction to imported rum and its raw material varied within Europe. The French brandy lobby secured a prohibition on the distilling of syrup and molasses, in both France and its colonies. This raised the price of brandy at home and abroad, and encouraged French sugar refiners to export sugar to the Dutch. Holland became the most advanced center of the distilling industry. Production rose rapidly from the 1640s on, and the towns of Rotterdam, Delftshaven, and Schiedam made and distributed gin regionally and even internationally, with exports beginning as early as 1604. In Holland, the government regulated spirits and taxed them less than beer.

By 1700, spirits occupied a major place in alcohol consumption in northern Europe. Excise statistics for England and Wales show the consumption of British spirits rising from 527,000 gallons in 1684 to a peak of 8.203 million gallons in 1743. The attention focused in England on the "gin mania," mainly an urban phenomenon, obscured the fact that rum and brandy imports were also increasing. The growing consumption and commercialization of spirits, with their transition from a commodity with use value to one with exchange value, made them increasingly attractive to states for revenue raising. In Russia, an official monopoly over production and retailing of vodka was claimed as early as 1478 and would be reasserted frequently thereafter until the collapse of the Soviet Union. The state might tax raw materials, the finished product, or the capacity of the still, or collect licensing duties from wholesalers and retailers. All approaches were tried in Britain before 1823, when a successful excise system was established.

The British fiscal state has been seen as particularly efficient, but taxing spirits proved a protracted affair with long-term effects on the distilling industry's structure. Private or household distilling had to be prohibited first. In Scotland this happened in 1781, provoking resistance in the Highlands where malt whiskey (spirit made solely from malted barley) was widely used by the peasantry and was a means of converting poor-quality grain into a more

DISTILLERY. *Distillation,* engraving by Giovanni Stradano (1523–1605). (Bibliothèque Nationale, Paris/Giraudon/Art Resource, NY)

highly valued product that paid the rent. In the Scottish Lowlands the excise system initially sought to copy the English system by concentrating production in a few large-scale licensed distilleries that could be easily policed. This policy was undermined by illicit (or untaxed) whiskey smuggled from the Highlands. From 1786 on, a duty was levied on the capacity of the still, which encouraged distillers to develop rapid distillation techniques by adopting large-diameter, shallow-depth stills. From an original level of £1.10 per cubic gallon, the still capacity duty increased to £54 in 1798. By then some Lowland distillers had cut their work times from the assumed once a day to eight minutes. By 1815, excise duties in the United Kingdom raised £29.5 million or 37 percent of total revenue. Over two-thirds came from taxation of alcoholic drinks and their raw materials. Resistance to taxation also occurred in the United States, where the Excise Act (1791) led to the Whiskey Rebellion in western Pennsylvania in 1794.

Technological Developments. Before 1830 the most widely used distilling vessel was the pot still, whose great virtue was that it produced a full-flavored spirit. It also had several weaknesses as it was (and is) a discontinuous (or batch) process. The first distillation produced a weak concentration of alcohol, and a second or even third distillation was needed to raise the alcoholic strength, thus increasing the cost of fuel and labor. Securing a proper fractionation of the spirit, so that the final product did not contain too large a proportion of secondary constituents, was difficult. The

pot still was heated by fire, and raising the contents to the boiling point was a slow process. Continuous distillation attempted to overcome these limitations.

Technologically, continuous distillation sought to produce a highly concentrated, pure form of alcohol. However, repeated concentration (or rectification) robbed the spirit of flavor, the very factor that made pot-still whiskey attractive to consumers. There was, then, a conflict between low prices and product quality. Although much experimentation occurred after 1780, especially in Britain and France, to increase the speed of distillation, involving preheaters, partial condensers, and new still shapes, continuous distillation was not achieved until 1830 when Aeneas Coffey, a retired Inspector General of the Irish Excise patented his still. Coffey's still was extraordinarily efficient, for it produced a concentrated spirit containing between 86 and 96 percent alcohol in a continuous and rapid operation. It was steam-heated, and heat exchange cut fuel costs. It had an enormous productive capacity compared to the pot still, and could use a mixed-grain mash in which unmalted cereals displaced more expensive malted barley.

Production and Marketing. The Coffey (or "patent") still symbolized the transition to factory distilling and created a marked contrast between pot and patent-still distillers. In 1854, when the output of patent-still distilleries passed that of pot distilling, there were thirteen patent-still distilleries in Scotland, whose combined output was over 7 million proof gallons (m.p.g.). Pot-still distilleries numbered 119, a reduction of 41 since 1840, and they shared an output of 4.75 m.p.g. The position was little different in the United Kingdom as a whole. In 1860, some 27 m.p.g. of spirits were distilled, of which 63 percent came from patent stills, concentrated in twenty-eight distilleries. From 1856 on, Lowland distillers sought to control the productive capacity of the Coffey still by forming restrictive cartels, which ultimately resulted in the formation of the Distillers Company Limited in 1877. A similar process was evident in the United States, where the Distillers and Cattle Feeders' Trust, modeled on the Standard Oil Trust, was formed in 1887 to rationalize the industry. By producing a cheap, relatively homogenous spirit, the patent still also provided the means to create a new type of whiskey, blended whiskey, by mixing grain spirit with malt or pot-still whiskey, an innovation attributed to Andrew Usher in 1853.

Scarcely known in England in the early nineteenth century, whiskey was the national drink of Scotland and Ireland. Irish distillers were the first to develop sales in England in the 1860s but were soon overtaken by Scotch whiskey blenders, who carved out a distinctive niche, first in England and then in international markets, by creating proprietary blends and standard brands. Scotch whiskey displaced brandy, gin, and rum in England and by 1914, some 10 m.p.g. were being exported, mainly to countries within the British Empire although the United States was also an important market.

In most industrializing countries, per capita spirit consumption rose in response to increased income; but as the supply of consumer goods widened, additional increases in income shifted away from spirits and other alcoholic beverages. Simultaneously, the social consequences of spirit consumption attracted increasing concern, and the sale of spirits was increasingly regulated by law. During World War I, the antidrink movement was international in character: Russia prohibited vodka; France prohibited absinthe; Germany prohibited the sale of spirits in industrial areas; Denmark and Switzerland made it illegal to use potatoes and corn for distilling; Norway prohibited spirits at the end of 1916; the United States prohibited the manufacture and import of spirits in the autumn of 1917; Australian states curtailed hours of sale; Canada banned the sale of liquor with a greater alcoholic strength than 2.5° proof; and British dominions copied the restrictive measures imposed in the United Kingdom.

After 1918, declining home markets, tariff barriers, and antidrink campaigns in export markets accelerated the trend toward merger and concentration in the Scotch whiskey industry. In 1925, the Distillers Company acquired the "big three" blending firms—Buchanan, Dewar, and Walker. The new DCL Group thus created, accounted for 60 percent of Scotch whiskey sales. There were other responses to the interwar depression. One was direct investment in overseas production facilities, for example, in Canada (1927), Australia (1929), and the United States (1934). In Canada and Australia, DCL's object was to circumvent duties and tariffs that favored domestic production. DCL's Canadian investment was in association with the Bronfman brothers, who subsequently built one of the world's largest beverage firms, the Distillers Corporation-Seagrams. Seagrams, like DCL, became an early entrant into the U.S. market following the repeal of Prohibition in 1933. Another response was diversification into the chemical industry via the production of industrial alcohol and its derivatives. Until displaced by oil after World War II, industrial alcohol (made from molasses) was a feedstock for the organic-chemicals industry. This response was pioneered in the United States, where the distilling industry, faced with Prohibition, thus made a transition from "the Whiskey Age" to "the Alcohol Age" with this diversification.

World War II disrupted the spirits industry again. Scotch whiskey consumption, at home and abroad, did not pass its peak of 42.8 m.p.g., established in 1900, until 1965. Recovery was based on exports, particularly to the buoyant North American market. By the 1960s, Scotch whiskey, like all the leading types of spirits, had become an internationally tradable product. With major shifts occurring in consumer preferences—for example, vodka consumption in the United States grew from 1.8 m.p.g. in 1952 to 18.0 m.p.g. in 1960—leading firms sought to acquire portfolios of brands. By the late 1980s, the spirits industry was dominated by global corporations, owning and marketing internationally recognized brands.

BIBLIOGRAPHY

Aerts, Erik, and Richard Unger. "Brewing in the Low Countries." In *Production, Marketing and Consumption of Alcoholic Beverages*, edited by Erik Aerts, Louis M. Cullen and Richard G. Wilson, pp. 92–101. Louvain, 1990.

Christian, David. *"Living Water": Vodka and Russian Society on the Eve of Emancipation*. Oxford, 1990.

Cullen, Louis M. *The Brandy Trade under the Ancien Régime: Regional Specialisation in the Charente*. Cambridge, 1998.

McCusker, John J. *Rum and the American Revolution: The Rum Trade and the Balance of Payments of the Thirteen Continental Colonies, 1650–1775*. New York, 1989.

Pokhlebkhin, William. *A History of Vodka*, translated from the Russian by Renfrey Clarke. London, 1991.

Underwood, A. J. V. "The Historical Development of Distilling Plant." *Transactions of the Institute of Chemical Engineers* (1935), 34–62.

Weir, Ron B. *The History of the Distillers Company, 1877–1939*. Oxford, 1995.

RON WEIR

DOMESDAY BOOK is a survey of England ordered by William I at Christmas 1085 and mostly compiled during the following year. The survey was entrusted to seven regional groups of commissioners who operated slightly differently from each other but with a tight specification of their duties. Each group collected information through inquiries conducted in county courts and returned its findings to Winchester. The information was recompiled into two registers, one (Little Domesday Book) for Essex, Suffolk, and Norfolk, and the other (Great Domesday Book) containing in more condensed form the data from the other thirty counties surveyed. No attempt was made to survey the far northern counties of Westmorland, Cumberland, Northumberland, and Durham; and the commissioners could not produce satisfactory returns for the larger towns, failing altogether with London and Winchester. In its final form the survey is compiled county by county. Within each county, properties (usually designated manors) are listed according to their owners, starting with those of the king and then moving in turn to those of his ecclesiastical and lay tenants. Properties are located by reference to the townships where the owners owed land-tax (geld); but since such townships often contained numerous lordships, as well as subsidiary settlements, the evidence relating to a particular place is commonly scattered. For each unit of property the survey records its assessment for land-tax, the number of its plows, the number and rank of its peasant subtenants, its woodland, meadow, and pasture, its mills and fishponds, and its "value," the latter being the sum for which it could be leased. Little Domesday Book has additional information about livestock. Details of land use are rarely expressed in acreages and require careful interpretation. Some information was required for both 1066 and 1086.

Undoubtedly the compilation of Domesday Book was intended to satisfy the needs of William I and his clerks for information about royal rights, especially entitlement to income. The fact that the survey was organized by counties and tenants implies that it would have been useful for establishing what was due when a tenant died without adult issue or suffered forfeiture for treason. However, Domesday Book's appropriateness for this purpose cannot have lasted long, and as an aid to administration it was intrinsically flawed. In later years the same type of information was collected (more usefully) when needed, notably in inquests postmortem following the deaths of the king's tenants.

Although Domesday Book is a stupendous source of information, using it to establish aggregate economic estimates is inherently problematic because of uncertainties concerning its comprehensiveness. It is doubtful, for example, how far the enumeration of subtenants should be treated as censuslike material, and what margin of error to allow. There is hardly any detail about peasant incomes, rents and services, prices, or wages. Grave doubts surround any statistical information for 1066, reconstructed by royal command twenty years later. The temptations of Domesday Book as a source of statistical data are irresistible, but the demands of analysis inevitably strain against the limits of what it is reasonable to attempt.

BIBLIOGRAPHY

Bates, David. *A Bibliography of Domesday Book*. Woodbridge, 1986.
Darby, H. C. *Domesday England*. Cambridge, 1986.
Holt, J. C., ed. *Domesday Studies*. Woodbridge, 1987.
Lennard, Reginald. *Rural England, 1086–1135: A Study of Social and Agrarian Conditions*. Oxford, 1959.
Roffe, David. *Domesday: The Inquest and the Book*. Oxford and New York, 2000.

RICHARD H. BRITNELL

DOMESTIC INDUSTRY. A simple but limited definition is a system of industrial organization that existed before the Industrial Revolution and the factory. A wide range of consumer goods was manufactured in the homes of the workers. The English historian Arnold Toynbee (1852–1883), who more than anybody else was responsible for popularizing the idea of the Industrial Revolution, wrote that "the all-prominent fact … [of the Industrial Revolution was] the substitution of the factory for the domestic system." Others have described domestic industry. The use of the word *system* implies something more structured than "domestic industry"; there are also such labels as "cottage industry," "the putting-out system," "industries in the countryside," and from the 1970s, "proto-industry" or the more abstract "proto-industrialization." The multiplicity of names is evidence that not one captures fully the intricacies of pre-factory-based forms of industry.

A factory is a centralized place of manufacture, where people go to work together, to tend machinery that is driven by a nonhuman power source. The factory system was at the heart of Britain's Industrial Revolution; it was largely the creation of the textile-industry inventions of James Hargreaves (the spinning jenny, 1770), Richard Arkwright (the water frame, 1769), Samuel Crompton (the mule, 1779), and James Watt (the steam engine, patented in 1769). The first three machines were initially developed for the spinning of wool, but they were particularly suitable also to the spinning of cotton yarn. The steam engine provided the source of power, although for a long time the water wheel was used as well. The machines were housed either in buildings converted from other uses, such as grain mills (hence the name woolen or cotton mill), or they were in custom-built premises. The principle of the factory system was capital intensiveness; fixed capital was invested in the buildings and plant, and circulating capital was invested in the raw materials that underwent processing. The capital requirements were greater than the resources of the individual workers, who were employed as wage laborers by the entrepreneurs, or capitalists, who financed and controlled the business.

DOMESTIC WORK. Lace makers in a tenement kitchen, New York City, 1911. The woman at right works with a child asleep on her lap. (Prints and Photographs Division, Library of Congress)

By contrast, small-scale units of production, located in the homes of craftsmen, characterized domestic industry. The fixed capital requirements were small—a hand-operated or a foot-operated spinning wheel or a loom for weaving—cheap to construct and inherited from generation to generation. Raw materials, such as fleece wool, were bought in small lots at weekly markets, then carded, spun, and woven at home, using family labor. The woven cloth was sold in local markets to merchants who might then organize further processing, such as dyeing, before selling the product.

The Economics of Domestic Industry. Two important features of domestic industry have been identified. First, it was labor intensive, not capital intensive. Second, production in the domestic cottages was for markets beyond the cottage door, perhaps beyond the immediate locality. Using the manufacture of woolen cloth to illustrate domestic industry has obscured a third feature—that widespread cottage production was also usual in the early stages of the European cotton industry. Domestic production had been commonplace in the manufacture of, for example, metalware, such as nails, pins, files, hinges, buckles, buttons, bridles, and bits. Leather goods, including gloves, saddles, boots, and shoes, were also produced that way, as were the rude utilitarian clocks that saw service in church towers and the fob watches that were tucked into waistcoat pockets. A few historians have even suggested that simple forms of mining may be characterized as domestic indus-

try, since all that was required was an accessible seam of coal or ore, a few sturdy picks and shovels, buckets and ropes, and a good deal of sweat and brawn. Too deep a hole, however, demanded drainage, ventilation, haulage equipment, and light, which sent capital costs soaring.

The requirements of labor, capital, and markets have been investigated, and the domestic industry was known to harness family labor—husbands, wives, children, other relatives, too, and the occasional hired hand. For the most part, the labor was unpaid for traditional skills that were learned as needed. Some exceptions include the operators of the damask looms who wove fine linens for the tables and bedrooms of the wealthy and the watchmakers who produced precision timepieces and accurate astronomical instruments. Still, most domestic workers were what one English social commentator in the early seventeenth century dismissed as "mere mechanicals."

Within households tasks were often specific to sex and age. Glovemaking and stocking-knitting gave employment to thousands of women and children. Weaving was almost always done by men and spinning by women. Carding and combining wool were often jobs for children, who began at about age six or seven. Their contribution to family income was meager but important, not least because it began to offset the costs of childrearing. The widespread gender-based division of labor is more difficult to explain; it cannot be accounted for by manual strength, since farmers' wives often engaged in heavy field labor and during the nineteenth century women toiled in coal mines. During the eighteenth century, as the demand for cottage labor increased, the traditional gender divisions became eroded as women took to the loom and were as likely as men to make cutlery. For some tasks, women's work was influenced by the life cycle. Young women, with babies and toddlers to attend, and washing and cooking, were doubtless busy by day and frequently interrupted; perhaps it was easier to leave the distaff and the spinning wheel than the loom unattended for a while or until evening. Still, custom and practice do account for the original gender division of labor.

Cheap labor was important where market competition depended on price, not quality. Specialty goods, such as fine silks, delicate laces, patterned linens, or sheer woolens held their own in markets in which skill was more important than the cost of labor. Yet basic consumer goods—fustian coats, linen undershirts, knitted hosiery, domestic pottery, iron pots and pans, wooden bowls—sold on price. Cottage labor was not paid well, especially if it was rural labor that moved from farming to manufacturing according to the rhythm of the agricultural year, as encapsulated in the phrase "industries in the countryside," the title of an important essay by Joan Thirsk (1961). Much rural labor in Europe before the Industrial Revolution was underemployed—where labor could move out of agriculture, at least for a season, without depressing output, to spin, weave, make woolen clothing, or small metal goods. In principle, the opportunity costs of this labor when used in manufacture was zero.

There are several reasons for farm labor to be underemployed. First, the size of farms in many regions had become so small, because of partible inheritance and subdivision, that farming alone was insufficient. Second, the soil had become too poor to yield a living income. Third, some forms of farming—pastoral farming, for instance—had slack periods, especially in the winter, that could profitably be used for manufacturing. Fourth, families conventionally provided support for members, even when they were surplus to strict economic requirements. Thirsk (1961) qualified her essay on industries in the countryside to explain that she did not cover all cases. For example, the important eighteenth-century linen industry in Ireland was located principally in County Armagh in the northeast; that region produced some of the highest quality cloth exported throughout Europe and to North America, yet much of the county produced food crops. Similarly, in France, the Pays de Caux in Upper Normandy was a crop-growing area that also developed an extensive cotton industry in the 1720s. Both exceptions reveal another reason for the existence and development of domestic industry: the growth of population.

From the late fifteenth or early sixteenth century, the population of western and central Europe grew after a century and a half of decline. Even now it is not clear why the recovery occurred, but the virulence of the post–Black Death epidemics was waning, temporarily at least. Since labor had become scarce in the mid-fourteenth century, standards of living had improved somewhat (the increase should not be exaggerated), with the result that people were healthier, living longer, and reproducing. Yet domestic industry contained its own demographic dynamics. The additions to family income boosted its welfare—which also opened the possibilities for earlier marriage and new family formation. An economic niche was required for marriage, and when a farm could not supply it, then cottage industry or combined farming and manufacturing might. The labor of the children was important to the family economy, and parents were reluctant to lose some of their labor supply, so production was often spread across more than one household, with young marrieds working for both family farms. Studies of eighteenth-century domestic industries in Western Europe have suggested that the earnings of women from domestic manufacture gave them some independence and reduced their economic need for a husband—especially for widows who had to support children.

The Putting-Out System. A development of cottage industry that gave it added vitality over several centuries was called the putting-out system. Putting-out was a method that combined capital with labor and linked producers in an efficient fashion. The main capital requirements in domestic industry were the stocks of materials for processing or, for semimanufactured goods, those parts that needed the various phases of processing. A small-scale clothmaker or nailmaker could survive and even make a comfortable living by buying small quantities of wool or iron rods by the week. The farmer-weavers of South Ulster (Ireland) produced good quality linens in that way; they transported them weekly to one of the many small market towns and sold them from the doorways of shops and inns to bleachers or drapers, who attended to the more capital-intensive stages of bleaching and finishing before sending them to their final destinations. Such an independent life could be precarious—if the manufacturing processes extended over many days, if illness or bad weather disrupted production, or if there were few buyers in the market. Even worse, the price obtainable for the finished product might not cover the cost of the materials. Reliance on an entrepreneur to supply the materials on credit minimized such difficulties. Suppliers or their agents traveled the countryside to bring supplies to the manufacturers and gather the finished product—paying for the output, less the cost of the materials. In the European woolen industry, that was the role of the clothier, a pivotal figure before the Industrial Revolution. Similar entrepreneurs existed for all the domestic industries.

The putting-out system had many advantages, the first of which was to draw supplies from wide areas. Although the eighteenth-century farmer-weavers of South Ulster grew much of their own flax, they also relied on flax and spun linen yarns made in North Connacht. In seventeenth-century England, the small-scale woolen manufacturers in the West Riding of Yorkshire worked with local wool, but the fine cloth manufacturers of the West of England and East Anglia used wool from sheep grazed in the Midland counties of Leicestershire, Lincolnshire, Northamptonshire, and Cambridgeshire. Some of the best wool-producing regions were, then, not regions of cloth productions; instead, clothiers transported the wool, sometimes over long distances, to places where labor was abundant and cheap. Wool is not a homogeneous commodity. Even wool from the same sheep varies according to whether it comes from the back or the belly and according to the animal's age. Different breeds produce different qualities; wool from hardy upland sheep is not the same as the wool shorn from sheep that grow fat on lush lowland grass. Clothiers were thus able to buy, sort, and mix wools, depending on market requirements.

The putting-out system exploited the benefits of the division of labor to the full. In the several production stages for woolen cloth, fleeces require washing to remove the grease; they require combing or carding to straighten the fibers and the loosely twisted ropes, a process known as roving. Then there is spinning into yarn, which is woven into cloth. The finished fabric may then be fulled (i.e., felted and shrunk); it might also be stretched or sheared. The wool, the yarn, or the cloth may be dyed. The manufacture of linen also involves several stages. Farmer-weavers often grew their own flax, and once harvested, the plant stems had to be retted (i.e., rotted) and hackled, to separate the inner fibers from the outer stalk. Then the fibers were washed, dried, and separated before the spinning and weaving. The resulting brown linens were usually bleached to whiten them, a time-consuming, capital-intensive operation usually beyond the means of most farmer-weavers. Many brown linen cloths were purchased by bleachers who possessed bleach greens and the water-powered machinery used for beetling (i.e., beating with wooden hammers to give the finish, or sheen). The production of metal goods took the division of labor even farther, as the eighteenth-century economist Adam Smith demonstrated, using pin manufacture to illustrate the benefits of the system. Smith identified eighteen operations, from drawing out the wire to attaching the completed pin to the paper for sale. Smith reckoned that dividing the labor for each could increase productivity tenfold.

The putting-out system made the best use of the labor supply in the domestic industries when all the processes—carding, roving, spinning, weaving, and so on—were under one roof. Still, it exploited the advantages of regional specializations. The farmer-weavers of South Ulster supplemented their own supplies of yarn with yarn spun in Connacht; the serge weavers of the southwest of England and the new drapery manufacturers of Norfolk imported woolen yarn from the southeast of Ireland; in the linen districts of northwestern and central Europe, some regions specialized in spinning, others in weaving and finishing. Such specialization did not have to involve long distances but could link neighboring households, perhaps even keeping families together as a production unit. In the woolen-producing town of Carrick-on-Suir in southeastern Ireland at the end of the eighteenth century, there were several households sharing the same family name that operated as a single business. Above all, the putting-out system was flexible; entrepreneurs could take on or lay off labor according to market demand. Even before the Industrial Revolution, the business cycle lurked in its formative phase—as an integral element of a market economy. If food prices soared because of a poor harvest, there was less to spend on clothing, bed linen, tableware, or weddings. Fashions changed, especially in the textile market, so the demand for one kind of fabric might be at the expense of another. Wars and rumors of wars disrupted trade. In the early 1620s, exports of woolen cloth from England were severely restricted because of currency devaluations in central Europe. As demand changed, merchants had to be adept at reading market signals and adjusting production and supply.

The disadvantages of the putting-out system included manufacturers who risked losing their investments and independence. An early nineteenth-century observer of the Ulster linen industry, where most producers were still farmer-weavers, extolled the independence of such men who were "free agents, whose employments are diversified and rational." The people who depended on entrepreneurs did not inevitably become wage labourers, but if they became bound to their suppliers by a web of credit that they could not repay, they were well on the way. Much of the evidence suggests, however, that families employed in rural industry did have higher incomes than their neighbors who depended on farming alone. The entrepreneurs faced two drawbacks. First, there were the costs of acquiring and distributing materials throughout a wide area of the countryside, then of collecting the product. They were however, spared the expense of providing central places of production. Second, cottage workers were not disciplined or regimented workers and could be fickle in their work habits. In the eighteenth century, the observation of "Saint Monday"—an alcoholic binge at the weekend, followed by a hangover on Monday—was common. When the demand for labor was high, cottagers might work for several masters at once or embezzle from their suppliers by substituting inferior materials for the ones that had been "put out" to them. A body of legislation grew in eighteenth-century Europe to impose penalties on manufacturers who attempted to defraud their suppliers.

The domestic industries were widespread throughout Europe and in non-European societies before the Industrial Revolution. They survive today in many handcrafted goods that are sold as luxury items, souvenirs, art, and so on. Originally located in farmers' cottages, it also exists and existed in towns, either as population growth overstocked them with laborers or where producers wanted control over specialty or skilled labor.

Domestic industry has been important wherever labor was the greatest element of production costs, and that proportion varied from industry to industry, place to place, and time to time. Domestic producers developed technical skills that were learned as needed, using robust, hand-made tools and machines powered by human minds and muscle. To develop, domestic industry needed and still needs a market for its output. In virtually every peasant household there has been some production—knitting, weaving, sewing—purely for subsistence. Yet domestic or rural industry—whether in Europe, Africa, Asia, the Middle East, or the Americas—was and is part of a market economy.

Proto-Industrialization, Industrialization, and Deindustrialization. A Neo-Marxist view of the word recognizes the feudal era in medieval Europe that was crumbling by the end of the fifteenth century. By the late eighteenth century, there had emerged European industrial capitalism, associated with the factory system. In between, there was a loosely defined era of merchant capitalism, when such merchants as clothiers organized Europe's manufacturing for distant markets. The rise of Europe's population from the late fifteenth century onward generated the supply of labor essential to the development of the domestic industries. It did two other things as well: (1) increased the demand for consumer goods; (2) depressed the price of labor, making the economics of cottage industry all the more attractive.

By definition, the term *proto-industrialization* refers to an initial or formative stage of industry. It implies that the factory system was the result, the fully developed form of industrial organization that grew from an earlier, less developed stage. It follows, therefore, that the domestic industries, rural industry, cottage industry, "industries in the countryside" were eventually superseded by full-blown industrialization—but did this occur and, if so, how and why?

As the domestic industries mobilized surplus labor into the production of manufactured goods for distant markets and grew, they also absorbed that surplus. As the opportunity costs of labor rose, it became more expensive to employ people in industry. The part-time manufacturers began to devote more time to spinning, or weaving, or so on, and less time to farming. The survival of regions with proto-industry, therefore, depended on there being supplies of food available from other regions that remained agricultural producers. As regional specialization became more pronounced, some concentrated on specialized agriculture, others on specialized manufacturing. Such specialization had always existed, alongside the regions of mixed agriculture and industry, but by the late 1700s and early 1800s, that became more pronounced. Industries in Europe's countryside also became victims of their own successes. As production expanded, they exhausted any comparative advantage—cheap labor—and prompted entrepreneurs to think of new ways to keep production costs low. One obvious strategy was to cast their net over wider regions of the countryside in the search for labor, but that increased the costs of distribution and collection. Another way was to set up a centralized manufactory, where workers could be supervised (and so have less opportunity to embezzle raw materials), where there might be the possibility of connecting a series of looms to a water wheel for power. All depended on whether the greater capital charges were justified by the savings on distribution costs. A more fundamental step was to replace labor by capital—that is, to develop and invest in new machinery. That brought about the classical Industrial Revolution, pioneered by the British textile industry.

In the eighteenth century, woolen weavers in Britain were expanding their demand for yarn faster than spinners could increase their output. The jenny, the water-frame, and the mule were machines that were invented to increase the supply of yarn. Initially, the jenny was scarcely more than a modified spinning wheel, capable of spinning of several yarns simultaneously; it fit in cottages and domestic workshops and was operated manually. The water-frame worked by passing the combed or carded wool through a series of rollers; it required an external source of power provided at first by water wheels. Richard Arkwright, the man most associated with the water-frame although probably not its inventor, has some claim as the founder of the modern factory system since he set up a manufactory at Cromford in Derbyshire, using water drawn from the River Derwent. The mule, a more sophisticated machine, was capable of producing fine counts of yarn, suitable for the weaving of high-quality fabrics; it had the two advantages of lowering unit cost of production and enhancing quality. The steam engine eventually displaced water as the source of energy. Neither the water-frame nor the mule was suitable for cottage production, and both required investments beyond the means of most rural workers. The mechanization of weaving lagged behind that of spinning (with the exception of the flying shuttle in 1733), since it was technically more difficult and the economic pressures were less severe. These technical developments in the 1700s were a response to problems in the woolen industry, but they were adaptable to Britain's formative cotton industry. British demand for cotton fabrics had been stimulated by the import of calicoes and muslins from India during the late 1600s. Cotton fabrics were smooth and more comfortable against the skin than woolens, took color and patterns well, and could be washed and dried more easily than woolens. The demand for cottons increased as the quality of English products improved and prices fell. By the early 1800s, the traditional woolen and linen fabrics of Europe, and even up-market silks, had a serious competitor in cotton. The new spinning machinery that was developed in the final decades of the eighteenth century for wool and cotton was not well suited to flax spinning, except for the coarsest counts of yarn, so serious mechanization was delayed in linen production until the introduction of wet-spinning in the 1820s.

As rising labor costs motivated British industry to move into the factory phase, labor shortages, nationally, became severe in the middle decades of the eighteenth century, when population growth slackened. Then from the 1770s onward, population growth accelerated and real wages fell, though there remained acute shortages of labor in the most rapidly industrializing areas. The productivity gains of the new methods of production were so great that they probably overwhelmed the one-time advantages of rural industry.

The process of industrialization in other regions of Europe offer similar warning against making simple connections between industrialization and the price of labor. The northern provinces of the Low Countries (Holland) was an area of high earnings, in which economic activities were concentrated on commercial agriculture and maritime trade. Their local industries, however, were ailing, and they did not innovate—so their advantages did not lie with manufacturing. The southern provinces of the Low Countries (Belgium), in contrast, possessed extensive rural industries that produced woolen textiles, linens, and metalwares. Population was growing rapidly and labor was cheap—yet the region adopted the English textile inventions with enthusiasm, the investment being financed from the profits of domestic industry. The combined benefits of low labor costs and productivity gains from technical innovation then shaped the future of their economic development.

During the nineteenth century, in some places, proto-industry remained just that and never moved into the stage of factory production. Elsewhere, where factories were established, cottage industry withered—a process that has come to known as "deindustrialization." Britain has many localities that lost their traditional cottage industries during the nineteenth century: the Weald of Kent and Sussex, large areas of Wiltshire and Gloucestershire, the Forest of Dean, and East Anglia. In Ireland, the hand-loom weaving of linen became contracted into East Ulster, near Belfast, and its smoking spinning mills. The once prosperous linen industry conducted by the so-called serf-weavers in Silesia (a German-Polish border state) was hampered by political turmoil in the mid-1800s and succumbed to competition from the newly mechanized cotton and linen factories of northwestern Europe.

The simple definition of domestic industry, as presented at the start of this article, stresses that manufacturing took place in domestic cottages and workshops, using household and family labor. The domestic industries were widespread throughout Europe and elsewhere and exist even today. Many materials were and are processed—wool, linen, silk, cotton, clothing, various metals, woods, leather, ceramics, wicker, and other basketmaking fibers. It endures because it suits certain economic and technical circumstances. It fits the social realities of communities built on families and households. It did not disappear in the nineteenth century but contracted as the factory system grew in Europe and worldwide. The phrase fails in capturing the nuances of the system—that it was commonly but not exclusively found in the countryside; that it was often but not always organized by merchant-capitalists; that the manufacturers were basically wage earners; that is sometimes but not inevitably was the first (proto-) stage of industrialization. Whatever the label, domestic industry as discussed has been a central feature of economic history.

[*See also* Factory System *and* Mass Production.]

BIBLIOGRAPHY

Clarkson, Leslie A. *Proto-Industrialization: The First Phase of Industrialization?* London, 1985.

Coleman, Donald C. "Proto-Industrialization: A Concept Too Many." *Economic History Review* 36.3 (1983).

Kriedte, Peter, Hans Medick, and Jürgen Schlumbohm, eds. *Industrialization before Industrialization.* Translated by Beate Schempp. Cambridge, 1981.

Mendels, F. F. "Proto-Industrialization: The First Phase of the Industrialization Process." *Journal of Economic History* 32 (1972) 241–261.

C. Ogilvie, Sheilagh, and Markus Cerman, eds. *European Proto-industrialization.* Cambridge, 1996.

Thirsk, Joan. "Industries in the Countryside." In *Essays in the Economic and Social History of Tudor and Stuart England*, edited by F. J. Fisher. Cambridge, 1961.

L. A. CLARKSON

DOMESTIC SERVICE. The turn of the twenty-first century has witnessed the reemergence of familiar forms of domestic service in Western economies. A phenomenon once widespread but recently thought to have been rendered superfluous by technological and social change, it has made a small but noteworthy comeback after an absence of some two generations. Just as the writings of Shakespeare, Molière, Austen, Flaubert, Tolstoy, and Wodehouse portray domestic servants ever present but subverting as much as attending to the needs and whims of their masters and mistresses in the domestic environment, middle-class employers of hired help perceive a "servant problem" once more.

In Latin America, Africa, and large parts of Asia there is widespread employment of domestic servants in the homes of those with the incomes to afford them, not least expatriate Westerners. For the superrich everywhere live-in servants never disappeared. Domestic service's apparent continuity throughout history and across continents is far more remarkable than its temporary near-disappearance in the developed West for sixty years. It would not be unreasonable to speculate that the institution of domestic service is as old as that of the family, albeit just as vulnerable to the contingencies of time and place. Indeed, the term *family* embraced not just immediate blood kin but also domestic servants within middle-and higher-ranking households in premodern western Europe, testifying to their significance in histories (urban histories in particular) of demography and of work.

Slavery and Service. Such a large and economically significant component of past societies must be satisfactorily defined and delimited without trampling on its variety of guises. Domestic service first must be distinguished from captive labor, or slavery. In preclassical Greece it may have been difficult to distinguish between slaves and servants within the households of landowning families (not least because Homeric sources do not usually allow such nice distinctions to be made); but in most other slaveholding societies since, several observable characteristics set servants apart. Fundamentally, slaves were unfree members of households who not only performed servile labor but had distinct constraints on movement, could be traded or exchanged (given that they were usually appropriated from foreign lands), and were also unwaged. Domestic servants may well have served in similar fashion, and to have contracted for periods that restricted their mobility. Though they sometimes may have changed households through arrangements made by their employers—within an aristocratic network of kin or friendship, for instance—the vast majority were part of an often active labor market. They were never bound to a family such that they could not choose their employers, who in almost all cases were contractually bound to pay them wages.

Slavery and service had long coexisted in Europe, but slavery in the Caribbean and the Americas—where the abominable practice has had its longest legacy—was arguably the continuation of an ever-westward trend of sugar plantations tended by slave labor. Begun in the medieval period by Moors on Mediterranean islands such as Sicily and embraced by the Spanish in the Balearics and the Canaries, it was really in the wake of the fifteenth-century Spanish Reconquista that slavery became associated with (initially) non-Christians of color from exotic foreign lands.

In northwestern Europe, sixteenth-century Reformations encouraged the clear conceptual separation of slavery from service, at least within domestic jurisdictions, demonstrated in the English case by two contrasting examples. First, the abject failure of mid-Tudor legislation to introduce the enslavement of English vagrants within the body of regulations known as the Poor Law was confirmed by the repeal of the law in 1550, only three years after its introduction. Second, throughout the seventeenth century a variant of apprenticeship known as indentured servitude was employed as a part of colonial policy in the Caribbean and the Americas to encourage poor young men and women to bind themselves contractually to a settler for a term usually of seven years. Unlike slaves (whom they often supervised in the fields), these servants had at least the chance to build capital and establish themselves at the end of their term.

The side-effects of slaveholding within the British Empire and the beginnings of the campaign for abolition led to a case that exemplifies continuing Western ambiguity on this issue. Lord Chief Justice Mansfield succumbed to the persuasive arguments of barrister Francis Hargrave (who published his account of the case in 1772) that his client, runaway slave James Somersett, was entitled in England to have the freedom of mobility and the contract of a servant rather than the absence of these freedoms of a slave. Mansfield released Somersett from the threat of being sent back to Virginia to be sold as punishment by his putative owner, confirming in his case the dictum of celebrated eighteenth-century English legal commentator William Blackstone that slavery could not lawfully exist on English soil; but he refused to extend his judgment to a general principle, which would have effectively involved the release of all slaves in England. This was the same LCJ Mansfield who took into his household Dido, his nephew's illegitimate daughter by a slave woman, and treated her as a favorite domestic servant (albeit one to whom he was related).

In his will he declared that she be forever freed from slavery, leaving a question mark over her previous status as relative and servant, and left her substantial sums in gift and in annuity. Unfortunately, ambiguities in the differences between slavery and service within popular contemporary perception are rarely recorded; but presumably since so many of the young poor engaged in service early in their working lives, it may have been an issue materially more clear in their minds than those of elite legal circles.

SERVANTS. *While the Sunday Lunch is Laid (Interior of the Architect Carlsberg's Home).* Painting by Pehr Gustaf von Heideken, c. 1835. A servant sets out lunch (*left*). (The Stockholm City Museum, Sweden)

The issue of service, slavery, and race is far too large to be satisfactorily addressed here, yet doubtless the confluence of these factors explains much more than Mansfield's apparently contradictory responses within the context of eighteenth-century Britain. Twentieth-century service in societies with significant domestic histories of slavery, such as Brazil or parts of the United States, are fractured by race in ways that significantly influence employer–employee relations in a context of subordination and mastery more potent than that of class alone. It skews demographic dynamics toward the spatial segregation of urban environments between servant-employing suburbs and the shanty towns to which servants between jobs return (even where their families dwell); distorts domestic-service labor markets, creating ghettoized service sectors demarcated by racial origin; and generates (as at least one historian of twentieth-century U.S. domestic service has opined) politically correct anguish among East Coast liberals who employ illegal Asian immigrants as maids while acknowledging the freedom this gives the employers as working women.

In South Africa it is impossible to understand domestic service during (and possibly even beyond) apartheid without acknowledging the comprehensive influence of the statutory racial divisions and culture of violence that prevailed. In this context, concepts of "the family" are distinctly limited in their embrace, signaling the degree to which this sector stood as a perpetual domestic reminder of the schizophrenic character of the South African economy between 1948 and 1994: the archaic or preindustrial within the postmodern.

Records and Sources. Although economic historians are interested in the quantification of social phenomena, it is not always easy to garner reliable statistics on the numbers of domestic servants in historical populations when they must rely so often on state or ecclesiastical surveys generated for fiscal, civil, or military purposes. Domestic servants were subordinate members of society usually in the employ of someone of higher status, and rarely in a position themselves to be taxed or otherwise identified years after the fact. This reason, and an earlier historical literature absorbed by elite voices and deeds, led to accusations of the deliberate erasure of servants (and other lower-order groups) from economic and political history. Yet while the prejudices and preoccupations of many professional historians may have led to narrow record selection, the absence of servants from orthodox accounts was also partly due to record availability. Record offices, libraries, and museums have made increasing numbers of record sets available and accessible. Moreover, with an increasing catholicity of taste in source material fostered by new theoretical approaches, the alleged "invisibility" of servants is no longer an appropriate starting point.

The taxation and counting of householders in, for example, the fourteenth-century London poll taxes, the fifteenth-century Florentine *catasti*, the late-seventeenth-century Marriage Duties Assessments in England, or the range of national censuses in the modern period provide some idea of the sizable minorities of (particularly female) domestic servants in urban populations, if only sometimes by default. Those records that provide far greater detail on individuals and events—such as diaries, memoirs, or witnesses' depositions in criminal and, in particular, church courts—add a qualitative richness to those quantitative sources. At their best, for instance the London ecclesiastical court depositions from the seventeenth century, they even can contribute to the question of numbers.

Service and Demography. Clearly, overall demographic stimuli (such as the incidence of epidemic disease), political conditions (most obviously the occurrence or absence of war or siege), the state and the nature of a town or a region's growth trajectory, and its relative economic fortunes will cause figures of the incidence of servants to vary. Research studies of the former by French and British historians especially have firmly established the persistence of a western-European demographic regime—evident from at least as early as the sixteenth century, and broken only in the nineteenth century—in which servants played a pivotal role.

In summary, the central driver of demographic history in the long run was found to be the rate of marriage and, in particular, changes in the age of female first marriage rather than the death rate. The age at which women on average married for the first time prior to the nineteenth century was found to be far later than originally thought, resulting in fewer children and therefore slower population growth; and that age was largely governed by the institution of life-cycle service. Late adolescence and early adulthood were spent by most young people in a period of subordinate labor outside their households of birth, which was intended to broaden the mind, inculcate work discipline, and lead to the acquisition of skills and, for women, the saving of a dowry in cash and/or kind to assist in the formation of a new household upon marriage. These findings helped explain why historical demographers kept finding sizable numbers of servants in the populations of western-European communities, and why those servants were predominantly in their late teens and early twenties.

However, those groundbreaking studies were largely based on findings from the populations of rural communities; and genuine difficulty arises in trying to identify specifically domestic servants, who in the countryside frequently are indistinguishable in the historical record from agricultural servants (in the English context, "servants in husbandry"). This ambiguity is illustrated in Richard Gough's *The History of Myddle* (1701), which chronicled the author's home parish of Myddle in rural Shropshire, one of the English midland counties bordering Wales. Convinced that the sixteenth-century Reformation of European Christianity had changed all social life as he had known it, Gough provided a snapshot of the social structure of an English rural community on the brink of the changes that many economic historians believe would transform it for ever.

Most striking to the modern eye, his account included a plan view of the seating arrangements in the local parish church drawn as if he had removed the roof and gazed down on the congregation. It outlined the hierarchical order of farms and families with the most eminent seated nearest the altar and pulpit; but it also included separate pews allocated to larger farms' servants, set considerably nearer their august employers (and therefore altar and pulpit) than other parish freeholders and tenant farmers occupying whole farms. Servants held economic and social significance in rural Myddle, but their working roles are not so distinct: how often, and under which circumstances, were dairy maids deputized as kitchen maids between milking rounds; or did reapers and mowers double as informal footmen on occasion? Perhaps historians' preoccupation with strict and enforceable categorical parameters overshadow the fluid boundaries between tasks and roles.

Urban Domestic Service. Domestic servants are much easier to pinpoint in urban settings than in rural communities. Risking sweeping generalization, one may note that larger towns and cities under relatively settled conditions have tended to contain proportions of domestic servants at around 8 to 12 percent of their total populations, though only a little in excess of 5 percent in smaller urban settlements. Rates of in- or out-migration are particularly good indicators (cause and/or effect) of numbers of servants in an urban population, for example, in medieval York and Prato in the aftermath of plague, when servant influxes rose appreciably.

In the early decades of the eighteenth century, when it became the largest city in Europe, London attracted huge numbers of young people into service. A quarter of working women and approximately 7.7 percent (between 35,000 and 50,000 people depending on population estimates) of the total population of the burgeoning metropolis were domestic servants, with four out of five of them female and most born outside London. The operation of the iron demographic law of life-cycle service is confirmed in this urban context by the finding that in excess of three-quarters of the female domestic servants were under the age of thirty, almost all of them yet to marry.

In 1851, when London was the heart of a global empire, the proportion of domestic servants in the total population was about 8.5 percent (albeit of a far larger number of

Londoners), the overwhelming majority of whom were female. Even with the knowledge that any attempt to quantify over a millennium and across vast geographical distances is doomed to imprecision, these proportions are large and represent significant groups within female—and to a lesser extent male—urban labor forces. Though not clearly visible in the records penned by or for elites, domestic servants were ubiquitous in the societies of their historical contemporaries.

Domestic Service and Gender. From this account so far, it is clear that gender plays a large role in our comprehension of domestic service in the past. Rural communities, particularly manorial households and the largest landowning families, may have employed sizable numbers of male servants, but their roles throughout history have been far more geared to agricultural labor than to domestic work; most identifiably domestic servants usually worked in the smaller urban households.

As a general rule, the smaller (i.e., the less the wealth or lowlier the status of) the household, the fewer the servants and the greater the likelihood that the servant(s) would be female; and historians of this subject frequently are surprised by how far down the social scale servant-employment occurred. Even within the ancient walls of the City of London, where some of Europe's wealthiest residents traditionally have lived, nearly four in five of servant-employing families had only one or two servants in the 1690s, and almost all of those were female.

Male domestic servants in most societies have been able to command higher wages than those of female servants, thanks to several factors: widespread patriarchal labor-market forces valuing male labor more highly than female; males' superior strength for manual tasks; their donning of livery (*la livrée*) or other uniforms as part-time military retainers and/or to mark specialized roles performed within or outside the house; and the related status symbolism for employers seen with what Thorstein Veblen described as the "conspicuous consumption" of idle luxury (the footman and flunky best embody this cultural manifestation in the West). Despite the tangle of cause and effect, their higher wages confined male servants to a few households and confirmed domestic service as "women's work" in most minds. The "upstairs–downstairs" cliché of employer–employee relations—spatial separation within the household, in effect separate realms for servant and served—is relevant only to the tiny minority of the largest landowning houses.

As the term suggests, domestic servants predominantly lived and worked within the homes of their employers. The diary of Samuel Pepys (1660–1669), a London resident, is a fascinating window into a small servant-employing urban household, which expands as household income rises. It makes frequent reference to the succession of boys and especially girls or young women who both lived and served in the household, and provides prosaic evidence of Pepys's and his wife Elizabeth's largely uncomplicated cohabitation with young people only rarely related to them. Complications could and did arise, as when two servants—Ashwell, Elizabeth's close "companion," and cook-maid Hannah (on the verge of dismissal for theft)—left within a day of each other in 1663; the unhappy episode when Pepys's younger sister joined the household; or the occasion when his wife caught Pepys kissing another of their female servants.

Living-in gave significant scope for abuses by masters and mistresses. Written in the fourteenth century, *Le menagier de Paris* was an early example of the European treatise or household manual advising on the proper roles of master and mistress, in this case calling on the wife to manage the servants and the husband to manage the wife. Relations within households were patriarchal power relations, and only recently has physical chastisement of resident subordinates been frowned upon.

Disorderly households also potentially presented a problem in the community; and many towns, particularly the largest ones with sufficient fiscal resources, developed sophisticated legal and institutional frameworks to deal with unruly servants. Houses of correction grew up in a number of towns and cities in late-medieval and early-modern Europe, such as London's Bridewell (1522), which largely existed to punish servants and apprentices. Masters' sexual abuses of female domestic servants seem to have been far more likely to be dealt with by community sanction (if at all) rather than legal punishment, emblematic of the power asymmetry of household relations in general.

Conclusion. In seeking to elaborate the salient factors and themes of domestic service's economic, social, and cultural history over the long term, this survey had to do serious injustice to a complex collection of phenomena. Nonetheless, if there is an overriding theme, it is that of continuity over change. Some historians have argued for a process of proletarianization in the nineteenth and twentieth centuries; but evidence for the medieval and early-modern periods suggests that most domestic servants in European towns—where most domestic servants resided and worked—were poor in-migrants from the countryside, as they were later on, and that they remained among the lower social orders upon leaving service. Others have portrayed modern domestic service as the result of feminization, or a growing preponderance of girls and women over time, therefore resulting in service's diminution in status and remuneration and contributing significantly to a new harsher regime of gender relations and the subordination of women; but women formed the vast majority of urban domestic servants from the fourteenth century onward, according to the extant evidence, which fails to demonstrate any female "golden age" in premodernity.

Linked to the feminization thesis has been that of "separate spheres," positing that an increasingly managerial mistress distant from the maid was central to class formation in the nineteenth century; but, again, modernity exhibits little novelty, as by the seventeenth century there is a vast literature advising mistresses on servant-management, affirmed in the archives. This view may sit ill with orthodox interpretations of change in economic history, but it need not deny their validity in other spheres of economic life. It does, however, allow scholars to temper their surprise at the complexities raised by domestic service's reemergence in the twenty-first century.

BIBLIOGRAPHY

Barret-Ducrocq, Françoise. *Love in the Time of Victoria: Sexuality, Class and Gender in Nineteenth-Century London*, translated by J. Howe. London, 1991. Refreshing antidote to overly schematic portrayals of (among other relationships) mistresses and servants.

Chaney, Elsa M., and Mary G. Castro, eds. *Muchachas No More: Household Workers in Latin America and the Caribbean*. Philadelphia, 1989. Wide-ranging and largely sociological collection on a subject neglected in English.

Clark, Alice. *Working Life of Women in the Seventeenth Century*. London, 1919. Pioneering text, neglected for over sixty years, whose "golden age" thesis still attracts many.

Earle, Peter. *A City Full of People: Men and Women of London, 1650–1750*. London, 1994. Subtle archival study of early-modern Londoners that brings domestic servants and their contemporaries alive.

Fairchilds, Cissie. *Domestic Enemies: Servants and Their Masters in Old Regime France*. Baltimore, 1984. Interesting if ideologically driven study of domestics in southwestern French towns, using a wide range of sources.

Goldberg, Peter J. P. *Women, Work and Life Cycle in a Medieval Economy: Women in York and Yorkshire, c. 1300–1520*. Oxford, 1992. Splendid and thorough account of domestic service within the context of women's work in general, firmly grounded in revealing sources.

Gutton, Jean-Pierre. *Domestiques et serviteurs dans la France de l'ancien régime*. Paris, 1981. Classic thoughtful study of French domestic service, rich in source material.

Hall, Catherine, and Leonore Davidoff. *Family Fortunes: Men and Women of the English Middle Class, 1780–1850*. London, 1987. Monumental statement of the "separate spheres" thesis that places mistress–servant relations at the heart of emerging class relations, hampered by the then lack of in-depth archival research on the early-modern period.

Hecht, Jean J. *The Domestic Servant Class in Eighteenth-Century England*. London, 1956. For far too long the only monograph on its subject, an elegant but limited assembly of elite anecdote and prejudice that overemphasizes male domestics.

Higgs, Edward. "Domestic Service and Household Production." In *Unequal Opportunities: Women's Employment in England, 1800–1918* edited by A. V. John. Oxford, 1986. Intense scrutiny of English census material that successfully undermines naive class analyses.

Hill, Bridget. *Servants: English Domestics in the Eighteenth Century*. Oxford, 1996. Stimulating if eclectic collection of essays that more often than not concerns the nineteenth century.

Marshall, Dorothy. *The English Domestic Servant in History*. London, 1949. Classic early survey of English domestic service across three centuries.

Maza, Sarah. *Servants and Masters in Eighteenth-Century France: The Uses of Loyalty*. Princeton, 1983. Fascinating contrast to Fairchilds, which overstresses servants' separation from wider French society but is extremely well written.

McBride, Theresa. *The Domestic Revolution: The Modernisation of Household Service in England and France 1820–1920*. New York, 1976. Comparative study that has been almost entirely superseded but is valuable to the growth of the modernization debate.

Meldrum, Tim. *Domestic Service and Gender, 1660–1750: Life and Work in the London Household*. Harlow, 2000. Attempt to redress the imbalance of histories written from the employers' point of view by focusing clearly on the working lives of servants in their words.

Mitterauer, Michael. *A History of Youth*. Translated by G. Dunphy. Oxford, 1992. Brave and wide-ranging synthesis that situates domestic servants in the context of youth.

Palmer, Phyllis. *Domesticity and Dirt: Housewives and Domestic Servants in the United States, 1920–1945*. Philadelphia, 1989. Revealing study of interwar America with interesting observations on mistress–servant relations.

TIM MELDRUM

DOWRY. *See* Inheritance Systems *and* Marriage Payments.

DOWRY FUND. Two changes paved the way for the emergence of dowry funds in medieval Europe. In twelfth-century Italy, Roman dowry was substituted for husbands' gifts to wives as the chief transfer of wealth at marriage. This was a Roman *dos*, or Falcidian quarter, that satisfied daughters' claims on fathers' estates. Dowries were awarded in cash, leaving patrimonial lands for surviving brothers.

Venice established a dowry fund under the authority of the Procuratoria di San Marco and the Grain Office, which invested government funds. By law, dowry was a woman's property and a husband could invest it only if its value was secured. Until 1233 that value was secured by real estate; thereafter gold or silver plate could be substituted, releasing the cash value for investment. Procurators invested dowries in local securities. By 1316 the Grain office was allowed to borrow dowries lying idle in the Procuratoria, with the city-state providing surety as required by law. In 1329 dowry assets were rendered more accessible to the state: a new law stated that all dowries on deposit could be given to the Grain Office, which provided surety. The office paid the same rate that it paid on forced loans, somewhat higher than the normal rate paid to Venetians and foreigners at the Grain Office (4 percent and 3 percent, respectively).

Dowries were not deposited when higher returns were available elsewhere, but moneys left with the procuratoria for orphans, even fines levied on rapists, were made available to a government strapped for cash. This system lasted until the Grain Office ceased payments; at this point, in the fifteenth century, the senate stepped in to aid persons who could not secure the return of capital.

Florence created a more elaborate system for employing dowry funds to solve the state's liquidity problems. The Monte della Doti, launched in 1424–1425, gained speculative and actuarial elements over time that made it attractive to private investors. By 1433 a model deposit of 60 florins produced a 500 florin dowry in fifteen years, provided that the girl was still alive (the original deposit was returned if she entered a convent). Florentines were willing to bet on daughters' life expectancies: 879 deposits were made over two months, providing the state with 67,231 florins, a sum equivalent to more than one-third of the carrying charges on the funded debt. The Monte's conditions were revised continually, in the areas of amounts deposited, maturation dates, and whether or not capital was returned to surviving male kin.

By January 1435–1436, dowry deposits could be used to purchase Monte credits, which were transferred to a new account in the endowed girls' names. Interest was paid to this account and new Monte credits added. At the due date officials cashed in the number of credits necessary to raise the dowry. The Monte delle Doti became a revolving fund, financed by dowry deposits, interest, and communal savings on debt service. In March 1440–1441 all deposits became Monte credits, making the link between the fund and the public debt direct. To protect capital, investors were drawn into the administration of state debt. Monte credits could be purchased in the marketplace, and by the 1450s there were almost 3 million florins in Monte accounts.

BIBLIOGRAPHY

Kirshner, Julius, and Anthony Molho. "The Dowry Fund and the Marriage Market in Early Quattrocento Florence." *Journal of Modern History* 50 (1978), 403–438.

Molho, Anthony. *Marriage Alliance in Late Medieval Florence.* Cambridge, Mass., 1994.

Mueller, Reinhold C. *Money and Banking in Medieval and Renaissance Venice*, vol. 2, *The Venetian Money Market: Banks, Panics, and the Public Debt, 1200–1500.* Baltimore, 1997.

Susan Mosher Stuard

DRAFT AND PACK ANIMALS. Before mechanization, animals were the most important form of physical capital. For centuries, both draft and pack animals were the primary means of transportation and the source of raw power to agriculture, industry, and commerce. Few forms of capital were used so unfailingly for so many centuries. Even today, many people in developing countries rely on draft animals as their primary motive power. Their efficient use in the context of local customs and institutions greatly affected the economic outcome of many societies.

The task at hand would indicate the type of animal used. Draft animals were used mainly for pulling machinery or transportation devices, whereas pack animals would generally carry a load. In this regard, pack animals were a substitute for human porters. Draft and pack animals became so important to the development of economies that they could greatly influence whether or not a particular region became rich or poor. Indeed, Jared Diamond argued, quite forcefully, that one of the main reasons Africa failed to develop as fast as other continents was that, unlike virtually every other part of the world, Africa had a wealth of animals, but not one was able to be domesticated as draft animals (1998, pp. 157–175).

The type of draft or pack animal used in a given location depended on the local labor market institutions, trade routes, the area's biodiversity, climate, as well as a host of other factors. Many different types of draft animals were used around the world, including reindeer, Indian elephants, water buffalo, dogs, llamas, and camels. However, most people are more familiar with horses, mules, and oxen as draft and pack animals. In Western economies, these three animals made up the bulk of draft animals used. Yet, why were different animals used in different contexts?

The answer to this seemingly simple question has become an area of increasing interest for economic historians. Although there is no simple answer, one can divide it into two parts. The first part deals with an animal's physiological ability to perform the draft or pack duties required. Two examples illustrate this point. First, the llama thrives in the extreme highlands of South America because of its extraordinarily high red blood cell level. This enables the llama to more efficiently use the small amount of oxygen available at high altitudes and is thus essentially the only option available to those living in the region. A second example is the use of camels in desert regions. Their ability to store water internally makes them uniquely qualified to act as draft and pack animals in hot and dry conditions. The second part of the overall answer, and perhaps the more economically interesting, deals with the availability of two or more types of animals. In this case, when there is more than one option, the economic agent must decide which animal to adopt.

In order to understand the economic decision to adopt a particular type of draft animal, one must realize that there is a context in which this decision is made. Many economic and social institutions form the structure of this decision. These institutions include such things as the manner in which labor is organized, cultural norms of behavior, and so on. In addition, while the economic agent, say, the farmer, has a choice between competing types of draft animals, it does not mean that the animals are identical as work animals. An illustrative case involves the choice

PACK ANIMALS. Caravan on a journey through the Pamirs, Central Asia, 1982. (© Roland and Sabrina Michaud/Woodfin Camp and Associates, New York)

faced by farmers in the United States in the late nineteenth and early twentieth centuries. The two main types of draft animals used in the primary agricultural areas (the South and what is now the Midwest) were the horse and the mule. Interestingly, there was a striking pattern in the adoption of the mule and horse in these two areas. The mule was used to a much greater extent in the South than in the North. For instance, in the 1910 U.S. Census of Agriculture there were only six mules for every one hundred horses in the census-defined area covering the upper Midwest. However, in the South the numbers were dramatically different: nearly one mule for every horse used in many areas of the South (1913).

This, of course, raises the question: Why the differential adoption of this form of capital? Although, of course, no theory or explanation can account for the adoption of each and every draft animal, one reason might have been that the existing social and economic institutions in the two areas of the United States helped to determine which type of draft animal was used. For instance, agriculture in the North was organized quite differently than it was in the South. Broadly speaking, the North was characterized by family farms where little outside labor beyond that of the family was used. In the South, however, plantations were common and accounted for a large proportion of the agricultural output of the region. Within the plantation system, labor was hired and remunerated in several ways. Essentially what developed was a hierarchical system of

labor hiring, which became known as the agricultural ladder (Alston and Kauffman, 2001, pp. 372–374). Beginning with the lowest "rung," the categories included the wage worker, sharecropper, share tenant, cash tenant, and owner. The two lowest-ranked occupations (wage worker and sharecropper) essentially only provided their labor services to the production of agricultural output on the plantation. The next two higher-ranked occupations (share tenant and cash tenant) also provided their labor services, as well as increasing amounts of capital (such as draft animals, tools, fertilizers, etc.). At the top, the owner provided all of the inputs to the production of his or her own crops.

On most plantations, wage workers and sharecroppers constituted the majority of workers. Thus, the plantation owner had to provide capital (including draft animals) to most of his workers. This, of course, presented a dilemma for the plantation owner. The owner would issue the capital, say, the draft animal, to the employee who then used the capital on an almost daily basis and often in isolation. In economics, this is referred to as a principal-agent problem. The principal (in this case the plantation owner) wanted to preserve the overall value of the capital (the draft animal). However, because the agent (say, the sharecropper) does not own the animal and is simply using his employer's animal, there is less incentive for the agent to treat the animal with extra care. This is not out of maliciousness but is rather similar to renting a car. Few people treat rental cars as well as they treat their own. Given the principal-agent problem, the principal must decide which type of animal to issue to his employees. Finally, note that Northern farmers largely did not face such a principal-agent problem, given that the people working the draft animals were family members, and thus all who worked the animals also effectively owned them.

One must now look at the choice of draft animals that the farmers in the North and the South had at their disposal: the horse and the mule. From a basic accounting framework, horses and mules are highly substitutable. The amount of raw input, such as feed, and the amount of raw output, such as pulling power, are similar. However, there are a number of significant differences that distinguish the two animals in important ways (1993b). Mules are the sterile hybrid of a male donkey and a female horse. The result is an animal that exhibits traits of both parents as well as others that neither parent possesses. For instance, mules require much less monitoring during feeding time. They will not overeat or overdrink, something that horses can do, which may lead to serious problems, sometimes even death. Also, mules are self-monitoring in terms of their work pace. The stubbornness that mules are famous for is more an internal regulating mechanism that prevents them from exhausting themselves. Again, horses will not refuse to work if tired and, as a result, may fatally harm themselves. These are but two examples of how mules tend to self-monitor, whereas horses need greater care and oversight.

Finally, there was a clear difference in the average price of a horse and a mule. Generally speaking, between 1867 and 1947 mules were between 5 and 20 percent more expensive to purchase than horses (U.S. Bureau of the Census, 1975). This difference, perhaps, partly reflected the self-monitoring aspects of the mule along with other factors, such as the lower fertility levels of mares carrying mule foals.

Therefore, the Southern plantation owner had to issue a draft animal to his or her employee, knowing that the employee would not care for it like it was his own. Given the inherent self-preservation characteristics of the mule, the extra cost often made good economic sense. Although this overarching model of draft animal use is reasonable, one would expect the premium that Southern plantation owners were willing to pay for the mule's "abusability" to be limited at some upper bound. Also, it might have been the case that the monitoring of employees at some of the plantations was extremely good or that the owners had such a good relationship with the workers that they did not need to pay the higher premium for the mules and instead could get by successfully with horses. Or still for other owners, it might have been more cost-effective to use the less expensive horse and suffer the expected losses associated with the agency problem in places where mules were not available or were too expensive.

This one example of draft animal adoption in the United States illustrates how economic factors, when viewed through the lens of existing economic and social institutions—in this case local labor-market hiring practices, were powerful tools in determining the pattern of draft animal use when farmers had a choice of animal to adopt.

Of course, no one explanation is able to depict the whole story; surely other factors were at play as well. Other cultural and economic factors could also help explain the choice of a horse or a mule in particular situations. For instance, once the regional pattern became clear and horses were much more plentiful in the North, perhaps even owners with a large workforce issued horses to their laborers because of a dearth of affordable mules in their area. This does not suggest that the basic model described above is incorrect; it says there are many aspects to a complicated economic system.

Beasts of burden have played an important role in all societies and economies for many millennia. Still today in many parts of the developing world, draft animals are an important input into the workings of a viable economic system. Thus, it is vital to understand the economic reasoning behind their adoption and diffusion. These lessons could help shed light on the adoption and diffusion of many other forms of capital as well.

[*See also* Horses.]

BIBLIOGRAPHY

Alston, Lee J., and Kyle D. Kauffman. "Croppers and Competition: A View from Plantations in the Early Twentieth Century; Were Postbellum Southern Agricultural Labor Markets Competitive?" *Explorations in Economic History* 38 (2001), 181–194.

Diamond, Jared. *Guns, Germs, and Steel.* New York, 1998.

Kauffman, Kyle D. "Why Was the Mule Used in Southern Agriculture?: Empirical Evidence of Principal-Agent Solutions." *Explorations in Economic History* 30 (1993a), 336–351.

Kauffman, Kyle D. "The Use of Draft Animals in America: Economic Factors in the Choice of an Early Motive Power." Ph.D. diss., University of Illinois, 1993b.

United States Bureau of the Census. *Thirteenth Census of the United States: 1910*, vol. 6, *Agriculture*. Washington, D.C., 1913.

United States Bureau of the Census. *Historical Statistics of the United States*. Washington, D.C., 1975.

KYLE D. KAUFFMAN

DRAINAGE AND HYDRAULIC WORKS. *See* Water Engineering.

DUCAT. The ducat was the sole gold coin of Venice from its inception, by edict of the Council of Forty, on 31 October 1284 (but first minted in March 1285), until the introduction of other gold denominations in the early sixteenth century. In the early modern period, the coin continued to be minted under the name *zecchino* with virtually no changes in weight, fineness, or appearance until the end of the Venetian Republic in 1797, and the name *ducat* was applied to a large silver coin. As one of the most important coinages of medieval Europe and the Mediterranean, the ducat served as the prototype for numerous other issues and remained the basis of the accounting system of many states well into the modern era.

Venice was relatively late in issuing a gold coin; for its trade and internal economy from the eighth through most of the thirteenth century, it relied on its own issues of base silver pennies and (after about 1200) fine silver *grossi* and on the gold coins of its Byzantine and Islamic trading partners. In 1252, Florence and Genoa became the first states of northern Italy to issue gold coinage (the florin and the *genovino*, respectively), following the lead of Frederick II and his Norman predecessors in the south. Venice based the standards of the ducat explicitly on those florin, but differences in the weight systems of the two cities resulted in the ducat weighing slightly more than the florin (3.545 modern grams compared with 3.536 grams); both were expected to be made from gold refined as pure as contemporary technology allowed (about 23.875 carats, or 99.47 percent pure). The name *ducat*, signifying a coin issued by a state led by a duke, was applied to the coin almost immediately.

By the time Venice introduced the ducat in 1284–1285, the florin had become established as the standard European gold coin; it was in the eastern Mediterranean that the ducat first established itself. Turkish emirs of Asia Minor issued imitation ducats in the late fourteenth century, and in 1425 the Mamluks of Egypt based their new issues of gold *ashrafi* on it. As Venice expanded its territory and power on the European mainland in the early fifteenth century, the ducat began to rival the florin there as well. It was the basis for the *cruzados* of Portugal struck from newly acquired African bullion and for gold portrait coinages introduced in Milan and Naples in the 1460s and in Aragon in the 1470s. In 1497, Ferdinand and Isabella, as the monarchs of the recently unified kingdom of Spain, established their new coinage of *excelentes* as double ducats.

Within Venice, the ducat became the basis for the local accounting system in the course of the fourteenth century, with a value of $3\frac{1}{5}$ that of the silver-based lira (pound) of account. When the relative value of gold and silver moved apart, the term *ducat* became applied both to the coin and to the value it had held in the local monetary system. The physical coin came to be called the mint ducat or *ducato di zecca*, which was shortened to *zecchino* in the sixteenth century and corrupted into *sequin* in English. By midcentury, new supplies of silver from America and central

Europe, as well as new technology for the striking of large coins, led Venice to issue the silver ducat, a coin of about 33 grams worth $6\frac{2}{5}$ lire of account. The new ducat took its place in the early modern silver-based coinage of thalers, crowns, scudi, and pieces of eight, while the *zecchino* carried on the physical characteristics of the original gold ducat.

[*See also* Money and Coinage, *subentry on* Money and Coinage before 1750.]

BIBLIOGRAPHY

Lane, Frederic C., and C. Reinhold Mueller. *Money and Banking in Medieval and Renaissance Venice*, vol. 1, *Coins and Moneys of Account*. Baltimore, 1985. Traces the monetary background for the ducat, within Europe and the Mediterranean as well as in Venice itself.

Ives, Herbert E., and Philip Grierson. *The Venetian Gold Ducat and Its Imitations*. The American Numismatic Notes and Monographs 128. New York, 1954.

Papadopoli, Nicolò. *Le monete di Venezia*. 4 vols. Venice, 1893–1919. Reprint. Bologna, 1997. The definitive catalog of Venetian coins with much monetary history.

Spufford, Peter. *Money and Its Use in Medieval Europe*. Cambridge, 1988. Presents an excellent overview of the development of European coinage up to about 1500; there is no equivalent work for the modern period.

Stahl, Alan M. *Zecca: The Mint of Venice in the Middle Ages*. Baltimore, 2000. In addition to details on minting, treats the volume of production and the circulation of the Venetian ducat.

ALAN M. STAHL

DUISBERG, CARL (1861–1935), chemist and industrialist.

A celebrated and controversial German chemist and industrialist and godfather of the infamous IG Farben chemicals concern (1925–1945), Carl Friedrich Duisberg rose to prominence in the final decades of the nineteenth century in Bayer & Co., one of the leading German organic chemicals firms, and ended his career as the national spokesman for German big business during the Weimar Republic (1918–1933). In that capacity, he labored unsuccessfully to stem the rise of Nazism and the economic ideology it represented, dying before events revealed that the corporate giant he had helped create was to become a mainstay of the Third Reich's murderous power.

Born in Barmen into the family of a ribbon weaver and educated in chemistry at the universities of Göttingen and Jena, Duisberg owed his prominence to volubility, self-confidence, and boundless energy. He made his reputation early as a creative researcher in Bayer's laboratories, then married Johanne Seebohm (1864–1945), the niece of one of the firm's owners, and went on to plan Bayer's pathbreakingly massive and integrated plant at Leverkusen, on the east bank of the Rhine near Cologne. Influenced by American trust-building, he wrote two persuasive memoranda in 1904 and 1915 that pulled the eight largest

German manufacturers of dyes and other carbon-based chemicals into successive rounds of consolidation. Prior to World War I, he was a prominent advocate of free trade in pressure groups such as the Hansa-Bund, the chemical industry's umbrella association, and in the National Liberal Party; but during the conflict he took a hard-line stance, opposing peace negotiations with the Allies and advocating the conscription of Belgian workers for labor in Germany. Faced in 1918–1919 with both the armistice and the overthrow of the German monarchy, he opted, as he put it, "to save what is saveable" by cooperating with the new republic and accepting the terms of the Versailles treaty.

As the first chairman of IG Farben's supervisory board (1925–1935), and president of the National Association of German Industry (1925–1931), Duisberg was less important to the firm's development than was Carl Bosch (1874–1940), his cofounder from the former BASF corporation; but he stood out as the business world's leading paternalist toward labor and pragmatist in politics. He pioneered in the development of company-subsidized benefit programs and social activities to keep his workers content, even as he criticized the costs of the Weimar Republic's social welfare legislation. A vigorous advocate of the Dawes and Young plans for paying German reparations and of the principle of free trade, he urged German executives to pursue their interests through patient negotiation with their adversaries at home and with the victors of 1918, and to stand by the moderately conservative parties and governments that ruled Germany during the Depression. In 1932, he served as one of the national chairmen of President Hindenburg's reelection campaign against Hitler. Already retired by the time the Nazi führer came to power, in his few public comments or appearances thereafter Duisberg ventured the hope that the "renewal of 1933" would succeed. His activities and views may be traced in his two-volume *Abhandlung, Vorträge und Reden* (Berlin, 1923 and 1933) and his memoir, *Meine Lebenserinnerungen* (Leipzig, 1933).

Though Duisberg, like many other German executives of his era, was often imperious, heavy-handed, and nationalistic, what stands out in his final years are the instances in which contemporaries failed to heed his moderation. He labored unsuccessfully to keep IG Farben a loose and internally competitive federation of firms, to persuade it to abandon the production of fuel from coal that gave the firm and the Nazi regime a common interest, to defeat Hitler's bid for power, and to discredit ideas that Germany could prosper by pursuing autarky, dominance in eastern Europe, or a government-directed economy. However, he also betrayed a reflexive patriotism and a fundamental misunderstanding of democratic politics that made him, and others like him, inept in the face of the demagoguery and ruthlessness of National Socialism.

BIBLIOGRAPHY

Flechtner, Hans-Joachim. *Carl Duisberg—vom Chemiker zum Wirtschaftsführer*. Düsseldorf, 1960.

Haber, L. F. *The Chemical Industry during the Nineteenth Century*. Oxford, 1958.

Haber, L. F. *The Chemical Industry, 1900–1930*. Oxford, 1971.

Hayes, Peter. *Industry and Ideology: IG Farben in the Nazi Era*. New York, 1987, 2001.

PETER HAYES

DUKE, JAMES BUCHANAN (1856–1925), American industrialist and philanthropist.

James Buchanan Duke was born on 23 December 1856 in Orange County, North Carolina. Early details are sketchy, but by his twenties Duke had become a partner in the family firm W. Duke, Sons and Company. During the early 1880s, the firm expanded into production of newly popular cigarettes. Problems arose as an 1883 tax decrease from $1.75 to $0.50 per thousand cigarettes caused retailers to withhold orders. While competitors hesitated, Duke cut his price in half, provided that retailers agreed to accept at least three-quarters of the shipment after 1 May, when the tax decrease went into effect. The retailers bought thousand of cigarettes from Duke. In 1884, Duke, as president of W. Duke, Sons and Company, negotiated a contract with the Bonsack Machine Company for the use of a cigarette-manufacturing machine. Several other companies had contracted with Bonsack or other companies for such machines, but the early machines were very unreliable. Duke's engineers improved their machines' performance, and Duke soon negotiated for its exclusive use.

Later based in New York, Duke, using his company's cost advantage and clever advertising, captured an increasing share of the cigarette market during the 1880s. By 1890, Duke successfully organized a number of competitors into the American Tobacco Company. As president of American Tobacco, he created an enormous corporation that used economies of scale and scope, national advertising, advanced accounting methods, and complicated contracts with distributors to dominate first cigarettes and then the entire tobacco industry. Success in the United States led Duke to Europe, where American Tobacco joined with British tobacco manufacturers in 1902 to form British-American Tobacco.

Between 1904 and 1912, Duke was extremely busy, both personally and professionally. In 1904, Duke married Lillian McCreedy. In 1905, he established the Southern Power Company with his brother Benjamin N. Duke and their longtime associate George W. Watts. In 1906, he divorced McCreedy; and in 1907 he was remarried, to Nanaline Holt Inman. Beginning around 1907, American Tobacco was coming under increasing scrutiny from the

JAMES BUCHANAN DUKE. Portrait (c. 1922) by John da Costa (1867–1931). (National Portrait Gallery, Smithsonian Institution, Washington, D.C./Art Resource, NY)

federal Bureau of Competition because of its enormous market share and allegedly unscrupulous business practices. Reports of these business practices diminished, but federal and state antitrust cases wore on, culminating in 1911 in the U.S. Supreme Court's dissolution of American Tobacco. Interestingly, the Court allowed Duke to design the breakup of American Tobacco into four companies. His division allowed the four—R. J. Reynolds, American Tobacco, Pierre Lorillard, and Liggett & Myers—to remain dominant, so much so that in the 1940s the government brought another antitrust suit against the four companies. In 1912, Duke's only child, Doris, was born.

After 1912, with his tobacco career largely behind him, Duke focused his efforts on electrical power and philanthropic efforts. In the electrical realm, much of his effort was directed toward development of hydroelectric power on the Saguenay River in Quebec, an enormous project. The best-known of his philanthropic efforts were the Duke Endowment and Duke University, the former established in 1924 to fund educational and religious charities in the Carolinas. A significant benefactor of the Duke Endowment was Trinity College, founded as Brown's schoolhouse in 1838. With Duke's blessing, Trinity was renamed Duke University after his father and his family. In 1925, Duke died in New York at age sixty-eight.

BIBLIOGRAPHY

Burns, Malcolm R. "Outside Intervention in Monopolistic Price Warfare: The Case of the 'Plug War' and the Union Tobacco Company." *Business History Review* 56.1 (1982), 33–53.

Burns, Malcolm R. "Economies of Scale in Tobacco Manufacture." *Journal of Economic History* 43.2 (1983), 461–474.

Burns, Malcolm R. "Predatory Pricing and the Acquisition Cost of Competitors." *Journal of Political Economy* 94.2 (1986), 266–298.

Campbell, Tracy. *The Politics of Despair: Power and Resistance in the Tobacco Wars.* Lexington, Ky., 1993.

Cooper, Patricia A. *Once a Cigar Maker: Men, Women, and Work Culture in American Cigar Factories, 1900–1919.* Urbana, Ill., 1987.

Cunningham, Bill. *On Bended Knees: The Night Rider Story.* Nashville, Tenn., 1983.

Duke, B. N. Papers, Benjamin Duke Collection. Duke University, Durham, N.C.

Duke (James Buchanan) Papers, 1777–1990. *Register of the James Buchanan Duke Papers, 1777–1990.* <htpp://scriptorium.lib.duke.edu/dynaweb/findaids/dukejb/>.

Durden, Robert Franklin. *The Dukes of Durham.* Durham, N.C., 1975.

Durden, Robert Franklin. *A Lasting Legacy to the Carolinas: The Duke Endowment, 1924–1994.* Durham, N.C., 1998.

Jacobstein, Meyer. *The Tobacco Industry in the United States.* New York, 1907.

Jenkins, John Wilber. *James B. Duke, Master Builder.* New York, 1927.

Massell, David Parera. "Amassing Power: J. B. Duke and the Saguenay River, 1897–1927." *Studies on the History of Quebec.* Montreal, 2000.

Nall, James O. *The Tobacco Night Riders of Kentucky and Tennessee, 1905–1909.* Louisville, Ky., 1939.

Porter, P. G. "Origins of the American Tobacco Company." *Business History Review* 43.1 (1969), 59–76.

Scott, J. "No Monopoly on Freedom: A Study of the American Tobacco Company from 1890 to 1911." Senior honors thesis, Duke University, Durham, N.C.,1990.

Tennant, Richard B. *The American Cigarette Industry: A Study in Economic Analysis and Public Policy.* New Haven, 1950.

Tilley, Nannie M. *The R. J. Reynolds Tobacco Company.* Chapel Hill, N.C., 1985.

U.S. Bureau of Corporations. *Report of the Commissioner of Corporations on the Tobacco Industry.* 3 vols. Washington, D.C., 1909–1915.

U.S. Bureau of Corporations. U.S. National Archives. Records of the Federal Trade Commission. Record Group 122. "Files of the Bureau of Corporations."

U.S. Industrial Commission. *Report of the Industrial Commission on Trusts and Industrial Combinations*, vol. 9. Washington, D.C., 1901.

KAREN CLAY

DUNLOP, JOHN (1840–1921), Scottish inventor.

Dunlop's significance was as the inventor of a pneumatic cycle tire, patented in Britain in 1888, and a detachable pneumatic tire, in 1891. Although the 1888 patent was swiftly undermined by the rediscovery of Robert W. Thomson's 1845 patent, it provided the basis for the establishment of the Dunlop Rubber Company, one of the industry's leading multinational enterprises during the twentieth century.

John Boyd Dunlop was born on 5 February 1840 in Dreghorn, a lowland Scottish village, into a farming family. He attended the local school and then boarded at

Irvine's Academy in Edinburgh and continued his education at Edinburgh University, where he qualified as a veterinary surgeon in 1859. In 1867, Dunlop migrated to Belfast, establishing a veterinary practice in Gloucester Street that apparently flourished and, reputedly, remained his principal source of income. Dunlop married in 1876 and he and his wife had a son, Johnny, whose tricycle served in the early tire experiments, and a daughter, Jean, who published a volume of her father's memoirs in 1923.

Dunlop began experimenting with air-filled, or pneumatic, tires in 1887, wrapping canvas around an air-tube and fixing it onto a wooden wheel. There was a famous trial in the backyard of the Dunlop home to compare the prototype pneumatic tire with a conventional solid-rubber tire, then used on carriages and cycles. On 28 February 1888, two pneumatic tires were tested on Johnny Dunlop's tricycle during a late-night ride in Belfast. In July 1888, Dunlop applied for a patent for the tire, which was granted on 7 December 1888. To exploit his patent, Dunlop contracted with the North British Rubber Company, based in Edinburgh, to supply tires that were sold on bicycles through Edlin and Company, cycle makers in Belfast.

As with many cycle innovations, demonstrated successes in local cycle races publicized the value of the novel tires. Moreover, through racing circles, Dunlop met William Harvey DuCros, who would be the key entrepreneur in the formation and the expansion of the Dunlop tire business. DuCros became managing director of the Pneumatic Tyre and Booth's Cycle Agency, with Dunlop as a stockholder and director, in 1889. The inventor agreed to sell his patent for £500 plus £3,000 in stock in the business. Effective control passed fully to DuCros, however, as he bought out the original business. Dunlop continued to promote the new tire and developed a dozen additional patents, notably those for a cushion tire (1890) and a detachable rim design (1891). By 1890, however, competitors had undercut the value of Dunlop's original patent by making use of Thomson's "aerial wheel" patent of 1845, which embodied the principle of an elastic tube for a tire.

With the original competitive advantage lost, DuCros defended the company's position by acquiring other rim patents, which were important for tires that were secure but not impossible to replace. He also purchased a rubber works in Birmingham in 1896, beginning the firm's crucial move into tire, and general rubber goods, production rather than simply cycle assembly. Subsequent financial dealings and commercial success in adding motor-tire manufacture built Dunlop into the dominant British rubber company and a major international force. John Boyd Dunlop played no role in this phase, having moved to Dublin in 1892 and resigned from the company in 1895, selling his stock in the business. The business continued to bear his name and to use the story of his invention, and

his son's cycle ride, in its advertising, but Dunlop resented aspects of his portrayal. He continued to be acknowledged as a major inventor, attended cycle events, and was guest of honor at a cycle and motor trade dinner in 1909. Dunlop maintained local business interests in Dublin, where he died on 23 October 1921, a year after his son's death.

BIBLIOGRAPHY

Donnithorne, Andrey G. *British Rubber Manufacturing: An Economic Study of Innovations*. London, 1958. A systematic appraisal of innovations, including tire designs.

DuCros, Arthur. *Wheels of Fortune: A Salute to Pioneers*. London, 1938. Early Dunlop history by one of the key early entrepreneurs.

Jennings, Paul. *Dunlopera: The Work and Workings of the Dunlop Rubber Company*. London, 1961. A broad history produced by the company.

Schidrowitz, Philip, and Thomas R. Dawson. *History of the Rubber Industry*. Cambridge, 1952. Comprehensive overview of the international rubber industry and trade.

MICHAEL FRENCH

DU PONT FAMILY. The du Pont family was one of America's richest and most influential industrial dynasties in the past two centuries. Emigrating from France to the United States in the beginning of the nineteenth century, the family established a small mill that produced gunpowder, which soon became the largest in the country. The founder's sons and grandsons subsequently diversified the company's operation, eventually making DuPont the largest chemical corporation in the United States.

The father of the family, Pierre S. du Pont de Nemours (1739–1817), was a French economist and politician. He served as inspector general of commerce and was granted by Louis XVI a patent of nobility for his efforts to achieve freer trade among France, Great Britain, and the United States. Pierre was active in the French Revolution before he immigrated to America in 1800 with plans to establish a self-sufficient colony. Once in the United States, he advised President Jefferson to purchase the Louisiana Territory from France instead of fighting over it, contributing to the conclusion of a Franco-American treaty in 1803.

His son, Éleuthère Irénée (1771–1834), who apprenticed in France under the famous chemist Antoine-Laurent Lavoisier, soon discovered that the gunpowder market in the United States was underdeveloped and founded a powder plant on the Brandywine River in Delaware. Although the new company grew rapidly, it soon found itself with large debts. Sales increased during the War of 1812, as DuPont was a major supplier of gunpowder to the United States. Ironically, this was not the last time a war saved the company. Irénée later served as a director of the Bank of the United States.

Upon Irénée's death, his son-in-law led the company for three years before the founder's children took control and managed the family business as a partnership. Between 1837 and 1850, Alfred Victor, Irénée's eldest son, was the manager in practice. His younger brother, Henry du Pont (1812–1889), succeeded him and led the company from 1850 to 1889. "Boss Henry," as he was nicknamed, and his chemist nephew Lammot du Pont (1831–1884), were both in charge of the company's remarkable success in the second half of the nineteenth century. The Civil War in America, which created huge demand for gunpowder, together with the development of railroads in the Midwest were external events that sparked DuPont's growth. But growth also came from within. In 1857, Lammot patented the "soda powder," making the production of powder cheaper and more reliable. In 1880, he founded Repauno, a chemical company designed to produce the powerful explosive dynamite, which was invented by the Swedish manufacturer Alfred Nobel. By that time, DuPont was dominating the explosives industry. Upon Henry's death, Eugene du Pont (1840–1902) became the head of the family business. Under him, the company did relatively well but didn't grow much. He lacked the energy and power of his uncle and was unable to rule the business and the family as Henry did.

The beginning of the twentieth century saw a decline of the DuPont empire. The board of directors had decided to sell the company when Alfred du Pont, together with his cousins Thomas Coleman and Pierre du Pont (1870–1954), all under forty, purchased it for a low price. Complementing each other in skills, the three cousins turned the family partnership into a corporation and further centralized the explosives industry. This led to the first, albeit not the last, antitrust suit for violation of the Sherman Act. In 1913, an agreement was reached, under which the company was to split into three. Nevertheless, this traumatic experience, together with the recognition that the war-created demand for explosives was short-lived, revealed the company's need for diversification. By 1919, when Pierre resigned as president, DuPont had transformed itself from an explosives company to a diversified chemical enterprise. Based on existing materials (e.g., nitrocellulose) that could be used both in production of explosives and in other nonmilitary chemicals, the company moved into the fields of solvents and paints, celluloid film, artificial leather, and automobiles. In 1917, acquiring the basic technology from a British company, DuPont entered the dyestuff field and became the largest company in the industry a decade later, reducing U.S. dependence on European production. The two factors making the diversification strategy possible were the huge profits from World War I, during which DuPont was the largest supplier of military explosives, and the successful investment in General Motors.

After resigning, Pierre engaged in philanthropic activities and headed a reform in Delaware's public school system to improve attendance in the state's schools. He spent $5 million on Delaware schools and $2 million on the local college, which later became the University of Delaware. Pierre's brother and successor, Irénée du Pont, contributed generously to the Red Cross and other relief programs for war victims. He also made contributions to medical research and to hospitals.

The 1920s witnessed growth and expansion of the DuPont Company. In 1923, DuPont, together with two French firms, began producing cellophane and artificial silk. The company further developed (through Charles F. Kettering, GM's head of research) tetraethyl lead, which reduced the "engine knock" in automobile engines, and quick-drying lacquers for automobiles. By the mid-1920s, DuPont had penetrated the photographic, glass, and U.S. rubber industries. When entering a new field, DuPont's strategy was to approach the leading firm in the industry, then integrate with it or buy its partner. Irénée's younger brother, Lammot du Pont, became president in 1925 and headed a policy of basic internal research. By the mid-1930s, DuPont's own scientists had developed a synthetic rubber, neoprene, and a synthetic fiber, nylon, which had both civilian and military uses. In 1943, Teflon, a heat-resistant plastic, was invented and was used in raincoats, exhaust systems of airplanes and autos, pots and pans, and coated metals. The 1950s and 1960s saw the beginning of heavy foreign investment by the company as well as the development of polyester, wrinkle-resistant synthetics, flame-resistant fabric, and other materials.

The role of the du Pont family in the corporation diminished over time. In the mid-1970s, a director outside of the family was appointed for the first time, and family members represented only 20 percent of the board. Once a company controlled by the family, it is now a conventional corporation.

BIBLIOGRAPHY

Carr, William H. A. *The DuPonts of Delaware*. New York, 1964.
Dorian, Max. *The DuPonts: From Gunpowder to Nylon*. Translated by Edward B. Garside. Boston, 1962.
Duke, Marc. *The DuPonts: Portrait of a Dynasty*. New York, 1976.
Gates, John D. *The DuPont Family*. New York, 1979.
Landau Arora, Ashish, Ralph, and Nathan Rosenberg, eds. *Chemicals and Long-Term Economic Growth: Insights from the Chemical Industry*. New York, 1998.
Taylor, Graham D., and Patricia E. Sundik. *Du Pont and the International Chemical Industry*. Boston, 1984.
Wilkinson, Norman B. *Lammot du Pont and the American Explosives Industry, 1850–1884*. Charlottesville, Va., 1984.

RAN ABRAMITZKY

DYE CROPS. The production of textiles answers a basic need of mankind. Coloring textiles answers further universal needs: aesthetic, symbolic. It implies the discovery of coloring matters and techniques of application suited to the great variety of fibers. Before the 1856 invention of the first synthetic dye, mauve, by the young English chemist Sir William Henry Perkin, most dyes were extracted from plants and animals (mollusks, insects). Since each one contained little coloring matter, large numbers were needed. They had to be collected in their natural environment, or cultivated, or reared (cochineal, lac-dye insects).

The first solution prevailed until the development of textile industries in various parts of the world gave dye sources a strategic importance in international policies and made the large-scale cultivation of selected dye plants necessary to ensure a regular supply. Sources of fast yellow, red, and blue dyes—the three basics of the dyer's art—such as weld, madder, and indigo plants were the first and the last to be cultivated. But many natural dyes could not or did not need to be cultivated. New stations of purple-producing seashells and orchil lichens had to be looked for ever further from the antique centers of their use in the eastern Mediterranean, where they were becoming rare.

On the contrary, a great variety of dyes were plentiful: brown, gray, and black shades were obtained from many tannin-rich trees and bushes. Yellow dyes, present in most herbs and leaves, also were gathered in wastelands. The best among the most abundant were chosen. These included dyers' broom or greenweed, which until the nineteenth century was an important source of income for the poor of Bristol, who supplied it to the dyers of the town. Following the discovery of America and sub-Saharan Africa by the Europeans, such dye woods as old fustic and logwood from Central America, quercitron from North America, brazil-wood from Brazil, and barwood and camwood from Africa brought a mass of new, cheap coloring matters mostly procured by careless exploitation of natural forests. Especially after the Industrial Revolution, the huge textile industries of Europe and North America relied more and more on these imports: around 1895, they were devouring 305,000 tons of logwood yearly.

Agriculture provided not only complements, but important ingredients. Weld, which gave the fastest and most beautiful European yellow dye, was cultivated from Roman times and figures among the archaeo-botanical remains of Viking York. It was a major crop in the south of France (Languedoc) and in Italy (Marches, Puglia) by the fourteenth century. Just before Perkin's breakthrough, France, then the first producer in the world, yearly exported hundreds of tons of dry plant on top of its own, far greater, consumption. Fast bright reds were extracted from the roots of madders (*Rubia*) in the Old World, of related plants (*Galium, Relbunium*) in North and South America. Dyers' madder was the species most widely cultivated, spreading from the Middle East to Mediterranean Europe in Roman times.

The rise of numerous centers of woolen-cloth industry in medieval Europe stimulated its cultivation in regions where it survived to this day (the Netherlands, southern France) or flourished more briefly (Lombardy in North Italy, during the twelfth to thirteenth centuries). Associated economic activities also developed including drying installations (recorded since the fourteenth century in Bruges and Lille) and the grinding of the roots in wind or water mills. Within the Muslim world, the diversity and high level of textile production during the medieval ages encouraged the cultivation of madder in many regions. From the tenth to the sixteenth centuries, the countries around the Caspian Sea and Yemen also exported it to India, whose production of dyed and printed cotton cloth needed even more red dyes than available on the sub-continent.

Fast blues equal indigo, indispensable also because blue shades are the basis for greens, purples, grays, browns, and black. Indigo is prepared from many different plants, grown from America to eastern Asia. In Europe, its only indigenous source was woad, *Isatis tinctoria*. By the end of the medieval ages, whole regions in present-day England, Belgium, Germany, Italy, Spain, and France were dedicated to its intensive cultivation, using manure and repeated hoeing and weeding. The leaves were crushed in mills and transformed into woad balls and couched woad, concentrated in indigo through a process of double fermentation. Vast quantities were traded all over Europe.

In the sixteenth century, the most prominent woad millionaires, the de Bernuys, emigrés from Burgos to Toulouse, yearly dealt with 1,790 tons of processed woad. This economy did not collapse, as was previously thought, with the growing imports of Indian indigo resulting from the discovery of direct sea routes around Africa: It declined progressively because woad was used to start the indigo vats used in the woolen-cloth industry until the adoption of synthetic indigo around 1900.

Exotic indigo, extracted from *Indigofera* plants, first came mostly from India, where it was cultivated from Vedic times, and from the Muslim world, where its cultivation spread westward to southern Spain and Morocco. In the seventeenth to eighteenth centuries, the colonial systems established by the Spanish, English, and French in America and the West Indies ensured the supremacy of their indigo, produced in large plantations, mostly by slave labor (four African slaves per five acres, from an English source of the time). During the nineteenth century, India, under British rule, regained its ancient leadership in indigo production.

The evolution of the dye-supply policy in industrialized societies thus reveals the leading part natural dyes played in the development of an intensive agriculture focused on cash crops. It also reveals the durable dependence of a major industry on wild natural resources, with consequences yet to be fully evaluated.

BIBLIOGRAPHY

Balfour-Paul, Jenny. *Indigo*. London, 1998. Scholarly synthesis and very beautiful book on of the most fascinating natural dyes. Extensive bibliography.

Cardon, Dominique. *Le monde des teintures naturelles*. Paris, 2003.

Cardon, Dominique. *The World of Natural Dyes*. London, forthcoming.

Chenciner, Robert. *Madder Red*. London, 2000. Enthusiastic study of another mythic dye, especially useful by the publication in appendices of hardly accessible Russian sources.

DOMINIQUE CARDON

E

EAST AFRICA *[This entry contains two subentries, on the economic history of East Africa during the precolonial period and during the colonial and modern periods.]*

Precolonial Period

Continental East Africa, covering the modern states of Kenya, Uganda, and Tanzania, is broadly divisible geographically as well as historically between the high plateau and the narrow coastal fringe. Before the eighteenth century the two regions developed somewhat independently in terms of their economic history, but they were deeply integrated with the development of the world capitalist economy after the middle of the eighteenth century.

East Africa has been described as the cradle of mankind, and it was inhabited by bands of hunters and gatherers until the late Stone Age. There has been some debate about the dynamics of change in the precolonial period. Contrary to the views of Thomas Malthus, who argued that population growth was dependent on inelastic agricultural productivity, Ester Boserup proposes that with population growth there was a progressive development of technology to increase productivity of the land, which in turn led to elaboration of land tenure and social and political systems.

Domestication of certain plants and animals and introduction of others, notably bananas, from as far as Southeast Asia and later maize from the Americas permitted the development of pastoralism and agriculture in East Africa. Within the last three millennia late Stone Age agriculturists from Ethiopia, Nilotic pastoralists, and Bantu-speaking Iron Age agriculturists etablished new food production systems to exploit the varied and sometimes marginal environments. There was considerable development of iron and other industries and the exchange of such essential commodities as hoes and salt over considerable distances. Highly centralized kingdoms developed in certain favorable areas, especially around Lake Victoria, where reliable rainfall coupled with mixed agriculture permitted the production of adequate surplus to support craft specialization and the emergence of ruling classes.

The coast was also populated by Cushitic- and Bantu-speaking peoples, but for more than two thousand years it also has looked out to the sea, trading with South Arabia and Egypt during the Roman period. Following the rise of Islam there was an enormous expansion of transoceanic trade with Arabia and beyond. Although the hinterland was somewhat limited by the harsh Nyika bushland in Kenya, deeper linkages were established further south between Mozambique and the gold fields of Zimbabwe. Based on the export of ivory, slaves, gold, foodstuffs, and mangrove poles and the import of Indian cloth and chinaware, a mercantile Swahili civilization developed along the coast. It attained a high level of material achievement, and some city-states, such as Kilwa and Zanzibar, even minted their own copper and silver coins from the eleventh century.

This civilization came to grief during the sixteenth century, when it was brutally but only partially integrated into the Portuguese seaborne empire, but its commercial links with the northern rim of the Indian Ocean were never completely broken. The Portuguese were eventually expelled at the end of the seventeenth century by the Swahili and their Omani allies.

During the eighteenth century small numbers of slaves were exported by the Arabs to supply date plantations and pearl fisheries in Oman and the Persian Gulf. During the last third of the century they were joined by the French, who wanted to supply their sugar islands in the southwestern Indian Ocean. However, the Napoleonic wars, culminating in the capture of Mauritius by the British in 1810, disrupted the export of slaves to the south. Slave trade to the south was prohibited in 1822 and to the north in 1845, while all slave trade by sea was embargoed in 1873.

Faced with the collapse of external markets, traders diverted the slaves to the internal market to develop clove plantations on Zanzibar and the production of sesame on the coast of Kenya for export to Europe. Thus all efforts to restrict the export of slaves from East Africa had the ironical effect of internalizing the slave economy with a much greater potential for expansion. By the 1860s more than twenty thousand slaves reached the coast annually, but a small proportion of them was smuggled to areas outside East Africa. Most were captured in the southern hinterland between the coast and Lake Malawi. As areas closer to the coast were depopulated, traders pushed deeper into the interior, effectively integrating the two regions.

119

The second sector of the economy was commerce. With the fruition of the Industrial Revolution came an enormous increase in the demand in Europe and North America for ivory to manufacture piano keys and cutlery handles and gum copal to produce varnish. The price of ivory rose steadily throughout the nineteenth century, and by 1859 Zanzibar exported 250 tons of ivory annually. The main imports were manufactured goods, especially textiles, metal wires, and guns, whose prices declined as a result of mechanization. The diverging price curve was a powerful engine for growth of the caravan trade, which integrated the coast with the deep African interior.

Zanzibar emerged as the capital of a vast commercial empire based on the twin foundations of plantation agriculture and commerce. To centralize trade in Zanzibar, Sultan Said (1806–1856) set up a customs structure that prohibited foreign merchants from trading directly on the mainland, taxed heavily the most productive central part of the coast to collect maximum revenue, and charged coastal traders lower duties to facilitate their penetration into the interior in competition with the African traders. Thus Zanzibar became a prosperous entrepôt where foreign diplomatic missions and firms were based.

This, however, was a commercial empire without an elaborate administrative or military structure to sustain it in the face of determined colonial expansion. Between 1885 and 1890 the whole hinterland of Zanzibar was partitioned between the colonial powers, and Zanzibar itself was declared a British protectorate in 1890. This was followed by what Helge Kjekshus describes as an ecological disaster as a result of the colonial wars, a rinderpest epidemic, and various human diseases and famines that followed in the wake of colonial expansion. The noted demographer R. R. Kuczynski concluded that the population of the region actually declined during the early colonial period.

BIBLIOGRAPHY

Boserup, Ester. *The Conditions of Agricultural Growth.* London, 1965.
Iliffe, John. *A Modern History of Tanganyika.* Cambridge, 1979.
Kjekshus, Helge. *Ecology Control and Economic Development in East African History.* London, 1977; 2d impression, 1996.
Kuczynski, R. R. *Demographic Survey of the British Colonial Empire.* 2 vols. London, 1949.
Malthus, Thomas Robert. *An Essay in Population.* London, 1798; reprint, London, 1960.
Oliver, Roland. "The East African Interior." In *The Cambridge History of Africa,* edited by Roland Oliver, vol. 3, pp. 621–669. Cambridge, 1977.
Sheriff, Abdul M. H. "Tanzanian Societies at the Time of the Partition." In *Tanzania under Colonial Rule,* edited by M. H. Y. Kaniki, pp. 11–50. London, 1979.
Sheriff, Abdul M. H. "Social Formations in Pre-Colonial Kenya." In *Kenya in the Nineteenth Century,* edited by Bethwell A. Ogot, pp. 1–32. Nairobi, Kenya, 1985.
Sheriff, Abdul M. H. *Slaves, Spices, and Ivory in Zanzibar.* London, 1987.
Sutton, John E. G. *A Thousand Years of East Africa.* Nairobi, Kenya, 1990.
Zwanenberg, Roger, and A. King. *An Economic History of Kenya and Uganda.* London, 1975.

ABDUL SHERIFF

Colonial and Modern Periods

The economic history of East Africa encompasses the economies of the mainland states of Kenya, Tanzania, and Uganda and Madagascar, Mauritius, and Seychelles on the Indian Ocean. These states were incorporated into the European colonial economy at different periods. However, by 1900 all of them had come under formal colonialism. A unique feature of East African colonial economy was that the states were ruled by only two colonial administrations: the mainland by Britain (Tanganyika was transferred from Germany to Britain during World War I) and the islands by France. Thus the two groups of states were governed like federations, thereby encouraging a high level of cooperation across national boundaries as well as the implementation of similar economic objectives. By 1960, for example, the per capita income was £26.3 in Kenya, £22.7 in Uganda, and £17.2 in Tanzania. The estimated population at the time was 8.1 million in Kenya, 6.7 million in Uganda, and 10.3 million in Tanzania.

Agricultural Economy. The foundation of the East African colonial economy was laid in the period between 1896 and 1920. During this period measures such as direct taxation and wage employment were introduced to shift the economy to one that better served colonial needs. Except in Seychelles, agriculture was the mainstay of the economy. The colonial economy began around 1896 with the construction of the East African railway from Mombasa in Kenya to Kisumu on Lake Victoria in Uganda. The main aim of the £8 million project was to tap the rich resources of Kenya and Uganda agricultural fields. With the completion of the railway, the government embarked on an export drive geared toward the production of sisal, coffee, and tea in Kenya and cotton in Uganda. Two major agricultural systems operated in East Africa. The most widespread was peasant agriculture, in which small-scale farms were established. These farms were worked by family labor, and the main target was to produce enough for the family and a small surplus for sale. On these farms men were generally responsible for the initial clearing of land, while cultivation of food crops was left to the women. The second type of agriculture was plantation farming. Since African farmers were not producing enough materials and parts of Kenya were considered suitable for European habitation, British settlers in large numbers moved into the most fertile parts of Kenya. White settlement was backed up with the 1915 Ordinance, which allowed each settler to occupy a plot for a period of ninety-nine years. Settlers increased from about one hundred in 1910 to two thousand in 1935 and four thousand in 1953. The settlers occupied parts of the Kenyan highlands, and the original Kikuyu occupants were forced out. The process of land alienation increased white-owned estates from 4.5 million acres in 1915 to 7.3 million acres in 1953. Each farmer had an average of twenty-four hundred acres. The government also introduced various measures to make labor available on white farms. For instance, Africans were prevented from producing export crops. In 1923 the Tariff Amendment Ordinance placed protective duties on a wide range of temperate-climate foodstuffs produced on white-owned farms. Also the hut and poll taxes paid by Africans were raised from ten to sixteen Kenyan shillings, while white settlers paid virtually no tax. In addition a 70 percent tariff was imposed on imports, while exports attracted only a 30 percent tariff. These measures created a demand for cash on the part of Africans, and since they received low prices for their crops, they were forced to work for wages.

Besides land alienation and policies geared toward labor supply, white settlers also raided the Masai and Nandi Districts for livestock. For example, in 1905 they raided about 50,000 cows and 600,000 sheep and goats, which the owners were compelled to sell at cheap prices to white farmers. In between peasant and plantation farms were farms owned by Asians and some wealthy Africans. These farms were always bigger than the peasant farms but not as capital intensive as the plantations. In Uganda, for example, Asian farms dominated sugar production. Apart from farm size, another difference in these farms was that, while the plantations specialized in specific crops, peasant farmers tended to cultivate several crops on their farms.

Racial discrimination had important implications for agriculture. In 1913 Africans produced about 70 percent of exports, but this fell to only 20 percent in 1928. As shown above, plantation farmers' preferences for export crops further tilted economic advantages in their favor. Shortly after World War I wages and prices of goods paid to African farmers were reduced. In Kenya this led to pockets of protests. For instance, Harry Thuku founded the Young Kikuyu Association, which demanded the abolition of the newly introduced pass system, the reduction of the poll tax, and the return of Kikuyu lands. These demands did not last long, as the 1920s brought an era of economic boom arising from expanded production and good wages.

In Nyanza Province of Kenya cotton production rose from one million pounds in 1930 to twenty-four million pounds in 1937–1938. During the depression of 1929–1930 Kenya farmers, unlike those in Uganda and Tanganyika, suffered less because the capitalist farmers received support from financiers who moved in quickly to protect their investments. One of the ways of cushioning the effects of the depression was to alleviate the debt burden of capital farmers, which enabled them to carry on with production.

In contrast, peasant farmers were increasingly turned into laborers on white farms.

World War II had a huge impact on Kenyan white farmers' coffee production. For instance, the value of coffee production dropped from about 40 percent to only 20 percent of domestic exports. But this was still much better than the 10 percent for Uganda and 7 percent for Tanganyika. Efforts were made between 1945 and 1960 to revive agricultural production. Over £46 million were invested in the Kenyan highlands through private and public finance, making possible a considerable increase in agricultural output. Reforms included further land alienation and increased peasantization of African farmers. Farm extensions and their implications for landholdings and labor supply triggered the Maumau revolt of the early 1950s. In 1953 the East African Royal Commission was appointed to inquire into the conditions of land tenure and use. After the commission reported, small landowners were ordered to consolidate their lands into larger units to produce more. By the 1950s white farmers produced about 95 percent of Kenyan agricultural exports or one-third of the total farm output.

In Uganda there was no conscious effort at racial discrimination, but the economy produced some results similar to those in Kenya. Government agricultural drive was geared toward cotton and coffee production. Unlike in Kenya, plantation agriculture and white farms were few, and where they existed, they were smallholdings. For example, Uganda plantations averaged 40,000 hectares in the 1960s, compared with 200,000 hectares in Kenya and 300,000 hectares in Tanzania. The colonial government in Uganda had little trouble coercing the peasant labor force by means of taxation and other measures, because, according to British colonial policy, each territory must pay for its own development.

Owing to the unreliability of the American cotton supply, Britain opted to establish the British Cotton Growers Association (BCGA) with a take-off capital of £500,000. Subsequently the Kenya-Uganda railway line was built, along which buying stations and ginning and baling factories were established. Therefore cotton growing benefited the textile industries, the iron and steel manufacturing companies, the banks, the merchants, and other small British businesses servicing the big monopolies, the colonial bureaucracy, and the clergy, who shared the surplus produced by the peasants. For example, the BCGA imported 1.5 tons of three different types of cottonseed that were distributed through the chiefs to peasant farmers in Buganda, Busoga, and Bunyoro. In return European investors set up gins in major locations. The use of African agents resulted in high cotton harvests. Uganda produced about 1,000 bales of cotton in 1905–1906, but this rose to 222,000 bales in 1916, 180,000 bales

INDIAN TROOPS IN EAST AFRICA. Large-scale production of iron and steel at the renowned Indian firm of Tata, early 1940s. Like Tuaregs, the veiled men of the Sahara, the workers cover their faces to protect themselves from the heat given off by the sheets of red hot metal which litter the floor of the mill. (Prints and Photographs Division, Library of Congress)

in 1926, and 420,000 bales in 1965. In 1904 Uganda exported cotton to the tune of £43,000, but this increased to £307,000 in 1911. As a result government revenue rose from £60,000 in 1904–1905 to £191,000 in 1910–1911. Those who benefited were involved in shipping, insurance, and banking.

Efforts by white farmers to establish themselves in Uganda failed, because Africans were able to grow coffee at a much cheaper cost. Arabica coffee was first tried on Mount Elgon in 1912 among the Bagisu peasants and later among the Bamba in the west. By 1929 Uganda was prosperous in its peasant economy. As late as the 1950s Uganda was one of the major producers of coffee and cotton in the commonwealth. As in Tanganyika, the Asian merchants (Ralli Brothers) were active in the cotton trade in Uganda. In Uganda as well Asian traders were the intermediaries between the producers and monopoly buyers. However, after World War II, the British Ministry of Food and the British India Office, like in Tanganyika, set up Agricultural Marketing Boards through which they bought Uganda's coffee and cotton. The target of the boards was to stabilize prices by preventing sharp price fluctuations. In reality, however, the boards paid low prices to the farmers and

helped the government rake in what they considered excess profit to farmers, which was retained in a stabilzation fund. In this manner, the Ugandan government realized £10.55 million between 1940 and 1948. The fund increased to £119 million by 1960, which meant that about half the price that should have been paid to Ugandan producers accrued to the colonial government.

In Tanganyika (modern Tanzania) prior to German colonization, the natives were focused on the production of food for subsistence. The Germans built a railway line from Tanga to Usumbara between 1893 and 1905. Another line was built between Dar es Salaam and Mongoro between 1905 and 1907. Between 1907 and 1912 the line was extended to Lake Tanganyika and Mount Kilimanjaro. To pay for these projects, taxes were raised and new agricultural rules were introduced to encourage the production of cotton, rubber, coffee, groundnuts, tea, and sisal. This was to reduce Germany's dependence upon North America, and Mexican products. Cotton production suffered a major setback in 1905, when low prices, taxation, and drought led to a poor cotton yield. This degenerated into local discontent, manifested in the Majimaji uprising. During the revolt many farmers destroyed their cotton farms and attacked several colonial infrastructures. As soon as the revolt was suppressed, cotton production was resumed, and in the 1940s and 1950s it employed over 70 percent of the labor force. German farmers also established plantations for large-scale production of cash crops, especially sisal, coffee, and cotton.

Cash crops in Madagascar include coffee, sugar, sisal, tobacco, vanilla, cloves, and of course, rice. Until the 1940s, about eighty percent of the population was engaged wholly or partly in agriculture, largely for their own subsistence with a small portion for cash sale. In 1970 agriculture was still Madagascar's main source of economy; it provided 55 percent of the GDP. This figure includes animal husbandry, forestry, and fisheries. In 1967, 45 percent of the export products came from robusta coffee and vanilla. Mixed farming was practiced because of the monsoon season, which was needed for irrigation. In the 1960s maize was introduced in the island. Between 1964 and 1965 Japanese methods and equipment to cultivate and grow rice were introduced in Madagascar, thus increasing the island's ability to produce rice. Madagascar possesses a huge cattle population. By 1961 the estimated number of cattle was about ten million. Between 1913 and 1929 exports of hides were estimated at 700,000 to 1 million per annum. However, from 1929 to 1939 the supply of hides fell to 360,000 units per annum, forcing farmers to sell their animals. By 1937, the number of cattle fell to about 7.7 million. In 1939, with the aim of stopping the decline of the animal population, the government limited the export of hides and skin to 4,000 and 360,000 units per annum, and forbade the slaughtering of cows or animals less than four years old. Owing to these measures and the improved treatment of animal diseases, the national herd slowly increased.

As in South Africa, an inadequate labor supply encouraged the inflow of migrant workers into East Africa. The earliest migrants were East Indians, who were imported in the 1890s to construct the Mombassa-Uganda railway line. Similarly white plantations in Kenya attracted labor from the Kikuyu and Luo Districts as well as from Uganda and Tanzania. Workers entered Uganda from Rwanda and Burundi. Rubber production in Tanganyika, for example, employed about 70,000 migrant workers in 1909 and 172,000 in 1913. These workers were engaged on a contract basis ranging from one to two years.

Industries. East Africa has a low industrial base, about half of which is located within Kenya. In 1960 Kenya's output was valued at £32 million (15 percent of the GDP), Uganda's output was valued at £17 million (11 percent of the GDP), and Tanzania's output was valued at £18 million (10 percent of the GDP). The concentration of industrial concerns in Kenya was related to the existence of larger markets for most goods there than elsewhere. Until about 1960 European concerns, such as Lever Brothers and the East African Company, handled the bulk of East African import-export trade. During the same time Indians controlled wholesale and retail trade. In the 1960s several import-substituted industries with special interests in beverages, textiles, breweries, and spare parts were established. In Kenya the manufacturing sector employed about sixty thousand workers at the time of independence, with the majority working in metal, textile, printing, and cement firms. However, like most other African economies, the manufacturing sector was concentrated in a few locations, Nairobi and Mombasa in Kenya. In 1963 Nairobi had 42 percent of the industrial establishments, while Mombasa had 13 percent. By 1968 Nairobi's portion had increased to 53 percent, while Mombasa's remained unchanged. The position of Mombasa as the second most important town in Kenya is linked to its position as the major port town, charged with handling the import and export trade.

Until 1960 the Ugandan economy was more or less an extension of Kenya's, which handled most of its exports and imports. Revenue generated from peasant agriculture, such as coffee and cotton, between 1945 and 1960 exceeded £231.9 million. This money was invested in the Nile hydroelectric plant, marking the beginning of a conscious effort at industrialization. The primary industrial concerns were tobacco, cement, and textile factories. To get raw materials into these factories and to facilitate the distribution of their products into the countryside, £364,000 and £1.886 million were spent in 1947 and 1951, respectively, on new buildings and road development. By 1957 about 1,176 enterprises were listed and operating under the Factories Ordinance of 1952. More than in other parts of East Africa, there were many Asian investors in the Ugandan economy. By 1960 they controlled local retail markets, while European establishments dominated the export-import trade. Outside retail stores, Asians also invested in oil mills, soap factories, confectioneries, and breweries. By 1960 the Uganda economy was a reflection of the history of the British imperialist economy.

In Tanzania the major factories were in the textile and metal sectors. There was also some mining, especially diamonds. Dar es Salaam combined the functions of Nairobi and Mombasa, thus it controlled about 50 percent of Tanzania's industrial concerns. In Tanzania industrial production contributed 15 percent of the GDP in the 1960s, but economic crises reduced this to only 5 percent in the 1970s and 4 percent in 1988. Like Kenya, Tanzania emphasized primary production of goods that were hitherto imported. Manufacturing was only 10 percent of the GDP in 1970 and 4 percent in 1988, while factories operated at one-third of installed capacity.

Industries in Madagascar have been only small-scale factories. Most industries deal with agricultural products, such as rice and tapioca, derived from dried cassava. The most-modern and best-equipped agricultural industry is the sugar industry, which is controlled by four French companies. Madagascar oil-processing industries treat groundnuts and cottonseed for local consumption. Madagascar produces thirty thousand to forty thousand tons of groundnuts a year. A meat factory was established around 1889 in Antongombato, and subsequently many more meat industries were established, especially corned beef industries, which supplied the French army. One of the hindrances to industrial development in Madagascar is the lack of proper roads and a reliable transportation system. The roads are broken up far more by the weather than by the traffic.

Part of the industrial problem in the region is attributed to the lack of integration between the different sectors of the economy. As an agricultural state, the processing of farm crops remained the most industrial activity. However, the rice mills processed less than one-third of local production, leaving the farmers to hull the remaining two-thirds in rural machines for local consumption. Similarly, in the 1940s and 1950s, while Malagasy farmers produced several thousand tons of cassava, only 25,000 tons were processed locally, forcing farmers to import animal feeds made from cassava from Germany. The most developed industrial sectors were sugar, fiber and textile production, and oil refining, which were all controlled by French firms. It was the demands for the reduction of expatriate control of the economy that promoted some of the political crises that degenerated into a military coup and the nationalization of the financial shipping and oil refineries in 1975. Foreign institutions, such as the International Monetary Fund (IMF), the World Bank, and other donors, financed most of the local industries. However, the industries did not meet the envisioned prospects of economic development. For example, industrial food production for 1974 was 136,148 tons, in contrast to 1982 production of 88,591 tons. Cement production in 1974 was 61,447 tons, in contrast to 1982 production of 35,921 tons. Industrial development in Mauritius was a direct consequence of its sugar production. In 1958 Mauritius planted about 200,000 acres of sugar, half planted by millers and the other half shared by tenant planters and large and small free planters. Sugar production increased gradually from 456,691 metric tons in 1950 to 533,341 metric tons in 1955 and 579,880 metric tons in 1959. Most of the crops were exported, while only about 4 percent of annual products were processed locally. Seychelles had little agricultural or industrial base. Its major revenue sources were tourism and fishing.

The colonial economy impacted differently on the people of East Africa. Export crop production increased the roles of women and children in food production as more men moved into cash crops. Similarly East African regions were divided into export, food, and labor producing regions. Therefore in migrant societies (labor producing), for example, there emerged a high level of female heads of households. In Uganda emphasis shifted to the production of bananas, which required less labor to manage. By the 1960s Kenya relied heavily on imported foodstuffs to meet its staple requirements. In Mauritius sugar production increased its dependence on Asia for food imports, especially rice and maize. Since industries were concentrated in a few cities, there emerged a huge rural-urban disparity. Rural communities became labor-exporting regions, while industrial and port towns became cosmopolitan communities. Similarly labor recruitment both onto farms and into manufacturing centers increased the level of urbanization. Indeed cities such as Nairobi, Mombasa, Dar es Salaam, and Kampala were essentially colonial creations, drawing people from the countryside. There emerged around Nairobi and white farms squatter slums occupied by migrant workers and those who had moved into the city for urban employment. In Uganda a perceived oppression of African workers by European and Asian workers resulted in racial antagonisms, racial attacks, and the eventual expulsion of Asians in 1972.

BIBLIOGRAPHY

Brett, E. A. *Colonialism and Underdevelopment in East Africa: The Politics of Economic Change, 1919–39*. London, 1973.

Cooper, Frederick. *From Slaves to Squatters: Plantation Labor and Agriculture in Zanzibar and Coastal Kenya, 1890–1925*. New Haven and London, 1980.

Cooper, Frederick. *On the African Waterfront: Urban Disorder and the Transformation of Work in Colonial Mombasa*. New Haven and London, 1987.

Covell, Maureen. *Madagascar: Politics, Economics, and Society*. London and New York, 1987.

Hazlewood, Arthur. *Economic Integration: The East African Experience*. Nairobi, Kenya; Ibadan, Nigeria; and Lusaka, 1975.

Heseltine, Nigel. *Madagascar*. New York, Washington, D.C., and London, 1971.

Iliffe, John. *A Modern History of Tanganuika*. London, New York, and Melbourne, 1979.

Issacman, Allen, and Richards Roberts, eds. *Cotton, Colonialism, and Social History in Sub-Saharan Africa*. Portsmouth, N.H., and London.

Keller, C. *Madagascar, Mauritius, and the Other East African Islands*. New York, 1901.

Meade, J. E., et al., eds. *The Economic and Social Structure of Mauritius*. London, 1968.

Nabudere, Wadada D. *Imperialism in East Africa: Imperialism and Exploitation*, vol. 1. London, 1981.

Nabudere, Wadada D. *Imperialism in East Africa: Imperialism and Integration*, vol. 2. London, 1982.

Ogot, B. A., and J. A. Kieran, eds. *Zamani: A Survey of East African History*. Kenya, 1968.

Saul, S. John. *The State and Revolution in East Africa*. New York and London, 1979.

OMAR ENO AND OJO OLATUNJI

EAST INDIA COMPANIES. *See* Joint-Stock Trading Companies.

EASTMAN, GEORGE (1854–1932), American inventor and industrialist.

George Eastman democratized photography, transforming it from a "black art" undertaken by experts using expensive mechanical contrivances and chemicals into a pastime for the masses. Eastman purchased his first camera and its associated equipment on 13 November 1877, for $49.58. He paid another $5.00 for photography lessons. In 1900, the Eastman Kodak Company brought out the Brownie camera. It cost $1.00, the associated equipment consisted only of film, which cost $0.15, and it required no lessons. As the famous slogan for this spectacularly successful new product introduction put it, "You push the button and we do the rest."

In the process of democratizing photography, Eastman became one of America's wealthiest citizens. His career illustrates a number of themes in American economic history, including entrepreneurship, the role of the large corporation, and the development of an economy characterized not only by the acquisition of basic "needs" but also by the satisfaction of "wants."

Eastman was born into a family of moderate means in Waterville, New York, on 12 July 1854. His childhood was brief. His father became chronically ill in 1857 and died in 1862. From that time on, Eastman was regarded as the man of the household, and it was a household in grave difficulty. When the father's ill health prevented him from earning an adequate living, the family began a stark economic descent. It settled permanently in Rochester, where, after Eastman's father's death, his mother took in lodgers to make ends meet.

Eastman, whose business success occurred in one of the most technology-intensive industries of his time, had only seven years of formal schooling. The family needed money, and in 1868 he got a job as an office boy at an insurance firm for $3.00 a week. He progressed quickly in the business world, moving on to the Rochester Savings Bank, where, by 1875, he was making $1,000 a year as second assistant bookkeeper.

In 1877, an acquaintance suggested that Eastman purchase photographic equipment to record a trip. His fascination with photography was immediate and permanent. By chance, Eastman had become interested in this field at a technological inflection point in its history. Experimenters were inventing chemicals and mechanical equipment that made it steadily simpler to take pictures, and young Eastman devoured technical articles on photography and conducted experiments on his own. At first his only goal was to facilitate his hobby, but soon he began to think about selling his inventions to others.

While experimenting with photography, Eastman continued to hold a full-time job at the Rochester Savings Bank. By 1880, he had made $4,000 running the Eastman

GEORGE EASTMAN. Eastman with a Kodak on the S.S. *Gallia*, circa 1890. (Courtesy George Eastman House, Rochester, N.Y.)

Dry Plate Company and was also drawing a salary of $1,400 a year at the bank. The following year would be pivotal. Passed over for promotion at the bank because of nepotism, he quit his job and decided to devote himself to his own company.

As a full-time entrepreneur, Eastman had to create a company amid the uncertainties of a rapidly evolving industry. He gained access to investment capital, hired talented people, and developed a vision of the business potential of photography. It is a significant statement about the United States of the 1880s that there was no "place" to which Eastman was confined by either law or custom. He had little else going for him but his own talent and capacity for hard work—but that was all he needed.

Eastman soon understood that the future of photography lay in mass marketing. This required mass production, research and development, and an organized, fully staffed corporation through which these functions could be coordinated and managed. Just as his personal economic upward mobility was a sign of the time and place in which he lived, so was his creation of a mass market for what was once a mysterious, "class" item.

In the words of economist Joseph A. Schumpeter: "Queen Elizabeth owned silk stockings. The capitalist achievement does not typically consist in providing more silk stockings for queens but in bringing them within reach of factory girls for steadily decreasing amounts of effort." Schumpeter's observations could be a summary of Eastman's career.

Eastman's vehicle for achieving this result was the corporation. He grew his small firm into a global industrial giant that dominated its industry for almost a century. The Eastman Kodak Company combined all the functions needed to lower costs. As costs dropped, prices declined, volume soared, and the company made money on volume.

Eastman began to leave active management to others after World War I, devoting himself to numerous philanthropies and travel. One of the few American big-businessmen who never married, he became lonely as he grew older, and his companions passed away. On 14 March 1932, an ailing and depressed George Eastman took his own life. His suicide note was brief and to the point: "To my friends: My work is done; why wait?"

BIBLIOGRAPHY

Brayer, Elizabeth. *George Eastman: A Biography.* Baltimore, 1996. The authoritative biography.

Jenkins, Reese V. *Images and Enterprise: Technology and the American Photographic Industry, 1839 to 1925.* Baltimore, 1975. A comprehensive history of the industry.

Martin, Albro. "George Eastman." In *Encyclopedia of American Biography*, edited by John A. Garraty. New York, 1974.

Tedlow, Richard S. *Giants of Enterprise: Seven Business Innovators and the Empires They Built.* New York, 2001. See especially the chapter "George Eastman and the Creation of a Mass Market."

Weisberger, Bernard. "You Press the Button, We Do the Rest." *American Heritage* 23.6 (October, 1972). Interesting and thought-provoking.

RICHARD S. TEDLOW

ECCLESIASTICAL ESTATES. The Christian church in the Middle Ages needed a substantial income. It had a staff of thousands of clergy, and its most expensive buildings, the large cathedrals and monastic churches, were expected to be impressively large and ornate structures with splendid furnishings. The highest ranks of the clergy, such as bishops and abbots, signaled their importance by living as well as lay aristocrats with appropriate houses, servants, food, clothing, and hunting grounds. They could be distinguished from the laity, certainly from the thirteenth century, by their celibacy, so their wealth was not hereditary, but their lands, houses, and parks belonged to their office and passed to successors in unbroken succession.

Wealth was needed by the leading churchmen to carry out their duty of governing the church. They also owed taxes to both the state and the papacy and were expected to dispense charity and to pay for some public works. After about 1100 they did not normally ride to war themselves, but they had to reward warriors who fought in the armies of the state.

The church was funded with offerings, gifts, and legacies; fees for specific services; and above all tithes, a tenth of all produce. The church at all levels held land, "ecclesiastical estates," that could be as modest as a few acres of glebe land attached to a chapel or parish church or as substantial as the great territories held by bishops and monasteries.

The church's large endowments of landed property began when Christianity became the official religion of the Roman Empire. The head of the church, the bishop of Rome (the pope), received enormous estates in Italy in the fourth and fifth centuries, and more modest quantities of land went to the bishops established in every city of the empire. From the sixth century the movement to found monasteries depended on further grants of property. Monastic life was based on a number of traditions, including those carried by Irish monks across the European Continent. But the most influential monastic rule in the West was that devised in the sixth-century by Saint Benedict, whose community at Monte Casino led a simple rural life, based on self sufficiency, with contributions to agricultural work from the monks themselves. Many monasteries founded in the seventh and eighth centuries, for example, in Gaul (France), were provided with tracts of land on which peasants and slaves lived and did the work. Saint-Bertin Abbey, for example, in northern France, was granted more than forty large pieces of land between 649 and 745 BCE, and by the mid–ninth century its possessions amounted to eleven thousand hectares. Lavishly funded monastic houses spread into the previously pagan parts of northern and eastern Europe as these areas were converted between the sixth and eleventh centuries. Monastic estates occupied some of the best land, for example, in the valleys of the major rivers, such as the Seine and the Rhine.

The great nobles and kings who gave land to the monasteries expected spiritual advantages. The monks prayed for the souls of the donor and his or her family, and the family used the monastic church as the family mausoleum. The prestige of the lay family was reflected in the grandeur of the monastery. But sometimes they expected more tangible benefits and could even own a monastery (a proprietary monastery). Others appointed the abbot, who could be a layman. More often a local noble acted as the monks' legal representative and exercised strong influence over the estates. Monasteries came under increasing pressure from predatory laymen in the ninth and tenth centuries. They were compelled to grant benefices (substantial pieces of land, often running to hundreds of hectares) to aristocratic warriors. As the Carolingian Empire, which ruled over most of continental western Europe until the late ninth century, was succeeded by petty states, unrestrained lay greed led to the loss of much church land.

When church property was being eroded toward the end of the first millennium, a church reform movement began in Burgundy in 910 with the foundation of a lavishly endowed monastery at Cluny. Cluniac monks, together with other reformers, influenced the papacy to set new boundaries between the church and the secular world. Under the leadership of such ardent reformers as Gregory VII (who died in 1085), it became inappropriate for laymen to own churches or monasteries or for clergy to buy church offices (and the landed incomes that went with them). The church became powerful enough to put a stop to the theft of church land.

In the following religious revival around 1100, a number of new monastic orders—Cistercians, Carthusians, and Augustinians together with crusading orders, such as the Templars and Hospitallers—attracted so much lay patronage that hundreds of new religious houses were founded, and many thousands of hectares of land were again passing from the laity to the monks. By 1152, for example, 328 Cistercian houses had been created. These new orders were not granted vast estates of prime agricultural land. The Cistercians, who had an austere mission to establish themselves away from the sinful world, were granted underdeveloped woods, moors, and marshes. As the twelfth and thirteenth centuries were a period of internal colonization, the monks joined in a campaign of clearance and drainage that converted wastes into wealthy estates. A number of Augustinian houses were founded in or near towns and were given pieces of urban property when towns were growing in size and prosperity. The Augustinians also received many parish churches with their tithes, which at a time of increased production of grain and rising prices became profitable assets.

The growing commercialization enabled the church to buy property. For example, a monastery negotiated to purchase plots from lay families in a village where it already had an estate in order to extend and consolidate a block of land. The land market became exploitative when a layman who had fallen into debt was "rescued" by a monastery that settled the debt and took the land. In short, by the early thirteenth century the church had participated successfully in a period of economic growth and had increased its share of property until in many regions it held more than a third of the land.

After 1200 a brake was placed on founding new monastic orders, and the number of large grants to the church diminished. The new religious foundations of the next three centuries were often quite small in scale and required only modest endowments. Many chantries (institutions to fund priests praying for the souls of the departed) and fraternities (collective chantries) were provided with houses and rents in towns, worth a fraction of a monastic endowment. Many colleges, almshouses, and hospitals were similarly funded with a handful of properties.

Lay aristocrats came to resent aspects of the church's wealth, which they felt was taking assets away from them. Legislation required the permission of rulers for churches to acquire more property. Lawyers used the word *mortmain* ("dead hand"), referring to the grip the church gained over land, holding it by secure tenures, and as an undying institution, never relinquishing it. Radical criticism of

church property came from the friars, such as the Franciscans (founded about 1206–1210) and the Dominicans (founded 1216), who lived in the manner of Christ's apostles by begging alms from the faithful. The church defended its position, and the extreme Franciscans, who advocated a doctrine of poverty and regarded church property as sinful, were condemned as heretics. Calls for the disendowment of the church came from laymen and radical clerics from the late fourteenth century. Land was transferred within the church when, during the long-running war between England and France, the estates of French monasteries in England were used to endow more fashionable institutions, such as colleges. When the church's lands were confiscated in great quantities in the Protestant Reformation in the sixteenth century, monasteries and chantries bore the brunt, and bishops and parish churches retained at least part of their property.

Church landlords kept careful records, and much knowledge of the medieval economy depends on the charters, surveys, and accounts preserved in the archives of bishops and monasteries. From these emerge the structure of estates and the management methods. They differed from one institution to another. Monastic estates were often grouped near the house, as the monks had to stay put, and food was carted to them. Bishops' scattered estates enabled the lord to travel round his diocese. Church landlords were faced with a series of dilemmas—should they live on food from their land directly or sell the produce and buy supplies for their households? Transport costs could make self-sufficiency expensive, and using the market might be more convenient and flexible. Should the land be managed directly by the lord's officials or farmed out? Again direct management could be most profitable, especially in a rising market, but leases were easier to administer and left the headaches of organizing cultivation and sales of produce to someone else. Should the demesnes (land reserved for the lord's use) be cultivated with labor services, or should the peasants be required to pay rents in cash and wage-earners hired to do the work?

The abundant documents from church estates have given the impression that the lords were especially efficient managers. The Cistercians in particular have gained a reputation as innovators who invested in improvements and ran their compact granges like modern farms. In fact the Cistercians were not so advanced and often depended on rents just like other medieval landlords. In general church estates and their management resembled closely those of lay lords: all were faced with similar problems and choices. Not all church estates were large: many monasteries and nunneries were endowed with scattered parcels of land, and indeed not all bishops were rich. A high proportion of church property consisted of parish glebes that resembled peasant holdings, and chantries were funded with limited accumulations of land. So church and lay lords alike held both large and small estates. The method of exploiting church estates developed in much the same way as those of other lords. In the early middle ages they often collected tribute from the population of extensive territories, but by the ninth century demesnes were cultivated by peasant labor services. In subsequent centuries agriculture became more intensive. In the late Middle Ages lords leased land and withdrew from direct management. In the early Middle Ages they invested in mills, and in the twelfth and thirteenth centuries they founded their share of new towns.

Did Christian ideas influence the management of church lands? The church lords sought the highest returns and worked within the prevailing values of their society. They owned slaves (before 1100), imposed serfdom, wielded powers of private justice, collected debts, foreclosed on mortgages, and generally behaved like any other landlord of their time. They were capable of some sharp practices, such as concocting or altering charters to defend their right to land. The distinctive character of the lordship of the larger church estates arose from their position as old institutions. They gained a grip on the land and tenants from centuries of continuous ownership, which gave them more serfs and greater jurisdictional controls than many other lords. For the same reasons they tended to resist change, with the result that some of the famous struggles between peasants and lords are found on great church estates. Monks in particular moved cautiously because they were conscious that they belonged to an institution with a long history, and their successes and failures would be remembered for generations to come.

The control by the church of such a high proportion of productive resources neither accelerated development nor hindered it greatly. The church participated in the economy and responded to its stimuli, even if slowly at times.

BIBLIOGRAPHY

Donkin, Robert A. *The Cistercians: Studies in the Geography of Medieval England and Wales*. Toronto, 1978.
Duby, Georges. *Rural Economy and Country Life in the Medieval West*. London, 1968.
Harvey, Barbara. *Westminster Abbey and Its Estates in the Middle Ages*. Oxford, 1977.
Herlihy, David. "Church Property on the European Continent, 701–1200." *Speculum* 36 (1961), 81–105.
Postan, Michael M., ed. *The Cambridge Economic History of Europe*, vol. 1, *The Agrarian Life of the Middle Ages*. 2d ed. Cambridge, 1966.
Southern, Richard W. *Western Society and the Church in the Middle Ages*. Harmondsworth, 1970.
Swanson, Robert N. *Church and Society in Late Medieval England*. Oxford, 1989.

CHRISTOPHER C. DYER

ECONOMIC CONVERGENCE AND DIVERGENCE.

Over time economies grow and slow. The analysis of growth differentials can lead to insightful patterns of convergence and divergence of levels of economic performance between regions and countries. Typical cases of convergence include the narrowing in per capita income among the twenty-five-odd richest countries in the world economy since World War II as well as among a range of emerging economies in East and Southeast Asia during the last quarter of the twentieth century. At the same time, however, living standards across a wider range of countries in the world diverged strongly. Over longer periods of time convergence and divergence trends have also led to changes in economic leadership. Examples include Europe's rise from its nadir to overtake China around the middle of the second millennium and the forging ahead of the United States relative to Britain in the nineteenth century. The economics of convergence and divergence provides insights into such patterns and the causes behind them.

History of the Catch-Up and Convergence Debate. The interest in studying the causes of international differences in growth performance dates back to the work of classical political scientists, including David Hume, Adam Smith, and Friedrich List. With greater availability of macroeconomic performance measures, the study of cross-country differences in growth rates boomed during the second half of the twentieth century. Thanks to the work of empirical economists, including Colin Clark (1940), Simon Kuznets (1966), Edward Denison (1967), Angus Maddison (1972, 1982), and Robert Summers and Alan Heston (1991), rich data sources were developed that could be used for international comparisons. In conjunction with the work of economic historians, including Alexander Gerschenkron (1962) and Moses Abramovitz (1986), basic hypotheses on the causes of convergence and divergence in the long run were formulated. In a seminal contribution to the debate on growth differences, William Baumol (1986) coined the term *convergence club* to describe a group of countries between which productivity levels converge. Bradford de Long (1988) argued that the sample selection of countries in convergence clubs should take place ex ante and needs to be based on an analysis of initial characteristics at the beginning of the period studied. These notions led to the convergence debate being captured by economists in their quest for the conditions under which countries would belong to particular convergence clubs. The cross-section regression approach is characteristic of most of the recent empirical work on testing convergence and divergence hypotheses, of which the work by Robert Barro and Xavier Sala-i-Martin (1995) is among the most widely quoted. Meanwhile economic historians have continued to stress the diversity of the forces behind convergence and divergence, being dependent on time and place.

Concepts of Convergence and Divergence. Although the concepts of convergence and divergence may refer to a wide range of economic variables, including prices, production structures, or consumption patterns, it mostly is related to a measure of living standards, for example, per capita income, (labor) productivity, or wages. Loosely defined, convergence refers to a narrowing of the gap in living standards between rich and poor countries. Divergence implies a widening of this gap. During the 1980s the convergence concept became defined more precisely. For example, William Baumol, Richard Nelson, and Edward Wolff (1994) distinguish between homogenization and catch-up. Homogenization refers to the phenomenon that the cross-country dispersion in terms of a pertinent variable declines over time. Catch-up refers to the case in which laggard countries narrow the distance separating them from the leading countries. Barro and Sala-i-Martin refer to homogenization as σ-convergence, whereas catch-up may be called β-convergence. These concepts are interrelated but by no means equivalent. For example, a steady decline in the dispersion of per capita income levels indicates homogenization, but this does not necessarily mean this group of countries is catching up with the country having the highest per capita income level. Hence homogenization is neither necessary nor sufficient for catch-up and vice versa. Related concepts to catch-up and convergence are leapfrogging, forging ahead, and falling behind. Falling behind is the counterpart of catching up and indicates a widening of the gap between a leader and the followers. Forging ahead refers to the phenomenon where productivity or income levels in the leader are being surpassed by a follower. Leapfrogging refers to the same phenomenon but puts the emphasis on the leader losing its leadership position because of a lock-in in obsolete technology (David, 1975; Brezis, Krugman, and Tsiddon, 1995).

Historical Patterns of Convergence. Based on the long-term quantitative evidence on per capita income, productivity, and wages, several stylized facts on patterns of catch-up, forging ahead, convergence, and divergence in the world economy have been derived. Maddison (2001) provides a detailed account of long-term growth patterns in the world economy in which he documents relative per capita income levels between countries and regions for two millennia. Although there is continued debate about the exact timing and speed at which western Europe took over economic leadership from China, Maddison argues that European leadership emerged rather early, around the fourteenth century, and advanced slowly to a level twice as high as in China by the nineteenth century. Indeed the possibility of a sharp acceleration in the pace of advance of per capita income in western Europe around 1500, when Europeans encountered America and made a direct entry into the trading world of Asia, is increasingly

seen as unlikely. But other histories of China (for example, Pomeranz, 2000), have disputed the view of gradual change and have argued that the gap between western Europe and China opened up only after 1750. But other parts of the world, notably Africa, Latin America, and large parts of Asia, clearly fell behind western European per capita income levels.

Cross-country growth differences became more pronounced during the nineteenth century, when western Europe and its offshoots entered the epoch of "modern economic growth." Western Europe and North America forged ahead of the rest of the world and experienced unprecedented growth rates in per capita income. These developments were in response to a combination of technological progress and institutional innovations to capture the benefits of the rise of knowledge and increased mobility of factor inputs (labor and capital) and trade. Indeed Jeffrey Williamson (1996) stresses the importance of globalization forces, in particular during the late nineteenth century and early twentieth century, exemplified by movements of people and capital between the Old World and the New World. Within the group of advanced countries, patterns of homogenization, catching up, and forging ahead took place. Britain, which had captured economic leadership from the Dutch Republic during the eighteenth century, lost ground to the United States and eventually was overtaken. The forging ahead of the United States is related to rapid capital formation, an increase in applied scientific research, and new forms of business management leading to greater standardization of products and enlargement of markets (Nelson and Wright, 1992).

Meanwhile, while losing ground to the United States, most Western European countries caught up with Britain in a process of homogenization during the period from 1870 to 1913. Between the two world wars the convergence process lost much of its force, but after 1950 a strong process of convergence in productivity levels occurred among advanced nations, in particular in western Europe. European integration of product and factor markets and the substantial rise in intra-European trade accounts for much of this convergence process. Moreover, and in contrast to the previous period, almost all countries caught up rapidly with the United States. Up to 1973 European catch-up is to a large extent related to the effects of postwar reconstruction, but the process continued, though at a slower pace, until the mid-1990s.

The most rapid catch-up episode of the postwar period relates to Japan. Catching up on the United States continued beyond the world growth boom from 1950 to 1973 but came to a standstill around 1990. The Japanese catch-up experience suggests that the technological and institutional infrastructure that helped it in narrowing the gap relative to the economic leader, that is, the United States, did not necessarily mean it could forge ahead. After the 1960s a group of lower-income Asian countries experienced growth rates well above the average for those countries belonging to the Organization for Economic Cooperation and Development (OECD). Indeed East and Southeast Asia were the fastest growing parts of the world economy during the latter half of the twentieth century, outperforming all other regions and gaining back some of its relative standing of the period before 1500. In contrast, because of important institutional failures, Latin America failed to live up to its expectations. Most countries in Africa and, since the fall of the Berlin Wall, in eastern Europe and the former USSR have also fallen seriously behind the average level of productivity and living standards of the advanced world.

Conditions for Convergence. The strong version of the convergence hypothesis claims the bigger the gap in performance levels, the faster the growth in follower countries will be. This "unconditional" convergence hypothesis is based on the assumption that follower countries catch up by bringing into production a large backlog of unexploited technology, which has public good characteristics so the benefits of that technology accrue to any potential user. This raises the question of under which conditions can nations exploit, as Gerschenkron (1962) stated it, their advantages of backwardness.

The original neoclassical growth model of Robert Solow (1956) predicts convergence of per capita income across countries, given similar saving rates and population growth rates. The mechanism driving convergence is the assumption of a single global production function featuring decreasing marginal returns to capital. Hence the higher the level of capital per head, the lower the additional increase in per capita income for a given amount of investment. However, Mankiw, Romer, and Weil (1992) show that only about half of the worldwide variation in per capita income can be explained by differences in savings rates and population growth. New growth theories in the 1980s explicitly addressed the possibility of divergence through endogenizing the public good effect of technical change. This was done either indirectly through physical or human capital formation or directly through recognizing knowledge as an input variable. Divergent trends, alongside convergence, have become a possibility depending on the strength of national and international spillovers (Grossman and Helpman, 1991). According to Jan Fagerberg (1994), the advantages to backwardness do not necessarily outweigh the disadvantages of being backward. In the technology gap approach, the technologically most advanced countries possess unique strengths in skills, experience, and knowledge to develop new technologies, which makes it more difficult for the follower countries to assimilate the new technologies, so catch-up will not take place. Economic historians have focused their attention more ex-plicitly on the diversity of institutional starting conditions. In his own work Gerschenkron, who focused on the conditions for the catch-up of late-developing continental European countries with Britain during the late nineteenth century, stresses the importance of centralization of institutions dealing with capital accumulation and administration. These included the development of vertically integrated enterprises, a major role for government in coordinating investment decisions, support investment banking, and in general a resolution of problems concerning asymmetric information on finance for industrialization, mobilization of savings, and development of infant industries. A similar latecomer model was adopted in many East and Southeast Asian countries and may be referred to as the developmental state model (Johnson, 1982). Abramovitz (1986) makes a distinction between the potential for catch-up and the realization of this potential. As with the unconditional hypothesis, the potential for catch-up is larger the more backward the country is. But this potential is restricted by the degree of technical congruence and the social capability to catch up. Technical congruence relates to the characteristics of the technologies to be exploited on the one hand and the natural resource endowment and market size of a country on the other hand. Social capability relates to the technological competence of a country's people, including the level of human capital, but also to the general state of a country's political, commercial, and financial institutions and the existence of an extensive physical infrastructure. Hence the opportunities for catch-up provided by technological backwardness may be offset by social backwardness. Structural changes induced by the introduction of new technology can have severe costs for some groups in society. They may be retarded by resistance of vested interests and by traditional relationships between employers and employees. Without a strong developmental state, the possible losers may oppose many of the potentially beneficial changes. But any social constraint on catch-up may also be overcome by the very opportunities generated by the backlog of technologies themselves. Ultimately catch-up and convergence depend on the political and ideological setting of a country. Economic policies and the social climate in a country together with historical accidents, including foreign shocks and developments in the international order, are the features of the "ultimate" causality of growth and catch-up.

[*See also* Economic Development; Economic Growth; Industrial Revolution; *and* Living Standards.]

BIBLIOGRAPHY

Abramovitz, Moses. "Catching Up, Forging Ahead, and Falling Behind." *Journal of Economic History* 46.2 (1986), 385–406.

Barro, Robert, and Xavier Sala-i-Martin. *Economic Growth*. New York, 1995.

Baumol, William. "Productivity Growth, Convergence, and Welfare: What the Long Run Data Show." *American Economic Review* 76 (1986), 1072–1085.

Baumol, William, R. R. Nelson, and E. N. Wolff. "Introduction: The Convergence of Productivity, Its Significance, and Its Varied Connotations." In *Convergence of Productivity: Cross-National Studies and Historical Evidence*, edited by William Baumol, R. R. Nelson, and E. N. Wolff, pp. 3–19. New York, 1994.

Brezis, E., P. R. Krugman, and D. Tsiddon. "Leapfrogging in International Comparisons: A Theory of Cycles in National Technology Leadership." *American Economic Review* 83.5 (1995), 1211–1219.

Clark, Colin. *The Conditions of Economic Progress*. London, 1940.

David, P. *Technical Choice, Innovation, and Economic Growth*. Cambridge, 1975.

De Long, Bradford. "Productivity Growth, Convergence, and Welfare: Comment." *American Economic Review* 78 (1988), 1138–1154.

Denison, Edward. *Why Growth Rates Differ: Postwar Experience in Nine Western Countries*. Washington, D. C., 1967.

Fagerberg, Jan. "Technology and International Difference in Growth Rates." *Journal of Economic Literature* 32 (1994), 1147–1175.

Gerschenkron, Alexander. *Economic Backwardness in Historical Perspective*. Cambridge, Mass., 1962.

Grossman, G. M., and E. Helpman. *Innovation and Growth in the Global Economy*. Cambridge, Mass., 1991.

Johnson, C. *MITI and the Japanese Miracle: The Growth of Industrial Policy*. Stanford, Calif., 1982.

Kuznets, Simon. *Modern Economic Growth*. New Haven, 1966.

Maddison, Angus. "Explaining Economic Growth." *Banca Nazionale del Lavoro Quarterly Review* 102 (September 1972), 211–262.

Maddison, Angus. *Phases of Capitalist Development*. Oxford, 1982.

Maddison, Angus. *The World Economy: A Millennial Perspective*. Paris, 2001.

Mankiw, Gregory, David Romer, and David N. Weil. "A Contribution to the Empirics of Economic Growth." *Quarterly Journal of Economics* 107 (1992), 407–437.

Nelson, R. R., and G. Wright. "The Rise and Fall of American Technological Leadership: The Postwar Era in Historical Perspective." *Journal of Economic Literature* 30 (1992), 1931–1964.

Pomeranz, Kenneth. *The Great Divergence: China, Europe, and the Making of the Modern World Economy*. Princeton, 2000.

Solow, Robert. "A Contribution to the Theory of Economic Growth." *Quarterly Journal of Economics* 70 (1956), 65–94.

Summers, Robert. and Alan Heston. "The Penn World Table (March 5): An Expanded Set of International Comparisons, 1950–1988." *Quarterly Journal of Economics* 106 (1991), 327–368.

Williamson, Jeffrey G. "Globalization, Convergence, and History." *Journal of Economic History* 56 (1996), 277–306.

BART VAN ARK AND MARCEL TIMMER

ECONOMIC DEVELOPMENT [*This entry contains two subentries, a historical overview and a discussion of development policies.*]

Historical Overview

The term *economic development* came into use in the late 1940s in response to the recognition that a few countries of the world had achieved relatively high gross domestic product (GDP) per person, while many others still had per capita GDP little higher or possibly lower than a hundred years earlier. Economic development therefore identifies the area of inquiry addressed to this question of why some countries are rich and others poor. "Development" was applied to those countries long poor seeking to begin to grow, and "growth" (of GDP per capita) to those countries that seemed to have had in place for some time an economy in which increasing output per capita occurred as a consequence of the routine operations of their economies. The objective of development, in very broad terms, was to modify the nongrowing economy such that its routine functioning produced rising per capita GDP.

Development then became much broader than growth, and imposed on analysts the necessity to extend and deepen their analyses beyond the usual boundaries and depth of conventional textbook economics. The narrow theory of growth of GDP was relevant, but that theory had to be set in an institutional, cultural, religious, political, historical environment that, having evolved in the context of widespread poverty and the absence of growth, was, in general, quite alien to its achievement.

The fact that currently rich countries began to grow in the early to mid-nineteenth century is an important part of the story. If some countries could grow, why could not all countries? A simple argument indicates that the conditions of growth should be very easy to achieve. Technical (and other) knowledge may be looked upon as a public good available to all, and capital assumed to flow around the world in search of the highest returns. These primary sources of growth were—or should be—more or less the same everywhere. That such a process seemed to apply to only a few countries made clear to most observers that the developmental issue was quite different from the growth issue, and required, as already noted, a wider net of both explanation and policy prescription.

Planning. Economists initially attributed the existence of a development problem to market failure. The market had failed in certain countries while seeming to function well in others. This view led to the obvious conclusion that planning of some sort was necessary, and during the 1950s most of the nongrowing countries put in place some kind of planning apparatus. Plans varied widely in scope and in sophistication. Some were mere lists of hoped-for investment projects while others were much more formal and reflected a detailed grasp of basic economic principles.

The necessity of planning was recognized by almost all economists and lending institutions. The World Bank and other aid agencies often required plans before loans or grants would be forthcoming. The emphasis on planning followed from the view that the market that had worked so well in western Europe, northern North America, Australia, and New Zealand, could not solve the development problems of the long-poor countries. This view was widely held despite the fact that few economists, trained in the textbook economics of the time, had much understanding and essentially no experience in creating and implementing a plan.

Within the context of planning there were many more specific approaches to understanding and policymaking in the 1950s. The most influential was that of Sir W. Arthur Lewis, (1915–1991) set forth in his article "Economic Development with Unlimited Supplies of Labor" (*The Manchester School* 22 (May 1954), 139–191). In this article, Lewis argues that the nongrowing economy was characterized by a very small "modern" sector and a very large "traditional" sector. In the latter sector, there was little capital (except land), and labor was so abundant and the technical knowledge so primitive that its average product was extremely low and its marginal product possibly zero. The market was little used in this sector, and output was assumed to be shared more or less equally among the members of the community. The modern sector was a scaled down version of the economies of the rich countries of the North.

Modern versus Traditional Sector. The basic idea of development in the Lewis model was to expand the modern sector and allow the traditional sector to disappear. All investment would take place in the modern sector, and knowledge would be imported from the rich North, so that this traditional sector would become a clone of the North. Labor would be pulled into the modern sector as it expanded without penalizing output in the traditional sector. When sufficient capital had been created in the modern sector to employ all available labor, the country would be declared developed and textbook economics would apply. The traditional culture, institutions, and values, were replaced, and the new rich society was created by this process of imitation. An expanded and more formal version of this basic idea of development was worked out by John Fei and Gustav Ranis (*Development of the Labor Surplus Economy: Theory and Policy*, Homewood, Ill., 1964).

The idea that development meant replacing the indigenous with the imported is fundamental to the model formulated by Lewis. This characteristic made the theory more nearly a theory of displacement than of development. A theory of development should account for the process by which the long nongrowing economy changed itself into one in which growth occurred regularly over extended periods of time. The Lewis model also relied heavily on physical capital formation as the principal source of increased capacity, largely because of the assumption that modern technical knowledge would be imported, along with the physical capital, from the rich North and applied directly.

Lewis also assumed that individual laborers would remain in the traditional sector until jobs were actually created in the modern sector. This in fact turned out quite wrong, and labor moved in large numbers from the rural to urban areas whether jobs were available or not. The ensuing unemployment created considerable difficulties and gave rise to what was called the "informal" sector. This sector had characteristics that were neither modern nor traditional but sometimes provided employment and other sources of sustenance for large numbers of people.

The ideas of development underlying the Lewis framework were widely accepted during the 1950s, and indeed continue to have considerable influence at the beginning of the twenty-first century. In particular, the idea of equating the replication of the North to "development" remains widespread. The main practical result of acceptance of this model however, seems to have been the creation of enclaves of modern economic activity within the economy, with little effect on the economy in its entirety.

Economic Structure. There were other ideas that emerged in the 1950s and that affected policies to some extent. In Latin America, a number of economists at the Economic Commission for Latin America argued that the structure of these economies constituted the basic barrier to sustained growth. Structure referred to the composition of output—mainly agricultural and mineral—and to the form of economic organization and to technology. The countries of the North were predominantly industrial with highly productive and constantly improving technology that allowed wages to rise. A quite different structure in Latin America had evolved as a consequence of foreign trade and investment and had kept the countries tied to agriculture and mining where technological change was much more modest and world demand grew much more slowly. The terms *peripheral* and *center* came to be used to identify the developing agricultural and mineral countries on the one hand and the industrial countries of the North on the other. The consequence for the peripheral countries was slow and irregular growth of GDP, deteriorating terms of trade, constant balance-of-payments problems, and widespread unemployment.

The objective became that of changing the structure of the economies, and this task required stronger medicine than the marginal adjustments brought about by a market mechanism. The only way out, it was argued, was to protect the economies from international trade, and to effect changes in structure by specific government action of one kind or another. To "de-link" from trade with the North became a common summary of the policy position of this group of economists and policymakers.

The structural argument had great influence in Latin America, but far less in other parts of the world. There were certain similarities between the structural model and the labor surplus model. The protection called for by the structuralists was, in effect, to result in an enlargement of the modern sector and to move the economy away from heavy dependence on agriculture. In both there is the implicit assumption that the traditional sector cannot grow, and hence must be replaced by imported institutions and technology.

"Big Push" Theory. Another idea that emerged in the 1950s to explain why some countries could not grow was identified as the "Big Push" or "Critical Minimum Effort." It was argued that individual investments could hardly succeed unless there was a great deal of investment going on at the same time. Therefore, a Big Push was essential if any investment at all was to take place, and growth must be "balanced" over a wide range of sectors. A Big Push was difficult for a weak economy with an inexperienced government and poor infrastructure to pull off. Again, such an argument reflected lack of confidence in the market to resolve the problem.

Evidently capacity to export would have solved the problem. A further assumption was therefore necessary, namely, that it would not be possible for newly created activities to export without some learning time behind protection from foreign producers. Since exports were assumed not possible, at least for a period of time, and protection was necessary, the Big Push issue was deemed to be of significance.

Unbalanced Growth and Hidden Rationality. Somewhat in response to the Big Push and Balanced Growth ideas, arguments developed showing that *unbalanced* growth was not only possible, but indeed preferred. There were several variations of the unbalanced growth argument, but the one of Albert Hirschman attracted the most attention. In his book *The Strategy of Economic Development* (New Haven, 1958), Hirschman argued that unbalanced growth was important to create a continuing flow of investment opportunities because potential entrepreneurs lacked the capacity to identify profitable investment projects. Government investments in particular should be aimed at creating bottlenecks, because bottlenecks were clear-cut investment opportunities. Hirschman introduced the term *linkages* among sectors to show how investment in one sector could create readily identifiable opportunities in another sector. The argument assumed that there would be no saving or finance problem and no shortage of capacity to carry out the investment necessary to break the bottleneck. If such problems did emerge, the bottlenecks would remain bottlenecks, and other investments would not be forthcoming. There does not appear to be any country that explicitly followed Hirschman's advice, but the notion of linkages became part of the vocabulary of development economics.

Another notion of Hirschman's is more important. In several places he speaks of "hidden rationality" (e.g., *Journeys Toward Progress*: *Studies of Economic Policy and Policy Making in Latin America*, New York, 1968). He emphasized that there is a rationality in the traditional society that has evolved over long periods of time and that is peculiar to a particular society. This rationality affects what can be done, even what can be thought, and how it can be done, and is often appreciated, even by nationals, only when efforts to change things are made. To seek to impose change from outside on a society without recognition of this "hidden rationale" is to (or may) violate the existing order to the extent that instability is created, and thereby the attainment of the objective sought is defeated. This notion represented an important insight, and is a forerunner of the idea and role of institutions in development. Institutions is a broader notion but does have direct links to the Hirschman notion.

This argument about hidden rationalities is one of the few early ones that is relevant to the question of why all countries did not begin to grow when the countries of the North began. Such rationalities reflect deep-seated characteristics of the society, characteristics that have been long in place and that evolved slowly in societies where change is rare, poverty rampant, and the idea of progress absent. Often religious convictions are directly relevant, as is the question of political power. Such characteristics are themselves frequently sources of well-being, and the absence of change may be looked upon with favor. Any fundamental change in such a situation is sure to take time and to be resisted in many ways, and outside sources of change are often suspect. Especially questioned are those new technologies that somehow appear to be controlling, or seeking to control, nature. In such an environment, ideas and things that spread quickly and easily in the North may face vastly higher hurdles elsewhere. It is this interpretation of "hidden rationalities" that makes the Hirschman notion so important.

There were other ideas, of course. Walt Rostow's stages of growth theory attracted attention. The take-off stage was discussed often, but had very little effect on general thinking or on policy. Hollis Chenery suggested a "Two Gap" barrier to growth, consisting of domestic saving and foreign exchange, rather than just the one conventional gap, saving. Such an approach came along just when the profession seemed to be moving away from structuralism and other sources of rigidities, and therefore had less influence than it might have had had it appeared in the 1950s.

Import Substitution and Outward Orientation. While no generally accepted model of development appeared in these years, there did emerge from these ideas, insights, and arguments a development strategy that reflected many of them and that was widely practiced. The strategy came to be called "import substitution," or IS. The IS strategy was simple: Protection would be afforded to a wide range of consumer durables, presently imported, in order to induce their domestic production. Physical capital to produce the consumer durables would be imported and was widely subsidized through interest-rate controls and an overvalued exchange rate. Protection was in the form of tariffs, quotas, exchange control, and outright prohibition. Technology would be embodied in the imported physical capital and in the organization that the new capital imposed, so it too was imported. Import substitution was intended to replace imports, but at the same time it was heavily import dependent. Rather than helping to resolve balance-of-payment problems, it in fact exacerbated them because of the necessity to import capital and the inability to export the new manufactured goods.

The IS strategy led to improvements in a wide range of characteristics of numerous countries. Rates of growth of GDP were higher during IS than was the case earlier in many countries, investment rates and exports rose among a number of countries, manufacturing activities increased absolutely and as a proportion of GDP, and literacy rates improved, as did life expectancy and other aspects of living conditions. Even so, problems began to appear by the mid-1960s. Growth began to slow, distortions in the economy became increasingly damaging, inflation seemed everywhere, poverty and unemployment, and underemployment were affected hardly at all. To many observers it was becoming increasingly clear that IS was a dead end and a different strategy must be sought.

By the end of the 1960s, Taiwan and South Korea had demonstrated great capacity to grow at impressive rates for sustained periods of time. The most obvious difference between these two countries and others that had long been poor and nongrowing was that the former two countries had achieved exceptional rates of growth of nontraditional exports. It also appeared at first glance—although later researches were to show otherwise—that in these two countries the role of the government in the economy was insignificant. Largely as a consequence of the experiences of Taiwan and Korea, plus the difficulties increasingly faced by those countries that had pushed IS hard, prevailing opinion began to shift sharply away from the ideas of the fifties and early sixties and the policies that those ideas had brought into being. The new strategy that gained rapid favor emphasized openness to world trade and finance, more or less free trade, the possible subsidizing of exports, and primary reliance on the market with minimal role of government in the economy.

This approach, called "Outward (or Export) Orientation" gained favor mainly because of the evident failure of IS in most countries and the apparent success of Taiwan and Korea in employing other policies and strategies. There was little theoretical discussion that led to the new strategy. As it became widely accepted, rationales appeared in various forms, but basically it has remained a strongly pushed policy with little theoretical support, except the old one that getting prices right was all that was necessary to grow. The empirical support for Outward Orientation is also quite mixed and open to doubts. On the other side, questions are being raised about the capacity of an outward orientation strategy to solve the development problem as that problem was defined in the first paragraph of this essay.

One additional topic needs to be touched on in a historical survey, namely the content of well-being. Growth of GDP was usually defended on the grounds that it allows a society to acquire more and more of what it wants, and what it wants is, virtually by definition, the source of well-being. If there were no poverty or incomes were fairly equally distributed among the population, this would be a fairly convincing argument. These latter conditions are rarely met, so by the end of the 1960s, poverty alleviation had become a major source of well-being. Similarly, as it became clear that growth did not generally solve the unemployment problem, job creation became a further widely held objective, distinct from growth. So too arguments developed to show that some preferences were "better" than others, and taking existing preferences as the basic criterion for the allocation of resources needed further thought. More generally, it became clear that the very content of well-being was vastly more complex than was thought to be case in the early 1950s.

Changes in Economic Thinking. When concern with development began in the late 1940s and early 1950s, it was generally believed that its achievement would be quite simple. For the poor countries to grow, all that was necessary was an investment rate of 15 to 20 percent and access to the technical knowledge of the already-rich countries. The most unambiguous thing that the brief history of development economics has taught us is that the process of development is vastly more complex than was thought to be the case at the beginning.

The basic issue is knowledge accumulation and application, and, while developing countries can learn from developed countries, we now see that there must be a fundamental commitment to searching and learning that is basically indigenous. For such a commitment to emerge in long-poor countries imposes deep-seated changes in ways of thinking and ways of being and provides many opportunities for upheavals of all kinds. To understand how these changes come about or can be induced pushes the analysts into much deeper, more complex, more society-specific investigations than was thought the case at the outset. These are the issues with which the more recent researches are concerned.

[*See also* Economic Convergence and Divergence; Economic Growth; Economic Imperialism; Labor Surplus Models; *and* Living Standards.]

BIBLIOGRAPHY

Chenery, Hollis, and Allen M. Strout. "Foreign Assistance and Economic Development." *American Economic Review* 56.4 (1966), 679–733. The two-gap theory is worked out here.

Coale, Ansley J., and Edgar M. Hoover. *Population Growth and Economic Development in Low-Income Countries*. Princeton, 1958. Influential early model on relationship between demographic change and economic development.

Edwards, Edgar O., ed. *Employment in Developing Countries*. New York, 1974. A collection of diverse views on the employment issue in developing countries.

Kuznets, Simon. *Economic Growth and Structure*. New York, 1965. An important early collection and discussion of the economic data of low-income countries by one of the great figures of empirical economics.

Lall, Sanjaya, and Paul Streeten. *Foreign Investment, Transnationals, and Developing Countries*. London, 1977. A review of the theory and empirical evidence of the role of foreign direct investment in development.

Leibenstein, Harvey. *Economic Backwardness and Economic Growth*. New York, 1957. A spelling out of the Big Push and Critical Minimum Effort notions.

Lewis, W. Arthur. *The Theory of Economic Growth*. London, 1955. The first major treatise on growth and development by one of the major figures in the early years of development economics.

Little, I. M. D., and J. M. Clifford. *International Aid*. London, 1965. A discussion of the many sides of the early experience with foreign aid to low-incomes countries.

Meier, Gerald M., and Robert E. Baldwin. *Economic Development, Theory, History, Policy*. New York, 1957. The first book designed specifically to be a text in development economics.

Meier, Gerald M., ed. *Leading Issues in Economic Development*. New York, 1964. A collection of articles and experts of articles on a wide variety of topics related to development.

Morawetz, David. *Twenty-Five Years of Economic Development: 1950–1975*. Baltimore, 1977. A survey of data and theory on the beginning years of development economics.

Myrdal, Gunnar. *Asian Drama*. New York, 1968. A three-volume study of development in Asia, with much attention to India.

Rostow, Walt. *Stages of Economic Growth*. Cambridge, 1960. An effort to divide history into several stages, the most interesting of which was the so-called "take-off."

Turnham, David. *The Employment Problem in Less Developed Countries: A Review of the Evidence*. Paris, 1971.

United Nations, Economic Commission for Latin America. *The Economic Development of Latin America and Its Principal Problems*. New York, 1950. The earliest statement of problems created by the existence of a "periphery" and a "center."

Waterston, Albert. *Development Planning: Lessons of Experience*. Baltimore, 1965. A major survey of the early planning efforts of many developing countries.

HENRY J. BRUTON

Development Policies

Economic development policies have gone through several marked shifts since World War II, reflecting changing theories of development and the failures of earlier policy efforts. The first generation of development policies (roughly covering the period 1945–1970) stressed the constraints put on development by scarce capital and by scarce foreign exchange. According to the so-called "Two-Gap Model" formalized by Hollis Chenery, built on earlier work by Arthur Lewis and Evsey Domar, developing countries faced a Leontief production function with fixed requirements for capital, labor, and imported inputs. Labor was assumed to be in excess supply, so what was crucial was the amount of financing available for investment (through domestic saving) and for imports (through exports and foreign aid). Government policy was necessary to increase saving and investment, such as by taxing consumers to finance public investment projects. Government planning was necessary to identify the key bottlenecks to be relieved by public investment, and many national planning departments throughout developing countries date from this era. State-owned enterprises (SOEs) were set up to implement these investments. These SOEs were particularly popular in newly independent Africa, where most of the private sector firms were owned by ex-colonials or other ethnic minorities.

As far as generating the imports necessary to fuel growth, increases in foreign aid helped but were not thought to be sufficient. Exports were constrained by the slowly growing world demand for primary commodities (the "export pessimism" school of Raul Prebisch), so government policies were also necessary to induce producers to economize on imports. This worldview inspired Latin America to pursue import-substituting industrialization behind high import tariff barriers in the 1950s and 1960s, with imitators scattered somewhat more widely throughout Africa and South Asia.

The second generation of development policies (roughly the decade of the 1970s) shifted the emphasis away from growth to income distribution and social concerns, like health and education, although this second generation was seen as supplementing rather than rejecting first-generation policies. A wave of populist governments came to power in developing countries, like Salvador Allende in Chile, Z. A. Bhutto in Pakistan, and Luis Echevarria in Mexico. For example, Echevarria, between 1970 and 1976, implemented a big expansion in public spending on social programs to foster redistribution with growth. The World Bank under Robert McNamara promoted poverty reduction and "integrated rural development" schemes to address the perception that growth in the 1950s and 1960s had benefited principally the landowning and manufacturing elites. The world population scare of the early 1970s also fostered increased emphasis on family planning policies.

The reckoning for the first two generations of development policies came with the debt crisis of the early 1980s in both low- and middle-income developing countries. The investment financed with foreign debt turned out not to have been sufficiently productive to service that debt. For example, in Mexico the government social programs under Echevarria and his successors had led to large government deficits and foreign borrowing. Social programs did not generate the kind of immediate payoffs to service the debt. Even Mexican public investment did not generate payoffs, since much of it was squandered on low-return projects, like the notorious state-owned Lazaro Cardenas steel mill that produced little steel despite billions of dollars of investment.

The early opportunities for substituting for light manufacturing imports in Latin America were exhausted fairly quickly, so import substitution began to drift into capital-intensive sectors in which Latin America was not efficient. Imports were increasingly financed with foreign borrowing rather than "substituted" in the 1970s. The day of reckoning came in August 1982, when the government of Mexico announced it could no longer service its debt and was quickly followed by most of the rest of Latin America and other middle-income countries, like Ivory Coast, Kenya, Morocco, and Nigeria. The result was a subsequent "lost decade" of growth.

At the same time the state-owned enterprises in Africa turned out to be sinkholes for political patronage and corruption, leading to excessive government deficits and debt for low-income countries in Africa. Growth had already been mediocre in the 1970s in Africa, but as it slowed further in the 1980s, Africa started to experience severe difficulties servicing its debt.

India in the 1980s expressed dissatisfaction with the low "Hindu rate of growth" under the import-substituting industrialization strategy. However, India did not develop a debt crisis.

The collapse of growth and crisis in debt servicing prompted a rethinking of development policies throughout Latin America, Africa, and Asia in the early 1980s. A third generation of development policy, the Washington Consensus, was born. This third generation of development policy marked a move back toward mainstream neoclassical economics. Statist development policies were out, market-friendly policies were in. Expansionary fiscal and monetary policies were out, and macroeconomic adjustment (fiscal and monetary austerity, often combined with currency devaluation) was in. Import substitution and protectionism were out, outward orientation and free trade were in (influenced in large part by the high export-led growth of East Asia, which escaped the debt crisis). State enterprises were out, privatization was in. The International Monetary Fund (IMF) and the World Bank supported this large change in development policies with the so-called "structural adjustment loans," which were supposed to tide countries over while they switched gears, enabling a return to high growth.

Empirical research on policies and growth in the 1990s supported claims that statist policies were associated with poor growth, although the mechanisms and causal directions underlying such associations were not clearly established. This empirical research mostly used data from the 1970s and 1980s. If the associations were interpreted as causal and reflecting a direct link from policies to growth, then developing countries would be predicted to enjoy rapid growth after reform.

Unfortunately for the typical developing country these predictions did not come to pass. In the first two decades after its adoption, the Washington Consensus did not live up to expectations. Progress toward adopting the policy reforms was halting and uneven, although most countries had finally adopted substantial reforms by 2000. Economic growth for most developing countries remained mediocre throughout the 1980s and 1990s, frustrating the key objective of structural adjustment loans—to restore growth. Progress on nonincome measures of well-being, like literacy and infant mortality, was steadier, but not tightly linked to policy reforms.

In the 1980s and 1990s Africa continued to stagnate, and Latin America lurched from crisis to crisis. Structural adjustment lending was so unsuccessful in Africa that the IMF and the World Bank agreed to forgive part of the loans in the "Heavily Indebted Poor Countries" initiative begun in 1996. An attempt to rapidly move to markets in the ex-communist countries of eastern Europe and the former Soviet Union was marked by a strikingly deep initial output depression. China and India experienced much more positive outcomes with rapid growth in the 1980s and 1990s, but their policies were not much in tune with the Washington Consensus (India and China both moved in the direction of free markets and free trade but stopped short of a market-friendly environment, compared to other developing countries).

Already by the early 1990s development economists were calling for yet another generation of reforms that would address corruption, make governments more efficient at delivering public services, and make governments more democratically accountable to their citizens. Research in the late 1990s gave empirical support to the importance of these institutional reforms. However, institutional reform is a slow process, and it is still an open question whether or not this generation of development policy will be any more successful than the previous ones. Perhaps the frequent disappointments with policy fads over the past fifty years should make development economists much more humble in making new policy recommendations.

[*See also* Economic Convergence and Divergence; Economic Growth; Economic Imperialism; Labor Surplus Models; *and* Living Standards.]

BIBLIOGRAPHY

Arndt, H. W. *Economic Development: The History of an Idea*. Chicago, 1987.

Easterly, William. *The Elusive Quest for Growth: Economists' Adventures and Misadventures in the Tropics*. Cambridge, Mass., 2001.

Easterly, William. "The Ghost of Financing Gap: Testing the Growth Model of the International Financial Institutions." *Journal of Development Economics* 60.2 (1999), 423–438.

Kapur, Devesh, John P. Lewis, and Richard Webb. *The World Bank: Its First Half Century*, vol. 1, *History*. Washington, D.C., 1997.

Meier, Gerald, and Joseph E. Stiglitz, eds. *Frontiers of Development Economics: The Future in Perspective*. New York, 2002.

Pearson, Lester B. *Partners in Development: Report of the Commission on International Development*. New York, 1969.

Perkins, Dwight H., Steven Radelet, Donald R. Snodgrass, Malcom Gillis, and Michael Roemer. *Economics of Development*. 5th ed. New York, 2001.

World Development Report: The Challenge of Development. Washington, D.C., 1991.

WILLIAM EASTERLY

ECONOMIC GROWTH. This essay considers four questions: (1) What is meant by "economic growth" and how well can we measure it? (2) What has been the experience of economic growth since the Industrial Revolution? (3) What have been the proximate sources of the rate of economic growth? and (4) Why have growth rates differed over time and across countries? These issues are central to the research program of economic history and are, to some extent, controversial. There has, however, been rapid progress in the recent past in terms of the development of new theoretical ideas and much better empirical evidence is now available.

What Is Economic Growth? Economic growth is the increasing ability of a society to produce goods and services and to satisfy consumer wants. Growth of productive potential results in part from the accumulation of more factors of production (capital, labor, etc.) through investment in machines and in skill formation and in part from increases in productivity (output per unit of factor input) derived from advances in technology, organizational efficiency, and so on. The most frequently used measure of economic growth is the rate of growth of real gross domestic product (GDP) per person in percentage points per year based on the national income accounts. This is obtained by totaling the monetary value added of everything produced each year and adjusting these nominal totals to real values using an index of prices.

Long-run economic growth has involved large increases in the level of real GDP per person. This typically involves substantial changes in the structure of the economy and the composition of output. As economies become richer, resources are shifted out of agriculture into industry and then to services, a higher share of GDP is saved and invested, the labor force is better educated, and technological capabilities improve. Over the past two centuries, the process of economic growth has been technologically progressive and has been characterized by the proliferation of new products and new techniques.

Gross domestic product is measured in national currencies. For international comparisons, these have to be converted into a common metric. It is generally accepted that the use of prevailing exchange rates is not the right way to do this. Instead, it is desirable to obtain an estimate of the "purchasing power parity" exchange rate, that is, of the outlay in the two currencies to buy a common basket of goods and services. Historical comparisons, as in Maddison (2001), are made by establishing a base year purchasing power parity level of real output per person in each country and then working backward and forward from there, using internal estimates of real GDP per person growth.

Real GDP is a measure of production rather than national income. The latter is usually defined as the amount that a society can consume this year while ensuring that the same level of consumption will be available in all future years. The associated national accounts concept is real net national product (NNP). Net rather than gross product means that resources are set aside to make good depreciation of the capital stock through replacement investment, and national rather than domestic product takes account of adjustments for income flows to and from the rest of the world. The traditional national accounts allow only for depreciation of physical capital, whereas, in principle, depletion of natural resources should also be included. In some circumstances, this might be a serious omission, for example, in the case of countries with substantial oil industries. In practice, it is generally assumed that GDP growth, which is much easier to measure, is a good proxy for NNP growth.

The measurement of long-term economic growth in these terms encounters serious index number problems. The price index numbers used to convert nominal to real GDP are weighted averages of prices where the weights depend on the relative importance of the component items in production. The weights that would be appropriate will vary over time and across countries and conversion of nominal to real values and the calculation of purchasing power parity may be sensitive to the choice of weights. Moreover, prices should be quality adjusted, and a procedure has to be adopted to deal with changes in the range of goods and services available over time. Generally speaking, these difficulties are greater in the economy of today than in that of the far distant past, in particular, as product innovation has accelerated and services have become a bigger share of economic activity, and are also more serious the longer the period over which growth is to be measured.

If, however, our concern in measuring economic growth is with living standards, the production-based approach of the national income accounts has further weaknesses. Ideally, we would wish to estimate how much income consumers need now to achieve a level of satisfaction (utility) equal to that of a base year given changes in prices, entry of new goods, and exit of old goods, recognizing that it is possible to trade off consumption of different goods one for another. This would inform us of the "true cost of living." If

TABLE 1. *Real GDP/Person, 1700–1998*

A) LEVELS ($1990 INTERNATIONAL)

	1700	1820	1870	1913	1950	1973	1998
W. Europe	1,024	1,232	1,974	3,473	4,594	11,534	17,921
U.K.	1,250	1,707	3,191	4,921	6,907	12,022	18,714
U.S.A.	527	1,257	2,445	5,301	9,561	16,689	27,331
China	600	600	530	552	439	839	3,117
India	550	533	533	673	619	853	1,746
Japan	570	669	737	1,387	1,926	11,439	20,413
East Asia				909	921	2,108	5,505
S. America	529	665	698	1,511	2,554	4,531	5,795
Africa	400	418	444	585	852	1,365	1,368
World	615	667	867	1,510	2,114	4,104	5,709

B) RATES OF GROWTH (% PER YEAR)

	1500–1820	1820–70	1870–1913	1913–1950	1950–1973	1973–1998
W. Europe	0.2	1.0	1.3	0.8	4.1	1.8
U.K.	0.3	1.3	1.0	0.9	2.4	1.8
U.S.A.	0.4	1.3	1.8	1.6	2.4	2.0
China	0.0	− 0.2	0.1	− 0.6	2.9	5.4
India	0.0	0.0	0.5	− 0.2	1.4	2.9
Japan	0.1	0.2	1.5	0.9	8.0	2.3
East Asia				0.0	3.7	3.9
S. America	0.2	0.1	1.8	1.4	2.5	1.0
Africa	0.0	0.1	0.6	1.0	2.1	0.0
World	0.05	0.5	1.3	0.9	2.9	1.3

Note: East Asia comprises Hong Kong, Indonesia, Malaysia, Philippines, Singapore, South Korea, Taiwan, and Thailand.
SOURCE: Maddison (2001).

new goods and services are imperfect substitutes for old ones in the sense that they offer additional new characteristics, then conventional price indices tend to exaggerate the rate of inflation (and underestimate the rate of growth of real consumption) because they fail adequately to allow for the value of these new attributes (Hausman, 1999).

More generally, if we wish to measure economic growth in terms of satisfaction of consumer wants rather than production, then it is appropriate to measure national income in terms of a utility-based concept (Nordhaus, 2000). This would represent the maximum amount that a nation can consume while ensuring that current utility levels are sustained in the future. But in this case, national income would have to be supplemented by the consumption equivalent of aspects of the quality of life not included in the national accounts. For example, in European countries over the past century, life expectancy has doubled and time spent in market work has halved. These improvements in living standards are worth a good deal in terms of the additional material consumption that would have to be given

to workers to compensate them for giving up lower mortality and longer leisure. An estimate of the growth of utility-based national income would augment the national accounts concept by embracing a valuation of such changes. Generally speaking, however, trying to measure growth in terms of a wider concept of income raises even more serious index number problems with regard to the weights to be applied to the various components.

A widely used measure of economic development is the human development index (HDI) proposed by the United Nations. This is actually a measure of the distance that a country has progressed in terms of an average of income, life expectancy, and education rather than of the speed of its advance. Its underlying rationale is that economic welfare depends not only on private consumption expenditures but, in most societies, also on state provision, for example, of education and health services. As many commentators have noted, HDI actually embodies an implicit set of weights that are nowhere explicitly set out or justified, including, of course, assigning a weight of zero to other aspects of well-being that are excluded. Nevertheless, HDI is an influential concept that offers a broader measure of the escape from poverty than do the national accounts, and it can be a useful supplement to conventional measures of economic growth.

What Has Been the Experience of Economic Growth? Table 1 reports estimates of rates of growth of real GDP per person and income levels for selected periods in constant prices adjusted for purchasing power parity. The chronology is also taken from Maddison (2001); although not ideal for all purposes, the periodization in Table 1 is quite convenient here. These growth rates exhibit a number of striking features.

First, it is clear that economic growth was very slow by later standards prior to the early nineteenth century. That said, there clearly were episodes of faster growth, for example, in Song China, but they were not well sustained over the long run of many centuries. Eventually, western Europe did open up a distinct gap in terms of income levels prior to the Industrial Revolution. Even when the pace then quickened, growth rates in the leading countries were at first modest compared with those observed after World War II.

Second, the first era of globalization in the pre-1914 period saw an additional acceleration of world growth and a widening spread of faster growth, notably to Latin America and to Japan, but this was followed by slower growth in the 1913–1950 period of global disintegration and World Wars. In these years, economic decline in China and India meant that by 1950 their income levels were much further behind the United States than in 1913.

Third, after World War II, there was a period of exceptionally rapid growth which, at least for the Organization for Economic Cooperation and Development (OECD) countries is generally described as a "Golden Age." This period ended in the mid-1970s, just as another era of what was to become much more profound globalization was on the way. Slowdown after the Golden Age was quite general except for China, India, and East Asia, while Africa and Latin America recorded slower growth than in any period since 1870.

Fourth, very rapid economic growth occurs during periods of catch-up growth, where a country initially has a productivity gap with the leaders and succeeds in reducing it rapidly during a period of high investment, industrialization, and technology transfer. The most famous example is that of Japan during the "Golden Age," but the leading East Asian "tiger" economies have also grown spectacularly since about 1960, as has China since the late 1970s. Rapid catch-up growth is by its very nature a transitory phase even if it lasts for a few decades. For advanced economies, 2 to 3 percent is as good as it gets.

The estimates reported in Table 1 are based on conventional national income accounting procedures. As such,

they need some qualification, as is apparent from the earlier discussion of concepts. Even on their own terms, they are subject to some error. In particular, the post-1973 slowdown in the OECD countries is probably overstated for two reasons. As the Boskin Commission pointed out, there has been a growing tendency for the national accounts to overestimate the rate of inflation (and thus to underestimate the rate of real output growth); by the 1990s, this may have led to American growth being understated by between 0.5 and 1 percent per annum. Also, since the 1960s, in response to high levels of regulation and taxation, there has been a major expansion of the shadow economy in many OECD countries, which may well have reduced recorded growth by 0.5 percent per year or even a little more (Schneider and Enste, 2000).

Probably more significant are the differences between growth of real national income per head based on a production-based concept as in Table 1 and a utility-based concept. Two aspects of this have attracted some empirical effort, namely, the gains from longer life expectancy and those from reductions in time spent in market work during the twentieth century. With regard to the former, Nordhaus (1998) provides a methodology and estimates for the United States that suggest that taking into account the consumption equivalent of the gain in longevity would more than double the growth rate of real consumption per person shown by the national accounts for that period. With regard to the latter, if wage rates are used to estimate the value of extra leisure, Crafts (2000) estimated that this would add about 0.3 percent to the typical OECD country growth rate prior to 1950 and about 0.5 percent post 1950.

Obviously, some other adjustments to the national income accounts would go in the other direction, for example, allowing for pollution, crime, and depletion of natural resources. Nevertheless, it seems very likely that, for the twentieth century, real living standards in the OECD grew more rapidly than the national accounts suggest. This was probably not, however, true for the pre-1850 period.

The experience of economic growth as captured in the national accounts has been described as "divergence big time" (Pritchett, 1997). Table 1 suggests an explanation, given the massive widening of income gaps over time between the poorest and richest areas of the world that the modern phase of economic growth has delivered. However, it should be noted that the recent acceleration of growth in China and India has ended the rapid advance of world income inequality that characterized the period from 1870 to 1970 (Crafts, 2002b).

In this context, it is also worth considering trends in the human development index (HDI), as reported in Table 2. Here perhaps the most notable feature is the rapid progress registered by Africa, China, and India since 1950. Even in Africa, average HDI by the late twentieth century

TABLE 2. *Human Development Index*

	1870	1913	1950	1999
North America	0.504	0.643	0.774	0.934
Western Europe	0.421	0.580	0.707	0.918
China			0.225	0.718
India		0.143	0.247	0.571
Japan	0.248	0.466	0.676	0.928
Africa			0.271	0.527

SOURCE: Crafts (2002b).

was above the late-nineteenth-century west-European level. The main reason for this progress is the enormous improvement in life expectancy prior to the onset of AIDS, which even in the worst-off countries had seen longevity above the level that Great Britain enjoyed in 1870. This reinforces the point that conventional measures of economic growth underestimate the advance of living standards during the twentieth century. Taking account of HDI also makes the twentieth-century experience of economic growth less one of divergence.

What Are the Sources of Growth? A useful distinction is that between the proximate and the ultimate sources of growth. The former relates to the contributions made by increases in factor inputs and productivity. A method of quantifying these proximate sources of growth widely used by economic historians is that of growth accounting. The latter refers to aspects of the social and economic environment that influence the rate at which inputs and productivity grow. In particular, they are grounded in the microeconomic foundations of the growth process in terms of institutions and policies that affect the incentives to invest and to innovate.

The standard growth accounting formula is the following

$$\Delta Y/Y = \alpha\Delta K/K + \beta\Delta L/L + \Delta A/A$$

where Y is real output, K is capital, L is labor, and A is total factor productivity (TFP) growth, while α and β are the elasticities of output with respect to capital and labor, respectively. Improvements in the quality of inputs (for example, in the skills of the labor force) can be explicitly included in the factor input terms if sufficient data are available, but if they are not, their contribution will be captured by TFP. Total factor productivity is measured as a residual after accounting for all the other terms in the equation and will reflect contributions to growth from better technology (unless this is accounted as better quality capital inputs), from economies of scale, and from improvements in the use of resources. The technique is especially useful as a method of benchmarking growth performance across countries, in which case it is often helpful to work with common values for α and β.

When this approach was pioneered in the 1950s, the original results were that almost all the growth of real output per person was accounted for by the residual. Similarly, the advent of "modern economic growth" was identified by Kuznets (1966) as an epoch where growth came to be driven by scientific and technological advance and the initial growth accounting estimates for the Industrial Revolution seemed to confirm the experience as a triumph of invention. Subsequent research has substantially modified these findings.

Table 3 reports selected estimates from the growth accounting literature, adapted to facilitate benchmarking. Assertions that the TFP residual is of overwhelming importance are clearly not valid, especially if directed to the growth of output rather than that of labor productivity. In fact, the contribution made by TFP growth has varied over time and across countries, as has that of factor inputs. The TFP estimates reported in Table 3 tend to exaggerate the impact of pure technological change since they also include the effects of education in raising the quality of the labor force and of improvements in the utilization of resources.

The following points should be noted from Table 3. First, in the United States, the contribution of capital seems to have been stronger in the nineteenth century than in the twentieth century, both absolutely and proportionately; and in the former period, capital intensity growth accounts for the vast majority of labor productivity growth, with TFP playing a minor role. In Great Britain during the Industrial Revolution and through the long nineteenth century, all sources of growth made quite modest contributions by later standards.

Second, TFP growth in the United States was much greater between 1913 and 1973 than either before or since. That acceleration of TFP growth, linked to the "second industrial revolution" and its new general-purpose technologies, went well beyond anything achieved by Great Britain during the first Industrial Revolution. In part, this reflects not only the less-powerful and more-prolonged impact of steam, the general purpose technology of that earlier era, but also the innovative capabilities of mid-twentieth-century America, which greatly exceeded those of Industrial Revolution Great Britain. In addition, the direct impact of education through labor force quality contributed almost 0.5 percentage points to the American acceleration in TFP growth.

Third, in the post-1950 Golden Age of growth, such countries as West Germany and Japan experienced exceptionally rapid TFP growth as well as strong capital accumulation. This growth owed a great deal to postwar recovery, which put underemployed factors of production back to work, together with the better allocation of resources based on trade liberalization and the contraction of agriculture. A

TABLE 3. *The Proximate Sources of Growth (% per year)*

	GDP	LABOR PRODUCTIVITY	CAPITAL	LABOR	TFP
Early Nineteenth Century					
GB 1780–1831	1.7	0.4	0.6	0.8	0.3
GB 1831–1873	2.4	1.1	0.9	0.8	0.7
USA 1800–1855	4.0	0.5	1.5	2.1	0.4
1871–1911					
Germany	2.8	1.4	1.1	0.8	0.9
U.K.	1.7	0.8	0.8	0.5	0.4
U.S.A.	4.3	1.5	2.4	1.6	0.3
1913–1950					
Germany	1.3	1.0	0.3	0.2	0.8
Japan	2.2	1.8	1.2	0.3	0.7
U.K.	1.3	1.6	0.4	− 0.2	1.1
U.S.A.	2.8	2.4	0.6	0.2	2.0
1950–1973					
Germany	5.4	5.3	1.8	0.1	3.5
Japan	9.2	7.8	2.8	1.0	5.4
U.K.	2.7	3.0	1.4	− 0.2	1.5
U.S.A.	3.6	2.4	1.1	0.9	1.6
1973–1995					
Germany	2.1	2.6	0.8	− 0.4	1.7
Japan	3.4	3.1	1.7	0.2	1.5
U.K.	1.7	2.3	0.7	− 0.4	1.4
U.S.A.	2.3	0.8	0.8	1.1	0.4
1960–1994					
East Asia	6.8	4.3	3.5	1.6	1.7
South Asia	4.2	2.3	1.8	1.2	1.2
Latin America	4.2	1.5	1.9	1.8	0.5
Africa	2.9	0.3	1.7	1.7	− 0.5
Middle East	4.5	1.6	2.5	1.9	0.1

Notes: The estimates have been adjusted to a common format and therefore in some instances differ slightly from those reported in the original sources. Labor quality is part of the TFP contribution. For benchmarking purposes, factor share weights have been standardized as follows: pre-1911: $\alpha = 0.4$, $\beta = 0.6$; advanced countries, 1913–1995: $\alpha = 0.3$, $\beta = 0.7$; developing countries, 1960–1994: $\alpha = 0.35$, $\beta = 0.65$. Germany is West Germany between 1913 and 1995. Post-1911 labor-force measures are based on hours worked, pre-1911 on persons in the labor force.

SOURCES: GB, 1780–1873: Crafts (1995); U.S.A., 1800–1855: Abramovitz and David (1999); 1871–1911: worksheets underlying Broadberry (1998); 1913–1950: Maddison (1991); 1950–1973 and 1973–1995: O'Mahony (1999); 1960–1994: Collins and Bosworth (1996).

detailed analysis can be found in Maddison (1996). Rapid catch-up also benefited from much-enhanced technology transfer in this period as American technology became more cost effective in other countries and those countries became better at assimilating it (Nelson and Wright, 1992).

Fourth, the very weak TFP growth in the United States after 1973 is a puzzle, especially in the context of advances in information and communications technology (ICT) and further increases in resources devoted to innovation. Developments after 1995, when a revival of TFP growth began, suggest that this may in part have reflected the long

gestation period before a new general purpose technology has a significant impact on productivity. This suggestion also seems to be consistent with earlier experience both of steam and electricity. Nevertheless, the weakness of late-twentieth-century American productivity growth is an important challenge to growth economics.

Fifth, the recent fast growth in East Asia looks rather different from that in western Europe's Golden Age. Table 3 reflects a very strong contribution from both capital and labor input growth such that, although TFP growth has been respectable, it is total factor input growth that has been unprecedented. Rapid labor-force growth has resulted from a demographic transition that led to favorable changes in age structure and in which, unlike Europe, hours of work per year have been sustained. Impressive capital stock growth has been based on high savings rates together with unusually low capital-to-output ratios.

Sixth, compared with Africa, which has represented a serious case of growth failure in the recent past, East Asia has had both much stronger TFP growth and more capital-per-worker growth. Africa's very weak labor productivity performance has been fundamental to an inability to keep up with the rest of the third world, let alone catch up the OECD countries. The post-colonial African growth experience has been very disappointing in terms both of capital accumulation and innovation.

Why Have Growth Rates Differed? The traditional workhorse model of economic growth was developed by Robert Solow (1924–) in the 1950s. Suppose that the economy can be represented as having a Cobb-Douglas production function such that

$$Y = AK^{\alpha}L^{1-\alpha}$$

where the notation is as before. This can, of course, be used as a theoretical justification for standard growth accounting. In this pure case, A will represent the state of technology, which is treated as exogenous and universal (manna from heaven). Here, α is less than 1, so there are diminishing returns to capital accumulation although there are constant returns to scale if both capital and labor increase by the same proportion.

If growth throughout the world were described by this setup, several important results would follow. First, long-run growth of output per worker is proportional to $\Delta A/A$, the rate of technological progress. Second, increasing the investment rate does not permanently raise the growth rate because it is eventually offset by capital productivity. Third, there should be no differences in TFP across countries. Fourth, if capital is fully mobile, it should flow from countries with high capital per worker to those with low capital per worker such that an automatic process of catch-up and convergence ensues. This catch-up is based on eliminating factor-intensity gaps.

Three pieces of empirical evidence are worth noting at this point. First, the assumption of diminishing returns to capital is correct (Oulton and Young, 1996). Second, capital has not flowed massively from rich to poor countries, as this model predicts (Lucas, 1990). Third, differences in income levels across countries are far too big to be explained only by capital per worker and reflect large differences in TFP (Parente and Prescott, 2000). The last two of these observations do not correspond to the traditional Solow model but would not surprise economic historians who have addressed the issue of how to explain economic growth.

Economic historians have traditionally focused on the ultimate sources of growth in the sense that they have sought to understand the reasons for differences in investment and innovation both over time and across the world. And in so doing, they have always stressed that institutions and economic policies matter. This is a common theme among writers as apparently diverse as Abramovitz, Gerschenkron, North, and Rostow.

Thus, Rostow (1960) in his famous stage theory of economic growth argued that there were prerequisites for take-off into sustained economic growth that included the advent of governments that would promote rather than obstruct growth and institutions that mobilized capital and entrepreneurship, that is, advanced a market economy. In exploring the scope for development from "backwardness," Gerschenkron (1962) explored the possibility that the state could intervene to create "unorthodox" institutions to substitute for missing "prerequisites." This involved a greater role for hierarchy and intrafirm decision making rather than reliance on markets and might be seen by later microeconomics as a possibly justified response to problems of transactions costs and asymmetric information that can impede investment and innovation in the early stages of development. This perspective is valuable in thinking about the role of the "developmental state" in East Asia.

Abramovitz (1986) emphasized the roles of technological congruence and, especially, social capability for successful catch-up growth. The former concerns the absence of obstacles to technology transfer arising from lack of cost effectiveness; for example, in the early twentieth century, it was often not profitable to adopt American technology, developed in conditions of cheap natural resources and mass markets, in European countries. The latter relates to the ability to assimilate advanced technology, which requires not only human capital but also institutions and political systems that do not undermine incentives or block reform. This perspective can fruitfully be applied to explaining the advent of the European postwar Golden Age.

Abramovitz was more pessimistic than Gerschenkron about the role of the state, seeing it as frequently part of the problem rather than the solution. North (1990) developed this point much further. Well-defined, enforceable property rights that reduce transactions costs in the form of exposure to opportunism and underpin investment and innovation lie at the heart of his view of the growth process. This implies a requirement for strong but limited government, able to promote the rule of law but constrained not to expropriate the returns to private enterprise. What is unclear is how these desirable attributes can be achieved. North pointed out that not only is there no natural selection process that ensures the replacement of inefficient with efficient institutions, but that network externalities, informal constraints, and the vested interests that surround existing arrangements tend to make institutional change a slow, incremental process and give it a path-dependent character. A central message is that achieving social capability is difficult.

The so-called new growth economics connects with these concerns in that it takes seriously the microeconomic foundations of investment and, especially, innovation. The models that are of most interest to economic historians are those in which innovation is endogenous, that is, where technological progress (including diffusion of technology and technology transfer) is influenced by economic factors. Some of these models also have the property that growth is endogenous, that is, that an improvement in economic policy or institutions can have a persistent growth rate effect rather than be offset by diminishing returns to capital as in traditional models where seeking to raise investment is the only policy lever.

Barro and Sala-i-Martin (1995, ch. 6) set out a model that illustrates this point. In their specification

$$Y = AL^{1-\alpha}NK^\alpha$$

where N is the number of varieties of capital goods, each of which in equilibrium is employed at the same level and can be measured in a common unit. This can be written as

$$Y = AL^{1-\alpha}(NK)^\alpha N^{1-\alpha}$$

where (NK) is the aggregate flow of capital services. This equation says that diminishing returns set in when K increases for given N but not when N rises for given K.

Here technological progress in the form of continuing increases in N can provide the basis for endogenous growth, but whether improved policy/institutions deliver this result depends on whether devoting more resources to innovative activities can escape periods of diminishing returns. If the model is applied to American experience as the leading twentieth-century economy, it appears from the record of TFP growth that this is not always true and that technological progress is more episodic than this.

What determines the rate of innovative activity in a model of this type? This generally depends on its profitability based both on costs (for example, the supply price of research and development inputs, attractiveness of alternatives) and expected revenues, which are related both to market size and, crucially, to the appropriability of returns. With regard to imitation by others, this may be enhanced by such devices as patents or by long lead times. In other respects, however, the issue is more one of ability to withstand opportunism perhaps by workers, or suppliers, or even predatory governments, and this links to a Northian view of technological progress. This may seem most obviously to apply to countries in which the rule of law is not firmly established but, for example, "hold-up" by multiple trade unions was probably a significant reason for weak

TFP growth in British manufacturing in the 1960s and 1970s (Bean and Crafts, 1996).

Broadly speaking, analysis along these lines is consistent both with much traditional discussion by economic historians of the "rise of the West"; in particular, both the expansion of markets and the development of effective property rights would be seen as positive for a breakthrough to modern economic growth. At the same time, these ideas also help explain why growth, even in the most advanced economies of the day, was much lower during the first Industrial Revolution than in the twentieth century, since at the time markets were relatively small, traditional rent-seeking occupations were highly lucrative, protection of intellectual property was insecure, and scientific education was minimal (Crafts, 1995).

Looking at the onset of sustained and significant growth of per capita income through this lens, it might be argued that a key feature of the world prior to, say, 1750 was that negative feedback effects generally resulted from episodes of growth. In particular, these were associated with weak institutions that were unable to restrain opportunistic behavior, which undermined incentives. If economic history is seen as a struggle between a propensity for growth and one for rent seeking (Jones, 1988), then most of the time the latter prevailed.

If appropriation is a key determinant of endogenous innovation, this might seem to reinforce the claim by economist Joseph Schumpeter (1883–1950) that market power is good for productivity growth. However, this is by no means always the case. Innovations are implemented by managers who may well find such changes costly in terms of the effort required. In enterprises with "agency problems," that is, where shareholders cannot easily control or monitor management, competition may enhance the adoption of innovations by revealing to shareholders that managers are underperforming and allowing shareholders more strongly to incentivize managers. This argument applies especially strongly to state-owned enterprise. Empirical investigation of British firms shows that increases in competition almost always raise the rate of innovation and suggests that British growth performance was undermined in the mid-twentieth century by a retreat into protectionism and cartelized markets (Crafts, 2002a).

The pioneers of the 1960s, for example, Simon Kuznets, were seeking to establish regularities in the pattern of modern economic growth. In the last fifteen years or so, growth regressions have become a popular tool for this kind of exercise, but, especially since the mid-1990s, these have been used to consider ultimate as well as proximate sources of growth. Indeed, an interesting aspect of this literature is that it has attempted to take into account institutional quality in terms of property rights, enforceability of contracts, the rule of law, and so on (as reflected in surveys of risk for international investment), and has attempted to quantify their importance for growth.

Growth regressions are statistical exercises that relate the rate of growth of income per capita for a cross-section of countries to a set of right-hand-side variables that reflect policy stance, institutional arrangements, exposure to world market shocks, and so on. The literature is voluminous, and some studies are undoubtedly beset by econometric problems, especially simultaneous equations and omitted variables biases (Temple, 1999). Nevertheless, some robust messages have emerged, and Table 4 reports results from a recent study that sought to establish an encompassing model and to decompose the gap between East Asian growth and that of other parts of the developing world.

Table 4 can be thought of as an attempt to quantify the role of social capability in catch-up growth. It confirms that institutions and policy have important effects. On average, autocracy is bad for growth, as is a failure to respect the rule of law. Exposing the economy to international competition and access to foreign markets has positive effects that outweigh any downside from exposure to adverse trends for primary producers in world markets. Fiscal responsibility has a payoff in terms of growth, as does better schooling. When all these things are taken into account, regional differences in growth are pretty well explained. The positive impacts of good institutions and openness for growth revealed here are consistent with their effects on levels of income across countries established, respectively, by Hall and Jones (1999) and Frankel and Romer (1999).

Broadly speaking, the evidence from growth regressions offers a strong vote of confidence to those economic historians who have always stressed that institutions matter for economic growth. In so doing, this literature also supports the thrust of new growth economics that incentives to invest and to innovate are central in explaining why growth rates differ. Given that many countries have had and still have very weak institutions, the failure of rapid catch-up growth to spread across the world becomes readily comprehensible. Globalization offers new opportunities, especially through better access to foreign capital, but only to those with good governance.

[*See also* Economic Convergence and Divergence; Economic Development; Industrial Revolution; *and* Living Standards.]

BIBLIOGRAPHY

PRIMARY SOURCES

Aghion, Philippe, and Peter Howitt. *Endogenous Growth Theory*. Cambridge, Mass., 1998. The best textbook treatment of growth based on endogenous innovation.

Barro, Robert J. "Notes on Growth Accounting." *Journal of Economic Growth* 4 (1999), 119–137. A clear account of the theoretical basis of growth accounting using either traditional or new growth economics.

Gerschenkron, Alexander. *Economic Backwardness in Historical Perspective*. Cambridge, Mass., 1962. A classic that is still valuable for its insights into the role of hierarchy as opposed to markets in the early stages of development.

Hall, Robert E., and Charles I. Jones. "Why Do Some Countries Produce So Much More Output per Worker than Others?" *Quarterly Journal of Economics* 114 (1999), 83–116. A careful econometric study that demonstrates that institutions have a large impact on productivity outcomes.

Jones, Eric L. *Growth Recurring*. Oxford, 1988. A very useful discussion of "pre-modern" growth and its episodic character.

Maddison, Angus. *The World Economy: A Millennial Perspective*. Paris, 2001. The standard source for historical estimates of economic growth.

Nordhaus, William D. "New Directions in National Economic Accounting." *American Economic Review Papers and Proceedings* 90 (2000), 259–263. An ideal starting point for thinking about how to augment conventional measures of national income.

North, Douglass C. *Institutions, Institutional Change and Economic Performance*. Cambridge, 1990. The classic statement of how institutions matter for economic growth and why they are hard to reform.

Rostow, W. W. *The Stages of Economic Growth*. Cambridge, 1960. A book that stimulated a great deal of useful research but is now part of the history of economic thought.

Temple, Jonathan. "The New Growth Evidence." *Journal of Economic Literature* 37 (1999), 112–156. A good guide to recent empirical work by growth economists.

SECONDARY SOURCES

Abramovitz, Moses. "Catching Up, Forging Ahead, and Falling Behind." *Journal of Economic History* 46 (1986), 385–406.

Abramovitz, Moses, and Paul A. David. "American Macroeconomic Growth in the Era of Knowledge-Based Progress: The Long-Run Perspective." Stanford Institute for Economic Policy Research. Discussion Paper No. 99–3, 1999.

Barro, Robert J., and Xavier Sala-i-Martin. *Economic Growth*. New York, 1995.

TABLE 4. *Explaining Per Capita Income Growth Rates Relative to East Asia, 1965–1990 (% per year)*

	SUB-SAHARAN AFRICA	LATIN AMERICA
Initial Income	+ 0.61	− 1.42
Human Capital	− 1.20	− 0.11
Age Structure	− 0.47	− 0.14
Institutions	− 1.05	− 0.80
Fiscal Policy	− 0.43	− 0.22
Openness	− 0.61	− 0.38
Prebisch/Singer	− 0.41	− 0.31
Residual	− 0.12	− 0.24
Total	− 3.68	− 3.62

SOURCE: Derived from Bleaney and Nishiyama (2002). Some variables are composites of the originals: "human capital" is schooling and life expectancy effects, "institutions" comprises both institutional quality and democracy, "fiscal policy" comprises government saving and consumption, and "Prebisch/Singer" comprises terms of trade effects and reliance on primary product exports.

Bean, Charles, and Nicholas F. R. Crafts. "British Economic Growth since 1945: Relative Economic Decline . . . and Renaissance?" In *Economic Growth in Europe since 1945*, edited by Nicholas F. R. Crafts and Gianni Toniolo, pp. 131–172. Cambridge, 1996.

Bleaney, Michael, and Akira Nishiyama. "Explaining Growth: A Contest between Models." *Journal of Economic Growth* 7 (2002), 43–56.

Broadberry, Stephen N. "How Did the United States and Germany Overtake Britain? A Sectoral Analysis of Comparative Productivity Levels, 1870–1990." *Journal of Economic History* 58 (1998), 375–407.

Collins, Susan M., and Barry P. Bosworth. "Economic Growth in East Asia: Accumulation versus Assimilation." *Brookings Papers on Economic Activity* 2 (1996), 135–203.

Crafts, Nicholas F. R. "Exogenous or Endogenous Growth? The Industrial Revolution Reconsidered." *Journal of Economic History* 55 (1995), 745–772.

Crafts, Nicholas F. R. "Globalization and Growth in the Twentieth Century." IMF Working Paper No. 00/44, 2000.

Crafts, Nicholas F. R. *Britain's Relative Economic Performance, 1870–1999*. London, 2002a.

Crafts, Nicholas F. R. "The Human Development Index, 1870–1999: Some Revised Estimates." *European Review of Economic History* 6 (2002b).

Frankel, Jeffrey, and David Romer. "Does Trade Cause Growth?" *American Economic Review* 89 (1999), 379–399.

Hausman, Jerry. "Cellular Telephone, New Products, and the CPI." *Journal of Business and Economic Statistics* 17 (1999), 188–194.

Kuznets, Simon S. *Modern Economic Growth*. New Haven, 1966.

Lucas, Robert E. "Why Doesn't Capital Flow from Rich to Poor Countries?" *American Economic Review Papers and Proceedings* 80 (1990), 92–96.

Maddison, Angus. *Dynamic Forces in Capitalist Development*. Oxford, 1991.

Maddison, Angus. "Macroeconomic Accounts for European Countries." In *Quantitative Aspects of Postwar European Economic Growth*, edited by Bart van Ark and Nicholas F. R. Crafts, pp. 27–83. Cambridge, 1996.

Nelson, Richard R., and Gavin Wright. "The Rise and Fall of American Technological Leadership." *Journal of Economic Literature* 30 (1992), 1931–1964.

Nordhaus, William D. "The Health of Nations: Irving Fisher and the Contribution of Improved Longevity to Living Standards." Cowles Foundation Discussion Paper No. 1200, 1998.

O'Mahony, Mary. *Britain's Productivity Performance, 1950–1996*. London, 1999.

Oulton, N., and G. Young. "How High is the Social Rate of Return to Investment?" *Oxford Review of Economic Policy* 12.2 (1996), 48–69.

Parente, Stephen L., and Edward C. Prescott. *Barriers to Riches*. Cambridge, Mass., 2000.

Pritchett, Lant. "Divergence, Big Time." *Journal of Economic Perspectives* 11.3 (1997), 3–17.

Schneider, Friedrich, and Dominik H. Enste. "Shadow Economies: Size, Causes, and Consequences." *Journal of Economic Literature* 38 (2000), 77–114.

NICHOLAS F. R. CRAFTS

ECONOMIC IMPERIALISM.

The term *imperialism* is generally used to mean foreign control of assets and decisions, including where such control exists in fact but not in law. Empire may be "formal" or "informal" (Gallagher and Robinson, 1953), "colonial" or "neocolonial" (in the terminology of dependency theory). This essay considers economic causes and effects of imperialism.

There is a long and geographically widespread history of rulers using force to enhance their fiscal and military potential by appropriating territory, subjects, or tribute from their neighbors. The literature on "economic imperialism," however, mainly concerns the last five hundred years. Its focus has been the causal relationships between the political and economic expansion of western Europe overseas and the consequences of European expansion for the economies of the rest of the world. This requires broadening, in recognition that the expansionary processes that emanated from Europe were extended, mainly by societies which themselves stemmed from earlier phases in these processes, such as the United States and Australia, but also by others on which Western imperialism had impacted from outside, notably Japan.

Types and Periods. Imperialism has taken diverse forms, often historically interrelated. But it is reasonable to make a basic distinction between the wholesale appropriation of territory, involving the demographic and political displacement of any previous occupants, and control over societies that, however reshaped, remained in occupation of much or all of the land.

Territorial appropriation and demographic displacement have occurred widely and recurrently, but in global terms the major example is the conquest and settlement, by west Europeans and people predominantly descended from them, of three already inhabited continents plus the previously uninhabited one, Antarctica. This process, begun with Columbus's arrival in the New World in 1492, was not essentially completed in North America and Australasia until the late nineteenth century. In South America in parts of the Amazon Basin, it was not quite finished by 2000. In the majority of these territories, the new societies, dominated by settlers or by Creole elites, won independence (for example, the United States, the republics of Latin America). Those British colonies of settlement established late enough for the imperial power to avoid the U.S. outcome became self-governing while retaining constitutional and political links with the "mother country." Haiti was an exception—a state created not by settlers but by a revolution (in the 1790s) of African slaves who had been imported to work the Europeans plantations.

Imperialism without anything approaching a demographic takeover also has an ancient and geographically widespread history, as when states were forced to pay tribute to foreign rulers. But in the context of the "economic imperialism" literature, two main subcategories may be identified.

One is informal: the use of force to secure or open foreign markets. This applies to the establishment by the Portuguese (from the fifteenth century), then (from the seventeenth century) by the Dutch, French, and English, of armed seaborne trading networks, with supporting shore bases, along much of the coasts of Africa and Asia. Naval power was used where possible to establish commercial hegemony over the existing Asiatic networks; characteristically, in each national case, a royal or chartered company monopoly was formed to export goods to Europe, while European company employees were permitted freely to engage in intra-Asian trade. The notion of "informal empire" also applies, conversely, to what Gallagher and Robinson called the "imperialism of free trade": the use of military and political pressure to coerce countries that were politically weaker and seemingly less competitive economically into opening their markets to foreign goods. The main era of this campaign was the mid-nineteenth century. It was practiced, arguably, by the British in Latin America and most especially in East Asia. Notable examples are the Opium Wars (1839–1842, 1858–1860), fought by Great Britain partly to oblige China to allow unrestricted imports of the drug from British India, and U.S. Commodore Matthew Perry's dictation to Japan in 1854 of an end to its self-imposed commercial isolation from the West.

The "formal" variant of imperialism without demographic takeover was colonial rule over predominantly indigenous populations. The main period of this may be dated from the British East India Company's establishment of control over the land revenue of Bengal in 1765. The trend was at its most intense in the late nineteenth century, when tropical Africa and much of Southeast Asia were partitioned among European powers. In the twentieth century, the process was braked, not only by lack of remaining opportunities, and in some cases by the emergence of powerful independence movements, but also by changing opinions in the imperial legislatures and in international gatherings. Thus, when Germany's colonies, plus the Arab provinces of the former Ottoman Empire, were divided between the victors of World War I, they were held on mandate from a new kind of international organization, the League of Nations. The sense that the appropriation of alien territory was increasingly regarded as illegitimate was signaled in the 1930s by the widespread international denunciation, by public opinion as well as governments—including Western imperialist countries—of the Italian and Japanese invasions of Ethiopia and China, respectively. Even so, the overwhelming consensus in the imperial polities was still that empire, as such, was morally acceptable and would endure. Yet, the west European retreat from colonies came relatively precipitately after 1945, most colonies gaining independence within twenty years, and was virtually complete by 2000.

Finally, it is important to note that the basic distinction drawn in this section is an analytical construct: the history was often less clear-cut, especially in Latin America and Africa. In much of what became Latin America, demographic displacement went beyond what the colonists had originally intended, while in certain cases that displacement was limited. The Spanish colonists initially intended to extract labor and tax from the local populations and polities they encountered; the rapid shrinking of indigenous populations went far beyond any military plans. Conversely, in some countries Native American numbers partly recovered in the seventeenth and eighteenth centuries. In Africa, certain colonies were envisaged as settler domains. But, in contrast to North America and Australia, settler economies always depended on African labor; and while the majority of the land was generally appropriated for white use, a portion was designated to be left in African hands with the intention that retired and future laborers would be fed by subsistence farming. Even in the country with the largest proportion of whites, South Africa, the vast majority of the population was always of African descent. In that sense, the "settler" economies ultimately belonged in the category of colonization without total displacement.

Theories of Economic Imperialism. The most influential economic theories of the causes and effects of imperialism all relate imperialism to the development of a capitalist-led world economy. Despite notable liberal contributions, the major tradition of theoretical writings on "economic imperialism" has been the Marxist-dependency one, against which critics such as Gallagher and Robinson have reacted. For Marx, imperialism was a form of "primitive accumulation," the use of a mixture of coercive and market methods to acquire resources that could be reinvested in the process of creating an advanced capitalist economy. It thus contributed to economic development in the imperial economies themselves. Yet, writing on British India, Marx took a paradoxically optimistic view of the impact of industrial-capitalist imperialism on less advanced economies. Colonialism was exploitative and brutal, but the logic of capitalist development ultimately accepted no frontiers. Motivated by the search for profit and propelled by competition among themselves, capitalist firms and the governments that (he argued) represented them would destroy precapitalist indigenous institutions (for example, in land tenure) and replace them with capitalist arrangements. Again, in pursuit of profit, they would introduce the most advanced transport technology available: in the nineteenth century, the steam railway. Greedy and initially destructive as the colonial rulers and firms would be, the ultimate result would be to advance India from what he considered a stagnant form of precapitalist economy on to a capitalist path of development.

A powerful development of the first half of Marx's analysis was provided by the West Indian historian Eric Williams. In *Capitalism and Slavery* (1944), Williams put forward the thesis that the Atlantic slave trade and plantation slavery in the New World provided reinvestable profits and cheap raw cotton on a scale essential for the British Industrial Revolution.

Dependency-theory writers broadly accepted the first half of Marx's analysis—and the Williams thesis—but rejected the second. They argued that the same process that brought development to the homelands of capitalism and to North America and Australasia simultaneously brought "underdevelopment" to the rest of the colonized world, trapping previously autonomous societies in poverty that was self-perpetuating because any significant profits made in them was extracted by Western firms or rulers (Frank, 1978). An important feature of dependency theory was the proposition that the end of colonialism was apparent rather than real, "decolonization" being really a transition to "neocolonialism," in which foreign capital continued to exploit the local population but with protection from a local client-state rather than from European officials. This analysis was built upon in left-wing critiques of U.S. government policy as well as of transnational corporations (Magdoff, 1969). Immanuel Wallerstein, in his *The Modern World-System* (1974, 1980, and 1989), which covers around 1500–1840, and elsewhere (*The Capitalist World Economy*, 1979) elaborated from the classic "dependency" argument in his own "world system" framework. This, however, envisaged some scope for upward economic mobility for underdeveloped countries. This provided some recognition of a reality that was then becoming increasingly clear: that industrialization was underway in formerly "underdeveloped" countries of East Asia in the 1960s to 1980s, while there had also been long-term growth of manufacturing in certain other parts of the third world, most notably Brazil. The economist Fernando Cardoso and others argued that, contrary to early dependency theory, *dependent development* was not a contradiction in terms but an accurate description of the dynamics of the Brazilian economy in the late twentieth century: an economy driven by a triple alliance of the national government, local capitalists (the junior partner), and foreign capitalists, the latter being mainly U.S. transnational corporations (Cardoso and Faletto, 1979). Meanwhile, Marx's "optimistic" (if also tragic) view of the consequences of imperialism for its victims was updated and restated, in a formidable polemic against dependency theory, by Bill Warren (Sender, 1980).

If Marxist and dependency writers have provided the most striking theories of the economic effects of imperialism, liberal writers have offered more on the motives and mechanisms of territorial and other forms of imperialism. Admittedly, Lenin made a much-cited contribution, *Imperialism: The Highest Stage of Capitalism* (1916 and 1942). But, written during World War I, this was primarily intended to explain the internecine aggression of industrial-ized capitalist states as the final stage of capitalism. He argued that in those countries in which capitalism was most advanced, the endeavor to sustain the rate of return on investment had led to the formation of monopolistic firms in the home market, who correspondingly encouraged their governments to use force to secure markets and raw materials abroad. Much of the inspiration for Lenin's formulation came from a liberal free trader, J. A. Hobson, whose classic *Imperialism: A Study* (1902, revised 1905, 1938) was a critique of what he saw as the economic interests behind Great Britain's recent pursuit of war with the Afrikaner republics. I will discuss how these theories have fared in the light of subsequent historical research.

Economic Causes of Empire. It is important to note three preliminary complications. First, the issue of economic elements in the causes of imperialism is a matter not only of the aims of the empire but also of its net costs. The latter affected the capacity of states to conduct imperialism even when the motivation for empire was noneconomic. Second, analysis of the motives for an empire has to take account of the fact that, almost always, more than one level of decision taking was involved. Just as Columbus needed a sponsor before he could sail, annexations were often authorized in the imperial capital "in response" to an initiative by a local commander or official. Conversely, much might depend on how the "man on the spot" interpreted his instructions, which had to be implemented after substantial delay (given the limits of communication technology in the period concerned) in an often unpredictable setting. Third, any satisfactory explanation of an annexation, for instance, must be structured: there were permissive and facilitating conditions as well as proximate causes. These complications help explain why analyses of the causes of specific imperial acquisitions or retentions often seem inconclusive. This rest of this section is organized in three parts. One enlarges on the methodological issues. The second reviews economic motives in the different forms and phases of imperialism outlined earlier, relating them to the evolution of economic development in a global context. The third comments on the changing costs of empire.

Analysis of motivation: methodological considerations. What kinds of economic motives have contributed to the acquisition and maintenance of empires, and how important were they compared to noneconomic motives? The following observations should be made.

A frequent motif in the historiography is the argument that the annexation of a particular place was determined on the spot rather than in the metropole. Logically, however, "peripheral" explanations can never be sufficient because, by definition, the local representatives of an imperial power could be overruled. Therefore, an adequate analysis must account for the different attitudes of

European governments toward the enthusiastic aggression of subordinates on the ground.

A common objection to economic explanations of metropolitan manifestations of imperial expansionism is that the prospective colony concerned accounted for only a small percentage of the prospective colonizer's overall trade and investment. This argument fails on marginalist logic. In economic terms, the question was surely whether the incremental cost of annexation compared with nonannexation was expected to be exceeded by the incremental benefits from trade and investment in the territory if it was colonized, compared to if it was not. Thus, the most significant aspect of the share of trade with Africa in the overall foreign trade of Great Britain, France, and Portugal in 1875, virtually on the eve of the "scramble for Africa," was not that it was small, but rather that it became much greater after the establishment of colonial rule (see Table 1).

Equally, that a territory's economic involvement with a particular European economy should have increased after annexation does not prove that this was the aim of annexation. Trade and investment could follow the flag even when the flag was imposed from noneconomic motives. The fact that the area was now a colony presumably reduced transaction costs for firms from the colonizing country. Meanwhile, the new colonial administration needed to justify its existence by trying to attract investment and by raising tax revenue—which was most easily obtainable via greater output for the market, and especially for export.

Finally, to resolve issues of motivation it is helpful to be able to examine the unpublished papers of the decision makers. Even so, care must be taken to check for consistency of purpose. If a private company wanted an imperial government to annex the country with which it was trading, it was in its interests to use whatever arguments it considered most likely to sway the decision—whether or not those arguments represented its own priorities. Conversely, a government that decided on an annexation for, say, political reasons might well have a political interest in allowing those who had petitioned for the annexation on commercial grounds to believe that the decision was specifically a favor to the petitioners.

Economic aims in imperialism. It would be unrealistic to expect to find a consistent set of aims for imperialism, even when the inquiry is "limited" to half a millennium of mainly Western domination. The noneconomic motives varied with cultural and political context. Thus if militant Christianity did much to inspire Iberian colonists in the New World, this hardly applies—certainly not in the same way—to the Dutch and English trading companies in the seventeenth and eighteenth centuries and is irrelevant to the French colonial annexations of the late nineteenth century, under the strongly secular Third Republic. Again, rivalry within Europe affected the behavior of European states overseas, but in varied, even opposite, ways depending on the position of the individual polity concerned. Following the Franco-Prussian War of 1871, French governments may have acquired vast spaces in Africa (from 1879) in part as perceived compensation for the loss of smaller but more highly valued space at home. But, by definition, such reasoning cannot explain why Germany (in 1884) acquired four African colonies itself. Economic aims were often important. But they, too, varied in patterns that are most plausibly understood as relating to the changing economic interests of the countries concerned—and especially of their decision-making business and political elites—in the context of international economic relations and development.

For the Iberian pioneers of expansion beyond Europe, the search for wealth appears to have been a powerful incentive, though it was necessarily realized in different forms: precious metals as loot for the invaders themselves, institutionalized flows of gold and silver from mines and taxes from Spanish America to the Spanish crown, and trading profits (some of them monopolistic) for Portuguese traders. The latter was the official purpose of the chartered companies created by northwestern European countries in subsequent centuries. In India, the transition of the British East India Company from merchant to ruler of most of India (by 1818) was, at one level, a series of piecemeal responses to crises in or with particular indigenous states that destabilized trading conditions (crises themselves partly the result of earlier British interventions). At a higher level of decision making, the main reason the East India Company directors overcame their reluctance to accept further territorial responsibilities was financial: the prospect of additional land revenue.

It seems clear that the "imperialism of free trade," whatever its ideological justification, was underpinned by the calculation that the Industrial Revolution had given Great Britain, and then other Western producers, a competitive edge in manufactured goods in overseas markets, notably in Asia. This is not the full story, however: Great Britain's

TABLE 1. *Share of Trade with Sub-Saharan Africa in Total Trade of Great Britain, France, and Portugal, 1875–1920 (selected years)*

Exports (Imports)	1875	1890	1905*	1920
Great Britain	2.9 (2.6)	4.3 (3.5)	8.3 (6.9)	6.7 (6.6)
France	1.5 (1.2)	0.8 (1.4)	0.5 (0.8)	2.0 (3.4)
Portugal	5.0 (2.5)	6.0 (2.5)	15.0 (3.5)	13.0 (4.5)

*In the British case, 1906.
SOURCE: Austen Ralph. *African Economic History*, pp. 277–278. London, 1987.

existing colonial interests in India were reflected in the name *Opium Wars*.

Less clear, and much disputed, are the reasons for the round of territorial annexations between 1875 and 1910. One point now established in the literature is that the Hobson-Lenin approach is largely irrelevant. Although there was indeed a vast outflow of capital from Great Britain and France in the period, little of it went to the countries that now came under colonial rule. Much stronger cases, however, have been made for the pertinence of other economic interests.

In Portugal, the least industrialized of the European countries that "scrambled" for Africa, the acquisition of further territory was seen as economically advantageous, though the economic imperialists disagreed over whether this advantage could be maximized by, in effect, leasing colonial resources and markets to foreign firms or having Portuguese companies exploit the opportunities themselves (Clarence-Smith, 1979).

British, French, and German merchants trading on the West African coast lobbied their respective governments, using chambers of commerce and members of their elected legislatures, for annexations to reduce the risks and costs in their dealings with African traders and rulers—problems that had increased because of a depression in the export trade of oil-palm products to Europe (Hopkins, 1973). For South Africa, it is necessary to explain why the British were willing to accept the independence of the Boer republics as late as 1881 (when the first war between the British and Afrikaners ended because Prime Minister Gladstone declined to pursue what was essentially a local quarrel), yet fought a major war to conquer them in 1899–1902. Economic hypotheses have centered on the discovery of gold on the Witswatersrand in 1886. For example, it has been argued that British mining companies sought to engineer a British annexation because they feared that the Afrikaner authorities would put the interests of Afrikaner farmers over those of British mine owners when it became a competition for African labor (Marks and Trapido, 1979, pp. 43–57; Porter, 1990, pp. 43–57).

In responding—selectively, albeit usually favorably in this period—to calls for annexations from economic interest groups operating in the countries concerned, policy makers in the imperial capitals had broader political and economic considerations. The influence of the latter can be seen in the role played by Joseph Chamberlain, the British colonial secretary from 1895 to 1903 and, therefore, a key figure in the final phase of British annexations in West Africa and in the origins of the South African War. Chamberlain, who had himself been a screw manufacturer, was to go on to champion the cause of commercial autarky for the British Empire. In office, he sought to extend the "undeveloped estates" of the British Empire in Africa

BRITISH EMPIRE. An 1887 advertisement for Pears' Soap assures British consumers "even if our invasion of the Soudan has done nothing else it has at any rate left the Arab something to puzzle his fuzzy head over." (The Fotomas Index, U.K.)

and elsewhere, not just to deny them to France or other rivals but to provide markets and investment opportunities for British private investment. This was in anticipation of a future in which Great Britain faced growing commercial competition from the industrial advances being made in Germany and the United States.

The most provocative and influential contribution of recent decades to the debate about the sources of British imperialism is P. J. Cain and A. G. Hopkins's *British Imperialism* (1993). They argue that, throughout the whole history of British overseas expansion, the decisive interest groups behind it were "gentlemanly capitalists," concentrated in London and the "home counties." Thus, not only was seventeenth- and eighteenth-century British imperialism pushed by landowners and merchants, but they were also succeeded in this, not by the northern manufacturers associated with the industrial revolution, but by City of London financiers. Cain and Hopkins's analysis has attracted controversy, which shows no sign of diminishing (Dumett, 1999;

Akita, forthcoming). What is now needed is a systematic effort to place the British debate in a full comparative context.

Economic costs of empire. Economic gain, whether for the "metropolitan" economy as a whole or for a sectional interest with influence over policy, may be an aim of empire. But the costs of acquiring and maintaining control, and the capacity of the metropolitan economy to meet those costs, are relevant to any analysis of the causes of empire, even when the motivation for imperialism is political and cultural rather than economic. In this context, the following observations should be made.

European capacity to create overseas empires—on a scale totally unprecedented in world history—was not invariably or necessarily founded in an overwhelming economic superiority, which enabled them to meet costs that would have been prohibitive to others. At the base of European imperial expansion were the advances in navigation and gunnery, which enabled small numbers of Portuguese ships to dominate much of the Indian Ocean; guns and horses, which assisted tiny numbers of Spanish to overwhelm the Aztec and Inca empires; and the numbers and quality of firearms that British and other European forces brought to bear around the world over several centuries, usually keeping ahead of efforts by their opponents to catch up by imports and improvisation. The diseases that the Europeans brought with them also helped in the conquest of the Americas. In the tropics, on the other hand, pathogens tended to raise rather than lower the net cost of conquest, at least until (starting in the 1850s), the Europeans began to make use of quinine against malaria.

The material and human costs of maintaining political control were a major determinant of the longevity of empire. In much of imperial history, European governments avoided many of these costs by leaving empire to private (or joint private-state) enterprise. The major form of this was the chartered company. Such arrangements lasted often until the company concerned was unable to prevent or suppress indigenous resistance, at least not without major subsidy and/or bad publicity to embarrass the imperial government. The British East India Company was abolished by the British Parliament following the South Asian Revolt of 1857, and a similar fate befell chartered companies in the German colonies in Africa.

Even when imperial governments assumed responsibility over the territories concerned, it might be possible to save money, again by delegation, but this time to indigenous employees and authorities. Thus, in British West Africa, military and police forces were small and mainly recruited within the region, while lower-level judicial and executive functions were delegated to African chiefs. When colonies were cheap, it was easier for the imperial power to leave aside the issue of whether they made a net contribution to the exchequer. Conversely, British India

had a major army, but the costs were borne by Indians, and its existence was considered a major military and political asset in Great Britain's global profile. The other way to limit the costs of coercion was to avoid policies likely to provoke large-scale resistance. Thus, after 1857, the British government of India followed a cautious policy in rural areas, eschewing land reforms that might upset vested interests (which officials believed to have been a cause of the uprising) and collecting land tax with a much lighter hand.

Finally, rising costs contributed to the end of empire after 1945. For France in Indochina and Algeria, as for the Netherlands in what became Indonesia, the costs of war against armed independence movements became unsustainable. In Portugal, the costs of fighting liberation wars in its African colonies (including increasingly long periods of conscription for young men) contributed greatly to the revolution that overthrew the dictatorship in Lisbon in 1974. Costs were also relevant in the much more peaceful context of the British and French withdrawal from tropical Africa. In the mid-1950s, both imperial governments concluded that colonial rule was increasingly expensive because it was now politically essential—in the colonies themselves, in the imperial legislatures, and in the context of Cold War competition—to be actively "developmental." This was expected to entail heavy metropolitan investments in infrastructure and education in the colonies. Both in London and Paris, such investments were no longer considered worth the likely return to the imperial economies (Cooper, 1996).

Economic Results of Empire for the Colonized. The consequences varied with the nature and context of the imperial relationship. Where imperialism involved demographic displacement, indigenous populations generally experienced catastrophe: huge losses of lands and population and a long-term struggle to secure a share of the modern economies that were eventually created in their old territories.

The early modern trading empires had mixed results, depending partly on the nature of the commodity. Despite the monopolistic behavior of each European company, there was competition between (effectively) independent European traders in the intra-Asian trade. For much of the eighteenth century especially, there was competition on the West African coast and in the Indian Ocean between various European-chartered companies, while each company faced independent European "interlopers." Particularly, though not exclusively, where the Europeans' trading partners—the merchants and rulers they dealt with in Africa and Asia—remained politically independent during the period, those partners (and, indirectly, their partners' suppliers) could gain from the overseas markets to which the European merchants gave them access. Thus, Indian cloth was sold, for example, in West Africa and Mexico.

African trading elites acquired revenue and imported trade goods, even while African economies absorbed the external costs of commerce based on the capture and export of people. In Asia, the Europeans had to pay for goods mostly with bullion: the coins issued by the Mughal emperors in the seventeenth century were made of American silver. The implication of this exchange was that the trade enlarged the output and income of Indian producers without subjecting them to the competition that imported goods would have represented (Prakash, 1998).

The impact of the informal imperialism of free trade was again limited to the extent that the countries affected remained politically sovereign. For Japan, the external challenge acted as a wake-up call. For China, though the Opium Wars resulted in increased consumption of the drug, the British were foiled in that the Chinese market was soon supplied largely by import-substituting Chinese producers.

A broad contrast may be drawn between the new economies created in the territories in which Europeans had largely displaced earlier populations and those colonies that remained mainly occupied by indigenous populations. The distinction can be put in terms of the import of factors of production; of the material and technical means to raise productivity by establishing new and higher production functions (new techniques, tools, and organisms); and of the institutional means for doing so, especially in the form of changes in property rights in factors of production. Generally, the colonies—and their successor states—taken over by European immigrants had relatively high rates of import of capital and labor, the latter including African slaves, in the New World. A qualification should be entered for Spanish America, where the flow of bullion to Spain seems to have largely bypassed opportunities for investment in colonial agriculture, at least until the late eighteenth century. Freed by the mid-nineteenth century from mercantilist restrictions, whether through the achievement of independence, or by imperial reforms, the new economies went on to attract most of the capital that flowed out of Europe, including during the golden era of such investment (c. 1870–1914). The interrelated process of conquest, settlement, and trade led not only to the transfer of tools and techniques but also to extensive exchange of animal and plant species between continents (Crosby, 1986). On the whole, productivity in the "countries of recent European settlement" was boosted by these biological introductions: Australia benefited from the sheep more than it lost from the rabbit, for instance, while Native Americans as well as European settlers made effective use of the horse. More generally, by 1900 it was clear that, as a result of some combination of these successful importations, these economies had expanded greatly for the most part since the creation of the original colonies. The exceptions were mainly in Latin America, but even there

Argentina was becoming one of the richest (per head) economies on earth, while by 1914 Brazil had a substantial light-manufacturing sector.

European settlers and their descendants generally adopted—and went on to change—rules of economic life derived from a model in their native continent. In this context, differences between empires may be as important as the shared experience of imperial rule. It has been argued that much of the economic success of North America is attributable to a favorable legacy of growth-conducive institutions from Great Britain, especially individual property rights, defined and secured both at micro level and in constitutional law and political process. By contrast, the argument continues, the institutional legacies of Latin America were less conducive to economic growth, and this accounts for the slower post-independence growth of the Latin American states. This view is plausible but surely insufficient. Alternative explanations relate not only to differences in factor endowment but also to the fiscal costs of achieving independence: whereas the costs of the American Revolution were borne partly by the French, the South American republics had to pay all their own expenses, a burden that denied them the opportunity to emulate the United States in moving fairly swiftly into self-sustaining economic growth (Bernecker and Tobler, 1993; Coatsworth, 1998).

African and Asian colonies attracted relatively small inflows of colonial capital and labor. India had only about 10 percent of British overseas investment by 1913. European agricultural techniques were tried, but in the tropics they often proved inefficient in the different climatic as well as economic conditions. Industrial-Revolution technology enabled British firms not only to take over the overseas markets that European ships had previously opened to Indian spinners and weavers but also to make great inroads into the domestic markets of handicraft industries in Asia and Africa. On the other hand, European sea trade gave African and Asian farmers the chance to try American plants, such as the cocoa tree with the result that—primarily through indigenous enterprise—West Africans became the main cultivators of this Amazonian species. In some colonies, notably in West Africa and Southeast Asia, export agriculture brought substantially higher—if fluctuating—real incomes to broad sections of the population. Even in industry, by 1914 Indian factory owners had taken over much of the market share that handicraft producers had lost to imported cloth. Colonial governments generally concentrated their investments on transport infrastructure, notably railways. The effect was to encourage export orientation in agriculture.

At an imperial level, colonies were expected to specialize in the production of primary commodities, and their administrations rarely did much to promote manufacturing. But some qualifications should be noted. A modern textile industry developed in North Vietnam from 1894 (under French ownership), based on cheap labor and defended by French tariffs, while in the Dutch East Indies, textiles led a varied manufacturing sector (under European, Chinese, and American ownership) that emerged strongly, also behind a tariff wall, in the 1930s. Even the government of British India became gradually more supportive of manufacturing during its last fifty years, partly because of pressure from nationalists (as with the introduction of a provision for "infant industry" protection in 1924). As of 1950, India was the tenth-largest producer of manufactured goods in the world. But Korea, under Japanese rule, was the only colony to have a substantial heavy industrial sector built on its soil. Finally, Kaoru Sugihara links the observation that the City of London "was a vital facilitator of technological transfer from the West to East Asia" with Cain and Hopkins's argument that British imperialism was driven by financial rather than industrial interests (Sugihara, forthcoming). This suggests an element of complementarity between British economic imperialism and the industrial development of Japan.

European institutions were much less widely adopted in the colonies of predominantly indigenous habitation than in those of mainly European settlement. In the early decades of British colonial rule east and south of the Mediterranean, it seemed that Great Britain was determined to refashion land tenure along British lines. In Bengal in 1793, Governor Cornwallis sought to create an English-type structure of landlords and tenants, in which the former would theoretically have an interest in encouraging improved methods of cultivation by the latter. Following the annexation of Lagos in 1861, the colonial government created individual titles in land to facilitate the capital as well as land markets. But such institutional radicalism was soon halted in India and West Africa: subsequent British policy was more cautious and generally sought to preserve what the administrations defined as the "traditional" land tenure system. An exception was lands reserved for white settlers in certain colonies. Otherwise, during the colonial twentieth century, tendencies toward stronger individual rights in land tenure and to the buying and selling of cultivation rights generally emanated from market forces or "informal" indigenous adaptations of existing practices, rather than from formal colonial intervention.

Colonial regimes generally adopted a similarly cautious approach to the reform of labor institutions. Europe's mercantilist empires in much of the New World had been based on slave plantations. When Europe partitioned Africa, the imperial powers committed themselves to abolishing slavery wherever they found it. Yet in practice, colonial governments usually took years or even decades before effectively prohibiting the various forms of slavery

and debt bondage that they encountered south of the Sahara.

This widespread reluctance of colonial regimes to impose contemporary European models of land and labor law on African and Asian societies stemmed partly from budget constraints: lack of revenue to pay for compulsory land titling or compensate owners of freed slaves. But more fundamentally, colonial administrators tended to put maintaining social order ahead of reform. Individual ownership of land and individual ownership of their own labor power could result in a breakdown of social control, as poor peasants lost their land through debt or sale, and/or as former slaves left their masters for an uncertain wage-labor market. When colonial governments encouraged wage labor, mainly for European employers (mines, plantations, or settler farms), it was usually in the halfway form of seasonal migration rather than full-scale dependence on the market. Yet by the end of colonial rule, Marx's "modernizing" view of capitalist imperialism had come at least half true. Partly in response to changes in demand for factors of production rather than because of colonial policies on land and labor as such, land tenure was often more commercialized, while labor was recruited from outside the family more often than before and, above all, was obtained on relatively free markets.

Economic Results of Empire for the Colonizers. It is questionable whether the possession of empire contributed to economic growth or structural development in the early modern era (to c. 1815). Spanish miners, shippers, and the monarchy and its payroll all benefited in real terms. But the orientation of imperial commerce toward the annual shipment of bullion to Spain was at the cost of inflation—transmitted throughout Europe but highest in Spain—and was associated with (though did not directly or sufficiently cause) lagging industrial expansion in Spain. Even in the Dutch economy, whose relatively advanced market orientation equipped it to take advantage of a trade-based empire, commercial expansion was not converted into sustained development of manufacturing. For France, the overseas adventures of the early modern era contributed greatly to the fiscal burden, which helped bring the ancien régime to crisis.

Great Britain was, arguably, the one early modern European economy to derive sizable net gains from empire, and it was the one with by far the largest trade with other continents. Yet, the importance of these gains has been much disputed. Patrick O'Brien argued that such commerce made a quantitatively insignificant contribution to the reinvestable surplus even of Great Britain, let alone of western Europe generally (O'Brien, 1982; compare Wallerstein, 1983). Meanwhile, research on the genesis of that revolution has emphasized domestic sources of investment and the importance of domestic and European

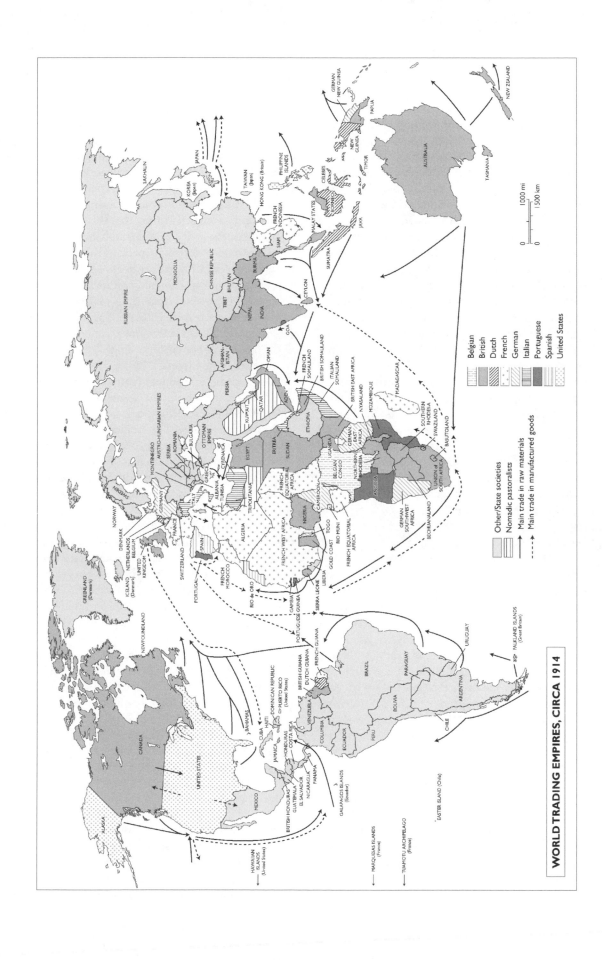

WORLD TRADING EMPIRES, CIRCA 1914

Belgian
British
Dutch
French
German
Italian
Portuguese
Spanish
United States

Other/State societies

Nomadic pastoralists

Main trade in raw materials

Main trade in manufactured goods

ALASKA

HAWAIIAN ISLANDS (United States)

MARQUESAS ISLANDS (France)

TUAMOTU ARCHIPELAGO (France)

EASTER ISLAND (Chile)

CANADA

UNITED STATES

MEXICO

BRITISH HONDURAS
GUATEMALA
EL SALVADOR
HONDURAS
NICARAGUA
COSTA RICA
PANAMA

GALAPAGOS ISLANDS (Ecuador)

BAHAMAS
CUBA
JAMAICA
HAITI
DOMINICAN REPUBLIC
PUERTO RICO (United States)

COLUMBIA
ECUADOR
VENEZUELA
BRITISH GUIANA
DUTCH GUIANA
FRENCH GUIANA

PERU
BRAZIL
BOLIVIA
PARAGUAY
CHILE
ARGENTINA
URUGUAY

FALKLAND ISLANDS (Great Britain)

GREENLAND (Denmark)

ICELAND (Denmark)

NEWFOUNDLAND

NORWAY
SWEDEN
DENMARK
UNITED KINGDOM
NETHERLANDS
BELGIUM
GERMANY
FRANCE
SWITZERLAND
PORTUGAL
SPAIN
ITALY
ALBANIA
GREECE
MONTENEGRO
SERBIA
BULGARIA
ROMANIA
AUSTRO-HUNGARIAN EMPIRE

RUSSIAN EMPIRE

MONGOLIA

CHINESE REPUBLIC

TIBET
NEPAL
BHUTAN
INDIA
BURMA

SIAM
FRENCH INDOCHINA

SAKHALIN
KOREA (Japan)
JAPAN
TAIWAN (Japan)
HONG KONG (Britain)
PHILIPPINE ISLANDS

MALAY STATES
SUMATRA
BORNEO
CELEBES
JAVA
TIMOR

NEW GUINEA
GERMAN NEW GUINEA
PAPUA

AUSTRALIA
TASMANIA

NEW ZEALAND

AFGHAN-ISTAN
PERSIA
OTTOMAN EMPIRE
CYRENAICA
TRIPOLITANIA
TUNISIA
ALGERIA
FRENCH MOROCCO
RIO de ORO

QATAR
KUWAIT
OMAN
ADEN

FRENCH SOMALILAND
BRITISH SOMALILAND
ITALIAN SOMALILAND
BRITISH EAST AFRICA

EGYPT
SUDAN
ERITREA
ETHIOPIA
UGANDA

FRENCH EQUATORIAL AFRICA
BELGIAN CONGO
GERMAN EAST AFRICA
NORTHERN RHODESIA

GOA
CEYLON

MADAGASCAR
MOZAMBIQUE
NYASALAND
SOUTHERN RHODESIA
SWAZILAND
BASUTOLAND
UNION of SOUTH AFRICA
BECHUANALAND
GERMAN SOUTH-WEST AFRICA
ANGOLA

FRENCH WEST AFRICA
GAMBIA
PORTUGUESE GUINEA
SIERRA LEONE
LIBERIA
GOLD COAST
TOGO
NIGERIA
CAMEROON
RIO MUNI
FRENCH EQUATORIAL AFRICA

1000 mi
1500 km
0

markets, rather than colonial trade. Clearly, possession of an overseas empire was unnecessary for an industrial revolution, as was demonstrated by nineteenth-century Germany. Neither was it sufficient, as was demonstrated by the slow economic development of Portugal and Spain after their acquisition of empires.

Recently, Kenneth Pomeranz (2000) has reemphasized the importance of empire to the eighteenth-century British economy. He argues that what finally enabled Great Britain (and, by extension, the West as a whole during the nineteenth century) to industrialize when China did not was that whereas Chinese growth ran into diminishing returns caused by a shortage of land and fuel, the British took advantage not only of their own coal but of the availability—thanks to colonialism—of North American natural resources. Thus, if the British economy escaped an ecological bottleneck, an essential contribution was made by cheap fuel and food from across the Atlantic, as well as by cheaper raw material for textiles, thanks to the combination of American land and African slaves.

The contribution of formal colonialism without demographic takeover to the "metropolitan" economies has been similarly controversial. The Dutch economy derived major benefit from its territorial empire in the nineteenth century following the establishment, from around 1830, of the Cultivation System, under which Javanese were forced to grow selected export crops on a large scale. In the heyday of the system, the 1850s and 1860s, the financial surplus from the Dutch East Indies constituted more than 30 percent of Dutch public revenue; but the system was dismantled during the late nineteenth century under domestic criticism (Brown, 1997). The French economy appears to have benefited, though relatively modestly, from colonies in Algeria and Indochina, though not necessarily from France's sub-Saharan possessions before 1945. The Portuguese economy arguably obtained net gains in the 1930s–1950s from more systematic exploitation under the Salazar regime—before the gains were swallowed by the costs of fighting independence movements. Part of the problem for European empires is said to have been that possession of "captive" markets deflected metropolitan firms from the central task of adapting to remain competitive with the new industrial leaders, including those with relatively minimal colonial empires—the United States and Germany.

That thesis would seem least applicable to the largest empire, the British, because of the British commitment to free trade until 1931. Even so, the fullest quantitative balance sheet of the British empire concluded that the British economy was the poorer for empire, though private investors, especially those from London and from the social elite, were the richer (Davis and Huttenback, 1986; compare O'Brien and Prados de la Escosura, 1999). Davis and Huttenback's analysis has been strongly disputed: their

finding of a net loss depends, for instance, on the problematic issue of how much the defense of Canada cost the British treasury. If the calculation were redone to allow for Canadian and other overseas imperial contributions to the British war efforts from 1914 to 1918 and from 1939 to 1945, the overall picture could look different (Offer, 1993).

Ironically, Great Britain's colonies in tropical Africa made their most valuable contributions to the imperial current account within what turned out to be the last twenty years of colonial rule, as commodities such as West African cocoa earned dollars that the metropolitan economy desperately needed. Malayan rubber was of diminishing importance in this respect in the late 1940s, as U.S. purchases of natural rubber declined. Crucially, there was a broader trend in the mid-twentieth century, rooted in changes within the Western economies, for European countries to trade even more among themselves and with other industrialized economies, while commercial links with remaining or recent colonies relatively declined (Marseille, 1984; Lipietz, 1983).

Conclusion. Since the virtual end of formal overseas empires around 1960, much necessary revisionism has taken place: discrediting some of the earlier analyses of economic motivation for empire and developing new or more refined ones; attempting to quantify the gains and losses to the metropolitan economies; and reshaping the context in which European imperial history should be understood—by showing that the world on which Europe burst out in the fifteenth to eighteenth centuries was by no means uniformly backward economically and by revealing the previously understated extent of indigenous economic initiatives within certain African and Asian colonies in the nineteenth and twentieth centuries. This essay has sought to illustrate the variety of historical experience and of available interpretation. It is appropriate to end by underlining the importance of the topic in a different context. Much of the history of global economic integration, including the reduction of transaction costs that provided the framework for price convergence in goods and eventually in factor markets, has been the history of imperialism. In principle, the results of empire might be distinguished from those of peaceful migration and trade: but the distinction is meaningless when conquest was a precondition of foreign settlement, or for mercantilism, or where free trade was imposed by foreign guns. That the populations of Australasia and the Americas speak European languages would not have happened without the violent seizure of overseas territory. Empire has been central to both the fact and the form of integration in the global economy during the last five hundred years.

[*See also* Economic Development; Geographical Expansion; International Migration; *and* Settler Economies.]

BIBLIOGRAPHY

THEORIES AND DEBATES

Brewer, Anthony. *Marxist Theories of Imperialism: A Critical Survey*. 2d ed. London, 1990. Excellent presentation and discussion of Marxist, dependency, and world-systems approaches.

Cain, Peter J., and Mark Harrison, eds. *Imperialism: Critical Concepts in Historical Studies*. 3 vols. London, 2001. Valuable set of readings; volumes 1 and 2 focus on economic imperialism.

Mommsen, Wolfgang J., and Jürgen Osterhammel, eds. *Imperialism and After: Continuities and Discontinuities*. London, 1986. Geographically wide-ranging essays, focused on nineteenth and twentieth centuries.

Owen, Roger, and Bob Sutcliffe, eds. *Studies in the Theory of Imperialism*. London, 1972. Influential and much reprinted collection with still useful annotated bibliography.

Robinson, Ronald, and John Gallagher, with Alice Denny. *Africa and the Victorians: The Official Mind of Imperialism*. London, 1961. Classic follow-up to their famous article (cited in text).

HISTORICAL SURVEYS

Burkholder, Mark A., and Lyman L. Johnson. *Colonial Latin America*. 4th ed. Oxford, 2001.

Clarence-Smith, William G. *The Third Portuguese Empire, 1825–1975: A Study in Economic Imperialism*. Manchester, 1985.

Fieldhouse, David K. *The West and the Third World: Trade, Colonialism, Dependence, and Development*. Oxford, 1999.

Fisher, John R. *The Economic Aspects of Spanish Imperialism in America, 1492–1810*. Liverpool, U.K., 1997.

Holland, Roy F. *European Decolonization 1918–1981: An Introductory Survey*. London, 1985.

Louis, William Roger, ed. *Oxford History of the British Empire*. 5 vols. Oxford, 1998–1999.

Myers, Ramon H., and Mark R. Peattie, eds. *The Japanese Colonial Empire, 1895–1945*. Princeton, 1984.

Osterhammel, Jürgen. *Colonialism: A Theoretical Overview*. Princeton, 1997. An extremely useful typology and periodization of colonialism; despite subtitle, not really theory but a succinct historical analysis.

Scammell, Geoffrey V. *The First Imperial Age: European Overseas Expansion, c. 1400–1715*. London, 1989.

Subrahmanyam, Sanjay. *The Portuguese Empire in Asia, 1500–1700: A Political and Economic History*. London, 1993.

Tracy, James D., ed. *The Political Economy of Merchant Empires: State Power and World Trade, 1350–1750*. Cambridge, 1991.

OTHER REFERENCES

Akita, Shigeru, ed. *Gentlemanly Capitalism, Imperialism and Global History*. Forthcoming.

Bernecker, Walther L., and Hans Werner Tobler, eds. *Development and Underdevelopment in America*. Berlin, 1993.

Brown, Ian. *Economic Change in South-East Asia, c. 1830–1980*. Oxford, 1997.

Cain, P. J., and A. G. Hopkins. *British Imperialism*. 2 vols. Harlow, U.K., 1993.

Cardoso, Fernando Henrique, and Enzo Faletto. *Dependency and Development in Latin America*, translated by Marjory M. Urquidi. Berkeley, 1979.

Clarence-Smith, William G. "The Myth of Uneconomic Imperialism: The Portugese in Angola, 1836–1926." *Journal of Southern African Studies* 5.2 (1979), 165–180.

Coatsworth, John H. "Economic and Institutional Trajectories in Nineteenth-Century Latin America." In *Latin America and the World Economy since 1800*, edited by John H. Coatsworth and Alan M. Taylor, pp. 23–54. Cambridge, Mass., 1998.

Cooper, Frederick. *Decolonization and African Society: The Labor Question in French and British Africa*. Cambridge, 1996.

Crosby, Alfred R. *Ecological Imperialism: The Biological Expansion of Europe, 900–1900*. Cambridge, 1986.

Davis, Lance E., and Robert A. Huttenback, with Susan Gray Davis. *Mammon and the Pursuit of Empire: The Political Economy of British Imperialism, 1860–1912*. Cambridge, 1986.

Dumett, Raymond E., ed. *Gentlemanly Capitalism and British Imperialism: The New Debate on Empire*. Harlow, U.K., 1999.

Frank, Andre Gunder. *Dependent Accumulation and Under-Development*. London, 1978.

Gallagher, John, and Ronald E. Robinson. "The Imperialism of Free Trade." *Economic History Review* 6.1 (1953), 1–15.

Hobson, John A. *Imperialism: A Study*. London, 1902. Revised 1905, 1938.

Hopkins, Anthony G. *An Economic History of West Africa*. London, 1973.

Lenin, Vladimir Ilich. *Imperialism: The Highest Stage of Capitalism*. London, 1942.

Lipietz, Alain. "Towards Global Fordism?" *New Left Review* 132 (1983), 33–47.

Magdoff, Henry. *The Age of Imperialism: The Economics of U.S. Foreign Policy*. New York, 1969.

Marks, Shula, and Stanley Trapido. "Lord Milner and the South African State." *History Workshop Journal* 8 (1979), 43–57.

Marseille, Jacques. *Empire colonial et capitalisme français: Histoire d'un divorce*. Paris, 1984.

O'Brien, Patrick. "European Economic Development: The Contribution of the Periphery." *Economic History Review* 35 (1982), 1–18.

O'Brien, Patrick, and Leandro Prados de la Escosura. "Balance Sheets for the Acquisition, Retention and Loss of European Empires Overseas." *Itinerario* 23.3–4 (1999), 25–52.

Offer, Avner. "The British Empire, 1870–1914: A Waste of Money?" *Economic History Review* 46 (1993) 215–238.

Pomeranz, Kenneth. *The Great Divergence: China, Europe, and the Making of the Modern World Economy*. Princeton, 2000.

Porter, Andrew. "The South African War [1899–1902]: Context and Motive Reconsidered." *Journal of African History* 31.1 (1990), 43–57.

Prakash, Om. *European Commercial Enterprise in Pre-Colonial India*. Cambridge, 1998.

Sugihara, Kaoru. "British Imperialism, the City of London and Global Industrialisation." In *Gentlemanly Capitalism, Imperialism and Global History*, edited by Shigeru Akita. Forthcoming.

Wallerstein, Immanuel. *The Capitalist World Economy*. Cambridge, 1979.

Wallerstein, Immanuel. *The Modern World-System*. 3 vols. New York, 1974.

Wallerstein, Immanuel. "European Economic Development: A Comment on O'Brien." *Economic History Review* 36.4 (1983), 580–583.

Warren, Bill. *Imperialism: Pioneer of Capitalism*, edited by John Sender. London, 1980.

Williams, Eric. *Capitalism and Slavery*. Chapel Hill, N.C., 1944.

GARETH AUSTIN

ECONOMIES OF SCALE. A technology may be characterized as exhibiting economies of scale, or increasing returns to scale, if a proportionate increase in all inputs leads to a more than proportionate increase in output. On the cost side, increasing returns are associated with a decreasing average cost curve over some range of output.

One may distinguish between scale economies internal to an establishment and those at the industry- or economy-wide level due to economies external to the plant or the firm.

Adam Smith, in *The Wealth of Nations* (Oxford, 1976), famously identified specialization or division of labor as a source of increasing returns and thus of increases in output per worker. A second familiar source of internal increasing returns involves indivisible inputs. If a production input, such as a machine, cannot be physically divided, it represents a cost that is fixed rather than variable with output, up to its capacity. As that fixed cost is spread over more and more units of output, average fixed cost declines. If marginal cost does not rise too steeply, falling average fixed costs may pull average total costs down, so that decreasing costs will be exhibited up to capacity. Although any ordinary establishment's U-shaped cost curve exhibits some range of increasing returns, changes in their extent and the forces underlying such changes have been of considerable historical import.

Both these factors were at work in the transformation of nineteenth-century American manufacturing. Before the Civil War, efficiency gains from specialization in transitions from small artisanal shops to nonmechanized factories were significant but relatively modest. However, the last half of the century, in particular the years after the War, witnessed much more dramatic increases than the earlier gains, in establishment size, productivity, and industry concentration due to increasing returns. Smith also observed that "the division of labor is limited by the extent of the market" (Book 1, Chap. 3). Technical change in transportation (i.e., the railroad) turned many formerly local or regional markets into national ones, allowing for the exploitation of greater ranges of increasing returns. In addition, labor-saving, or capital-deepening, technical change within manufacturing increased the capital–output ratio and hence increased the range of decreasing costs in many industries. The modest amount of quantitative evidence that has been brought to bear on this issue, either through direct estimation of production functions or by examination of surviving establishment sizes over time, generally supports the picture of technical-change-driven increasing returns in this period.

An increase in size of the minimum-efficient-size establishment clearly leads to a decrease in the number of optimal-size plants a given market can support, other things being equal, and hence leads to higher levels of industry concentration. An impulse toward increased market concentration at the end of the nineteenth century, due to larger, more capital-intensive plants, was reinforced at the firm level by the diffusion of a new means of virtually instantaneous communication, the telegraph, which permitted coordination and control of many different units or plants within a single firm. If there were also economies of joint production or distribution, the multi-plant firm could enjoy economies of scope in addition to economies of scale (at the plant level). Consequently, it was in this period that the modern business enterprise, a multi-unit firm staffed by a hierarchy of managers, developed.

As U.S. manufacturing moved from smaller firms to larger firms over the nineteenth century, in agriculture the reverse occurred. Robert Fogel and Stanley Engerman (1974) found that slavery, long thought to be an inefficient mode of production based on unwilling and uncooperative workers, was actually highly efficient, much more so than free farming. They attributed this result to the division of labor on large plantations associated with the gang system. This discussion in turn led to a vigorous and prolonged debate about the nature and the extent, if any, of economies of scale in slave agriculture, which is too lengthy and convoluted to allow succinct summary here. The most recent quantitative work comes from Elizabeth Field-Hendrey (1995), who, based on a stochastic frontier production function approach, argues that slavery *per se* did not make agriculture more efficient. Small slave farms were not technologically better than nonslave ones, but large slave farms were technologically superior to both small slave and Southern nonslave farms, a result consistent with the gang system having been crucial for scale economies. On the other hand, in free agriculture, although mechanization, (e.g., the adoption of the reaper) increased the range of decreasing costs for the individual farm (to the extent that the machine was truly indivisible and could not be shared by a large number of owners), the range was still modest relative to that of slave plantations.

In addition to falling average fixed costs, the average cost curve may be pulled down by declining marginal costs. Most notably, Paul David (1975) has argued that declining long-run marginal cost curves due to learning by doing were crucial factors in nineteenth-century development. Whether learning-based economies were internal or external depended on the extent to which they were appropriable, that is, the degree to which technical knowledge derived from production experience could be readily applied by new entrants with little or no production experience.

Another factor contributing to increasing returns is positive feedback, or network effects, in which the larger the number of agents already using a particular technology or a firm's product, the more attractive it becomes to potential new adopters, and the more likely it becomes that they will choose it also. In such a case, a particular firm or a technology can come to dominate a market even if no technical economies of scale are present. In the case of competing firms, this leads to a "natural" monopoly not necessarily based on cost advantage. In the case of competing technologies, reinforced by learning effects, the adoption process could lock in, perhaps as a result of relatively insignificant historical events, on whichever technology got the better start, even if it ultimately proved to be inferior to the alternative. Thus regrets are possible about the technological path followed, which might not be remediable by private actions. Industrial history thus may not be quite so technologically deterministic as the first part of this essay might imply.

Finally, taking a longer-term perspective, external economies resulting from the production of knowledge are the basis of the so-called new growth theory. If knowledge is not totally appropriable, Paul Romer (1986) argues that creation of knowledge by one firm has a positive external effect on production possibilities of other firms. Knowledge then may have an increasing marginal product, leading to increasing returns in the economy as a whole. In such a world of increasing returns, per capita output levels across countries need not converge, for example.

[*See also* Integration *and* Mass Production.]

BIBLIOGRAPHY

Arthur, W. Brian. *Increasing Returns and Path Dependence in the Economy*. Ann Arbor, 1994.

Atack, Jeremy. "Economies of Scale and Efficiency Gains in the Rise of the Factory in America, 1820–1900." In *Quantity and Quiddity*, edited by Peter Kilby, pp. 286–335. Middletown, Conn., 1987.

Chandler, Alfred D. *The Visible Hand*. Cambridge, Mass., 1977.

David, Paul A. *Technical Choice, Innovation and Economic Growth*. Cambridge, 1975.

Field-Hendrey, Elizabeth. "Application of a Stochastic Production Frontier to Slave Agriculture: An Extension." *Applied Economics* 27.4 (1995), 363–368.

Fogel, Robert, and Stanley Engerman. *Time on the Cross*. Boston, 1974.

James, John A. "Structural Change in American Manufacturing, 1850–1890." *Journal of Economic History* 43.2 (1983), 433–459.

Romer, Paul M. "Increasing Returns and Long-Run Growth."*Journal of Political Economy* 94.5 (1986), 1002–1037.

Sokoloff, Kenneth. "Was the Transition from the Artisanal Shop to the Nonmechanized Factory Associated with Gains in Efficiency? Evidence from the U.S. Manufacturing Censuses of 1820 and 1850." *Explorations in Economic History* 21.4 (1984), 351–382.

JOHN A. JAMES

ECONOMIES OF SCOPE. Economies of scope in production are present when there are cost savings that result from the scope rather than the scale of the enterprise—it is less costly to combine two or more product lines in one firm than to produce them separately. Sharing or joint utilization of inputs by two or more product lines without congestion implies economies of scope. For example, a fixed factor of production such as a stamping machine may be used to produce inputs for two different outputs, such as cars and light trucks. The stamping machine would thus be the public input. The public input may also be the hierarchy of middle and top managers in a firm, which makes the activities and operation of the whole enterprise more than the sum of its operating units. The notion of economies of scope is a powerful modeling tool for the study of industry structure because it summarizes both the production and the organizational cost savings from combining two or more product lines in one firm.

When a firm exploits economies of scope and produces more than one output, it is considered multiproduct. Multiproduct firms can often start and terminate the production of one of their outputs in a relatively short period of time. For this reason, markets with a small number of firms may still be highly competitive. The theory of contestable markets analyzes this situation in which there are few firms that compete fiercely.

In some other situations there exists a trade-off between economies of scope and economies of scale, and thus many firms are present in the industry. This is the context of multiproduct competitive industries. The central question in the literature of multiproduct competitive industries is whether both specialized and integrated firms can be present in a competitive equilibrium. Panzar and Willig (1981) show that in a competitive industry, the existence of economies of scope is a necessary and sufficient condition for the existence of multiproduct firms in equilibrium. Baumol, Panzar, and Willig (1982), MacDonald and Slivinski (1987), and Eaton and Lemche (1991) show that specialized companies are also present in equilibrium when multiproduct firms alone cannot cover the demand of both outputs by themselves. In particular, Baumol et al. (1982), MacDonald and Slivinski (1987), and Eaton and Lemche (1991) show that the industry composition—the number of specialized and integrated firms—is determined by the size of the aggregate demand of one product relative to the size of the aggregate demand of the other products.

Chandler (1990) and Bailey and Friedlaender (1982) provide historical examples of industries where economies of scope existed in the production and distribution.

[*See also* Integration *and* Mass Production.]

BIBLIOGRAPHY

Baumol, William J., John C. Panzar, and Robert D. Willig. *Contestable Markets and the Theory of Industry Structure*. San Diego, 1982.

Bailey, Elizabeth E., and Ann F. Friedlaender. "Market Structure and Multiproduct Industries." *Journal of Economic Literature* 20.3 (September 1982), 1024–1048.

Chandler, Alfred D. *Scale and Scope: The Dynamics of Industrial Capitalism*. Cambridge, Mass., 1990.

Demsetz, Harold. "The Cost of Transacting." *Quarterly Journal of Economics* 82.1 (February 1968), 33–53.

Eaton, B. Curtis, and S. Q. Lemche. "The Geometry of Supply, Demand, and Competitive Market Structure with Economies of Scope." *American Economic Review* 81.4 (September 1991), 901–911.

MacDonald, Glenn M., and Alan Slivinski. "The Simple Analytics of Competitive Equilibrium with Multiproduct Firms." *American Economic Review* 77.5 (December 1987), 941–953.

Panzar, John C., and Robert D. Willig. "Economies of Scope (in Sustainability Analysis)." *American Economic Review* 71.2 (May 1981), 268–272.

FEDERICO CILIBERTO

ECUADOR. *See* American Indian Economies; Andean Region; *and* Spain, *subentry on* Spanish Empire.

EDISON, THOMAS A. (1847–1931), American inventor and manufacturer.

The most prolific inventor in American history, Thomas Edison played a major role in the communications, electric power, and entertainment industries. Just as important, he broadened the notion of invention to encompass what is now called innovation—invention, research, development, and commercialization—and invented the industrial research laboratory. Moreover, his canny sense of the emerging influence of the popular press helped to make him one of the most famous people in the world.

Edison began his inventive career in the telegraph industry in 1868, and during the first half of the 1870s he established himself as the foremost telegraph inventor in America. Several companies competed for control of his work. He made major improvements in printing telegraphs used as stock tickers and for private lines, as well as for other urban telegraph services such as fire and burglar alarms and central-station systems. He was a contract inventor for the Gold and Stock Telegraph Company, the leading supplier of market reports, and later for Western Union, which acquired control of the business. He also worked for a Western Union competitor on a system of automatic telegraphy, and for Western Union on multiple telegraphs. His quadruplex telegraph, which enabled four messages to be sent simultaneously, was an important invention that became embroiled in an attempt by the notorious financier Jay Gould to build a network that would compete with Western Union. A year after successfully developing the quadruplex in 1874, Edison agreed to a contract with Western Union that assigned all his work in multiple telegraphy to that company.

Edison's contracts and patent royalties enabled him to set up several telegraph manufacturing shops in Newark, New Jersey. In the nineteenth century, such shops were the loci of inventive activity, providing skilled machinists and resources for building and modifying inventions. In 1875, Edison began to develop a new combination shop and scientific laboratory separate from manufacturing, an effort that culminated a year later with the construction of his famous laboratory at Menlo Park, New Jersey. The Menlo Park laboratory and a larger one Edison built in West Orange, New Jersey, became models for other inventors.

They demonstrated how invention, when properly organized, could become an industrial process with significant long-term benefits to a sponsoring corporation. During the 1880s and 1890s, independent inventors and leading companies in the electrical industry, such as General Electric and Bell Telephone, established similar laboratories.

In a remarkable five-year period from 1876 to 1881, Edison developed three major inventions. The first of these was the carbon transmitter, which made Alexander Graham Bell's telephone a viable commercial technology. Second was the cylinder phonograph, which so astounded the world that it made Edison an international celebrity, although the technology required another two decades of development before the sound-recording industry emerged. Third, and most important, was Edison's work on electric light and power. The resources of his laboratory enabled Edison to develop a complete system, rather than just a light bulb, which became the foundation of the electric light and power industry.

During the 1880s, Edison developed central-station technology and set up manufacturing and operating plants for electric light and power. He continued to make important improvements in the technology, but most of this work took place at the manufacturing plants until he set up his new and larger laboratory at West Orange in late 1887. By the early 1890s, however, Edison's low-voltage direct-current (DC) electrical system was being supplanted by high-voltage alternating current (AC). The Edison company merged with Thomson-Houston, a leading AC company, to form General Electric in 1892. The merger, negotiated without Edison's involvement, left the top executives of the better-managed Thomson-Houston Company in charge. Although he remained on the board of directors, Edison had little to do with the company. By the time of the merger, his inventive interests increasingly lay outside of electric lighting, and he subsequently devoted most of his attention to other technologies, although he performed some experimental lamp work for General Electric in the mid-1890s.

In the late 1880s and 1890s, Edison developed the basic technology for two new entertainment industries—sound recording and motion pictures. Edison's ability to conduct research and development at his laboratory enabled him to pioneer in developing the early commercial technology in these industries, and his companies became their leading firms. However, as the focus of innovation shifted from the technology to the artistic side of these businesses, Edison and his companies found it more difficult to compete. Edison and his staff developed improved sound recording and duplicating technology as well as better-quality phonographs around the turn of the century, which enabled him to become the industry leader. After 1907, however, his company began to lose market share to the Victor

THOMAS EDISON. Edison, with Henry Ford and Harvey Firestone, tests synthetic rubber in the laboratory on his Fort Myers, Florida, estate, circa 1931. (Prints and Photographs Division, Library of Congress)

Company, which developed the disc phonograph and focused its business strategy on recording and promoting major musicians and singers. Although Edison developed a technically superior disc record and phonograph, they were incompatible with the equipment of other manufacturers, and the Edison company continued to lose market share. This decline was exacerbated by Edison's decision personally to select recording artists, and his company went out of business in the late 1920s. In the motion picture business, Edison used his control of key patents to form a cartel known as the Motion Picture Patents Company, which dominated the industry until it was broken up by the government in 1915. Unable to compete with the stars and the artistic quality of films produced by its competitors, the Edison company went out of business three years later.

Edison's other major inventions are not so well known and had a relatively limited impact on their respective industries. Edison's most important failure was his effort to develop a process for mining low-grade iron ore, during the 1890s. Although technically successful, this process proved a commercial failure, thanks in part to the discovery of rich ores around Lake Superior at the end of the decade. In the first decade of the new century, however,

Edison was able to use the same technology to develop a process for manufacturing cement. His major innovation in this field was the long rotary kiln, which, although widely adopted, led to overproduction and price depression in the industry. During these same years, Edison developed an alkaline storage battery for electric automobiles; but by the time it appeared, those vehicles had largely lost out to cars with internal combustion engines. Instead, the Edison battery was used for a host of industrial applications, including railroad signals and switches, lighting for ships and railway cars, submarines, ship radios, backup power for central stations, isolated house lighting, miner's lamps, and electric trucks.

In 1927, at the end of his life, Edison undertook one last major research effort, to find a natural substitute for rubber that could be produced rapidly in case of war. By this time, Edison and his laboratory were no longer in the forefront of research and development; although he did develop such a substitute, it was made impractical by industrial researchers who developed artificial rubber while working at new laboratories established by other companies. The growth of such research laboratories throughout American industry became a lasting tribute to his influence.

BIBLIOGRAPHY

Bazerman, Charles. *The Languages of Edison's Light*. Cambridge, Mass., 1999.

Friedel, Robert, and Paul Israel. *Edison's Electric Light: Biography of an Invention*. New Brunswick, N.J., 1986.

Hughes, Thomas P. "Edison's Method." In *Technology at the Turning Point*, edited by William B. Pickett, pp. 5–22. San Francisco, 1977.

Israel, Paul. *Edison: A Life of Invention*. New York, 1998.

Jenkins, Reese, Bob Rosenberg, Paul Israel, et al. *The Papers of Thomas A. Edison*. Baltimore, 1989–.

Millard, Andre. *Edison and the Business of Innovation*. Baltimore, 1990.

Musser, Charles. *Before the Nickelodeon: Edwin S. Porter and the Edison Manufacturing Company*. Berkeley, 1991.

Pretzer, William S., ed. *Working at Inventing: Thomas A. Edison and the Menlo Park Experience*. Dearborn, Mich., 1989.

Thomas A. Edison Papers. <http://edison.rutgers.edu> Includes original documents, patents, bibliographies, and chronologies.

PAUL ISRAEL

EDUCATION. A significant long-term trend within the industrialized economies has been the sustained growth of educational enrollment, durations, and qualifications, and an accompanying growth of skills and literacy/numeracy qualifications in the work force. This trend began many centuries ago: it has been estimated that by the mid-seventeenth century, more than half of the adult population of large Western cities was literate. By middle to late nineteenth century most of western Europe and North America had extensive formal education systems and had achieved literacy rates of 50 percent or more for the population as a whole (Aldcroft, 1996, p. 11). In the twentieth century the most obvious trend was a sustained increase in access to secondary and tertiary education. A natural historical question concerns the links between education and the persistent productivity growth of the last two centuries. This entry describes some broad dimensions of the growth of educational enrollments and attainments and of the interpretations that have been put upon that growth in terms of the link between education and economic growth.

Literacy. The historical development of education systems should be seen in the context of the growth of literacy and the advantages that were perceived to flow from it (see Vincent, 2000, for an overview). Literacy and numeracy remain major objectives of education systems, although neither has an unambiguous definition. Literacy exists along a spectrum from basic comprehension of simple formulations to the ability to read and compose complex text. Likewise, numeracy extends from simple counting to sophisticated mathematical routines. The extension of literacy in Europe had a variegated geographical distribution and was shaped by economic, social, cultural, religious, and gender statuses and relationships—in general, men became literate before women, the rich before the poor, urban residents before the rural population, and the north before the south. Measurement is difficult because of definitional ambiguity, but taking the ability to sign formal documents as an indicator of literacy, literacy rates began to grow from around 1500 in Europe. Virtually all members of the English gentry were literate by 1600. By the middle of the nineteenth century, more than 50 percent of the broadly northern European populations (France, the Low Countries, Germany, the United Kingdom, Switzerland, and the Nordic countries) were literate. By the early twentieth century, the Mediterranean countries, the Balkan region, and most of central and eastern Europe had achieved these rates (see Houston, 2001, for an excellent survey of the data and interpretive issues regarding literacy). Much of the growth of literacy was achieved outside any formal education system—and indeed in the absence of schools at all—by teaching within the family or other informal local contexts. The emergence of schools was a haphazard process, with schools being promoted by a variety of agencies with often different and competing purposes. Religious bodies or associations, workers' associations, and local communities established increasing numbers of schools from the early nineteenth century. Many of these agencies saw literacy in terms of personal empowerment, political development, and economic advantage, and so education was highly valued independently of any state provision and grew before any involvement by states. But this does not mean that schooling was widely available—the supply of schools was uneven, and fees were often prohibitive for poor parents (West, 2001, pp. 48–68).

Education Provision and Enrollment. School "systems" developed relatively late in Europe and the United States, usually around the mid-nineteenth century, although the principle of state education sometimes emerged as early as the late eighteenth century. In Austria, for example, primary school education was brought under state control in 1774, and the principle of compulsory education was introduced at the same time. But it was not until 1869 that eight years of compulsory education was established in that country. The earliest serious provision of primary education was in the Netherlands, which had a full primary system under state control from 1806, and Scandinavia, with full state-funded primary education in Denmark from 1814, Norway from 1827, and Sweden from 1842. In Belgium, communities were required to provide primary education from 1842, with state control of secondary schools beginning in 1850. In France, the principle of public schools under civil control was established with the revolution, but it was not until 1882 that a secular, free access system was introduced. In Germany, Prussia had eight years of compulsory education by 1763; an education ministry was established in 1808. But for Germany as a whole, the establishment of a primary and *mittelschule* system came in 1872, offering ten years of compulsory education.

The timing of state control was sometimes an outcome of major political changes, such as unification of Germany and Italy or the emancipation of the serfs in Russia in 1861. Each of these events was ultimately followed by the establishment of a full national system of primary education. England and Wales were relatively late—governments were reluctant to become involved in education, although a regulatory framework was established from 1833. But free primary education was not introduced in principle until 1893 and not fully implemented until after World War I.

Generally, state involvement in Europe took the form of measures to control, simplify, systematize, and coordinate schools already in existence. The entry of the state into educational provision usually meant that schooling became compulsory, and this resulted in a significant extension of schooling provision and literacy in the second half of the nineteenth century. Numbers in primary education grew consistently through that period, with primary school enrollment and teacher numbers roughly doubling in most European countries from 1850 to 1900, as Table 1 indicates. The figures in Table 1 need in some cases to be treated with care. For example, the rapid jump between 1850 and 1860 in the United Kingdom may well reflect the entry of preexisting schools into the state school system rather than the expansion of the state system itself. Nevertheless, the sustained upward trends are found across all counries.

In Europe, the establishment of full primary education was followed by the development of secondary and tertiary education systems. In the twentieth century, significant proportions of the population were engaged in such education, as Table 2 shows. The key point here is that the proportions rose dramatically, usually by orders of magnitude, from 1875 to 1975. Of course, most of the growth is concentrated in the post–World War II period, but this should not obscure the almost equally significant growth in the 1920s and 1930s.

These trends for Europe are even more pronounced in the United States. In terms of schooling, the educational picture in the United States is one of a sustained rise in enrollments, first in elementary schools, then in high schools. In 1880, the enrollment ratio for those between the ages of 5 and 17 was 72 percent, but virtually all of this enrollment was in elementary schools. In the course of the following century, there was a continuous rise in years of schooling, focused mainly on secondary schooling; by 1988, 85 percent of the U.S. labor force had a high school diploma. This was accompanied by a similar sustained rise in tertiary education, so that by 1988 more than a quarter of the labor force had four or more years of college or university education and 45 percent had some form of tertiary education (Abramovitz and David, 1996). Goldin points out that the United States had significantly higher rates of enrollment in secondary education than all European counries until well into the second half of the twentieth century, although this partly reflects the fact that European countries maintained significant part-time education in technical schools for working students (Goldin, 2001, pp. 267–269). She shows that the late twentieth century saw major convergence toward U.S. enrollment levels in secondary schools, and therefore "even today's currently poor nations and their people invest in secondary schooling to a far greater degree, in terms of enrollment rates, than did the currently rich countries in the past" (Goldin, 2001, p. 272).

The evolution of education provision within the United States showed strong regional variation. The period 1910 to 1940 saw major growth in high school education in the United States, particularly in what Goldin and Katz have called the "education belt"—a band of states comprising Utah, Colorado, Nebraska, Kansas, Iowa, Indiana, and New England. In seeking to explain the rise in high school provision and graduation, Goldin and Katz (2001) have gone beyond the human capital approach, looking not only at individual economic returns to education (although they do show that these were high) but also at factors prompting community funding of education. Their key point is that when communities fund public education, they are in effect funding an intergenerational transfer system: one generation in effect is lending money to another. Goldin and Katz have integrated social capital theory with the human capital approach. "Social capital" refers to those features of social organization—such as social networks and their associated norms and values—that create externalities for communities. This usually involves networks or community organizations that promoted trust, cooperative behavior, transparency in government, and the like. In a quantitative analysis, Goldin and Katz have showed that "the areas of the country with the greatest tangible wealth and seemingly greatest intangible wealth, or social capital, witnessed the earliest and the most rapid diffusion of the high school movement" (Goldin and Katz, 2001, p. 330). They also have showed that the forms of social capital that drove early commitments to education have persisted over time and continue to play a role in human capital formation in the present.

Education and Its Impact: Economic Growth. It often has been suggested that there is a strong connection between education and economic development, but the content, mechanisms, and outcomes of the link remain a matter of debate. Most historians and economists take a view that runs roughly as follows: economic development is closely connected to the creation, diffusion, and adaptation of technology. Technology is best conceptualized as knowledge—that is, as a combination of abstract and practical understandings and capabilities related to productive transformations. At least from the time of the Industrial

TABLE 1. *Primary School Enrollment (P) and Teacher Numbers (T) (thousands)*

	AUSTRIA		BELGIUM		FRANCE		GERMANY		IRELAND		ITALY	
	P	T	P	T	P	T	P	T	P	T	P	T
1830												
1840	1,365	27.3	453									
1850	1,426	28.4	487	8.9	3,322				271	4.9		
1860	1,656	27.6	516	9.2	4,437	114			263	6.0	1,009	28.2
1870	1,821	35.3	619	9.8					359	8.8	1,605	41.0
1880	2,438	48.4	8.3	25.7	5,049	123			469	10.7	2,003	48.3
1890	3,157	63.2		28.4	5,594	146			489	11.1	2,419	59.0
1900	3,693	79.9		31.3	5,526	158	8,966	147	478	11.9	2,708	65.0
1910	4,534	110		35.5	5,655	157	10,310	187	496	12.8	3,309	72.8
1920	868	31.4	968	50.8	3,697	119	8,894	196	182		4,166	105
1930	793	22.2	871		4,635	133	7,590	190	421	13.6	4,595	105
1940	716	27.5	939		4,913	154			389	13.3	5,213	127
1950	867	36.4	780		4,726	159	6,330	131	382	12.9	4,640	170
1960	744	34.6	969		5,708	226	5,291	145	431	13.9	4,418	200
1970	964	44.5	1,029		5,147	198	6,347	188	453	14.9	4,841	222
1980	831	63.6	823		5,017	198	5,044	248	503	18.8	4,423	

	NETHERLANDS		NORDIC COUNTRIES		SPAIN		SWITZERLAND		UNITED KINGDOM	
	P	T	P	T	P	T	P	T	P	T
1830			178	2,142						
1840			180	2,236						
1850	397	6.5	196	2,575	1,005				282	
1860	401	8.4	238	3,533	1,252				920	
1870	467	11.0	811	11,974					1432	16.8
1880	541	14.2	953	17,787	1,769		456	8.8	3,560	59.6
1890	643	18.1	1,342	19,992			470	9.5	4,643	93.2
1900	740	24.7	1,559	26,576	1,526		485	10.8	5,722	141.8
1910	904	30.1	1,748	35,312	1,812		559	13.0	6,122	185.6
1920	1,032		1,795	46.3	1,800		536	13.5	5,833	184.9
1930	1,183	36.1	1,901	54.8	2,262	49.2	472	13.4	5,525	188.5
1940	1,143	30.4	1,737	57.5	2,410	51.1	453	13.5	4,119	177
1950	1,216	34.4	1,904	86.1	2,123	59.9	476	14.5	4,562	152.9
1960	1,416	41.6	2,417	48	3,387		557	17.7	4,722	164.1
1970	1,462	49.2	2,237	51.8	4,749				5,659	211.2
1980	1,333	56.5	2,576	69.1	6,789				4,896	220.5

SOURCE: Compiled from Mitchell, B.R., *International Historical Statistics, Europe 1750–1988*, 3d ed., London, pp. 855–885.

Revolution, technologies (and their underlying knowledge bases) have become complex enough to require either high standards of literacy and numeracy or more specific training in relevant disciplines (such as basic sciences or technological disciplines such as electrical or chemical engineering) if they are to be operated successfully. From this perspective, education is seen as a key input to the advanced economy. More specifically, education is the investment process through which "human capital" is created, and this is increasingly seen as the central input to growth.

There are further underlying ideas that should be made explicit to understand the impact of education on economic performance. One key view in analyzing the impact of education is that growth is a broad process of social, institutional, and economic change—that is, it is not a matter simply of a few leading sectors or technologies, but of more or less sustained advance across the spectrum of economic activities. In this case, the focus tends to be on general participation in education and on average attainment levels—on access to formal schooling and on literacy rates, for example. On the other hand, development is sometimes seen in terms of specific areas of technological change, and education is then often seen in the context of specific forms of training and/or research. An emphasis on capital goods production and engineering technologies as drivers of growth has led some to focus on modes and

TABLE 2. *Students in General Secondary and Higher Education, 1861–1975 (% of total population)*

	AUSTRIA	BELGIUM	DENMARK	FINLAND	FRANCE	GERMANY	IRELAND	ITALY	NETHERLANDS	NORWAY	SWEDEN	SWITZERLAND	ENGLAND AND WALES	SCOTLAND
1861	0.3								0.1					
1870–1871	0.3						0.4		0.2					
1875		0.5			0.2						0.4			
1880–1881	0.4						0.5	0.3	0.2	0.5	0.4			
1885						0.6								
1890–1891	0.4	0.6			0.3		0.6	0.4	0.3	0.7	0.4	0.8		
1895–1896						0.6						0.8		
1900–1901	0.6	0.6		0.7	0.3				0.3	0.8	0.5			
1910–1911	0.8	0.7		0.9	0.4	1.1		0.4	0.5	0.9				
1918–1919	1.2	0.9												
1920–1921				1.1	0.7	1.3		0.6	0.7	1.3	1.3	1.1	0.9	1.3
1925–1926		0.8	1.6		0.8							1.2		
1928–1929	1.2						1.0				1.3			
1930–1931				1.6	1.1	1.3		0.6	1.7	1.1			1.1	2.0
1935–1936	1.4		1.9				1.4					1.4	1.2	2.1
1938–1939		1.3		2.4	1.5	1.1		1.3	2.2	1.4	1.6			
1945–1946			2.1				1.7	1.7		1.6		1.4	3.3	
1950–1951						1.9			2.6					5.2
1955–1956		2.3	2.8	3.6	2.2	2.5	2.4	2.4	3.2	1.8	2.7	1.4	5.0	4.9
1964–1965	2.1	4.5	4.3	6.8	6.4	3.2	4.1	5.8	4.8	5.1	5.7		7.1	4.3
1975	3.7	7.3	6.9	9.1	9.3	6.4	7.2	8.8	7.4	7.8	7.3	2.5	9.3	8.9

SOURCE: Compiled from data in Flora, P., et al., *State, Economy and Society in Western Europe, 1815–1875*, Vol. 1, *The Growth of Mass Democracies and Welfare States*, London, Frankfurt, and Chicago, 1983, pp. 553–633.

levels of engineering education: for instance, it is common now to hear that education in information technologies is critical for growth. A view from this perspective is that "the spread of technological knowledge, narrowly considered, is not a matter of mass education but of the training of a small elite" (Parker, 1961, p. 1).

Beyond this contrast between mass and elite education are related debates concerning the functions of education: does it consist of imparting technologically relevant knowledge, or is it a process of inculcating attitudes and behavioral characteristics that are in some sense appropriate for modern economic production? (Such issues are overviewed and discussed in Anderson and Bowman, 1965.) A more radical perspective—from a range of authors beginning in the 1830s and continuing to the present—is that education is closely connected to work discipline and social control. It is in part a form of social conditioning, establishing habits of punctuality, respect for authority, and so on that are integral to the disciplinary structure of capitalist production (see Mitch, 1993, pp. 295–299 for a discussion of the literature on this issue).

The first of these approaches—growth as a broad process resting on wide access to formal schooling—often is taken in discussions of how and why currently developed economies took off, while the second—growth as a narrow process requiring technological elites—usually forms part of analyses of changing industrial leadership or major structural change. Insofar as there is a conceptual framework for thinking about how precisely education affects economic performance, it is usually through the concepts of "human capital" and "signaling," and it is to those concepts we turn first.

Human Capital and Signaling. Classical economics, particularly in the writings of Adam Smith, placed a clear emphasis on the development of skills and specialized knowledge as core components of economic growth and as explanations of income distribution. On the one hand, the division of labor, in Smith's view, rested on the acquisition of specialized skills. On the other, the division of labor extended to knowledge itself; Smith saw the emergence of knowledge-intensive specialized activities as a contributor to growth. Modern human capital theory, developed over the past quarter of a century, extends and formalizes these long-standing views in economics. Not only is it a theory of the demand for education, but it also has implications for how education affects the growth process.

Human capital refers to the person-embodied knowledge, skills, and capabilities of people. The term *capital* is relevant here because the theory sees the development of such knowledge and skills strictly as an investment process, producing both individual benefits (in the shape of higher incomes) and economic outcomes (in the form of higher productivity) over future time periods. The invest-ment model is followed rather rigorously, and the demand for education is seen in terms of a return-on-investment approach in which the costs of education are related to the marginal benefits of enhanced incomes.

Development of this concept is directly related to the economics of growth and technological change. Early quantitative analyses of long-term growth in the United States, particularly by Moses Abramovitz and Robert Solow, produced a well-known puzzle: only a relatively small part of U.S. growth was explained by increased inputs of capital and labor, leaving a large unexplained "residual." One broad explanation of this, still widely accepted, is that the unexplained component of growth results from technological change that dramatically enhances the combined productivity of other inputs. However, T. W. Schulz, Edward Denison, and John Kendrick took a different approach, arguing that the residual reflects hitherto unobserved and unmeasured qualitative improvements in inputs. On the labor side in particular, there are investments in human capital, taking the form of education and training. Kendrick was the first to explore the rate of return on human capital investments (that is, returns on education and training costs in the form of enhanced incomes) and showed that they approximate returns on investments in physical capital. These ideas were developed most notably by Gary Becker (particularly in Becker, 1964) into large-scale theories of the supply of and demand for education, income distribution, demographic effects on incomes, gender differences in pay, and so on.

The human capital approach sees education as directly inculcating productive forms of knowledge and skill. Becker distinguished between two forms of this: general skills and capabilities that are applicable across many activities, and firm-specific human capital in the form of localized technical, organizational, or other abilities. An alternative view is that education provides little in the way of specifically productive skills. Rather, it is a "signaling" system, conveying information about general abilities, summed up in the ability to acquire educational qualifications (Spence, 1973). These views of course have different implications for the contribution made by education to economic performance. In the first approach, educational inputs are extremely important since they directly enhance technological knowledge and productivity. In the second, education is simply a screening process, selecting and channeling capable people into appropriate positions, without necessarily playing any direct role in enhancing knowledge capabilities and productivity: "On this interpretation educational attainment . . . is not an indicator that the individual thus educated has acquired cognitive knowledge that will raise his or her productivity when employed, but, rather, signals that the person is likely to be readily (hence less expensively) trainable" (Abramovitz

TRADE SCHOOL. Five men making and repairing shoes, Hampton Institute, Virginia, circa 1900. (Frances Benjamin Johnston Collection/Prints and Photographs Division, Library of Congress)

and David, 1996, p. 52). There is no reason that education should not fulfill each of these functions, with the balance varying according to subjects and disciplines. But it should be noted that these perspectives imply different conclusions about the role and place of education in knowledge generation.

Literacy, Educational Attainment, and Economic Development. Sustained economic development began in a number of Western countries and Japan. An obvious starting point in empirically oriented explanations of this is to look for distinguishing features of those societies. One of these is basic education, and specifically the impact of the changing literacy levels sketched above.

Easterlin (1981) presents perhaps the most systematic argument concerning the links between basic education and growth, seeking to explore what is surely a major issue for economic historians: the existence and persistence of large income and wealth disparities between the regions and countries of the world.

In Easterlin's view, the problem of explaining growth differences is one of explaining limits to rapid technological change. It is clear from a wide range of studies that this is primarily a problem of diffusion: growth on the world scale is not so much a matter of developing indigenous technologies as of accessing, adapting, and using technologies from others. The technologies of the advanced economies are common technologies, striking more for their similarities than their differences. The question, then, is, what is involved in the process of technology diffusion? Again, we have some robust empirical knowledge here: diffusion is not a matter of simply accessing and implementing blueprints available from others. Technological knowledge—contrary to some of the claims of the new growth theory—is not a public good that spreads unproblematically and rapidly (and thereby creates externalities). On the contrary, it requires significant levels of personal contact and occurs through sustained processes of practical learning, involving demonstration, training, imitation, on-the-job experience, and so on. This is, according to Easterlin, "an educational process, in which a new and difficult subject—'modern' technology—must be taught and learned" (Easterlin, 1981, p. 4).

So the question then becomes, what kinds of factors facilitate or inhibit this process of learning? The potential list of relevant factors here is large, and certainly includes institutional structures, incentive systems, and so on. But there also is a prior capability constraint within the population as a whole that, in Easterlin's argument, shapes the possibilities for exploiting and developing new institutions and incentives. This capability is fundamentally a matter of formal schooling. In most cases, the available data suggest that increases in schooling are independent of the growth process itself and precede increases in growth rates. Easterlin's argument is that the link between education and economic outcomes primarily involves the ways in which education shapes attitudes—secular, rationalist education accords with skill acquisition and positive attitudes toward change, which promotes technological adaptation, an approach that accords with the broad interpretation of the nature of economic development.

Easterlin's argument is open to the objection that it contains no formal statistical exploration of the links between enrollments, literacy, and income levels or growth rates. In fact, given the limitations of the available data, only recently has such an analysis been possible. However, Easterlin's general hypothesis was further developed by Lars Sandberg, who explored the effects of formal schooling, assembling data on education and the growth of income for a range of European economies from the mid-nineteenth century to 1970 (Sandberg, 1982).

Sandberg looked at a range of western, central, and eastern European economies, ranking them in terms of literacy in 1850, and looked at the evolution of income from 1850 to 1913 and then to 1970. The countries fall into three literacy groups: high (above 70%), medium (above 50%), and low (less than 50%). Literacy rates in 1850 correlated poorly with income: the Nordic economies and Germany ranked very high in literacy and low in gross national product (GNP) per capita. Low-literacy countries (e.g., Spain, Italy, Greece, and Hungary) were also in the low-income categories. By 1913, the high-literacy countries had significantly outstripped the income levels of the low-literacy countries and were approaching the income levels of the previous leaders (England and Wales, Scotland, and Switzerland). By 1970, the income rankings corresponded closely to the initial literacy rankings. Sandberg concluded that the literacy rates of 1850 were "an amazingly good predictor of per

capita income in the 1970s": countries with high literacy levels reached high per capita income levels even if they were very poor in 1850. Sandberg's argument does not rest simply on these correlations: his view is that literacy also is closely linked to a more commercially minded population, and thus to the size and growth of the banking system and financial services generally. This in turn has important implications for the financing of industrialization.

These ideas subsequently have been explored for a number of other countries, and authors have generally supported Sandberg's ideas (see, e.g., Tortella, 1990, for a range of papers on these themes). Recent work has sought to test these hypotheses more formally. O'Rourke and Williamson (1995), for example, explored various explanations of the catching-up process through which Sweden became wealthy, and in the process tested Sandberg's propositions for a number of European countries. They assembled school enrollment rates and two literacy-rate estimates for fourteen European economies plus Argentina, Australia, Canada, and the United States for the years 1870 to 1890. Then they regressed the growth of real wages and gross domestic product (GDP) per worker separately on these two schooling variables, concluding:

> The contribution of schooling to GDP per worker growth and real wage growth is statistically significant in every case, supporting the view that schooling was important to late nineteenth century growth. As predicted by Abramovitz, Easterlin, Sandberg, Tortella and the new growth theorists, schooling levels "conditioned" real wage convergence in the late nineteenth century. Poor countries well endowed with schooling caught up faster than those poorly endowed, presumably because their "social capabilities" were better established. That is, they were better able to exploit the open economy and globalization effects . . . . (O'Rourke and Williamson, 1995, p. 301)

What emerges from these studies is that there is a robust association between wealth and the educational attainments, especially literacy but also presumably numeracy, that flow from elementary education. But it is little more than an association. One difficult issue in this area is that the direction of causality is not necessarily clear—education can be seen not only as an investment for growth but also as a consumption good for which demand rises as income grows. Moreover, there is little research on how and why these educational achievements actually have effects, how educational contents are related to technological requirements, or how education and technology taken together relate to specific growth paths. For an attempt to relate these factors into an approach to growth, we must look to the United States.

Long-Run Dynamics of Education and Growth: The United States. In general, there have been few attempts to analyze in detail the long-term dynamics of education, technology, and growth for any country within a comprehensive theoretical context. An important exception is the work of Abramovitz and David (1996).

The changes in the duration and level of education in the United States have important economic implications purely in terms of the resources used to achieve them. In the late nineteenth century, it was legal for many children to enter full-time work as early as age eleven, so the direct costs of education (expenditures by households, nonprofit organizations, and government) should be augmented by the value of foregone earnings by households. In the last decade of the nineteenth century, total resource use for education was already over 4 percent of augmented GNP (that is, GNP including foregone income); by the early 1960s, this had reached 6.3 percent of augmented GNP. This implies that a large and increasing part of U.S. savings flowed toward education. Education has become the largest component of nontangible investment (the other main components being investments in health and safety and in research and development). In 1929, total nontangible capital stocks were approximately half the size of total tangible capital stocks (structures and equipment, inventories, and natural resources). Over the ensuing sixty years, the education share rose dramatically, so that by 1990 intangible stocks were greater than tangible (U.S. $32.8 billion versus U.S. $28.5 billion), and education and training stocks made up 41 percent of U.S. capital stocks as a whole (Abramovitz and David, 1996, pp. 39–42).

How does this relate to the evolution of technological change and the growth path of the U.S. economy? Abramovitz and David showed that over the very long run, from 1800 to 1966, the residual share of output growth (that is, the growth of output per worker not accounted for by increasing capital per worker) rose from 48 percent to 84 percent; in the period from 1966 to 1989, it fell back to 53 percent. The argument is that this trend rests on significant improvements in labor quality and is therefore linked to the educational investment trends sketched above.

But how does this relate to the characteristics of technological change? As Abramovitz and David argued:

> Perhaps the single most salient characteristic of recent economic growth has been the secularly rising reliance on *codified* knowledge as a basis for the organization and conduct of economic activities, including among the latter the purposive extension of the economically relevant knowledge base. (Abramovitz and David, 1996, p. 35)

Abramovitz and David saw education and training as the mechanism through which access is gained to these growing codified knowledge bases, with both private and social benefits flowing from such access. If this is correct, it implies a bias in technological change favoring the intangible investments outlined above. "Technological change tended to raise the relative marginal productivity of capital formed by investments in the education and training of the labour force at all levels" (Abramovitz and David, 1986, p. 37). This is difficult to check statistically, since the benefits of intangible investments often accrue to both capital and labor; but the underlying technological dynamic could account both for sustained investments in education, as well as the fact that rates of return to education have not fallen significantly despite the dramatic expansion of education.

This is one of the few attempts to relate education to the nature of technological advance over the long run. In many ways, the case that is made is suggestive rather than conclusive, and considerable future research is needed on these issues, not least on whether the argument can hold for other advanced economies.

Education and Economic Performance: Britain. Britain is one of the few economies for which there has been a wide-ranging debate on the relation between education and economic performance. However, much of this debate has been focused on the idea that Britain has experienced a long-run "decline" and that the problem therefore is to explain the causes of this decline (for a general overview of educational issues in British industrialization culminating in a discussion of the "decline" debate, see West, 2001).

The most comprehensive and balanced overview of this debate is Sanderson (1999) (but see also Aldcroft, 1990). Britain has certainly been in relative decline compared with other advanced economies since the mid-nineteenth century, in the sense that it has had lower long-run growth rates and has therefore been overtaken in GNP per worker or per capita. At the same time, it has continued to grow, and national income rose sixfold from 1879 to 1989. The notion of Britain's decline actually began to surface in the late nineteenth century and stems from such phenomena as poor performance in international exhibitions, increasing imports of manufactures from Germany and the United States, and the emergence of completely new industries in other economies (such as chemical dyestuffs, based on breakthroughs in organic chemistry in Germany). Much of the public attention on these developments focused on the emergence of new educational institutions in trading partners: technical high schools in Germany and the *grands écoles* in France, for example. These developments, as well as claims of actual or impending decline, were forcefully emphasized by an emerging lobby arguing for an expansion of industrially oriented education.

Questions concerning the role of education in British growth in fact extend back to the first Industrial Revolution, beginning in the late eighteenth century. In a comprehensive survey, David Mitch (1993) showed that educational provision and literacy rates did not rise ahead of or during the Industrial Revolution, although a more complex division of labor may have required greater educational background in some work categories. He concluded that despite an increasing knowledge intensity in many technologies of the Industrial Revolution, there was "little evidence to suggest that education played a central role in England's Industrial Revolution" (Mitch, 1993, p. 303), which may in turn be related to British economic performance as technologies became more complex.

Claims concerning education became a standard part of explanations of decline for the nineteenth century. These have tended to take two basic forms. On the one hand, there is the argument that technical education in Britain was more or less deficient, especially in comparison to Germany. This led to the development of more engineers in Germany. Associated with this was a general reluctance to employ well-educated engineers in Britain (Sanderson, 1999, pp. 19–21). These phenomena led to major weakness in engineering education and research, and such writers as Corelli Barnett have placed great weight on these factors in shaping decline and relatively weak performance (Barnett, 1985, 1986).

The second explanation for decline concerns the nature of elite education in the United Kingdom. The system of public schools and the focus on Oxford and Cambridge as the pinnacle of the university system implied on the one hand a concentration on nontechnical subjects such as classics and on the other a set of social values that denigrated commercial pursuits and valorized the professions (such as the law), the military, and government service. In an analysis that resonated particularly with right-wing politicians in the 1980s, Martin Wiener interpreted these developments as factors in Britain's decline, having caused a "decline in the industrial spirit" that had allegedly characterized early Victorian growth (Wiener, 1981). It should be noted that there tends to be a division within this literature, between accounts that tend to make rather sweeping claims concerning Britain's decline and those that seek detailed analysis of the links between technical education and the performance of specific industries (such as Wrigley, 1986).

There are a number of objections frequently raised to the citing of education as a cause of decline. First, the system of apprenticeship, in which young men spent up to five years at minimal incomes learning trades, was a widespread and important element in human capital formation in the first Industrial Revolution (Mitch, forthcoming, p. 5). Second, there was an increasingly active technical education system in Britain after 1850. From 1850 to 1876, five new universities were created, all deeply involved in technical education and all closely related to the industrial specializations of their localities: Manchester, Leeds, Sheffield, Liverpool, and Bristol. Local industrialists often generously funded these and other civic universities. From the 1880s, many polytechnical and engineering colleges were created. The Technical Instruction Act of 1889 allowed councils to levy local taxes to build colleges, and within ten years 160 such

colleges were created. By 1911, there were 708,000 students attending evening classes in technical colleges (Sanderson, 1999, pp. 26–29). A third objection is centered on the fact that dramatic changes took place after 1890, making it therefore misleading to regard the whole period from 1850 as characterized by a single system or even single set of educational values. The supposed advantages of the German system also have been challenged, with the idea that the British system represented one rational solution to a complex education problem. Finally, it is not clear that the problems of specific British industries could have been remedied by more or better education.

The framework of decline shapes much of the literature on education and growth in Britain, but if this framework is misleading, then some of the questions asked may be weak or wrong (see Edgerton, 1996, for a trenchant attack on ideas of decline). These issues are unlikely to be resolved in the near future and illustrate plainly some of the continuing difficulties and challenges associated with analyzing the relationships between education and economic change.

Technical Education and Industrial Performance in Europe. The late nineteenth century was characterized by the extensive development of technical education throughout western Europe. Technical schools and colleges were created on an extensive scale. In many cases, these originated in the previous century as training institutions for civil and military engineers in the service of the state—this occurred most notably in France, but also in Britain, Spain, the German states, and Scandinavia (Grelon, 1993, p. 42). During the nineteenth century, the focus of attention on such institutions changed as the demands of training for industry came to the fore, driven partly by the formation of national states (in Italy and Germany), partly by military considerations (such as the catastrophe of 1870–1871 in France), and partly by more general considerations of nation building (in Scandinavia, for example). In France, forty-two engineering schools were founded from 1880 to 1913 (Grelon, 1993, p. 44). In Germany, eleven *Technische Hochschulen* were established from 1820 to 1910, as well as a wide range of intermediate schools providing vocational training (König, 1993, pp. 66–68). Smaller countries also took part in this expansion, though often a little later. In the early twentieth century, Belgium created seventeen engineering schools, Sweden two (although these two were large-scale technological universities in Stockholm and Göteborg) plus a system of technical secondary schools, Spain nine (at university level), and Italy seven (also as part of the university system) (see chapters by Ahlström, Baudet, Guagnini, and Riera I Tuèbols in Fox and Guagnini, 1993).

This widespread creation of technical education systems reflected a conscious attempt to create a human resources infrastructure for industrialization in these countries: trade associations, professional organizations, and governments were usually very explicit in seeing the link between such education and industrial objectives. Although there was a considerable amount of intercountry imitation and flow of particular participants, what emerged was a complex, diverse, heterogeneous system in Europe. This seriously complicates any assessment of impacts of different systems or different levels of provision on economic performance.

Certainly there are some spectacular examples of schools generating major enterprises or even whole industries. For example, Giovanni Batista Pirelli trained at the newly founded Istituto Tecnico Superiore in Milan in 1867 and 1868 (see Francesca Polese, 2001). After a thorough training at which he excelled, Pirelli won a grant from the institute to travel in Europe for the purpose of visiting factories. His travels lasted about ten months, finishing in September 1871. During that time, he visited 138 factories of all types and sizes, in Switzerland, France, Germany, and Belgium. He applied for permission to visit almost every rubber plant in these countries, and actually visited seven. He came back with a full notebook and a collaboration agreement with a major French manufacturer and engineer, Antoine Goulard. Pirelli established his first factory the following year, in 1872, and Pirelli's company became one of the major forces in Italy's industrialization.

In Pirelli's case, there is a clear link between education and industrial impact. In most cases, however, these links are difficult to establish. This does not prevent more tentative conclusions. Available studies suggest extensive diffusion of engineers from the schools established in the nineteenth century into the industries and regions that characterized European growth. Although we may wish to question the nature and direction of causal impacts, the association between engineering education and European growth seems clear and sharp.

The expansion of educational provision and attainments in the advanced economies has continued more or less uninterrupted for centuries. Although it cannot be concluded that enhanced educational attainment was necessary for early industrialization in Britain, it does appear to have been central in the ability of follower economies to take off, and in the continuation of productivity growth over time in advanced economies. As well as raising fundamental questions about the nature of economic growth and the role of human skills and capabilities, this long-standing role of education ought to provoke questions about continuity and change in advanced economies. There are many at present who argue that advanced economies in the late twentieth century entered a new phase of "knowledge-based" development. But in terms of human capabilities, the knowledge-based economy appears to have been with us for a long time, particularly if literacy, numeracy, and technical capability are connected. So the knowledge-based economy is far from new: it is in fact a basic form of capitalism and has persisted for several centuries.

However, the links between knowledge, education, and growth deserve deeper research. Often research has taken the form either of case studies of particular societies or of statistical associations between measures of educational attainment and measures of economic performance. One fruitful way forward in this area may be to address the problem of knowledge far more directly than has been done up to now in studies of education. We have relatively little in the way of studies that link forms, cognitive content, and application of knowledge. Mokyr (2002) is an attempt to do this, by developing a theory and history of "useful knowledge" not only in terms of its acquisition, storage, and transmission but also in terms of its links to technology. This requires both an understanding of the knowledge contents of science and of a wide range of less formal knowledge that feeds into the capabilities to produce and innovate—that is, a distinction between "knowledge" as the invention of a set of instructions for doing something and "competence," as in the ability to implement those instructions. This approach may well provide a way of understanding the integration of elite education with more general educational attainments. As Mokyr remarks, "Even if very few individuals in a society know quantum mechanics, the practical fruits of the insights of this knowledge to technology may still be available just as if everyone had been taught advanced physics. For the economic historian, what counts is clearly *collective* knowledge" (Mokyr, 2002, p. 5). But these high-level forms of knowledge still require a range of other knowledge (spatial, logical, numerical, and so on) to be able to operate in the world of practical technology, and this is the realm in which the vast bulk of education expenditure, time, and attainment occurs. From this perspective, the notion of the "knowledge economy" certainly has meaning, but we might argue that this would encompass the whole of the modern economic era and its associated growth in education.

[*See also* Human Capital *and* Literacy.]

BIBLIOGRAPHY

Abramovitz, M., and P. David. "Technological Change and the Rise of Intangible Investments: The US Economy's Growth-Path in the Twentieth Century." In *Employment and Growth in the Knowledge-Based Economy*, pp. 34–65. Paris, 1996.

Aldcroft, D. H. *Education, Training, and Economic Performance, 1944–1990.* Manchester, 1990.

Aldcroft, D. H. "Rich Nations—Poor Nations: The Penalty of Lateness." In *Rich Nations—Poor Nations: The Long-Run Perspective*, edited by D. H. Aldcroft and R. E. Catterall, pp. 19–37. Cheltenham, U.K., 1996.

Anderson, C., and M. Bowman. *Education and Economic Development.* Chicago, 1965.

Barnett, C. "Long-Term Industrial Performance in the United Kingdom: The Role of Education and Research, 1850–1939." In *The Economic System in the United Kingdom*, edited by D. J. Morris. Oxford, 1985.

Barnett, C. *The Audit of War.* London, 1986.

Becker, G. *Human Capital*. New York, 1964.

Easterlin, R. "Why Isn't the Whole World Developed?" *Journal of Economic History* 41.1 (1981), 1–19.

Edgerton, D. *Science, Technology and British Economic Decline, 1870–1970*. Cambridge, 1996.

Fox, R., and A. Guagnini, eds. *Education, Technology and Industrial Performance in Europe, 1850–1939*. Cambridge, 1993.

Goldin, C. "The Human-Capital Century and American Leadership: Virtues of the Past." *Journal of Economic History* 61.2 (2001), 263–292.

Goldin, C., and L. Katz. "Human Capital and Social Capital: The Rise of Secondary Schooling in America, 1910–1940." In *Patterns of Social Capital: Stability and Change in Historical Perspective*, edited by R. Rotberg, pp. 295–335. Cambridge, 2001.

Grelon, A. "The Training and Career Structures of Engineers in France, 1880–1939." In *Education, Technology and Industrial Performance in Europe, 1850–1939*, edited by R. Fox and A. Guagnini, pp. 42–64. Cambridge, 1993.

Houston, R. A. "Literacy." In *Encyclopedia of European Social History from 1350 to 2000*, edited by Peter N. Stearns, vol. 5, pp. 391–407. New York, 2001.

König, W. "Technical Education and Industrial Performance in Germany: A Triumph of Heterogeneity." In *Education, Technology and Industrial Performance in Europe, 1850–1939*, edited by R. Fox and A. Guagnini, pp. 65–87. Cambridge, 1993.

Landes, D. "The Creation of Knowledge and Technique: Today's Task and Yesterday's Experience." *Daedalus* 109 (1980), 111.

Mitch, D. "The Role of Human Capital in the First Industrial Revolution." In *The British Industrial Revolution: An Economic Perspective*, edited by J. Mokyr, pp. 267–307. Boulder, San Francisco, and Oxford, 1993.

Mitch, D. "Education and Skill of the British Labour Force between 1700 and 1860." In *The Economic History of Britain*, edited by R. Floud and P. Johnson, forthcoming.

Mokyr, J., ed. *The British Industrial Revolution: An Economic Perspective*. Boulder, San Francisco, and Oxford, 1993.

Mokyr, J. *The Gift of Athena: Historical Origins of the Knowledge Economy*. Princeton, 2002.

O'Rourke, K., and J. Williamson. "Education, Globalization and Catch-Up." *Scandinavian Economic History Review* 43.3 (1995), 287–309.

Parker, W. "Economic Development in Historical Perspective." *Economic Development and Cultural Change* 10 (1961), 1–7.

Polese, Francesca. "The Value of Foreign Knowledge in the Creation of an Innovative Firm: The Preparation and First Step of the Pirelli Rubber Company (1870–1880). Paper presented at the Fifth EBHA Conference, Oslo, 2001.

Rotberg, R., ed. *Patterns of Social Capital: Stability and Change in Historical Perspective*. Cambridge, 2001.

Sandberg, L. "The Case of the Impoverished Sophisticate: Human Capital and Swedish Economic Growth Before World War I." *Journal of Economic History* 39.1 (1979), 225–241.

Sandberg, L. "Ignorance, Poverty and Economic Backwardness in the Early Stages of European Industrialization: Variations on Alexander Gerschenkron's Grand Theme." *Journal of European Economic History* 11 (1982), 675–697.

Sanderson, M. *Education and Economic Decline in Britain, 1870 to the 1990s*. Cambridge, 1999.

Spence, M. "Job Market Signaling." *Quarterly Journal of Economics*, 87.3 (1973), 355–374.

Tortella, G., ed. *Education and Economic Development since the Industrial Revolution*. Valencia, Spain, 1990.

Vincent, D. *The Rise of Mass Literacy: Reading and Writing in Modern Europe*. Cambridge, 2000.

West, E. G. *Education and the Industrial Revolution*. Indianapolis, 2001.

Wiener, M. *English Culture and the Decline of the Industrial Spirit, 1850–1980*. Cambridge, 1981.

Wrigley, J. "Technical Education and Industry in the Nineteenth Century." In *The Decline of the British Economy*, edited by B. Elbaum and W. Lazonick, pp. 162–189. Oxford, 1986.

KRISTINE BRULAND

EDUCATIONAL LAND. The term refers to landed endowments (*xuetian*, literally "school land" in Chinese) that were created by extended kinship groups (lineages) beginning in the eleventh century. The concept of an estate that was owned jointly by all lineage members seems to have been borrowed from Buddhism. Since lineage land could not be sold without the consent of all members, the wealth could be passed on to future generations without diminution, unlike private or household wealth, which was divided among all sons upon the death of the father. In central and south China during the eighteenth and nineteenth centuries, corporate estates provided a significant and sometimes the majority of household income for members of selected local lineages.

The incentive to invest lineage resources in education was heightened during the eleventh century, when the civil service examinations, which required advanced levels of education and mastery of classical texts, became the primary means of entering the bureaucracy. Families exerted themselves to prepare their talented sons to sit for the examinations. Over centuries, acquiring the advanced examination degrees required for appointment to office took longer and longer, raising the educational costs.

One of several types of landed endowments attached to lineages, the rent revenues of "school land" were used to finance schools open to the sons of lineage members. Some lineages also presented cash subsidies and school supplies to those attending school. Others gave money to students who could not attend the clan school so that they might be educated. Some wealthy lineages provided scholarships to advanced scholars who had to travel to the provincial or national capital to take the civil service examinations. Many lineages presented cash awards to successful degree winners as well. The funds to pay for educational support came not only from the "school land" but also from ritual and charitable land revenues: some lineages earmarked a stipulated percentage of these other revenues to be spent on education.

Before the twentieth century, elementary schooling in China was primarily private. In regions in southeast and south China where strong lineages enjoyed sizable incomes from corporate estates, lineage schools played significant roles in contributing to the examination success of their kinsmen. Studies have shown that some surname groups in the densely urbanized Yangzi River delta were able to produce outstanding individuals who capped the examination lists for generation after generation, thanks in large part to their lineage schools. Divisions among Confucian scholars also frequently tended to be formed along regional and lineage lines, and the perpetuation of Confucian traditions was thus intertwined with the success of kinship-based groups.

Private academies (*shuyuan*), which became significant centers of scholarship from the eleventh century onward, also acquired landed endowments and used the revenues to support activities such as editing and publishing select editions of Confucian works as well as providing advanced education for scholars with the first civil service (*shengyuan*) degree. More broadly, landed endowments became by the nineteenth century a widely accepted means of supporting voluntary associations in Chinese society such as orphanages, widows' welfare associations, and other charitable organizations.

BIBLIOGRAPHY

Elman, Benjamin A. *A Cultural History of Civil Examinations in Late Imperial China*. Berkeley, 2000.
Elman, Benjamin A. *Classicism, Politics, and Kinship: The Ch'ang-chou School of New Text Confucianism in Late Imperial China*. Berkeley, 1990.
Hu, Hsien-chin. *The Common Descent Group in China and Its Functions*. New York, 1948.
Rawski, Evelyn S. *Education and Popular Literacy in Ch'ing China*. Ann Arbor, 1979.

EVELYN S. RAWSKI

EGYPT [*This entry contains two subentries, on the economic history of Egypt during ancient and classical times and during the Islamic and modern periods.*]

Ancient and Classical Periods

About 3200 BCE, Egypt became one of the first centralized states, and irrigation from the Nile River provided for its farming economy, beginning as early as 8,000 years ago. Ancient Egypt does not fit neatly into economic theory, yet its history is a key to understanding market history, as well as the relationship of the origins of the state to economic growth. Archaeologists have established that the Nile Valley was one of the most densely populated regions of ancient times. On average, the fertile soil of the Nile's alluvium, deposited in annual floods, produced a seed-to-yield ratio of 1:10 on grain-bearing land.

The Nile River flows into the Mediterranean Sea through the Nile Delta, a broad fertile plain. The breadth of the cultivation zone in the Nile Valley was about fifteen miles. A separate branch of the river fed the Fayyum Depression, to the west, in the Sahara, a very productive region in ancient times. Nile agriculture had irrigation works that fed water onto terraced basins—a system used until the 1970 completion of the High Dam at Aswan,

which eliminated the annual flooding. The Nile, which began flooding in June, at Aswan, replenished the soil with nutrients; the flooding receded in late August, at which time broadcast sowing of crops began.

The virtually flat gradient of the river from Aswan to the Delta allowed for local management of the irrigation canals. Emmer wheat (*Triticum dicoccum*), barley (*Hordeum vulgare*), and flax (*Linum usitatissimum*) were the main crops. The basic diet for all levels of society was bread and beer; linen cloth was used for clothing. Agricultural technology remained relatively constant until the introduction of the water-lifting pole and bucket *shaduf* during the New Kingdom, which enabled the watering of both gardens and marginal high-lying land.

Population figures for ancient Egypt are educated guesses, based on the estimated carrying capacity of the land and the extent of its cultivation, often worked back from classical references and secure modern figures. For the height of the New Kingdom, Egypt's maximum exploitation of the land before the Greco-Roman period, the accepted figure is about 3 million. An estimate of 3 to 5 million for the Greco-Roman period is based in part on immigration from the Greek world of some 250,000 to 500,000, plus two new cities—the port city of Alexandria and the southern city of Ptolemais.

State Structure and the Economy. At the beginning of Egypt's political unification, during the Old Kingdom, centralizing ideology with extensive territorial claims by a divine king was already established. This overarching ideology, however, should be distinguished from the regional character of Egypt's political organization, in which upper Egypt and Lower Egypt (the Delta) maintained their sociocultural differences. Still, there were some continuous features in the overall economy. In that early theocracy, the connection between the central administration, the local elite, and the land formed a network that included the palace, the temples and shrines, and the local officials. Egyptian ideology of the divine king as chief officiant in the religious cults linked the central state to local organizations of production. Private rights in land (not full private ownership in the sense of Roman law) and conveyance of land and wage labor (for pyramid and tomb building; for agricultural labor at harvest time) were documented. The state's building projects and the concomitant requisition of a labor force by the local elite served to convey royal domination in the provinces. Strong forces of state unity included the control of writing by royal scribes and the control of the "social cage," the lands of the Nile Valley. The royal city of Memphis (to the south of present-day Cairo) served as the first political capital. It was located at the approximate midpoint of the north-south arable land. The residence of the king was, however, moved from dynasty to dynasty. Ancient Egypt's administrative units are today called "nomes" (after the Greek word of the Ptolemaic era). Their origin is debated, but they were likely in existence by the Old Kingdom. There were traditionally forty-two nomes, although their actual number varied with time. Records of their administration and produce were kept, as well as their taxation. Redistribution of both produce and taxes went from the producers to the administrators, both civil and religious. New studies indicate that market exchange was, however, the main mode of the allocation of resources.

State Bureaucracy. During the New Kingdom, in its fully developed form, the bureaucracy consisted of two main branches, the military and the royal treasury. The treasury linked village officials to regional officials, the monarch's, and to central bureaus in the capital. Most of that bureaucracy was administered land tenure, land measurement, and land taxation. Major temple estates played a key role in the local agrarian administration, and their officials provided record keeping, long-term grain storage, and local employment (to both the part-time priests, and the support staff of herdsmen of the sacred flock, bakers, carpenters, etc.).

Real property, in private hands from the Old Kingdom onward, was established in writing, could be conveyed by private document, and could be inherited. Land was given to local officials by the king in exchange for service to the state. Unlike the ancient Near East, Egypt's legal system was not codified but functioned through royal decrees and self-help at the local level. Records of court cases have survived, which were heard by the local elite. The office of vizier (established in the Old Kingdom but only well-documented in the New Kingdom) was an important state post, with special responsibilities for legal administration, including land registration and property records. At times, there were two such officials, in charge of maintaining at least the appearance of social justice; they traveled the country to hear petitions, and they provided instruction in legal cases.

Markets. Transactions in the private economy were, until the Greco-Roman era, concluded by barter. The process is well documented in Middle Kingdom writings and in extensive documentation from the royal tomb builders' village at Thebes during the New Kingdom. The price of a good was established relative to a fixed measure of exchange—usually reckoned in units of oil, grain, silver or bronze/copper weights (the *deben*). During eras of strong state centralization, local grain redistribution operated through the temples that employed monthly shifts of priests and laborers; in this way, the state functioned as a major employer. Increasingly, private demand for goods was stimulated by elaborate burial customs; those required not only tomb building and burial goods for the provincial elite but tombs and goods for even the middle classes, such as wooden coffins, stone funerary stelae, funerary papyri, and various ceramic jars and statuary. During the New Kingdom, considerable intertemple exchange of surplus taxes and rents suggest robust market mechanisms.

Taxes. Ancient Egypt imposed taxation in grain, with an overall tax rate of some 10 percent of total production, but higher on some classes of land. The harvest tax, probably one of the earliest, was enforced by an official annual crop survey. The Old Kingdom's state taxation regime included a biennial cattle census and corvée labor for the canals. By the Greco-Roman era, that had been elaborated and partially monetized.

Early Dynastic Egypt (c. 3000–2686 BCE). Historians of ancient Egypt tend to stress the three major eras of political centralization—the Old, the Middle and the New Kingdoms—before the Greco-Roman era. The decline of all three periods is usually attributed to a combination of political and environmental decline, as well as (in the last two periods) foreign incursion. Each was followed by an Intermediate period, characterized by political fragmentation, regional artistic styles, and so on. The impact of low Nile floods at the end of the Old Kingdom and start of the First Intermediate period, and the subsequent reports of famine, are still debated by historians. The threat of famine caused by inadequate Nile flooding must always have loomed.

Upper and Lower Egypt were unified as a territorial state about 3200 to 3000 BCE by a process, still little understood by scholars, that began in the southern region (called Upper Egypt for the upper reaches of the Nile). The pace of state formation and even the historicity of political unification are still debated (see Ian Shaw, ed., *The Oxford History of Ancient Egypt*, Oxford, 2000). The archaeology of the eastern Delta region and adjacent Israel-Palestine suggests extensive trade contacts and social networks; there were also early trade contacts between southern Egypt and northern Nubia (Sudan) by late predynastic times.

Most of the evidence for the early state comes from elite cemeteries, in which royal tomb complexes, jar labels, and seal impressions attest to royal estates and domains that supported the funerary complexes and their priests. The early state economy was organized around such royal foundations that funded the king and court, into which taxes in kind were paid. The ideology of divine kingship and central control enabled the early Egyptian state to administer hinterlands otherwise sparsely populated, as was the case in the western Delta, where many royal foundations had been established. Central control was effected by record keeping, and the royal annals from the early state suggest a census—then, from the second dynasty on, a biennial cattle count. The collection, storage, and redistribution of revenues were coordinated by the state treasury.

ANCIENT EGYPT. Men and women at work in grain fields. Wall painting. (Giraudon/Art Resource, NY)

The kings of the first dynasty were buried in royal mortuary complexes at Abydos, in the central Nile Valley, and their elaborate burials demonstrate the considerable expense of the ritual burial of Egypt's divine kings.

Old Kingdom (2686–2125 BCE). The first monumental use of stone was for the funerary complex of King Djoser, third dynasty, when large pyramidal tombs were first built. A new office—vizier—coordinated all aspects of centralized state bureaucracy. Those coordinated efforts were used to build the pyramid complexes of the fourth dynasty kings at Giza and for the mining expeditions to the quarries at the Wadi Hammamat, Hatnub, and elsewhere. An Egyptian presence was established in the mining regions to the north at Sinai, and trade routes were expanded into sub-Saharan Africa. Political developments from the fourth dynasty to the sixth include the gradual move from family ties to a bureaucratic structure and, then, from centralization at the capital in Memphis to a decentralized governing system, with increasing power going to local elites. The ever-increasing bureaucracy was paid in grants of land. An important fourth dynasty legal case, recorded in the tomb of an official, suggests the large-scale private ownership of agricultural land among the upper echelons of the elite. The Palermo Stone, a fifth dynasty document about much of the Old Kingdom, records the biennial cattle census as one of the key state institutions. The earliest account records detail the income and expenditures of some pyramid-temples at Abusir; they are fifth dynasty writings on papyrus.

Middle Kingdom (2055–1650 BCE). After the First Intermediate period, central control was reestablished by the eleventh dynasty at Thebes, the new capital, and with it came the renewal of state-directed building projects. Powerful local elites were brought under royal authority by the twelfth dynasty. The royal residence was established in the Western Desert (Sahara) near the Fayyum Depression, which was for the first time developed by Egypt's kings. Significant new features in the social organization include the larger and more articulated bureaucracy, divided into northern and southern groups, with a system of corvée labor that was enforced by a new bureau of the central government for public works. Egypt's internal expansion was likely driven by a population increase. The power of the nomarchs—local governors—grew so extensively that by the end of the twelfth dynasty their power had to be curtailed by the king. The Hekanakhte correspondence (private letters and accounts that probably date from the twelfth dynasty) are the first documentary source for private farming activity and business strategy—with details of the private lending of grain; renting rather than the buying of land; and the purchase of land and commodities by barter with copper, oil, and linen.

New Kingdom (1550–1069 BCE). After the disruptions of the Second Intermediate period, the New Kingdom rulers consolidated Egypt once again, along with Nubia in the south and the Syria-Palestine region in the north. A gradual political and economic shift occurred toward the Delta, from about 1400 BCE onward. The desire to control

Near Eastern trade routes sent many New Kingdom rulers on active military campaigns there, which brought considerable wealth to Egypt in the form of booty and slave labor. Much of the wealth was deposited in the temples, principally the great Theban state temple of Amun-Re at Karnak. Temples were then major land-owning institutions; their role as legitimizers of the imperial regime was a major factor in the New Kingdom's economy. Considerable price data is known from the *ostraca* (marked limestone sherds used for recordkeeping) excavated at the workman's village, Deir el-Medina, a state-funded project for building the rulers' tombs. The payment of the state land tax in gold, documented a few times, suggests an attempt at monetization.

Third Intermediate Period. After two thousand years of Egyptian civilization, the political decline of the New Kingdom was marked by the invasion of the Sea Peoples (Phoenicians, Philistenes, Mediterranean traders), who came in the wake of the Hittite Empire's collapse. The general economic and social deterioration of the time was marked by very high grain prices recorded in some documents, which suggest at least local failures in the agricultural system. Egypt became divided into several smaller polities, so the Egyptian economy as a whole cannot be known. About 700 BCE, the Nubian kings based at the southern city of Napata restored order to the Nile Valley. Aided by higher Nile floods, they resumed a building program in Egypt. The Assyrian invasion of 671 BCE, however, brought Egypt into the Assyrian Empire of the Near East.

Saite/Persian Period (664–332 BCE). Little is known of the structure or extent of Egypt's economy during this time, but Greeks came in large numbers as soldiers and as traders. The Greek trading community at Naucratis was established by Amasis in about 620 BCE; the first smelting of iron in Egypt was attested here by the Greeks, and Greek wine and silver were imported through this trading point. Much of the Saite period was concerned with the reassertion of central control across Egypt and Egypt's incorporation into the Persian imperial system. As part of the Persian Empire, Egypt (and Cyrenaica to its west) paid an annual tribute; some attempt at economic improvement was made, by granting imperial estates to officials. Under Darius I, a canal was built from the Nile to the Red Sea, probably as much to affect ease of communications with Persia and easier troop transport as for trade. Little in the way of economic structure was changed under Persian rule; however, the new writing system—Demotic—was part of the process of political consolidation. The use of demotic for private legal agreements shows a change in the law of contracts. Egypt lagged behind Greek regions in the use of coinage, but coinage came with the Greek merchants and soldiers.

Greco-Roman Period: Ptolemaic (332–30 BCE), Roman (30 BCE–312 CE) and Late Antique (312–642 CE). Alexander the Great's general Ptolemy ruled Egypt and began the Ptolemaic dynasty. Large numbers of documentary papyri in Demotic and in Greek are known. The hierarchical market structure was evident in the villages, in the district capitals, and in the great new port city of Alexandria, built by Alexander the Great. The use of money became widespread, and market activity increased in the villages and towns. Trade guilds were the means by which the central administration controlled prices in the key sectors of manufacture. Skilled laborers and craftsmen, although working in the earlier periods, were widely documented in papyri. Alexandria became one of the main commercial centers of the Mediterranean world and in it was built the greatest of the ancient libraries. In Ptolemaic times, coinage was produced in Alexandria, and the central government imposed an economic order designed to maximize tax revenues.

The Ptolemaic dynasty was established along ancient Egyptian lines—for acceptance and authenticity. New economic institutions were then gradually installed to better exploit local agricultural production. Among the most important were the following: widespread use of coinage to pay taxes; the tax-farming system; a system of monopolies that set the price of raw materials in key industries; the use of public auctions to dispose of derelict property; the issuance of tax receipts; and a banking system, used in the main to collect tax payments. A poll tax (called the "salt tax") was imposed, and taxes on most forms of production were exacted. Under royal patronage, a land-reclamation project in the Fayyum Depression trebled the amount of arable land there. New crops were introduced, including the important new strain of northern Mediterranean wheat, *Triticum durum*, and more extensive viticulture was practiced for the wine trade.

In 30 BCE, by military defeat, Egypt became an imperial province of the Roman Empire. The emperor Augustus reorganized Egypt's fiscal and social structure. Basic local features of the Ptolemaic economy were retained, but they were modified to suit Roman fiscal and taxation practices. Private ownership of land was greatly increased. The province of Egypt was subject to direct taxation, and an annual poll tax (*laographia*) was introduced. The closed currency of Egypt came to an end in 296 CE, when the Alexandrian mint stopped producing the *tetradrachm* coin. Egypt was thereby more easily integrated into the empire. A series of late devaluations of Roman coinage led to an empire-wide currency crisis, and the response by the emperor Diocletian was to regulate prices (the so-called Edict of Maximum Prices), by 301 CE. Then in 313 CE, a new 15-year tax cycle was introduced. The key to understanding the change in the economic structure was the growth of the Christian church in both political and economic power in those years. The emperor Constantine's conversion to Christianity in 312 CE and his reorganization of the economy allowed the church to acquire vast amounts of wealth in the form of land. Much would be changed by the Islamic invasions of the mid-600s.

BIBLIOGRAPHY

Baer, Klaus. "An Eleventh Dynasty Farmer's Letters to his Family." *Journal of the American Oriental Society* 83 (1963), 1–19.

Bagnall, Roger S. *Egypt in Late Antiquity*. Princeton, 1993.

Bowman, Alan K. *Egypt after the Pharaohs*. Rev. ed. Berkeley, 1996. Overview of the Ptolemaic, Roman, and Late Antique periods. Chapter four contains an excellent general account of the economy and economic trends.

Bowman, Alan K., and Eugene Rogan, eds. *Agriculture in Egypt: From Pharaonic to Modern Times*. Oxford, 1999. Papers presented at a conference in Oxford, England, which contain an up-to-date (but incomplete) account of land tenure in ancient Egypt as well as in Ptolemaic, Roman, and Early Christian times.

Bowman, Alan K., and Dominic Rathbone. "Cities and Administration in Roman Egypt." *Journal of Roman Studies* 82 (1992), 107–127. Survey of the changes and continuities in the economic and social organization of Roman Egypt.

Butzer, Karl. *Early Hydraulic Civilization in Egypt: A Study in Cultural Ecology*. Chicago, 1976. A central study of the relationship of the environment to long-term Egyptian history.

Husson, Geneviève, and Dominique Valbelle. *L'État et les institutions en Égypte des premiers pharaons aux empereurs romains*. Paris, 1992.

Janssen, Jac. J. *Commodity Prices from the Ramessid Period*. Leiden, 1975.

Kemp, Barry. *Ancient Egypt: Anatomy of a Civilization*. London, 1989. Focus is on material culture, but there is a survey of Egyptian social structure. Chapter 6, "The Birth of Economic Man," summarizes the basic structure of the ancient Egyptian economy.

Préaux, Claire. *L'économie royale des Lagides*. Brussels, 1939. Still the classic assessment of the royal economy under the Ptolemies.

Rathbone, Dominic. *Economic Rationalism and Rural Society in Third-Century A.D. Egypt*. Cambridge, 1991.

Shaw, Ian, ed. *The Oxford History of Ancient Egypt*. Oxford, 2000.

Trigger, B. G., B. J. Kemp, D. O'Connor, and A. B. Lloyd. *Ancient Egypt: A Social History*. Cambridge, 1983.

Warburton, David A. *State and Economy in Ancient Egypt: Fiscal Vocabulary of the New Kingdom*. Freibourg, 1997. A Keynesian (!) interpretation of the economy of the New Kingdom; contains a good general discussion of the structure of the Egyptian state. The most sophisticated account of Egyptian economy (in the New Kingdom) in English. An excellent overview (absent Weber's views, however) of previous theory of the Egyptian economy is given on pp. 73–111.

Wilkinson, Toby A. H. *Early Dynastic Egypt*. London, 1999. Survey of the Egyptian economy and social structure and the institutions of the early Egyptian state, covering the first, second, and third dynasties.

J. G. MANNING

Islamic and Modern Periods

From the Islamic invasion of the 630s CE to the present, Egypt's economic history combined great stability with repeated transformations. As in earlier times, Egypt's agricultural wealth—based on the Nile River, its annual floods and its irrigation—was its economic stabilizer, the basis for its strong political regimes and the lure that drew foreign interest and intervention. Egypt's ruling elites sought to control its agricultural production, its foreign trade via the Mediterranean Sea and Red Sea, and its influence in its many areas: the Mediterranean region, North Africa, sub-Saharan Africa, the Middle East, and the increasingly interconnected world economy. The long continuities in Egypt's economic history were affected by the specifics of changing markets, regional power struggles, evolving institutions, new technologies, and the patterns of demographic change.

The Arab invasion of the 630s had many economic consequences for Egypt. Within two hundred years the economy had shifted from the Byzantine Empire's institutional framework to the new Islamic patterns of the Arab caliphs. Muslim administrators and merchants instituted Islamic practices in government and trade, collected taxes, and paid debts in the new coinage; the conquerors relied on agricultural land taxes and on a poll tax for non-Muslims. In time, the land tax revenues decreased, owing to corruption, emigration, or poor administration. As Egyptians converted to Islam, the poll taxes also decreased. Alternative revenues had to be found. As a conquered province, Egypt's status changed several times. It was an independent state and, on occasion, the center of empire. Such political changes affected the flow of resources into or out of the country. From 868 to 884, Egypt obtained a degree of financial independence from the Ummayyad caliphate in Baghdad; Ibn Tulun (Ahmad b. Tulun) built a new capital city near Cairo, strengthened Egypt's army with Turkish, Greek, and Sudanese slave troops, and occupied Syria. Details of Egypt's fiscal organization then are few, but Ibn Tulun increased the security of land tenure and increased the cultivated area through land grants.

The Fatimid dynasty (969–1171 CE) flourished at the center of an Egyptian empire. Fatimid rulers not only established the capital city of Cairo and al-Azhar, its renowned Islamic university, but also took measures to improve agriculture and industry. Wheat and flax were Egypt's principal crops, both for internal consumption and international trade. To pay military officers, the government granted *iqta*'s to them, grants that began as an assignment of revenues from agricultural land without giving manorial jurisdiction or administrative functions. With time, the term *iqta'* was variously interpreted by the grantees and by successive regimes. Property holders could place their estates in a pious (religious) trust, *waqf*, for charitable purposes, which removed them from state intervention or control.

During both the Fatimid and Ayyubid (1171–1250 CE) dynasties, there was considerable long-distance trade between the lands of the Indian Ocean and Egypt. Spices and silks were traded by Karimi merchants, who joined in partnerships to spread their risks as they provided the necessary ships. The Ayyubids provided military protection, supplied warehouses, and improved ports. Despite the interruptions of the Crusades, when European armies tried to retake the Holy land for Christendom, a European merchant community settled at Egypt's Mediterranean port of Alexandria to handle the Mediterranean trade. Textiles were imported from Europe, while niter and alum from Egyptian mines were exported, as well as with Indian Ocean goods. Through the assignment of *waqf* revenue, Ayyubid leaders supported immigrant and local Muslim scholars, who served as judges, administrators, and market inspectors.

Egypt remained independent under the Mamluks (1250–1517 CE), as Baghdad and much of the region fell to Mongol invaders. The Indian Ocean trade, via the Red Sea and the Nile River, remained outside Mongol control, a source of revenue to the Mamluk rulers. The Mamluks, a dynasty of military slaves, relied on the further import of slaves from the Black Sea area. To ensure this supply, carried in part on ships from Genoa, diplomatic maneuvering and occasional military intervention were necessary along the key trade routes. Egypt had inherited the responsibility for the protection of Islam's holy cities, Mecca and Medina, in the Arabian Peninsula across the Red Sea; that emphasized the importance of the Red Sea route but increased Egyptian interest and intervention in Upper Egypt (the South) and adjacent Nubia, alternative sources of slaves and gold. The bubonic plague struck Egypt in 1347 and, repeatedly, until about 1500. Its impact was strongest in the cities, where manufacturing declined with the loss of artisans and apprentices, and the military strength of Egypt was reduced by the plague deaths of young Mamluks in their barracks. By the fifteenth century, royal monopolies were established in the Indian Ocean trade and on sugar exports, to make up for Egypt's revenue losses in other sectors. By the end of the century, Mamluk rulers were confiscating private fortunes and property, the revenues of *waqfs*, and, eventually, the *waqf* title-deeds. A factor in the financial crisis was their need to supply the army with expensive artillery and firearms, since the Ottoman Empire soon became the major threat to any Egyptian independence.

Given its strategic position and full granaries, Egypt had always been a desirable and contested prize. In the sixteenth and seventeenth centuries, conflict began between the Iberian and Ottoman Empires over dominating the Mediterranean and the Red Sea. Later, the long rivalry of the eighteenth century and early nineteenth began, between France and Great Britain, culminating in the Napoleonic Wars. The Ottoman-Iberian competition was economic as well as military; Spain's advantage was the massive influx of silver from the newly discovered and dominated Americas, as well as Portugal's challenges to the Arab trade networks in the Red Sea and Indian Ocean. In Egypt, price inflation undermined the economic security of Ottoman troops and others on fixed salaries,

which decreased their loyalty to the state. Egyptian merchants then lost much of their income from trading spices and, later, coffee—since New World coffee was marketed in Europe and in the Ottoman Empire. The Napoleonic invasion of Egypt in 1798, designed to block Britain's shortest route to India, was a proof of Europe's growing influence on the Egyptian economy; Europe then transformed Egypt from a key trading entrepôt to a provider of grain and other cash crops. The French rediscovered the ancient Egyptian monuments and studied them sytematically, which brought scholars, adventurers, and tourists to the Nile Valley. Egyptology became an important field of study and Egyptomania, as a stylish presence, swept through Europe and the United States.

From 1517 to 1805, Ottoman economic practices and policies had been established in Egypt. Since the Ottoman Turks had accepted Islam, many of their practices were similar to those of the earlier Muslims. Under the Ottomans, the notion was restored that all land belonged to the state. After a survey, *iltizam* (tax-farming rights) were auctioned; the tax farmers had to forward the taxes on the villages under their control, maintain local irrigation works, and foster agricultural prosperity—in exchange for the right to make a profit. The central government in distant Istanbul soon lost control over tax rates, revenues, and even the land, when *iltizam*s became inheritable in the late 1600s. A land-owning class then developed in Egypt, composed not only of state officials but also of military leaders, merchants, and scholars.

From about 1800, four themes have dominated Egypt's economic history: a search for economic independence; a rapidly growing population; urbanization; and an increased integration into the world economy. Muhammad Ali Pasha (1807–1848) was an Ottoman governor who was determined to make Egypt into a prosperous and powerful country on its own. He actively sought to build up its population, its army, and its economy. He introduced up-to-date health services, which began Egypt's steady demographic growth. He increased the size of its army and navy, then deployed his military in Arabia, in Sudan, and in the Mediterranean often without Ottoman sanction. To develop the Egyptian economy, he set out to transform agriculture first—investing in irrigation works and promoting cotton, indigo, and sugar as cash crops. He established Egyptian trading monopolies in those crops and in the trade goods from Sudan. He sought European advisors in all key fields, particularly in the creation of cotton mills, indigo printing factories, and sugar refineries, and for import-substitution manufacturing schemes in military supplies. He began the process of transforming land tenure in Egypt by abolishing *iltizam*s, replacing them with the direct taxation of peasant landholdings.

After 1820, wealthy peasants and notables gradually gained land by paying its back taxes. Privileged estates were granted to Muhammad Ali Pasha's family and to state officials as tax-exempt holdings. Those trends were to continue under his descendants, who ruled Egypt for the rest of the century, as if it no longer belonged to the Ottoman Empire. They tried to capitalize on his policies. During the American Civil War (1861–1865) Egypt's cotton growing expanded fivefold as the world price for cotton quintupled. It resulted in making cotton Egypt's leading export, into the twentieth century; by 1900, it had led to a rise in the general standard of living, although great disparities in income persisted and continue to persist.

Britain's economic interest in Egypt began because of its strategic location on the shortest sea route from Europe to India and from its crucial role as a source of cotton during the American Civil War. With the building of the Suez Canal by a French company, Britain became a key investor. From 1882 to 1922, Britain controlled Egypt's economic affairs completely, but after World War I a monarchy was established, over which Britain retained great economic influence until 1952. The volume of Egypt's cotton exports had increased twentyfold from 1850 to 1910, with similar growth in value and purchasing power; a huge investment in infrastructure included the following: an expansion of irrigation and the completion of the Aswan Dam of 1902; improvements in transportation and the creation of a railroad system; the completion of the Suez Canal in 1869 and development of the ports of Alexandria, Suez, and Port Said. Apart from the large landowners, the top of Egypt's economy was in European hands, with control of the banks, insurance companies, cotton manufacturing and export firms, transportation, utilities, and the best professional posts. Some technical, administrative, and commercial skills were supplied by other Middle Eastern minorities (Jews, Syrians, Lebanese, etc.). That bourgeoisie blocked the development of an indigenous economy until after World War II. Borrowing for infrastructure improvements by the British-controlled Egyptian monarchy also led Egypt into a massive debt burden. Under those conditions, capitalism was increasingly viewed as foreign and debilitating to the Egyptian people, and the monarch was ousted in 1952. Most of the Jews left for the new State of Israel, which was established in 1948 but was attacked by Egypt and the armies of the Arab League until 1949—and several times since. With the end of the first Arab-Israel war, the Arab League placed an economic boycott on Israel that lasted until the late 1990s.

Between 1912 and the revolution of 1952, Egypt encountered three key economic problems: agricultural expansion had nearly reached the limits of available land, although new dams and perennial irrigation mitigated the problem; in the late 1920s and the 1930s, cotton prices fell, and Egypt's terms of trade declined, as did the world economy during the Great Depression; but Egypt's population

CAIRO. City scene, 1986. (© Robert Frerck/Woodfin Camp and Associates, New York)

had doubled. Only in the 1930s did the new monarchy begin to respond, as Egypt regained control over its own tariffs and fiscal powers. The strategy chosen was industrialization for import substitution, with tariff protection for the new industries. World War II only reinforced this strategy, as supply lines from Europe were cut and Allied troops stationed in Egypt increased the demand for manufactured goods.

Nationalism favored Egyptian education, the development of an Egyptian bourgeoisie, and the expanded employment of Egyptians at all levels of the economy. The 1952 revolution, led by General Mohammed Naguib, gave control to an army junta led by Gamal Abdel Nasser, who addressed the perceived economic problems of Egypt by embracing "Arab socialism." He nationalized the Suez Canal and, later, the banks, insurance companies, and other international businesses. Reforms transferred one-sixth of all land from large landowners to small farmers and many people benefited from rent reduction. The new

Aswan High Dam of the early 1960s, built with Russian assistance and moneys, provided flood control, irrigation, and hydroelectric power, while creating new environmental problems throughout the Nile Valley and around the dam-created reservoir, called Lake Nasser.

Since Nasser's death in 1970, his successors reversed many of his policies—casting off Soviet support and abandoning Arab socialism for the capitalist way. In 1977, government subsidies for food were dropped on the advice of the International Monetary Fund (IMF), and riots broke out in Cairo; food subsidies were restored. At the end of the twentieth century, agricultural gains were overcome by population growth, and grain imports rose markedly. Egypt's population is more than 65 million, and Cairo is one of the world's largest cities. Egypt signed a peace treaty with Israel in 1979, and Egyptian leaders have tried to broker peace between the Palestinians and Israel several times, making safe meeting places available. Egypt was badly affected by the expenses and disruptions of the Arab-Israel wars; by the rise and decline of the Arab-dominated OPEC oil cartel; by the rise of fundamentalist Islam and its politico-economic prescriptions and aspirations; and by a growing dependence on foreign aid from the United States.

BIBLIOGRAPHY

Baer, Gabriel. *Studies in the Social History of Modern Egypt*. Chicago, 1969.

Bowman, Alan K., and Eugene Rogan, eds. *Agriculture in Egypt: From Pharaonic to Modern Times*. Proceedings of the British Academy, 96. New York, 1999.

Cuno, Kenneth M. *The Pasha's Peasants: Land, Society, and Economy in Lower Egypt, 1740–1858*. Cambridge, 1992.

Daly, Martin W., ed. *The Cambridge History of Egypt*, vol. 2: *Modern Egypt, from 1517 to the End of the Twentieth Century*. New York, 1998.

Dols, Michael. *The Black Death in the Middle East*. Princeton, 1977.

Marsot, Afaf Lutfi al-Sayyid. *A Short History of Modern Egypt*. Cambridge, 1985.

Owen, E. R. J. *Cotton and the Egyptian Economy, 1820–1914: A Study in Trade and Development*. Oxford, 1969.

Petry, Carl F., ed. *The Cambridge History of Egypt*, vol. 1: *Islamic Egypt, 640–1517*. Cambridge, 1998.

Redford, Donald M., ed. *The Oxford Encyclopedia of Ancient Egypt*. New York, 2001.

Rivlin, Helen Anne B. *The Agricultural Policy of Muhammad Ali in Egypt*. Cambridge, Mass., 1961.

Walz, Terence. *The Trade between Egypt and Bilad as-Sudan, 1700–1820*. Cairo, 1978.

GEORGE MICHAEL LaRUE

ELECTRICAL INDUSTRY. A continuous current of electricity became available in 1800, when Alessandro Volta (1745–1827) described Volta's pile, which, with another arrangement called the crown of cups, were the first electric batteries. The first mass-produced battery was designed by William Cruickshank (1745–1800), who soldered copper and zinc plates together in pairs and sealed them with wax in a wooden trough filled with acid. Most electrical research in the first third of the nineteenth century depended on Cruickshank batteries, which remained the best practical source of electricity until 1836, when John Frederic Daniell (1790–1845) invented a cell with a constant output.

Humphry Davy (1778–1829) established the science of electrochemistry and isolated several new elements by electrolysis of their compounds. He introduced the idea that the force binding the atoms in a chemical compound is electric. In his work Davy demonstrated the brilliant light produced by an arc between two pieces of carbon connected to a high-voltage supply. He used the heat of the arc, but it was never developed into a practical method of illumination in his lifetime.

Electricity and magnetism were linked in the winter of 1819–1820, when Hans Christian Oersted (1777–1851) discovered that a current in a wire could deflect a compass needle. Following that, J. S. C. Schweigger (1779–1857) found that, if the wire was wound into a coil around the needle, then the deflection was greatly increased. This arrangement became known as Schweigger's multiplier. Its application as a current detector was obvious, and the name galvanometer was introduced in 1821.

The most important figure in early electrical history is Michael Faraday (1791–1867), who began his scientific career as Davy's assistant. Following Oersted's discovery of the circular magnetic force around a wire, Faraday made two devices that could be called electric motors in September 1821. In one a bar magnet was fixed vertically in a basin of mercury. A wire with a cork on its lower end was loosely suspended from a point above the magnet. When a battery was connected between the suspended wire and another wire dipping into the mercury, the lower end of the suspended wire moved in circles around the magnet. In the second device one end of the magnet was tied to the bottom of the basin, but the other end was free (a steel magnet floats in mercury). A fixed wire dipped into the center of the mercury. When current flowed in the fixed wire, the free end of the magnet moved in circles around it. The experiment was repeated widely and brought Faraday into prominence.

If an electric current could produce magnetic effects, could magnetism produce electricity? Ampère suggested that magnetic effects were owed to circulating currents within the magnet. Faraday reasoned that, if two wires were side by side, then a current in one should produce some effect in the other. He eventually succeeded on 29 August 1831 with two coils wound on a soft iron ring. The coils were in several parts, so the number of turns could be varied. When a battery was connected to one coil, then a galvanometer connected to the other coil showed a brief deflection as the battery circuit was being made or broken.

A change of current in one coil produced a current in the other. When the number of turns in the coils was changed, the deflection of the needle varied.

That experiment was important, being the basis of the transformer, but Faraday had not produced electricity from magnetism. Experimenting with a variety of coils of wire, magnets, and pieces of iron, he first observed magnetoelectric induction (the production of electricity from magnetism) on 24 September 1831. Two bar magnets and a piece of soft iron were arranged in a triangle. The soft iron was surrounded by a coil connected to a galvanometer, and when the iron was pulled away from the magnets, he observed a deflection of the galvanometer. His own magnets were of limited strength, so Faraday arranged to use a powerful magnet belonging to the Royal Society and on 28 October 1831 made a copper disc rotate between its poles. A galvanometer connected between metal brushes pressing on the edge and the center of the disc showed that a continuous electric current was produced. This disc generator was the first electric generator, but its output was small because only one conductor was passing through the magnetic field. In the following year the French instrument maker Hippolyte Pixii (1808–1835) made the first generator using coils rather than a single conductor, and many designs of generator were developed in the following decades.

The First Exploitation of Electricity. Electricity was first exploited commercially in the electrochemical industry and in the telegraph. By 1844 the Birmingham firm of Elkington's was electroplating articles on a commercial scale. A massive wooden-framed magnetoelectric machine driven by a steam engine was the source of electricity. A related process that also flourished industrially was electrotyping. Small objects, such as coins and medals, were copied by coating a wax impression with an electrically conducting layer, such as carbon paste, and then electrodepositing metal. Electrolytic refining of metals, especially aluminium and copper, did not begin commercially until the end of the nineteenth century, when cheap electric power became available.

Many people tried to make an electric telegraph, but the first used commercially was that patented by Cooke and Wheatstone in 1837. William Fothergill Cooke (1806–1879) had seen a telegraph demonstration and resolved to exploit it. He made experimental telegraphs that worked in a laboratory and found a customer in the new railways. Unfortunately his telegraphs would not operate through very long lengths of wire. A search for scientific advice led him to Charles Wheatstone (1802–1875), who was professor of experimental philosophy at King's College London from 1834 until his death. The son of a musical instrument manufacturer, Wheatstone was interested in the transmission of sound through solids. Might it be possible to send messages between towns by transmitting sound vibrations through stretched wires? Experiment convinced him that it was not practical, and he turned to electricity. Using several miles of wire, he investigated how to obtain the maximum effect on instruments at a distance, which led him into the study of electrical measurements.

Cooke with his business acumen and Wheatstone with his scientific understanding should have made a splendid partnership, but they quarreled. They succeeded, however, in installing the first commercial telegraph along the Great Western Railway west from London in 1838. Cooke arranged the installation, but the instruments were Wheatstone's design with moving needles pointing out letters on a panel. The system was used both for railway business and for sending messages for the public for a fee. The telegraph developed slowly for a few years, then rapidly. Cooke recorded the sums involved. Between 1836 and 1844 he paid out £31,000. The Electric Telegraph Company was set up in 1846 to raise capital for further lines.

While Cooke and Wheatstone were developing their telegraphs in Britain, Samuel Findlay Breeze Morse (1791–1872) was working in the United States. Morse, a painter and sculptor, conceived the idea of a telegraph that sent signals by an intermittent current using a code. Morse sought the help of Alfred Vail (1807–1859), who helped with the manufacture of equipment. Vail devised the code of long and short signals known as Morse code. Morse obtained a U.S. patent in 1837 but failed to obtain an English patent because his work had already been published. He erected a telegraph line between Baltimore and Washington, D.C., that first worked in 1843 and was opened as a public service on 1 April 1845. Thereafter Morse quickly gained financial backing, and telegraph circuits spread throughout the United States. New York and San Francisco were linked in 1861.

In 1868 there were 80,000 miles of telegraph wire in the United Kingdom, and more than 5.6 million messages were sent. In addition almost 800,000 messages were sent overseas, to Europe and to America, using the cable that opened in 1866. The usual charge for sending a message up to one hundred miles in 1868 was one shilling (5p) for twenty words and up to twice that for longer distances. The price did not change greatly until 1915.

The telegraph brought enormous changes to the world, but equally significant was the impact on electrical science and technology. The terms *electrical engineer* and *electrical engineering* were not in general use until the end of the nineteenth century (the pioneers called themselves *electricians*), but the science, technology, industry, and profession of electrical engineering all grew out of the telegraph. The early scientific understanding of electric circuits arose from the study of telegraph operation, and the telegraph pioneers worked out such practical matters as how to insulate wires and run them from point to point. The industry that could manufacture cables, coils, electromagnets, instruments, and mechanisms was already in existence when needed for electric lighting.

The first professional organization for what are now called electrical engineers was the Society of Telegraph Engineers, formed in 1871 with C. W. Siemens as president. The Society's journal records that at the opening meeting on 28 February 1872, a leading telegraph engineer prophesied, "This Society will . . . develop more into an electrical society than into a society of telegraphy proper." By 1879 it was taking an interest in electric lighting, and in 1880 the title was broadened to the Society of Telegraph Engineers and of Electricians. The present title, the Institution of Electrical Engineers, was adopted in 1888. Many pioneers of electricity supply, including Sir William Thomson (Lord Kelvin) (1824–1907) in Britain and Thomas Alva Edison (1847–1931) in the United States, first entered the electrical engineering profession as telegraph engineers. A similar body in the United States, the American Society of Electrical Engineers, formed in 1884, is now part of the Institute of Electrical and Electronics Engineers.

Electricity Supply and the "Electrical" World. Electric lighting was possible using batteries, but that was always expensive. Large-scale lighting had to await the development of electricity supply. But there was no market for an electricity supply until lamps were available, so the two developed together. The arc light demonstrated the possibility of lighting by electricity. Individual units, however, were too bright and too bulky for domestic use. The filament lamp provided an ideal light for the home, but it needed a more finely regulated supply. Once public electricity supply was established, other uses of electricity developed rapidly.

The electric arc lamp. The first electric lights in practice were arc lamps, utilizing the brilliant light produced by an electric spark or arc between two pieces of carbon. The carbons must be in contact initially but then drawn apart quickly when the current is turned on. Since the carbon burns away in the heat, some mechanism is essential to keep the spacing constant. Much ingenuity went into early arc lamps, which were the first mass-produced automatic electrical equipment. The movement of the carbons should be smooth to avoid flicker. Renewal of the carbons must be easy even if the lamp normally operates high in the air, and the mechanism must be robust, reliable, and cheap.

An arc lamp that needed no mechanism was the Jablochkoff candle. Although used for only a few years for street lighting, it brought electric lighting to public notice. Paul Jablochkoff (1847–1894), a Russian telegraph engineer, went to Paris and met Louis Bréguet (1804–1883), who was interested in arc lighting and the practical electric generators developed recently by Zénobe Théophile

Gramme (1826–1901). Jablochkoff's candle consisted of two parallel carbon rods separated by a thin layer of plaster of paris. A thin link of graphite joined the upper ends. When the circuit was switched on, the current fused the connecting link, and an arc was struck between the ends. As the carbons burned, the plaster crumbled away. Typically sixteen lamps were connected in series to one generator, and each gave seven hundred candlepower. A disadvantage was that, once the light had gone out, for whatever reason, the candles had to be replaced before the light could be switched on again. The Jablochkoff candle was superseded when reliable automatic regulating mechanisms became available.

Jablochkoff candles and other arc lights were exhibited at the Exposition Universelle in Paris in 1878 and enjoyed great popular success. The candles were adopted for street lighting in the avenue de l'Opéra in Paris. Several lighting installations were then set up in London.

Many designs of arc lamp mechanism were made in the 1880s and 1890s. All had an electromagnet connected in series with the arc whose function was to pull the carbons apart initially and so strike the arc. Either the same electromagnet or another one regulated the spacing of the carbons. Usually the upper carbon fell under gravity but was restrained by a brake under the control of the regulating electromagnet. The first English electric lighting engineer and arc-lamp manufacturer was R. E. B. Crompton (1845–1940). His first electric lighting product was a portable steam engine and generator on a horse-drawn trailer and a lamp mounted up a pole. He hired equipment for events such as the Henley Regatta, for contractors working at night, and for farmers wishing to harvest after dark. Indoor use, however, required a smaller light source that did not need frequent attention.

The filament bulb. There was no single inventor of the filament bulb. The basic ideas were old, but it was only in the late 1870s that advances in materials and in air pumps made it possible to construct a practical bulb. The filament material had to be carbon because the only available materials that could stand the heat were carbon and platinum, and platinum was too expensive. Platinum had to be used for the lead-in wires connecting to the filament because it was the only electrical conductor with a coefficient of expansion approximately the same as that of glass and so could be sealed through the glass without cracking. All the first bulb inventors made carbon filaments from strips of organic material that were "carbonized" by heating in a closed furnace to drive off the oxygen and hydrogen present.

Filament bulbs were first shown on a large scale at the International Electrical Exhibition in Paris from August to November 1881. Four inventors displayed their products. The best known were Joseph Wilson Swan (1828–1914) from Britain and Thomas Edison from the United States, but another Englishman, St. George Lane Fox (1816–1896), and another American, Hiram Maxim (1840–1916), also had lamps on display. The Exhibition Jury made measurements of the efficiencies of the bulbs. Edison's were the most efficient, though not by much, and he was not satisfied with the life of his bulbs. The main thing that distinguished the different inventors was the choice of starting material for their filaments. Swan used a cotton thread that had been treated in sulphuric acid, which smoothed and hardened it. Edison adopted a fiber from a variety of bamboo.

Swan had tried to make a filament bulb in the 1840s but failed for want of an adequate vacuum pump. On hearing of the Sprengel air pump, he resumed his bulb experiments. He also realized that part of the reason he had not obtained an adequate vacuum was that gas was absorbed on the carbon filament and on the inner surface of the glass and then released when the bulb became hot. It was necessary to heat the bulb while the pumping continued. Edison only became interested in electric lighting toward the end of 1877 but had already made his name as a designer of telegraph instruments and inventor of the phonograph. Edison reasoned that commercially successful electric lighting needed to have similar characteristics to the existing gas lighting. The bulbs should have the same candlepower as gas jets, and electrical energy should be distributed in such a way that each lamp could be operated independently.

Electric generators. The simple generators developed from Faraday's disc generator of 1831 all used permanent magnets. The "self-excited" generators, invented independently by several people and demonstrated publicly in 1867, used electromagnets energized from the output of the generator itself. With this arrangement the output was no longer limited by the strength of available permanent magnets, and there was no fundamental limit to the electric current that could be generated. The Belgian engineer Gramme, working in Paris, made the first really practical generators around 1870, and his machines supplied many of the early electric street lighting installations. The Siemens brothers, Werner Siemens in Germany and Carl Wilhelm Siemens (later Anglicized to Charles William) in Britain, were soon making generators in both countries. The first major British manufacturer was Crompton, and in the United States, Edison also manufactured generators. His early machines had long poles, whereas the early European ones were all squat. The consulting engineer John Hopkinson (1849–1898), who advised both Edison and the British manufacturers, provided the first scientific rationale for generator design with his concept of the magnetic circuit of the machine.

Most early generators were driven either by reciprocating steam engines or by water turbines, leading to genera-

tor speeds of a few hundred revolutions per minute (rpm). It was therefore appropriate to use multipolar machines, especially in alternating current systems, where the frequency of the supply is the product of the number of poles and the speed in revolutions per second. The steam turbine, developed by Charles A. Parsons (1854–1931) in the 1880s, ran much faster than other prime movers. Generators were developed for it with only one pair of poles. The steam turbine is more efficient than the reciprocating engine, and the efficiency of generators increases with their speed. Consequently the combination of a turbine and a two-pole generator has been the standard for power station generators ever since, whether the heat for the boiler comes from coal, oil, gas, or a nuclear reactor.

Public electricity supply—the technical issues. The earliest electric lighting schemes all had their own generators, which was fine for street lighting and even for large country houses, where the owner could employ someone to run the machines in the evening. If electric lighting was to be available to everybody, however, there had to be a system of supply from a central generating station to private houses. This first happened on a small scale in the autumn of 1881 in the Surrey town of Godalming. The streets had been lit by gas, but the town council and the gas company failed to agree on terms for the coming winter. A small company stepped in and offered to install and supply electric street lighting if it could also supply private houses.

Early in 1882 the English Edison Company set up its first supply system from a power station on Holborn Viaduct in central London. The location had the advantage that cables could be taken to several dozen premises without digging up the streets. Later the same year Edison established his first American power station at Pearl Street in New York City. Many similar small schemes were set up in the following few years. The Kensington Court Company, which supplied direct current in west London, was run by Crompton, who also built a power station in Vienna. The resistance of the mains resulted in "volts drop," which had two disadvantages: it was wasteful of power, but more important, customers farther from the power station experienced a lower supply voltage—and therefore dimmer lights—when demand was heavy.

The problem of volts drop could be reduced by distributing electricity at a higher voltage and converting it locally to the desired supply voltage. This was easy with alternating current (AC) systems once transformers were developed. In London the Grosvenor Gallery Company, originally established to light a picture gallery, was soon supplying alternating current to houses over a large area of west London. The distribution system operated at twenty-four hundred volts, and transformers converted this to one hundred volts for the customers. The Grosvenor Gallery

Company is known best for the man who became its chief engineer in 1886, Sebastian Ziani de Ferranti (1864–1930), an Englishman of Italian descent. Ferranti pioneered the idea of building a large power station out of the city and transmitting electricity into the center at high voltage. His power station at Deptford in southeast London began generating in 1889 and transmitted electricity at ten thousand volts to substations in central London. Ferranti's scheme was a brilliant technical achievement but a commercial disaster because he grossly overestimated the potential load. A comparable scheme in Italy in 1892 transmitted electricity from a hydroelectric power station at Tivoli into the center of Rome. It proved a great success, showing that Ferranti's basic ideas were sound.

For lighting it did not matter whether the supply was AC or direct current (DC), but the first motors required DC. Until satisfactory AC electric motors were developed, many people preferred to have a DC supply notwithstanding the advantages AC gave in distribution. The technical debate that raged between the proponents of DC supply and the supporters of AC was called "the battle of the systems." The dominant names associated with the DC side were Edison and Crompton, while George Westinghouse (1846–1914), Nikola Tesla (1856–1943), and Ferranti were leaders of the AC school. From about 1900 virtually all new supply systems used AC (but at a variety of different frequencies and currents), while existing DC systems continued to supply direct current. As systems were expanded and interconnected, standardization of voltage and frequency became essential. A frequency of fifty hertz (Hz) was adopted in Europe and sixty hertz in North America. The voltage adopted was usually about 240 in Europe and 110 in North America. Most countries followed one of those standards, though in a few, such as Japan, both are in use.

The politics and economics of electricity supply. In 1888 Crompton addressed the Institution of Electrical Engineers analyzing the costs of building and running a power station. He thought the maximum economic size of a station was one that could supply one thousand houses with a total of ten thousand lamps. That was correct with the technology of the time, where the distribution mains and the supply to individual customers were all at the same voltage. Once electricity could be transmitted at a higher voltage and then converted to the customers' voltage near the point of use, it became economic to generate on a much larger scale. The conversion was usually done by transformers on AC systems and by motor-generator sets on DC systems.

Initially the public demand for electricity grew quite slowly. By the end of the nineteenth century about 3 percent of households in the United States and less than 1 percent of those in Britain were connected. Since electricity cannot easily be stored in large quantities, it has to be generated as required. The first public supplies of electricity were exclusively for lighting, so most of the demand was concentrated into a few hours each evening. If a daytime load could be found, then power stations could increase their sales without having to install additional equipment. Such an off-peak load was found in heating and cooking, and for many years electricity undertakings offered customers a power circuit, metered separately from the lighting circuit and charged at a lower rate. As uses other than lighting developed, the time of day when the demand was less changed. Since the 1920s the minimum demand has been during the early hours of the morning, and in Britain and many other countries electricity is available during the night at less cost than during the day.

In Britain the Electric Lighting Act, 1882, provided a legal framework for electricity supply, including such provisions as the right to dig up the streets to lay cables. It also allowed local authorities to purchase an electricity undertaking in their area after twenty-one years (amended in 1888 to forty-two years). This is said to have discouraged investment in electricity supply, though it can also be argued that investors in a completely new industry would be seeking to recover their investment in much less than twenty-one years. From 1900 a number of power companies were permitted by special Acts of Parliament. These did not supply customers directly but generated electricity in large, more efficient power stations and sold it to local supply undertakings. This was clearly the way forward, though local undertakings were reluctant to give up their autonomy. In 1925 a government committee under Lord Weir (1877–1959) found that Britain had 432 power stations. They recommended that fifty-eight stations should be selected (forty-three existing and fifteen new ones), connected together in a network that became known as the National Grid, and the remainder closed. In the United States the Rural Electrification Act of 1936 established the Rural Electrification Commission, which was given federal funds to promote rural electrification and the supply of electricity to areas not currently receiving an electricity supply.

In 1945, after struggling for many years with independent and uncooperative undertakings, the British Government decided to take the whole industry into public ownership in effect from 1 April 1948. The British Electricity Authority, which took over the power stations and the grid at nationalization, sold electricity to fourteen area electricity boards, who were responsible for local distribution and sales and also for establishing electricity supply in parts of the country as yet unreached. By the early 1960s virtually the whole of Britain had electricity supply. Whether the electricity supply industry of a country should be a public enterprise or the work of private companies has always been a political decision. In some countries, including

Britain, the industry has been through both nationalization and privatization. In all countries, however, governments have introduced legislation giving them considerable regulatory powers.

Electric Power. The origin of electric motors may be traced back to Oersted's discovery of the deflection of a compass by the electric current and Faraday's production of continuous motion by electromagnetism. During the nineteenth century many electromagnetic engines were designed and made, but despite the hopes of their promoters and the support of the technical press, none achieved lasting success as a source of power. However, the research and development work that went into these machines increased the understanding of electrical technology and prepared the way for practical motors.

The first person to appreciate that electromagnetism might be used to provide mechanical power was probably the American Joseph Henry (1797–1878). In 1831 he made a machine in which a straight electromagnet was mounted horizontally on a pivot with vertical bar magnets under each end. The electromagnet coil was connected to two pairs of wires that dipped into mercury cups when their end was down. A battery was connected to each pair of mercury cups. When one end of the bar was depressed, the electromagnet was energized in such a way that the bar rocked in the other direction. Thus a reciprocating motion was established.

The following year William Sturgeon (1783–1850) made a motor incorporating a commutator, the first to do useful work—it turned a roasting spit. A typical machine of the 1840s was W. H. Taylor's motor, which was enthusiastically written up by *Mechanics Magazine*. It was a simple arrangement of four electromagnets on a frame surrounding a wooden wheel with seven soft iron armatures on the periphery of the wheel. A simple commutator on the axis switched the four electromagnets sequentially. Taylor's claim to novelty was quickly disputed by supporters of the Scotsman Robert Davidson (1804–1894), who in the winter of 1841–1842 ran an electrically driven four-wheeled carriage weighing five tons on the Edinburgh and Glasgow Railway.

Economic considerations were heavily against the electric motor. In 1849 the U.S. commissioner of patents, Thomas Ewbank, included in his annual report to Congress some thoughts on the subject of electric motors, adding, "The belief is a growing one that electricity, in one or more of its manifestations, is ordained to affect the mightiest of revolutions in human affairs." In 1850 the U.S. Congress gave $20,000 to Charles Page of Salem, Massachusetts, to develop electromagnetic engines, apparently with the U.S. Navy mainly in mind. Page stated in a report that he had made machines of one and four horsepower (hp) and asked for further funds to build a one hundred horsepower motor. He did not get any more money,

though in 1854 he built an electric locomotive weighing about 12 tons that ran at 19 miles per hour (30.6 kilometers per hour) on the level.

Practical electric motors. Most generator manufacturers in the 1870s were aware that a direct current electric generator will run as a motor if electricity is fed into it. Electric motors were demonstrated at several exhibitions, including the Philadelphia Exhibition in 1875 and the Loan Collection of Scientific Apparatus in London the same year. Electric plowing was tried in France in 1879 using an arrangement similar to that used for steam plowing. Electric motors with winding drums were mounted on wagons on each side of the field, and the plow was hauled by ropes. Exhibits at the International Electrical Exhibition in Paris in 1881 included several electrically driven sewing machines, a lathe, a drill, and a printing press. The Siemens company exhibited a passenger lift in the building and a tram running along the Champs Elysées.

The first permanent electric railway was built by Siemens at Lichterfelde, Germany, in 1881. In 1883 Magnus Volk (1851–1937) built a railway on the seafront at Brighton, England, which still runs for the benefit of tourists. The first practical tramway system opened in 1888 by Frank Sprague (1857–1934) at Richmond, Virginia, with forty cars running over twenty kilometers of streets. The supply was by overhead conductor wires, though some of the tram cars were also equipped with storage batteries.

Existing horse-drawn tramways in Britain were slow to convert to electric operation, though after 1890 most new tramways were electric. The London Underground railways had been steam powered from their inception in 1863, but they were only just beneath the surface with frequent ventilation holes. Electric traction made possible the deep "tube" railways, the first of which, the City and South London Railway running from Stockwell to the Bank, opened in 1890. The first main line railway to use electric traction was the Baltimore and Ohio Railroad in 1892.

The railways and tramways just described and most later ones have direct current series motors, so-called because the field coils and the armature are in series. These motors exert maximum torque on starting. On starting two (or more) motors are connected in series, so each experiences only half the supply voltage. Series resistances are also used to reduce the voltage further and give smooth starting. Most electric trains have the traction motors distributed along the length of the train, built into the coach bogies with one end of the motor supported on the axle and the other held by springs. This construction was introduced by Sprague, who also introduced in 1895 the multiple unit control system, by which motors throughout the train are controlled from the driver's cab with control wires along the train, but the power cables do not have to go through the cab.

For applications requiring constant speed, or speed control independent of the load, shunt DC motors are preferred. In these the field coils are connected in parallel with the armature or even supplied separately. Important early applications of shunt motors were in lifts and in industrial drives, such as rolling mills.

Powerful AC motors were made possible through the work of Nikola Tesla, born in what was then Austria-Hungary. He emigrated to the United States, where he worked for a few years for Edison but then joined Westinghouse, one of the leading proponents of AC systems. Tesla's major achievement was to combine two alternating magnetic fields produced by alternating currents in two coils in such a way that the resultant field was rotating. A permanent magnet pivoted in the magnetic field would then rotate at the speed of the field. This is the synchronous motor. If the rotor is magnetic, but not a permanent magnet, then a current is induced in the rotor and creates a magnetic field that interacts with the rotating field to produce a turning force. This is the induction motor, which runs at a speed just below the speed of the rotating field. Both synchronous and induction motors are therefore essentially fixed-speed machines, but they are simple to make, robust, and efficient. Most importantly they provided a motor that could be run from AC mains and thus remove the principal disadvantage of AC supply systems.

By the end of the nineteenth century about 5 percent of mechanical power in American factories was provided by electric motors, a figure that rose to 50 percent in the period up to 1920. Comparable figures are not available for Britain as a whole, but in some areas, such as Tyneside, where electrical development was promoted vigorously, electric motors were widely adopted in heavy industry such as shipbuilding. Hugo Hirst (1863–1943), the founder of the General Electric Company, began the manufacture of induction motors in a new factory at Witton, Birmingham, in 1900, and the price of motors fell rapidly in the following few years. A 10-horsepower motor cost £65 in 1901 but only £30 in 1905. At first the electric motors were used to replace steam engines, driving a line shaft from which machines were driven by belts. The real advantage of electric drives was realized as machines began to be driven by individual motors of appropriate size that were independently controlled. Electric drives were widely used in the many factories developed around London in the 1920s and 1930s for light manufacturing industry.

Domestic electrical appliances. Electric cookers and other heating appliances were not reliable because the heating elements, initially made of iron wire, did not last long. Nevertheless the supply undertakings were eager to promote their use, and appliances were often hired out for a small charge to be paid with the electricity bill. The City of London Electric Lighting Company in 1894, for example, would sell a small electric cooker for £7.10s or hire it for 7 shillings (35p) per quarter. The alloy nichrome does not oxidize in air even when red-hot and has been used for most of the heating elements in cookers and space heaters since its invention in 1906. Electric lamps were often used as the heating element in early space heaters. The very concept of electric cooking had to be sold. Crompton equipped the School of Electric Cookery in London in 1894, and in 1912 a combination restaurant and sale room for electric cooking equipment was opened in London's Oxford Street.

By the 1930s the pattern of demand had changed so that the off-peak period, or time of minimum demand, was during the night. Night storage heaters were introduced then. These had a mass of brick or similar material in a well-lagged casing that was heated at night by electricity charged at a reduced off-peak price. A system of air ducts through the brick allowed heat to be released at will during the day. The system was revived in the 1960s, so by 1976 about 9 percent of British households used storage heaters, although the proportion has since fallen, probably because other central heating systems can be adjusted more quickly in response to changes in the weather.

Electric motors made many domestic electrical appliances possible. The first important one was the vacuum cleaner. A young civil engineer, Cecil Booth (1871–1955), set up his Vacuum Cleaner Company in London in 1901. This company had horse-drawn vans carrying a suction pump driven by a petrol engine. Long hoses were taken from the van into a customer's house to clean carpets and furniture. By 1905 Booth was selling portable vacuum cleaners, either operated manually or driven by an electric motor.

The largest users of electrical energy in the home are refrigeration, freezing, and air conditioning. Ice was a readily available domestic commodity in the nineteenth century in both Europe and the United States. Initially blocks of ice were transported, often by ship, from colder regions, but toward the end of the century steam-driven refrigeration plants came into use. From early in the twentieth century electrically driven refrigerators were made on a small scale for the domestic market, but there were problems because the working fluids used were sometimes dangerous and always unpleasant if they leaked. In 1928 the Frigidaire company introduced the use of chlorofluorocarbon as the working fluid, and the refrigerator market grew rapidly. From midcentury the refrigerator became commonplace in American homes and soon after in Europe and Japan. Air conditioning, which uses refrigerator technology to cool the air but also has equipment to control the humidity, was a logical development. Some air conditioning was introduced in large public buildings in North America

ELECTRICAL PLANT. Circuit breaker at Lake Lynn Hydroelectric Power House & Dam, Cheat River, West Virginia, 1968. (Prints and Photographs Division, Library of Congress)

in the 1920s, but it only became commonplace in American homes after 1950. In Europe large shops and commercial buildings now routinely have air conditioning. It remains rare in private homes, though suitable equipment is on the market.

Before World War II washing machines were rare in Britain although more common in the United States. Normally they had no heaters and were just tubs containing electrically driven agitators. Often a wringer was attached, and a system of gears permitted the motor to drive the wringer rather than the agitator. Spin dryers, for removing water from the washing by centrifugal force, only became common after about 1960.

Motor control—power semiconductors. The ideal electric motor would be as easily controlled as a DC machine and yet operate from an AC supply. The American engineer H. Ward Leonard (1861–1915) developed an arrangement in which a motor (which could be AC or DC) drove a generator producing DC to supply the motor that had to be controlled. The output of the generator could be closely controlled by adjusting the relatively small current in its field winding, and in this way the speed of the final motor could be regulated. Ward Leonard systems were used for high-power drives in industry and for special applications where the cost of three machines was acceptable. The system

could not be used in electric trains. A few railways, mainly in Italy and Switzerland, ran on AC supplies early in the twentieth century, but almost all used DC until first mercury arc rectifiers and then controlled semiconductor rectifiers became available.

The mercury arc rectifier is essentially a high-power version of the thermionic triode used in radio. They began to be used industrially in the 1930s and were used on some trains, so the external power supply to the train could be AC while the train had traditional DC motors.

The introduction of power semiconductor devices opened new possibilities. Initially semiconductor devices just replaced the mercury arc, giving a rectifier of much higher efficiency. The controlled semiconductor rectifier, also known as the thyristor, available from 1960, could regulate the current in a circuit as well as rectify it. By 1970 semiconductor devices were available that could carry one thousand amps and switch up to twenty-five hundred volts. Twenty years later both those figures had more than doubled, and development continues. Furthermore the devices can be connected in series and parallel banks, so there is no limit to the power that can be controlled. Thyristors can be operated as inverters, converting direct current into alternating current, and they can do so at any desired frequency. When supplied through a variable frequency inverter, the simple and robust induction motor becomes a variable-speed drive. Such drives are widely used in modern industry, enabling cumbersome and expensive systems, such as the Ward Leonard control, to be replaced by a relatively small control unit. The motor and its control unit are often sold as an item, not as separate components. Modern high-speed electric railways, including the Channel Tunnels trains, all use this technology.

Semiconductor devices also feature in the power distribution networks of many countries. High-voltage direct current links were introduced during the 1960s into the power systems of several countries where it was desired to transmit large powers over long distances. Examples are the link across the English Channel, the link carrying power from a hydroelectric plant in the South Island of New Zealand to the more populous areas of the North Island, and the Pacific Intertie in the United States. Such links originally had mercury arc rectifiers, but these are gradually being replaced by banks of thyristors.

Modern Electric Lighting. The efficiency of filament lamps depends on the filament temperature, and the limit with carbon is about 1,600°C. Several high melting-point metals were tried, including vanadium and niobium. Metals have a lower electrical resistance than carbon, so metal filaments have to be longer and thinner. Furthermore the refractory metals are brittle and difficult to draw by conventional wire-drawing techniques. The solution adopted initially was to use the metal in powder form, mix it with a binder, squirt the mixture through a fine die, and then heat the resulting thread to drive off the binder and sinter the metal particles together. Sintered osmium lamps were made for a few years from 1902 and were used mainly in Europe. Tantalum can be drawn into a fine wire and was used from 1905, but it quickly becomes brittle in use.

Tungsten has the highest melting point of any metal, 3,410°C, and tungsten filament lamps were first produced in Vienna by Alexander Just and Franz Hanaman using a sintering process. A method of drawing tungsten into a fine wire was developed by William Coolidge, in Cleveland, Ohio. His process was one of compressing tungsten powder, heating it, and hammering it. Drawn tungsten has been the standard filament material since 1911.

Early lamps all had the bulb evacuated as completely as possible, but it was found that the presence of a little gas discouraged evaporation of the filament, increasing the life of the lamp. The gas, however, tended to cool the filament by convection and reduce the overall efficiency. Irving Langmuir found that, although the rate of heat loss is proportional to the length of the wire, it is not much affected by the diameter. This led to the idea of winding the filament into a tight coil so that, from the cooling point of view, the filament was much shorter. The first gas-filled, coiled-filament lamps were marketed in 1913, the gas be-

ing nitrogen. Subsequently argon has been used because it is denser and has a lower thermal conductivity.

Until the early 1920s lamps were evacuated through the end opposite the cap and lead-in wires, leaving a characteristic "pip" where the bulb was sealed. This pip was easily broken, and lamps are now evacuated through a tube at the cap end so the seal can be enclosed within the cap. From 1934 the coiled filament was often coiled again upon itself, giving the modern "coiled coil" filament.

An ordinary metal filament lamp lasts, with only a little loss of efficiency, until the day it fails. Attempts were made as early as 1882 to prevent the blackening of the bulb by including a small amount of chlorine. The idea was that the chlorine would react with the evaporated carbon and form a transparent compound. The idea was not very successful with carbon lamps but has proved useful in extending the life or the efficiency of tungsten filament lamps. Any of the halogens will react with tungsten vapor in the bulb, and if the conditions are right, the compound formed will break down in the region near the filament. Consequently material that has been evaporated from the filament is returned automatically and redeposited on or close to the filament. Halogen lamps were made for floodlighting in 1960, and since about 1990 they have been sold for domestic use, both as general-purpose, mains-voltage lamps and as low-voltage spotlights, usually working at twelve volts and rated at fifty watts, to give a compact source of bright light.

Discharge lamps. The electric arc and the filament lamp are not the only ways of producing light by electricity. An electric discharge through a suitable gas at low pressure will also produce light. Most practical discharge lamps use either mercury vapor or sodium vapor. Mercury lamps were tried in the early years of the twentieth century but were not very successful. They were more efficient than contemporary filament lamps, but their light was blue.

About 1930 discharge lamps were being made to give light of various colors for floodlighting. They needed a high-voltage circuit to start but could then be run from the 230 volt mains. The color of the light depended on the gas filling. Neon gave an orange-red light, neon or argon together with mercury gave a blue light, and helium gave a yellow light. It was known that sodium vapor offered the theoretical possibility of an efficient yellow lamp, but the chemical problems posed by the high reactivity of hot sodium vapor had not been solved. The main research effort, with the General Electric Company in Britain at least, was concentrated on these other lamps. In France the Claude Company used just two lamps, one with neon giving red light and the other with mercury giving blue-green light, to produce a white effect. Georges Claude (1870–1960) used neon lamps at the Grand Palais in Paris in 1910, the beginning of the ubiquitous neon and other discharge lamps in advertising.

Two major advances occurred almost simultaneously in 1932. The General Electric Company developed the high-pressure mercury vapor lamp, which has a much better color than the low-pressure lamp, and installed them for street lighting on the road outside their central research laboratories at Wembley, Middlesex. At about the same time the Phillips company at Gindhoven, Netherlands, solved the chemical problems and developed a viable low-pressure sodium lamp. The low-pressure sodium lamp gives a pure yellow light, but it is the most efficient of all electric lights and therefore popular for street lighting.

The color of mercury lamps has been improved by the addition of other elements into the discharge tube, and a wide range of discharge lamps are now available, giving a choice of color and efficiency. The low-pressure sodium lamp has been gradually replaced since about 1970 by the high-pressure sodium lamp, which has a much better color spectrum.

Fluorescent lamps. The electric light most commonly found in shops and offices is the fluorescent tube, available in a wide range of shapes, sizes, and colors. The basic principle is that a discharge in mercury vapor produces ultraviolet light, which is converted to visible light by a phosphor coating inside the tube. As with all discharge lamps, the fluorescent lamp needs special control equipment to limit the current through the lamp and provide a high-voltage pulse for starting. This inevitably makes their initial cost much greater than that of filament lamps. Although efficient, early fluorescent lamps were unpopular because of their poor color rendering and tendency to flicker, especially when old. The best modern fluorescents have largely overcome these problems by using semiconductor-based control circuits rather than the heavy iron-cored inductances previously used.

By 1930 it was known that under the right conditions a discharge through a mixture of mercury vapor and another gas was phenomenally efficient in converting electrical energy into ultraviolet light. If the mercury vapor and the other gas, usually argon, were at the optimum pressures, as much as 60 percent of the electrical energy in the discharge could be radiated at a single wavelength, 253.7 nanometers (nm), which is in the ultraviolet part of the spectrum. Cold cathode fluorescent tubes, operating at several thousand volts, were introduced for general indoor lighting about 1938, quickly followed by the familiar hot cathode tube. Cold cathode tubes were up to three metres long and were favored for situations such as railway stations, where long life was of value and the high voltage equipment could be high up and out of reach.

The basic construction of a fluorescent lamp did not require any new technology except the process of coating the inside of the tube with fluorescent powder. This was done by pushing a sponge soaked in adhesive through the tube, pouring the fluorescent powder into the tube so that a layer of it sticks on the glass, and then tipping the surplus material out. The commercial exploitation of fluorescent lighting was delayed by World War II, and although it was used in factories, the general public did not see much of it until the late 1940s. A major obstacle to widespread adoption of the fluorescent lamp when first developed was the fact that it could not replace the filament lamp directly. It could not be put straight into incandescent lamp sockets, and the cost of the associated control gear was a discouragement to potential purchasers. As fluorescent lamps gradually proved themselves in service, the value of their much greater efficiency led to their widespread adoption.

Until the early 1970s nearly all fluorescent tubes were made with a diameter of thirty-eight millimeters because that was found to give the greatest efficiency. From 1975 slimline fluorescent tubes, twenty-six millimeters in diameter, were introduced. These have krypton rather than argon filling and require about 10 percent less electricity for the same light output. Twenty years later even slimmer tubes, sixteen millimeters in diameter, were introduced. The first phosphors used in fluorescent lamps were based on fluorescent minerals. Better phosphors were considered so important that research into them continued during World War II, and a new group of chemicals, the halophosphates, were discovered in 1942 by British lighting researchers. From 1970 alkaline-earth silicate phosphors have been developed. The latter are more efficient than the halophosphates, but whereas the halophosphates give a broad spectrum of light, the newer materials usually give light with a single-line spectrum. In most fluorescent lamps a mixture of several fluorescent materials is used in order to obtain the desired color and efficiency. There is inevitably an element of compromise between color and efficiency. Lamps of high color-rendering ability are not the most efficient, while the most efficient lamps do not give the best color.

The compact fluorescent lamp, launched in 1980, was a direct replacement for a filament lamp. It required only one-quarter of the electrical input of a filament lamp giving the same light and had five times the life. The control equipment was semiconductor-based and so small it could be fitted inside the cap of the lamp. The new lamp could therefore be put directly into the holder that had previously held a filament lamp. Although a direct descendant of the long fluorescent tube, the compact fluorescent is virtually a new lamp and has been marketed vigorously as the energy saving lamp. Manufacturers have avoided calling them fluorescent lamps, presumably feeling that name would not encourage sales. From 1990 they were readily available, and by 1995 half the households in Britain were using at least one. They were even more popular in continental Europe, and their market share continues to increase.

The cost of light. Electrical equipment in general has fallen in price year by year, though the cost of electricity has both fallen and risen, often in response to political decisions. Comparisons of cost over long periods of time are difficult, but careful studies have been made of the cost of lighting. The economist William D. Nordhaus made a detailed study of light sources from ancient times to the modern compact fluorescent lamp, seeking to find the relative cost of light at different times. His results show that candles cost between U.S. 20 and U.S. 90 cents for 1,000 lumen hours of light. Early gas lights, where the source of the light was a gas flame, cost about 50 cents for 1,000 lumen hours. With early gas mantles, the cost was 52 and by 1916 had reduced to 0.34 cents. The price of light from an electric filament lamp varied between 2.3 and 0.17 cents per 1,000 lumen hours in twentieth-century America, depending mainly on the cost of electricity. The lowest price Nordhaus found was in 1970. The more efficient compact fluourescent lamp gave 1,000 lumen hours of light for 0.124 cents in 1992, about one-quarter of the price at the time of light from a filament lamp.

Early advertising for electric light stressed its advantages of cleanliness and convenience but not its price. There was some price competition in advertising in the 1920s and 1930s, but electric lighting was so obviously superior to all other lighting that price soon ceased to be mentioned. Cost became an issue again in the 1990s, when manufacturers of the compact fluorescent lamp needed to convince customers that it was worth paying for the costlier lamp in order to spend much less on electricity.

BIBLIOGRAPHY

Bowers, Brian. *A History of Electric Light and Power.* London, 1982. The quotations in the text are taken from this book.

Bowers, Brian. *Lengthening the Day: A History of Lighting Technology.* Oxford, 1998.

Brown, Deward Clayton. *Electricity for Rural America: The Fight for the REA.* Westport, Conn., 1980.

Byatt, I. C. R. *The British Electrical Industry, 1875–1914: The Economic Returns of a New Technology.* Oxford, 1979.

Corley, T. A. B. *Domestic Electrical Appliances.* London, 1966.

David, Paul A. "The Hero and the Herd in Technological History: Reflections on Thomas Edison and the Battle of the Systems." In *Favorites of Fortune: Technology, Growth, and Economic Development since the Industrial Revolution,* edited by Patrice Higonnet, David S. Landes, and Henry Rosovsky. Cambridge, Mass., 1991.

Hirsh, Richard F. *Power Loss: The Origins of Deregulation and Restructuring in the American Electric Utility System.* Cambridge, Mass., 1999.

Hughes, Thomas P. *Networks of Power: Electrification in Western Society, 1880–1930.* Baltimore, 1983.

Hughes, Thomas P. "The Electrification of America: The System Builders." *Technology and Culture* 20 (1979), 124–161.

Nye, David E. *Electrifying America: Social Meanings of a New Technology, 1880–1940.* Cambridge, Mass., 1990.

Nordhaus, William D. "Do Real-Output and Real-Wage Measures Capture Reality? The History of Lighting Suggests Not." In *The Economics of New Goods,* edited by Timothy F. Bresnahan and Robert J. Gordon. Chicago, 1997.

Weiher, Sigfrid von, and Herbert Goetzler. *The Siemens Company: Its Historical Role in the Progress of Electrical Engineering.* Berlin and Munich, 1977.

BRIAN BOWERS

ELECTRONICS INDUSTRY. The electronics industry consists of two main sectors: components (vacuum tubes, semiconductors, connectors, and so on) and equipment (computers, audio and video, television, and the like). The industry has been marked by the influence of government, often military, agencies, the establishment of a broad and deep research and development foundation, technological upheavals, and relatively free dissemination of technical and scientific information through licensing, personnel mobility, and government decrees. With roots in the nineteenth century, electronics by the late twentieth century grew into one of the most important industries in the world, essential to almost every other industry and central to the creation of modern society.

Radio. "Wireless" transmission of information began in the late nineteenth century; radio pioneer Guglielmo Marconi achieved transatlantic transmission by 1901. Early radio attracted the attention of companies such as General Electric (GE) and Westinghouse in the United States, as well as that of European naval officers, who saw the advantages of wireless communications with and between offshore vessels. The United States Navy, initially reluctant, also soon adopted wireless technology.

Early sound radio relied on so-called "cat's whisker" radio sets that used crystal diodes of galena, silicon, and other materials to rectify the signal. Their fickle unreliability notwithstanding, crystal sets, enthusiastically assembled by amateurs, fostered the first sound radio broadcasts. The two-element vacuum tube, invented in 1905 by English physicist John Ambrose Fleming (though with roots in earlier work by Thomas Edison), and the triode (three-element) tube, invented the following year by American Lee De Forest, formed the basis for the modern electronics industry. These tubes generated, detected, and amplified radio waves, making possible commercial radio broadcasting and receiving.

In the wake of World War I, the United States military feared falling behind in competition with foreign development. First encouraging General Electric to purchase the American holdings of the British Marconi Radio Telegraph Company, the government then pushed the establishment of the Radio Corporation of America (RCA) as a pool for the patents of General Electric (GE), AT&T, and Westinghouse. RCA's dominant patent position in radio, and later television, had profound consequences for the United States and world electronics industry.

By 1930, over 14 million United States homes had radio sets. At prices up to $200 each, radios represented a major new industry; dozens of manufacturers entered the industry, each paying RCA license fees. The major makers of vacuum tubes were GE, RCA, Sylvania, Columbia Broadcasting System (CBS), Philco, Tung-Sol, and Westinghouse, with other, smaller manufacturers focused on specialty tubes and other components. Manufacturing centered on the East coast and Middle Atlantic region, with an important outpost catering to the military in northern California. Foreign subsidiaries of United States companies established radio and component manufacturing in European countries and Japan. European radio and tube makers included the Dutch Philips concern, which traced its roots to light bulb manufacturing, and Siemens, a German electrical equipment firm with nineteenth-century origins. Even so, RCA held essential patents that these companies licensed.

Extension and Growth. Recognizing the importance of scientific research and seeking to protect and extend their patent positions, firms founded Research and Development laboratories early in the twentieth century. AT&T's Bell Telephone Laboratories, General Electric, RCA, and Westinghouse Electric were prominent among these, with many smaller firms joining the trend. Including university and military labs, the United States developed a broad and deep foundation in electronics science and technology, marked by a notably practical and commercial orientation.

By the end of the 1930s, vacuum tube amplifiers had found applications in many areas: home and car radios, early television, phonographs, telephone repeaters, hearing aids, burglar alarms, and scientific and medical instruments and measuring equipment, among other applications. Electronic communication—radio, recorded sound, and movies—lay at the heart of the emergence of a new "mass culture."

Television research was well established by the mid-1920s; like radio, the earliest television technology was the work of inspired amateurs; it was soon picked up by corporate labs. RCA gained particular importance when its electronic black and white television was established as the industry standard by the FCC.

After World War II, television, radio, and other consumer electronics became a large industry; few technologies have spread faster than television, and the coming of home stereo spurred a great expansion in the market for electronics, as did the 1950s introduction of color television by RCA. In the United States RCA dominated, though the television industry had other large players such as Magnavox, Motorola, and Westinghouse. RCA's strong patent position and its policy of licensing its patents as a package provoked anti-trust charges. In reaction, the company increased its foreign licensing. RCA's failed diversification program drove it out of television manufacturing; no other United States firm could pick up the slack. Foreign companies, notably the Japanese, soon dominated the industry. In the 1990s, Korean and Taiwanese companies, often with Japanese aid, entered the industry and gained a significant market share.

Solid State. While vacuum tubes made inroads into new areas, semiconductor electronics was in its infancy. Semiconductors, first explored in the nineteenth century by European scientists, defied accurate scientific comprehension until the development of the quantum theory of solids in the early decades of the twentieth century. Spurred by this theory and empirical investigations, scientists in the 1930s predicted that the electronic properties of crystals could be harnessed, in other words, solid-state electronics.

In the mid-1930s Bell Laboratories formed a solid-state physics research group. Focused mainly on silicon and germanium, Bell Labs research quickly yielded increased understanding of these materials' electrical characteristics and the importance of junctions between N- and P-type semiconductor materials. This work coincided with the buildup to and outbreak of World War II.

If World War I was the first fully mechanized war, World War II was the first electronic war. Radar, mobile communications, command and control systems, the proximity fuze, and early electronic computers all aided the Allied victory. The radar project, run through MIT's Radiation Laboratory, in particular influenced the nature and structure of the post-war electronics industry. The efforts of a wide array of commercial firms, university laboratories, and government research establishments accelerated both practical and theoretical understanding of semiconductor materials and created a community of semiconductor researchers.

Semiconductors. In late 1947, three researchers at Bell Labs created a transistor from a piece of germanium. John Bardeen, Walter Brattain, and William Shockley shared the 1956 Nobel Prize in physics for their work; Shockley then discovered a much improved type of transistor and formed the first semiconductor company in what would become Silicon Valley. Bell Labs disseminated transistor information through seminars in the early 1950s, first for corporate and university defense contractors, and then, under pressure from a federal anti-trust suit, to any firm paying a modest license fee. Licensees included existing American, European, and Japanese firms in three categories: tube makers, existing firms wishing to work with the new technology, and firms formed to enter the semiconductor industry.

The military supplied the largest initial market for semiconductors; government procurement accounted for more than 50 percent of the industry's output throughout the 1950s and into the 1960s. The government also supported semiconductor Research and Development widely in industrial and university laboratories. Many manufacturing processes resulted from the broad investment. Particularly important in the 1950s were AT&T Bell Labs, Texas Instruments, the United States Army's Diamond Ordnance Fuze Laboratories, and Fairchild Semiconductor.

A spinoff from Shockley's semiconductor company in Palo Alto, California, founded in 1957, Fairchild established the semiconductor industry in northern California. With an intensely commercial focus, Fairchild developed its own processes and equipment as well as adapting others' and quickly introduced a new, important electronic structure, the planar transistor. The same processes made it possible, by the late 1950s, to make all the elements of a circuit on a single piece of silicon, the integrated circuit. Spinoffs from Fairchild populated the industry in what became known as Silicon Valley. The valley's commercial orientation emphasized process innovations as well as ever-decreasing component size, which aided not only electronic performance, but also the economics of production. The industry, again following Fairchild's lead, actively sought new applications for solid-state electronics, enlarging their market while making their products increasingly ubiquitous. Aggressive pricing strategies and wild booms and busts marked the formative years of the industry.

During the 1950s Japanese firms, at the urging of the government, began a program of semiconductor research and development. By the late 1950s they produced large numbers of transistors, as well as equipment using them. Sony, Toshiba, Mitsubishi, and other companies established themselves in the industry. Though Japanese exports increased hugely, United States companies remained dominant through the 1970s.

By the early 1960s United States companies began to move transistor production to foreign countries, including Taiwan and Hong Kong. Starting with mechanical assembly, over time more sophisticated processes were transferred abroad, spreading expertise and establishing a technical and scientific foundation for these countries.

During the 1960s solid-state electronics expanded beyond defense and space applications into consumer goods and general-purpose computers. Integrated circuit applications expanded with the development of solid-state memory. These chips became the center of international competition, the United States industry yielding leadership to the Japanese by the mid-1980s. Intel Corporation, founded in 1968 by some of Fairchild's founders, pioneered the microprocessor, the "computer on a chip," fostering an industry growth spurt. Semiconductor manufacturing required the highest standards of precision of any industry in all inputs and processes.

European attempts to establish indigenous semiconductor manufacturing generally failed in spite of generous government subsidies. European semiconductor scientists, though, made significant contributions, at Siemens in particular. In the early 1970s Taiwan's government promoted semiconductor manufacturing with some success; Korean efforts have also had largely positive results. In the late 1990s The People's Republic of China targeted the semiconductor industry and welcomed foreign investment therein. India and Brazil also promoted semiconductor manufacturing, with less success.

Much of the spread of the industry after about 1985 resulted from the vertical disintegration of semiconductor manufacturing. Once unified, design and manufacturing steps and processes became separate industries, typified by "silicon foundries," which specialize in manufacturing integrated circuits designed elsewhere.

The electronics industry remains of central importance to world economy. It is widely perceived to be an important multiplier industry, the core around which other industrial development can occur.

[*See also* Computer Industry.]

BIBLIOGRAPHY

Aitken, Hugh G. J. *Syntony and Spark: The Origins of Radio*. New York, 1976.

Aitken, Hugh G. J. *The Continuous Wave: Technology and American Radio 1900–1932*. Princeton, 1985.

Braun, Ernest, and Stuart MacDonald. *Revolution in Miniature: The History and Impact of Semiconductor Electronics*. 2d ed. Cambridge, 1982.

Fagan, Melvin D., ed. *A History of Engineering and Science in the Bell System: National Service in War and Peace (1925–1975)*. Murray Hill, N.J., 1978.

Fisher, David, and Marshall Jon Fisher. *Tube: The Invention of Television*. New York, 1997.

Graham, Margaret. *RCA and the Videodisc: The Business of Research*. Cambridge, 1986.

Malerba, Franco. *The Semiconductor Business: The Economics of Rapid Growth and Decline*. Madison, Wis., 1985.

Morris, Peter Robin. *A History of the World Semiconductor Industry*. London, 1990.

Reich, Leonard S. *The Making of American Industrial Research: Science and Business at GE and Bell, 1876–1926*. Cambridge, 1985.

Reid, T. R. *The Chip: How Two Americans Invented the Microchip and Launched a Revolution*. New York, 1985.

Riordan, Michael, and Lillian Hoddeson. *Crystal Fire: The Birth of the Information Age*. New York, 1997.

DANIEL HOLBROOK

EMIRI LANDS. *Emiri land* is an Ottoman Turkish term for state-owned land. The term was used throughout the Ottoman Empire until 1919. *Emiri* land falls into the five categories of the Ottoman Land Code of 1858:

1. *mamluk* or *mulk*, milk land—in Egypt, privately owned land
2. *emiri*, *miri*, or *amriyya* land—state-owned land that is leased to individuals

3. *matruka* land—common land or land reserved for public purposes
4. *mawat* land—dead land
5. *waqf* land—land that has been established as pious endowment

Emiri land is recognized by contemporary analysts as the land that has been conquered by the Ottoman sultan through military expedition. This definition also applies to all state-owned land under the control of a Muslim ruler or the state outside the Ottoman Empire.

The origin of *emiri* land can be traced to the pre-Islamic Persian impact on Muslim political theory. This influence was based on the concept of the supremacy of the state, which Muslim jurists were said to have incorporated into the philosophy that gives the ruler significant power over the sources of revenue for the administration of the state. *Emiri* land, therefore, incorporates the legal ownership of land that is vested on the *bait-ul-mal* (the treasury) comprising all arable fields, meadows, pasturing grounds of all seasons, and woodland whose disposition lies with the state government.

Emiri land was leased to the peasants during the Ottoman period to ameliorate the impact of military conquest if the owners of the land were killed or did not flee. Peasants, therefore, enjoy *tasarruf* (usufruct right) over the land allocated to them based on the payment of the *kharaj* land tax, based on the belief that it would be of strategic concern should the empire attempt to dispossess the peasants of their arable land. The cultivator of *emiri* land has the status of quasi-ownership: He may sell, let, mortgage, or give away; but he is restricted in inheritance because the land cannot be bequeathed by will if there are no heirs. The state's control over *emiri* land is usually supervisory by nature because the land is theoretically given to cultivators or occupants on the conditions that the recipient must cultivate it and must also pay taxes.

According to Dr. James Heyworth-Dunne (*Land Tenure in Islam, 630 AD–1951 AD* Cairo, 1952) *emiri* land falls into the following categories:

1. *miri khali*—a vacant land
2. *miri that at-tasarruf*—private usufruct state land
3. *miri matrukah murafaqah*—communal profit-à-prendre state land
4. *miri matrukah mahiyah*—common easement or servitude state land
5. *Mahlul*—escheated state land
6. *Waqf ghair sahih* or *takhsisat waqf*—usufruct land owned by the state where state revenues are assured to pious foundations

The reforms presented in the 1858 Ottoman Land Code transformed the status of *emiri* land throughout the empire. The Code rescued and corrected many aspects of land ownership and clarified the extent of *emiri* land control. Official consent was made mandatory before emiri land can be sold or divided as presented in Articles 25 and 31 of the Code. Provision was made whereby *emiri* land that is abandoned for a period of three years shall be transferred to the state. Many aspects of the Code, such as prohibition of collective ownership and record keeping of the *emiri* land, were said to be nominally adhered to. The term *emiri land* in modern Middle East and other Muslim states is usually applied to unoccupied or uncultivated land.

[*See also* Mulk Lands *and* Waqf.]

BIBLIOGRAPHY

Fisher, Sir Stanley, ed. *Ottoman Land Laws Containing the Ottoman Land Code and Later Legislation Affecting Land with Notes and an Appendix of Cyprus Laws and Rules Relating to Land.* London, 1919.

Gibb, Hamilton Alexander Rosskeen, et al., eds. *The Encyclopaedia of Islam.* New ed. Leiden, 1960.

Liebesny, Hebert J., and Majid Khadduri. *Law in the Middle East*, vol. 1, *Origin and Development of Islamic Law.* Washington, D.C., 1955.

Liebesny, Herbert J. *The Law of the Near and Middle East: Readings, Cases, and Materials.* Albany, N.Y., 1975.

IBRAHIM HAMZA

EMPLOYERS' ASSOCIATIONS.

With industrialization, employers' associations (EAs) emerged across the developed economies of the world and came to play a significant role in capital-labor relations. However, organizational structure, power, and strategies varied considerably across different nation-states. In essence, such bodies were the capitalist equivalent of the workers' trade unions and were frequently formed in reaction to strikes and/or collective organization by employees. There was a fairly strong symbiotic relationship operating here. Employers' associations protected and pursued the interests of their members in the area of labor relations, as distinct from trade associations and the chambers of commerce, which focused on trade and commercial matters.

Some organizations, however, combined these functions and others evolved to specialize in particular services to employers, such as antisocialist propaganda (e.g., the Economic League in the United Kingdom) or the provision of "free labor" and strikebreakers (e.g., the British National Free Labour Association). Market pressure and the growth of state intervention in economic and social affairs were the other two main interlocutors, facilitating the drift from individualism toward collective organization of employers in developed economies. While there was no monolithic capitalist reaction, associational activity invariably represented a response by employers to a perceived external threat to profitability. To some commentators, their emergence has been interpreted as an expression of sharpening class consciousness, while others emphasize the relative weakness of EAs—their fragmentation and inherent disunity.

Among the earliest employers' associations were those formed in Great Britain in the eighteenth century. Adam Smith (1723–1790) identified a number of semiclandestine masters' combinations operating in his classic treatise *The Wealth of Nations* (1776). The master tailors, for example, formed an organization in London in 1764 and imported more than a thousand new workers to break a strike in that year. Formal associations dealing with labor-relations matters proliferated throughout the nineteenth century in the United Kingdom, first at the local level and later at regional and national levels. Among the earliest and most powerful were those of the coal masters and the textile mill owners. Employers' associations also emerged across Europe and in the United States as their economies industrialized, especially in manufacturing, mining, and the "heavy industries." The range and complexity of such bodies defies generalization. However, there was a marked tendency in this early period for such organizations to be aggressively antilabor. Their role was invariably coercive and confrontational. They coordinated strikebreaking, victimized workers for their membership in unions, and enforced the "open-shop" principle, employing a whole arsenal of weapons to starve workers into submission, including the multiemployer lockout, which evolved as a tactic largely in response to sectional strikes by unions, picking off employers one by one.

The surge in trade union membership and the increasing militancy and power of organized labor from the late 1880s to World War II led to a massive proliferation of EAs in Europe and the United States. In Great Britain, the numbers of associations grew from 336 in 1895 to 1,487 in 1914 and to 2,403 in 1925. By World War II, it was estimated that more than half of all British workers were employed in companies that were members of employers' associations. During this period, EAs in some countries (e.g., Scandinavia and the United Kingdom) pioneered a new approach to the labor problem, recognizing the trade unions and working with them to forge collective agreements on wages, working conditions, and disputes procedures. The Brooklands Agreement in British cotton spinning in 1893 and the Terms of Settlement that ended the national lockout in engineering in the United Kingdom in 1898 were pivotal examples. This heralded the germination of the modern system of industrial relations, substituting more subtle procedural and bureaucratic forms of control over labor for the more provocative methods of coercion and confrontation that characterized the nineteenth century. In the United States during this period, however, employers' associations tended to remain anti-union, sometimes fiercely so. The National Metal Trades Association and the National Manufacturers' Association were in the vanguard of a concerted counterattack against the trade unions and the drift toward collective bargaining in the United States in the 1900s. This commitment to the "open-shop" principle was sustained in the United States up until the New Deal reforms in labor law, including the Wagner Act, in the late 1930s.

By the mid-twentieth century, a complex matrix of employers' associations existed within most developed Western economies, the United States, Australia, and Japan. The two world wars acted as significant additional catalysts as employers felt pressured to organize more effectively to lobby legislatures and enable the voice of capital to be heard. This was increasingly necessary, too, as a counterpoise to the growing political muscle of organized labor as voting franchises were extended to incorporate working men and women. In the United Kingdom, for example, the first confederations of employers emerged around the turn of the century (Employers' Parliamentary Council), though the first really effective grouping came just after the end of World War I with the formation of the National Confederation of Employers' Organisations in 1919. This later combined with the Federation of British Industries in 1965 to form the Confederation of British Industries (CBI), which continues to represent the interests of British employers today. Even in Japan, recent research indicates a long history of associational activity and suggests an important role was played in industrial relations and policy making in the post-1945 period by the industry employers' associations and their coordinating federation, Nikkeiren.

Internal divisions of interest, the variety of company forms and strategies, the competitive relationship that existed between employers, and the growth of multinational corporations has placed great strains upon associational activity. Centripetal pressures co-existed with centrifugal ones, and conflicting interpretations abound in the literature on just how influential, powerful, and united such organizations were in different national contexts. What is clear, however, is that employers' associations have transmogrified over time from belligerently antiunion, strikebreaking agencies to collective-bargaining institutions, playing a pivotal role in the modern industrial relations systems of developed nations. Lately, their role as government pressure groups representing the interests of capital and as advisory bodies providing a range of services to their members on such issues as labor law and workmen's compensation has become more important.

[*See also* Bargaining, Collective; Industrial Relations; *and* Unions.]

BIBLIOGRAPHY

Gospel, Howard F. *Markets, Firms and the Management of Labour in Modern Britain*. Cambridge, 1992.
Jacoby, Sanford M., ed. *Masters to Managers*. New York, 1991.
Johnston, Ronald. *Clydeside Capital, 1870–1920*. East Linton, Scotland, 2000.

McIvor, Arthur J. *Organised Capital*. Cambridge, 1996.

McIvor, Arthur J. *A History of Work in Britain, 1880–1950*. London, 2001.

Tolliday, Steven, and Jonathan Zeitlin, eds. *The Power to Manage*. London, 1991.

Windmuller, John P., and Alan Gladstone, eds. *Employers' Associations and Industrial Relations: A Comparative Study*. Oxford, 1984.

ARTHUR J. MCIVOR

ENCLOSURES, a method of land reform that prevailed in those parts of Europe that once practiced the system known as open-field agriculture. Although the open-fields system had also been practiced in Scandinavia and the German lands, the best-known enclosure movement swept over England (and marginally Wales) in the eighteenth and nineteenth centuries. Enclosure changed the agricultural practices that had operated under systems of cooperation in communally administered landholdings, usually large fields that were devoid of physical territorial boundaries. After enclosure, such practices became essentially noncommunal and therefore individual, and man-made boundaries (hedgerows in the lowlands and dry stone walls in the uplands, and a mixture of hedgerows and drainage ditches on land liable to periodic flooding) separated one person's land from his neighbors. An open-field farming and landownership structure was thus replaced by individual initiative and individual landownership plots. Individual property rights prevailed and common property obligations, privileges, and rights were declared null and void for all time. As often as not, there was also a counterpart enclosure of the otherwise nonagricultural common land and waste land.

Parliamentary Enclosure. Although this kind of land reform took place over a long period and across a wide geography, economic historians have emphasized particular periods of enclosure. For example, they have identified the so-called depopulating enclosures of the fifteenth and sixteenth centuries, when much of lowland England was transformed out of communal open-field arable husbandry into grazing country. The popular aphorism of the day was that "horn and thorn shall make England forlorn." The horned sheep and cattle, regulated in fields separated by hawthorn hedges, eventually led to the forced or circumstantial desertion of villages unable to support a population that depended on the produce and income from livestock cultivation alone; this was a protracted process. The enclosures that have attracted more attention from economic historians were the parliamentary enclosures of the eighteenth and nineteenth centuries. They are called "parliamentary," because they employed judicial means. They were important, because they form direct links to debates about the timing and outcome of the agricultural revolution and general links to agricultural change, the demography, and the industrial transitions. There are two major concerns: whether there were agricultural productivity gains arising from the land reform; and whether there were resulting serious social dislocations. First, the geographical extent and the temporal emphasis of parliamentary enclosure must be discussed.

Until recently, it was assumed that parliamentary enclosure was the most important of all enclosure movements in England and Wales. In a crude way, it is possible to define the progress of enclosure from the Middle Ages onward, using the records that have survived. These include land transaction documents, court proceedings and judicial enquiries, and the vestigial remains on the ground of some former agricultural practices. By about 1500, perhaps 45 percent of England was already enclosed. At first sight, this looks like an impressive figure—but it includes parts of England that may never, strictly speaking, have been in open fields or commons. This includes much of Celtic Britain, and also the county of Kent with its land-development origins from the Jutish (Danish) settlements rather than the Anglo-Saxon. There are also parts of Britain that today are not enclosed by boundaries identifiable on the ground, such as the moors scattered over the many highlands. That is not the same as saying that such lands are communally owned—they are not in the main. From that base in 1500, perhaps another 2 percent was enclosed in the sixteenth century (the seventeenth century is considered below). In the eighteenth century, another 11 percent was enclosed, principally through parliamentary means. In the nineteenth century, another 11 to 12 percent was enclosed, almost entirely by parliamentary enclosure. Finally, in about 1914 perhaps 4 to 5 percent of England was still in commons. This accounting leaves a residual of 24 percent of the land area of England, whose attribution has been hotly contested. Some attribute it to the seventeenth century, in which case England's most intense enclosure era took place relatively silently; the surviving records do not support such a history (but that may be due to the English Civil War, the Restoration, and the Glorious Revolution and its aftermath—all of which disrupted English life in the 1600s). Instead, it is likely that far more enclosure by agreement took place, without the intervention of the judiciary, than we have discovered yet in the documentary record. In particular, much of it was almost certainly concentrated in the period parallel with the parliamentary enclosures. Therefore much of this residual enclosure contributes to the contested ground in which economic historians are particularly concerned, the twin questions of productivity gain and social cost.

Yet, in England, the main wave of enclosure was even more concentrated than these statistics suggest. Parliamentary enclosure may be traced to 1604 (Radipole in

Dorset) or even as early as 1545 (the enclosure of Hounslow Heath), and it may have been continued until 1914 (Elmstone Hardwicke in Gloucestershire). In total, some 5,250 individual parliamentary enclosure acts touched parts of almost one half of all English parishes. They accounted for 21 percent of the land area of England, or 6.8 million acres, initially thought to be in the ratio of two-thirds open-field arable and one-third common land and waste land. A very detailed analysis of a 10 percent sample suggests that perhaps 7.3 million acres was enclosed by act, and that much common meadow and pasture were mistakenly cataloged as open-field arable. More significantly, 18 percent of England was enclosed in two short bursts of activity—first in the 1760s and 1770s; then during the French wars of the 1790s and 1800s. In the 1760s and 1770s, much of central England was enclosed as a response to relative price movements between arable and animal crops. Much of that land tumbled to grass, as was the case with the dense lands of the relatively contiguous counties of Leicestershire, Warwickshire, and North Buckinghamshire. Then in the 1790s and 1800s, enclosure activity took place in most counties (including those already mentioned), mainly in response to the high grain prices of the wars with France. This encouraged both investment in existing arable cultivation and an extension of the arable lands, by ploughing up or improving the common lands and waste lands. In 1803, at the resumption of the Napoleonic War, the exhortation by Sir John Sinclair, Member of Parliament and president of the Board of Agriculture, was not to be "satisfied with the liberation of Egypt, or the subjugation of Malta, but let us subdue Finchley Common; let us conquer Hounslow Heath, let us compel Epping Forest to the yoke of improvement." It was taken up enthusiastically, and the most intensive enclosure activity took place from 1800 to 1814.

Enclosure and Modernization. Traditionally, some very important and enduring themes have been central to economic and social historians regarding enclosures. Originally, enclosure was thought to be the modernizing vehicle in English agriculture; the dissolution of the open-field system transformed the small-scale independent peasant base into a large-scale capitalist enterprise and, by this process, agriculture was thought to be made more productive. The resulting increase in production, it was said, was a fundamental prerequisite for the burgeoning Industrial Revolution—among other ways, by releasing labor from primary food production and thus providing the workforce of the Industrial Revolution. That interpretation endured claims and counterclaims in the historiography of the twentieth century, but it came under serious assault by the 1970s.

The latest research established that the open fields were not as backward as generations of historians had believed.

The apparent rigidity of two crops and a fallow season in a three-field system actually allowed great adaptability, by adjustments to rules and by-laws that governed the communal way of husbandry. In England, this even allowed areas of permanent or semipermanent grass to be introduced into what were otherwise entirely arable fields. An alternative interpretation of the apparent flexibility has been suggested—one that signaled a resource crisis, a land hunger, and a desire to increase the amount of animal husbandry that could be practiced. If this was the case, then it was the response to the change in the trade price terms between grain and livestock-based products. The overproduction of grain, relative to the growth of England's population in the half century or more before 1750, had depressed prices.

Enclosure and Productivity. A second area of scholarly debate was whether the elimination of the open fields did in fact lead to an increase in productivity. The aphorism of the early nineteenth century, that "enclosure made a good farmer better but a bad one worse," suggested that the communal farming arrangements held back the more innovative and industrious, whose personal enterprise might be released after the imposition of enclosure. Alternatively, the open-fields system protected the improvident or unlucky, who could be sustained with a low level of output. The study of crop yields in both open-field and enclosed situations indicates a land productivity gain after enclosure. The yields of wheat, barley, and oats in enclosed fields were greater by 20 to 26 percent than yields in the open fields. There might not have been an improvement of that magnitude had it not been for relatively inferior grain lands that went out of production after enclosure, thus raising the average yield. The land released from grain crops could then be used for animal husbandry (grazing), thus increasing the variety of output. Through comparative land advantage, then, total output was increased. The increase in animal husbandry soon led to an increase in natural fertilizer, which closed the circle of improvement by providing for increased crop yields. Some studies have disputed the level of improvement after enclosure in England, but even the most sceptical recognize some improvement. The major fault with all such studies so far is that they have not yet looked at a fixed area of land and analyzed it in its open-field state, then as enclosed farms.

The traditional timing of England's agricultural revolution is the eighteenth and nineteenth centuries, with enclosure at its heart. In that view, agriculture developed more or less in tandem with both the demographic and industrial transitions, and it did so in a capitalist, market-oriented atmosphere, through the industry and enterprise of landlords. The independence of the yeoman farmer in England was eroded, and he was reduced to a dependent tenant, whose next step on the agricultural ladder might be as a landless laborer, unless he could respond to the demands of his landlord. A revised view of the agricultural revolution is now emerging, connected to the revised assessment of enclosure: its role is now played down, and the ultimate research heresy is even proposed—was enclosure necessary? The new view suggests that the main thrust of England's agricultural improvement took place well before 1770 or even 1750. The course of crop yields from medieval times onward partly supports such a view. The extension of this argument is that if agriculture made its decisive contribution before the main thrust of industrialization, then it came about through the industry and enterprise not of the landlords but of the yeoman farmers. Thus began the idea of two revolutions—the yeoman revolution and the landlord revolution—in which the new emphasis was placed on the deeds of the farmer.

Enclosure and Tenure. If this view prevails then it also emphasizes the importance of the yeoman's independence, embodied in the contractual arrangements he had with the owners of the soil, the landlords. Under a system of archaic leases and copyhold tenures, there was every incentive for the yeoman to improve his farm's output, because his obligations to his landlord were weighted in his own favor. In particular, his rental payments were relatively fixed, subject to review only after long intervals. The landlord was not particularly disadvantaged by such a situation, as long as general price levels did not change very much. Then, in the mid-to-late eighteenth century, this situation changed. There was a general price inflation that became a severe inflation after the French Revolution, during the Napoleonic Wars. This coincided with the periods of greatest enclosing activity.

During a period of rising prices, the fixed nominal rents that prevailed under long leases were a declining real cost to the tenant, as well as a declining real income to the landlord. If the landlords could find a way to renegotiate the leases, they could recoup a proportion of the rent surpluses that their tenants enjoyed. In the new scholarly interpretation, enclosures are viewed as the landlords' device to break those lease contracts. The individual Acts of Parliament for nearly all parliamentary enclosures contained a clause that allowed existing rack rents to be declared null and void. In their legislative language, they allowed the renegotiation of rack-rent leases, but not all leases. Parliamentary enclosure made no inroads on archaic leases and copyhold tenancies. On the contrary, every act that contained the clause regarding the nullification of rack rents also contained a clause safeguarding the integrity of other than rack-rent contracts. The yeoman may still have been the architect of a pre-1750 English agricultural revolution, but enclosure was not, with certainty, the device set up supposedly for his demise. Furthermore, copyhold tenures lingered on until legislation was introduced in the 1840s for enfranchising the fee-simple element of the tenure (but usually, as it turned out, by transferring it to the copyholder not to the lord), and this enfranchisement process lingered into the twentieth century.

Enclosure and Social Change in the Countryside. The study of enclosures has been motivated by a concern for their economic consequences and for their social repercussions. A historiographical tradition that still attracts attention suggests that enclosure was a pure enough case of class robbery. The majority of landowners or, more correctly, the landowners of a majority of the land, obtained the necessary legislation for enclosure—regardless of the wants and desires of the remainder of landowners, who may have had a numerical majority. Enclosure was an expensive business. It is suggested that the various costs involved—to satisfy the manorial obligations, to commute the tithes owners, as well as the physical and administrative costs—led many of the smaller landowners to sell. The choices open to them were stark: they could become landless laborers; they could go to the towns and become industrial laborers; or the more fortunate could become tenant farmers on short-term leases. The same historiographical tradition bestowed a worse fate on those rural dwellers whose only toe on the agricultural ladder was a landless laboring toe, with just the enjoyment of common rights.

That traditional story has never been properly overturned. It has been tempered at the edges by suggesting that common rights were not so common and widely owned as the name implies and, therefore, that the landless had nothing to lose in the first place. Yet even attempts at smoothing the rough social edges of enclosure cannot deny that legally or otherwise the landless did enjoy many moral common rights. They might glean in the open fields after harvest, they might trap rabbits on the commons and wastelands, they might pick berries from plants on the commons. They played on the commons and generally availed themselves of its use. Enclosure robbed them of these uses; any tangible or even intangible sense of ownership and independence was thus removed by enclosure. Equally important, the villages that were once communities of seasonal activity and general participation were also changed by it, irrevocably. A more commercial, enterprising spirit in agriculture, of which enclosure was but one aspect, eroded that sense of community. Enclosure did not put people out of work; the agricultural labor force continued to expand until long after the main thrusts of enclosure had passed. Yet by changing the structure of rural society and by closely defining property rights, the propertyless majority did become a more biddable labor force for town and country alike.

[*See also* Open-Field System *and* Property Rights in Land, *subentry on* Communal Control.]

BIBLIOGRAPHY

Allen, Robert C. "The Efficiency and Distributional Consequences of Eighteenth-Century Enclosures." *Economic Journal* 92.4 (1982), 937–953.

Allen, Robert C. *Enclosure and the Yeoman: The Agricultural Development of the South Midlands, 1450–1850*. Oxford, 1992.

Chapman, John. "The Extent and Nature of Parliamentary Enclosure." *Agricultural History Review* 35.1 (1987), 25–35.

Neeson, J. M. *Commoners: Common Right, Enclosure, and Social Change in England, 1700–1820*. Cambridge, 1993.

Snell, K. D. M. *Annals of the Labouring Poor: Social Change and Agrarian England 1660–1900*. Cambridge, 1985.

Turner, Michael E. *Enclosures in Britain, 1750–1830*. London, 1984.

Turner, Michael E. "English Open Fields and Enclosures: Retardation or Productivity Improvements." *Journal of Economic History* 46.3 (1986), 669–692.

Turner, Michael E. "Benefits but at Cost: The Debates about Parliamentary Enclosure." *Research in Economic History* Supplement 5, Part A (1989), 49–67.

Wordie, J. R. "The Chronology of English Enclosure, 1500–1914." *Economic History Review* 36.4 (1983), 483–505.

MICHAEL TURNER

ENCOMIENDA AND REPARTIMIENTO describe various aspects, relating especially to labor procurement and tribute, of the general Spanish attempt in the Americas to employ indigenous mechanisms, relatively unchanged. Usage of the terms varied greatly, though the terminology has become standard among scholars.

The Spaniards originally settled mainly among sedentary peoples who had rulers with various kinds of authority over their subjects. The first serious Spanish attempt to take advantage of the situation was to assign to prominent Spaniards the rights that would accrue to the local ruler of a particular entity, the granting of which was an *encomienda*. It varied with the assets of the region and the rights of the ruler, but everything was channeled through the traditional indigenous authority.

Originally, in the Caribbean, the *encomendero* (holder of a grant) received primarily draft seasonal labor. Then in Mexico and the Andes tribute products were added, based on the practices of that region. Some of the tribute was directly or indirectly valuable to Spaniards; some was not. A process began immediately of restricting tribute to things useful to Spaniards and getting payment in precious metal, or even money if possible.

As ever more Spaniards immigrated, viable markets arose for many new products, especially Spanish crops and livestock, bringing on more direct Spanish intervention. *Encomenderos* began to establish enterprises on the *encomienda* territory, getting special grants of land, using draft labor from the *encomienda* and also permanent personnel, both non-Indians and permanent indigenous employees outside the legal framework of the *encomienda*. *Encomenderos* became the center of almost all kinds of business except import-export; they and their employees were the core of the local Spanish market.

Encomenderos continued to have full rights to draft labor, used in the silver mines and all their other enterprises. But this system, with the sedentary indigenous populations and mining for precious metals at its base, attracted large numbers of Spanish immigrants who could not be readily absorbed within it. Starting in the 1540s, the crown in Spain began for various reasons to try to end the labor rights of the *encomienda* and restrict it to a specified schedule of tribute in kind or money. Such efforts were successful only in areas like Mexico and Peru, where a large Spanish population existed outside the *encomienda* system.

In the second half of the sixteenth century a system arose in these central areas that took indigenous draft labor away from the *encomienda* and let government officials distribute it temporarily to all Spaniards according to their enterprises. Through this system, called the *repartimiento*, the silver mines were gradually weaned from the *encomienda*. Outside the mines, however, the *encomenderos* as large entrepreneurs continued to command a very large proportion of the supply of temporary draft labor. Draft labor was still procured by traditional indigenous mechanisms; in Peru the whole system was called the *mita*, the Quechua word for draft labor obligations. Still, many more Spaniards and other nonindigenous people were involved in direct supervision than before.

The combination of a drastically decreasing indigenous population because of epidemic disease and a sharply increasing Spanish sector gradually made the *encomienda* vestigial in the central areas by various times in the seventeenth century. Tribute income had become insignificant, and direct labor power was lost. Instead, landed estates called haciendas, serving city markets and owned and operated entirely by Spaniards, became the dominant estate form, although many of their structures went back to the *encomienda*. The *repartimiento* draft labor also weakened in time, becoming so inefficient that Spaniards went around it and hired temporary laborers directly. The process was slower in the Andean region than in central Mexico, partly because of exceptionally strong preconquest draft labor traditions in the Andes.

In areas outside Mexico and Peru, with less sedentary indigenous peoples organized in smaller units, and with little or no draft labor, things were very different. *Encomiendas* were much smaller and often could deliver neither tribute nor labor without direct Spanish intervention. In many cases, a *repartimiento* separate from the *encomienda* was never established. Poor and outside the international mining economy, these areas received little Spanish emigration, and hence there was no pressure to change the *encomienda*. It lasted in many peripheral regions far into the eighteenth century, although, because of the nature of local indigenous society, it took very different shapes than in the central areas.

BIBLIOGRAPHY

Bakewell, Peter J. *Miners of the Red Mountain: Indian Labor in Potosí, 1545–1650*. Albuquerque, 1984.

Lockhart, James. *Spanish Peru, 1532–1560: A Social History*. 2d ed. Madison, Wis., 1994.

Lockhart, James, and Stuart B. Schwartz. *Early Latin America: A History of Colonial Spanish America and Brazil*. Cambridge and New York, 1983.

Service, Elman R. *Spanish-Guarani Relations in Early Colonial Paraguay*. Ann Arbor, 1954.

Zavala, Silvio A. *La encomienda indiana*. Madrid, 1935.

JAMES LOCKHART

ENERGY REGULATION. Energy regulation is a recent phenomenon. Its development in the nineteenth century coincides with a dramatic increase in the magnitude and intensity of energy use. Energy regulation played a significant role in industrial economies with the discovery of natural gas and then oil and the advent of electricity in the late nineteenth century. This survey addresses the development of electricity, natural gas, and oil price regulation in the late nineteenth and early twentieth centuries. In some countries energy industries have been subject to nationalization, although that trend reversed in the 1980s.

Electricity and Natural Gas Regulation. Both electricity and natural gas were initially produced for local use, and in the nineteenth century both were products of coal. During the nineteenth century first natural gas and then electricity grew in popularity, entry into the industry was common, and entrepreneurs created new products for customers and profits for producers. This pattern occurred particularly in the United States and Europe and tracked industrialization. Elsewhere home heating and lighting continued to depend on other resources, such as wood and coal, with electricity and natural gas entering the home heating and lighting market late in the nineteenth century.

As these industries evolved, local governments saw natural monopoly characteristics in the distribution of natural gas and then later in the generation and distribution of electricity. Increasing economies of scale in these activities were seen as examples of natural monopoly theory, the theoretical foundation of electricity and natural gas regulation. In economic theory a natural monopoly exists if production by a single firm is the least-cost way to meet demand (Viscusi et al., 1998, p. 351; Primeaux, 1986). In such a case monopoly pricing would lead to inefficient production, but full competition is unlikely because it would lead to a market in which the participants would not be able to earn a profit. This conundrum provided the justification for municipalities to award franchises for electric and natural gas utilities.

In common law countries (for example, the United Kingdom, Canada, and Australia) regulation of the electricity and natural gas industries has been supported through a government's ability to regulate industries in the public interest. In the United States, for example, the Supreme Court's decision in *Munn* v. *Illinois* (1877) reinforced the state's right to regulate in the public interest under common law doctrine. According to the "public interest" theory of regulation, concern about the market power implications of the economies of scale in electricity led governments to introduce rate and service area regulation under public utilities commissions (Bonbright, 1961). The rent-seeking theory, on the other hand, argues that utility regulation arose out of the interests of incumbents in protecting their industry from competition. Gregg Jarrell (1978) found that, in the United States between 1900 and 1920, the states that initially adopted electric utility regulation actually had lower prices and profits, not monopoly prices, a result consistent with a rent-seeking theory of regulation. A third argument for the industry embracing regulation is that it would help them raise capital, an argument that is also consistent with rent seeking (Hausman and Neufeld, 2002).

By the beginning of the twentieth century private companies provided electric service to municipalities under nonexclusive franchises. These franchises allowed companies to compete, provide different services, or install systems using different frequencies or voltages over small or large areas. Some customers also provided their own power using coal-fired generators. Competition and entry eroded profits by the early twentieth century in many countries. Fragmentation and the competing standards of direct current and alternating current created messy operating environments for electric companies, particularly in the United States. The chaos gave entrepreneurs such as Samuel Insull opportunities to consolidate multiple small companies into one holding company. Insull believed that electricity generation was a natural monopoly and looked to local and state government to block entry and grant legal protection to his company. In 1907 Wisconsin and New York extended their existing railroad regulation to electric utilities in an effort to counteract possible monopoly power on the one hand and ineffectual or corrupt municipal officials on the other. By 1914 forty-five states had enacted state public utility regulation.

In countries with federal government structures, such as the United States and Germany, regulation began at the local and state levels. Federal involvement in utility regulation in the United States did not truly occur until the Federal Power Act was amended in the 1930s and the Public Utilities Holding Company Act of 1935 increased federal regulation of the corporate structure of electric utilities. In Germany the electricity industry remained decentralized and fragmented, with vertically integrated firms and competing regional and local distributors, until the federal government passed the energy law of 1935 (Müller and Stahl, 1996, p. 277). This law centralized federal regulation (implemented under the Nazi regime), stipulated regulated or frozen rates, and created exclusive franchises over geographic territories for electric utilities.

The United Kingdom and Japan experienced similar patterns of economic regulation of the electricity industry. The United Kingdom's industry was decentralized, with generation done by both private and municipal companies and governed by local statutes, until 1926 and the establishment of the Central Electricity Board. In 1948 the government nationalized both the electricity and coal industries. The industry was nationalized until 1990, when the United Kingdom was the pioneer in electricity industry privatization and regulation that is more focused on supporting competition than on managing and controlling the industry. In Japan regulation began in 1891, with further regulations through 1931. Japan also shifted the industry's organizational structure to regional regulated monopolies (Navarro, 1996, pp. 235–237).

Natural gas has also experienced price regulation. Natural gas is often found near oil deposits, and for centuries it was used as an indicator of where to look for oil. Natural gas has often been burned off (flared) or reinjected to maintain pressure in deposits, because the transportation and use of natural gas was a more expensive alternative. High transportation costs have limited natural gas use in many countries, except for the United States and Russia and other Caspian countries. Before 1955 natural gas represented less than 1 percent of total energy consumption in western Europe, largely owing to high transportation costs and the capital requirements of pipeline construction (Estrada et al., 1988, p. 9).

U.S. federal regulatory involvement in the natural gas industry began with the Natural Gas Act of 1938, after the states unsuccessfully attempted to regulate interstate pipelines in violation of the interstate commerce clause of the Constitution. Federal jurisdiction increased in 1954, when the Supreme Court's decision in *Phillips Petroleum* v. *Wisconsin* extended regulation back to wellhead gas prices. Deregulation began to unravel these precedents when the Natural Gas Policy Act of 1978 brought markets back into the pricing and allocation of pipeline access and the energy commodity itself.

Oil: National Security and Nationalization in the Twentieth Century. In the nineteenth century the U.S. oil industry was the world leader after the original U.S. oil discovery in Pennsylvania in 1815 and kerosene distillation in 1849 created a vibrant world market for crude oil. U.S. producers used domestic crude oil deposits to compete against Dutch and British entrepreneurs shipping oil from the Caspian Sea starting in the 1880s and retained substantial global market share into the twentieth century as demand shifted from kerosene to gasoline and fuel oil. The oil industry was increasingly seen as crucial to national security, which led to government regulation or ownership of the industry in many nations.

The timing and progression of World War I both jettisoned oil into the role of the leading energy source and convinced countries like Germany, Britain, France, and the United States that having access to stable and plentiful sources would be important for national security. Technological change and the conversion of military technology from coal and steam to oil-fired vessels, such as the famed German submarines and the British dreadnought navy ships, increased military demand for oil dramatically, creating concern about the availability of oil. During World War I the U.S. concern about oil supplies for the war effort went as far as government-imposed rationing and appeals for voluntary "gasolineless Sundays." In the interwar period Japan's concern about its lack of domestic oil deposits led to efforts in the 1930s to secure supplies in Southeast Asia, and the ensuing conflicts in Asia led to Japan's entry into World War II.

Although many countries experienced these concerns, government approaches to the supply question varied. The United States relied on voluntary price controls and supply rationing while leaving the industry private and without substantial additional economic regulation. France, on the other hand, looked vigorously to the Middle East, particularly Mesopotamia (now Iraq), to get drilling concessions for the French government. Britain took a more hybrid approach, with the government owning shares in British oil companies operating in Mesopotamia after World War I and having contracts with those companies that guaranteed supplies for the British military. These ownership forms largely persisted until late in the century, with French oil nationalized, U.S. oil private, and British oil largely private.

Nationalization also occurred in European countries in electricity and natural gas either between the wars (for example, Germany and France) or after World War II (for example, Britain). Political unrest, the threat of encroaching communism, and rising Arab nationalism during Gamal Abdel Nasser's administration in Egypt brought about a spate of nationalism of oil properties (and the Suez Canal) in the three decades after World War II. The other notable example of nationalization was in the Soviet Union and its subsequent iron curtain neighbors, in which state ownership of economic entities was required. Generally nationalization was motivated by concerns over monopoly power and the belief that government ownership would secure stable, reliable production at competitive prices. Britain's famous series of privatizations in the 1990s led the way for European countries to sell off their nationalized industries, although they are still subject to economic regulation (of either price or rate of return, depending on the industry and the country).

Oil Proration, Import Restrictions, and Price Controls in the United States. By 1930 production efficiencies and new discoveries had driven crude oil's market price to five cents per barrel in the United States. Falling demand during the Great Depression exacerbated low and volatile prices, and the industry appealed to President Franklin D. Roosevelt for assistance in March 1933. The resulting "Petroleum Code" created oil prorationing, a system of interstate production quotas on oil-producing states. State regulatory commissions allocated their quotas among producers; as a result crude oil prices increased to $1.08 per barrel by October 1933. Texas bore a disproportionate share of the production decreases because of its low-cost deposits, and its allocation of the quota reflected the political interests of higher-cost producers (Libecap and Smith, 2001). The Interstate Oil Compact of 1935 solidified interstate regulation, which persisted until 1972, when increasing domestic production was seen as a way to control the market power of the Organization of Petroleum Exporting Countries (OPEC).

As oil's use increased after World War II, the federal government in the United States saw a national security interest in restricting oil imports and supporting domestic production. Under the authority of the 1958 Trade Agreements Extension Act, and building on a voluntary import restriction program, President Dwight D. Eisenhower instituted the Mandatory Oil Import Program (MOIP). Under the MOIP, refiners received import tickets in proportion to their crude refining capacity. Tickets were allocated regardless of whether or not a refiner imported, which led to a vigorous informal market for tickets among refiners. In the wake of rising oil prices and the loopholes in the MOIP, President Richard M. Nixon replaced it with an import fee system in 1974.

President Nixon also instituted wage and price controls in 1971 in an attempt to combat inflation. These controls imposed a price ceiling on domestic oil producers. Furthermore, suppressing market adjustments through price mechanisms barred the U.S. economy from adjusting to the relatively small output restrictions that OPEC pursued in 1973 and 1974 and from the disruptions with the fall of the shah of Iran in 1978–1979. In 1981 President Ronald Reagan repealed the price controls on oil and refined products, and as suppliers brought more domestic oil to the market, uncontrolled prices fell.

This brief overview of developing energy regulation reveals some general patterns. The industries had entrepreneurial beginnings. In all cases the regulatory environment evolved from local statute governance to increasing state and then federal involvement. These cases also indicate the ongoing interplay between regulation motivated by serving the public interest and regulation as rent seeking, to serve the interests of industry participants in reducing competitive pressures.

BIBLIOGRAPHY

Bonbright, J. *Principles of Public Utility Rates.* New York, 1961.

Castaneda, Christopher. *Invisible Fuel: Manufactured and Natural Gas in America, 1800–2000.* New York, 1999.

Estrada, Javier, Helge Ole Bergesen, Arild Moe, and Anne Kristen Sydnes. *Natural Gas in Europe: Markets, Organisation, and Politics.* London, 1988.

Hausman, William, and John Neufeld. "The Market for Capital and the Origins of State Regulation of Electric Utilities in the United States." *Journal of Economic History* 62 (2002): 1050–1073.

Jarrell, Gregg. "The Demand for State Regulation in the Electric Utility Industry." *Journal of Law and Economics* 21 (1978): 269–295.

Libecap, Gary, and James Smith. "Political Constraints on Government Cartelization: The Case of Oil Production Regulation in Texas and Saudi Arabia." Working paper, Southern Methodist University, 2001.

Lyon, Thomas. "Capture or Contract? The Early Years of Electric Utility Regulation." Working paper, Indiana University, 2001.

MacAvoy, Paul. *The Natural Gas Market: Sixty Years of Regulation and Deregulation.* New Haven, 2000.

Müller, Jürgen, and Konrad Stahl. "Regulation of the Market for Electricity in the Federal Republic of Germany." In *International Comparisons of Electricity Regulation,* edited by Richard Gilbert and Edward Kahn, pp. 277–311. Cambridge, 1996.

Navarro, Peter. "The Japanese Electric Utility Industry." In *International Comparisons of Electricity Regulation,* edited by Richard Gilbert and Edward Kahn, pp. 231–276. Cambridge, 1996.

Newbery, David, and Richard Green. "Regulation, Public Ownership, and Privatisation of the English Electricity Industry." In *International Comparisons of Electricity Regulation,* edited by Richard Gilbert and Edward Kahn, pp. 25–81. Cambridge, 1996.

Primeaux, Walter J., Jr. *Direct Electric Utility Competition: The Natural Monopoly Myth.* New York, 1986.

Viscusi, Kip, John Vernon, and Joseph Harrington. *Economics of Regulation and Antitrust.* Cambridge, Mass., 1998.

Yergin, Daniel. *The Prize: The Epic Quest for Oil, Money, and Power.* New York, 1991.

LYNNE KIESLING

ENGEL'S LAW. In 1857, the statistician Ernst Engel (1821–1896) published an analysis of the budgets of 153 Belgian families. Engel divided them into three social groups of increasing income and compared the shares of spending on different commodities. He concluded that the fraction of income spent on food declined as income increased. This generalization is known as Engel's law. In 1875, the American statistician Carroll Wright reprinted Engel's table and added more generalizations that have become further elaborations of Engel's laws: the shares of income devoted to clothing and to housing did not vary with income, while the share of outlays beyond food, clothing, and housing increased with income.

Subsequent statisticians have subjected these Engel's laws to many tests. In modern formulations, they are usually expressed in terms of income elasticities of demand: the income elasticity of demand for food is less than one, while the income elasticities of demand of housing and clothing equal one, and the elasticity of "everything else" is greater than one. These generalizations have been substantially verified. In an article marking the centenary of Engel's law, Houthakker reviewed forty budget surveys from thirty countries and concluded that the income elasticity of demand for food was 0.6, the income elasticity of housing was 0.8, that of clothing was 1.2, and "everything else" was 1.6. Budget studies for developing countries indicate an income elasticity of demand for food of about 0.6, as do late eighteenth- and early nineteenth-century working-class budgets for Great Britain.

Engel's law is important in explaining the long-run decline of agriculture during modern economic growth. Since the fraction of income spent on food decreases as income rises, the demand for food grows less rapidly than the economy as a whole. Conversely, the demand for manufactures and services grows more rapidly. The allocation of labor and capital follows these changes in demand, and agriculture declines as a fraction of the economy.

Engel's law is of use to economic historians in several respects. It can be applied in measuring the standard of living: Since the fraction of income spent on food declines as income rises, income levels can be gauged from that fraction. If food comprises a large share of consumption, one may conclude that the standard of living is low. A rise in the share of expenditure devoted to food signifies a fall in the standard of living, while a decline in that share indicates that real incomes are increasing.

Engel's law also guides the choice of parameters in many economic models of historical events. For instance, agricultural output can be computed from a demand curve for agricultural products (Crafts, 1983; Allen, 1999). In these calculations, demand depends on income and prices. As noted earlier, Engel's law indicates that the income elasticity of demand should be about 0.6. Computable general equilibrium models of whole economies require that demand curves be specified to represent consumer behavior. Engel's laws govern the values chosen for the income elasticities in these formulations.

BIBLIOGRAPHY

Allen, Robert C. "Tracking the Agricultural Revolution in England." *Economic History Review* 2d series, 52.2 (1999), 209–235. Uses a demand curve and Engel's law to estimate the growth in agricultural output from 1520 to 1850.
Crafts, Nicholas F. R. "British Economic Growth, 1700–1831: A Review of the Evidence." *Economic History Review* 2d series, 36.2 (1983), 177–199.
Clark, G., M. Huberman, and P. H. Lindert. "A British Food Puzzle, 1770–1850." *Economic History Review* 2d series, 48.2 (1995), 215–237. Verification of Engel's law with budget studies from the British Industrial Revolution.
Houthakker, H. S. "An International Comparison of Household Expenditure Patterns, Commemorating the Centenary of Engel's Law." *Econometrica* 25.4 (1957), 532–551. Favorable assessment of Engel's law based on comparison of budget studies from many countries.
Philips, L. *Applied Consumption Analysis*. Amsterdam, 1974. Clear exposition of Engel's law in the context of modern consumer theory.
Stigler, G. J. "The Early History of Empirical Studies of Consumer Behavior." In his *Essays in the History of Economics*, pp. 198–233. Chicago, 1965. Precise discussion of Engel's procedures and conclusions and the way in which he and others reformulated them.

ROBERT C. ALLEN

ENGLAND *[This entry contains two subentries, on the economic history of England during the early and medieval periods up to 1500 and during the early modern period. For a continuation of the economic history during the British Empire and during the modern period, see* Great Britain.*]*

Early and Medieval Periods up to 1500

Throughout the early history of England, trading possibilities were limited by the country's location at the edge of the Eurasian landmass. Trade westward and northward, with Wales, Ireland, and Scotland, could supply some agrarian and marine products (grain, wool and wool fleeces, cattle, dairy produce and hides, fish), but was always less valuable than trade with continental Europe. Under the Romans the principal harbors were on the southern and southeastern shores. Dover and Richborough communicated with Boulogne, but traders also passed from Gaul to the estuaries of the Colne, the Thames, the Itchen, and the Exe. These routes were discontinued during the fifth century, but as trade recovered England was better provided than before with ports facing eastward and southward. By 1200 a long line of ports stretched from Newcastle in the northeast to Plymouth, Bristol, and Gloucester in the southwest. Some English trade passed through the small Welsh ports, but north of the Severn estuary the only major western port was Chester. During the thirteenth century, a native merchant class became sufficiently well established to participate in local government and to represent their towns in parliaments summoned by the king, but English overseas trade always depended heavily on foreign merchants.

The commercial advantages of southern and eastern England were augmented by the distribution of arable land. The borders of the medieval kingdom extended to the hills of Wales and Scotland, but even within these bounds there were uplands unfavorable to arable farming in the north and west, including the Cheviots, the Pennines, the Lake District, the Peak District, and Dartmoor. These regions could supply pastoral produce and minerals, and sustained enough arable farming to feed their inhabitants, but their development was constrained by poor soils. In southern and eastern England, the land supported higher population densities. Around 1300, there were five hundred inhabitants to the square mile on the fertile soils of eastern Norfolk. In 1086, about 29 percent of the rural population of England lived in the four east-coast counties of Lincolnshire, Norfolk, Suffolk, and Essex, and their percentages remained at 17 percent in 1377, following the development of northern England in the intervening centuries. Given the advantages of better access to Europe, richer agricultural resources, and denser rural populations, it is not surprising that towns became larger and more numerous in southern and eastern England than elsewhere. Even at the height of medieval urban development in about 1300, probably all the largest fifty English towns except Chester lay south and west of a line drawn from Plymouth in the southwest to Newcastle in the northeast.

English trade was facilitated by coastline and river communications, although there were technological and political limits to the extent to which water transport was cheap and easy. Travel to foreign ports by a direct route was made hazardous by the dangers of bad weather and piracy. Trade from southwestern ports to Spain, or from east-coast ports to Scandinavia and the Baltic, was risky at all times. The location of some of the largest later-medieval ports at the head of river systems (Newcastle on the Tyne, Hull on the Humber, Lynn on the Ouse, London on the Thames, Bristol on the Severn) indicates the importance of inland waterways for the conveyance of merchandise. Some inland towns, like York and Cambridge, had quays to serve river trade. Historians disagree, though, about the extent of inland navigability. The interests of river trade competed with landlords' plans to construct mills and fisheries, so that in the course of time the quality of navigation probably deteriorated, particularly during the thirteenth and fourteenth centuries.

Meanwhile, the development of trade also depended heavily on overland transport. The construction of a road system by Roman engineers after the conquest of 43 CE, and its subsequent improvement and maintenance through 360 years or more, was an investment of lasting value, despite the deterioration of the system after the collapse of Roman authority in the early fifth century. The medieval revival of inland trade was facilitated by its existence, a fact attested by the number of Stratfords (street fords), like Stony Stratford and Stratford upon Avon, that were developed by their lords as market towns in the twelfth and thirteenth centuries. The ancient roads, especially when improved by the substitution of bridges for fords, were wide, level, and firm enough to permit increasing wagon and cart traffic.

Political and Social Institutions. Both under the Romans and again from the reign of King Edgar (959–975 CE), English economic activity was constrained by a single unifying political and legal structure. Roman currency in England, mostly from continental mints, was of a common imperial standard. After the long period of political fragmentation between the fifth and tenth centuries, English kings created new national standards. From about 973 onward, the English penny, known as the sterling (from "easterling") from as early as around 1078, was normally minted to a common standard across the kingdom, and it acquired an international reputation both for the quality of its silver and the reliability of its weight over long periods. When a gold currency was minted in England from 1344, it too was minted to a high and relatively stable standard.

Control of weights and measures, though somewhat less successful, was nevertheless an object of intrusive and persistent royal attention, especially from the late twelfth century, and the elimination of serious deviations from royal norms was a major achievement of the crown from this time on. Policing trade and providing standard procedures for the recovery of debt were made subject to national rules. From the later twelfth century, many larger towns obtained charters authorizing them to choose their own judicial and financial officers, but any such administrative independence was always granted on the understanding that they were subject to national legislation. Towns had no rights to regulate industry and trade beyond their narrow territorial boundaries unless empowered to do so by the king, and in practice the crown discouraged regional industrial or trading monopolies, and contributed, through numerous grants of exemption, to the reduction of urban tolls on internal trade.

The benefits of such measures of national uniformity can easily be overstated; some of the wealthiest regions of Europe, like Lombardy and Tuscany, were the most politically fragmented. However, to the extent that standardization lowered trading costs, it is likely that political unification permitted a higher level of trade than would otherwise have been the case. Wars in pursuit of dynastic rather than commercial interests, notably under Edward I (r. 1272–1307), Edward III (r. 1327–1377), Henry V (r. 1413–1422), and Henry VI (r. 1422–1461 and r. 1470–1471), are unlikely to have been more costly than those that burdened Europe's principal trading regions in northern Italy, northern France, and the Low Countries. It is probable, in other words, that the benefits of political unification outweighed the costs.

Customs regulating relations between powerful men and their tenants in rural society were very localized. How much continuity they preserved from the Iron and Romano-British Ages through to the Middle Ages has long been disputed. Similarities of structure between some complex lordships, especially in the north, and institutions of royal administration in Wales and Scotland, have encouraged the hypothesis that rural institutions of Celtic origin persisted through the Romano-British period and the Anglo-Saxon conquests. Such "multiple estates" were characterized by a central hall and farmlands under a lord's direct control, with dependent laborers and rent-paying tenants in subordinate townships nearby. But by the time rural institutions became well documented in the eleventh century, many of these lordships had fragmented into a number of independent manors, and it is impossible to reconstruct how widespread they had been in earlier times.

As this implies, the origins of tenurial custom are mostly unknown. The complexity of manorial money rents, produce rents, and labor services is daunting. Even within the same settlement, tenants related to overlords with different obligations. It has been surmised that triumphant Norman landlords reshaped peasant renders on many estates after 1066, to the disadvantage of tenants. Local servile custom, increasingly written down from the twelfth century on, determined many peasant dues until the fifteenth century. However, in the course of time, landlord-tenant relations became more standardized, first through the operations of a royal legal system that from the twelfth century reformulated the characteristics of free tenure, then through the multiplication of free tenures during the twelfth and thirteenth centuries, and later still from the decline of serfdom.

Despite the widespread survival of local customs, from the eleventh century English lordship departed from the feudal mold characteristic of much of Europe in two related ways. The independence of lay and ecclesiastical landlords was curtailed through their subordination to royal legislation and the institutions of central government. The bishops of Durham and earls of Chester did little more than supervise the king's administration within their so-called palatinates. In the second place, even the greatest noblemen exercised little territorial control, since most large estates were widely scattered.

Though the characteristic medieval English rural settlement is usually represented as a nucleated village with regulated arable fields and commons, such institutions were the outcome of a long development and were far from universal at any period. Even at the peak of medieval population growth around 1300, less compact and less highly regulated forms of settlement were widespread, especially in the more pastoral regions of the kingdom. Iron Age and Roman Britain were settled in a rich variety of settlement forms that included both permanent nucleated settlements and hamlets. The growing density of population in the first and second centuries CE was accompanied both by the creation of towns and villages and by a wider scattering of hamlets and isolated villas. In the age of Anglo-Saxon settlement, average settlement sizes shrank considerably, as both towns and larger rural settlements decayed. The nucleated pattern of the Middle Ages was largely a reconstruction of the later Saxon and Norman periods, even where villages made use of earlier territorial boundaries.

To this later period also belongs the rationalization of pasturing practices to create two- and three-field systems in a zone that stretched from the south coast of Hampshire and Dorset through the Midlands to Yorkshire and southern Durham. Many new nucleated settlements became sites of parish churches in this period, and the duty of villagers to pay tithes to the church was rationalized by drawing parish boundaries.

If the Iron Age populations of Britain resembled those of Wales and Ireland in later centuries, ties of kinship were a powerful determinant of both tenurial and settlement structures. Such patterns were broken up perhaps under the impact of Roman rule, and certainly at the hands of the Germanic invaders. By the eleventh and twelfth centuries, family attachments were significantly less important to rural families in England than they were in the lands of Celtic tradition. Even if the original Anglo-Saxon settlers lived in scattered family groups, that pattern was undermined as larger units of settlement were formed, and by the eleventh century, it could not be assumed that neighbors and kinsmen were the same.

Siblings were more likely to remain as neighbors in adulthood if they inherited jointly, or if their parents provided them with land, but these forms of provision were far from universally possible. The practice of primogeniture on freehold lands, and on many customary lands, often drove younger sons from home to seek their fortunes. Landlords tolerated some fragmentation of agrarian units in the course of population growth between the eighth and the thirteenth centuries, and this might temporarily have enabled families to stay together. Such splitting could not proceed indefinitely, though, and the resulting reduction in the size of tenements made it increasingly difficult for them to accommodate more than a nuclear family. Thirteenth-century and later evidence shows that households characteristically comprised a single married couple with their offspring; even dependent elderly relatives were unlikely to be housed under the same roof as their children and grandchildren. The migration of country people in search of land or employment contributed throughout this period to the occupation of new farmland, to the growth of towns, and to the colonization of territories outside England altogether in Wales, Ireland, and Scotland.

The Course of Change. Economic development in England, as elsewhere in western Europe, followed a very uneven course between the Iron Age and the year 1500. Some positive development between the start and finish of this period is apparent in the growth of technical and commercial knowledge, the enormous elaboration of legal and commercial institutions, and improvements in normal standards of living. In all these respects, however, development was far from continuous. In particular, the economy suffered catastrophic deterioration in the centuries following the collapse of Roman administration and the invasion of peoples from outside the Roman Empire. The two periods of most remarkable economic development were in the first and second centuries under the Pax Romana, and again between the tenth century and the thirteenth. Most of the considerable gains of the first period were lost in the crumbling of Romano-British civilization, and only the road system and those parts of the urban structure capable of being revivified at a later date constituted assets of lasting significance. By contrast, the economic development of the late Anglo-Saxon period onward has led without serious institutional disruption or loss of knowledge and expertise into the economic development of the present day.

Even before the Roman Conquest, there is evidence of agrarian development and population growth among the British kingdoms of southern England, but between the first and early fourth centuries, the impact of Roman unification and administration was phenomenal. The country was opened up to trade by new roads and military security, and attained unprecedented levels of settlement and cultivation. A recent estimate of the population of Roman Britain in the first half of the fourth century, based on observed densities of settlement and the size of towns, places the figure at about 3.7 million (Millett), of which about 90 percent was rural and 6.5 percent urban. The remainder was in the army. Innovation was apparent on every front, not only at the level of state investment in conquered territory but also in less visible developments in agriculture and industry. The multiplication and expansion of towns, growth of grain exports, expansion of the coinage in circulation, and rapid multiplication of consumer goods on rural sites, all imply a very rapid commercialization of agriculture. By the second century CE, coinage circulated in quantities comparable with those of other western provinces of the Empire. These developments required new traditions of management, accounting, and record-keeping, both at the highest level of government administration and in the control of larger rural enterprises.

The economy of Britain was relatively little affected by external challenges to Roman rule until late in the fourth century. However, archaeological evidence suggests an abrupt collapse between 390 and 410 CE, best indicated by a sudden cessation of pottery manufacture. The use of coinage was discontinued from about 420. By the mid-sixth century, the economy had regressed to levels of output probably lower than those on the eve of the Roman Conquest, and archaeological evidence implies that trading patterns were similarly circumscribed. Trade with continental Europe had petered out. Signs of commercial revival, and a significant increase in the use of money, are in evidence from the later seventh century, when trading activity expanded both in some former Roman centers and at newer waterside sites such as Ipswich and Southampton (Hamwih). In the course of this early expansion, new coinages were devised based on silver as the normal monetary medium. However, the revival of monetary circulation and trade made little impact in many rural areas before the ninth century.

Population growth and commercial development between the eighth century and the thirteenth were interrupted by the impact of Viking invasions, by heavy taxation (geld) in the early eleventh century, by local destruction in the wake of the Norman Conquest, and by destructive civil war between 1139 and 1153. Nevertheless, urban growth was already impressive before the Norman Conquest of 1066 in towns like Canterbury, Winchester, and Lincoln. Not only did existing towns continue to grow after 1066, but urbanization spread northward and westward as kings and lords created new ones. The north experienced rapid urban development for the first time between 1080 and 1250.

The success of kings and landlords in promoting the growth of internal trade is attested by the expansion of currency in circulation from a normal level of about £25,000 in the eleventh century to about £1,100,000 in 1311. By the late twelfth century, at least, a market economy was developed enough for prices to fluctuate with supply. Urban growth was largely supported by the growth of rural demand, but a simultaneous expansion of overseas trade is apparent from the rapid development of ports at Newcastle upon Tyne, Hull, Boston, King's Lynn, London, Portsmouth, and elsewhere. English exports included wool, hides, grain, and minerals. Some woolen cloth was exported during the twelfth and early thirteenth centuries, though this trade was subsequently undermined by Flemish competition, and even more by disruptions in Flanders's chief markets, in the Mediterranean basin (c. 1280–c. 1330).

The growth of rural demand from the mid-Saxon period on implied increasing agricultural output and sales. There were direct links between agrarian expansion and aggregate demand for manufactures since some traded goods, such as salt and various types of ironware for construction, tools, and plow parts, were necessary for effective agriculture but difficult to substitute through domestic crafts. In addition, agrarian expansion permitted the incomes of landlords and some peasants to grow, and the volume of trade responded to their higher living standards. Increased output of food and raw materials was achieved by clearing forests and moors and by draining land from the sea, river estuaries, fens, and marshes. It was also facilitated by increases in the productivity of land, which in regions of advanced practice such as Norfolk owed something to improved cropping and manuring, though in general a rise in labor inputs may have been more important.

The rate of population growth is uncertain, since estimates of total population range widely. Respected estimates of England's total population for 1086 are in the

ENGLAND. Women tending sheep. Illustration commissioned by Geoffrey Luttrell (1276–1345) for the *Luttrell Psalter*. (British Library, London/Art Resource, NY)

region of 1.75 to 2.25 million, and for 1300 they range between 4.5 and 6 million (Hatcher). Lower rates of growth would be easier to explain than higher ones, since the wide extent of arable land recorded by Domesday Book in 1086 discourages optimistic estimates of the amount available for new cultivation, at least in southern England. It is likely that the proportion of the English population predominantly employed in trade and industry increased in this period both in towns and villages. English towns were characteristically small; London, with its unique combination of commercial and political advantages, probably had more than 60,000 inhabitants by 1300, but there were probably no more than sixteen others with more than 10,000. On the other hand, there were hundreds of small market towns below that size, and the urban proportion of the population at that time was conceivably as high as 15 to 20 percent.

Despite differences of emphasis between different analytical traditions, there is little disagreement that by 1300 in most parts of England, economic development was approaching a production possibility frontier, to be defined by some combination of limited resources, technological constraints, institutional rigidities, and seigniorial power. Resource constraints meant that forest clearance and drainage decreased markedly after 1250, despite rising prices for agrarian produce and the prevalence of low wage rates, apparently because reserves of readily attainable arable land were becoming scarce. Any available new agrarian technology was restricted by commercial viability to particular contexts, such as the exceptional soils and market opportunities of eastern Norfolk and Kent, and there was little provision, outside the management of individual great estates, for the dissemination of ideas. Institutional rigidities—in particular, the prevalence of very small peasant farms—in turn hampered the ease with which

food producers could respond to a rising price level through changes in technique and land use. Seigniorial power allowed kings and lords to raise rents, fines, and taxes as money incomes grew, thereby distorting the pattern of demand away from both consumption and productive investment among small producers.

However, none of the overarching models employed to explain the limits to growth has provided convincing explanations of the subsequent course of change. Population growth and agrarian expansion, having been arrested around 1300, were then thrown into reverse. The level of population was reduced by famine from 1316 to 1318, and then more severely by the plague epidemic of 1348–1349 (the Black Death), which perhaps reduced the population at a stroke by as much as 40 to 50 percent. By 1377, the population of England was no more than 2.5 to 3 million, and it fell further to around 1.8 to 2.3 million in the 1520s. By that time, some slow recovery was probably under way, so that it seems likely that at its nadir, in the mid-fifteenth century, the total population had been substantially under 2 million. At the same time, not surprisingly, between 1315 and 1500 the area of arable cultivation contracted as land reverted back to rough pasture, often in new enclosures more appropriate to pastoral farming.

Since England shared this history of falling population and contracting arable with much of the rest of Europe, it is inappropriate to explain it in exclusively English terms. The strongest explanation remains the high incidence of crisis mortality, resulting from disease, particularly bubonic plague. Epidemics were numerous and severe enough to offset the recuperative capacity of the population, so that peaks in the death rate were not offset by corresponding surges in the number of births. England also suffered from periodic international problems of deficient demand associated with shortages of the gold and silver that constituted the monetary medium, particularly between 1395 and 1415 and again between 1440 and 1460. Currency problems induced successive governments from the mid-fourteenth century to pursue bullionist policies in attempting to attract precious metals to English mints.

Notwithstanding the drop in population to perhaps a third of its former level between 1300 and 1450, historians are no longer as prepared as they once were to interpret the economic and social history of the period in negative terms as one of economic failure, decaying institutions, and cultural collapse. Many of the welfare implications of declining population and structural change will bear a positive interpretation. Greater availability of land combined with greater scarcity of labor to favor a transfer of commercial farming from large estates to small family farms, and permitted higher average incomes among the peasantry. Having been exceptionally slow among western European populations to allow serfdom to fade away—one of the less attractive results of their centralized legal system—the English experienced a dramatic decline in the incidence of labor services and servile dues after about 1380. This was partly an outcome of social conflict, but happened chiefly because landlords and employers in search of tenants and workers created opportunities for serfs to move about, and so escape their former terms of tenure.

Despite legislation from 1349 designed to curb wage increases, higher rates of pay, coupled with higher normal employment rates and a tendency for prices to fall, permitted improved standards of living for wage earners. The widespread rise in living standards created new opportunities for specialization that sometimes offset the tendency for urban populations to decline. The strong growth of exports of woolen cloth in the later fourteenth century, and again from 1470 on, constituted a further source of employment, though the towns benefiting from the later textile boom were not the same as those that had pioneered the first one. Average annual textile exports rose during this period from 6,413 cloths a year (1351–1360) to 81,562 (1501–1510). Partly because of the greater availability of resources per capita, and partly through changes in their deployment, average levels of labor productivity rose substantially in this period. Any reduction in the national output of goods and services between 1300 and 1500 (and such a reduction can only be hypothetical) was probably substantially less than the decline in population.

BIBLIOGRAPHY

Astill, Grenville, and Annie Grant. *The Countryside of Medieval England.* Oxford, 1988.

Bolton, James L. *The Medieval English Economy, 1150–1500.* London, 1980.

Britnell, Richard. *The Commercialisation of English Society, 1000–1500.* 2d ed. Manchester, 1996.

Britnell, Richard, and John Hatcher, eds. *Progress and Problems in Medieval England.* Cambridge, 1996.

Campbell, Bruce M. S. *English Seigniorial Agriculture, 1250–1450.* Cambridge, 2000.

Dyer, Christopher. *Standards of Living in the Later Middle Ages: Social Change in England, c. 1200–1520.* Cambridge, 1989.

Hatcher, John. *Plague, Population, and the English Economy, 1348–1530.* London, 1977.

Hatcher, John, and Mark Bailey. *Modelling the Middle Ages: The History and Theory of England's Economic Development.* Oxford, 2001.

Miller, Edward, and John Hatcher. *Medieval England: Rural Society and Economic Change, 1086–1348.* London and New York, 1978.

Miller, Edward, and John Hatcher. *Medieval England: Towns, Commerce, and Crafts, 1086–1348.* London and New York, 1995.

Millett, Martin. *The Romanization of Britain: An Essay in Archaeological Interpretation.* Cambridge, 1990.

Palliser, David M., ed. *The Cambridge Urban History of Britain, I: 600–1540.* Cambridge, 2000.

Salway, Peter. *Roman Britain.* Oxford, 1981.

Sawyer, Peter H. *From Roman Britain to Norman England,* 2d ed. London, 1998.

Thirsk, Joan, ed. *The Agrarian History of England and Wales.* Vols. 1–3. Cambridge, 1972–1991.

Richard H. Britnell

Early Modern Period

In 1500, the island of Great Britain was still dominated by primary production, apart from its extensive textile and some mineral exports, with an economy displaying only modest levels of integration. By comparative European standards, its towns were equally limited; population was little changed from the depressed state of around 1400, if beginning to grow; shipping was probably weaker than a century earlier; and there were few long-distance trading linkages. By contrast, in 1760 it had the fastest-growing urban sector in Europe, widespread industrial development (extractive and manufacturing), a highly advanced service economy, and high levels of political and economic integration, both internally and within an extensive extra-European empire in the formal and informal sense. It was increasingly populous, but its economy's demand for labor grew even faster and would shortly embark upon the economic miracle of the first industrial nation, even if transition to modern developed nation was not yet absolutely guaranteed. The routes of this transformation were neither linear nor simple and represented the complex outcome of institutional change, factor endowments applicable to development at existing levels of technology, a polity favorable to economic welfare, and the beneficial consequences of political actions that might easily have led in opposite directions.

Demographic Characteristics. For much of the period, Great Britain shared the demographic experience of its European neighbors with some variations, and to around 1700 its pattern appeared to be that of the homeostatic cycle: a significant period of growth starting around 1480 saw England's population rise from around 2.4 million in 1520 to 4.1 million in 1600 and 5 million in 1670 and slow to 5.1 million in 1700. Growth then resumed to reach 5.8 million in 1750 and continued to 8.7 million in 1801. Over the whole period, 1550–1820, the population of Scotland and England grew more quickly than any part of Europe with the exception of Ireland. Wrigley and Schofield's analysis (1981) emphasized the role of fertility in this growth: rising nuptiality and, above all, a fall in the age at first marriage for women are now seen as the predominant forces in the demographic revolution of Great Britain within the eighteenth century, accounting for perhaps 80 percent of growth. Great Britain distinctively shifted from a high-intensity regime of fertility and mortality in the sixteenth century, through an adjustment period of low intensity in the seventeenth, to a unique path of growth sustained throughout the eighteenth. Improved real wages, changes in economic organization, and the development of new employment opportunities were the overall determinants of this distinctive population history.

The spatial distribution of the population over this period may suggest only modest change: 94.5 percent of England's population (there is no comparable data covering Scotland and Wales, but their inclusion would certainly have increased this figure) was rural in 1520, 92 percent in 1600, 86.5 percent in 1670, and 79 percent in 1750. This has often been taken to demonstrate an unchanging hegemony of agriculture in Great Britain's occupational structure, but these figures apply a stringent test of the urban (those in towns of more than 10,000) and disguise the reality of a substantial nonagricultural population in the countryside. Thus, in 1520, four-fifths of the rural population was engaged in agriculture, or 76 percent of the total population; by 1670, it had fallen to 70 percent, 60.5 percent in all; and by 1750, it dropped to 58 percent, 46 percent of a total population that had more than doubled. Extensive structural change thus occurred in the period: agriculture became significantly more productive, meeting most home food needs; the population of towns quadrupled; and the nonagricultural population living outside the largest towns doubled. By 1800, little more than one-third of England's work force was occupied in agriculture.

Property Rights and Agriculture. Agriculture's transformation encompassed two fundamentals of British economic development, the first of which, the reordering of property rights, has generic application. A key characteristic of the enhanced productivity of farming lay in the strong reinforcement of landlords' property rights. Earlier forms of tenure, such as copyhold, the successor to servile tenures of the medieval manor, were displaced by more "modern" forms, above all leases, through which landlords could extract a full Ricardian share of the product of land. By so doing, they supplied the incentive to the tenant to innovate

and become more productive. Leasehold was a central force behind improvement of farming and helped break the inertia of traditional cropping and husbandry. The innovation was contested, at times strongly. Though the historiography has recently been largely optimistic, this was the core of the agrarian problem of sixteenth-century England, of the disputed parliamentary enclosures of the eighteenth century, and of the attack on clan tenure and the crofting system in eighteenth- and nineteenth-century Scotland, the Highland Clearances. Enclosure was an important structural change but in no sense a single transforming innovation; it is better considered as an integral element of the wider redefinition of property rights. Manorial tenures and open fields survived into the nineteenth century, some with rents paid in part in carrying or other labor services, notably in the north and west of England. But the institutional frameworks developed by British lawyers in this period had the effect of generalizing the landlord-tenant leasehold system and relocating farmsteads from village community to individual units within enclosed fields. Market forces led to the gradual decay of feudalism from the middle years of the fourteenth century, but tenants' acquisition of personal freedom did not in general convey freehold property rights. Central to the history of early modern Great Britain is this landlords' revolution in property rights.

For much of the sixteenth century, farming experienced the tensions imposed by shifting demand, with production of wool to supply a buoyant textile industry and corn to feed a growing population, which proved incompatible in midland England. Increased demand from English towns helped to develop cross-border livestock trades with Wales after 1450 and Scotland from 1600 and helped intensify farming in these most peripheral parts of Great Britain. Agriculture thus responded increasingly to changed market conditions. Redefinition of the sixteenth-century legislative constraints enhanced agriculture's capacity to respond. The abolition and subsequent restoration of the statutes in amended form against enclosure in the 1590s exactly demonstrated this institutional change. When the laws were applied under Archbishop Laud in the 1630s, it was primarily for fiscal purposes.

Between 1640 and 1670, Great Britain moved from fear of famine to worries about surplus. Legislation to support corn growers through export bounties was introduced in 1673 and made permanent from 1689. Increasing urban demand, concentrated outstandingly in London, produced a shift toward meat and dairy produce sparked by consumers enjoying rising real incomes. New farming systems emerged to raise the physical productivity of the land and output per head. Market incentives for barley production stimulated the replacement of fallows by fodder crops in much of East Anglia and the development of the sheep fold on the downlands of the Thames Valley. Greater livestock herds further improved the fertility of soils. In midland England, grass leys in arable fields facilitated the shift toward grazing and foreshadowed enclosure of open fields for commercial livestock production. In many parts of the west and north, dairying developed significantly from the later seventeenth century, often carried on in association with rural industry. Sheep and cattle rearing in Wales and Scotland generated major interregional trades. British agriculture raised productivity through modest technical improvements—effective use of spring grains, improved cropping systems, and higher labor inputs from proportionately fewer workers—and by intensifying regional specialization. Average corn yields even in 1760 probably did not exceed best practice of the Middle Ages, but Great Britain was thus able to feed itself largely without imports and continued to do so throughout the eighteenth century.

Industry. Throughout this period, the distinction between agriculture and industry remained more relative than absolute. Even in mining, the work force was often by-employed on the land or had some access to land on which to produce food. From 1500, miners of tin in Devon and Cornwall and lead in Derbyshire and the Yorkshire Dales and many exploiting outcropping inland coal worked both land and mines. The miner-smallholder, exploiting mines and quarrying on a permission basis, was an increasingly common feature of much of early modern Great Britain. For some, such low-intensity industry provided a subsistence regime in regions of poor or inadequate land resources: hill lands such as the lead-mining Mendips (Somerset), the forests of Kingswood and Dean (Gloucestershire), and the stone-quarrying Isle of Portland (Dorset), where partible inheritance fragmented but preserved arable strip fields for the underlying mineral rights.

Alongside these extensive systems, Great Britain developed some extractive industries of advanced character and capital intensity, above all in coal mining centered upon Newcastle upon Tyne. Tyneside coal made intensive use of river and coastal shipping. Its landowners invested in waggonways from the mid-seventeenth century as pits closest to water were worked out. The industry adopted steam pumping to tackle drainage problems and kept its focus on the distant London market. This made Newcastle the core of Great Britain's first industrialized region before 1700, though its relative growth slowed in the eighteenth century as others caught up. This model was followed after 1700 in south Lancashire—centered on the Mersey River and the communities of Wigan, Prescot, and Orrell—and by 1750 in Durham, around Sunderland and the Wear River, inland in the valleys of the Severn and Trent Rivers, and in south Wales. Coal traffic was central to the profitability of the subsequent canal system. Before 1750, waterways were critical to the scale of mining. Access to local coal and Baltic iron had led Ambrose Crowley to relocate his manu-

facturing business to the northeast around 1700 and to adopt centralized production in place of the outwork he had used in the west midlands. Industries such as salt boiling and glassmaking, located in South Shields in order to use coals that could not command distant markets, and access to water-borne coal released industrial potential, as in the salt production of Lymington (Hampshire). Coastal trade to Ireland created the new coal town of Whitehaven (Cumberland) in the 1680s and stimulated the development of the south Wales and Ayrshire industries and the mines around the Firth of Forth, trading along the coast and into the North Sea region. Great Britain's coincidence of exposed coalfields and water transport led to early exploitation and permitted coal to fuel urban growth. Output of around 227,000 short tons in 1560 rose to 2.6 million in 1700 and reached 5.2 million short tons in 1750, trebling again by 1800. Coal displaced wood for most urban domestic uses and many industrial activities by 1700, as Hatcher indicated (1993), releasing Great Britain early from the shackles of dependence upon timber or peat fuels.

Coal, too, underpinned the advance of several of Great Britain's early industrial regions. From the later sixteenth century, the relocation of iron smelting from the Kent and Sussex Weald toward the midlands and the north (with development of new blast furnaces), eased the move of small metalware manufacture toward the coalfields and the development of dual economies of manufacture and small-scale farming. In the west Midlands during the seventeenth century, edge-tool manufacture developed in Worcestershire and Shropshire; iron wares, ranging from horse furniture, boxes, and toys to locks and chains were produced in the Black Country to the west of Birmingham, where the ten-yard seam of coal outcropped; and nail making flourished as a domestic industry, engaging large numbers of women in the manufacturing process. South Yorkshire, around Sheffield and Rotherham, also mixed craft-workshop manufacture of edge tools and cutlery with easily available coal and a wider network of nail manufacture that made petty holdings on poor lands viable family units. In south Lancashire, the Prescot region came to specialize in the domestic manufacture of parts for watchmaking, supplying the London workshops and applying the same factor supply to advantage. Coal permitted population to thrive where lands were poor and thus laid the foundations of two of Great Britain's principal industrial regions.

Textiles provided a parallel linkage of domestic economy, modest access to land, and circulating capitals and entrepreneurship of towns—the core of regional development. The textile industries of the older corporate towns had declined from the later Middle Ages and continued to suffer from rural competition into the middle years of the sixteenth century. Great towns such as York lost their manufacturing role and sustained the perception of an urban crisis. From the 1550s onward, rural labor was the fundamental force to British textile industries, with towns acting as the economic hubs of manufacturing districts, providing most mercantile and finishing services. Places such as Exeter, Stroud, Bradford and Trowbridge, Norwich, Shrewsbury, Halifax, and Leeds all fulfilled these functions, though in differing ways. From the knitting district of Dent in the Yorkshire Dales to the valleys of Wiltshire and Gloucestershire, pastoral regions were the primary sources of labor supply for textile manufacturing. This form of production consolidated in the sixteenth century and established a model for rural textile development that endured until the third quarter of the eighteenth century. Changes took place within this classic pattern of domestic industry. Regions such as the traditional broadcloth areas of Wiltshire, Gloucestershire, and Suffolk lost foreign markets in the mid-sixteenth century and gradually adopted new products; some minor textile districts, like The Weald of Kent and Sussex, effectively deindustrialized in the years before 1650; Norfolk textiles fell out of fashion after 1700 and lost ground among the textile regions; and others, notably Yorkshire, Lancashire, and parts of Scotland, carried this protoindustrial system through to the Industrial Revolution.

Work's Effect on Social Structure. Work in early modern Great Britain was fundamentally a family activity, with all capable members contributing to the generation of income. In textiles, children assisted preparatory tasks, women spun, and men wove or worked stocking frames; both men and women manufactured metalwares, with edge-tool making and grinding reserved to males; both knitted. In arable farming districts, both might clean crops with the hoe and reap with the sickle, while plowing and threshing were predominantly male activities; children were employed seasonally as bird scarers, stone pickers, and gleaners. A large proportion of adolescents were placed in residential service as apprentices in varying trades and as domestic or farm servants, learning trades with less institutional formality. Some of them succeeded through marriage, patronage, or effective application of acquired skills to independent callings such as shopkeeping, innkeeping, and other retailing. As Prior (1985) showed, many women, perhaps increasingly in the second half of the period, conducted businesses in widowhood, despite apparent legal limitations on the holding of property, and not merely as caretakers for juvenile children.

The experience of work was fairly universal outside the upper levels of society, but it was certainly less intense than in the modern world. Farming was dominated by seasonal patterns, with only part of the work force employed all year, increasingly as farm servants in the later seventeenth and eighteenth centuries; others worked regularly on arable farms for parts of the year; and a third group labored only at harvest or haymaking time. Industries dependent upon water power—paper manufacturers of the Thames River basin, the grinding, milling, and fulling of cloth—probably lacked the water to work for more than half the year. Major processing industries, such as brewing and later distilling, stopped work for the summer months, when ambient temperatures threatened the spoilage of wash. Major trades also displayed significant seasonal patterns: coal shipments peaked in the summer months and corn in the late winter and early spring. Problems of labor discipline were met largely within the family or in residential master-servant relationships, and even in 1700, wages functioned imperfectly as incentives to full regular work. Later, as new goods raised the incentive to consume and better nutrition enhanced the capacity of the work force for sustained labor, Great Britain experienced the gains of what de Vries (1984) has called "the industrious revolution," and by midcentury new systems of work, power sources, and means of adjusting the natural environment further altered the labor process.

Work was not confined to the primary and secondary sectors of the economy. Services in many forms were fundamental and grew significantly with urbanization. The impact of London's rapid growth reached throughout the island and beyond, creating handling, carrying, and distributional work, and was replicated by the lesser towns. Alehouses and inns developed essentially with the domestic transport trades from the later sixteenth century. Rivers were improved by navigation and roads by turnpiking from the middle of the seventeenth century. And in addition to scheduled carrying services by wagon or stagecoach, huge intermediate transport and handling systems were implicit in the protoindustrial economy. Shops reached even modest village communities by 1750. By the early eighteenth century, for example, iron might be imported from Pennsylvania and carried to a Shropshire or Yorkshire forge for slitting, rods distributed by middlemen to cottage nailers, and the finished nails collected for distribution by wholesalers to ultimate markets, which again could be colonial America. Other industries, exemplified by London watchmaking, made still greater demands: parts were supplied from south Lancashire, and clock cases were provided by provincial specialists such as Gillow at Lancaster. And in the West Yorkshire woolen manufacture in 1588, these intermediate carrying and supply services occupied one-tenth of the entire work force.

Such factors explain first the recovery and then the major growth of Great Britain's urban sector, as transport, services, and resort came to supplant the lost manufacturing role of towns. Led by the dramatic growth of London—from around 100,000 in 1500 to 200,000 in 1600, 400,000 in 1650, 575,000 in 1700, and 675,000 in 1750—Great Britain became the second-most urbanized country of Europe during the early modern period. It dominated Europe's urbanization in a period in which, as de Vries has shown (1984), growth tended to be concentrated in the large towns of more than 10,000 persons. Between 1600 and 1750, England alone moved from 6.1 to 17.5 percent in such towns, whereas the rest of northwest Europe grew to only 12.1 percent and Europe as a whole only 9.4 percent. England accounted for 40 percent of all of Europe's urban growth between 1600 and 1750, and the rate of gain was accelerating: it made up two-thirds of Europe's urban growth in the eighteenth century as a whole. Symbolic of these new and critical urban functions were Manchester and Liverpool, ranking 12 and 24, respectively, in England's urban hierarchy in 1700. They both placed in Europe's top ten by 1850, the only cities within this group that were not national capitals. Reflecting the rapid growth of Great Britain's commercial-industrial complex in the period, its towns reinforced the processes of social, cultural, and behavioral change. Cultures of consumption, new tastes, new habits, and new aspirations for improvement all were fostered within Great Britain's rapidly growing urban sector.

Government's Role. Early modern Great Britain was able thus to change because even in 1500 it was economically better integrated than its European neighbors. It was an effective political unity, with unions with Wales in 1542 and Scotland in 1707. Before 1600, it had few internal customs barriers or other controls on commodity flows. And even the enlarged "Great Britain" after 1707 was a polity of a scale with which communications systems dependent upon sail, horse, and oar could cope. Government did strongly attempt to control and direct economic activities up to the end of the sixteenth century. Legislation covered a wide range of industries: acts against the enclosure of farmland began in 1485 and, after abolition in 1593–1594, were reinstated in 1597; in 1549, a Poll Tax on sheep attempted to curb excess grazing; "political lent" of 1563 introduced a second mandatory fish day to the week to stimulate seafaring; middlemen were subjected to controls in 1555 and 1563; and the labor market was regulated by the Statute of Artificers in 1563 and the poor law of 1597 and 1601. Many of these statutes lasted beyond 1750, but from the 1680s they were less enthusiastically and consistently enforced, as the doctrine of "trade as the child of freedom" gained currency. By the middle of the eighteenth century, textile workers could be found requesting justices to enforce minimum wage regulation and women in the market towns demanding a moral economy in which forestallers were prevented from raising prices and engrossing supplies. Intervention in commodity markets had become a matter of need, not regular habit.

By the first half of the eighteenth century, then, Great Britain was no haven of economic liberalism, since an extensive arsenal of tariff barriers, commodity-specific prohibitions, and corn laws were employed against the outside world. Domestically, however, it was unified, enjoying effective transport systems and sufficient economic freedom to permit the reallocation of its resources fully to secure potential gains from comparative advantage, the second fundamental of early modern Great Britain's development. Well before 1750, it enjoyed an economically efficient urban system and an unusual flexibility in the employment of its factor endowments.

In the demands made by its government, Great Britain differed little from its neighbors for most of this period. The paradox of its "financial revolution" from the 1690s was its subsequent capacity to sustain a larger "public sector" and higher taxation than its neighbors at lower political cost. From 1500, Great Britain experienced the normal problems of revenue raising and war finance, acutely revealed in its new subsidy of 1524–1525, the sales of the seized monastic lands from the 1540s, currency manipulation (as in the "great debasement" of the same period), wobbly borrowing from trade companies and monopolists until late in the seventeenth century, and chronic debt and recurrent financial crises, such as those of the 1590s, 1620s, and 1640. The removal of the king's head in 1649 took with it some of the more extreme financial expedients but did not end them, and it was the decades after the Crown's bankruptcy of 1672 that forced change. The use of an effective new tax, the excise, based on the Dutch model; customs revenues buoyed by expanding international trade; and the three great funding operations for public debt between 1694 and 1720—by the Bank of England, the East India Company, and the South Sea Company—combined to transform Great Britain's public finances and the domestic capital market. The political economist Postlethwayt (*Great Britain's New System*, 1757) was still able to perceive threats to liberty in the national debt and the unavoidable taxation it demanded, but he was almost the last major critic.

Since the 1680s, the new system of Great Britain's public revenues had created an effective stock market, reduced the market rate of interest from around 10 percent to 3.5 or less, and fostered banking agencies through the process of revenue raising. More the outcome of serendipity than design, and catch-up rather than European leadership, the system nonetheless distinguished the British economy and attracted the Dutch—the inspiration and model for many of these innovations—to the holdings of British public debt. On the expenditure side, seapower supported the growth of Great Britain's international trade, and supply needs stimulated a range of industries from bacon curing to cannon founding. On both sides of the public accounts, then, the new regime from the 1680s fostered capital formation, trade, and growth in industrial scale.

Great Britain shared many of the experiences of its neighbors between 1500 and 1760, and was little distinguished from them, except initially in relative isolation and backwardness. However, from the 1680s it displayed a striking social, personal, and economic fluidity and struck most visitors as distinctly different. Its social elite was more open than most in Europe, with few rigid barriers between the mercantile and commercial world and the old wealth of land. Marriage could take place freely between the two without serious loss of status. The social position of women was relatively strong: they were regarded as freer than their European sisters in behavior and movement, if disadvantaged by property laws. The country's middling sorts were major agencies of improvement, through turnpike road or river navigation or in the aspirational public sphere of assembly room, infirmary, or circulating library. And its artisans were robustly independent, extensively literate, and much given to the public reading of newspapers in alehouse or coffee shop. Long before the advent of industrialization, Great Britain was following a rather different path from that of the nonconstitutional monarchies of mainland Europe.

BIBLIOGRAPHY

Aldcroft, D. H., and M. J. Freeman, eds. *Transport in the Industrial Revolution*. Manchester, 1983.

Berg, Maxine. *The Age of Manufactures, 1700–1820: Industry, Innovation, and Work in Britain*. 2d ed. New York, 1994.

Brewer, J., and R. Porter, eds. *Consumption and the World of Goods*. London, 1993.

Chartres, J. A. *Internal Trade in England, 1500–1700*. London, 1977.

Chartres, J. A., ed. *The Industrial Revolutions*, vol. 1, *Pre-industrial Britain*. Cambridge, Mass., 1994.

Clark, Peter, ed. *The Cambridge Urban History of Britain*, vol. 2, *1540–1840*. Cambridge, 2000.

Clay, C. G. A. *Economic Expansion and Social Change: England, 1500–1700*. 2 vols. Cambridge, 1984.

Corfield, P. J. *The Impact of English Towns, 1700–1800*. Oxford, 1982.

De Vries, Jan. *European Urbanization, 1500–1800*. London, 1984.

Dickson, P. G. M. *The Financial Revolution in England: A Study in the Development of Public Credit, 1688–1756*. London, 1967.

Epstein, S. R. *Freedom and Growth: The Rise of States and Markets in Europe, 1300–1750*. New York, 2000.

Flinn, Michael W. *The History of the British Coal Industry*, vol. 2, *1700–1830: The Industrial Revolution*. Oxford, 1984.

Hatcher, John. *The History of the British Coal Industry*, vol. 1, *Before 1700: Towards the Age of Coal*. Oxford, 1993.

Hudson, Pat, ed. *Regions and Industries: A Perspective on the Industrial Revolution in Britain*. Cambridge, 1989.

Landes, D. S. *A Revolution in Time*. Cambridge, Mass., 1985.

Mathias, Peter. *The Transformation of England: Essays in the Economic and Social History of England in the Eighteenth Century*. London, 1979.

Overton, Mark. *Agricultural Revolution in England: The Transformation of the Agrarian Economy, 1500–1850*. Cambridge, 1996.

Prior, Mary, ed. *Women in English Society, 1500–1800*. London, 1985.

Thirsk, Joan, ed. *The Agrarian History of England and Wales*, vol. 4, *1500–1640*. Cambridge, 1967.

Thirsk, Joan, ed. *The Agrarian History of England and Wales*, vol. 5, *1640–1750*. Cambridge, 1985.

Weatherill, Lorna. *Consumer Behaviour and Material Culture in Britain, 1660–1760*. 2d ed. New York, 1996.

Woodward, D. M. *Men at Work: Labourers and Building Craftsmen in the Towns of Northern England, 1450–1750*. Cambridge, 1995.

Wrigley, E. A., and R. S. Schofield. *The Population History of England, 1541–1871*. London, 1981.

Wrigley, E. A. *People, Cities, and Wealth*. Oxford, 1987.

JOHN CHARTRES

ENTREPRENEURSHIP. The entrepreneur is a leading character in many accounts of economic growth. He appears in business biographies as a charismatic founder of a company; in industry studies as a prominent innovator, or a leading figure in a trade association or cartel; and in general economic histories as one of the hordes of self-employed small business owners who confer flexibility and dynamism on a market economy. Entrepreneurship is not confined to the private sector; it can also be discerned in the personalities of people who establish progressive charitable trusts and reform government administration.

Yet this very ubiquity of the entrepreneur is a cause for concern. Entrepreneurship means different things to different historians. It is rarely defined explicitly, and controversies over entrepreneurship often involve questions of semantics as well as fact. Few definite hypotheses have been deduced from theory, and few lawlike generalizations have been advanced from case-study evidence.

Economic Theories of the Entrepreneur. The term *entrepreneur* appears to have been introduced into economic theory by Richard Cantillon (1759), an Irish economist of French descent. According to Cantillon, the entrepreneur is a specialist in taking on risk. He "insures" workers by buying their output for resale before consumers have indicated how much they are willing to pay for it. The workers receive an assured income (in the short run, at least), while the entrepreneur bears the risk caused by price fluctuations in consumer markets.

This idea was refined by the U.S. economist Frank Knight (1921), who distinguished between risk, which is insurable, and uncertainty, which is not. Risk refers to recurrent events whose relative frequency is known from past experience; uncertainty relates to unique events whose probability can be only subjectively estimated. Knight thought that most of the risks relating to production and marketing fall into the latter category. Since business owners cannot insure against these risks, they are left to bear them by themselves. Profit is a reward for bearing this uninsurable risk: it is the reward of the pure entrepreneur.

Popular notions of entrepreneurship are based on the heroic vision of Joseph A. Schumpeter (1934). The entrepreneur is visualized as someone who creates new industries, thereby precipitating major structural changes in the economy. The entrepreneur innovates by carrying out new combinations. He is not a pure inventor, because he adopts the inventions made by others; nor is he a financier, because he relies on bankers to fund his investments.

The entrepreneur makes the crucial decision to commit resources to the exploitation of new ideas. An element of calculation is involved, but it is not pure calculation because not all of the relevant factors can be accurately measured. He is motivated by profit, but not purely by profit: the other motivators include the "dream and the will to found a private kingdom"; the "will to conquer: the impulse to fight, to prove oneself superior to others"; and the "joy of creating."

Schumpeter was concerned with the "high level" kind of entrepreneurship that historically has led to the creation of railways, the development of the chemical industry, and the growth of integrated oil companies. His analysis left little room for the much more common, but no less important, "low level" entrepreneurship carried on by small firms, particularly by those in the wholesale and retail trades. Alfred Marshall (1919) described the role of these firms in some detail but omitted them from his formal analysis of supply and demand.

The essence of low-level entrepreneurship can be explained by the Austrian approach of Friedrich A. von Hayek (1937) and Israel M. Kirzner (1973). Entrepreneurs are middlemen who provide price quotations as an invitation to trade. While bureaucrats in a socialist economy have little incentive to discover prices for themselves, entrepreneurs in a market economy are motivated to do so by profit opportunities. They hope to profit by buying low and selling high. In the long run, competition between entrepreneurs arbitrages away price differentials; but in the short run, such differentials, once discovered, generate a profit for the entrepreneur.

Judgmental Decision-Making. The insights of these economists can be synthesized by identifying an entrepreneurial function that is common to all approaches. This is the exercise of judgment in decision making (Casson, 1982). Thus, a middleman who buys before he knows the price at which he can resell must make a judgment about what the future price will be, while an innovator must assess whether a new product will prove attractive to consumers.

If information were freely available and could be costlessly processed, then there would be no need for judgment, and no mistakes would ever be made. But in practice, information is costly. Decision makers cannot afford to collect all the information they need, and so they have to act under uncertainty. But the uncertainty faced by one person may be different from the uncertainty faced by another. Sources of primary information are highly localized; for example, only people "on the spot" can directly observe an event. Different people in different places will therefore have different perceptions of any given situation. They may therefore make different decisions. The nature of the decision thus depends on the identity of the person who makes it. The entrepreneur matters because his or her judgment of a situation is potentially unique.

If a situation recurs frequently, it is worthwhile investigating it carefully in order to derive a suitable decision rule. The information required to implement the rule can then be collected on a regular basis. Once this optimal decision rule has been specified, there is no further need for the entrepreneur. Now consider the opposite case of an entirely novel situation, which is complex to analyze and where a decision has to be made quickly. It is so unusual that it never pays to investigate it fully. Nobody knows the correct decision rule. To improvise a decision quickly, people have to rely on their intuition and on any relevant information that they can retrieve from their memory. Different intuitions, combined with different memories, lead to different decisions.

The greater the cost of a mistake, the greater the importance of finding the appropriate person to make the decision. The cost of a mistake depends upon the value of the resources involved and the extent to which an erroneous decision can be reversed before it is too late. The greater the "sunk costs" involved, the more important the quality of judgment becomes, and the more important it is that the decision is made by a fully competent entrepreneur.

The Supply of Good Judgment. People differ in their quality of judgment. In a free society, people are allowed to decide for themselves whether their judgment is good. In choosing their occupations, people who are confident that their judgment is good will tend to gravitate to jobs that call for intensive use of judgment, while those who believe that their judgment is bad will gravitate to jobs where other people make decisions for them. On this view, entrepreneurs will *specialize* in making judgmental decisions. Specialization is rarely complete, however: most entrepreneurial roles also involve some minor routine, as well as ritual activity, such as making speeches. Specialization in entrepreneurship is not total, therefore, but a matter of degree. Although everyone makes judgmental decisions from time to time—such as whether to marry, or change jobs, or relocate—entrepreneurs specialize in making these decisions on behalf of other people.

Not all entrepreneurs are successful. There is a strong bias in the historical literature toward successful entrepreneurs, for fairly obvious reasons: Successful entrepreneurs make an impact on the national economy; they are inclined to self-promotion; and the enterprises they create survive long enough to leave good records. The successful entrepreneurs are those whose confidence in their judgment turns out to be well placed. For every high-profile success, however, there are numerous failures. Small start-up businesses are notoriously prone to failure in the first two to three years. Failures are often caused by overconfidence—though bad luck may also play a part.

Entrepreneurship is a scarce resource, and so it is important to know whether its supply can be increased. This raises the question of whether entrepreneurs are "born" or "made." There is little evidence that entrepreneurial ability is inherited: the evidence on family firms suggests that sons usually display less initiative than the fathers they succeed. There is some support for the idea that entrepreneurial qualities are incubated in adversity. Fatalistic acceptance of poverty is certainly not an entrepreneurial characteristic, but determination to reverse an economic setback often seems to be (Brenner, 1983). Many entrepreneurs claim to be "self-made," but it is impossible to know whether, in making this claim, they are simply unwilling to give credit to parents, teachers, and others who have helped them along the way.

The Contractual Position of the Entrepreneur. A good deal of historical evidence is based on the archives of firms; and in applying the theory of entrepreneurship, it is obviously important to know which members of a firm are entrepreneurs—the owner, the chief executive he employs, or both?

In a market economy, specialization by entrepreneurs takes two main forms. In the first, the entrepreneur is an employee, and in the second he or she owns a firm in which others invest. Looked at from the point of view of an entrepreneur, the problem is how to gain control of resources on a significant scale with modest personal means. One method is to obtain a job that gives scope for the exercise of judgment over how the employer's resources are used; the other is to become self-employed and borrow sufficient funds to buy the requisite resources.

Many business biographies clearly demonstrate that entrepreneurial initiative is often supplied by imaginative and committed employees. It is a mistake to regard the archetypal entrepreneur as the owner of a small firm. Many successful owner-entrepreneurs have first acquired their experience by exercising their talents as someone else's employee—often in a large professionally run firm. They left their previous employment to found their own business only when their self-confidence had grown to the point where they felt that the constraints upon them had become too great, and that the prospective rewards for success were too small.

Information Synthesis. Decision making normally requires the synthesis of different types of information. The high-level entrepreneur of the Schumpeterian type, for example, needs to synthesize information about new inventions with information about trends in product demand, and in the prices of raw materials, in order to determine whether an innovation is worthwhile. If the entrepreneur does not possess this information himself, then he must know where to acquire it. If some of the information is confidential, then it will have to be acquired through personal contact rather than from published sources. The entrepreneur, therefore, needs to create a network of social contacts that can feed him the information that he requires.

Location in a major metropolis is a great advantage from this point of view. This is the place where travelers often call first when arriving from overseas; it is where journalists collect information for their stories, and where groups of people assemble to make important decisions—politicians in parliament, business leaders at their headquarters, and so on. Entrepreneurship is a distinctly urban activity.

Geographical Mobility of the Entrepreneur. It was noted above that everyone makes decisions from time to time. Entrepreneurs will reveal their qualities by the kind of choices they make. Young people have to decide, at some stage, whether to remain in the place they grew up or to move elsewhere. Entrepreneurial people are more likely to move and nonentrepreneurial people to stay. Isolated rural areas where there are few opportunities for profit tend to selectively lose their more entrepreneurial young people. Conversely, large cities tend to attract entrepreneurial young people.

"Push" as well as "pull" factors may stimulate migration—an extreme example being the expulsion of ethnic minorities by totalitarian political regimes. This may range from the persecution of religious sects, to the dispossession of peasants, to the expropriation of a wealthy merchant class. While such measures do not discriminate between entrepreneurs and nonentrepreneurs in terms of whether people move, they may well discriminate in terms of where the migrants terminate their travels. The least entrepreneurial may well stop at the first place of refuge, while the more entrepreneurial may continue in search of the most promising location.

While immigrants who have been expelled from other countries might be thought to be, on balance, less entrepreneurial than the purely "economic" migrant, the effect of their adversity on their motivation should not be overlooked. If loss of wealth and status stimulates a desire to restore the family's fortunes, then expulsion may turn into a very powerful motivator of success.

The Institutional Framework. Entrepreneurs who are prepared to move long distances have a choice of political regimes under which to operate. The regimes that are most attractive to mobile entrepreneurs are likely to possess the classic institutions of the liberal market economy. They will have some or all of the following characteristics:

- Private property, which is freely alienable, subject to certain minimal restrictions;
- Freedom of movement and freedom to associate with business partners;
- Confidentiality of business information, especially regarding relations with customers and suppliers;
- Protection of creative work through patents, copyright, design protection, and so on;

- Access to impartial courts, which will enforce property rights and which have the competence to settle complex commercial claims;
- A stable currency, based on prudent control of the money supply;
- Democratic government, with sufficient balance of power between opposing interests to reduce the risks of Draconian interventions in industry and commerce;
- Openness to immigration by entrepreneurs and skilled workers (and possibly other groups as well).

Entrepreneurs not only move between industries within the private sector: they also can move between the private sector, the nonprofit sector, and the government sector. Choice of sector will reflect the entrepreneur's preferences. Some entrepreneurs consider the importance of pecuniary rewards and the scope for innovative behavior in the private and public sectors.

Occupational Mobility of the Entrepreneur. The relative mobility of the entrepreneur applies to occupation as well as to location. Young men who remain behind in a locality may well follow their father into the same line of business. Where father is an employee, they follow him "into the works" or "down the pit." To those with narrow horizons and a parochial outlook, any long-standing local industry may appear secure. Such nonentrepreneurial workers may eventually join the ranks of the "structurally unemployed."

The same mechanism applies in a family firm (Church, 1993). "One day all this will be yours," the father tells the son, and the son feels morally obliged to succeed his father, even though his interests lie elsewhere. A more entrepreneurial son might turn down the offer and set up his own business in a different industry, forcing the father to look outside the family for a successor—possibly with beneficial results for the firm.

Business owners who remain behind in a declining industry or region may join forces to lobby for protective tariffs or industrial subsidies. They harness organizations, such as trade associations, which originally may have been established to provide training, for price-fixing purposes instead (Olson, 1982). A secretive and conspiratorial business culture develops, reflecting the entrepreneurial weaknesses of the business group. Similarly, craft guilds or trades unions may try to "protect jobs" by resisting technological change. Inflexible attitudes within a region may deter entrepreneurs in "sunrise" industries, who move away to areas where they have more freedom of action. This suggests that successive waves of innovation will move around a country, avoiding areas where earlier innovations have stagnated and ossified the business culture (Pollard, 1981). Only the metropolis will remain vibrant because of its continuing ability to attract young entrepreneurs. If the me-

tropolis, too, goes into decline, then the outlook for the entire national economy is likely to be bad.

Historical Applications of the Concept of the Entrepreneur. Early academic writers on British economic and social history employed the concept of the entrepreneur mainly as a social stereotype. The Victorian entrepreneur was a member of an upwardly mobile lower middle class, imbued with the bourgeois values of proprietary capitalism. The Victorians themselves seem to have been more impressed with their own engineering feats than with their entrepreneurial achievements; thus it was the civil and mechanical engineers, rather than the railway promoters or the company secretaries, that were seen as the heroes of the Railway Revolution (Smiles, 1862). More generally, it was the creation of the empire, rather than an entrepreneurial domestic economy, that was the main political preoccupation. Modern interest in Victorian entrepreneurship is more a reflection of a desire to recover something that has been lost than the continuation of a concern that the Victorians themselves expressed.

In the United States, a powerful mythology developed around the "rags to riches" entrepreneur (Sarachek, 1978), but detailed investigations (see, for example, Taussig, 1915) highlighted the middle-class professional origins of many successful entrepreneurs.

Schumpeter (1939) provided one of the earliest economic applications of entrepreneurial theory. He identified five main types of "new combinations" effected by entrepreneurs: new products, new processes of production, the development of new export markets, the discovery of new sources of raw material supply, and the creation of new forms of institution, such as the cartel or trust. Schumpeter's classification fits well with the major forms of innovation that occurred in Europe during the "Age of High Imperialism," from 1870 to 1914. The large-scale entrepreneurial exploits of the "robber barons" of the late nineteenth century—Cornelius Vanderbilt, E. H. Harriman, John D. Rockefeller, and so on—also conform well to Schumpeter's model. Schumpeter claimed that his schema fitted any economy that made extensive use of credit—from the growth of Mediterranean trade during the Renaissance onward. He also claimed that he could explain Kondratieff "long waves" of fifty to sixty years' duration by the periodic clustering of innovations since the Industrial Revolution. Unfortunately, however, the empirical basis of Schumpeter's speculations on long waves has not stood the test of time very well (see Solomou, 1987).

Pursuing the Schumpeterian theme, Hughes (1965) examined the influence of the "vital few" in promoting economic growth. Hughes's approach is mainly biographical, emphasizing the personality factor in entrepreneurship. The great value of his contribution lies in the fact that he recognizes the role of the entrepreneur in the public as well as the private sector, although he sees the public sector entrepreneur as heavily implicated in the growth of bureaucracy. The policy implication of Hughes's study appears to be that people with entrepreneurial personalities need to be attracted into the private sector where, thanks to competitive markets, the incentives are better aligned with the long-run public interest.

A rather similar conclusion arises from Jones's (1981, 1988) studies of long-term world economic growth. Adopting an international comparative perspective, Jones argues that entrepreneurship is a natural feature of human behavior that government can either encourage or suppress. Encouragement is provided by a regime of freedom under law, which allows people to carry out experiments in commercial and industrial organization at their own expense. Suppression is effected by governments that fall into the hands of elites, who think they know best which experiments are socially desirable and which are not. They subsidize prestigious experiments out of taxes, and repress ordinary experiments because they are seen as either useless, immoral, or politically subversive.

The Debate on Entrepreneurial Decline. The most substantive recent discussion of entrepreneurship has focused on the alleged decline of entrepreneurship in Great Britain after 1870 (see, for example, Aldcroft, 1964; Sandberg, 1981). This decline is seen as having both technological and cultural roots (Wiener, 1981). One of the major symptoms of failure is said to be lack of investment in new technologies in key industries. It has been correctly pointed out, however, that good entrepreneurship does not always mean deciding to invest, for in many situations the correct decision is not to invest at all. Nor is innovation always an indicator of good entrepreneurship; it sometimes pays to let others make the first move, and to learn from their mistakes.

A complete analysis of Britsh entrepreneurial decline needs to embed the issue within a wider perspective. In late-Victorian Great Britain there was significant emigration of entrepreneurial individuals who left to colonize the growing empire. The London capital market played a major role in channeling resources to their overseas ventures. The great railway and mining entrepreneurs did not so much disappear as transfer their skills overseas once the domestic railway system had matured and traditional mining deposits had become exhausted. Supplies of entrepreneurship are finite, and migration is a selective process. It is therefore hardly surprising that the limited group of less entrepreneurial businessmen who remained behind in Great Britain, and inherited family businesses, concentrated their efforts on managing their existing Imperial export trade, rather than pioneering new industries, in the manner of entrepreneurs in countries that were attempting to "catch up" with Great Britain. Moreover, insofar as there were deficiencies in U.K. technological innovation, these may have more to do with the limitation of the English university system than with the quality of entrepreneurship per se—thus Clydeside entrepreneurs, drawing on the academic engineering expertise of Scottish universities, were very active in high-technology shipbuilding throughout the period of "decline."

The Market for Entrepreneurs. The demand for entrepreneurship, like the demand for any other factor of production, is a derived demand. Unlike more conventional factors of production, however, the demand for entrepreneurship derives not from the overall level of product demand, but rather from the volatility of such demand. Volatility generates novel and complex situations that call for improvised decisions. When volatility increases, there is an increase in the demand for entrepreneurs and a corresponding decline in the demand for managers. This is normally reflected in the formation of more small firms and the restructuring of large firms. The large firms may disappear through bankruptcy, or be split up through management buyout and "asset-stripping"; alternatively, they may be reorganized in a more flexible form, as a coalition of entrepreneurs. Greater competition to hire entrepreneurial employees means that the rewards of entrepreneurship will rise. Pay structures will tend to become more flexible because it will no longer be possible to offer both entrepreneurial employees and nonentrepreneurial employees the same rates of pay.

Enterprise Culture. When there is a general perception in a society that volatility has increased, social and political attitudes may change as well. This is what appears to have happened in many Western industrial countries toward the end of the 1970s. Increasing awareness of global competition, and the failure of large-firm "national champions" to respond effectively, led people to believe that future job creation would come from small business. Start-up entrepreneurs became popular role models, creating a new set of myths about the "rags to riches" entrepreneur, and encouraging young people to make their careers in the private sector.

Considered as a historical phenomenon, the enterprise culture of the 1980s and 1990s was a natural reaction to some of the antientrepreneurial attitudes that had taken root in the West in the early postwar period. It should not be inferred, however, that this enterprise culture was based on a correct understanding of the role of the entrepreneur. The highly competitive and materialistic form of individualism promoted by "enterprise culture" did not accurately represent the dominant values of successful entrepreneurs of previous generations. For example, the Victorian railway entrepreneurs operated through social networks based in Great Britain's major provincial towns and cities. The limited amount of historical evidence that has been collected and analyzed in a systematic way suggests that successful entrepreneurship is as much a cooperative endeavor, mediated by social networks, as a purely individualistic and competitive one.

BIBLIOGRAPHY

Aldcroft, Derek. "The Entrepreneur and the British Economy, 1870–1914." *Economic History Review* 2d ser. 17 (1964), 113–134.

Brenner, Reuven. *History: The Human Gamble*. Chicago, 1983.

Cantillon, Richard. *Essai sur la nature du commerce en générale*, edited with an English translation by Henry Higgs. London, 1931.

Casson, Mark. *The Entrepreneur: An Economic Theory*. Oxford, 1982.

Church, Roy. "The Family Firm in Industrial Capitalism: International Perspectives on Hypotheses and History." *Business History* 35. 4, (1993), 17–43.

Hayek, Friedrich A. von. "Economics and Knowledge." *Economica* new ser. 4 (1937), 33–54.

Hughes, Jonathan R. T. *The Vital Few: The Entrepreneur and American Economic Progress*. New York, 1965.

Jones, Eric. *The European Miracle*. Cambridge, 1981.

Jones, Eric. *Growth Recurring*. Oxford, 1988.

Kirzner, Israel M. *Competition and Entrepreneurship*. Chicago, 1973.

Knight, Frank H. *Risk, Uncertainty, and Profit*. Boston, 1921.

Marshall, Alfred. *Industry and Trade*. London, 1919.

Olson, Mancur. *The Rise and Decline of Nations*. New Haven, 1982.

Pollard, Sidney. *Peaceful Conquest*. Oxford, 1981.

Sandberg, L. G. "The Entrepreneur and Technological Change." In *The Economic History of Britain since 1700*, edited by R. Floud and D. McCloskey, vol. 2, *1860 to the 1970s*, pp. 99–120. Cambridge, 1981.

Sarachek, B. "American Entrepreneurs and the Horatio Alger Myth." *Journal of Economic History* 38 (1978), 439–156.

Schumpeter, Joseph A. *The Theory of Economic Development*. Translated by Redvers Opie. Cambridge, Mass., 1934.

Schumpeter, Joseph A. *Business Cycles*. New York, 1939.

Smiles, Samuel. *Lives of the Engineers*. London, 1862.

Solomou, Solomos. *Phases of Economic Growth, 1850–1973*. Cambridge, 1987.

Taussig, Frank W. *Inventors and Moneymakers*. New York, 1915.

Wiener, Martin J. *English Culture and the Decline of the Industrial Spirit*. Cambridge, 1981.

MARK CASSON

ENVIRONMENT [*This entry contains two subentries, a historical overview and a discussion of environmental policies and regulation.*]

Historical Overview

With respect to the natural environment, the main concerns for economic historians are the opportunities and costs for settlement and production afforded or imposed by variations in the initial conditions of different ecosystems; the impact of human occupation; and the consequences or "kickback" of the drastic modifications that have taken place. The environment is taken here as comprising the whole human habitat: geology, landforms, and soils; deserts, forests, and plains; rivers and seas; the climate; competing and collaborating species, including those that make up the "disease environment"; and the "built environment" of cities. Much economic history explicitly or implicitly discusses waves of human occupation of various habitats, and the stages by which their use, or the use of elements within them, has repeatedly been intensified. The number of interactions is enormous and has changed kaleidoscopically. Nevertheless, economic historians have not paid nearly as much attention to the environment as ecologists, geographers, and adherents of the belief that there is a global environmental crisis.

Human Impact and Responses. Originally, humans resided as small groups in vast untouched savannas and forests; next, for several millennia, humans dwelt alongside nature, dominating only a few habitats such as large townscapes; lastly, in the industrial nineteenth and twentieth centuries, humans surrounded nature, often reducing pockets of relatively unaltered vegetation to enclaves and corralling wildlife in reserves. This suggests a crescendo of unpleasing changes but that is a one-sided view: modern economies have created enough wealth to encourage a taste for "wild" nature, formerly ignored or abhorred, and provided the wherewithal to reserve areas of natural land in which to house it. They have also become rich and interested enough to conserve once-threatened species and to bring about the numerical recovery of some of them, at times to pest proportions. A "Kuznets curve" has been found in the forested area of Thailand, meaning that forests shrank in the early stages of development but began to expand again once high levels of income were attained. The crossover point from deforestation to reafforestation came c. 1973 at a per-capita GDP of U.S. $1,000. In several European countries an equivalent crossover may have taken place around 1890 at a per-capita GDP level of about $1,750.

That one species, *Homo sapiens*, has become so numerous and virtually ubiquitous in its distribution, as well as a heavy user of an infinite range of natural products, has created almost tautologically a massive impact. Other species have been moved aside, reduced in numbers, and sometimes driven to extinction. In the process habitats have been altered, often becoming simpler, though with their energy flows expanded. The main agency has been the replacement of natural vegetation by higher and higher yielding crops specially bred to maximize such desirable properties as food and fiber. Although the agricultural area has been immensely extended, the damage to the diversity of species has often been surprisingly slight. For example, 90 percent of the Amazonian forests in Brazil was cleared with no loss of species. Everywhere the mix and populations of nonhuman species have been transformed, yet claims that large numbers of extinctions are still occurring are often propaganda by nongovernmental organizations acting as "green" firms and competing for subscriptions by announcing one alleged threat or loss after another.

Environmental activism began in the nineteenth century; the roots of the green movement, like those of the Nazis, go back to the holistic ecology of Haeckel. But since 1970 the rise of environmentalism has been prodigious. This seems to reflect the decline of alternative ideologies (Marxism, organized religion) rather than genuinely worsening environmental ill-health in the rich countries in which it mainly emerged. Complex changes nevertheless continue to be described as signs of historically unprecedented, irreversible pressure on the entire global environment. Certainly, cultural preferences have sometimes lagged behind development and reinforced this opinion: the "East Asian economic miracle" was so successful between 1960 and 1995 that the Japanese, for example, were able to consume infinitely more traditional animal products, such as whales and ivory, depleting the stocks of distant regions. But this emphasis is correcting itself; as an instance, conservation has already permitted many whale populations to rebound. Industrialization has usually been accompanied by an "environmental cycle." Industrial economies initially emit much pollution and use huge volumes of raw materials. But as their industrial structure matures and incomes grow, they shift to resource-saving technologies and abandon the most polluting industries. They start to exert a taste for clean surroundings and accept farmed substitutes instead of the products of hunting, gathering, and fishing.

Consequences for Species and Habitats. Generalizations founded on detailed research into the economic history of forestry, fishing, or whaling have been far fewer than popular assertions about environmental harm. Serious work has been done on urban settlement, factory industry, agriculture, and mining, but ecologists have attended most to the environmental implications. The upgrading of habitats has received proportionately less attention. Here, two major effects may be mentioned. First, there have been fundamental translocations of species, as in the Arab Agricultural Revolution, which carried productive crops from India as far west as Spain; the "Columbian Exchange," which took corn, potatoes, and peanuts from the Americas as far afield as Africa and China; the spread of European farm plants and animals to the prairies, pampas, veldt, and outback; and the more ornamental results of the nineteenth-century acclimatization societies, which expanded the range of the flora and fauna in Europe's colonies. Second, lumbering and clearing land for agriculture has opened up dense forests and increased the "ecotone" (the edge between two types of habitat, favored by many species for breeding and feeding). Thus the net effect of habitat changes was not necessarily the devastation commonly reported: songbirds in eastern North America became commoner than they were in the early nineteenth century and there are now more trees in Australia than at the time of Captain Cook.

Premodern activity, using less potent tools (except for fire) and at far lower human population densities than today, brought about relatively greater changes without the compensations that increased wealth has made possible. The first major impact may have been the "Pleistocene Overkill" during which the largest mammals—the megafauna—were exterminated. Although human agency in that extermination is disputed, large animals were certainly slaughtered en masse in much more recent times—e.g., when American Indians drove herds of bison over cliffs. More evidence, in the form of the fossil record, survives about a wave of extinctions that eliminated more than two thousand bird species through the human occupation of tropical islands in the Pacific before 1000 CE. This assault reduced the number of bird species in the world by 20 percent, leaving the subsequent European "discoverers" with only mopping-up operations.

The literature typically portrays premodern and non-European humans as natural conservationists. Some communities—including many in the Western world—did conserve edible species in order to sustain the harvest. Alternatively, the catch was regulated to share out the resource, or private property rights were established. An example relates to colonies of the Edible-Nest Swiftlet in Indonesia, the salival nests of which make birds'-nest soup. Regulation may have had conservational effects, but the aim was sometimes to reserve preferred species, such as turtles in Tahiti, for the elite. And, at the same time, communities the world over did engage in wasteful slaughter, as during "ring shoots," when animals were driven together and massacred. Often the aim in part was pest control—understandable, since a significant effect of human modification of the environment, notably cropgrowing, is to provide excellent food and breeding sites for adaptable species like deer, monkeys, and weaverbirds, which thereupon explode in numbers.

Intensified Human Uses. The European colonization from the end of the fifteenth century represented a wider diffusion of dense human populations than ever before. Walter Bagehot, nineteenth-century editor of *The Economist*, called these colonists the "conquering *swarm*." They often made explicit searches for natural resources, such as for beavers, whose pelts were used to cover hats; and for whales, for lamp and lubricating oil. Overall European occupation transformed habitats across the world: clearing forests, ploughing grasslands, introducing the entire European "living entourage" of domestic animals besides the associated pests and weeds, and founding great cities where none had existed. Only with respect to a few cities that the Soviets established in northern Siberia, and which Russia cannot perhaps afford to provision, is there any sign that humanity may retreat.

Global population growth and development mean that even areas beyond the frontiers of former European empires have witnessed all the changes associated with dense urban-industrial living. Cities replaced farmland, which in turn replaced native vegetation. Human populations drew food, fuel, and fiber from distant fields, woods, mines, and oilwells and thus initiated land-use changes on the far side of the world. Closer to home they crowded out native flora and fauna, brought in exotic species to make parks and gardens, and let others come in free-riding with trade goods. The translocation of species is now beyond unscrambling. The costs associated with the human impact, even desertification, salination, and urban pollution, all of which had historical forerunners or extended existing trends, have nevertheless proved less than the benefits. The physical manifestations are more visible than the economic consequences.

The exception most discussed is the warming of the earth's atmosphere through the emission of carbon dioxide (CO_2). This emission constituted the first global "insult" when agricultural clearances simultaneously burned vegetation on several continents in the late nineteenth century, although the anthropogenic origin of the present elevated CO_2 levels remains uncertain. In other respects air quality in the richer countries has improved: solid particles in the atmosphere of American cities have been declining since 1914. Where the trend is otherwise, as in China, economic growth will presumably make better technologies affordable and increase demands for cleanups of the type demanded in other countries once their incomes rose. Economic history permits us to view environmental change as a series of overlapped, long-term processes involving considerable self-correction. The record shows net losses of species and natural habitats but, where the market prevails, countervailing tendencies that have rescued many species and created historicized landscapes of types long familiar, and well loved, in Europe. The record is more damning in sometime command economies like Maoist China and the former Soviet Union, where the failure to require the managers of state-owned enterprises to internalize their costs and rein in negative externalities meant fifty or seventy years of unrestrained pollution.

Rather than climatic distress, the most disturbing element in ecological globalization is probably the disease environment. Global epidemics have occurred before, notably influenza, which may have killed 20 million people in 1918–1919; international ones like the medieval Black Death (bubonic plague); and "virgin soil" outbreaks like the diseases that were carried overseas by colonialists and weakened the resistance of indigenous populations. Transport connections are now so pervasive as to dwarf these precedents and another flu pandemic is confidently, if morbidly, anticipated.

Major Economic Effects. It is not easy to demonstrate that differences in the environment from place to place, or fluctuations in conditions such as warming or cooling of the climate over time, have really played a determining role in economic activity. For example, the late-medieval climatic deterioration was accompanied by falling, not rising, grain prices. Population and hence demand trends have been left out of account, as have ingenuity, adaptability, and inventiveness.

But some people still argue that differential endowments have been the key to economic experience. One argument is that mammals capable of becoming beasts of burden differed among the continents, thus permitting development here but not there. Another is that the indented coastline of Europe indicated a landscape variety that led to the rise of multiple political units, and that competition among these generated an economic growth not secured in the blander landscapes of Asia. The leaps between endowment and outcome in these interpretations by natural scientists are not characteristic of economic history itself.

The most prominent of the relevant debates surrounds Karl Wittfogel's thesis of "Oriental despotism." Wittfogel urged that the imperatives of irrigated farming in the great river valleys of the Middle East and Orient stultified development. To coordinate digging channels and embanking thousands of miles of rivers, as well as allocating water to farming communities one after the other down each valley, necessitated a central authority. The social contract notionally agreed between the peasantry and the central authority required that peasants cede power to, say, the Chinese emperor. Yet by agreeing, as it were, to an emperor's right to dragoon labor corvées for irrigation works, and to draft their sons into his army, they ceded too much. The ruler became all-powerful and commandeered all surplus revenues for luxurious living at his court. The peasantry could never hold back enough to raise its own consumption, much less accumulate capital for nonagricultural investments. The system was trapped in a low-level environmental equilibrium.

This thesis fitted the stereotypes of long-run Chinese history. For Cold War purposes, Wittfogel extended it to explain the sterility of command economies. However, it does not fit less stylized versions of Chinese or other histories. Irrigation works were organized by local gentry, for cash. Peasants were able to retain some of the harvest, which they converted, so to speak, into slow, continual population growth. A feature of the Chinese empires is also how little tax reached the emperor and the extent to which his function was symbolic.

The Wittfogel thesis was embroiled in a bitter dispute within Marxism. Stalin vehemently rejected the idea that the environment determined, or even restricted, human activity. Soviet man, he declared, could conquer nature and achieve whatever he undertook. The classical economists, too, had inclined to point out that bananas could be grown at the North Pole. What both these "possibilist" strands of thought underplayed was the matter of costs, which returns us to the likelihood that different endowments did shape, though not determine, economic history.

Although few will deny that the costs of occupying marginal environments like deserts or snowfields are high, and that natural conditions do thus have an effect, the point is minor. Marginal habitats are marginal, and most economic history has taken place elsewhere. A more significant case is the topics, where indigenous populations can be dense but development remains elusive. Old arguments have been disinterred that there is an inherent "tropical deficit." Counterclaims say that the environment is secondary and what matters is good policy arising from good government, which could find ways of overcoming difficulties. One example was in the nineteenth century, when quinine conquered the malaria that had made West Africa the "white man's grave." The question of whether the political deficit itself was and is a function of the natural environment has not been resolved.

A related manner in which the environment may have had some influence was through the differential incidence of disasters like earthquakes, volcanic eruptions, epidemics, or epizootics. These have all been associated with interrupted development, most plausibly in Central America. Disasters are by definition sharp shocks to which adaptation is difficult. However, few of them are truly natural, and their force is muffled or amplified by the technology, materials, finance, and social organization available to the affected populations. Unless we can show, as is probable only in extreme cases, that the social weakness results directly from the shocks, the full independence of environmental considerations is again compromised.

Environment and Religon. An even more prominent debate concerns the degree to which Christianity was responsible for a drive toward "Faustian mastery" over the environment. The defining text was a 1967 article by Lynn White, "The Historical Roots of Our Ecologic[al] Crisis." With its presupposition that there is such a crisis, this paper caught the mood of the 1970s. The case it made chimed with other arguments that blamed Europeans for the alleged environmental destruction of the postmedieval world; it replaced triumphal optimism about the Industrial Revolution and the American frontier with eco-pessimism.

Other authors found that the crucial turn from the animistic worship of nature to its untrammeled exploitation came earlier, in Mesopotamia, ancient Israel, or the classical world. However, the point is unclear: animists have usually found it acceptable to fell trees, mine mountains, or dam brooks once they have placated the spirits in charge. Temples may preserve original vegetation in the sacred groves they stand in, but this only reveals that most of the forest has been cleared. To give an illustration from an Eastern religion, Shinto may raise nature to the level of humanity but the unexpected corollary is that nature is required to look after itself. For practical purposes there is little sensitivity here to counterpoint Christianity's purported license to use nature as it likes.

The case that Christianity is responsible for the altered environment of recent centuries superficially accords with the occupation of the earth by intrusive European populations and their inevitable displacement of many nonhuman species (though scarcely with their synthesis of agreeable new humanized landscapes). The argument suffers from several defects. It is at odds with what the Bible actually says about Christian stewardship. It relies on particular textual readings without evidence that these were what actually motivated peasants grubbing out trees and burning the bush. In addition, it lacks "controls" in the economic history of non-Christian civilizations, and instead contrasts Western destructiveness with a fictitious Eastern tenderness. In several publications, Tuan countered Lynn White by showing that China's environmental record was not benign, whatever the imperial pronouncements claimed. The Chinese cleared 670 million acres of forest, promoted the erosion of hillsides, and brought about the silting of their river systems. In this debate, as in so much of environmental history, fashionable opinion has submerged research-based generalizations. Mainstream economic historians have put up little serious resistance. The situation, fortunately, differs with respect to the economic history of natural resource use.

BIBLIOGRAPHY

Budiansky, Stephen. "Chaos in Eden." *New Scientist* (14 Oct. 1995), 33–35. Succinct exposé of the misuse of ecological concepts in interpreting the long-run course of environmental change.

Cronon, William. *Changes in the Land: Indians, Colonists, and the Ecology of New England.* New York, 1983. Pioneering work, already a classic, on the environmental impact of different cultures.

Crosby, Alfred W. *The Columbian Exchange.* Westport, Conn., 1972. Pioneering work, now a classic, on a major early international translocation of crops.

Crosby, Alfred W. *Ecological Imperialism: The Biological Expansion of Europe, 900–1900.* Cambridge, 1986. Detailed analysis of the environmental changes produced by European settlement overseas.

Dubos, René. *Wooing of Earth.* London, 1980. Classic modern work establishing the human origin of many supposedly "natural" landscapes.

Jones, E. L. "The History of Natural Resource Exploitation in the Western World." *Research in Economic History* Supp. 6 (1991), 235–252. Detailed examination of the actual treatment of the environment by European, ancient, and Asian civilizations.

Mather, A. S., et al. "Environmental Kuznets Curves and Forest Trends." *Geography* 84.1 (1999), 55–65. Presents evidence of dip, then recovery, in area under woodland during economic development.

Newbigin, Marion L. *Man and His Conquest of Nature.* London, 1922. Survey of the human environmental impact treated, characteristically for the period, as an achievement.

Richards, J. F. "World Environmental History and Economic Development." In *Sustainable Development of the Biosphere,* edited by

W. Clark and R. Munn, pp. 53–74. Cambridge, 1986. Serious, wide-ranging, survey of the human impact.

Simmons, Ian G. *Changing the Face of the Earth: Culture, Environment, History*. Oxford, 1989. Massive, one-man successor volume to the standard collection edited a generation earlier by W. L. Thomas. Contains a very long and immensely useful bibliography.

Simon, Julian L., ed. *The State of Humanity*. Oxford, 1995. Major analyses, including those by economic historians, with important data on status and trends in environmental indicators.

Smil, Vaclav. *The Bad Earth*: *Environmental Degradation in China*. London, 1984. Early volume of original research exposing the environmental costs of collectivist economics in China.

Steadman, David W. "Prehistoric Extinctions of Pacific Birds: Biodiversity Meets Zooarchaeology." *Science* 267 (1995), 1123–1131. Evidence and discussion of massive species losses as a result of prehistoric human occupation.

Thomas, William L., ed. *Man's Role in Changing the Face of the Earth*. 2 vols. Chicago, 1952. The *locus classicus* of environmental history.

Tuan, Y. "Discrepancies between Environmental Attitudes and Behavior: Examples from Europe and China." *Canadian Geographer* 12 (1968), 176–191. Counter, often overlooked, to the unhistorical view that Europeans were uniquely destructive of the environment.

White, Lynn, Jr. "The Historical Roots of Our Ecologic[al] crisis." *Science* 155 (1967), 1203–1207. Seminal text for those who argued that Christianity came to license unbridled human use of the environment.

Wittfogel, Karl. *Oriental Despotism: A Comparative Study of Total Power*. New Haven, 1957. Seminal text for those who argued that eastern empires were condemned never to develop on their own because of their dependence on centrally administered river irrigation.

ERIC JONES

Environmental Policies and Regulation

Environmental and natural resources have served in three main capacities throughout the span of human history: they have been consumed as final goods; they have been inputs in the production of other market or nonmarket goods; and they have absorbed waste. The environment is inextricably tied to the economic productivity and welfare of nations. Economists separate the study of such concerns into resource economics and environmental economics. Resource economics focuses on the flow of resources into the economy, attempting to quantify the human use of nature. Environmental economics examines quality aspects of this use by considering the impact of the flow of residuals back into the environment. This discussion is concerned mainly with the latter.

Some of the earliest environmental legislation is found in the religious restrictions in Judaism and Hinduism regarding sanitary measures, set thousands of years ago. From these origins on into the twentieth century, environmental regulations mainly were localized attempts to alleviate air and water pollution and community overuse of natural resources. Legislative efforts became better organized as environmental damages became more severe. The Bubonic plague in Europe led to legislation aimed at improving public sanitation and imposing quarantines, from the mid-1300s through the seventeenth century.

Beginning in the 1800s and escalating since World War II, there has been a growing appreciation of the problems of pollution across borders and of global pollution, requiring international cooperation. Widespread dissemination of environmental ideas may have developed first through conservation advocate James Audubon in the 1830s. The writings of Americans John Muir and Gifford Pinchot at the turn of the twentieth century spread the ideas of conservation and preservation. Muir developed ideas that valued preservation for its own sake. Pinchot saw conservation as a tool for anthropocentric value. This split in ideology continues today.

Development of Environmental Legislation. As communities have grown to reach the carrying capacities of the environment, they have required social constructs to address the economic consequences presented by these constraints. The constructs can take many forms; the two main classes are command-and-control techniques and incentive-based techniques. Command-and-control techniques set explicit requirements for pollution output levels, abatement, or pollution control technology through government mandate. Command economies rely entirely on such techniques, but market economies also have used command and control more frequently than any other mechanism. Examples include the original Clean Air Act of 1970 in the United States or King Edward I of England's 1306 ban on burning coal in London while Parliament was in session.

Incentive-based techniques attempt to align the incentives of private firms and individuals with socially beneficial outcomes. Taxes, marketable permits, and deposit-refund systems are examples of incentive-based techniques. They each serve to internalize the cost of damages from environmental or resource degradation to the polluter's profit-maximizing problem. Tradable permits allow cost-effective reductions of sulfur dioxide and nitrogen oxide emissions in the United States under the 1990 Clean Air Act Amendments, and lobster trap permits in Australia create marketable commodities that establish incentives to reduce pollution. Effluent fees, or taxes for emitting pollutants, establish a cost for damages to waterways. China, among other nations, is adopting wide-scale pollution taxes to alleviate its high levels of pollution. Ideally these costs will equal the damages inflicted upon society by the pollution.

Governments can actively participate in pollution prevention. For example, by the beginning of the second millennium BCE, records indicate that the kingdom of Mari (in present-day Syria) had taken significant protective measures to guard its forests and prevent the soil erosion, drought, and salt buildup that had plagued the Sumerian empire (in present-day Iraq). In a similar vein, the Persian ruler Artaxerxes attempted to restrict the widespread cutting of cedar trees in Lebanon in 450 BCE. Papal prohibitions tried to prevent the export of timber from the Venetian empire in the thirteenth century.

Governments can provide or mandate technological solutions to existing pollution problems. In the Canary Islands in the fourteenth century, complex irrigation systems were built to replenish the water lost when forests were despoiled by the newly established European plantation agriculture.

A further step available to governments is the direct production of environmental resources. In the eleventh century, Egyptian rulers began vast replanting schemes; in the fourteenth century, Germany's rulers reclaimed agricultural land for forests; and in the fifteenth century, the Council of Ten in Venice ordered replanting along streamsides in an attempt to protect the lagoon from siltation. Many of these command-and-control policies failed. It was not to the personal benefit of individual peasants to protect downstream, societal interests. Therefore, their interests did not coincide with the state interest in resource protection. Without providing tangible net benefits for these individuals, the group goals were not achieved. In Venice, and later in India and African colonies, local peasant opposition to forest conservation policies even inspired sabotage and civil unrest.

Only recently have policy makers actively attempted to match individual incentives with social goals. In the United States, the 1990 Amendments to the Clean Air Act created a system of marketable permits for sulfur dioxide and nitrogen oxide emissions to lower abatement costs. Ideally, firms with high costs of abatement will buy permits from firms with lower costs so that pollution abatement will occur at the lowest cost. Regulators will not have to discern the costs of abatement for any firm. The U.S. experiment with sulfur dioxide permits has shown that permit markets should include as many participants as possible, and they should allow the retirement of permits by groups willing to pay more to retire a permit than firms are willing to pay for the permission to pollute. This latter condition will assist in the trial-and-error iterations necessary to establish the optimal pollution reductions with imperfect information on costs. Transactions costs and the limited number of permit holders will limit the gains from this system.

Environmental Regulation: Performance- and Technology-Based. Much environmental legislation is structured to achieve certain levels of environmental quality. For example, ambient air quality standards set the acceptable levels of pollutants measurable in the atmosphere, but methods for attaining these levels of air quality may vary across nations. In the United States, today's national ambient air quality standards were first set in 1970 under the Clean Air Act. Individual states became responsible for developing state implementation plans for achieving the standards.

In 1972, efforts by an environmental group, The Sierra Club, to prevent deterioration in air quality in pristine environments, forced the U.S. government to set higher standards in areas of considerably higher air quality than the standards that had been enacted. To accompany these higher standards, the United States added technological requirements to the performance-based standards. New pollution sources in pristine environments must use the best available control technology (BACT), regardless of cost. Then, in the 1977 amendments to the Clean Air Act, the requirements for regions that still remained below the national standards became even stricter. New sources in the nonattainment regions may not pollute above the lowest achievable emission rate (LAER), the lowest emission rate included in any state implementation plan regardless of whether any source is currently achieving that rate. Thus new sources of pollution might be required to use technologies that never have been commercially tested (Tietenberg, 2000).

The type of environmental legislation implemented has long-term effects on technology as well. As shown, command-and-control techniques may be technology-forcing. The invention of the catalytic converter is an example of successful technology-forcing; the inability of the United States to reach Clean Water Act–mandated goals of zero emissions for water pollution by 1985 or even 2001 represents a failure to force the development of the needed technology.

Legislative restrictions on technology began mainly with controls on the types of fuel energy that people could use. In 1603, James I of Britain switched from bituminous coal to cleaner-burning anthracite coal to alleviate air pollution.

Even slight differences in legislation can have many ramifications. In Europe, the United States, and Asia, recent legislation has placed new taxes on gasoline use. These taxes will raise prices and should lower consumption. European and Asian taxes average more than twice U.S. taxes. Although Americans have not lost their taste for low-mileage, large automobiles, Europeans have, and the average automobile's fuel economy in Europe or Japan is significantly higher than in the United States. Gasoline tax revenues in Europe are spent on efforts to achieve cleaner air. In Korea, many automobile manufacturers and owners have switched to significantly lower-taxed diesel fuel (Banaszak et al., 1999). In the United States, gasoline taxes are spent on maintaining and improving roads; but as the roads improve, the miles driven increase, and American fuel consumption increases even more. Poorly set legislation can severely limit incentives for technology development. In particular, legislation that does not allow for market growth and entry by new firms with better pollution control will slow technological advances. Existing firms will face lower levels of competition and have reduced incentives to innovate.

With respect to technology, environmental legislation has historically favored existing firms over new ones. To gain political acceptance by existing firms, more flexible standards often are applied to the adoption of new technology by existing firms than are applied to entering firms. This new-source bias has slowed adoption of the most effective control technology in the U.S. electricity industry. The Japanese electric power industry faces similar concerns as it chooses between low-cost power production with higher levels of carbon dioxide emissions and higher-cost adoption of new technology with lower emissions.

Models of command economies suggest that the social planner should easily be able to determine and mandate efficient levels of pollution abatement, as individual incentives become secondary to the overall welfare of the state. However, eastern Europe, China, and the republics of the former Soviet Union face some of the worst pollution excesses in the world. Command economies have not chosen to mandate environmental protection, instead favoring cheaper cost outputs.

The Aral Sea, a freshwater inland sea fed by rivers in the republics of Uzbekistan, Tajikistan and Turkmenistan, is disappearing at a tremendous rate, leaving chemical and pesticide pollution and economic devastation in its wake. In the late 1950s Soviet state planning diverted the rivers for agriculture. The sea has since shrunk by 75 percent of its 1960 volume, and agricultural opportunities there have dried up.

Command economies have an advantage when populations are small. The limited resources available on small oceanic islands have shaped much of the history of the Polynesian, Melanesian, and Micronesian peoples. In particular, vast ocean voyages undertaken to alleviate population congestion were influenced by their search for resources. These limited resources forced early development of societal regulations regarding resources and the environment. Generally subject to a single ruler, these communities used taboo systems to maintain stocks of timber, reef fish, and other marine resources. Under the taboo systems, kings or chiefs essentially managed the environmental resources as private property and provided limited access to the resources in order to maintain future production. The colonial influence of Western political and legal systems has eroded the taboo systems and has led to increased environmental pressures.

Regional and Global Concerns. Even nations that have invested money and efforts in significant environ-

DEATH OF THE ARAL SEA. The diversion, ordered by the government of the former Soviet Union, of the Amu Darya and Syr Darya Rivers for the purpose of irrigating cotton fields has not only caused severe environmental damage in the region, but has also had serious social, economic, and humanitarian consequences. Fisherman leaning against a stranded fishing boat looking at abandoned freighters in the desert, 1989. (© Novosti/Lehtikova/ Woodfin Camp and Associates, New York)

mental legislation over the past half century have not sufficiently addressed problems of transboundary pollution. A series of deaths from smog in the late 1940s and early 1950s (Donora, Pennsylvania, 1948; London, 1952 and 1956; New York, 1953; and Los Angeles, 1954) led to the first international air pollution conference in 1955. No international agreements emerged. Local pollution often can be passed off to one's neighbors. In 1804, Pittsburgh alleviated its air pollution problems by building taller smokestacks and sending its pollution out of the area. With countless similar cases over the last two hundred years, much of the U.S acid precipitation–causing emissions has landed in Canada. Only in 1991 did the affected countries sign the Canada–U.S. Air Quality Agreement.

Polluted water also flows through countries. In 1924, Gifford Pinchot, who had helped Theodore Roosevelt establish and develop the National Forests and National Park Service to conserve valuable resources, worked successfully with the National Coast Anti-Pollution League to get an international oil-dumping treaty to protect the coastlines of New England from others' wastes. Much of eastern Europe faces cleanup due to a long history of transboundary water pollution problems, affecting navigability, toxicity, public health, and wildlife conservation. The United Nations Development Programme (UNDP) is trying to resolve many longstanding regional environmental conflicts, including pollution in the Dnieper River basin and the Black Sea that includes runoff and waste from Belarus, Georgia, Romania, the Russian Federation, Turkey, and Ukraine.

Much environmental legislation comes after scientific inquiry discovers that the human use of environmental resources has unintended and not apparent side-effects. A lack of information and uncertainty about the carrying capacity of the global environment, as well as the uneven global distribution of negative effects of resource use, make attempts at united action for change extremely challenging. The idea that human action could affect the climate originated at the local level in Greece when Theophrastus of Crete posited that deforestation was causing a decline in rainfall. The European experience with colonial islands in the Caribbean and Pacific Oceans from the 1300s forward revived this theory.

Theories of climate change continued to develop throughout the industrial age. In 1997, the Kyoto Protocol established global goals for the reduction of greenhouse gas emissions; but the agreement is fraught with difficulties that were not apparent in the Montreal Protocol of 1987, a global agreement to eliminate chlorofluorocarbons (CFCs). The benefits and costs of reducing global pollutants are not evenly distributed. Although CFCs may be relatively easily phased out of use by substitutes and prohibitions on production (as part of a highly concentrated industry), greenhouse gases include methane (CH_4) and carbon dioxide (CO_2), which are essential to much life on earth. Additionally, automobile exhausts, forest fires, and other non–point source emissions contribute extensively to the release of these gases, and are very difficult to regulate.

The uneven distribution of costs and benefits across economies is particularly acute in this case. Small Pacific islands, which will be inundated by rising ocean levels, have the most to lose from climate change and are at the same time the smallest producers of greenhouse gases. China's coal use makes it the largest national emitter of CO_2. However, China's status as a developing nation means that in the existing framework for global emissions control, the Kyoto Protocol, the nation has no required abatement or limitations on the growth of this use—although China has begun to limit its use of coal because of domestic air pollution problems. The release of greenhouse gases that will occur if China does not curtail coal use could overwhelm global efforts to reduce the effects of global warming.

Burden of Compliance. Frequently industrial interests argue against environmental regulation such as the Kyoto Protocol for fear that they will bear all the costs of compliance while receiving few of the benefits. This question has been analyzed for many industries, and the results are mixed. In some industries, including chemicals, plastics and synthetics, fabric, and leather tanning, both productivity and international competitiveness have been enhanced by stringent environmental legislative standards. The compliance costs frequently have been lower than expected for new environmental policies as firms have boosted their productivity after installing the required new technologies. For example, in the pulp and paper sector in the United States, expected costs of compliance with the Clean Air Act of 1970 were $16.40 per ton of abatement, but actual costs were around $4.00 to $5.00 per ton (see Bonson et al., 1988).

Unions and champions of labor have criticized environmental legislation for its propensity to reduce jobs. Again, studies have shown that, worldwide, for the first two decades of a comprehensive environmental policy setting, in the 1960s and 1970s, labor experienced a net gain from pollution control requirements. For each $1 billion of pollution control spending, sixty thousand to seventy thousand jobs were created on average. This is higher than the average fifty thousand jobs created by each $1 billion increase in GNP (Haveman, 1978).

Environmental Protection versus Economic Growth. Communities and nations frequently have perceived trade-offs between environmental quality and the cheap production of market goods and services. Protection of the environment often has been presented as a luxury good. Certainly, countries with greater disposable income are today spending greater amounts than poorer countries on using and developing clean technologies or restricting production that increases environmental damages.

Less-affluent developing nations guiding economic development must choose between more expensive "green" technologies and the cheaper tools of industrialization that the United States, Europe, and others used to achieve rapid economic growth in the nineteenth and twentieth centuries. The economic incentives facing a developing nation may favor increased pollution. Many of the damages that these nations would create through the use of cheaper but dirtier production will be felt outside their borders. The economic gain from cheap production, however, mainly will be reaped inside these nations. So, incentives for developing environmental regulations are limited.

Between 1880 and 1920, the United States increased the relative intensity with which it used nonreproducible natural resources such as petroleum, coal, and minerals. This intense resource use explains a highly significant portion of the rapid increase in manufacturing and the country's rise to the top of global industrial output in this time period (see Wright, 1990). The lure of similar economic growth could lead to large increases in pollution for developing nations with large natural resource reserves. These sorts of economic conflicts have pushed environmental legislation onto the international stage over the past half century as borders have opened and trade has increased. In 1972, the United Nations formed the UN Environment Program; and the Montreal Protocol came from this program. This agreement has met with tremendous success. A clear international consensus on the dangers of ozone depletion and highly concentrated industrial sources of CFCs made its implementation politically attractive and economically feasible. Technological innovations have enhanced the protocol's enforceability. A lack of consensus on global warming, as well as the difficulties described earlier, has hindered the adoption of the Kyoto Protocol.

BIBLIOGRAPHY

Amagai, Hisashi, and PingSun Leung. "The Trade-off between Economic and Environmental Objectives in Japan's Power Sector." *Energy Journal* 12.4 (1991), 95–104.

Banaszak, Sara, Ujjayant Chakravorty, and PingSun Leung. "Demand for Ground Transportation Fuel and Pricing Policy in Asian Tigers: A Comparative Study of Korea and Taiwan." *Energy Journal* 20.2 (1999), 145–165.

Bonson, N. C., Neil McCubbin, and John B. Sprague. "Kraft Mill Effluents in Ontario." Report prepared for the Technical Advisory Committee, Pulp and Paper Sector of MISA, Ontario Ministry of the Environment, Toronto, Ontario, Canada, 29 March 1988.

Grove, Richard H. *Green Imperialism: Colonial Expansion, Tropical Island Edens, and the Origins of Environmentalism, 1600–1860.* Cambridge, 1995.

Hahn, Robert W. "Economic Prescriptions for Environmental Problems: How the Patient Followed the Doctor's Orders." *Journal of Economic Perspectives* 3.2 (1989), 95–114.

Haveman, Robert H. "The Results and Significance of the Employment Studies." In *OECD Employment and Environment*, pp. 48–53. Paris, 1978.

Levinson, Arik. "Grandfather Regulations, New Source Bias, and State Air Toxics Regulations." *Ecological Economics* 28.2 (1999), 299–311.

Priest, W. C. *Risks, Concerns, and Social Legislation: Forces That Led to Laws on Health, Safety, and the Environment.* Boulder, 1999.

Porter, Michael E. *The Competitive Advantage of Nations.* New York, 1990.

Porter, Michael E., and Claas van der Linde. "Toward a New Conception of the Environmental-Competitiveness Issue." *Journal of Economic Perspectives* 9.4 (1995), 97–118.

Schmandt, J., J. Clarkson, and H. Roderick, eds. *Acid Rain and Friendly Neighbors: The Policy Dispute between Canada and the United States.* Durham, N.C., 1988.

Tietenberg, Tom. *Environmental and Natural Resource Economics.* 5th ed. New York, 2000.

Wright, Gavin. "The Origins of American Industrial Success, 1879–1940." *American Economic Review* 80.4 (1990), 651–658.

BROOKS KAISER

EPIDEMICS are sudden outbreaks of disease that spread rapidly within and between human communities. Often, but not always, the diseases involved are infectious, and thus transmitted directly between humans (e.g., tuberculosis, smallpox, measles, and syphilis). Other epidemic diseases can be transmitted to humans by insect vectors (e.g., bubonic plague, malaria, typhus, yellow fever). Still others are transmitted by water (e.g., cholera, typhoid) or foodborne toxins (e.g., ergotism). Widespread vitamin-deficiency diseases such as scurvy can appear to erupt suddenly in a particular population. Any epidemic disease can be either new to a community or endemic to it, that is, part of both the normal disease environment and the background level of mortality.

At present, sophisticated surveillance systems make it possible to detect epidemics before they take many lives. In the past, the fact that an outbreak of disease was recorded for posterity generally meant that it killed a considerable number of people in a short period of time, thus causing a substantial degree of economic and social disruption.

Until the last few centuries, information about epidemics as mortality crises came from narrative sources, both official and unofficial. These sources have predictable limitations, which make the number of lives actually lost during an epidemic highly uncertain. The survivors of an epidemic might have described it as killing tens of thousands; later historians may question their estimates and reduce the number of fatalities. Narrative sources are most likely to inflate the number of victims when those who fled an epidemic are included among the dead. In every case, evaluating the available evidence for past epidemics always requires careful interpretation of a wide range of sources.

Under some circumstances, it has proved possible to reduce uncertainty about past epidemics by supplementing informal descriptive sources with archaeological data. See, for example, R. Duncan-Jones's (1996) resourceful reconstruction of the Antonine plague in the Roman Empire, 166 CE. Contemporaries described that epidemic as exceptionally deadly. A sharp reduction in the amount of land under cultivation in Egypt and a reduced volume of trade and taxation show they were not exaggerating.

The descriptions found in traditional narrative sources usually provide information on the symptoms associated with a specific outbreak, but they rarely permit certain identification of a specific disease with a modern equivalent. From an economic perspective, however, it is probably more important to have information on the age groups

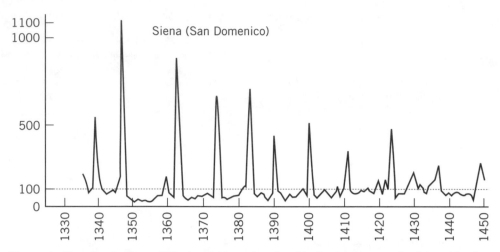

FIGURE 1. Mortality in Siena, Italy, involving outbreaks of bubonic plague and other epidemics, 1330–1450. The period average = 100. Therefore the outbreak of bubonic plague right before 1350 involved many deaths, more than ten times the average. SOURCE: L. de Panta, 1980.

most affected rather than the specific disease involved. The impact of a severe epidemic on the economy will differ markedly if it kills mainly children and/or the elderly instead of working-age adults, including men in arms.

Those epidemics that caused mortality crises in western Europe after circa 1400 CE can be studied in quantitative detail by using the bills of mortality (as kept in selected cities) or the deaths recorded as burials in both urban and rural parishes. Figure 1 is a reconstruction, using various data sources, of the mortality crises associated with sudden outbreaks of disease in Siena, Italy, from 1335 to 1450. As with all mortality crises, those graphed differ according to frequency, amplitude, and duration; but none of these quantitative differences points to a specific disease. Moreover, it is entirely possible that some mortality crises involved two or more epidemic diseases erupting simultaneously. Epidemics also differ according to their geographical scale. Most outbreaks are highly localized, but some involve one or more continents. The large-scale outbreaks (pandemics) are relatively infrequent and exceptionally disruptive.

Because epidemics come in different sizes and geographical patterns, something as basic as counting past epidemics is not a simple exercise. A two-page list of epidemics in history (Cliff et al., 1998, Table 1.4) contains no instances of epidemics in Asia. Yet for China alone traditional sources have been used to compile a long list of epidemics occurring between 243 BCE and 1911 CE, and this list is far from complete because it excludes small-scale, localized epidemics (see McNeil, 1976).

Although no exhaustive historical account of epidemics has been attempted, Del Panta (1980) has reconstructed major epidemics in various Italian cities over five centuries. Biraben (1975) focuses on epidemics in medieval and early modern France. English epidemics are the subject of Creighton's (1891) classic, mostly descriptive, two-volume history. Wrigley and Schofield (1981) take a more quantitative approach, focusing on smaller-scale outbreaks. Epidemics in Asian history finally have begun to receive serious historical attention in English-language research (Janetta, 1987; Benedict, 1996; Watts, 1997). Because published historical research is unstandardized, it is difficult to make cross-cultural and over-time comparisons that are more than casually descriptive.

The Origins of Epidemic Disease. Sudden outbreaks of disease have been part of the evolution of most life forms and thus of biological history in general. In animal populations, sudden outbreaks of disease are called epizootics. Over one hundred diseases found in bird and wild-animal populations can jump the species barrier and cause human epidemics. Among domesticated animals, at least three hundred epizootic diseases can cause human outbreaks. Whether frequent or infrequent, mild or severe, local or widespread, epidemics have been part of human history from its beginnings, although certain contexts have been more conducive to them than others.

The importance of animal reservoirs in human disease history has led to the hypothesis that when all human beings lived in small, highly mobile hunter-gatherer groups, they were infrequently struck by epidemics because hunting did not involve close, continuous contact with animal populations or other human populations. During the transition to agriculture, new diseases evolved and took epidemic form, especially among groups who shared their living space with domesticated animals. This implies that, as settled life became the norm in any one area, and epidemics became more frequent, life expectancy fell. Subsequently, with the development of large cities, high-density living ensured that epidemics, particularly airborne and waterborne diseases, would break out with even greater frequency.

Before the modern mortality transition (see below), epidemics took many more lives than they do now, at least in developed countries; but the proportion of lives lost to epidemic disease versus endemic disease remains uncertain. Whether epidemics were a major or a minor cause of premature death in the past matters in explaining the mortality transition. In any case, calculating the proportion of lives lost to epidemic disease before the twentieth century depends on specifying the criteria for a mortality crisis. If the threshold for a mortality crisis were set at a relatively high level (crisis mortality is defined as a death rate at least five times normal), then death by epidemic would be a relatively infrequent event in most places and times. The lower the threshold is, the greater the proportion of deaths occurring during sudden outbreaks of disease. The most deadly epidemics in history were pandemics, whose scale and ferocity suggest that these outbreaks are best regarded as exogenous shocks occurring independently of economic conditions, including those involving food shortages.

Bubonic Plague. Perhaps the most researched epidemic/pandemic in history is the outbreak of bubonic plague in medieval western Europe. Although this particular pandemic has been studied extensively for more than a century, nothing about its causes or consequences has achieved the status of undisputed fact. Controversies that were already well developed in the 1970s remain unresolved. Since any disease outbreak could be called plague in medieval Europe, it is possible that the bacterial pathogen *Yersinia pestis* was not solely responsible for all the sudden outbreaks of disease attributed to it by later historians.

Any residual biological uncertainty notwithstanding, it appears that a great many Europeans died in the large-scale outbreak of disease (or diseases) that swept over Europe from 1347 to 1352 CE. Contemporaries often wrote as if the dead outnumbered the living; but later estimates put losses at 20 to 70 percent of continental Europe's population, and most estimates have the population of Europe reduced by a third after the first major outbreak between 1347 and 1352. In subsequent decades, several more continent-wide outbreaks followed (1368, 1375), and by the mid-1400s continuing pandemics of "plague" probably had reduced the population of Europe to half its former level. Population growth had resumed by 1500 or 1520 (at the latest), but the levels achieved by circa 1300 may not have been reached again until 1600 or 1700.

To some economic historians, epidemic-induced population decline remains an unmitigated economic disaster associated with a sustained decline in Europe's per capita gross domestic product, but other historians continue to argue that those who survived the epidemic had a higher standard of living than its victims. Although a great deal of human capital was lost in the form of adult lives, other forms of tangible capital were left largely intact—arable land, houses, tools, barns, the urban infrastructure, and so on. In that sense, the survivors were left better endowed with the cooperating factors of production. After the initial and very disruptive shocks wore off, by the 1370s, most of the evidence indicates that the resulting shortage of labor caused rising real wages and falling rents for a century or more.

At present, it is conventional to stress the extent to which population growth itself stimulates innovation. But as Mokyr (1990) points out, "population decline should be equally conducive to technological change" (p. 190). If in "the two centuries before 1500, Europe's technological creativity had become increasingly original" (p. 57), then, at the very least, the recurrent epidemics that prevented demographic recovery in Europe between circa 1350 and 1500 did not prevent continuing technological progress.

In England, serfdom disappeared as the least advantaged people capitalized on the shortage of labor to secure their freedom. Brenner (1985) argued that the struggle to escape forced labor in England led to a revolution in property rights and markets that gave its economy a long-run dynamic edge over those of other European countries. In eastern Europe, however, disease-induced scarcity of labor led to an intensification of serfdom. These very different outcomes highlight the importance of the overall institutional context in which epidemics cause a major loss of life.

Although data-quality problems will ensure continuing debates, pessimistic interpretations generally overlook the fact that Europeans became better educated in the century and a half after the first outbreak of "plague." Between 1100 and 1350, twenty (pre-plague) universities were founded in Europe to train secular professionals in medicine and other fields. From 1351 to 1500, another thirty (post-plague) universities were founded that offered medical degrees (Nutton, 1995). In short, a population cut in half was able to support more than twice the number of universities. The post-plague demand for higher education among elites was paralleled by the spread of more basic forms of education among the less privileged. Many skilled workers became both literate and numerate in the century after the first major outbreak of "plague." More women may have been taught to read as well, but universities were closed to them. Recently, the century and a half after the first outbreak of plague has been described as a period of creative destruction in which responses to disease-induced disruption led to the formation of modern states in western Europe (Epstein, 2000).

Although the long-run economic effects of Europe's greatest mortality crisis remain a matter of speculation, in

CHOLERA. Citizens of Marseille dance around a fire that has been lit to destroy the pestilence. Wood engraving, *Harper's Weekly*, 18 November 1865. (Courtesy of the National Library of Medicine, Bethesda, Maryland)

the short run all major epidemics/mortality crises were economically and politically disruptive. As tens of thousands died and/or fled, urban economies virtually shut down, and the resulting economic distress among the survivors often led to rioting and rebellion. Even after order was restored, city governments were forced to support more dependent survivors on a reduced tax base. For a variety of reasons, ruling elites had strong incentives to consider minimizing the disruption caused by sudden outbreaks of disease. As a more secular, less fatalistic mentality took hold among Europe's ruling elites, they considered new approaches to disease management, often consulting physicians, whose interests generally favored naturalizing disease processes.

By 1600, the outlines of modern public health were clearly visible in Italian cities, in the form of both local surveillance systems and the imposition of comprehensive quarantine measures in response to a rapid rise in the number of reported deaths. Eventually, local surveillance systems expanded to include international information networks designed to provide European governments with advance warning about distant outbreaks of "plague," particularly those likely to spread to Europe via trade routes. In major port cities, the spread of epidemic disease eventually was contained through strictly enforced quarantine measures, but outbreaks of plague in Turkey also spread overland to central Europe. Eventually, cordon sanitaires

extending over hundreds of miles were constructed to halt the flow of goods and people during epidemic outbreaks. Coincidentally or not, as the management of plague became a matter of national security in western Europe, outbreaks became less frequent and less severe. The last potential pandemic of bubonic plague in western Europe (Marseille) was successfully contained in 1720.

Whether or not primitive public health reforms were effective, they were efficiently enforced by the most authoritarian governments. When quarantine measures disrupted trade, merchants lost money. Ordinary people suffered as well when they found themselves unemployed and/or incarcerated in their own homes during quarantines. Powerful elites were willing to ignore the objections of both merchants and ordinary people. Not surprisingly, it has been argued that as proactive governments assumed greater control over individual behavior during an epidemic, ordinary human welfare, economic and social, probably was compromised for the sake of elite welfare.

Because the human management of disease has implications for health policy, even historical research remote from the present can become covertly political, in which case the evidence is given a strong spin in the desired direction. Generally, a belief in the increasing efficiency of epidemic control measures in western Europe between 1500 and 1800 is frequently, but not inevitably, associated with a sympathy for governments willing to limit individual freedom (economic and social) for the sake of saving lives. In contrast, the argument that early modern epidemic control measures did not work, or that they did more harm than good, is generally associated with the conviction that government interference is inherently inefficient or harmful, especially when elites act to protect their own interests.

From either standpoint it is relevant to note that none of the Islamic countries adopted plague-control measures; and, coincidentally or not, they continued to be struck by major outbreaks of bubonic plague long after western Europe appeared to be free of them. In Turkey, major outbreaks of plague continued until the 1840s, when the government finally adopted some European-style reforms.

The New World Holocaust. Medieval pandemics may or may not have stimulated the economic development of western Europe, but the pandemics that swept the Americas were undoubtedly as beneficial to European invaders as they were disastrous for the native Amerindians. Pomeranz (2000) argues that Europe's "epidemiological luck" gave it an "ecological windfall" (in the form of the New World's extra land and resources) that assured its subsequent rise to global economic dominance.

"Epidemiological luck" refers to the fact that for thousands of years those human beings who lived in the Americas had been isolated from exposure to the set of killer epidemic diseases long shared by Europeans, Asians, and Africans. Thus, once exposed to new epidemic diseases, Amerindians were bound to be exceptionally hard-hit. For reasons not well understood, the inhabitants of the New World did not have any major epidemic diseases to export to Europe, with the possible exception of syphilis.

New World demography is a politically sensitive topic, precipitating debate over the rights and wrongs of European imperialism/colonialism. In politically charged scholarship, it is hard to sort out fact from fiction. Currently, the dominant story is that within a century or so after contact with Europeans began, some 90 to 95 percent of New World natives had died from newly introduced infectious diseases (smallpox, measles, tuberculosis) and vector-borne diseases such as yellow fever, to which they had not been previously exposed (Stannard, 1992). This figure has acquired the status of fact, though it is based simply on the presumption of homogeneity (every group of Amerindians was effected to the same drastic extent by unfamiliar diseases) and guesstimates about the size of precontact populations that seem invariably to favor the highest possible figures (see McCaa, 2000, on Mexico).

Like all human populations, those located in the Americas had the biological capacity to recover from epidemics, provided that fertility could rebound once death rates returned to normal; but demographic recovery required maintaining effective political control over land and its re-

sources. When invading Europeans fought defeated local elites, as they did in Mexico and Peru, the political and cultural basis for economic continuity was destroyed. Many native cultivators were expropriated, and others were reduced to brutal servitude. Sometimes colonization was accompanied by drastic environmental changes that economically marginalized the surviving native peoples. In other cases, European colonists encouraged warfare between rival native groups, which left the Europeans free to colonize lands vacated by the defeated. Even in the absence of the most brutal forms of conquest, the economic and cultural disruption caused by Europeans could be sufficiently severe to keep native birth rates from returning to normal levels between epidemics (see Crosby, 1992, on Hawaii).

Although epidemic disease gave Europeans a critical advantage over Amerindian populations, it took more than pure "epidemiological luck" to conquer, dispossess, and/or displace them. Despite contact shock, a surprising number of local populations managed to adapt and survive as viable demographic/economic entities. As new research begins to replace the "holocaust" model of decline, careful case studies have begun to reveal an unexpected amount of diversity. In a very real sense, each surviving people had its own, fairly individualized experience of postcontact demographic and economic history. Their responses displayed adaptive intelligence in many different forms.

Although most of the surviving indigenous peoples had a difficult time, a few exceptional groups flourished. By trading with Europeans, they enjoyed a temporary period of prosperity and even population growth, sometimes for as long as a century or more. In what later became the American South, some native populations managed to establish a flourishing trade with Europeans that prevented rapid population decline. When epidemics did not result in depopulation, and native groups managed to adapt and survive (as did the Cherokee), Americans forcefully removed them, and replaced them as cultivators of the land. In short, although epidemic disease played a major role in Europe's successful invasion of the Americas, for hundreds of Amerindian groups life continued. Much more research is needed on how these surviving populations coped with contact shock by adapting to new and stressful circumstances.

Malthus and the "Average" Epidemic. The ordinary epidemics that punctuate human history neither transformed nor destroyed the populations they struck. According to Malthus (1766–1834), what might be thought of as the typical epidemic was part of a system of positive checks that kept human numbers in approximate equilibrium with material resources, especially the food supply Malthus assumed that since sexual desire drove human reproduction independently of reason (which operated in the form of preventive checks such as delayed marriage or abstinence), populations tended to grow more rapidly than the food available to feed them. As poverty increased, rising mortality reduced population growth, and eventually the additional positive checks—epidemics, wars, and famines—suddenly reduced absolute numbers to a more sustainable level.

In Malthus's economically driven theory of mortality crises, sudden shocks hit the poorest people with the greatest force, thus temporarily reducing poverty. To some of his contemporaries, this implied that epidemics and/or famines were natural correctives that governments would be well advised to leave alone, unless they wished to be overwhelmed by increasing poverty. It is more than possible that Malthus's logic influenced government policy during the reform of the English Poor Law in the 1840s. Benefits were cut and made harder to obtain in order to discourage fecklessness, including early marriage and high fertility. Malthus's reasoning may have also influenced the practical management of famine in Ireland during the 1840s, and in India, even as late as the 1890s.

Since Malthus's time, much has been learned about epidemic disease as a check on population growth. Today, epidemics seem more important than ever as the prime force that regulated population growth in traditional agrarian societies such as those found in western Europe. In addition, epidemic disease probably has made all wars and famines more deadly than they otherwise would have been. However, Malthus, like his contemporaries, knew next to nothing about the biology of epidemic disease, and thus overestimated the role played by poverty in such disease.

Those diseases that take epidemic form are differentially, not equally, sensitive to the nutritional status of the people exposed. Some diseases are classified as nutrition-insensitive, including bubonic plague, smallpox, and malaria. A few infectious diseases, often associated with nonspecific "fevers," are more likely to kill the rich than the poor, for example, any bacterial disease that benefits from reproducing in iron-rich blood—a common side-effect of a high-protein diet—will flourish among the rich; whereas relatively undernourished hosts, who usually suffer from anemia, have a biological advantage. Even those epidemic diseases most likely to kill the malnourished can kill privileged individuals, although to a lesser degree. Thus, no group of human beings is entirely safe from epidemics.

Depending on the mix of epidemic diseases that dominated a disease environment at any point in time, quantitative indicators of the food supply will appear more or less important as determinants of mortality crises. During the 1400s, when real wages were relatively high and Europe's food supply was relatively abundant, "plague" outbreaks were frequent, along with epidemics of dysentery and ergotism. In this environment, demographic recovery was prevented by disease outbreaks alone, despite the relatively favorable economic context.

In contrast, pulmonary tuberculosis (TB) is classified as one of the most poverty-sensitive diseases. Wherever TB (in epidemic or endemic form) was a leading cause of death, poverty itself was invariably implicated as a critical predisposing cause. Nevertheless, biologically vulnerable individuals from both wealthy and middle-class families could develop cases of tuberculosis severe enough to cause their deaths. Typhus also tends to spread rapidly in conditions where social upheaval (sometimes related to war or famine) disrupts the economy and increases poverty, often encouraging mass migration among the poorest victims of social disruption.

Because Malthus assumed that all epidemics reduced poverty (at least temporarily), he ignored the ways in which they could increase it as well. Parish officials in eighteenth-century England could see that after a local epidemic of smallpox, tax-supported-poor rates rose because some dead adults left behind helpless dependents, and some surviving workers were left disabled by blindness, or too weak to work. In the hope of saving money on poor relief, parish officers were willing to inoculate the entire parish against smallpox, once the cost of treatment had been reduced by medical innovators, from pounds to pennies per person.

Encouraged by monarchs, ministers, and leading physicians, parish officials in England conducted what amounted to a large-scale, rural public health campaign in the mid- and late eighteenth century. Smallpox epidemics routinely killed between 10 and 15 percent of a local population; so when outbreaks failed to recur, parish populations increased more rapidly than otherwise, sometimes creating the surplus labor and low wages that Malthus found problematic by 1800. Eventually, the money saved by preventing smallpox epidemics may well have been spent on relief for underemployed and unemployed agricultural workers; but what Malthus blamed on timeless sexual drives and a failure to control reproduction by delaying marriage (the preventive check) may well have been a side-effect of recent advances in public health, combined with a stagnant economy in many rural parishes.

Given that specific epidemic diseases differ in their sensitivity to preexisting poverty and malnutrition, it is not surprising that quantitative research supports the conclusion that up to half of all epidemics in Europe broke out independently of food shortages and high prices. In specific cases, a steep rise of grain prices could precede, parallel, or lag behind the sharp rise in death rates associated with epidemic disease. Although the study of short-term fluctuations is dedicated to modeling systematic relationships between grain prices and mortality, it seems unlikely that one model will ever fit all contexts in early modern Europe or elsewhere.

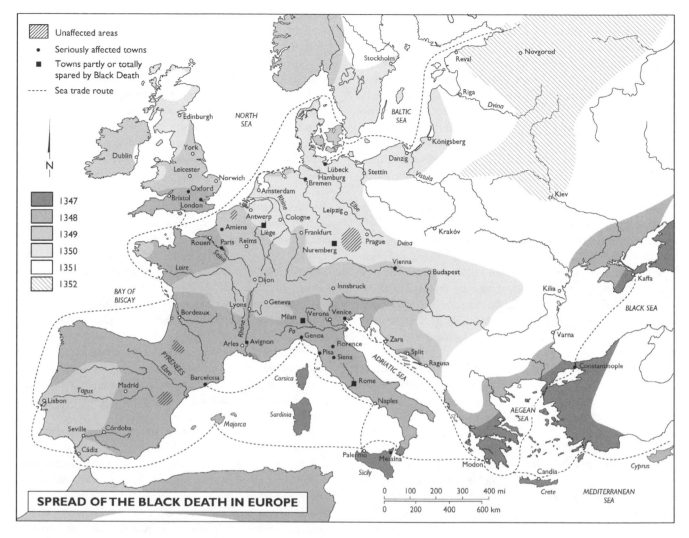

SPREAD OF THE BLACK DEATH IN EUROPE

Legend:
- Unaffected areas
- Seriously affected towns
- Towns partly or totally spared by Black Death
- Sea trade route

- 1347
- 1348
- 1349
- 1350
- 1351
- 1352

In the spirit of Malthus, many economic historians have continued to believe that poverty is causally implicated in all disease, epidemic and endemic. Thus they assume that when per capita incomes rise, death rates should fall, and thus life expectancy should rise. Since the process of economic development increases per capita income levels, development itself is presumed to be capable of causing a sustained fall of mortality/rise of life expectancy. Once again, this ignores the complex biology of epidemic disease; but, more important, it ignores the relationship between development, rising incomes, and urbanization.

Although Malthus showed little awareness that economic development was transforming the England in which he lived, he knew that cities almost always had higher death rates than rural communities. In his time, it was conventional to describe cities as "graveyards" or "eaters of men" because their death rates were much higher than their birthrates. If cities survived, it was only by attracting migrants from rural areas. Wrigley (1967) has shown that the particularly rapid growth of London during the seven-

teenth century absorbed most of rural England's normal surplus of births over deaths.

Urban historians still speak of the law of natural decrease (meaning that before the late nineteenth century, cities of ten thousand or more inhabitants invariably had higher death rates than birthrates). To the extent that the percentage urban remained a historical constant, Malthus did not need to consider urbanization itself as a positive check on population growth; but when he began to write, England had begun to urbanize, and by 1850 over half the nation's population lived in large cities. In all these cities, death rates were higher than the national average, partly because epidemics were both more frequent and more deadly in cities than they were in rural areas and small towns.

As germ theory began to reduce uncertainty about the biological causes of disease (c. 1870–1900), it became apparent that urban living itself facilitated the spread of all the airborne infectious diseases, whereas water pollution encouraged outbreaks of diseases such as cholera and typhoid fever. Because new susceptibles (in the form of migrants) were particularly abundant in towns, most of the epidemic diseases normally were present in endemic form. However, migrants themselves could introduce new, quickly spreading diseases to which even seasoned urban residents proved susceptible, just as returning migrants could carry urban diseases back to the countryside. Insect-borne disease also flourished in some cities. In America, yellow fever epidemics terrorized urban populations, and its general insensitivity to poverty assured that this disease would continue to cause death, even as development raised standards of living. Moreover, since foodstuffs imported from the countryside were imperfectly stored, contaminated food continually encouraged urban outbreaks of the gastrointestinal diseases.

Although cities had long been associated with disease and death in the popular mind, migration from the countryside continued as long as urban employment was more abundant and/or better paid. Thus, when development stimulated urbanization in England, it generally depressed local life expectancy levels while raising wages. As density increased, even higher wages could not prevent more frequent epidemics.

The same thing was true in Japan, where very high-quality data can be used to track the statistical relationship between income levels and mortality levels during the entire process of economic development. In the late nineteenth century, when good data became available, higher-than-average income levels in developing areas were clearly correlated with higher-than-average death rates at the provincial level. It took decades of public health reform before Japan's urban (high-income) areas lost their traditional mortality disadvantages compared to poorer, rural areas.

In the United States, death rates also tended to rise as development accelerated. Because personal and economic liberty was highly valued in this democracy, government intervention, even in the form of traditional public health methods, was feared and loathed. Thus American economic development/urbanization after 1800 proceeded for decades without much urban public health reform. It now seems clear that as the percentage urban doubled between 1840 and 1860, American death rates rose substantially. From a Malthusian perspective, development combined with rising mortality is still problematic or paradoxical. When the biology of epidemic disease is taken into account, however, rising mortality becomes a predictable outcome of development when urbanization is unaccompanied by public health reform.

In the developing United States, where migration was actively encouraged, the Malthusian assumption that population growth increased poverty had never seemed relevant to the country's special circumstances. Thus American economists may have easily appreciated the extent to which epidemics could destroy human capital, disrupt economic life, and reduce profits. In 1878, a deadly outbreak of yellow fever occurred in Memphis, Tennessee, spreading rapidly down the Mississippi River and killing twenty thousand people in a few months. Soon economic estimates were produced, indicating that this one outbreak cost the nation's economy more than $200 million in terms of lost production and disrupted trade. Once epidemics seemed too expensive to tolerate for the sake of freedom from government interference, and germ theory made the epidemic diseases seem like specific biological problems with technological solutions, U.S. resistance to public health reform collapsed.

In New York City, health reforms were so concentrated and efficiently enforced in the last decades of the nineteenth century that by 1907 the city's crude death rates achieved equality with those of the state's rural areas. This death rate parity came during a period in which New York was growing rapidly by absorbing thousands of low-wage immigrants who lived in miserable tenements. Those crowded conditions, otherwise ideal for the epidemic diseases, were now effectively countered by methods of disease management that could prevent or contain eruptions of disease at earlier and earlier stages.

Cross Cultural Comparisons. When Malthus theorized about the positive and preventive checks that kept human numbers in line with resources, he made cross-cultural comparisons using traditional descriptive sources. From them, he gleaned the idea that Europeans married later and less frequently than Asians, and he therefore assumed that fertility was lower, and population growth slower, in Europe compared to Asia. According to Malthus's model, this implied that epidemics and famines had to break out more frequently and with greater force in Asia than in Europe, to keep the numbers in line with resources.

China was Malthus's favorite example of an Asian country in which poverty was more extensive and therefore mortality crises (particularly famines) were more frequent than in Europe. Once again, however, modern research has failed to confirm his reasoning. China, for example, had its own system of proactive cultural controls on both fertility and mortality. Infanticide was extensively practiced, even within marriage, and through it mortality (especially female mortality) was artificially raised to keep reproduction in line with economic resources. Epidemics and famines broke out in China, as they did everywhere, but, thus far, there is no empirical basis for concluding that these crises were more frequent and/or deadly than those in Europe.

On the other hand, traditional epidemics continued to break out in China far longer than they did in Europe. As late as 1900, bubonic plague could still become a major threat to life; but following the adoption of urban public health measures, plague was eventually contained in China.

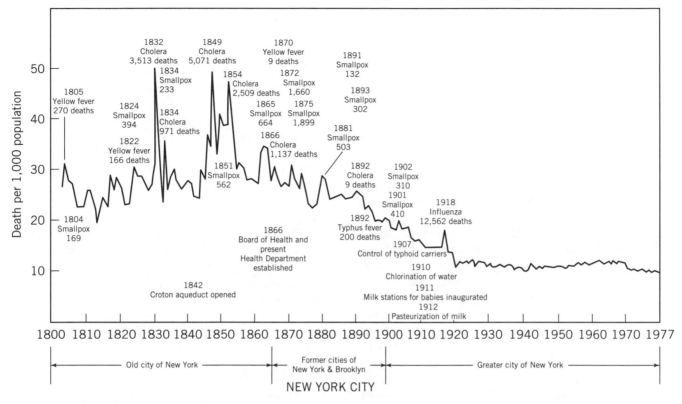

FIGURE 2. Crude death rates in New York City, 1800–1977. Crude death rates appear to be rising in New York City until the 1850s. SOURCE: Omran, A. R. "Epidemiologic Transition." In *International Encyclopedia of Population*, New York, 1982.

The Epidemiologic Transition. At a global level, the mortality transition involves a sustained rise of life expectancy at birth from values in the low range of twenty to forty years to values in the high range of sixty to eighty years. Conventional graphs of this transition often depict the rise of life expectancy as a smooth process, thus inadvertently obscuring the role played by the gradual retreat of epidemic disease in the modern decline of mortality. In contrast, when the mortality transition is seen as an "epidemiologic transition" (Omran, 1971), attention is explicitly focused on the gradual disappearance of the traditional mortality crises associated with famines and epidemics. According to Omran, as both types of mortality crisis became less frequent, death rates lost their traditional volatility, and life expectancy levels rose. Figure 2 shows how Omran linked the decline of mortality in New York City to public health reform.

Modern cause-of-death data strongly suggest that, at life-expectancy-at-birth levels below fifty years, at least half of all deaths are caused by infectious and parasitic diseases, both endemic and epidemic. This relationship in turn suggests that any measures designed to reduce the diseases' incidence and prevalence (for example, immunization or water purification) also would reduce the frequency of epidemic outbreaks. By extension, control of

epidemic outbreaks will reduce the incidence and the prevalence of infectious disease. In the world's least-developed countries, where the infectious diseases still comprise half of the top ten causes of death, epidemics continue to break out. What is known about them is limited because the countries most vulnerable to epidemic disease are also the countries where vital registration systems remain underdeveloped or nonexistent. Thus in African countries, especially those south of the Sahara, epidemics can be described by observers but not tracked with great precision, even in the case of acquired immune deficiency syndrome (AIDS). The recent history of epidemics continues to rely on descriptive sources supplemented with somewhat exact local data.

In the developed countries, traditional epidemics linked to major mortality crises disappeared by the 1930s. As national-level death rates stayed low and flat decade after decade, it was widely supposed that epidemics were a thing of the past. In the United States, it was argued that health policy should begin to focus on the chronic diseases, not the infectious diseases long associated with epidemics. This idea had several biological shortcomings, the major one being that as long as there are microorganisms, epidemic disease will remain a potential biological threat to human life everywhere. In recent years, new or newly discovered epidemic diseases have continued to turn up at the rate of six to seven per decade; but when these new (or newly resurgent) epidemics break out in the developed countries, most of them are detected and contained so quickly that comparatively few lives are lost.

AIDS is the great exception to this pattern. First recognized as a new epidemic disease in 1981, AIDS was killing about fifty thousand Americans a year by 1994–1995; but even this tragic loss of life to a single disease was not sufficient to create a traditional mortality crisis at the national level. Thus, all through the AIDS epidemic, American death rates remained low and flat; and the slow rise of life expectancy at birth continued at the national level.

By historical standards, even this deadly epidemic disease was quickly brought under limited medical control. In the 1980s, most persons with AIDS died within two years of being diagnosed; presently, AIDS patients who receive appropriate drug treatment can expect to live for decades. Since treatment is expensive (ten to twenty thousand dollars per person per year), only developed countries can afford the best medicine. Unless costs can be reduced quickly, millions of lives in the developing countries, especially Africa, will continue to be lost prematurely to an epidemic disease because an effective drug treatment, which is available, is not affordable.

Scholars may debate the effect that bringing AIDS under control would have in the poorest countries. Malthusian perspectives suggest that an epidemic such as AIDS can be considered a natural consequence of rapid population growth and increasing poverty; but at present, it is unacceptable to argue that nature should take its course and be allowed to "correct" overpopulation. In the development literature, all diseases (endemic or epidemic, infectious or chronic) are defined as barriers to development. Since epidemics are assumed to perpetuate poverty, rather than reduce it, their elimination is all to the good. To suggest otherwise is not acceptable. As a consequence, regardless of any merits Malthus's arguments once may have had, or still may have, they have become empirically and ethically unacceptable.

To the extent that political and moral constraints influence quantitative estimates, the "what ought to be" continues to overwhelm the "what is (or was)." As long as it does, the role of epidemic disease in history, including economic history, will remain too poorly understood to replace controversy with consensus.

[*See also* Diseases.]

BIBLIOGRAPHY

Axtell, James. *The Indians' New South: Cultural Change in the Colonial Southeast.* Baton Rouge, La.,1997.

Benedict, Carol. *Bubonic Plague in Nineteenth-Century China.* Stanford, Calif., 1996.

Biraben, Jean Noël. *Les hommes et la peste en France et dans les pays européens et méditerranéens.* Paris, 1975.

Bloom, Khaled. *The Mississippi Valley's Great Yellow Fever Epidemic of 1878.* Baton Rouge, La., 1993.

Brenner, Robert. "The Agrarian Roots of European Capitalism." In *The Brenner Debate: Agrarian Class Structure and Economic Development in Pre-Industrial Europe,* edited by T. H. Ashton and C. H. Philpin, pp. 213–327. New York, 1985.

Cliff, Andrew, Peter Haggett, and Matthew Smallman-Raynor. *Deciphering Global Epidemics: Analytical Approaches to the Disease Records of World Cities, 1888–1912.* Cambridge and New York, 1998.

Cohen, Mark N. *Health and the Rise of Civilization.* New Haven, 1989.

Creighton, Charles. *A History of Epidemics in Britain from AD 664 to the Extinction of the Plague.* 2 vols. Cambridge, 1891.

Crosby, Alfred. "Hawaiian Depopulation as a Model for the Amerindian Experience." In *Epidemics and Ideas,* edited by Terence Ranger and Paul Slack, pp. 175–202. Cambridge, 1992.

Del Panta, Lorenzo. *Le epidemie nella storia demografica italiana.* Turin, 1980.

Duncan-Jones, Richard. "The Impact of the Antonine Plague." *Journal of Roman Archaeology* 9 (1996), 108–136.

Easterlin, Richard. "How Beneficent is the Market? A Look at the Modern History of Mortality." *European Review of Economic History* 3 (1999), 257–294.

Epstein, Steven R. *Freedom and Growth: The Rise of States and Markets in Europe, 1300–1750.* New York, 2000.

Ewald, Paul. *Evolution of Infectious Disease.* Oxford, 1994.

Flinn, Michael. *The European Demographic System, 1500–1820.* Baltimore, 1981.

Fox, Daniel M. *The Failure and Future of American Health Policy.* Berkeley, 1993.

Haggett, Peter. *The Geographical Structure of Epidemics.* Oxford, 2000.

Haines, Michael. "The White Population of the United States, 1790–1920. In *A Population History of North America,* edited by Michael Haines and Richard Steckel, pp. 305–369. Cambridge, 2000.

Hardy. Anne. *The Epidemic Streets.* Oxford, 1993.

Hatcher, John. *Plague, Population and the English Economy, 1348–1530.* London, 1977.

Henderson, John. "Epidemics in Renaissance Florence: Medical Theory and Government Response." In *Maladie et société (XIIe–XVIIIe siècles),* edited by N. Bulst and R. Delort, pp. 165–186. Paris, 1989.

Herlihy, David. *The Black Death and the Transformation of the West.* Cambridge, Mass., 1997.

Himmelfarb, Gertrude. *The Idea of Poverty.* London, 1984.

Jannetta, Ann B. *Epidemics and Mortality in Early Modern Japan.* Princeton, 1987.

Johansson, S. Ryan. "Food for Thought: Rhetoric and Reality in Modern Mortality History." *Historical Methods* 27 (1994), 101–125.

Johansson, S. Ryan, and Carl Mosk. "Exposure Resistance and Life Expectancy: Disease and Death during the Economic Development of Japan, 1900–1960." *Population Studies* 41 (1987) 207–235.

Karlen, Arno. *Plague's Progress: A Social History of Disease.* London, 1996.

Kiple, Kenneth. "The Ecology of Disease." In *Cambridge Encyclopedia of Human Disease,* edited by Kenneth F. Kiple, vol. l, pp. 357–381. London, 1993.

Kunitz, Stephen. *Disease and Social Diversity: The European Impact on the Health of Non-Europeans.* New York, 1994.

Landers, John. *Death and the Metropolis: Studies in the Demographic History of London, 1670–1830.* Cambridge, 1993.

Le Bras, Hervé. "Malthus and the Two Mortalities." In *Malthus Past and Present,* edited by J. Dupaquier, A. Fauve-Chamoux, and E. Grebenik, pp. 31–43. London, 1988.

Lee, James, and Wang Feng. *One Quarter of Humanity: Malthusian Mythology and Chinese Realities, 1700–2000.* Cambridge, Mass., 1999.

Livi-Bacci, Massimo. *The Population of Europe: A History.* Oxford, 1999.

Malthus. Thomas R. "An Essay on the Principle of Population." In *The Works of Thomas Robert Malthus,* edited by E. Wrigely and D. Souden. London, 1986.

Matossian, Mary A. K. *Poisons of the Past: Molds, Epidemics and History.* New Haven, 1989.

McCaa, Robert. "The Peopling of Mexico from Origins to Revolution." In *A Population History of North America,* edited by Michael Haines and Richard Steckel, pp. 241–304. Cambridge, 2000.

McNeil, William H. *Plagues and Peoples.* Garden City, N.Y., 1976.

Mercer, Alex. *Disease Mortality and Population in Transition.* Leicester, 1990.

Mokyr, Joel. *The Lever of Riches: Technological Creativity and Economic Progress.* New York, 1990.

Mosk, Carl, and S. Ryan Johansson. "Income and Mortality: Evidence from Modern Japan." *Population and Development Review* 12 (1986), 415–440.

Nutton, Vivian. "Medicine in Medieval Western Europe, 1000–1500." In *The Western Medical Tradition,* edited by L. Conrad, M. Neve, V. Nutton, R. Porter, and A. Wear, pp. 139–206. Cambridge, 1995.

Omran, Abdel R. "The Epidemiologic Transition: A Theory of the Epidemiology of Population Change." *Milbank Memorial Fund Quarterly* 49 (1971), 509–538.

Palloni, Alberto. "On the Role of Crises in Historical Perspective: An Exchange." *Population and Development Review* 14 (1988), 145–158.

Pomeranz, Kenneth. *The Great Divergence: China, Europe, and the Making of the Modern World Economy.* Princeton, 2000.

Preston, Samuel. *Mortality Patterns in National Populations.* New York, 1976.

Preston, Samuel, Nathan Keyfitz, and Robert Schoen. *Causes of Death: Life Tables for National Populations.* New York, 1972.

Reff, Daniel T. *Disease, Depopulation, and Culture Change, Northwestern New Spain, 1515–1764.* Salt Lake City, 1991.

Riley, James C. *Rising Life Expectancy: A Global History.* Cambridge, 2001.

Saris, P. "The Justinian Plague: Origins and Effects." Manuscript. Trinty College, Cambridge, 2001.

Scott, Susan, and Christopher J. Duncan. *Human Demography and Disease.* Cambridge, 1998.

Snooks, Graeme D. *The Dynamic Society: Exploring the Sources of Global Change.* London, 1996.

Stannard, David E. *American Holocaust: Columbus and the Conquest of the New World.* New York, 1992.

Szreter, Simon, and Graham Mooney. "Urbanization, Mortality, and the Standard of Living Debate: New Estimates of the Expectation of Life at Birth in Nineteenth-Century British Cities." *Economic History Review* 51 (1998), 84–112.

Timaeus, Ian. "Mortality in Sub-Saharan Africa." In *United Nations Symposium on Health and Mortality,* pp. 367–392. Brussels, 1997.

Twigg, Graham. *The Black Death: A Biological Reappraisal.* London, 1984.

Watts, Sheldon J. *Epidemics and History: Disease, Power, and Imperialism.* New Haven, 1997.

Weinberg, Eugene. "Iron and Infection." *Microbiological Review* 42 (1978), 45–66.

Wrigley, Edward A. "A Simple Model of London's Importance in Changing English Society and Economy, 1650–1750." *Past and Present* 27 (1967), 44–70.

Wrigely, Edward A., and Roger Schofield. *The Population History of England, 1541–1871: A Reconstruction.* Cambridge, Mass., 1981. See Appendix 10.

Zurbrigg, S. "Evolution of Colonial Asian Population History." IUSSP Conference on Asian Population History, Taipei, Taiwan, 4–8 January 1995.

S. RYAN JOHANSSON

ERICSSON, L. M.

ERICSSON, L. M. (1846–1926), Swedish mechanic and entrepreneur.

Only a few details of Ericsson's early years are known. Having lost his father at age twelve, he began work as a smith's apprentice two years later. In 1866, at age twenty, Ericsson moved to Stockholm, where, for six years, he worked at Öllers & Co., the first workshop of the electromechanical industry in Sweden. There he acquired a reputation as a particularly industrious and skillful instrument maker.

Like many other promising industrialists at that time, Ericsson obtained a government travel grant, enabling him to train, study, and work in some of the more industrially developed European countries. He journeyed to Germany and Switzerland to acquire practical experience in electrotechnology, and he worked at one of the most prominent electromechanical engineering companies in Europe, Siemens & Halske of Berlin. Probably few grants of this type have paid off so well for a country.

In 1876, Ericsson was ready to strike out on his own and set up a small electromechanical workshop. The firm, LM Ericsson & Co., repaired telegraph instruments. In the same year Alexander Graham Bell invented the telephone, and Bell telephones began to show up in Ericsson's shop for repairs. In 1878, he began to produce telephones himself, marking the start of LM Ericsson as a telecommunications company. Ericsson did not invent the telephone, but he proved to be an entrepreneurial and mechanical genius in improving existing inventions and giving telephone instruments an attractive design.

At that time, the international Bell group of companies, in practice, had a monopoly on manufacturing telephones and distributing operating services. They could charge their subscribers high rates, which prevented the spread of telephones. A Swedish engineer, Henrik Tore Cedergren, led reaction against this monopoly. To carry out his vision of "a telephone in each home in Stockholm" he formed Stockholm's Public Telephone Company in 1883, relying on Ericsson to design and produce the high- quality equipment necessary to compete with the Bell companies. In turn, Ericsson, in 1885, provided the practical design and engineering used for the first hand sets combining receiver and transmitter in a single unit. Cedergren's and Ericsson's fruitful cooperation made Stockholm the world's leader in telephone density in 1886.

L. M. Ericsson retired from his company and severed all formal connections as manager and owner in 1903. In 1924, he contracted an illness that made him so shaky that he no longer could read or write, and two years later he died.

Before the outbreak of World War I, LM Ericsson already was a multinational firm. Despite great difficulties in the interwar period, the firm survived and prospered during World War II, starting a recovery that has lasted into the twenty-first century. Ericsson, as Lars Magnus Ericsson's firm is called today, is one of the largest and most advanced telecommunications companies in the world. Now quoted on several stock exchanges, it was the dominant firm on the Stockholm Stock Exchange during the 1990s.

BIBLIOGRAPHY

Attman, A., J. Kuuse, and U. Olsson. *LM Ericsson: 100 Years*. Örebro, Sweden. 1977.

Hubendick, E. "Ericsson, Lars Magnus." *Svensk biografiskt lexikon*, vol. 14. Stockholm, 1951–1952.

Johansson, Hemming. *Lars Magnus Ericsson: några biografiska data*. Stockholm, 1946.

Johansson, Hemming. *Telefonaktiebolaget L. M. Ericsson*. Stockholm, 1953.

Meurling, John, and Richard Jeans. *A Switch in Time*. London, 1995.

KARL GRATZER

ERITREA. *See* Ethiopia.

ESPIONAGE, ECONOMIC AND INDUSTRIAL.

Espionage is the stealing of secrets and is conventionally associated with military conflict. But commercial organizations also have their secrets and their theft is a form of espionage—industrial espionage. Economic espionage is a less common term and refers to the threat to national security posed by the theft of commercial secrets; such theft undermines not the military strength of a country, but its economic competitiveness. United States export controls to prevent the flow of high technology information to the Soviet bloc during the cold war deftly confused economic with military threat in the notion of dual-use technology (technology with both civilian and military application), a notion that nicely included the Japanese in the military threat to the United States.

In its military derivation, espionage is akin to many other management terms. The theme of the leader rallying the forces of an organization to defeat an external enemy is long established, especially in strategy. Military metaphor is less appropriate to new forms of organizational structure. The virtual organization, the network organization, and a general appreciation that firms cooperate as they compete do not easily accommodate a fundamental model of us versus them. Nor are they compatible with the traditional idea of espionage.

As the economy becomes more information-intensive, it becomes increasingly obvious that information is a valuable resource. The organization tends to hoard and guard something so precious, judging its capacity to innovate and compete to be a function of how much information it has and how little its competitors have. This is information mercantilism and it is unsustainable. Information is not like other goods. Organizations must give information if they are to receive information. As chatelaine of an information fortress, the senior manager has trouble with this concept. Though disclosed information is inevitably retained, the manager sees disclosure as the organization's loss and the competitor's gain, a perception encouraged by the "competitive intelligence" community.

> Many businessmen fail to appreciate the extremely wide range of corporate data that could be useful to a competitor and thus harmful to their own company. (Edwards, 1987, 18–19).

Measures taken to prevent the loss of information may well disrupt transactions that acquire information (especially tacit and uncodified information) from the outside world. In the midst of organizational and market failure, such transactions are often effected by individual employees exchanging information in their own personal networks. These employees are trading in information on their own account and primarily for their own benefit, and may be incapable of distinguishing between the organization's information and their own, so it is hardly surprising that their activities are often confused with espionage. This is not to say that the organization should make all its information available to competitors. Far from it; some information should be kept secret because it is critical to strategy, or because it is easily transferred and does not require complex exchange transactions in the personal networks of key employees. Sales figures might be an example. There is nothing sophisticated about the simple sale of explicit information by employees who know only that the information is valued by others. Why, then, are the two processes so readily confused? An historical interpretation is helpful.

Modern observers can be taken aback by the often casual attitude toward espionage displayed by the entrepreneurs of the British Industrial Revolution. Managers knew full well that Continental visitors were often spies and still showed whatever there was to see, arguing that their own innovation would be faster than that of any imitator. But they were also practical, appreciating as much as the modern entrepreneurs of Silicon Valley that only a knowledgable market will buy new technology. The same understanding persuaded British exporters of new machinery, first the threshing machine and then the steam engine, to allow skilled mechanics to accompany their machines and to train local workers in their use and maintenance. In contrast, the British government generally sought to prohibit the loss of the information embodied in man and machine. Governments have always been much more anxious to acquire information for innovation than to part with such information.

It is sometimes argued that the innovations of the Industrial and Agricultural Revolutions depended on technique rather than science, that innovation is now derived from government policy and corporate strategy rather than individual endeavor, whether artisan or professional. Innovation is presented as the product of system—political, organizational, managerial. As a threat to innovation, espionage supports beliefs that innovation is an output of scientific qualifications, of large organizations, of R&D laboratories, of investment in research, of managed process.

Thus, for example, the patent system, which suits the need of large chemical and pharmaceutical firms to protect information that cannot easily be kept secret, is preserved and strengthened not only because it facilitates their innovation, but also because it is compatible with prevailing beliefs about innovation. Notions of network and information transactions, of individual responsibility for information exchange, of information as personal rather than corporate property are inimical to these beliefs. So, too, is the experience of organizational collaboration and international development demonstrating that innovation is actually rather hard to achieve, even when information transfer is intended. Instead, the beliefs support a myth in which the slightest lapse in procedure results in the theft of organizational information and its instant use by competitors. It follows that every effort must be made to prevent this leakage.

Secrecy and need-to-know regimes impede information flow and transactions in personal networks, and would ultimately force organizations to innovate in isolation. Avoiding this fate requires the admission that most information for innovation comes from others, that this information cannot be acquired unless information is given in return, and that individuals are best equipped to effect these transactions. These individuals are also well able—as organizational innovation systems apparently are not—to distinguish between a transaction that exchanges tacit information for other tacit information and one that purchases extremely explicit information with an envelope stuffed with banknotes. The information transaction of the former, together with mobility of human containers of information, is as essential to innovation now as it was two hundred years ago: the information transfer of the latter is primitive and unlikely to contribute much to innovation. Yet it is the former that attracts the attention of the spy catcher.

Espionage in industry is a growing menace to the prosperity of our country. Never discuss secret work in public places. Keep our secrets secret. (British Cold War poster)

When these constraints are recommended even for Silicon Valley, where innovation and competitiveness have long been acknowledged to be dependent on personal information networks, the irony is complete.

There is no way to know who is listening … . One experienced listener remarked about *The Lion and The Compass*, a popular Silicon Valley bar: "If you really want to spy, just pull up a stool and listen." (Bronson, J. G., 1987, 173–178).

BIBLIOGRAPHY

Augsdorfer, Peter. *Forbidden Fruit: An Analysis of Bootlegging, Uncertainty, and Learning in Corporate R&D.* Aldershot, U.K., 1996.
Bronson, J. G. "Unfriendly Eyes." *IEEE Transactions on Professional Communication* 30.3 (1987), 173–178.
Bruland, K. *British Technology and European Industrialisation.* Cambridge 1989.
Edwards, E. "Corporate Espionage: Legal but Usually Dishonest." *Management Accounting* 65.10 (1987), 18–19.
Harris, J. R. "Industrial Espionage in the Eighteenth Century." *Industrial Archaeology Review* 7.2 (1985), 127–138.
Hodkinson, K. "Spies, Brain Drains, and Allied Problems: Reflections on English Industrial Espionage Law." *International Journal of Technology Management* 3.1–2 (1988), 87–103.
Jeremy, D. J. "Damming the Flood: British Government Efforts to Check the Outflow of Technicians and Machinery, 1780–1843." *Business History Review* 51.1 (1977), 1–34.
Macdonald, Stuart. *Technology and the Tyranny of Export Controls: Whisper Who Dares.* London, 1990.
Macdonald, Stuart. "Nothing Either Good or Bad: Industrial Espionage and Technology Transfer." *International Journal of Technology Management* 8.1–2 (1993), 95–105.
Macdonald, Stuart. "Industrial Espionage and Innovation." *Interdisciplinary Science Reviews* 21.3 (1996), 209–214.
Mathias, Peter. "Skills and the Diffusion of Innovations from Britain in the Eighteenth Century." *Transactions of the Royal Historical Society* 25 (1975), 93–113.
Sugihara, Kaoru. "The Development of an Informational Infrastructure in Meiji Japan." In *Information Acumen: The Understanding and Use of Knowledge in Modern Business*, edited by Lisa Bud-Frierman. London, 1994, 75–97.
Tann, Jennifer. "Marketing Methods in the International Steam Engine Market: The Case of Boulton and Watt." *Journal of Economic History* 38.2 (1978), 363–389.
Woolrich, A. P. *Mechanical Arts and Merchandise: Industrial Espionage and Travellers' Accounts as a Source for Technical Historians.* Eindhoven, Netherlands, 1986.

STUART MACDONALD

ETHIOPIA. The economic history of northeast Africa, which now includes the nation-states of Ethiopia, Eritrea, and Somalia, has taken its contours from the exigencies of both geography and environment. In geopolitical terms, the region includes the north-south axes of the Nile Valley in the west and the Red Sea on its eastern side. Its long-term trade and cultural contacts thus reflect connections to the Mediterranean world as well as to the Persian Gulf and Indian Ocean trade complexes. In ancient as well as modern times, these long-distance economic networks have been defined by the region's political economy and its cultures.

The regional economy of the Ethiopia/Eritrea region is a product of the politically dominant highland zones and the complementary human and physical ecology of surrounding lowlands below the eastern and western escarpments. Highlands above 1,500 meters (about 5,000 feet) cover over 40 percent of the region and make up almost half of Africa's highland area. Rainfall is the key "limiting factor" in agriculture and directly reflects elevation, ranging from 1,200 millimeters (30 inches) per year in the highlands to below 400 millimeters (10 inches) in the lowlands. Transsected by river valleys and mountain ranges, the highlands contain numerous microecologies as well as areas affected by rainfall shadows. The result has been a history of agricultural productivity juxtaposed with historical patterns of drought revealed in a historical record that spans approximately three millennia.

Economic Foundations. The macroeconomic patterns are twofold. First, the political economy of the region over time shows a distinct pattern of economic extraction in peripheral areas (lowlands and southern highlands) by the politically and militarily dominant northern highlands, including the empire state of Aksum and the later Solomonic empire that built its hegemony on Christian tradition and ox-plow agriculture. Extraction included long-distance trade goods such as ivory, frankincense, gold, gum arabic, and slaves, all commodities exported into wider trade networks in the Mediterranean and Indian Ocean areas. This long-distance trade also led in the late eighteenth and early nineteenth centuries to the rise of several small kingdoms—Kaffa, Jimma, Gera, and others—in the southwest part of the region, where the trade commodities had originated.

The second foundation of economic production, in the highlands, was (and is) ox-plow agriculture carried out on smallholder farms. The technology of the single-tine ox-plow has remained in place since at least 500 BCE, and has been most commonly associated with expansion of the historical Christian tradition of the Aksum Empire (c. 500 BCE–1000 CE). However, its annual-crop, cereal-based farming system has crossed the highlands into lands that include Christian and Muslim populations and Semitic and Cushitic languages. The system includes the simple but effective plow, skills of animal husbandry, and a package of crops that include several endemic cereals and pulses (Eragrostis teff, Niger seed, and many distinct cultivars of sorghum and barley). Because of its base in annual crops and ox traction, the farming system required land clearing and land use that is historically more extensive than intensive. Its labor efficiency historically produced surplus food, which allowed the growth of state and ecclesiastical hierarchies ranging from the central Solomonic Christian kingdom of the central highlands to smaller kingdoms and states to the west (Wallega), and states that embraced Islamic influence in the southwest (Jimma, Gera, Kaffa) and the southeast (Harer, Yifat). Traditions of pastoralism and animal husbandry in the agricultural highlands and pastoral lowlands have given the Ethiopian region Africa's highland livestock population.

Shaping the Modern Economy in the Age of Imperialism, 1869–1916. Nation-states in northeast Africa, like their counterparts in Europe and Asia, took their modern form during the last quarter of the nineteenth century. For Ethiopia this process took place with the expansion of the Shawan kingdom of Menilek II (also Menelik) from its base in the central highlands to its successful efforts to control the extractive trade of the southwest and the east. Shawa expanded its political control over the regional economy by playing off expansionist European powers, concentrating its control over regional trade, and monopolizing firearms obtained from international trade. In the far north, however, the Italians managed to establish a colony (Eritrea) north of the Merab River in the 1890s. By the time of the emperor's death in 1913, the Shawan-dominated state had established a permanent capital at Addis Ababa, built a rail link to the French Red Sea port of Djibouti, and begun the process of shifting its extractive economic base to cash crops (coffee, cotton). For its part, the Italian colony of Eritrea began to build a reexport economy that depended on cross-border trade with Ethiopia and the Sudan and on attempts to construct plantation agriculture. By 1913, Addis Ababa also had become the symbolic and economic center of an ethnically diverse empire that stretched from the Eritrean colonial border to the borders of British East Africa and the Anglo-Egyptian Sudan. Addis Ababa now is Ethiopia's commercial center and has developed an elaborate system of urban food supply, relying upon a combination of commercial agriculture, adaptations of its older landholding system, and an emerging mercantile sector.

External trade was small but significant, though constrained by lack of a currency and formal banking, as well as a revenue base dependent on in-kind transfers that flowed to regional authorities rather than the national treasury. The long-distance trade originated in southwest Ethiopia and flowed out to the Red Sea ports of Massawa, Tajura, Zeila, and Berbera. In 1892, Menilek issued a decree that transferred the traditional *asrat* (tithe) from the support of local churches directly to the support of the state. In 1895, silver coins bearing his likeness began replacing the silver Maria Teresa thalers that had served as the major currency in the Red Sea economy since the beginning of the nineteenth century. In 1907, the emperor established the first cabinet, including a ministry of finance, a ministry of agriculture and labor, and a ministry of foreign affairs and trade. In 1917, the railway begun two decades prior by Menilek's government and French partners finally reached Addis Ababa. Telephone and telegraph lines followed the railway line to Addis Ababa and eventually reached regional capitals and markets by the 1920s.

The Modernization of Tradition: Haile Sellassie, 1916–1974. In 1916, a young aristocrat named Tafari Makonnen assumed power as the regent of the Empress Zawditu. Educated at a French mission in the eastern city of Harer, Tafari began a systematic policy of centralizing power in Addis Ababa and putting a modern economic infrastructure in place. To do this, he began to appoint his own loyalists to regional customs posts, authorized the foundation of a national bank, and surrounded himself with educated "young Ethiopians" who served as the shock troops of modernization of the nation's political economy. Fundamental to the economic transition was the arrival of an increasing number of expatriates of Indian, Armenian, Greek, Yemeni, and European origin. These small-scale entrepreneurs contributed to the expansion of the import-export trade, processing plants, and informal credit. The royal family and the aristocracy also played key roles in controlling economic concessions for mining, transportation, and agriculture; and, by the early 1930s, the emperor had hired foreign financial advisers, monetized much of the exchange economy, and continued building an economic infrastructure to move goods internally and into international trade. Crowned king in 1928, Tafari assumed the throne as Emperor Haile Sellassie (also spelled Haile Selassie) in 1930, and began a full-scale modernization program that he hoped would forestall Mussolini's imperial designs. In 1932, he took direct control of Jimma, an important coffee district, and built Ethiopia's first modern commercial road. He also authorized America's Sinclair Oil Company to begin explorations in the Ogaden region, in an attempt to draw the United States into a more direct role as a potential patron. Nevertheless, in 1935 Mussolini's troops invaded and quickly defeated Ethiopia's fledgling modern army. Italy's embattled occupation of Ethiopia (1936–1941) failed to transform the country's rural economy. Attempts to introduce a colonial currency, develop wheat production for the Italian market, and resettle "surplus" Italian peasants in the Ethiopian highlands failed. Yet the occupation set up a system of roads and bridges and an urban infrastructure still visible today.

The Italian colonial episode ended in 1941. In the postwar years, Emperor Haile Sellassie's government began the process of aligning itself internationally with the United States and the United Nations and new multilateral donors such as the World Bank. In 1952, Haile Sellassie signed a military assistance agreement with the United States to replace its dependence on the British, and he negotiated with the United Nations to place Eritrea under Ethiopian control as a federation. In this way, Ethiopia obtained control of Eritrea's important mercantile skills and an industrial base in light manufacturing, brewing, and transport. In the private sector, Addis Ababa's growth reflected the expansion of sectors such as transportation, insurance, and manufacturing, in which the aristocracy had a major role.

By the mid-1960s, Ethiopia's urban expansion led its economic growth. Ethiopia, including Eritrea, sported some two hundred towns, which held almost 10 percent of its population and grew at an annual rate of 7 percent. The towns and the cities housed landowners, state functionaries, and merchants, who dominated the marketing of food and agricultural inputs, though urban residents still exercised little direct control over food production.

A series of five-year plans beginning in 1957 set priorities in urban infrastructure, import substitution, and housing for a growing urban bureaucratic class. Investments in agriculture constituted only 6 percent of the total budget and consisted of surveys to develop potential irrigation schemes for export production. In later plans, agricultural investments increased but emphasized export production in cotton and livestock from large commercial farms rather than smallholders, who made up over 90 percent of the population.

In 1962, Haile Sellassie's imperial government abrogated the federation with Eritrea, making it a province of Ethiopia. The program of integration led to the migration of human capital from Eritrea's capital Asmara to Addis Ababa, though Eritrea's fundamental reexport economy continued to benefit from its access to the Red Sea and to internal trade with northern Ethiopia. Capital investment, which had peaked in the 1930s under Italian colonial rule, steadily declined in the following decades. Declining investment in infrastructure and in industry in Eritrea became one of several causes for the growth of Eritrean separatism, which began in the early 1960s and culminated in 1993 with Eritrea's formal separation as an independent state.

Ethiopia's 1974 revolution was a major historical event in both economic and political terms. The early 1970s had witnessed several economic shocks, including international publicity about a major famine in the country's northeast and the effects of the 1973 oil crisis, which hit Ethiopia's transport sector hard. After a 1973 military coup, the new government, by Mengistu Haile Mariam, directed a revolution led by new urban classes and military leaders who sought to usurp state power from the aristocracy. To do this, the military government (the Derg) in 1975 attempted a process of socialist transformation that included major land reform, which broke the rural links of

ETHIOPIA. Farmer plows the land to prepare it for the next crop, 1999. (© Betty Press/Woodfin Camp and Associates, New York)

the governing class and, at least initially, sought to return "land to the tiller." Even though land reform brought major change to the country's political economy, the revolution was fundamentally an urban phenomenon in which young military officers and ideologues followed the land reform by nationalizing banks, transport, and large private businesses and attempted to control grain marketing. A war with Somalia followed Ethiopia's political realignment with the Socialist bloc. Its foreign aid, per capita, dropped to the world's lowest rate.

In the agricultural sector, the government attempted to lead a social revolution based on major land reform and formation, especially in the south and east, of Soviet-style producer cooperatives and cooperative marketing organizations. These coercive rural policies, forced labor on development projects, and new policies in the ministry of agriculture changed Ethiopia's food supply. Formerly dominant crops of teff, barley, and sorghum gave way to maize as the country's number one food crop, despite consumer preferences for the traditional crops. Urban food prices jumped dramatically as farmers shifted their cropping strategies away from the controlled food crops and coffee; government shops attempted to control scarce commodities such as grain, bread, and fuel.

Although the land reform was enormously popular in rural areas, the forced villagization/resettlement and the state intervention in grain marketing upset smallholding peasants, particularly in the north. In and around the region of Tigray, the Tigrayan Peoples Liberation Front

(TPLF) gained ground in a guerilla war that gradually drew in a disaffected peasantry from other regions. In 1984, a devastating famine hit the north, exposing the politics of food as a weapon and also the depleted foreign exchange coffers in Addis Ababa. In an attempt to control rural populations and provide concentrated services to rural people in the mid-1980s, the government instituted a program of massive resettlement and the construction of centralized villages. Economic policy based on forced rural labor and nongovernmental organization (NGO) food-for-work programs dominated environmental policy. Such programs built terraces and roads and reforested hillsides, though few of these efforts succeeded in the long term. In Eritrea, military offensives, sometimes accompanied by spurious economic development campaigns, failed, and central government forces steadily lost ground, exhausting foreign exchange reserves. In 1991, the combined forces of the TPLF and other regional groups (now called the Ethiopian Peoples Revolutionary Democratic Front or EPRDF) captured the capital and recognized the victory in Eritrea of the Eritrean Peoples Liberation Front, which had long sought independence from Ethiopia.

Since 1991, the EPRDF-led government has sought to implement a policy of ethnic federalism and economic liberalization and a structural adjustment program. Although rural land remains in control of the state, marketing of agricultural inputs (fertilizer, improved seed, and equipment) ostensibly has been privatized, and there has been substantial urban economic growth, especially in the service sector. The economic effects of federalism are unclear. There is continuing debate over the degree of centralization of state revenues. Growth in agricultural production in the early 1990s seems to have been the result of good rains, but also perhaps an aggressive "green revolution" package program based primarily on production of maize.

In 1993, Eritrea gained its official independence from Ethiopia. Initially, cross-border trade and a common currency with Ethiopia spurred economic growth in Eritrea's reexport economy. Eritrean merchants imported goods and purchased commodities under favorable Ethiopian exchange rates and reexported them at the two Red Sea ports under Eritrea's control. Eritrea's economy also sustained itself by remittances paid by economically successful expatriate Eritreans in Europe and North America. In 1997, however, Eritrea issued its own currency unit, the nakfa. In a change in policy, Ethiopia did not accept the new currency at parity with the birr and demanded hard currency in bilateral transactions. These economic issues led to tense relations between the two countries, and in May 1998 a border dispute broke out as a major war. Massive spending by both countries on military hardware has clouded the immediate economic future, as has evidence of a new drought/famine that has affected the eastern escarpment of the region.

BIBLIOGRAPHY

Bekele, Shiferaw, ed. *An Economic History of Modern Ethiopia*. Dakar, Senegal, 1995.

Clapham, Christopher. *Transformation and Continuity in Revolutionary Ethiopia*. Cambridge, 1988.

Crummey, Donald. "Abyssinian Feudalism." *Past and Present* 89 (1980), 115–138.

Donham, Donald, and James Wendy. *The Southern Marches of Imperial Ethiopia*. Cambridge, 1986.

Erlich, Haggai. *The Struggle over Eritrea: War and Revolution in the Horn of Africa*. Stanford, Calif., 1983.

Marcus, Harold G. *A History of Ethiopia*. Berkeley, 1994.

Marcus, Harold G., *Haile Sellassie I: The Formative Years, 1892–1936*. Lawrenceville, N.J., 1995.

McCann, James C. *People of the Plow: An Agricultural History of Ethiopia*. Madison, Wis., 1995.

Selassie, Bereket Habte. *Conflict and Intervention in the Horn of Africa*. New York, 1980.

Tamrat, Taddesse. *Church and State in Ethiopia*. Oxford, 1972.

Zewde, Bahru. *A History of Modern Ethiopia, 1855–1991*. Oxford; Athens, Ohio; and Addis Ababa, 2001.

JAMES C. MCCANN AND SHIFERAW BEKELE

EURODOLLAR. The "Euromarket" and the "Eurodollar" refer to the pool of unregulated and uncontrolled capital that emerged and grew rapidly over the course of the 1960s, first in dollars, and then, much later, in other currencies used for financial operations outside their national areas—first in Europe and then in many other offshore centers. This new pool took the form of deposits, credits, increasingly syndicated bank credits, and, later, of securitized instruments, Eurobonds and short-term promissory notes, called Euronotes.

It would be misleading to think of this as simply a post-1945 development. Already in the interwar years, deposits and loans in non-national currencies had provided an element of competition between currencies. There had been British, Dutch, and Swiss dollar loans to Central Europe.

The postwar Eurodollar market began in the late 1940s, when the new Chinese communist government placed its dollar earnings with a Soviet bank in Paris (the Banque Commerciale pour l'Europe du Nord). In the early 1950s, after Yugoslav gold in New York was sequestered by the U.S. government, the Soviet Union and China made a consistent practice of not depositing dollars derived from export earnings with American banks. The Federal Reserve Board's Regulation Q, limiting interest payments on U.S. domestic bank deposits, and the 1965 program of voluntary restraint on capital exports, which later became mandatory, added an American incentive to leave dollars abroad. U.S. capital exports and military spending resulted in additional accumulations. In the early 1960s, the majority of Eurodollars were held by central banks. After exchange controls on current transactions were lifted in 1958, Swiss and British commercial banks were free to accept foreign-currency deposits and could offer more favorable rates than those on the U.S. domestic market. A much larger and more active private market developed after 1966 as U.S. money-market interest rates rose above the levels permitted on bank deposits under Regulation Q. Once the market had reached a certain size, it generated transactions no longer necessarily limited to outflows from the United States. By 1971, it was estimated that half the Eurodollars originated in Europe. In 1967, private banks began a practice of rolling over short-term deposits into what were effectively long-term loans. In 1963, the first postwar dollar bond issues outside the United States were concluded. As a result of these developments, during the course of the 1960s, the Eurodollar market grew to a very substantial size: from $1,500 million in 1959 to $46,000 million at the end of 1970. Since there were by then other currencies than the dollar used for extraterritorial transactions, the total "Euromarket" was larger: $57,000 million for 1970 and $71,000 million for 1971.

The development of the Eurocurrency markets meant a definitive end of the Bretton Woods attempt to create an internationally controlled money supply. Some observers blamed the Eurodollar for an inflationary development, analogous to the role of banks in providing a domestic money multiplier; but most academic analysis rejected this interpretation. But by increasing the options available for the transfer of money, it also inevitably made for greater instability on currency markets, undermined attempts at capital control, and thus also helped to make unviable the fixed parity regime of Bretton Woods.

BIBLIOGRAPHY

Johnston, R. B. *The Economics of the Euro-market: History, Theory, Policy.* London, 1983.

Swoboda, Alexander. *Credit Creation in the Euromarket: Alternative Theories and Implications for Control.* New York, 1980.

HAROLD JAMES

EUROPEAN MONETARY SYSTEM. The European Monetary System (EMS) was instituted in 1979 among a group of European Union (EU) countries (Belgium, Luxembourg, Netherlands, France, Germany, Ireland, Denmark, and Italy). This group was later enlarged to include Spain, Portugal, Sweden, and the United Kingdom. The creation of the EMS came as a reaction to the great volatility of the major exchange rates during the 1970s, and the threat that this was perceived to pose for trade relations within the EU.

The EMS had two features, the Exchange Rate Mechanism (ERM) and the European Currency Unit (ECU), the ERM being the more important feature. In this system participating countries committed themselves to keep their bilateral exchange rates within a prespecified band 2.25 percent above and below the bilateral central rate. (Italy and later Spain and Portugal profited from a larger band, 2×6 percent. See Gros and Thygesen, 1998, and De Grauwe, 2000.) In order to sustain this agreement a system of short-term financing was instituted. If, say, France had to intervene in the foreign exchange market to prevent the franc (FF) from dropping below its lower limit against the deutsche mark (DM), the Bundesbank would lend unlimited amounts of the German mark to the Banque de France to make this intervention possible.

The second feature of the EMS was the creation of the ECU, a new currency unit defined as a basket of the national currencies of the countries participating in the EMS. At the start it was hoped that the ECU would become a parallel currency that would gradually displace the national currencies, but this objective was not realized. The use of the ECU remained quite limited to the issue of international bonds.

The first years of the EMS were characterized by turbulence and frequent crises. The participating countries experienced very different rates of inflation, so that the ERM frequently came under pressure. As a result, the central rates were often adjusted. The high point of these crises was in 1982 to 1983, when serious doubt emerged as to French commitment to the system. In the end the view that France should stay in the EMS prevailed, with the French government making a U-turn on its economic policies away from socialist-inspired programs toward orthodox

economic policies based on fiscal and monetary restriction.

During the 1980s the EMS developed into a more stable system with fewer crises. That was also a time when high-inflation countries used the fixed exchange rate with the strong German mark as an instrument to lower inflationary expectations and to move toward a low-inflation path. (For an analysis of credibility issues in the EMS, see Padoa-Schioppa, Giavazzi and Giovannini, Giavazzi and Pagano, and Fratianni and Hagen.) By the end of the decade, France and other high-inflation countries had achieved this objective.

An important policy shift occurred in 1987, leading to the so-called Bale-Nyborg agreements, which contained a number of technical agreements on the operation of the ERM (e.g., that the participating central banks would be allowed to perform intramarginal interventions using each other's currencies). More important, there was a new political commitment to keep the central rates fixed. Thus, the EMS moved from a system of fixed but frequently adjustable exchange rates into a system in which the central rates would remain fixed. Another important change occurred a little later, around 1990; as a result of the internal market program, EU countries abolished the controls on capital movement. These two changes led to a new type of EMS characterized by rigidly fixed exchange rates and an increasing degree of capital mobility.

The major occurrences in Europe in the early 1990s were the opening up of Eastern Europe and German unification. These events shook the new EMS, creating major asymmetry within the system. On the one hand the United Kingdom, which had joined the EMS in 1990, and France experienced a strong recession. On the other hand, Germany continued to experience a demand-led boom due to a major expansion of German government spending, which itself was the result of unification. This led to conflict over desirable monetary policies. The British and French authorities made it no secret that they desired a more expansionary monetary policy; but because of their peg to the German mark, they were unable to relax monetary policies. The Bundesbank, concerned about the inflationary pressures that existed in Germany, would not yield. This policy conflict between the major participating countries weakened the credibility of the fixed-exchange-rate commitment of UK and French authorities. (For an analysis of the instability of the EMS see Eichengreen and Wyplosz, 1993; see also Walters, 1986.)

In September 1992 a massive speculative attack broke out, forcing the United Kingdom and Italy to leave the system. The FF-DM fixed peg could be maintained, but not for long. In August 1993 a new speculative attack forced the ministers of finance to radically change the system. The permissible band of fluctuation was raised from 2×2.25

percent to 2 × 15 percent. As a result, the total band of fluctuation became 30 percent, transforming the system into a quasi-flexible exchange rate regime. This system of wide bands turned out to be much more manageable than the rigid system with relatively narrow bands that existed before the crisis.

The last phase of existence of the EMS had begun and would continue until 1 January 1999, the date of the start of the European Monetary Union (EMU). On that date the exchange markets within the EMU were abolished, and the EMS ceased to exist. The ECU was transformed into the euro.

This transitional stage was remarkably stable, with a total absence of speculative crises. One reason was undoubtedly the existence of wide margins. Another reason was the Maastricht convergence dynamics. Most EU countries made a strong political commitment to monetary unification and started a program of economic convergence of inflation rates, interest rates, and budgetary policies. This convergence process certainly had the effect of stabilizing the foreign exchange markets. In the end it was successful in helping the EU countries (those willing to do so) to smoothly enter the EMU.

BIBLIOGRAPHY

Begg, D., F. Giavazzi, J. von Hagen, and C. Wyplosz. *EMU: Getting the End-Game Right, Monitoring European Integration 7.* London, 1997.

De Grauwe, Paul, and Lucas Papademos, eds. *The European Monetary System in the 1990s.* London, 1990.

De Grauwe, Paul. *Economics of Monetary Union.* 4th ed. Oxford, 2000.

Eichengreen, B., and C. Wyplosz. "The Unstable EMS." CEPR Discussion Paper 817. London, 1993.

Fratianni, Michele, and Jürgen von Hagen. *The European Monetary System and European Monetary Union.* Boulder, 1992.

Giavazzi, Francesco, and Alberto Giovannini. *Limiting Exchange Rate Flexibility: The European Monetary System.* Cambridge, Mass., 1989.

Giavazzi, Francesco, and M. Pagano. "The Advantage of Tying One's Hands: EMS Discipline and Central Bank Credibility." *European Economic Review* 32 (1988), 1055–1082.

Gros, Daniel, and Niels Thygesen. *European Monetary Integration: From the European Monetary System towards Economic and Monetary Union.* 2d ed. London, 1998.

Ludlow, Peter. *The Making of the European Monetary System.* London, 1982.

Padoa-Scioppa, T. "The European Monetary System: A Long Term View." In *The European Monetary System*, edited by F. Giavazzi, S. Micossi, and M. Miller. Cambridge, 1988.

Walters, Alan. *Britain's Economic Renaissance.* Oxford, 1986.

PAUL DE GRAUWE

EXCHANGE RATES. An exchange rate is the relative price of two moneys. Exactly what is being exchanged has, of course, varied with the assets that were used as money at any point in time. In ancient times and into the early part of the twentieth century, money generally consisted of a full-bodied metallic coinage of one sort or another. In the past two centuries, it has come increasingly to consist of currency notes and, more importantly, bank deposits. Exchange-rate arrangements have varied from systems in which exchange rates are rigidly fixed to ones in which they could vary freely with market forces.

In discussing exchange rates, it is useful to distinguish between nominal and real exchange rates. The nominal exchange rate is simply the actual rate in the foreign exchange market. The real exchange rate, in contrast, is the rate at which a market basket of goods in one country can be exchanged for a market basket of goods in the other. It is, therefore, a theoretical construct rather than something that is directly observable.

The discussion that follows provides a chronological survey of exchange-rate behavior, exchange market practices, and exchange-rate regimes from the classical era forward. It concludes with an overview of the current foreign exchange market.

Greco-Roman Era. In ancient Greece and Rome, the analog of the foreign exchange markets of today were the markets in which one type of coin was exchanged for another. The principals in these markets were the money changers. In the Athens of the fourth century BC these money changers were known as *trapeziate*, so named because of the bench-like tables (*trapeza*) that they used for their transactions. In Rome they were termed *argentarii*. The *argentarii* plied their trade throughout the Roman world, exchanging the foreign gold and silver coins that came to Roman lands against the large Roman bronze coins, the *aes grave*, that made up the domestic Roman coinage during the Republican period.

The details of what went on in these early markets, including those surrounding the course that exchange rates actually followed, are murky. As in any monetary system in which a metallic coinage serves as money, prices of the various metals must have played a major role. Doubtless also of importance were changes in the metallic content of those coins. Such changes could come about as the result of normal wear and tear, of clipping, or of policies of debasement that altered the fineness or weight of the coinage. The last was an occasional occurrence during the time of the Roman Republic and then became completely commonplace under the later Empire.

Two additional items to note in connection with exchange-market practices during this period are what appear to be the beginnings of a market based on financial instruments rather than specie—in this instance, letters of transfer—and the issuance of what was perhaps the first truly international currency, the Roman gold aureus.

Early Middle Ages. The Early Middle Ages suffers from an even greater dearth of information with regard to exchange rates and to monetary conditions than the classical era. Doubtless, a major reason was the breakdown of the money economy in western Europe that occurred after the fall of the Western Roman Empire and the increased use of barter in place of money that followed. Very likely another reason was the diminished level of international trade that characterized the early centuries of that era.

However, a good deal is known about one set of developments during this period. It was the introduction of a full-bodied, stable gold coinage for use in large transactions throughout the Mediterranean region. The earliest such coin, known variously as the *solidus*, the *bezant*, and the *nomisma*, got its start early in the fourth century under the Emperor Constantine. It kept essentially the same gold content until well into the eleventh and continued to be coined in Byzantium until the thirteenth century. This remarkable stability has gone unmatched since. The *nomisma* was a true international currency—"the dollar of the Middle Ages," as one scholar has put it. It did not, however, enjoy a monopoly. From the end of the seventh century, it shared its position with a similar coin introduced in the Moslem world, the *dinar*. Like the *nomisma*, the *dinar* kept a stable metallic content for centuries, and was not debased until three hundred years later.

Thirteenth-Century Commercial Revolution. The thirteenth century was extraordinary in a number of ways. By all accounts it was a time of great learning and of considerable scholarly interchange. It was the start of a European commercial revolution, the chief manifestation of which was substantially increased trade, not only within Europe itself but between Europe and the rest of the world. It was, moreover, a time of considerable financial innovation, including the return to gold coinage in Western Europe.

International trade was centered around the fairs that were held regularly throughout Europe; the fairs of Champagne were the most important. These fairs naturally became centers of foreign exchange activity, and money changers were a regular fixture. Initially the money changers' role was confined mostly to changing one type of coin for another. Then, as bills of exchange increasingly came into use, the money changers, and also certain of the merchants themselves, began to branch out and become intermediaries in this market. As time wore on some of these merchants actually began to specialize in this activity— whence the origin of the term "merchant banker."

The purpose of these bills of exchanges was to eliminate the need for specie to be shipped each time goods were bought and sold. The mechanism was simple and evidently also effective, since the bill of exchange remained the major form in which foreign exchange transactions were effected throughout most of the nineteenth century, and indeed survives today in modified form when coupled with letters of credit.

Here is a typical scenario involving the use of a bill of exchange. Taylor, a London merchant, wants to buy cloth from De Vries, a Bruges exporter. To pay for this transaction and to avoid having to ship specie, Taylor purchases a bill of exchange from Evans, an English merchant banker. The bill of exchange is then sent as payment to De Vries, who ships the cloth and remits the bill to Koedijk, a Flemish merchant banker. Koedijk pays De Vries in groten and settles with Evans. This settlement might simply be a bookkeeping transaction, Koedijk canceling offsetting obligations to Evans, or it could involve a shipment of specie, to take place perhaps at a time in the future agreed upon by the two as the date for reconciling their books.

In the fifteenth century, the fairs became year-round ventures and the cities that housed them financial centers. In northern Europe first Bruges and later Antwerp occupied such positions. In southern Europe, the Tuscan cities of Florence, Lucca and Siena, were the major centers initially; Venice took over from all three later. Italians, moreover, became the banker class of Europe.

The reintroduction of a western European gold coinage took place in 1252 with the striking of two full-bodied gold coins in northern Italy—the genoin of Genoa and then a few months later the fiorina (or florin) of Florence. For the next century and a half these two coins, the florin particularly, were the world currencies. In the fifteenth century, their place was taken by the ducato of Venice. Not surprisingly, given the economic and financial changes that occurred during the thirteenth century, it is at that time that exchange rate data start to become available. Throughout Europe smaller denomination silver coins and coins of various baser metals were used in most internal transactions. A good overview of exchange rate behavior, therefore, can be had by examining the rates of exchange between these coins and the gold coins used as international money. Table 1 presents such data, using the Florentine florin as the numeraire. Listed in the table are indices of exchange rates for eight currencies relative to the florin at half-century intervals over the period 1252 to 1500.

What stands out is the upward trend in all these exchange rates. In each instance the domestic currency depreciated in value relative to the international currency, the florin. A major factor engendering these movements was the series of debasements that took place in all of the European countries throughout this era. A second influence was the discovery and subsequent mining of silver in several countries of Europe during the fifteenth century. The modern notion that a metallic money is a stable money is clearly not borne out by these data.

A third point is the difference across countries in the pace at which the exchange-rate depreciation occurred. The English pound sterling, for example, showed relatively little movement, a drop in value of 0.2 percent per year over these two and a half centuries; the Castilian marivedi, in contrast, registered a decline of 2.0 percent per year over the two hundred years for which data on it are available.

TABLE 1. *Indices of Exchange Rates Relative to the Florentine Florin*

	1252	1300	1350	1400	1450	1500
Austria	90	100	141	225	333	495
Castile		100	431	1137.9	2586.2	6465.5
Cologne	37.5	100	336.3	630	915	1680
England	80	100	100	96	121.3	146.7
Flanders		100	128.3	255.2	373.3	609.5
France	80	100	250	220	312.5	387.5
Rome	58.8	100	138.2	214.7	290.2	382.4
Venice	75	100	100	145.3	181.3	193.8

SOURCE: Spufford, 1988.

The depreciation of these currencies does not seem to have been matched by increases in the various countries' price levels. The likely reason is that increases in money supplies were themselves matched at least to some degree by increases in production and in desired quantities of money demanded.

Sixteenth-Century Price Revolution and Exchange-Rate Theory. In the sixteenth century, however, European price levels did increase, and although the magnitudes of those increases appear to have differed across countries, the overall trends in price levels appear to have been similar. A major factor underlying these increases was the increase in money supplies that took place as a result of inflows of specie—silver in particular—from the Spanish colonies in America to Europe. These inflows naturally came to Spain first, causing Spanish prices to rise and Spanish exchange rates to depreciate to the limits set by the cost of transporting the specie abroad. From Spain the specie and associated inflation spread to the rest of Europe and eventually to the rest of the world.

The philosophers and moral theologians associated with the University of Salamanca displayed a particular interest in these developments. Indeed, the writings of this "Salamanca School" contain what are now regarded as the earliest statements of the quantity theory of money and of the purchasing power parity theorem, both major underpinnings of modern exchange-rate theory.

The first of these, the quantity theory, posits a relation between money supply and the price level as follows:

$$M = kPy,$$

where M is the money supply, k is the desired ratio of money to nominal income, a measure of the real quantity of money demanded, P is the price level, and y is real income. Suppose, as was the case in sixteenth-century Spain, that M increases as a result of specie discoveries. Suppose further that k is not affected and that the increase in M exceeds any increases in y caused by the normal forces of economic growth. The result then will be an increase in P.

The second relation, purchasing power parity, can be seen by considering the following equation linking nominal and real exchange rates and the price levels of the two countries in question:

$$Q = E/(P/P^*),$$

where Q is the real exchange rate, the rate at which a domestic market basket of goods exchanges for a foreign market basket, E is the nominal exchange rate, the domestic currency price of the foreign currency, and P and P^* are the domestic and foreign price levels, respectively.

Suppose now that P increases and that Q is unaffected. The result will be an increase in either E or P^* and, in certain circumstances, both. If E is rigidly fixed, as it would be under a specie standard or if a currency union such as the one currently in existence between Panama and the United States prevails, then the increase in P will be reflected in a corresponding increase in P^*. If, in contrast, E is floating, as it has in many countries over the past three decades, E will increase commensurately with the increase in P, and P^* will be unaffected.

This difference between systems of floating exchange rates and systems of fixed exchange rates has important implications with regard to the links among economies. It implies that under fixed rates monetary disturbances will be transmitted internationally, while under floating rates nominal exchange rates rather than variables like the balance of payments and price levels will adjust following a monetary disturbance.

In sixteenth-century Spain, as P increased because of the specie inflows, both E and P^* felt the impact. The increase in E, however, would have been limited to a narrow band set by the costs of transporting the specie abroad. Most of the increase in P would, therefore, have translated into an increase in P^*.

Martín de Azpilcueta, a professor and canon-lawyer, known also as Navarrus, was the first to write on the subject. In 1556, he wrote *Commentario resolutorio de usuras* (as cited in Grice-Hutchison, 1978, p. 104):

> And even in Spain, in times when money was scarcer, saleable goods and labour were given for very much less than after the discovery of the Indies, which flooded the country with gold and silver. The reason for this is that money is worth more where and when it is scarce than where and when it is abundant.

In 1601, the philosopher and theologian Luís de Molina summarized the developments of the previous century in similar terms. In his *Disputationes de Contractibus* (as cited in Grice-Hutchison, 1993, p. 165) he wrote:

> Other things being equal, whenever money is most abundant, there it will be least valuable for the purpose of buying goods

EXCHANGE HOUSE. The courtyard of the Amsterdam bourse after its renovation in 1668. Painting by Job Berckheijde. (Amsterdams Historisch Museum, Amsterdam)

and comparing things other than money . . . . Thus we see that in Spain the purchasing power of money is far lower on account of its abundance than it was 80 years ago . . . . We likewise see that money is far less valuable in the New World (especially in Peru, where it is most plentiful) than it is in Spain.

Seventeenth through Early Nineteenth Centuries. The distinguishing feature of the seventeenth and the eighteenth centuries from the standpoint of exchange rate history was the institutional development that took place. During the seventeenth century Amsterdam became the world's principal financial center and market for foreign exchange. A century later London began its ascent, and by the early nineteenth century it had completely eclipsed Amsterdam in both regards. The other important financial innovations during this period included development of an active secondary market for bills of exchange, development of a financial press providing regular quotes for foreign exchange rates and prices of financial assets, and the founding of the Bank of Amsterdam, an institution that had as one of its major functions facilitating the settlement of foreign exchange transactions.

Over most of this time, exchange rates and price levels showed little or no long-term movement. That, however, changed abruptly in the late eighteenth century as first

France and then England abandoned specie standards and adopted paper money. In France, from 1789 through 1796, the money supply grew at rapid and accelerating rates, inflation soared, and the exchange rate depreciated dramatically. In England, where money growth, inflation, and exchange-rate depreciation were much more muted, the movement began a year after the French one had ended but lasted much longer.

In the meantime, interest in exchange-rate theory increased. To explain the depreciated currency, Henry Thornton, John Wheatley, and a number of other "bullionist" writers used the quantity theory coupled with the purchasing power parity theorem. In so doing, they echoed the Salamancan writers of two centuries earlier, although they were apparently unaware of the previous work.

Nineteenth-Century Gold Standard. England returned to the gold standard in 1821 and remained on the gold standard continuously until the outbreak of World War I. As the nineteenth century wore on, more and more countries joined England. Germany, the Netherlands, and the Scandinavian countries switched to gold in the 1870s, while Belgium, France, and Switzerland, the former members of the Latin Monetary Union, switched in 1878. The United States, which prior to the Civil War had been on the gold standard de facto, went on it de jure in 1879. Japan adopted the gold standard in 1897.

Under the gold standard, bank notes and deposits increasingly were used as money but both were redeemable in gold. Gold, in turn, circulated domestically as money and could be used in international transactions too.

The late nineteenth century also was a period of considerable international economic and financial integration, and in the United States, in particular, a period of considerable economic growth. Some would argue that the degree of integration experienced during that period has only begun to be matched during the last decade.

In the mid-nineteenth century, the telegraph came into use, and in 1867 the Atlantic cable was laid. The immediate result was an increased information flow in the foreign exchange and other financial markets. These improvements in communication also altered the way in which the foreign exchange market operated. What had been a market centered around organized exchanges eventually became a strictly over-the-counter market. Transactions were conducted via telegraph and cable and then later over the telephone instead of on the trading floor of an exchange.

Twentieth Century. The interwar years saw an attempt to resurrect the gold standard, but that effort was both halfhearted and short-lived. Ultimately it floundered under the pressures of the Great Depression. In place of gold, countries adopted various expedients, ranging from floating rates to the rigid foreign exchange controls instituted by National Socialist Germany.

During World War II such practices spread, and Allied governments too became highly interventionist, both domestically and internationally. In international finance, the devices used included capital controls, tariffs, quotas and other restrictions on trade, and multiple exchange rates. In a number of countries, such restrictions remained in place for well over a decade and a half after the end of the war.

In 1944 in Bretton Woods, New Hampshire, the major Allied powers drew up plans for an international monetary system of fixed exchange rates in which the United States dollar would effectively be the reserve currency. As it turned out, the system was of short duration. It was 1959 before many industrial countries allowed their currencies to become fully convertible and the system became fully operable. Then in the summer of 1971 it started to break down, and by early 1973 it had done so completely. The reason for its demise, as with the gold standard four decades earlier, was the ease with which shocks got transmitted internationally under these two sets of exchange-rate arrangements. In the 1970s, the culprit was overly expansive U.S. monetary policy, which resulted in worldwide inflation; in the 1930s it had been the overly restrictive U.S. policy, which caused a cyclical contraction in the United States to take on a worldwide dimension.

The floating exchange rates that took the place of the Bretton Woods system were a device for insulating countries that wished to avoid importing the inflation then being generated by U.S. policy excesses. In this regard, they clearly have worked. The only problems have been in the

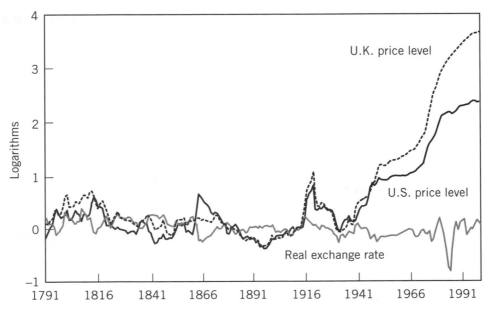

FIGURE 1. U.K. and U.S. price levels and real exchange rate, 1791–1998. SOURCE: Lothian and Taylor, 1996.

area of exchange-rate behavior itself. For a decade and a half following the move to floating rates, nominal and real exchange rates varied exceedingly, much more than most observers had expected. Questions were raised about how applicable existing exchange rate theory was to this new world of floating exchange rates. Purchasing power parity, in particular, was widely viewed as having broken down.

This assessment turned out to be much too pessimistic. The behavior of price levels, during both the floating-rate period and the decade or two leading up to it, has, in fact, differed markedly from earlier historical experience, but the behavior of real exchange rates has been roughly the same, at least when viewed over the long term. This is clear from Figure 1, which plots annual data for the price levels of the United Kingdom and the United States and for the corresponding real exchange rate for the long period from 1791 to 1998. Prior to World War II, price levels and the real exchange rate appear trendless. After World War II, the picture changes dramatically for the price levels, both countries exhibiting substantial upward trends. For the real exchange rate, however, it does not alter at all.

Exchange Rates and the Foreign Exchange Market at the Start of the New Millennium. Today the traditional foreign exchange market is almost totally an over-the-counter market. It is dominated by commercial and investment banks and certain other financial and nonfinancial corporations. Trading takes place over the telephone and by electronic communication.

The foreign exchange market is currently the largest financial market in the world. In April 1998, the latest date for which data are available, the estimated average daily turnover in the foreign exchange market was $1.5 trillion. This was one and one-half times the size of the next largest market, the U.S. government bond market, and two and one-half times the size of the foreign exchange market a scant decade earlier in 1989. Roughly 60 percent of the turnover in 1998 involved forward transactions and only 40 percent spot, almost the exact opposite of the situation in relative shares of the two in 1989.

The dominant positions of the United Kingdom and the United States—in essence London and New York—in this market have remained virtually the same over this period, however. The United Kingdom accounted for 26 percent of the turnover in 1989 and 32 percent in 1998; the United States for 16 percent and 18 percent in 1989 and 1998, respectively.

In addition to these traditional markets, moreover, markets now exist for over-the-counter and exchange-traded foreign-exchange derivative products. Measured in terms of average daily turnover neither is large relative to the traditional foreign-exchange market. Measured in terms of notional amounts outstanding, however, they are sizable—$22.1 trillion.

[*See also* Bretton Woods System; Gold Standard; *and* Monetary Standards.]

BIBLIOGRAPHY

Bank for International Settlements. *Central Bank Survey of Foreign Exchange and Derivative Markets Activity, 1998*. Basel, May 1999.

Bordo, Michael D. "The Bretton Woods International Monetary System: A Historical Overview." In *A Retrospective on the Bretton Woods System*, edited by Michael D. Bordo and Barry Eichengreen, pp. 3–104. Chicago, 1993.

Center for Medieval and Renaissance Studies, University of California, Los Angeles. *The Dawn of Modern Banking*. Los Angeles, 1979.

Chown, John F. *The History of Money from AD 800*. London, 1994.

Cipolla, Carlo M. *Money, Prices, and Civilization in the Mediterranean World, Fifth to Seventeenth Century*. New York, 1967.

Cross, Sam Y. *All About the Foreign Exchange Market in the United States*. New York, 1998.

Darby, Michael, and James R. Lothian. "International Transmission Afloat." In *Money, History and International Finance: Essays in Honor of Anna J. Schwartz*, edited by Michael D. Bordo, pp. 203–243. Chicago, 1989.

Darby, Michael, James R. Lothian, et al. *The International Transmission of Inflation*. Chicago, 1983.

Einzig, Paul. *The History of Foreign Exchange*. 2d ed. London, 1970.

Feavearyear, Albert Edgar. *The Pound Sterling: A History of English Money*. 2d ed., rev. by E. Victor Morgan. Oxford, 1963.

Grice-Hutchinson, Marjorie. *Early Economic Thought in Spain, 1177–1740*. London, 1978.

Grice-Hutchinson, Marjorie. *Economic Thought in Spain: Selected Essays*, edited and with an introduction by Laurence S. Moss and Christopher K. Ryan. Translated from Spanish by Christopher K. Ryan and Marjorie Grice-Hutchinson. Aldershot, U.K., 1993.

Hamilton, Earl J. *American Treasure and the Price Revolution in Spain, 1501–1650*, Cambridge, Mass., 1934.

Kindleberger, Charles P. *A Financial History of Western Europe*. 2d ed. New York, 1993.

Lopez, Robert S. *The Shape of Medieval Monetary History*. London, 1986.

Lothian, James R., and Mark P. Taylor. "Real Exchange Rate Behavior: The Recent Float from the Perspective of the Past Two Centuries." *Journal of Political Economy* 104.3 (1996), 488–509.

Officer, Lawrence H. *Between the Dollar-Sterling Gold Points: Exchange Rates, Parity, and Market Behavior*. Cambridge and New York, 1996.

Officer, Lawrence H. *Purchasing Power Parity and Exchange Rates: Theory, Evidence, and Relevance*. Greenwich, Conn., 1982.

Phelps Brown, Henry, and Sheila V. Hopkins. *A Perspective of Wages and Prices*. London, 1981.

Spufford, Peter, with the assistance of Wendy Wilkinson and Sarah Tolley. *Handbook of Medieval Exchange*. London, 1986.

Spufford, Peter. *Money and Its Use in Medieval Europe*. Cambridge and New York, 1988.

Thornton, Henry. *An Enquiry into the Nature and Effects of the Paper Credit of Great Britain* [(1802) together with his evidence given before the Committees of secrecy of the two houses of Parliament in the Bank of England, March and April, 1797, some manuscript notes, and his speeches on the bullion report, May 1811]. Edited and with an introduction by F. A. von Hayek. London, 1939.

Wheatley, John. *Remarks on Currency and Commerce*. London, 1803.

JAMES R. LOTHIAN

EXCISES. *See* Taxation, *subentry on* Taxation and Public Revenue.

F

FACTORY SYSTEM. One of the most important economic and social changes associated with the Industrial Revolution was the emergence of the factory system. The location of production was transferred out of the household or adjacent artisan shop and centralized into a spatially distinct plant. The basic nature of work was altered as employees were subject to supervision, coordination, and discipline. The functioning of families and households changed; these no longer served as the main arena for production. In strict economic terms, the factory system enabled firms to lower production costs through economies of scale and increased efficiency, to more easily deal with informational asymmetries in production, and to more effectively utilize more complex production technologies.

There is some debate regarding the exact characteristics that truly define a factory. The literature has identified at least four that help to differentiate the factory system from older domestic or artisan modes of production. First, there is centralization and increased scale of production. Factories represented much larger agglomerations of people, plant, and equipment under one roof than was typical of the traditional modes of production. Second, there is technology. The modern factory system has become the primary locus for technological change involving mechanization of production processes and the use of inanimate sources of power. Third is organization. Factories have traditionally been associated with the institution of direct work-process supervision, the promulgation of work rules enforcing strict "factory discipline," and innovations in manipulating worker incentives through different forms of compensation. Fourth, factories have been associated with a more extensive division of labor. Subdivision of work creates interdependencies among workers, requiring greater coordination of production processes, and may permit tasks to be mechanized more easily.

Protofactories before the Industrial Revolution. Some centralized workplaces did exist even before the Industrial Revolution. One class of such enterprises involved production processes too large or energy intensive to be performed in the home or small shop. Fulling mills serving the European woolen industry, charcoal iron-blast furnaces and hammer forges, glassworks, breweries, and early paper mills were either furnace industries and/or required waterpower to operate, even before 1750.

More important to the development of the modern factory system were the "protofactories," agglomerations of workers using more or less traditional hand technologies. Calico printing shops, wool scribbling and finishing mills, and handloom weaving sheds in England, France, and preindustrial Japan; early centralized metalworking establishments such as Matthew Boulton's Soho works; Swiss watchmakers' workshops; and early American waterpowered woodworking and clock-making shops all fall into this category. The primary rationale for these centralized workplaces was organizational. Direct process supervision allowed better quality control, enforcement of a more intensive work pace, and improved design of work tasks to exploit the division of labor. Many of these shops also enhanced productivity through the introduction of small-scale machinery and waterpower and by relying on cheaper female and child labor (Sokoloff, 1984; Berg, 1994).

Birth of the Factory System in the Industrial Revolution, 1770–1870. The genesis of the modern factory system can be traced to the eighteenth-century British textile industry, with the new powered preparatory, spinning, and weaving machinery. The first waterpowered textile mills were set up in Derbyshire for silk throwing in 1717. Richard Arkwright's cotton-spinning mills of the 1770s, the archetype of the early modern factory, utilized sophisticated waterpower systems and a planned layout of machinery to create a nearly continuous flow of materials through the plant. By 1800, the efficient new cotton-spinning technologies had virtually eliminated single-spindle handicraft spinners. Other textile sectors followed cotton toward mechanization with varying rates of diffusion.

In the worsted trade, an adapted version of Arkwright's water-frame made spinning a factory industry by 1820. During the 1830s, the development of the "wet spinning" process fostered the rapid mechanization of flax spinning. Wool was the slowest branch of the textile industry to become a factory industry. As late as the 1840s, a substantial amount of woolen yarn continued to be spun on hand-powered jennies in the homes of domestic handloom weavers. The diffusion of mechanized cloth weaving in Great Britain proceeded more slowly than did spinning. In all the textile branches, hand-loom weaving remained common well into the nineteenth century, as late as the 1880s in the case of wool cloth production.

In continental Europe, developments in the mechanization of textiles lagged those in Great Britain. By the 1830s, an advanced cotton-spinning industry had been established in French Alsace, where firms specialized in the production of high-quality fabrics for luxury markets. Alsatian cotton weavers were relatively quick to adopt the power loom as well, so that by 1840, handloom weavers were working only the finest cloths. Overall, though, there was still a substantial French handloom-weaving sector as late as 1870. As in Great Britain, the pace of mechanization was much slower in French wool production, with the scale of plant much smaller than in cotton. The first large French silk factories, integrating throwing and steam-powered weaving, were set up after 1875.

Mechanization of Swiss cotton spinning occurred between 1800 and 1820. By 1850, the Swiss cotton-spinning industry was the second-largest in Europe after Lancashire, with the number of cotton spindles and yarn output per capita second only to Great Britain's. In cotton weaving, power looms were used only for plainer cloths before the 1850s.

In Germany, the first mechanized cotton-spinning mill, explicitly modeled on Arkwright's early factories, was set up in 1784 near Elberfeld in the Rhineland. Further mechanization in the region came slowly, however; it was not until the 1850s that hand spinning was completely displaced in some areas. In Saxony, which developed into an important center of high-quality cloth production, the first water-driven mule-spinning cotton mill was set up in 1799; by 1831, there were eighty-four mills. Most of the weaving, though, was by handloom until after 1860. In the major wool-producing centers, Rhineland and Brandenburg, the factory system grew rapidly after 1840. By 1895, most German wool spinners worked in factories, while the handloom weavers held on tenaciously.

The American cotton-spinning industry began in 1790 when Samuel Slater smuggled the design for Arkwright's water-frame into Rhode Island. The first textile mill to integrate spinning and weaving was built in Massachusetts by Francis Cabot Lowell, who brought the design for the power loom from Great Britain in 1814.

Two major innovations transformed the scale and organization of the British iron industry: coke smelting and Henry Cort's puddling and rolling process (patented in 1784). Coke smelting, which required larger redesigned blast furnaces and mechanized material handling, increased the capital intensity and minimum efficient scale of pig iron production. The puddling and rolling process, while greatly extending the division of labor, permitted nearly continuous-flow production of wrought iron. In continental Eu-

rope, British iron-making techniques began to diffuse only after 1830, when the processes were adapted for use with the region's coal deposits. In the United States, adoption of British coke-smelting techniques awaited the perfection of the "hot blast" technique in the 1840s, which allowed blast furnaces to use the anthracite coal that was so abundant in the eastern part of the country.

In British metalworking, leading large-scale engineering works such as Maudslay's and Nasmyth's employed several hundred workers, pioneered the use of steam-powered machine tools and mechanized material handling inside the plant, and were well organized with an extensive division of labor, process supervision, and a carefully designed workshop layout that foreshadowed later developments in flow production. Most British engineering workers, however, remained relatively independent and craft-oriented. After 1815, the factory system also made inroads into traditionally artisan-based metalworking industries such as Sheffield cutlery and the Birmingham metal trades. German engineering expanded rapidly in the 1850s, based on demand for steam engines and locomotives. Unlike some of the more advanced British engineering works, though, German machine shops of this era were typically organized as collections of workshops with little division of labor.

In the pottery industry, British entrepreneurs such as Josiah Wedgwood pioneered large-scale factory production, and the use of innovative production techniques including transfer printing, steam-powered lathes, and mechanized clay-cutting equipment. His Etruria works exhibited an extensive division of labor, systematic work organization, and factory discipline. In papermaking, the diffusion of the Fourdrinier machine in Great Britain transformed what had been a small-scale centralized industry into true mechanized factory production.

Factory Discipline and Organization. Nearly all factory owners, regardless of industry or location, were concerned with imparting a new type of work discipline to their labor forces that was alien to artisan and household production systems. The combination of a more extensive division of labor, expensive capital equipment, interdependent production processes, and the need for improved quality control standards meant that factory employers wanted fixed work hours for all employees, punctuality and consistent attendance, high levels of work effort, an emphasis on accuracy of work and uniformity of the finished product, and proper use and care of expensive production equipment and raw materials. In smaller factories, direct process supervision and face-to-face contact between supervisors and workers were sufficient to establish rudimentary levels of discipline. In larger establishments, where direct communication and control were infeasible, factory discipline regimes were codified into work rules that might deal with disciplinary matters and specify standards of output, quality, and care of machinery. Enforcement of discipline relied on deterrent mechanisms such as corporal punishment or, more usually, the threat of dismissal and stiff fines for violating the factory rules. Later, factory owners turned to positive incentives to elicit high levels of discipline and work effort, including piece-rate pay or bonuses tied to high productivity, overtime, or firm profits. Employers in all countries tried to engender loyalty and acceptance of the disciplinary regime by offering their workers various paternalistic fringe benefits— housing; sickness, accident, and disability insurance; pensions; medical care; and educational, religious, and recreational facilities.

Supervision regimes took two basic forms. Where large amounts of skilled labor were used, as in mule spinning, iron production, or engineering, employers would often rely on subcontract systems. Master craftsmen or machine operators would be responsible for hiring, supervising, disciplining, firing, and paying their own workers. The masters would also often be responsible for setting up and maintaining their own machinery and have substantial power to determine the work pace. The masters would generally be paid piece rates and pay their underlings time wages.

In Great Britain, subcontracting systems were used early and often and eventually evolved into craft control of work processes by skilled labor that lasted well into the twentieth century. Early French textile factories also used subcontracting extensively, as did Meiji-era Japanese ironworks and engineering shops. In the United States, many nineteenth-century metalworking establishments used a form of subcontracting called the inside contracting system. Although subcontracting has been referred to as a means of evading management responsibilities, it should also be seen as a potentially efficient response to information asymmetries. When skilled workers had more knowledge about the production process than did their employers, it may have made sense to delegate some control over the production process, especially in an era when managerial ability was in scarce supply.

When substantial portions of the labor force were unskilled or semiskilled, as in nineteenth-century British and American water-frame or throstle cotton-spinning factories, shop-floor management was typically carried out by a group of foremen who formed the lowest level of the managerial hierarchy of the firm. After 1850, many American, German, and French factories in textiles, iron and steelmaking, and others adopted some form of the foreman system. Foremen in such establishments typically grew powerful by the late nineteenth century, with authority over personnel matters, including in some cases establishing promotion and wage policies, setting up machinery, determining the work pace, and coordinating work flows,

in addition to the normal supervisory tasks of enforcing discipline and pushing workers to achieve ever-higher levels of output.

Industrial Organization in the Mid-Nineteenth Century. By the mid- to late nineteenth century, the factory system was extensive and growing rapidly in most industrialized countries. Factories were far from ubiquitous, however, as many small-scale forms of production continued to operate in many industries and regions. In the United States from 1850, factory production was standard in iron and steel, engineering, metalworking, and woodworking and was beginning to transform traditional work relations in shoemaking and clothing as well. In urban areas, pockets of domestic industry still existed, such as the textile trades in Philadelphia, where artisan and domestic outworkers coexisted with factories.

By 1860 in Great Britain, the progress of mechanization led to a sort of "industrial dualism" in many industries. Production processes in industries such as pottery, brewing, metalworking, and engineering became increasingly polarized between concentration in factories and decentralized, labor-intensive subcontracting, outwork, and sweatshop systems. Consumption industries such as tailoring, milling, shoemaking, brewing, wheel making, and blacksmithing were mostly performed in small shops.

France also exhibited a dualistic industrial structure in which capital-intensive centralized production developed alongside labor-intensive domestic and workshop manufacturing. The French small-scale workshop sector was actually much larger than the factory sector and continued to grow up to the 1860s. The workshop sector produced most consumption goods, including food and clothing, shoes, and furniture. German industry, too, was characterized by a dual industrial structure. Concentrated industries such as mining, mechanical and electrical engineering, chemicals, and textiles each had more than two-thirds of its employees in plants with more than fifty workers by 1882. Industries that remained as small-scale workshops or putting-out enterprises included clothing, food processing, wood products such as furniture, and leather products.

The Evolution of the Factory System after 1870. The development of the so-called American System revolutionized factory organization and management in many industries after 1850. In the American System, complex products were assembled from mass-produced individual components. High-quality, specialized machine tools were used to fabricate the components, which were designed and produced to be interchangeable, along with precise jig and fixture systems to ensure accuracy and uniformity and with improved gauges and measurement devices to guarantee quality control. The assembly process involved an extensive division of labor and sequential movements of

FACTORY. Steelworkers at Biermeister and Wain, painting (1885) by Peter Severin Kroyer (1851–1909). (Statens Museum for Kunst, Copenhagen/Snark/Art Resource, NY)

work in process from stage to stage. Finished products could thus be assembled by less-skilled labor without costly hand fitting at a much lower cost than possible with traditional handicraft methods.

At first, goods made with interchangeable parts were actually more expensive than those made by traditional methods, and so the American System was adopted by organizations for which quality was the primary consideration—naval shipyards or military armories. By 1800, the British navy's block-making plant at Portsmouth, designed by the renowned engineer Marc Brunel, was producing nearly perfectly identical pulleys for ships using many of the elements of interchangeability and flow production. In the United States, interchangeable-parts manufacture was pioneered by the federal armories at Harpers Ferry, Virginia, and, especially, Springfield, Massachusetts.

Outside of the armories, interchangeable-parts manufacture found its earliest elaboration in the U.S. wood-

working industry prior to 1850. From there, the American System spread to commercial firearms production and then to the metalworking industries such as sewing machine production between 1850 and 1880, bicycle manufacturing after 1890, and, finally, the automobile industry after 1900. Techniques worked out in these industries were applied to a broad range of other industries—clocks, locks, pumps, agricultural machinery, typewriters, and engines.

Outside of the United States, the spread of interchangeable-parts manufacture was a slow and uneven process. The basic barrier was the fragmented, heterogeneous nature of the European market, which militated against the efficiency of mass production processes before World War I. Bicycle producers in Great Britain and France were typically among the quickest to introduce the new methods. German volume machinery producers, Swiss watchmakers, and Japan's Toyoda Loom Works all introduced variants of the American System as well.

Continuous-Flow Processes and the Assembly Line.
In industries such as petroleum refining, chemical production, and agricultural processing (especially grain milling and meat packing), continuous-flow processes, in which workers remained in fixed locations while mechanized material-handling systems moved work in process between workstations, were developed after 1850.

Henry Ford's Model T plant at Highland Park, Michigan, combined the ideas of interchangeable parts with continuous-flow production. Ford mass-produced some components using high-quality machine tools and new steel alloys to improve precision in manufacturing. For other parts, Ford borrowed the steel press and punch-work processes that had been developed in the bicycle industry. For the assembly process, Ford's production engineers designed a material movement system from conveyors, rollways, and gravity slides to move work in progress at a predetermined rate between fixed workstations manned by specialized personnel.

The assembly line made mass production in metalworking a nearly continuous-flow process. These techniques were subsequently applied to a wide range of products, including radios, telephones, refrigerators, washing machines, motors, and tractors. After World War II, mass-production processes in the automobile industry were refined still further, as "Detroit-type automation" used automatic work transfer and positioning devices to link together the operation of successive machines. This enabled companies to fabricate huge volumes of identical parts at low cost. The switch from steam to electric power after 1900 helped greatly in the design of such systems, as machinery could now be located wherever it was most efficient.

Although some European automobile producers such as Opel and Citroën experimented with assembly line systems during the 1920s and 1930s, full adoption of mass production in Europe did not occur until after World War II. In Germany, the Volkswagen Beetle was manufactured by mass-production techniques, as were products in consumer electronics, electrical goods, and agricultural, sewing, office, and construction machinery. British automobile producers, too, adopted mass-production techniques such as assembly lines and automated transfer machinery and body shops.

Not all industries were good candidates for efficient mass production, of course. In particular, the engineering industries all over the world that produced the machinery for heavy industry, the American System, and assembly-line mass production were custom or small batch "specialty" industries that made most of their goods to order. Specialty engineering firms tried as best as they could to "rationalize" production by standardizing parts across models where possible and by reorganizing production processes. But there were limits to what could be done in such industries.

Systematic Management. The increasing complexity of production processes in heavy industry and metalworking required a revolution in factory management techniques. The changes, adopted in various forms by both mass producers and specialty producers, were basically threefold: first, the reform of shop management and production control systems; second, the development of cost accounting; and third, the modification of compensation systems to properly motivate workers to high levels of effort.

Traditional foreman-based control systems were inadequate to coordinate and manage the complex new processes developed in volume production of machinery. To solve this problem and to provide the data needed for accurate cost accounting, firms developed shop ticket systems. The tickets would indicate through which departments a given order would pass and what parts would be fabricated and assembled for it; provide a record of labor costs and material usage, offering an accurate picture of the operating costs of each department; and serve as the authority to perform work and requisition materials. These systems allowed plant managers to take production planning and coordination out of the hands of foremen, while providing statistical controls with which to evaluate processes and workers. Mass and specialty producers in the United States, Germany, and elsewhere adopted variants of this system. Later, systems were also devised to accurately determine and allocate overhead costs to specific products, a problem that was not addressed by shop ticket systems.

The third problem involved how to design compensation systems so that workers and foremen would be motivated to both use the new production control and cost accounting systems properly and maintain high effort levels. Foremen and powerful inside contractors strongly resisted the new centralized planning and personnel departments that curbed their authority over production control and wage determination. Factory managers hoped to gain their acquiescence by adopting profit-sharing plans.

A system adopted by many firms was to pay workers a time-base wage plus a premium to those who exceeded a standard output. One of the cornerstones of Frederick Taylor's scientific management theory was that production standards in profit-sharing plans should not be measured against historical data but rather against a "scientifically" determined standard time and output for each task, to be deduced through detailed task analyses and time-and-motion studies. These ideas spread like wildfire to factories the world over throughout the twentieth century.

Modern Manufacturing: Flexible Mass Production.
In the 1950s and 1960s, Japanese automobile producers

such as Toyota and Nissan pioneered a system known as lean production that allowed the manufacture of high-quality products at low prices. This represented a real departure from the usual mass-production approach to manufacturing involving rigid, single-purpose machinery, an extensive division of unskilled labor, and long runs of standardized products. The principles of the system included worker self-monitoring of the production process and product quality, "just-in-time" inventory replenishment, cross-functional training and job rotation, more flexible machinery with reduced setup times, and simultaneous engineering of new products by teams that included all the important functional groups—marketing, engineering, production, and suppliers. The goals of this system were to reduce waste by reducing inventories, identifying bottlenecks more quickly, and tightening quality control. In addition, the system helped to increase design and production flexibility by making it economical to introduce new products more frequently and produce them in smaller batches. It remains to be seen whether flexible mass production represents the future of the factory system in the advanced industrial economies.

Understanding the Triumph of the Factory System.
Traditionally, the factory system has been understood as the result of technological changes (expensive machinery, centralized power sources) that strengthened the importance of fixed capital in production. The deepening of fixed capital inputs increased minimum efficient plant scales, making production processes too large to fit into households or small artisan shops (Clark, 1994; Landes, 1986; Mantoux, 1983).

Given that many centralized workplaces before the Industrial Revolution used neither power nor machinery, however, technological change clearly cannot explain every aspect of the transition to factory production. Therefore, radical economists (Marglin, 1975) have argued, there is no efficiency justification for the factory system. Division of labor and hierarchical management, the radicals contend, were strategies by capitalists to ensure themselves an essential role in the production process as integrators of artificially separate operations into a finished product. Capitalist owners could then expropriate more of the enterprise surplus for themselves. This view, which disregards traditional arguments for the efficiency of specialization, has not made much headway among mainstream economic historians.

Another efficiency rationale for the factory system suggests that supervision and factory discipline are mechanisms to overcome asymmetric information problems. If workers' marginal productivities are difficult to measure (perhaps due to the increasing importance of team production as the division of labor has progressed), then supervision and factory discipline may serve as mechanisms

to improve the employer's knowledge of productivity or effort level (Langlois, 1999).

Product quality is another aspect of production processes that may be difficult to measure. Some quality characteristics of a good (for example, standardization) may be difficult or impossible to improve without close supervision over production processes. This would allow factory owners to gain information about how workers use raw materials and how they perform tasks (Szostak, 1989). Such explanations, however, often fail to explain why the progress of the factory system typically corresponded closely with that of mechanization.

The technological and organizational characteristics of flexible mass production interact with each other in such a way that engaging in any one of the activities individually increases the marginal return to engaging in each one of the other aspects of the strategy as well, according to Milgrom and Roberts (1990). This complementarity effect means that the productivity increase generated by adoption of the entire flexible mass production system is larger than just the sum of the productivity increases accruing to any single practice. This type of complementarity effect may have been working during the late eighteenth and early nineteenth century to make the factory system, understood as mechanization and process supervision together, more productive than simply introducing machinery or process supervision by themselves (Geraghty, 2002). This effect might explain why factory organization and mechanization developed together, even though in some cases centralization and supervision occurred initially without machinery.

Joel Mokyr (2002) suggests that the centralization of work into the factory system was a direct consequence of the increased complexity of technology. The amount of knowledge needed to build, operate, and maintain the complex technologies of the Industrial Revolution simply grew too large for an individual artisan or household to master. In an era of high communication costs, it was much more efficient to move specialized workers to the job than to try to communicate all of the necessary information to nodes in a decentralized production network; hence, process centralization and the factory system.

This hypothesis, as Mokyr suggests, has an interesting implication. With the recent reduction in the cost of communicating information due to modern information processing technologies, do current trends toward telecommuting and increased homework mean the end of the factory system?

[*See also* Domestic Industry *and* Mass Production.]

BIBLIOGRAPHY
Berg, Maxine. *The Age of Manufactures, 1700–1820: Industry, Innovation, and Work in Britain*. 2d ed. London, 1994.

Chandler, Alfred D. *The Visible Hand: The Managerial Revolution in American Business*. Cambridge, Mass., 1977.

Clark, Gregory. "Factory Discipline." *Journal of Economic History* 54.1 (1994), 128–163.

Floud, Roderick, and Donald McCloskey. *The Economic History of Britain since 1700*. 2d ed. 3 vols. Cambridge, 1994.

Geraghty, Thomas M. "Technology, Organization, and Complementarity: The Factory System in the British Industrial Revolution." Ph.D. diss., Northwestern University, 2002.

Herrigel, Gary. *Industrial Constructions: The Sources of German Industrial Power*. Cambridge, 1996.

Hounshell, David. *From the American System to Mass Production, 1800–1932: The Development of Manufacturing Technology in the United States*. Baltimore, 1984.

Kocka, Juergen. *Industrial Culture and Bourgeois Society: Business, Labor, and Bureaucracy in Modern Germany*. New York, 1999.

Landes, David. *The Unbound Prometheus: Technological Change and Industrial Development in Western Europe from 1750 to the Present*. Cambridge, Mass., 1969.

Landes, David. "What Do Bosses Really Do?" *Journal of Economic History* 46.3 (1986), 585–623.

Langlois, Richard N. "The Coevolution of Technology and Organization in the Transition to the Factory System." In *Authority and Control in Modern Industry*, edited by Paul L. Robertson. London, 1999.

Mantoux, Paul. *The Industrial Revolution in the Eighteenth Century: An Outline of the Beginnings of the Modern Factory System in England*. Chicago, 1983.

Marglin, Stephen A. "What Do Bosses Do? The Origins and Functions of Hierarchy in Capitalist Production." *Review of Radical Political Economy* 6.2 (1975), 60–112, and 7.1 (1975), 20–37.

Mathias, Peter, and M. M. Postan. *The Cambridge Economic History of Europe*, vol. 7, *The Industrial Economies: Capital, Labor, and Enterprise*. Cambridge, 1978.

McCraw, Thomas K., ed. *Creating Modern Capitalism: How Entrepreneurs, Companies, and Countries Triumphed in Three Industrial Revolutions*. Cambridge, Mass., 1975.

Milgrom, Paul, and John Roberts. "The Economics of Modern Manufacturing: Technology, Strategy, and Organization." *The American Economic Review* 80.3 (1990), 511–528.

Milward, Alan S., and S. B. Saul. *The Economic Development of Continental Europe, 1780–1870*. London, 1973.

Milward, Alan S., and S. B. Saul. *The Development of the Economies of Continental Europe, 1850–1914*. London, 1977.

Mokyr, Joel. *The Gifts of Athena: Historical Origins of the Knowledge Economy*. Princeton, 2002.

Pollard, Sidney. *The Genesis of Modern Management: A Study of the Industrial Revolution in Great Britain*. Cambridge, Mass., 1965.

Rosenberg, Nathan. *Technology and American Economic Growth*. Armonk, N.Y., 1972.

Scranton, Philip. *Endless Novelty: Specialty Production and American Industrialization, 1865–1925*. Princeton, 1997.

Sokoloff, Kenneth L. "Was the Transition from the Artisanal Shop to the Non-Mechanized Factory Associated with Gains in Efficiency?" *Explorations in Economic History* 21 (1994), 351–382.

Stearns, Peter N. *Paths to Authority: The Middle Class and the Industrial Labor Force in France, 1820–1848*. Urbana, 1978.

Szostak, Richard. "The Organization of Work: The Emergence of the Factory Revisited." *Journal of Economic Behavior and Organization* 11 (1989), 343–358.

Yamamura, Kozo, ed. *The Economic Emergence of Modern Japan*. Cambridge, 1997.

THOMAS M. GERAGHTY

FAIRS *[This entry contains two subentries, on European fairs and emporia and bazaars.]*

European Fairs

Fairs were among the oldest market forms, organized with regular intervals in fixed places where goods and services could be concentrated and exchanged between sellers and buyers, particularly on or near major trade routes. But economics was by no means the only factor responsible for the origin of fairs. Politics were important as well. A great number of fairs owed their establishment simply to a decision by the prince or the local lord who wanted to extend his jurisdiction and control over certain rights in a given region. Finally, religion, too, had its influence since in quite a significant number of places fairs originated from religious festivals and ecclesiastical feasts to honor a local saint or celebrate an important event.

Commercial Fairs. It is now commonly accepted that the Germanic invasions in the fourth and fifth centuries did not extinguish commercial life. Even after the disappearance of the Roman Empire, trade survived, though greatly reduced, and so did towns, markets, and fairs. Fairs certainly existed in some parts of Merovingian Gaul and Visigothic Spain. One of the most famous fairs in that period was located at Saint-Denis, near Paris. This fair was established around 634 by the Merovigian king Dagobert. Trade in agricultural products was clearly predominant. Although regular markets increased during the Carolingian period, fairs remained few in number. If some of the great emporia or trading centers in Scandinavia or in the Rhine-Meuse-Scheldt delta had fairs, they were devastated by Viking raids after 830.

When long-distance trade received a new impetus from the end of the tenth century, and new towns began spreading all over Europe, fairs too became much more numerous. Saint-Denis received a second fair, the Lendit fair, at the beginning of the eleventh century. In the same period, or even earlier, the first traces appeared of the Flanders fairs, foreshadowing the important role that this region was going to play in long-distance trade. The oldest fair was at Saint-Omers (ninth century), followed by the fairs of Douai and Ghent (early eleventh century), Torhout and Messines (end of the eleventh century), Ypres (Ieper), Lille, and Bruges (early twelfth century). Some of these fairs found their origins in an initiative taken by the counts of Flanders, while others were associated with religious festivals. All of them were highly stimulated by the growth of the local woolen-cloth industry. The latter became famous as the "five great Flemish fairs" when they became integrated into a regular cycle during the thirteenth century.

The Flemish fairs attracted merchants from Flanders and northern France itself, but also from other principalities in

MEDIEVAL FAIR. Fair of Lendit at Saint-Denis, France. Late-fourteenth-century miniature from *Grandes Chroniques de France,* folio 122v. (Musée Goya, Castres, France/Giraudon/Art Resource, NY)

the Low Countries and even from Italy, Germany, Spain, and to a lesser extent England. Still, recent research has pointed out that regional activities and retail trade may not be excluded from the picture. The fairs indeed were not only visited by important merchants but also frequented by a great variety of persons, belonging to very different groups of the population. Apart from the usual commercial transactions, some of the fairs were renowned for financial transactions.

The Ypres fair especially maintained a lively business in so-called *lettres de foire.* These documents were transferable to a third party, redeemable in cash or in merchandise at one or more of the fairs (hence the expression "de foire en foire" or "aux cinq foires de Flanders"), but also payable at one of the Champagne fairs.

The Champagne fairs were undoubtedly the most important set of fairs in medieval Europe. Their apogee in the thirteenth century coincided completely with the most powerful development of long-distance trade overland. As such, the four fairs of Lagny-sur-Marne, Bar-sur-Aube, Provins, and Troyes in northeastern France symbolized the era with probably the most pronounced economic growth from the medieval period. At the beginning of the twelfth century, fairs were still largely agricultural markets; but by the end of

that century, a regular cycle of six weeks for each fair had been introduced, covering in a regular rhythm of mutual alteration the whole year. This organizational progress helps to explain their expansion in the next century.

The success of the Champagne fairs did not, however, have much to do with their geographic location. For much more important was the protection and security offered by the counts of Champagne, later the kings of France. Every product known in the medieval economy, from common bulk goods to the most costly articles, coming from all parts of Europe, northern Africa, and the Middle East, was bought and sold at these fairs. As at the fairs of Flanders, the Champagne fairs also offered an excellent opportunity for financial transactions. These involved not only promissory notes (letters obligatory) but also investment contracts (such as the *instrumentum ex causa cambii*). So important were these transactions and so sophisticated were the book transfers for the settlement of debts that the Belgian-American scholar Raymond de Roover (1904–1972) labeled the Fairs of Champagne as "the major money market and clearing center of Western Europe" in the thirteenth century.

Several theories have been formulated to explain the decay of the fairs at the end of the thirteenth century. One of the most influential hypotheses sees the establishment of new, direct sea routes between Italy and northwestern Europe as a primary factor. Recently, John Munro has cogently argued that the upswing of new alternative maritime trade routes via Gibraltar was more the consequence than the cause of the decline of the fairs. He refers to the consequences of increased warfare from the 1290s that dramatically increased the transaction costs for overland traffic, which led to a profound crisis in one of the main commodities traded via these fairs, the relatively much cheaper and light semiworsted textiles, whose commerce so rapidly declined, as did the trade in such textiles in the English Midlands fairs (St. Ives, etc.), which went through a similar crisis. The fourteenth century, and especially the difficult second half, also witnessed the disappearance of several other English fairs. This is quite a contrast with the prosperous period between 1200 and 1350 when more than 1500 new regional fairs were established.

The decline of the Champagne fairs, in many respects permitted the subsequent development of new international fairs, such as those of Besançon, Geneva, and Lyons. The Geneva fairs, which had operated as regional fairs in the thirteenth century, gained an international reputation in the later fourteenth century and realized their best years in the first half of the fifteenth century. After 1460, their role was taken over by the fairs of Lyons, largely as a result of a number of political measures by the kings of France. By that time, following a long contraction in the aggregate volume of transcontinental trade, some degree of economic revival, especially in Italy, had led to a vigorous revival of international trade, but now via new overland routes, starting in North Italy and linking southern Germany over the Rhineland with Brabant in the Low Countries and via Lyon with Castile.

Along with those new commercial axes, new fairs came into being: in Germany the *Messe* of Frankfurt am Main and Leipzig, in Spain the *ferias* of Medina del Campo, Villalón, and Rioseco, in Brabant the fairs of Bergen op Zoom and Antwerp. The Brabant Fairs especially enjoyed an important role in these new routes. According to the Belgian economic historian Herman van der Wee, between 1500 and 1570 Antwerp formed the heart in a complex network of overland contacts that encompassed the whole of Europe.

Financial Fairs. At the end of the Middle Ages, a trend became visible that would be typical for the fairs of the early modern period: Fairs became increasingly incorporated in the public finance of the central state. New national states, such as France and Spain, used the money market of the fairs to finance military expenditure. In the short term, this phenomenon stimulated activities on the fairs. Viewed from the long run, this evolution was less positive. A series of moratoria and state bankruptcies of the Span-

ish government between 1557 and 1612 ruined the south German bankers and seriously afflicted the Antwerp money market. In the same way, the bankruptcy by France in 1558 meant the end of the financial fairs at Lyon.

Another trend that started at the same moment was the development of purely financial fairs (fairs of exchange, *foires de change*). Already at the fairs of Lyon, a clear distinction was made between the commercial and financial fairs. On the latter, no goods were traded. All attention went to international payments and clearing operations and to arbitrage on the exchange rates. To facilitate exchange, a number of financial innovations were introduced, such as the use of one single money of account or a basket of such moneys as a key currency for all payments at the fair. In the course of the seventeenth century, most financial fairs would also develop other functions, for example, the extension of facilities for investment credit. A good example of these financial fairs were the Besançon fairs that emerged from the collapse of the Lyon fairs and after 1579 were held at Piacenza (hence the name "Bisenzone" fairs).

Financial fairs survived until the middle of the eighteenth century, gradually facing more competition from modern money markets (e.g., Amsterdam, Hamburg, London) and banks with branches, agents, and correspondents all over Europe. Commercial fairs did not disappear. Some of them even gained significance. In the eighteenth century, the fairs of not only Frankfurt am Main and Leipzig, but also those of Breslau and Frankfurt an der Oder became very important for long-distance trade over land. Leipzig was the central place for export of textiles to the Middle East.

Still, with the improvement of transportation and communication, the explosive growth of population and consumption, and the increasing internationalization of the economy, many commercial fairs declined as well. "Wholesale trade overflowed the narrow canals of fairs," wrote the famous French historian Fernand Braudel. In the nineteenth century, the world exhibitions (the first was organized in London in 1851) for a great part took over the functions of the international fairs. On a regional and local level, year-round shops, boutiques, and stores replaced the former role of fairs in the distribution channels.

Importance of Fairs. Fairs were of crucial importance. Thanks to fairs, greater numbers of consumers could enjoy foreign products or luxury goods unknown in their own region. As such, fairs contributed to the rise of consumer markets, regional specialization, and the growth of market integration. Through fairs, the countryside became linked to the urban network. Fairs created financial services and new monetary techniques or instruments. For the local community of the organizing places, fairs acted as a sort of multiplier effect on aggregate income, since many people attending the fairs had to be fed and given shelter. But the most important contribution of fairs to the process of economic growth, however, seems to have been their effect in reducing transaction costs. Fairs indeed offered more security and safety, facilitated communication and exchange of information between the different parties, reduced risks, made prices more transparent, and, above all, allowed for scale economies by spreading fixed costs over a great number of transactions. The importance of fairs went further and certainly was not limited to economic activities. At the fairs, people from all quarters of the world exchanged the latest news, passed on new intellectual ideas, propagated different religious convictions, spread new artistic concepts, and introduced different economic and social customs. As such, for many people the great world became a bit smaller.

[*See also* Staple Markets and Entrepôts.]

BIBLIOGRAPHY

Bautier, Robert-Henri. "The Fairs of Champagne." In *Essays in French Economic History*, edited by R. Cameron, pp. 42–63. Homewood, Ill., 1970.

Boyer-Xambeu, Marie-Thérèse, Ghislain Deleplace, and Lucien Gillard. *Private Money and Public Currencies: The 16th Century Challenge*. New York and London, 1994. Fascinating theory; not always accurate with facts.

Braudel, Fernand. *Civilization and Capitalism: 15th–18th Century*. vol. 2, *The Wheels of Commerce*. New York, 1979.

Cavaciocchi, Simonetta, ed. *Fiere e mercati nella integrazione delle economie europee secc. XIII–XVIII*. Istituto Internazionale di Storia Economica "F. Datini" Prato. Serie II—Atti delle "Settimane di Studi" e altri Convegni, 32. Florence, 2001. Impressive volume with numerous contributions in English.

Epstein, Stephen. "Regional Fairs, Institutional Innovation, and Economic Growth in Late Medieval Europe." *Economic History Review* 47:3 (1994), 459–482.

Johanek, Peter, and Heinz Stoob, eds. *Europäische Messen und Märktesystemen in Mittelalter und Neuzeit*. Cologne, Vienna, 1996.

Koch, Rainer, ed. *Brücke zwischen den Völkern: Zur Geschichte der Frankfurter Messe*, 3 vols. Frankfurt, 1991.

Moore, Ellen W. *The Fairs of Medieval England: An Introductory Study*. Pontifical Institute of Mediaeval Studies. Studies and Texts, 72. Toronto, 1985.

Munro, John H. "The 'New Institutional Economics' and the Changing Fortunes of Fairs in Medieval and Early Modern Europe: The Textile Trades, Warfare, and Transaction Costs." *Vierteljahrschrift für Sozial- und Wirtschaftsgeschichte* 88.1 (2001), 1–47.

Van der Wee, Herman. *The Growth of the Antwerp Market and the European Economy (Fourteenth–Sixteenth Centuries)*, vol. 1, *Statistics*; vol. 2, *Interpretation*; vol. 3, *Graphs and Indices*. Leuven, Paris, and The Hague, 1963.

Van der Wee, Herman. "Monetary, Credit, and Banking Systems." In *The Cambridge Economic History of Europe*, edited by E. E. Rich and C. H. Wilson, vol. 5, pp. 290–392. Cambridge, London, New York, and Melbourne, 1977.

Verlinden, Charles. "Markets and Fairs." In *The Cambridge Economic History of Europe*, edited by M. M. Postan, E. E. Rich, and E. Miller, vol. 3, pp. 119–153. Cambridge, London, New York, and Melbourne, 1963.

ERIK AERTS

Emporia and Bazaars

Emporia and bazaars refer to types of marketplaces. Emporia (from the Greek *emporos*, meaning traveler, a merchant) are large trading centers, coastal or inland, associated with the availability of imported goods and the residence of foreign merchants. Asian emporia, including both caravan cities and port towns, stretched from the Islamic Mediterranean to the expansive Indian Ocean. The attraction of emporia, especially for foreign merchants, rests in the size and diversity of markets and the consequent ability to spread business risk. The broad availability of commercial intelligence and access to credit also drew in a range of buyers and sellers.

Bazaars, by contrast, do not necessarily imply the presence of goods imported from afar or the residence of foreign merchants. *Bazaar*, a word of obscure Persian origin, is the classic "Oriental" market, referring to marketplaces across North Africa, the Middle East, and Central, South, and Southeast Asia. A bazaar, or *sūq* as it is called in the Arab world, often links production in the hinterland with town or urban patterns of consumption. A bazaar can be permanent or periodic. Bazaars can thrive in small provincial towns or in emporia, thereby linking hinterland production with distant consumers.

The evolution of coastal emporia correlates in large measure to changes in maritime trade. K. N. Chaudhuri (1985, p. 102) explains that emporia in the Indian Ocean are clustered within three natural segments, which were determined by the annual monsoon cycle. The first segment encompassed the Red Sea and the Persian Gulf to Gujarat and the Malabar Coast. The second segment arose from the annual voyages from coastal India to the Indonesian archipelago. The third linked trading ports in the archipelago with those in the South China Sea. Chaudhuri emphasizes the aggregate stability of emporia trade between the tenth and early sixteenth centuries, a period that witnessed the broad diffusion of Islam over the Indian Ocean. This pattern included Hormuz and Aden in the western region, Cambay and Calicut in the central, and Malacca (also Melaka), Canton (Guangzhou), and Zaiton (Quanzhou) in the eastern.

The pattern of emporia trade shifted after 1600, according to Chaudhuri. Aden and Hormuz declined while Mocha and Bandar 'Abbās prospered. Surat and Goa emerged on India's western coast, and Madras (now Chennai), Masulipatnam (now Machlipatnam), and Hugli developed along the Bay of Bengal. Malacca's preeminence became counterbalanced by the rise of Acheh, Bantam, and, most notably, Batavia (present-day Jakarta). Canton, by contrast, maintained its pivotal position in East Asia. By the eighteenth century, the so-called "Muslim-controlled trade pattern" (Risso, 1995, p. 95) had shifted decisively toward port cities established or controlled by the Dutch and English. Thus despite the regularity of the wind system, the terminal points of the Indian Ocean sea-lanes switched considerably over time.

Explaining the fluctuations in Asian maritime trade from the fourteenth to the eighteenth centuries has proved controversial. The rise of Muslim political hegemony, the settlement of hinterlands, the introduction of new crops, and the incidence of plague each played a role in the shaping of emporia trade. The factor that has received the most historical attention, however, is the arrival of the Portuguese and, more importantly, the northern Europeans. Steensgaard (1973) maintains that by redirecting the overland traffic between Asia and Europe to the sea route around the Cape of Good Hope, the northern Europeans precipitated an Asian trade revolution. The Europeans achieved this in the early seventeenth century, he argues, through superior commercial organization built upon the internalization of protection costs. However, scholars with access to Asian language sources have shown Steensgaard to be incorrect on a number of points, including his timing of the demise of the caravan trade and his characterization of Asian merchants as peddlers. Many have convincingly argued that superior force and the willingness to use it to pursue economic objectives are the real explanations for European commercial expansion in Asia.

The dichotomy between forced and "free" trade raises the following question: Was Afro-Asia an international free-trade zone before the arrival of the Europeans circa 1500? Usually yes, but not always. Free trade does not suggest the total absence of either direct taxes on merchants or governmental regulation of trade. Instead free trade indicates the presence of a competitive economic order. Where political elites ensured the physical protection of merchants and their cargoes, where merchants were subject to a more or less regular system of taxation and customs, competitive trade thrived. In stateless societies too, commercial transactions were often made possible by social institutions that enabled foreign merchants to operate peacefully. Referring to the Mediterranean during the classical Geniza period (969–1250), S. D. Goitein (1967, pp. 29, 70) describes it as a time of relatively free trade in which Muslims and Christians, upon paying customs for their goods, circulated unmolested in each other's territories. Indian Ocean scholars likewise consider maritime commerce during the pre-Portuguese period, the first half of the second millennium, as free of coercion.

Such characterizations are qualified by well-documented cases of piracy (including privateering), expulsions, and violent treatment by rulers, in addition to frequent monetary "exactions." One example of a state attempting strict controls of trade was the Hindu-Buddhist kingdom of Srivijaya during the seventh to thirteenth centuries. It was based in Palembang, Sumatra, and spread across the Malay Peninsula and parts of the islands of Borneo and Java. The monsoon dictated that ships plying between India and China pass through the Strait of Malacca. The naval fleet of Srivijaya patrolled the narrow passage, apprehended merchant vessels, and extorted payments for protection. In the eleventh century, the Cholas of southern India sent naval expeditions to pursue their "politics of plunder and expansionism." Much later in the seventeenth and eighteenth centuries, English sources were replete with bitter and self-serving complaints of the arbitrary decisions and venal character of Indian rulers insensitive to maritime trade. Such descriptions, believed literally by nineteenth- and early-twentieth-century writers, typify the "Oriental despot" approach to trade.

Neither forced nor free, a more flexible reading of trade policies from 1400 to 1700 describes them as broadly mercantilist. Sanjay Subrahmanyam (1999, p. 51) observes that states that depended on maritime commerce often participated directly in trade using whatever means available to influence producers and trade partners. The Persianized rulers of states in the Bay of Bengal were not disinterested onlookers of flourishing commerce. They promoted trade even as they intervened actively, reserving lucrative or prestige markets for themselves and unevenly regulating the activities of diasporic trading communities. A famous example of such a state is the sultanate of Malacca situated on the Malay Peninsula along the strait bearing the same name. In Malacca during the late fifteenth century, the sultans participated in trade through ship ownership and deploying a large staff of slaves to pursue the state's business interests. They regulated foreign trade through the office of the *shahbandar*. Each of the four major communities trading in Malacca—Gujaratis, Tamils, Javanese, and Chinese—had its own *shahbandar* who met arriving ships, helped settle merchants and their cargoes, and ensured that the government's customs were collected. The Gujaratis and Tamils paid a flat duty of 6 percent, whereas the Javanese and Chinese paid no duty. Instead, they were required to sell to the state and purchase from the state a part of the cargoes. Another example comes from the West African kingdom of Kong in the Volta river basin. In the early nineteenth century, elite Kong merchants maintained amicable relations with the military that controlled the state. The state concentrated "military force on protecting trade routes and posting garrisons to key points. In effect, they created a reasonably close parallel to the kind of overland trading post empire being developed in this same period in North America by the French *courers de bois* or the Hudson's Bay Company" (Curtin 1984, p. 45). Thus Subrahmanyam's mercantilist paradigm characterizes well the policies of Kong, Malacca, and many other states.

EMPORIUM. Ebute Ero market, Lagos, Nigeria, 1959. (Eliot Eliso-
fon/Eliot Elisofon Photographic Archives/National Museum of
African Art, Smithsonian Institution, Washington, D.C.)

Though smaller and more numerous than emporia,
bazaars exhibited a similar vibrancy in the range of traders
and transactions. Itinerant traders, hawkers, petty retailers, commission agents, bill brokers, moneylenders, jewelers, smiths, cobblers, and wholesalers all rubbed shoul-
ders in the marketplace. In many cases, specific castes,
religious, or ethnic communities often specialized in the
trade of a specific commodity or with a specific region. In
colonial Calcutta, the import and export of produce was
largely conducted by Marwaris, Kutchi Muslims, and Europeans. Local caste groups were widely represented in
small retailing and peddling activities. In wholesaling and
capital-intensive retail trades, distinct communities (for
example, the Bhatias) that had large networks of commission agents and a strong tradition of migration tended to
dominate. Through the bazaar, tribal people and herdsmen engaged the cash economy. Agriculturalists and artisans transformed their produce in specie for their own

consumption and to meet their tax burdens. Futures contracting and all manner of commodity, service, and credit
transactions took place amid the din and cramped lanes of
the bazaar.

Bazaars appeared as contiguous lanes of shops and
stalls, or they were contained within large roofed buildings, such as the nineteenth-century Crawford Market in
Bombay (now Mumbai). Alternatively, they were arranged
around a large open square, such as the Fatehpur Sikri
bazaar built during the reign of the Mughal emperor Akbar
(1556–1605). Bazaars were also adjoined to a larger complex, such as a caravansary, fort, or mosque. In Istanbul,
the L-shaped Misîr Carsisi, or Egyptian market, was built
in the seventeenth century next to Yeni mosque. Permanent bazaars were built on lands deeded by their original
owners for the benefit of their coreligionists. Bazaar merchants paid rents and taxes rather than owning their place
of business. Ruling families or religious officials associated with local mosques often used the rental receipts to establish hospices, maintain tombs, or support Qur'ānic education.

In the bazaar membership in a specific linguistic group,
caste, or religious group, often provided commercial advantages. Group membership aided the cultivation of specialized human capital across generations. Thus, the Ar-
menians of the late seventeenth century established a
trade school on the outskirts of Eşfahān (Iran) to train
their youth in accountancy, foreign weights, and currencies. Group membership aided the resolution of conflict
through institutions such as the Parsi *panchayat*. In North
Africa, oasis-centered religious orders, such as the nineteenth century Sanusiyya, provided lodges for their merchant members and storage for their goods. The Sanusiyya
order furthermore founded a new trade route across the
Sahara (Curtin 1984, pp. 51–52). In other cases, group
membership provided insider access to capital and initiated newcomers into established relationships of trust.
Thus, intricate social and religious affiliations sustained
and were sustained by business transactions in the bazaar.

Not surprisingly many scholars conceive the bazaar as
categorically different from "the market". To such scholars
the bazaar, with its close reflection of local ethnic, social
and gender hierarchies, bears little resemblance to a scientific notion of the market shore of cultural attributes. The
bazaar is often used to conceptually distinguish the modern from the traditional, factory-made from handicraft,
the formal from the informal. In European imperial historiography, for example, the bazaar is typically the counterpoint to the colonial market, with its august banks, corporations, factories, and import-export firms.

But what makes the bazaar distinct from the market?
For anthropologist Clifford Geertz (1979, p. 125) the search
for information is the central experience of life in the

bazaar. Specifically, buyers and sellers in the bazaar have highly skewed information about important attributes of transactions. For example buyers often lack explicit information about product availability, prices, and quality suggests Geertz. The costly search for information produces features unique to bazaars such as intense price bargaining, the importance of personal reputation, and stable clientship ties between buyers and sellers. Within firms too, several features of the bazaar, such as greater traditionalization of occupations, make it qualitatively distinct.

Economic anthropologists and economic historians have debated whether or not such distinctions imply that the usual truisms of economics do not operate in the bazaar. Most notably Karl Polanyi (1957) and his disciples (Dalton, 1968) of the "substantivist" school have insisted that transactions are socially embedded and are therefore not subject to the laws of supply and demand. "Formalists" by contrast reject the nation that economic analysis applies only to modern industrial economies but not to "primitive-subsistence" ones. Scott Cook (1966), for example, believed it was merely a romantic idealization of the "primitive" and a distinct anti-market ideology that prevented the fruitful application of formal economic theory to historical and cross-cultural settings.

Nearly a half-century later, the evidence has gone against the substantivists. In case after case, the initial enthusiasm for the Polanyi school has ended in yet another demonstration of the universality and antiquity of market behavior. An individual bazaar is indeed a unique social landscape, embedded in geography, language, ethics, and information constraints. Yet within the bazaar, market principles, common to both the village tailor and Wall Street trader, still affect behavior.

[*See also* Staple Markets and Entrepôts.]

BIBLIOGRAPHY

Chaudhuri, Kirti N. *Trade and Civilization in the Indian Ocean.* Cambridge, 1985.
Cook, Scott. "The Obsolete "Anti-Market" Mentality: A Critique of the Substantive Approach to Economic Anthropology." *American Anthropologist* 68.2 (1966), 323–345.
Curtin, Philip D. *Cross-Cultural Trade in World History.* New York, 1984.
Dalton, George, ed. *Primitive, Archaic, and Modern Economies: Essays of Karl Polanyi.* Garden City, N.Y., 1968.
Geertz, Clifford. "Sūq: The Bazaar Economy of Sefrou." In *Meaning and Order in Moroccan Society: Three Essays in Cultural Analysis*, by Clifford Geertz, Hildred Geertz, and Lawrence Rosen. Cambridge, 1979.
Goitein, S. D. *Mediterranean Society*, vol. 1. Berkeley, 1967.
Gray, Richard, and David Birmingham, eds. *Pre-Colonial African Trade: Essays on Trade in Central and Eastern Africa before 1900.* London, 1970.
Lombard, Denys, and Jean Aubin, eds. *Asian Merchants and Businessmen in the Indian Ocean and the China Sea.* New Delhi, 2000.
Polanyi, Karl, Conrad M. Arensberg, and Harry W. Pearson, eds. *Trade and Market in the Early Empires: Economies in History and Theory.* Glencoe, Ill., 1957.
Ray, Rajat Kanta. "The Bazaar: Indigenous Sector in the Indian Economy." In *Business Communities of India,* edited by Dwijendra Tripathi, pp. 241–267. New Delhi, 1984.
Risso, Patricia. *Merchants and Faith.* Boulder, 1995.
Steensgaard, Niels. *Carracks, Caravans, and Companies: Structural Crisis in the European-Asian Trade in the Early Seventeenth Century.* Copenhagen, 1973.
Subrahmanyam, Sanjay. "'Persianization' and 'Mercantilism': Two Themes in the Bay of Bengal History, 1400–1700." In *Commerce and Culture in the Bay of Bengal 1500–1800,* edited by Om Prakash and Denys Lombard, pp. 47–85. New Delhi, 1999.

SANTHI HEJEEBU

FAMILY POLICIES. Family policies are difficult to define. Four main issues have been raised in the literature. First, it has been strongly argued that the concept is not useful and that it is instead appropriate to talk of education, health, and welfare policies as they affect families. Indeed, the call for all policies to undergo a "family audit" as a fundamental element of "family policy" grew strong during the last quarter of the twentieth century.

Second, critics have taken issue with the idea that the term *family policy* or policies implies that assumptions are being made about the nature of "the family." During the last quarter of the twentieth century, family change in many Western countries was extremely rapid, with increasing rates of divorce, unmarried motherhood, and cohabitation (especially in western and northern Europe and North America) resulting in larger proportions of single-mother families. Historically, it can be shown that most welfare states have assumed the existence of a male breadwinner model family, in which there are two parents, and in which men take primary responsibility for earning and women for care. However, it is part of the complexity of modern welfare states that policies have endeavored to support the traditional family but also have facilitated changes in family form because of the payments made to single-mother families. The balance of the evidence does not support the idea of a causal relationship.

Third, there is a question as to how explicit family policy has been. The English-speaking countries in particular have tended not to make explicit reference to family policies, largely because state intervention in the private sphere of the family has been deemed inappropriate unless and until there is evidence of gross abuse. However, in France, the state adopted a pro-natalist policy in the early nineteenth century, and social provision in general was explicitly structured around the support of families with children (rather than the poor, as has been the case in the English-speaking countries). It was thus an easy step for the French government in the twentieth century to try to "reconcile" employment and family responsibilities, a matter that became increasingly problematic as female labor-market participation increased and the male-bread-winner model eroded. However, in the United States and the United Kingdom, governments remained reluctant to make such an issue a matter for public policy.

Finally, it is far from clear which family members are included under the heading of family policies. Most of the literature, historical and sociological, has focused on policies for the financial maintenance and support of children; but the family has been the most important source of provision of care for older dependent adults as well, although there is little historical work on this topic. It is also the case that policies addressing children usually make assumptions about, and therefore affect, the role of their main caregivers, mothers. In contrast, fathers were not the subject of family policies for most of the twentieth century. At the beginning of the century there is evidence of concern about the willingness of working men to maintain their families, for example, in the debate over the provision of school meals in the United Kingdom in 1906, and again at the end of the century there was considerable anxiety, verging on moral panic, about father absence and father distance.

Welfare States and Family Responsibilities. The relationship between the family and the state has been fundamental to the development of modern social provision. The male-breadwinner model underpinned the core programs of the modern welfare state, based on social insurance. The aim was primarily to protect the male breadwinner against sickness and unemployment and "first class" social insurance benefits tended to go to regularly employed, white men, while widows, divorcees, and unmarried mothers and their children resorted to "second class" social assistance payments, which in many Western countries descended from Poor-Law systems. These took many different forms, remaining available to anyone on a means-tested basis in the United Kingdom, but taking the form of a categorical benefit (Aid to Families with Dependent Children) in the United States. Nevertheless the question of how to treat the male breadwinner's dependants was raised early in the twentieth century. In many countries dependants' allowances were paid, increasing women's economic dependency on men. The position of children raised additional questions about the function of the wage, posed most acutely by Eleanor Rathbone in *The Disinherited Family* (London, 1924), and the role of collective as opposed to individual/family responsibility. By World War II, all Western countries except the United States had developed some system of family allowances, operated via a tax and/or benefits system. The motives behind this singular development were many and varied. Feminist arguments for the recognition of women's caregiving work through the payment of allowances to the mother, pro-natalist concerns, especially during the 1930s when the birth rate in western European countries was very low; left political parties' wish to promote a living wage and address child poverty; Catholic trade unions' desire to promote the family; and the interests of firms and governments in limiting wage bills—all played a part in the debates to differing extents in different countries.

A larger issue behind the debates over the introduction of family allowances was the question of how far the family should bear the burden of supporting and caring for its members, which in great measure explains why the United States did not enter this policy arena, and why allowances were much more generous in 1940s France than in 1940s Britain. This has been the most important continuing theme. Thus, in the late twentieth century, social assistance payments to unmarried mothers increasingly were questioned in the English-speaking countries and particularly in the United States, and legislation was to try to secure child support payments from "absent fathers." As the populations of Western countries have aged, so also have questions been raised about the care and support of older people; in some countries, for example Germany, there is still a legal obligation for children to support their elderly parents financially.

The issue of collective versus individual responsibility for care has, if anything, been especially controversial. From the 1970s on, the decision in Sweden to provide extensive public, high-quality child care was linked to the decision to draw more married women into the labor market, as well as to ideas about what was best for children. In France too the widespread provision of child care was considered part of the state's responsibility. However, in the United Kingdom, where the male-breadwinner model eroded rapidly after World War II, child-care arrangements were considered a private matter and left primarily to the family and the market. Women's labor-market participation is high in all three countries. Indeed, the period of development for modern welfare states has been a period of increasing individualization for adults. There is evidence, however, that in countries where the support and the care of dependents has been most readily accepted as a collective responsibility, the welfare of children, measured by the rate of child poverty, has been greatest.

BIBLIOGRAPHY

Bock, Gisela, and Pat Thane, eds. *Maternity and Gender Policies: Women and the Rise of European Welfare States, 1880s–1950s.* London, 1991.

Gordon, Linda. *Pitied but Not Entitled: Single Mothers and the History of Welfare, 1890–1935.* New York, 1994.

Kiernan, Kathleen, Hilary Land, and Jane Lewis. *Lone Motherhood in Twentieth-Century Britain.* Oxford, 1998.

Koven, Seth, and Sonya Michel, eds. *Mothers of a New World: Maternalist Politics and the Origins of Welfare States.* London, 1993.

Macnicol, John. *The Movement for Family Allowances, 1918–1945.* London, 1980.

Michel, Sonya. *Children's Interests, Mothers' Rights: The Shaping of American Child Care Policy.* New Haven, 1999.

Pedersen, Susan. *Family Dependence and the Origins of the Welfare State in Britain and France, 1914–1945*. Cambridge, 1993.

Skocpol, Theda. *Protecting Soldiers and Mothers: The Political Origins of Social Policy in the US*. Cambridge, Mass., 1992.

JANE LEWIS

FAMILY STRUCTURES AND KINSHIP.

Essential concepts for social analysis include family structures, kinship systems, and households. Each culture defines kin and kinship in its own way.

The term *kinship* refers to human societal systems of mutual rights and obligations, and their symbolic representations, which link social actors with respect to consanguineal, affinal, ritual, or "kinship-like" relations—that is, consanguinity ("blood"), affinity (marriage), customs like godparenting, as well as adoption, fostering, and metaphorical extension (fictive kinship). These are not mutually exclusive: some persons may marry, adopt, or be godparents to blood relatives; then, too, cultural dicta may proscribe some relationships, as in taboos on marriage between certain consanguines.

The term *family structures* refers to systems of grouping social actors according to cultural principles and units that have especially intense or enduring expectations of mutuality, including economic or ritual corporacy (joint interest). The various levels of family structure exhibit different intensities of expectation or corporacy. *Lineages* are mutually exclusive family structures defined by descent through only one sex (e.g., patrilineages by agnatic descent or matrilineages by uterine descent). *Clans* are lineages defined by putative or legendary descent. *Kindreds* are overlapping family structures defined by bilateral (cognatic) descent.

The term *household* refers to units of social actors who are usually coresidents and have a relatively high degree of common consumption, with often some degree of common production. Households are subsets of family structures, but they are not necessarily the smallest and are usually an intersection of two families; for example, a conjugal pair (husband and wife) is often smaller than its household and is an intersection of the families from which each spouse came. The terms *family* and *household* are often used interchangeably, but they are best distinguished in the senses given above.

The ways that individuals classify persons and think about membership in categories of kinship or families or households is complex; these may vary over the life course. For example, a young bride may become a member of her husband's household but not yet be thought of as a member of his family; in later years, with children of her own, she would be considered a member both of his household and of his family, and he of hers. The meaning of her phrase, "my family," will differ in her two life stages. Family systems vary in the degree and timing with which in-marrying persons are incorporated. In some patrilineal systems, wives are never incorporated into their husband's lineage—in others they are.

EXTENDED FAMILY. Head of the Bakhtiari tribe with his wives and children, Iran, 1984. (© Tony Howarth/Woodfin Camp and Associates, New York)

Family systems can vary over short spans of time in a single locus, as when rapidly changing rates of extramarital cohabitation lead to different local understandings of household and family or when increasing rates of divorce and remarriage lead to complex webs of kinship. Variability increases in complex societies with class differentials in culture and social organization and in multiethnic societies. Dangers of misunderstanding by Western observers are substantial outside the social systems within which most were socialized or outside those that have a written economic history. A typical analytical error occurs in demographic surveys for societies characterized by polygyny (several wives), joint or extended households, or strong lineage systems. In such societies, the assumption that decisions about reproduction, maternal and child health, and human capital investment will be made by a conjugal pair, or its male head, fails to recognize the broader corporacy of interest and control characteristic of such systems.

Kinship Systems. The study of kinship systems can be concerned (1) with the mutual rights and obligations among kin, as locally defined, or (2) with the mechanisms of language that name and classify kin. These two approaches often stand in theoretical opposition. Particularly disputed are (1) the degree to which genealogical connection may be taken as an analytic tool and (2) whether application of a kinship term, like *uncle*, to a person not genealogically related is part of a core definition or is a metaphorical extension.

Kinship Terminologies. The way in which local languages classify kin is often a clue to local ideas of kinship roles. Western historians are familiar with terminologies in which, for example, father and his brother are named by different terms ("father," "uncle"), yet mother's brother and the husbands of the parents' sisters are all "uncles" too. Such systems signal the primacy of conjugal units, and they differentiate those with whom a person ("ego") lives from all those in which ego does not. Some languages and cultures have different systems: in Slavic languages, father's and mother's brothers are often differently named and the wife of each is called by a feminine form of their husband's term—but the sisters of both parents have the same term and their husbands a derivative of it. This suggests a strong differentiation of the mother's and father's lineage and of both of these from ego's own household, as well as the primacy of links through males. In English, *brother* and *cousin* are terminologically distinct, but in Slavic they are often not. In some terminological systems, the strength of lineage organization is so great that some individuals of different generations are co-classified under one term, for example, mother's brother and mother's father, a version of which is seen in Latin, *avus* ("grandfather"), *avunculus* ("little grandfather, the mother's brother") versus *pater* ("father"), *patruus* ("father's brother"), exemplifying the strong patrilineal bias of Roman social organization.

Kinship as Reciprocal Obligation. Some studies of kinship structures may be concerned only with systems of mutual rights and obligations. For example, Anglo-Saxon kinship structure specified the degree of responsibility and compensation in feuds. Social actors may also be regarded as bundles of separable rights and duties. In some African systems, the rights of a husband in his wife with respect to sexual services, labor, and her children are each separate and contingent on the stage of the marriage process. He may have no right to count her children within his lineage until the full brideprice has been paid, and when it is, he may have that right no matter who was the genitor of her child. In Latin America, nonmarital cohabitation may carry all customary obligations of fatherhood found in formal marriage, except that of endowing (in terms of inheritance) the children of the union. Where systems of fostering are strong, as in much of Africa, the costs and benefits of childbearing are more widely shared than when children are raised only in their natal households. Recognition of these situations are crucial to economic interpretations of fertility behavior. Similar interpretations may be given to systems in which children leave home early as servants or apprentices; a substantial part of their maintenance and of investment in them occurs outside the natal household.

Classification. Attempts to classify kinship structures have had varying success. Terminological systems have been characterized by the pattern of naming parents and their siblings, or of siblings and cousins, or of the nature and extent of cross-generational merging. To simplify, the following symbols are introduced: H = husband, W = wife, F = father, M = mother, B = brother, Z = sister, S = son, D = daughter, C = child; thus MBS = mother's brother's son, etc. The classifications (see Table 1) have been in common use (Murdock 1949); however, empirically observed terminological systems combine some of the features shown. More refined approaches (componential analysis and transformational analysis, both derived from formal linguistics), using a set-theoretical approach and a specialized algebra, are more capable of capturing the internal logic of terminological systems (see Goodenough 1956, Hammel 1965, Kroeber 1909, and Lounsbury 1964).

Descent Theory. Systems of social organization have been characterized by the kind and degree of lineage organization and their patterns of corporacy and inheritance (see Fortes 1953, Goody 1969, and Radcliffe-Brown 1952). Membership in social units can be unilineal or cognatic (see Table 2).

Few if any societies can be characterized as entirely within one of these categories. More commonly, different corporacies and memberships are reckoned in different ways. For example, in strongly patrilineal societies, bonds of affection or mutual obligation may be especially strong and even ritualized between a boy and his mother's brother, the senior male relative who is not in his patriline but in his mother's; in such systems, a famous or sole female survivor may found a patriline, may marry a "ghost" to properly place her children, may marry a woman to claim that woman's children for her lineage, and so on. In many societies some kinds of property pass along agnatic links, sometimes differentially to sons and daughters, while other kinds pass only from mothers to daughters. Special obligations to the parental lineage to which one does *not* belong (e.g., to mother's patriline in a patrilineal system) are called "complementary filiation."

TABLE 1. *Classification of Kinship Terminological Systems*

EQUALITIES AND DIFFERENCES	COMMON DESIGNATION	MAJOR CHARACTERISTICS
F = FB = MB M = MZ = FZ	"Hawaiian"	Grouped by generation and sex
B = MBS = FBS = MZS = FZS Z = MBD = FBD = MZD = FZD	"Polynesian"	Grouped by generation and sex
F ≠ (FB = MB) M ≠ (MZ = FZ)	"lineal"	Collaterals grouped, separate from lineals, by sex
F ≠ FB ≠ MB M ≠ MZ ≠ FZ	"bifurcate collateral"	Distinguished by lineality, collaterality, sex
(F = FB) ≠ MB (M = MZ) ≠ FZ	"bifurcate merging"	Grouped by sex of links and of the relative
B ≠ (FBS = MBS = FZS = MZS) Z ≠ (FBD = MBD = FZD = MZD)	"Eskimo"	Collaterals other than siblings grouped
(B = FBS = MZS) ≠ (FZS = MBS) (Z = FBD = MZD) ≠ (FZD = MBD)	"Iroquoian"	Grouped by sex of links, cross (MBC, FZC) vs. parallel (FBC, MZC) cousins
MF = MB = MBS...	"Omaha"	Grouped across generations within the mother's patriline
FM = FZ = FZD...	"Crow"	Grouped across generations within the father's matriline

TABLE 2. *Types of Descent Systems*

TYPE	CHARACTERISTIC
Unilineal: Patrilineal	Membership through agnatic (male) links only
Unilineal: Matrilineal	Membership through uterine (female) links only
Unilineal: Double Descent	Membership through simultaneous combination of agnatic and uterine links
Unilineal: Ambilineal	Membership by individual choice in the lineage of either the father or the mother
Cognatic	Membership by genealogical degree regardless of sex of links

Alliance Theory. While some theorists have focused on descent systems, others (see Dumont 1957, Leach 1982, Levi-Strauss 1969, and Needham 1974) have emphasized the relationships between descent units, principally through marriage. Many descent groups are exogamous (marriage cannot be between members), typically requiring an exchange of persons for social and other goods at marriage, such as brideprice for brides. The nature of the rules of exogamy may be closely linked to the kinship system and may result in highly patterned systems of marriage exchange. Some scholars distinguish "elementary" and "complex" marriage systems. In elementary systems, rules specify which kin are marriageable; and some researchers have distinguished between prescriptive and preferential

forms of such rules. In complex systems, rules specify which kinds of kin are not marriageable. For example, in Iroquoian systems where siblings and parallel cousins are classed together, persons classified as cross cousins are the only possible spouses. In Dravidian systems (a subset of Iroquoian), the term for cross cousin is also that for spouse. Systems in which women of two groups are exchanged as wives in the same generation are said to be characterized by symmetrical cross-cousin marriage, and marital transactions are usually between social equals. There are two kinds of asymmetrical cross-cousin marriage, matrilateral and patrilateral, the former common, the latter rare. If marriage is prescriptively or preferentially between a man and his MBD (or other more distant cousin similarly classified), the system may be circular, with women traveling in one direction to join their husband's patrilocal households on marriage, and counter-prestations traveling in the other direction. Some such systems are not closed but socially hierarchical, commonly with women marrying up the social scale (hypergyny), their natal kin often assuming a client status to the kin of their husbands. In patrilateral cross-cousin marriage, brides move to an adjacent group in the system, but their daughters then move back in the next, in delayed reciprocal exchange. Some systems of marriage favor endogamy to consolidate diverging branches of a lineage; for example, in some Semitic groups and some groups heavily influenced by Islam, marriage with the father's brother's daughter is preferred; it reunites, as the interests and property of a new conjugal pair, the interests and property of their paternal grandfather, which were diverged to their own respective fathers.

Family Structures. Grounded in the broader kinship system and existing at different levels are family structures. Most Europeans, having a cognatic kinship system, think of concentric circles of kin, each next outer circle characterized by lower levels of mutuality. In unilineal systems, there is an inverted tree of levels, defined by the genealogy (both biological and socially recognized). The broadest units, with the deepest roots, may only recognize common ancestry or ritual obligation, and corporacy in respect of production, consumption, and mutual obligation increase inversely as genealogical depth. Specification of corporacy is crucial, especially in respect of productive property. In some systems, all members of a wide kin group have usufruct, but the property is inalienable; access to it follows the local rule of kinship reckoning. In other systems, access may be restricted to narrower groups, such as siblings or cousins. The practices may differ for different kinds of property in the same society.

The nature and the correlates of different family structures are important as mechanisms for the transfer of wealth and power between generations. Kinship structures that are strongly unilineal tend to be characterized by homogeneous devolution; access to resources depends on membership in the unilineal kin group—and such systems are common in sub-Saharan Africa and some parts of East Asia and South Asia. Strongly cognatic kinship structures are characterized by diverging devolution; rights to resources are brought together in the inheritances of two spouses as a conjugal estate, then devolved again to their children of either sex, as inheritance or dowry—and such systems are most common in northern and western Europe, Oceania, and parts of Asia. Somewhat intermediate are systems with descent groups that appear to be unilineal, because of agnatic filiation in last names or access to political position, but in which productive property is cog-

natically transmitted—and Scottish clans and Semitic lineages are example. For these, however, inheritance is often restricted; in some European and Middle Eastern societies, daughters may receive only a part of the share that sons receive or may be excluded altogether (except for household dowry). Then, too, inheritance may be equal for all children (or all males), as in systems of partible inheritance, or it may be restricted to one child, either by primogeniture or ultimogeniture rule or by testamentary disposition.

The nature of inheritance rules is important for understanding the economic strategies of reproduction, child care, and human capital investment of both families and households. They may also affect the more general economy and the society. The traditional system of marriage and family in northern and western Europe from the fall of the Roman Empire until the eighteenth century restricted marriage to persons holding a niche in the occupational structure, which incidentally kept population in check. As imported New World crops permitted those Europeans subsistence on smaller plots, and as employment in labor and manufacturing became more common with the Industrial Revolution, a greater proportion of the population could marry and marry earlier, leading to an increase in population. It was this phenomenon that led to Thomas Malthus's theories of population and overpopulation (*An Essay on the Principle of Population*, 1798; rev. ed., 1803).

Households. Persons join households by marriage and birth (or its equivalents, like adoption) and leave by death, divorce, or migration. Household structures are extremely variable and are distinguished according to whether they contain one, more than one, or no conjugal units, as well as the ways that multiple conjugal units are related, whether they contain additional kin other than members of conjugal units, and the way in which a new conjugal unit sets up a household on marriage (see Hammel and Laslett 1994, Skinner 1997, and Netting et al., 1984; see also Table 3).

Household formation may be flexible and mutable, often following a regular cycle of household development. In many societies (often patrilineal in some degree), a new spousal pair may live with the husband's father (patrivirilocal residence) in a patrilocal extended family, which may contain other married sons of the father. Then, with the father's death, the household may persist with the widow (and children) resident, ultimately becoming a fraternal joint family. It may even fragment into a series of nuclear households. Household structures also vary seasonally, with shifts to accommodate climate changes and/or economic necessities.

Marriage. In many societies, marriage is less an event than a process, joining not only two persons but also their families. Conjugality takes many forms, including some

TABLE 3. *Common Household Classifications*

CLASSIFICATION BY TYPE OR RULE OF RESIDENCE	HOUSEHOLD CONTAINS OR IS LOCATED AS
Solitary	One person (e.g., a widow)
Nuclear ("simple")	Spouses with or without children, or remnant thereof (e.g., widow with children)
Extended	Two conjugal units or remnants thereof, in different generations (e.g., patrilineal extended family, father and mother with one or more married sons)
Joint	Two conjugal units or remnants thereof, in the same generation (e.g., fraternal joint household, of married brothers and nuclear families)
Neolocal	Spouses establish a new household on marriage
Virilocal	Wife lives at husband's locale
Uxorilocal	Husband lives at wife's locale
Patrilocal	Spouses live with the father of one, usually virilocally
Matrilocal	Spouses live with the mother of one, usually uxorilocally
Avunculocal	Spouses live with the wife's brother or mother's brother, usually uxorilocally
Duolocal	Spouses live in their natal households, meeting for sexual purposes

socially legitimized forms of sexual access that do not involve the formalities of marriage; these may occur simultaneously in a society.

Social custom may result in each person marrying only once (if at all). It may permit dissolution of marriage, by formal or informal means. If marriages are dissolved or ended by death, remarriage may be encouraged differently for widows and widowers. If monogamous dissolution and remarriage are frequent, the result is called "serial" monogamy. Social custom may permit polygamy—the marriage of one or more persons to one or more other persons. Polygyny permits multiple wives and is common in many regions; nevertheless, even where it is encouraged, most men are monogamous, since the acquisition of wives is expensive. Polyandry permits multiple husbands. It is rare (Himalayas, South Asia, Polynesia, Africa) and never the only marital form. Polygynandry (a simultaneous combination of polygyny and polyandry) is even rarer (Himalayas, Polynesia). Among the matrilineal Nayar of Malabar (India) a formal and early marriage is soon deactivated, and women, continuing to reside in their natal household, take lovers who are the genitors of their children but who are not their social fathers. Even more extreme practices occur among the Moso of southern China.

The classifications discussed above are only a survey of the observed variety of custom, law, and practice. Nevertheless, the lesson for the economic historian is clear. Features of kinship terminologies, of family systems, and of the construction and cycling of households have important implications for understanding socioeconomic behavior.

[*See also* Children; Family Policies; Household; *and* Marriage.]

BIBLIOGRAPHY

Barnes, John A. *Three Styles in the Study of Kinship*. Berkeley, 1971. Theoretical overview of anthropological studies of kinship.

Dumont, Louis. "Hierarchy and Marriage Alliance in South Indian Kinship." Occasional papers, Royal Anthropological Institute of Great Britain and Ireland; no. 12. London, 1957. Seminal work on hypergyny and alliance.

Fortes, Meyer. "The Structure of Unilineal Descent Groups." *American Anthropologist* 55 (1953), 17–41. Important definitional work.

Fox, Robin. *Kinship and Marriage*. Princeton, 1967. General introduction.

Goodenough, Ward. "Componential Analysis and the Study of Meaning." *Language* 35 (1956), 195–216. Seminal work in formal semantic analysis of kinship terminology.

Goody, Jack. *Production and Reproduction*. Cambridge, 1953. Overview of family systems in Africa and Eurasia.

Goody, Jack. *Comparative Studies in Kinship*. Stanford, Calif., 1969. Important theoretical overview.

Goody, Jack. *The Development of the Family and Marriage in Europe*. Cambridge, 1983. Important for the economic history of Europe.

Hammel, Eugene, ed. "Formal Semantic Analysis." *American Anthropologist* 67.2.5 (1965). Papers on the formal analysis of kinship terminologies.

Hammel, Eugene, and Peter Laslett. "Comparing Household Structure over Time and between Cultures." *Comparative Studies in*

Society and History 16 (1974), 73–109. Definitional outline of household types.

Kroeber, Alfred. "Classificatory Systems of Relationship." *Journal of the Royal Anthropological Institute* 39 (1909), 77–84. Seminal analytic paper on native principles of kinship classification.

Laslett, Peter, ed. *Household and Family in Past Time.* Cambridge, 1972. Contains analyses of historical household forms in Europe and Asia.

Leach, Edmund. *Social Anthropology.* New York, 1982. General introduction, stressing alliance theory.

Lévi-Strauss, Claude. *The Elementary Structures of Kinship.* Translated by James Harle Bell, John Richard von Sturmer, and Rodney Needham. Rev. ed. Boston, 1969. Seminal work in the French structuralist tradition.

Lounsbury, Floyd. "A Formal Account of the Crow- and Omaha-type Kinship Terminologies." In *Explorations in Cultural Anthropology*, edited by W. H. Goodenough. New York, 1964. Formal semantic analysis of kinship terminology systems with generational skewing.

Morgan, Lewis Henry. *Systems of Consanguinity and Affinity of the Human Family.* Washington, D.C., 1870. The earliest compendium and analysis of kinship terminology systems.

Murdock, George. *Social Structure.* New York, 1949. General introduction, now dated, but giving classifications still in common use.

Needham, Rodney. *Remarks and Inventions: Skeptical Essays about Kinship.* London, 1974. Important theoretical work, especially regarding alliance theory.

Netting, Robert M., R. Wilk, and E. J. Arnould, eds. *Households: Comparative and Historical Studies of the Domestic Group.* Berkeley, 1984. Articles on theory, analysis, and description of household forms.

Radcliffe-Brown, A. R. *Structure and Function in Primitive Societies: Essays and Addresses by A. R. Radcliffe-Brown.* London, 1952. Important early contributions to descent theory.

Schneider, David M., and Kathleen Gough, eds. *Matrilineal Kinship.* Berkeley, 1961. Fundamental survey of such kinship systems.

Skinner, G. William. "Family Systems and Demographic Process." In *Anthropological Demography: Toward a New Synthesis*, edited by David Kertzer and Tom Fricke. Chicago, 1997. Important overview paper on effects of family systems on demographic behavior.

Wall, Richard, ed. *Family Forms in Historic Europe.* Cambridge, 1983. Analyses of many but not all historically known family forms in Europe.

E. A. HAMMEL

FAMINE RELIEF. In premodern times, kings and other rulers were frequently judged on their ability to provide relief during times of famine. The model was in the Bible—that the pharaoh of Egypt had wisely placed Joseph the Israelite in charge of his granaries to ration and thereby forestall a predicted famine. Monarchs were expected to emulate this biblical example with emergency supplies that were provided by taxation and tribute, and they were accorded popular legitimacy in proportion to their success. State-organized famine relief at such times entailed the distribution of handouts from state granaries, the organization of grain imports, the provision of monetary relief, the prohibition of hoarding by merchants, and the forcing of dealers to sell their produce at fair prices. Similar considerations applied in all civilized societies, as in imperial China, where the ruler and his officials were expected to act as "father and mother" of the people. They were to do their best to prevent famine through the provision of land and irrigation and by maintaining food stores that helped the peasantry when harvests failed. In Mughal India during famines, the state waived taxes, organized the distribution of free food, and punished profiteers.

In the Middle Ages, famine relief was also provided by religious bodies and by merchants. In medieval Europe, church foundations—monasteries, almshouses, and hospitals—provided sustenance. In India, rich merchants paid for cooked food to be fed to the starving in the streets, a practice that encouraged the poor to flock to the towns at such times and kept them from stealing and rioting. Rural moneylenders and usurers might also sustain their clients through credit advances. In eighteenth-century Europe, with the growth of trade and commerce and with improvements in agricultural techniques, governments sought to free themselves from the obligation of providing the bulk of relief. This was justified in a number of ways. In Britain, the political economist Adam Smith argued that state interference at such times upset the workings of market forces which, left to themselves, would remedy the situation. Smith reasoned that the high prices of a year of dearth ensured that merchants would import large stocks of food and thus provide for the people. The 1798 *Essay on the Principle of Population* by Thomas Malthus was also invoked, to state that famine indicated that population levels had become unsustainable and that nature should be left free to eradicate the indigent and weak. The Utilitarians recognized that some relief was required, but they argued that the poor should always be made to work for their sustenance; they prescribed the establishment of public works during famines, for which the poor would be paid minimal wages for their labor.

These principles informed the response of the British government to the great Irish famine of 1846 to 1851 (when a potato blight destroyed the subsistence crops). In practice, the refusal to provide any checks on the market led to grain being exported freely, as the local poor could not afford to buy it—and that revealed the limits to Smith's theory. State relief was grudgingly provided, mainly through public works. The rest was left to private charities. By 1847, however, the continuing destitution, starvation, deaths, and suffering of the people who could not emigrate forced the British government to provide more generous outdoor relief. Eventually, a blight-free potato was introduced. The Utlilitarian doctrines were applied also in British Colonial India, which during the nineteenth century became the archetypal "land of famine," depicted in harrowing photographs of skeletal famine-victims. There, the British broke with tradition by refusing to countenance the fixing of market prices and banning of grain exports during

FAMINE RELIEF. Bags of American corn being delivered to relieve famine in Sudan, 1998. (© Betty Press/Woodfin Camp and Associates, New York)

famines. Although relief was provided in work camps, wages were so low and sanitary conditions so poor that epidemics of cholera and typhoid erupted, killing millions. Clearly, concentrating large numbers of malnourished people in such camps was an invitation to disaster, which suggested that dispersed, hygienic relief was needed. Despite this, relief camps have continued to be established in famines throughout the world, often with continuing tragic consequences in undersupervised conditions.

The experience of devastating famines in India in the 1860s and 1870s led to a rethinking of British colonial policy. More resources were put into public irrigation works, with a network of canals constructed and paid for largely by loans from Britain. A vast railway network was constructed that would, it was believed, take food to the most remote areas. A famine code was created in 1880, which the historian David Arnold described as "one of the most significant administrative measures devised during the entire period of British rule in India" (*Famine*, London, 1968, p. 96). The code established clear guidelines for officials, so that they might act rapidly in famine situations, providing adequate relief through labor camps. The government also resolved to provide loans for India's peasants, to allow them to carry out local relief works—such as digging wells—and to rebuild their lives after the crisis was over. The code did not, however, allow any checks on the market, so in the famines of the late 1890s, produce continued to be exported from the worst-hit areas, which on occasion led to grain-riots. After 1900, the famine code was implemented more generously, and serious famine was averted for the rest of the British period (with the notable exception of the great Bengal famine of 1943—caused by a breakdown in relief arrangements during World War II—which might have been averted with more foresight).

Famine relief work by private charities became more systematized during the nineteenth century and the twentieth. In particular, the Christian missionaries who went into the areas of European colonialism endeavored to raise emergency funds, goods, and services for relief during famines. By providing food handouts, work and education on mission stations, and housing and schooling for famine-orphans, they gained grateful converts—the so-called rice-Christians of China and elsewhere. With the growth in communications, the print and the photographic media, famines in remote parts of the world were publicized in distressing detail in the West. This helped create a Western demand for effective, internationally organized relief initiatives; governments and private donors were enjoined to provide funds for famine relief in distant parts of the globe. The response tended, however, to reinforce the view that the "dynamic" West was coming to the aid of passive and often fatalistic "victims" in the East—in Asia and Africa. The structural disruptions caused by imperialism and the globalization of capital that had in many cases caused these famines in the period after 1800 were largely ignored.

After World War I, Western governments began to provide international aid as a counter to possible socialist revolution in poor countries. The intent was to provide a vivid demonstration of the superiority of the capitalist economy—which generated a large food surplus—as well as to emphasize the benefits of the West's commitment to liberal and humanitarian values. Thus the United States provided aid for eastern Europe and Russia during the famines that followed the collapse of the tsar and the Russian Revolution. This helped to check the advance of communism in parts of eastern Europe, though not in Russia. A similar strategy was adopted by the United States after World War II, when relief (the Marshall Plan) was provided on a massive scale for the hungry and starving of Europe so as to win people away from the Soviet Union. A similar approach has been applied by the West globally since then, as a tool of winning the Cold War (1945–1991). Food aid was withheld from Communist-led countries, in the hope that the famine-stricken would reject that form of rule. Food aid was provided to countries run by governments of which the Western powers approved. International food aid, it may be noted, has also served to open up vast new markets for U.S. grain, further helping to strengthen the U.S. economy.

During the twentieth century, private, or nongovernment organizations (NGOs), have become increasingly important in organizing international famine relief. Several emerged from Christian mission organizations, such as the China International Famine Relief Commission (1920), which raised funds internationally to help China; it also funded public works to provide a more long-term insurance against famine. Of such organizations, the best known is perhaps Oxfam, which was formed in 1942 to relieve the severe food shortages that affected Europe during World War II. Such organizations stood for the ideal of humanitarian neutrality in disaster-relief operations. Implicitly, they were critical of the often politically motivated relief work of governments. Since 1945, and backed by fund-raising initiatives like Band Aid, they have become major players in contemporary famine relief.

Relief work has frequently been hampered by the active promotion of famine by certain sectional interests. For example, in Sudan, food supplies for famine victims have been obstructed so as to undermine the resistance of rebels in the South. Elsewhere, various rebel groups have deliberately created famine situations to fan discontent and encourage outside intervention. In some cases, as in Brazil, rural elites have appropriated relief supplies so as to sustain famine and bring still more relief to their doors. The generally approved strategy of targeting the most destitute victims has little chance of success in such circumstances; in such cases, the chief emphasis has to be on political solutions before relief can be effective.

[*See also* Famines *and* Irish Famine.]

BIBLIOGRAPHY

Ambirajan, S. *Classical Political Economy and British Policy in India*. Cambridge, 1978. Examines the effect of the theories of the eighteenth-century economist Adam Smith in relation to famine relief policies in India.

Arnold, David. *Famine: Social Crisis and Historical Change*. Oxford, 1988. One of the best short introductions to the topic.

Black, Maggie. *A Cause for Our Times: Oxfam the First 50 Years*. Oxford, 1992. A history of a leading modern nongovernment organization (NGO) dedicated to famine relief and prevention.

Cathie, John. *The Political Economy of Food Aid*, Aldershot, U.K., 1982.

Clay, Jason W., Sandra Steinberger, and Peter Niggli. *The Spoils of Famine: Ethiopian Famine Policy and Peasant Agriculture*. Cambridge, Mass., 1988.

De Waal, Alexander. *Famine That Kills: Darfur, Sudan, 1984–1985*. Oxford, 1989. Chapter 8 is on relief, and De Waal distinguishes between famine as widespread social and economic disruption and "famine that kills"—in the former case, relief in a form other than food is more appropriate. Some criticisms of famine work by nongovernment organizations (NGOs) are addressed, and the huge complexities of relief work are emphasized.

De Waal, Alexander. *The Sudan Famine Code of 1920: Successes and Failures of the Indian Model of Famine Relief in Colonial Sudan*. London, 1989.

Deng, Francis M., and Larry Minear. *The Challenges of Famine Relief: Emergency Operations in the Sudan*. Washington, D.C., 1992.

Drèze, Jean, and Amartya Sen. *Hunger and Public Action*. Oxford, 1989. Examines the role of public policy in protecting or failing to protect "entitlements" (for this concept, see Sen, 1981, below).

George, Susan. *How the Other Half Dies: The Real Reason for World Hunger*. New York, 1976; rev. ed., 1986.

Halstead, Paul, and John O'Shea, eds. *Bad Year Economics: Cultural Responses to Risk and Uncertainty*. Cambridge, 1989. Examines how people react to such disasters as famine and how they modify their behavior accordingly, so as to prevent such occurrences in the future.

Jordan, William Chester. *The Great Famine: Northern Europe in the Early Fourteenth Century*. Princeton, 1996. A detailed and readable examination of famine in medieval Europe, with analysis of famine relief in chapters 6 and 9.

Keen, David. *The Benefits of Famine: A Political Economy of Famine and Relief in Southwestern Sudan, 1983–1989*. Princeton, 1994. An important study of the organization of relief. Argues that during recent famines in Sudan, Ethiopia, and Somalia, certain groups actively promoted the famine for their own benefits. Suggests that the solution to famine has to be political in such cases.

Sen, Amartya. *Poverty and Famines: An Essay on Entitlement and Deprivation*. Oxford, 1981. A seminal work on the causes of famine—attributed to the lack of "entitlement" of the poor to food. In such a light, famine relief must above all involve the creation of such entitlement.

Vaughan, Megan. *The Story of an African Famine: Gender and Famine in Twentieth Century Malawi*. Cambridge, 1987.

Wallerstein, Michael B. *Food for War—Food for Peace: United States Food Aid in a Global Context*. New York, 1980.

DAVID HARDIMAN

FAMINES. Defining famine remains a controversial issue. On the one hand, famines that produce excess mortality usually represent only peaks in a chronic or endemic malnutrition that renders "normal" mortality high. On the other, famine deaths are often difficult to distinguish from deaths that are due to epidemics such as malaria or cholera. It follows that the dividing line between crises that reduce the resistance of the poor to disease and harvest shortfalls that result in literal starvation is not clear-cut. Here our main focus will be on "famines that kill." By this definition, the Third Horseman has been a looming presence since the dawn of history.

Why Famines? Throughout history natural disasters such as volcanic eruptions or floods resulting in poor harvests were often the proximate cause of famines. Well-known examples include the eruptions of Laki (Iceland in the 1780s) and Tambora (Indonesia in the 1810s), potato blight (in Europe in the 1840s), and the El Niño drought (Asia in the late 1870s). The worst famines were due to back-to-back or repeated crop shortfalls, such as those in Ireland in the 1840s, India in the 1890s, and China in 1958–1960. Big famines were rarely the product of live-stock deaths alone.

Yet history suggests that famines had a more deep-seated cause than such exogenous shocks. Invariably they were the product of both backwardness on the eve of the crisis and the relative severity of the harvest shortfall. Cross-section statistical analyses of the incidence of famine mortality losses across regions and countries confirm that the poorest areas suffered most. However, the mortality could be exacerbated or mitigated by other factors. The effectiveness of relief undoubtedly played a role; so did the quality of the bureaucracy, the size of the voluntary sector, and the threat or presence of warfare in the affected area. Throughout history, famine has often been exacerbated by war; in postcolonial sub-Saharan Africa it repeatedly converted distress into famine.

When T. R. Malthus described famines in 1798 as "the last, the most dreadful resource of nature" he would influence both the policy and the analytical response to famines for a long time to come. For Malthus "gigantic inevitable famine" was the response when other sanctions failed: "with one mighty blow [it] level[ed] the population with the food of the world." The connection between famine and overpopulation—defining overpopulation here as a state in which a significant proportion of the population is close to the margin of subsistence—may have been looser than Malthus asserted. But there can be little doubt that throughout history overpopulation increased vulnerability to famine. The reason is obvious: those close to subsistence were in no position to save or to trade down to more economical foods, or to guard against attendant infectious diseases.

It is hard to imagine a famine for which more transfers of purchasing power from the rich to the poor would not have reduced mortality. Famines, like wars, highlight man's inhumanity to man. The unequal impact of famines across socioeconomic groups is a reminder of the role played by shifts in income distribution or entitlements. Although all famines involve such shifts, in recent decades increasing emphasis has been placed on the impact of market-induced shifts, quite apart from harvest-induced reductions in food availability. Amartya Sen applied an entitlements approach first to the Great Bengali Famine of 1942–1943, arguing that hoarding and speculation on the part of producers at the expense of the landless poor, rather than a significant harvest shortfall *per se*, were responsible for the crisis. This, claimed Sen, was an instance of starvation amid adequacy, if not plenty. Since then, several other famines have been interpreted from the same perspective.

The thesis that, by performing poorly or perversely, markets exacerbate famines runs counter to a tradition going back to the French enlightenment and Adam Smith, which maintains that well-functioning markets minimize both the risk of famines and the damage they do when they occur. Reacting against an earlier tradition of interventionism, French *économistes* held that free markets increased steady-state output levels, and thus reduced the damage imposed by any proportional shortfall, while Smith highlighted the roles of both intertemporal and spatial arbitraging between markets. Note too, however, that well-functioning markets can more effectively remove food from the needy because the needy lack purchasing power: when the markets were exporting food (as in the early stages of the Irish famine and also in Bengal in 1942) it merely dramatized a more general phenomenon.

Hard historical evidence on these issues is limited. Two classic studies, Sen's on the Bengali famine and Martin Ravallion's sophisticated econometric analysis of the Bangladeshi famine of 1973, make the case for market failure. On the other hand, markets seem to have operated in classic textbook fashion in Ireland in the late 1840s and in Finland in the late 1860s. Research on how markets function during famines is still thin, however. The claim that they perform as usual runs counter to popular belief as reflected in fictional accounts such as that in Alessandro Manzoni's *I promessi sposi*. Understandably, the victims of famine in backward market economies have usually failed to distinguish between high prices caused by a crop shortfall and high prices caused by speculation and hoarding. That is why governments have often acted to control markets in times of crisis.

Demographic Impact. Despite the publicity attending modern famines (useful from a humanitarian aid standpoint) the demographic impact of famines today is minor. The number of lives claimed by, for example, the Great European Famine of 1315–1317 will never be known, even approximately. Famine has not been a significant factor demographically in England since the sixteenth century,

FAMINE OF 1709. Henri-François d'Aguesseau, attorney general to the Parlement of Paris, authorizing the removal of grain from a storage facility. Colored aquatint from *Portraits des grands hommes, femmes illustres, et sujets mémorables de France: Gravés et imprimés en couleurs,* 1792. (Prints and Photographs Division, Library of Congress)

though in France more than one-tenth of all mortality in the half-century or so before 1710 was caused by famine. Much of Europe was subjected to famine in 1740–1741 and 1817–1819. In Ireland the famine of 1740–1741 killed proportionately more people than the more famous potato famine of the 1840s. Europe's last major subsistence crisis was the Finnish famine of 1868. Today, for the first time in history, only pockets of the globe, such as Afghanistan, North Korea, and parts of Africa, remain really vulnerable to the threat of famine.

Famines that kill more than a few percent of the population are unusual. The eruption of a volcano at Laki in Iceland in June 1783 led to the "haze famine," which killed one-fourth of the population. In the mid-1850s one-fourth of the population of Cape Verde died of famine. But these famines occurred in small places. Even the Chinese famine of 1958–1960, so atrocious in absolute terms, removed only at most 2–3 percent of the total population of China.

Since famines have nearly always occurred in backward economies, their human toll is often difficult to measure. In Ireland in the nineteenth century, as in the Ukraine and in China in the twentieth, the wilder upper and lower

bounds tend to be set by ideologues. Estimates of excess mortality in the Ukraine in the 1931–1932 famine range from 2 to 8 million, while those of deaths from the Chinese Great Leap Forward famine range from 15 to 43 million. Claims that the Chinese famine was the largest in history gloss over uncertainties about its true toll, and ignore estimates of 20 to 30 million deaths from famine in China between 1876 and 1900 and a further 12 to 20 million deaths in India over the same period. Twentieth-century famines were for the most part "small."

Most famine victims die not of literal starvation but of infectious diseases, such as typhoid fever, typhus, malaria, and dysentery. In Ireland in the 1840s, for example, only about one in ten of the famine's victims died of starvation, and that includes deaths from oedema (or "dropsy") and marasmus. Typhoid fever and cholera killed one in three, and dysentery or diarrhea another one in four. The remainder were attributable to a wide range of partially hunger-sensitive diseases. Famines kill the very young and the very old disproportionately, but these groups are the most vulnerable in normal times also. The decline in the birthrate that invariably accompanies famines reduces the proportion of infants in overall mortality. Women tend to resist famines better—mainly, it seems, for physiological reasons. Births decline, because of reductions in sexual activity and in womens' capacity to bear children (famine amenorrhea). The trough in births typically lags behind the peak in deaths by about a year. When the worst of the crisis is over, deaths fall below trend for a year or two and births rise above it. Presumably demographic reckonings that include averted births during famines should also include averted deaths and births induced in its wake. Migration may exacerbate famine by spreading infectious disease; alternatively it may act as a form of disaster relief by reducing the pressure on resources.

The role of medical science in reducing the number of deaths from infectious diseases is an interesting issue. Long before the discoveries of Robert Koch and Louis Pasteur, the risks associated with being near fever victims was well understood, though the mechanisms of contamination were not. Moreover, there was a long lag between scientific diagnosis and curative measures with penicillin and electrolytes. In the twentieth century there were famines in which infectious diseases were the main killers (e.g., in Bengal in the 1940s and in Ethiopia in the 1970s), and famines in which they killed few (e.g., on Mykonos in 1942–1943 and in the western Netherlands during the "Hungerwinter" of 1944–1945). The message seems to be that where infectious diseases are endemic in normal times, they bulk large when famine strikes. In such instances, Thomas McKeown's connection between medicine and mortality rules in reverse. McKeown argued that in nineteenth-century Europe the decline in mortality preceded major progress in medical technology; in the twentieth century third world contagious diseases such as typhoid fever and cholera persisted despite the medical knowledge available to deal with them.

Famines are now largely confined to sub-Saharan Africa, where they are no longer caused by land hunger or food availability in the strict sense. We have the medical and nutritional supplies that would prevent deaths, but not the means of getting them to the victims. African famines, which owe more to Mars than to Malthus, are postcolonial in the sense that the departing imperial powers left a political vacuum. Eliminating famine in the future rests more on political than on economic factors.

Public Action. Threatened with famine, the poor relied in the past on compassion on the part of the ruling class and its fear of contagion and social unrest. Rarely were such sentiments enough. In the ancient world, capital cities tended to be best organized for famine relief. Christian ideology may also have helped marginally, since it expected the rich to be charitable. Though Malthus denied the right of the hungry citizen to subsistence, rulers have long implicitly acknowledged a responsibility to help.

Relief came through a variety of strategies: the maintenance of public granaries, institutionalized care through poor laws, workfare, improvised soup kitchens, migration schemes. Private charity has rarely been enough in times of severe harvest failure, however. The record suggests that particularly when a crisis persists, compassion fatigue sets in. Today international relief, both governmental and nongovernmental, supplements local effort, but with the attendant danger that it lets local elites and oligarchs off the hook.

For early disciples of Malthus, famines were a providential response. Too much kindness entailed moral hazard in the sense that it might lead to even worse famines later. In Ireland in the 1840s and in India in the late 1870s there was thus a tension between Malthusian ideology and interventions that would minimize mortality. In practice public action was, and is, often complicated by the problem of agency. Antisocial behavior is an inevitable concomitant of famine: theft increases and hospitality diminishes. Informal systems of mutual help may work at first, but their effectiveness is not lasting. Controversy about how best to ensure that the poor are the beneficiaries of relief revolved around this problem. Some cheating and free riding were inevitable. The Irish experience is illustrative in this respect. In the 1840s, relief through a system of unproductive public works was initially seen as the best way around such problems. But the public works were ill geared to help the weak, and exacerbated contagion from infectious diseases. When replaced by food aid, the food was distributed in nonresalable form in order to minimize free riding. Once the worst of the crisis was deemed over, the onus shifted back to relief within the workhouse on the basis of "less eligibility." Elsewhere, as in Ireland, worries about free riders ended up hurting the vulnerable.

Today the choice between public works schemes and food aid is still a matter of debate. One of the problems with food aid, such as through the U.S. PL480, is that it runs the risk of damaging indigenous agriculture.

Postfamine Adjustment. Seen as a Malthusian positive check, famine was a blunt remedy because in most cases its horrors were not reserved exclusively for "poor devils only" (as Karl Marx described the victims of the Irish famine). Before the twentieth century, the not-so-poor who lived near the poor had no effective defense against infectious diseases such as typhoid fever. It was also arguably an ineffective remedy to the extent that population growth tends to restore the demographic vacuum left by famine. In Finland, for example, population grew much faster after the major famine of 1868 than before it, filling the void left by famine deaths within a few years. In France the demographic dent made by the major famines of 1693–1694 and 1708–1709 was repaired within a few years. Ireland is an exception to this pattern, since the population decline that began with the Great Famine of the late 1840s persisted for decades. That decline was partly due to a "friends and neighbors" effect that magnified the postfamine outflow, and partly to the resulting reduction of the domestic market, entailing less specialization, and thus also less population. In any event, the rising demand for labor in the United States would probably have reduced population in the long run.

Postfamine adjustment remains an underresearched area. Population tends to recover in the wake of famines, but this does not rule out some demographic "learning." Ireland's increasing recourse to the Malthusian "preventive check" after 1850 through later and less frequent marriage is well known. Whether the Irish took this route because of the famine remains a moot point, however. Recent survey-based research on Ethiopia suggests some reduction in marital fertility in the 1990s in some of the areas worst hit in the 1970s and the 1980s: only time can tell whether the effect persists. This is a topic worth further investigation.

Since famines usually reduce population, but leave the land endowment and physical capital largely intact, their effect on living standards seems clear-cut: an improvement in the lot of surviving workers relative to farmers and landowners. The impact on landowners might be intensified by the incidence of relief spending falling mainly on them. However, if the chaotic conditions that often precede famines prevent them from fully enforcing their property rights they too may find their incomes rising once normality has been established.

[*See also* Crop and Plant Diseases; Crop Failures; Crop Yields; *and* Irish Famine.]

BIBLIOGRAPHY

Davis, Mike. *Late Victorian Holocausts: El Niño Famines and the Making of the Third World*. London, 2000.

Drèze, Jean, and Amartya K. Sen. *Hunger and Public Action*. Oxford, 1989.

Dyson, Tim, and Cormac Ó Gráda, eds. *Famine Demography: Perspectives from the Past and the Present*. Oxford, 2002.

Jordan, William C. *The Great Famine: Northern Europe in the Early Fourteenth Century*. Princeton, 1996.

Le Roy Ladurie, Emmanuel. *Times of Feast, Times of Famine: The History of Climate since the Year 1000*. London, 1972.

Ó Gráda, Cormac. *Black '47 and Beyond: The Great Irish Famine in History, Economy and Memory*. Princeton, 1999.

Ravallion, Martin. "Famine and Economics." *Journal of Economic Literature* 35.3 (1997), 1205–1242.

Riskin, Carl. "Seven Lessons About the Chinese Famine of 1959–61." *China Economic Review* 9.2 (1998), 111–124.

CORMAC Ó GRÁDA

FARM CAPITAL. The capital employed in farming is traditionally defined as the difference between the sale value of an operating farm and the sale value of the land in its natural state. Capital is thus the value of the resources that have to be invested to take land from its natural state and transform it into a complete farm operation. Farm capital in this definition includes investments in land clearing, fencing, draining, and roads and buildings, as well as investments in tools, animals, animal feed, seed, and wages embodied in growing crops and animals.

Because capital is such a comprehensive collection of crops in progress, animals, tools, and land improvements it is very hard in practice to measure the amount of capital employed in different agricultural systems, and such estimates are rare before the twentieth century. Fruit trees and vines planted on land are capital, for example, as are the dykes of the Low Countries, the rice terraces across the hills of Java, and the vineyards hacked into the south-facing slopes of the Alps in northern Italy. Also, different types of capital depreciate at different rates. Leveling land or removing stones may last forever, but cows get old and unproductive after a few years, and seed sown lasts only a year.

To complicate matters further the fertility of the soil itself is a form of capital. In temperate latitudes uncultivated soils accumulate large stocks of organic compounds that facilitate plant growth. It is possible to increase yields in the short run by depleting this stock of natural fertility. As A. D. Hall (1914) noted of England,

> Fen farming is a case of exploiting the natural resources of the soil without any return being made; crop after crop is taken and sold away . . . . Slow as the process may be, one cannot live on capital indefinitely; and this land will run out, just as the black soils of the middle west of America have begun to show a noticeable decline in fertility.

Thus the amount of soil nutrients left in the soil by various farming practices should properly also be regarded as a form of capital. Therefore, we must modify the traditional definition of farm capital as the difference between the land in its natural state and its value as an operating farm. Instead it is the difference between the land exhausted of depletable nutrients and its value as a farm.

Capital can be employed more or less intensively in producing agricultural output. One way to measure the capital intensity of an agricultural system is to measure the ratio of capital to output. Table 1 shows a rough calculation of the elements in the capital of English farms in the 1870s from contemporary estimates. The capital is divided into that owned by the landlord—the buildings, roads, fences, drains, and organic capital embodied in soil fertility—and that owned by the tenant. Farm workers' cottages have been excluded; though these were often owned by the landlord, they were not really part of the agricultural enterprise.

The major components of landlords' capital in England were the organic residues in the soil that enhance fertility. Soil freshly broken up for cultivation in England has been

TABLE 1. *Farm Capital in England, 1870s and 1300s*

TYPE OF CAPITAL	VALUE PER ACRE (£), 1870s	VALUE PER ACRE (s.), 1300s
Landlord's Capital	**28.8**	**12.5**
buildings (including threshing machines)	7.0	4.6
fences, roads, drainage	3.0	6.4
soil fertility	18.8	1.5
Tenant's Capital	**12.3**	**5.3**
work animals	1.5	1.2
livestock	6.2	1.4
implements	1.5	0.6
crops in progress	3.1	2.1
All Capital	**41.1**	**17.8**
Value of Net Output per Acre	4.5	3.1

SOURCES: Squarey, Elias P. "Farm Capital." *Journal of the Royal Agricultural Society of England* 14 (1878), 425–444. Wratislaw, Charles. "The Amount of Capital Required for the Profitable Operation of a Mixed Arable and Pasture Farm in a Midland County." *Journal of the Royal Agricultural Society of England* 14 (1861), 425–444.

estimated to contain about 5,000 pounds of nitrogen in organic material. Land under continuous grain cultivation without any manuring for a hundred years had only about 1,400 pounds of nitrogen at Rothamsted experimental station. The nitrogen in organic material aids plant growth. Its value can be estimated by considering the amount of farmyard manure that would have to be added to depleted land to restore this amount of nitrogen, and the cost of that manuring. Assuming that farmland manure in the 1870s cost 2 s. per ton, it would cost £25 to restore the nutrients in depleted soil.

Half of the land in England was then pasture and would still have had nearly the full complement of soil nutrients. For arable land in the 1870s the soil organic capital was much less, probably halfway between full depletion and wilderness conditions. In this case the average organic capital per acre in England in the 1870s would be about £19 per acre. Thus the total of the landlord's capital was £29 per acre. Since average land rents in the 1870s were £1.75 per acre (including taxes paid by tenants), and the return on capital invested in land was 2.5 percent, the numbers in Table 1 imply that about 40 percent of land rent in England in the 1870s was actually a return to the landlord's capital, rather than to "the original and indestructible powers of the soil."

Table 1 also implies that the ratio of capital to output in agriculture would be about nine in England in the 1870s. Notice that even in the 1870s machinery was a very unimportant type of capital, constituting less than 5 percent of the total. "Crops in progress" refers to the expenditure by the farmer on labor, land rent, and animal feed for crops not yet sold.

These numbers for England in the 1870s suggest that unless we have information about buildings per acre and about the capital embodied in soil fertility, we can only guess at the capital for most agricultural systems in history. For medieval England we do have some records, however. They allow for a crude estimate of the amount of capital per acre and per unit of output circa 1300. The big difference is in the estimated amount of capital embodied in organic material in the soil. In medieval England more than 80 percent of land was depleted arable with very low fertility. Based on the rent differential between this arable and the fertile meadow, the value of the organic material even on the meadowland was low. Thus the capital output ratio in medieval England is estimated at about six, lower than in later years. Since output per acre was so much less in 1300 than in the 1870s, the amount of capital per acre was only about a quarter of its later level.

These figures imply that traditional agriculture in England, even in the Middle Ages, actually had a much higher capital-output ratio than modern industrial society. Thus Charles Feinstein estimates the net stock of capital in Britain in the 1860s, when Britain was already largely industrialized, at just above double GDP. Even in modern economies the capital-output ratio is typically less than three. Ironically, the rise of capitalism in Europe at least was associated with the declining importance of capital in production because of the falling share of agriculture in total output.

The capital intensity of agricultural systems, the amount of capital employed per acre of per unit of output, varied greatly. The Dutch of the seventeenth century wrested land from the sea with dykes and windmills in a very capital-intensive form of agriculture. The gauchos on the pampas of Argentina in the late nineteenth century herded cattle on land that was very little changed from its natural state. Most other systems seem to have been less capital intensive than England in the nineteenth century. Thus Atack and Bateman's estimates for agriculture in the mid-nineteenth century in the United States suggest much lower capital output ratios, in the order of 2.5 (making no allowance, however, for the capital embodied in the fertility of the soil). These estimates and their components are shown in Table 2. Since output per acre was much less in U.S. agriculture than in Britain, the amount of capital per acre was probably at least five times as great in Britain, even ignoring capital embodied in soil fertility.

The explanation for this variation for believers in neoclassical economics would lie mainly in the ratio of the costs of unimproved land to the costs of capital. The higher that ratio the more capital will be employed per acre (assuming

TABLE 2. *Farm Capital in the United States, 1860, 80-Acre Farm*

TYPE OF CAPITAL	MIDWEST VALUE PER ACRE ($)
Landlord's Capital	**8.1**
land clearing	3.2
buildings	2.3
fences, roads, drainage	2.6
soil fertility	—
Tenant's Capital	**9.0**
livestock	3.5
implements	0.8
crops in progress	4.7
All Capital	**17.1**
Value of Net Output per Acre	7.0

SOURCE: Atack and Bateman (1987), pp. 121–145.

that other factors are kept constant). The reasoning is that the amount of capital employed on farms will be such that the last unit of capital employed adds just enough net output to cover the interest and depreciation cost of the capital so employed. If fencing, for example, costs $20 per foot, and the interest and depreciation cost per year is 10 percent of this, the last foot of fencing built on a farm should increase net output by $2.

Thus in neoclassical theory the real interest rate is an important determinant of the capital per unit of output. Similarly, the cost of another unit of land, the rent of unimproved land, has to equal the increase in net output that one more acre would bring; output per acre will be high where unimproved land rents are high for land of a given natural fertility. These propositions together imply that the amount of capital invested per acre will—other things being equal—be proportionate to the ratio of land rents to real interest rates. Paul Rhode's article (1995) is a nice illustration of the application of this neoclassical theory to explain the change from wheat to fruit farming in nineteenth-century California.

Thus part of the explanation for capital-intensive agriculture in seventeenth-century Netherlands would be that capital was so abundant, that its real return fell as low as 2 percent, while unimproved land was costly. The explanation for scant capital on the pampas would be the very small rental values of unimproved land and the high interest costs of capital. Again, at least a partial explanation for the scant capital in medieval English farms would be the high real interest rate of about 10 percent, and the very slight value of unimproved land.

Different systems of farming distribute ownership of this capital differently. In the typical English arrangement of fixed-rent farming the landowner contributed the capital embodied in land improvements and buildings while the tenant contributed that embodied in animals and crops in progress. Under sharecropping in the southern United States in the nineteenth century the landlord might also contribute some of the capital embodied in crops and animals, claiming in return a larger share of the output. Tenant ownership of all the movable capital limits competition for land to tenants with significant property of their own. Landlords may thus supply some or all of the movable capital. But landlord ownership creates monitoring costs. The tenant with no capital can more easily default on the rental at the end of the term. Where laborers were hired by the year and received part of their pay only at the end, they were also contributing some of the capital to the enterprise. Where they were paid by the day or the week, the capital costs of their labor fell on the land cultivator.

FARM. A farm in Owyhee county, Idaho, circa 1909. (Geo R. Lawrence Co./Prints and Photographs Division, Library of Congress)

With well-operating markets the form of the ownership of capital and of the organization of agriculture should have no impact on the amount of capital used; this will be determined by equating costs and marginal outputs if cultivators seek to maximize their economic return from farming. But many historians, like Roger Ransom and Richard Sutch, have argued that financial and other institutions such as the form of tenancy can change the calculus of investment from the simple neoclassical one discussed above, and can significantly reduce the capital intensity of agriculture. Ransom and Sutch argue that postbellum Southern agriculture in the United States experienced much less investment than would be warranted by the respective costs and benefits of capital. They say that the curbs on investment were a result of sharecropping, which was itself, they argue, a legacy of the slave system. Others have argued that peasant agriculture, where the land is owned and operated by small holders, typically results in underinvestment in capital because of the constraints on peasant saving.

[*See also* Agriculture, *subentry on* Technological Change; Draft and Pack Animals; *and* Fertilizing.]

BIBLIOGRAPHY

Atack, Jeremy, and Fred Bateman. *To Their Own Soil: Agriculture in the Antebellum North.* Ames, Iowa, 1987.

Clark, Gregory. "The Cost of Capital and Medieval Agriculture Technique." *Explorations in Economic History* 25 (July 1988), 265–294. Discusses the effects of high rates of return on capital on agriculture in medieval England.

Clark, Gregory. "The Economics of Exhaustion, the Postan Thesis, and the Agricultural Revolution." *Journal of Economic History* 52 (March 1992), 61–84. Discusses soil fertility as a form of capital.

Feinstein, Charles, and Sidney Pollard, eds. *Studies in Capital Formation in the United Kingdom, 1750–1920.* Oxford, 1988. Gives estimates of the capital stock in English agriculture for these years.

Hall, A. D. *A Pilgrimage of British Farming, 1910–1912.* London, 1914, p. 76.

Rhode, Paul. "Learning, Capital Accumulation, and the Transformation of California Agriculture." *Journal of Economic History* 55.4 (1995), 773–800.

Ransom, Roger, and Richard Sutch. *One Kind of Freedom: The Economic Consequences of Emancipation.* Cambridge, 1977.

GREGORY CLARK

FARMING INTENSITY. Intensification occurs when the amount of variable inputs per unit of fixed input increases over time. This term is normally used to describe the introduction of agricultural chemicals, higher-input varieties, and irrigation to increase output per unit of land. Intensification has been largely responsible for humanity's ability to sustain a sixfold increase (from one to six billion) in population between 1800 and 2000 without a proportional increase in utilized land. Acreage harvested in the United States in 1995 (320 million acres) was smaller than in 1920 (350 million acres), while agricultural production in 1955 was 3.3 times greater than in 1920 (*Historical Statistics of the United States,* 1975; *Statistical Abstract of the United States, 1980,* 1980; *Statistical Abstract of the United States, 1998,* 1998). Between 1950 and 2000 global population increased from 2.6 to 6 billion, grain production per person increased by 12 percent, but arable acreage increased by less than 20 percent (Brown, Gardner, and Halweil, 1999). Increase in food demand in the nineteenth century was mostly owed to expansion of arable land, but especially from 1950 onward, most of the expansion of food production was owed to intensification. This included increased irrigation, adoption of chemical pesticides and fertilizers throughout the developed world and part of the developing world, and adoption of high-yielding crop varieties that were developed as part of the Green Revolution. During the last fifty years U.S. corn yields per acre increased eightfold, and similar results have been observed with other crops throughout the world.

Agricultural intensification has been a continuing process that coevolved with technological change and increased knowledge in agriculture, population growth, health, and other sectors. Ester Boserup (1965) argued that the transition from slash-and-burn agriculture toward more intense cropping systems has been driven by increased population intensity. D. H. Perkins (1969) provided a similar take on intensification of farming in China over five centuries ago. Innovations outside agriculture (for example, in pumping and conveyance) were crucial to the expansion of irrigation that led to multiple cropping in India and other countries. Irrigated agriculture has been especially productive because it enabled expansion of production in locations (deserts) and seasons (dry) with vast solar radiation that led to high productivity and diversified crop selection.

Most of the economic literature on agricultural productivity models outputs as well-behaved functions of applied inputs. Various studies found that productivity of inputs increases over time. The selection of improved varieties has significantly enhanced the capacity to utilize irrigation, withstand disease, and take advantage of other complementary inputs, for example, water, fertilizers, technology, and so forth (Evenson and Huffman, 1993). Significant increases in farming system productivity have also been associated with improved management and integrated crop systems, such as biological control, which has been especially effective with cassavas in Africa and integrated pest management (Norgaard, 1976).

Microlevel studies elucidate deeper mechanisms at work in the process of intensification (Mundlak, 2001; Khanna and Zilberman, 1997). They model output as a product of distinct technologies, each of which may be embodied in specific capital goods and crop varieties, with parameters governing the use of variable inputs. With this approach, analysis of intensification emphasizes adoption choices. There is a growing literature on adoption in agriculture (see Sunding and Zilberman, 2001). In many models the decision is not whether or not to adopt but the extent of technology adoption. For example, within a farm, adoption of high-yield varieties may be gradual. At the beginning a small number of acres will be allocated to the new technology, and over time the acreage will be increased. Factors that retard adoption include uncertainty about the technology, lack of credit, and human capital.

Larger farms with better access to credit were earlier adopters of Green Revolution varieties in India, but risk diversification considerations may explain why over time relative adoption is larger on smaller farms. Policies to enhance adoption include subsidization of new inputs, extension, improved terms of credit, and subsidization of output. For example, W. W. Cochrane (1958) argues that agricultural support programs have been a major contributor to intensification in developed countries. Introduction or liberalization of water and land markets may also be important factors that tend to accelerate adoption of a new resource-augmenting technology.

While intensification has led to a significant increase in agricultural output, it may also be associated with adverse environmental effects. The use of chemical pesticides and fertilizers has in many instances led to deterioration of water quality and damaged human and environmental health (DDT was banned because of the damage it caused to fish, birds, and other wildlife). In some cases intensification may have a negative long-term effect on productivity, for example, by building resistance to chemicals or depletion of soil or groundwater resources (Carlson, Zilberman, and Miranowski, 1993).

Recognition of some of these impacts has led to development of institutions and policies to reduce the environmental side effects of intensification. These include introduction of polluter-pay principles or direct controls that limit use of inputs with negative side effects. For example, to prevent the buildup of resistance to genetically modified varieties, farmers are required to maintain refugia, acreage dedicated to traditional varieties. Furthermore new technologies (sometimes termed precision technologies) may have higher input use efficiency, thus reducing polluting residues while increasing output (Khanna and Zilberman, 1997). Such technologies enable the substitution of chemicals or water for computer and human expertise.

Adoption of precision technologies is not always justified, and its extent and timing will depend on agroecological conditions, human and physical capital, and institutional capacity. Pollution control regulations, subsidization of precision technologies, and education and research

activities may affect the intensification process by inducing the development of new technologies. For example, increased scrutiny of chemical pesticides was a major contributor to the evolution of genetically modified varieties and biological control strategies.

Intensification serves not only to expand physical output but also to increase product quality, value added, and product differentiation in agriculture. Increased differentiation associated with intensification has contributed to a transition toward contract farming and vertical integration.

BIBLIOGRAPHY

Boserup, Ester. *The Conditions for Agricultural Growth.* London, 1965.

Brown, Lester, Gary Gardner, and Brian Halweil. *Beyond Malthus: Nineteen Dimensions of the Population Challenge.* New York, 1999.

Carlson, Gerald A., David Zilberman, and John A. Miranowski, eds. *Agricultural and Environmental Resource Economics.* New York, 1993.

Cochrane, W. W. *The Development of American Agriculture.* Minneapolis, 1958.

Evenson, Robert E., and Wallace Huffman. *Science for Agriculture: A Long-Term Perspective.* Ames, Iowa, 1993.

Historical Statistics of the United States, pts. 1–2, *Colonial Times to 1970.* U.S. Bureau of the Census. Washington, D.C., 1975.

Khanna, Madhu, and David Zilberman. "Incentives, Precision Technology, and Environmental Quality." *Ecological Economics* 23.1 (October 1997), 25–43.

Mundlak, Yair. "Production and Supply." In *Handbook of Agricultural Economics*, vol. 1A, edited by Bruce L. Gardner and Gordon C. Rausser, pp. 3–85. Amsterdam, 2001.

Norgaard, Richard B. "Integrating Economics and Pest Management." In *Integrated Pest Management*, edited by L. Apple and R. F. Smith, pp. 17–27. New York, 1976.

Perkins, D. H. *Agricultural Development in China, 1368–1968.* Chicago, 1969.

Statistical Abstract of the United States, 1980. 101st ed. U.S. Bureau of the Census. Washington, D.C., 1980.

Statistical Abstract of the United States, 1998. 118th ed. U.S. Bureau of the Census. Washington, D.C., 1998.

Sunding, David, and David Zilberman. "The Agricultural Innovation Process: Research and Technology Adoption in a Changing Agricultural Sector." In *Handbook of Agricultural and Resource Economics*, vol. 1A, edited by Bruce L. Gardner and Gordon C. Rausser, pp. 207–261. Amsterdam, 2001.

DAVID ZILBERMAN

FARM MANAGEMENT. Two issues fall under the heading of farm management. First, who did the organization of production in agriculture? Was it peasant families, commercial tenants under fixed-rent tenancies, or estate managers working for wages? Second, what rules did cultivators employ to determine what to produce and what inputs to use?

Economists have assumed that in general, no matter the managerial structure, cultivators can be assumed to maximize the implied profit from the enterprise, meaning the difference between the value of the output and the values of the inputs of land, labor, and capital. This simple assumption of profit maximization carries a raft of implications about how much labor and capital managers will employ per unit of land and about how production decisions will change in response to changes in wages, interest rates, and the prices of various outputs. This assumption is, however, contentious. Historians, sociologists, and anthropologists have frequently argued that the objectives of the managers of enterprises are socially determined and quite different from profit maximization. Thus Karl Marx in *Capital* argues that in precapitalist economies landowners wanted to maximize their political power by creating the large bodies of retainers. Others have argued that in peasant society family labor will be employed well beyond the point where the implied profits are maximized and indeed often to the point where the output from some of the labor is close to zero.

If peasants failed to profit maximize in the way of commercial farms, their farms would show lower output per worker or per acre and consequently a lower measured total factor productivity. This would mean that the transition from peasant to commercial agriculture could be associated with such things as increases in output per worker in agriculture and a flow of labor out of the agricultural sector. The institutional structure of agriculture would matter to its economic performance.

One source of evidence on the objectives of cultivators is the literature on farm management that appears in the case of England as early as the thirteenth century. The most extensive tracts are *Walter of Henley* (c. 1280) and *The Seneschaucy* (c. 1276). These treatises instructed people holding the office of steward or bailiff on large estates how to conduct the operations of a farm. Later works on farm management, such as Arthur Young's in the late eighteenth century and those of John Morton and Henry Stephens in the nineteenth century, are addressed mainly to the substantial tenant farmer.

In the case of large agricultural estates run by managers, the evidence that they ever pursued objectives other than maximizing the profit, explicit or implicit, derived from the estate is minimal. The medieval estate manuals are clearly focused on how to maximize the profits derived from estates, with no other objectives given any weight. Thus *The Seneschaucy* states with reference to pigs: "He who will keep pigs throughout the year entirely at the expense of the grange will lose twice as much as he will gain. Let him reckon the cost of their food, the provision and the wage for the swineherd, and the damage the pigs will do to the corn during the year: he who will reckon this up will see the truth" (*Seneschaucy*, ch. 8, p. 60). The records of estates in Roman Egypt in the first three centuries CE similarly suggest that maximizing profits was the main objective. Thus an estate owner, Appianus, wrote circa 250 CE to one of his administrators, Heroninos, that "what you

sent up was not worth the wasting of the time of a man and an ass, all for four little baskets of bitter little figs." Elsewhere in his letters there is concern that draft animals should not "be idle" (Rathbone, 1991, p. 273).

By the eighteenth century in England books of advice on farm management, such as those of Arthur Young, routinely assumed that the aim of the farmer was to maximize the surplus derived from the farm. In discussing the introduction of threshing machines, for example, the only consideration Young gives is to "the profit of their use" (Young, 1793, p. 251). There is no discussion of their possible effects on the employment of the rural population, even though the 1790s were a period of increasing social concern about the rural landless. In the world of Young and his successors, profit is the measure of all things.

These books, however, were directed at substantial tenant farmers. The smallholder, the traditional peasantry, using only family labor, may have employed a different calculus. It has been argued, for example, that peasant households tended to employ family labor beyond the point that maximized profits. The value of output produced by their labor at the margin was less than the cost of that labor measured by the wage it could earn on the labor market. One reason that more than the profit maximizing amount of labor was employed was that children considering migrating from the farm into the city would balance the wage they could earn in the city with the share of family output they would get in the countryside. But since their share of output was greater than their marginal contribution to the farm output, the marginal product of labor in peasant agriculture tended to be less than the wage it could earn on the labor market.

The peasantry was also, it is claimed, undercapitalized. The return from further investment on family farms was higher than the cost of borrowing agricultural capital. Finally, the peasantry was supposed to choose outputs that were biased toward the subsistence needs of the family and biased away from what was most profitable, measured by the market values of the various outputs. These last two alleged deviations from profitability are explained as stemming from a desire of peasant households to minimize the fluctuation of their consumption from year to year.

Undercapitalization and lack of specialization by peasant households would lead to a reduced value of output per acre from their holdings. The absence of documentation for peasant holdings before the twentieth century makes it hard to assess these claims that peasants generally did not profit maximize. Without detailed farm records, it is impossible to assess whether or not inputs and outputs were at a level that maximized the implied profits from the holding.

[*See also* Agriculture, *subentry on* Agricultural Inputs, Productivity, and Wages.]

BIBLIOGRAPHY

Morton, John C. *A Cyclopedia of Agriculture, Practical and Scientific.* London, 1875.

Oschinsky, Dorothea, ed. *Walter of Henley and Other Treatises on Estate Management and Accounting.* Oxford, 1971. Translations of four English medieval estate management manuals with commentaries.

Petrusewicz, Marta. *Latifundium: Moral Economy and Material Life in a European Periphery.* Translated by Judith C. Green. Ann Arbor, c. 1996.

Rathbone, Dominic. *Economic Rationalism and Rural Society in Third-Century A.D. Egypt.* Cambridge, 1991.

Stephens, Henry. *The Book of the Farm.* Edinburgh, 1844.

Young, Arthur. *The Farmer's Guide in Hiring and Stocking Farms.* London, 1770.

Young, Arthur. "Some Farming Notes in Essex, Kent, and Sussex." *Annals of Agriculture* 20 (1793).

GREGORY CLARK

FARM SCALE. Refers to the size of the operational farm unit. Academic and political debate about the desirability of small versus large farms has continued literally for centuries, with sharply opposing views united only in the shared assumption that farm size matters for economic growth and income distribution. Although this debate is primarily focused on the operating size of farms, in important instances it extends to the size of ownership units, with the understanding that the scale of ownership is an important determinant of the operational farm size.

A key point of departure in the farm-size debate is the family labor farm hypothesis, which posits that farms that are sufficiently small to be operated primarily by the family labor of the farm operator (who has a residual claim on output) have a labor cost advantage over larger farms that must rely on wage labor (note that the physical area that defines small under this definition depends on living standards and so forth). Two arguments underlie this hypothesis. The first is the Chayanovian perspective (named for the Russian economist A. V. Chayanov, whose work is discussed in more detail below) that rural labor markets are either missing or so thin that farm households face off-farm–labor sales constraints. On smaller farms, with more abundant family labor, the shadow price of labor of otherwise unemployable labor will be lower, and the labor intensity of cultivation subsequently will be higher. The distributional side of this proposition is that households with poor land access will find it difficult to secure a livelihood.

Complementing this Chayanovian perspective is the labor-extraction argument that the intrinsic nature of agricultural production makes it difficult to assure that hired laborers diligently carry out their work. It is difficult to "extract" labor effort from hired labor in agriculture because the geographic dispersion of agricultural production makes direct, contemporaneous supervision costly, whereas the random nature of agricultural production makes it difficult *ex post* to infer effort. The efficiency wage cost of hired labor (cost per unit of effective labor effort) is thus hypothesized to be higher than that of family labor that has incentives to work hard based on its role as a residual claimant on the production process.

Ancient History and the English Enclosures. Supported by either or both of these arguments, the family labor farm hypothesis has been used to support the claim that the optimal farm size is small. Karl Wittfogel (1957) notes that operational farm size in ancient economies was always small because of the extraordinary advantage enjoyed by small-scale peasant farming. In environments as diverse as China and Peru, ruling elites found no need directly to organize production on land under their control, and instead used taxes to extract income from a sector of small-farm operators.

Although the family labor farm advantage was decisive in the ancient world by Wittfogel's estimation, he questions its modern relevance by noting that in postfeudal Europe many landlords took to directly cultivating their land on a large scale in order to employ scientific methods. Matching this skepticism is a massive body of historical literature on the English enclosure movement of the sixteenth through the eighteenth centuries. The enclosures undercut the land rights of traditional small-scale family labor farms by reducing the land they had available for cultivation as well as by eliminating the commons or communal areas that were part of the peasants' livelihood. Contemporary observers of the enclosures, as well as historians ranging from Marx to Polanyi (1944) to Brenner (1985), have argued that the increased farm sizes brought by enclosures were the *sine qua non* of the agricultural productivity growth needed to fuel the British Industrial Revolution. Without the enclosures, labor and other resources would not have been freed to serve the emerging industrial economy. Whatever the labor cost advantages enjoyed by the family labor farms, this enclosure perspective sees them as overwhelmed by the superior growth and technological adoption capacity of larger-scale farms. Although many historians have emphasized the human cost of this transformation, it was above all socially necessary from this pro–large-farm perspective.

The revisionist historiography of Robert Allen (1992), among others, has come to dispute this perspective on the historic role of the enclosures. Allen argues that rates of technological progress by the small-scale family labor (yeoman) farms that survived enclosure were in no measure inferior to those of large-scale manor agriculture. While Mark Overton (1996) and others have questioned the statistical basis for this conclusion, Allen's argument implies that the advantage of large-scale farming was specious, and the enclosures served the interest of no one beyond those who used them as a vehicle to extinguish traditional land rights.

Lenin, Chayanov, and the Soviet Debate. Paralleling the historiographical debate over the enclosures was a real-time policy debate over farm size in Russia and the Soviet Union. Well before the October revolution of 1917, A. V. Chayanov became locked in debate with Lenin over the future of small-scale, peasant, or family labor farm agriculture. The heart of Chayanov's argument was that the labor cost advantage enjoyed by small farms gave them a decisive advantage over large-scale, labor-hiring farms. He further argued that small scale farms could cooperate to realize the benefits of any economies of scale, located outside the agricultural production process *per se* (e.g., in crop marketing or technology access). Small-scale farms were thus both desirable and economically stable, according to Chayanov.

In opposition to Chayanov's so-called agrarian populist position, Lenin (1899/1977) argued that large-scale agriculture was a technological imperative whose weight could already be seen in the form of emerging polarization in the Russian countryside as large farms began to displace and proletarianize the peasantry. Although Lenin identified several roads by which an economy might arrive at a large-scale farming structure, his analysis left no doubt concerning the final destination of the process of agricultural modernization.

The mobility studies of Chayanov and others disputed the claim that the contemporaneous farm survey data identified the patterns of class differentiation that Lenin claimed, but the collectivization of agriculture begun in 1928 under Stalin decisively resolved the farm-size debate in favor of large farms. Although much has been written on both the brutality and the ambiguous economic effects of large-scale, collectivized agriculture in the Soviet Union, the presumptive superiority of large-scale agriculture drove collectivization of agriculture throughout the post–World War II communist world. It was only the collapse of the Soviet Union in 1990s that led to a restoration of family-farm agriculture. A similar restoration had taken place a decade earlier in China with spectacular results (Putterman, 1992).

Farm-size in the Post–World War II Third World. The debate over small versus large farms also emerged in the post–World War II third world. The agrarian populist position early on was buttressed by statistical findings from the Indian farm management studies that seemed to identify a pronounced inverse relationship between farm productivity and farm size. Although some contributors to this literature recognized the statistical frailty of many of the early studies that failed to control adequately for a variety of factors beyond farm size that might explain the inverse relation (Sen, 1975, summarizes this earlier work), the inverse relationship itself rose to the status of stylized fact (Berry and Cline, 1979, codify the inverse relation-

ship). The work of Chayanov, rationalizing such a finding, was itself resurrected and published in English in the mid-1960s.

The inverse relationship soon came to play an important part in the economic case for land reform designed to break up large farms and redistribute them as small-scale, owner-operated farms. In an influential book, Johnston and Kilby (1975) added further weight to the call for an agriculture comprised of uniformly sized family labor farms (what they called a unimodal structure) by drawing on Japan's historical success at industrializing off the base of very small family labor farms. In contrast, they argued that countries that had pursued seeming scale economies in agriculture by creating or subsidizing large-scale farms (Mexico and the Soviet Union) created economic failure.

Despite these arguments, many academics and policy makers remained unconvinced. Empirical support for the inverse relationship weakened as econometric analysis became more sophisticated (see Benjamin, 1995). The Chayanovian logic of the small-farm, agrarian populist position came under often withering criticism (see, e.g., Patnaik, 1979). As with other variants of the farm-size debate, the critics argued that small farms were incapable of adopting new technologies and adapting to the vagaries of the market. The assumption that small farms had the same technology and market access as large farms was argued to be the fundamental flaw in the Chayanovian logic.

The notion that large, not small, farms were the key to future economic growth remained strongest in Latin America where large-scale farm ownership units (haciendas) dominated the agrarian structure. In the estimation of some historians (Duncan and Rutledge, 1977, summarize the debate), the increasing commercialization of Latin American agriculture would bring along the destruction of the peasantry as large estates ceased to rent out land to internal sharecroppers and other small farmers and took up large-scale direct cultivation based on wage labor. It was certainly the case that when serious land-reform efforts took place in Latin America during the 1960s and 1970s, commercial and export agricultural activity was concentrated in large farm units. Rightly or wrongly convinced of the benefits of large-scale farms, the continent's most significant land-reform programs (those in Cuba, Chile, Peru, Honduras, Nicaragua, and El Salvador) devised cooperative institutions to redistribute land rights while preserving the large scale of cultivation that typified the inherited agrarian structure. Without exception, large-scale cooperative farms floundered across Latin America—seemingly belying the notion of scale economies—and in nearly all instances, they have been subdivided into small-scale, privately owned units (see Thiesenhusen, 1989). Debate continues over whether these newly created family labor farm units will prove competitively viable and stable, or whether they will be swallowed up by large-scale commercial units. Evidence from recent agro-export booms suggests that they may not be viable (Carter et al., 1996), and that at best Latin American agriculture may become dominated by middle-sized "capitalized family farms" that strike a balance between the advantages of large- and small-scale farming (Lehman, 1982).

Emerging Theoretical Perspectives. The continued relevance of debates over farm size in contemporary low-income countries has motivated a growing theoretical literature that tries to make sense out of the farm-size question. Eswaran and Kotwal (1986) structure a theoretical analysis that highlights countervailing forces that advantage one size of farm over another: labor-extraction costs advantage small over large farms, whereas wealth-biased access to the working capital needed to finance labor and land rental costs advantages larger farm units. The latter force, which is rooted in the economic theory of credit rationing, provides an endogenous economic explanation for the presumption of unequal small-farm access to technology that is central to Marxist and other criticism of the populist, small-farm perspective. The central result of the Eswaran and Kotwal analysis is a provocative one in the context of the long debates on farm size. They find that although small farms potentially will produce the most from a given resource base, wealth-biased capital access may prevent the economy from reaching a small-farm–based agrarian structure. The performance of the agrarian economy is in effect sensitive to the distribution of ownership rights, with less equal distribution resulting in a less productive economy.

Subsequent theoretical work has extended this analysis, with rich portrayals of technology, risk, and dynamic behavior. Carter and Zimmerman (2000) show that an endowment-sensitive economy will tend toward a small-farm agrarian structure as low-wealth households sacrifice consumption and accumulate the working capital needed to finance modern, capital-using production. Other work shows that risk, subsistence constraints, and fixed costs associated with agricultural activities can defeat this process, and that the market can create exclusionary growth processes not unlike those associated with the English enclosures. The underlying lesson of this theoretical literature is perhaps one of historical contingency, in the sense that it is impossible to say which farm size will be either dominant or most desirable, independent of initial conditions, market structures and imperfections, and agro-climatic conditions.

Farm Size from Past to Future. At the dawn of the twenty-first century, farm size continues to be an important issue in a number of countries. In China, some worry that farms are so small that mechanization and future productivity growth will be blocked. In locations as far flung as southern Africa and Brazil, governments search for market-based agrarian reform mechanisms that will redistribute land rights while preserving the economy's productive and export base. In the countries of eastern Europe and the former Soviet Union, agriculture appears mired between the remnants of large state and collective farms and an emergent, yet apparently dysfunctional, family labor farm structure. Across all these locations, as with the English enclosures centuries ago, the way the economics of farm size play out will shape the well-being of the rural people who continue to comprise the largest and least well-off group of people on the globe.

BIBLIOGRAPHY

Allen, Robert. *Enclosure and the Yeoman*. Oxford, 1992.

Benjamin, Dwayne. "Can Unobserved Land Quality Explain the Inverse Relationship?" *Journal of Development Economics* 46.1 (1995), 51–84.

Berry, R. Albert, and William Cline. *Agrarian Structure and Production in Developing Countries*. Baltimore, 1979.

Brenner, R. "The Agrarian Roots of European Capitalism." In *The Brenner Debate: Agrarian Class Structure and Economic Development in Pre-Industrial Europe*, edited by T. H. Ashton and C. H. E. Philpin. Cambridge, 1985.

Carter, Michael, Bradford Barham, and Dina Mesbah. "Agricultural Export Booms and the Rural Poor in Chile, Guatemala and Paraguay." *Latin American Research Review* 31.1 (1996), 33–65.

Carter, Michael R., and Frederick Zimmerman. "The Dynamic Cost and Persistence of Asset Inequality in an Agrarian Economy." *Journal of Development Economics* 63.1 (2000), 265–302.

Chayanov, A. V. *The Theory of Peasant Economy*. Homewood, Ill., 1966.

Duncan, Kenneth, and Ian Rutledge. "Introduction: Patterns of Agrarian Capitalism." In *Land and Labour in Latin America*, pp. 1–19. Cambridge, 1977.

Eswaran, Mukesh, and Ashok Kotwal. "Access to Capital and Agrarian Production Organization." *Economic Journal* 96.2 (1986), 482–498.

Johnston, Bruce, and Peter Kilby. *Agriculture and Structural Transformation: Economic Strategies in Late-Developing Countries*. New York, 1975.

Lehman, David. "After Chayanov and Lenin: New Paths of Agrarian Capitalism." *Journal of Development Economics* 11.1 (1982), 133–161.

Lenin, V. I. *The Development of Capitalism in Russia*. 1899. Reprint. Moscow, 1977.

Overton, Mark. *Agricultural Revolution in England: The Transformation of the Agrarian Economy, 1500–1850*. Cambridge, 1996.

Patnaik, Utsa. "Neo-Populism and Marxism: The Chayanovian View of the Agrarian Question and Its Fundamental Fallacy." *Journal of Peasant Studies* 6.4 (1979), 375–420.

Polayni, K. *The Great Transformation*. New York, 1944.

Putterman, Louis. *Continuity and Change in Rural China*. Cambridge, 1992.

Sen, Amartya K. *Employment, Technology and Development*. Oxford, 1985.

Thiesenhusen, William. *Searching for Agrarian Reform in Latin America*. Boston, 1989.

Wittfogel, K. *Oriental Despotism*. New Haven, 1957.

MICHAEL R. CARTER

FASHION INDUSTRY. Fashion is a complicated category of cultural and economic life. It displays the characteristics of an art form, a social process, and an industrial product. Its study can include the consideration of a chain of events whereby the sketch of a designer, informed by historical precedent or contemporary influences, is translated into an object of refined beauty. It can be defined as the ritualistic adorning of the body by a subject whose choice relates to aesthetic and sociological contexts. Or it can be viewed as the mechanical transformation of textiles into garment, replicated according to customer size and wealth, displayed for sale in the retail sphere, and given meaning for the potential consumer by its reproduction in the promotional images of film and print media. All of these interpretations are linked by the concepts of "modishness" and ephemerality that pervade the field. Fashion is distinct from clothing because its defining features rely on the prioritization of temporal notions of style over functional considerations of wear and tear. It is a symbolic commodity whose power resides in its ability to anticipate and generate trends in visual and material culture, taste, and behavior.

The Emergence of Fashion. The conditions for the rise of the modern fashion industry in Europe were the same as those that paved the way for the emergence of a consumer society. (It should be noted that definitions of fashion in other regions are specific to place and period, but anthropologists have identified similar processes in play in ancient civilizations and in early modern China and Japan.) These included an intensification of urban culture and class distinction, the reorganization and partial mechanization of production methods in manufacturing, improvements in communication systems, an increased level of visual and textual literacy, and a concurrent "democratization" of supply. Such conditions ensured that by the middle of the nineteenth century, many consumers in Europe and North America had access to a high turnover of fashionable garments whose proliferation and range was undreamed of by their ancestors. This was the outcome of a process that had been gathering steam since the fourteenth century. But it was in Paris and London during the 1850s that the potential for a sartorial revolution on an unprecedented scale really took hold, influencing the growth of the global fashion system that prevails in the twenty-first century.

The Italian city-states of the Renaissance witnessed the first stirrings of sartorial competition. This competition initiated a speeding up of style change, which was connected to the profound reorientation in the construction of garments that took place during the 1340s and 1350s. From the Classical era to the Middle Ages, clothing was generally draped across the body or cut in a loose "T" shape and gathered in with belts and ties. Social status was marked by the intrinsic quality of the textile, its color, and its surface decoration rather than its form. The basic structures of dress thus remained fairly static for several centuries and changes in style or taste were marked through subtle amendments on the surface.

In the early fourteenth century, Florentine and Venetian tailors began to introduce figure-hugging items that emphasized the contours of the body through the cut of the cloth rather than its fall. This potential for radical manipulation opened up a new scenario in the styling of elite wardrobes and a vastly expanded repertory of fashionable shapes. At about the same time, the word *fashion*, originally a simple verb describing the process of making, began to take on its modern meaning as a description of a mode of behaving and appearing according to contemporary social dictates. New "fashionable" clothing forms spread rapidly through Europe. The ruling houses of Burgundy and then Spain emerged as important centers for the promotion of fashionable innovation from the fifteenth to the seventeenth centuries. Their years of sartorial dominance reflected those periods during which these respective courts enjoyed an unparalleled level of political and military influence. Instructive conduct books and miniature dolls dressed in the latest styles advanced toward subservient centers, promoting the rules of courtly taste.

Paris, though a significant center for the production of luxury goods, held no early monopoly on dictating fashion trends; its association with any particular ruling dynasty was too tenuous to make an impact on the rest of Europe. In the late seventeenth century, the court of Louis XIV played host to the most concerted effort yet to harness the idea of fashion as propaganda for dynastic and nationalistic ends. State sponsorship of the textile and decorative arts industries and the consolidation of the court at Versailles as a carefully managed symbol of absolutism were strategies that helped to promote French fashion and utilize its power as a means of social control. Ambitious subjects were kept in check by a complex system of sumptuary laws, and foreign competitors were awed into submission by the spectacular staging of ostentatious examples of fashionable consumption.

The manufacture of fashionable goods was still based in Paris, benefiting from a concentration of craft skills. As the eighteenth century progressed, the multitude of weavers, embroiderers, tailors, dressmakers, and milliners employed there in the service of the court established themselves as an alternative center of sartorial knowledge. Similarly, the demimonde of wealthy courtesans and actresses at home in the city were able to subvert the stranglehold of court etiquette while drawing on the same material resources. In this manner, Parisians found their unique and directional tastes promoted above the fossilized ceremonial of official culture in the new magazines and fashion plates that anticipated and recorded life à la mode. This style sense lent a heightened visibility and greater importance to the activities of their tailors and dressmakers.

The French clothing industry was complex in its organization. The *marchand de mode* traditionally supplied the trimmings that marked shifting taste while the *maitresses couturières* were responsible for cutting and constructing of the basic and more slowly changing garment. In 1675, the *couturière*'s role was restricted under trade guild rules to the production of specific elements of the female wardrobe. This restriction protected the business of the tailor, whose practice extended across men's and women's dress. The *marchand de mode* fell under the jurisdiction of a competing guild and found it easy to encroach on the couturière's compromised status.

The most successful *marchand* was Rose Bertin, who capitalized on the high profile of her première client, Marie Antoinette. Bertin's carefully managed reputation as a domineering dictator of fashion arguably formed the prototype from which later popular definitions of the fashion designer developed. As with her successors, her expertise lay in her knack of juxtaposing existing patterns, colors, or decorations in surprising combinations and an ability to flatter and anticipate the tastes of her elite clients, rather than in inventing completely new lines. Any assessment of Bertin's influence on the development of the modern fashion industry also relates to a broader discussion concerning the contradictory nature of consumer culture itself and the relationship between supply and demand. It could be argued that the desire for innovation and differentiation that the *marchand de mode* fed upon arose from intellectual and social currents among the professional citizens of Paris, for increasingly the wealthy bourgeoisie, rather than the aristocracy, articulated progressive taste in dress. Alternatively, entrepreneurial figures like Bertin could be viewed as reactionaries who traded on social snobbery while stamping their signatures on the rash of new products that improved manufacturing and marketing practices had encouraged.

Modern Fashion. Whatever the reasons for the successful rise of fashion trade personalities, by the start of the nineteenth century the control of fashionable style had been wrested from the court (aided in no small part by the upheaval of political revolution) and was now identified with the practices and products of a select group of style leaders, secure of their hegemony in the commercial sphere of Paris. Beyond the prestigious showrooms and aristocratic clients of the rue Saint-Honoré, the rue de Richelieu, and the rue de la Paix, this powerhouse of fashion came to incorporate the Palais Royal with its reputation for supplying opulent ready-made goods to tourists, and the rue Saint-Denis, which was associated with the respectable purchases of the lower middle classes. By the 1850s, all of these areas proclaimed the supremacy of Paris fashion, and the trading names of future tenants would become synonymous with that same phenomenon. This local business context fostered the emergence of grand couture. It provided the raw materials, labor, and inspiration for a succession of fashion giants, beginning in the mid-nineteenth century with the Englishman Charles Worth (who brought with him the experience of a retail training in London) and moving in the first half of the twentieth century through the careers of designers including Paul Poiret, Coco Chanel, Madeleine Vionnet, and Elsa Schiaparelli. The tradition culminated in the postwar output of Christobal Balenciaga, Christian Dior, Hubert Givenchy, and Yves Saint Laurent, before declining in the face of a global fashion system that by the 1960s looked beyond Paris to designers, entrepreneurs, and consumers in London, New York, Milan, and Tokyo for its aesthetic and economic leads.

Names like Worth, Chanel, and Dior may loom large in published histories of modern fashion, but as active makers their contribution toward fashion as material product was disproportionately small. Their huge influence rides on the backs of millions of uncredited workers whose labor translated provocative ideas into three-dimensional materiality. At all levels, modern fashion has always been industrial in scale. For idea to become profitable commodity, the industry depends on both the mechanical processes of construction and the technology of reproduction. Much of the work involved in that transition, though often a source of pride and creative fulfillment, has also been repetitive, uncomfortable, undervalued, and poorly paid.

This is the reality that lies behind, and partly explains the rise of, the named designer, a figurehead employed to impart a more sophisticated patina to a trade that has generally lacked the finesse that fashion likes to claim for itself. The creativity credited to celebrated couturiers lay firmly in the realm of promotional and styling skills. Thus Charles Worth reinvented himself as an autocratic genius whose public image was closer to that of the Renaissance painter than the ex–shop assistant. His oeuvre recalled the romanticism of eighteenth-century imagery, transforming the women of Parisian society into figures from a Watteau canvas. Paul Poiret engineered commercial collaborations with Fauvists like Dufy, utilizing his vivid designs in printed textiles. He also borrowed orientalist motifs from the success of the Ballet Russe to create scandalous but publicity-garnering collections. And Coco Chanel traded in the language of architectural modernism, producing items whose pared-down simplicity made deliberate references to iconic modernist objects such as the Model T Ford motor car. By allying the clothing industry to the phenomena of artistic avant-gardism and an eroticized exoticism in this way, the more mundane circumstances of its production could be hidden while its cultural value increased.

The maintenance of the myth into the second half of the twentieth century was helped by the stratification of the industry into distinct sectors whose organization

HAUTE COUTURE. Fashion Week in the garment district, New York City, 1984. (© Marvin Newman/ Woodfin Camp and Associates, New York)

underpinned the useful characterization of fashion as an elitist pursuit. At the top end of the trade, the couture house produced the most expensive, directional, and exclusive goods. Fine hand sewing, bureaucratic control, and a heightened creative vision ensured commercial success. Here rich customers were guaranteed ownership of an inimitable artifact, unsullied by the reproduced glamour of cheaper fashions, yet innovative enough in its effects to inspire future copies. The customer entered into a seemingly individual consultation with the couturier, who would advise on a selection from his current collection. Outfits were arranged on a seasonal basis that followed the social calendar and were generally promoted to selected clients via the theatrical trappings of the fashion show. The couturier was aided by a saleswoman who managed the running of the public areas of the salon. Once the client was measured by a fitter (over several fittings), three ranks of seamstresses would work to equip her with a perfect dress that hugged the body like a glove. A buyer would ensure that the house had access to appropriate textiles (silks, brocades, velvets, fine wools, and exquisite trimmings), negotiating a network of small local businesses whose wares were sourced to achieve the sense of individuality central to the identity of couture. Such a pattern was replicated beyond Paris in the elite dressmaking establishments of many capital cities, but between 1850 and 1960 Paris set the tone and attracted the most important custom.

The running costs of a couture house in terms of intensive labor and luxurious materials was high in comparison to the level of output achieved (at least as far as bespoke dresses were concerned), making it an anachronistic organization. In some ways, the coordination of work was similar to that experienced in other sectors of the industry, such as high-class men's tailoring. The sophisticated machinery and improved mass-production methods by the 1920s had rendered factory-made items such as underwear and hosiery superior to equivalent handmade items. They had also introduced the profitable idea of the made-to-measure suit to the menswear trade and sportswear to America. However, the language and methods of the production line were (on the surface) taboo in the rarefied philosophy of couture.

Made-to-order and ready-made enterprises did share an interest in the area of marketing. In this sphere, the couture house could reasonably claim to be remarkably modern. Despite its antiquated working practices and craft ethos, high fashion maintained a monopoly on the concept of desirability that was supported through the promotion of the couturier as a dictator of trends. Extraordinary copies of garments paid their way, in tandem with the selling of toiles for copying by mass producers, in-house diffusion lines (known from the 1950s as prêt-à-porter), and a diversification into other aspirational products such as perfume. These strategies vindicated the economic sense in encouraging a fantasy of narcissistic individualism that lies at the heart of the fashion trade and fostered tie-ins with other leisure industries, including Hollywood, popular women's magazines, and the department store.

Fashion and the Mass Market. From the 1960s onward, marketing and publicity skills became ever more important to established fashion businesses. The preeminence of traditional couture was challenged by a democratization of taste fostered through the more accessible activities of the film, retail, and publishing industries. This more egalitarian fashion scene ended the notion of a singular high-fashion vision that emanated from Paris at strategic moments of the year. The proletarian energy of urban life and of a more visible youthfulness embodied in the figures of the American and British teenager, together with the emergence of alternative fashion spaces, including London's Carnaby Street and San Francisco's Haight-Ashbury district, reordered received ideas about the formation of tastes and trends. Fashionable innovation thus became more dispersed and more pluralistic. Running parallel to this shift was a growing need for the industry to recognize global markets, the potential of new synthetic materials, increased competition, and mass dissemination as the keys to economic survival.

While the old couture houses witnessed the shrinking of their traditional markets and a decline in their functional and cultural relevance, a new generation of designers, stylists, retail buyers, and journalists within the field of high fashion were still able to retain control of trend directions and sales. The symbolic power they wielded aided the continuation and growth of the business of luxury first pioneered by Bertin and Worth. Successive mergers and takeovers in the sector from the 1970s on have meant that the majority of those houses established as independent concerns in the early twentieth century were, a century later, owned by just two corporate giants. But these older names have been joined by the Italians Gucci, Armani, and Versace, the Japanese Issey Miyake and Rei Kawakubo (Comme des Garçons) and the Americans Ralph Lauren, Calvin Klein, and Donna Karan. Similarly, the focus of production has shifted from the narrow provision of couturier clothing to the mass selling of branded fragrance, luggage, accessories, and licensed items that aspire to partake of the mythology of distinction that has always characterized this segment of the industry.

It could be argued that the rise of the logo, the designer jean, and the training shoe provides a suitable metaphor for understanding the increasing importance placed on the role of the fashion process in the general operation of today's capitalist system. Many writers on modern culture have seen a broad shift from a society that focuses on the utility of products to one that places much greater value on their symbolic and associative worth. The early twenty-first century offers a scenario in which the carefully manipulated associations of the brand and a keen attention to the vagaries of style have transformed the humble equipment of contemporary living into the ephemeral props of ever-changing lifestyle concepts. Fashion in the present has expanded well beyond the design, manufacture, and acquisition of a new garment to incorporate a symbol of desire on a global scale.

[*See also* Clothing Trades; Cosmetics Industry; Cotton Industry; Jewelry Industry; Linen Industry; Silk Industry; Textiles; *and* Wool Industry.]

BIBLIOGRAPHY

Boucher, François. *A History of Costume in the West*. Rev. ed. London, 1996.
Breward, Christopher. *The Culture of Fashion: A New History of Fashionable Dress*. Manchester, 1995.
Bruzzi, Stella, and Pamela Church Gibson. *Fashion Cultures: Theories, Explorations and Analysis*. London, 2000.
Bruzzi, Stella. *Undressing Cinema: Clothing and Identity in the Movies*. London, 1997.
Burman, Barbara. *The Culture of Sewing*. Oxford, 1999.
Craik, Jennifer. *The Face of Fashion: Cultural Studies in Fashion*. London, 1994.
Crane, Diana. *Fashion and Its Social Agendas*. Chicago, 2000.
Davis, Fred. *Fashion, Culture and Identity*. Chicago, 1992.
De la Haye, Amy, and Elizabeth Wilson. *Defining Dress: Dress as Object, Meaning and Identity*. Manchester, 1999.
Entwhistle, Joanne. *The Fashioned Body: Fashion, Dress and Modern Social Theory*. Cambridge, 2000.
McDowell, Colin. *McDowell's Directory of Twentieth Century Fashion*. London, 1987.
Mendes, Valerie, and Amy de la Haye. *Twentieth Century Fashion*. London, 1999.
Roche, Daniel. *The Culture of Clothing: Dress and Fashion in the Ancien Regime*. Cambridge, 1994.
Steele, Valerie. *Paris Fashion: A Cultural History*. Oxford, 1988.
Tarrant, Naomi. *The Development of Costume*. London, 1994.
White, Nichola, and Ian Griffiths. *The Fashion Business*. Oxford, 2000.
Wilson, Elizabeth. *Adorned in Dreams: Fashion and Modernity*. London, 1985.

CHRISTOPHER BREWARD

FEDERAL RESERVE SYSTEM. *See* Central Banking *and* United States.

FEDERAL TRADE COMMISSION ACT. *See* Antitrust.

FERTILITY. Fertility is a fundamental aspect of the demography of all populations. Mammals (and birds), in contrast to other animal species, achieve reproduction by having relatively few offspring, spaced at long intervals. Further, sexual dimorphism is essential to the process, increasing chances for genetic mutation, both favorable and unfavorable. Humans, being relatively large mammals, have a long gestation period, few multiple births, and an extended period of breast-feeding and care for the young.

In the course of this article, the topics of methods and measurement, theories of fertility transition and differential fertility, and the historical study of fertility will be covered. Since the topic of marriage is closely related to the study of fertility, some aspects of nuptiality will be treated.

Methods and Measurement. Since females actually bear and nurse children, it has become common to relate fertility to women. Women also have a more circumscribed reproductive period than men. Menarche (the onset of menstruation) now happens in early teenage years in well-nourished populations with low incidence and prevalence of infectious and parasitic diseases. Menopause commonly occurs in the late forties or early fifties of life. It can occur significantly earlier but usually not much later. Historically the age of menarche came rather later, often in the late teens. Even when young women begin to menstruate, they are usually not fully fecund. About 5 to 10 percent of all women are wholly or largely sterile. *Fecundity* is defined as the capacity to conceive and bring a child to term. *Fertility* is defined as the actual event of bearing a child.

To measure fertility, two types of data are commonly required: vital statistics (records of births) and census or survey data to provide the base population at risk. Some historical studies, for example the parish register analyses of early modern Western societies, use baptisms rather than births. Using baptisms presents problems since some children die before being baptized or named. Other studies have used continuous registry data, family books, and genealogies (for example, for Germany, Japan, China, and the United States). These micro sources make it possible to calculate more precisely the person years at risk in a time interval.

The simplest measure of fertility is the crude birth rate (CBR), live births (that is, excluding stillbirths) per one thousand population per year. Ideally the population at risk for any rate is in terms of person years of experience in a time interval, but often the mid-period population is simply used. In the case of the CBR, the whole population is clearly not directly at risk of producing a live birth. Consequently more refined measures are related to the female population. The general fertility rate (GFR) is usually defined as live births per one thousand women in the childbearing ages, often ages fifteen to forty-nine or fifteen to fifty-four, though the age groups frequently depend on the age categories available in published data.

Since fertility varies dramatically by age of woman, being highest in the late teens or early twenties and declining thereafter to menopause, age-specific fertility rates are useful. This requires data on births by age of mother and the population of women in those ages, either by single years of age or in age groups (commonly five-year groups, such as fifteen to nineteen, twenty to twenty-four, fifty to fifty-four). A common method of summarizing this large amount of information is the total fertility rate (TFR), obtained by summing the age-specific fertility rates over all ages of women. If this is done for a cross section at a point in time, it is known as a "period TFR." It is interpreted as the number of births an average woman would have, whether married or unmarried or in a reproductive union or not, if she experienced the same set of rates over her life as prevailed in the cross section. If the rates are calculated for the same group of women as they age over time (known as an age cohort), it is called a "cohort TFR." For the rate to apply actually to the same group of women, the cohort must be closed to in- and out-migration. Historically the TFR has been observed above 10.0 and is currently below 1.5 in some developed European nations.

A further refinement of the TFR is the gross reproduction rate (GRR), which confines the age-specific birthrates to female births only. This is still further refined into the net reproduction rate (NRR), which makes allowance for the survival of female infants to the ages of their mothers at the time of the infants' births. This has the intuitive interpretation. An NRR of 1.0 means that a population is exactly reproducing itself, while an NRR above or below 1.0 implies that the population will be growing or declining (from natural increase) over the long run. The long run is about sixty or seventy years when the age structure becomes stable. At modern mortality rates in developed countries, an NRR of 1.0 implies a TFR of about 2.1.

The age structure of the population depends largely on the level of fertility because births affect the age pyramid only at the bottom, whereas mortality operates at all levels of the age structure. Hence a high fertility population is more heavily weighted toward young people and has a lower median age. The reverse is true for a population with low birthrates. For example, the median age of the American population was about sixteen years in 1800, when the TFR for the white population was about seven births per woman. The median age rose to about 35 years in 2000, when the TFR had fallen to about 2.1 births per woman.

All of the previously mentioned fertility measures can be refined to cover overall, marital, and nonmarital fertility. Historically marital and nonmarital fertility have often been labeled legitimate and illegitimate fertility. Some of the rates (TFR, GRR, NRR) can be calculated for actual age cohorts. All of the rates can be calculated separately for different population subgroups, such as rural-urban residence, region of residence, race, ethnicity, language group, education, occupation, or labor force status of the father or mother. All this depends on having the appropriate published tabulations or the ability to retabulate the original census and vital statistics data.

Vital statistics are not always available and, if available, may be seriously incomplete. Other measures and methods have been designed for these circumstances. One common measure is the child-woman ratio, a wholly census-based measure. It takes the ratio of surviving young children (for example, aged zero, zero to four, zero to nine) per one thousand women in the childbearing ages (for example, fifteen to forty-nine). It requires population tabulations by age and sex, a commonly published result. This has been extensively used for the United States historically, since that nation has had a decennial census since 1790 but was not fully covered by vital statistics registration until 1933. Another census-based measure is based on a question of the number of live births to an adult woman in her lifetime. This question began to be asked in the late nineteenth century in a number of nations and gives a measure of completed or cumulative fertility (parity) when tabulated by age or marriage duration of a woman. It also allows the calculation of parity-progression ratios, that is, the probability of a woman moving from one parity to the next.

A relatively straightforward set of indexes of fertility and nuptiality were developed by Ansley Coale for the study of the European fertility transition. They consist of I_f (the index of overall fertility), I_g (the index of marital fertility), I_h (the index of nonmarital fertility), and I_m and I_m^* (the indexes of proportions married). The virtue of these indexes for historical work is that they have relatively moderate data requirements: aggregate birth data by legitimacy status and census data by age, sex, and marital status. There is also an intuitively appealing interpretation. For example, I_f gives the ratio of actual births for a given population of women to the births that the same group of women would have experienced if they had had the fertility of married Hutterite women in the United States in the 1920s (the highest fertility group ever observed). I_g measures the same for married women in the given population, and I_h provides an index for unmarried women. The fertility indexes (I_f, I_g, I_h) thus furnish a form of indirect standardization with a value of 1.0 being historically close to maximum human reproduction. I_m and I_m^* are different, being ratios of the weighted age distributions of married women in the given population to the weighted age distribution of total women (or the sum of the Hutterite weights in the case of I_m^*) in the given population. These indexes have been widely used, most particularly by the European Fertility Project at the Office of Population Research at Princeton University, for which indeed the measures were developed. Monographs and articles have been produced for Portugal, Spain, Italy, Germany, Austria-Hungary, France, Belgium, Britain, Switzerland, and Russia. A volume has been prepared that summarizes a number of the major overall findings (see Coale and Watkins, 1986). While the Coale indexes are only a form of indirect standardization, the modest data requirements, easy intuitive interpretation, and ease of calculation have insured a current wide utilization.

The issue of the Hutterite birth schedule points to the question of natural fertility. This is defined as fertility not subject to deliberate limitation or control or, more technically, as the situation in which the behavioral (as opposed to the biological) probability of moving from one parity (that is, achieved number of children ever born) to the next parity does not depend upon parity already achieved.

This has found application in models of fertility that attempt to measure the extent of fertility control. The most widely used of these is the Coale-Trussell model, which assumes an average pattern of natural fertility (from contemporary and historical data), natural fertility for all women at ages twenty to twenty-four, and a model pattern of deviation from natural fertility at other ages. It generates two parameters: the overall level of natural fertility at ages twenty to twenty-four and the degree of departure from natural fertility, interpretable roughly as the degree of fertility control. One problem is difficulty in inferring family limitation behavior from age-specific fertility data when spacing as well as stopping behavior occur early in fertility decline, which produces a nonstandard pattern of deviation from natural fertility. Also when nuptiality patterns are quite different from those of the populations underlying the model, marriage duration effects may intervene and produce poor parameter estimates. Early in a fertility transition it is more common to have stopping behavior, in which parents cease childbearing when they reach a desired, or at least tolerable, number of live births or surviving children. Later in the transition parents must also resort to spacing, which involves lengthening birth intervals deliberately in order to achieve a small completed family.

The study of birth intervals (the period between successive births) is often accomplished with the analysis "proximate determinants" of fertility behavior. These methods are designed to break down the female reproductive period and birth intervals into measurable, distinct, and meaningful components: age at marriage or entrance into a sexual union, age at menopause, duration of gestation, duration of postpartum infecundability, time added by spontaneous intrauterine mortality, and waiting time to conception. Waiting time to conception may be subdivided into effects of contraception, induced abortion, breast feeding, and biological subfecundity. Such variables operate between fertility outcomes and the socioeconomic variables which are hypothesized to influence fertility differentials, fluctuations, levels, and trends. The chief historical populations studied with this approach have been natural fertility groups in small communities in Europe (England, France, Belgium, Germany), North America (colonial United States and French Canada), and Asia (China and Japan).

Theories of Fertility Behavior and the Fertility Transition. The historical study of fertility and marriage has often used the "theory of the demographic transition" from high to low levels of fertility and mortality. The more conventional "ideal type" of this model (since it really is not a theory in the scientific sense) identifies a pretransition stage with high and reasonably stable natural fertility and high and fluctuating mortality. This is followed by a reduction in mortality variation and then a decline in mortality, followed in turn by a stage of fertility decline, and finally succeeded by an era of low mortality and low but fluctuating fertility. Socioeconomic forces are seen to play a central role in this process: urbanization, the movement of work outside the home, increased population mobility, the increased importance of the nuclear family, the increased importance of education and human capital, declining infant and child mortality, changing roles of women, and increased rationality in individual and family decision making.

Empirical evidence is not always consistent with this view. These structural variables are often good at predicting differentials in fertility but poor in explaining the timing and pace of the fertility transition. The European Fertility Project is an example. Analyzing subnational geographic units (usually provinces) and utilizing the Coale indexes, a number of essential descriptive findings were put forward. With the exception of France, an early decliner, and some isolated small geographic areas and particular groups, the decline in European fertility took place after about 1870 and was largely complete by 1960. Declines in marital fertility exceeded declines in overall fertility, and indeed changes in marital fertility were the driving force. Nuptiality, after about 1930, actually moved to offset declines in marital fertility as age at marriage fell, the proportions of women married at various ages rose, and the proportion of the female population remaining permanently celibate fell. Once the decline by province began, it almost never stopped or reversed until a low level of marital fertility had been reached, and the decline and geographic spread were relatively swift. The decline diffused across Europe much like an "epidemic," generally from west to east, but the geographic pattern was complex. Geographically adjacent areas often experienced quite different patterns, the difference often being linguistic and cultural rather than strictly economic. For example, in Belgium, French-speaking Walloon areas showed early declines, while adjoining and socioeconomically similar Flemish-speaking areas had later declines and initially higher fertility levels.

Beyond the European fertility project, analysis of population aggregates and small local area studies for Germany, France, and England have revealed natural fertility to have been the rule in western Europe prior to the mid-nineteenth century. But there were also significant variations from place to place and over time. Many of these differences were unrelated to economic factors and were more closely associated with such things as differences in breast-feeding practices. The work of Edward A. Wrigley and Roger S. Schofield (1981) shows that variations in marriage were quite important, causing, for example, the gross reproduction rate in England to vary between 1.81 and 3.06 during the period 1541 to 1871. Moreover nuptiality and natural fertility likely interacted in a homeostatic fashion to keep pretransition population growth rates at relatively low levels.

John Knodel and Etienne van de Walle (1982) have attempted to identify threshold levels of various indicators of modernization and socioeconomic development relevant to the date of an irreversible 10 percent decline in marital fertility. They concluded that the marital fertility decline took place under a wide variety of social, economic, and demographic conditions. At the date of permanent 10 percent decline, the percentage of the male labor force in agriculture ranged from 13 percent in Scotland and 15 percent in England and Wales (1892) to 70 percent in Bulgaria (1912) and 73 percent in Hungary (c. 1890). The percentage of the population that was rural ranged from 85 percent in Finland (1910) and 84 percent in Hungary (c. 1890) to 26 percent in the Netherlands (1897) and 28 percent in England and Wales (1892). The percentage of the population in cities of over 20,000 inhabitants ranged from 7 percent in Bulgaria (1912) and France (c. 1800) to 57 percent in England and Wales (1892) and 49 percent in Scotland (1894).

Nor has the relationship between education and fertility been regular historically. Percentages of the population aged 10 or 15 and over who were illiterate ranged from quite low in such countries as Germany (1890), Switzerland (1892), Denmark (1900), and Norway (1904) to 60 percent in Bulgaria (1912), 46 percent in Spain (1918), and 49 percent in Hungary (c. 1890) at the date of 10 percent decline in marital fertility. There is strong evidence in the late twentieth century of an inverse correlation between parents' education and fertility, but the relationship is less clear historically, especially when literacy is used instead of the number of years of school completed. Some historical studies have seen no relation or even a positive one instead of the expected negative relation between parental literacy and fertility. Some authors believe the role of literacy is seriously underestimated.

John C. Caldwell (1982) has proposed that the rise of modern mass education has had an important influence on fertility decline, particularly by increasing the diffusion of middle-class values and knowledge of family limitation practices but also by increasing child costs. As parents invest more in the human capital of their children, the net flow of resources switches from children to parents over to parents to children. Net child costs rise, and fertility declines. Caldwell's notions of intergenerational resource and wealth transfers are not easy to test empirically, however.

Related to this are the views of Gary Becker (1991) that parents choose fewer children and more "quality" per child over time because of the decline of the implicit price of child "quality." The reduced price of child quality in turn has been caused by increased returns to human capital (education and health) in the course of economic growth and development. Fertility declines seem to occur at a time of a relatively high level of primary school enrollment and the beginning of rapid increases in secondary school enrollments.

The supply and demand model of Richard Easterlin and Eileen Crimmins (1985) proposes that, as long as the demand for children remains at or above the level of natural fertility (supply), birthrates will not decline. The demand for children is also not for live births *per se* but rather for children surviving to adulthood. Once the demand for children begins to fall toward fewer and higher-quality surviving children, eventually supply exceeds demand. Then families begin to limit and space births. Reductions in infant and child mortality play an important role by increasing the number of live births who survive to adulthood. Also improvements in women's health may actually increase the level of potential supply (natural fertility).

Another major characteristic of the fertility decline in Europe was that apparently knowledge of effective family limitation practices was absent or imperfect in many areas before the fertility transition. That is not to say that it was not possible to limit family size. Knowledge of contraception was present even in the ancient world. It was simply quite difficult to achieve effective family limitation with the technology and knowledge available. Sustained fertility declines did take place earlier among particular groups, such as the Jews of Italy and the bourgeoisie of Geneva, and in both the United States and France from at least 1800. As late as the 1890s and 1900s, however, it was a problem to achieve a small family size in a regime of inefficient contraceptive technology. Both spacing and stopping behavior were required. The result was a substantial amount of unwanted fertility. Empirical work with micro data sets for Germany and England reveals relatively little evidence of stopping or deliberate spacing among most of the population until the late nineteenth century. Although some of this evidence comes from the use of the Coale-Trussell model, which may be limited, there is other supporting information, such as mean birth intervals, mean age of mother at last birth (adjusted for mothers' mortality), and proportion of childbearing by women beyond age thirty. Additional evidence is that both marital and nonmarital fertility rates declined together. Since the motivation for fertility control presumably was greater among unmarried women, this is interpreted as evidence of technological limitations.

Infant and child mortality (for example, survival to age fifteen or twenty) played an ambiguous role in historical fertility decline. Declines in infant and child mortality should lead to reductions in fertility because a biological mechanism tends to lengthen birth intervals (partly through prolonged lactation) and also because parents perceive that fewer births are necessary to obtain a target surviving family size. The historical evidence is mixed. Marital fertility declined in Ireland well after the onset of a decline in infant mortality. This was not true in Germany and Belgium, where levels of infant mortality remained high while fertility was declining. The prolonged fertility decline in the United States prior to the Civil War may have taken place despite rising mortality rates. If child survival had an effect on fertility decline, one certainly would have expected substantial changes in infant and child mortality prior to or at least accompanying fertility decline. Such was not universally the case. Cross-sectional results for small geographic areas (for England, Wales, and Prussia) have given mixed results on the relationships between infant mortality and either overall or marital fertility. Nevertheless some historical micro data do reveal that child deaths were partially replaced.

Thus the influence of the socioeconomic context on fertility, so forcefully spelled out by the theory of the demographic transition, has not proven to be predictable or strong. This has been shown especially true for aggregate data for smaller geographic areas for which, as a statistical matter, such relationships should be quite marked. In particular cases and in the cross section, the relationships may be strong, highly correlated, and in the predicted direction. But the results are not consistent across countries. In some instances, such as Germany and Belgium, the effect of region alone was an extremely powerful predictor of decline. In Russia it was often not the Western nationalities themselves who were responsible for lower fertility and earlier decline but the characteristics of areas and regions in which Western nationalities were present.

An important modification to transition theory focuses on cultural values. According to Ron Lesthaeghe (1983), a good predictor of fertility differentials and change in Belgium since 1880 was an index of industrialization and urbanization and of secularization (measured as the percentage voting socialist or liberal in 1919). The idea of secularization has been expanded to include fundamental changes in the ideational structure of societies in which fertility control becomes a choice variable only when the cultural context permits it. Once this is true, the technology of family limitation permits, and it becomes socially and economically advantageous to control fertility, declines proceed rapidly. The hypothesis that a change in ideology from one emphasizing community and family authority and exchange patterns to one exemplifying individual choice and rationality fostered decline is consistent with the evidence of rapid and irreversible fertility decline occurring in Europe across a wide variety of socioeconomic situations within a relatively short span of time (roughly thirty years). Advances in the technology of family limitation only assist this process, since both France and the United States were already experiencing declines with existing, inefficient technology prior to most of Europe. Advances in urbanization and industrialization also made family limitation in some cases more advantageous, but the cultural context appears to have been crucial.

A model of the costs and benefits of children is related to most of the other theories of fertility transition. In the case of England and Wales it is argued that differential child costs were important in explaining cross-sectional differentials in legitimate fertility in 1911 and that changes in child costs were important in explaining the fertility decline between 1877 and 1938. Economic structure (for example, female labor force activity, proportions of the labor force in mining and textiles) was also significant. A considerable literature on current developing nations has used the cost and benefit analysis to study the actual or prospective fertility transitions in the third world. And yet the concept of child costs must embody subjective elements—perceptions of future benefits as well as present and future costs, which influence investment in the human capital of children.

Three of the most interesting cases of fertility decline are those of France, the United States, and English-speaking Canada in the nineteenth century. They are cases in which changes in the costs and benefits of children may provide insights. Fertility decline preceded substantial industrialization and urbanization. Present evidence points to fertility declines in France and the United States from the late eighteenth century. These were largely agrarian societies that nevertheless experienced a prolonged and dramatic sociodemographic change—a possible lesson for developing nations today. They are, however, quite different cases, since the United States and Canada were land abundant, relatively literate, and newly settled, while France was long settled and much less literate. The leading theory of American fertility decline before about 1860 is the land availability hypotheses: fertility was highest when there was an abundance of cheap improved land, presumably making it easier to endow children with adequate farm sites nearby. Canada seems an analogous case. Alternate views stress more conventional socioeconomic variables, including the marriage market, urbanization, and education. Another approach emphasizes a model of life cycle fertility, savings, demand for old-age support, bargaining within the family, and the development of urban, nonagricultural labor market opportunities for farm children to explain the rural American fertility decline, rather than the gradual erosion of the frontier and the disappearance of inexpensive bequests of land. Postbellum fertility decline in the United States and Canada follows the structural model quite well.

Differential Fertility. Research on historical fertility differentials for the presently developed countries has revealed, in general, higher fertility in rural than in urban areas; higher fertility among manual than among white-collar and professional occupations; higher fertility among lower income and wealth groups; higher fertility among the illiterate and less-educated groups; lower fertility among wage-earning women (though not necessarily among self-employed workers in the home); and higher fertility among certain religious, racial, and ethnic groups, such as blacks in the United States, Catholics in Germany and the United States, and the French Canadians.

The actual historical record is not as clear, however. The study of differential fertility by literacy status in historical studies has led to ambiguous results, with differing directions of the relationship and often statistically insignificant results. Information on number of years of schooling, which has produced much more consistent inverse correlations with fertility among contemporary populations, is frequently unavailable in historical data. Although ecological correlations sometimes are strong, it is not clear that what is observed at present was also true in the past. For example, occupation and class differentials in fertility in England and Wales appear to have become more pronounced during the fertility decline before closing up again. While fertility in urban areas was often lower than in rural places, it depended upon the type of urban place. For instance, cities based on mining and heavy industry have frequently had higher fertility than surrounding rural environments, in contrast to cities based on commerce and administration. While the foreign-born in the United States often had higher fertility than that of the native population, there were exceptions.

Most of the theory related to differential fertility has to do either with differences in the relative costs and benefits of children or with issues of norms or tastes. The issue of norms or tastes can be posed as one of constraints or of costs, such as the additional psychological cost of fertility regulation among Roman Catholics (Easterlin and Crimmins, 1985). For example, why do fertility differentials exist between racial and ethnic groups? One viewpoint, the socioeconomic characteristics hypothesis, states that, once all relevant socioeconomic differences are taken into account, fertility differences by race and ethnicity should disappear. Since income, wealth, education, occupation, residence, and other factors are frequently highly correlated with race or ethnic background, this is a plausible view.

A competing view is the minority group status hypothesis, which states that minority groups may "protect" themselves by either having many children or having relatively few high-quality children. The problem here is that the effect of minority status on fertility can be in either direction. The fertility pattern of American blacks has attracted much attention, with relatively high rural fertility and surprisingly low urban fertility. Fertility differentials among the native and foreign-born populations of the United States have historically attracted similar interest. The persistence of high fertility among French-speaking Canadians, followed by a precipitous decline in birthrates in the late twentieth century, is another interesting case.

The variant occupational and rural-urban differentials in fertility are also problematic. The effect of economic structures can be crucial. Mining and heavy industry create economic structures (which can be interpreted as microeconomic constraints) that provide incentives for particular areas, occupations, and groups to have higher fertility. It is generally argued that urban areas encourage smaller families because of greater density, scarcer and more expensive housing, fewer child labor opportunities (in contrast to agriculture), more wage labor opportunities for women, and better enforcement of child labor laws and compulsory education statutes. Child costs thus are thought to be higher in urban areas, as also might be the rewards to greater investment in human capital (quality per child). But much depends on the actual circumstances. For instance, mining and heavy industrial areas had few female labor force possibilities while providing good opportunities for children. Male wages peaked early in the life cycle and were relatively high, encouraging early marriage and shorter mean length of generations. Differential net in-migration of young adult males (in response to the same labor demand factors) biased sex ratios in favor of earlier and more extensive marriage of women. Higher child mortality tended to shorten birth intervals. All this combined to favor both higher (female) nuptiality and greater marital fertility in those areas and among occupational groups most affected. Hence in late-nineteenth-century Europe some industrial cities had higher fertility than the surrounding rural areas. In contrast, textile centers, which made extensive use of female labor, and urban areas, with a greater demand for female domestic workers, tended to have late and less-extensive marriage among females and possibly lower marital fertility because of higher child costs owing to a greater opportunity cost of women's time.

Cycles in Fertility. An area that has generated some attention in fertility analysis has been the study of cycles in fertility (and marriage) behavior. Perhaps the most notable is Easterlin's explanation of the post–World War II baby boom in the United States and elsewhere as a product of long swings in economic activity, migration, and cohort size phenomena. In the immediate post–World War II period fertility unexpectedly rose in the United States (from a TFR of about 2.5 in 1945 to one of about 3.7 in the late 1950s), peaking in about 1960 before declining to today's levels. Several other but not all developed nations also experienced this in greater or lesser degrees. The economic explanation involves a strong postwar labor market, small cohorts of younger workers (caused by earlier fertility declines), restrictions on international migration, and modest expectations for material living standards among those younger workers. Supply and demand factors thus interacted to provide a favorable environment for young families to have both more children and a rising material standard of living. This remains the dominant theory.

BIBLIOGRAPHY

Alter, George. "Theories of Fertility Decline: A Non-Specialist's Guide to the Current Debate on European Fertility Decline." In *The European Experience of Declining Fertility, 1850–1970*, edited by John R. Gillis, Louise A. Tilly, and David Levine, pp. 13–27. Oxford, 1992.

Becker, Gary S. *A Treatise on the Family*. Enlarged ed. Cambridge, Mass., 1991. See especially chap. 5, "The Demand for Children."

Bongaarts, John, and Robert G. Potter. *Fertility, Biology, and Behavior: An Analysis of the Proximate Determinants*. New York, 1983.

Bulatao, Rodolfo, and Ronald D. Lee, eds. *Determinants of Fertility in Developing Countries*, vol. 1, *Supply and Demand for Children*. New York, 1983.

Bulatao, Rodolfo, and Ronald D. Lee, eds. *Determinants of Fertility in Developing Countries*, vol. 2, *Fertility Regulation and Institutional Influences*. New York, 1983.

Caldwell, John C. *Theory of Fertility Decline*. New York, 1982.

Cleland, John, and John Hobcraft, eds. *Reproductive Change in Developing Countries: Insights from the World Fertility Survey*. Oxford, 1985.

Coale, Ansley J., and Susan Cotts Watkins, eds. *The Decline of Fertility in Europe*. Princeton, 1986.

The Determinants and Consequences of Population Trends: New Summary of Findings on Interaction of Demographic, Economic and Social Factors. United Nations. New York, 1973.

Easterlin, Richard A. *Population, Labor Force, and Long Swings in Economic Growth: The American Experience*, pt. 2, *Fertility Analysis*. New York, 1968.

Easterlin, Richard A., and Eileen M. Crimmins. *The Fertility Revolution: A Supply-Demand Analysis*. Chicago, 1985.

Gillis, John R., Louise A. Tilly, and David Levine, eds. *The European Experience of Declining Fertility, 1850–1970: A Quiet Revolution*. Oxford, 1992.

Haines, Michael R. "Economic History and Historical Demography: Past, Present, and Future." In *The Future of Economic History*, edited by Alexander J. Field, pp. 185–253. Hingham, Mass., 1987.

Haines, Michael R., and Richard H. Steckel, eds. *A Population History of North America*. New York, 2000.

Indirect Techniques for Demographic Estimation. United Nations. Manual 10. New York, 1983.

Knodel, John, Aphichat Chamratrithirong, and Nibhon Debavalya. *Thailand's Reproductive Revolution: Rapid Fertility Decline in a Third-World Setting*. Madison, Wis., 1987.

Knodel, John, and Etienne van de Walle. "Fertility Decline: 3. European Transition." In *International Encyclopedia of Population*, edited by John A. Ross, pp. 268–275. New York, 1982.

Leete, Richard, and Iqbal Alam, eds. *The Revolution in Asian Fertility: Dimensions, Causes, and Implications*. Oxford, 1993.

Lesthaeghe, Ron. "A Century of Demographic and Cultural Change in Western Europe: An Exploration of Underlying Dimensions." *Population and Development Review* 9.3 (1983), 411–435.

Livi-Bacci, Massimo. *A Concise History of World Population*. 2d ed. Malden, Mass., 1997.

Preston, Samuel H., Patrick Heuveline, and Michel Guillot. *Demography: Measuring and Modeling Population Processes*. Malden, Mass., 2001.

Shryock, Henry S., Jacob S. Siegel, and Associates. *The Methods and Materials of Demography*. U.S. Bureau of the Census. Washington, D.C., 1971.

Wrigley, E. A., and R. S. Schofield. *The Population History of England, 1541–1871: A Reconstruction*. Cambridge, Mass., 1981.

MICHAEL HAINES

FERTILIZING. The normal growth of plants requires the presence of at least sixteen different elements, three of which—nitrogen (N), phosphorus (P), and potassium (K)—are commonly depleted by crop growth and thus are the principal constituents required in manures and fertilizers. Manure is the feces and urine of farm animals, often combined with bedding material such as straw, although manure from human sources (usually known as nightsoil) has been and still is extensively used. The nutrient content of manure is relatively low; even the most concentrated, poultry manure, only contains about 2 percent N and P and 1 percent K. Organic fertilizers are more concentrated, with hoof and horn meal and dried blood containing 12 to 14 percent N. The range of such materials used in the past was enormous; guano, gas lime, fish, blubber, "greaves" (candle-makers' waste), furriers' clippings, feathers, wool, linen rags, shoddy, fellmongers' poake (carcass remains), and rape dust all appeared on a list compiled in 1860. Inorganic fertilizers are the most concentrated, with available nutrients accounting for up to half the weight of the material applied. Lime, which is not a fertilizer but reduces soil acidity, also is required on many soils. Many materials, from burnt lime to marl and shell sand, have been used for their lime content.

Farmers always have had to cope with shortages of crop nutrients. Shifting cultivation was one approach to the problem, and sedentary farmers in the Nile delta from earliest times had the benefit of the mineral-rich silt brought by the annual flood; but most relied upon manure, often in short supply. In many parts of South America and Africa, pastoral and arable farming were not well integrated, so the available manure did not always reach the land on which it was most required. Farmers in China, where animals played a relatively minor role in agriculture, went to great lengths to conserve nutrients. Chhen Fu, an agricultural writer of the Song period (tenth to thirteenth centuries CE), gave a detailed explanation of the construction of a manure house in which sweepings, ashes, husks and chaff, chopped straw, and fallen leaves were combined

FERTILIZERS. Spreading lime for fertilizer, Jasper County, Iowa, 1940. (John Vachon/Prints and Photographs Division, Library of Congress)

with nightsoil and pig dung and allowed to compost before use. By the time of the Ming dynasty (fourteenth to seventeenth centuries CE), hemp waste, oil cake, and bean curd waste all were being used as manures, and, as in Japan and Europe at the same time, any potentially compostable material was worth selling and transporting. In the early centuries of Islam, Arab farming writers had much to say on the value of various kinds of dung, animal products such as blood and powdered bones, olive oil sediment, leaves, rags, shavings, ashes, sand, marl, and broken tiles. They also knew that some crops, such as legumes, restored soil fertility, as too did Roman authors such as Columella, who pointed out the value of lupines and vetches when ploughed in as green manure. In Europe, increased use of leguminous fodder crops such as lucerne, sainfoin, and clover from the sixteenth century onward not only fixed nitrogen in the soil but also allowed more animals to be kept, and thus more farmyard manure to be produced. Similarly, expenditure on purchased feedingstuffs for stall cattle in the nineteenth century was, at first, justified by the increased manurial value of their dung.

Scientific arguments about the way in which plants obtained their nutrients opened up the whole question of inorganic fertilizers and their function in agriculture just when a greater range of such materials was becoming available. The first of these "concentrated portable manures" (as they were called at the time) was Peruvian guano, the first cargoes of which reached Liverpool, England, in 1840. It was not itself an inorganic fertilizer, but the dried droppings of seabirds, built up over centuries on the rainless coast of Peru and containing both nitrogen and phosphorus. At about the same time trade developed in sodium nitrate mined in Chile. Ground animal bones had long been used as a fertilizer, and in 1840 Liebig demonstrated that their fertilizing value (meaning, essentially, their solubility) could be increased by treatment with sulfuric acid. In 1842 Lawes patented the treatment of ground phosphate rock with sulfuric acid to produce what he called superphosphate, the first of the truly artificial fertilizers. Initially, in Britain, the phosphate was derived from mining fossilized animal remains called coprolites. The deposits had been exhausted by 1900, but by then numerous other sources were available. Phosphate rock mining began in the United States in 1868, and since the 1890s the United States has been the world's biggest superphosphate producer. Subsequently, mines were also developed in Morocco (in the 1920s), the Kola Peninsula in Russia and Kazakhstan (in the 1930s), and China and Jordan (after World War II).

Superphosphate was the principal fertilizer in the late nineteenth and early twentieth centuries, but not the only one. Beginning in the 1880s, the use of basic slag, a by-product of steel making and another phosphate source,

spread rapidly throughout Europe. From the 1860s, when the Stassfurt (Prussia) potash mines were opened, the state-run Potash Syndicate had a world monopoly of potassium fertilizers until 1914. Thereafter, American sources gradually were developed. There were soon several sources of nitrogen to compete with Chilean nitrate: ammonium sulfate, a by-product of gasworks, from the 1870s: cyanamide, introduced in Germany in 1898; and the Birkeland-Eyde electric arc process, which was first established in Norway in 1903 and needed very cheap hydroelectricity to be competitive. Most modern nitrate fertilizer production replicates (using natural gas) the Haber-Bosch process for fixing atmospheric nitrogen, developed in Germany between 1905 and 1913. Much of the product was initially sold as ammonium sulfate. By the 1960s, it had been almost entirely superseded by ammonium nitrate, urea, and anhydrous ammonia.

By the beginning of the twentieth century, the fertilizer industry was securely established. Its subsequent history is one of expansion and concentration: expansion of production and international trade, and concentration in the number of firms and factories involved. Table 1 demonstrates the rapid increase in world fertilizer output, especially in the second half of the twentieth century. This increase has not been evenly distributed, however. Although average fertilizer consumption in Africa, for example, doubled between 1969–1971 and 1988, it was still only 20 kilograms per hectare (total NPK) at the latter date; and countries such as Botswana, Mozambique, Niger, and Somalia continued to use little if any inorganic fertilizer. Japan and Taiwan, in contrast, were using over 300 kilograms per hectare by 1950.

In its early years, the fertilizer industry consisted of numerous small firms. The 1861 census of England and Wales listed 581 manure manufacturers; ten years later there were 1,210, of which, it was estimated, a dozen or more produced about 50,000 tons each per year, while the rest accounted for between 1,000 and 20,000 tons each. The 47 establishments in the U.S. fertilizer industry in

TABLE 1. *World Fertilizer Production (million tons of nutrient)*

	NITROGEN	PHOSPHATE	POTASH
1870s	0.1	< 0.5	0.1
1900–1913	0.4	2.5	0.9
1930s	1.0	3.8	2.8
1948–1953	4.5	6.1	4.8
1975–1976	43.8	26.1	23.5
1997–1998	90.1	34.9	24.9

SOURCE: Collins, 1947; Cowie, 1951; FAO, 1948; Gray, 1944; Smil, 1990; and Wright, 1909.

1859 had grown to 550 by 1909. As in other branches of American industry, there was much merger activity at the end of the nineteenth century, with several firms in the Northeast combining to form the American Agricultural Chemical Company, and the larger firms in the South, which was the main fertilizer-using area, combining into the Virginia-Carolina Chemical Company. In 1908 J. P. Morgan put together the International Agricultural Chemical Company. However, in this period, ease of entry, advantages in near-market location, and a wide range of inputs prevented any single firm from dominating the American market, which by 1944 consisted of about 1,100 establishments operated by between 800 and 900 manufacturing, distribution, and sales companies.

The increasing importance of nitrogenous fertilizers and compounds (i.e., containing combinations of N, P, and K) in the second half of the twentieth century, in whose manufacture there were considerable economies of scale, led to further concentration of the industry. The 1990s saw further merger and consolidation in the United States; in Europe the process began earlier. By 1990 five firms, all at least half state-owned, such as Norsk Hydro (Norwegian) and Kemira (Finnish), accounted for over half of western European fertilizer sales. The U.K. Fertilizer Manufacturers' Association had sixty-eight members in 1959 but only thirty in 1998, by which time the U.K. market was dominated by Norsk Hydro, Kemira, and Terra Nitrogen (a U.S.-based company). Efficiency increases, overinvestment, and the availability of cheap supplies from the former Eastern bloc countries (both the United States and the European Union applied antidumping tariffs in the 1990s) led to chronic overproduction in Europe in the late twentieth century. There were also attempts to restrict fertilizer use in some areas. In part, this was a response to their environmental impacts, but since the 1920s there also had been a conscious rejection of fertilizers by the organic farming movement. However, increasing fertilizer use was paralleled by increasing world population, from 1.2 billion in 1850 to 2.4 billion in 1950 and about 6 billion in 2000. The maintenance of world food supplies with current technology thus might prove difficult in the absence of continued applications of nitrogen, phosphate, and potash.

[See also Agriculture, subentry on Technological Change and Soil and Soil Conservation.]

BIBLIOGRAPHY

Brassley, Paul. "Plant Nutrition." In *The Agrarian History of England and Wales*, vol. 7, *1850–1914*, edited by E. J. T. Collins, pp. 533–547. Cambridge, 2000. Surveys the use of both manures and fertilizers, and concludes that the former were more important than the latter in the period considered.

Bray, Francesca. *Agriculture*, vol. 6, Part 2 of *Science and Civilisation in China*, edited by Joseph Needham. Cambridge, 1984. See especially pp. 289–298. Excellent on the nineteenth century and earlier but contains little on inorganic fertilizer use in the twentieth century.

Brock, William H. *Justus von Liebig: The Chemical Gatekeeper*. Cambridge, 1997. See especially Chap. 6. Standard biography of one of the scientists responsible for elucidating the theory of plant nutrition.

Collings, Gilbeart H. *Commercial Fertilizers: Their Sources and Use*. London, 1947. Not primarily a history, but a detailed source of contemporary commercial practice in the United States.

Cowie, George A. *Potash: Its Production and Place in Crop Nutrition*. London, 1951. The source of the pre-1948 data for K in Table 1.

Food and Agriculture Organisation (FAO). *Fertilizer Yearbook* and *Production Yearbook*, Rome, annual series. Both containing statistics on output, use and so on, since 1948, and the sources of the post-1948 data in Table 1.

Fussell, George E. *Crop Nutrition: Science and Practice before Liebig*. Lawrence, Kans., 1971. Largely derived from agricultural literature.

Gray, A. N. *Phosphates and Superphosphate*. London, 1944. Mostly descriptive of the contemporary industry, but with much historical data on phosphates, including pre-1948 data in Table 1.

Grigg, David B. *The Agricultural Systems of the World: An Evolutionary Approach*. Cambridge, 1974.

Mathew, W. M. *The House of Gibbs and the Peruvian Guano Monopoly*. London, 1981. Appears to be limited to a single firm, but in fact contains much material on the U.K. market as a whole in the nineteenth century.

Smil, Vaclav. "Nitrogen and Phosphorus." In *The Earth as Transformed by Human Action*, edited by B. L. Turner II et al., pp. 423–436. Cambridge, 1990. Contains material on both fertilizer output and the environmental effects of fertilizers.

Thompson, F. M. L. "The Second Agricultural Revolution, 1815–1880." *Economic History Review* 2d series, 21.1 (1963), 62–77. A classic paper on the impact of fertilizers (and feedingstuffs) in the U.K.

Wines, Richard A. *Fertilizer in America from Waste Recycling to Resource Exploitation*. Philadelphia, 1985. Covers the U.S. industry to the beginning of the twentieth century, arguing that by then it had changed from a recycling industry to a resource-exploiting and energy-consuming industry.

Wright, Robert P., ed. *The Standard Cyclopedia of Modern Agriculture and Rural Economy*, vol. 1, pp. 209–210. London, 1909.

PAUL BRASSLEY

FEUDALISM *[This entry contains three subentries, a historical overview and discussions of the manorial system and taxation during feudal times.]*

Historical Overview

The English word *feudalism* is one of those many "-isms" recognized only after the event. "Feudalism" was something that European scholars of the Enlightenment saw as an old-fashioned, outmoded socioeconomic and legal system whose survival and perseverance—in France, for example, until the 1789 Revolution—was a major impediment to human progress. These notions, which tended to see "feudalism" as an all-encompassing label for a particular type of social organization, found further expression in the nineteenth- and twentieth-century Marxist historical tradition: one that pictured feudalism as the precursor of capitalism and defined it as a means of production that could profoundly influence the structure and culture of a given society. The expansiveness of this definition meant that in non- and post-Marxist writing, "feudalism" was (and still is) used, often in a rather thoughtless manner, in reference to a particular period of time when the social and economic features associated with the term were thought to prevail. In relation to Europe, "feudal" thus became another way of saying "medieval." Modern usage has become especially sloppy in the sense that both these terms are now often laden with value judgments: "feudal" and "medieval" are used in the sense of "primitive" or "backward."

Since the term can be applied to social organization at particular phases in its development, those who inhabited societies that historians have identified as "feudal" did not, unsurprisingly, say so at the time. It is in the nature of the human experience that feudal societies have had little or no experience of alternative forms and regard the social structures arising out of their economic systems to be naturally or divinely appointed. The most famous and apposite example of this is the medieval European notion that society was structured into three "orders" or "estates," organized in a hierarchy: at the top, "those who pray" (the professional clergy, who were closest to God and whose task it was to save the souls of all humankind); "those who fight" (professional warriors, who were supposed to defend the rest of society from outside attack); and "those who work" (peasants, who provided manual labor on the estates held by the first two groups and thus generated the wealth that sustained those clerical and lay elites). Early European social thought thus implicitly and succinctly demonstrated the link between economic production and the structure of society. By representing this in terms of "orders" rather than "classes," it attempted to suggest that the three estates, rather than being in a perpetual state of potential conflict with each other, were strongly interdependent. Priests needed peasants for their labor as much as peasants needed priests for salvation. Indeed, the accommodation of this functionalist paradigm into the tradition of liberal historical and social analysis has helped to perpetuate "feudalism" as a concept in academic writing and debate and (at least in informed and scholarly circles) to rescue it from its popular usage as a term of contempt.

Military Feudalism. There are two principal ways in which feudalism is currently defined and understood. The first, and more specific, application is in relation to the dependent or conditional tenure of property (usually real estate). In this respect, feudalism denotes a tradition whereby an individual in possession of the means of wealth offers a portion of his assets to another in return for various forms of service. By undertaking this arrangement, the original holder of the land, the lord, retains a residual claim over the property and can reclaim it if the tenant fails to provide the forms of service agreed or understood by local convention to be reasonable. The European tradition applies certain specific words to the players and terms of this arrangement. The original holder is the suzerain or lord (*seigneur* in French, and thus the adjective *seigneurial*); the individual who holds land from him in a specific form of dependency is the vassal; and the land held in conditional tenure is the fief (in Latin *feodum*, the word from which the modern *feudalism* derives).

This same tradition places emphasis on the nature of the "contract" made between lord and vassal. It was unwritten, determined by custom rather than individual negotiation; it was made between men of free status (the term *vassal* in its medieval European usage may denote subjection, but certainly did not denote servitude); it was sealed by a formal ceremony (the act of vassalic commendation); it was made for the life of either party, and might be renewed by the heir and successor to either party, but only through a formal renewal of the bond. It was also exclusive in the sense that, while the lord might take as many vassals as he wished, no vassal could hold of more than one lord. Finally, the European tradition identifies the primary form of service—and, indeed, the essential purpose of this particular form of feudalism—as military: the vassal is required, within particular conventions and restraints, to provide his lord with the service of his own body (and/or that of others) when circumstances require and the demand is made. While the vassal was also commonly required to provide his lord with counsel and with financial aid, the lord's primary reason in handing over tenure of the fief was therefore to provide his vassal with the economic means through which he might equip himself appropriately to serve the lord in war.

Since the earliest evidence of this particular form of military organization in Europe comes from Frankish Gaul in the seventh and eighth centuries CE, and therefore coincides with the early use of cavalry—mounted horsemen—as the preferred and predominant military force in Europe, the development of feudalism is usually seen as intimately linked to the emergence of the medieval knight. And since the social status of knights tended to increase during the high Middle Ages, so that these men were seen to form part of the nobility in most parts of Europe, the particular institutions and conventions involved in feudal-vassalic relations have been represented as a socially exclusive, "upper-class" affair, involving only a very small number of people and intended only for a very specific purpose. They are also seen as giving way by the later Middle Ages to forms of "bastard" or "decayed" feudalism that were much more like early-modern forms of patron-client contract, which differed from the "classic" form of feudalism by substituting cash for the fief, by accepting fixed-term, as well as life contracts, and by allowing the retainer to make contracts with any number of lords for a wider variety of forms of military, administrative, political, and ceremonial service.

Manorial Feudalism. The second, broader definition of feudalism found in the historiography of the European Middle Ages is that which sees feudalism as the social, economic, and legal framework through which the elite established its control over the peasantry. In the theory of the three orders, "those who work" (that is, those whose responsibility it was to provide physical labor on the land) were not necessarily seen as the dependents of the clerical and military elites merely because they happened to be socially inferior to them. The circular tour of responsibility in this conceptual framework allowed for the category of laborers to include the genuinely free as well as the servile. Nevertheless, the tendency in medieval society was toward the assumption and acquisition of title to real estate by the upper orders of society and the reduction of those who lived and worked on that land to a dependent status. To generate the wealth required to support their specialist functions (praying and fighting), the ecclesiastical and military elites required those occupying their lands to devote a proportion of their yields and/or labor to the lord as rent in money and kind.

The classic economic-administrative unit within which the lord asserted and collected such rights and rents was the manor. Although a multiplicity of different forms of peasant tenure existed in the European Middle Ages, scholarship has been preoccupied with the basic distinction between free and unfree tenancies, the former often defined by an annual money rent, and the latter by the exaction of regular (often weekly) unpaid labor on the lord's own lands within the manor. (The holders of this latter type of tenancy were those recognized as having given up their free status and become serfs, dependent on the lord.) What particularly defines such dependent peasant tenancies as "feudal," however, is the particular form of jurisdiction that they accorded to the lord of the manor. Free and unfree tenancies were made and monitored in the manor court, the private court of the lord, which dispensed customary law under the authority not of some higher public authority but of the lord himself. The seigneurial authority thus asserted and tested by the lord in his own court came to be seen as the most characteristic and abiding, as well as pervasive, forms of feudalism by those who campaigned for their abolition in the seventeenth and eighteenth centuries.

In England, "feudal" tenures were formally abolished in 1660; in France, seigneurial rights continued to be upheld by law until the Revolution of 1789. This more expansive notion of feudalism—what might otherwise be called manorialism—obviously contains within its grasp a much larger proportion of the society claimed as "feudal" than does the exclusive, military form outlined above, and might therefore be seen as a more socially relevant definition of the term. It was in this spirit that the *Annales* school of social historians in the early twentieth century turned their attention back to feudalism and generated in Marc Bloch's *Feudal Society* (originally published in French in 1939), the book that remains the classic statement of this expansive characterisation of the medieval experience of feudalism.

There is no correct answer as to which of the two forms—the military and the manorial—provides the more accurate characterization of "feudalism" in the European experience. The matter is so subjective, indeed, and the terminology so fraught, that since the 1970s some scholars, especially those in the Anglophone tradition, have proposed the complete abandonment of the term *feudalism* in relation to the European Middle Ages on the grounds—as the American scholar E. A. R. Brown has put it—that "feudalism" is a mere construct that has tyrannized historians for too long. Such an argument depends partly on a more questioning and thorough scheme of empirical research that is no longer content merely to reinforce existing models but highlights the variety of experience, even to the extent of suggesting that the exceptions to the "feudal" rule might themselves be seen as establishing a new norm. In terms of military organization, for example, it is well established that very few rulers of the Middle Ages could rely simply on the feudal host to provide all the heavy cavalry required to make up an effective fighting force. Not only was feudal service limited to certain theaters of war and periods of time (often forty days), but the practice of subinfeudation (the phenomenon whereby fiefs were subdivided to create further, second-tier, dependent tenancies) made it increasingly difficult to regulate and guarantee feudal services.

Consequently, the later medieval "innovation" of supplementing or replacing feudal cavalry with paid, contracted forces is now recognized as having been in place for a long time before the available documentation allows us to chart its existence in detail. Similarly, in relation to manorialism, it is now acknowledged that the classic forms of servile tenure and seigneurial authority associated with feudalism tended to be concentrated in grain-producing areas, where large-scale enterprises dominated by powerful ecclesiastical institutions and noble families tended to create particular types of peasant dependency; in pastoral zones, and in regions where lordship was fragmented and exercised by the lesser aristocracy, serfdom was a good deal less viable, relevant, or prevalent.

The Influence of European-Style Feudalism on Non-European Societies. Feudalism in the senses in which it has been defined here may be said to have been the predominant form of social organization during much of the

Middle Ages in France, western Germany, parts of Spain and Italy and (through its importation and imposition by the Normans) in England. Historians trained in both the Marxist and the Western liberal traditions have also attempted to identify features of European-style feudalism in non-European societies. As a result, for example, it has been argued that Byzantium and Iran underwent an inevitable and simultaneous transition into a feudal mode during the sixth and seventh centuries CE as a result of the adoption of a system of dependent military tenures by farmer-warriors (known in the case of Byzantium as the "theme" system).

Although this model of development has been disputed, it is still generally accepted that feudal-vassalic institutions developed in the empires created by these powers, as for example in the Balkans under Byzantium and in Armenia and Georgia under Iran. Much has also been written of the similarities between Western feudalism and the Japanese form of military organization developed by the shoguns and their retainers, the samurai, from the late twelfth century CE. It is a mistake to push such comparisons too far: in both Byzantium and Japan, for example, feudal forms of military tenure developed after, and continued to exist alongside, enduring traditions of centralized and bureaucratized civil administration. Here then, rather as in England (a country of "imported feudalism"), feudalism was something essentially managed by states, rather than emerging, as supposedly in continental Europe, as an organic and pragmatic response to the collapse of central authority. Ironically, however, it has recently been argued by the British historian Susan Reynolds that the institutionalized system of dependent tenure that emerged between rulers and nobles in Europe during the twelfth and thirteenth centuries was not of a natural development from earlier, more protean, forms of social and military organization but was, in itself, a fundamentally new structure created by emergent bureaucratized states: in this case, even European feudalism can no longer necessarily be assumed to have been a "natural" stage in social and economic development, or to have had a continuous history during the medieval period.

[*See also* Serfdom.]

BIBLIOGRAPHY

Anderson, Perry. *Passages from Antiquity to Feudalism.* London, 1974.
Bloch, Marc. *Feudal Society.* Translated by L. A. Manyon. London, 1965.
Brown, E. A. R. "The Tyranny of a Construct: Feudalism and Historians of Medieval Europe." *American Historical Review* 79 (1974), 1063–1088.
Brown, R. A. *The Origins of English Feudalism.* London, 1973.
Ganshof, F. L. *Feudalism.* Translated by P. Grierson. London, 1964.
Hicks, Michael. *Bastard Feudalism.* London, 1995.
Hyams, P. R. *Kings, Lords and Peasants in Medieval England.* Oxford, 1980.
Reynolds, Susan. *Fiefs and Vassals: The Medieval Evidence Reinterpreted.* Oxford, 1994.

W. M. ORMROD

Manorial System

Although the manor is often regarded as a fundamental characteristic of feudal systems, it existed before, and survived after, the particular military-political institutions that are regarded as having generated feudalism itself. The manor may be defined as an economic unit under the lordship of a single individual (or institution). In the medieval European experience, the manor was not necessarily conterminous with the nucleated village: townships recognized as cohesive units for the purposes of public administration could often be split into two, three, or more manors. Nor was it coterminous with the basic ecclesiastical administrative and economic unit, the parish, though lords of manors were often responsible for the original foundation (and sometimes the subsequent upkeep) of parish churches. Rather, the existence of a manor was most obviously demonstrated (and tested) by the presence of a manor court: that is, a forum in which the lord's jurisdictional rights over his tenants were expressed through the policing of economic obligations and the dispensing of justice.

The origins of the manor are fraught with definitional, evidential, and historiographical problems, and it is easier to identify than to explain the emergence of manorialism in early medieval Europe. According to many historians, the Germanic tribes that invaded and settled the Roman Empire from the fifth century CE responded to the logistical challenges posed by their conversion from raiders to farmers by developing agrarian enterprises that were staffed, controlled, and managed not by single families but by extended communities. This communal form of agriculture was then subject to organizational change during the Viking, Saracen, and Magyar attacks of the ninth and tenth centuries, when local lords increasingly took advantage of the collapse of centralized political authority to assert lordship over peasants and their agricultural enterprises. Documentary sources indicate that, by the ninth century, the economic unit known as the *villa* (which may, in turn, have had its origins in Roman agricultural organization) had developed into two distinct sections: the "demesne" (*mansus indominicatus*), which was cultivated directly by the lord; and a series of holdings (*mansi*) operated by peasant tenants. The collapse of the Roman agrarian system, with its heavy reliance on slave labor, had produced a new dispensation, whereby those claiming control of land were prepared to dispense with the responsibility of direct cultivation in return for rents, while prospective tenants were prepared to accept terms that involved the rendering of tributes, including labor and/or military services, for their newly acquired lands because they needed the sanction and protection provided by nascent feudal lords.

A further important development occurred between the ninth and the thirteenth centuries, when the *mansi* developed into two distinct types: free and unfree. Some peasant tenants held by forms of free service that required little more than the payment of an annual rent, but others were subjected to more extensive forms of social and economic control that turned them and their descendants into serfs. It is the existence of unfree *mansi*, or servile tenancies, that tend to give the manorial system a particular character, though it should be understood that manors could exist, and could function perfectly well, without serfs.

The emergence of feudal lordship over the manor and its tenants had two consequences. On the one hand, it fragmented fundamental economic autarchy, in the sense that authority over land and its disposal was now exercised at the local level of the manor. In this respect, it is worth contemplating the fact that great landholders, who held many manors, encountered considerable logistical challenges in attempting to manage agricultural enterprises that were unconnected in managerial, as well as merely geographical, terms. On the other hand, manorialism arguably helped to create a high degree of coherence and integration at the local level by involving all those living upon and subject to the manor in the process of cultivation and the maintenance of social order. The significance of manorial systems may therefore be pursued both in agricultural and in jurisdictional terms.

Manorialism and Its Effect on Agriculture. In terms of agricultural enterprise, manorialism provided a means of guaranteeing a ready workforce for the lord's demesne. In some cases, it was possible for lords to maintain significant numbers of workers as landless servants (*famuli* or *ministeriales*). These servants lived in the lord's household or in cottages provided by him and generated a resource of labor especially for the more permanent demands of the local economy, such as the tending of animals. It was also possible to buy labor on a commercial basis, according to need, by making short- or long-term contracts for wages with smallholders and landless cottagers living in the vicinity of the manor (and sometimes under its jurisdiction). This form of labor supply was important in regions where serfdom was insignificant, and became an increasingly frequent and important recourse with the collapse of serfdom in western Europe during the later Middle Ages.

Until the fourteenth century, however, the agrarian economy of much of Europe relied significantly on the ability of lords to mobilize those holding tenancies on the manor in the process of cultivating his demesne. The labor thus extracted was rendered without payment, and was seen as part of the rent or return that the tenant made for the continued possession of his holding. Free tenants tended to provide such labor services only at harvest time, when the whole community of the manor might in effect be called upon to assist in bringing in the year's crops. Although they were said to do such services out of love for their lord (in England they were referred to as "boon works"), the latter in fact sometimes rewarded such service, if only symbolically, by providing a harvest supper. Servile tenants, by contrast, could in theory be obliged to provide "week work" (*corvées*, as they were known in France), that is, a set number of days' labor each week on the demesne, for which no wage or other reward needed to be given. It is important to appreciate that week work was levied on the household, not on heads of population. A peasant family holding a servile tenancy would not necessarily find the cultivation of its own holding jeopardized by the requirement that one of its members serve one or more days of the week on the lord's demesne.

It is also true that manorial custom went to some length to define the content of a day's work in terms of plowing, sowing, weeding, and so on. Once the work was done, the representative of the servile holding was entitled to spend the rest of the day on his own holding. On the other hand, the number of days of week work required by lords inevitably fluctuated and was greatest at precisely those times of year when families holding tenancies might otherwise have expected all hands (literally) to the plow or scythe. It is not surprising, therefore, that resentment, and a certain amount of disruption, was created by the necessity of giving the lord's work priority.

The other particular characteristic of the agricultural organization associated with manorialism is that of the open fields and related systems of crop rotation. Open fields may have predated the development of manorialism, and may be associated with the practices of the Germanic invaders and settlers at the end of the Roman Empire. They represent a high level of communal organization. A single settlement ordered its land into a number of large blocks, with two and, later (from about the tenth or eleventh centuries), three fields for the cultivation of crops and further areas for grazing. The fields were subdivided into long, thin plots or "strips," with the strips set high on land piled up by generations of plowing, separated from each other by ruts, which acted as drainage ditches. (This characteristic corrugated topography of "ridges and furrows," which continued to operate in certain areas until the eighteenth century, can still sometimes be seen in European landscapes.) Each strip was assigned to a particular farmer, whose holdings were therefore scattered across the open fields and distributed in such a way as to reflect either equity or hierarchy in the allocation of the best available plots. Essentially, feudal manorialism stamped itself onto

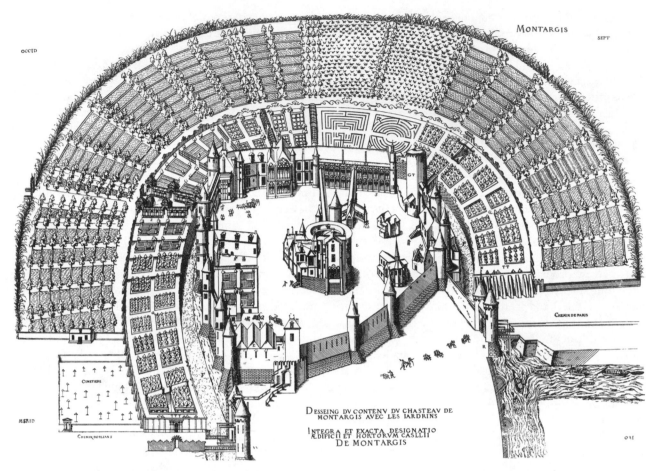

MANOR. Château of Montargis, France. (North Wind Picture Archives)

this open-field system by allowing the lord to appropriate old and newly cultivated land for the demesne and requiring the holders of other strips in the open fields to provide him with rents and labor services.

The advent of lordship did little in itself to alter the system of crop rotation, which was based on the observation that yields are best maintained by prudent exploitation and that a proportion of the cultivated land ought to be allowed to lie fallow in order to enhance its fertility. In northern and eastern Europe, a three-field system tended to dominate. The classic rotation was an autumn-sown crop in one year, followed by a spring-sown crop in the next, followed by a year of fallow. In southern Europe, however, spring-sown grains tended not to be successful, since they had insufficient time to ripen before they were burned off by the hot summer sun; consequently, the tendency here was to adopt a two-field system, in which an autumn-sown crop alternated with a year of fallow. By the thirteenth century, the sustainability of these rotational systems was being threatened. A high level of population encouraged overintensive cultivation and provoked some farmers to give up long-established principles of husbandry and to

cultivate all the available land every year. The results are demonstrable in the extant records of some manors, where more frequent cropping resulted in a gradual decline in annual yields.

The emphasis on the production of cereals and pulses is a reminder that manorialism was best suited to, and was largely confined to, the agrarian sector. In upland regions, where there was little or no cultivation of crops and the local economy depended on pastoralism, there was inevitably much less utility to be derived from the systematic parceling out of land in small units, and with fewer nucleated settlements and a scattering of hamlets and isolated farmsteads, the characteristic forms of manorialism were a good deal slower to develop, if they emerged at all.

Effects of Feudal Lordship on the Manorial System. The imposition of feudal lordship onto the forms of manorialism that had existed and developed, at least since the collapse of the Roman Empire, had a fundamental impact on the forms of jurisdiction exercised over, and within, the manor. In essence, feudalism meant the appropriation by the lord of the manor of a wide range of local customs concerning the regulation of economic and social life, with the result that, in many places, customary law was in effect subsumed into the private, "seigneurial" jurisdiction of the lord. This practice of appropriation was tolerated because the collapse of public and central authority in many parts of Europe during the ninth and tenth centuries made local nobles and churchmen the only effective sources of authority and order.

Furthermore, the restoration of public authority in the form of newly powerful monarchies in certain parts of Europe during the eleventh and twelfth centuries, far from threatening or impinging on seigneurial authority, actually reinforced it. In France and (to a lesser but still significant extent) in England, kings found that the only effective means of guaranteeing the loyalty of aristocratic families and ecclesiastical institutions was to allow them to exercise various forms of jurisdiction that were otherwise regarded as royal prerogatives.

These "immunities," "franchises," or "liberties" usually fell short of the right to dispose of the free property of free men, but they not infrequently included the right to provide a court of first instance for a wide range of civil actions and all but the most serious of criminal offenses. In particular, public law reconciled itself to the new realities of serfdom by acknowledging that the unfree were completely under the jurisdiction of seigneurial law and could not (except in very rare cases) pursue actions either against their lords or against other parties in the king's courts.

The place where the lord's rights of jurisdiction were exercised and tested was the manor court. It was an essential principle of manorialism (and a feature that helps to explain its distinction from other kinds of economic organization based on conditional tenure of land) that those who held of a lord owed him not only rents and services but also "suit of court," that is, attendance at, and subjection to the decision of, his court of the manor. Because the manor court dispensed so many functions deriving from its responsibilities in relation to both customary and public law, powerful lords could sometimes assume that the whole population living within the manor was subject to seigneurial justice. There was a wide variety of practice in terms of the frequency of sessions of the manor court: some might be held every few weeks, others only once a year. Sessions were often held in the open air, though the more ambitious and assertive the lord, the more likelihood that he might provide a room or hall for the conduct of his business. While the obligations of freemen varied, serfs were invariably bound to attend the manor court and could be fined for failure to do so. The manor court was the place of appointment (sometimes by election and/or acclamation) of the lord's agent for the manor, who himself might be of servile status. (The terminology here is vague: "bailiff" is a generic term for such officials, but the

more specific English word for this office is "reeve.") In those manors where the lord claimed the right to dispense justice derived from public law, the court might be the place of judgment upon local infractions of the standard for weights and measures or the quality controls for bread and ale, the infringement of rights of free passage on the highway or by river, and even the declaration of the death penalty for serious offenses, such as theft of goods.

It is in terms of the exercise of customary jurisdiction, however, that the records of these courts reveal most about the economic regulation of the manor. Because it accommodated both the rights of the lord and the custom of the locality, the manor court used the authority of the former to enforce the communal interests associated with the latter. Thus, the manor court was not only the place where the lord asserted and defined his rights to the labor services of unfree tenants, but was also the forum in which the community resolved disputes over the allocation of strips in the open fields, the management of common grazing, or the exploitation of woodland. It is quite wrong, therefore, to consider that the lord's court was merely an instrument of tyranny. On the other hand, the actions of such courts were legitimate only because they were made through the agency of the lord, and they therefore had the tendency of constantly reinforcing his rights.

Thus, for example, the practice known as pannage, whereby peasants were allowed to put their pigs out in the woodland during the autumn to fatten them on nuts and other forage, might be raised in the manor court in terms of a private complaint against a tenant who abused the privilege in some way, and might be resolved in terms of a restatement of that tenant's obligations to his neighbors. In the process, however, *all* those needing grazing for their swine would be reminded that they had the right only at the will of their lord. Similar striking assertions of seigneurial authority are found in the manor court's regulation of behavior and morality. A serf who committed adultery and was thus fined by an ecclesiastical court, or the daughter of a serf who lost her virginity outside marriage, were both considered to have deprived the lord of his economic assets and were thus required to compensate him through money penalties levied in the manor court. It was the manor court that also enforced the lord's monopoly rights by enforcing the charges he made on his tenants for the right to use his mills, ovens, fishponds, and woods.

Long-Term Effects of the Manorial System. The manorial system can thus be seen, from the European example, to represent a combination of communalism (a highly integrated system of land management regulated by local custom) and lordship (the exercise of rights of ownership in parts of the manor and of jurisdiction over all of it). It provided an economic framework that proved remarkably enduring: for example, whereas the direct farming of the demesne largely ceased in western Europe after the Black Death, it continued to be the norm in eastern Europe until the abolition of serfdom in the late eighteenth and nineteenth centuries; and even in western Europe, the characteristic open-field system survived into the same period. It is easy to be dismissive about the economic capacity of manorialism, which could be argued to have perpetuated a barter economy and a protectionist view of production, to have stalled the development of agricultural specialization or diversification and the effective integration of markets, and to have favored communal self-sufficiency over individualism and capitalism. But the manorial system should also be recognized for the fundamental contribution that it made to the longer-term development of entrepreneurialism, commercialization, and the application of science and technology in the agricultural economy.

[*See also* Serfdom.]

BIBLIOGRAPHY

Astill, Grenville, and Annie Grant, eds. *The Countryside of Medieval England*. Oxford, 1988.

Cheyette, Frederick L., ed. *Lordship and Community in Medieval Europe*. Huntingdon, U.K., 1975.

Bennett, H. S. *Life on the English Manor: A Study of Peasant Conditions, 1150–1400*. Cambridge, 1937.

Bloch, Marc. *Feudal Society*. Translated by L. A. Manyon. London, 1965.

Duby, Georges. *Rural Economy and Country Life in the Medieval West*. Translated by C. Postan. London, 1968.

Hyams, Paul R. *Kings, Lords and Peasants in Medieval England*. Oxford, 1980.

Maitland, Frederic William. *Collected Papers*. Cambridge, 1911.

Pounds, N. J. G. *An Economic History of Medieval Europe*. 2d ed. London, 1994.

Postan, M. M. *The Medieval Economy and Society: An Economic History of Britain in the Middle Ages*. Harmondsworth, U.K., 1975.

W. M. ORMROD

Taxation

Feudal taxation has fundamental importance in economic history both in terms of its contribution to the organization of the basic unit of production (the manor) and of its significance to the emergence of public finance in nascent states. Although there is a great diversity of experience in the detail, the relevant economic systems may be said to have observed a core set of principles and practices that are characteristic manifestations of, if not indeed essential to the very definition of, feudalism.

Feudal systems were historically founded on the assumption that those who exercised lordship could, under certain circumstances, extract dues from their tenants and dependants over and above any regular rents that might be charged for the tenure of land. In this sense, the term *taxation* is used here in relation to extraordinary levies occasioned by particular conditions. It is important to remember that servile and free peasant tenants were subject to a whole range of levies associated with particular seasons and functions: for example, the requirement to work on the lord's estates at harvest. In addition, the lord had the right to enforce a series of monopolies (*banalités*) that also generated forms of income for him. He could, for example, impose the requirement that peasants grind their corn or bake their bread in his mills and ovens and pay him a charge for the use of such facilities, or that they render him a certain number of swine every year in return for the right of "pannage" (the grazing of pigs during autumn in the lord's woodland). In western Europe, by the thirteenth century, when many forms of labor service were being commuted to cash rents, it is often unclear whether peasants or lords distinguished coherently between levies that were regular (calendar-driven) and those that were occasional (determined and exacted at the discretion of the lord). What *is* clear, however, is that peasant unrest was often precipitated by attempts to revive old fiscal exactions and to invent new ones.

Within the repertoire of levies available to lords at all levels in the feudal hierarchy, some of the most significant were those associated with the life cycle of the tenant. Perhaps the most easily explicable of these is the succession tax and entry fine: a payment payable to the lord by the heir of a deceased dependent in order to effect the transfer of property and/or rights from one generation to the next. These levies went by a wide variety of names, and the vocabulary often distinguished (though not especially consistently) between the tax payable by peasants (*mainmorte* in French, *heriot* in English) and that payable by free and aristocratic tenants (*rachat* in French, *relief* in English). The form of the payment also inevitably varied, but was often linked symbolically to the nature of the services that were owed from the relevant land. Peasant heriots often took the form of a surrender of the tenant's best beast, while those holding in knight service often rendered a horse bridle or other military accoutrement. In emergent money economies, efforts were made by ambitious lords to translate such dues into cash fines. In England, the attempts of the Angevin rulers of the late twelfth century to extract very high entry fines led the baronial opposition to force a definition (and thus a limitation) of the rate of feudal reliefs in the Magna Carta (1215). In general, however, entry fines were not very sensitive to the real market value of the relevant holding, and were important as much for the way that they upheld the theoretical rights of lords: their residual survival in relation to servile tenancies (for example, in France until the Revolution) was in particular a marker of feudal forms of social control.

Another series of life-cycle taxes arose from the rights claimed by feudal lords to control the heirs to fiefs and holdings under their lordship and to extract payments for

FEUDAL TAXES. The cadastre (tax record) of the Monastery of Monte Luce, 1361, folio 148v–149r. (Archivio di Stato, Perugia, Italy/Alinari/ Regione Umbria/Art Resource, NY)

the assets that such heirs and other offspring represented. In aristocratic feudal societies, it was conventional that, when a tenant died leaving an heir still under age, both the heir and the associated lands were taken into the wardship (custody) of the lord and help until the heir was old enough to enter the property and provide the services due from it. Although there was also a convention that estates in custody ought to be managed benevolently, they were often exploited either by the direct lords or by those to whom those lords decided to sell the right of wardship. Similar practices were pursued in exercising the right to arrange the marriage of such an heir; and the families of prospective marriage partners could be made to pay dearly for the right to choose a wife or husband for minors in wardship. The sums levied by the original lord as compensation for his alienation of such rights are known in the English tradition as "fines": these were not judicial money penalties but levies assessed and imposed at the discretion of the lord. In servile tenancies, certain customary rights were built on similar notions of compensation due to the lord for the alienation of persons over whom he had direct rights. For example, many medieval landlords exercised the right to impose *merchet* (in France, known as *formariage*): the exaction of a fine to permit serfs to marry off their daughters to serfs residing in other manors, to recompense the lord for the loss of the young woman's labor from leaving the manor, and, more important, the loss of labor from generations of her offspring.

If life-cycle taxes can be seen to have applied to free and unfree, high- and low-status tenants, then there was also a particular form of levy, *tallagium* (known as *tallage* in English and *taille* in French), that was confined to, and a characteristic of, servile tenancies. The right to tallage was an appropriation of the sovereign's public authority to extract tribute from his followers. Indeed, in some part of later medieval Europe, kings themselves continued to claim the right to tallage their own demesnes and (as in England) their chartered towns on the grounds that these otherwise privileged sectors ought to compensate the ruler appropriately for the dispensation of his grace. However, the arbitrary and unilateral nature of tallage—imposed from above without consultation from below—made it a mark of servility and one associated particularly with manorial fiscality and the special rights that a lord might claim over his unfree tenants. In practice, the right to tallage one's serfs "at will" was often more theoretical than real: local custom, as well as local politics, tended to turn tallages into annual fixed sums. But there always remained the possibility that the rate and frequency of tallage might be increased, and it was this sense of uncertainty, and the absence of legitimate means of resistance, that generated so much hostility to the charge among peasant communities in medieval Europe.

Another fiscal relic of the appropriation of public power by private lords during the Middle Ages was the aid (*auxilium*), which could be demanded of both unfree and free tenants. Aids, in turn, were of two kinds: "customary" and "gracious." Customary aids were fiscal obligations associated with the circumstances of the lord's family (specifically, the knighting of his eldest son and the marriage of his eldest daughter) and with the enterprise of war (specifically, the undertaking of Crusade). Because the lord was considered to be permitted to demand these levies as of right, the imposition of such taxes did not (at least in theory) require consent. The subsidies associated with the knighting of the eldest son and the marriage of the eldest daughter clearly indicate the survival of a much older system of tribute exaction associated with symbolic (and expensive) moments in the life of the lord. But the inclusion of Crusade from the twelfth century, as one of the circumstances allowing the collection of a customary aid, indicates that new influences—in this case, the concern of the church adequately to resource its project for the recovery of the Holy Land—could serve to extend and reinforce existing seigneurial rights.

It also demonstrates an increasing awareness of the desirability of money over (often inadequate) supplies of manpower. It was during the twelfth century that the characteristic form of service required in military feudalism, knight service during war, also began to be commuted into a money fine, *scutagium* (*scutage* in English; and literally meaning "shield money"). This general tendency to convert services in kind into money payments (evident also in peasant tenures) was further advanced by the expansion of the money economy in the thirteenth century.

Gracious aids differed from customary aids in that they were levies to which a lord had no established right and which therefore had to be represented by him to the potential payers as reasonable, and negotiated with his free tenants in order to seek their formal consent. The most obvious circumstance in which the lord might request a gracious aid was for the making of war. In some traditions, the customary aid for Crusade was enlarged to accommodate war in general. This may be explained partly in terms of the more general application of the ideology of Crusade to local and secular conflicts during the high and later Middle Ages (for example, in Spain), and partly in terms of the absence of significant political agencies that could constrain the extension of the fiscal authority of princes (for example, in Germany). In other cases, however, it was established that lords who wished to collect aids for war needed to obtain consent. In 1297, in opposing what they saw as a war subsidy imposed without proper consultation, a group of English barons commented that such practices had the effect of turning an aid into a tallage, and thus of reducing them and all other liable free men to the status of serfs.

It was this tradition of consent that also facilitated the development of aids that were levied not just on those holding in feudal service of a ruler but (potentially) on all his subjects. From the thirteenth century, political theory and (to a greater or lesser extent) political practice in large parts of Europe stipulated that, in order to impose a gracious aid (whether it was specific to his feudal tenants or extended to his subjects at large), a ruler needed to demonstrate the appropriate circumstance, defined as "urgent necessity" and usually experienced as the need for military defense against imminent invasion. So long as he demonstrated these circumstances and sought some form of consent, there was in fact comparatively little that his subjects could do to challenge his right to the tax (though this did not prevent them from resisting its actual collection). In the late Middle Ages, as forms of taxation previously associated with the extraordinary circumstances of war became more and more regular, some European rulers (for example, in France) were able to obviate the need for consent and to impose general taxes at will—often making them permanent in the process. One of the things that eased the path to this assertion of fiscal authority was the very fact that such taxes tended to be avoided by nobles, either because they enjoyed an explicit exemption or because the nature of assessment and collection tended to underrate the assets of the landed elite. Indeed, nobles often ended up closely involved in this process of extraction by fulfilling the role of tax regulators in their own regions. As private lords found it more difficult, in the adverse economic circumstances that ensued after the Black Death, to extract their own feudal dues from peasants, they therefore began to cooperate with rulers in collecting state taxes, which would in due course often be used to pay the salaries and other benefits of local elites.

[*See also* Serfdom.]

BIBLIOGRAPHY

Bloch, Marc. *Feudal Society*. Translated by L. A. Manyon. London, 1965.

Bois, Guy. *The Crisis of Feudalism: Economy and Society in Eastern Normandy, c. 1300–1550*. Cambridge, 1984.

Bonney, Richard, ed. *Economic Systems and State Finance*. Oxford, 1995.

Brown, E. A. R. *Customary Aids and Royal Finance in Capetian France*. Cambridge, Mass., 1992.

Duby, Georges. *Rural Economy and Country Life in the Medieval West*. Translated by C. Postan. London, 1968.

Postan, M. M. *The Medieval Economy and Society: An Economic History of Britain in the Middle Ages*. Harmondsworth, U.K., 1975.

Pounds, N. J. G. *An Economic History of Medieval Europe*. 2d ed. London, 1994.

W. M. ORMROD

FIBER CROPS. Man has long used fibers extracted from the stems and leaves of plants to make cloth, rope, and other goods. Some of the oldest surviving textiles are pieces of linen from ancient Egyptian tombs. While hemp and, to a lesser extent, flax have been widely used since antiquity, many of the other so-called hard fibers were confined to their native areas until they entered global commerce in the nineteenth century. This was true of jute in India, ramie in China, abacá (or Manila hemp) in the Philippines, and sisal (or henequen) in the Yucatán. Until surpassed by jute in the late nineteenth century, flax and hemp were the most important of these fibers.

The hard fibers have certain common characteristics. Extracting the fiber is a major step in the production process. Flax, for example, must be soaked and beaten to break up the surrounding plant matter, which must then be combed out. These preparatory processes were usually carried out in the countryside by farmers or rural craftsmen. Even when mechanical methods were slowly introduced in the nineteenth and twentieth centuries, flax and other hard fibers remained costly to prepare for spinning. The hard fibers are not very elastic; hence they tend to break easily. Fine yarn and cloth could be made only with great care, and mechanization of spinning and weaving proved difficult and costly, except for the coarsest products. Although the Chinese created some remarkable machines to spin hemp in the fourteenth century, they proved to be a technological dead end, perhaps because they could produce only coarse yarns.

From antiquity to the late eighteenth century, flax and hemp were widely cultivated in Europe and North Africa, primarily for local production of basic textiles. Yet some areas were noted for production of these fibers. From antiquity, Egypt was a major producer of linens and in the Middle Ages exported flax to North Africa and Italy. Constantinople drew on western Greece, as well as Egypt, for its flax supplies. From the late Middle Ages, Flanders and northwestern France became the most celebrated flax-growing area in northern Europe, and they remain major centers for high-quality flax production. Poland, and from the eighteenth century, Russia, became major suppliers of lower-quality flax and hemp.

During the first half of the nineteenth century, the advent of cheap cotton goods undermined local production of linen and hempen cloth and with it cultivation of flax and hemp in the eastern United States and in many parts of Europe. From mid-century, the rising agricultural wages in western Europe also discouraged farmers from planting these labor-intensive crops. Production of flax and hemp for fiber became overwhelmingly concentrated in the northern part of European Russia, so that by the early twentieth century, this area accounted for nearly 90 percent of world output. In western Europe, only production of high-quality flax persisted in northern France, Belgium, and the southern Netherlands. A similar concentration of high-quality hemp production survived in Italy around Bologna.

From the late eighteenth century, burgeoning industrial demand led to the development of global markets in what had hitherto been local crops in parts of America and Asia. From the 1790s the British East India Company tried to encourage use in England of Sunni hemp and jute. Jute proved to be the more successful. By the 1860s, Dundee producers of cloth for sacks and packing were using more jute than flax or hemp. During the late nineteenth century, abacá from the Philippines was increasingly substituted for European hemp in rope production, and sisal from Mexico was the dominant raw material for making binder twine.

During the twentieth century, there was little growth in the use of hard fibers. Flax cultivation probably reached its peak near 1914. World War I and the civil war in Russia totally disrupted flax supplies, and linen gave way increasingly to easier-to-maintain fibers. Flax cultivation and use remained important only in Eastern Europe and declined sharply from the early 1990s. Producers of hemp, abacá, sisal, and jute suffered from the stagnation of international commerce between the wars. The markets for these fibers also became overcrowded as their cultivation spread from traditional centers to other countries in Africa, Asia, and South America. After World War II, paper and plastic increasingly replaced natural fibers in the manufacture of packaging and cordage, which led to severe falls in the cultivation of hemp and sisal and almost no growth in abacá and jute production.

BIBLIOGRAPHY

Dewilde, Bert. *Flax in Flanders throughout the Centuries*. Tielt, Belgium, 1987. Well-illustrated discussion of the techniques of cultivation and processing.

Goswami, Omkar. *Industry, Trade, and Peasant Society: The Jute Economy of Eastern India, 1900–1947*. Delhi, 1991. A good introduction to the economic and social context of jute cultivation.

Owen, Norman G. *Prosperity without Progress: Manila Hemp and Material Life in the Philippines*. Berkeley, 1984. One of the few books on this industry.

Stewart, Gordon T. *Jute and Empire: The Calcutta Jute Wallahs and the Landscape of Empire*. Manchester, 1998. The best recent work on jute manufacture in India and Scotland.

Warden, A. J. *The Linen Trade, Ancient and Modern*. London, 1864; reprinted 1967. An indispensable compendium of information on flax and jute.

Wells, Allen. *Yucatán's Gilded Age: Haciendas, Henequen, and International Harvester, 1860–1915*. Albuquerque, 1985.

PETER M. SOLAR

FILM INDUSTRY. Three functions define the film industry in any country: production, presentation, and distribution. With stars, stories, and special effects, production creates the first copy of a film on celluloid, which then can be recopied. Despite its great publicity, production is the riskiest function because of the inability of entrepreneurs to predict the public's tastes. Presentation—too often misleadingly referred to simply as theatrical exhibition—is the means whereby the public sees movies. Movie viewing was a purely theatrical experience until the arrival of television. By the close of the twentieth century, advertising-supported broadcast TV and pay-TV, plus home video, offered the dominant means of film presentation.

Distribution is invisible to the average movie fan, but is the basis of any powerful film industry. In some nations (i.e., France, Germany, Japan, and India), film industries have used regional distribution to reap economies of scale; but the U.S. film industry—Hollywood—has long dominated world cinema because, since the 1920s, it has reaped the greatest economies of scale. Worldwide distribution has long been the key to Hollywood's power, as no other national film industry has been as far-reaching as Hollywood. It pioneered "global media" and thus achieved dominance, both when films were shown primarily in theaters and, since the 1950s, from streams of income from TV.

Beginnings of the Modern Film Industry. The movies as a new technological form were invented during the latter half of the nineteenth century, with innovations added as the twentieth century commenced; but it was only during the late 1910s and early 1920s that a small number of companies based in Southern California began to dominate the world film industry. During the 1910s, the successful companies, led by Famous Players-Lasky (later renamed Paramount), developed a system for manufacturing popular, feature-length films. Through the principles of classic narrative production featuring notable stars, Hollywood taught the world how to make motion pictures popular and profitable in a global marketplace. Many contributed to the development of Hollywood, but Paramount's Adolph Zukor led the way.

Zukor took the star system and classic story telling and, in a factorylike system, produced films that Paramount could sell in diverse cultures throughout the world. Simultaneously, Zukor revolutionized the motion picture industry by building a set of Paramount distribution outlets, first across the United States and then throughout the

BOLLYWOOD. Hoardings with film posters, Bombay (Mumbai), 2000. The Indian film industry produces more than 700 films a year; more than 300 films are produced in Bollywood. (© Catherine Karnow/Woodfin Camp and Associates, New York)

world. Zukor reasoned that once a film was made, the majority of its cost had been accumulated. If he led the way with worldwide distribution, expanding the market territory to include greater and greater portions of the world, additional revenues would overwhelm any extra costs. This is a simple application of economies of scale. With other national cinemas increasingly restricted to their own countries, the Hollywood motion picture industry took on the world as its proper marketplace.

Zukor took advantage of disruptions in world trade caused by World War I to surpass European rivals. The formerly strong French film industry was particularly hard-hit; not only was the economy in shambles, but for a time all motion picture theaters were shut down. Zukor's other main rival, the German film industry, also ceased as materials and people were devoted to the war effort. Simultaneously, Paramount set up distribution offices in Asia, Africa,

Canada, Central and South America—indeed throughout the world.

By the end of the war, Hollywood, led by Paramount, settled into a comfortable world economic hegemony. Only the Soviet Union, Germany, and Japan were even able to keep the Hollywood companies at bay. The Hollywood motion picture industry formed a trade association, the Motion Picture Producers and Distributors Association of America, and hired Will H. Hays to facilitate conditions of open trade so that Hollywood could continue to dominate. By 1925, in Great Britain, Canada, and Australia, Hollywood controlled some 85 percent of screen time, and in France, Poland, Hungary, Yugoslavia, and Rumania about two-thirds. The situation was the same in South America, the Caribbean, and Central America. Filmmakers in other nations simply struggled to take a small share from Hollywood, by some sort of "cultural bettering" of the classic narrative tales emerging from the Hollywood studios.

Technological Change. The coming of sound during the late 1920s seemed to promise change in the world's film industries. Would not non-English-speaking nations be able finally to establish important film studios? Would Hollywood's market share decline? Remarkably, Hollywood remained dominant. Through the remaining technological changes in the film industry Hollywood rarely lost market share, and more often than not increased its comparative advantage, despite efforts by government after government to subsidize and prop up native film industries.

What the coming of sound—and later technological changes—accomplished was to determine the small number of Hollywood companies that defined Hollywood. Since Warner Bros. Pictures, Inc., and the Fox Film Corporation introduced sound to films, no other major studios have emerged to define Hollywood as they did. What other technological change did was to penalize those companies that could not adjust; and, like MGM with broadcast television and United Artists (UA) with pay-TV and home video such companies simply dropped from the ranks of Hollywood's elite.

In 1925, Warner Bros. sought a way to grow and to challenge Paramount. Starting in 1926, Warner Bros. began to make short subjects with sound, and then feature-length talkies. Although Al Jolson's *The Jazz Singer*, released in October 1927, is recognized as the first feature-length talkie, it was Jolson's *The Singing Fool* (1929) that set a box-office record that stood until toppled a decade later by *Gone with the Wind*.

William Fox did not believe there existed a future for feature-length talkies, but the veteran showman reasoned that the public might prefer newsreels with sound. The premiere of Fox Movietone News came on 30 April 1927; a month later, sound footage of the takeoff of the transat-lantic flight of Charles Lindbergh caused a sensation. By 1930, Fox had joined Hollywood's leading companies.

The other major movie companies, led by Paramount, did not ignore the innovative activities of Warner Bros. and Fox. After months of haggling over terms, early in May 1928 Paramount began to innovate with talkies. Thereafter, widespread adoption of motion pictures with sound—their diffusion—took place within a remarkably brief time span. The major Hollywood companies had too much at stake to procrastinate. The movie going public's infatuation with talkies set off the greatest rush to the box office in the history of U.S. movies. At its peak, every person over the age of six in the United States went to the movies on average once a week (Gomery, 1986). Profits for the major Hollywood companies soared. Film industries outside the United States took longer to catch up, and lost more and more ground to Hollywood's domination.

Hollywood's Golden Age. Remarkably, dubbed films from Hollywood proved the world's most popular throughout the 1930s and 1940s. As an international film industry leader, Hollywood had four key corporations: Paramount Pictures, Loew's (parent company for the better-known MGM), Fox Film (later Twentieth Century Fox), and Warner Bros.

Paramount Pictures was the most profitable and powerful Hollywood company. Its international distribution arm resembled a second "Department of State" for the United States, and its chain of more than one thousand theaters further boosted corporate might. A former Chicago theater man, Barney Balaban used his accounting training to set up a Hollywood operation as "modern" as any business in any industry. Hiring as many lawyers and MBAs as movie stars, he maintained tight cost controls, requiring management approval for every expenditure from a wig for Bing Crosby to setting up a separate distribution office in New Zealand. Balaban's conservative corporate management strategies worked, and in 1946 Paramount earned a record $40 million profit, a figure that would stand unmatched for two decades.

Metro-Goldwyn-Mayer ranked right behind Paramount. From a purely business perspective, MGM functioned as a successful unit within the larger enterprise of Loew's, Inc. A fully integrated movie company, Loew's owned a movie studio, a network for international distribution, and a highly profitable theater chain. Loew's management, led by Nicholas M. Schenck, ran the company as if it were simply a chain of movie houses supplied with MGM's films. In Culver City, California, a suburb of Los Angeles, MGM operated a classic "movie factory" with twenty-seven sound stages on 168 acres.

Twentieth Century Fox ranked behind Paramount and MGM. The Great Depression did not prove kind to the fortunes of William Fox, and his successors merged Fox Film with Twentieth Century Pictures in 1935. The new management team of Joseph M. Schenck and Darryl F. Zanuck quickly remade Twentieth Century Fox into a Hollywood powerhouse. Studio boss Zanuck was a more public figure than CEO Schenck, but Schenck kept the international hegemonic apparatus humming.

Warner Bros. represented the sole old-fashioned, family-run operation among the major movie studios, with oldest brother Harry as president, middle brother Abe supervising distribution, and youngest brother Jack heading the studio in Burbank, California. The Warners pioneered in a number of film genres, notably the gangster film, and aped Paramount's innovative business methods; but in the 1930s and 1940s they never matched Barney Balaban's operation in terms of profits and power.

Postwar Changes. The Golden Age saw Hollywood flourish, but significant changes after World War II—suburbanization in the United States, the forced sale of theaters, and the introduction of television—shook the film industry to its roots. Throughout the 1950s, these changes seemed to herald the end of Hollywood domination; however, although non-U.S. film industries did thrive at times, new Hollywood business leaders adapted to change and reinvented the studio system. By 1960, the Hollywood major companies had survived and prospered, except for MGM and UA.

Around the world, only in the rare nation did Hollywood not capture more than half the film business. At considerable expense, the Hollywood major studios maintained offices around the globe, with their representatives in constant contact with the heads of the dominant theater chains, and later pay-TV outlets as well as home video retailers. Hollywood's regular production of hit films provided a strong incentive for foreign theater, pay-TV, and home video companies to consistently deal with the six major companies rather than gamble on a true independent. This effort has led, in recent years, to joint deals with foreign companies to build theaters in Britain, Australia, Germany, Spain, and France, and to run cable TV networks all over the world. Through all the new technologies of presentation, the Hollywood studios placed themselves at the center of profit-maximizing strategies, to the chagrin of policy makers seeking to protect native-culture industries.

As the major Hollywood companies maintained their economic power and influence, filmmakers outside the United States long struggled to find their place in their national cinemas, often requiring government assistance. Only sporadically have large nation-states—France, Italy, Japan, and India, in particular—been able to mount a studio system as an alternative and a serious rival to Hollywood even in their own countries, let alone elsewhere.

After the advent of blockbuster films, it became harder for foreign governments to subsidize a native cinema industry, most choosing to focus on television instead. However, Germany and Australia, for example, for a while in the 1980s created enough different types of popular productions for a long-enough time to be discovered as the latest "new wave." Japan had long had a studio system, but the coming of television and the takeover of Hollywood studios by Sony, and temporarily, Matsushita, ended the importance of that native industry. In another example, India was still able to maintain native popular cinema, complete with a star system and defined genres like those of Hollywood; but its films were intended for domestic consumption, with minimal export possibilities. Community viewing in Indian cities and poor areas alike continued to flourish.

The New Hollywood. Warner Bros. began its transition into Time Warner when, in July 1956, founding brothers Harry and Abe Warner sold their shares to a syndicate headed by Boston banker Serge Semenenko and New York investment banker Charles Allen. The new owners cut the company's ties to the past, and quickly embraced television production, with pioneering series including 77 *Sunset Strip* and *Maverick*. But during the remainder of the 1950s and into the 1960s, the company struggled, and so in July 1969 sold out to Steven J. Ross's Kinney National Services, Inc., a New York conglomerate engaged in parking lots, car rentals, and funeral homes. Ross and chief assistant Gerald Levin reinvented Warner, principally by pioneering Home Box Office (HBO) as a new revenue stream, with viewers around the world. In 1989, Ross merged Warner with Time, and the modern Time Warner corporate colossus was born.

Paramount Pictures slowly adapted to the new film business as Barney Balaban continued to run "his" company as he had in the salad days of the 1930s and 1940s. Profits fell, and during the fall of 1966 a giant conglomerate, Charles Bluhdorn's Gulf & Western Industries, bought Paramount. Bluhdorn hired former press agent Martin Davis to run his latest acquisition, and under studio boss Barry Diller the "new" Paramount prospered so much that, in 1989, Gulf & Western became simply Paramount Communications. Four years later, Sumner Redstone's National Amusements acquired Paramount and enveloped it in Viacom, Inc.

Twentieth Century Fox began its transition with the mid-1950s resignations of long-time CEO Joseph Schenck and studio boss Darryl F. Zanuck. The company did well as it pioneered renting recent hit features to the TV networks for prime-time showings, commencing with NBC's *Saturday Night at the Movies* in 1963. Thereafter, the company struggled until its initial blockbuster, *Star Wars* (1977), produced so much profit that less than a decade later Australian billionaire Rupert Murdoch's News Corporation acquired Twentieth Century Fox.

Columbia Pictures had been a small player during Hollywood's Golden Age, led by brothers Harry and Jack Cohn, who worked on Hollywood's margins until each died in the mid-1950s. Their former assistants, Abe Schneider and Leo Jaffe, did far better than the Cohns as they produced both hit feature films and hit television series. However, the 1970s were not kind to Columbia; the studio lost $30 million in 1971, and cost cutting became the order of the day. In 1972, Columbia sold its studio lot and moved in to share operations at Warner's Burbank studio. Less than a decade later, in 1980, Columbia sold out to Coca-Cola, but the soft drink giant did not adapt to Hollywood's home video revolution. In the early 1990s, Coke sold the company to Japan's electronics giant Sony.

Although these companies did adapt, MGM and United Artists did not. By the 1990s, they were functioning at the edge of the Hollywood system. In contrast, the greatest success story of late-twentieth-century Hollywood proved to be one of the smallest studios of the 1930s and 1940s. Former agent Lew Wasserman transformed the Universal studio over several decades, redefining the film industry as much as Adolph Zukor had done a generation earlier. Beginning in 1962, Wasserman showed the U.S. film industry how to use a flexible system of production, how to exploit television, and how to increase its market share in nation after nation around the world.

Numerous achievements rank Wasserman as the leading executive of his age. First, Wasserman initiated "independent" production, whereby others, principally agents, developed and produced films for clients including stars such as James Stewart and directors such as Alfred Hitchcock. Wasserman then "green-lighted" those he reasoned Universal's distribution arm could best sell around the world. In the process the studio as "film factory" disappeared, and Universal accumulated a library of film titles, to sell and resell to broadcast TV and pay-TV, and, in the 1980s and beyond, as home videos.

Second, Wasserman pioneered movies made for television premiers. With TV movies, Universal became the largest supplier of network-broadcast television programming, reaching a crest in 1977 by providing *Roots*, the most popular TV movie of its era.

Wasserman also pioneered the blockbuster motion picture, beginning with *Jaws* (1975). Universal's record-setting *E.T.: The Extraterrestrial* (1982) generated gross revenues measured in the billions of dollars, with the movie sold in a variety of forms. He coupled mass, saturation advertising on television with simultaneous bookings in cineplexes across the United States, and later in all developed countries of the world. Advertising on television became the key to turning a feature film into a blockbuster, enabling the studio distributor to reap millions and millions of dollars from "ancillary rights," such as sales of toys, alliances with fast-food chains, and in all manner of deals converting a blockbuster feature film into a billion-dollar payoff when successful. When Lew Wasserman retired in 1990, he sold his company to Japanese electronics giant Matsushita, which five years later sold it to Seagrams, Inc.

Another great Wasserman influence was to inspire the Disney family to hire Michael Eisner and ask him to make the Walt Disney Company into a company like Universal. Starting in 1984, Eisner did just that, and Disney prospered. Eisner added new "brand names" such as Touchstone, Miramax, and Hollywood Pictures, reinvested in feature-length animated blockbusters, and synergized the company's products in a manner far surpassing what Wasserman had done.

Merger Mania and New Venues for Presentation. Lew Wasserman and Michael Eisner pioneered in the new Hollywood film industry. In doing so, they set off a merger mania in which, during the 1980s and 1990s, new owners paid billions of dollars for the right to own one of the Hollywood studios, and to infuse it their with own version of corporate energy. These mergers included the Rupert Murdoch 1985 acquisition of Twentieth Century Fox and, in the 1990s, the Sony of Japan takeover of Columbia, the Seagrams of Canada acquisition of Universal, Viacom's merger with Paramount, and Time's joining Warner.

With all this ownership change, the function of Hollywood as film industry around the world actually changed little. Year in and year out, the major studios controlled between 80 and 90 percent of the expanding U.S. movie business, and a bit less than that in the rest of the world. Every few years a couple of bold pretenders—during the 1980s Orion and New World and in the 1990s Dreamworks, SKG—emerged to challenge the leaders, but none survived in the long run. As the twentieth century ended, Dreamworks was still trying to defy this pattern; but with its distribution handled by Warners, and its long-promised new studio headquarters never built, Dreamworks, SKG remained an experiment in progress—despite its fabled owners, including Steven Spielberg.

The major studios worked through their trade association, the Motion Picture Association of America, to maintain their world distribution hegemony. Jack Valenti, head of the MPAA throughout the final third of the twentieth century and into the twenty-first century, did his job well.

To maximize revenues from all venues, the major studios have long worked together to enforce a system of classic price discrimination in presentation. A generation ago the process was simple: features opened with big premieres and publicity; then they played off from first-run to second-run to third-run, so on down the line; pay-TV and home video added to the windows of revenue that price discrimination opened. By 1990, Hollywood released films in the following presentation order: theaters, home video, pay-per-view, pay cable, and, finally, broadcast and basic cable television. Each window was an exclusive one. A new window opened only when all value of the previous window had been captured. Customers knew that if they waited, the cost they paid at the new window would be lower than that at the prior one. Home video also allowed customers to view films whenever they desired. Anyone who waited long enough could purchase a blank tape and copy a film from free, over-the-air, broadcast television. It is no wonder that, by the turn of the twenty-first century, although theatrical premieres received the most publicity, most of the moneys paid for film viewing came from home video purchases or rentals.

Although broadcast TV channels had been showing old films since the mid-1950s, by the early 1980s it was Time Warner's HBO that revolutionized the world film business as people paid a monthly fee to see uncut, full-length, non censored versions of feature films that had completed their theatrical runs. Viewers finally had an alternative; they could subscribe to HBO and see uncut, uncensored, uninterrupted films outside a movie house. Yet the demand for pay-TV would crest and stabilize in 1990, as home video grew steadily more important.

HBO began as a microwave service in 1972; but not until 1975, when it went to satellite, hence world, distribution, did HBO spark interest in cable television. In one of the most productive investments in television history, Time Inc. gambled $7.5 million on a five-year lease to put HBO on RCA's satellite, Satcom I, even before the satellite service had been launched. HBO commenced satellite national distribution on 30 September 1975, and from a base of 300,0000 subscribers moved, within five years, to six million. With subscribers given uncut, uninterrupted movies a few months after they had disappeared from theaters, HBO's growth during the late 1970s and into the early 1980s proved nothing less than spectacular. Via satellite, movie fans around the world could see HBO presentations.

The most important transformation in movie viewing during the late-twentieth century was caused by the video cassette recorder (VCR). Again the consistent financial winners were the Hollywood studios, as the after-market revenue stream from VCR use ranked as their largest single source of revenue. The history of the home video industry offers a prime example of technological innovation. In little more than a decade after the 1976 introduction of the Betamax and the VHS alternative, rentals and sales of movies on tape surpassed the theatrical box-office proceeds. Home video combined the best of the box-office approach with the convenience of television watching at home. Unlike advertising-based broadcast and cable television, in which the presentation of films is geared to the desires of advertisers, home video serves the desires of the individual viewers. Home video also proved superior to pay-TV because the customer could choose when to play the tape.

None of these presentation innovations diminished Hollywood's power. By the turn of the twenty-first century, the major Hollywood studios had discovered how to dominate home video. Revenues soared, as did profits. People around the world seemed to prefer simply going to the local video store and renting a film. The coming of home video added an additional window (in industry terms), and with skillful adjusting of the windows and time between them, the major Hollywood companies employed a skilled use of admission-price discrimination to extract optimal amounts of moneys from the fan base.

Nothing threatened to change the Hollywood film industry's power as the twenty-first century dawned. As technology had not done so in the past, it seemed unlikely that it might someday. Numerous governmental policies had been tried, but in the end non-Hollywood (i.e., non-U.S.) industries—often subsidized by governments—still struggled to fit into market segments that Hollywood simply did not want. The economic history of the world's film industry remains a Hollywood story, possibly its greatest production.

BIBLIOGRAPHY

Compaine, Benjamin, and Douglas Gomery. *Who Owns the Media?* Hillsdale, N.J., 2000.

Gomery, Douglas. *The Hollywood Studio System*. New York, 1986.

Gomery, Douglas. *Shared Pleasures*. Madison, Wis., 1992.

Guback, Thomas. *The International Film Industry*. Bloomington, Ind., 1969.

Lardner, James. *Fast Forward: Hollywood, the Japanese, and the Onslaught of the VCR*. New York, 1987.

Morin, Albert, ed. *Film Policy: International, National, and Regional Perspectives*. London, 1996.

Moser, James D., ed. *International Television and Video Almanac*. New York, annually.

Neale, Steve, and Murray Smith, eds. *Contemporary Hollywood Cinema*. London, 1998.

DOUGLAS GOMERY

FINANCIAL PANICS AND CRASHES. The forces of supply and demand usually do a credible job moderating excesses in asset prices. However, from time to time, and for a variety of reasons, an asset type will generate a fever of unsustainable interest, driving its price to excessive levels; or pessimistic expectations may drive prices well below their market fundamentals. A boom, or surging growth, in an asset or in an entire economy may be well underway before it is generally recognized. If the boom concentrates in a particular asset type, it can produce an investment bubble, or an unsustainable appreciation in value. A bust, or a crash—or rapid decline in value—may soon occur. A panic, or a period of irrational fear, sometimes follows a crash. Busts or crashes can be very dramatic, closely watched, and inspire terror and awe. Unless there is a lender of last resort to provide liquidity and restore confidence, panics may be followed by economic depressions.

Panics and crashes are part of recurring economic cycles that mark the course of both securities markets and the economies that undergird them. No panic or crash ever looks exactly like another one, yet most seem to share some similar attributes. Panics and crashes have occurred many times and in many places throughout recorded economic history. While they have not occurred with every economic cycle, they have been triggered, oftentimes by financial excesses and economic shocks. It is important to remember that accurate and reliable knowledge about bubbles, crashes, and panics is possible only in retrospect.

To understand the effects that panics and crashes can have on economies, one needs to consider psychological, as well as economic, factors that influence individual and group behavior. Confidence, once shaken, can be difficult to restore.

Exogenous shocks can inflict disproportionate damage on an economy when they affect expectations and induce investors and consumers to adopt more cautious behavior. Such a pessimistic outlook can become self-fulfilling and drive the economy to a different equilibrium. While in the very long run asset prices may be constrained by market fundamentals, deviations from these fundamentals can be prolonged. In the wake of certain shocks, even highly advanced economies have sometimes stumbled badly.

Nations throughout history have faced their own panics and crashes. Most, until our modern, globally interconnected era, have been localized phenomena. More recently, a crash, and its possible ensuing panic have had the potential to affect economies around the world.

Early Asset Price Bubbles. The market for tulip bulbs in early-seventeenth-century Holland has ever since then held the imagination of investors and moralists, and remains a fitting place to begin this discussion of asset price bubbles. The importance of the tulip mania lies not in its macroeconomic impact, for it was minor and concentrated largely to the environs of the cities of Haarlem and Amsterdam, but rather to the unusual character of the asset (tulip bulbs) and the trading techniques (informal futures trading) that undergirded the increase of prices. The tulip bulb is incapable of rapid multiplication, and its seventeenth-century popularity as an exotic and beautiful flower caused demand to far outstrip supply, raising bulb prices. Added to this was the discovery that some bulbs produced petals of contrasting colors—flamed or striped tulips—rather than solid colors. Such bulbs were infected with a mosaic virus, but this was not known at the time. These unusual bulbs were highly prized, and the hope that they would produce similarly infected secondary growths generated a speculative interest. A futures market emerged in planted bulbs, which were delivered after they flowered in the spring.

In the winter of 1636–1637, this market, until then mainly confined to growers and connoisseurs, spread broadly to novices engaging in futures trading in taverns. The rare flamed bulbs traded for hundreds, even thousands of guilders each, and even ordinary bulbs rose steeply in price. Then, for reasons that remain obscure, the market collapsed in February 1637. The futures contracts were legally unenforceable, and town officials declined to intervene on behalf of the trade. Moralizing pamphlets ridiculing this greed-fueled mania soon appeared; and two centuries later, Charles Mackay offered a strongly embellished account in his *Extraordinary Popular Delusions and the Madness of Crowds* of 1841. Ever since, the tulip mania has been a staple of business journalism.

If the tulip mania was the first commodity bubble based on futures trading, the first international financial panic is generally considered to be the simultaneous South Sea (British) and Mississippi (France) Bubbles of 1720. In both Great Britain and France, the long wars preceding 1713 left a legacy of public debt and monetary weakness. While the details varied greatly (and John Law's project in France had many intriguing dimensions), both countries established joint-stock companies whose ostensible commercial activities were secondary to their financial functions. The companies took state debt in payment for company shares (debt-for-equity swaps) and encouraged this process by artificially supporting the share prices. The governments' stakes in the success of these companies was great and was reinforced in Great Britain by the liberal distribution of options and bribes to members of Parliament. In the summer of 1720, share prices of the South Sea Company reached £1,000 as speculators crowded the coffeehouses of London and Paris—and Amsterdam, Hamburg, and Geneva—to exchange rumors and trade shares. Later that year, investor confidence in Law's enterprises, which now controlled all government debt, collapsed, leading to financial panic and Law's flight from the country. The panic spread to every financial center, where all manner of joint-stock enterprises had been established in the hope of benefiting from the craze in shares. It also dragged down the South Sea Company, where it appears that the rumor of insider trading—company directors selling their own shares while still offering new shares to the public—ignited panic selling. The British government's stake in the company quickly led it to promulgate the Bubble Act. The initial motivation of forbidding the formation of new joint-stock companies except by explicit parliamentary legislation was to suppress competition in the hope of shoring up the existing South Sea Company, the Bank of England, and the British East India Company, all critical to the state's fiscal well-being. Until its repeal in 1854, the Bubble Act's lasting impact was to restrict the formation of new joint-stock companies.

THE GREAT FINANCIAL PANIC. Closing the door of the New York Stock Exchange, 20 September 1873. Illustration from *Frank Leslie's Illustrated Newspaper*, 4 October 1873, vol. 37, no. 940, p. 66. (Prints and Photographs Division, Library of Congress)

Panic of 1825. If the bubbles of 1720 had a pan-European character, England's stock market crash and banking panic of 1825 was perhaps the first crisis with an intercontinental reach, involving "emerging markets."

With the end of the Napoleonic Wars in 1815, the Bank of England began the painful, postwar work of deflating a nation's economy after years of easy money to fight Napoleon. By 1821, a period of rapid expansion commenced, leading to booms in both investment and exports. Feeding the boom in exports were newly opened markets in Latin America. At the same time, in England and the European continent, projects involving gas lighting, railroads, and canals sopped up huge stores of investment funds. Financing these activities was done through the sale of stock, gold and silver from real (and fraudulent) mines in Latin America, and from government debt issued by both European and Latin American nations. The easy money stoked an enormous stock market boom and economic expansion that bid up prices of real and imaginary

assets everywhere from Great Britain to the fictitious South American Republic of Poyais. Real firms fought for available funding and found it difficult to obtain except at premium rates. Banks infected with the euphoria appeared more eager to make risky loans to secure "a piece of the action" than to finance long-established firms.

In April 1825, when the end of the bubble came, the stock collapse triggered the failure of many enterprises, as well as a number of smaller country banks that had become active lenders during the mania. The banking collapse then spread to some large London banks, and full-fledged panic arose. The Bank of England staunched further deterioration at home only after lowering its discount rate and by becoming one of financial history's earliest "lenders of last resort." Also, it got France to suspend gold convertibility on English notes. Still, a serious recession swept Great Britain in 1826, which then spread to Europe and Latin America, prompting general defaults on some sovereign debt.

Blame for the crisis was laid upon the many small banks that participated in financing the boom, as well as on the Latin American issuers of sovereign debt and mining stocks. But the real culprit was likely the Bank of England, without whose expansionary policies the boom would not have occurred, nor without whose monetary tightenings and belated actions as a lender of last resort the bubble might not have ended as badly as it did.

Panic of 1837. The underlying cause of the Panic of 1837 was a speculative mania in land in the United States. But several other circumstances contributed to the resulting large debts incurred by the public sector to finance an early overexpansion of canals and railroads, crop failures in both 1835 and 1837, and an excess of imports over exports, causing a serious trade imbalance that was made worse by the outflow of "specie," gold and silver. England stopped exporting capital to the United States in late 1836, demanding payment in hard currency for new exports and sharply curtailing its demand for American cotton. These actions pinched credit availability and caused many prices to collapse in America.

With the termination of the Second Bank of the United States, funding for many ill-guided speculations became available through the state and "wildcat" banks that grew quickly in the 1830s. Land—and borrowing for land purchases—was at the top of this speculative frenzy, affecting everyone from investors to small farmers. But speculation continued in private land nationwide, from Maine to Michigan. By the time Andrew Jackson (1767–1845) left office in the spring of 1837, his protégé and successor, Martin Van Buren (1782–1862), inherited a severely strained economy. That strain exacerbated tensions and rivalries between sections of America right up to the Civil War.

Panic of 1847. Panics can contribute to larger social and political revolution, as did the Panic of 1847. Arising in part from crop failures in grains and potatoes as far back as 1845, the Panic of 1847 laid siege to Europe, fueling political revolution that touched almost every nation. Agriculture dominated the economies of much of the developed world at the time. Yet industrialization was growing in importance, and along with it, a growing need for credit and investment.

The dawn of industrialization created a search for capital by a few, and poverty for masses of artisans and craftspeople. Capital formation, focused on stocks and bonds, produced many exciting but ill-advised investments. At first, only the wealthy and entrepreneurial were affected by the misallocation of capital, but soon the middle classes were affected as well. Railroad construction, employing public funds, and the development of its supplier iron industry created an infatuation with railway and mining stocks, captivating banks and individuals alike. The ill effects of these investments destroyed public and private confidence and produced a crisis in 1847, exposing the inadequacies of early capital formation to the needs of a new industrial economy. Bankruptcies struck public companies and banks. Emigration, civil unrest, and credit crises arose across Europe, overwhelming the incipient industrial sector, burdened already with investments and indebtedness. Millions could not find work. Public works projects, initiated to employ the jobless, halted as the value of industrial production shrank by half.

The crisis lessened toward the end of 1847, when wheat prices fell toward normal levels. Signs of recovery surfaced in commerce and industry, but the crisis had raised question of government legitimacy that played a part in setting the stage for a series of revolutions that would sweep across Europe in 1848, bringing upheaval everywhere except Russia and England.

Panic of 1873. In June of 1873, a financial crisis hit Vienna; while in the United States, railroad construction boomed. After the Civil War, railroads had become America's largest nonagricultural employer. Banks and other industries saw railroads as excellent investments. So when the banking firm of Jay Cooke, a firm heavily invested in railroad construction, closed its doors in September 1873, a major economic panic swept the nation.

Cooke's firm had been the government's chief financier of the Union military during the Civil War. It also became a federal agent in the government financing of railroad construction. But railroad building involved huge amounts of money—and risk. No sooner had the nation's first transcontinental railroad been completed in 1869 than a second was planned—the Northern Pacific. Cooke's firm became the financial agent for this venture, and poured its own money into the project. Yet the firm realized it had overextended itself and declared bankruptcy on September 18.

By 1877, the continuing depression set off railroad strikes. In response to wage cuts and working conditions, workers across the country struck, preventing trains from moving. The new President, Rutherford B. Hayes (1822–1893), was forced to send federal troops to quell the strikes. In the end, fighting between strikers and troops left more than one hundred people dead and many more injured. The depression did not abate until 1879.

The Panic of 1873 brought a general end to an expansion in the world economy that had begun in the 1840s.

Panic of 1893. Like most major financial downturns, the depression of the 1890s was preceded by a series of shocks that undermined public confidence and weakened the economy. In the final days of the presidency of Benjamin Harrison (1833–1901), the Reading Railroad, a major eastern rail line, declared bankruptcy. Soon, hundreds of other banks and businesses dependent upon the Reading and other railroads failed along with it. The stock market plunged. Fearing further collapse and feeling their own financial stress, European investors pulled their funds out of the United States. Recession had come to Europe earlier in the 1890s from many sources, including monetary stringency and the collapse of many speculations in Argentina, South Africa, and Australia, sharply affecting European bankers. An ongoing agricultural depression in the American West and South also deepened, spreading misery to those regions as well.

Although thousands of businesses failed and more than 4 million people became unemployed, President Grover Cleveland (1837–1908), Harrison's successor, did little. He believed, as did many enlightened leaders of his day, that the business cycle—the economy's swing between boom and bust—was a natural occurrence and should not be tampered with by politicians.

One economic matter that did concern President Cleveland deeply, however, was the nation's gold reserve, which had been steadily declining during the last years of the Harrison administration. Cleveland acted to stop the outflow of gold, but in the process divided his own Democratic Party and alienated the silver forces of the South and West.

Many business consolidations followed the upsurge in failures and bankruptcies. The depression of the 1890s did not end until 1897.

Panic of 1907. The Panic of 1907 was the last and perhaps most severe of the bank panics that plagued the "National Banking Era" of the United States. Bank panics were characterized by the widespread appearance of bank runs, attempts by too many depositors to withdraw their deposits simultaneously from the banking system. Two things set the Panic of 1907 apart from earlier panics: The banking panic was worldwide, striking New York City and its trusts companies particularly hard; and it was "the last straw," leading to the creation of the Federal Reserve System in the United States.

The panic began in October, with the collapse of F. Augustus Heinze's attempt to corner the stock of the United Copper Company. Although United Copper was only a moderately important firm, the collapse of Heinze's scheme exposed an intricate network of interlocking directorates across banks, brokerage houses, and trust companies in New York City. The close associations between bankers and stockbrokers raised anxiety in already nervous depositors and investors.

Heinze was forced to resign his presidency of a New York bank after his failure to corner the stock of United Copper. His resignation began a run on his bank by its depositors, as well as runs at other banks controlled by Heinze's friends and business associates at other New York banks.

Systemic panic did not, however, strike the New York banking system until another New York City bank announced that it would stop clearing checks for the Knickerbocker Trust Company, the third-largest trust in New York City. Knickerbocker's president was also reported to have been involved in Heinze's copper scheme.

Ominously, the next week The New York Times ran a front-page story on the Trust Company of America, the second-largest trust company in New York City, right next to the story of the run on the Knickerbocker Trust. The president of Knickerbocker was also a member of the board of directors of Trust Company of America. A run then began on the Trust Company of America.

Realizing that the failure of several trust companies in New York City would endanger the New York money market, five leading trust company presidents formed a committee to assist trusts needing cash. J. P. Morgan and John D. Rockefeller, among others, became involved, fearing the collapse of several large New York trusts would be disastrous to the local and national economy. Even the U.S. Treasury decided to help by depositing funds in the ailing trusts, but its own anemic working capital made the city's major financiers better rescuers.

With the bank runs continuing, by late October call money on the New York Stock Exchange was nearly unobtainable. Call moneys were funds lent to buy stock, with the underlying stock serving as collateral for the loan. Call loans could be called in at any time. Runs on the trust companies had forced them to liquidate their most liquid assets: call loans, which, if sold en masse, would maul the stock market. What had begun as a run on one bank now involved the fate of the capital markets, unless the panic could not be stopped and confidence restored.

Confidence was restored through loan certificates issued by the New York Clearinghouse Association, which acted like the Federal Reserve would less than a decade later. The Clearinghouse provided needed liquidity to the banking system, which reassured investors and depositors.

The 1907 panic may have enriched those who took the risk of lending money amid the fury of its storm. Still, the risks it had posed turned out to be far more severe than its rescuers may have initially anticipated. Even if Morgan, after the fact, made money in the Panic of 1907, the expectation of higher default risk made the possibility of lending in future panics unattractive to all who might be able to. Perhaps this is what the New York bankers relized, causing them to abandon their role as de facto lenders of last resort and setting the groundwork for the establishment of the Federal Reserve System.

Crash of 1929. The stock market soared during the 1920s. Despite an agricultural depression, economic life was good in the decade following the end of World War I. A worldwide mania with making "easy money" gripped people of means and people just filled with hope. A land boom occurred in Florida in the middle of the decade. Investors bought up—sight unseen, at just 10 percent down—well-marketed, but questionable land, in the hope of participating in arise of land values. A vigorous market arose, not merely in the land, but in "binders"—contracts to buy land at fixed prices as the land market soared. But by 1926, buyers hesitated, and with a hurricane's final shove, the Florida land boom came crashing down.

The land boom's collapse should have served as a cautionary tale to investors of the 1920s, but instead the frenzy for making easy money simply shifted to stocks. With the help of margin buying, investors could own stock for 50 percent down, borrowing the rest, while leaving the stock as collateral with a broker. Call loans to finance these stock purchases were supplied by banking firms from around the world at 5 to 14 percent. When stocks doubled and more in a single year, a 12 percent loan seemed to be a bargain.

Adding significantly to the investment froth were the arrival and growth of investment trusts (i.e., mutual funds), first appearing in England. Trusts relieved investors of the challenges of stock selection and ongoing management of a portfolio. During the 1920s stock mania, trust managers were seen as geniuses, fortunately able to be hired by the common man. Initially, the trusts comprised only stocks and bonds. But, in time, they frequently included other trusts. Furthermore, leverage—in this case, buying more stock with other assets—was often used to enhance dramatically a trust's ability to take advantage of the favorable market environment. As is often the case in a bubble, investors did not know what was in a trust, nor how it worked—nor did they seem to care, as long as the market continued to rise.

By the summer of 1929, however, fundamental economic conditions had deteriorated. Industrial production and home building were but the leading edges of a softening economy that would take the stock market down from its precipitous heights in the fall of 1929. That a vicious, worldwide depression would follow was not foreseeable. The boom in credit, which so often accompanies a bubble's rise, may have actually intensified the speed with which it fell and the severity of its aftermath. The Federal Reserve, and other central banks following its lead, raised rates to try to gently deflate the stock bubble. But by so doing, they affected worldwide business activity, drawing it into recession before stock speculators decided to sell.

The Internet Bubble of 1998–2000. The Internet Bubble of the late 1990s rose out of the belief that the world's economy had fundamentally changed. In the past, industrial companies had made products that cost money to make, sell, and deliver. In the so-called "New Economy," the claim was made that intangible, intellectual assets would dominate. Lower costs and higher profits and a previously unthinkable, endless, national prosperity would turn the "Old Economy" into a quaint relic. The Internet Bubble ended with a crash in the spring of 2000.

[*See also* Business Cycles *and* Great Depression.]

BIBLIOGRAPHY

Bulgatz, Joseph. *Ponzi Schemes, Invaders from Mars, and More Extraordinary Popular Delusions and the Madness of Crowds*. New York, 1992.

Carswell, John. *The South Sea Bubble*. Palo Alto, Calif., 1960.

Dash, Mike. *Tulipomania: The Story of the World's Most Coveted Flower and the Extraordinary Passions It Aroused*. New York, 1999.

Garber, Peter. *Famous First Bubbles: The Fundamentals of Early Manias*. Cambridge, Mass., 2000.

Galbraith, John Kenneth. *The Great Crash*. Cambridge, Mass., 1961.

Kindleberger, Charles. *Manias, Panics, and Crashes: A History of Financial Crises*. New York, 1996.

Malkiel, Burton. *A Random Walk Down Wall Street*. College ed. rev. New York, 1975.

Mackay, Charles. *Extraordinary Popular Delusions and the Madness of Crowds*. New York, 1980.

Palgrave, R. H. *Dictionary of Political Economy*. London, 1926.

JAMES M. O'DONNELL

FINLAND. *See* Nordic Countries.

FIRE CONTROL. In his book *Fire and Civilization*, Johan Goudsblom writes that the ability to control fire has in many ways made life in human societies easier and safer than in earlier times, but at the same time it has created new constraints and risks. Archaeological evidence suggests that *Homo erectus* was tending fires, rather than relying on them to occur naturally, as long as half a million years ago. For Goudsblom, adaptation to the presence of fire in human groups was a central component in the process of "civilization," as new behaviors were learned, shared, and transmitted. Control of fire gave humans a competitive advantage over large predators and encouraged the humans to use it to clear land to assist in food production. Cooking increased the range of foods that could be consumed. Controlled fire provided heat, light, protection, and a focus for group life and security.

The domestication of fire by groups of hunters and collectors was a precondition for the eventual domestication of plants and animals, which began around ten thousand years ago. Societies extended their care and control over fire to care and control over selected plants and animals. The ability to control fire, which is unique to humans, gave them the power to control certain species and keep wild animals away from crops and herds. The ability to cook turned various types of grasses and cereals into staple foods. The result was greater productivity in food production, which permitted considerable increases in population. Specialist users of fire, notably potters and smiths, produced objects that were essential to the creation and the growth of military regimes. Using clay pots for storage enabled greater supplies of food to be transferred from producers to rulers. Rising agricultural productivity made a greater proportion of the population available for conscription into armies or the building of public works. Metallurgy had several uses, some of which raised agricultural productivity further, and its use for weapons permitted a greater scale of military organization that expanded the command element of economies. This encouraged the growth of trade and the rise of cities.

In preindustrial times, artisans used fire to make products such as iron and glass. In the eleventh century, Chinese ironmasters began to use coke, obtained from abundant coal deposits, to fuel their blast furnaces, rather than charcoal, obtained from scarce timber reserves. The results were a surge in iron output and increased production of weapons, farm implements, and tools for manufacturing, which affected production in other industries. Gunpowder was used for fireworks in China as early as the ninth century, but it was Europeans who explored its military applications, through the development of guns in the fourteenth century. The Industrial Revolution itself involved the discovery of new uses for untapped sources of energy, stored in coal, and later in oil and gas. Steam power entailed a further refinement in human control over fire, as fires and their fuel could be transported to the most efficient location for them, freeing manufacturers from the need to locate facilities close to the running water required to power water mills. Steel, steamboats, railroads, and guns—the tools of European imperialism—were all products of a sophisticated level of control over fire. That control was monopolized by industrialized European nations, and helped them to subdue the indigenous population of the New World and the tropics and to secure access to a range of important foods and raw materials.

Control of fire was thus an important component of the structural changes that took place in economies as they grew and matured. Where the domestication of plants and animals was done successfully, efficient agriculture encouraged population growth and the transfer of resources from primary production to the manufacturing sector. Cities and their workplaces grew, thus encouraging the primary sector that supplied them with food and raw materials to become more commercialized and productive. For people in their hinterlands, cities could provide sufficient job opportunities to mop up surplus or displaced land workers. Cities were, and are, good places to do business and fertile settings for technological change because they provide clusters of labor with diverse skills, as well as locations and transport facilities that give access to large markets. When such structural change takes place, rising incomes encourage allocating an increased proportion of total spending to services. Yet cities can prosper only if these economic advantages are not offset by congestion costs that arise from the need to house and service concentrations of people; no city can remain an effective place to work and do business if the advantages of doing so are outweighed by the congestion costs—one such cost being the risk and the incidence of large-scale fire disasters.

Throughout history, fire disasters have been common in towns dominated by closely built wooden housing. Fires were a menace in preindustrial towns in northwest Europe, Scandinavia, and eastern Europe because, as Daniel Defoe wrote of early eighteenth-century Coventry in *A Tour through the Whole Island of Great Britain* (1991), the townscapes there were dominated by "timber-built houses, projecting forwards and towards one another, till in the narrow streets they were ready to touch one another at the top." Disastrous fires were thus a consequence of the use of flammable building materials, and the conventional explanation for a significant reduction of the problem in the eighteenth and nineteenth centuries has centered on improvements in building technology. Studies by E. L. Jones and others have identified a process of postfire rebuilding in which bricks and tiles replaced timber and thatch or shingles as the predominant building materials. During the eighteenth and early nineteenth centuries, economic growth, a cheapening of the cost of bricks relative to timber, and the charging of much higher premiums by fire insurance companies for timber houses than for brick ones encouraged the building of less flammable cities. Less flammable buildings created fire breaks and helped to confine fires to small districts. As new, durable houses replaced the old ones that burned down, cities moved toward a longer-life, fire-safe stock of buildings. As Europe industrialized, the towns that grew most rapidly were crowded

FIREFIGHTERS. Félix Faure, president of France, observing firefighters in action. Anonymous color engraving from *Le Petit Journal*, 28 February 1898. (Snark/Art Resource, NY)

and dirty places, but with few exceptions they were fairly fire-safe.

Major fires persisted in North America long after the problem had been brought under control in Europe, as timber was cheap in America. In frontier and gold-rush towns, fires were frequent because most building was done roughly and cheaply with flammable materials such as timber and canvas. In Chicago after the fire of 1871, new brick houses cost twice what those built of timber did, and most workers could not afford to build or rent houses constructed of materials other than wood. Attempts to redevelop fire-damaged cities by building wider streets and more fire-safe buildings usually were fruitless; and only the introduction of downtown fire zones, where timber building was forbidden, and the spread of low-density suburbs, where houses were built of timber but less crowded together, brought about a decline in the number of multibuilding fires.

The problem of fires also persisted in Asian cities throughout the nineteenth century. It was usual for Asian houses to be crowded together and built of wood and bamboo, with thatched roofs, as these simple houses were usually much cheaper than those built of brick or stone and were all ordinary city-dwellers could afford. Such houses had a further advantage in that they would bend and sway, rather than collapse, during earthquakes. In large cities such as Edo (Tokyo), Hankow (part of modern Wuhan), and Constantinople (Istanbul), several factors added to the fire risk: a high population density; the predominance of narrow streets and alleys, which made fire fighting difficult; the unreliability of water supplies; the presence of large numbers of wooden bridges and boats; the use of charcoal-burning braziers, which could easily topple over during earthquakes, for cooking and heating; and the storage of combustible items in commercial warehouses. Fire disasters occurred on a regular basis in Edo and Hankow, and hardly anyone who visited Constantinople and wrote of the experience failed to record having watched a big fire.

Although the threat of fire in Asian cities was constant, and people anticipated that their houses and commercial buildings would need to be rebuilt at unpredictable intervals, the cities were too economically valuable to be abandoned. People rebuilt and got back to business quickly. One might infer from this phenomenon that the shocks of fires and other natural disasters were of minor economic significance and therefore ephemeral, but a more likely explanation for the fast rebuilding of these cities is that people were able to develop strategies that prevented complete devastation when disaster occurred: they tended to build and furnish their houses cheaply, so that destruction would keep losses of capital to a minimum; in Edo, they kept the savings they would need to pay for rebuilding in fireproof containers; and merchants kept reserves of timber waterlogged in rivers to be available for immediate rebuilding. When buildings were destroyed by fire, however, they were rebuilt of the same flammable materials, which would provide fuel for the next fire. Also much investment in these cities was unproductive, as people tended to hoard their savings rather than invest in productive forms. The fires ultimately caused considerable economic harm, although most of it was not due directly to the fires themselves but to loss of the income forgone as people developed ways of coping with the problem.

Today the problem of fires in urban areas has been brought under control to a considerable extent by improvements in firefighting techniques, fire regulations, building materials, and the dispersal of much of the population into detached suburban houses. Such procedures tend to be less well developed in the Third World, however, and the risk of fire damage there remains high. In the developed world, when fires occur, they are less likely to spread to other buildings and cause major losses of life and capital than has been the case in the past. However, the sprawl of cities has created a new fire hazard, as areas of suburban growth encroach onto natural bush or forested land, where the risk of fire is very high.

BIBLIOGRAPHY

Defoe, Daniel. *A Tour through the Whole Island of Great Britain*, abridged and edited by P. N. Furbank and W. R. Owens. New Haven, Conn., 1991.

Frost, Lionel. "Coping in Their Own Way: Asian Cities and the Problem of Fires." *Urban History* 24.1 (1997), 5–16. Analysis of the economic consequences of fire disasters in Asian cities and their implications for modern Third World city growth.

Goudsblom, Johan. *Fire and Civilization*. London, 1992. Broad survey of the relationship between control of fire and the evolution of human societies. The most useful general introduction to the topic.

Jones, E. L., and M. E. Falkus. "Urban Improvement in the English Economy in the Seventeenth and Eighteenth Centuries." In *The Eighteenth Century Town: A Reader in English Urban History*, edited by P. Borsay, pp. 116–158. London, 1990. The most accessible of Jones's many articles on fires and English towns, it considers the reduction of the fire problem as part of a general process of improvement in the urban environment.

Jones, E. L., S. Porter, and M. Turner. *A Gazetteer of English Urban Fire Disasters, 1500–1900*. Norwich, U.K., 1984. Important data source on the extent of the fire problem in English towns.

McNeill, William H. *The Pursuit of Power: Technology, Armed Force, and Society since AD 1000*. Oxford, 1982. Survey of the impact of changing military technology on economic life.

Rosen, Christine M. *The Limits of Power: Great Fires and the Process of City Growth in America*. Cambridge, 1986. Study of the process of replanning and rebuilding the urban environment, including fires disasters in Chicago in 1871, Boston in 1872, and Baltimore in 1904.

Rowe, William T. *Hankow: Commerce and Society in a Chinese City, 1796–1889*. Stanford, Calif., 1984.

Rowe, William T. *Hankow: Conflict and Community in a Chinese City, 1796–1885*. Stanford, Calif., 1989. Rowe's excellent books on this important city contain much information about the problem of fire and people's responses to it.

Weaver, John C., and Peter de Lottinville. "The Conflagration and the City: Disaster and Progress in British North America during the Nineteenth Century." *Histoire Sociale—Social History* 13 (1980), 417–449. Study of the problem of fire control in Canada, with a useful list of major town fire disasters.

Lionel E. Frost

FIRM *[This entry contains two subentries, on the firm before and after 1800.]*

The Firm before 1800

Historians often have struggled to categorize firms before 1800. Attempts by Hubert Bourgin in 1914 and Edward Lipson in 1931 offered little more than a taxonomic veneer to the study of industrial organization. The search for natural relationships distinguishing and linking historical firms has not proved fruitful, and most economic historians today rely instead on prevailing legal distinctions among firms, such as sole proprietorship, family firm, partnership, and corporation. These legal conceptions of firms vary in terms of four basic features: legal personality, transferability of interest, managerial structure, and limitation of liability. Thus the distinction between legal conception and analytical features provides a historically grounded framework with which to sample the rich variety of firms occurring from the economic revival of the eleventh century to the late eighteenth century.

The most ubiquitous form of organization was the sole proprietorship, in which the firm was the individual. Sole proprietors would include hawkers, peddlers, commission agents, and jobbers, and did not involve common ownership of capital. Capital was under the control of the owner-manager, who was his own master, subject to market conditions. Village bakers, blacksmiths, and cobblers are classic examples of such independent business people.

Another popular form of business organization, which has not attracted the historical attention it deserves, is the family firm. As Frederick Lane wrote, "In most societies, at most times, it has been the great family which by its wealth, power, prestige, and presumption of permanence has been the outstanding institution in private economic enterprise" (1966, pp. 36–37). Family firms could range in scale from the village dry goods store to international banking institutions such as the House of Rothschild. Unique among types of organizations, however, the family firm depended less on external laws than on family traditions and values. Ron Harris (2000, p. 28) describes the features of family firms: "Management was based on the generational hierarchy within the family. All family members contributed the whole of their labor capability to the firm and enjoyed the use of family capital. Profits were distributed according to need and tradition, or plowed back in to the firm. Interest in the firm was transferred from one generation to the next by way of succession, according to family and inheritance laws, and regional and class customs." Such flexible features avoid conflicts of interest between owners and managers and enable rapid decision making in information-scarce environments.

At the same time, such features allowed a family's social aspirations to merge with its economic ones, thus leading some scholars to believe that family firms fall outside the logic of profit maximization. Mary Rose (1995, p. xiv) explains that business historians have often regarded family firms as "forces of conservatism and backwardness" despite their "extraordinary persistence and dynamism." Among the criticism leveled against family firms is the charge that they often fall prey to their own success. As Rose puts it, "business success encouraged gentrification and consequent neglect of or withdrawal from business"

(1995, p. xv). This is the so-called Buddenbrooks syndrome, named after Thomas Mann's 1901 classic tale of a Lübeck-based merchant family. Certainly some family firms before 1800 overcame the dilemma. One distinguished German example is the Möller Group, which began in 1762 in Westfalen. Originally the family ran a successful copper-works in Bielefeld. Today they are a leading electrical equipment manufacturer specializing in power distribution and automation systems, with operations in seventy countries worldwide. The long-term dominance of family firms in India, Japan, and China further suggests that the Buddenbrooks syndrome is not the foreordained fate of family firms.

Family enterprises often were well suited to markets in which commitment of permanent resources to a single, specialized activity was considered too hazardous. This was the case of the Pisani *fraterna* or family partnership in early sixteenth-century Venice. Venetian businesses depended upon a broad spectrum of international commerce, and the Pisani interests included ownership in merchant galleys, the wool and cloth trade, international banking, local real estate, and government bonds. Venice's persistence in family capitalism and its reliance on overseas trade can be viewed as mutually reinforcing, the flexibility of the former ameliorating the vagaries of the latter. The advantages of flexibility apparently were greater than the disadvantages of gentrification.

A third class of firms was the partnership, which like the family firm, represented a pooling of effort and resources for a common purpose. The partnership involved a formal division of profits and responsibilities within the organization. Profits were divided in proportion to each partner's contribution to the capital stock, and liability for losses was unlimited. The general partnership had its origins in the Roman *societas* and the Italian *compagnia* of the late Middle Ages. The largest of the great Italian partnerships, the medieval "supercompanies," were the Bardi, Peruzzi, and Acciaiuoli of Florence. These partnerships were semi-permanent; when a partner died or when capital shares were adjusted, the business was immediately reorganized. It would continue, write Hunt and Murray, "without interruption, carrying on through numerous reorganizations over decades" (1999, p. 105). Permanence was projected through the direct management of foreign branches by partners and through the use of a company logo. The prestige of the leading family, which gave a partnership its name and its chairman, carried over to the organization.

The limited partnership by contrast did not aspire to permanence, but was a firm that lasted only for the duration of a contractual relationship. The *commenda* contract, for example, was the basis of a partnership that lasted for the duration of a specific voyage to a specific destination. One partner provided capital, the other labor, and both agreed to a prespecified division of the profits. Other varieties of "sea loans" included *respondentia* and bottomry. The former was used to acquire cargo for a specific voyage, and the latter to acquire a vessel. Such partnerships brought together an active manager and a passive, often anonymous, investor. The active partner, usually a ship's master, controlled all the operational details of the undertaking, whereas the passive partner waited quietly for news of the outcome of the venture. The passive partner enjoyed limited liability against losses, but the active partner did not. Such partnerships were common across continental Europe and provided a way for nobility discreetly to participate in trade while evading its social taint.

The opportunity for passive investment with limited liability also attracted capital to another business form: the corporation. Originating in medieval guilds and livery companies, the corporation was the least common form of business organization before 1800, with a separate legal identity bestowed by the state and independent of the lives of any set of investors. In England, business corporations aimed at generating profit began to appear in the sixteenth century and were of two types, joint-stock and regulated. Joint-stock companies, or *sociétés par actions*, as they were called in France, operated with a common capital stock managed by professional directors and salaried employees. Interest in a joint-stock company was freely transferable and did not impact the quotidian operations of the firm. Indeed, key features of the early joint-stock corporations survived through the first and second industrial revolutions, remaining integral to the giant industrial corporations of the twentieth century.

Regulated companies differed from joint-stock companies in at least two ways. First, members of the company traded on their own accounts and not on behalf of the firm. Second, their smaller, joint stock was not used in the service of specific transactions, but was instead aimed at providing "public goods" for all members of the firm. The regulated companies levied entrance fees, annual payments, and duties on their members. As Harris explains: "Money collected in this way was used to provide facilities for its members, such as factories, embassies and consulates, and convoys. Thus, while each member performed routine trading separately, on his own account, much of the infrastructure was common, or in the form of joint stock" (2000, p. 32).

A few of England's early corporations were industrial, domestic enterprises; but many specialized in foreign trade, their charter or letters patent granting them exclusive access to overseas markets. Among the earliest industrial corporations were the Mines Royal (1561) and the Mineral and Battery Works (1565). As Sidney Pollard (1965) has observed, both seemed likely to succeed, given their skilled workforce, high capitalization, and legal monopoly. Yet both failed miserably, unable to overcome technical difficulties and curb wasteful expenditures. As for trading companies, the regulated companies included such fabled names as the Merchant Adventurers (1505–1689), the Muscovy (1555–1746), and the Levant (1581–1753) companies. The joint-stock trading companies included the East India (1600–1858), Royal African (1672–1752), and Hudson's Bay (1670–present, but monopoly abolished in 1869) companies. Interestingly, many trading firms switched between regulated and joint-stock organizations over time.

Preeminent among the early trading companies were the English East India Company and its Dutch counterpart, the Verenigde Oostindische Compagnie or VOC (1602–1799). These great rivals were each massive enterprises reaching from Canton to Calcutta, Bombay to Bandar Abbas. At the London and Amsterdam headquarters, elected bodies called the Court of Directors and the Heeran XVII, respectively, managed global operations. They specified the goods to be purchased from the "East Indies" and fitted out great men-of-war called East Indiamen for the roughly nine-month transcontinental trip. Salaried employees stationed overseas exchanged bullion for Asian manufactured and raw goods, such as nutmeg, mace, pepper, calicoes, muslins, raw silk, porcelain, lacquerware, and tea, which fetched handsome prices in Europe. Such goods yielded stable dividends to investors and whetted the appetite of European consumers for "colonial products." Through their systematic operating procedures, managerial hierarchies, and transferable interests, one glimpses clear precursors to the modern industrial firm.

Some features distance the English and Dutch East India companies from modern firms. Older institutions such as the family and the state played a much more significant role in these early corporations than they did in twentieth-century corporations. Nepotism was common in the period, and families such as the Harrisons of London and the Bickers of Amsterdam retained influential positions within top management for generations. Admission into the companies' service depended as much upon social access to the directors and the Heeran XVII as on objective qualifications, in contrast to the more merit-based organization of modern firms.

The role of the state in corporate life was more apparent than in modern firms. These early companies' complex relationships with their governments muddled the public and private characters of the enterprise. One issue was their legal monopoly over trade with Asia. Governments often grant monopolies over specific trades or industries because doing so serves a public purpose; but what public benefit could be attributed to the import of cotton cloth? Critics of the companies argued that the monopoly status benefited only the merchant elite involved in the trade, and that the greater (public) good would be served by free trade with the Indies. The companies also had specific financial obligations to their governments at home and embodied the delegated political authority of their governments abroad. This meant that the English company had on several occasions to lend money to the British Crown in exchange for continuance of its charter. It also meant that the Dutch company was specifically enjoined to implement and extend the anti-Portuguese policies of the United Provinces in Asian waters. One of the most important consequences of this unique public-private duality was that commercial engagement with Asia by the mid-eighteenth century degenerated into imperial expansion.

With such a variety of firms before 1800, observers may ask what impact the technological advances of the nineteenth century had on their organization. Did the spread of the steam engine, the locomotive, and the telegraph transmogrify firms into something without precursors in agrarian economies during the age of sail? For Alfred Chandler (1977) the answer is unequivocally yes. He argues that the technological revolution did precipitate a managerial revolution. The new industrial innovations required management that was professional, technically trained, and increasingly independent of the original owners. The integrated, industrial firms were created by large, self-perpetuating heirarchies that could organize economic activities at lower unit cost using internal, administrative controls rather than market mechanisms. For Chandler, managerial and technical innovations were closely aligned and thus impossible in an earlier era.

Researchers who specialize in pre-1800 businesses might take issue with this view. The closer one looks at "traditional" enterprises in an era of slow communication and hazardous travel, the more one is impressed with the earlier arts of profit maximizing and the creative efforts and vigilance of everyday managers, from medieval to early modern times. The organizational achievements of managers such as J. Edgar Thomson of the Pennsylvania Railroad cast no shadow on the achievements of Mayer Amschel Rothschild or on the managers of the English East India Company. Both before and after 1800, firms proliferated in a variety of organizational forms suited to the markets they served and the technical and institutional constraints they faced.

[*See also* Entrepreneurship.]

BIBLIOGRAPHY

Braudel, Fernand. *The Wheels of Commerce Civilization and Capitalism, 15th–18th Century,* vol. 2, translated by Siân Reynolds. New York, 1979.

Chandler, Alfred. *The Visible Hand.* Cambridge, Mass., 1977.

Curtin, Philip D. *Cross-Cultural Trade in World History.* Cambridge, 1984.

Harris, Ron. *Industrializing English Law.* Cambridge, 2000.

Hunt, Edwin S., and James M. Murray. *History of Business in Medieval Europe, 1200–1550.* Cambridge, 1999.

Lane, Frederic C. *Venice and History: The Collected Papers of Frederick C. Lane.* Baltimore, 1966.

Lipson, E. *Economic History of England,* vol. 2, *The Age of Mercantilism.* 6th ed. London, 1956.

Pollard, Sidney. *The Genesis of Modern Management.* Cambridge, Mass., 1965.

Rich, E. E., and Wilson, C. H., eds. *Cambridge Economic History of Europe,* vol. 4. Cambridge, 1966.

Rose, Mary, ed. *Family Business,* Aldershot, U.K., 1995.

SANTHI HEJEEBU

The Firm after 1800

Although historically the word *firm* referred to the name (or style) under which a commercial partnership conducted its affairs, as business enterprises evolved and assumed new organizational forms, the meaning of the word expanded to include businesses of all types—from small single proprietorships to giant multinational corporations. The particular forms that businesses (and hence firms) could take, however, have always been a function of legal rules, the substance of which have varied considerably across space and time. These variations have been important because they determined what firms were able to do. For example, in order to capture economies of scale or scope, firms had to be able to raise outside capital. But it was difficult to raise outside capital if the legal rules made all investors fully liable for the obligations of the enterprise. Similarly, it was difficult to raise capital if insiders in a firm could exploit the informational advantages they had over outsiders.

Partnerships. The importance of the legal rules governing firms can be seen by examining the simplest type of collective enterprise—the partnership. Under Anglo-American common law, partnerships could be formed freely but were not legal persons. No written contract or notice was required to create a firm, and partnerships could not sue and be sued as entities but only in the names of the individual parties involved. In continental Europe partnerships could be organized informally in much the same manner as in Great Britain or the United States. But they also could be organized more formally under the terms of the French commercial code or one of its continental variants by writing a contract and publishing the salient details (form of organization, identity of the partners, capital, and so on) in the appropriate newspaper of record. Partnerships organized in this way, unlike partnerships under Anglo-American law, were legal persons and could sue and be sued in their own names.

Legal personhood might seem to be a matter of trivial importance for firms made up of small numbers of people, but the implications of possessing this attribute were in fact profound. For example, lack of personhood made Anglo-American partnerships much less flexible than their continental counterparts. In Great Britain and the United States, each member of a firm had full ownership rights and could incur debts on behalf of the enterprise without consulting the other partners, yet each partner was fully liable for obligations thus assumed. Although many partners negotiated copartnership agreements that restricted the ability of one or more members to enter into debts on behalf of the firm, these contracts were not binding with respect to third parties that did not know of their existence. Because there was no general provision for notification (indeed, no requirement that there even be written contracts), the standard attributes of the form dominated.

In continental Europe, things were different. Because they included descriptions of the main features of the contracts, the public notices required for the creation of new legal persons made it possible for partnerships to organize themselves in a variety of ways. Thus, agreements could specify that only certain partners had the right to bind the firm, that debts could not be incurred unless all of the partners jointly signed the note, or even that the firm could not go into debt. As a result, members of partnerships were able to protect themselves from some of the risks associated with unlimited liability—particularly the risk of being held liable for debts that the partners had no knowledge of and would not have approved if they did.

Whether or not partnerships were legal persons had ramifications for other forms of organization as well. In continental Europe, the commercial code allowed business people to organize their enterprises as *commandites*, or limited partnerships, consisting of one or more general partners who managed the firm and were unlimitedly liable for its debts, and one or more special partners whose liabilities were limited to their investments and who did not play a role in management. This form of organization was difficult to square with the Anglo-American common law, especially partnerships' lack of legal personhood. Therefore, its spread depended on the passage of permissive statutes.

In Great Britain, Parliament did not provide for the formation of limited partnerships until 1907. In the United States, New York, and Connecticut passed enabling statutes as early as 1822, and most other states followed suit within the next couple of decades. But the statutes were restrictively drawn and were interpreted by courts committed to common-law principles in ways that exposed special partners to unlimited liability in a variety of circumstances beyond their control. Not surprisingly, businesspeople in the United States rarely made use of the form. In continental Europe, however, limited partnerships flourished and grew more complex and sophisticated over time. For example, in France by the late 1820s there were increasing numbers of what were called *commandites par action*—that is, limited partnerships in which the shares of the special partners could be traded on the market. Such enterprises had many of the advantages of the corporate form; indeed, when the managing partner had little wealth, they were largely indistinguishable from corporations from the standpoint of creditors.

Corporations. Under Anglo-American law, the only way to form an entity with the attributes of legal personhood was to organize a corporation. During the early nineteenth century, this step required explicit permission from the government in the form of a corporate charter. Such permissions initially were difficult to obtain, but over time governments became increasingly liberal, ultimately routinizing the process of forming a corporation. The shift occurred first in the United States.

After the American Revolution, state legislatures chartered corporations to encourage investment in infrastructure projects that states could not, either for economic or political reasons, undertake with government funds. In order to make such investments more attractive, they often included in the charters privileges, such as limited liability, that are now generally associated with the corporate form. Because the grant of a corporate charter required a special legislative act, these privileges became objects of contention. Opponents charged that only those who were politically well connected could obtain them, and the most extreme critics proposed abolishing corporations entirely as a result. Others, however, advocated opening up the granting process to make charters freely available to all who wanted them.

In the end, this more moderate policy won out—in part because there was broad support for economic development and interest in participating in corporate ventures, and in part because incorporation fees were so lucrative that states that chartered large numbers of corporations could reduce the property-tax burden on their citizens. By the middle of the century, therefore, most states had regularized the process of granting charters by passing general incorporation laws.

In Great Britain, incorporation policy was much more restrictive until the second half of the century. Common-law tradition required firms to secure authorization from the state in order to organize as corporations, and Parliament reinforced this rule in the early eighteenth century. Responding to the South Sea bubble, a burst of speculative trading in the shares of companies formed to exploit overseas opportunities, it made it illegal for firms to adopt attributes of the corporate form, such as tradable shares, without a charter from Parliament. Such charters were difficult (and costly) to obtain, and only a small number were granted before the early nineteenth century, when a deluge of requests spurred Parliament in 1825 to repeal the so-called Bubble Act. The common-law prohibition still applied, however, so businesses seeking some of the advantages of the corporate form still had to resort to cumbersome trust agreements or elaborate partnership contracts (called joint-stock companies) to achieve their ends. Finally, pressure from business spurred Parliament to pass the Companies Act of 1844, making it possible for firms to organize as entities with legal personality and transferable shares simply by registering under the act. Not until the passage of additional legislation in 1855 and 1856, however, were firms able to secure limited liability without a specific grant from Parliament.

With the exception of Belgium, general incorporation came a bit later in continental Europe. Under the French *Code de Commerce*, which underpinned commercial law in most of western Europe, corporations (*sociétés anonymes*) could only be formed with the express consent of the government. In France, an 1863 law allowed corporations below a certain threshold size (capital of less than 20 million francs) to incorporate through a registration process, but larger firms still required specific state authorization. In 1867, the capitalization limitation was removed, and general incorporation became available to firms of any size. Germany passed similar legislation in 1870; Italy, Spain, and Switzerland did so in the 1880s.

Even after the spread of general incorporation laws, considerably more corporations were chartered in Great Britain and especially in the United States than on the European continent—perhaps because British and American firms had effectively only two organizational choices, the partnership or the corporation, whereas continental firms could adopt an intermediate form, the limited partnership. Although the advantages of the corporation for large-scale enterprises are obvious, they are not so clear for the small- and middle-sized, often family-run, firms that took out most of the charters, again especially in the United States.

Whatever funds such firms raised on the outside typically took the form of debt rather than equity, yet limited liability could increase the cost of borrowing. Indeed, stockholders of these more modest-size firms often found that they had to endorse personally their companies' debts in order to secure loans at affordable rates. In addition, although the corporate form helped businesspeople involved in small- or medium-size enterprises avoid some of the agency problems they faced as a result of the limited efficacy of side contracts in partnerships, it sometimes exacerbated other kinds of agency problems, particularly in the United States, where general incorporation laws specified majority-rule governance based on one vote per share.

This point can best be seen by imagining a case in which members of a firm have serious disagreements about the direction the company should take. If the business was organized as a partnership, and the partners could not agree, then one member of the firm could move to dissolve the partnership, thereby forcing the others either to buy him out or to bear proportionately the costs of liquidating firm-specific assets. The ability to exit thus provided an incentive for partners to resolve their differences in a mutually satisfactory way. This incentive did not exist in the case of corporations. If the majority followed policies that minority stockholders felt were wrongheaded and detrimental to their interests, they could do little but grin and bear it (unless the actions were so egregiously exploitative as to justify intervention by the courts). Minority shareholders could not force a dissolution nor could they easily exit by selling their shares. Indeed, in the case of closely held corporations, often the only buyers for their shares were the same majority shareholders with whom they were in conflict.

More Flexible Forms. This problem of governance of small closely held corporations was not as serious in Europe (including Great Britain) as it was in the United States, in large measure because general incorporation statutes were more flexible, permitting a range of voting rules as alternatives to the one-vote-per-share specified by most legislation in the United States. Moreover, because certain aspects of the general incorporation statutes (particularly those requiring registration of detailed financial information) proved burdensome to small firms that did not plan to issue publicly tradable shares, many European governments passed legislation creating a special version of the corporate form for small privately held enterprises.

Germany led the way in 1892 by providing for formation of what were essentially limited liability associations (*Gesellschaften mit beschränkter Haftung*), in which all members of the firm have limited liability but the capital is not divided into tradable shares. In Great Britain, a revision of the Companies Acts in 1908 distinguished small family-run "private" corporations from "public" companies whose securities would be sold on the market. A new French law in 1925 similarly provided for the creation of *sociétés à responsabilité limitée*, essentially small limited-liability associations similar to those earlier legalized in Germany. In all three countries, the majority of firms that incorporated chose the private-company option.

In the United States, legislative recognition of the need for more flexible organizational forms for small enterprises did not occur until the last third of the twentieth century. From the late 1960s to the early 1980s, two major waves of legislation took place. The first created in most jurisdictions a separate legal status for "close" corporations, and the second protected minority interests in small corporations by defining (and establishing legal remedies for) "corporate oppression" and other similar torts. Beginning in the late 1980s, states also began to pass legislation increasing the available menu of organizational choices. The first wave of statutes made possible the formation of limited liability companies (LLCs) similar to their German predecessors; the second created limited liability partnerships (LLPs)—partnerships in which all members had limited liability. The result of all these changes was to give businesspeople in the United States much the same range of organizational choice that their European counterparts had long enjoyed.

Regulation of the Large Corporation. The advantages that the corporate form held for large-scale enterprises were much clearer than for small- and medium-sized firms because incorporation provided a means of raising funds from a broad pool of investors and yet, at the same time, permitted an efficient concentration of managerial authority. These advantages did not accrue to firms automatically, however. For example, before external investors were willing to invest in a corporation, they had to be assured that their funds would be used well and that they would reap their fair share of the firm's profits. Periodic scandals from the South Sea bubble of the early eighteenth century to the Enron and WorldCom debacles of the early twenty-first indicated that whatever personal interest promoters and managers had in the ongoing life of their enterprise was not sufficient in and of itself to prevent abuse.

As a result, the scandals spurred governments to make repeated efforts to reform corporate governance. In France, the first such statute actually predated passage of the nation's general incorporation law. A wave of scandals involving firms organized as *commandites par action* led in 1856 to the passage of legislation that aimed to protect the interests of outside investors. These safeguards plus a few others were then embodied in the general incorporation act of 1867. They included the requirement that a company could not go into business until all of its capital had been subscribed, at least one-quarter of the whole had actually been paid in, and subscribers had formally approved the firm's governance structure and the evaluation of its assets. The legislation also mandated that a firm maintain 10 percent of its capital in a reserve fund, that managers publish periodic financial statements, that the firm's accounts be audited annually by a committee of its stockholders, and that stockholders' elected *conseil* provide ongoing oversight of the firm's affairs.

In Germany, a perceived connection between abuses by corporate promoters and the Panic of 1873 led to the passage of a new statute in 1884 (revised and updated to conform to the nation's new Commercial Code in 1897). This statute provided more stringent protections for outside investors, including provisions making both organizers of corporations and the bankers who handled their share issues personally liable for the correctness of the venture's initial financial statements. Although German incorporation law was in large measure based on the French model, it had gone beyond its predecessor to set up a novel two-tiered governance structure. Accordingly, firms were managed by an executive board (*Vorstand*), which was in turn overseen by a supervisory board (*Aufsichtsrat*). (French firms were given the option of a similar two-tiered structure only in 1966.) The 1884 reforms strengthened the powers of the supervisory board over the executive board. Legislation in 1937 attempted to limit further the extent of managers' control of German corporations, and subsequent initiatives after World War II mandated that employees also have substantial representation on their firms' supervisory boards.

In Great Britain, similar concern about abuse by corporate insiders led to the passage of the Companies Act of 1900, which required corporations to file audited balance sheets each year with the government's Board of Trade, and to legislation in 1908 and 1929 (and subsequently), strengthening this provision and mandating the dissemination of accounting information to stockholders. In the United States, however, the trend for many years was in the opposite direction. Although some early general incorporation laws (most notably New York's widely copied 1848 statute) had required corporations to issue annual financial reports, statutes became increasingly lax as competition among states to charter corporations heated up.

Indeed, by the turn of the century, American general incorporation laws rarely included mandates either to publish annual statements or to maintain reserve funds, except in the case of special types of corporations such as banks. Not until a wave of scandals following the 1929 stock market crash led to the creation of the Securities and Exchange Commission was there much in the way of government protection for external investors. Until that time, such regulation was largely private and affected only those corporations that sought listing on the New York Stock Exchange or one of the regional securities markets.

The ability to attract investment from a broad pool of external investors enabled corporations to grow large, to exploit new capital-intensive technologies, and to expand the geographic scope of their operations. Moreover, because they were legal persons, corporations could own stock in other corporations. (In the United States, though not in Europe, such ownership required special legislative sanction and was first granted by the state of New Jersey during its 1888–1889 legislative session.) This ability enabled corporations to merge with other firms in the same industry, to integrate backward into raw material production and forward into distribution, to diversify into new economic activities, and to expand across national boundaries. Corporations were thus versatile institutions that could range from simple single-unit firms to complex multinational enterprises with chains of subsidiaries producing a wide variety of goods in a number of different locations.

Organizational Forms throughout the World. Western organizational forms diffused through the rest of the world in a number of different ways. European institutions had spread to Spanish America during the period of conquest. But it was only after independence that liberal, reform-minded governments embraced French civil law and, with it, the partnership and limited-partnership forms of organization. During the late nineteenth century, the success of large corporations in Europe and the United States encouraged these nations to take the next step of passing general incorporation laws, usually based on the French model. In Brazil, the pattern of adoption was a little different because the Portuguese monarchy was not overthrown until 1889. The government of the First Republic moved quickly, however, to adopt a general incorporation law and promote the growth of securities markets to facilitate the flow of capital to industry.

In India and throughout much of Africa, the diffusion of Western forms of organization was part of the process of colonization. Indian merchants, for example, formed partnerships in order to exploit new business opportunities to mediate between local producers and European trading firms. After passage of a series of company acts during the 1850s and early 1860s, the largest Indian firms began to reorganize as corporations. African businesses went through a similar evolution, though somewhat later and somewhat less successfully. In both India and Africa, however, as in most places throughout the world, the vast majority of businesses continued to be household or kinship-based enterprises conducted much as they had been for centuries.

The success of Western business enterprises also encouraged a number of Asian nations never subject to European colonization to pass legislation enabling their citizens to organize corporations or to adopt other Western forms of business organization. The ease with which these transplants took root depended in large measure on the extent to which the preexisting culture was receptive to the idea of granting a firm legal personhood. In the Middle East, Islamic beliefs tended to be inhospitable to such a notion. Although in the Middle Ages Arab traders had exploited partnership forms that were sophisticated by contemporary European standards, these enterprises were not legal persons. They had no existence independent of the people who made them up, and Islamic inheritance rules forced firms not only to dissolve but to liquidate their assets upon the death of any partner. Conscious adoption of European business forms by Turkey and other nations in the nineteenth century eased the problem somewhat, but these forms coexisted uneasily with Islamic tradition.

In East Asia, the situation was just the opposite. Confucianism had long subordinated the interests of the individual to those of the group—albeit a group defined in terms of kinship. Hence, family businesses had a status that was a kind of legal personhood. As these enterprises grew larger, they retained their identification with particular kinship groups, even though the familial element became increasingly fictitious. This identification provided a cover that enabled business enterprises to operate in ways that were remarkably similar to corporations. Not surprisingly, there was relatively little interest by Chinese businesses in attempts by the nationalist government to introduce Western-style corporate law in the early twentieth century.

The suppression of older forms of family capitalism after 1945 made the passage of a new general incorporation law in 1994 a more significant spur to enterprise, however. This law, which provided for the formation of private limited-liability associations as well as of publicly traded corporations, borrowed extensively from Western models. But it also incorporated elements from the family capitalism of the past, especially those that were compatible with socialist doctrine. Thus, the officers of a Chinese corporation are supposed to operate the firm in the interests of its employees as well as of its owners.

In Japan, the zaibatsu (groups of diversified businesses, each controlled by a particular "family") took advantage of a new general incorporation law, passed during the 1890s by an imperial government intent on encouraging industrialization on the Western model, to reorganize their operations and position themselves to take advantage of the government's largess. Although many of the earliest corporations were not in fact associated with zaibatsu, the spurt of enterprise formation (particularly in textiles) that followed the passage of the law demonstrated the utility of the form. Consequently, the zaibatsu moved quickly to charter many of their subsidiary enterprises as corporations and also to reorganize their core businesses as holding companies. After World War II, the occupying American forces attempted to suppress the zaibatsu, but similar groups soon reemerged and assumed positions of dominance in the economy. As in China, the merging of traditional family forms of organization with the Western corporation meant that managers had broad social responsibilities beyond the duty to earn profits for the firm's owners.

Although there has been a considerable amount of convergence over time in the legal rules governing firms in different parts of the world, substantial differences remain—both in the menu of organizational choices that are available to firms and in the success with which businesses have been able to exploit their various options. Because most giant multinational firms are corporations, scholarly attention has tended to focus on the development and spread of the corporate device. Although this form certainly has advantages for attracting capital on a large scale, it is not necessarily well suited for the smaller enterprises that have traditionally been responsible for much of the job creation in any economy. Indeed, even in the United

States, where the corporate form was more widely used than anywhere else, state governments devoted considerable effort by the late twentieth century to providing small- and medium-sized enterprises with a more flexible array of organizational choices. Developing countries might also find it useful to experiment with adopting these more humble forms in order to encourage business-people to enter into productive relations with each other on a small as well as a large scale.

[*See also* Entrepreneurship.]

BIBLIOGRAPHY

Baskin, Jonathan Barron, and Paul J. Miranti. *A History of Corporate Finance*. Cambridge, 1997.

Bernstein, Jeffrey R. "Japanese Capitalism." In *Creating Modern Capitalism: How Entrepreneurs, Companies, and Countries Triumphed in Three Industrial Revolutions*, edited by Thomas K. McCraw, pp. 439–489. Cambridge, Mass., 1995.

Bishop, Carter G. "Unincorporated Limited Liability Business Organizations: Limited Liability Companies and Partnerships." *Suffolk University Law Review* 29.4 (1995), 985–1058.

Cadman, John W. *The Corporation in New Jersey: Business and Politics, 1791–1875*. Cambridge, Mass., 1949.

Charkham, Jonathan P. *Keeping Good Company: A Study of Corporate Governance in Five Countries*. Oxford, 1994.

Clark, Rodney. *The Japanese Company*. New Haven, 1979.

Dunlavy, Colleen A. "From Citizens to Plutocrats: Nineteenth-Century Shareholder Voting Rights and Theories of the Corporation." In *Crossing Corporate Boundaries: History, Politics, and Culture*, edited by Kenneth Lipartito and David B. Sicilia. Forthcoming.

Evans, George Heberton. *Business Incorporation in the United States, 1800–1943*. New York, 1948.

Fear, Jeffrey. "German Capitalism." In *Creating Modern Capitalism*, edited by Thomas K. McCraw, pp. 135–184. Cambridge, Mass., 1997.

Freedeman, Charles E. *Joint-Stock Enterprise in France, 1807–1867: From Privileged Company to Modern Corporation*. Chapel Hill, N.C., 1979.

Freedeman, Charles E. *The Triumph of Corporate Capitalism in France, 1867–1914*. Rochester, N.Y., 1993.

Freyer, Tony. *Regulating Big Business: Antitrust in Great Britain and America, 1880–1990*. Cambridge, 1992.

Fruin, W. Mark. *The Japanese Enterprise System: Competitive Strategies and Cooperative Structures*. Oxford, 1992.

Gates, Hill. *China's Motor: A Thousand Years of Petty Capitalism*. Ithaca, N.Y., 1996.

Gower, L. C. B. "Some Contrasts between British and American Corporation Law." *Harvard Law Review* 69.8 (1956), 1369–1402.

Haber, Stephen. *Industry and Underdevelopment: The Industrialization of Mexico, 1890–1940*. Stanford, Calif., 1989.

Haber, Stephen. "Financial Markets and Industrial Development: A Comparative Study of Governmental Regulation, Financial Innovation, and Industrial Structure in Brazil and Mexico, 1840–1930." In *How Latin America Fell Behind: Essays on the Economic Histories of Brazil and Mexico, 1800–1914*, edited by Stephen Haber, pp. 146–178. Stanford, Calif., 1997.

Handlin, Oscar, and Mary Flug Handlin. *Commonwealth: A Study of the Role of Government in the American Economy; Massachusetts, 1774–1861*. Cambridge, Mass., 1969.

Hanley, Anne Gerard. "Capital Markets in the Coffee Economy: Financial Institutions and Economic Change in São Paulo, Brazil, 1850–1905." Ph.D. diss., Stanford University, 1995.

Hannah, Leslie. "Mergers, Cartels, and Concentration: Legal Factors in the U.S. and European Experience." In *Law and the Formation of the Big Enterprises in the Nineteenth and Early Twentieth Centuries*, edited by Norbert Horn and Jürgen Kocka, pp. 306–316. Göttingen, 1979.

Harris, Ron. *Industrializing English Law: Entrepreneurship and Business Organization, 1720–1844*. Cambridge, 2000.

Hartz, Louis. *Economic Policy and Democratic Thought: Pennsylvania, 1776–1860*. Cambridge, Mass., 1948.

Hawkins, David F. "The Development of Modern Financial Reporting Practices among American Manufacturing Corporations." In *Managing Big Business: Essays from the Business History Review*, edited by Richard S. Tedlow and Richard R. John, pp. 166–169. Boston, 1986.

Hetherington, J. A. C., and Michael P. Dooley. "Illiquidity and Exploitation: A Proposed Statutory Solution to the Remaining Close Corporation Problem." *Virginia Law Review* 63.1 (1977), 1–62.

Hirschmeier, Johnannes, and Tsunehiko Yui. *The Development of Japanese Business, 1600–1980*. 2d ed. London, 1981.

Hopkins, Anthony G. *An Economic History of West Africa*. New York, 1973.

Horn, Norbert, Hein Kötz, and Hans G. Leser. *German Private and Commercial Law: An Introduction*. Translated by Tony Weir. Oxford, 1982.

Howard, Stanley E. "Business Partnerships in France Before 1807." *Accounting Review* 7.4 (1932), 242–257.

Howard, Stanley E. "The Private Business Corporation under Modern French Law." *Accounting Review* 9.2 (1934), 105–113.

Hunt, Bishop Carleton. *The Development of the Business Corporation in England, 1800–1867*. Cambridge, Mass., 1936.

Hurst, James Willard. *The Legitimacy of the Business Corporation in the Law of the United States, 1780–1970*. Charlottesville, Va., 1970.

Jeremy, David J. *A Business History of Britain, 1900–1990s*. Oxford, 1998.

Karjala, Dennis S. "The Board of Directors in English and American Companies through 1920." In *Law and the Formation of the Big Enterprises in the Nineteenth and Early Twentieth Centuries*, edited by Norbert Horn and Jürgen Kocka, pp. 204–226. Göttingen, 1979.

Kuhn, Arthur K. *A Comparative Study of the Law of Corporations with Particular Reference to the Protection of Creditors and Shareholders*. New York, 1912.

Kuran, Timur. "The Islamic Commercial Crisis: Institutional Roots of Economic Underdevelopment in the Middle East." Research paper C01–12, University of Southern California, Center for Law, Economics, and Organization, 2001.

Lamoreaux, Naomi R. "Constructing Firms: Partnerships and Alternative Contractual Arrangements in Early-Nineteenth-Century American Business." *Business and Economic History* 24.2 (1995), 43–71.

Lamoreaux, Naomi R. "Partnerships, Corporations, and the Limits on Contractual Freedom in U.S. History: An Essay in Economics, Law, and Culture." In *Crossing Corporate Boundaries: History, Politics, and Culture*, edited by Kenneth Lipartito and David B. Sicilia. Forthcoming.

Lamoreaux, Naomi R. "Partnerships, Corporations, and the Theory of the Firm." *American Economic Review* 88.2 (1998), 66–71.

Lamoreaux, Naomi R., and Jean-Laurent Rosenthal. "Organizational Choice and Economic Development: A Comparison of France and the United States during the Mid-Nineteenth Century." Unpublished paper, 2001.

Lamoreaux, Naomi R. "Business Organization." In *Historical Statistics of the United States, Millennial Edition*, edited by Susan B. Carter, et al. Forthcoming.

La Porta, Rafael, et al. "Law and Finance." *Journal of Political Economy* 106.6 (1998), 1113–1155.

Lydon, Ghislaine. "On Trans-Saharan Trails: Trading Networks and Cross-cultural Exchange in Western Africa, 1840s–1930s; Mali, Mauritania, Morocco, Senegal. Ph.D. diss., Michigan State University, 2000.

Macharzina, Klaus. "Corporate Forms and Limited Liability in German Company Law." In *Limited Liability and the Corporation*, edited by Tony Orhnial, pp. 44–72. London, 1982.

Maier, Pauline. "The Revolutionary Origins of the American Corporation." *William and Mary Quarterly* 50.1 (1993), 51–84.

Okazaki, Tetsuji. "The Role of Holding Companies in Pre-War Japanese Economic Development: Rethinking *Zaibatsu* in Perspectives of Corporate Governance." *Social Science Japan Journal* 4.2 (2001), 243–268.

O'Neal, F. Hodge. "Developments in the Regulation of the Close Corporation." *Cornell Law Quarterly* 50.4 (1965), 641–662.

O'Neal, F. Hodge. "Close Corporations: Existing Legislation and Recommended Reform." *The Business Lawyer* 33.2 (1978), 873–888.

Payne, Peter L. "Industrial Entrepreneurship and Management in Great Britain." In *The Cambridge Economic History of Europe*, edited by Peter Mathias and M. M. Postan, vol. 7, pt.1, pp. 180–230. Cambridge, 1978.

Pineda, Yovanna. "The Firm in Early Argentine Industrialization, 1890–1930: A Study of Fifty-Five Joint-Stock Companies' Owners, Finance Sources, Productivity, and Profits." Ph.D. diss., University of California, Los Angeles, 2002.

Roy, Tirthankar. *The Economic History of India, 1857–1947*. Oxford, 2000.

Roy, William G. *Socializing Capital: The Rise of the Large Industrial Corporation in America*. Princeton, 1997.

Ruskola, Teemu. "Conceptualizing Corporations and Kinship: Comparative Law and Development Theory in a Chinese Perspective." *Stanford Law Review* 52.6 (2000), 1599–1729.

Stover, Fallany O., and Susan Pace Hamill. "The LLC Versus LLP Conundrum: Advice for Businesses Contemplating the Choice." *Alabama Law Review* 50.3 (1999), 813–847.

Wallis, John Joseph, Richard E. Sylla, and John B. Legler. "The Interaction of Taxation and Regulation in Nineteenth-Century U.S. Banking." In *The Regulated Economy: A Historical Approach to Political Economy*, edited by Claudia Goldin and Gary D. Libecap, pp. 121–144. Chicago, 1994.

Yamamura, Kozo. "Entrepreneurship, Ownership, and Management in Japan." In *The Cambridge Economic History of Europe*, edited by Peter Mathias and M. M. Postan, vol.7, pt. 2, pp. 215–264. Cambridge, 1978.

NAOMI R. LAMOREAUX

FISHERIES AND FISH PROCESSING. Fishing—the recovery (search and capture) of food and other valuable resources from bodies of water—is an ancient enterprise. Archaeological finds indicate that marine shellfish manually harvested from along the seashore were among the early foods of humans. For centuries the fish-rich coastal, continental shelf regions of the world's major oceans and marginal seas have provided most of the catch for both subsistence and trade. Fish was and still is an important part of the world food supply.

Fishing is a highly uncertain activity in which people increasingly must compete for limited, open-access, renewable (nevertheless exhaustible) resources. Commercial fishing (organized fishing for profit) includes everything from small-scale, traditional local fisheries employing small vessels—at the end of the twentieth century artisanal fisheries remained responsible for half the total world catch—to the distant, deep-sea, diesel-powered, steel-hulled multipurpose factory vessels usually associated with industrial fishing.

The variability of supply and the extreme perishability of all fishery resources once caught necessitated techniques for preserving fish. Demand was, and still is, for fish products rather than fish *per se*. In all times and cultures, males normally conducted the fishing, and females played critical economic, shore-based roles processing and distributing fish.

European commercial harvesting and preservation techniques expanded with the organization of European ocean bulk fisheries for North Atlantic herring and cod in the Middle Ages. In the second half of the nineteenth century, fishing nations attempted to extend the total productivity of the oceans by all possible means: exploiting existing fisheries more intensely, developing untapped fishing grounds or previously underused species (fishing down the food chain), engaging in aquaculture, and applying advanced food-processing methods to preserve the catch. Industrial fisheries spread into the North Pacific, with the canning of salmon, sardines, and tuna, and the freezing of salmon and halibut.

With post–World War II expansion into the fishing grounds of the Southern Hemisphere, between 1945 and 1985, the world catch quadrupled. The rise of a multinational reduction fishery, producing fishmeal and fish oil for nonfood use, accounts for much of the increase. Postwar fisheries and advanced processing centered in low-income areas to meet demand in more highly developed economies. The fisheries of the older fishing nations of Europe, such as France, Germany, and Great Britain, faced decline, whereas, through its reduction fishery, Peru emerged as a leading world fishing nation in terms of tonnage. Japan continued to be a major international producer, but largely to meet domestic demand, which it still could not satisfy without massive imports.

The intensity of commercial fishing after the mid-nineteenth century gave rise to national and international fisheries-research programs and prompted institutional changes for managing fisheries. Research on the ecological effects of fishing has been driven by strong economic and political interests. With the post–World War II development of resource economics and the expansion of national sovereignty over the high seas by coastal states, economists brought the economic issues of supply and demand into fisheries-policy development. Modern management regimes and international treaties and conventions altered fishing patterns, and thus the types of vessels used by many countries. The gear rivalry and ethnic conflict surrounding fisheries internationally is also present within nations between various commercial and noncommercial "user" groups, including fish-based immigrant communities and indigenous economies that claim an aboriginal right to traditional resources such as fish.

Demand. Commercial fishers have always competed for the relatively few species for which there are known markets and clear demand. The availability, regularity, and nature of fish products over time have conditioned tastes. World demand in terms of the per capita human consumption of fish products rose following World War II, when fish gained importance in the diet, and a wider variety of ocean, freshwater, and propagated fish products was consumed.

Demand for fish products has never been uniform among nations. After World War II, the major traditional fish-eating countries of Japan, Portugal, Iceland, and Norway led in the per capita consumption by live landed round (undressed) weight, edible (dressed) weight, and percent of total calories or of total animal protein in the diet. Japan, other parts of Asia, western Europe, and Africa led in the total consumption by edible weight. However, consumers differentiate between species of fish, as well as between kinds of and variations in processing—and always have done so.

Preserving fish by drying them in the sun, wind, or frost, or over wood fires is the oldest preservation method. The rock-hard stockfish produced by Iceland and Norway was a staple on European sea voyages, and Mediterranean and African markets for stockfish survived into the twentieth century. The ancient art of smoking fish was also important on its own for curing oily species or in conjunction with drying or salting to add distinctive flavor.

Salt curing proper dates to the Middle Ages. Dry salting (dressing, packing in salt, draining off the brine thus produced, and drying the fish) was suitable for preserving white fish (notably cod), and pickle curing (packing in brine in airtight barrels) was used for fatty fish such as herring. The dry salting of northern Atlantic cod in the "banks" fisheries of North America involved producing wet stacks (salting and draining in piles in the open), followed by open-air drying on beaches or racks (flakes) to produce a heavy or hard cure. Various products of the fisheries of the region found specific markets. The Spanish, for example, preferred large cod cured in cool weather in New England; slaves in the West Indies consumed the cod taken in summer and cured in Nova Scotia. Pickled herring produced in the North Sea–Baltic fishery provisioned the armies and beleaguered towns of Europe in the Middle Ages. Salt curing has declined in terms of world production, but it remains important in low-income countries.

The use of industrial, "advanced" processing to inhibit microorganism growth and overcome the constraints of time and distance on marketing fish began after the mid-nineteenth century with the canning of firm-fleshed, flavorful species of seafood products such as Pacific salmon, sardines, and smoked oysters. Canned fish is a durable, unique-tasting, ready-to-eat product, and thus a relatively high-priced food item. Wide-scale applications of artificial cooling and freezing were introduced in the twentieth century, in the interwar decades, for marketing fresh fish. Frozen fish competed directly with fresh fish, demand having increased because of railway and later air transportation, and, after World War II, fish farming; and the flash-freezing technology available after World War II also created a range of novel products, such as precooked frozen fish sticks. Because fresh/frozen fish and fish products require a "cold chain" from processing plant to market and home, demand for these items has been restricted to high-income countries. The nonfood use of fish as a fertilizer dates at least to Roman times, but after World War II fish reduction boomed, once fish meal found additional industrial markets as feed for livestock and farm-raised fish and mink.

In low-income countries, a lack of capital and infrastructure has meant that the fish consumed are caught locally in artisanal fisheries and cured or eaten fresh. Even in certain high-income countries, culturally generated preferences for specific traditional fish products have proved highly resilient. In Japan, Norway, and Iceland, and in fish-based indigenous societies, traditional fish products remain sources of social standing and identity, and symbols of wealth.

The Productivity of Oceans and the Fishery Resource. Western nations long assumed that the ocean was a vast underused resource, a cornucopia. However, as most fishing people have always known, and Western scientific research has demonstrated, the ocean lacks uniformly high fertility. The interplay of surface and bottom ocean waters and of ocean waters and freshwater runoff from land creates conditions of light and oxygen that support large biological production on the fishing grounds of the continental shelves and embayments, as well as in the areas of current-induced upwelling in the northern and southern extremes and wind-induced upwelling along the western continental coasts. Linking the specific zones of concentrated plant nutrients and fish populations are complex local food webs.

The Atlantic Ocean has a large drainage area and broad areas of continental shelf. Areas of coastal upwelling of cold, nutrient-rich deep water off western Africa, on the Grand Banks of Newfoundland and the waters surrounding Iceland, in the Mediterranean and the Gulf of Mexico, and off the coasts of southeastern South America and southern Africa have generated much of the Atlantic's rich fish life. The Pacific Ocean occupies a third of the surface of the terrestrial globe and has the most varied complement of plants and animals of the world's oceans. Conditions in the North Pacific and the Bering Sea, the Sea of Japan, the East China Sea, and the South China Sea have produced outstanding harvesting grounds, and the Sea of Okhotsk has been one of the most biologically productive in the world. The Indian Ocean is the smallest, youngest, and physically most complex of the major oceans. The seasonal upwelling caused by the monsoon regime in specific areas causes nutrients to concentrate in surface waters to nurture large populations of commercially valuable fish, and the fertile estuary of the Bay of Bengal and the coralline structures of the tropical coasts shelter numerous species.

Within fertile areas of the oceans there are limits to the productivity of fish populations. Fish is a differentiated resource varying in size, location, depth, density, seasonal availability, and ease of capture. Commercial fishers typically seek abundant, conveniently located concentrations (to lower fishing effort, hence supply costs) of marketable species. Natural fluctuations and fishing pressures create wide differences among fish stocks in their vulnerability to capture and to depletion (measured as a decrease in the total catch and/or the catch per unit of effort).

Fluctuations in stocks are a reality with which fishing societies have always coped. Beginning in the late nineteenth century, industrial nations devised strategies for scientifically managing depletion in commercially valued stocks in their territorial waters. The earliest such measures were designed to protect reproduction potential (closing nursery grounds, operating fish hatcheries); later measures regulated the catch (controlling the amount and the effectiveness of gear and/or the amount of fishing "effort"; imposing catch quotas and seasonal and weekly limits on fishing, preventing bycatches, and limiting the number of producers).

The Fishing Process. Although catching methods, which involve fishing gear and its use, with or without vessels, have been standardized and mechanized over time, they have not changed in fundamental ways. Collecting by hand or hand tools such as rakes, or by diving or using hunting animals, is the simplest and oldest method. Others include the use of grappling, wounding, and impaling gear, such as harpoons (for large fish and aquatic mammals) and spears, clubbing, and attracting with fire and lures. Fish traps involve various ingenious customized impounding devices that aquatic creatures can enter but, once inside, not escape.

Line fishing employs natural or artificial bait or lure and usually hooks. Included are hand lines, long or set lines (such as bottom-baited and anchored longlines for halibut), drifting, and trolling. Industrial-era long liners are larger than handliners (which are small, open or decked, for inshore waters), and have a mechanical system for baiting and removing fish and chilled seawater tanks for storing them.

Encircling gear includes bag nets kept vertically open by a frame and held stationary, pushed, or dragged against the current. Trawl nets (large cone-shaped bags of netting dragged along the seabed or towed in midwater between seabed and surface) have become the most important fishing gear of the industrial fisheries of northwest Europe. The Japanese experimented with factory (processing) trawlers in the interwar years of the twentieth century. Factory trawlers are the largest type of fishing vessel today, second only to purse seines in total world production. Seine nets surround pelagic fish from both sides and underneath, preventing escape. Seiners range from hand-operated canoes to deep-sea vessels with powered net-handling equipment.

Entangling nets, fixed or free, form a barrier to intercept the moving shoals of fish; tides and water clarity influence their use. Before the invention of midwater trawls, drift nets were a principal gear for pelagic fisheries and the main technique for deep-sea fishing in northern Europe. Gill nets are a variant adapted for inshore waters to intercept bony fishes on their one-way spawning "runs"; gill-netters provision the Canadian and U.S. Pacific salmon canneries.

The widening range of ocean harvesting led to size increases, expansion in scope of fishing, and standardization in design of fishing vessels in the twentieth century. Multipurpose (combination) fishing boats for two or more different types of fishing accommodated seasonal fishing and short seasons. Artisanal fishing boats powered by sails, oars, or outboard motors are still standard for fishing inshore waters in low-income countries. Freshwater vessels everywhere are smaller and lighter than ocean vessels, and adapted to local and unique fishing conditions.

Industrial-era saltwater fishing strategies reflect the compromises fishers face between their aims and constraints, and reflect levels of state support. Many strategies exist for small-scale (low-investment) fishers who provide local seasonal sources of protein-rich (sometimes oil- and vitamin-rich) food and jobs for fishing communities and their hinterlands, as well as a substantial portion of the world catch. Small-scale fisheries are characterized by a high diversity of target species and flexibility of boat and gear, and are labor-intensive. They are dominated by fishing generalists who may switch to alternative species, hence, to multispecies trawl boats or combination boats (trawler/seiner), for example, or even leave fishing as the season progresses, if and when alternate opportunities present themselves. Fishers may quit fishing once they

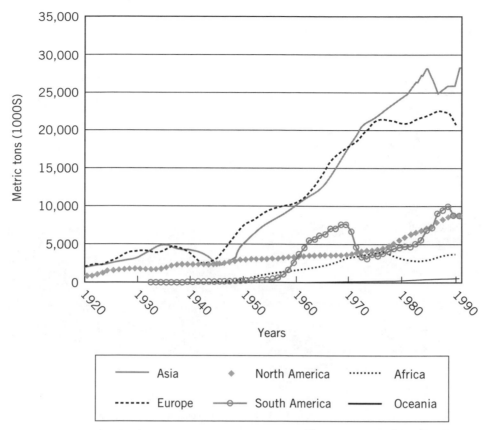

FIGURE 1. World fish landings, 1920–1990 (Fresh-Round Weight, Five-Year Moving Average). The data include all domestic landings of marine fish in the round (whole, not dressed) by all boats belonging to each country, so include the catches from foreign fishing (though exclude amounts landed in foreign ports). For some countries for some years, fish other than the main commercial species are excluded. Because the data for China are highly incomplete and include the large freshwater catches, they have been excluded from the calculations for Asia. SOURCE: Mitchell, 1998a, pp. 275–278; Mitchell, 1998b, 396–399; Mitchell, 1998c, pp. 326–331.

reach their target for food or income, even if allowed to continue. Others might need to continue for a certain number of days in financially unprofitable fisheries simply to qualify for employment insurance or to maintain membership in fishing cooperatives, or because of substantial state subsidies and loans for vessels and processing operations.

Supply. In world terms, fishing effort or output (supply) varies with the degree to which different nations are dependent on their fisheries—that is, the degree to which the economy is dependent on fish, or to which fish and fish products account for national exports, and the average percentage of the labor force engaged in fishing and fish processing. Iceland is at one extreme, scoring high on all counts. Canada scores low on all counts. However, Canada has always had low domestic demand for fish; so it has always ranked high in terms of the percentage of the catch exported. Figure 1 shows fish landings from 1920 to 1990, in different parts of the world.

Most fishing countries have access to more than one ocean coast, and many have operated both distance (for foreign fishing) and domestic fleets. The major fishing grounds of the Atlantic Ocean and its major seas have long been the most productive and utilized of all the oceans. Bulk harvesting has included the northern cod Grand Banks fishery of Newfoundland conducted by the English (West Country), French (Basque, Brittany), and Portuguese. The five-century history of that fishery inspired a major early economic study, Harold Adams Innis's *The Cod Fisheries: The History of an International Economy* (Toronto, reprinted 1978), and it influenced his staples thesis of economic development, that is, the way economic development is directed toward concentration on staples for export to more highly industrialized regions. For twentieth-century Newfoundlanders, new harvesting technologies and the introduction of quick-freezing in the late 1930s enabled state-subsidized frozen fish production in centralized plants eventually to supplant household

FISH. *Dutch Herring Fleet*, painting by Pieter Vogelaer (1641–1720). (© Rijksmuseum-Stichting, Amsterdam)

production of saltfish by Newfoundland families. In the 1950s and 1960s, after it joined with Canada, Newfoundland was the single largest supplier of frozen groundfish to the U.S. market. The northern cod fishery off Newfoundland collapsed unexpectedly and ceased operating in 1992.

Herring fisheries were the first great European marine fisheries, lasting from the twelfth century to the twentieth century. Hansa merchants organized the original seasonal herring production on the Scania Peninsula, and the prominent position of the Hanseatic League in the commerce of northern Europe was largely due to its control of the herring fisheries. A second great fishery flourished in the sixteenth and seventeenth centuries, capitalizing on late-fourteenth-century innovations in the "Dutch cure" method for pickling and packing herring at sea that had ultimately allowed the Dutch to control a high-quality, salt herring export industry. The seventeenth century saw development of the Great Fishery, which extended fishing to the shores of England and Scotland. Great Britain (mainly Scotland) ruled supreme in the North Sea fisheries for the next two centuries.

The twentieth-century commercial fisheries of the Pacific Ocean were substantially larger than those of the other oceans, and until recently furnished three-fifths of the total world catch. Japan and Russia, although not fishing exclusively in Pacific waters, had the largest fisheries in the world as measured by tonnage caught. The Pacific Ocean and most of its major marginal seas surround Japan, where all local seafood is important in the diet, as are freshwater and propagated species. In spite of Japan's dominant international position, Japanese foreign fleets have faced restrictions from international treaties and more recently the extension of territorial seas in all national coastal waters.

The United States, Peru, Chile, South Korea, and Indonesia (with Japanese involvement) are also among the world's major fishing nations today, with all or much of the catch coming from the Pacific. Pacific salmon fisheries were central to the fish-processing (canning) industries of Japan, Russia, Canada, and the United States between the late nineteenth century and the 1940s. After World War II, tuna fishing and tuna canning became important to the small island nations of the Pacific, using technologically advanced vessels belonging to Japan, the United States, South Korea, and Taiwan. California's intensive sardine fishery and canning industry, which began as an off-season opportunity for albacore and squid fishermen in the early 1900s, peaked in the late 1930s and then collapsed spectacularly in 1952. The postwar demand for fish meal for animal feed drove U.S. businesses to tap undeveloped sources of supply such those in northern Chile, Morocco, and, most successfully, Peru. Peruvian fish production has declined and rebounded at least twice since the 1960s. Fish farming is a growing industry in countries such as Peru and Chile.

In the Indian Ocean, fish of high value are taken by the world's major fishing nations (Japan, South Korea, Russia, and Taiwan), all located outside the waters of the Indian Ocean. Shrimp is the most valuable commercial species for coastal countries, with India leading in the commercial catch.

In 1990, freshwater fish, taken in the major inland lakes and prominent rivers, composed only 5 percent of the total catch of water products of the world. Nevertheless, the freshwater catch is important in the domestic (household and restaurant) trade and community livelihoods in China, South Asia, Southeast Asia, tropical Africa, and Arctic regions. Much of the freshwater catch for household consumption is dried, salted, or smoked.

Fishery Science and Management. The scientific study of the variability of catches (an area known since the beginning of the twentieth century as fishery science or fishery biology, and later, as a coherent study area, fish population dynamics), with linkages to the fields of ecology and oceanography, began with Norway's 1860s investigation of North Sea cod fluctuations. Research and management of a "flow resource" such as fish always has required international cooperation. Effective international agencies have included the International Institute of Agriculture in Rome, established in 1902 by convention, whose functions the Food and Agriculture Organization (FAO) of the United Nations took over after World War II.

By the interwar decades, fisheries agencies and marine biological institutes had developed the research approaches and measurement tools needed to confirm that some fisheries were "exhaustible" and rapidly becoming impoverished. Scientists theorized about suitable size limits, offered reasons why fish populations decline over time (examining factors of age and spawning behavior), determined cycles of abundance (to predict fish catches in advance of a season), and suggested steps to counter the effects of harvesting. Using the methods of actuarial science, fisheries biologists provided a concrete meaning for the long-discussed idea of an "optimum catch."

Three partial theories about achieving optimal catch crystallized in the period 1940–1955: maximizing the total production each year (surplus production and its corollary, maximum sustainable yield); maximizing the number of spawners returning from each year's spawning (spawner recruit); and maximizing the yield obtained from whatever young fish appear each year (yield per recruit). Also championed was the significant role of natural fluctuations in the abundance of stocks, although the idea had been promoted by a leading American zoologist, W. F. Thompson, since the 1920s and had been around since at least Great Britain's influential fisheries exhibition in 1883. Omitted in the various debates of fisheries biologists, however, was the need to study the economic side of fishing.

Canadian economist H. Scott Gordon saw the problem of rational fishing as primarily economic. He was critical

FISH. Boy and man cleaning fish in a cannery, Eastport, Maine, 1911. (Lewis W. Hine/Prints and Photographs Division, Library of Congress)

of the biologists for their too-narrow focus on the biological aspects (hence, the production side, ignoring the cost side) of fishing, and even more critical of economists for their lack of input. In his influential paper, "The Economic Theory of a Common-Property Resource: The Fishery" (*Journal of Political Economy* 62 (1954), pp. 124–142), Gordon argued against both the popular idea of maximizing the raw catch and the unspoken assumption that humans existed outside the ecosystem. He argued that a "modern" formulation of the fisheries problem must include fishermen, because "large numbers of fishermen permit valid behavioralistic generalization of their activities along the lines of the standard economic theory of production." He proposed maximizing the economic return from fishing rather than the raw yield of fish (maximum economic yield). Market forces properly channeled under a limited-entry (exclusive) rather than the existing common-property (inclusive) regime would tend to reward ecologically prudent behavior and thus work automatically to conserve the resource. At base was the need to exclude entrants and adjust harvesting effort to maximum economic advantage.

Economists view property rights as restricting the rules of the game and creating incentives to direct individual behavior. Economics discourse extends the concept of property to systems of open access and to resources that are not owned at all, under the label "common property." In their pioneering study of the economic and institutional characteristics of industrial fisheries, *The Common Wealth in Ocean Fisheries: Some Problems of Growth and Economic Allocation* (Baltimore, 1965), the North American resource economists Francis T. Christy and Anthony D. Scott defined common property natural resources as: "those resources that can be used by more than one user at the same time. No single user can control the output of other users, or prevent the entry of new users. Under these conditions, the industry tends to attract too many producers or to stimulate an overly rapid rate of production, or both." Thus, the common-property nature of modern fisheries had led to economic inefficiency in the industry and the overfishing of stocks because in a competitive economy the indefiniteness of ownership mitigates against self-regulation. It was the fisherman's inevitable problem that a fish left in the water will be taken by (thus profit) competitors.

In his 1968 paper, "The Tragedy of the Commons" (*Science* 162, 1243–1248), the American biologist Garret Hardin famously cast the fisherman's problem in terms of a group of farmers grazing cows on a common pasture. Inevitably—tragically—everyone goes broke. The Gordon-Hardin "tragedy of the commons" analysis has since the 1960s fueled fisheries policy debates and modern management regimes.

The modern concept of a "territorial sea" evolved into a formal claim to an extended sovereignty of coastal states that had by the early 1980s created an exclusive zone within two hundred miles of land: the two hundred–mile limit. Coastal states then began creating private rights in the fish stocks (individual transferable quotas) to eliminate inefficiencies and overcapitalization in the fisheries and allow market mechanisms to handle the sticky problem of individual allocation. Heated challenges to the privatization of the fisheries abound. Members of traditional fishing communities, marine anthropologists, environmentalists, and others point to a global history of good management of living resources by traditional and contemporary societies making rational choices about weighing individual short-term needs against the community as a whole over the long run. Many argue that the term common property cannot begin to capture the diversity of rights held in common by resource users. At the beginning of the twenty-first century, with many major fisheries having collapsed, the direction of fisheries research and state management continues to be subject to transitory economic and political forces, addressing needs of the moment, needs subject to change.

[*See also* Common Goods *and* Whaling.]

BIBLIOGRAPHY

Acheson, James M. *The Lobster Gangs of Maine.* Hanover, N.H., 1988. An important monograph for understanding property–rights issues in traditional inshore trap fisheries.

Alexander, David G. *The Decay of Trade: An Economic History of the Newfoundland Saltfish Trade, 1935–1965.* Saint John's, Newfoundland, 1977. A respected early study of the modern decline of salt cod markets.

Cadigan, Sean T. *Hope and Deception in Conception Bay: Merchant-Settler Relations in Newfoundland, 1785–1855.* Toronto, 1995. An examination of resource endowment rather than external demand, which argues that merchant capital was a long, rational, mutual adaptation of merchant-fishing-family dependence on salt-cod markets in a region with, at the time, no economic alternatives.

Ciriacy-Wantrup, S. von. *Resource Conservation: Economics and Policies.* 3d ed. Berkeley, 1968. Published first in 1952, a pioneering study in resource economics and conservation.

Crutchfield, James A., and Giulio Pontecorvo. *The Pacific Salmon Fisheries: A Study of Irrational Conservation.* Baltimore, 1969. An influential early application of the theory of maximum economic yield.

Cutting, C. L. *Fish Saving: A History of Fish Processing from Ancient to Modern Times.* London, 1955. The essential guide to the history of processing from a European-Atlantic perspective.

Food and Agriculture Organization of the United Nations. *Atlas of the Living Resources of the Seas.* 4th ed. Rome, 1981. A unique global overview in maps and biographical references.

Gregory, Hommer E., and Kathleen Barnes. *North Pacific Fisheries: With Special Reference to Alaska Salmon.* Reprint. New York, 1976. An indispensable economic history of the U.S. canned salmon industry, which first appeared in 1939, when Alaska was the leading world producer.

Holdsworth, Edmund William Hunt. *Deep Sea Fishing and Fish Boats: An Account of the Practical Working of the Various Fisheries around the British Islands, etc.* London, 1873. One of the few useful histories of the North Atlantic fisheries and fishing techniques.

Jenkins, James Travis. *The Herring and the Herring Fisheries*. London, 1927. The standard general introduction to the history of Atlantic herring fisheries.

McCay, Bonnie J. "'That's Not Right': Resistance to Enclosure in a Newfoundland Crab Fishery." In *Fishing Places, Fishing People: Traditions and Issues in Canadian Small-Scale Fisheries*, edited by Dianne Newell and Rosemary E. Ommer, pp. 301–320. Toronto, 1999. Taking the theoretical perspective of economic anthropology, an essay that provides an early assessment of community response to the recent trend in private-rights–based management of industrial fisheries to create private rights in fish stocks (individual transferable quotas). In a traditional fishing community, local traditions, social practice, folklore and narratives, and customs for passing on knowledge, gear, and harvesting spots have proved to be highly tenacious—socially embedded.

McEvoy, Arthur F. *The Fisherman's Problem: Law and Ecology in the California Fisheries, 1850–1980*. New York, 1986. An indispensable work that provides the ecological and legal background to the development of California's historically rich and varied marine fisheries. Topics include fisheries depletion, the theory and politics of resource management (in which Pacific Coast scientists led the way), "immigrant" and indigenous fisheries, and the rise and fall of the California sardine industry, which the American writer John Steinbeck celebrated in his early novel *Cannery Row*.

Miller, David. "The Evolution of Mexico's Spiny Lobster Fishery." In *Common Property Resources: Ecology and Community-Based Sustainable Development*, edited by Fikret Berkes, pp. 185–198. London, 1989. A useful contribution to the common-property-dilemma debate, a case study that looks at the individual ownership of fishing grounds in Mexico's important Yucatan Peninsula fishery.

Mitchell, Brian R. *International Historical Statistics: The Americas, 1750–1993*. 4th ed. London, 1998a.

Mitchell, Brian R. *International Historical Statistics: Europe, 1750–1993*. 4th ed. London, 1998b.

Mitchell, Brian R. *International Historical Statistics: Africa, Asia & Oceania, 1750–1993*. 3d ed. London, 1998c.

Nadel-Klein, J., and D. L. Davis, eds. *To Work and Weep: Women in Fishing Economies*. Saint John's, Newfoundland, 1988. A rare historical study of gendered contributions to fishing economies. See also Newell (Toronto, 1997) and Pálsson (Manchester and New York, 1991).

Newell, Dianne. *Tangled Webs of History: Indians and the Law in Canada's Pacific Coast Fisheries*. Toronto, 1997. An examination of the history of Canada's regulation of the West Coast fisheries, looking at the salmon-canning industry and at Indian participation in it and other regulated fisheries. Canadian fisheries traditionally have been among the most regulated in the world, and Indian nations of the Northwest Pacific Coast were the major fishing peoples of aboriginal North America.

Ommer, R. E. *From Outpost to Outport: A Structural Analysis of the Jersey-Gaspé Cod Fishery, 1767–1886*. Montreal and Kingston, 1991. Using a generalized development approach, an examination of the role of external demand and the truck system in retarding economic development in the previously neglected Gulf of Saint Lawrence (Quebec Gaspé) cod fishery.

Pálsson, Gísli. *Coastal Economies, Cultural Accounts: Human Ecology and Icelandic Discourse*. Manchester, U.K. and New York, 1991. A fine anthropological study of the evolution of Icelandic fishing and fish processing that includes a discussion of folk explanations of differential fishing success in Iceland, especially the much debated "skipper effect."

Smith, Tim D. *Scaling Fisheries: The Science of Measuring the Effects of Fishing, 1855–1955*. Cambridge, 1994. An essential history of fisheries science, which examines how, for example, economic pressures affected the science of measuring the effects of fishing. Included are substudies of historic fisheries that have influenced particular scientific theories such as maximum sustained yield.

Taylor, Joseph III. *Making Salmon: An Environmental History of the Northwest Fisheries Crisis*. Seattle, 1999. A well-researched, thorough history of Columbia River salmon fisheries and the failure of technological "fixes" to overcome fluctuations in supply.

Wolff, Thomas. *In Pursuit of Tuna: The Expansion of a Fishing Industry and Its International Ramifications: The End of an Era*. Tempe, Ariz., 1980. A useful study of the historical legal, legislative, and diplomatic aspects of this twentieth-century high-value, deep-sea fishery, including the Inter-American Tropical Tuna Commission, which emphasizes the California–Latin America connection.

Wright, Miriam. *A Fishery for Modern Times: The State and the Industrialization of the Newfoundland Fishery, 1934–1968*. Don Mills, Ontario, 2001. A study in the political economy of the frozen-fish trade in groundfish fisheries and of the role of the state in structuring modern fishing economies that provides the other half of the story told by Alexander (Saint John's, 1997).

DIANNE NEWELL

FLEXIBLE SPECIALIZATION. The notion of flexible specialization gained currency among economic historians and other social scientists in the early 1980s, when it was defined as the inverse of mass production. Mass producers make standardized goods by using large dedicated machine systems tended by unskilled or semiskilled workers; flexibly specialized firms produce heterogeneous goods by employing general-purpose machinery and skilled workers. This contrast in the organization of production and labor is above all a response to different market conditions. Mass producers face a relatively homogeneous and predictable demand for their products; flexibly specialized firms cater to highly differentiated markets and rapidly changing tastes.

Flexibility and specialization are linked at two distinct but related levels. At the level of the single unit of production, workers use their skills and accumulated knowledge to adapt the technologies of production to the rapidly changing desires of the firm's customers. At the more general level of the industry, single firms concentrate on the kinds of expertise that give them a distinctive competitive advantage and develop relationships with other firms that specialize in complementary tasks. This division of labor among related units of production allows networks of firms to respond to market changes quickly and flexibly. The economies of scale that provide the rationale for vertical integration in mass production are replaced by economies of scope and external economies enjoyed by connected agents. Thus, flexible specialization denotes a less hierarchical and more cooperative form of industrial organization than mass production. Flexibly specialized agents achieve coordination neither through detailed contracts nor through hierarchical control. Instead, they regulate competition by creating institutions meant to monitor trust within loosely defined communities of producers.

Evidence for the historical development of flexible specialization has come from two main sources: case studies of preindustrial and early industrial clusters of specialized producers, and more recent examples of industrial restructuring in the wake of the global economic crisis of the 1970s. In criticizing linear and deterministic interpretations of industrialization, many scholars began to recast a wide variety of historical industrial experiences in a new light. Instead of viewing local artisanal economies as mere exceptions to the classic British model of industrialism or as vestiges of an older economic order, they placed the multiplicity of paths to industrial modernity at the center of their interpretation and pointed to the lasting success of craft industries in the eighteenth and nineteenth centuries as proof of the validity of their thesis. Evidence for the existence of viable alternatives to mass production came from the histories of the silk industry of Lyon, the cutlery manufacturers of Sheffield and Solingen, the hardware traders of Birmingham, and the textile producers of Philadelphia and Rhode Island. Although some of these industries did not survive the competition of mass producers, others adapted to new market conditions by creating niches for high-quality and custom-designed goods. In these revisionist narratives, the consolidation of mass production first in late-nineteenth-century America and then elsewhere after 1945 loses its aura of inevitability and becomes a contingent response to specific environmental conditions peculiar to the United States and a consequence of its political and military power after World War II.

The joint crisis of Fordist mass production and Keynesian regulation in the 1970s and 1980s provided the proponents of flexible specialization with further evidence and political clout. While many large-scale industrial corporations underwent long and painful processes of restructuring, often leading to the deindustrialization of entire regions, flexibly specialized producers thrived. Examples of success included the fashion-related industrial districts of northern and central Italy, the textile and engineering companies of Baden-Württemberg, the furniture and shipbuilding clusters of firms in western Denmark, and the pioneers of electronics production in Silicon Valley and Route 128 around Boston. These clustered networks of firms proved more apt than Fordist companies to take advantage of the unprecedented volatility of market demand and the retrenchment of state protection. This contrast led Michael Piore and Charles Sabel, followed by others, to view flexibly specialized networks of firms as harbingers of an imminent post-Fordist era.

The interpretations of capitalism's recent history centered on the notion of flexible specialization have not gone unchallenged. Many Marxist regulation theorists, for example, have argued that the contrast between mass production and flexible specialization replaces technological determinism with market determinism by envisioning scenarios in which adaptation to customer demand is the prime mover of economic change and social conflict is incidental at best. Ash Amin and other geographers have pointed out that localized clusters of firms are far from common and that the importance of massive multinational corporations actually increased during the recession of the 1970s and 1980s, paving the way for the globalization of economic activity in the 1990s. Also as a response to these critiques, Charles Sabel and Jonathan Zeitlin have refined their position by rejecting the evolutionary bias of their original thesis in favor of a conception of industrial change that stresses the coexistence of different modes of organization in the historical actors' repertoire of strategic choices. In adopting hedging strategies, economic agents expand their cognitive possibilities and actively shape the context for their action.

BIBLIOGRAPHY

Amin, Ash, ed. *Post-Fordism: A Reader*. Oxford, 1994.
Hollingsworth, J. Rogers, and Robert Boyer, eds. *Contemporary Capitalism: The Embeddedness of Institutions*. Cambridge, 1997.
Piore, Michael, and Charles Sabel. *The Second Industrial Divide*. New York, 1984.
Sabel, Charles, and Jonathan Zeitlin, eds. *Worlds of Possibilities: Flexibility and Mass Production in Western Industrialization*. Cambridge, 1997.

DARIO GAGGIO

FLOOD CONTROL. *See* Water Engineering.

FLORENCE. The story of Florence's economic development is intrinsically linked to its cultural and artistic achievements. Florence emerged in the fourteenth, fifteenth, and early sixteenth centuries as both a commercial and industrial leader of Europe and the home of the Renaissance.

The beginnings of Florence's economic expansion are not well documented. The city benefited from the great demographic surge of the high Middle Ages (1000–1350). The population of the city quadrupled in that time. A small but vibrant merchant community traveled to international trade fairs in France and did business throughout Italy and the Mediterranean. As late as the twelfth century, however, Florence was still a relatively minor town, less populous and wealthy than its maritime neighbor Pisa. Florence possessed few inherent geographical advantages. Although situated on the Arno River, the city lay inland, off the main highway linking France to Rome. Its hilly rural lands were only moderately fertile. The city needed to import grain to feed its growing population.

In the middle of the thirteenth century, Florence supported the pope and the French House of Anjou in their wars in southern Italy. The pope rewarded the Florentines by allowing them to manage his revenue. This provided a crucial boost to the city's economy and remained a bedrock of Florentine prosperity for years after. Similarly, the French, after installing themselves as rulers of Naples in 1269, employed Florentines to collect taxes and manage the Neapolitan grain trade. The trade in foodstuffs was southern Italy's most remunerative export industry, and the Florentines soon established a monopoly over distribution.

Enterprising Florentine merchants exploited their advantage to establish a dominant position in banking and trade. The late thirteenth century and early fourteenth century saw the rise of merchant banks, international in scope and able to facilitate the movement of money across national borders. The three largest have been called super companies. They were grander in scale than any before or after in the Middle Ages. The Peruzzi bank (the second largest) maintained fifteen branches spread across Europe, northern Africa, and the Levant. It derived much of its profits from the Neapolitan grain trade and the import of raw wool from England. The bank collapsed in 1345, taking the others with it. But Florence maintained its hegemony in the banking industry. A new generation followed, led by the Medici family. The new banks organized themselves differently. While the super companies had been highly centralized, the Medici bank resembled a modern holding company. Each branch was a distinct legal entity, owned separately with its own capital and own books. When one branch failed, the others remained unaffected. The Medicis focused their business more squarely on the pope. They earned more than 50 percent of their profits from their papal branch.

Alongside its business in banking, Florence established a strong manufacturing sector. The city became the European-wide leader in the production of woolen cloth. Local

FLORENCE. View of the the city, with the cathedral at left and the Palazzo Vecchio in the distance at the right. (Alinari/Art Resource, NY)

entrepreneurs began first by "finishing" imported Flemish cloths and then exporting them elsewhere. This brought considerable profits and paved the way for a native wool-cloth business. Here, the city skillfully exploited its one resource, the Arno River, which ran through its urban center. The river was used to clean the raw wool, an important initial step in the long process. At its height, the Florentine wool firms purportedly produced 100,000 pieces of cloth a year, worth 1.2 million florins. The industry employed some 30,000 people, nearly one-third of the local population.

By the middle of the fourteenth century, Florence was well established as an economic powerhouse. Internally, the activities of the various trades were regulated by guilds. These were not, however, especially restrictive, nor did they cover all professions. Wealth accumulated through trade, and manufacturing became invested in the countryside, as rich Florentines bought up rural estates. There is little evidence, however, that the flow of money produced major innovations in the agrarian sector.

Florence's success owed in no small measure to its innovation in the field of public finance. In 1345, city officials established a funded public debt, the so-called *monte* (mountain). The act consolidated all outstanding loans drawn from citizens and fixed repayment at a single rate of 5 percent. Officials allowed credits to be transferable, thus opening up a secondary market for wealthy speculators. The reform helped tie the wealthy classes more firmly to the state. In 1427, the Florentines worked to ensure a fairer tax assessment of citizens by enacting the famous *catasto*. The legislation involved a comprehensive rendering of the taxable wealth of all the inhabitants of the Florentine state by means of a complicated formula that allowed for deductions for dependents and exemptions for movables and business profits. Apart from its utility to the government, the *catasto* has proved a gold mine of information for modern-day social and economic historians.

The advent of the Black Death of 1348 altered the Florentine economy. The plague claimed between 50 and 80 percent of the city's population. To offset decline in production, entrepreneurs moved more forcefully into the manufacture of higher priced commodities such as luxury cloth and silk, which were still in great demand. The silk business proved particularly remunerative, routinely turning profits of 20 percent and more on capital investment. The overall balance sheet however, is hard to determine, and economic historians continue to debate the issue. The task is complicated by the fact that the city also faced frequent crop failures and perpetual war.

One certain result of the crises was that Florence gained relative to its neighbors. It used its economic hegemony to create a "territorial" state, seizing surrounding towns and eventually all of Tuscany. Florence's domination produced variable results, encouraging economic development in some sectors, damaging prospects in others.

By the late fifteenth century, Florence had begun to lose its place in the broader European economy. The banking industry suffered a severe crisis in the 1490s. The French invaded Italy in 1494 and spent the first half of the next century fighting its wars with Spain on Italian soil. Meanwhile, Florence's supremacy in the woolen cloth industry was being challenged by first Venetian and then English producers. By the seventeenth century, Florence was all but eliminated from the international marketplace. The city reverted to the largely regional economy and tourist center that it is today.

BIBLIOGRAPHY

Brucker, Gene. *Renaissance Florence*. New York, 1969.

Goldthwaite, Richard. *The Building of Renaissance Florence*. Baltimore, 1980.

Goldthwaite, Richard. *Wealth and the Demand for Act in Italy, 1300–1600*. Baltimore, 1993.

Hunt, Edwin S. *The Medieval Super Companies*. Cambridge, 1994.

Molho, Anthony. *Florentine Public Finances in the Early Renaissance, 1400–1433*. Cambridge, 1971.

Roover, Raymond de. *The Rise and Decline of Medici Bank*. New York, 1966.

WILLIAM CAFERRO

FLORIN. According to Giovanni Villani, writing in the 1330s, the florin was first struck in Florence in November 1252. Unlike earlier European gold coins, the florin's standard of weight and fineness (3.54 grams, with 23.875 carats, 99.48 percent fine) did not depend on north-African originals. Initially designed to fit into the Florentine monetary system, it contained enough gold to pass for a lira of Florentine silver piccoli (i.e., a pound of 240 pence). However, it rapidly passed into international trade, first with the Levant and then with north Africa. In the thirteenth century, its standard of weight and fineness, although not its type, was imitated by other Italian commercial cities, from Genoa within months to Venice as late as 1284–1285. In Italy during the thirteenth century, Florentine and other "florins" replaced north-African coin and west-African gold dust that circulated by the ounce in leather bags for larger payments. For even larger payments, florins themselves were put into sealed bags, to prevent the erosion of their gold contents.

The heyday of the Florentine florin was in the fourteenth century after 1320, when the Kremnica gold mines began producing for the kings of Hungary. The number of florins minted in Florence rose to 352,000 a year in 1344–1345. In Hungary itself when king Charles Robert began striking his own gold coins in 1328 from the newly mined ore, he made them not only identical in weight and fineness with the Florentine florins but also very similar in appearance, with the lily of Florence on one side and Florence's patron saint, John the Baptist, on the other, substituting only his own name for that of Florence.

Florentine florins now began to circulate widely in western Europe outside Italy, and even as early as the 1320s they had reached distant England. This largely came about because of the higher value placed on gold (in terms of silver) in northern than in southern Europe, so that the relative bimetallic ratios made it sensible to make payments in gold in the north, and in silver in the south. Northern Italian merchants, whose commercial networks stretched to London, Bruges, and beyond, now generally quoted international exchange rates between local silver currencies and the Florentine florin.

As a consequence, many of the first gold coins to be struck by rulers and cities outside Italy were of the same weight and fineness as the Florentine florins, and many of them, like the florins of the king of Hungary, imitated the types as well. The king of Aragon, for example, chose to imitate the Florentine florin rather than the Castilian *dobla*, as did the pope at Avignon, the emperor, and the Rhineland electors (Archbishops of Mainz, Trier, and Cologne, and the Count Palatine, from 1354 on).

Gradually the Florentine types were abandoned, but the weight and fineness remained. On his florins Hungarian king Louis I (1342–1382) and his successors replaced the Florentine lily by the royal arms and St. John the Baptist by St. Ladislas of Hungary. The emperors and the Rhineland electors did the same.

In Aragon, although the Florentine type was retained, the fineness and weight were reduced. In Germany the emperor and the electors also reduced the weight and the fineness of their florins or gulden from 1385 onward (the latter from 23.5 carats to 18.5 carats by 1490, thereafter remaining unchanged until its last issue in 1626). By 1400 there were two major monetary areas in Europe, one based on the electoral and imperial florins in northern Europe and one based on the florin, and increasingly the Venetian ducat in the south. The increasing commercial and industrial importance of the south-German cities such as Frankfurt, Nuremberg, and Augsburg was reflected in the wide circulation of the imperial gulden minted there.

In those parts of Europe for which the original florin remained the standard, the Venetian ducat gradually replaced the Florentine florin as the key international currency in the fifteenth century. However, since the Venetian ducat was effectively of the same weight and fineness as the Florentine florin, it was really a continuation of the dominance of the florin.

As in the fourteenth century international exchange rates had generally been quoted against the Florentine florin, so in the fifteenth century they were increasingly quoted between local silver currencies and the Venetian ducat or the German gulden. As the fifteenth century progressed, the Rhine and imperial gulden spread their influence more widely. The Burgundian rulers of the increasingly commercially important Netherlands changed from a Florentine florin standard to a Rhineland standard in 1466. In Florence itself the florin as a gold coin came to an end in 1533, although the "florin" standard continued in Venice until the last ducats were struck around 1840.

From the thirteenth to the sixteenth century, the florin was the key measure of value in Europe and beyond, as the gold sovereign, the pound sterling, was to be in the more globally integrated world of the nineteenth century, replaced after World War I and for the remainder of the twentieth century by the U.S. dollar. The Dutch florin or gulden, derived from the Rhine gulden, survived in a slowly transformed fashion until the introduction of the euro at the beginning of the twenty-first century.

BIBLIOGRAPHY

Bernocchi, Mario. *Le monete della repubblica fiorentina.* 4 vols. Florence, 1974–1978.

Cipolla, Carlo M. *The Monetary Policy of Fourteenth Century Florence.* Bologna, 1982. English translation. Berkeley, 1983.

Cipolla, Carlo M. *Money in Sixteenth-Century Florence.* Bologna, 1987. English translation. Berkeley, 1989.

Goldthwaite, Richard A., and Giulio Mandich. *Studi sulla moneta fiorentina (secoli XIII–XVI).* Florence, 1994.

Spufford, Peter. *Money and Its Use in Medieval Europe.* Cambridge, 1988.

PETER SPUFFORD

FOGEL, ROBERT, born in New York City on 1 July 1926, is a major pioneer of what has come to be called cliometrics, or the new economic history.

Fogel, with another innovator, Douglass C. North, was awarded the 1993 Nobel Prize in economic science for this work. After attending New York's prestigious Stuyvesant High School, Fogel attended Cornell University, graduating in 1948. After several years as a political activist and organizer, he returned to graduate school in economics at Columbia University. There he wrote his master's thesis under the supervision of Carter Goodrich. This thesis was published in 1960 as *The Union Pacific Railroad: A Case in Premature Enterprise.* The book combined detailed primary research with an imaginative use of economic theory to evaluate the risk of this government-subsidized project. Fogel then attended The Johns Hopkins University, receiving his Ph.D. in 1963. His thesis, written under Simon Kuznets, led to the publication, in 1964, of *Railroads and American Economic Growth: Essays in Econometric History,* a book that triggered many debates regarding its historical methods and substantive conclusions.

Railroads and American Economic Growth was based on an extensive amount of empirical information concerning the railroad and its impact on the economy. The concept of social saving, an estimate of the differential costs of shipment of goods by railroads as opposed to alternative means of transportation, was used to structure the question of how large the railroad's contribution to economic growth had been in the years leading up to 1890. This task involved asking "what if" or counterfactual questions. Perhaps surprisingly, given the general reliance of historians on this approach, the use of counterfactuals led to much of the subsequent controversy. Some questioned the appropriateness of particular counterfactuals; others attacked the general use of the approach. As it evolved in subsequent decades, the role of counterfactuals has been explicitly understood as a general part of the historian's approach to the past. Fogel's finding of what seemed, at the time, to be a smaller than expected contribution to American growth remains debated, but studies of technical change have drawn upon the argument that any one innovation can have only a relatively small impact on the economy. The fruitfulness of Fogel's analysis of the railroad is seen in a number of country studies that have been based on his methods.

Fogel's next major project concerned the economics of slavery in the United States South, leading to several books and numerous articles by Fogel, his colleagues, and his students. The first major publication, *Time on the Cross* (co-authored with Stanley Engerman), was a two-volume work that presented findings from numerous types of primary data located in southern archives, and was based on a style of research—using many assistants to collect a lot of primary data—that was not then typical in either history or economics. Because of its methods and some of its conclusions about the profitability and efficiency of slavery, the relatively favorable material treatment allowed slaves, and the relatively favorable economic position of the South before the Civil War, *Time on the Cross* attracted an unusual amount of attention for an academic publication, and led to a lengthy controversy and series of disputes on many of the questions studied. As with the railroad book, some of the debate was on the nature of the questions that should be asked and some on substantive analysis. In 1989, Fogel published a new study of slavery in the United States, *Without Consent or Contract*, which went over many of the aspects of the debate, while still presenting most of the basic positions of his earlier work on slavery. In 1992, three edited volumes of papers and notes by Fogel and others were published, providing much of the analysis and data featured in the primary volume.

Beginning in the 1980s, Fogel has been working principally on another big project, one that requires extensive data retrieval and collaborative work with many scholars from different disciplines. This project focuses on long-term issues related to mortality, health, and labor productivity as influenced by nutrition, work effort, and disease. Variables employed include such measures as life expectation, height, and body mass. By using records of the military and related sources that go back several centuries, the pattern of height differences and changes over time has been used to complement other measures of economic well-being. The great availability of anthropometric and demographic data in many countries has meant that, following the earlier work of Fogel and others, economic historians and economists have studied these issues widely, contributing greatly to our knowledge of the past.

We have focused on three of Fogel's major research projects, but he has made many other valued contributions to economic history, to the study of historical method and methodology, and to the study of the relation between religious and political change.

Fogel has taught at the University of Rochester, the University of Chicago, and Harvard University, and has been Charles R. Walgreen Distinguished Service Professor of American Institutions at the University of Chicago since 1981. Honors, besides the Nobel Prize, include membership in the National Academy of Science and the American Academy of Arts and Sciences; presidencies of the Economic History Association, the Social Science History Association, and the American Economic Association; the Bancroft Prize; and the Pitt Professorship of American History and Institutions, University of Cambridge. He was the first director of the Development of the American Economy program of the National Bureau of Economic Research, and chairman of the Committee on Mathematical and Statistical Methods in History of the Mathematical Social Science Board.

BIBLIOGRAPHY

Fogel, Robert W. *The Union Pacific Railroad: A Case in Premature Enterprise.* Baltimore, 1960.

Fogel, Robert W. *Railroads and American Growth: Essays in Econometric History.* Baltimore, 1964.

Fogel, Robert W. "Nutrition and the Decline in Mortality: Some Additional Findings." In *Long-Term Factors in American Economic Growth*, edited by Stanley L. Engerman and Robert E. Gallman. Chicago, 1986.

Fogel, Robert W. *Without Consent or Contract: The Rise and Fall of American Slavery.* 4 vols. New York, 1989.

Fogel, Robert W., and Stanley L. Engerman. *Time on the Cross: The Economics of American Negro Slavery.* 2 vols. Boston, 1974.

Goldin, Claudia, and Hugh Rockoff, eds. *Strategic Factors in Nineteenth Century American Economic History: A Volume to Honor Robert W. Fogel.* Chicago, 1992.

O'Brien, Patrick, ed. *Railways and the Economic Development of Western Europe.* New York, 1983.

STANLEY ENGERMAN

FOOD PROCESSING INDUSTRY *[This entry contains four subentries, a historical overview, and discussions of technological change; industrial organization, markets, and trade; and food safety regulation.]*

Historical Overview

The food processing and manufacturing industries in most industrial economies have received little attention from historians compared to many other industrial sectors, despite their evident economic, social, and strategic importance. Few studies of the Japanese economy in the postwar period, for example, have emphasized the role of food processing, which during the mid-1980s accounted for 11 percent of national industrial production, employed 1.2 million people, and was integral to the operations of the six largest *keiretsu* conglomerates. In the United States, by the same date, food processing was the largest single component in manufacturing, representing 14 percent of total manufacturing production, although this position was a significant decline from its apogee of 26 percent around 1909. Most existing studies of the sector concentrate on individual firms or specific branches of what has always been an extremely diverse industry. They also focus on the growth of large enterprises in the United States and to a lesser extent in the United Kingdom and continental Europe. This has left little space for discussion of the many small- and medium-sized enterprises or of initiatives in cooperative business organization that have retained an important role into the twenty-first century in food processing as well as agricultural production.

Preserved and processed foodstuffs have been items of commerce since antiquity, when the demands of urbanization and new technological developments, especially in milling, provided incentives to commercial production and distribution. The subsequent development of the food-processing industries has remained closely connected to the development of new technologies, both in food processing and distribution, and to the demands of urban populations lacking the resources to produce and preserve food for themselves.

In medieval and early modern Europe, food processing artisans, such as bakers, butchers, millers, and brewers, worked from relatively small workshops or their homes, employing family labor and selling their goods mostly at local markets. They were organized much like other medieval craftspeople, in craft guilds that set the quality standards and the guidelines for the training of apprentices. The distinction between the manufacturing and commercial aspects of food processing was as yet underdeveloped, and the various "mongers" and "grocers" carried out both functions. Much of the processing of food, however, was carried out in the household itself, especially in rural areas with less access to specialized merchants and artisans.

During the medieval and early modern periods, incremental improvements in food processing technologies were stimulated by the demands of growing urban populations, and extensive processing facilities were frequently found in major port cities, such as London. These provided for the local population and for those embarking on lengthy sea journeys. Preserved fish was produced on a large scale and was an important commodity from the tenth century, but few other processed or preserved foodstuffs were traded in large quantities because of high transport costs. Those that were traded retained their luxury status and were affordable only by the richest members of society. The opening up of new sources of supply in the New World combined with more efficient production technologies meant that sugar was one of the first commodities to undergo the transformation from luxury to necessity in the European diet. In the United Kingdom consumption in 1800 was fifteen times that of a century earlier.

Mid-Nineteenth Century to Early Twentieth Century. The convergence of a number of developments toward the end of the first half of the nineteenth century contributed to the emergence of large-scale food processing enterprises that came to dominate some sectors of the industry, especially in the United States and the United Kingdom, by the end of the century. On the demand side rapid urbanization combined with rising real wages among the urban working classes to increase the number of potential customers, while the advent of the railroad began to remove barriers to nationwide distribution first in the United Kingdom and later in the United States. This provided manufacturers with incentives for technological innovations capable of generating economies of scale and for the development of advertising and marketing techniques to promote their products. The opening up of new territories to agriculture in the American West and in Britain's formal and informal empire combined with improvements in land and sea transport to reduce the cost of the agricultural raw materials required by processors. The impact of these trends is clearly seen in the history of the U.S. meat-packing industry, centered in Chicago, which effectively combined innovations in processing, transport, and distribution to supply national and international markets with its products. A listing of the largest U.S. firms in 1917 included two meat packers, Armour and Swift, among the top ten enterprises. By the end of the nineteenth century sugar refining, roller milling, powdered milk, and canning had joined the ranks of large-scale corporations. In the United Kingdom biscuits, preserves, and chocolate were also capital-intensive industries engaged in mass production for the urban working classes. Many of the firms

FOOD PROCESSING. Worker operates a machine that cores and slices apples in preparation for drying them for making apple pie, 1944. (Prints and Photographs Division, Library of Congress)

involved were family businesses whose owners became famous for their industrial paternalism as well as for their products. Outside of these sectors the industry continued to be dominated by small and medium-sized firms operating in local and regional rather than national markets.

The growing economic and social importance of food manufacturers was reflected in the growth of efforts to regulate their activities. These have been well documented on both sides of the Atlantic. Regulation came earlier to the United Kingdom, starting in the 1870s after lengthy campaigns. In the United States the Pure Food and Drug Act of 1906 is closely associated with Harvey Wiley, chief chemist of the Department of Agriculture, and with the campaigning journalism of Upton Sinclair, whose novel *The Jungle* (1906) exposed working conditions in the Chicago slaughterhouses. In fact the success of legislation in both countries depended crucially on the support of food manufacturers, notably H. J. Heinz in the United States and George Cadbury in the United Kingdom, who saw regulation as a way of raising barriers to entry and reducing competition.

During the 1920s mergers in both the United States and the United Kingdom increased levels of concentration, allowing firms to further exploit economies of scale in processing technology and advertising. Historians of the British case have suggested that the experiences of World War I, where large numbers of people were introduced to new foodstuffs while serving in the armed forces, led to lasting changes in taste that helped foster a national market for food manufacturers. One of the main firms to emerge from this merger wave was Unilever, formed from the British Lever Brothers and the Dutch Margarine Unie. Firms later benefited from the decline in prices of raw materials in the early 1930s. These combined with increased mechanization to reduce the relative prices of many of their products and to extend their markets further down the income scale. By 1935 in the United Kingdom the largest three units produced more than 60 percent of net output in seven sectors: chocolate (66 percent), preserved meat and fish (67 percent), pickles (61 percent), sausages (62 percent), condensed milk (94 percent), margarine (90 percent), and sugar (78 percent). This means that the history of these sectors can be told largely by reference to just a few firms. Similar trends were evident in the United States, but in continental Europe, with a few significant exceptions, such as the German chocolate industry, there was much less concentration of production. Little is known about commercial food processing elsewhere, except where it was carried out by the affiliates of U.S.– or U.K.–based multinational enterprises, a trend that intensified during this period. There is limited evidence of overseas manufacture by British firms before the conflict, but rising barriers to trade encouraged them to consider overseas manufacture after it. A few U.S. firms, including Heinz, were already well established in Britain prior to World War I, but many more joined them during the two decades after. The chocolate industry yields some of the most well-documented examples of these developments. The two dominant British manufacturers, Cadbury Bros. and Rowntree's, both expanded production to the Dominions, and Mars, one of the preeminent U.S. confectionery firms, established a plant near London on the new industrial estate at Slough. Other U.S. firms that made major investments in the United Kingdom during this period included Kellogg's (Trafford Park, Manchester), Kraft Cheese (Hayes, Middlesex), Quaker Oats (London), and Wrigley (London). The Canadian Garfield Weston had a significant impact on the biscuit industry from his Associated British Foods plant in Edinburgh.

After World War II. For two decades after World War II the industry, especially in the United States, enjoyed a period of relative stabilization and widespread public and government approval, highlighted in the report of the National Commission on Food Marketing, set up by Congress in 1964 to investigate the industry. In the United Kingdom government controls over the manufacture and distribution of foodstuffs during and after World War II combined with rapidly increasing levels of concentration in food retailing to increase the existing tendency toward concentration and a more unified national market. This was reinforced by the increasingly capital-intensive nature of the industry as it shifted from batch to continuous-processing technologies and adopted automatic control technologies. During the mid-1960s most commentators expected concentration to increase, but few predicted the extent to which "merger mania" would grip the industry on both sides of the Atlantic later in the decade or how long it would last. The result was the emergence of an oligopoly, where the largest four firms had 55 percent or more of the market in every major food category in the United States by the mid-1980s. In canned soups and breakfast cereals the figure was 90 percent, and the top fifty processors made 75 percent of all profits in the sector. The European industry was also becoming increasingly polarized, and by 1991 the three largest food companies, Philip Morris,

Nestlé, and Unilever, accounted for 36 percent of the combined sales of the fifty largest firms. British firms continued to dominate the list of the largest European food manufacturers, contributing eleven of the largest fifteen by turnover in the mid-1990s. Many of these firms had substantial investments overseas, including in the United States, reflecting the internationalization of food manufacture despite the relatively small volume of international trade in processed food products. In Japan the picture moved in a similar direction with particularly high concentration ratios in edible oils (86 percent), processed meat (76 percent), cheese (87 percent), chocolate (77 percent), and soups (78 percent). These sectors were dominated by the food-processing affiliates of the Keiretsu conglomerates, and in other sectors small enterprises remained common, with an average of 14.5 employees per firm across the industry as a whole.

The pursuit of economies of scale through increasing concentration represented one part of the industry's response to its recognition that consumers in Western industrial nations had reached saturation levels of food consumption by the 1950s. Another was vertical integration, and some manufacturers moved into institutional feeding operations, supermarkets, and restaurant chains. Most considered farming too risky a venture, and especially in the United States, they maintained supplies through the type of production contracts pioneered in the canning industry during the nineteenth century. This practice was adopted much later in Europe. Firms also sought to expend their markets geographically, moving beyond western Europe and North America to operate on a global scale, often with profound consequences for dietary habits. Ironically, the convergence of diet in technologically advanced societies and elsewhere that these developments fostered occurred at the same time that the characteristic dishes of local food cultures were adapted and reborn as part of the voracious search for novelty that also preoccupied these firms.

This search reflected another response to this situation: diversification into a widening range of value-added products. In the United States between 1947 and 1982 value-added in food processing increased by seven times, and the price of manufactured foods ceased to reflect trends in the price of agricultural products. Food preparation increasingly moved away from the home and into the factory, a development often linked to rising levels of employment among married women, although one should be wary of simplistic correlations between these trends. It certainly meant an increasing diversity of products, up from six hundred items in a British corner shop of the 1950s to eighteen thousand in a superstore during the 1990s. Manufacturers introduced large numbers of new food products and variations on existing lines, a trend that accelerated during the

1980s in the United Kingdom from one thousand a year at the start of the decade to over three thousand by its close, a figure close to the estimate of thirty-five hundred in the United States by the same date. Although 75 to 85 percent of these new products failed to retain their presence after a single year, around 25 percent of food sales were of products introduced in the preceding five years. The priority of the industry in developed food economies was to tailor foods to markets in terms of taste, nutrition, health, and lifestyle. By the end of the twentieth century some commentators talked of the problem of "overchoice" and blamed the food manufacturing industry and its products for the explosion in the problem of obesity that now afflicted more people worldwide than malnutrition.

BIBLIOGRAPHY

Brenner, Joël Glenn. *The Chocolate Wars: Inside the Secret Worlds of Mars and Hershey.* London, 1999. A valiant attempt to examine the histories of the two secretive firms that have dominated chocolate manufacture in the United States for decades.

Burns, Jim, et al. *The Food Industry: Economics and Policies.* London, 1983. Economic survey of food manufacturing and processing in the United Kingdom.

Conner, John M., et al. *The Food Manufacturing Industries: Structure, Strategies, Performance, and Policies.* Lexington, Ky., 1985. Economic survey of food manufacturing and processing in the United States.

French, Michael, and Jim Phillips. *Cheated Not Poisoned? Food Regulation in the United Kingdom, 1875–1938.* Manchester, 2000. A comprehensive evaluation of Britain's food laws that identifies the role of the food industry in the law-making process.

Goodall, Francis, et al., eds. *International Bibliography of Business History.* London, 1997. A useful source for tracking down the histories of individual enterprises.

Jeremy, David J., ed. *Dictionary of Business Biography: A Biographical Dictionary of Business Leaders Active in Britain in the Period 1860–1980.* 6 vols. London, 1984–1986. Contains details of the careers of most major figures in the British industry, including their philanthropic activities.

Levenstein, Harvey. *Revolution at the Table: The Transformation of the American Diet.* Oxford and New York, 1988.

Levenstein, Harvey. *Paradox of Plenty: A Social History of Eating in Modern America.* Oxford and New York, 1993. Contains details of the role of food manufacture in dietary change.

McCorkle, Chester O., Jr. *Economics of Food Processing in the United States.* San Diego, Calif., 1988. Economic survey of food manufacturing and processing in the United States.

Rothacher, Albrecht. *Japan's Agro-Food Sector: The Politics and Economics of Excess Protection.* Basingstoke, U.K., 1989. Provides a welcome perspective in a literature dominated by consideration of the United States and western Europe.

Schlosser, Eric. *Fast Food Nation: The Dark Side of the All-American Meal.* New York, 2001. One of many critiques of the impact of the domination of food production in the United States by large corporations.

Wilson, Charles. *The History of Unilever: A Study in Economic Growth and Social Change.* 3 vols. London, 1954, 1970. Impressively detailed study of one of Europe's largest food manufacturers.

Young, James Harvey. *Pure Food: Securing the Federal Food and Drug Act of 1906.* Princeton, 1989. A detailed account of the battle for this legislation.

SALLY M. HORROCKS

Technological Change

Food processing and preservation were practiced before settled agriculture or the domestication of animals. They rendered foods more palatable and easier to digest and allowed people to enjoy a diet that transcended the confines of what was immediately available in the local environment, both temporally and geographically. Archaeological evidence of labor-intensive processing of plant food exists in Europe during the Upper Paleolithic period. In Central and South America the native populations developed the processes necessary to remove the poisonous prussic acid from cassava (manioc), which became a staple of their diets. The origins of the traditional food preservation techniques of drying, salting, pickling, the use of honey or sugar, smoking, curing, fermentation, and cold are obscure and cross boundaries of region and culture. Certainly most of these techniques were practiced in ancient Egypt, where large-scale processing and storage installations were integral to the growth of the state. The storage of grain on a large scale was also practiced in China from earliest times. By the late Roman Empire numerous tools and machines had been developed to apply these techniques, including significant advances in milling. The spread of this technology to China from the Middle East was important for the development of commercial noodle production, for which there is evidence in Han China around 100 CE. Many of the advances of the Greco-Roman period necessitated large capital investment and encouraged the production of a substantial salable surplus. Preserved fish, especially from the Black Sea, was one of the most extensively traded food items, and like others it benefited from improvements in technologies of storage and transport. It is important to remember, however, that the vast majority of food processing and preservation was carried out domestically for household consumption.

Processing. Although few wholly new techniques of processing and preservation were introduced, at least in the West, until canning in the nineteenth century, there were many improvements to the existing processes, some of which were carried out on a considerable scale. Of particular importance were improvements in the application of power sources to milling, especially waterpower. Wind power was first harnessed in Europe around 1185, and with the emergence of the post mill in the Low Countries during the fifteenth century, all the main types of mill were established. The mechanization of bolting (the process by which the fine flour is separated from the other products of milling) took place during the sixteenth century, and there were also improvements in gearing that increased the efficiency of mills. In China by this date water wheels powered batteries of trip hammers that were used for a variety of food processing purposes, including milling rice and extracting juice from sugarcane. At the same time in Europe the advent of the printing press had a major impact in spreading information about food processing and preservation.

While the scale of food processing operations certainly increased in medieval and early modern Europe, absolute size tended to be limited by that of local markets, as high transport costs made it uneconomical to transport produce long distances, especially overland. The most striking exception was preserved fish, an important commodity for religious reasons. Stockfish, or dried cod from Norway, was widely traded by the tenth century, and pickled and smoked herring were produced on a large scale, the latter in extensive smokehouses, from at least the thirteenth century. After the European "discovery" of Newfoundland by John Cabot in 1497, salted dried cod was produced from the abundant North American cod stocks. This highlights the changes to the European diet after the fifteenth century that resulted from access to new sources of supply and new foodstuffs from the East as well as the New World. Sugar quickly became an important crop in the New World, and sugar refining, based on techniques pioneered by the Persians in the seventh century, was carried out on an unprecedented scale. Improvements in cane-milling machinery, possibly based on technologies already used in the extensive Chinese sugar industry and imported to South America via the Philippines, were also significant as sugar began its transformation from luxury to necessity. In Britain total sugar consumption increased fifteenfold between 1700 and 1800. By this date incremental improvements and new power sources had transformed the scale of production in some branches of food processing. In Naples, for example, the adoption of an improved screw press with interchangeable die plates had considerably increased the efficiency of pasta production.

The advent of canning in the early nineteenth century is generally seen as the first wholly new food preservation technique to have emerged in the West since antiquity, although it can be regarded as an example of preserving food by sealing, a technique with a much longer history. Bottled fruit was sold as a luxury in Britain during the seventeenth century, and in its early years canning was a craft industry catering to a limited market, retaining much in common with its predecessor. The foundation of the food-canning industry is generally attributed to the work of the Frenchman Nicholas Appert, who perfected a technique for bottling that earned the approval of the French government and disseminated it through his book *L'Art de conserver* (1810). Appert's name has remained synonymous with the technique despite the strong claims of others, such as the London-based Bryan Donkin, whose work developed along similar lines around the same time and who pioneered the use of tinned iron containers in place of glass jars. Early canning techniques involved filling the container and sealing it before heating it in a water bath to cook the food. Initially canned foods were a luxury or were prepared for special purposes, especially for the British navy.

This began to change in the mid-nineteenth century, when large-scale canneries for meat were established in both South America and Australia. Although their products were regarded as significantly inferior to fresh meat, exports increased dramatically, and canned meat became part of the diet of the industrial working class in Europe, especially Britain. It was in the United States, however, that the industry really came of age, starting with canned tomatoes in the late 1840s. It relied on the developments of new techniques in processing foodstuffs prior to canning, changes in the way the canned foods were processed, and new ways of producing cans. Also important was the way in which canneries secured continuous supplies by contracting directly with farmers for their produce rather than relying on the vagaries of the market. Only later, at the end of the nineteenth century, was the new science of bacteriology applied systematically to solve long-standing problems in the industry. Initially foodstuffs were processed in a labor-intensive manner, using the same tools as in a domestic kitchen. Gradually some of the steps became automated as specific devices, such as the automated corn kernel remover (1875) and the pea sheller (1883), were developed along with devices for filling cans and labeling them. Various techniques for increasing the processing temperature and reducing production time dramatically increased the output of canneries. The addition of calcium chloride to the heating liquid was particularly successful in this regard and became the standard technique before it was replaced by the autoclave (pressure retort).

Improvements in the technology of can production initially involved automating elements of the production process and culminated in the double-seam can patented by Max Ames of New York in 1896. This removed the need to solder the seam. Ames also developed a machine for producing his design automatically. These developments contributed to the rapid growth of the industry, especially in the United States, where firms such as Heinz, Campbells, and Libby grew rapidly, and consumers began to enjoy the same choice of fruits and vegetables throughout the year.

Developments in the preservation of food by cold were also of considerable social and economic importance during the nineteenth century and played a role, alongside canning, in securing supplies of meat for the urban populations of Europe and North America. This highlights the extent to which innovations in food processing and preservation were stimulated by urbanization and industrialization. Natural ice had long been used to preserve foodstuffs, and during the early nineteenth century an international trade in ice extended the use of natural ice to new territories. Mixtures of natural ice and salt were used to transport foodstuffs, especially fish and meat, by rail in specially insulated carriages, but the technique was inevitably limited. The advent of mechanical refrigeration extended dramatically the territories from which chilled or frozen meat could be transported to Europe and the distances it could travel within the United States. Mechanical refrigeration was based on the technique of evaporating and condensing a suitable fluid by compression to use the latent heat of evaporation for refrigeration, and land-based refrigeration was developed commercially in the United States by the 1850s, although there were difficulties in finding an effective nontoxic refrigerant. Successful extension of the technique to ships took until the late 1870s. Frozen meat from Australia was successfully transported to Britain on the SS *Strathleven* in 1880, heralding the start of an extensive trade.

In the United States, primarily Chicago, during the 1870s and 1880s the meat-packaging industry made use of these developments in mechanical refrigeration combined with the mechanized processing—the "disassembly" line—to produce meat for consumption on a wholly unprecedented scale. Here carcasses were hung on a moving conveyer for bleeding, skinning, dressing, and trimming before moving directly to coolers or for further processing before canning. Subsequent developments maintained this basic pattern but included the use of power tools. The success of the big six meat processors—Armour, Swift, National, Cudahy, Morris, and Schwartzchild and Sulzberger—depended not only on their mastery of these processes but on vertical integration, which saw them developing refrigeration facilities in the commercial and transport chain so their products could reach the public not only in the United States but also in Europe in optimum condition.

Significant innovations in techniques for processing and preserving milk can also be traced to the second half of the nineteenth century. In Britain in particular the growth of the railway network, combined with refrigeration, stimulated the trade in liquid milk. Pasteurization, which uses heat to kill microorganisms in the milk, remained controversial well into the twentieth century, despite claims that it prevented the spread of tuberculosis. In 1877 the Swede Gustav Laval introduced his centrifugal cream separator. In widespread use by the end of the 1880s, it transformed butter production, especially when combined with Alfa discs and Babcock's test for butter fat content. In most of Europe cheese making continued to be a relatively small-scale craft industry, although a growing share of the British market was secured by factory-produced cheeses from Australia, Canada, and the United States. Dried milk

has probably been produced in India for centuries, but the first British patent was granted in 1855. This included several additives, including sodium carbonate and sugar, and was produced by open evaporation. Later vacuum pans were used. Dried milk without additives appeared on the U.S. market in 1898, and roller driers came to be the preferred technique before the advent of spray drying. Vacuum technology was also important in the production of evaporated milk, pioneered by Gail Borden of Connecticut. His patent was granted in 1856, and manufacture expended rapidly during the Civil War. J. B. Meyenberg, working for the Anglo-Swiss Condensed Milk Company, was responsible for developing Borden's process to include sterilizing the products in its can. Canned milks were an integral part of the British working-class diet by the end of the century.

Processing. Alongside these developments in preservation techniques were significant changes in processing. The advent of roller milling was perhaps the key nineteenth-century innovation. In contrast to existing techniques, in which grain was ground between horizontal grinding stones, the roller mill passed the grain between pairs of fluted rollers arranged in series and followed by pairs of plain rollers, grinding the grain in stages and allowing the miller to produce a number of different grades of flour from the same wheat. It emerged in Hungary possibly as early as the 1820s and became more widespread after 1840. The adoption of roller milling in the United States was rapid after around 1880, when German and Hungarian engineers were imported to develop the new technology, especially around Minneapolis and Saint Paul, which became an important milling center. In Britain uptake was slower, and the transition was still not complete by the outbreak of World War I. Roller milling substantially lowered the cost of white flour, and its product could be kept for an extended period after milling. These factors contributed significantly to the growth of national and international markets for what had previously been a local commodity. The production of flour on a large scale was accompanied by the addition of artificial improvers to reduce variations in quality.

The mechanization of bread making, baking, and other means by which flour was processed before consumption all occurred during the second half of the nineteenth century in Europe and North America. Steam power was used to drive a whole range of specially designed machines, reducing the labor required to make bread, and in Britain the firm of Huntley and Palmer pioneered biscuit making on a factory scale. A key development in this industry was that of the "traveling oven," which allowed continuous baking rather than the batch operations of a conventional oven and was first used by the firm in 1850. The transition from batch to continuous production significantly increased output and was the trajectory eventually followed by other branches of the industry. This was certainly the case for the Italian pasta industry. British-made kneaders, extruders, and cutters were adopted for use during the 1880s, continuous extrusion was established during World War I, and the first completely mechanized production line was introduced by the Braibanti company in 1933.

Like milling, sugar production underwent considerable change during the nineteenth century. Its scale increased dramatically, and ownership of the industry concentrated in fewer and fewer hands. The key innovations were the introduction of the vacuum pan, dramatically shortening boiling times, and of the centrifuge, already used in other industrial processes, to dry the sugar. Experiments with decolorizing agents also brought significant improvements. Raw sugar from cane-growing areas was exported to the main population centers in Europe and North America for the final stages of processing. The failure of Chinese producers to adopt the new techniques led to a dramatic fall in China's sugar exports after the 1890s. Chinese sugar was rapidly displaced in its domestic market by cheaper and more highly refined imports, and sugarcane cultivation slumped dramatically. Another nineteenth-century development was the production of sugar from beets on a commercial scale, starting in France and later spreading widely in Europe. Refining processes used first on cane sugar were later adapted for use with beets. Britain was by far the largest domestic market for sugar during the nineteenth century. Its largest firms, Henry Tate and Sons and Abram Lyle and Sons, later merged to form Tate and Lyle and dominated the industry.

Alongside these changes in preservation and processing techniques need to be placed two other changes that can also be dated to the second half of the nineteenth century. The first was the development of wholly new foodstuffs and radically new ways of consuming existing ones. These include margarine, breakfast cereals, chocolate, and custard powder. The second was the transition from domestic to factory production of foodstuffs, such as pickles and preserves, previously made primarily for domestic consumption or on a small scale for the luxury trade. Hippolyte Mège Mouriès invented margarine in France in 1869 as a cheap substitute for butter made from beef fat, skimmed milk, and water. Factory production was initiated in 1870, and by the end of the century the product had spread to other European countries and North America. The development of commercial fat hydrogenation processes based on the catalytic reaction patented by Paul Sabatier and Jean Baptiste Senderens allowed manufacturers to use a wide variety of fats and oils for margarine production. Breakfast cereals were pioneered in the United States by health food advocates, such as Sylvester Graham, John Harvey Kellogg, and Charles W. Post. Most were produced

by processing maize, wheat, or rice by some combination of baking, grinding, or puffing and were eaten with milk. The majority of the major brands still popular in the early twenty-first century were on sale by 1910. Chocolate production was transformed by the van Houten press, patented in 1828, which removed about two-thirds of the cocoa butter from the bean and allowed the production of cocoa free of the fatty residue with which it had previously been associated. The British firm Cadbury Brothers sold block chocolate, produced by adding the cocoa butter residue to the ground beans, by 1842. Swiss manufacturers pioneered other significant innovations. Rudolphe Lindt developed the process of conching, where the chocolate is worked in a trough shaped like a shell to improve its texture, and Daniel Peter is credited with producing the first milk chocolate in 1876.

By the end of the nineteenth century there had been significant technological development in both food processing and preservation. Not only had new techniques been developed but existing ones had been modified and increased dramatically in scale. Also important to the technological development of the industry were innovations in transport and packaging. The most successful companies integrated these with new techniques of marketing and retailing. During World War I they played an important role provisioning military and civilian populations, bringing their products to the attention of many people who had never tried them before. By this date many had also begun to employ scientists, although scientific explanations of new processes or techniques were frequently forthcoming only long after they had been in commercial use for some time. Initially the U.S. and British food manufacturers employed scientific expertise, but others followed in western Europe, notably in the Netherlands, Denmark, and Germany, and elsewhere, including the notable case of the Colonial Sugar Refining Company in Australia. In most firms scientists were employed first to carry out quality control work, which became increasingly important as the scale of production increased. They rapidly developed substantial expertise in the raw materials with which they were dealing and began to generate new knowledge, frequently using their scientific understanding of existing processes to effect improvements in them. They also worked closely with engineers to develop new machinery and to facilitate increased levels of mechanization.

Probably the first major innovation in food preservation of the twentieth century was the development of quick freezing, which made it viable to freeze fruit and vegetables on a large scale without them completely loosing characteristic texture when thawed. The American Clarence Birdseye is generally credited with solving this problem, although he was not alone in developing new freezing techniques during the 1920s. Equally important

FOOD PROCESSING. Workers separate egg yolks from whites at a plant in Shanghai, China, circa 1890–1923. (Frank and Frances Carpenter Collection/Prints and Photographs Division, Library of Congress)

was his collaboration with the DuPont chemical company to produce moisture-proof cellophane that facilitated quick freezing. The use of waxed cardboard to retain the shape of defrosted foods was also important in overcoming the negative image they had in the eyes of many consumers. In 1929, shortly before the stock market crash, Birdseye sold his company to General Foods. The Great Depression and then World War II stalled the subsequent development of the industry, but it grew rapidly in the United States from the second half of the 1940s and in Europe, particularly as a result of the activities of Unilever, from the 1950s. The commercial success of frozen foods depended not only on the development of techniques of production but also on distribution and marketing. Initially frozen food was stored in the freezers of shopkeepers and purchased for almost immediate consumption. Later the spread of the domestic freezer encouraged the storage of frozen food at home. The advent of the microwave oven bolstered the industry during the 1980s and encouraged the development of frozen meals. Frozen food was quickly adopted by the catering industry, reducing preparation times and costs dramatically. It underpinned the menus of the nationwide restaurant chains that emerged in the United States after World War II. These took the labor-saving possibilities of frozen foods a step further and attracted large numbers of Americans unwilling to spend time preparing foods for themselves.

Innovations in dehydration were also significant during the mid-twentieth century. Freeze drying was first used during the 1930s for pharmaceutical and biological materials. This technique uses the fact that ice can change from solid to water vapour without passing through the liquid phase and has the advantage that its products do not need cold storage. Foods are quick frozen then put in a vacuum chamber and slightly warmed to encourage sublimation before being packed in airtight containers. This technique tends to be reserved for small and high-value items, such as peas and prawns, and for liquids, such as coffee. The first large-scale plant for freeze drying meat and fish was established in the USSR in 1954. Dehydration techniques were the subject of extensive research by government-funded scientists in both Britain and the United States during World War II. Spray drying was the most important new development. In this technique, which can be used for liquids and semiliquids, including milk, eggs, and instant coffee, the liquid is sprayed into a chamber into which hot air is also blown, and it collects as a fine powder. The ability of spray-dried powders to reconstitute can be improved dramatically by rewetting and agglomerating the particles to form larger particles. Many spray-dried products entered the commercial area during the 1950s, although meals based entirely on powders proved to have little commercial appeal. Instead, a limited range of products, including soup and topping mixes, became popular.

Topping mixes (Angel Delight in the United Kingdom, Miracle Whip in the United States) exemplify the extent to which the 1950s became the "golden age of food chemistry" as chemists developed hundreds of new additives to assist in processing and preserving food. The mixes were produced from vegetable fat, protein, and carbohydrate combined with surface-active agents, flavors, colors, and usually a stabilizer and had a long shelf life. Their resemblance to any agricultural product was slight indeed. The same could be said for many of the snack foods manufactured by extrusion and for the various processes developed to cement meat pieces together and restructure them or to produce simulated meats from soya protein. One estimate suggests that 7,500 new food products were introduced to the British market alone between 1959 and 1975. Many of these embodied the latest developments in food technology and were heavily marketed, but only a few were commercially successful.

Also during this period food manufacturers, especially in the United States, were faced with the reality that consumers had reached saturation levels of food consumption and that food expenditure constituted a declining proportion of household budgets, even if total spending continued to rise. They responded to this by seeking economies of scale and by turning to products offering value added. Food processing became an increasingly capital-intensive industry with machines replacing humans at all stages of processing. Automatic control technologies allied with computer facilities for processing the data they generated and robots capable of complex tasks meant that people almost disappeared entirely from the most modern food factories by the end of the twentieth century. This trend favored the large companies with the technical expertise and capital resources to maximize its potential and reinforced other factors favoring concentration, especially in the United States and the United Kingdom. By the late twentieth century the large food manufacturers had developed into global enterprises whose products were sold in every continent.

After World War II it was increasingly common for food processors to work with agricultural scientists to develop foods with characteristics that made them better adapted to processing. A prime example of this was the development of new breeds of battery chicken in the United States. These were meatier with broader breasts, thicker drumsticks, and fewer blemishes than their free-range ancestors. Fruit and vegetable varieties were also selected for their processing characteristics, but the enhancement of desired attributes was frequently a lengthy process. This changed during the last quarter of the twentieth century as the techniques of biotechnology offered the prospect to tailor crops rapidly to the needs of processors, often reducing the need for artificial chemical additives, and replacing them with specific qualities. During the 1990s, for example, scientists predicted that within a decade corn would be produced that was targeted with specific nutritional enhancement for animal feed or with processing qualities that made it ideally suited to produce corn syrup. These developments brought firms in other sectors where biotechnology was being developed much closer to the food industry. In addition links were forged between small biotechnology firms and the major food companies, who had been slow to develop their in-house capabilities because of their traditional focus on chemistry. Some consumers, especially in Europe, resisted these developments, which fed into existing concerns about the food supply.

There can be no doubt that by the end of the twentieth century the activities of food manufactures and changes in food processing technologies had contributed to significant changes in diet and to when and how food was consumed. The same abundant and varied diet could be enjoyed throughout the year without limitations of geography and climate, and some items were accessible, at a cost, in most major cities around the world. Critics insisted that these changes had been detrimental to the quality of food and to the health of the consumer. Those inside the food manufacturing industry argued that its activities delivered to consumers a wealth of choice unprecedented in human history and, by removing the labor required to prepare food in the home, had freed up time for other activities. Any assessment of these claims needs to proceed with caution and cannot be made in isolation from the many other factors contributing to food choice.

BIBLIOGRAPHY

Chalmin, Philippe. *The Making of a Sugar Giant: Tate and Lyle, 1859–1989.* Translated by Erica E. Long-Michalke. Chur, Switzerland, 1990. A meticulously detailed history of the firm and its predecessors that pays considerable attention to technical developments.

Curtis, Robert I. *Ancient Food Technology.* Leiden, 2001. Detailed account of food-processing technology from prehistoric times to the end of the Roman Empire.

Davidson, Alan. *The Oxford Companion to Food.* Oxford, 1999. An essential reference work with aspirations to global coverage and with a substantial bibliography.

Levenstein, Harvey. *Revolution at the Table: The Transformation of the American Diet.* Oxford and New York, 1988.

Levenstein, Harvey. *Paradox of Plenty: A Social History of Eating in Modern America.* Oxford and New York, 1993.

Mintz, Sidney. *Sweetness and Power: The Place of Sugar in Modern History.* New York, 1985.

Needham, Joseph. *Science and Civilization in China,* vol. 6, pt. 3, *Biology and Biological Technology,* by Christian Daniels and Nicholas K. Menzies. Cambridge, 1996. The section by Daniels provides a detailed account of sugarcane production and processing, including the transfer of Chinese sugar-making technology to other parts of Asia and possibly to South America.

Singer, Charles, E. J. Holmyard, A. R. Hall, and Trevor I. Williams, eds. *A History of Technology.* Oxford, 1957. Each volume includes an essay on food processing and preservation, although these vary considerably in coverage and detail. Other essays, especially those on milling, also contain information relevant to food processing.

Thorne, Stuart. *The History of Food Preservation.* Kirkby Lonsdale, U.K., 1986. Despite its title, this concentrates almost exclusively on canning.

SALLY M. HORROCKS

Industrial Organization, Markets, and Trade

In modern economic growth, food processing industries are among the first to emerge. Developing countries typically are largely agricultural, and as such it is appropriate that the initial industries are associated with that sector. The rise of the food processing industries is closely tied to the historical development of international trade in grains, livestock, and meat, and this trade, in turn, is importantly affected by declining transportation costs and the introduction of new technology that facilitates long-distance shipping of perishable items. Finally, declining transportation costs that extend markets and new production and energy technologies that introduce economies of scale in food processing bring changes in optimal firm size and industry composition. The political reaction to these structural changes, however, has been important in the development of antitrust and other forms of government regulation. Regulation also has been stimulated by the demands of consumer and producer groups to monitor food quality when it is shipped in long-distance trade. With remote sellers, consumers have less opportunity to observe the quality of food production and preservation.

Flour Milling Industry. The major food processing industries in historical economic development in western Europe and North America were flour milling and meat packing. By the mid-nineteenth century, in England the flour milling industry consisted of a large number of small-scale enterprises dispersed across the country (Perrin, 1990). Until the spread of railroads, most wheat was consumed in the local farming district where it was grown and milled into flour. Early water transport was not very effective because of moisture damage to flour. Adoption of steam power and new rolling techniques in milling after 1850 brought economies of scale, and together with the expansion of the rail system, consolidation occurred as flour mills grew in size. The overall domestic market in England and Wales did not grow dramatically between the 1870s and the start of World War I, so the growth in the size of flour milling firms meant that small firms were displaced. Moreover, English mills gradually switched to hard winter or spring wheat imported from the United States and Canada that could be ground using new technology into a clean, high-quality white flour.

In the United States, as early as 1850, flour milling accounted for almost 10 percent of all industrial establishments and over 13 percent of the value of all industrial products. By the turn of the twentieth century, flour milling had dropped in relative importance, but it remained a vital part of the economy, accounting for almost 5 percent of all manufacturing establishments and over 4 percent of the value of all industrial production (U.S. Department of the Interior, 1850, 1900). The same process of consolidation and shift to hard wheat that occurred in Britain took place in the United States. Eastern mills that had relied on soft wheat felt competition from larger western millers based in Minneapolis and other Midwestern cities that used new machinery to grind the hard wheats that predominated in the Midwest. As a result, the center of the American industry shifted westward during the latter part of the nineteenth century (Perrin, 1990). With an expanding rail system, flour milling could be concentrated and product shipped to markets throughout the country. By the end of the nineteenth century, American and Canadian flour exports to Britain had grown steadily, forcing additional adjustments within the British industry toward larger and more efficient mills.

Meat Packing Industry. Similarly, the meat packing industry emerged as an important contributor to early industrialization, especially in the United States after 1880. Prior to the introduction of refrigeration, the industry was characterized by small wholesale slaughterhouses and packing plants, located near or in urban areas. They slaughtered both local livestock and those shipped from the Midwest. In 1880, there were 872 slaughter and packing firms, some with retail outlets (U.S. Department of the Interior, 1883). Production units were small, entry was easy, and the industry was very competitive at the wholesale and retail levels. Production and demand were seasonal, with most slaughtering of cattle and hogs in the winter, curing and shipping in the spring. Although production was widespread, around Cincinnati there was a concentration of hog raising and pork packing. Pork, more readily than beef, was cured into hams, bacon, and sausages for shipment. Expansion of the rail system allowed for broader shipment of meat products and for the transport of cattle to the stockyards around Chicago in the 1840s and 1850s. These factors did not dramatically change the industry. Refrigeration, however, introduced after 1870, did.

Refrigeration allowed for the centralized, large-scale slaughtering of cattle in Chicago or other leading western packing centers and the shipment of carcasses to eastern markets and export. Centralized slaughtering offered economies that the older, live cattle trade with local butchering could not match (Yeager, 1981). Transport costs were lowered by two-thirds; large-scale production brought economies of scale in processing; and refrigeration allowed for the year-round consumption of meat. In the United States, Chicago packers pioneered the use of refrigeration and centralized slaughter. These companies invested in refrigerated railroad cars and wholesale branch outlets with refrigeration for storing meat. The new Chicago packers quickly changed the structure of the meat packing industry and dominated trade in livestock products in the United States.

As early as 1884, 84 percent of the cattle slaughtered in Chicago were by four packers: Swift, Armour, Morris, and Hammond. Other meat processing centers were in Omaha, East Saint Louis, Kansas City, South Saint Paul, and Fort Worth, where the Chicago firms opened large branch plants. Between 1880 and 1910, the average capital in slaughter and packing plants grew by more than a factor of ten (Libecap, 1992, p. 248). Retail prices of beef fell and consumption grew, displacing cured meat such as ham and other pork products.

Although consumers benefited from these technical and organizational innovations, small producers, who were displaced by the new competition, did not. Small slaughterhouses attempted to discredit refrigerated beef as unhealthy because of the alleged use of diseased animals, but their claims were without merit and not accepted by domestic consumers. These health concerns, however, were used by European producers to justify trade restrictions on low-cost American meat imports (Libecap, 1992). Small U.S. packers organized the Butchers National Protective Association in 1886 and lobbied for state and federal government regulation of the industry. They were joined by cattle raisers, who feared the potential monopsony power of the Chicago packers. The packers periodically attempted to form pools to purchase livestock and to divide markets between 1886 and 1901. The pools had formal structures (the Allerton and Veeder pools), and the number of members was small. Even so, any impact on cattle prices appears to have been short term. The pooling agreements were unstable with new entry and unauthorized expanded production by member firms. Nevertheless, the political reaction to declining cattle prices after 1884 helped motivate cattle raisers to seek antitrust controls on the packers. They also sought to increase livestock and meat exports through government inspection and health guarantees.

Regulation took two forms, antitrust and meat inspection. Beginning in 1889, twenty states adopted antitrust laws, in part to constrain the market power of the packers. Local meat inspection statutes also were adopted initially to inspect the "dressed beef" products of the Chicago packers as a means of protecting local butchers and secondarily to provide consumers with information. In 1890, Congress adopted the Sherman Antitrust Act, and in 1891, the first federal meat inspection law was enacted.

The Beef Trust played a prominent role in congressional hearings on the impacts of trusts in the economy. Between 1888 and 1890, there were three major congressional hearings on trusts on sugar refining, oil refining, whiskey production, cotton bagging, and the Chicago packers. The report on the Beef Trust was the most lengthy and was introduced during debate over the Sherman Act. Disputes over an amendment to directly regulate the Beef Trust delayed final adoption of the act.

The Meat Inspection Act of 1891 was enacted to encourage meat exports to Europe, which had been damaged by the internal political debate over the wholesomeness of refrigerated beef and the market power of the packers (Libecap, 1992, pp. 258–259). Federal government inspection of food products initiated by the Meat Inspection Act was extended by the 1906 Meat Inspection Act made popular by the publication of Upton Sinclair's *The Jungle* and his allegations of unsavory conditions in the Chicago packing houses.

Expansion of Trade. Besides the rise of the food processing industry in the mid-nineteenth century in the United States and Europe, international trade in agricultural commodities, especially wheat and livestock, also grew, demonstrating the expansion of domestic and global markets during the period. In the late nineteenth century, after the adoption of refrigeration, the United States dominated livestock and meat product exports that primarily went to western Europe. American imports were opposed by small, high-cost local firms, and various European countries enacted protective trade restrictions from time to time. After 1900, however, U.S. livestock and meat production increasingly was aimed at the domestic market, and the pampas of Argentina and Uruguay became the primary sources of cattle and beef trade between the Americas and Europe. American packers, such as Armour and Swift, opened packing plants in Montevideo and Buenos Aires. Export earnings in those countries stimulated economic growth and higher per capita incomes at least through 1920.

Similar trade expansion occurred in grains. Before the 1840s, most countries were more or less self-sufficient in the production of their principal bread grains. But by the start of World War I, western European countries, as a whole, imported in excess of 30 percent of their wheat consumption, with over three-quarters of domestic consumption in Britain imported. Much of the grain that was imported came from Russia, Argentina, Romania, the United States, Canada, and Australia, which were the world's major grain exporters. By 1960, the United States predominated in grain exports, with significant sales from Canada, Australia, and Russia. Western European and, as the century progressed, Asian countries were the major importers (U.S. Department of Agriculture, 1912, 1962).

Between 1850 and 1910, the price of wheat in Chicago and London converged as the world market became more integrated with expanded trade. This convergence took place as the price of transportation over land and sea declined, through more efficient steam engines, and new rail and ocean shipping designs. Technological changes in flour milling also allowed for the relatively hard North American wheat to be milled as satisfactorily as the softer English wheat. The growth of trade brought a decline in wheat prices in consuming regions, a rise in producing regions, and increased specialization in production (Harley, 1980). Production specialization increasingly was in newly settled regions, the American Midwest and Great Plains, the Canadian Prairies, Argentina, and Australia. Movement into these areas occurred during periods of high wheat prices and new investment in transportation and other infrastructure. Export-led economic growth associated with the wheat boom was particularly important in these areas between 1890 and 1920 (Ankli, 1980; Williamson, 1980). High yields and high prices brought rising levels of per capita gross national product, which in turn attracted immigration and further settlement and investment. As supplies expanded beyond demand growth, prices fell and output growth moderated, initiating a cycle of production, exports, and wheat-based income.

Price cycles were damaging to farmers who held mortgages and other agricultural debt. One of the sharpest declines was in 1921, following the end of World War I. When farmers defaulted on loan payments, banks in the United States, particularly in the upper Great Plains, foreclosed on loans and often closed. In Canada, where branch banking dominated, the banking system was much less vulnerable to agricultural distress. Grain prices rebounded somewhat in the 1920s before falling during the Great Depression of the 1930s. Agricultural regulations, which included setting target prices, adopting production controls, providing income supplements, and granting export subsidies, were put into place in western Europe and North America to mitigate the problem of low agricultural prices and incomes. These regulations were unprecedented in their scope. They remained in force even after prices rose after World War II. Agriculture became the most regulated and subsidized sector in developed economies (Libecap, 1998). Furthermore, international agreements among exporting countries were put into place after World War II to dampen price cycles. The International Wheat Agreement outlined a system of export and import quotas to fix market shares for each country (Malenbaum, 1953).

BIBLIOGRAPHY

Ankli, Robert E. "The Growth of the Canadian Economy, 1896–1920: Export Led and/or Neoclassical Growth." *Explorations in Economic History* 17 (1980), 251–274.

Harley, C. Knick. "Transportation, the World Wheat Trade, and the Kuznets Cycle, 1850–1913." *Explorations in Economic History* 17 (1980), 218–250.

Libecap, Gary D. "The Rise of the Chicago Packers and the Origins of Meat Inspection and Antitrust." *Economic Inquiry* 30 (1992), 242–262.

Libecap, Gary D. "The Great Depression and the Regulating State: Federal Government Regulation of Agriculture, 1884–1970." In *The Defining Moment: The Great Depression and the American Economy in the Twentieth Century*, edited by Michael D. Bordo, Claudia Goldin, and Eugene N. White, pp. 181–224. Chicago, 1998.

Malenbaum, Wilfred. *The World Wheat Economy, 1885–1939.* Cambridge, Mass., 1953.

Perrin, Richard. "Structural Change and Market Growth in the Food Industry: Flour Milling in Britain, Europe, and America, 1850–1914." *Economic History Review* 43.3 (1990), 420–437.

U.S. Department of Agriculture. *Yearbook of Agriculture.* Washington, D.C., 1912, 1962.

U.S. Department of the Interior. "Flour and Grist Mill Products." *Census of Manufacturers.* Washington, D.C., 1850, 1900.

U.S. Department of the Interior. *Census of Manufacturers.* Washington, D.C., 1883.

Williamson, Jeffrey G. "Greasing the Wheels of Sputtering Export Engines: Midwestern Grains and American Growth." *Explorations in Economic History* 17 (1980), 189–217.

Yeager, Mary. *Competition and Regulation: The Development of Oligopoly in the Meat Packing Industry.* Greenwich, Conn., 1981.

GARY D. LIBECAP

Food Safety Regulation

Food processing is a sector of immense complexity and diversity in terms of its products, firms, and customers. Its importance in society is reflected in a variety of regulations, whether local, national, or international, that affect food production, prices, and quality. Food-safety regulations usually are designed to protect consumers against unsafe products or to provide information on which purchasing decisions may be made, thereby supplementing or requiring information supplied by producers through advertising, branding, and labeling. In this respect, there has been a long tradition of regulating the price and the quality of basic foodstuffs, notably bread, where opportunities for fraudulent or hazardous adulteration have existed. Popular pressures, through protest campaigns at times of high prices or shortages, periodically have reinforced the significance of such controls. In addition, states have used regulations to raise revenues through taxation of commodities, particularly alcoholic beverages and luxury items. During the nineteenth and twentieth centuries, regulation focused primarily on meat and milk as major commodities, on concerns about public health, and on the implications of new processes and ingredients. Agricultural policies also had a major impact on the food processing industry.

During the eighteenth and nineteenth centuries, there was some relaxation of earlier regulations of food processing, though activities such as milling and baking were subject to controls intended to protect farmers and consumers against fraud by millers and bakers, respectively. Where, as in Britain, free trade and "cheap food" policies came to dominate, a laissez-faire presumption limited the effectiveness and the impact of regulations. Paradoxically, however, a combination of rapid urban growth and an expanding international commodity trade made state regulation increasingly attractive to reforming professionals and some commercial interests. A "public interest" campaign for food-safety laws centered on claims that adulteration defrauded consumers or threatened their health, and that professional expertise, whether of doctors, chemists, or veterinarians, was essential to inform and protect consumers against their own ignorance. In Britain, such campaigns achieved major publicity from the *Lancet*'s Analytical Sanitary Commission from 1851 onward and initiated a cycle of exposés, official inquiries, and legislation from the 1860 Adulteration Act to the key Sale of Food and Drugs Acts of 1875 and 1899. Similar coalitions of chemists, doctors, and public officials were behind national food legislation across Europe from the 1870s on, including the French law of 1905, and, along with women's organizations, sustained the long campaign that led to the U.S. Pure Food and Drugs Act of 1906.

Generally the food processing industry resisted regulation, arguing that branded goods, its own self-interest, and new technologies were the best guarantees of safe foodstuffs. Such arguments limited the impact of regulations, especially as enforcement remained largely a local matter. However, some business interests actively supported regulation, usually as a way to disadvantage a competitor or a rival product, especially where the threat was external. Thus, coffee planters supported restrictions on adding chicory to coffee, and, in many states, dairy farmers and butter producers were successful in obtaining laws on margarine, designed to disadvantage the new product. Danish laws on margarine were strict, designed to protect the reputation of the butter export trade, and in Canada oleomargarine was prohibited from 1923 to 1951. National standards could be a form of protection against imports or, in the United States, a defense against state-level controls, used to facilitate trade.

The links between consumer health, professionalization, and commercial interest were particularly evident in the case of meat and milk. From the 1840s on, the incidence of cattle plague led to tighter frontier controls, especially on traffic in live animals, which intensified in the 1870s and early 1880s with a scare over trichinosis in American meat imported into Europe. The result was new regulations, including veterinary inspections, and a slow move toward municipal slaughterhouses. For American meatpackers, European controls and consumer fears threatened their export trade. During the 1890s, large producers supported

regulation of meat processing, designed to improve food safety, in part on the assumption that compliance costs would disadvantage their smaller domestic rivals. Kolko (Chicago, 1967) has argued that such commercial motivations accounted for the passage of the U.S. Pure Food and Drugs Act in 1906. As meatpacking became increasingly capital-intensive in production and distribution, firms supplied national and international markets, but incurred greater sunk costs that required maximum production. The protracted "public interest" campaign was intensified by Upton Sinclair's journalistic exposé of conditions in the Chicago stockyards that revived European fears about imported meat products. According to Kolko, leading U.S. packers "captured" the resulting regulatory process, ensuring that inspections would be financed by the federal government and in the hope of restoring consumer confidence. Once the law was enacted, other business interests sought alliances with key officials, notably Harvey S. Wiley, in the hope of defining their own products as legitimate and disadvantaging rival commodities.

The Chicago episode consolidated a trend toward national food-safety legislation and gave further momentum to a series of international congresses on food issues, including an 1897 proposal for an International Codex Alimentarius. Yet the effects of regulation were limited: enforcement remained essentially a local matter and agricultural policies were more influential than food safety. For milk, where health risks and adulteration were most significant, some local health officials established controls over production, distribution, and sale while local courts and national regulations gradually restricted the use of chemical additives; but commercial resistance, scientific disputes, and official caution combined to delay national laws to make pasteurization compulsory. In some countries national governments regulated prices and supplies, either directly or, as in the United States, through dairy cooperatives. From 1910 to 1945, food-safety regulations were temporary wartime measures or reactions to new food scares, as was the case with the U.S. Pure Food and Drug Act of 1938, signifying that neither "public interest" nor "capture" was a powerful force. In other cases, the state's influence came through other types of regulation, as in the use of U.S. antitrust laws to undermine the meatpackers' cartel in 1921. Indirectly too, federal grading of meat from 1927 slowly weakened the barriers to entry created by the major packers' own systems of grading.

A new phase of development was apparent after World War II. National governments exerted greater influence, at least as forums for discussion between food industry trade associations, officials, scientists, and health professionals. The transition from wartime scarcity to a postwar emphasis on maximizing agricultural output provided a context for the rapid adoption of new technologies in food production and processing, including new scientific developments. Within the regulatory process, trade associations were more numerous and linked to government, often through highly specialized commodity groupings. The result was greater inspection and regulation, especially in relation to public health concerns, and powerful corporatist arrangements in some sectors, especially milk production, where price and output were tightly controlled. Yet the pace of innovation in food production and distribution was a fundamental challenge to the regulatory system. Regulation provided the parameter within which such new innovations were legitimized through the state's role as agent for the consumer. International initiatives also continued, notably through the World Health Organization and the Food and Agriculture Organization; the 1964 Codex Alimentarius Commission established international norms although national standards retained much of their protectionist effect. In Europe, agricultural policies took precedence over food-safety issues, and even the proliferation of European food-safety regulations from 1973 were largely voluntary and allowed the persistence of national practices. An approach of developing broad policies and then relying on national-level implementation became a deliberate strategy to avoid the immense complexities of seeking detailed agreement among all nations.

Producers continued to emphasize their own commitment to food safety and the importance of innovation to satisfy consumers' wants. The major food retailers increasingly identified their role as protecting consumers' interests through low prices, choice, and quality. In sectors such as meat, the packers' earlier control over distribution declined, allowing private transactions between wholesalers and retailers greater influence over prices and quality. These developments and confidence in foodsafety regimes were challenged by revived consumer movements from the 1960s on, which resembled the late-nineteenth-century reform campaigns. There was demand for regulations to address health concerns, such as the nutritional value of foods, their associations with the incidence of cancer and heart disease, and fears about the consequences of new technologies (e.g., use of pesticides in the food chain and artificial colorings and preservatives). In part, the increasing provision of both exotic and fresh foods increased the technological challenge of ensuring food safety. Reformers criticized regulatory frameworks as being "captured" by producers rather than representing consumers, and they challenged scientific expertise, whereas conservative advocates of "deregulation" proclaimed the effectiveness of relying on private enterprise, especially large-scale retailers. Where, as in the U.S. meat and milk sectors, the structure of the industry was changing, retailers or cooperatives did exert increased influence.

Conflicting pressures thus created scope for change, especially in Britain, where the 1980s and 1990s saw recurring food scares about food poisoning rates, *Salmonella*, *Listeria*, and BSE (Bovine Spongiform Encephalopathy) and the new variant CJD (Creutzfeldt-Jacob Disease) as well as concerns about new technologies, such as genetically modified foods. As in the nineteenth century, the response was a series of public inquiries, new legislation, and the establishment of a Food Standards Agency in 2000, for the purpose of giving priority to consumer interests and restoring public confidence in food safety. With plans for a similar European initiative, the structures of food-safety regulation have shifted substantially, strengthening emphasis on consumers within a framework dominated by representatives of business and governments and health professionals. The regulatory developments of the nineteenth and early twentieth centuries suggest that the new forums are likely to see intensive and protracted debates with rather limited practical effects on food safety.

BIBLIOGRAPHY

Atkins, P. J. "Sophistication Detected, or the Adulteration of the Milk Supply, 1850–1914." *Social History* 16 (1991), 317–339.

Burnett, John. *Plenty and Want: A Social History of Food in England from 1815 to the Present Day*. London, 1989. Major study that includes discussion of late-nineteenth-century legislation.

Burnett, John. *Liquid Pleasures: A Social History of Drinks in Modern Britain*. London, 1999.

Burnett, J., and D. Oddy, eds. *The Origins and Development of Food Policies in Europe*. London, 1994. Valuable articles on European regulations.

Campbell, J. L., J. R. Hollingsworth, and L. N. Lindberg, eds. *Governance of the American Economy*. Cambridge, 1991. Work that includes articles on meat and milk sectors in nineteenth and twentieth centuries.

French, M., and J. Phillips. *Cheated Not Poisoned? Food Regulation in the United Kingdom, 1875–1938*. Manchester, U.K., 2000. Study of politics of food regulation, 1875–1938.

Grant, Wyn, ed. *Business Interests, Organisational Development and Private Interest Government: An International Comparative Study of the Food Processing Industry*. Berlin, 1987. Detailed studies of European industry and relations to governments, 1950s–1980s.

Jackson, C. O. *Food and Drug Legislation in the New Deal*. Princeton, 1970. Key account of 1938 law.

Kolko, Gabriel. *Triumph of Conservatism: A Reinterpretation of American History, 1900–1916*. Chicago, 1967. Classic revisionist interpretation of business-related regulations, including meat laws.

Okun, M. *Fair Play in the Marketplace: The First Battle for Pure Food and Drugs*. DeKalb, Ill., 1986. Appraisal of diverse interests in late-nineteenth-century U.S. campaigns for food-safety laws.

Paulus, Ingeborg. *The Search for Pure Food: A Sociology of Legislation in Britain*. London, 1974. Impressive sociological study of nineteenth-century debates and laws concerning food.

Wood, Donna. *Strategic Uses of Public Policy: Business and Government in the Progressive Era*. Pittsburgh, 1986.

Young, J. H. *Pure Food: Securing the Federal Food and Drug Act of 1906*. Princeton, 1989. Authoritative study of key U.S. legislation.

MICHAEL FRENCH

FORD, HENRY (1863–1947), American industrialist.

Henry Ford was a mechanic turned automobile manufacturer who had one of the great commercial ideas of the twentieth century and implemented its production faithfully. In the end, this brought him both triumph and catastrophe. He is remembered as a great champion of the mass market for consumer durables, a central figure in the development of mass production methods, an important figure in the history of welfare capitalism, and a cautionary figure in the history of corporate change.

Ford was born in rural Michigan during the Civil War. His father was a farmer. Henry showed mechanical aptitude as a child and preferred pursuing this to agriculture. He trained as a machinist and found early employment in Detroit, the nearest city. He moved from job to job in the early years of his career, repairing watches and clocks to make ends meet; married; and started a family. By 1893, he was the chief engineer of the Edison Illuminating Company. He was also tinkering in his garage with primitive internal combustion engines and early automobiles. He built his first car in 1896 and by 1899 had quit Edison to devote himself to automobiles full time.

Ford's first company lasted only two years and ended in bankruptcy. His second was more successful. The Ford Motor Company was founded in 1903 by Ford and eleven other investors. The company's cars sold from the first, but the designs also evolved. In the course of debate over the direction this evolution should take, Ford gained control of the company and with the famous Model T set it going down an unusual path. Most cars on the market at that time were large, heavy, and expensive enough that only the well-to-do could afford them. Ford thought that there would be a large market for a modest lightweight model and that with a large enough market, he could make such cars inexpensively enough for the multitudes to afford them. He proved to be correct.

Automobile manufacturing was a custom-oriented, craft-intensive activity at this time. Ford saw that the key to low-cost production lay in the standardization of product and the routinization of work. American-system interchangeable-parts manufacturing had theretofore commonly been deployed on small and simpler products, but Ford eventually adopted it root and branch and made important innovations. In the popular consciousness, the Ford company invented the moving assembly line. It certainly became well known for highly fragmented job tasks with low skill content, its dedicated machine tools, and centralized control of pace. It also became by an order of magnitude the largest firm in the industry. Ford dropped its price steadily and a mass market, in the countryside as well as the city, did indeed emerge. Mass ownership of automobiles, in turn, had many profound and long-lasting effects on the character of American life.

HENRY FORD. Portrait, circa 1919. (National Photo Company Collection/Hartsook/Prints and Photographs Division, Library of Congress)

In 1914, at the crest of the development of the manufacturing methods and with the company's product selling hundreds of thousands of units a year, Ford became well known for its employment policies as well. At a time when the country was slipping into a deep recession, its principle owner announced that he would more than double the modal wage in his factory to the then-grand sum of five dollars a day. This was coupled to home inspections and part of an initiative that included Americanization classes for the many immigrant employees and a trade school. In the mornings just after the announcement, there were roughly as many people lined up outside the employment office looking for jobs as there were actually working in the factory (around twelve thousand in this period). Fire hoses were required on the first day to clear the way for the incoming shift. The real value of the wage was allowed to fade over the years, as were the programs; but the initial gesture provoked great debate. This only seemed more salient as Ford invested in a massive and highly vertically integrated plant on the River Rouge outside Detroit, at its peak one of the largest industrial establishments in the world.

The American automobile market changed a great deal during the 1920s, but the Model T did not. Ford's competition also changed. The most important of the competitive changes concerned the General Motors Corporation (GM), by the mid-1920s a multidivisional firm that could place economies of scope as well as scale behind the product it put up against the Model T. General Motors also believed in marketing and planned change, whereas Ford clung relatively stubbornly to an increasingly dated design and look. Perhaps most important, GM's organizational innovations facilitated investment analysis and strategic thinking. Ford remained a sometimes willful autocracy.

By the second half of the 1920s, GM was rising and the not-much-changed Model T was in marked decline. The end came in 1927. In essence, the Ford company then replaced the single old product with a single new one, the Model A. The Model A was indeed better suited to its times and the public's tastes than was its predecessor. But the Rouge plant and its equipment were not well suited to the Model A. The plant was essentially shut down for refurbishment for more than six months and roughly half the machine tools were rebuilt or replaced. The costs of this and new machine tool acquisition alone ran to $18 million. The total costs of the changeover, including the opportunity costs of the shutdown, are thought to have totaled about $250 million.

Ford's clarity of vision and decision-making authority were valuable in the earliest years, but they were an increasing burden to the company as time passed. Product and production decisions entirely aside, Ford made decisions that embittered dealers in the early 1920s and labor relations in the 1930s. Many talented managers fled, much to the advantage of Ford's competitors.

Henry Ford died in 1947, having buried his son and heir, Edsel, four years previously. His company survived him (in both senses), though not without wrenching transitions. It never regained the market dominance it had once possessed, though it did subsequently prosper.

BIBLIOGRAPHY

Arnold, Horace L., and Faye L. Faurote. *Ford Methods and the Ford Shops*. New York, 1915. Drawn from contemporary articles in a trade journal, this gives a detailed and illustrated view of Ford manufacturing methods about 1914. Long out of print but sometimes available in research libraries.

Hounshell, David A. *From the American System to Mass Production: The Development of Manufacturing Technology in the United States*. Baltimore, 1984.

Stephen C. Meyer III. *The Five-Dollar Day: Labor Management and Social Control in the Ford Motor Company 1908–1921*. Albany, N.Y., 1981.

Nevins, Allan. *Ford: The Times, the Man, the Company*. New York, 1954.

Nevins, Allan. *Ford: Expansion and Challenge 1915–1933*. New York, 1957.

Nevins, Allan, and Frank Ernest Hill. *Ford: Decline and Rebirth 1933–1962*. New York, 1962.

DANIEL RAFF

FORESTS AND DEFORESTATION. From earliest times, humanity has had an ambivalent relation with forests. For hundreds of thousands of years, people have needed wood to cook their food and to heat their homes. They therefore have had to burn and destroy the very resource on which they have depended for survival.

Importance of Forests and Uses of Wood. Throughout history, hunters have relied on forests to shelter the game that they eat. Yet they burn forests to flush out their prey. Destroying habitats in this way has led to the extinction of many local species. Faced with declining natural food supplies, many societies began domesticating animals as a substitute for the loss of game. Pasturing these animals led to further forest loss both by the animals' foraging habits (they feed on roots, shoots, and seeds, limiting the forests' ability to regenerate) and by the herders' habit of burning down forests to encourage the growth of grass for better pasturage.

Trees and their litter also make the soil in which they grow more fertile. Its fecundity has lured farmers to consider planting there. But first, the very agents of the soil's enrichment, the trees, have to be removed to make room for crops.

As societies became more complex, they needed forests as never before to supply them with fuel and building material. Yet to survive and grow, these societies had to destroy trees in increasing numbers for these supplies. Burgeoning populations demanded more wood for household fuel. When it was found that metals made superior tools and weapons, wood fuel was used to supply the heat to separate the metal ores from the rock in which they were found. Until the early nineteenth century, wood fuel in the form of charcoal provided the necessary heat metallurgists required. The heat from wood fuel transformed useless mud into pottery and building materials such as brick, limestone, and plaster. Wood was also used to heat foodstuff to make it edible.

Wood has been the primary building material for most societies. Their growth requires trade, which depends on transport. Merchants over the millennia have relied on ships to carry most of their goods. To keep shipping lanes safe and trade flowing, great powers have depended on their warships. Until the last 150 years, wood composed every ship from fore to aft, from hull to mast. In fact, in the days when timber was the sole material for shipbuilding, the Italian word for wood, *legno*, could also mean "ship," because wood and ship were so intertwined.

Other forms of transport before the coming of railroads and motor vehicles, such as chariots, carts, and wagons, were made of wood. The Lakota word for wagon translated as "wood on wheels." Even railroads depended on wood for ties and trestles, and in the United States, for fuel well into the latter part of the nineteenth century.

DEFORESTATION. Aerial view of parts of the Ituri Forest cleared for farming, Zaire, 1989. (© Jose Azel/Woodfin Camp and Associates, New York)

Mines would have collapsed without their wooden posts. Almost every type of building relies on wooden beams and rafters for support. Wooden handles for tools increase their range of use.

With all these demands for wood, no wonder the ancient writers observed that forests have always receded as civilization developed and grew. The great Roman poet Ovid wrote, for instance, that before civilizations took root, "not yet had the pine tree been felled on its mountainside;" but when the Iron Age (Ovid's term for early civilization) began, all the pine were cut down.

The ancients had no doubt why this happened: they recognized the use of wood as the primary agent that propelled humanity from a stone-and-bone culture to its civilized state. Plato, for example, observed that all arts and crafts were derived from forestry and mining. And metals, according to the Roman natural philosopher Lucretius, could not have been extracted from ores without wood fuel. More than a thousand years later, the seventeenth-century English writer Gabriel Plates made a similar discovery: that all "tools and instruments are made of wood and iron." But of the two materials, wood took precedence because without wood fuel, "no iron can be provided."

Language, too, recognized the primacy of wood in our ancestors' lives. *Hulae* and *materia*, the Greek and Roman words for "wood," soon evolved in popular discourse to mean "primary matter." This etymological transformation demonstrates that those living in classical times regarded wood as primary to their lives and to their society. The Latin word *mater* ("mother") originally referred to the growing trunk of a tree. In other words, the Romans saw the tree as the creator of life on earth as they lived it.

History of Early Deforestation. History bears out the ancients' contention that forests decline as civilization progress. It therefore should come as no surprise that the first evidence of large-scale deforestation arose in Asia, one area where civilization first began. All the founding legends in this part of the world tell of humans' attack on the forests. *The Epic of Gilgamesh*, the world's oldest surviving written saga, tells of Mesopotamia's founding king, Gilgamesh, and his followers "stripping the mountains of their cover." During the third millennium BCE, kings in that region bragged in boasts written in cuneiform and preserved in clay how they, too, "made a path into the cedar mountain and felled its cedar down with great axes." The logs were floated down the Euphrates and its tributaries, ending up in southern Mesopotamia as building material for the great temples or for the cargo ships that conducted trade between the cities in the region and in Arabia and India.

Once the Mesopotamians began felling large quantities of trees near the banks of the upper courses of the Euphrates, Tigris, and Karun rivers and tributaries, salt and silt filled the waters heading south as the exposure of steep, deforested hillsides directly to sun, wind, and rain accelerated erosion. Coinciding with peak deforestation in

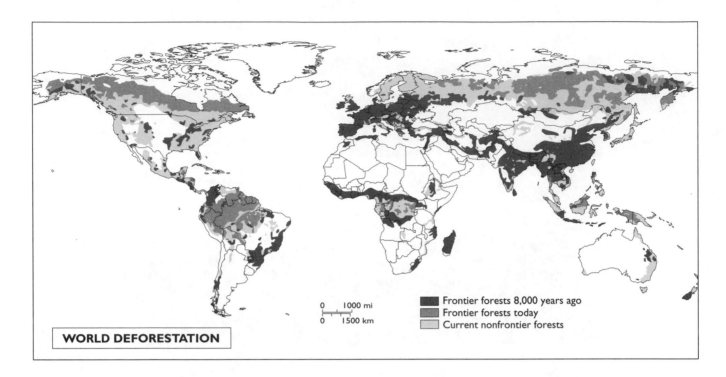

Frontier forests 8,000 years ago
Frontier forests today
Current nonfrontier forests

WORLD DEFORESTATION

the north, silt accumulated in the south at a dangerous pace, forever threatening to clog up the irrigation canals.

Deforestation also dominates the founding legend of historical China. According to the ancient Chinese philosopher Mencius, China's first emperor, Yao, felt great anguish to see the land overgrown by vegetation and crowded by swarming birds and beasts. Yao's handpicked successor, Shun, acted to rid the landscape of what had so offended his mentor by ordering his forester, Yi, to set on fires the forests and vegetation on the mountains and in the marshes, "so that the birds and beasts fled away" and all kinds of grains could then be planted. Mencius personally viewed the continuation of China's war against the trees when he saw "the trees of Niu mountain . . . hewn down" and therefore "bare and stripped."

In the *Mahabharata,* the Sanskrit Hindu epic, the ancient Aryan heroes Krsna, Vasudeva, and Arjuna help the fire god devour the great Khandava forest in northern India and make sure none of the fleeing creatures survive. The heroes want the forest cleared to assure their new kingdom of sufficient farmland.

Unlike Mesopotamia, China, and India, ancient Egypt lacked forests of any size in its immediate territory. Its rulers made up for this deficit by exploiting the cedars growing in nearby Lebanon. The timber trade between Egypt and Byblos, on the coast of present-day Lebanon, began about 4,600 years ago. While the pharaohs held hegemony in the Near East, they demanded the cedars of Lebanon as tribute. They needed timber to outfit their navy as well for supports for large buildings. As Egyptian

power waned, the Phoenicians demanded large quantities of silver from the weakened Egyptian rulers, enriching Phoenicia, which became the great maritime power of the Mediterranean during the latter part of the second millennium BCE.

On their voyages, the Phoenicians discovered great amounts of copper and pine on the island of Cyprus. The combination of abundant ore and fuel allowed the Phoenicians to oversee the smelting of copper in large quantities. Alloying the copper with small amounts of tin to produce bronze, the Phoenicians conducted a highly profitable trade in bronze throughout the Mediterranean world. As the alloy proved stronger and more durable than mere copper, the Homeric heroes armored themselves with bronze and fought with bronze weaponry. Once the Cypriot copper mines ran out of ore, metallurgists discovered that the slag contained great amounts of iron, which they could easily remove by hammering. People soon discovered the superiority of this new metal. Hence, the deforestation of Cyprus inadvertently pushed humanity into the Iron Age.

The deforestation of Cyprus brought other changes to the island. With the majority of the forests cover along the coast and hillsides cleared, pigs, which thrive in a moist, woody habitat, could no longer thrive, giving way to sheep and goats, which flourish in a relatively barren environment. With the forest cover gone, silting of major harbors and an increase in floods and mud slides on urban sites ensued.

The Athenians in their heyday, like the Egyptians, lacked trees of great size. Their power, though, relied on naval supremacy. They therefore went to great lengths to control timber growing in northern Greece. When they lost control of this region, the abundant forests lured them to Italy and Sicily. Forests near Rome were so thickly wooded that no Romans dared to enter for fear they would lose their way and never be found. But as Rome grew and the Roman lifestyle took on great affluence, forest by forest fell. The Roman natural historian Pliny observed the destructive effect on the welfare of the earth when trees were cut. When rain fell on denuded hillsides, Pliny observed, devastating torrents resulted, carrying much of the surrounding topsoil into streams and rivers. Although felling wood close to the Tiber and its tributaries facilitated its transport to Rome, large amounts of earth also came down these waterways. Eventually, the mouth of the Tiber silted up and rendered Rome's harbor at Ostia useless for large vessels, forcing the Roman fleets to anchor in the open sea and unload their cargoes onto smaller boat that could still sail to Ostia.

When Theodoric, the barbarian king of sixth-century Italy, referred to that country as "abounding in timber," he did not have in mind the Tiber watershed. He was referring instead to the Po basin and the land north of it, much of which later came under the control of the Venetian Republic. The Venetians, the great power of southern Europe from the thirteenth to the sixteenth centuries, acknowledged their debt to wood for their affluence. As a state whose wealth was based on sea power, Venice regarded its forests as "the very sinews of the republic." Others living in Venetian territory needed the same wood to fuel the growing industries in Venice, such as its famous glass industry. Farmers valued the same woodlands as space for pasture- and cropland. They therefore had no compunction to cut down the big trees growing in the foothills and mountains above Venice and set fire to the remaining brush. Without the protective forest covering, according to Venetian forester Giuseppe Paulini, "there is no vegetation to retain rainwater and the snow lies exposed to the sun. In an instant after a storm, water will precipitously swoop down from the mountains and will carry such enormous quantities of debris as to break pasture land, devastate the countryside, destroy buildings and sometimes ruin entire towns." By the sixteenth century, Venetian ship builders had to search far and wide for suitable timber. The rising cost of wood put the Venetians at a disadvantage to powers in northern Europe that had access to the great timberlands of Poland, the Baltic States, and Scandinavia, allowing them to build large fleets at relatively low cost to take advantage of the great opportunities offered by the opening of transoceanic commerce.

Developments in the New World. It cannot be overstated the sea change for life in Africa, America, and Europe brought about by the discovery and exploitation of the East Indies and the New World by Europeans. The lengthy voyage from Europe to the East Indies set Christopher Columbus on his quest for a faster route to the East. Once in the New World, the wild game living in the forests sustained the Europeans, whether conquistadores, pirates, or settlers. Fuel from the trees smelted the silver and gold from the Americas, which then came back to the Old World in ships built or repaired from the New World's great trees. Much of the booty stolen from the Spanish fleet by English pirates such as Sir Francis Drake helped finance England's first Industrial Revolution fueled by woods from the English counties of Sussex, Kent, and Surrey. When these trees gave out, England turned to coal, initiating the era of fossil fuels.

The forest soils of the West Indies and Brazil nurtured more sustainable wealth–in the form of sugar than either silver or gold generated. The wood from trees cut down to make way for sugar plantations built the mills where the sugar was processed. Wood from adjoining forests fueled the kettles in which the cane juice was boiled down into sugar loaves, ready for export to Europe. Money from the sugar sold on the European market brought great wealth to Europe, providing the capital that helped finance the second Industrial Revolution, which began in the early 1800s and continues to this day.

The clearance of the tropical forests to support the sugar industry forced those gathering its fuel to go great distances looking for wood. The renowned explorer and scientist Alexander von Humboldt also observed that "the clearing of forests, the want of permanent springs and the existence of torrents are three phenomena closely connected together."

Farther north, the forests of New England provided the capital for the Puritans and other settlers to establish businesses and farms. Vintners on the "wine islands" (the Canaries and Madeira) willingly traded wine for staves from New England from which they made casks. New Englanders traded the wine in England for manufactured goods, which they sold in America.

The coasts of New England also attracted shipbuilders who could turn out vessels cheaper from forests full of higher quality and more abundant wood than that found in the England and sell for a hefty profit boats made in America to ship across the Atlantic. New England timber also found many buyers among sugar mill owners in the West Indies, who had destroyed their forests to plant and process sugar cane but needed more wood to continue operating. This need on the part of the West Indian planters brought great wealth to New England and developed a trade vector that became known as the Evil Triangle: New Englanders shipped wood down to the Indies. There they picked up rum and headed for Africa. In exchange for rum, they took African slaves. Back to the Indies with their human cargo, the New Englanders bartered the slaves for molasses, sugar, and rum. Much of that went to England in exchange for manufactured goods, which were eventually sold in America at a huge profit.

Thanks to its forests, New England became the most powerful and wealthiest part of British North America. But this abundance also introduced several inevitable conflicts with far-reaching consequences. The British and other Europeans had depleted the best trees in Europe for masting their great warships. The only remaining timber fir for masting these huge ships grew in New England. England's archenemy, France, allied itself with the local Native Americans to harass English naval procurement teams in the forests where these large white pines grew. To protect its naval assets, the British finally decided to take up arms, expelling the French from North America in 1763.

Whereas the English took efforts to husband the timber in New England for their current and future naval needs, the colonists wanted to cut down the trees and sell them at home and abroad for startup capital to establish their own farms. The conflict over timber between the British and the colonists developed into the first irresolvable conflict between England and the American colonies. The tensions led to conflict, which only independence resolved. The English came to fear America as a consequence of its forest resources. Many concluded that a country so endowed with timber and pitch for naval pursuits, as well as plentiful wood fuel and iron to turn out artillery and shot, could easily take on militarily the less-endowed mother country. Likewise, knowing the power their timber assets gave them, many Americans came to wonder why they should subject themselves to a country that had come to depend on them for its naval supremacy.

After independence, tens of thousands of Americans migrated to the densely forested area bounded by the Allegheny Mountains and the Ohio and Mississippi rivers, formerly closed to their settlement by the British. The settlers came onto a forested land comparable only to the Amazon. Settlers came upon oaks more than 140 feet (43 meters) tall, walnut trees almost 7 feet (2 meters) in girth, and sycamores with a circumference of over 40 feet (12 meters). Soon these trees were cleared for farmers to plant in the rich soil the forests had nurtured over thousands of years. The farmers sold much of the wood to cart wrights, coopers, and shipbuilders. Steamboats and later railroads that carried crops to market, making farming in this region economically possible, also used wood for fuel. Others suffered irrevocable harm, however. Native animals, including more than three million bison that roamed Indiana, Ohio, and Michigan, robbed of their habitats, either died or fled west. A parallel fate befell the regions' indigenous populations, who were dependent for survival on the forests and the animals that foraged within.

Pattern of Deforestation. And so America became part of a cycle repeated in so many lands and ages before and after: an Old World once new, fully forested, and abounding in animals both big and small, turned sterile, stripped of its great trees and robbed of its bountiful game. The quest for new frontiers, long thought peculiar to the American experience, turns out to be just a repetition of an age-old process that has occurred again and again through the millennia.

Before humanity began its war on the forests 10,000 years ago, six million hectares of the earth's land was forested. The area of forestland has now shrunk to three and a half million hectares. The areas that first lost their forests were the Middle East, the Mediterranean watershed, South Asia, and the Far East. Since 1850, forest destruction has accelerated. Currently, about 14.8 million hectares of forestlands are lost annually. The clearing of so many trees has released such large amounts of carbon into the atmosphere as to become, along with industrialization, a major contributor to global warming.

[*See also* Timber and Logging Industry.]

BIBLIOGRAPHY

Bryant, D., D. Nielsen, and L. Tangley. *The Last Frontier Forests: Ecosystems and Economics on the Edge.* Washington, D.C., 1997.

Myers, N. "The Present Status and Future Prospects of Tropical Moist Forests." Environmental Conservation 7.2 (1960), 101–114.

Perlin, J. *A Forest Journey: The Role of Wood in the Development of Civilization.* Cambridge, Mass., 1991.

Richards, J., and R. Tucker, eds. *World Deforestation in the Twentieth Century.* Durham, 1988.

Smil, V. *The Bad Earth.* London 1984.

Tucker, R., and J. Richards, eds. *Global Deforestation and the Nineteenth-Century World Economy.* Durham, 1983.

JOHN PERLIN

FOSSIL FUELS. Ours is the first civilization energized primarily by fossil fuels. Although they were known, and in some places used, since antiquity, their rise to dominance and their gradual displacement of traditional biomass energies (wood, charcoal made from it, crop residues, in some places also grasses and dried dung) that supplied heat and light for all premodern societies are relatively recent. Coal became the largest source of the world's total primary energy supply (TPES) during the 1890s, and it yielded its primacy to crude oil only during the 1970s. Natural gas now supplies about as much energy as coal. In aggregate, fossil fuels account for nearly 90 percent of the world's commercial TPES, with the rest coming from primary (hydro- and nuclear) electricity. If the still important use of mostly noncommercial biomass energies in low-income countries is added, then the fossil fuels provide about 80 percent of the global TPES.

Concentrated energy released by the combustion of fossil fuels has stimulated an era of unprecedented technical innovations and remarkable social opportunities that have revolutionized every aspect of modern economies and radically reshaped industrial, residential, and transportation infrastructures (Smil, 1994). Electricity generation (currently about 60 percent of it comes from the combustion of fossil fuels) has been perhaps the most far-reaching innovation because of its transformation of industrial production (electric motors became its key prime movers) and provision of effortless residential comforts (lighting and air conditioning) and services (cooking, refrigeration, washing, and cleaning).

Coal and steam engines energized the first century of industrial advances, and the subsequent availability of refined liquid fuels has made it possible to deploy internal combustion engines. Their mass deployment ushered in two critical transformations: the mechanization of field and processing tasks in agriculture (tractors, combines, irrigation pumps, and dryers) and the creation of new means of public and private transportation using buses, trucks, passenger automobiles, and airplanes. Flying was further transformed by the invention of gas turbine and the resulting affordable intercontinental travel on jets.

Fossil fuels are energy sources as well as feedstocks for a multitude of chemical syntheses, ranging from nitrogen fertilizers, whose availability is a key to raising crop yields, to many kinds of plastics, whose ubiquity in our lives is now taken for granted. Fossil fuels have also transformed modern wars by fueling the machines of high mobility (tanks and planes) and by enabling syntheses of more powerful explosives. The quest for a reliable supply of high-quality fossil fuels, particularly of crude oil, has emerged as a major factor of international economics and politics. Modern society, however, has paid a serious environmental price for its reliance on fossil fuels, as their extraction, transportation, and conversion have contributed to land degradation and water pollution and as their combustion generates various atmospheric emissions. Production of carbon dioxide, a greenhouse gas, is the most important reason for growing concerns about global warming taking place at a rate unprecedented in human history.

Varieties and Properties. First, a qualifier regarding the adjective *fossil*—it clearly implies that all such fuels are the products of converting solar radiation into biomass whose underground transformation yielded, after 10^6 to 10^8 years, various types of solids, liquids, and gases. Recently, and controversially, some geologists have come to believe that some oils and gases have abiotic origins in the earth's crust (Gold, 1999). Fossil fuels span such a range of appearances, properties, and qualities that it is misleading to see them as singular commodities. Coals are basically carbon solids adulterated with incombustible matter. Now rare, anthracites are nearly pure carbon. In contrast, some lignites have more ash and water than carbon, and hence

may contain less energy than air-dried wood. Today's global coal production is dominated by bituminous (black) coals that contain typically about 10 percent ash and 2 percent sulfur and have only about half as much energy per mass as crude oil. Peats are only partly fossilized remains of phytomass, and hence inferior even to lignites.

Crude oils are mixtures of complex hydrocarbons with mere traces of ash. Most common varieties are relatively heavy and sometimes also waxy with as much sulfur as in bituminous coals; rarer light and low-sulfur (sweet) crudes are priced higher on the international market. Refining of crude oils produces a variety of liquids for specific uses: gasoline and jet and diesel fuel for transportation, and fuel oils for heat and steam generation; residues go into lubricants and paving materials. Some natural gases are nearly pure methane; others contain ethane and propane. They are the least-polluting fossil fuels, but because their energy density under normal pressure is only 1/1,000 that of crude oil, their use as portable transportation fuel is limited.

History of Coal Use. Coal seams outcrop in many parts of the world, and hence were known and locally used since antiquity, when coal's most important application was in iron making during the Han dynasty (Needham, 1964). European extraction is documented in Belgium in 1113; the first shipments of coal to London date to 1228 (Nef, 1932). Almost all of the English coalfields that fueled the country's industries until the mid-twentieth century were already exploited between 1540 and 1640. Serious regional wood shortages, caused not only by rising demand for fuelwood and charcoal but also because of large needs for construction and shipbuilding timber, were the reason that England was the first country to shift from wood to coal. Its output approached 10 million tons by the end of the eighteenth century (Flinn et al., 1984–1993). However, it was not the first country to shift from biomass to fossil fuels; that primacy belongs to the seventeenth-century Netherlands, where the golden age of the country's economy and creativity was energized largely by domestic peat (DeZeeuw, 1978).

All traditional coal mining was a matter of heavy and dangerous labor in extremely dusty, poorly ventilated, and confined spaces. Boys as young as six to eight years did many lighter tasks, and women were often employed to carry coal to the surface by ascending steep ladders (Ashton and Sykes, 1929). Donkeys and small horses were used for underground transport after 1650. Gradual deepening of coal pits (some reached more than 200 meters [656 feet] after 1770) needed more energy for water pumping and ventilation as well as for hoisting of coal. Waterwheels, windmills, and horses used for these tasks were only slowly replaced by Thomas Newcomen's (1664–1729) very inefficient steam engines that converted a mere 0.5 percent of coal into useful motion. Extracted coal was moved in horse-drawn wagons over shorter distances and exported to large cities, and overseas, by boats and ships.

Households, forges, and producers of bricks, tiles, and soap, among others, were the principal early users of coal. Glassmaking was added after 1610 following the invention of heat-reflecting furnaces, and although coke was first prepared from coal around 1640, it was only in 1709 that Abraham Darby succeeded in smelting pig iron with coke. However, widespread replacement of charcoal began to take place only after 1750. Blast furnaces charged with coke were bigger, raising productivity and creating more demand for the fuel. But by far the greatest boost for coal extraction came with James Watt's (1736–1819) improved steam engine, patented in 1769. Its greatest innovations were the addition of a separate steam condenser, an air pump maintaining vacuum in the condenser, and an insulated steam jacket around the cylinder. These improvements increased the engine's efficiency four- to sixfold compared to Newcomen's machines, and by 1800, close to 2,000 engines were in operation. Their average power was about 20 kW (27 hp), a capacity more than five times higher than the mean for typical contemporary watermills, and nearly three times larger than that for windmills.

Soon after the expiration of Watt's patent in 1800, the steam engine was rapidly adopted by many industries and further improved by the introduction of high-pressure boilers. The first seagoing steam ship was launched in 1802, the first public railway opened in 1830, and the first Atlantic crossing unassisted by sails came in 1833. By the mid-nineteenth century, the steam engine became the world's first ubiquitous, economic, and reliable converter of chemical energy into motion (reciprocating or rotary) that was powering not only entire old and new industries but, after it was installed on locomotives and ships, also the first inanimate means of affordable and reliable land and water transportation. By the end of the century, the largest machines operated under pressures a hundred times higher and were about thirty times more powerful and ten times more efficient than their predecessors in 1800.

U.S., German, French, Russian, and Japanese transitions from biomass to fossil fuels also started with coal, but greater availability of wood and water power made the process slower than in Great Britain. For example, in Germany, the switch required state measures in favor of coal. The American TPES was dominated by wood until the 1880s, the Russian until the early twentieth century. The United States and the Soviet Union then proceeded faster in switching from coal to oil and natural gas, as did post–World War II Japan and Germany. Most Asian, African, and Latin American countries skipped the coal stage entirely by turning to imported crude oil.

Great Britain's dominance of coal extraction lasted until the 1890s, when the U.S. production became the world's largest, and it was surpassed by Soviet output during the 1950s. Global coal production expanded from 10 million tons in 1810 to 1 billion tons in 1910 and to more than 4.5 billion tons during the 1990s. This large increase was made possible by rapidly rising mining productivity and accompanied by fundamental restructuring of final demand. Virtually complete mechanization of underground extraction and higher shares of the fuel extracted in surface mines have transformed the modern coal industry. Coal from large mines is often burned in adjacent power plants or moved to distant markets by special trains.

The main reasons for coal's relative retreat were the steam engine's inherent limitations: it could not remain the leading prime mover of the twentieth century because it was too heavy for any nonrail applications on land and too inefficient. The modern coal market is dominated by the combustion of bituminous coals and lignites for electricity generation (about 85 percent of the total) and by production of metallurgical coke. Widespread use of coal in households and by industries is now limited only to China (now the world's largest coal producer) and India and, to much a lesser extent, parts of Europe.

Crude Oil and Refined Fuels. Because of seepages of the fuel and bitumen pools, common in many areas of the Middle East, crude oil, like coal, was also known since antiquity, but its practical uses, for heating or lubricants, were rare. The proximate reason for the large-scale introduction of liquid fuels was the mounting slaughter of whales that made whale oil more expensive. Lamp kerosene was first distilled in 1853 by Abraham Gesner (1797–1864) in London, and before the decade's end, in August 1859, Colonel E. L. Drake's (1819–1880) workers, using a mechanized version of an ancient Chinese technique whereby their percussion drill was driven by a small steam engine, completed the first oil-producing well in Oil Creek, Pennsylvania (Brantly, 1971).

Before the end of the nineteenth century, oil fields in Romania (Ploeşti), Russia (Baku area on the Caspian Sea), and Sumatra joined those in Pennsylvania, California, and Texas in producing crude oil for the first refineries that began supplying fuel for the newly invented internal combustion engines (Perrodon, 1985). Nikolaus Otto (1832–1891) built the first four-stroke cycle engine running on coal gas in 1876, and the first light gasoline-powered single-cylinder vertical engine was patented by Gottlieb Daimler (1834–1900) in 1885. In the same year, Karl Benz (1844–1929) built the world's first car powered by a much slower horizontal gasoline engine. A different mode of fuel ignition, using high compression without sparking, was introduced by Rudolf Diesel's (1858–1913) invention patented in 1892. Diesel engines are heavier but inherently more efficient (over 40 percent vs. 25 percent for the Otto cycle) and can use cheaper liquid fuel.

FOSSIL FUELS. Gas station in Chapultepec Heights, Mexico City, early 1900s. (Prints and Photographs Division, Library of Congress)

Mass production of cars was under way in Henry Ford's (1863–1947) factories by the first decade of the twentieth century, when lightweight internal combustion engines also began to be used, following the Wright brothers' pathbreaking trials in 1903 to power flying machines heavier than air (Wright, 1953). Paved roads, freeways (which first developed in Hitler's Germany in the 1930s; the U.S. interstate program began only in the 1950s), and popular car models—epitomized until 1927 by Ford's Model T, then by Ferdinand Porsche's Volkswagen, initially designed in 1932, and recently by Soichiro Honda's best-selling Civics and Accords, launched in the 1970s—made gasoline-fueled cars the signature machines of the twentieth century (Womack et al., 1991). The introduction of jet airplanes in the 1950s and wide-bodied jets a decade later (the Boeing 747, in 1969) transformed flying from a rare privilege to an affordable way of travel.

The petroleum industry's success in supplying these new large and still far from saturated markets has rested both on new discoveries and on incessant technical innovation. The rolling cutter rock bit, introduced by Howard Hughes in 1909, opened the way for universal adoption of rotary drilling (Brantly, 1971). Most of the post-1960 discoveries were made possible only because of remarkable advances in geophysical exploration, and production benefited from new capabilities for deeper, directional, horizontal, and offshore oil well drilling. Transportation has matched the high-volume production thanks to the introduction of large-diameter seamless pipes for long-distance pipelines and, after World War II, the construction of progressively larger oil tankers (whose growth eventually stabilized with

ships capable of carrying 500,000 tons of crude oil). The world's longest pipelines were built in the 1970s to deliver Siberian oil to European markets. Catalytical cracking, introduced by American refiners in 1936, made it possible to produce lighter, high-octane distillates (above all, gasoline) from intermediate and heavy compounds.

Major twentieth-century discoveries came before World War I in Mexico, Trinidad, and Venezuela. The interwar years brought the first large finds in Iraq and Saudi Arabia. The most important post–World War II finds led to the exploitation of giant oil fields in the Persian Gulf region (the area that contains about 65 percent of the world's known oil reserves), in European and Siberian parts of Russia (before its collapse, the Soviet Union was the world's largest producer of crude oil), in China, and, after 1960, in the North Sea. Global oil production rose from about 20 million tons in 1900 to nearly 500 million tons in 1950 and to about 3.5 billion tons by 2000. By the end of the twentieth century, the five largest crude producers were Saudi Arabia, the United States, Russia, Iran, and Mexico. The United States, Japan, and Germany were the largest importers.

New oil discoveries and constant innovations in the twentieth century guaranteed decades of stable, even declining, crude oil prices, a trend that was abruptly terminated by the temporary exercise of oligopoly powers by the Organization of Petroleum Exporting Countries (OPEC), as the cartel quintupled the price of its oil in 1973–1974 (in the wake of the Yom Kippur War), then more than tripled it again in 1979–1980 (during the fall of the Iranian monarchy and the rise of a fundamentalist regime whose mullahs still rule the country a generation later). Much higher crude oil prices resulted in a massive transfer of capital to the OPEC countries, but much of this temporary windfall was wasted (Smil, 1987). Moreover, the rise in prices stimulated the search for oil in non-OPEC countries, led to unprecedented savings of crude oil, and motivated the development to other energy sources. As a result, world crude oil prices collapsed in 1985. Except for several short-lived spikes, the average price of crude has remained, when compared in constant monies, between $15 and $25 per barrel, which is not far above the pre-1973 level (BP, 2002).

Natural Gas. From the beginning of the Han dynasty (200 BCE) until the latter half of the nineteenth century, the Sichuanese were the only people that extracted natural gas, distributed it by bamboo pipelines, and used it mainly to evaporate brines, as well as for lighting and cooking. This gas extraction was made possible by the invention of percussion drilling, with teams of laborers raising, then letting fall, heavy iron bits attached to long bamboo cables from bamboo derricks (Needham, 1964). Incredibly, in 1835, the deepest well reached a depth of 1 kilometer (0.62 mile) (Vogel, 1993). Large volumes of natural gas became available only toward the end of the nineteenth century with the development of the modern petroleum industry, but most of the fuel was flared. Long-distance transfers of natural gas became common only after World War II with the introduction of seamless, high-pressure, large-diameter pipelines.

The subsequent rapid increase of natural gas extraction has been driven by demand for nonpolluting fuel for residential and institutional uses, for both fuel and feedstock for many chemical syntheses (from ammonia to polyvinyl chloride), and, most recently, for electricity generation using highly efficient gas turbines. Conversion of residential heating from coal and fuel oil to natural gas has reduced air pollution in European and North American cities, and the same process is now under way in China. Russia is both the world's largest producer and the largest exporter of natural gas, thanks mainly to its giant fields in western Siberia. U.S. extraction is not far behind, followed by Canadian and North Sea production (BP, 2002). Exports from the gas-rich countries of the Middle East, as well as from Algeria, Nigeria, and Indonesia, are limited by the necessity of expensive liquefaction of the gas for overseas shipment in special tankers.

Concerns Ahead. The dominant energy source shapes the technical, economic, and social contours of every civilization; ours is so obviously the product of fossil fuel combustion. Highly uneven access to this energy (the United States alone claims a quarter of it; G7 countries burn about 45 percent, whereas the poorest quarter of the world's population uses less than 3 percent) is one of the two major concerns of the twenty first century. The other is not the amount of remaining fossil fuel reserves (there are large unexploited resources of every fuel) but rather the environmental consequences of their combustion, above all the emissions of carbon dioxide. Atmospheric concentrations of this gas rose from 280 parts per million (ppm) in the mid-nineteenth century to 370 ppm in 2000. Together with other greenhouse gases, these concentrations have already begun affecting the global climate. Accelerated transition to nonfossil energy sources is thus the most prudent course to follow.

[*See also* Mining *and* Oil Industry.]

BIBLIOGRAPHY

Adshead, Samuel A. M. *Salt and Civilization*. New York, 1992.
Ashton, Thomas S., and Joseph Sykes. *The Coal Industry of the Eighteenth Century*. Manchester, 1929.
Brantly, John E. *History of Oil Well Drilling*. Houston, 1971.
British Petroleum. *Review of World Energy*. London, 2002.
DeZeeuw, J. W. "Peat and the Dutch Golden Age." *AAG Bijdragen* 21 (1978), 3–31.
Farey, J. *A Treatise on the Steam Engine*. London, 1827; reprint, 1971.
Flinn, Michael W., et al. *History of the British Coal Industry*. 5 vols. Oxford, 1984–1993.
Forbes, R. J. "Bitumen and Petroleum in Antiquity." In *Studies in Ancient Technology*, vol. 1, pp 1–24. Leiden, 1964.
Gold, Thomas. *The Deep Hot Biosphere*. New York, 1999.
Harris, J. R. *The British Iron Industry, 1700–1850*. London, 1988.
Kanefsky, J., and J. Robey. "Steam Engines in Eighteenth-Century Britain: A Quantitative Assessment." *Technology and Culture* 21 (1980), 161–186.
Needham, Joseph. *The Development of Iron and Steel Industry in China*. Cambridge, 1964.
Nef, U. *The Rise of the British Coal Industry*. London, 1932.
Perrodon, A. *Histoire des grandes decouvertes petrolières*. Paris, 1985.
Sieferle, R. P. *The Subterranean Forest*. Cambridge, 2001.
Smil, Vaclav. *Energy Food Environment*. Oxford, 1987.
Smil, Vaclav. *Energy in World History*. Boulder, Colo., 1994.
Smil, Vaclav. *The Earth's Biosphere*. Cambridge, Mass., 2002.
Vogel, H. U. "The Great Wall of China." *Scientific American* 268.6 (1993), 116–121.
von Tunzelmann, G. N. *Steam Power and British Industrialization to 1860*. Oxford, 1978.
Womack, J. P., et al. *The Machine That Changed the World*. New York, 1991.
Wright, Orville. *How We Invented the Airplane*. New York, 1953.

VACLAV SMIL

FRANCE *[This entry contains five subentries, on the economic history of France during the early and medieval periods, the early modern period, the modern period, the French Empire to 1789, and the French Empire between 1789 and 1950.]*

Early and Medieval Periods

The German nations who settled in present-day France during the fifth century CE inherited a decaying Roman economy. From the southwest to northern Gaul, beginning as early as the second half of the third century CE, natural vegetation encroached significantly on cultivated land as the climate became wetter and colder (a trend that lasted well into the seventh century) and agricultural production fell when the population shrank (by 25 percent from the second century). Migrations of Visigoths, Burgundians, and Franks to Gaul did not reverse the demographic decline: they accounted for only 3 to 4 percent of a population of 5 million. The situation worsened in the sixth century when plague epidemics decimated seriously the south (Marseilles, Narbonne) and famine threatened the north.

Infancy (Early Middle Ages). During the sixth and the seventh centuries, the Franks occupied old Roman sites and settled new areas. Although free peasant landholdings remained in some regions (for example, in Maine, Rouergue, and Brittany), in general during this period of great insecurity, the classic model of the Roman *villa* persisted, though it was transformed. The *villae*, ancient aristocratic properties and, now more commonly, royal assets (*fisc*) utilizied to secure lay loyalty and clerical support, expanded to become villages and small towns (*vici*) as they attracted peasants seeking personal and economic protection (*coloni*). These *coloni* were allotted tracts of land (tenures) apportioned from their masters' domains (manorial manses) as dwindling supplies of specie became insufficient to pay free labor.

The rural landscape dominated the early medieval economy. A vast majority of the population (95 percent) lived in the countryside, characterized by self-sufficiency and land concentration. Peasants practiced complementary activities (wheat crops, wine, cattle raising, and so on), adapting German and Gallo-Roman methods. Low levels of agricultural production promoted human mobility and consequent habitat instability, leading to commercial and urban stagnation. However, a luxury exchange persisted between Mediterranean Gaul and the East to satisfy small numbers of the lay and ecclesiastical elite. Yet, as early as the sixth and seventh centuries, Celtic, Anglo-Saxon, Frisian, and Frankish tradesmen stimulated interregional commerce in northern Gaul.

Signs of recovery appeared first in northern France in the seventh century and in the south by the late eighth to ninth centuries. As population increased, new villages emerged from Paris to Marseilles. The Carolingian *polyptiques* (inventories) point to a family average of five to six children surviving infancy after more favorable agricultural returns followed climatic warming; thus, for example, one sack of grain now easily yielded more than four sacks. Large-scale production was undertaken in the south by the combined efforts of small landholders. In the north, holders of great estates, the church and, to a lesser extent, lay nobles, propelled the agricultural revival and introduced major technical improvements: three-field crop rotations, with spring-sown cereals and nitrogen-fixing legumes; bet-

ter use of the heavy wheeled plow; the proliferation of watermills, and so on. Surpluses were sent to market by such prosperous landlords as the monks of St. Denis, whose fair near Paris attracted a regular flow of northern traders. Other monastic houses turned directly to the North Sea to sell their products. There international trade flourished, particularly at Quentovic and Dorestad, where the early Carolingians extended their fiscal control, and built a mint to coin the royal silver (*denarius*). Signaling a new era, the *denarius* replaced the *nomisma* (Byzantine gold coin) in international and local trade.

Takeoff (High Middle Ages). In spite of Viking, Magyar, and Saracen invasions (ninth to the tenth centuries), the collapse of the Carolingian Empire (843 CE), and the ensuing political anarchy, northern rural markets spread in the shadow of the monastic economy. In the south, land clearance and coastal maritime trade reactivated urban life. The fortification movement ("castral revolution") in the tenth and eleventh centuries, accompanied by widespread land clearances (14–31 percent of new soils were conquered), led to the creation of new villages, burgs, and towns throughout France. The Parisian region alone saw five hundred villages founded between the eleventh and the thirteenth centuries, with the assistance of a new royal dynasty, the Capetians (from 987 CE).

During this period, slaves progressively gained personal freedom, and their new status grew closer to that of the serfs. The latter were both former *coloni* and free peasants who had fallen under the authority of feudal lords and thus suffered the generalization of *mauvaises coutumes*, that is, arbitrary payments in kind, specie, and human labor (*corvée*). The moderating climate (especially north of the Alps) and wider use of the new agricultural technology allowed lords to mobilize and control both human and material resources and intensify their demands upon the peasantry. Although serfdom spread, small landholders, organized around the village community, retained higher profits for themselves, providing the force for a general increase in agricultural production, the key, in turn, to high birthrates and continuous demographic expansion (for example, families in twelfth-century Picardy averaged 5.4 children). The French population doubled between the tenth and the twelfth centuries (from 5 to 9.2 million); by 1328, this nation of 22 million inhabitants was the most populous in Europe.

Agricultural surpluses were exchanged for commodities and luxury goods from Asia and other European countries, which were export markets for cereals and wine from Burgundy and the Atlantic regions, and textiles from the northern provinces (including Artois and Flanders). That produced the most extensive international fair circuit of the time. In the twelfth century, foreign merchants traveled en masse, especially to the fairs of Champagne and the fairs of Flanders, under the special protection of their counts. This intensification of commercial activities, combined with higher agricultural yields, stimulated the creation of new cities (Lille, La Rochelle, Montpellier) and the expansion of the economy of older towns. Artisans and merchants contributed to the increased mobility of capital and the extension of international commercial networks, especially in textiles. Cloth manufacture emerged in Flanders and Artois (Arras, Amiens, Saint-Omer, Hesdin, Douai, and then Lille, Ypres, Bruges, and Ghent) from the eleventh and twelfth centuries and, by the next century, in Normandy, Picardy, and Champagne. By the turn of the fourteenth century, the north clearly offered the most dynamic and diversified economy, despite the decline of international trade gatherings in Champagne, which foreshadowed more somber realities.

Crisis and Recovery (Late Middle Ages). From the middle of the thirteenth century in the most populated areas (Paris, Picardy, Haute-Provence, Normandy), and elsewhere during the first half of the fourteenth century (Brittany and the Southwest), land occupation reached critical saturation levels, affecting all facets of society. By the early 1300s, cereals barely yielded four to one ratios, except in the rich soils around Paris and in northern France (eight to one). Coinage debasements (from 1296) and the consequent inflation threatened the aristocracy's main source of income: rents fixed by custom. In response, landlords resorted either to leasing their estates to enriched peasants and bourgeois, or to increasing commutation rights. Facing new fiscal demands (feudal and royal), and already overcrowded and underfed on their narrow tenures, countless peasants joined the masses of agricultural and urban laborers who worked for wages that could hardly meet the rising cost of living. In the early fourteenth century, when crops rotted during an unusual wave of humid, cold weather, successive years of deadly famine ensued, especially in northern regions.

In the decades following the Great Famine (1315–1322), economic and demographic stagnation worsened dramatically with the onset of the Black Death in 1348—with frequent recurrences of the plague—and of international warfare (Hundred Years' War, 1337–1453), regional conflict (Franche-Comté, Toulousain, Provence, Flanders), brigandage, urban and peasant revolts, and general insecurity. France lost one-third of its population—50 percent of Parisians died—in the demographic catastrophe from which it did not recover until the 1470s (or later). This major crisis induced the reconfiguration of the economy. Some villages were abandoned; most rural communities were consolidated for further physical and economic protection. After a short-lived price and wage increase immediately following the Black Death, deflation characterized the period from the 1360s to the 1470s, with some regional variations. Cereal and wine production suffered, while cat-

tle raising grew, dependent on newly available pasture land. The woolen cloth industry declined in Flanders, but developed (c. 1400) in other regions, such as Normandy, Provence, and Brittany.

At the close of the Middle Ages, the French economy was slowly convalescing. With the return of peace, regional centers rebuilt their economies (Marseilles, 1440; Île-de-France, 1445; Normandy, 1475). Recovery, however, did not extend to the rest of the country before 1520, partly because of conservative values, attitudes, and behavior. In the countryside, the manorial economy revived at the initiative of traditional lords and bourgeois nouveaux riches, through widespread *métayage* (sharecropping) and *bail à cheptel* (livestock lease) arrangements. Peasant holdings remained small; only a handful of prosperous villagers were able to accumulate tenure land. Although serfdom had significantly receded since 1350, lords increased lease rates in some regions (Limousin); in others areas, they reduced the personal freedom of their tenants, especially where the population grew after 1470 (Burgundy). In towns, craft guilds became increasingly protectionist, closed to both local journeymen and foreign artisans. The merchant class remained reluctant to invest its capital in land or in large-scale commercial ventures; international trade deserted French fairs and moved eastward, beyond the Rhine valley (Geneva). At the turn of the fifteenth century, as it entered the age of Great Discoveries, France had yet to develop its "commercial genius."

BIBLIOGRAPHY

Alexandre, Pierre. *Le climat en Europe au Moyen Âge: Contribution à l'histoire des variations climatiques de 1000 à 1425, d'après les sources narratives de l'Europe occidentale.* Paris, 1987.

Amouretti, Marie-Claire, and Georges Comet. *Hommes et techniques de l'Antiquité à la Renaissance.* Paris, 1993.

Bois, Guy. *La grand dépression médiévale XIVe et XVe siècles: Le précédent d'une crise systémique.* Paris, 2000.

Bourin, M., and R. Durand. *Vivre au village au Moyen Âge: Les solidarités paysannes du XIe au XIVe siècle.* Paris, 1984.

Carpentier, Élisabeth, and Michel Le Mené. *La France du XIe au XVe siècle: Population, société, économie.* Paris, 1996.

Contamine, Philippe, Marc Bompaire, Stéphane Lebecq, and Jean-Luc Sarrazin. *L'économie médiévale.* Paris, 1997.

Duby, Georges. *The Early Growth of the European Economy: Warriors and Peasants from the Seventh to the Twelfth Century.* Translated by Howard B. Clark. New York, 1974. From: *Guerriers et paysans, VIIe–XIIe siècles: Premier essor de l'économie européenne.* Paris, 1973.

Fossier, Robert. *Enfance de l'Europe: Aspects économiques et sociaux (Xe–XIIe siècles).* 2 vols. Paris, 1982.

Fourquin, Guy. *L'histoire économique de l'Occident médiéval.* 2d ed. Paris, 1990.

Heers, Jacques. *L'Occident aux XIVe et XVe siècles: Aspects économiques et sociaux.* 2d ed. Paris, 1990.

Jordan, William C. *The Great Famine: Northern Europe in the Early Fourteenth Century.* Princeton, 1996.

Spufford, Peter. *Money and Its Use in Medieval Europe.* Cambridge, 1988.

F. G. MICHAUD

Early Modern Period

In the early modern period (1500–1789) France became one of the most powerful and influential countries in Europe. Its rise to power began with a long military struggle against the Habsburg dynasty, which started in Italy in 1494 and continued intermittently in various parts of central and western Europe until 1714. Yet the ascendancy of France was not simply military; it was intellectual and cultural, too. By the eighteenth century, French writers had come to wield enormous influence throughout Europe, and French was widely spoken as a second language by European elites.

Despite all the triumphs in the military and cultural spheres, France's economy was something of a disappointment. In a Europe that was still largely agricultural, France was handicapped by farmers who could not produce as much as their Dutch or English counterparts, and French workers lagged behind as well. To make matters worse, in the late eighteenth century England, not France, gave birth to the Industrial Revolution. This article begins with a description of early modern France and its economy. Then it lays out the evidence for the slower economic growth in France between 1500 and 1789 and seeks to explain why the country's economy stagnated.

Base of the Economy. Like many other kingdoms, France had been assembled by a process of accretion as French monarchs cobbled provinces together. When they acquired a new province, they usually tried to win its allegiance by offering their subjects assorted privileges, which might include confirmation of existing laws and institutions and even tax exemptions. As a result, the legal and political structures varied from place to place, and so did tax rates. There were even internal tolls and customs duties on trade within France. In some parts of the country, local representative bodies had the right to consent to taxation, and many regions had their own sovereign law courts that ruled upon appeals in civil and criminal cases and could at times even judge the admissibility of new royal legislation. The law these courts drew upon was a blend of customary law, Roman law, and royal legislation, but the mix differed from province to province. Customary law, which was peculiar to a region (or even a city or village), played a more important role in the north of France than in the south, where Roman law settled many legal questions. Throughout the kingdom, royal legislation could change the law altogether.

France's economy was just as variegated as its legal and political structures. True, most of the kingdom was agricultural (as one would expect of any country whose per capita income was low). Perhaps 73 percent of the labor force engaged in agriculture in 1500 versus 61 percent in 1750. Yet despite the importance of farming, crops and livestock differed enormously from region to region and even from village to village. The variation reflected soil conditions, transportation costs, and, more generally, comparative advantage. On the rich soil of the northern plains, the typical farmer grew grain and raised sheep to fertilize crops. Farmers tilled narrow strips of arable land scattered through the open fields, plowing and manuring the ground one year, sowing a winter grain like wheat the next, and a spring grain like oats after that. Farther south, the typical farmer's fields were wider and bore crops one year out of two instead of two out of three. And in contrast to the north, they were often dotted with orchards, vines, or gardens. In the west of France, plots of arable land were hedged in and surrounded by prairie, heath, or waste, where livestock grazed. A particular plot might be cultivated for several seasons and then allowed to revert to waste for a number of years. Even these generalizations gloss over many other forms of agriculture, such as the orchards and gardens in the Loire Valley, the vines planted here and there throughout the country, or the cattle and sheep herded in the Alps, the Pyrenees, and the elevated plateau in the country's center.

Crops and livestock did not just change from place to place, they changed over time, too. In parts of western France, for example, farmers began to specialize in raising livestock for markets such as Paris. Near Paris, they planted pulses and sowed artificial meadows to feed their own animals and then sold their hay and straw to Parisian stable owners, who in turn provided the farmers with manure. But the greatest change in agriculture no doubt came in wine production. Vines were grown in many places to furnish wine for local consumption; elsewhere they fed long-distance trade. The wine for the long-distance trade came not just from territories where grapes are still grown today but also from many parts of northern France, where in the Middle Ages vineyards that have long since vanished were producing wine for sale in northern Europe. These northern vineyards began to disappear in the seventeenth century, after Dutch merchants arrived in western France and started shipping local wine to northern Europe through ports such as Nantes and Bordeaux. The lower shipping costs drove the northern vineyards out of the international market and in some cases out of the wine business altogether. Those that survived did so by shifting their production to wine of low quality for domestic consumption. That was not the only change, for from the late seventeenth century onward, merchants and wine makers in Bordeaux and Champagne were taking the first steps toward producing high-quality wines. They began clarifying wine, aging it, and selling it in bottles instead of in barrels. With grapes from Champagne, they started producing sparkling wines. The movement toward quality was not finished in 1789 but continued in the nineteenth century.

Commerce and Industry. Commerce and industry were varied as well, and not surprisingly, they too changed over time. By and large, manufacturing was spread out over city and countryside. For example, textiles—the major industry in Europe at the time—were produced throughout France. Linen production tended to concentrate in the northwest, where the climate was suitable for preparing flax. For similar reasons, most silk production was localized near Tours and in the southwest, particularly near Lyon. Woolens, the most common form of cloth, were made nearly everywhere, although certain provinces and urban centers—the southern province of Languedoc and the northern tier of the country stretching from Normandy in the west to Champagne in the east and north to the cities along what is now the Belgian border—came to dominate the wool trade.

Over time, more and more manufacturing moved into the countryside in the early modern period. In sixteenth-century Rouen, for example, weavers began to move to small nearby towns, and merchants started to organize rural production of stockings, a thriving business in the first half of the century. The shift to rural production continued throughout much of France during the next two centuries for two reasons. First, the shift made it possible to tap a cheap supply of labor in the agricultural off-season, an example of comparative advantage that was particularly important for products that made intensive use of unskilled labor. (In some instances, pockets of highly skilled workers developed in the countryside, as with clock makers in the foothills of the Alps in eastern France.) Rural industry also allowed manufacturers to escape restrictions imposed by the guilds that existed in many (though not all) cities. The guilds typically limited entry and created monopolies, often with the government's support, since the monarchy could then share the profits.

Long-distance trade in manufactured commodities tended to concentrate in cities that rose and fell with the commerce in particular goods. Because it was relatively expensive to haul commodities over land and was cheaper to transport them by boat, these cities either were ports or were located on the banks of navigable rivers. In the sixteenth century, for example, ports such as Marseille on the Mediterranean and Bordeaux, La Rochelle, Nantes, and Rouen on the Atlantic were centers of a thriving international trade in textiles, metals, paper, spices, raw materials, and agricultural products, such as alum, salt, wool, and wine. At the same time, the inland city of Lyon, which stood at the confluence of two navigable rivers, dominated a growing traffic in silks and luxury goods from Italy. Lyon also had the advantage of fairs every three months, which helped reduce the costs of transacting business. At the fairs, merchants could trade items without paying import and export duties, and commercial disputes could be set-tled in a swift and low-cost judicial system that bypassed the sluggish royal courts. In the sixteenth century, Lyon's fairs attracted a large number of foreign merchants and bankers, particularly Italians, and they made the city an international center of banking and short-term finance, which even the French monarchy tried to tap.

As the sixteenth century drew to a close, many of these commercial centers experienced difficulty. Trade declined as banks failed, fighting raged between Catholics and Protestants, and taxes and other exactions increased, in particular, manipulations of coinage. There were some exceptions to this dismal trend, notably in Marseille, whose merchants did a booming business in the Mediterranean. Commerce and industry seem to have picked up again in the early seventeenth century, especially along the Atlantic, where Dutch merchants were active, but business then stagnated and fell in the last half of the seventeenth century.

The eighteenth century brought a revival of both trade and industrial output, and enough figures are available to make estimates about rates of growth. The value of exports (in currency of constant silver value) rose at roughly 2 or 3 percent per year over the eighteenth century, and the value of imports (including goods shipped from French colonies) increased at an even faster rate of perhaps 3 or 3.5 percent per year, fueled by the popularity of coffee and of sugar imported from the French Antilles. Bordeaux and Nantes prospered from this trade and from the traffic in slaves and supplies shipped to the Caribbean. Meanwhile, industrial output expanded at 1.5 to 1.9 percent a year, with the most rapid growth in silks and cotton textiles. Agricultural output rose, too, though much more slowly, some 0.3 percent per year in the eighteenth century, a figure not much higher than during the previous centuries.

Population and Urbanization. At that rate of growth, agricultural output just kept pace with the population in the eighteenth century. Earlier, particularly in the sixteenth century, it may have even fallen behind. The figures for the country's population in the early modern period are of course uncertain, and they depend upon whether the population is calculated for France's current frontiers or for the smaller contemporary ones. For its current frontiers, a reasonable estimate is that France had a population of 13.5 million in 1500, 19.3 million in 1600, 21.5 million in 1700, and 28.4 million in 1780. Population growth thus was rapid in the early sixteenth century—almost 0.4 percent annually. It slowed, though, in the seventeenth century and even declined slightly, only to pick up again after 1700.

As elsewhere in early modern Europe, mortality rates were high, especially among the poor and in cities, and couples postponed marriages when times were tough. Despite the high urban death rates, the fraction of the population living in cities probably increased substantially in the sixteenth and seventeenth centuries only to level off thereafter.

Urban growth was striking in Paris, which doubled in population between 1550 and 1700 from perhaps 250,000 inhabitants to more than half a million. Paris in fact became such an important center of finance, consumer demand, and political affairs that few other cities could rival it, and the rest of France never developed the sort of widespread urbanization found in the Low Countries.

Explaining the Performance of the French Economy. How then did the early modern French economy perform? The answer has long been that it lagged behind the English economy. Even in the eighteenth century observers deplored the performance of French agriculture, the largest sector of the economy, with its open fields and seemingly archaic crop rotations. And later observers pointed to the lack in France of an English-style Industrial Revolution with rapid technical and structural change. But evidence of this sort does not really prove beyond a doubt that France fell behind. Recent research has shown that enclosing fields had little effect on agricultural productivity. The technical and structural change of the Industrial Revolution did not immediately bring rapid growth in per capita income to England. Indeed, estimates by Patrick O'Brien and Caglar Keyder (1978) indicate that per capita income growth in France in the century after 1780 was just as rapid as in England.

Although per capita income in France may have grown as rapidly as in England, its level in 1780 does seem to have been lower. It may have been lower at the end of the seventeenth century, too, if the conjectures of Gregory King (1648–1712) can be trusted. Here wages provide a more reliable gauge than the per capita income figures; they too point to lower income levels in France. When measured in silver, wages in Paris were in fact significantly lower than in London throughout the eighteenth century, a sign of lower marginal productivity of labor. The wage gap first opened in the second half of the seventeenth century, and it implies that France did experience slower economic growth than England, although the slower growth came well before the Industrial Revolution.

Wages in Paris in 1789 were lower than in Amsterdam, too, and while it could be misleading to extrapolate from Paris to the rest of France, estimates of agricultural labor productivity for France as a whole suggest that French farmers produced less that their English and Dutch counterparts. At the end of the eighteenth century, agricultural labor productivity in France was only some 58 percent of what it was in England and the Netherlands, and in the case of England, the productivity gap opened up in the seventeenth century, just as with wages. Since agriculture was such a large sector of the economy, it is likely that labor productivity as a whole was lower in France, too.

Why had the French fallen behind the English and the Dutch? Historians have advanced a number of possible causes. One explanation invokes population growth and diminishing returns in agriculture. The argument is that a growing population began to press upon resources in the late sixteenth century and early seventeenth century, leading to small, inefficient farms. Yet there are two difficulties with this story. First, larger farms turn out not to have had significantly higher productivity. Second, both England and the Netherlands experienced roughly the same population growth as France. Why did they not run into diminishing returns? And why did wages in both countries rise relative to wages in France? Although population growth may explain movements in relative prices and in relative incomes, it does not seem to account for France's slower economic growth.

Another possible cause of economic stagnation in France also involves agriculture—namely peasant farming and property rights. The peasants, it is said, were too concerned with subsistence to innovate, and they resisted reforms of property rights (in particular, enclosures) that would have boosted agricultural efficiency. Yet appealing though this line of reasoning may seem, it is open to criticism. To begin with, there is considerable evidence that peasants in fact would innovate if the incentives were correct. Furthermore, enclosures turn out to have had little effect on productivity either in England or in France. Property rights did hinder growth in agriculture when externalities were involved (as with drainage and irrigation), but the overall impact on the economy as a whole was relatively small.

A third conceivable explanation derives from Max Weber's Protestant ethic. France, so the argument would go, fell behind England and the Netherlands because it chased out its Calvinists, thus losing thousands of thrifty and innovative entrepreneurs. Yet this argument too collapses on closer inspection. Historians of early modern religion have cast doubt on Weber's account of the differences between Calvinism and early modern Catholicism, and by studying Calvinists and Catholics who lived side by side in France in a time of relative toleration, the historian Philip Benedict (1996) has refuted the claim that Calvinists were thriftier than Catholics.

Some scholars contend that the lack of nationwide representative institutions hobbled the French economy. Since France had nothing like the English Parliament, some claim, the country was likely to be a poor credit risk. As a result, a secondary market for government securities developed slowly, and private entrepreneurs would ultimately suffer because they could benefit from a secondary market that already existed to trade government bonds.

This argument, however, is just as vulnerable as the others. France was a poor credit risk, but its fiscal problems had more to do with politics and taxes than with secondary markets and representative institutions. Indeed, the French government managed to raise immense amounts of money in the eighteenth century despite its defaults and the lack of a national assembly, and private entrepreneurs found it equally easy to float loans. Investors were simply not frightened away by the government defaults. Even disasters, such as the experiment with paper money and a state bank during the Law affair (1716–1720), did not drive them away for long.

A better way to understand France's economic failings is to start with the political institutions that affected investment and transaction costs. (Here transaction costs include all the expenses involved in coping with obstacles to exchange, from taxes and inefficient courts to expensive transport and poor information.) Transaction costs seem to have been high in France, which is perhaps one reason the country never developed the dense network of cities that existed in Belgium and the Netherlands. The higher transaction costs were not just the result of geography. Because the early modern monarchy spent most of its revenues on wars, it had little left over for building canals, and the roads it built facilitated not trade but rather the movement of troops and emissaries in and out of Paris. Fragmented property rights and a cumbersome judicial system placed great obstacles in the way of private road and canal building, and high tariffs (especially those levied against the Dutch in the late seventeenth century) strangled international trade. The net effect was to increase the cost of transportation and trade, and the ultimate causes were political.

Investment also suffered. Taxes were no higher in France than in England, but their effect at the margin could discourage private investment. Tax exemptions encouraged wealthy savers to put their funds in government offices, which had the added advantage of giving the purchasers noble status. Private investment suffered as a result. Government regulation of guilds and trades discouraged innovation, and the monarchy's frequent wars destroyed considerable capital, especially in agriculture. In short, if the French kings had spent less on war and more on transportation and if they had designed the fiscal system to facilitate trade and investment, then their kingdom's economy might not have performed so poorly in the early modern period. That possibility would have required very different political choices from the kings of France.

BIBLIOGRAPHY

Allen, Robert C. "The Great Divergence in European Wages and Prices from the Middle Ages to the First World War." *Explorations in Economic History* 38 (2001), 411–447.

Allen, Robert C. "Economic Structure and Agricultural Productivity in Europe." *European Review of Economic History* 4 (2000), 1–25. Estimates of agricultural labor productivity in various European countries.

Benedict, Philip. "Faith, Fortune, and Social Structure in Seventeenth-Century Montpellier." *Past and Present* 152 (1996), 46–78.

Braudel, Fernand, and Ernest Labrousse. *Histoire économique et sociale de la France.* 4 vols. Paris, 1970–1982. Although the contributions are untouched by economic theory and now somewhat dated, vol. 1 and 2 (which cover the early modern period) are still essential references.

Brennan, Thomas. *Burgundy to Champagne: The Wine Trade in Early Modern France.* Baltimore, 1997.

De Planhol, Xavier, and Paul Claval. *An Historical Geography of France.* Translated by Janet Lloyd. Cambridge, 1994.

Grantham, George. "The French Cliometric Revolution: A Survey of Cliometric Contributions to French Economic History." *European Review of Economic History* 1 (1997), 353–405. Excellent overview of recent work in French economic history.

Hoffman, Philip T. *Growth in a Traditional Society: The French Countryside, 1450–1815.* Princeton, 1996. Agricultural productivity.

Hoffman, Philip T., Gilles Postel-Vinay, and Jean-Laurent Rosenthal. *Priceless Markets: The Political Economy of Credit in Paris, 1660–1870.* Chicago, 2000.

Hoffman, Philip T., and Jean-Laurent Rosenthal. "New Work in French Economic History." *French Historical Studies* 23 (2000), 439–453.

Mathias, Peter, and Patrick O'Brien. "Taxation in Britain and France, 1715–1810: A Comparison of the Social and Economic Incidence of Taxes Collected for the Central Administration." *Journal of European Economic History* 5 (1976), 601–650.

O'Brien, Patrick, and Caglar Keyder. *Economic Growth in Britain and France, 1780–1914: Two Paths to the Twentieth Century.* London, 1978.

Rosenthal, Jean-Laurent. *Fruits of Revolution: Property Rights, Litigation, and French Agriculture, 1700–1860.* Cambridge, 1992.

Velde, François, and David Weir. "The Financial Market and Government Debt Policy in France, 1746–1793." *Journal of Economic History* 52 (1992), 1–40.

Weir, David. "Life under Pressure: France and England, 1670–1870." *Journal of Economic History* 44 (1984), 27–47.

PHILIP T. HOFFMAN

Modern Period

The French economy grew at a slow but steady rate during the eighteenth century, largely thanks to its integration into world trade. The break caused by the Revolution and the Empire had far-reaching consequences. France turned inward, first on itself then on Europe. This resulted in twofold isolation, both commercial and technological. Political turmoil was responsible for the sudden disappearance or flight of many merchants. The wars ruined colonial trade, removing France from the boom of the Atlantic economy during the 1800s. This, in turn, weakened the ports, excluding the country from the trend toward innovation that was feverishly underway in Great Britain, despite France's industrial renewal that had begun during the Empire, particularly in the textile and chemical industries. By the end of the Napoleonic wars, a part of France's establishment realized how far the country had fallen behind with respect to Great Britain and wished to catch up by all means.

Thus, beginning in the 1820s, French society began to move into action. The economic history of France was marked by three cycles of medium- to long-term growth and depression: 1820–1896, 1896–1947, and 1947–1996 (Table 1).

After the brilliant start of the 1830s to the 1860s, a major slowdown lasted until 1896, when the French economy resumed its growth. This continued beyond the war until 1930. The crisis of the 1930s and World War II assumed the dimensions of a real national catastrophe. But the recovery of 1945–1949 was quick. From 1949 to 1973, the French economy ranked among the leaders in European growth. The slowdown that marked the years 1973–1994 once again raised doubts about the future of the French economy. In reality, it was accompanied by an unprecedented effort at economic restructuring.

Long-Term Growth. Growth during the years 1830–1870 was based initially on the completion of major public works programs, begun in the 1820s. The development of transportation—roads, waterways, ports, and railways—permitted an unprecedented intensification of trade. New urban markets were thus opened to specialized agricultural production. This growth, which had begun in the 1820s, continued for forty years (Table 2). It was based on the introduction of new methods of agriculture. The practice of leaving land fallow was replaced by the cultivation of fodder crops or sugar beets. Specialized zones were developed, such as vine culture in the Languedoc region or milk production in Normandy. The underemployed workforce of agricultural day laborers was put to work, and rural emigration developed. Soil yield and labor productivity increased. But this progress met with limits in several regions beginning in the 1870s because of less favorable natural conditions or agrarian institutions that were too dispersed to be well adapted to needs.

The rapid industrial expansion was supported by the dynamism of the domestic market, due to increased agricultural and urban revenues and to the strong increase in exports. Large-scale industries developed, sheltered by customs barriers, thanks to the importation of the technologies of the first Industrial Revolution. It involved the iron and steel and chemical industries as well as the mechanical engineering, textile and paper-making industries. But dispersed small-scale industries, whether crafts or production at home or in small workshops, continued to develop. It produced quality products such as silk from Lyons or *articles de Paris*, generally destined for foreign markets. In fact, industrial growth owed more to the increase in the labor supply than to any rapid rise in investments, which were limited, if not negligible.

Starting in 1870, French economic growth decelerated. The agricultural sector became a drag on overall performance as agriculture prices—subject to changes in world prices—plummeted, and with them farmers' incomes. Nonetheless, French agriculture continued its transformation: Output of livestock farming was still increasing, while rural emigration continued. The crisis of the agricultural economy, stagnant demographics, reduced dynamism in basic investments after completion of the main railway network, and, finally, the near stagnation of exports all brought on a reduction in industrial markets. French industry was unable to adapt to the changes in world demand. Whole parts of the system collapsed. The rural industries underwent a massive decline. Overall, the performance of the French economy slid: The growth of total-factor productivity was halved, falling from 1 to 0.5 percent.

The recovery of the 1890s was most importantly linked to an increase in domestic demand. Real wages tended to rise beginning in the 1860s and benefited significantly from the general decrease in prices after 1872. In the cities, a middle class was slowly forming, whose consumption was increasing and becoming more diversified. Industrial growth thus no longer depended on the prosperity of agriculture. To that was added a recovery in exports, allowing France to reconquer some of the markets lost since 1870. In 1913, France had become the second financial power in the world. It held 20 percent of all international investments and 12 percent of direct foreign investments. This position was entirely destroyed by World War I. During the 1920s, inflation favored the rise in domestic demand as well as in exports, which collapsed in the 1930s.

TABLE 2. *Labor Force and Employment by Sector: Total Labor Force, 1806–1896*

	AGRICULTURE	INDUSTRY AND CONSTRUCTION	SERVICES	TOTAL
1806	65.1	20.4	14.5	100
1896	42.5	31.4	26.1	100

TABLE 1. *Stages of Growth in France: Average Annual Growth Rates in Percentages*

PERIOD	GROSS DOMESTIC PRODUCT	AGRICULTURE	INDUSTRY AND CONSTRUCTION
1831–1866	1.7	1.1	2.1
1866–1896	0.8	0.5	1.3
1896–1911	1.5	0.7	2.1
1911–1931	3.6	1.1	5.6
1931–1949	0.9	1.2	0.7
1949–1973	5.1	2.9	6.4
1973–1995	2.2	1.1	1.1

SOURCE: Claude Thélot, Olivier Marchand. *Le travail en France, (1800–2000)*. Paris, 1997.

MODERN FRANCE. *Factory on the Oise at Pontoise*, painting (1873) by Camille Pissaro (1830–1903). (Collection of Mr. and Mrs. Paul Mellon, © Board of Trustees, National Gallery of Art, Washington, D.C.)

French industry managed to maintain its rank in the boom of the second Industrial Revolution. While during the 1880s and 1890s French industry began to lag seriously behind in the areas of electricity and organic chemistry, it caught up quickly starting in 1906, thanks to the import of foreign technologies. French industry was able to create and develop new sectors such as electrochemistry and electrometallurgy, the automotive industry, and aeronautics. In addition, during the 1900s and 1920s, the whole of French industry undertook an immense effort to modernize and reequip, largely linked to the labor shortage created by the war and by the reduction in working hours imposed by the state. Growth in the agricultural sector was distinctly weaker. The transformation of agrarian structures was slowed because of the protectionism instituted in 1891. But the movement toward regional specialization was accentuated, and the increase in labor productivity continued. Overall, global performance of the French eco-nomy improved notably. But rural France had difficulty keeping up with the rate of the urban sector's development, and regional disparities in growth tended to become more pronounced.

The economic crisis of the 1930s, prolonged in France by a poorly adapted monetary policy and, more importantly, by World War II, brought about an unprecedented downturn in the French economy. At the end of the war, France suffered not only from destruction and pillaging but also from the technological lag that the country's isolation had caused. The economic recovery of 1945–1949 was rapid, but it was accompanied by galloping inflation, and the accumulated lag was far from overcome.

The extraordinary growth of the gross domestic product between 1950 and 1973, even while the labor force remained almost stable, resulted from France's ability to attain American productivity levels. In 1950, these had been more than twice as high as those of France. The French workforce was skilled enough to adopt new technologies, and French consumers were impatient to begin enjoying the benefits of mass consumption. Starting in 1967, the effect of catching up with American levels was assisted by a more independent process of growth. But inflation, which since 1945 had never been effectively contained, took up its course. Strong growth made it possible to reconcile the increase in investment rates with that of income levels. During the 1960s, following the opening of the common market in 1959, France was able to integrate itself without difficulty not only into the European economy but also into the world economy, which was then in the process of liberalization. The marked increase in productivity involved agriculture as well as industry.

A long slowdown that generated mass unemployment marked the years 1973–1996. In France as in the rest of the world, the slowdown was characterized by an inflationary phase during the 1970s, followed by a long and painful stabilization and by a marked decrease in the productivity growth rate. But in France, the inflation of the 1970s was particularly strong, and the slowdown of the period 1981–1996 was pronounced despite the brief and brilliant recovery of 1987–1990. A serious disequilibrium in foreign trade began in 1973. External constraints forced the socialist government, which took power in 1981, to abandon its policy of boosting the economy and to adopt a policy of monetary and fiscal austerity in 1983. This policy of "competitive deflation" certainly threw many businesses into bankruptcy, but starting in 1990 it caused a spectacular recovery in the balance of payments, thanks to the return of competitiveness (excluding the effect of price differentials). Nonetheless, the austerity policy was maintained through the 1990s because of threats against the franc, clearly shown during the crisis of 1992. Everything was sacrificed to make the European monetary policy succeed and to establish the euro.

In reality, the French economy underwent a radical technological and organizational change. As one hundred years beforehand, entire sectors of the industrial system collapsed. But new sectors, particularly in services, were developed. As in the United States, the recovery was carried forward by the spread of information technologies. It was also the fruit of the effort at rationalization undertaken by French business beginning in the 1970s.

What is most striking overall in the economic destiny of this country is, first of all, the extent and the gravity of the recessions (1866–1896, 1931–1946, and 1973–1996). To understand this, one must take into account the negative effects of the economic and monetary policies adopted by successive governments. During the interwar period, inflationary measures of the 1920s were followed during the 1930s by deflationary measures, which slowed down the economy. France's establishment, having turned to economic liberalism during the 1860s, began to adopt points of view starting in the 1880s that increasingly favored state intervention. Thus, policymakers opted for protectionism at the end of the nineteenth century, for neocorporativism in the 1930s and 1940s, and finally for a planned and *dirigiste* economy during the 1950s and 1960s. The organization of the financial markets provides one of the best illustrations of the negative effects of heavy state intervention. Starting in 1942, these markets were subjected to strict controls and only became free from them starting in 1978 and especially in 1983. Heavy state intervention largely explains the survival into the 1970s of archaic structures in numerous sectors. This made the restructuring of the 1980s and 1990s all the more painful.

But what also is striking is the atypical way French society has evolved, explaining the slowness of transformations noted up to World War II.

Growth and Social Change. During the first half of the nineteenth century, the growth of the French population was already distinctly lower than that of other European countries, but it was still increasing (+0.55 percent per year from 1816 to 1846). This modest growth decelerated further for nearly a century, eventually falling below zero. After World War II, there was a spectacular renewal: The French population grew by 47.4 percent between 1946 and 1997. This evolution was primarily caused by natural changes. The decrease in the fertility rate, which had already begun before 1789, accelerated during the Revolution and Empire, particularly in the countryside. It then reached a threshold, but accelerated again starting in the 1870s. This profound and early demographic weakness led to an aging of the population. In addition, while until the 1860s the growth of the labor force was ensured by the disappearance of the hidden male unemployment, after that it was necessary to increasingly turn to female labor and immigration. The female labor force participation rate reached 36 percent in 1913. The proportion of foreigners in the population was 3.6 percent in 1911 and 7.2 percent in 1936.

A recovery of the birth rate began at the end of the 1930s and continued until 1963. It fell sharply between 1964 and 1976 and then began to decrease much more slowly after that. In 1998, the French fertility-rate indicator of 1.75 was higher than that of Europe, 1.44. This development accompanied a radical change in the types of unions adopted since the mid-1970s. The proportion of births outside of marriage rose from 8.7 percent between 1911 and 1913 to 40 percent in 1997. The family was tending to break up. Immigration has continued. In 1946, 6.6 percent of the population was made up of foreigners, while in 1975 it was 9.1 percent. Since then, this percentage has stabilized. Until 1975, immigrants of European origin were in the majority, which was no longer the case in the 1980s and 1990s. After having fallen to 28 percent in 1962, the rate of female participation in the workforce increased to 38 percent in 1996.

Overall, the long sluggishness in population growth has reduced the prospects for growth. It has inhibited workforce mobility between economic sectors and has weakened the dynamism of the domestic market. On the other hand, starting in 1967 the "baby boom" of the 1940s and 1950s has prevented a decline in the working population and, since 1962, has reinforced the takeoff of household demand.

Structural changes in the French economy were gradual until World War II, whereafter structural change accelerated. Three indicators make it possible to illustrate this process: structures of the labor force, population distribution between city and country, and income change.

One notes a continuous and regular decline in the proportion of the labor force in agriculture, which decelerated strongly after 1950 (Table 3). Until 1974, its rate was multiplied by three. Until 1896, the increase in the proportions of the labor force in the industry and service sectors occurred at the same rate. After that date, the proportion in the service sector increased much more quickly, and accelerated after 1950 and again after 1974. On the other hand, the proportion of the labor force in industry, after a rather slow increase between 1949 and 1974, decreased sharply after that date. In fact, the development of the service sector was made possible by improved productivity in agriculture and industry, which occurred much more quickly than in the service sector.

The increase in overall employment came from that of wage earners and, after 1860, from the drop in the proportion of the self-employed. Wage earners made up 28 percent of the labor force in 1866, 51 percent in 1936, and 81 percent in 1982. Among the wage earners, workers represented the largest proportion until 1968. Managers and office workers, among whom women became increasingly numerous (55 percent in 1982), saw their numbers increase at the same rate as that of workers until 1950, and after that much more quickly (Table 4).

From these upheavals, one should note the dominant tendency toward increasing professionalization of society. A person's occupation became the individual's principal identifying feature. This tendency became pronounced starting in the beginning of the nineteenth century. Each occupation sought to acquire a status that would establish the rules for hiring, remuneration, retirement, and advancement. This process involved civil servants as well as self-employed professionals, managers, and certain privileged categories of salaried employees and workers, such as railway workers, postal workers, or electricians. Within each occupation, the hierarchies were fixed in a rigid manner and usually defined as a function of academic degrees earned. This organization made the labor market inflexible and slowed adaptations.

The education of the population, begun during the nineteenth century for primary schooling, spread rapidly after

TABLE 3. *Employment (Labor Force Excluding Unemployed), 1896–1996*

	AGRICULTURE	INDUSTRY AND CONSTRUCTION	SERVICES	TOTAL
1896	42.9	31.1	25.9	100
1949	29.6	33.1	37.3	100
1974	10.6	38.5	50.9	100
1996	4.5	26.0	69.5	100

SOURCE: Claude Thélot, Olivier Marchand. *Le travail en France, (1800–2000)*. Paris, 1997.

TABLE 4. *Number of Workers, Managers, and Office Workers at Different Dates (in thousands)*

DATES	WORKERS	MANAGERS AND OFFICE WORKERS
1866	3,462	827
1954	6,485	4,082
1982	8,263	10,771

SOURCE: Claude Thélot, Olivier Marchand. *Le travail en France, (1800–2000)*. Paris, 1997.

World War II to secondary education, then to higher education. The average number of years of school attended by people aged fifteen to sixty-four increased from seven in 1913 to almost ten in 1950 and sixteen in 1992. During the nineteenth century, illiteracy disappeared almost completely. Secondary education gradually became mass education. Before the war, those having obtained their bachelor's degree constituted 1–2 percent of their generation. In 1950, the figure was 5 percent and in 1996, 62 percent. Higher education has also been democratized since 1970. In 1950, one member of the labor force out of twenty held a higher-education degree. In 1996, the proportion was one out of five.

Technical training, designed for skilled workers, was put in place starting in 1860 and organized in a coherent manner in 1919. The École Polytechnique was created in 1791. Members of the major state technical corps were graduates of the Ponts et Chaussées and Mines. During the Empire (1804–1815), the Arts et Métiers schools were created. Active starting in the 1830s, they trained middle managers, many of whom became engineers. The École Centrale, founded in 1829, provided engineers with multiple skills. Starting in the 1880s, specialized schools were created, primarily in chemistry and electricity. They became more numerous after World War II. Overall, annual growth in the quality of labor was evaluated at 0.2 percent per year between 1831 and 1955 and at 1 percent between 1955 and 1996.

In 1850, one French person out of five lived outside of his *département* of birth; in 1913 it was one out of three. This increased mobility resulted from a transfer of population from rural villages (defined as groupings of less than 2,000 inhabitants) toward the cities. But it was not until 1931 that the number of city dwellers surpassed that of rural dwellers. The slowness of urbanization was a consequence of the low birth rate. Started in the eighteenth century, urbanization underwent a significant slowdown during the Revolution and empire. The percentage of city dwellers passed from 21.5 percent in 1790 to 17.5 percent in 1806. Urbanization in the nineteenth century benefited cities of more than 50,000 inhabitants. These cities accounted for 27 percent of the urban population in 1801 and 56 percent in 1911. Many small towns stagnated. A concentration occurred in the large industrial basins and in the ports. Four urban centers were particularly dynamic: Paris, Lyon, the Mediterranean coast, and the north-northwest of France, particularly the Lille-Roubaix-Tourcoing urban area. The trend toward urbanization slowed in the 1930s and 1940s, then accelerated abruptly after World War II, when the rural population represented only one-fourth of the total. Moreover, many village dwellers simply resided there and went to work in cities. Urban areas thus took form around the old cities. In 1995, France counted fifty-one urban areas of more than 150,000 inhabitants. The largest was Paris, which counted 10.6 million inhabitants, or 18.3 percent of the French population. Next came Lyon and Marseille with 1.3 and 1.1 million inhabitants, respectively. In fact, the urban structure inherited from the eighteenth century is still in place. But urbanization, marked among other things by the development of "new towns," has not been well managed. It has given rise to serious imbalances, in spatial as well as social terms.

The real income of French people has increased considerably over these two centuries, thanks primarily to the increase in purchasing power of wages—most particularly those of workers. During the first half of the nineteenth century, real wages, which were quite volatile, tended to decrease somewhat. But they increased, starting in the 1840s, for skilled workers and from the 1860s on for the working class as a whole. The increase continued at the long-term rate of 1.15 percent per year until 1996, with a very strong acceleration from 1946 to 1976 (+ 4 percent). High unemployment, both structural and hidden, which struck at the beginning of the nineteenth century, was eliminated by the 1860s. Unemployment as it has been counted since 1896 reached a first peak of 5 percent in 1936. It had almost disappeared at the beginning of the 1960s, reappearing in 1967 to take on an increasingly massive character (12.3 percent in 1996). Despite unemployment compensation, extreme poverty reappeared.

During the nineteenth century, the intermediate categories between great wealth and poverty, which had begun to spread over a series of successive levels, became increasingly numerous. Essentially, the middle class developed. The increase in real wages concerned all wage earners but in an unequal way. During the twentieth century, wage differences among the various occupations were considerably reduced. But the reduction in wage differences was statistically compensated for by the increase in highly skilled labor. The trend toward more equalized structures was not limited to wage earners. At the end of the nineteenth century, the inequalities of revenue were very high, which acted as a brake on growth. These inequalities were gradually reduced until 1950. They remained practically stable between 1950 and 1968. But the decrease resumed and accelerated between 1968 and 1985, when French income inequality was about average for industrialized countries. Concentration of individual fortunes was also significantly reduced during the twentieth century. The proportion of the total wealth held by the richest five percent of the population fell from 80 percent in 1902–1913 to 40 percent in 1997.

French Society and Innovation. French society was not as closed to novelty and as reticent with regard to innovation as has often been claimed. Since the end of the eighteenth century, there has been constant renewal in French entrepreneurial milieus. There has never been a lack of business vocations. The milieus of Parisian, Lyonnais, and Alsacian entrepreneurs are characteristic in this regard. During the first part of the nineteenth century, merchants, traders, and manufacturers in the domestic system contributed to the development of the textile industry; technicians, artisans, or workers to that of mechanical engineering. During the years between 1890 and 1929, high technology sectors such as electricity, automobile manufacturing, electrochemistry, or aviation were developed by new entrepreneurs. Young graduates of engineering schools gradually took their places among the founders of these industries. After World War II, the initiatives of the new entrepreneurs played an essential role in the renewal of productive activities. They challenged many oligopolistic practices and established new firms in industry, distribution, and services.

The management of large businesses was long based on undiluted employer power associated with paternalistic practices. The large multifunctional unit was late to appear. During the twentieth century, concentration was accomplished by creating holding companies, rather than large production units. After tending to diversify during the 1960s and 1970s, the groups recentered on their original activities and internationalized during the 1980s and 1990s. The slowdown of growth and the intensification of international competition forced large French businesses to rationalize their management, a process which bore fruit starting in the 1980s, making it possible to restore the competitiveness of the French economy. But this policy led to massive reductions in employment. Small- and medium-sized businesses became the only creators of jobs after the 1980s.

Large French businesses were late in creating big research laboratories that were integrated into their companies. But they always maintained contact with the world of research. In addition, innovation was one of the missions given to engineers, who were highly trained in the sciences. Nevertheless, the research laboratories that appeared in certain companies starting before World War I employed only a limited number of people in 1939. After World War II, development was explosive, as several big industrial laboratories were founded between 1945 and 1955. At the same time, the state made available financial support for university research and put into place specialized research centers such as the Centre de l'Énergie Atomique (Center of Atomic Energy), or CEA. The Centre National de la Recherche Scientifique (National Center for Scientific Research), or CNRS, created in 1939, was primarily oriented toward basic research. A highly voluntarist policy was put in place by President Charles de Gaulle starting in 1959, which particularly benefited big state laboratories and large businesses. During the 1970s, an attempt was made to reorient policy toward the needs of the market and to benefit medium-sized businesses. The development of research networks was also a goal, to encourage dialogue between public and private research in an increasingly European context.

Consumers were open to the change. Starting in the 1830s, the increase in income and the development of transport permitted the diffusion of new ways of living. Food products by households became more diverse. Semidurable products such as cottons, shoes, and household goods, but also newspapers and books, were spread through the whole of society. Thanks to the railway, the taste for travel and leisure conquered all classes of society. The middle-class French person favored expenses devoted to housing and to the education of children, while the worker sacrificed housing expenses in favor of food costs. The use of durable goods such as automobiles, household appliances, and radios spread quickly in the middle classes until 1939 without taking on the character of mass consumption. This stage was quickly left behind after World War II. The French then favored spending on health, transportation, travel, and leisure out of a preference for a lifestyle centered on the home. During the 1970s and 1980s, they welcomed without hesitation the (new) information technologies. But lifestyles became more diverse according to criteria that were not solely based on differences in income.

The development of the French economy thus corresponds to the general pattern of development of the Western economies, notwithstanding a few notable distinctive features. The Revolution and Empire interrupted the takeoff of international trade for a long time. The accumulated lag made the integration of France into world trade difficult. Slow population growth explains the slowness with which social change occurred until the 1950s. Agrarian structures long slowed the spread of the agricultural revolution. The slowness of urbanization limited the prospects offered by the domestic market. The economic policies adopted since the end of the nineteenth century were often poorly adapted. On the other hand, a business milieu in constant renewal was always able to find, after long periods of adaptation, new ways to innovate and to specialize

that were adapted to world demand. Consumers were receptive with regard to new products, and often even welcomed them with enthusiasm. Society, despite serious rigidities, was able to change. The profound trauma of World War II makes it possible to understand the speed of later changes and the ease with which they were accepted. At this time, French people experienced a humiliating feeling of decadence and wished to affirm their modernity.

BIBLIOGRAPHY

Aftalion, Florin. *The French Revolution: An Economic Interpretation.* Paris, 1990.

Braudel, Fernand, and Ernest Labrousse, eds. *Histoire économique et sociale de la France*, vol. 3 and 4. Paris, 1970–1982.

Breton, Yves, Albert Broder, and Michel Lutfalla. *La longue stagnation en France: L'autre grande dépression, 1873–1897.* Paris, 1997.

Cameron, Rando. *France and the Economic Development of Europe.* Princeton, 1962.

Caron, François. *An Economic History of Modern France.* New York, 1979.

Carré, Jean Jacques, Paul Dubois, and Edmond Malinvaud. *La croissance française: Essai d'analyse économique causale de l'après-guerre.* Paris, 1972.

Crouzet, François, ed. *The Economic Development of France since 1870.* 2 vols. Aldershot, U.K., 1993.

Daumard, Adeline, ed. *Les fortunes françaises au XIXe siècle.* Paris, 1973.

Heywood, Colin. *The Development of French Economy, 1750–1914.* Basingstoke, U.K., and London, 1992.

Levy-Leboyer, Maurice, ed. *Histoire de la France industrielle.* Paris, 1996.

Levy-Leboyer, Maurice, and François Bourguignon. *The French Economy in the Nineteenth Century.* Cambridge, 1990.

Levy-Leboyer, Maurice, and Jean Claude Casanova, eds. *Entre l'État et le marché: L'économie française des années 1880 à nos jours.* Paris, 1991.

Marchand, Olivier, and Claude Thélot. *Le travail en France, 1800–2000.* Paris, 1997.

O'Brien, Patrick, and C. Keyder. *Economic Growth in Britain and France.* London, 1978.

Price, Roger. *The Modernisation of Rural France.* London, 1983.

Toutain, Jean Claude. *Le produit intérieur brut de la France de 1789 à 1982.* Paris, 1987.

Toutain, Jean Claude. "Comparaison entre les différentes évaluations du produit intérieur brut de la France de 1815 à 1938." *Revue Economique* 47.4 (July 1996), 893–919.

Walton, W. *France at the Cristal Palace: Bourgeois Taste and Artisan Manufacture in the Nineteenth Century.* Berkeley and Los Angeles, 1992.

Woronoff, Denis. *Histoire de l'industrie en France du XVIe siècle à nos jours.* Paris, 1994.

FRANÇOIS CARON

The French Empire to 1789

To a significant degree, France's early imperial development paralleled that of Great Britain. Wide exploration but failed colonization in the sixteenth-century yielded to more sustained conquest and population growth as the seventeenth century progressed. The eighteenth century was marked by pronounced economic and demographic growth centered in the Caribbean and North America. The French Empire also had unique characteristics. When at its largest physical size in 1683, it was underdeveloped. Its impressive economic advance thereafter was accompanied by significant territorial reduction. Throughout the entire period, pervasive public disinterest, or even hostility to colonial ventures, reinforced low emigration rates. By 1789, the reduced but flourishing empire was important to sectors of the metropolitan economy yet peripheral to most French people's consciousness.

Repeatedly eclipsed by European affairs, French colonization began fitfully. From the early sixteenth century, some French exploited opportunities in the New World. They supplied textiles and slaves to the Spanish and Portuguese Empires, fished cod off Newfoundland, and bartered for fur on the North American continent—all activities that retained their importance. Yet the appeal of overseas ventures waned when neither bullion mines nor western routes to Asia were discovered, settlement schemes quickly miscarried, and the Wars of Religion (1562–1598) threw France into crisis. Only after 1600 was a territorially based French Empire gradually established. Private commercial initiatives loomed largest, but the desire of the Crown to strengthen the metropolitan economy and to improve France's strategic position, as well as Counter Reformation missionary impulses, also encouraged colonization. At the empire's apogee, France claimed some form of hegemony over vast areas around the globe. Predominantly settler colonies were established in the New World. They embraced a large swath of the North American mainland and nearby islands, stretching from Newfoundland to the Gulf of Mexico. In these colonies, sparse immigrant populations fished, gathered fur, and raised crops on mainly family farms, often in uneasy coexistence with more numerous Native Americans. Settler colonies were also found on a dozen Caribbean islands (e.g., the French Antilles) and Cayenne in South America, where plantations grew tropical crops for export to Europe; Louisiana also had numerous plantations. Entrepôts (*comptoirs*) in West Africa supplied slaves for Caribbean-area plantations. Similar trading posts in India mainly furnished cloth, much of it likewise destined for the slave trade.

The eighteenth-century empire coupled substantial growth—colonial populations more than quadrupled and French trade with its empire grew more rapidly than did that of its chief rival, Great Britain—with the loss of considerable territory. With the signing of the Treaty of Utrecht (1713), France surrendered claims to Hudson's Bay, Acadia, and Newfoundland to Great Britain; at the end of the Seven Years' War (1756–1763), France gave up all its remaining continental North American possessions, the smaller West Indian islands, and the African entrepôts

(restored in 1783). In India, dreams of French domination likewise ended in 1763, leaving France with a few trading posts on the subcontinent and, in the Indian Ocean, Île Bourbon (Réunion), Île de France (Mauritius), and the Seychelles, which were way stations that also raised tropical crops for export. In 1789, France retained possessions scattered across the seas, but the rich and dynamic West Indian sugar islands of Martinique, Guadeloupe, and Saint Domingue (western Hispaniola) now formed the core of its empire.

Tools of Empire. Mercantilist acts that were intended to foster both economic development and state power regulated much of the French imperial economy—again much like the British. Policies known collectively as the *Exclusif* mandated that all colonial products be sent directly to France on French ships and that colonists use only French goods (also carried solely on French ships), while sharply restricting colonial manufacturing. Frequently, however, these restrictions had to be violated, largely because the supply of necessary goods was recurrently interrupted. Chartered companies, granted trading monopolies for designated geographical areas, were repeatedly established and just as repeatedly failed. Undercapitalized, burdened with high costs and excessive central control and regulation, and outflanked by domestic and foreign interlopers, most companies did little to develop either colonial economies or imperial trade.

Many merchants (supported by some Crown officials) preferred to trade on their own, both within protected colonial markets and as interlopers. These forms of "free trade" were always important in the New World because of the proximity of vast Spanish-American markets and enterprising Dutch and British merchants on neighboring islands. After 1763, authorities sought to calm unrest among Antillean planters and merchants by opening some Caribbean ports to foreign ships, regularizing what had long been common practice. At that time, too, East Indian trade was liberalized. Still, the establishment of new chartered companies for Cayenne (1777) and Senegal (1785) and the revival of the recently abolished East India Company demonstrated the continuing hold of mercantilist approaches among powerful policymakers.

Economic Balance Sheet: France. Its first empire produced mixed results for France's economy. Together with Indian cottons, such "groceries" as sugar, coffee, and tobacco stimulated important processing industries and innovative consumption habits. According to some scholars, these changes promoted a "consumer revolution" in the 1730s and 1740s. Existing manufactures like textiles benefited from a growing—if predominantly enslaved—colonial customer base. And though its effects are hard to distinguish from those of nonimperial commerce and of fishing, colonial trade provided additional stimulus

1. Moulin. 2. Fourneaux 3. Fòrmes. 4. Vinaigrerie. 5. Cannes   SVCRERIE.   6. Gros 7. Latanir. 8 Pajomirioba 9. Choux   10. Cases   11 Figuir. 131.
    et Chaudieres.   de Jucre   Cocos. p 115. p. 111.   p. 92.   Caraibes.   de Negres.

FRENCH EMPIRE. Slave labor on a Caribbean sugar plantation, seventeenth century. From Jean-Baptiste Duterfe's *Histoire des Antilles*, Paris, 1667, vol. 2, p. 122. (New York Public Library/Art Resource, NY)

to shipbuilding and allied manufacturing, provisioning trades, maritime insurance and related services, and the building of port infrastructure. But just as for Great Britain, the rise of plantation slave colonies in the eighteenth century had the weightiest influence. Colonial trade grew at least twentyfold between 1716 and 1720 and 1784 and 1788, whereas French foreign trade as a whole tripled; by 1789, colonial trade formed a larger proportion of all foreign trade in France than in Great Britain.

Recent research suggests that many areas and industries initially participated in the imperial economy. But from the 1730s, a dynamic, export-oriented, largely Atlantic France pulled ahead of the stagnant, heavily agricultural interior. The empire heightened French regional disparities, even within the dynamic zone. A handful of ports controlled colonial trade; Bordeaux alone accounted for half. Yet their effects were not widely felt. In sharp contrast to Great Britain, the internal market for consumer goods grew slowly in France. So most port areas developed as enclaves focused on specific, usually external, markets, such as northern Europe, the destination of most processed groceries.

Merchants, too, benefited unequally from colonial trade. Slow debt collection and falling prices after trade liberalization in the 1760s increasingly squeezed profits; and by the 1780s, liquidity crises or even bankruptcy threatened many merchants, despite continuing rapid quantitative growth. Though commercial expansion had attracted numerous small firms, the biggest companies, which also often owned shipyards and colonial plantations, increasingly dominated.

Whether because of strong tenurial rights and masked attachment to the land, a generally immobile and backward economy, roadblocks put in the path of religious dissidents, or other factors, French emigration was by far Europe's lowest. In French North America, moreover, less than a third of migrants remained, a much higher rate of return than other European colonies witnessed. Thus the small size of nonslave colonial population and the poverty of the enslaved provided only limited stimulus to French manufacturing. Whereas in Great Britain colonies and metropole developed as complementary markets, French industrial growth depended on exports to Europe. By the late 1780s, half of French imports came from overseas and half from Europe, but three-fourths of exports went to Europe, with just a quarter going overseas. Ironically, Spanish America, reached either via Spain or directly (often as contraband), formed one of the leading colonial markets for French industrial products, particularly linen and woolen textiles.

Economic Balance Sheet: Colonies. Beginning in the late seventeenth century and accelerating once sugar became king in the 1730s, the Antilles experienced strong growth. Saint Domingue's sugar output grew eightfold in the eighteenth century; by 1780, all French islands' output exceeded that of their British competitors. On the eve of the French Revolution (1789–1799), Saint Domingue alone—source of two-fifths of world sugar production and half the world's coffee, and home to two-thirds of all the slaves in the entire French Empire—accounted for 40 percent of French foreign trade. Population in the French Antilles, half that of the British West Indies in 1700, was larger by 1790, and consumed a large proportion of all French exports, despite an extremely skewed wealth distribution that severely dampened demand among the nearly seven hundred thousand slaves. On balance, the Antilles most closely approximated the mercantilist ideal: producing only primary products, importing all manufactures, and raising only crops not grown in Europe, they had positive effects on the balance of payments and were relatively cheap to defend.

French North America also underwent pronounced growth in the eighteenth century. Population quadrupled, and from the 1730s exports diversified as an increasingly vigorous trade in grain and peas to the Antilles joined traditional furs, fish, and wood. Still, by 1760, on the eve of the British takeover, the seventy thousand or so French colonists represented less than 3 percent of the population of British North America, and they were dispersed over a vast territory suffering from weak economic, political, and military links. The economic base of French North America was also much narrower than that of the thirteen British colonies. Virtually all manufactures were imported; both official and private initiatives to develop cloth weaving, iron foundries, shipyards, and other industries using local raw materials came to grief. They fell victim to high costs, technological inadequacies, and settlers' preference, given relative prices, for arable agriculture. Furs remained the largest export item, accounting for half the value of goods sent to Europe even in the mid-eighteenth century. Gathering and exchanging pelts played a central role in the economies of numerous Native American nations living in areas over which France claimed what was usually a nominal sovereignty. These activities integrated natives into the Atlantic market economy yet also made at least some of them perilously dependent on the production

of one staple. Paradoxically, the fur trade became increasingly marginal to the settler economy, providing only a few hundred jobs for French fur traders, the middlemen between Amerindians and metropolitan merchants, processers, and consumers.

Though few and small, France's Asian and African entrepôts were integral to the imperial economy. French traders sought to obtain a variety of goods from throughout Asia; nevertheless, Indian cottons were always their main item. Exigent West African consumers demanded large quantities of blue cottons. White cottons were taken to France to be finished for reexport. To protect domestic fabrics, their sale was forbidden in the metropole, though fraud made them widely available even before restrictions were eased after the mid-eighteenth century. Since Asian consumers showed little interest in French or other European goods, gold and silver typically made up half or more of all cargoes sent there.

The African slave trade was as vital to the development of the French Antilles plantation economies as to the rest of the European Caribbean. Trade with Africa had, however, only limited effects on France. Its impact was largely confined to French merchants engaged in Asian trade, the source of the textiles that made up at least half of the cargoes used to buy slaves, and to the area around Nantes, far and away the premier slaving port and home to most manufacturers of "Negro cloths," cottons that imitated (poorly, in the eyes of many disdainful African consumers) Asian fabrics. As for the consequences for Africa of trade with France (and the rest of Europe), interpretations have changed. Historians once believed that this trade promoted major changes. Scholars now acknowledge that the production of goods and slaves remained in African hands: Because cloth and metals had long been known in Africa, imports, apart from firearms, neither created much new demand nor displaced existing commodities.

An Empire Suited to France. By 1789, then, the French Empire was considerably smaller than it had been a century earlier, having failed to compensate for the land ceded in North America with significant territorial gains elsewhere. Yet it retained an increasingly rich Caribbean nucleus as well as the African and Indian entrepôts needed to service that core's exigent labor demands. The dramatic growth in Franco-Antilles trade during the eighteenth century suggests that the French policy that had evolved in the face of British military prowess—namely, to hold on to tropical colonies that supplied groceries for processing and reexport to Europe rather than to cling to any and all territory—was well advised, given French capabilities.

BIBLIOGRAPHY

Ames, Glenn J. *Colbert, Mercantilism, and the French Quest for Asian Trade*. DeKalb, Ill., 1996. Good discussion of the problems besetting one of the main chartered companies, with wider implications.

Butel, Paul. "France, the Antilles, and Europe in the Seventeenth and Eighteenth Centuries: Renewals of Foreign Trade." In *The Rise of Merchant Empires: Long-Distance Trade in the Early Modern World, 1350–1750*, edited by James Tracy pp. 153–173. Cambridge, 1990. Useful account of French-language work on the core area of the French Empire in its most flourishing period.

Butel, Paul. *L'économie française au XVIIIe siècle*. Paris, 1993. Best analysis of the place of colonial trade within overall French commerce.

Clark, John G. *La Rochelle and the Atlantic Economy during the Eighteenth Century*. Baltimore, 1981. Excellent case study of the structure of French overseas trade.

Egnal, Marc. *New World Economies: The Growth of the Thirteen Colonies and Early Canada*. New York, 1998. Illuminating comparison of British and French North American colonies.

Engerman, Stanley L. "France, Britain, and the Economic Growth of Colonial North America." In *The Early Modern Atlantic Economy*, edited by John J. McCusker and Kenneth Morgan pp. 227–249. Cambridge, 2000. Brief but stimulating comparison from a different perspective than Egnal.

Price, Jacob. *France and the Chesapeake: A History of the French Tobacco Trade and of Its Relationship to the British and American Tobacco Trade*, 2 vols. Ann Arbor, 1973. A classic not only on the subjects announced in the title but also on the broader French New World colonial economy.

Quinn, Frederick. *The French Overseas Empire*. Westport, Conn., 2000. The first three chapters provide the most up-to-date English language summary of the French Empire as a whole.

Stein, Robert Louis. *The French Slave Trade in the Eighteenth Century: An Old Regime Business*. Madison, Wis., 1979. Casts much light on many aspects of French colonial commerce.

Stein, Robert Louis. *The French Sugar Business in the Eighteenth Century*. Baton Rouge, La., 1988.

ROBERT S. DUPLESSIS

The French Empire between 1789 and 1950

In 1789, France was on the verge of losing its entire "First Empire." The starting point was the revolt in Santo Domingo (Saint-Domingue), which has been erroneously represented as originating in French-English rivalry exacerbated by the French Revolution. The crisis was triggered by a slave rebellion led by Toussaint Louverture. Although as there were only 15,000 slaves in 1715, by 1789 there were 450,000—in other words, less than one white for twenty blacks. The colonists' only defense had become terror and racism, enslavement based on skin color. The proslavery members of the Constituent Assembly succeeded in maintaining the institution despite Robespierre's strong opposition ("As soon as you utter the word 'slaves' in one of your decrees, you will have pronounced your own dishonor and the undoing of your constitution" [*Archives parlementaires*, vol. 84, 13 May 1791, p. 60]). Under the impact of the rebellion, the Legislative Assembly extended voting rights to all "free persons of color"; the convention briefly abolished slavery two years later (1793), but Napoleon Bonaparte reestablished it in 1802.

The British blockade had cut off relations between France and its empire, temporarily ruining the sugar cane industry to the benefit of sugar beet growers. The Treaty of Vienna in 1815 left France only scattered remnants: Martinique and Guadeloupe in the Caribbean and the ports of Île de Gorée and Saint-Louis in Senegal. The English had abolished the slave trade during their occupation; its resumption was demanded in the name of free trade by the Creoles of Saint-Louis in the "register of grievances" submitted to the Assembly of the Estates General in 1789.

Preoccupied with its Industrial Revolution at home, France did not turn again toward empire until the second half of the century. The conquest of Algeria in 1830 was destined to turn the attention of the French public away from the domestic political problems of the ultraconservative government of King Charles X. Economic interests had a good deal to do with the conflict in Algeria, whose origins went back to the directory: a financial conflict had allowed the dey to demand reimbursement for a grain delivery along with interest on the unpaid amount. The expedition proceeded quickly: France landed five hundred ships with thirty-five thousand men from its expeditionary corps on 14 June 1830, and the dey capitulated on 5 July. The July Monarchy, which came to power at the end of July was undecided on what course to follow with the risky and potentially costly Algerian venture. At first, the monarchy considered an attempt to control the country without annexing it directly, via recognition by the Turkish authorities. But it nearly immediately proved impossible. Ministers temporalized, and the *ad hoc* and self-serving measures of local military commanders decided French policy. Characteristic of these actions was the looting of the treasury, confiscation of the property of expelled authorities, and sequestration of many *habous* (religious endowment property) that provided mosques and schools with independent revenues. The Parliamentary Commission on Africa acknowledged a devastating balance sheet for the operations in 1833 but nevertheless opted for colonization. A revolt organized by Abdelkader began in 1832, and lasted more than fifteen years.

The influence of Marseille merchants was equally decisive in West Africa. In 1843, on the Dahomey coast, the Marseille-based house of Régis gained control of palm oil, valued as the raw material for the burgeoning soap industry and as an industrial lubricant. Libreville was created on the Gabonese coast the same year. The political turning point came in 1851 with the report from the Commission on Trade and Commerce for the African Coasts (Schnapper, 1961). The so-called fulcrum policy was developed by Prime Minister Guizot in Parliament. In 1840, Bugeaud was named governor general of Algeria, and he raised the number of French troops to more than one hundred thousand in 1847—one soldier for every thirty inhabitants.

FRENCH COLONIALISM. Advertisement for travel in Algeria, *Le Petit Journal*, 1896. (SEF/Art Resource, NY)

The war was waged with unprecedented cruelty and violence. Abdelkader, a marabout intellectual with an urban background, sought to "found an Arab nationality in Algeria" (Émerit, 1951, pp. 148–149). But the loss of major ports, and the serious military defeats hampered his plans, and he surrendered to the French on 21 December 1847.

The conquest of the Kabyles began in 1851, that of the Djurdjura mountain region in 1857. The eastern Constantine region rebelled in 1852; the insurrection spread from the Oran region to the Constantine region in 1864–1865. The last large-scale revolt broke out in 1871, led by El-Mokrani, in Kabylia. In 1870 and 1873, and reinforced in 1887, the administrative system and the land laws that were adopted and applied made the colonists masters of the land. Individual confiscation of rebel leaders' property and, later, collective confiscation of property belonging to insurgent tribes brought the most fertile lands into the colonists' hands in record time. Full-scale colonization triumphed between 1880 and 1900. The *système de l'indigénat* (transferred to sub-Saharan Africa in the early twentieth century) gave colonial officials full latitude to exercise re-

pression; they could impose fines of up to 15 francs and five days in prison. Algeria was attached to the mother country in from 1881 to 1890; for the colonists, it became France.

However, the indigenous peoples were reduced to poverty on a broad scale. The Muslim population did not return to 1830 levels in the cities until the end of the century. The loss of livestock was estimated at 18 million sheep, 3.5 million cattle, and 1 million dromedaries, or three to five times as many heads as there were a century later. Many Algerian peasants were forced off their land by a combination of economic changes and deliberate legal measures. The Algerian population regressed in social terms as fellahs (peasants) came under the control of powerful feudal leaders to whom the colonial masters turned over tax revenues in exchange for their support. An 1873 law on property abolished joint ownership, recognizing only private property. (The law was adopted in French West Africa only in 1904.)

Earlier, Napoleon III had tried to set a new course by supporting an "Arab kingdom" policy. But the episode was too brief (1863–1869) and its bases too unstable, since the bases consisted of keeping the populations under military control to protect them from the colonists. The latter increased in number from less than 8,000 in 1833 to more than 500,000 in 1901, concentrated in the coastal cities and the wheat-producing plains. From then on, there were more Europeans born each year in Algeria than there were new immigrants. The indigenous population had begun to increase again: the Muslims, estimated at 3 million in 1830, had dropped to 2.7 million in 1860; they increased to 3.5 million in 1891 and 4 million in 1901 (nearly 5 million in 1921). Despite the introduction of some forms of assistance, such as the creation of indigenous mutual aid societies (a law instituting Sociétés indigènes de Prévoyance was passed in 1893)—here again an experiment that was passed on a generation later in sub-Saharan Africa—the Algerian peasantry saw themselves forced into the ranks of a burgeoning rural proletariat.

The Jules Ferry government launched its Indochina policy in 1883, against the advice of Parliament. All of West Africa and French Equatorial Africa were set up as two federations, as was Indochina, at the threshold of the twentieth century. The regime was autocratic, and the colonial economy was wholly controlled by white chiefs, except for some cash crops left in the hands of the natives.

The colonial fervor of the late nineteenth century has been much debated by historians. It seems clear that before World War I, on the whole, despite the illusions of the colonial expansionists of the era and especially those of the theoretician Paul Leroy-Beaulieu (his book *De la colonisation chez les peuples modernes* went through many printings), the first colonial phase was of little profit to the French state (Brunschwig, 1966). Still, it is not enough to explain this "scramble for Africa" solely in political terms, as Leroy-Beaulieu does, and particularly in terms of the need to salve France's wounded pride in the wake of the 1870 defeat by Germany. Colonial imperialism at the end of the century is explained by Western competition among rival powers, as each of the home countries sought to set aside "private preserves" at the expense of its neighbors' ambitions (Coquery-Vidrovitch, 1997).

The situation in Indochina was a little different: among all the colonial enterprises, it alone was profitable, producing rice, plantation-grown rubber, and lignite. In this case, the colonial budget was substantial enough to reimburse the costs of conquest. In overall terms, Indochina at the time absorbed as much in constant values in investment as North Africa did between the two wars or sub-Saharan Africa and Madagascar later on (Marseille, 1984). A working class emerged, and an elite developed thanks to a relatively open Franco-Vietnamese school system. Starting in the 1830s, to the great displeasure of the French government, including the Popular Front, these new social strata stirred up anticolonial protests a full generation before the other colonies.

The colonial economy was nevertheless undermined by a cautious and short-sighted policy adopted by Parliament starting in 1900: the so-called financial autonomy of the territories, which was supposed to adjust expenses to income. However, income was limited to the head tax (capitation) and, more important, customs revenues. Customs duties, which were low on goods leaving the country in order to favor expatriated firms that were exporting raw materials to France, bore heavily on goods imported into the colonies. They were most burdensome for the local populations, which were taxed indirectly. The necessity for colonial budgets to increase customs receipts condemned the territories to an import-export economy focusing outward. France's reluctance to industrialize the colonies privileged the exchange between primary export goods on the one hand and imported manufactured substitute goods on the other, to the detriment of imported goods and equipment intended for an industrial infrastructure. These were imported in insufficient quantities and at high cost. The only substantial mining industry was that of phosphate in Morocco and to a lesser extent in Algeria.

As early as 1917, with war raging, a first colonial conference had attempted to promote a more profitable policy, but it entailed conflicting attempts to increase production while at the same time supplying men for the battlefields of metropolitan France. The contradiction was resolved only through the use of forced labor; this was officially illegal, but it clearly existed, since a law was needed to suppress it (the Houphouët-Boigny Law of 1947). Forced labor and the imposition of specific crops made it possible to introduce certain cash crops that prospered later on, such

as coffee in the Ivory Coast. In 1919, an ambitious plan to invest in colonial infrastructures promoted by Albert-Pierre Sarraut, minister of the colonies, met with failure, since the postwar reconstruction of the national territory had priority (Sarraut, 1923). Reports and periodic conferences organized during the Great Depression in 1931, 1934, and 1936 did no better, for want of funding and because metropolitan industry heads were opposed to industrialization in the colonies, fearing competition. Only a few significant loans were granted, most notably in 1931, just enough to cover the deficits caused by the Depression. Meanwhile, poverty was increasing in rural areas during the crisis, owing to the drastic fall in export prices. Migration toward urban areas began just as jobs in cities were becoming scarce, at a time of heightened motivation to work—for in order to subsist, people had no choice but to seek a salary, no matter how wretched.

Even so, a change in direction did not come until the conference that was organized in 1944 by Free France in Brazzaville, where the same need for preliminary investments was reiterated. It led to the creation of the Fund for Social and Economic Investment and Development (FIDES) in 1947, with 45 percent of the financing supplied by France and the Central Bank of Overseas France (CCFOM); these were ancestors of the Fund for Aid and Development (FAC) and the Bank for Economic Cooperation. Between 1945 and 1947, the introduction of the franc-CFA was intended to compensate for the trade imbalance between primary export goods and imported industrial goods in the colonies, for prices had been frozen in the territories during the war while runaway inflation in metropolitan France had caused prices to skyrocket. But for Indochina, in full rebellion (1947–1954), it was too late. Stopgap measures were also used by French authorities in Algeria in their struggle against the Front de Liberation National (FLN) during the Algerian War of Independence (1954–1962). In 1958, Charles de Gaulle unveiled the Constantine Plan that aimed at staving off independence by developing industry, expanding education, and redistributing land.

For a few years (1947–1956), French efforts were focused on sub-Saharan Africa and Madagascar. Until 1940, half of all exports, in terms of value, still involved groundnuts from Senegal. Major hydroelectric works were undertaken at last. But investments in agriculture, concentrated on the efforts of the Office du Niger to establish cotton crops in the loop in the river, were disappointing, and private enterprises, which had always specialized in the import-export business, did not join in to any significant extent.

It became obvious that the empire was not—or was no longer—profitable, except for a limited colonial lobby. The politics of "imperial preserve" that had been followed between the wars, which made the colonial field a protected market that benefited only certain sagging metropolitan industrial sectors (primarily textiles and steel), caused these industries to lose even more ground in the long run, as it sheltered them from the open competition that could have forced them to innovate. Only the ideology of the Third and Fourth Republics, reinforced by the success of the 1931 International Colonial Exhibition in Paris, was inseparable from the empire, symbolically rechristened the French Union (Union française) in 1945. In Algeria, a million colonists resisted, inch by inch.

According to Jacques Marseille's thesis, widely accepted today, French public opinion began to defend the colonial ideology just when the empire was proving to be increasingly less profitable. This was especially the case in Algeria, where it took a *coup d'état* and the full authority of General Charles de Gaulle to convince France to recognize the inevitable: the end of the French Empire, which was no longer defensible, even from the standpoint of big business and industry at home.

The newly independent Vietnamese states became embroiled in a long and costly war with major American intervention; Algeria had been bled dry; despite belated reforms (administrative decentralization undertaken in the wake of the Brazzaville conference, promulgation of French labor laws in 1952, a framing law instituting universal suffrage in 1956), the independent African states and Madagascar manifested huge economic and social lags in 1960. All that remained, once again, were the former "confetti" colonies of the Caribbean, the Indian Ocean, and the Pacific, transformed into French departments or territories: Guadeloupe, Martinique, French Guiana, La Réunion, New Caledonia, and Tahiti.

BIBLIOGRAPHY

"L'Afrique et la crise de 1930." *Revue Française d'Histoire d'Outre-Mer* 63 (1976) 289–290.

Agora-Pocket 175, vols. 2 and 3. N.p., 1996. The best modern synthesis on French colonial policy.

Brocheux, Pierre, and Daniel Hémery. *Indochine, la colonisation ambiguë, 1858–1954*. Paris, 1995.

Brunschwig, Henri. *French Colonialism, 1871–1914: Myths and Realities*. London, 1966. An important revision of previous assertions.

Conklin, Alice. *A Mission to Civilize: The Republican Idea of Empire in France and West Africa, 1895–1930*. Stanford, Calif., 1997.

Coquery-Vidrovitch, Catherine, et al. *l'Afrique occidentale au temps des Français: Colonisateurs et colonisés, c. 1860–1960*. Paris, 1997.

Émerit, Marcel. *L'Algérie à l'époque d'Abd el Kader*. 2d ed. Bouchene, France, 2002.

Lacoste, Yves, André Nouschi, and André Prenant. *L'Algérie, passé et present*. Paris, 1960. Still the best comprehensive study on colonial Algeria.

Manning, Patrick. *Francophone Sub-Saharan Africa, 1880–1995*. 2d ed., rev. Cambridge, 1998.

Marseille, Jacques. *Empire colonial et capitalisme français: Histoire d'un divorce*. Paris, 1984. The major interpretive study on French imperialism.

Sarraut, Albert. *La mise en valeur des colonies françaises*. Paris, 1923. The model of the colonial welfare and development program for the interwar period.

Schnapper, Bernard. *La politique et le commerce français dans le golfe de Guinée de 1838 à 1871*. Paris and The Hague, 1961. Unequalled to date.

CATHERINE COQUERY-VIDROVITCH
Translated from French by Catherine Porter

FRANKLIN, BENJAMIN (1706–1790), American statesman, scientist, and philosopher, was born in Boston.

Franklin was apprenticed to his brother, who published a local newspaper. He moved to Philadelphia in 1723 and became a successful printer in his own right. After taking in a partner, he retired from active management of the business in 1748. But well before his retirement from business, Franklin had become a public figure. His prominence only increased in the ensuing decades. Broadly viewed, Franklin was a key figure in building early American society, and his bold actions and beliefs resonate down to this day.

A determination to improve colonial society and, not incidentally, to advance his own career, led Franklin to establish or reinvent several institutions. He helped found the American Philosophical Society, the Pennsylvania Hospital, and the Academy, which grew into the University of Pennsylvania. He created a volunteer fire company, a

BENJAMIN FRANKLIN. Portrait (c. 1785) by Joseph Siffred Duplessis (1725–1802). (National Portrait Gallery, Smithsonian Institution, Washington, D.C./Art Resource, NY)

volunteer militia, and the Library Company. After becoming deputy postmaster general in 1753, he made the colonial mail service both efficient and profitable.

Franklin's confidence in the efficacy of reason and his desire to better the lives of his fellow citizens made him a remarkably successful inventor and scientist. He invented bifocals and the Franklin stove, which heated homes more efficiently than existing stoves. His work with electrical phenomena, ably summarized in *Experiments and Observations on Electricity* (1751), demonstrated the unity of lightning and electricity. Characteristically, Franklin turned his discoveries to practical ends by developing "lightning rods" to protect buildings.

In his long career as a statesman, Franklin repeatedly demonstrated his belief in America's ascent. His 1729 tract on paper money argued that additional currency would promote growth. In 1754 he proposed a "Plan of Union" for the colonies. During the 1740s and 1750s he supported British efforts against the French and Indians, but warned Britain to treat her colonies fairly. Before the early 1770s he hoped America's growth could take place within the framework of the British Empire. During a lengthy stay in England, he worked to persuade leaders on both sides of the Atlantic to share these goals. But when reconciliation proved impossible, Franklin assumed his place among the first rank of patriot leaders. He helped write the Declaration of Independence, served as ambassador to France during the Revolutionary War, and took part in drafting the U.S. Constitution in 1787.

Last, Franklin was well known during his lifetime and since for his advice on getting ahead in the world. Franklin's wisdom appeared in various editions of *Poor Richard's Almanac*; in an oft-reprinted pamphlet, *The Way to Wealth* (first compiled in 1758): and in his *Autobiography*, published in its entirety in 1868. The watchwords of Franklin's teachings were *industry* and *frugality*. Such advice was apt for the eighteenth century, a time of slow but unmistakable economic growth. But Franklin's sayings and the story of his rise in the world would continue to inspire Americans (and others), particularly during the era of rapid industrialization after the Civil War.

BIBLIOGRAPHY

Baida, Peter. *Poor Richard's Legacy: American Business Values from Benjamin Franklin to Donald Trump*. New York, 1990.

Egnal, Marc. *A Mighty Empire: The Origins of the American Revolution*. Ithaca, N.Y., 1988.

Wright, Esmond. *Franklin of Philadelphia*. Cambridge, Mass., 1986.

MARC EGNAL

FREE TRADE. As it is usually understood, the term *free trade* refers to the free exchange of goods and services in international commerce without any artificial impediments in the form of taxes or tariffs, quotas, prohibitions, or subsidies.

More often observed in the breach than in fact, the merits and demerits of free international trade and its effects on economic growth, prosperity, unemployment, and political economy have been the subject of immense interest for several centuries, and are of particular importance for the economic history of the industrialized countries. Though early thinkers touched on some of these issues, the modern intellectual origins of the term derive from the writings of Adam Smith, while the pragmatic debates over policy have been especially marked since Great Britain worked to promote free trade as an ideal in the middle of the nineteenth century.

There is also another sense of the word, which was more prevalent during the eighteenth and nineteenth centuries. At that time, free trade also referred to domestic and internal trade, particularly the removal of interregional trading barriers and the minimization of the regulation and taxation of domestic commerce. However, this article is primarily concerned with the modern sense of free trade and its importance in economic history, rather than its intellectual origins.

Despite the stray comment or fragmentary discussion of something that foreshadowed trade theory, no extended treatment of the subject appeared until the eighteenth century, and particularly during the Scottish Enlightenment. Even more important from the standpoint of economic history is that no region or nation had ever made a concerted effort to promote or establish a free-trade regime. It would not have been difficult to argue, along with Arthur Young, that "a general free trade, as there has been no example of it in history, so is it contrary to reason."

But though free trade may have seemed unnatural, the importance of international trade in state policy began to loom large in the eighteenth century. It is remarkable that this interest in trade was accompanied by an upsurge in the desire to regulate and restrain commerce in the century preceding the appearance of Smith's *Wealth of Nations*. The rise of the modern nation state throughout much of western Europe led to frequent military conflict and a consequent need for large infusions of revenue. The necessity of maintaining large armies, the relative ease with which foreign trade could be monitored and taxed, the desire to excel economically, especially at the expense of one's rivals, and the limits of existing forms of income and wealth taxation made all foreign commerce a focus of regulatory and tax authorities.

Of all the great nations of the pre-Smithian period, perhaps only the Netherlands worked to promote a system of reasonably open trade with modest mercantile restrictions. Indeed, that nation's successful economic growth from about the end of the sixteenth century to the end of the seventeenth is usually attributed to the highly developed nature of its domestic and foreign trade, which led to even greater specialization and to Dutch dominance as the European entrepôt. Still, the Dutch were free traders only in comparison with the rest of Europe and for the most part relied on many of the same instruments—duties and excises—for its administrative needs.

Customs duties, and to a lesser degree, prohibitions and quotas, were the central tools of government intervention in trade. The revenues derived therefrom accounted for a significant share of the budgets of the leading Western powers. Of all these nations, Great Britain became especially dependent on customs and excise duties of various sorts, particularly on such goods as wines, linens, and silks, which featured prominently in the trade of its great rival, France.

This discrimination was not accidental. Great Britain had not always relied on customs for major revenues. Indeed, even in the last half of the seventeenth century, customs revenue played only the smallest part in the British budget relative to direct income and wealth taxes. However, a series of wars and conflicts with the France of Louis XIV led to the prohibition or, after the wars, the imposition of nearly prohibitive duties on French products, while differentially favoring British allies, Spain and Portugal. What began as a purely protectionist measure, however, soon metamorphosed into something essential to the well-being of the state.

When political circumstances moved Great Britain toward the promotion of free trade in the nineteenth century, the nation was hindered in these efforts by the importance of special interests arising from long-standing restrictions on trade. Efforts to lower tariffs dramatically began to take effect after the 1840s when a variety of agricultural restrictions known as the Corn Laws were removed. The following two decades saw the removal of virtually all the major tariffs, except those on coffee, tea, sugar, tobacco, and wine and spirits.

The last category weighed heavily on British trade and prevented agreement between Great Britain and France on a free-trade treaty in the 1840s. However, the rise of a French ruler sympathetic to free trade—Napoleon III—and the change in British willingness to compromise on wine and spirits led to the successful passage of the Anglo-French Treaty of Commerce in 1860. This landmark agreement, removing all French prohibitions and lowering tariffs in both nations, ushered in one of the most significant periods of free trade in Europe.

Other nations, fearful of being left out by the accord between the leading powers of Europe, quickly agreed to similar bilateral agreements with the two nations, granting each new partner most-favored-nation status. Of all the major world powers at the time, only the United States raised tariffs after the 1860s as a result of the changed makeup of Congress during the Civil War.

The U.S. case was especially notable because of its fervent protectionist stance throughout the nineteenth century. However, to some degree, this policy was undercut by American willingness to favor the free movement of labor from Europe as well as by the increasingly efficient system of capital markets that developed.

Increased conflict between the Great Powers in the early twentieth century was foreshadowed by agricultural unrest deriving from falling prices worldwide. This led to abrogation of the numerous trade agreements at the end of the nineteenth century and a partial return to protection in agriculture in France and Germany, though at levels considerably more liberal than at the beginning of the century. Great Britain alone was steadfast in promoting the most open trade regime possible.

The period of open trade was effectively destroyed by the advent of World War I and then by the Great Depression of the late 1920s and 1930s. Nations raised tariffs in response to domestic pressure and in retaliation for other nations' tariff increases.

The attempt to promote and coordinate freer trade did not emerge again until the period after the end of World War II, when international organizations were created to deal with trade on a multinational basis through such mechanisms as the General Agreement on Tariffs and Trade (GATT). From 1947 to 1994, the GATT was the primary forum for the creation of a worldwide trading system through negotiation of lower tariffs, removal of trade barriers, and establishment of nondiscriminatory trading rules, meeting with some success in enlarging the scope of world trade. Nonetheless, and despite the seeming openness of world trade, commerce in the second half of the twentieth century was interleaved with complicated restrictions and regulations, some ostensibly for quality-control purposes, many to serve as de facto trade barriers.

Still, rapid increases in the total volume of world trade, spurred on by technological change and the successful development of numerous countries outside of Europe and North America—notably Japan followed by Taiwan, South Korea, Singapore, and after the 1980s, China—led to an era of massive trade flows permitting increased cooperation and integration of industry on an international basis. Ironically, this "globalization" of international trade began to be seen as a target by some groups in the nations that benefited most from this trend. "Globalization" was blamed for ills as diverse and contradictory as depression of living standards worldwide, poor labor conditions in the third world, unemployment in the most-developed nations, and degradation of the environment. In fact, it is most likely that the source of discontent was the pace of modern technological change more than free trade *per se*, given the hit-or-miss nature of trade restrictions worldwide. Changes in living style brought on by modernization, the effects of worldwide intermigration, the freer flow of financial capital, and improvements in communication technology did as much if not more than free trade to promote the global village that seems to have arisen at the beginning of the twenty-first century. It remains to be seen whether the interplay of technological improvement and political conflict will usher in an even more open period of free trade—somewhat akin to the late nineteenth century, but this time for the whole world—or whether the variety of conflicts and resentments spill over into a new round of trade restrictions and movements toward autarky characteristic of the period between the two world wars.

In 1995, the GATT was succeeded by the World Trade Organization (WTO), which became the new organization for the resolution of trade disputes. While taking over the concerns of the GATT, the WTO also became heavily involved in such issues as dumping (or the supposed selling of goods below true cost), the effects of trade on the environment, and the problems of establishing coherent rules of intellectual property in an era increasingly devoted to trade in services or nontangible goods. This was particularly important for problems regarding trade in items of software, movies, and music, where the actual physical product (tapes and CDs) was of little value. The primary content was easy to copy and transfer, and conflicts over outright cases of piracy or more complicated disagreements over the appropriate scope of regulation loomed ever larger in negotiations over world trade.

Since the time of Adam Smith, there has also been an extended theoretical and intellectual debate on the merits of free trade. In general, the opinion of professional economists has been in favor of unfettered trade as a desirable ideal, with a few exceptional cases permitting tariffs on products of infant industries, or those with very large and pronounced economies of scale. Even so, the various exceptions to the doctrine of free trade have been quite limited and in general require that governments be even more farsighted and benevolent than any private enterprise. Indeed, this is a prominent case of near unanimity among economists, with scholars of very different political persuasions arguing for free trade in general and against many of the existing tariffs in practice. Unsurprisingly, many of the tariffs most often observed in the real world do not conform to any theoretically efficient regime and are better explained in terms of interest group politics rather than putative efficiency. Furthermore, the professional consensus notwithstanding, free trade has had very mixed public support throughout the last two centuries, and it remains to be seen how the world trading system will evolve over the course of the next century.

[*See also* Commercial Policy.]

BIBLIOGRAPHY

De Vries, Jan, and Ad Van Der Woude. *The First Modern Economy: Success, Failure, and Perseverance of the Dutch Economy, 1500–1815.* Cambridge, 1997.

Irwin, Douglas A. *Against the Tide: An Intellectual History of Free Trade.* Princeton, 1996.

Irwin, Douglas A. "Welfare Effects of British Free Trade: Debate and Evidence from the 1840s." *Journal of Political Economy* 96 (1988), 1142–1164.

Nye, John V. C. "The Myth of Free Trade Britain and Fortress France: Tariffs and Trade in the Nineteenth Century." *Journal of Economic History* 51. 1 (March 1991), 23–46.

JOHN V. C. NYE

FRIEDMAN, MILTON (born 1912), American economist.

The scholarly work of this University of Chicago professor and Nobel Prize winner has had a profound impact on economics. His policy proposals, both when they have been adopted and when they have been rejected, have influenced economies around the world. Within the discipline, his most influential works include *A Theory of the Consumption Function* (1957), which changed the focus of

MILTON FRIEDMAN. Bronze sculpture (1982) by Bonnie Veblen Chancellor. (National Portrait Gallery, Smithsonian Institution, Washington, D.C./Art Resource, NY)

research on consumption from current flows of income and consumption to long-run flows, and *A Monetary History of the United States, 1867–1960* (1963), written with Anna J. Schwartz, which changed the focus of research in macroeconomics from private investment and government spending, as stressed by Keynes, to the stock of money. In the public arena, Friedman's advocacy of many libertarian policies reshaped policy debates around the world. These policies included, but were not limited to: (1) floating exchange rates, (2) slow and stable growth of the stock of money, (3) the negative income tax, (4) the all-volunteer army, (5) the legalization of marijuana and other drugs, and (6) school vouchers. Friedman was not the first, in every case, to advocate these policies, but his unmatched ability to marshal the relevant evidence and to develop his reasoning in straightforward language made his arguments uniquely persuasive.

Friedman first advocated flexible exchange rates in "The Case for Flexible Exchange Rates" (1953). This essay, and his subsequent work on flexible rates, made a powerful impression. It is possible that in the early 1970s the United States would have devalued the dollar rather than floated it had it not been for the arguments for flexible exchange rates made by Friedman and his allies. It is possible, in other words, that the architecture of the international financial system at the end of the twentieth century could be traced in part to Friedman's advocacy of flexible rates. Friedman's arguments for a monetary rule—the stock of money should grow at a constant rate of, say, 3 percent per year—were laid out in *A Program for Monetary Stability* (1959). This policy was not widely adopted; but its cousin, the idea that the goal of monetary policy should be long-run price stability, has become the conventional wisdom among monetary economists and central bankers. The arguments for items (3) though (6), and similar policies, were developed in *Capitalism and Freedom* (1962). As the title of the book indicated, Friedman's advocacy of these policies ultimately flowed from his belief that individual liberty should be the primary aim of public policy, and that this goal could be achieved only in a capitalist economy. Capitalism in Friedman's view does not ensure freedom—it is all too easy to think of capitalist economies that have not been free—but it is a necessary precondition. When Friedman began writing along these lines, he was swimming against the prevailing intellectual tide. Few would have been willing then to predict that, by the end of the twentieth century, free market economics, the economics of Milton Friedman, would be ascendant.

BIBLIOGRAPHY

Friedman, Milton. "The Case for Flexible Exchange Rates." In *Essays in Positive Economics*, pp. 157–203. Chicago, 1953.

Friedman, Milton. *A Theory of the Consumption Function*. Princeton, 1957.

Friedman, Milton. *A Program for Monetary Stability*. New York, 1959.

Friedman, Milton, with the assistance of Rose D. Friedman. *Capitalism and Freedom*. Chicago, 1962.

Friedman, Milton, and Anna J. Schwartz. *A Monetary History of the United States, 1867–1960*. Princeton, 1963.

HUGH ROCKOFF

FUGGER BANK. The Fugger family dates back to fourteenth-century Augsburg, where they worked in the fustian business. In the following century, they founded the merchant house (*Handlung*) and entered with investments into silver and copper mining. They became famous in 1488, when they received the use of the silver mine at Schwaz in exchange for a loan of 150,000 florins to Archduke Sigismund the Münzreiche (the inventor of the *Taler*) of Tirol. They acquired a silver and later a copper monopoly in Tirol and Hungary (Slovakia), as neither Sigismund nor his successor Maximilian paid the growing debt back. This encouraged further lending activities of the Fuggers, led by Jacob Fugger II (1459–1525), called Reiche (Rich), in favor of Habsburg rulers.

In 1519, Jacob Fugger raised 543,585 florins of the bribes necessary for the royal election of the young King Charles (the later Emperor Charles V). The Welsers and Italian banking houses supplied the rest of it, a total of 308,333 florins. In this way, the Fuggers hoped to gain royal imperial support against the antimonopoly and antiusury campaigns directed by the German Reichstag to the South German merchant houses.

The imperial military expeditions against the Turks, France, and the Schmalkaldic League required new financial means. As the emperor had no regular income in Germany, he had to transfer his liquid and credit resources from the south via Antwerp to the place required. The Fuggers lent the Emperor money at Antwerp or supplied him with money via an exchange market elsewhere. The money was to be redeemed on the Castilian Fairs (Medina del Campo) or in Seville by assignments to Spanish fiscal income or the expected silver fleets. Moreover, the Fuggers received by way of redemption the farm of the *Maestrazgos*, the lands belonging to the Military Orders in Spain, including the mercury mines of Almadén.

With the savagery of the military conflicts in the 1540s and 1550s, the growing credit demands exceeded by far the amounts redeemed and the profits from the *Maestrazgos*. In this situation, Charles V pressed the Fuggers to provide another loan, the Villach *asiento* of 1552. Anton Fugger promised 100,000 ducats and guaranteed to raise another 300,000 scudi in Italy, at 12 percent interest. As security, the Fuggers received assignments to income of the Spanish crown, to a certain amount of American precious metals, and to state annuities *(juros)*. Moreover, they obtained permission to export, tax free, 400,000 ducats in coin or gold out of Spain. However, the money was wasted by the emperor in the fruitless siege of Metz.

New *asientos* and extensions of loans followed. In 1557, Philip II (1527–1598) issued the first state bankruptcy decree. All payments of assignments to fiscal income were suspended and the precious metals of the incoming fleets were confiscated. Although the Fuggers entered into an arrangement with the crown three years later, south German merchant houses never recovered from this blow. They had only two choices: to withdraw from the Spanish scene, writing the Spanish claims off; or to remain in contact with the Spanish crown, trying to realize at least some of the claims. That is why the Fuggers witnessed more losses in the following Spanish state bankruptcies of 1575 and 1607. However, they avoided the fate of the Welsers, who went bankrupt in 1614, as a result of the suspension of payments by France and Spain. Altogether the Fuggers' losses with the Habsburg rulers are estimated at 8 million florins, and that was a considerable part of their gains as a merchant house.

There was neither specialization nor an innovation in the business of the house of Fugger. The Fuggers represented, above all, the most-developed form of the late medieval family companies, differing from their predecessors with respect only to their worldwide activities and the concentration on Habsburg rulers. With regard to heir exchange business, they resembled the Italian merchant bankers of the Middle Ages. They maintained a widespread network of branches and factors in the major markets and exchange places of Europe, with the primary objective of advancing funds by bills of exchange, making big profits by exploiting the fluctuations of the money markets. They handled the money remittances of papal collectors and church dignitaries on behalf of the Roman Curia, and they had a foot in the international spice and precious metals trades. They enlarged their working capital by acquiring money from numerous depositors, ranging from Cardinal Melchior von Meckau of Brixen to small Augsburg savers.

When the Welsers finally failed and the Fuggers retired to their landed estates, they were replaced by other Augsburg merchant bankers, such as the Paler, who tried to combine foreign trade with (deposit) banking and industrial development, avoiding the risks of credits to a sole powerful debtor. However, loans to princes remained important with respect to metal production and metal trade. This shows the example of Nuremberg merchants, whose investments into Thüringen's Seigerhütten required licences by the dukes of Saxony and the counts of Mansfeld, but strengthened their leading position on the European copper market.

[*See also* Banking, *subentry on* Middle Ages and Early Modern Period.]

BIBLIOGRAPHY

Ehrenberg, Richard. *Das Zeitalter der Fugger: Geldkapitel und Kredite im 16. Jahrhundert*, vol. 1, *Die Geldmächte des 16. Jahrhunderts*. Hildesheim, 1990.

Hildebrandt, Reinhard. "Augsburger und Nürnberger Kupferhandel 1500–1619: Produktion, Marktanteile, und Finanzierung im Vergleich zweier Städte und ihrer wirtschaftlichen Führungsschicht." In *Schwerpunkte der Kupferproduktion und des Kupferhandels in Europa 1500–1650*, edited by H. Kellenbenz, pp. 190–224. Cologne and Vienna, 1977.

Kellenbenz, Hermann. *Die Fuggersche Maestrazgopacht, 1525–1542: Zur Geschichte der spanischen Ritterorden im 16. Jahrhundert*. Tübingen, 1967.

Kellenbenz, Hermann. *Die Fugger in Spanien und Portugal bis 1560: Ein Grossunternehmen des 16. Jahrhunderts*, vol. 1. Munich, 1990.

North, Michael. *Kommunikation, Handel, Geld, und Banken in der frühen Neuzeit*. Munich, 2000.

Pölnitz, Götz Freiherr von. "Jakob Fugger und der Streit um den Nachlass des Kardinals Melchor von Brixen." *Quellen und Forschungen aus italienischen Archiven* 30 (1940), 223–294.

Pölnitz, Götz Freiherr von. *Jakob Fugger: Kaiser, Kirche, und Kapital in der oderdeutschen Renaissance*, vol. 1. Tübingen, 1949.

Pölnitz, Götz Freiherr von. "Der Asiento Kaiser Karls V. vom 28. Mai 1552." *Historisches Jahrbuch* 74 (1954), 213–233.

Wee, Herman van der. "Monetary, Credit, and Banking Systems." In *The Cambridge Economic History of Europe*, vol. 5, *The Economic Organization of Early Modern Europe*. Cambridge 1977, 315–322.

MICHAËL NORTH

FUR TRAPPING AND TRADE. Throughout human history, animal furs have been used for clothing. Fur trapping was long part of the normal activities of a family or a group of families, with pelts and furs used for rudimentary types of apparel. Although furs undoubtedly were traded between groups, this early trade was an integral part of normal economic exchange, not a specialized activity. By the late Middle Ages, the native fur-bearing animals of Europe were sufficiently scarce that a specialized fur trade had begun, principally with Russia. The use of furs increasingly was a luxury. With the discovery of North America came a new source of supply, and a transatlantic trade quickly emerged. The fur trade in North America was one of the first major economic activities of European settlement, often the cause of settlement. It pushed back the colonial frontiers and became the trade of empire building. The early European fur traders, in the seventeenth century, were the Dutch, English, and French. Later, in the nineteenth century, the Russians established trading posts in the northwest parts of the American continent. Furs continued to be trapped throughout the world, but it was only in North America that the fur trade contributed significantly to economic development.

The principal fur-bearing animals at risk were beaver, whose skins were mainly used in the felting/hatting trades of Europe; but there was also a substantial trade in fox and lynx (as furs), deer skins (as parchment), and

Fᴜʀ Tʀᴀᴘᴘɪɴɢ. *Trapping Beaver*, painting (c. 1850) by Alfred Jacob Miller (1810–1874). (Walters Art Museum, Baltimore)

winter varieties of marten and fox (as fashion items). Later sea otter and fur seals were hunted for their pelts. Apart from clothing, furs were used for such purposes as traveling blankets, linings for wooden chests, and decoration. In felting, beaver pelts were of superior quality if previously used as garments by the American Indians, and then were called *castor gras* (literally "greasy beaver"). Use of the pelts as clothing wore away the guard hairs, making them desirable in the markets of London and Paris. The pelts of newly killed animals were known as *castor sec* ("dry beaver"), and required additional treatment in manufacture. Generally, the American Indians hunted and trapped the animals, whose pelts were then taken to trading posts, usually on an annual basis. This pattern continued into modern times. The trapping of furs for trade tended to make tribal property rights over traditional hunting areas more concrete than they had been; and because of the trade value of the animal resource, it was a source of conflict among the Indian tribes themselves, especially as the animal stocks dwindled. Within tribal or specific trapping areas, access to the resource was generally unlimited. It was a common-property resource.

In the early seventeenth century, the French established a great trading "fair" at Hochelaga (Montreal), and the Dutch traded at Albany in what is now upper New York State. The English took over the Dutch trade in 1664 although Americans of Dutch descent continued to play prominent roles. The English expansion from Albany in the mid-seventeenth century brought the Anglo-American traders into direct conflict with the French to the north, although in practice there was much smuggling of furs southward by independent-minded *couriers des bois*. The French fur trade was established at the port of Tadoussac (near Quebec City) with a loose association of traders who ultimately were subsumed into *La Compagnie de la Nouvelle France* and several successor companies. Since the principal market for furs was Europe, the trade required substantial economic commitment to inventories. The financing of trade goods (knives, pots, nails, textiles, beads, and alcohol) shipped from Europe, as well as their movement to the interior of North America and the reverse journey for the fur cargoes, often took up to three years. The original pattern of settlement and trading also established allegiances with native North Americans that tended to persist and become political. The Iroquois Confederacy was allied with the British and American colonists, and the Huron and Montagnais sided with the French. Other Indian nations involved in the seventeenth-century trade were the Ojibway, Algonquian, and Cree peoples.

The tendency to overcrop local animal populations, driving them down in numbers, raised the per-unit cost of harvesting and raised the offer price. As populations became less dense, the reaction of the traders was to expand into the adjacent fur-bearing areas. In the seventeenth century, some American Indians attempted to control trade with areas farther from the eastern markets, such the Huron control of the great Ottawa-Nippissing-French river system route to the west (north of the Great Lakes). However, this effort was temporary. The French were the most rapid in expanding the trade in the late seventeenth and early eighteenth centuries, especially after achieving a negotiated peace among the major Indian nations in 1701. The French pushed down through the Great Lakes, establishing an important fort at Detroit. This linked them to the Ohio-Mississippi river system with the central trading link at Fort Duquesne (Pittsburgh). Some of the great names of French exploration of North America are associated with this drive west and south: La Salle, Cadillac, and La Vérendrye. The vast but thinly settled French empire ringed in the British colonies of the seaboard.

The North American phase of the Seven Years War (the French and Indian Wars) of the mid-1700s was an attack on the French empire that led ultimately to the ceding of New France (sarcastically referred to by Voltaire as *quelques arpents de neige*, or "a few acres of snow") to the British. This broke the barrier to American expansion of the fur trade to the west, but, more important, it brought about a collapse of the French fur trade. Without a link to Paris and access to their traditional capital markets, the French fur traders could not survive in their historical form of organization. Into the economic vacuum came Anglo-American traders, who took over the old French fur-trade territory managed out of Montreal. Several distinct groups competed for dominance. This competition was mostly played out in the Old Northwest—the area to the south and west of the upper Great Lakes, where on one occasion a territory was deliberately denuded of fur-bearing animals in order to deny harvests to rivals. By forcing longer lines of communication and trade routes, the rivals pushed up the trade's fixed costs (because of the necessity of maintaining defensive forts/trading posts) as well as its variable costs (through a longer time commitment to inventories and labor costs). The eastern-based trade assumed many characteristics of a natural monopoly from a market or trading perspective. By the end of the American War of Independence, the various Montreal interests had assumed the form of a single company, the North-West Company.

In the mid-seventeenth century, two disaffected French fur traders approached the English for fur-trading rights in North America. King Charles II, with almost no control of the territory and little understanding of its scope, made the famous grant to Radisson and des Grosseilliers of all the lands drained by waters flowing into Hudson Bay, an area covering much of modern Canada and parts of what would be the northern United States. This was the origin of "The Governor and Company of Adventurers of England Trading into Hudson's Bay"—extant as the Hudson's Bay Company. The company was established on the shores of James Bay with several massive (stone) forts for trading and shipping purposes at Fort Albany and Moose Factory, and for almost a century it was content to trade "at the bay" with little permanent penetration of the hinterland. The combination of a new aggressive expansionary company policy in the late-eighteenth century and the emergence of the North-West Company as a force brought the two companies into conflict.

The competition of the two fur-trading giants saw the Hudson's Bay Company react to the presence of the North-West Company by establishing the Selkirk Settlement in southern Manitoba. It also introduced an efficient river carriage system using freight-carrying dories called York boats, for the York River flowing into James Bay. The settlement helped to enforce the territorial claim of the Hudson's Bay Company but also excluded the North-West Company from rich fur-trappings areas, forcing it to take longer routes into the prairie west and increasing the cost of finding local supplies—particularly of pemican (dried buffalo meat). The reaction of the North-West Company was to seek new trapping areas, and it entered a remarkable period of geographic exploration. Simon Fraser reached the Pacific Ocean by an overland route, and Alexander MacKenzie traveled to the western Arctic Ocean along a river that now bears his name. Although the North-West Company introduced many transportation refinements, such as the huge freight-carrying *canots de maître*, transport and inventory costs made them only marginally competitive. Friction between the two companies over both trapping areas and transport routes in western Canada was a constant feature of the rivalry in the early nineteenth century. At one stage, a full-scale battle erupted, the Battle of Seven Oaks, and the British government intervened, requiring the two companies to merge. The Hudson's Bay Company was the dominant partner to the merger in 1821, and the main fur trade thereafter was centered on the Hudson Bay route to European markets.

In the nineteenth century, the U.S. fur trade was conducted mainly from Saint Louis. As it pushed westward, the American trade, led by the Astor company, also ran into conflict with the Hudson's Bay company, particularly in lands that were to become the Oregon Territory. British claims to this area were eventually withdrawn after a British–U.S. settlement. By the mid-nineteenth century, U.S. fur traders followed an aggressive expansionary policy at sea, in search of sea otter and the North Pacific fur seals. Pursuits of these animal resources were a major reason for the 1867 U.S. purchase of the Russian-held territory Alaska. The land-based fur trade did not disappear, but continued to grow in absolute terms well into the twentieth century. Although its relative importance to the economies of North America became very small, it nonetheless remained an important part of the economic life of Native American, Déné, and Inuit communities.

The fur trade sold its products in luxury- and semi-luxury-goods markets, and the demand for the fur tended to be relatively price-inelastic but income-elastic. The trade and gathering of furs required a substantial commitment to inventories, the establishment and maintenance of transport routes and trading centers (forts), and territorial exclusivity. These needs were barriers to entry that became higher as the trade grew and expanded from the eastern seaboard. By the nineteenth century, the trade had taken on many characteristics of a natural monopoly—a market condition where one firm might survive, but two firms would both take losses. From a trapping perspective, although a renewable resource, the animal populations generally were harvested at a rate well beyond that which would maintain populations, because of the common-property attributes of trapping and hunting in distinct resource-gathering areas. This activity tended to put pressure on the traders to expand into newer, and more distant, resource areas.

BIBLIOGRAPHY

Carlos, Ann M., and Frank D. Lewis. "Property Rights, Competition, and Depletion in the Eighteenth-Century Canadian Fur Trade: The Role of the European Market." *Canadian Journal of Economics* 32.3 (May 1999), 705–728.

Innis, Harold A. *The Fur Trade in Canada.* New and rev. ed. Toronto and Buffalo, 1999.

Norton, Thomas Elliot. *The Fur Trade in Colonial New York, 1686–1776.* Madison, Wis., 1974.

Paterson, Donald G. "The North Pacific Seal Hunt, 1886–1910: Rights and Regulations." *Explorations in Economic History* 14.2 (April 1977), 97–119.

Ray, Arthur J. *Indians in the Fur Trade: Their Role as Trappers, Hunters, and Middlemen in the Lands Southwest of Hudson Bay, 1660–1870,* with new introduction. Toronto and Buffalo, 1998.

DONALD G. PATERSON

FUTURES MARKETS. Futures exchanges, such as the Chicago Board of Trade (CBOT), emerged in essentially modern form during approximately 1865 to 1885. Although the late twentieth century witnessed a substantial expansion of the items traded as well as the number of ex-

changes, all these extensions copied the idea of standardized, impersonal contracts traded among members. Although Osaka's rice market had independently developed many modern features by the early eighteenth century, it had become moribund by 1850. And many trading practices can be traced earlier. New York City, not Chicago, had an advanced grain market by the late 1840s, employing techniques known in eighteenth-century London and seventeenth-century Amsterdam. (Simple forward contracts in which one party agrees with a counterparty about an exchange on some future date can be traced thousands of years earlier.) But the 1870s marked a substantive change. As the period's improvements in storage and transportation increased shipments, the telegraph made it possible for shippers to instruct brokers far away in advance of arrivals. Those brokers, naturally congregating in major ports, founded informal associations, then formal exchanges.

Although futures exchanges are extolled today for their pricing transparency, low-cost arbitrage, and ease of risk transfer, those advantages exist only because nineteenth-century exchanges developed—not always intentionally and not always in line with prevailing legal doctrines—several mechanisms for enforcing contracts. Members' committees worked to standardize the contracts (predictability being a major advantage in general commercial law). In the mid-1860s, the Liverpool Cotton Brokers' Association, a forerunner of the Liverpool Cotton Exchange, prepared printed contracts for cotton to arrive from India. These printed contracts did not list specific loads on specific ships. Rather, they indicated a generic commodity arriving during a window of time. U.S. cotton exchanges worked, sometimes collectively, to define vague terms such as *middling* and to hire inspectors.

Even if acting as brokers for others, members began trading among themselves as principals, in large part because they were not in simple relationships with their own principals. A rural grain shipper's Chicago "commission merchant" would hold, by way of a railroad and a Chicago grain elevator, a negotiable warehouse receipt, which gave him effective title to the grain; meanwhile, he would be the creditor of the shipper, who would have paid farmers with checks "drawn on" his commission merchant. A comparable system of "advances" existed for cotton throughout the United States, (except that those lending the money were called "factors") and for coffee through Le Havre, where a futures exchange was established by the 1880s. In Liverpool, the transatlantic cable allowed brokers, who had represented those importing cotton, to deal directly with exporters in the United States in competition with their own clients.

To reduce cascades of defaults, members developed a mechanism known as "ringing out" to cancel redundant contracts ahead of the delivery date, adjusting for any difference in prices through a side payment. In the 1870s in Chicago, clerks traveled from one CBOT member's office to another, searching for rings of contracts, until it was realized that sending all the trading books to one large room would reduce the need for clerks. Later, all side payments were calculated against an official "settlement" price and dispersed through a common fund to further reduce the need for clerks. On the CBOT, ringing out was voluntary, while on the New York Cotton Exchange, it was compulsory. Objections to settling contracts ahead of delivery were raised in court cases usually brought by a broker's client who had lost money. Lawyers emphasized that agency law required a broker to consult his client about ringing out, for implicitly another counterparty was substituted. Such consultations, the courts eventually perceived, would make ringing out prohibitively cumbersome. Because courts do not help collect gambling debts, lawyers emphasized that money changed hands whenever prices moved. Settlement by the payment of monetary differences, the courts eventually perceived, derived from commercial convenience.

Members among themselves, as well as brokers with their customers, could demand a good-faith deposit as a margin for performance. More important, they could demand additional "margin" money whenever prices moved against the other party and, if it were not forthcoming, could close out the other party's position immediately. In general commercial law, a forward contract could not be declared as nonperforming until the delivery date nor could an agent eliminate his principal's contract.

For ringing out offsetting contracts, paying monetary differences, and collecting margin, it became convenient (while reducing the number of clerks) to treat each member as trading met with other members but with an entity called the clearinghouse. Clearinghouses also took on the role of passing documents, such as warehouse receipts. Liverpool created the Cotton Brokers' Bank in 1878; comparable formal institutions were present in the United States by the 1880s.

Futures exchanges encouraged, if not mandated, arbitration by quasi-judicial members' committees. The CBOT's new state charter in 1859 explicitly disallowed those members who had submitted to arbitration from appealing to the courts, an innovative doctrine of private law. The ultimate sanction soon became expulsion.

With each of these enforcement mechanisms, the counterparty to any contract became less and less important, to the extent that the contracts became fungible. It is as if the contracts themselves became the goods traded. Indeed, *futures* might just as easily have been called *contracts* markets. In the nineteenth century, the full phrase was *a contract for future delivery*. At that time, *delivered* referred to something in a warehouse, distinct from, say, *free on board*.

As futures contracts became fungible, most traders expected to offset their initial position rather than to make or take delivery. Some traders, soon named *scalpers*, began to specialize in holding positions for only a few minutes. (While seeking short-run profits, they provide futures markets' exceptional liquidity.) Some other traders, knowing that they could buy later what they had sold, began to engage in short speculation. Short speculation seemed to some farmers as a cause of low prices. That perception sparked efforts to outlaw futures trading in the United States in the 1890s (as succeeded in Germany) and again in the 1920s. Although shippers outside the main ports were slower to perceive the opportunities in using futures contracts as temporary substitutes for merchandising contracts to be arranged later, from the 1890s, futures prices—at least of grains and cotton—were providing seasonal storage and shipment signals to large numbers of commercial firms (and indirectly to producers). From at least 1900, traders nearly everywhere were quoting local grain prices as differentials based on the most active futures price. That system of "basis trading" has emerged eventually for all commodities in which futures trading has flourished, despite initial resistance.

In summary, futures markets evolved from groups of aggressive traders involved with a commodity in relatively abstract form, rather than from groups of conventional shippers or processors, let alone producers, all of whom considered futures a dubious innovation.

BIBLIOGRAPHY

Ellison, Thomas. *Gleanings and Reminiscences*. Liverpool, U.K., 1905. Recounts from the inside the origins of the Liverpool Cotton Exchange and illustrates well the sophistication of an earlier age.

Irwin, Harold S. *Evolution of Futures Trading*. Madison, Wis., 1954. The Chicago Mercantile Exchange's origins around 1900 through improved storage of butter and eggs.

Lipartito, Kenneth J. "The New York Cotton Exchange and the Development of the Cotton Futures Market." *Business History Review* 57.1 (1983), 50–72.

Lurie, Jonathan. *The Chicago Board of Trade, 1859–1905: The Dynamics of Self-Regulation*. Urbana, 1979.

Pashigian, B. Peter. "Why Have Some Farmers Opposed Futures Markets?" *Journal of Political Economy* 96.2 (1988), 371–382. An analysis of Senate votes in the 1920s to tax futures trading prohibitively.

Schaede, Ulrike. "Forwards and Futures in Tokugawa-Period Japan: A New Perspective on the Dojima Rice Market." *Journal of Banking and Finance* 13.3 (1989), 487–513.

Starr, Merritt. "The Clearing House in the Grain and Cotton Exchange." *American Law Review* 20 (1886), 680–697.

Taylor, Charles H. *History of the Board of Trade of the City of Chicago*. 3 vols. Chicago, 1917.

Williams, Jeffrey C. "The Origin of Futures Markets." *Agricultural History* 56.1 (1982), 306–316.

JEFFREY WILLIAMS

G

GABON. *See* Central Africa.

GAMBLING AND GAMBLING INDUSTRY. Gambling cannot easily be defined but may be taken to include staking money on an event over which the action has no direct influence (this would rule out stock market speculation). Intuitively, most people accept that gambling includes casino gaming (on cards, dice, and roulette and similar games), bingo, betting on sporting and other events (horse and dog racing most commonly but also other sports and even contests such as elections), and lotteries. It has a long history: Crude dice or counters as tokens of gambling have been found in Ancient Egypt or the pre-Columbian Americas. Medieval and early modern European records reveal repeated attempts to stop people from gambling although governments exploited the propensity to gamble to raise revenue through public lotteries. Areas of European settlement in the New World did much the same. The English Crown established a monopoly for lotteries in 1694 and operated them until 1826. States of the early American Union used lotteries but had nearly all abandoned them by the 1860s. In much of continental Europe lotteries were never completely abandoned, but other forms of gambling were attacked in law in the nineteenth century. Despite various attempts to restrict it, gambling has always continued, and in the twentieth century it became highly commercialized and internalized into corporate capitalism.

Early History. Gaming was hugely popular in most of eighteenth-century Europe. This period of license was followed by one of increased restriction, arguably associated with the influence of the Protestant work ethic. Gaming houses (casinos) had been outlawed in eighteenth-century England but with little effect, as the well connected were able to escape prosecution. A more effective restriction was introduced in 1854. Similarly, the states of the United States banned casinos; only some racecourse betting was permitted. After briefly allowing some casinos in 1806, France banned all gambling (save for that sponsored by the state) in 1836. Casinos for well-to-do tourists were allowed to operate in German states until 1873. The most famous European casino in the nineteenth century was in Monte Carlo; opened in 1862 by the Blanc brothers, it quickly became the most fashionable place to play. Its success caused the French government to allow tourist casinos in some resorts such as Biarritz and Deauville from 1907. World War I, however, brought financial difficulties, and the Monte Carlo casino's premises were taken over by the prince. Its glamorous reputation returned in the 1920s. Casinos remained illegal in Britain but were developed in some other parts of Europe as tourist attractions (they even were permitted again in Germany in 1933 by the Nazi regime), often to the exclusion of local residents.

Gambling in the United States. A development that was to prove far more significant was the establishment of gambling facilities in the U.S. desert state of Nevada in 1931 in a government-inspired attempt to revive local economic fortunes. It was not until World War II, however, that the business really began to grow. The El Rancho casino was opened in 1941; and in 1946 Bugsy Siegel and Meyer Lansky (reputedly aided by Mafia connections) opened the famous Flamingo casino in Las Vegas, thought to have been used for laundering money from organized crime. In an ironic development, a number of Mormon bankers (forbidden from gambling themselves) helped to finance later ventures. In 1957 the Riviera casino was bought by a Mormon-owned bank; similar acquisitions followed. This gave some propriety to the business, which was enhanced in 1966 when eccentric businessman Howard Hughes bought the Desert Inn. More significantly, the 1969 Corporate Gaming Act (of Nevada) permitted corporations to hold gaming licenses. Large companies such as MGM, Hilton, Holiday Inn, and Ramada subsequently made substantial investments and incidentally enhanced the respectability of the business. Nevada remained the only U.S. state where gaming (and off-track betting) was legal.

A decade later a second U.S. gaming center was opened in Atlantic City, New Jersey, a result of corporate lobbying, mostly by Resorts International but also by city hall, to support legal gambling to revive the ailing tourist resort. It is generally agreed that although the casinos have brought substantial corporate returns, they have done little for the people of Atlantic City. However, the growth of casino gaming was only just beginning. In 1988 the Indian Gaming Regulatory Act allowed gaming on Native American reservations and triggered widespread expansion of legal

FANTAN GAMBLING. Men playing fantan in Guangzhou (Canton), China, circa 1890–1923. Fantan is derived from the Chinese "fan," which means "to turn over" (a cup), and "tan," which means "to spread out" (a pile of buttons). (Frank and Frances Carpenter Collection/Ah Fong/Prints and Photographs Divsion, Library of Congress)

casinos and high-stakes bingo. Gambling gradually came to be accepted as a form of popular recreation. The states had themselves set an example by reintroducing public lotteries in the 1960s and 1970s as a disguised, politically acceptable tax. By 2000 thirty-seven states operated lotteries, and thirty-five allowed casino gaming in some form.

Gambling in Other Countries. Developments in other countries were similar. In Canada public lotteries for revenue production for provinces were considered in the 1970s. Some casinos were allowed to operate on a temporary basis for charitable purposes in the 1970s and in 1990 permanent commercial casinos opened in Winnipeg and Manitoba. First Nation tribes then established their right to open casinos on reserved land in Ontario. In Britain a series of legal measures allowed casinos and commercial bingo (as well as off-track betting) in the 1960s, subject to strict regulation and limited in number. By 1970 some 116 casinos were operating nationwide, with twenty in London, and in the 1990s further locations were licensed. Businesses with interests in other gambling or leisure activities soon were involved. Bingo clubs were opened under the same legislation. Britain and Spain quickly became the largest markets for commercial bingo in Europe. However, ready admission by tourists to either casinos or bingo

clubs was not possible, since all players had to become members in advance. In the Caribbean, the Middle East, and much of continental Europe, on the other hand, casinos were intended primarily for tourists, generally with the exclusion of local residents. This was the case in France, Germany, and Austria, the last extending its state monopoly to casinos in 1962. Similarly Netherlands in 1975, Spain in 1979, and Denmark in 1990 allowed casinos primarily for tourists. Even in Communist East Europe some "hard currency" casinos were allowed, in Bulgaria and Hungary. With the collapse of Communism in the Soviet Union, an early manifestation of commercial liberalization was the opening of casinos.

Elsewhere, casino gaming probably grew fastest of all in Australia and New Zealand. The first legal casino in Australia opened in 1972. Once again the experience of Australian state lotteries appeared to be influential, in demonstrating the revenue potential of popular gambling. Commercial gaming in casinos and clubs burgeoned in most parts of Australia. Gambling machines (known as poker machines) were already popular although often illegal. New Zealand for a while continued to prohibit casino gaming but allowed betting, lotteries, and charitable bingo. However, in 1990 a new legislative act endeavored to "promote the development of casinos." Gambling has always been popular in much of Asia. Communist China for years outlawed all gambling although it probably continued illegally; in 1987 the state itself introduced a social-welfare lottery. Paradoxically the take-over of Hong Kong in 1997 and Macao in 1999 allowed the continuation of established popular gambling in these territories (horse racing in Hong Kong, gaming in Macao).

History of Betting. Betting, like other gambling, was universally popular in eighteenth-century Britain, mostly on horse racing but also other sports such as foot races and cricket. To serve this interest, a cohort of bookmakers grew up ready to take bets on, and offer odds against, all runners in a race. By the early nineteenth century betting opportunities were available on racecourses are frequently off-track as well. In the 1920s importation, from the United States, of the idea of racing greyhounds in enclosed stadia added to legal, popular, and especially working-class betting opportunities. Cash betting shops had been closed by law in England in 1853, but illegal off-track cash betting with "street bookmakers" continued on a wide scale

GAMBLING. Roulette players, Las Vegas, Nevada, 1940. (Arthur Rothstein/Prints and Photographs Division, Library of Congress)

despite further restriction with the Street Betting Act of 1906. As this applied only to cash betting it was a class discriminatory measure, because the wealthy had always been able to bet on credit with a legal bookmaker. Cash betting shops were permitted in Ireland from the 1930s, and two decades later in Australia and New Zealand. In Britain they were once again permitted in 1961. This removed a legal anomaly and opened the way for oligopolistic corporate bookmaking to grow. Four major companies—Ladbrokes, William Hills, Corals, and Mecca—soon took a large share of the betting market, with a merger later reducing the number to three.

Betting markets in Britain and Ireland continued to be dominated by bookmakers, offering fixed odds; but in many other parts of the world, bookmaking was banned. It was permitted with restrictions in South Africa, Australia, Germany, Belgium, and some other markets but nowhere on the corporate scale that it came to occupy in Britain. In the United States, bookmakers were gradually outlawed by state legislatures shortly before World War I and later permitted only in Nevada. They were driven off racecourses in France in the 1890s and in New Zealand in 1921. Betting on horses and dogs, and some other events, became largely confined to parimutuel pool betting, a system developed in France in the 1860s whereby returns to winning bets were calculated after the event by dividing the pool after a deduction was made for operating costs and profit. The system was designed to provide a return to the promoters of racing, including the courses. Such betting was initially resisted in Britain, as it was in the United States. Introduced in Britain in 1929 (where it is known as the totalisator after the mechanical device invented in New Zealand for calculating the returns), it never became as popular there as elsewhere. In the United States as in most of the rest of the world in the twentieth century, however, racecourse betting was done exclusively on the pari-mutuel system. In Australia toward the end of the century some racetrack bookmakers faced bankruptcy as pool betting and alternative gambling outlets ate into their market.

Lotteries, Match-Fixing, and More. Throughout the twentieth century, gambling opportunities multiplied. In the years after World War I pool betting on football (soccer) matches began in Britain, and it followed in many other parts of Europe. The pools in Britain became dominated by a small number of large companies. The medium provided a remote chance of a big win for a modest outlay, as in a lottery; and in taxing them heavily, after World War II, governments treated them largely as others have used lotteries. Public lotteries were revived and became almost ubiquitous throughout the world in the late twentieth century, providing revenue for public expenditure without being regarded as a tax by the playing public. Total world lottery sales exceeded U.S. $79 billion in 1992, a figure added to significantly when Britain, one of the last major markets to introduce a national lottery, did so in 1994. Unusually in this market, the lottery was operated under license by a private business for profit.

Gambling has often been associated with crime, if only because much of it was illegal for many years. However, gambling also presented an opportunity for laundering the result of dishonestly obtained funds—in postwar Las Vegas or post-Communist Russia, for instance. Gambling has also led to illegal activity in fixing the results of races, or sports contests, through doping or bribery. In the 1990s bookmakers in the Far East were implicated in attempts to fix results in British soccer games on which large bets had been struck.

Such a mixed picture is perhaps inevitable. By the end of the twentieth century, however, gambling had become a highly respectable legitimate business and one of the most profitable industries. In the United States in 1994 the casino business alone produced annual revenues of U.S.$15 billion, providing net returns more than double those of manufacturing industry. The political acceptability of public lotteries and the promise of revenue have brought political and social approval to gambling as well as attracting large investment funds. However, at the dawn of the twenty-first century a new question has emerged: How far will the provision of gambling opportunities on the Internet, already booming, undermine established markets and practices?

[See also Lotteries.]

BIBLIOGRAPHY
Abt, Vicki, James F. Smith and Eugene M. Christiansen. *The Business of Risk: Commercial Gambling in Mainstream America.* Lawrence, Kans., 1985.
Ashton, John. *A History of Gambling in England.* London 1898.
Brenner, Reuven, and Gabrielle A. Brenner. *Gambling and Speculation: A Theory, a History and a Future of Some Human Decisions.* Cambridge, 1990.
Caldwell, Geoffrey, Brian Haig, Mark Dickerson, and Louise Sylvan. *Gambling in Australia.* London, 1985.
Dixon, David. *From Prohibition to Regulation: Bookmaking, Anti-Gambling and the Law.* Oxford, 1991.
Eadington, William R., and Judy Cornelius. *Gambling and Commercial Gaming: Essays in Business, Economics, Philosophy and Science.* Reno, Nev., 1992.
Grant, David. *On a Roll: A History of Gambling in New Zealand.* Wellington, 1994.
Goodman, Robert. *The Luck Business: The Devastating Consequences and Broken Promises of Americas Gambling Explosion.* New York, 1995.
Munting, Roger. *An Economic and Social History of Gambling in Britain and the USA.* Manchester, 1996.
O'Hara, John. *A Mug's Game: A History of Gaming and Betting in Australia.* Kensington, 1988.
Rosecrance, John D. *Gambling without Guilt: The Legitimisation of an American Pastime.* Pacific Grove, Calif., 1988.
Sternlieb, George, and James Hughes. *The Atlantic City Gamble.* Cambridge, Mass., 1983.
Vance, Joan. *An Analysis of the Costs and Benefits of Public Lotteries: The Canadian Experience.* Lewiston, N.Y., 1989.

ROGER MUNTING

GAS INDUSTRY. Broadly speaking, the output of gas for commercial purposes has taken place in two major technological phases. First, from the beginning of the nineteenth century until around the mid-twentieth century, most gas was manufactured from coal. The coal was distilled in retorts and distributed through pipelines from a central plant to consumers. In the process of manufacture, various by-products were produced, notably coke, and these became a significant associated industry. Second, especially from the 1960s, natural gas quickly, and almost completely, supplanted manufactured gas.

This sequence needs supplementing with a few caveats. First, from the beginning, various substances other than coal were used to produce gas. Gas was manufactured from wood, peat, and vegetable oil, for example. But coal held sway, and, especially where coal was abundant and cheap, coal gas had become a familiar source of lighting by the second half of the nineteenth century.

Second, new processes resulted in the development of new forms of manufactured gas. One was water gas, invented in America in the 1870s, where air was blown over coal or coke in a furnace. Water gas ultimately supplanted coal gas in America and was widely used as a source of peak load supply in the United Kingdom after World War II.

Third, from the 1950s, new distillations of oil (especially propane and butane) allowed conversions into gas at special catalytic converter plants. Such manufactured gas was of considerable importance in Britain and elsewhere in western Europe at a time when coal prices were rising and before the advent of large-scale natural gas.

Finally, we should note that although natural gas has become the main source of gas supply since the 1960s, the existence of natural gas has long been known. The use of natural gas for streetlights was recorded in America as early as 1821; and by the mid-1930s, natural gas sales had overtaken those of manufactured gas.

Significant changes have taken place in the market for gas. At first, in Britain and elsewhere, gas was demanded principally for lighting. Until World War I, lighting was by far the main use for gas, although at this time electricity was making rapid inroads into the lighting market. The earliest gas markets were found for street lighting and large industrial and commercial buildings. However, falling costs, associated with greater productivity and lower coal prices, allowed gas to be used increasingly for domestic lighting, initially among the wealthy, but by the end of the nineteenth century in working-class homes, also.

Gas cookers were designed in the 1820s, and several designs were displayed at the Crystal Palace Exhibition of 1851 in London. But only after the 1880s did the cooking and water-heating markets make significant headway.

The era of natural gas after 1960 dramatically altered the demand pattern for gas. Throughout Europe (mirroring a pattern already evident in the United States), gas found new industrial and commercial outlets. From being a minor source of energy, principally used by domestic consumers for cooking, by 1980 gas had become a leading supplier of primary energy in many countries. In western Europe as a whole, natural gas supplied only 2 percent of primary energy in 1965. By 1977 this had expanded to more than 17 percent. By the 1990s, natural gas was a principal fuel used in power stations in many countries.

The Beginnings. The gas industry had its origins in the British Industrial Revolution. Research has noted two paths by which the industry developed in Britain.

There was a long-felt need for better forms of light for commercial and industrial purposes than could be supplied by traditional candles and oil lamps. This was especially true for the textile mills of northern England, where night work was required and where existing forms of light were expensive, hot, and dangerous.

In 1792, a Scotsman named William Murdock (an employee at Boulton and Watts, the famous Soho foundry) successfully managed to produce, from coal, gas that could be used for lighting. The Soho works were illuminated with gas lamps in 1802, and in 1805 Murdock installed a gas-making plant at the large cotton mill of Phillips and Lee in Manchester. By 1815, several other factories and large buildings were illuminated in this manner. However, individual gas plants were never widespread and proved costly to install and maintain.

Even before Murdock's successful experiments, Philippe Lebon, a brilliant French engineer, experimented with making gas from wood. Lebon staged a public exhibition of his "thermolampes" in Paris in 1801, an exhibition witnessed by Friedrich Albert Winzer (1763–1830) from Brunswick, Germany. Winzer was a flamboyant publicist and entrepreneur who (now Winsor) came to London in 1803 to develop the invention. In 1807, he lit the first streetlamps in Pall Mall. Eventually, in 1812, Winsor promoted the first gas company, the Gas Light and Coke Company. This company, founded by Royal Charter, lasted until nationalization in 1949, though Winsor's role was short-lived.

Yet it was Winsor's, rather than Murdock's, pattern of gas development that became the norm for the progress of the gas industry—gas manufactured at a central source and supplied to consumers through pipes. In Britain, various towns soon followed London's lead: Exeter and Preston in 1816 and Manchester (the first municipal works),

Bristol, Liverpool, and Glasgow in 1817. By 1825, all British towns with a population in excess of twenty thousand had at least one gas company, while by 1850 even small towns with populations of five thousand or more usually had a gasworks.

Spread of the Industry. Manufactured gas for lighting began to appear in the United States and Europe within a few years of the founding of London's first company. In June 1816, the Gas Light Company of Baltimore was founded, and the first streetlamps were lit in February 1817. Boston's streets were lit by the Boston Gas Light Company in 1822, and the New York Gas Light Company started operations in 1825.

Europe also saw the first use of gas in streetlamps at about the same time: Paris and Brussels in 1819 and Hanover in 1825. During the 1820s and 1830s, major cities in France, Belgium, and Germany obtained gas companies. Some were constructed with British capital and technology, and prominent was the Imperial Continental Gas Association founded in 1834, which built several gasworks in Europe, including that at Cologne in 1841. By 1870, there were some 340 gasworks in Germany.

In Britain, the construction of gasworks broadly followed the trade cycle, with promotional booms in the mid-1820s, late 1830s, and late 1840s. By 1829, there were more than 200 gas companies operating in the country, and in 1882, despite amalgamations, more than 480.

By around 1860, most principal cities in America and western Europe had incorporated or municipal gas companies, and gas lighting was becoming familiar elsewhere. In America, for example, Louisville and New Orleans obtained companies in 1832, Philadelphia in 1834 (the first municipal company in America), Pittsburgh in 1836, Washington in 1848, and Chicago in 1850. Sydney, Australia, had a gas company in 1841, and Toronto, Canada, in 1847. During the 1840s, gas lighting appeared in Switzerland and Sweden, and during the 1850s, gas companies were found in Copenhagen, Madrid, Rome, Warsaw, Rio de Janeiro, Buenos Aires, Calcutta, and Mexico City. By the 1860s, there was gas street lighting in Moscow, Saint Petersburg, and other Russian cities; in Bangkok, Rangoon, Bombay, and a host of cities throughout the world. Japan obtained its first gas company in 1872 (Yokohama), and Tokyo followed in 1874. By 1912, there were some 75 gas companies in Japan. Most of these gas plants used coal, but other substances were also utilized. The Baltimore company, for example, distilled pine tar for the first five years of its existence.

Technology. By around 1820, many of the basic technological problems in the production and distribution of gas had been solved by trial and error. Methods of purification were developed by Heard (assistant to Winsor), who patented a dry lime process in 1806. Also in 1806, Samuel

Clegg invented the wet liming process. Clegg was the greatest of the early gas engineers. He had been an apprentice with Boulton and Watt, working alongside Murdock. He set up as an independent gas engineer in 1805 and became chief engineer of the Gas Light and Coke Company in 1812.

Storage of gas was achieved with the development of large gas holders (gasometers) set in water, while early meters, owing much to the work of Samuel Clegg and John Malam, were able effectively to record the consumption of gas by around 1820.

During the nineteenth century, there were many technical improvements in all aspects of gas operation and consumption, and developments came from European and American, as well as British, engineers. By the 1840s, growing gas productivity allowed significant price falls, and this spurred increased demand and the setting up of profitable gasworks in ever-smaller towns.

An important development was the Bunsen burner, a German invention in 1855. This was the principle used by the Austrian chemist Baron Von Welsbach in his invention of the incandescent gas mantle in 1885 and greatly extended the use of gas lighting at a time when competition from electricity was threatening. With the invention of the tungsten filament for electric bulbs in 1910, however, the era of gas lighting was finally doomed.

Another important development was the invention in England of the prepayment meter ("penny-in-the-slot") in the 1870s. This encouraged the use of gas further down the social scale, and helped develop the use of gas for cooking and water heating.

Government Regulation. A feature of the gas industry has been its status as a "public utility" and "natural monopoly." The industry has been subjected to various forms of government regulation. Usually, statutory gas companies have had restrictions placed on dividends, prices, and areas of supply. There has also been a strong municipal interest, and in Britain, America, and elsewhere, municipal gas undertakings have been established since the first half of the nineteenth century. In Britain, the gas industry was nationalized in 1948 and was operated by Area Boards and Regions until the industry reverted to private enterprise in 1986.

Natural Gas. Between 1950 and the 1970s, natural gas supplanted manufactured gas in many countries. The movement came first, and was most widespread, in the United States, the Soviet Union, and parts of western Europe. In Britain, conversion to natural gas was completed by 1977.

The world's first natural gas company was established at Fredonia, New York, in 1858, where natural gas has been known and utilized for several decades. But only in the interwar years did new discoveries and new pipeline technology enable significant expansion. A long-distance pipeline of 217 miles was constructed in 1925 by the Magnolia Gas Company of Dallas. In 1931, the first 1,000-mile pipeline was built from the world's largest natural gas field at Panhandle, Texas, to Chicago by the Natural Gas Pipeline Company. By the mid-1930s, sales of natural gas in the United States exceeded those of manufactured gas, although sales of the latter continued to expand until 1948. However, by the 1950s the dominance of natural gas was overwhelming, and, indeed, natural gas supplied more than half the energy consumption of the American domestic market and some 40 percent of industrial consumption.

In the Soviet Union, natural gas, usually associated with oil production, made significant headway before 1940, and from the mid-1950s, successive plans put emphasis on greater production and utilization of natural gas. During the 1970s, the Soviet Union became a major exporter of natural gas to eastern and western Europe.

Meanwhile, in western Europe, natural gas development was transformed by the discovery of the huge Groningen field in the Netherlands in 1959 and of North Sea gas in 1965. As a result, supplies of natural gas became abundant at a time when oil and coal prices were rising, and gas became increasingly significant as a domestic, industrial, and commercial source of energy. The Netherlands was converted to natural gas between 1964 and 1978, while in Britain a vast nationwide conversion program was started in 1967 and completed almost exactly a decade later.

[*See also* Public Utilities.]

BIBLIOGRAPHY

Falkus, Malcolm. "The Early Development of the British Gas Industry, 1790–1815." *Economic History Review* (May 1982).
Falkus, Malcolm. *Always under Pressure: A History of North Thames Gas since 1949.* London: Macmillan, 1988.
Peebles, M. W. H. *Evolution of the Gas Industry.* London: Macmillan, 1980.
Tokyo Gas Co. Ltd. *History of the Gas Industry in Japan.* Tokyo, 1978.
Williams, T. I. *A History of the British Gas Industry.* Oxford, 1981.

MALCOLM FALKUS

GATHERING. Gathering vegetable, insect, and small invertebrate foods has been important in human history ever since the divergence of the hominins and African apes and until the advent of effective agriculture. Even today, some subsistence agricultural societies make extensive use of wild plants for essential nutrients not abundant in domestic plants. Since our closest phylogenetic relatives are chimpanzees who subsist mainly on ripe fruit, early Australopithecines probably ate a diet based mainly on ripe fruit, nuts, roots, and insects. Later, when *Homo erectus* began to acquire significant amounts of hunted foods, a division of labor probably arose in which women and children continued to gather sessile resources, while men focused on hunting. Most probably, women did not hunt because it was incompatible with their main goal of providing effective care for vulnerable infants (Hurtado, et al., 1992).

Among modern hunting-and-gathering societies, many valuable food resources are collected by women and children. Most vegetable resources that humans exploit are calorically dense reproductive storage organs found in large patches. These include mainly roots, nuts, seeds, fruits, growing shoots, and stored starch in the trunk of palm trees. Surprisingly, however, fruits do not contribute more than about 5 percent of the energy in the diet of most modern hunter-gatherers (Kaplan, et al., 2000). This is mainly because most fruits are low caloric density (with high water content) and not available during many seasons of the year. Of the commonly collected vegetable foods, only nuts and seeds contain significant amounts of protein and lipids required for optimal human health. Because of these macronutrient requirements, women and children also collect insects and invertebrates, or engage in informal trade for meat with men who hunt during the day. The most commonly sought insects are larval forms of beetles and social insects. Aquatic invertebrates, such as shellfish and crustaceans, are also attractive. Finally, honey is an important resource collected in many places around the world.

Most important gathered resources require some processing to make them edible, including removing inedible parts, eliminating toxins, and cooking. Because collecting is often laborious and processing time can be considerable, the overall caloric return rate from gathering is usually not high. For example, mongongo nuts, a staple in the Kung bushmen diet, provide only 670 calories per hour when all travel and processing time is included in the cost of acquisition (Hawkes and O'Connell, 1985). More typically, return rates from gathering are measured after the collector has arrived at the resource patch. From a database of ninety-one resource types whose hourly return rate has been measured, the following averages can be calculated (given as mean, standard deviation): fruits 4750, 3900; roots 1380, 1560; nuts 1650, 1540; grass seeds 560, 370; starch extraction 1450, 740; growing shoots 1790, 360; insect larva 2040, 950; wild honey 17,230, 7470 (Hill, et al., 1987; 81–82). These numbers suggest that honey collection is the most profitable resource. Not surprisingly, this activity is often carried out by men rather than women and children. Fruit collection also gives high average returns but with high variability (large fruits have return rates about twice as high as smaller fruits). Grass seeds probably have the lowest return rate because of the extensive processing required (winnowing and grinding). Because of substantial travel time to collecting patches and the scarci-ty of the most calorically dense collected resources, women's overall return rate from gathering is often only about 600 calories per hour.

Women's daily time allocation to gathering resources varies among hunter-gatherer groups and is strongly affected by their reproductive status (Hurtado, et al., 1992), with new mothers spending very little time gathering compared to older post-reproductive women. The mean number of hours gathering per day from twenty-two foraging societies is about 3.8 hours. The biggest advantage of gathering over hunting is that it is less likely to fail to provide any food on a given day and it is an activity that children can engage in to provide some of their own food needs. Children's effectiveness at gathering is mainly dependent on whether gathered foods require complicated extraction techniques, or they can simply be collected from the environment. Since most fruits require no complicated extraction, children are nearly as efficient as adults in gathering fruits (Kaplan, et al., 2000), a finding that appears to have important implications for the divergence in life history between fruit-eating apes and early human ancestors.

[See also Hunting.]

BIBLIOGRAPHY

Hawkes, K., and J. F. O'Connell. "Optimal Foraging Models and the Case of the !Kung." *American Anthropologist* 87 (1985), 401–405.

Hill, Kim, Kristen Hawkes, Hillard Kaplan, and A. Magdalena Hurtado "Foraging Decisions Among Ache Hunter-Gatherers: New Data and Implications for Optimal Foraging Models." *Ethology and Sociobiology* 8 (1987), 1–36.

Hurtado, A., K. Hill, H. Kaplan, and I. Hurtado. "Tradeoffs Between Female Food Acquisition and Child Care Among Hiwi and Ache Foragers." *Human Nature* 3.3 (1992), 185–216.

Kaplan, H., K. Hill, J. Lancaster, and A. M. Hurtado. "The Evolution of Intelligence and the Human Life History." *Evolutionary Anthropology* 9.4 (2000), 156–184.

KIM R. HILL AND A. MAGDALENA HURTADO

GENDER RELATIONS. Since the 1970s, the value of gender analysis in understanding historical economic processes has become increasingly recognized. Informed by a complex and dynamic set of analytical perspectives, historians look closely at the relationship between men and women in all areas of social, political, and economic activity. Through insights derived from women's history, gender history, and most recently the history of masculinity[ies], the exploration of gender relations within economic history has been enhanced. From the vantage point of the early twenty-first century, it can be argued that gender has surpassed social class as a consideration in the analysis of historical transformation. This section will explore the significance of gender and indicate the ways in which it enhances an understanding of economic change over the past several hundred years. It uses the examples of Europe and the United States and identifies both the similarities and the key differences between them.

Early History. It is sometimes assumed that the process of industrialization created or cemented a particular pattern of gender relationships, but there is no doubt that in the preceding centuries men and women occupied unequal economic positions both in the workplace and in the home. Recent research has confirmed that women's work was more variable than men's across time and space, that gender relationships took various forms in urban and rural areas, across region and locality, and at different stages of economic cycles or according to family circumstances.

Urban settings. In medieval and early modern Europe, the nature of work both in the home and in the workshop, in the town and in the countryside, clearly took on gendered forms. In the typical artisanal family, most if not all skilled work was performed by the male head of household, assisted by male apprentices with the occasional and flexible contribution from the wife. In the towns and cities of early modern Europe, therefore, occupational categories for men and women were already differentiated. Men monopolized the skilled and high-status jobs, while women's work already conformed to a secondary labor market where employment was largely unskilled, low-status, poorly paid, casual, seasonal, and irregular. Such distinctions did not exist harmoniously and were often maintained with some difficulty. Although medieval women were not formally barred from all skilled occupations and indeed played an important part in such trades as goldsmithing, most urban guilds in most European economies attempted to restrict women's work opportunities and to define the proper spheres of productive and unproductive work in gender terms alone.

Such differentiated gender interests, and especially the exclusion of women from a range of occupations, was primarily an urban phenomenon. It was not rigorously practiced in all towns, however, and where regulation was weak, women were found either in specifically female trades, or sometimes working alongside men, or in the case of a husband's death, temporarily controlling the family business. Even in these cases, women did not enjoy equal status with men. They experienced less than equal opportunities when it came to training and apprenticeship and were welcomed into men's activities only when economic circumstances required it, or when men could not cope alone. Whether or not women actually did less skilful and specialized work than men, that is how it was perceived. Within the urban family production unit, parents and children toiled together and work was distributed according to the requirements of the enterprise and domestic or family commitments. Nevertheless, the domestic system of manufacture depended on the excessive and low-paid labor of women and children.

Rural settings. In the countryside, gender relationships were more fluid and more harmonious than those that prevailed in the towns, a characteristic that historians have identified in the context of the protoindustrial system. Evidence suggests that much of the labor force within protoindustrial activity consisted of family groups working at home and organizing industrial work around agricultural commitments. In many such groups—which are seen to have been flexible and cooperative—work and responsibility were distributed in a nongendered way. This was not always the case, however, and in some protoindustrial trades, a male-dominated hierarchy of labor existed; new research on masculinity appears to indicate that men occupied positions of authority in the household and did not engage seriously with domestic chores. Certainly there is evidence that female labor, despite its value, was relatively underrewarded and that manufacturing activity spread into the countryside from the late seventeenth century because of the prevalence of cheap and unregulated female labor.

Industrialization. The commentary of political and economic thinkers offers an alternative perspective on gender distinctions of labor. Some praised women for their industriousness, recognizing the contribution of their productive effort to the wealth of the nation as well as to individual families. For example, in the context of the shift to industrialization, the contribution of rural women to the family budget lay mainly in the mobilization of common resources, including gathering and scavenging, food processing, the care of livestock, and the cultivation of kitchen crops. It has been shown that by these and other activities, such as the very profitable gleaning, and the selling of brooms made from heath material, women could earn as much money in a year as their menfolk. In such an analysis, men and women shared in the creation of wealth.

But women's flexibility denied them access to the skilled and specialized work that came to be particularly valued from the turn of the century, partly the result of gendered apprenticeship patterns, which suggests a downgrading of female work and a narrowing of occupational opportunities for girls and women. During the early industrializing period of the later eighteenth century, the closure of a number of traditional female activities meant that women more than men had difficulty in making ends meet. Late-eighteenth-century commentators referred to the association of women with poverty. Eighty percent of those classed as poor were women, and by the turn of the century women became cast more as economic burdens than assets and ceased to be regarded as joint supporters of the laboring household. The outcome was a greater inequality in home and work. Therefore, the era in which the family economy dominated was by no means one in which gender relations were equitable and free of conflict.

DIVISION OF LABOR. An idealized fifteenth-century carpenter's shop portraying the wife spinning; spinning was probably the most widespread female occupattion. Painting by Jean Bourdichon (c. 1457–1521). (École des Beaux-Arts, Paris/Photo Bulloz/Giraudon/Réunion des Musées Nationaux/Art Resource, NY)

Matrimony. This was particularly true in the case of matrimony. Evidence that eighteenth-century marriage, especially in the middle-class groups, became more equal and affective needs to be balanced by evidence that in the context of marriage women lost control over their property and that in legal terms women's very existence depended on their family roles. In Great Britain, for example, married women had no civil existence under the provisions of the common law, and within the framework provided by Lord Hardwicke's Act of 1753, they owned no personal property, could not divorce their husbands, nor claim any rights over their children. In contemporary America, a similar system operated but was less rigidly enforced. On the continent, the legal basis of marriage typically took the form of a contract, which recognized the property rights of both men and women. Resisting its harshness, many working people in Great Britain operated outside of the law, however, mostly by cohabiting but also—as in the case

of some Owenite socialists who saw marriage as the "eternal prisonhouse of the wife"—by writing their own marriage contract. Although the solemnization of marriage was not practiced widely among the working class, pressure to establish a household with a sexual partner was irresistible. Women appear to have been subordinated in the majority of heterosexual cohabiting relationships and felt forced into dependent relationships because of low wages and limited employment possibilities. So although marriage and cohabitation comprised an economic unit for the mutual support or survival of all members of the family, gender relationships within it were unequal and sometimes oppressively so. The subordination of women within a marital relationship formed the basis of their subjection in the political and economic sphere. Women had few more legal rights in marriage than unpaid domestic servants. Although some women and men negotiated mutually satisfying relationships, gender conflict within the home and family became increasingly apparent.

The nineteenth century. In the nineteenth century, the process of industrialization in Europe and North America took place through a symbiosis between a centralized and high-productivity manufacturing industry, an informal economy of family production, and a growing outwork and sweating sector. In many areas, cheap female labor, using hand or intermediate techniques, was long preferred over mechanization. During the nineteenth century, married women in particular continued to work in less formal settings both in urban and rural areas, as opposed to the factory and mill, where the single woman predominated. Domestic industry and labor-intensive homework were integral to the development of numerous industries as the family economy continued to operate in new contexts. Within this complex organizational structure, differences between male and female social roles became more pronounced. The making of gender and gender relationships in the period of industrialization was neither automatic nor straightforward, and there was inevitable conflict. A variety of contests and compromises took place as new techniques and organizations of production were introduced. In the early stages of industrialization, employers hired as much female and child labor as possible, and although women were generally employed on unfavorable terms, male workers envied and felt threatened by their indispensability. As a result, from the early nineteenth century, exclusionary strategies practiced by skilled men, which resembled those of the early modern era, resurfaced. Rather than seeking to minimize gender differences and establish worker solidarity, male workers attempted to distinguish themselves from women workers as much and as often as possible. With the backing of male-dominated trade unions, men influenced the gendered use of new technology and orchestrated a gendering of skills. By restructuring notions of skill, craftsmen both avoided much of the deskilling potential of the new technology and further strengthened the perception of their own work as skilled and that of women as unskilled.

Domesticity. Also important in the shaping of gender identities and gender relationships was the construction of a new concept of domesticity. The obligations implied by domesticity combined to restrict women's freedom to engage in other social and economic activities, and in particular weakened their working position, yet many working-class people and organizations pursued domesticity in an attempt to enhance family living standards and material comforts. Although it was popular, it also created tensions, and ironically it split the interests of working women and men and divided women according to marital status. This was particularly reflected in the fight for the breadwinner wage, which formed an important plank of labor union demands through much of the latter part of the nineteenth century. Industrialization may have threatened the natural order of things, but by the later nineteenth century, domesticity had been created, recreated, and restored through political struggle.

Heterogeneity. These processes were common to many of the industrial regions of Great Britain, Europe, and the United States during the nineteenth century with some distinctions. Although married women formed a diminishing proportion of the formal labor force in all parts, at 5 percent they were particularly poorly represented in the United States, while in the French mill towns they were relatively numerous. Gender relations were everywhere informed by social class, and in the United States more than elsewhere, race compounded the heterogeneity of gendered experience. Racial minorities of both sexes found themselves segregated in low-status and low-wage jobs, though women's disadvantage was more pronounced. Following the end of slavery, black women, for example, were twice as likely as expected to work in farming or laundering and were more or less excluded from factories, and from clerical and shop work. Asian-American women were concentrated in agriculture, peddling, and the sewing trades. Variations in gender relationships existed both between economies and between regions of the same economy. Most evident were differences between town and countryside. In most urban industrial regions, the major employers of women were domestic service (exceptionally great in Great Britain), textiles, and garment making, while in rural areas, family farming enterprises (very common in France, but less so in Great Britain) coexisted with more traditional forms of manufacturing. In England, for example, men and women in the northern textile towns, especially in the cotton-weaving districts, enjoyed greater cooperation, both in the workplace and at home, than those in southern agricultural districts or in the coal-mining region of the northeast.

The twentieth century and beyond. Inequality in gender relations was clearly not created but was evidently restructured and cemented during the nineteenth century. Reflective of the patriarchal nature of many of the structures of industrial society, it was challenged from the early twentieth century. "First Wave" feminism, influential in achieving woman suffrage early in the twentieth century, encouraged the mobilization of working women into trade unions. It also raised issues of gender equality and was especially critical of the double standard—whereby acceptable behavior for men and for women were quite distinct—that existed within marriage. Late in the nineteenth century, women had gained more rights over their own property and person; and through the twentieth century, marriage became more companionate, and the easing of divorce law meant that unhappy marriages no longer had to be endured. Such improvements to gender relations did not apply to the workplace, however, where, except during the two world wars, women remained confined to low-status occupations. The ideology of domesticity and women's primary association in the home remained popular. "Second Wave" feminism of the 1960s and 1970s played an important part in encouraging equal rights at work and in the home and generally in empowering women. By the end of the twentieth century, there was clear evidence of "gender transformation"; and in principle and in law, there was equality in both the workplace and the home. But although women constituted 50 percent of the labor force in some parts of the industrialized world, they formed the majority of those in low-paid, unskilled, and part-time work and continued to bear the brunt of child care and other domestic chores. Both the extent and meaning of part-time work varied across Europe and the United States. In the United Kingdom, where female-dominated part-time work was more common than in Europe, the particular conditions of part-time work operated to maintain women in relatively disadvantaged positions in the labor market. Research in the Nordic countries, however, indicated that poor conditions are not inevitable for part-time workers and where part-timers are employed under the same conditions as full timers [which is European law], then part-time work can act as a bridge rather than a trap for women. Although gender relations in the early twenty-first century are less hostile than they once were, equality is still very far from a reality.

BIBLIOGRAPHY

Bennett, Judith. "Medieval Women, Modern Women: Across the Great Divide." In *Culture and History, 1350–1600: Essays on English Communities, Identities and Writing,* edited by David Ares, pp. 147–175. London, 1992.

Clark, Alice. *Working Life of Women in the Seventeenth Century.* London, 1982.

Clark, Anna. *The Struggle for the Breeches: Gender and the Making of the British Working Class.* Berkeley, 1995.

Davidoff, Leonore, and Catherine Hall. *Family Fortunes: Men and Women of the English Middle Class, 1780–1850.* London, 1987.

Frader, Laura L., and Sonya O Rose, eds. *Gender and Class in Modern Europe.* Ithaca, N.Y., 1996.

Honeyman, Katrina. *Women, Gender and Industrialisation in England, 1700–1870.* Basingstoke, U.K., 2000.

Rendall, Jane. *The Origins of Modern Feminism: Women in Britain, France and the United States, 1780–1860.* Basingstoke, U.K., 1984.

Scott, Joan. *Gender and the Politics of History.* New York, 1988.

Shoemaker, Robert B. *Gender in English Society, 1650–1850: The Emergence of Separate Spheres?* London, 1998.

Simonton, Deborah. *A History of European Women's Work: 1700 to the Present.* New York, 1998.

Tilly, Louise, and Joan Scott. *Women, Work and Family.* New York, 1978.

Valenze, Deborah. *The First Industrial Woman.* Oxford, 1995.

Vickery, Amanda. *The Gentleman's Daughter: Women's Lives in Georgian England.* New Haven and London, 1998.

Walby, Sylvia. *Gender Transformations.* London and New York, 1997.

KATRINA HONEYMAN

GENOA. Beginning with its recovery from a Muslim sack in 934/935 to the end of its independence in 1805, Genoa played a major role in Mediterranean trade and the economic development of Italy. The city, located at the best northern harbor on the Tyrrhenian Sea, was well suited to serve as an entrepôt connecting Lombardy and parts of northern Europe to the Levant. Along with Venice, Pisa, and Amalfi, Genoa was a leader in the "commercial revolution" of the Middle Ages. The Genoese, blessed with few natural resources, thrived by building ships and using them to move commodities from places of abundance to those of scarcity. The large number of early commercial contracts in the city's archives testify to its precocious role in the commercial revolution. These rich runs of documents, beginning in the mid-twelfth century, have been intensively studied because they offer a unique view of the earliest phases of economic development in the western Mediterranean.

Genoese merchants were already active in Egypt in the mid-eleventh century, purchasing such luxury items as pepper, cotton, and paper in exchange for silver, timber, and slaves. Genoese merchants mainly served as middlemen in this trade, gathering raw materials the Egyptians would purchase and exporting the bulk of the luxuries, via the fairs of Champagne, into northern Europe. Genoa's profits from this trade enabled the city's merchants to build more ships and extend their authority over most of the Italian Riviera from Monaco to Portovenere, and eventually the island of Corsica. Genoa actively participated in the Crusades (1095–1291) and acquired trading privileges and merchant colonies along the coast of Syria and the Holy Land. By the end of the thirteenth century, Genoese traders had established merchant colonies in the Black Sea, and intrepid merchants were already active in Persia.

(Tombstones from the next century reveal that some had gone as far as China, in the footsteps of Marco Polo.) The notarial cartularies reveal an increasingly complex system of law and contracts, based on sharing risks and pooling capital, that made these ventures profitable. Commenda contracts enabled traveling merchants to obtain capital from many investors, and shared profits (or losses) and expenses according to standard percentages. Genoa fought bitter, expensive trade wars against its main rivals, Pisa and Venice. To pay for these wars the city established a funded public debt in the 1250s whose shares were soon traded in an active market. Gradually Genoa established a series of funded public debts, backed by specific tax receipts, a precocious experiment in state finance that allowed it to pay for large navies to defend its interests in the Mediterranean. Around 1300 Genoa reached its medieval population height of about 100,000. The city would suffer in the plague of 1348 and subsequent outbreaks, and would not reach the 1300 figure again until 1850.

In the fourteenth century Genoa's naval power enabled it to establish durable merchant colonies in the Crimea at Caffa and on the island of Chios in the Aegean Sea. Trade from these places partly compensated for increasingly hostile relations with the Ottoman Turks and Mamluk Egypt. The city government turned over Chios to the group of investors who had sponsored the conquest in 1346. This famous company, the Maona of Chios, exploited the island's resources to pay dividends to the shareholders—another early example of colonial exploitation. This century also witnessed the further growth of Genoa's banking business and the appearance of some of the first insurance contracts in western Europe. In 1407 the city consolidated all the old debts from its previous wars to exchange them for shares in a new institution, the Casa of San Giorgio. This quasi-private financial house, run by its shareholders, became responsible for collecting a big share of the state's taxes. The Casa also attempted to function as a bank, advancing loans to shareholders and providing services for bills of exchange. The Casa tried to pay its promised 7 percent annual return, but bad loans to the government brought down the bank in 1444; however, the Casa continued to exist and pay its investors various rates of return until the end of the republic. Its share prices over five centuries, and its virtually complete records, are an excellent barometer of the city's financial health. This unusual institution was an amazing attempt to remove much of the city's taxes and finance from partisan squabbles and place them under the authority of the debt holders. The experiment, while durable, foundered on the state's incessant demand for credit and the incredibly complex record systems, which became unmanageable.

Genoa's seapower waned in the fifteenth century in the face of Venetian competition, thus encouraging able

GENOA. View of the city in 1481. (Museo Navale di Pegli, Genoa, Italy/Scala/Art Resource, NY)

mariners and mapmakers such as Christopher Columbus to serve foreign powers. Many Genoese ended up in distant parts of the world, lending their commercial and financial expertise to others but retaining sentimental ties to their native city. Under the formidable Andrea Doria (1466–1560) Genoa became a stable client state of Spain, supplying banking services and galleys for war. Genoese bankers initially profited from their ties to Philip II; it would be said that gold was born in the New World, died in Spain, and was buried in Genoa. The city played a key role in international exchange but lost a great deal of wealth in the Spanish monarchy's repeated bankruptcies. In the early modern period Genoa's naval and economic power gradually declined. By the mid-seventeenth century the city was reduced to buying and attempting to copy a Dutch sailing ship. Genoa's efforts to establish its own East Indies Company ended in disaster. Cut off from the Atlantic trade and from establishing colonies outside the Mediterranean, and facing stiff competition in its own sea from English, French, and Dutch traders, Genoa's aristocratic republic collapsed in 1797.

Fortunate to remain the most convenient port to Turin and Milan, Genoa benefited from Italian economic development and railroad construction in the late nineteenth century. Genoa regained its economic importance (unlike Venice and Pisa), and today is Italy's principal port and an important center for insurance and oil refining.

BIBLIOGRAPHY

Abulafia, David. *The Two Italies: Economic Relations between the Norman Kingdom of Sicily and the Northern Communes.* Cambridge, 1977.

Epstein, Steven A. *Genoa and the Genoese, 958–1528.* Chapel Hill, N.C., 1996.

Grendi, Edoardo. *La repubblica aristocratica dei genovesi.* Bologna, 1987.

Kedar, Benjamin Z. *Merchants in Crisis: Genoese and Venetian Men of Affairs and the Fourteenth-Century Depression.* New Haven, 1976.

Lopez, Robert S. *The Commercial Revolution of the Middle Ages.* Cambridge, 1976.

STEVEN A. EPSTEIN

GEOGRAPHICAL EXPANSION. The geographical expansion of Europe began with the Portuguese conquest of the North African trading city Ceuta (1415), and the fifteenth century ended with two further events that would change the future course of world history. The discovery of the New World by Christopher Columbus (1492) and the voyage of Vasco da Gama to India (1497–1498) around the Cape of Good Hope in South Africa not only transformed the medieval European thinking on cosmography but also brought into being a new discourse on the practical meaning of global space. As a result, the social identity of the occidental Christian world relative to its perception of the people of other religions and cultures also began to change. European expansion during the period from 1415 to 1800 represented an entirely new type of geographical and historical development, very different from the previous three world expansions—that of Islam, China, and the Mongols. This difference arose from an application of different social principles and self-identities to the organization of that expansion and from the invention of an entirely new technological base to human society in general. The application of artillery and gunpowder to the offensive and defensive capacity of long-distance cargo-carrying vessels was one aspect of that technological expansion. In time, it was to manifest itself through the innovations of the Industrial Revolution. Prior to 1400, the world of Islam had exercised enormous cultural and political dominance over large parts of the Old World and helped to separate a European identity from a Mediterranean, geographical identity. In the aftermath of the great plague epidemic of the fourteenth century, the internal weakness of the Islamic world system provided the preconditions for a resurgence of Western sea power in the Mediterranean and eventually in the Atlantic.

The two centuries from 1415 to 1600 mark the period when the Portuguese and Spanish model of maritime and territorial expansion was perfected and implemented; its ideology and logistics dominated both the Atlantic Ocean and the Indian Ocean in different ways. But that abstraction derived its rationale from the continuation and refinement of the old medieval order in Europe, in which warrior ethos and royal patronage were more important than

the logic of economic considerations. Although the Portuguese tried hard, they did not really succeed in diverting the centuries-long spice and oriental trade from the Middle Eastern routes to the Cape route. That task was accomplished by the Dutch and the British East India Companies in the period from 1600 to 1713. These two commercial institutions represented a totally new system of organizational control that eventually created the present-day capitalistic world system. The Dutch dismantling of the Portuguese maritime empire in the Indian Ocean, in Brazil, and in West Africa took a long time to accomplish, but by the middle of the seventeenth century, the Dutch East India Company had become a state within a state, able to impose its own objectives in Europe, Africa, and the Indian Ocean. The period of Dutch hegemony came to an end with the Treaty of Utrecht. In the period from 1713 to 1757, the British East India Company reversed its previous role and became the senior partner both in the race for naval supremacy and economic leadership. In 1757, Colonel Robert Clive, a man of legendary political and military skill, was sent out to recover Calcutta, which had been captured by Nawab Siraj ud-Daula, the Mughal governor of Bengal; Clive organized a spectacular palace revolution known as the Battle of Plassey. Siraj ud-Daula was defeated and killed, and a new puppet ruler under the political control of the British East India Company was installed as the governor of Bengal. Within a decade from

BRITISH EXPLORER. The English navigator James Cook (1728–1779) in Polynesia. (Image Select/Art Resource, NY)

1757, the political wheel turned inexorably toward the establishment of a great British empire in the Indian subcontinent. But the foundation and the fulfillment of British imperial order did not go without challenge from another European power, France. However, with the Battle of Waterloo (1815), the French were finally eliminated from the control of the high seas.

It is evident that the present-day perceptions of the chronology of European geographical expansion rest on a long historiography of Western thought. By the third quarter of the eighteenth century, European historians and thinkers identified correctly that there were two separate dimensions to the process of European expansion. On the one hand, the settlement and colonization of the New World created a new source of demand that was reinforced by the growing wealth of Spain, Portugal, Holland, England, and France. The rising level of demand for goods and consumer expenditures in the West was related causally to the discovery of new sources of supplies in the East. In the economic syntax of Adam Smith, the extension of markets was vital to the process of growth, and the main effect of the discovery of America and the navigation of the Indian Ocean, according to him, was to "raise the mercantile system to a degree of splendour and glory which it could never otherwise have attained to." The result of the fresh stimulus to demand was to encourage European trade and industry more than agricultural growth. Adam Smith's arguments were part of a sophisticated economic model that laid the foundation for the theory of international trade and international division of labor as developed by David Ricardo in the nineteenth century. But even in the sixteenth century, Portuguese, Spanish, and Asian observers were aware that European success in reaching the Indian Ocean represented a revolutionary change in the direction and organization of the ancient transcontinental trade. The Portuguese methods of control and overseas expansion in the South Atlantic and the Indian Ocean included three parts. First, sea power was used to create the theory and practice of controlling oceanic space. Second, the coastal fortress provided protection for the Portuguese colonizers in small enclaves throughout the areas of settlement. Finally, the *feitoria*, or factory, created the commercial countinghouse and the office to manage the trading and economic affairs. The armada, the fortress, and the factory were the triple instruments of European overseas expansion linked up with a distinct political ideology that would provide the Dutch and the English in the following centuries with a model that has remained in place to this day.

The foundation of the British and Dutch East India Companies in 1600 and 1602, respectively, would eventually bring ruin to the Portuguese power in the East and a slow erosion of Spanish economic power in the New World. The Habsburg hegemony in Central and South America rested not only on a systematic replacement of the indigenous political powers in the areas concerned but also on the establishment of a new economic order. The exploitation of the mineral and natural resources of the New World provided Spain with a substantial increase in its international purchasing power. From the 1550s, massive imports of silver bullion to Seville from the mines of Mexico and Peru began to reorient the mechanism of world bullion trade and banking systems throughout the Mediterranean and the Indian Ocean. The rise of Japanese silver mining in the later sixteenth century added to the volume of world monetary liquidity. It is doubtful that the spectacular expansion in Euro-Asian trade, which began from the middle of the sixteenth century and continued through the seventeenth and eighteenth centuries, could have been financed without the monetary resources of the New World and Japan.

For the seventeenth-century development, the significant point to note is that both Holland and England adopted very different methods of organizing their overseas trade from those of the Iberian empires. The initiative was taken by merchants and not by the agents of the state. It is true that both the Dutch and the British East India Companies were given monopolies in the national markets, but the two companies derived their economic and political rationale from those of market forces. Both were organized on the principle of joint-stock capital, and their organizational structure and system of decision making introduced an important capitalist principle. The general body of shareholders was separated from the Court of Directors, which was composed of professional merchants. Thus the ownership and the management of capital were separated in principle and in practice. The two companies became outlets for public investment either through the shares or the bonds market. At the height of their commercial fortunes, the two companies were multinational business organizations with financial and commercial power rivaling that of the state. In the supply markets, their purchasing policies introduced important innovations that anticipated the modern system of advanced planning by firms and their policy on inventory holding. In the consuming markets, the two companies became central distribution agencies working on capitalist profit-maximizing principles. The impact of the new development taking place in Amsterdam and London was to lay the foundation of the classic dual economy of the nineteenth century in which peasant and artisan producers were articulated to an organized capitalist market. The commodity markets of Amsterdam and London redistributing colonial products far surpassed anything Venice and Antwerp could offer in the past in terms of the volume of trade or its variety. Furthermore, while Amsterdam lost some of its economic importance later, London remained the world's leading economic center to the present time.

Just as the seventeenth and eighteenth centuries saw the emergence of important innovations in European commercial organization, the structure of demand and consumption similarly witnessed spectacular changes. Before and during the Portuguese period of trade, black pepper remained the most important single article imported from outside Europe, followed by items such as rare spices, indigo, raw silk, woven silk, and a variety of cotton textiles. During the seventeenth century, the consumer and commodity revolution in the European markets was brought about by the rising imports of Indian cotton and silk textiles. The flood of imports in the late seventeenth century reached such proportions that many European countries with a substantial textile industry were forced to impose high tariffs on the Indian imports or prohibit their use altogether. Furthermore, the re-export of Asian textiles to the Americas, Africa, and even to the Middle East, created a worldwide boom in the consumption of cotton fabrics. The imported cotton goods in turn provided a substantial stimulus in inducing an industrial revolution in Europe through the mechanization of weaving and spinning. The consumption and distribution of sugar, tobacco, tea, and coffee were just as spectacular as that of cotton textiles, and by the end of the seventeenth century, these new competitors in the domestic budget had replaced black pepper as articles of wider if not mass consumption. The conjunction of Chinese tea, West Indian sugar, and Chinese porcelain tea services represented a new cultural phenomenon—the social role of tea parties—an example of how commodities exchanged through trade can transform tastes and habits.

In conclusion, it is necessary to stress the fact that European geographical expansion in the period from 1400 to 1800 provided the basis of an exchange conducted through trade, an exchange that was discontinuous both in terms of space and time. It is because human settlements and communities are separated from one another in space, time, and degrees of technological knowledge and cultural preferences that merchants and traders are able to grasp the rationale of diffusion and profit from it. Although diffusion was by no means the sole source of technological innovations, many crop-growing techniques and industrial processes did in fact travel over wide distances. It is unlikely that such transmissions could have taken place without a conduit through which information or the actual trade objects could travel. The quantitative measurements of premodern trade might lead to the conclusion that as a proportion of agricultural activity, it was very small. But this neither tells us much about the motivation of merchants and traders engaged in trade nor does it explain the fact that trade was the only route to the acquisition of liquid wealth. The members of the ruling elites in turn wished to possess rare, luxury goods that could be obtained only through trade.

[*See also* Economic Imperialism.]

BIBLIOGRAPHY

Bethell, L. *The Cambridge History of Latin America*. Cambridge, 1984–.

Blussé, Leonard, ed. *Companies and Trade: Essays on Overseas Trading during the Ancien Regime*. Dordrecht, 1981.

Boxer, C. R. *The Dutch Seaborne Empire, 1600–1800*. London, 1965.

Boxer, C. R. *Dutch Merchants and Mariners in Asia, 1602–1795*. London, 1988.

Boxer, C. R. *The Dutch in Brazil, 1624–1654*. Hamden, 1973.

Boxer, C. R. *The Christian Century in Japan, 1549–1650*. Berkeley, 1951.

Boxer, C. R. *The Portuguese Seaborne Empire, 1415–1825*. London, 1969.

Brading, D. A. *The First America: The Spanish Monarchy, Creole Patriots, and the Liberal State, 1492–1867*. Cambridge, 1991.

Brading, D. A. *Miners and Merchants in Bourbon Mexico, 1767–1810*. Cambridge, 1971.

Braudel, F. *Afterthought on Material Civilization and Capitalism*. Baltimore, 1977.

Chaudhuri, Kirti N. *The Trading World of Asia and the English East India Company, 1660–1760*. Cambridge, 1978.

Chaudhuri, Kirti N. *Trade and Civilisation in the Indian Ocean: An Economic History from the Rise of Islam to 1750*. Cambridge, 1985.

Chaudhuri, Kirti N. *Asia before Europe: The Economy and Civilisation of the Indian Ocean from the Rise of Islam to 1750*. Cambridge, 1990.

Chaunu, P. *European Expansion in the Later Middle Ages*. Amsterdam, 1979.

Chaunu, P. *Les Amériques: 16è, 17è, 18è siècles*. Paris, 1976.

Crosby, Alfred W. *Ecological Imperialism: The Biological Expansion of Europe, 900–1900*. Cambridge, 1986.

Curtin, P. D. *Cross Cultural Trade in World History*. Cambridge, 1984.

Das Gupta, Ashin. *India and the Indian Ocean, 1500–1800*. New Delhi, 1987.

Davis, Ralph. *The Rise of the Atlantic Economies*. London, 1973.

Elliott, J. H. *The Old World and the New, 1492–1650*. Cambridge, 1972.

Fischer, Wolfram, Marvin McInnes, and Jurgen Schneider, eds. *The Emergence of a World Economy, 1500–1914*. 2 vols. Wiesbaden, 1986.

Furber, Holden. *Rival Empires of Trade in the Orient, 1600–1800*. Minneapolis, 1976.

Godinho, Vitorino Magalhaes. *Os descobrimentos e a economia mundial*. 4 vols. Lisbon, 1982–1987.

Haudrere, P. *La compagnie française des Indes au XVIIIe siècle, 1719–1795*. 4 vols. Paris, 1989.

Israel, J. I. *Dutch Primacy in World Trade, 1585–1740*. Oxford, 1989.

Israel, J. I. *The Dutch Republic*. Oxford, 1995.

Lach, Donald Frederick. *Asia and the Making of Europe*. 8 vols. Chicago, 1965–1994.

Marshall, P. J. *East Indian Fortunes: The British in Bengal in the Eighteenth Century*. Oxford, 1976.

Morison, Samuel E. *The European Discovery of America*. 2 vols. New York, 1971–1974.

Pohl, Hans, ed. "The European Discovery of the World and Its Economic Effects on Pre-Industrial Society, 1500–1800." Papers of the 10th International Economic History Congress. Stuttgart, 1990.

Prakash, Om. *The Dutch East India Company and the Economy of Bengal, 1630–1720*. Princeton, 1985.

Steensgaard, Niels. *Asian Trade Revolution of the Seventeenth Century: East India Companies and the Decline of Caravan Trade*. Chicago, 1975.

Subrahmanyam, Sanjay. *The Political Economy of Commerce: Southern India, 1500–1650*. Cambridge, 1990.

Tracy, J. D., ed. *The Rise of Merchant Empires: Long Distance Trade in the Early Modern World, 1350–1750.* Cambridge, 1990.

Wallerstein, Immanuel. *The Modern World System*, vol. 1. New York, 1974.

KIRTI N. CHAUDHURI

GEORGIA. *See* Central Asia *and* Russia, *subentry on* Russian Empire.

GERMANY *[This entry contains three subentries, on the economic history of Germany during the early and medieval, early modern, and modern periods.]*

Early and Medieval Periods

Medieval Germany can be defined as *regnum Teutonicum*, that is, the north alpine parts of the Holy Roman Empire. Modern Germany encompasses several natural regions, defined by geology, geography, and climate. These include the river valleys of the Rhine and the Main, the marshlands of the North Sea coast, the northern German plain, the central German forest belt, stretching from Thuringia to the Swabian Alps, and the high mountainous region of the Bavarian Alps. During the Middle Ages, these regions were further shaped in appearance by colonization, settlement, and the formation of territories.

Decisive for medieval Germany's long-term economic development, both rural and urban, was demographic change. Although population estimates are always risky to make for the medieval era, approximately 2.5 million to 3.0 million people lived in the *regnum Teutonicum* around 800 CE. Thereafter, population rose continuously, with annual rates of 0.3 to 0.5 percent until the early fourteenth century, then stagnated at about 13 million to 15 million people. In the mid-fourteenth century (1347–1351), the Black Death caused heavy population losses. About a quarter of the population, varying from region to region and town to town, fell victim to the first wave of bubonic plague and pneumonia. The overall population of Germany declined to about 10 million, perhaps as low as 7 million, in 1470. Despite this long-term decline, several cities such as Hamburg, Danzig, Nuremberg, Augsburg, and Leipzig enjoyed some growth in population because of favorable economic circumstances.

In general, demographic development and changes in agrarian production were interrelated. Whereas animal husbandry had dominated agrarian production at the beginning of the tenth century, a rising population favored cereal production and brought about changes in techniques and the organization of agrarian production during the eleventh and twelfth centuries: the wheeled plow with moldboard, three-course crop rotation, and the decompo-sition of the Carolingian villa (*villicatio*), followed by the transformation of the demesne. In some cases, estate officials, especially stewards, provosts, and foresters, usurped the demesnes of royal or ecclesiastical estates. In other cases, direct cultivation was abandoned so that the demesne or parts of it were parceled out among tenants. As a result, labor services (*corvées*) declined and were replaced to a large extent by rents in money and kind. With the gradual dissolution of the classical villa and the continuous waning of the *dominium directum* over the tenants, the latter eventually became in practice small or middle peasant proprietors, who benefited by the rise in the prices of agricultural products and by the growing urban markets. This process coincided with the German settlement and colonization of the Slavonic lands, from about 1150 on the middle and lower Elbe, spreading east and southeast until the second half of the fourteenth century, when German settlers reached Russia. Attracted by heritable tenure, personal freedom, stable rents in money and kind, and self-government of the village, the *Ostsiedlung* (German settlement east of the Elbe) formed an outlet—together with the interior colonization of the West Elbian territories—for Europe's growing rural population.

However, with the Black Death, the long-term expansion of agriculture and the continuous rise in the value of agricultural products were suddenly interrupted and reversed. Population decline led to considerable losses of farms and villages. Although we have to distinguish between deserted settlements and deserted arable land and, moreover, between region and region, a loss of four thousand settlements between 1300 and 1500 can be estimated. Population decline led to a falling demand for grain, a long-term fall in agrarian prices, shrinking agrarian incomes, and thus to migration from the land. As a result, this period of "agrarian depression" (Abel, 1978) experienced far-reaching changes in land use. Much arable land was converted to grazing land or reverted to woods in areas of poor soil. Other areas of good soil were more intensely cultivated with specialized crops. Cultivation of dyestuffs—madder on the Upper Rhine (area of Speyer) and woad in Thuringia (area of Erfurt)—expanded. Flax production in south Germany, Westphalia, and Lower Saxony also provided peasants with additional income. Viticulture and horticulture were also more intensively pursued during the fifteenth century, because they became more profitable than grain growing.

The impact of the agrarian crises on peasants and lords varied from region to region, manor to manor. Where peasants could specialize, they could maintain and even raise their standard of living. Where landlords depended on rents in kind and money, the tenants suffered from population losses and from sinking grain prices. Moreover, they had to make concessions (rent reductions) if they wanted to resettle and recultivate deserted lands. However, we witness different reactions with respect to local structures of lordship and seignorial rights. Some landowners tried to compensate for their income losses by putting heavier burdens on the peasant economy, demanding higher seignorial dues or raising *corvée* obligations. If possible, they used force to prevent peasant mobility. In the southwestern parts of Germany, the agrarian crisis led to strengthened bonds of personal servitude of peasants to their lords. In eastern Germany, the lords took deserted village lands into direct cultivation and extended their rights over the peasantry. Thus, the late medieval agrarian crisis provided the origins of the early modern manorial economy (*Gutswirtschaft*) in East Elbia.

Urbanization and industrial production were also subject to demographic change. Whereas in the early Middle Ages 95 percent of the population earned their living in agriculture, by the end of the Middle Ages, 20 to 25 percent of the German population lived in towns and cities. The emergence of cities and the process of urbanization in the *regnum Teutonicum* during the eleventh and twelfth centuries were based on rising agrarian productivity and demographic growth, which permitted a greater division of labor between city and countryside. Market production for the hinterlands and long-distance trade led to diversification and specialization in the urban industries, documented by the growing number of guilds (especially after 1250). This continued in the later Middle Ages when the shortage of employable people led to innovations and a further interregional division of labor.

Urban Landscapes (*Städtelandschaften*). Industrial specialties emerged, thus developing partly into *Gewerbelandschaften:* Rhineland, Upper Germany, Central Germany, and the Hanseatic coastal area. Although the areas of woolen cloth manufacture ranged from northern Swabia, through central Württemberg, the Middle Rhine to Cologne and Aachen, and eastward to Thuringia and Lusatia, the major center of production and distribution became Cologne, which used its quality seals to replace much Flemish and Brabantine cloth on the German markets. Cologne's merchant-entrepreneurs made use of the putting-out system (*Verlagssystem*) in cloth production, as did linen producers in the Lake of Constance area and in eastern Swabia. The major breakthrough of the putting-out system and merchant capitalism came with the development of the fustian industry in Upper Swabia from the late fourteenth century onward. Merchants imported the raw material (raw cotton) from the Mediterranean (chiefly Venice) and supplied spinners and weavers. From larger towns, such as Nördlingen, fustian manufacture spread to the countryside, where entrepreneurs, circumventing urban guild restrictions, found cheaper sources of labor. Therefore, not surprisingly, the Fuggers started their enterprise in the Augsburg fustian business, then founded

their merchant house and entered with investments into silver and copper mining in the late fifteenth century. The major technical innovation in the latter field was the invention of liquation (*Saigerverfahren*), whereby silver was extracted from argentiferous raw copper through the admixture of lead in smelting. This innovation, together with innovations in mechanical drainage and the discovery of argentiferous copper deposits in Thuringia (Mansfeld, Hettstedt), Tyrol (Schwaz), and Upper Hungary (Neusohl), produced the central European silver mining boom (c. 1460–1540). The Fuggers owned smelteries and maintained factories in these areas, just as they had acquired a silver and copper monopoly in exchange for loans to Habsburg rulers. The Fuggers channeled the metals on the European markets for precious metals via the Frankfurt and Antwerp fairs, and also into the workshops of Nuremberg metalworkers. Nuremberg was South Germany's most advanced industrial area, where such important inventions as metallurgical liquation, tinplating, and wiredrawing had been devised. The city and its entrepreneurs organized the hinterland into a zone for mass production. Craftsmen of the hinterland, using a putting-out (*Verlag*) system, supplied semifinished ironware for Nuremberg's finished manufactures (hooks, blades, knives, needles, armor, wires, etc.), destined for European markets. Thus, it was the combination of these different factors, in commerce, mining, and industrial production, along with technical innovations and the introduction of Italian bookkeeping and banking practices, that allowed this region of later-medieval Germany to gain economic superiority.

In commerce, only the Hanseatic trading system in the north had a comparable importance. The Hanseatic League, a powerful association of towns and cities, led by Lübeck, dominated trade, shipping, and politics in the North Sea and the Baltic from the fourteenth to the sixteenth century. Its trade ran on an east-west line from Novgorod-Reval-Riga-Visby-Danzig-Stralsund-Lübeck-Hamburg-Bruges-London. Its commerce was fundamentally based on the exchange of food and raw materials from northern and eastern Europe with manufactured goods from northwestern Europe, thus creating a prospering trading area. However, during the fifteenth and sixteenth centuries, this system, based on trade privileges and not on competition, was challenged by more aggressive rivals, especially the Dutch and the Upper Germans, and by emerging national states (England, Denmark, Sweden, Russia), which abrogated the privileges of the Hanseatic merchants. Thus, only such cities as Hamburg and Danzig, which could fulfill indispensable services (e.g., the grain supply) for the rising Atlantic economy and also successfully adapt western methods, succeeded in maintaining and promoting their position in international trade during the early modern period.

BIBLIOGRAPHY

Abel, Wilhelm. *Geschichte der deutschen Landwirtschaft vom frühen Mittelalter bis zum 19: Jahrhundert.* 3d ed., pp. 118–122. Stuttgart, 1978.

Abel, Wilhelm. *Agricultural Fluctuations in Europe: From the Thirteenth to the Twentieth Centuries.* London, 1980.

Ganshof, François Louis, and Adriaan Verhulst. "Medieval Agrarian Society in Its Prime: 1. France, the Low Countries, and Western Germany." In *The Cambridge Economic History of Europe,* vol.1, *The Agrarian Life of the Middle Ages,* edited by Michael Postan, 2d ed., pp. 291–339. Cambridge, 1966.

Hammel-Kiesow, Rolf. *Die Hanse.* Munich, 2000.

Holbach, Rudolf. *Frühformen von Verlag und Großbetrieb in der gewerblichen Produktion, (13.–16. Jh.).* Stuttgart, 1994.

North, Michael, ed. *Deutsche Wirtschaftsgeschichte: Ein Jahrtausend im Überblick.* Munich, 2000.

Pohl, Hans, ed. *Gewerbe- und Industrielandschaften vom Spätmittelalter bis ins 20: Jahrhundert.* Stuttgart, 1986.

Scribner, Bob, ed. *Germany: A New Social and Economic History,* vol. 1, *1450–1630.* London and New York, 1996.

Stromer, Wolfgang von. *Oberdeutsche Hochfinanz: 1350–1450.* 3 vols. Wiesbaden, 1970.

MICHAËL NORTH

Early Modern Period

German economic development in the early modern period conformed roughly to the general European pattern of the era. The sixteenth century was marked by demographic growth and consequent increasing output. The seventeenth century was a period of demographic and economic stagnation or even decline. The eighteenth century saw renewed demographic expansion and increasing output with the emergence of extensive rural industries, most notably in textiles, producing for regional, national, and international markets.

German developments differed from general European trends in at least three conspicuous respects. First, the territorial fragmentation of the Holy Roman Empire, the political frame for "Germany," meant that there was no coherent economic policy for Germany as a whole. The impetus for economic change and the effects of such changes were localized. Second, there was a broad social and geographical divide between the western German territories and those east of the Elbe River. Though both areas belonged to Germany, they developed in quite different directions during this era, west-Elbian German development aligning with that of France, the Low Countries, and Britain, east-Elbian German development aligning with that of Poland, Russia, and Czechoslovakia. And third, the general European decline and stagnation of the seventeenth century was accentuated in Germany by the impact of the Thirty Years' War (1618–1648), the greatest demographic crisis to afflict Europe after the Black Death.

"Germany" itself is difficult to pinpoint in this era. It was a cultural notion rather than a political or economic unit.

Historians usually treat Germany as coterminous with the Holy Roman Empire, but at the beginning of this period the Holy Roman Empire included Switzerland, the Netherlands, and Northern Italy as well as both German-speaking and non-German-speaking lands belonging to the House of Habsburg—lands that are, in varying degrees, tangential to the economic development of Germany as it unified in the nineteenth century. In the course of the early modern period, the Holy Roman Empire sloughed off these "extra" bits, and the empire itself dissolved in 1806, leaving a welter of small and midsized territorial states in its place. During the early modern period Prussia emerged from being an economic backwater to become the strongest military and economic power within Germany.

Early modern Germany was overwhelmingly rural. About 75 percent of the labor force was engaged in agricultural production, and foodstuffs formed the bulk of output. Yet most of the conspicuous economic and cultural activity took place in towns and cities. This relationship between the large weight of the agricultural sector and the strategic importance of the urban sector shapes most discussions of German economic development.

Agriculture. Agricultural production in Germany followed two different systems: small peasant proprietorship based in village communities and large, noble-owned landed estates. Historians often distinguish the two systems by the German names identifying the legal conditions by which land was controlled: *Grundherrschaft* for small peasant production and *Gutsherrschaft* for estate agriculture. Small peasant production tended to flow to local or regional markets, helping support a relatively dense urban network and higher overall populations. Noble estates often produced for an export market, contributing to the development of the Baltic Sea as a European trading center. Small peasant proprietorship dominated the agricultural landscape west of the Elbe in Germany, while large, noble-owned estates predominated east of the Elbe.

In east-Elbian Germany local nobles, called Junkers, consolidated their legal control over their estates during the sixteenth century, restricting peasant mobility and imposing serfdom. In west-Elbian Germany direct noble control over the land attenuated, leaving individual peasant households and village communities as the main organizers of agricultural activity.

In both east- and west-Elbian Germany agricultural producers sent at least some of their produce to market. Rents and dues were often paid in money rather than in kind, though one of the characteristics of *Gutsherrschaft* was to rely on labor services by serfs on noble domains. Coins were in general circulation. Peasants bought and sold not only foodstuffs, animals, and handicrafts but also property—actually for the use-right of the land rather than outright ownership, which remained in the hands of a lord

PEASANT REVOLT. Woodcut from Francesco Petrarca's *De remediis utriusque fortunae* in a German version of *Trostspiegel*, Augsburg, 1539. (Foto Marburg/Art Resource, NY)

under both *Grundherrschaft* and *Gutsherrschaft*. Local systems of credit were in place to facilitate purchasing. Creditors were often village residents. Agricultural techniques changed little, with the most significant innovation being the widespread cultivation of the potato in the late eighteenth century.

Urban Activities. The political fragmentation of the Holy Roman Empire fostered a strong independent urban sector. The empire itself made some attempts to regulate economic affairs, such as the Common Penny Tax of 1495 or the Imperial Trades Edict of 1731. But most economic policy was created by local sovereigns, either territorial princes or free imperial cities, self-governing towns with representation in the imperial diet. And enforcement of both territorial and imperial regulations was in the hands of local lords.

German towns were small in comparison to the leading cities in other parts of Europe. In 1500 there were only eight cities of more than twenty thousand inhabitants in the empire, the largest being Cologne with forty thousand. Thus no German city could play the role of regional or national economic engine that Paris or London played.

Towns were the trade and manufacturing hubs of the late medieval period. They asserted a monopoly on the right to hold markets and practice certain trades. Their influence was extended in urban leagues, the most notable of which was the Hanseatic League of North German cities. The political and economic influence of these urban leagues waned in the sixteenth century.

Urban manufacturing was shaped by guild organization. The master artisan–owned shop with perhaps some journeymen assistants was the norm. The underlying rationale of the guild system in most smaller German towns was to enforce quality control and job security for producers oriented to the local urban market and its hinterland. Already in 1500 some manufacturers had moved to a "putting out" system (in German, *Verlagsystem*), in which a merchant-entrepreneur forwarded raw materials and equipment to artisans for sale in the export market. The putting out system expanded in German towns throughout the early modern period. In the course of the sixteenth century it also extended to rural craftspeople, who sometimes competed with the guild system and who were sometimes co-opted into the guild.

The rise of the putting out system was undoubtedly connected to the emergence of "manufacturing regions" (*Gewerbelandschaften*) within Germany that specialized in different industrial products. These regions were responding to a larger shift in weight in international trade from the Mediterranean to the Atlantic, even though Germany itself played only a secondary role in either trade zone. Throughout the era Germany was noted for mining and metalworking. At the beginning of the sixteenth century central Europe supplied three-quarters of European silver. By 1530 it produced about fifty thousand kilograms per year. But central European production was swamped by the influx of American silver at the end of the century, and the industry did not recover. Germany also supplied around half of Europe's iron, doubling its output in the course of the sixteenth century. By 1800 Germany produced two million metric tons of iron. Solingen in the Rhineland became a center for the production of cutlery; Essen in the Ruhr and Suhl in Thuringia specialized in guns; Altena in the Sauerland specialized in needles. Linen also emerged as a major product, helping Westphalia and Silesia become two of the most economically advanced regions in Germany in the seventeenth and eighteenth centuries.

Demographic Tensions. By 1500 Germany had about nine million inhabitants. It had regained the population it had lost at the time of the Black Death. Increasing population during the sixteenth century placed pressure on the agricultural economy by increasing the proportion of landless and land-poor villagers. Some rural land-poor sought to supplement their agricultural incomes with small craft production. The same demographic trends also increased the proportion of permanent journeymen in the urban guild system. Demographic trends produced social tensions not only within the guild between masters and journeymen but also between urban journeymen and nonguild rural artisans as each group feared encroachment on its livelihood. By 1600 the German population had grown to sixteen million.

Partly as a consequence of expanding population and partly as a result of an increase in the amount of silver in circulation, the sixteenth century experienced a steady inflation, sometimes labeled a "price revolution." The price of grain in particular grew considerably, while wages for day laborers lagged. Primary beneficiaries of the price revolution were large-scale grain producers. Small landholders could not derive the same benefits because they had to consume most if not all of what they produced. The rise in the price of grain also exacerbated tensions between town and countryside.

Thirty Years' War. The Thirty Years' War reversed the economic trend of the sixteenth century. Inflationary pressures crested in a brief hyperinflation, called the *Kipper und Wipper* (1619–1623) after the coin clippers who were thought to have started it, at the outbreak of the war. Both industrial output and fiscal policy were redirected to support the war, sometimes by choice, sometimes by necessity. The war drove the overall German population back down to about ten million, because production was dislocated and disease was spread by marauding armies. The impact of the war varied from place to place, however. Much of northwestern Germany was relatively untouched during the war, while central Germany was repeatedly devastated. Some regions may have lost as much as 80 percent of their population for a brief period of time.

The economic center of gravity of Germany changed after the Thirty Years' War. It is difficult to say how much of the change was a result of the war or how much the war was a result of the same process that brought about economic change. The amount of death and destruction during the war is not an indicator of later economic developments. For example, Mecklenburg and Württemberg both belonged to the most grievously affected parts of the empire. Mecklenburg stagnated after the war, while Württemberg became one of the economically dynamic sections of the empire. But in marked contrast to the depopulation at the time of the Black Death, the Thirty Years' War did not precipitate the desertion of existing settlements or arable land. Economic recovery took place within the prewar political-legal framework of land tenure and jurisdictions, albeit with extensive displacement of individuals and families.

The most noticeable change induced by the war was that many of the leading free imperial cities began to stagnate or decline. For example, before the war the Swabian city of Augsburg, the financial hub of the Fugger and Welser families, was one of the largest and most powerful cities in the empire. After the war it became riven with pauperization and ceased growing. By 1800 it was an economic backwater of purely local significance with twenty thousand fewer inhabitants than in 1600. Innumerable other towns that had been regionally important declined into provincial hometowns, losing economic ground to their surrounding countryside. Frankfurt, Leipzig, and Hamburg, on the other hand, retained and even advanced their positions in the German economy. The first two were the locations of the two most important international trade fairs within the empire. And court cities, such as Munich, Dresden, and Berlin, began to play a more prominent economic role as the state gained greater control over taxation and the administration of justice.

Eighteenth Century. After the war the territorial states of Germany all pursued some form of mercantilist economic policy. German forms of mercantilism were called cameralism. With a few notable exceptions, such as the settlement of expelled Huguenot artisans in Brandenburg-Prussia or the establishment of the Meissen porcelain works in Saxony, these efforts had negligible economic impact. Cameralism did, however, play a significant role in expanding state fiscal power.

In some respects economic trends in Germany in the eighteenth century looked like a reprise of the sixteenth. The prewar population was regained in most regions by 1700. By 1800 the German population had grown to twenty-two million. Population growth once again led to an increase in the number of land-poor and permanent journeymen. But in the eighteenth century the emergence of intensified regional craft production absorbed much of the additional labor. For example, by 1800 there were some 400,000 looms in operation in Silesia and Lusatia. Industrial specialization in the *Gewerbelandschaften* was now irreversible.

Even though Germany experienced notable demographic and economic growth in the eighteenth century in comparison to the sixteenth century, by 1815 it was at an economic crossroads. Population again seemed to be pushing against Malthusian limits. But more strikingly German economic advance visibly lagged behind that of its neighbors. Agricultural relations continued to be regulated by *Grundherrschaft* and *Gutsherrschaft* rather than modern property rights. Noble interests dominated state fiscal and economic policy. Intensification of rural industry had not led to the development of factory-based industrialization. Territorial fragmentation inhibited the development of a national market—though Prussia's large size compensated for this limitation to some extent. The German economy would have to undergo wrenching changes in the period between 1815 and 1870 before it could be a major factor in the international economy.

BIBLIOGRAPHY

Achilles, Walter. *Landwirtschaft in der Frühen Neuzeit: Enzyklopädie Deutscher Geschichte*, vol. 10. Munich, 1991. This series is particularly recommended for its extensive bibliographies.

Friedrichs, Christopher. *Urban Society in an Age of War: Nördlingen, 1580–1720*. Princeton, 1979.

Gömmel, Rainer. *Die Entwicklung der Wirtschaft im Zeitalter des Merkantilismus, 1620–1800. Enzyklopädie Deutscher Geschichte*, vol. 46. Munich, 1998.

Mathis, Franz. *Die Deutsche Wirtschaft im 16. Jahrhundert. Enzyklopädie Deutscher Geschichte*, vol. 11. Munich, 1992.

McIntosh, Terence. *Urban Decline in Early Modern Germany: Schwäbisch Hall and Its Region, 1650–1750*. Chapel Hill, N.C., 1997.

North, Michael. *Kommunikation, Handel, Geld und Banken in der Frühen Neuzeit. Enzyklopädie Deutscher Geschichte*, vol. 59. Munich, 2000.

Ogilvie, Sheilagh. *State Corporatism and Proto-Industry: The Württemberg Black Forest, 1580–1797*. Cambridge, 1997.

Ogilvie, Sheilagh, ed. *Germany: A New Social and Economic History*, vol. 2, *1630–1800*. London, 1996.

Pfister, Christian. *Bevölkerungsgeschichte und Historische Demographie 1500-1800. Enzyklopädie Deutscher Geschichte*, vol. 28. Munich, 1994.

Reininghaus, Wilfried. *Gewerbe in der Frühen Neuzeit: Enzyklopädie Deutscher Geschichte*, vol. 3. Munich, 1990.

Robisheaux, Thomas. *Rural Society and the Search for Order in Early Modern Germany*. Cambridge, 1989.

Sabean, David Warren. *Property, Production, and Family in Neckarhausen, 1700–1870*. Cambridge, 1990.

Scribner, Bob, ed., *Germany: A New Social and Economic History*. Vol. 1, *1450–1630*. London, 1996.

Theibault, John. *German Villages in Crisis: Rural Life in Hesse-Kassel and the Thirty Years' War, 1580–1720*. Atlantic Highlands, N.J., 1995.

JOHN THEIBAULT

Modern Germany

The French wars (1792–1815) radically altered the political map of Germany. They led to the dissolution of myriads of mostly ecclesiastical micro-territories, brought down the Holy Roman Empire, and triggered legal and social reforms on a large scale. Traditional historiography (Nipperdey, 1994) has tended to regard Napoleon's impact as decisive for Germany's modernization in the nineteenth century. Under French occupation, feudal structures were uprooted, French civil law was introduced or imitated, and a customs barrier was erected that isolated Germany from England while the wars lasted.

However, even prior to the French Revolution, Germany had been less static than it often seems. In the second half of the eighteenth century, industrialization gradually took hold in the commercially advanced regions along the Rhine river and in Saxony (Pollard, 1981). Population size had just recovered the losses from the Thirty Years' War and kept growing steadily. Still, institutional reform advanced only slowly, with the Prussian Civil Code of 1794 and the Josefinian reforms in the Habsburg monarchy as the major exceptions.

The pace of reform changed after Prussia's defeat against France in 1806. Between 1806 and 1810, Prussia abandoned the guild system, introduced free enterprise, freed its peasantry, and reshaped its administrative system. Entry exams for Prussia's higher civil service were created that included Adam Smith in the list of required readings. An era of economic liberalism began that lasted into the 1870s.

Economic and institutional reform elsewhere in Germany often proceeded more cautiously. West of the Elbe River, liberation of the peasantry was less of an issue, as in many regions, the manor system hardly consisted in more than rental payments for farmers and in—usually detailed and restrictive—entitlements to the use of the village commons. Compensation schemes were drawn up, but full implementation was often delayed until the 1860s. On the other hand, this gradualist approach ensured the transition of property rights without much social disruption. This contrasted with the east where compensation often forced smallholders into selling off their land.

Industrial recovery from the war remained unbalanced and was often slow. High taxation to pay off the war debts combined with inefficient market size and British dominance in the markets for manufactures. Prussia combined its scattered territories in a customs union in 1818, which

GERMAN INDUSTRY. *Iron Rolling Mill*, painting by Adolf von Menzel (1815–1905). (Staatliche Museen zu Berlin–Preussischer Kulturbesitz Gemäldegalerie/Bildarchiv Preussischer Kulturbesitz, Berlin)

fostered industry but damaged the export interests of its agriculture. Successive enlargements soon widened this union to most of northern Germany, except for the coastal regions with their strong British trade links. A more protectionist southern German customs union formed in 1820 as a countervailing block. Significantly, it excluded the Habsburg monarchy, which stood to gain even less from agricultural exports and had opted for a high-tariff system.

Formation of the *Zollverein* in 1833, to go into effect in 1834, unified the north and south German customs unions. It involved, albeit limited, economic concessions by Prussia to the protectionist south, but also achieved the Prussian goal of excluding Habsburg and its Austrian territories.

Canals and roads continued to reduce transport cost and helped to exploit the possibilities opened by the new customs arrangements. Still, due to Germany's mostly uneven terrain, the railway boom may have been more important for the economic integration of Germany than in Britain or northern France. A railway industry quickly developed in the 1840s, followed by a growth spurt in heavy industry after 1850, when development of the coalfields north of the Ruhr began.

Prussian Dominance. Prussia's dominance in the *Zollverein* survived the failed revolution of 1848. A national assembly convened in Frankfurt during that year failed to resolve the rivalry between Prussia and the Habsburg monarchy. A strongly protectionist proposal by the Habsburg delegates antagonized the north, deepened the rift between Prussia and Austria, and contributed to the failure of attempted unification (Best, 1980). Low tariffs favored northern Germany with its proximity to the sea, and kept the door open for the coastal regions not yet in the customs union. In contrast, peasants and small-scale industry in landlocked southern Germany favored protectionism. Export interests of the landed aristocracy met with the railroad business that depended on imports for its expansion. Prussia's conquest of most of northern Germany in 1866 tipped the balance even further in favor of free trade. Indeed customs on iron and machinery imports were lifted in 1873.

Still, economic development remained imbalanced, as did the political map. Controlling most of Germany's nascent heavy industry, Prussia easily imposed its hegemony on Germany in the Austro-Prussian War of 1866, and achieved easy victory over France in the war of 1870. The

German Empire of 1871 reflected Prussia's unwillingness to share power. The new central government only received authority over customs and some indirect taxes and depended well into the 1890s on transfers from its member states. Parliament was elected through universal and equal male suffrage but had only limited prerogatives. It voted on the budget but could not impeach the chancellor. The military budget could only be approved as a global sum, effective several years ahead, while the details were left to the king of Prussia. With military expenditure consuming up to 80 percent of the budget, parliament's prerogatives had precious little value.

After 1870, Germany experienced another upswing fueled by abandoned restrictions on joint-stock companies, the French war indemnity, and a wave of business start-ups. The stock market crash of 1873 swept many of them away. It foreshadowed the end of the railway boom, marked the beginning of the depression, and changed the political climate. Excess capacity in metal industry made further imports of railway material unnecessary. Agriculture was affected by increasing American competition in the grain market. The structural crisis in south and west German peasant farming was aggravated by reduced possibilities for migrants in the industrial cities. This and depressed export markets created a new coalition of interests between Prussia's landed aristocracy, south German protectionists, and heavy industry (Klug, 2001).

The new tariff of 1879 introduced moderate to high levels of protection combined with export subsidies to compensate industry for its elevated raw material cost. Paradoxically this tariff strongly resembled the failed Austrian proposal of 1848. The new tariff indeed favored the south at the expense of the coastal north and contributed to a gradual southward drift of Germany's economic center of gravity.

Otto von Bismarck's turnaround in welfare policy reflected the same political pattern. The introduction of social security as a corporatist organization coincided with a ban on the Social Democratic Party and its trade unions in 1880 that lasted to 1890. Social democracy had its historical roots among journeymen in the trades and expanded into the skilled segment of the manufacturing labor force (Welskopp, 2000). These groups had long asked for a corporatist system resembling the old guilds. Austria and parts of south Germany had been more responsive to these demands than Prussia. The organization of social security in corporatist self-administration bodies was a first concession. The introduction of a corporatist system in the traditional trades with apprenticeships and other barriers to entry followed. Prussia's departure from a traditional policy stance again marked the beginning of a new trend. Vocational training through apprenticeship and access control to the workplace gained popularity in the 1920s

and was made almost universal after 1933. In weakened form, it survived into the postwar period.

Soon after 1871 Germany's fragmented financial sector began to centralize around large universal banks. Alongside these financial all-purpose companies, heavy industry trusts developed that integrated coal, steel, and machine building. Cross-ownership, long-term credit, and interlocking directorates established a tight network of control. Rudolf Hilferding (1981) argued that dependence on long-term credit gradually brought big business under the control of the Berlin banks. Restrictive stock market legislation beginning in the 1890s gave further importance to bank finance at the expense of the market for equity. Alexander Gerschenkron (1962) adopted a more optimistic perspective on the same theme: state intervention, monopolistic industry, and control through universal banks formed the basis of Germany's rapid catching-up on Britain as the European industrial leader. The tight network between universal banks and oligopolistic firms appeared to be Germany's way of overcoming backwardness and was seen as a historical model.

Recent research has cautioned on the power of universal banks. Smaller-scale regional savings banks, mostly in public hands, continued to hold a large market share in corporate bank credit. Also the power wielded by the big banks seems far from clear (Wellhöner, 1989; Fohlin, 1999). Nevertheless there exists a large body of research in support of the Gerschenkron hypothesis (Tilly, 1980).

Germany entered a new growth cycle in the 1890s. Fertility began to decline, population pressure diminished slowly, and emigration to the New World subsided. Still, almost 50 percent of the population worked in agriculture, although often in connection with occupation in manufacturing. At the same time the first immigrants began to arrive. Mostly these were Polish mine workers destined to the Ruhr district. Internal migration flowed from the east to the west and later to the coastal port cities. Germany's efforts to build up a commercial fleet and a navy created a sizable shipbuilding industry. This tied the economic interests of the main ports closer to the rest of Germany and led to the entry of Hamburg, Bremen, and Lübeck into the German customs union.

Germany's maritime ambitions went hand in hand with colonial aspirations and the desire to challenge Britain's naval superiority. Coming late, starting from a weak basis, and being at a locational disadvantage, these efforts were necessarily futile. But they tilted Germany's heavy industry basis toward unhealthy expansion, locking in its economic interests with the fate of German militarism. Around 1910 German mining and manufacturing enjoyed a clear productivity lead over Britain (Broadberry, 1997). However this armament boom created structures that could hardly compete in peacetime.

On the eve of World War I, Germany enjoyed elusive stability. Social revolt had been avoided, although the Social Democratic Party gained majorities in parliament without gaining power. The kaiser was popular, although much of his success in public was owed to fostering national chauvinism and creating international tension. Engineering and the sciences flourished, and Germany reaped a good share of the newly awarded Nobel Prizes each year. Still, the political basis of this prosperity was unsound, both internationally and domestically.

World War I. Germany triggered off World War I with the anticipation of a short campaign and without being prepared for a war of attrition. Niall Ferguson (1998) has argued that Germany's strategic stance was essentially defensive, while a large research tradition in the wake of Fritz Fischer (1967) has emphasized the radicalism of important factions of Germany's military leadership, which aimed at a continental empire and at German colonization of east central Europe. Contrary to any of these aspirations, Germany's war economy soon slipped into stagnation and decline. Total output stagnated and probably fell, and the Allied naval blockade caused severe food shortages. A peace treaty imposed on Russia in early 1918 did not alleviate these difficulties, although in an operation strangely foreshadowing World War II, German troops occupied the Ukraine and parts of southern Russia down to the Caucasus. Still, the collapse of the German war machinery in 1918 had military rather than economic reasons. Given the failure of the German public to realize this, it may be argued that armistice was granted to Germany too early. Germany asked for and obtained negotiations after meeting formally with demands for democratization and the abdication of its monarch. Yet the old elites successfully placed the economic and political burden of coping with military defeat in the hands of their democratic successors.

Germany emerged from the war burdened with the quest for social change and the reparation problem. The reparations bill of 1921 amounted to 132 billion gold marks, its realistic parts to 50 billion gold marks, which was roughly equivalent to its national income in 1913. A net indemnity of 12 billion served to compensate for war damage and a further 38 billion for inter-Allied debts. Relative to prewar national income, the net indemnity did not exceed the French indemnity to Prussia of 1871. At the root of Germany's reparation problem was lack of enforceability, arguably more so than Germany's capacity to pay. By modern standards Germany was overindebted, not because payments were unbearable but rather because in the given quantity they were not enforceable. Full payment of reparations seemed unlikely from the beginning, and the country remained close to foreign debt crises or in outright default to the early 1950s. Confiscation of German overseas assets and protectionism in the recipient countries further reduced the gains from cooperation and made a retreat into autarky seem more attractive. Germany soon tested the limits of enforcement by deferring payments and was declared in default by late 1922. French and Belgian troops occupied the Ruhr district in January 1923 to secure payments and to enforce German cooperation. The experiment ended with disappointing results for both sides and paved the way for a rescheduling arrangement under American aegis in 1924.

The paramount concern of domestic welfare policies was to ease workers' discontent, which had contributed to the revolution of 1918 and threatened to fuel a communist takeover in 1919. The Stinnes-Legien Agreement of 1919 between organized capital and labor introduced workers' representation at the factory level, the eight-hour day, and pay increases. In the national assembly a similar coalition worked out a centralized tax constitution for the new Weimar Republic. Tax authority and collection were for the most part centralized in the hands of the central government, and a redistributive tax code with a broad tax base was introduced. The system was designed to yield sufficient tax revenues to pay for substantial but "bearable" reparations. However, when rumors spread in late 1920 of the likely reparation burden, the new tax constitution came under public attack. The two architects of Germany's new fiscal and foreign policy, Matthias Erzberger and Walther Rathenau, found themselves exposed to shrill public campaigns and were assassinated within a year's time.

Weimar Republic. The Weimar Republic never solved the domestic policy problem posed by the reparation conflict. Cooperation with reparation creditors required austerity policies that produced trade surpluses to pay for reparations. Legitimacy in a weak democracy with deeply rooted social conflict called for income redistribution and welfare policies. Politicians were unable to cope with this two-sided principal-agent problem, whose solutions appeared to be mutually exclusive. The Weimar Republic only enjoyed relative prosperity when reparations were shifted abroad through foreign credit. Gerald Feldman (1993, p. 837) has referred to Weimar as a "mortgaged democracy."

Inflation was the way out of the dilemma in the short term. It concealed the distribution of the war burden, financed welfare through the printing press, and created a short-lived export boom that even permitted the transfer of parts of the reparations bill. Inflation also isolated the German economy from the international recession of 1920–1921 (Holtfrerich, 1986). Export surpluses also furthered the case against reparations in Britain, where cheap German imports were unwelcome. Until 1922 recovery was fast, and unemployment gradually disappeared. Only in early 1923 did inflation begin to have adverse macroeconomic effects. High subsidies to the idling industries in the occupied Ruhr district combined with a sharp recession to render further inflation unsustainable. Stabilization in late 1923 fixed a new currency unit, the *rentenmark*, later the reichsmark (RM), at 1000 billion to 1.

American mediation led to the Dawes Plan of 1924. It introduced a scheme of reparation annuities starting at low levels. An international loan provided working capital to restock the German economy. Germany's central bank, independent since late 1922, was put under international control. The new currency was pegged to the gold standard at the prewar parity of 4.2 RM to the dollar. A transfer protection clause prevented the transfer of reparations into foreign currency whenever a foreign exchange shortage threatened. De facto this rendered commercial debts senior to reparations. As a result Germany enjoyed spectacular capital inflows during the following years. Reparations were paid on schedule, albeit entirely on foreign credit. Even interest payments were rolled over by fresh money. Still, substantial trade deficits remained. Germany's foreign borrowing between 1924 and 1929 amounted to a third of its 1929 GNP. By opening the gates for foreign credit, Germany abused the protection clauses of the Dawes Plan to drive out reparations (Schuker, 1988).

Based on foreign credit, Germany enjoyed its own version of the Golden Twenties. However, the domestic basis of recovery remained unsound. Unit labor cost increased and soon exceeded the 1913 level. Fixed business investment remained disappointing and peaked in 1927, two years before the turnaround in the United States. Public budgets ran deficits, particularly at the levels of the states and municipalities. A new costly unemployment insurance scheme burdened the social security system.

When the foreign credit pyramid collapsed, Germany was left with the choice between paying reparations out of surpluses or resorting to debt default. To prevent future reparation payments on credit, the Young Plan of 1929 reduced reparations but tightened the terms of payment. As a result Germany switched to austerity in 1929, even before the international depression set in. An emergency cabinet under Heinrich Brüning formed in early 1930 and pursued a policy of forced austerity. Brüning has been charged with deflating the German economy on purpose to get rid of reparations. The defense of his policy argues that the public budget faced a binding credit constraint. The debate about these conflicting views has been summarized by Knut Borchardt (1990) and Carl-Ludwig Holtfrerich (1990), the main contenders in this controversy.

Under mounting domestic pressure to default on reparations, Brüning in June 1931 combined a new austerity package with a call for international renegotiations. Capital flight and a banking panic followed, and in July, U.S. president Herbert Hoover proposed a moratorium on reparations and war credits, which relieved Germany of half its reparation payments (James, 1986). Short-term credits extended to Germany were prolonged by half a year. Fearful of recurrent inflation and unwilling to go the full way toward autarky, Brüning avoided default on commercial debt and hoped for a reparation write-off that would restore Germany's international creditworthiness. Negotiations over such a settlement were overshadowed by Britain's departure from the gold standard. Elections in France and Germany in early 1932 caused further delay. In May 1932, Brüning's government fell because it lacked support from the nationalist entourage of the president. Just weeks later, the conference of Lausanne began, when most further reparations were forgiven.

Two short-lived successor governments oscillated between fiscal orthodoxy and credit expansion, activating off-the-shelf programs devised under Brüning for the day when reparations would be gone. Foreign trade policy turned increasingly to protectionism and diverted trade away from the main creditor countries. Domestic credit expansion and the retreat into autarky were strongly intensified after the National Socialists took power in January 1933.

National Socialism. National socialism had no clear-cut economic program of its own. Adolf Hitler appears to have believed in a racist version of Malthusian doctrines, according to which scarcity of land and food in the light of growing populations were a pressing problem that could only be overcome by wars of annihilation. Such ideologies did not bode well for the future. In addition, they had little advice to offer for day-to-day business-cycle policies. Indeed economic policy mostly remained in the hands of administrative experts from the Weimar Republic. Hjalmar Schacht, the former architect of Germany's return to the gold standard in 1924, was reappointed to the presidency of the Reichsbank in 1933 and later also served as interim head of the commerce ministry.

Germany declared partial default on its foreign debt in 1933 and applied the typical policies of a defaulting debtor country, ranging from split exchange rates to import substitution. Foreign exchange and trade control was embedded in a tight network of bilateral trade and exchange agreements. Germany diverted—trade away from the creditor countries, where sanctions threatened, and toward smaller trading partners in eastern Europe, aiming to establish dominance there.

Financed through a clandestine system of shadow budgets, an armament boom began as early as 1934, violating the Treaty of Versailles. Civilian work creation drew much public attention and was exploited for propaganda, but was quantitatively less important. Autobahn construction in particular only grew into sizable proportions in 1936, when high levels of employment had already been reached. The overall effect of public spending on recovery has probably been exaggerated: public deficits oscillated between 2.5 and 5 percent of national product, hardly an impressive amount even by the standards of the day (Ritschl, 2002). National product itself did not expand faster than in the U.S. recovery.

Economic policies consisted mainly of ad hoc measures typical of a war economy. However, there was also a large body of legislation that changed the deep parameters of the German economy. It regulated everything from banking and insurance to public utilities, introduced Germany's dual vocational training system to industry, established new regulations for the free professions, and shifted power towards company managers in joint-stock companies. Rather than relying on Soviet-style central planning, these laws remodeled Germany's economic system in a peculiar blend of corporatist and market elements. Remarkably most of these regulations survived the war and later formed the institutional fabric of market regulation in West Germany. Often their substance remained almost unaltered to the deregulation wave of the mid-1980s.

Labor relations were the major exception. Trade union headquarters were stormed in May 1933. A subsequent labor act introduced authoritarian structures at the firm level, and regulation kept wages down at the depressed levels of 1932. Living standards slowly recovered from the Depression, but lack of imported goods, extended workweeks at low wages, and lower nutritional and health standards were noticeable. The brutal oppression of the Jewish minority and of political opponents led to massive emigration and created shortages in all professions, notably among medical doctors. Those who had to stay were gradually driven out of their jobs and soon were reduced to misery through expropriation and confiscatory taxation.

World War II. The Four Years' Plan of 1936 introduced elements of central planning but badly failed to achieve its goals. Worried about excess capacity, business leaders resisted investment at the stipulated rates. A state-managed heavy industry conglomerate under Hermann Göring was built up to fill the gap. Still, Germany's economic preparation for war was only half-hearted. Autobahns were built through 1940, female labor market participation was minimal, and at the time of the attack on Russia, output of heavy armament stood at just a few pieces per day.

Conversion to a full-scale war economy came after the failed assault on Russia. Faced with another war of attrition, planners reinvigorated the capacity targets of the Four Years' Plan but left practicalities to industry associations. Germany drew heavily on capital goods looted abroad. A slave economy was established that forced about eight million foreign workers into Germany under often abysmal conditions. At the same time the abundant supply of forced labor from eastern Europe removed the last inhibitions that may have existed to completing the destruction of at least six million of Europe's Jews.

Exploitation of occupied Europe allowed Germany's output to grow through late 1944. By the time of the Allied victory, industrial capital stock, often composed of multipurpose machinery, exceeded prewar levels by one-third. In the subsequent years of stagnation, it remained higher than before the war in spite of losses due to depreciation, reparations, and dismantling. However, almost half of Germany's urban housing stock was destroyed, and the transport network was severely disrupted.

During the last weeks of war production in Germany almost ground to a halt. The Potsdam agreements divided Germany into four zones of occupation and introduced strict economic planning to dismantle the war economy. About twelve million refugees flowed in from the lost eastern provinces and southeastern Europe, while millions of displaced persons within Germany waited to emigrate or to be repatriated. Faced with growing transfers to the ailing German economy, occupation policy in both the Soviet and the western zones shifted away from restricting and dismantling capacity to promoting recovery, not without mutual accusations (Gimbel, 1976; Karlsch, 1993).

The Marshall Plan of 1947 made the shift in American policy manifest. Through U.S. commitment to a continuing military presence, political security against Germany and economic recovery in Germany could be disentangled from each other. Aid to the European countries was conditioned on accepting the economic unification of Germany and on cooperation in trade. This involved renouncing reparations and reprisals. To maximize acceptance of this policy in Britain and France, almost half the volume of transfers under the European Recovery Program went to these two countries. Marshall aid to West Germany was important in opening bottlenecks but probably worked more through its conditionality than its size.

The Soviets interpreted the Marshall Plan as a ploy to ensure American dominance in Europe and to foster a revival of German militarism. Its zone of occupation was prevented from participating, and both sides prepared for the economic split of the two Germanies. After unsuccessful negotiations on German currency reform, the military government mopped up the monetary overhang by introducing a new occupation currency in July 1948, called deutsche mark. Soon, this new brand name, and the company created along with it, became a stunning success. The Soviets reacted with their own currency reform and a blockade of West Berlin, the three western sectors of occupation in Berlin that were surrounded by the Soviet zone. In an operation of profound symbolic value for a whole generation of Germans, resources and food were airlifted into West Berlin for a full year, a nd the political division of Germany became official in 1949.

A Divided Germany. Recovery in divided Germany after that date was rapid, albeit from an extremely low basis. With annual growth rates of output around 10 percent, West German recovery was soon called an economic miracle, or *Wirtschaftswunder*. Still, the West German economy attained full employment only in the mid-1950s, when the economy gradually converged to its historical trend. At the same time, labor scarcity was felt in East Germany. Owing to successive waves of collectivization and rigid ideological control, professionals, business people, and farmers left for West Germany in droves. Growth in East German consumption fell short of output growth, largely because of forced deliveries to the Soviet Union, which had placed large parts of industry under its direct control. Strikes and anti-Soviet manifestations in 1953 were suppressed but convinced the Soviets to reduce economic pressure.

Epitomized by the firmly market-oriented commerce minister Ludwig Erhard, West Germany gradually abandoned wartime regulations and introduced antitrust measures. Partial trade liberalization in the European Payments Union from 1950 on gave West Germany access to Europe's markets (Kaplan and Schleiminger, 1989). By modern standards, however, the economy was still regulated rather tightly. The European Coal and Steel Community substituted political quotas and capacity targets for the old transnational cartels in mining and heavy industry. Investment planning to overcome bottlenecks in price-regulated public utilities was reintroduced for some time in 1951.

The West German currency reform of 1948 had converted prices and recurrent liabilities at par, annihilated domestic government debt, and converted other nominal claims at an average rate of 6.5 to 1. Real capital was left untouched, with only minor corrections in later tax reforms. As a consequence owners of real assets saw their property values skyrocket after 1950. A provisional central bank was converted into the independent Bundesbank in 1957. It completed West Germany's transition to full convertibility under the Bretton Woods system in 1958. Free of any sizable interest burdens, West Germany's public budgets were easily balanced. Twin surpluses appeared in the balance of payments and the public sector accounts. Unlike after World War I, West Germany began to transfer substantial resources abroad and became an engine of European recovery. Integration into the European Economic Community after 1957 deepened this process. However, it also perpetuated import protection against the rest of the world, particularly in agriculture.

East German reconstruction was based partly on the import substitution industries from the world wars, large parts of which were on its territory. Curtailed by West German sanctions, trade with West Germany was negligible,

except for a few raw materials. Trade with the countries of the Eastern bloc remained strangled by foreign trade monopolies and bilateral trade treaties. Systematic trade policies developed with the transition to closer cooperation within the Council for Mutual Economic Assistance (COMECON) but then evolved into almost complete specialization in production, involving a strong degree of trade diversion.

In 1961 the Berlin Wall closed the last escape to the West for East Germans. Without a continuing drain of human capital, East Germany experienced relative prosperity in the 1960s. However, domestic pressure toward economic and political reform now mounted, and attempts to implement a system of planning by shadow prices were made in 1963. As the reform movement threatened to get out of control, these reforms were successively reversed. In the late 1960s central planning was reinvigorated through the Soviet model of huge trusts, which were highly diversified and sometimes almost self-sufficient.

In West Germany the labor shortage increased after immigration from the East stopped. Hiring campaigns for "guest workers" from southern Europe and Turkey were launched, bringing in several million immigrants. After the beginning of détente in 1969, immigration brought in several hundred thousand people of German ancestry from Southeast Europe and the Soviet Union, later followed by waves of immigrants seeking political asylum. Without a systematic policy but with an eye to low fertility rates, West Germany converted into Europe's major destination for immigrants.

Economic growth remained high in the two Germanies to the mid-1960s and briefly resumed in the early 1970s. West Germany's export surpluses combined with increasing foreign exchange reserves. Upward pressure on the deutsch mark exchange rate had existed since the late 1950s, and a first realignment in 1961 brought only temporary relief. A recession after 1966 led to a major expansion in welfare spending, tighter labor market regulation, and a new tax constitution that required majorities both in parliament and in the chamber of state representatives for most changes. Increased public spending contributed to economic overheating in the early 1970s, when speculative foreign exchange inflows into Germany brought the Bretton Woods system to a collapse. As a consequence West Germany entered the international recession of 1973 with a growing fiscal burden that could only be reduced by joint legislation, an unlikely outcome under Germany's federal two-chamber system. Monetary policy after Bretton Woods cooperated with other European central banks under a crawling peg while floating vis-à-vis the dollar. Driven by monetarist orthodoxy, the Bundesbank pursued quantity targets, frequently clashing with Keynesian-minded governments.

East Germany experienced its own version of an expanding welfare state after 1970. International détente provided East Germany with access to substantial international credits, which were largely used to increase living standards. Chronic labor scarcity propelled employment, particularly female labor participation rates, to extreme levels. Extended child care facilities and preferential housing allowances for families were introduced to counteract the fertility decline since the 1960s, apparently with some success.

The two crises of 1973 and 1979 hit Germany both as an oil shock and as a monetary shock. West German unemployment increased without falling again. Structural problems in mining, steel, and heavy industry led the old industries of the Ruhr and northern Germany into decline. Low growth in total factor productivity had reappeared in the 1960s and now became chronic. Keynesian stabilization attempts doubled West Germany's national debt during the 1970s and again in the 1980s.

Increased oil prices initially afforded a privileged position to the COMECON countries, including East Germany, which benefited from subsidized Soviet oil. Often these deliveries were resold in the West at world market prices, relieving the pressure on the balance of payments and compensating for dwindling exports of its increasingly obsolete products. The tide turned in 1985, when the Soviet Union started to insist on payment for its oil deliveries in convertible foreign exchange.

While East Germany was struggling to make its international payments in the second half of the 1980s, West Germany experienced relative prosperity and another export boom under a strong but temporary increase in the dollar-deutsch mark exchange rate. East Germany renounced parts of its welfare commitments, lowered technical and safety standards, and made desperate attempts to substitute oil imports with domestic lignite. West Germany was still slow to reform its consensus model of political decision-making from the 1970s (Giersch, Paqué, and Schmieding, 1992). Gradual reforms, such as the privatization of West Germany's state-owned telecommunication and public transport monopolies, began only under the pressure of European Community directives.

Unified Germany. An ailing domestic economy, mounting foreign debt, and a lack of financial support from the Soviet Union, which was entangled in reform itself, accelerated East Germany's demise after 1987. East Germans greeted unification in 1990 as a way of importing the Western model together with its standards of social security. West German policy aimed at securing East German incomes and savings to prevent massive migration to the West. Currency holdings were converted at rather generous rates, and wages were permitted to increase rapidly (Sinn and Sinn, 1992).

Unification soon brought high unemployment in the east and pressure on government budgets, which borrowed heavily to bolster the effects of unification on the taxpayer. The Bundesbank increased interest rates considerably to resist the inflationary shock caused by an excessively generous conversion rate. This contributed to a series of currency realignments throughout Europe and an international recession in the early 1990s. Under a European commitment to budget stability and tighter monetary cooperation in the Maastricht Treaty of 1989, Germany agreed to a conversion of the European Monetary System into a currency union, to go into effect in 1999.

A decade after unification the rigidities and structural weaknesses of Germany's corporatist consensus system had become persistent. Created in times of high export growth and little concern about sustainability, the German welfare state proved slow to absorb the shocks from unification. While still strong in traditional sectors, Germany's economy has failed to deliver significant growth for over two decades. By the new millennium, the German economy appeared to have lost the leading role in European growth and development that it had set out to acquire around 1870.

BIBLIOGRAPHY

Best, Heinrich. *Interessenpolitik und nationale Integration, 1848–1849.* Göttingen, 1980.

Borchardt, Knut. "A Decade of Debate about Bruening's Economic Policy." In *Economic Crisis and Political Collapse: The Weimar Republic, 1924–1933,* edited by J. V. Kruedener, pp. 99–151. Oxford, 1990.

Broadberry, Stephen. *The Productivity Race: British Manufacturing in International Perspective, 1850–1990.* Cambridge, 1997.

Feldman, Gerald. *The Great Disorder: Politics, Economics, and Society in the German Inflation, 1914–1924.* Oxford, 1993.

Ferguson, Niall. *The Pity of War.* London, 1998.

Fischer, Fritz. *Germany's Aims in the First World War.* London, 1967.

Fohlin, Caroline. "Universal Banking in Pre-World War I Germany: Model or Myth?" *Explorations in Economic History* 36 (1999), 305–343.

Gerschenkron, Alexander. *Economic Backwardness in Historical Perspective.* Cambridge, 1962.

Giersch, Herbert, Karl-Heinz Paqué, and Holger Schmieding. *The Fading Miracle: Four Decades of Market Economy in Germany.* Cambridge, 1992.

Gimbel, John. *The Origins of the Marshall Plan.* Stanford, Calif., 1976.

Hilferding, Rudolf. *Finance Capital: A Study of the Latest Phase of Capitalist Development.* London, 1981.

Holtfrerich, Carl-Ludwig. *The German Inflation.* New York, 1986.

Holtfrerich, Carl-Ludwig. "Was the Policy of Deflation in Germany Unavoidable?" In *Economic Crisis and Political Collapse: The Weimar Republic, 1924–1933,* edited by J. V. Kruedener, pp. 63–80. Oxford, 1990.

James, Harold. *The German Slump: Politics and Economics, 1924–1936.* Oxford, 1986.

Kaplan, Jacob, and Günther Schleiminger. *The European Payments Union.* Oxford, 1989.

Karlsch, Rainer. *Allein bezahlt? Die Reparationsleistungen der SBZ/DDR 1945.* Berlin, 1993.

Klug, Adam. "Why Chamberlin Failed and Bismarck Succeeded." *European Review of Economic History* 5 (2001), 219–250.

Nipperdey, Thomas. *Deutsche Geschichte, 1800–1866.* Munich, 1994.

Ritschl, Albrecht. *Deutschlands Krise und Konjunktur, 1924–1934: Binnenkonjunktur, Auslandsverschuldung und Reparationsproblem zwischen Dawes-Plan und Transfersperre.* Berlin, 2002.

Schuker, Stephen. *American "Reparations" to Germany, 1924–1933.* Princeton, 1988.

Sinn, Gerlinde, and Hans-Werner Sinn. *Jumpstart: The Economic Unification of Germany.* Cambridge, Mass., 1992.

Tilly, Richard. *Kapital, Staat und sozialer Protest in der deutschen Industrialisierung.* Göttingen, 1980.

Wellhöner, Volker. *Großbanken und Großindustrie im Kaiserreich.* Göttingen, 1989.

Welskopp, Thomas. *Im Banne der Brüderlichkeit: Die deutsche Sozialdemokratie vom Vormärz bis zum Sozialistengesetz.* Bonn, 2000.

ALBRECHT RITSCHL

GERSCHENKRON, ALEXANDER (1904–1978), economic historian and teacher.

The winds of political revolution carried Alexander Gerschenkron from Russia to Austria to America, endowing him along the way with research tools and languages needed for the comparative study of European industrialization. He fled with his family from Russia to Vienna in 1920, earned a doctorate from the University of Vienna in 1928, and was forced to flee again as the Anschluss made life dangerous for a liberal intellectual with a Jewish father. With the assistance of a visiting American scholar, he received a low-level academic appointment at Berkeley in 1938. From there he moved to Washington in 1944 for a position with the European Section of the Federal Reserve, and, finally, to Harvard in 1948, where he taught until his retirement in 1975.

Gerschenkron's primary substantive research was a series of well-crafted indexes of industrial output for Italy (1881–1913), Bulgaria (1878–1939), and Soviet heavy industry (1927–1937). His reviews and critiques of the work of others on long-term growth in income and wealth almost constitute original research on their own. He was meticulous in his attention to problems of weighting and deflation, recognizing, for example, that a consistent base-year volume index requires given-year price indexes as deflators. He was an authority on "the index-number problem" across space and time; his name is often attached to the notion that advanced-country price weights lower growth estimates of backward countries relative to measured growth using the indigenous weights (if available) of the backward countries themselves.

On a more abstract level, the concept of relative backwardness provided Gerschenkron with a set of historical generalizations in the middle range between universal laws, Marxian or other, and individual narratives. Industrialization, he observed, begins with a great spurt in industrial output—the more backward the nation, the greater the kink. He abhorred the concept of necessary prerequisites for growth, preferring instead to search for substitution patterns by which a lack of, say, financing or skilled labor or social overhead capital could be overcome through institutional innovation, often governmental in origin, to allow industrial development to proceed. He presaged the evolutionary approach to economic change that values descriptive insights above predictive power.

Gerschenkron's scholarly output spread beyond the boundaries of economic history into political science, comparative literature, and linguistics, among other disciplines. His colleagues and students marveled at his lifelong ability to master additional languages; like Joseph Conrad, he wrote brilliantly in English, a language he first studied seriously in his thirties.

Perhaps his greatest legacy resides in those he taught and trained at Harvard. Nearly every graduate student during the third quarter of the twentieth century enrolled in Gerschenkron's course and faced the prospect of writing two long papers to be judged by an Olympian polymath with expectations of high performance. Individuals deemed worthy might be invited to join a weekly seminar that featured visitors from among the elite of the global economic history fraternity, and to complete dissertations under his kindly, but exacting, mentorship. His students, including several future presidents of the American Economic History Association, helped launch the New Economic History.

In the words of the Memorial Minute presented to the Harvard faculty in 1987, "He was one of the greatest historical economists of our time."

BIBLIOGRAPHY

Dawidoff, Nicholas. *The Fly Swatter: How My Grandfather Made His Way in the World.* New York, 2002. A biographical memoir of Gerschenkron's life and influence.

Gerschenkron, Alexander. *Economic Backwardness in Historical Perspective.* Cambridge, 1962.

Gerschenkron, Alexander. *Continuity in History and Other Essays.* Cambridge, 1968.

McCloskey, D. N. *If You're So Smart: The Narrative of Economic Expertise.* Chicago, 1990. Chapter 5 uses Gerschenkron as an exemplar of persuasion through economic storytelling.

Rosovsky, Henry, ed. *Industrialization in Two Systems: Essays in Honor of Alexander Gerschenkron.* New York, 1966.

WILLIAM WHITNEY

GHENT. A city in Belgium at the confluence of the Scheldt and Leie rivers and several canals, with a population (1991) of 230,000, Ghent arose where a Roman fortification, Ganda, and two monasteries originally existed, at the edge of a sandy coastal plain. The city developed after Viking attacks of the ninth century, from the merging of two merchant settlements, one on the Scheldt on the site of Ganda and a somewhat later nucleus on the Leie outside a castle of the counts of Flanders. The economy of Ghent was based initially on provisioning the counts' entourage and the monks, selling the agricultural surplus from the counts' and the abbots' domains, and manufacturing basic industrial goods. In addition to enjoying the advantages of a river junction, Ghent was on the land route leading from the Rhineland to the Flemish coast. Canals soon linked Ghent to Damme, the port of Bruges, and northeastern Flanders.

By 1100 Ghent also had a thriving textile industry, using mainly Flemish and northern French wool, and within a century cloth of Ghent and other Flemish cities dominated many overseas markets. In the late thirteenth century Ghent was the second largest (after Paris) city of northern Europe, with a population exceeding sixty thousand. As demand for cloth outstripped the supply of Flemish wool, Ghent's drapers switched to higher-quality English wool. Textile entrepreneurs of Ghent monopolized the English wool export and "put out" the actual manufacture of cloth to artisans who worked for a wage. By the late thirteenth century occasional interruptions of the English wool supply were throwing thousands out of work and exacerbated conflicts between the merchant-drapers and the artisans. Increased competition on international markets in the fourteenth century from cloth of Brabant, England, and the Flemish villages and small towns caused Ghent to concentrate on the production of heavy, luxury woolens that had no equal elsewhere. More than half the inhabitants of Ghent were supported by the textile industry as late as 1358; but plagues, warfare with the Flemish counts, and continued discord within the various trades and between feuding lineages led to a sharp drop in textile production in the second half of the fourteenth century. The industry recovered somewhat in the fifteenth century, but the foreign market for luxury cloth was inelastic, and cheaper foreign textiles competed with the native product even within Flanders.

Ghent's troubles were alleviated to some extent by a monopoly that the city's shippers were exercising by 1323 on grain entering Flanders along the Leie and the Scheldt, and after 1486 on their tributaries. Cargoes were taken to Ghent, where they passed customs and satisfied local demand, and the rest was reconsigned to northern Flanders. Ghent fought wars with Ypres and Bruges over attempts of those cities to build canals into the Leie to divert grain at a point south of where Ghent's monopoly took effect. A structural shift from an industrial economy dominated by producing textiles for export to one dominated by a regional market function was thus accomplished during the fourteenth century. By 1500 the grain staple had replaced the woolen textile industry as the main source of income for Ghent.

As Ghent declined in population and economic importance, its political privileges were gradually limited. Reli-

gious turmoil in the sixteenth century was costly, and the city began to recover economically only in the seventeenth. Ghent became the most important linen market of the southern Netherlands, and new industries developed, including pottery, glass blowing, mirror manufacture, brass making, ivory and ebony working, and ribbon weaving. A new canal linking the city with Bruges (1613–1624) revived the fortunes of the Ghent shippers.

Following a sharp recession in the early eighteenth century caused by declining demand for linens and the abolition of the grain staple, Ghent grew into a major European city after 1750, becoming the commercial as well as industrial center of Flanders, even before the establishment of independent Belgium in 1830. Linen manufacturing revived, and sugar refining and mechanical cotton printing, spinning, and weaving were introduced between 1770 and 1830. Ghent became a railway junction after 1837. The city also became the second largest port of Belgium with the reconstruction of the Sassevaart, a canal that linked Ghent to the Scheldt near Antwerp. With the industrial revolution came massive immigration into Ghent, with most newcomers settling in slums on the outskirts. Ghent became a center of the Belgian Socialist movement, although in the late nineteenth century the city undertook measures of public housing and poor relief that seem to have prevented the violence that occurred elsewhere.

Ghent recovered from the devastation of World War I in the 1920s, mainly through textiles and the port. Although linen manufacturing declined, in 1939 Ghent accounted for almost two-thirds of the production of cotton textiles in Belgium. Economic expansion has continued since 1945 with the arrival of chemical companies and oil refineries in Ghent and its northern suburbs.

BIBLIOGRAPHY

Decavele, Johan, ed. *Ghent: In Defence of a Rebellious City: History, Art, Culture*. Antwerp, 1989.

Fris, Victor. *Histoire de Gand, depuis les origines jusqu'en 1913*. 2d ed. Ghent, 1930.

Munro, John H. *Textiles, Towns, and Trade: Essays in the Economic History of Late-Medieval England and the Low Countries*. Aldershot, U.K., 1994.

Nève, J. *Gand sous la domination française, 1792–1814*. Ghent, 1927.

Nève, J. *Gand sous le régime hollandais, 1814–1830*. Ghent, 1935.

Nicholas, David. *The Metamorphosis of a Medieval City: Ghent in the Age of the Arteveldes, 1302–1390*. Lincoln, Nebr., 1987.

Nicholas, David. *Medieval Flanders*. London, 1992.

Pirenne, Henri. *Early Democracies in the Low Countries: Urban Society and Political Conflict in the Middle Ages and the Renaissance*. New York, 1963.

Scholliers, Peter. *Wages, Manufacturers, and Workers in the Nineteenth-Century Factory: The Voortman Cotton Mill in Ghent*. Washington, D.C., 1996.

Van Werveke, Hans. *Gand: Esquisse d'histoire sociale*. Brussels, 1946.

Verhulst, Adriaan. *The Rise of Cities in North-west Europe*. Cambridge, 1999.

DAVID M. NICHOLAS

GIFTS AND GIFT GIVING. Gifts are interpersonal transfers that are not mediated through the price system and are not part of a barter exchange. In 1922, the anthropologist Bronislaw Malinowski described and interpreted the "kula ring": this paradigm of reciprocity described long sea voyages in open canoes undertaken by South Pacific islanders in pursuit of ritual exchanges of decorative seashells. Malinowski influenced Marcel Mauss, whose enigmatic work *The Gift* is still the starting point of modern discussion. It features the potlatch, a competitive ritual exchange of goods by natives of the Pacific Northwest. For Mauss, gift giving was a "total" system of exchange, driven by implicit obligations to give, to receive, and to reciprocate. The obligation to reciprocate "with interest" could give rise to oppression. Following the sociologist Emile Durkheim, both scholars highlighted cultural and even transcendental aspects of gifting, while also allowing a functionalist interpretation.

Gifting was introduced into economic history in 1944 by Karl Polanyi, who posited a shift from gift to market relations gathering pace in eighteenth-century Britain. This notion of a premarket system of exchange has influenced writers especially on the left in the 1950s and 1960s, for example, Moses Finley on Homeric Greece and E. P. Thompson on the "moral economy" in eighteenth century Britain. In the same period, several American sociologists (e.g., George Homans and Alvin Gouldner) described social exchange as a system of reciprocity driven by norms. In the 1970s, Marshall Sahlins placed aboriginal gifting more precisely in two contexts, as a system of reciprocal exchange of decreasing intensity outward from a kinship core and as a system of redistribution through chieftains. These might be rationalized as protection against famine in simple societies. R. M. Titmuss described the voluntary donation of blood in modern Britain as a successful solution to a social dilemma, superior to market provision, anticipating the concept of social capital.

Writers in the Polanyi tradition have implied that reciprocal gifting is virtuous and is driven by norms that are desirable in themselves. This view came into conflict with the neoclassical economic vision of society as the productive interaction of self-interested individuals, and consequently attracted criticism from these quarters, as well as empirical challenges from economic historians. There are two issues at stake: (1) whether gifts are genuinely altruistic, which is difficult to reconcile with individualism, or perhaps even with rationality; and (2) whether, in some circumstances, social virtue may be more efficient than narrow self-interest. Both of these possibilities have attracted support from sociobiologists and game theorists, as well as from innovative market economists (e.g., Gary Becker and David Collard). Avner Offer and others have argued recently that gifting has efficient allocative properties that are comparable to those of markets.

GIFT GIVING. Tlingit man wearing a ceremonial potlatch hat indicating the number of gifts he has given (3), Angoon, Alaska, 1984. (© Cont/Jose Azel/ Woodfin Camp and Associates, New York)

Empirical and historical studies demonstrate that gifting has always been, and continues to be pervasive worldwide, in a variety of domestic, informal, and market settings, both archaic and modern, and that it can function as an effective substitute for enforcible contracts when institutions are simple or when goods are complex. As a form of exchange that is discretionary and delayed, gifting also acts to authenticate personal regard, over and above the gains from trade. Adam Smith ranked "sympathy" high among human rewards. It is difficult for impersonal markets to provide it credibly, which suggests another reason why reciprocity and gifting have endured through history and why they continue to flourish in developed market societies.

BIBLIOGRAPHY

Malinowski, Bronislaw. *Argonauts of the Western Pacific: An Account of Native Enterprise and Adventure in the Archipelagoes of Melanesian New Guinea.* London, 1922.

Mauss, Marcel. *The Gift: The Form and Reason for Exchange in Archaic Societies*. Paris, 1925.

Offer, Avner. "Between the Gift and the Market: The Economy of Regard." *Economic History Review* 50.3 (1997), 450–476.

Polanyi, Karl. *The Great Transformation*. Boston, 1945.

Sahlins, Marshall D. *Stone Age Economics*. Chicago, 1972.

Titmuss, Richard M. *The Gift Relationship: From Human Blood to Social Policy*. London, 1970.

AVNER OFFER

GLASS PRODUCTS INDUSTRY. Glass is a unique material whose appeal and value are derived principally from its special properties. For example, glass gradually softens with increasing temperature and can exhibit remarkable optical properties. Artisans over the millennia have exploited the properties of glass using a wide range of techniques to shape glass into a remarkable variety of luxury and utilitarian objects.

The history of glass manufacture differs from traditional ceramics, such as pottery or porcelain. In preindustrial times, glassmaking was a relatively high-tech undertaking compared to more traditional material technologies. The glass industry relied extensively on established trade networks for the movement of both raw materials and finished products. In short, glassmaking has historically required relatively stable political and economic circumstances to flourish.

Early Beginnings. There are numerous technological antecedents before the actual production of glass vessels. Glazes and faience are both vitreous materials that existed centuries before true glass production began around 1500 BCE in ancient Egypt and Mesopotamia. One common technique used for early vessel glassmaking began by forming a core from clay and sand around a metal rod. Artisans dipped the core into a crucible containing molten glass or trailed glass onto the core, sometimes adding decoration later. After the piece was cool, the artisans removed the core, leaving a hollow vessel behind. This technique was time and labor intensive but remained a common manufacturing method for more than fifteen hundred years. Other means of production included casting pieces in molds or slumping flat blanks of glass over molds in a kiln.

Scholars know comparatively little about the social and economic context of prehistoric glassmaking. Production often was centered around royally supported facilities. For example, archaeologists have found glass and faience beads in the context of Mycenaean palaces of the twelfth century BCE. Finds such as these reinforce the view of glass as a valuable material produced with the support and infrastructure of a ruling elite. Industrial output was primarily luxury oriented, including perfume containers, beads, and pendants. Glass production in the ancient Near East and the Mediterranean largely ceased for a few hundred years beginning about 1200 BCE due to trade disruptions.

More or less simultaneous with the establishment of Roman hegemony over the entire Mediterranean area, glassblowing was invented in the ancient Near East around the middle of the first century BCE. Glassblowing irrevocably transformed the nature of production and made glass cheap and common. Glass and glass production quickly spread throughout the Roman Empire within about a century, as attested by the writings of Roman authors. For example, a character in Petronius's *Satyricon* comments that he would prefer "a glass cup to one of bronze or gold had glass of late not become so plentiful." The relative political and economic stability of this time contributed to the rapid dissemination of glass technology. By 100 CE, artisans developed the glassmaker's basic tool kit, which has changed little right into the twenty-first century.

Roman artisans made a wide variety of glass products, as represented by the archaeological record, which shows a large amount of vessels, pitchers, beakers, bowls, and tableware. Much of this glassware was blown into molds because of the rapidity of the operation. This utilitarian glass—cheap, attractive, impermeable, and widely available—formed a new class of material culture that continues into the twenty-first century. Glass was widely used as a transparent window material, and artisans made magnifying lenses as well. Artisans also made fine luxury glass—the Portland Vase in the British Museum is a classic example of Roman cameo glass requiring skilled blowing and glass cutting. Comparatively little is known about the social organization of glassblowing during the Roman period. For example, glassmaking was sometimes connected to military and urban systems of control in Roman Britain.

As power and wealth shifted from Rome to Byzantium, so did the sites of luxury glass production. Artisans in the Byzantine period adapted the Roman technique of making mosaics with colored and gilded glass *tesserae* into stunning architectural decoration. These techniques spread to Italy, as seen in the intricate mosaics in Venice and Ravenna. From Byzantium, the spread of church decoration brought glassmakers to such cities as Kiev and helped create a medieval Russian glass industry. At the same time, medieval workers in northern Europe created new glass recipes with locally available materials, such as those recorded by the monk Theophilus in his famous treatise *On Divers Arts* (c. 1122). Because glassmakers in northern Europe often used a different suite of raw materials than that employed by artisans in the ancient Near East and in southern Europe, compositional differences allow scholars to classify glass remains and trace trade patterns.

Glassmaking in the ancient Near East has a very long and rich history. Court patronage and competition between wealthy emirs in the thirteenth century supported

GLASS BLOWING. Artisan blowing crown glass. Plate from Diderot and d'Alembert's *Encyclopédie,* 1762–1772

Islamic glassmakers, while a healthy trade in luxury goods between the Levant, Europe, and East Asia provided the stimulus of decorative influence and a trade infrastructure. Polychrome glass, enameling, and gilding were all characteristic features of Islamic glass production, while mosque lamps are some of the best-known pieces of Islamic glass production from this period. The principle centers of glass production in Syria in the thirteenth and fourteenth centuries were Aleppo and Damascus. These cities exported high-quality glassware to all parts of the Mediterranean but were later devastated by the Mongols; the destruction of Damascus by Tamerlane in 1400 effectively destroyed the once-strong Islamic glass industry.

Venetian and English Glassmaking. Renaissance Venice became the next major center of glass production, beginning in the mid-fifteenth century. The craft of glassmaking in Venice goes back at least to the tenth century. However, the prominent position of Venice in the fifteenth-century economy helped the city foster one of the few European manufacturing activities with "industrial" characteristics. Glassmaking in Venice featured relatively large capital investment, importation of raw materials and exportation of finished goods, factory-style production, and clearly defined and specialized labor categories. There was also considerable entrepreneurship as artisans experimented with new glass recipes and products. In response to consumer demand, a variety of technological changes in the glass industry occurred. These included an increased number of factories and the sudden appearance of more complex glass compositions and designs that necessitated a greater technical sophistication on the part of craftsmen.

Glassmaking in Venice was concentrated on the small island of Murano. This location reduced the risk of fires in the larger city of Venice and placed the industry where it could be better monitored by state and guild authorities. A relatively sudden revitalization of the Venetian glass industry occurred in the mid-fifteenth century with the production of fine luxury wares directed at the upper and middle classes of Renaissance society. The resurgence of the glass industry in the 1450s was sparked initially by the innovation of a new glass composition called *cristallo*, whose appearance evoked the visual qualities of much rarer and expensive rock crystal.

In the sixteenth and seventeenth centuries, Venetian glassmaking technology spread to other emerging centers of production in Europe, such as Florence, Amsterdam, and London. This transfer of technology occurred in two ways. The first was the migration of craftsmen who brought the production skills needed to make *façon de Venise* (Venetian-style) glass. A more subtle means was through the written word in the form of recipe books and technological treatises. The synergistic effect of these two mechanisms allowed other regions of Europe to create or improve local glass industries and offer effective competition to Venice's glass industry.

An example of this phenomena is the rise of the English glass industry in the late seventeenth century. Prior to this time, the domestic glass industry in England produced mostly utilitarian objects, such as relatively crude vessels and window glass. Gradually, demand for higher quality glass increased and English artisans attempted to manufacture it domestically. In 1674, George Ravenscroft secured a royal patent for the production of colorless lead crystal, a new composition. The addition of lead to glass enhances its brilliance and makes it easier to cut, both desired qualities for a glass that was often decorated by faceting and engraving. Lead glass was the foundation for the rise of the English and Irish glass industries beginning in the late seventeenth century. During the seventeenth and eighteenth centuries, English glassmakers refined lead crystal and diminished the demand throughout Europe for Venetian products. In England, the 1845 repeal of excise duties on glass led to further expansion of that country's industry. The Bohemian glass industry also refined a different potash-chalk composition and offered further competition in the luxury glass market.

New Technology. Before the nineteenth century, glassmaking was still largely a craft-based industry. By 1900, this knowledge had been supplanted by a greater understanding of the nature of glass as a material and how varying its composition would affect its properties. Glass chemists developed many new glass compositions for specific applications. For example, in the late nineteenth century, Ernst Abbé and Otto Schott led a research-and-development effort in the German city of Jena that resulted in more than eighty new types of optical glasses. The formation of professional societies, such as the American Ceramic Society (1898), also helped transform glassmaking from a craft to a science-based technology.

Also in the late nineteenth century, such engineers as Werner Siemens developed new reverberatory furnaces fired with gas and, later, electricity. Consequently, glass producers no longer had to rely on centuries-old methods of using wood or coal as fuel. Tank furnaces gradually gave way to continuous furnaces as workmen fed raw materials in one end and molten glass flowed from the other. Factory owners further mechanized production in the early twentieth century by introducing glass-forming equipment that quickly made tons of pressed and mold blown container goods. Michael J. Owens built the first fully automatic bottle-making machine in 1898, and soon such devices made more than twenty-five hundred bottles an hour. Similar developments in the manufacture of household glassware enabled production by pressing hot glass into molds, yielding a myriad of shapes and designs. While such technologies encouraged smaller workforces, producers and consumers enjoyed a close relationship, which played a prominent role in the development of new consumer goods by new American glass companies, such as Corning and the Homer Laughlin China Company.

In the early 1960s, Alastair Pilkington revolutionized the manufacture of flat window glass in England by the introduction of the float-glass process in which a stream of molten glass is poured continuously onto a shallow pool of molten tin. The glass floats on top of the molten tin and forms a smooth, solid layer as it gradually cools before being cut to size. Licenses to use the patented Pilkington method were granted by the mid-1970s and almost all of the early–twenty-first-century flat glass made and sold throughout the world is float glass.

Since World War II, researchers have provided a deeper scientific understanding of the relationship between glass structure and its composition and properties. As a result, commercial firms can now custom make specialty glasses for specific engineering applications. Established companies such as Corning Inc. stopped producing basic housewares and concentrate on sophisticated products, such as tempered glass and glasses for laser and fiber-optics applications. Engineers have also developed more precise controls for glass processing and manufacture, making possible the manufacture of extraordinary eight-meter-diameter mirrors for astronomical telescopes. These are but a few of the multiplying roles of glass in a consumer-oriented, technologically sophisticated society. A complete history with all its technological, social, economic, and political aspects and context has yet to be attempted.

BIBLIOGRAPHY

Blaszczyk, Regina Lee. *Imagining Consumers: Design and Innovation from Wedgwood to Corning*. Baltimore, 2000.

Charleston, Robert. *English Glass*. London, 1984.

Ellis, William. *Glass: From the First Mirror to Fiber Optics: The Story of the Substance That Changed the World*. New York, 1999.

Grose, David. "Innovation and Change in Ancient Technologies: The Anomalous Case of the Roman Glass Industry." In *High Technology Ceramics: Past, Present, and Future*, edited by W. D. Kingery, pp. 65–80. Columbus, Ohio, 1986.

Liefkes, Reino. *Glass*. London, 1997.

Macleod, Christine. "Accident or Design? George Ravenscroft's Patent and the Introduction of Lead-Crystal Glass." *Technology and Culture* 28.4 (1987), 776–803.

McCray, W. Patrick. *Glassmaking in Renaissance Venice: The Fragile Craft*. Aldershot, U.K., 1999.

Scoville, Warren. *Revolution in Glassmaking*. New York, 1972.

Tait, Hugh, ed. *Glass: 5000 Years*. New York, 1991.

W. PATRICK McCRAY

GLASS-STEAGALL ACT. The Glass-Steagall Act is a set of regulations enclosed in the Banking Act of 1933 aimed at preventing commercial banks from acting as investment banks and vice versa. Commercial banks operate with depositors and offer short-term loans in order to finance commercial transactions. Investment banks are expected to underwrite and trade securities issued by companies. The motivation for the separation was the suspicion that "insider trading" by banks acting as both commercial and investment banks made the Great Depression worse.

Section 16 limited commercial banks to trading securities only as mediators. Section 20 barred commercial banks from being affiliated with any organization that deals with security underwriting. Section 21 banned any investment bank from collecting deposits. Section 32 prohibited directors, officers, and employees of a commercial bank from having interlocking relationships with an investment bank.

The Glass-Steagall Act was considered necessary because, even after the formation of the Federal Reserve System in 1913, commercial banks had become more and more involved in the long-term credit business, in particular by establishing securities affiliates. Although looked upon with suspicion by the legislators, these affiliates were tolerated during the second half of the 1910s because of the need to raise the necessary funds to sustain the war effort, and for almost all of the 1920s, given the favorable economic conditions characterizing those years. After the Wall Street crash in 1929, the activities pursued by the affiliates were considered to be among the main reasons for the wave of bank failures. Congress instituted special committees and called hearings to shed light on mismanagement and bad practices conducted by the commercial banks and their affiliates. In particular, the affiliates system was accused of endangering the safety and soundness of the financial system by leading commercial banks to invest in risky assets. It was also blamed for an intrinsic conflict of interest between the role of banks and the investment affiliates: banks should objectively direct customers toward the most profitable investment, but through the affiliates they were also the promoters of the investment. The approach of the act was facilitated by the work of the congressional committees that disclosed fraudulent behavior, another wave of bank failures during 1933, and the determination of Senator Carter Glass (1858–1946).

After just two years, Glass recognized that the law was an overreaction to an extreme situation. In the postwar period, the act became a burden for commercial banks. It limited their possibilities of portfolio diversification and their competitiveness in the modern and deregulated financial markets. Moreover, Glass-Steagall increased the cost of raising external funds for private corporations and imposed on them a tighter liquidity constraint. Consequently, and in particular after 1970, the Federal Reserve eroded the act's effectiveness, allowing securities subsidiaries of bank holding companies to transact with securities before regarded as ineligible. However, it posted a limit on the revenue that such organizations could enjoy from the operations.

Modern research has not found any evidence that banks with both commercial and investment options aggravated the Great Crash or ensuing Depression; the correlation between bank failures and involvement in the security market is low. It has judged the law as an overreaction and unjustified, claiming that the hearings of the Congress did not take into account all the relevant evidence. Moreover, quantitative analysis showed low correlation between bank failures and involvement in the security market. After several attempts, the Glass-Steagall Act was finally repealed in 1999.

BIBLIOGRAPHY

Benston, John. *The Separation of Commercial and Investment Banking: The Glass-Steagall Act Revisited and Reconsidered.* New York, 1990.

Kelly, Edward J., III. "Legislative History of the Glass-Steagall Act." In *Deregulating Wall Street,* edited by Ingo Walter, pp. 41–65. New York, 1985.

Krozner, Randall S., and Raghuram G. Rajan. "Is the Glass-Steagall Act Justified? A Study of the U.S. Experience with the Universal Banking before 1933." *American Economic Review* 84.4 (1994), 810–832.

Mester, Loretta J. "Repealing the Glass-Steagall: The Past Points the Way to the Future." *Federal Reserve Bank of Philadelphia Business Review* (1996), 3–18.

Ramirez, D. Carlos. "Did Glass-Steagall Act Increase the Cost of External Finance for Corporate Investment?: Evidence From Bank and Insurance Company Affiliation." *Journal of Economic History* 59.2 (1999), 372–396.

White, Eugene Nelson. "Before the Glass-Steagall Act: An Analysis of the Investment Banking Activities of National Banks." *Explorations in Economic History* 23.1 (1986), 33–55.

FABIO BRAGGION

GOLD AND SILVER INDUSTRY *[This entry contains three subentries, a historical overview, and discussions of technological change and industrial organization. The bibliography for this entry can be found at the end of the last subentry.]*

Historical Overview

Gold and silver are so important historically because of their double status as commodities and money in many world cultures. In their long history, gold and silver have served as goods produced by mining (or mobilized through pillaging and recycling), means of exchange, and stores of value. For centuries before World War I, when gold began to lose its monetary functions, the expansion (or contraction) of trade increased (or reduced) the demand for gold and silver, while their availability and production costs affected the price levels of other commodities, albeit to varying degrees in different parts of the world. These price differentials in turn influenced international trade, thereby reinforcing or curbing the supply and demand of the precious metals themselves. Although this essay will focus on gold and silver as goods, the monetary functions of these metals have affected the economic life of large portions of humankind, especially after the world-wide expansion of European trade from the fifteenth century on.

Early History. The origins of the use of gold and silver for ornamentation and religious purposes are unknown. Gold jewelry dating to 4000 BCE has been excavated in modern Bulgaria. Around the same period, ancient Egyptians used small bars of precious metals for ceremonial exchange. In the ancient civilizations of the Middle East, the use of gold was largely a royal prerogative, which kept the demand for precious metals relatively low. Most of the gold known in biblical times was mined in Nubia (now encompassed by Egypt and Sudan), where production might have amounted to 30 kilograms a year. Nubia remained a major source of gold for Europeans until the Arab conquest of Egypt in the seventh century CE. Alluvial gold was also collected in Asia Minor (modern Turkey) as early as 3500 BCE. It was here that gold and silver coinage might have begun in the seventh century BCE. Herodotus credits Croesus, the last king of the Lydians, with introducing the first official currency in Greek history, the stater, in the sixth century BCE, together with official bimetallism at the ratio of 1:10. Precious metals, trade, and political power were to remained linked for the next twenty-five hundred years.

In addition to the Nubian mines, the Mediterranean civilizations of Greece and Rome could count on an increasing supply of precious metals. Athenians mined silver at Laurion; Philip II, Alexander the Great's father, opened up gold mines in Thrace and Macedonia; and the Romans relied on gold mined in northern Spain. In the first century CE, Diodorus described the appalling living conditions of the slaves who worked in the Nubian mines. The use of slave labor for mining was spread by the Romans throughout their empire. Around Diodorus's time, gold production had probably risen to five tons a year. Yet repeated episodes of currency debasement testify to the shortage of precious metals in Roman times. Constantine partly eased this shortage by authorizing the plunder of pagan temples after legalizing Christianity in 313 CE. Constantine also introduced the gold solidus, which evolved into the bezant and dominated Mediterranean trade for the next seven centuries.

The Middle Ages through the Eighteenth Century. As long-distance trade declined in Europe in the early Middle Ages, Arab expansion into Africa in the seventh and eighth centuries reopened a major source of gold which had first been tapped by the Carthaginians a millennium before. Three successive trading empires in western Africa (the Ghana Empire from the fourth to the tenth century, the Mali Empire from approximately 1240 to 1500, and the Songhai Empire in the fifteenth and sixteenth centuries) acted as intermediaries between the Arab traders from the north and the gold miners of the area south of the Sahara Desert that came to be known as the Gold Coast (present-day Ghana). Traders obtained most of the gold mined south of the Sahara through silent barter: salt and other goods were deposited in specifically dedicated sites, where African miners bartered their gold without direct negotiations. Around 1700, Akan-speaking groups unified the gold-producing territories of the Gold Coast by establishing the Asante State, which developed into a full-blown trading empire a century later. In thriving commercial centers such as Sijlemese in modern Morocco and Timbuktu and Jenne in modern Mali, gold from sub-Saharian Africa was traded for cloth, copper, silver, and slaves.

The Arabs had unsuccessfully tried to discover and conquer the gold mines located south of the Sahara. After 1400 the Portuguese followed in their footsteps. In 1415 Henry the Navigator conquered Ceuta (in present-day northern Morocco, the terminal point of one of the main commercial routes linking the Gold Coast to the Mediterranean. From there the Portuguese carried out a policy of aggression against African coastal cities, which culminated with the foundation of San Jorge da Mina (in modern Ghana) as a major post for the gold and slave trades. The Portuguese failed to discover the location of the gold mines, but by 1500 they managed to ship approximately 700 kilograms a year to the royal mint in Lisbon. After 1550 much of Portuguese gold was shipped directly to south and east Asia, where it was exchanged for spices, silk, and luxury goods. It is worth noting that the peoples of India and China did not regard gold as money. China had established a sophisticated system of paper money in the ninth century and used copper for coinage. However, the Indian and Chinese elites had an insatiable appetite for gold for hoarding and display. Therefore south and east Asia acted as a sponge for European bullion from the fifteenth to the eighteenth centuries.

In the fifteenth century, the Spanish began to compete with the Portuguese over the commercial routes to Africa and Asia. The American voyages of Christopher Columbus in the 1490s, for example, were largely motivated by the desire to discover new supplies of precious metals. Columbus found some gold in Hispaniola and soon afterward in Puerto Rico and Cuba. By 1525 the indigenous population of these islands had been wiped out by disease and ruthless exploitation in alluvial mines. The bulk of Spanish gold and silver, however, came from Peru, Columbia, and Mexico. Pizarro's conquest of Peru in 1533–1534 opened up enormous alluvial deposits of gold for mining. The

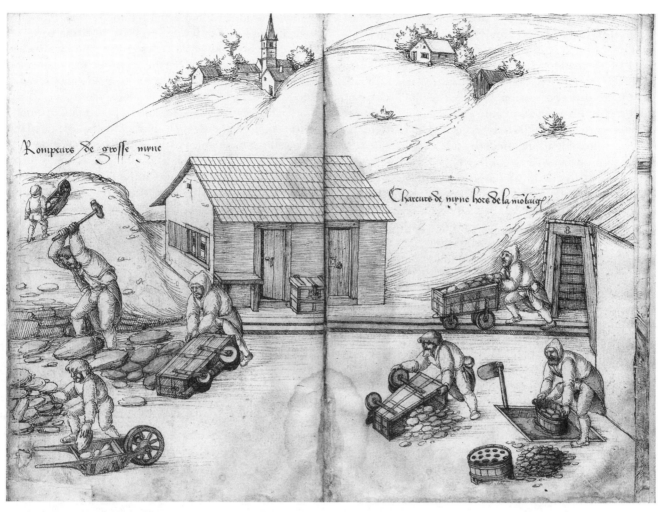

SILVER INDUSTRY. Workers in the silver mine of Saint Nicholas in Lorraine, France. Drawing by Heinrich Gross, sixteenth century. (Bibliothèque de l'École des Beaux-Arts, Paris/Giraudon/Art Resource, NY)

plunder of the Inca treasure alone yielded five tons of gold. At midcentury, deep-lying mines were also discovered in Buturica, in modern Columbia. The precious metal, mined first by Indian and then African slaves, was shipped to the coastal city of Cartagena de Indias and from there to the House of Trade in Seville. Cortés organized both alluvial mining and looting of gold in southern Mexico. As a result of these activities, by the end of the seventeenth century the gold stock in Europe was five times as large as in 1492. The increased availability of gold and its extremely low production costs prompted long-term inflation all over Europe, the so-called "price revolution."

After 1545 the American gold deposits began to show signs of depletion. The colonizers' attention then moved to silver. Enslaved Indians were put to work at Zacatecas, Guanajuato, and other sites in northern Mexico. However, the main site for silver production in the late sixteenth century was Potosì, in modern Bolivia. By the end of the cen-

tury, this remote village, located at an altitude of 4,000 meters, had mushroomed into a city of 160,000. Every village in the area was forced to provide young men for work in the mines, according to a system of labor conscription called *mita*. Despite the harsh conditions endured by miners in Potosì, many of these uprooted laborers decided to stay on after the end of their contract and work as *mingados* ("free workers") in hundreds of royal concessions. The cheapness of this labor force compensated for the transportation costs incurred in shipping the metal to Buenos Aires, 2,400 kilometers to the south. Approximately 300 tons of silver a year were mined in the Americas between 1560 and 1640. A little over half of the metal found its way to Spain, while the rest fueled commerce and further economic expansion in the colonies.

The economic decline of Spain and Portugal in the seventeenth century left room for the hegemony of Dutch and English trade. The Bank of Amsterdam, founded in 1609, regulated and distributed the stocks of precious metals used in international trade for more than a century, followed by the Bank of England, established in 1694. After a period of stagnation, the production of gold and silver picked up again in the eighteenth century, when Brazil, then a Portuguese possession, became the main source of gold. Prospectors from São Paulo systematically searched for gold deposits after 1700, triggering a "gold rush" in the area corresponding to the modern state of Minas Gerais. Tens of thousands of slaves were shipped from Africa to Brazil to work both in alluvial and deep-lying mines. Brazilian gold fueled a triangular trade between Portugal and England, with the latter getting the best end of the deal: most of the gold mined in Minas Gerais ended up in the Bank of England. The eighteenth century also saw the revival of the Mexican silver mines. While gold production subsided after 1750, silver mining proceeded unabated.

The Modern Era. In the nineteenth century, the age of the gold standard, there was an unprecedented boom in gold mining. A series of gold rushes across the world led to a veritable explosion in the availability of precious metals, especially in the second half of the century. By 1908 gold production was a hundred times as great as in 1847. The first rush of the nineteenth century took place in Russia. Large-scale prospecting and mining were first organized in the 1820s by Alexander I in the Ural Mountains, and then by big landlords in Siberia. Both the Russian monarchy and the landowners relied on the use of servile labor. By 1847, 60 percent of the world production of gold came from the Russian Empire. The Russian gold rush, however, pales in comparison to what took place in California after 1848. That year James Marshall, a carpenter working at Jonathan Sutter's sawdust mill, discovered gold by chance in the sand of the Sacramento River. In the next five years, more than one hundred thousand prospectors rushed to California from all over the world, panning their way first along the Sacramento River and its tributaries and then up the Sierras, where they discovered a belt of gold-bearing quartz rock stretching for over a hundred miles, the so-called Mother Lode. Production peaked at 93 tons in 1853, leading to widespread fears of worldwide inflation. Instead, the concurrent expansion of trade and careful institutional monitoring ushered in a period of relative price stability, which is all the more remarkable in light of the further expansion of gold mining after the California rush. In 1851 Edward Hargraves, a prospector returning from California, discovered gold in New South Wales, in eastern Australia. This discovery transformed Australian history forever: what had been a remote colony for British convicts only a few years before became the coveted destination of hundreds of thousands of immigrants. Both in California and Australia, diggers took less than ten years to scoop up most of the gold available near the surface. The Klondike Gold Rush in northern Canada, which began in 1897, lasted for even fewer years. By 1900 the best areas around the boom town of Dawson City had already been mined of all their gold. Smaller prospecting rushes took place in British Columbia in 1858, Colorado and Nevada in 1859, and Idaho in 1862.

Individual prospectors constituted the main promoters of the American and Australian gold rushes, but large-scale mining companies organized the exploitation of the immense South African deposits, destined to become the main source of gold throughout the twentieth century. In 1886 gold-bearing soil was accidentally discovered by George Harrison, who had been a prospector in Australia. Unlike the American and Australian alluvial deposits, the gold-bearing reefs of the Witwatersrand basin around Johannesburg were extremely low grade, containing on average one ounce (32.15 grams) of gold for each ton of soil excavated. In these circumstances, gold extraction called for massive amounts of capital, which was provided by the diamond miners of Kimberley in association with international financiers. Nevertheless, only the adoption of the MacArthur-Forrest cyanidation process after 1890 made gold mining profitable. Production rose from 14 tons in 1889 to almost 120 in 1898. In that year, South Africa surpassed the United States as the largest gold producer in the world. More than one-third of the present world stock of gold (approximately 125,000 tons) has been excavated in South Africa over the past century.

[*See also* Jewelry Industry *and* Mining.]

DARIO GAGGIO

Technological Change

Human societies have collected alluvial gold for millennia by using labor-intensive and relatively unchanging tools that sifted gold-bearing sand with water and took advantage of gold's high specific weight when subjected to rotating movements. Quartz veins and lodes have also been exploited at least since 4000 BCE. In this context an important innovation was hydraulicking, the use of powerful jets of water to expose and remove gold-bearing ground. This technique was introduced by the Romans in Spain and was still adopted two thousand years later during the California Gold Rush. In California, however, hydraulicking was outlawed in 1884 because of its damaging environmental impact. Silver, whose metallurgy is complex, appeared later than gold, probably among the Hittites of Asia Minor around 2000 BCE. Much of this early silver was obtained from galena, a mineral made up mostly of lead sulphide.

Many processes were adopted to extract gold and silver from the ores in which they are usually embedded. Some of these techniques are very old. Cupellation, the separation

Madagascar ~ Nord. ~ 18. - Mines d'or de l'Andavakoera RANOMAFANA. - Autre Chantier

Diégo-Suarez - Edition Chatar

GOLD MINES. Andavakoera, northern Madagascar, 1905. (Eliot Elisofon Photographic Archives/National Museum of African Art, Smithsonian Institution, Washington, D.C.)

of precious metals from base metals through the addition of lead, probably originated in Asia Minor in the third millennium BCE. Cupellation usually produced an alloy of silver and gold. A variety of methods were used to create silver compounds (usually sulphide or chloride) that left a button of refined gold. The silver could then be recovered through another round of cupellation. Liquation, a pro-cess used to extract gold and silver from copper ores by graded fusion with the addition of lead, was already known in the first millennium BCE. Liquation was usually followed by cupellation to separate gold and silver from lead.

The early methods to extract silver were very wasteful. At Laurion, for example, more than one-third of the silver mined by the Athenians was lost in the slag. Improving on traditional processes, the Romans introduced mercury amalgam to extract gold in Spain. Gold ores were crushed and mixed with mercury, the resulting amalgam was recovered by filtering it through leather, and the mercury was finally distilled off. In the fifteenth century, German miners applied a similar mercury amalgam process to the extraction of silver. They began to add mercury, copper sulfate (pyrite), salt, and water to crushed silver ore. The sil-

ver amalgamated with the mercury, creating a compound that could be easily separated. The mercury was then eliminated by evaporation. This laborious process was more energy-efficient than the traditional techniques, and therefore it was widely adopted in the Americas, where fuel was scarce. A German miner, Lomann, transferred it to Potosí, Bolivia, in the 1550s, leading to the exploitation of the huge mercury mines of Huancavelica, south of Lima, Peru. Around the same time, Georgius Agricola described sophisticated water-driven machinery to crush argentiferous ore. The metallurgy of silver became an increasingly capital-intensive pursuit that called for sizable investments both in Europe and the Americas.

The Industrial Revolution brought new and more efficient ways of extracting silver, which integrated cupellation. In 1829 H. L. Pattinson from Newcastle noticed that molten argentiferous lead produces lead crystals as it cools off. These crystals could be scooped up, and the process could be repeated in a series of adjacent castiron pots. The enriched lead was then refined by cupellation. An even more powerful process for the extraction of silver was pioneered by Alexander Parkes, another Englishman, in 1850.

Parkes's basic idea was to add zinc to argentiferous ore and let the zinc incorporate the silver. The silver-zinc crystals were then removed and the zinc was eliminated by distillation or with acids. The Parkes process produced a silver alloy of high purity, thereby replacing the Pattinson process in the late nineteenth century. Even in the case of the Parkes process, however, silver needed to be further refined. Several complex chemical processes involving the use of acids were introduced in the late nineteenth century to separate gold and silver to obtain almost pure metals. In 1863 Charles Watt realized that gold in a solution of chlorine could be subjected to electrolysis. By the turn of the twentieth century, the faster and more reliable electrolytic methods for refining gold and silver had replaced chemical processes worldwide.

The most important innovation in the long history of the gold industry is arguably the MacArthur-Forrest process, which allowed the profitable exploitation of the South African deposits after 1890. This method was patented in 1887 by John Stewart MacArthur, a chemist, and the Forrest brothers, Robert W. and William, two Glascow physicians. The fundamental idea consisted of the use of a diluted solution of cyanide and lime in which the crushed ore was mixed. Air was then blown into the solution until the gold was dissolved. This process produced an alloy whose gold content was as high as 90 percent, thereby making it profitable to extract gold from extremely lean ores, with gold content as low as 7.5 grams per ton. The MacArthur-Forrest process was transferred to South Africa by Allan James of the African Gold Extracting Company, who built a pilot plant in 1890. Soon afterward, a long controversy over patenting rights opposed the Rand Chamber of Mines, which argued against the originality of the method, and the British inventors. In 1896 the courts sided with the chamber, thereby facilitating the general adoption of the process and leading to an enormous leap in the productivity of the South African gold industry.

In the twentieth century, methods for extracting gold and silver have reached extremely high levels of precision and reliability. At the same time, gold and silver have become omnipresent. Gold is a very effective insulating material. In 1929 the first gold-plated building was erected in Los Angeles for Richfield Oil. Gold films are also used to coat space equipment, including the visors of astronauts. Almost all electric and electronic appliances contain gold-plated contact points. Silver is also used as an electrical conductor, as well as in photography.

DARIO GAGGIO

Industrial Organization

Despite the enormous increase of gold production and sales in the twentieth century, a relatively small number of key actors have controlled this worldwide trade. The first reason for this concentration of power lies in the increasing importance of one country, South Africa, as the site of the most productive mines in the world. Second, within South Africa, gold mining has grown into a monopolistic industry, with one company (Anglo-American) accounting for an ever-expanding share of total production. Third, gold marketing channels have been shaped by the tight collaboration between the South African producers and a handful of London-based merchant houses and international (especially Swiss) banks. However, this tight network of international actors controls only the early phases of commercialization. After the wholesale stage, a large portion of the precious metal—namely, the portion that does not replenish the reserves of the central banks—scatters. Further distribution is highly informal, often defying the monitoring efforts of regulatory agencies.

Corporate Collusion. Unlike the diamond industry, South African gold mining developed an oligopolistic structure rapidly, only a few years after the discovery of the Witwatersrand reef in the late 1880s. In 1886, three thousand people were prospecting in the Rand, where they established a diggers' committee to organize production and settle controversies. However, no limit was set to the number of claims any single miner could control. This form of miners' democracy was short-lived, largely because of the extremely low grade of the ores and the ensuing necessity of mechanization. Already in 1887 the first London-registered gold-mining house, Gold Fields of South Africa Limited, emerged from the consolidation of the claims of Cecil Rhodes and other diamond magnates. Other major houses were established in rapid succession. Eckstein, the house of G. and L. Albu, the company of Wernher and Beit, and the one of Messrs Ad. Goerz were all chartered in 1888. Johannesburg Consolidated Investments of Barney Barnato (another diamond magnate from Kimberley) followed in 1889. These mining houses proceeded almost immediately to promote the coordination of their activities. In 1889, they established the Witwatersrand Chamber of Mines, whose main tasks were the recruitment of labor and the pooling of technical information. Already at this early stage, competition among the major players was largely limited to prospecting: collusive practices remained a distinctive trait of the industry in the following decades.

The tendency toward concentration and collusion intensified in the 1890s, when the mining houses developed into holdings in which a parent house with two boards of directors—one in London and the other in the Transvaal—presided over the mining companies of the group by fulfilling financial and informational functions. This group system was meant to spread risk and reduce costs by achieving economies of scale and tighter technical collaboration. Thus Gold Fields became Consolidated Gold Fields of South Africa in 1892; Eckstein was transformed into Rand Mines in 1893; the house of Albu changed into General Mining in 1895; Wehrner Beit became Central Mining in 1905; and Goerz grew into Union Corporation in 1918. Only Johannesburg Consolidated Investments retained its original name. These six groups dominated gold mining in the Rand for decades, with General Mining taking the lead.

Collusion among these groups was particularly evident in the recruitment of labor. Workers were strictly stratified by skill and race: a small aristocracy of white immigrant labor faced a growing army of African immigrant workers. In 1890, already 8,750 out of a total of 15,000 African workers were hired in Mozambique on temporary contracts. The tight collaboration between the Chamber of Mines and the government led to several measures meant to curb upward pressures on wages. Most of these measures, such as the 1895 Pass Law, aimed at reducing the mobility of African labor. After the Boer War, the problem of labor supply was also tackled through the import of more than 63,000 Chinese workers between 1904 and 1906. By 1912, the mining groups employed 191,000 African workers, while the Chamber of Mines successfully established a monopsony over labor recruitment in Mozambique. The restrictive legislation enacted in the gold mining industry dovetailed with the policies implemented at the national level. The Lands Act of 1913 confined Africans to 8.8 percent of the territory, a decisive step toward the establishment of apartheid.

Labor Issues and Expansion. During World War I, the industry was crippled by shortage of equipment, which was still largely imported from Britain. The war was followed by a period of high inflation. In the face of these challenges, the mining groups set out to increase productivity by restructuring work relations and technical practices. However, workers actively resisted such efforts, thereby inaugurating a phase of intense class struggle. Black workers were the first to strike in February 1920. After defeating black labor, the mining groups proceeded to step up mechanization. Small jack-hammer drills operated by black workers replaced large reciprocating machines, while several white jobs were deskilled through the redefinition of the color bar in 1921. White mine workers reacted by calling a strike in January 1922. The ensuing repression caused 250 casualties among the workers. The mining groups' victory over labor was translated into increasing productivity, the relative decline in the number of white laborers, and widespread wage cuts.

The World War I period also saw the foundation of the Anglo-American Corporation, destined to become the financial and political pivot of the gold industry in South Africa and beyond. The company, sponsored by Ernest Oppenheimer, was another expression of the marriage of gold and diamonds. Through Dunkelsbuhlers & Company,

GOLD INDUSTRY. Goldsmith's workshop in the Studiolo of Francesco I (1401–1466), Florence. (Palazzo Vecchio, Florence/ Scala/Art Resource, NY)

Oppenheimer began to acquire interests in the companies prospecting for gold in the Far East Rand, which until then had only been exploited for coal. Anglo-American was established in 1917 to tap the U.S. capital necessary to finance this risky pursuit. By 1918, Anglo—still a subordinated member of the Dunkelsbuhlers Group—already controlled four of the eleven mining companies in the Far East Rand. Yet both Central Mining and Gold Fields held the lion's share of prospecting rights in the new mining area. It was Oppenheimer's successful onslaught on the diamond industry and his takeover of the chairmanship of De Beers in 1929 that fueled the further expansion of his group into gold mining.

The 1931 repeal of the gold standard in Britain was followed by a steep increase of gold prices, which greatly benefited the South African mining industry. The 1930s saw an unprecedented boom in gold production, both through increases in productivity due to mechanization and through successful prospecting in new areas. Two major companies were founded for prospecting in the Rand: West Witwatersrand Areas, controlled by Consolidated Gold Fields, and Western Reefs Exploration and Development, controlled by Anglo. The outcome was the creation of four new mines in the Far West Rand and Klerksdorp areas. But these developments were eclipsed by the discovery of an enormous gold field in the Free Orange State Province after 1936. During World War II, by relying on the exceptional profits accumulated in the diamond business, Anglo took the lead in the development of the new area, setting the stage for a major shift in the gold industry's structure. Over the 1940s and 1950s, Anglo developed into a diverse constellation of mining and manufacturing concerns controlled by the Oppenheimer family through the strategic financial location of E. Oppenheimer and Son, which replaced Dunkelsbuhlers in 1935.

World War II also saw a resurgence of black labor militancy in the gold mines in South Africa, which culminated with the general strike of August 1946. Despite the participation of almost one hundred thousand workers, the strike was brutally repressed by the police in less than a week. After this incident, the right to strike was severely curtailed for black workers, the labor mobility of black South Africans was further reduced, and the recruitment area for immigrant labor grew even larger. As a consequence, the percentage of foreign workers in the gold mines rose from 58.7 percent in 1946 to 63.3 percent in 1960, and to 75.8 percent in 1970. The defeat of labor paved the way for the development of the immensely rich deposits in the Free Orange State. This proved to be a very expensive undertaking, mostly because the gold-bearing reef, broken and uneven, lay at a minimum of 300 meters under the surface. The sum of £370 million necessary for this enterprise was provided both by international investors and through financing internal to the mining groups themselves, capable of directing funds from other activities (diamonds, copper mining, manufacturing, and so on) toward gold production.

A large portion of this money was invested in the mechanization and electrification of the mines. These improvements saved labor but also called for higher skills, developed through the implementation of training programs. This increase in human capital led to measures aimed at reducing labor turnover—above all, longer contracts. The mining groups also tried to allow semi-skilled black workers to settle with their families in the mining areas, which would have constituted a partial breach of the migrant labor system. But this measure was successfully countered by the government. While labor productivity rose by 43 percent between 1951 and 1959, this increase was not reflected in higher wages. Output doubled between 1951 and 1961, and rose by 37 percent in the following decade. In 1970, the South African mines crossed the threshold of one thousand tons of fine gold.

Consolidation, Continuity, and Challenge. As a result of its control over the most productive mines, located in the Orange Province and in the Far West Rand, in 1958 Anglo became the largest producer of gold in the world, surpassing Central Mining. Ten years later, the output value of Anglo's twelve mines alone represented more than 3 percent of South Africa's GNP. But Anglo and the other mining groups also had considerable interests in the mining of other materials, especially diamonds, uranium, copper, and coal, as well as in manufacturing. All together, the mining groups constituted a very sizable share of South Africa's economy. In the 1960s and 1970s, Anglo acquired minority shares in most of the other gold mining groups, thereby becoming the largest mining monopoly in the world. By the early 1980s, after placing a successful bid on a substantial minority share of Consolidated Gold Fields, Anglo controlled more than 60 percent of South African gold. Although gold, mined in 48 locations, held a privileged position within Anglo, other activities such as diamonds, coal, copper, nickel, oil, and platinum made up a growing share of the group's concerns. In 1976, Anglo alone had interests in more than 250 companies in 22 countries, half of which were located in Africa, from Namibia to Mauritania. Anglo and the other mining groups have strongly influenced the economic and political lives of many of these countries, often in problematic and less than transparent ways.

Relative concentration of power is also the hallmark of the history of gold distribution in the twentieth century. London acted as the preeminent market for gold from the early eighteenth century to the late 1960s. To strengthen this leadership position, a small group of London companies held exclusive rights on the marketing of South African gold until 1968. There was remarkable continuity among the protagonists of the gold trade. For more than two centuries, a small group of London-based international houses controlled gold distribution and refining. Mocatta & Goldsmid, whose history dates back to the second half of the seventeenth century, held a privileged position as the official gold broker of the Bank of England throughout the eighteenth century. Pixley & Company was founded in 1957 from the union of Sharps and Wilkins, who moved into gold in 1811, and Pixley & Abell, established in 1852. N. M. Rothschild & Sons Limited, established in 1804, convinced the Bank of England to discontinue its exclusive relationship with Mocatta & Goldsmid in 1840. The head of the Rothschild house also became the chairman of the gold price fixing club, established in 1919 after an agreement between Rotshchild itself and the South African producers. Johnson Matthey, founded in 1817, specialized in gold refinery: its gold bars soon became the most readily accepted in the world. The most recent member of this exclusive club, Samuel Montague & Company Limited, made its debut in 1853.

London market's position remained unchallenged until 1968, when the restructuring of the "gold pool," which had tried to anchor the price of gold at $35 an ounce throughout the 1960s, led to the aggressive move of a small group of Swiss banks (Swiss Bank Corporation, Swiss Credit Bank, and Union Bank of Switzerland). Not only did these banks make an offer to the South African producers to act as principals (the London houses were little more than brokers) but also promised them that they would absorb gold production under all circumstances. After 1968, Zurich was in a position to challenge London as the main market for physical gold. Around the same time, the Swiss banks also reached an agreement with the Soviet government to market Russian gold. The roots of this hegemonic position dated back to the post–World War II years, when the Swiss took advantage of the temporary closing of the London market to become the main suppliers to the European gold jewelry industry, concentrated in Italy and Germany. The Swiss have also challenged London's supremacy in the field of gold refining by opening large-scale plants in Neuchâtel and near Chiasso. But this concentration of control stops at the first stage of distribution. According to some estimates, 40 percent of the gold mined each year is smuggled for at least part of its journey to the final customer, in violation of import bans or simply to evade sales taxes. In the 1990s, international police forces have repeatedly investigated the link between drug smuggling, money laundering, and the international gold trade.

[*See also* Diamond Industry.]

BIBLIOGRAPHY

Ally, Russel. *Gold and Empire: The Bank of England and South Africa's Producers, 1986–1926.* Johannesburg, 1994.

Bernstein, Peter. *The Power of Gold: The History of an Obsession.* New York, 2000.

Fetherling, Doug. *The Gold Crusades: A Social History of Gold Rushes, 1849–1929.* Toronto, 1988.

Green, Timothy. *The New World of Gold: The Inside Story of Who Mines, Who Markets, Who Buys Gold.* New York, 1993.

Innes, Duncan. *Anglo American and the Rise of Modern South Africa.* London, 1984.

Jastram, Roy. *The Golden Constant: The English and American Experience, 1560–1976.* New York, 1977.

Marx, Jenifer. *The Magic of Gold.* New York, 1978.

Rawls, James, and Richard Orsi, eds. *A Golden State: Mining and Economic Development in Gold Rush California.* Berkeley, 1999.

Richards, J. F., ed. *Precious Metals in the Later Medieval and Early Modern Worlds.* Durham, 1993.

Rosenthal, Eric. *Gold. Gold. Gold.* London, 1970.

Stein, Stanley. *Silver, Trade, and War: Spain and America in the Making of Early Modern Europe.* Baltimore, 2000.

Sutherland, C. H. V. *Gold: Its Beauty, Power, and Allure.* London, 1959.

Wheatcroft, Geoffrey. *The Randlords.* London, 1985.

Vilar, Pierre. *A History of Gold and Money, 1450–1920.* London, 1976.

Wilks, Ivor. *Ashanti Gold: Essays on the Akan and the Kingdom of Asante.* Athens, Ohio, 1993.

Wilson, Francis. *Labour in the South African Gold Mines, 1911–1969.* London, 1972.

DARIO GAGGIO

GOLD STANDARD.

GOLD STANDARD. Between 1880 and the late 1930s a gold standard was the most common monetary arrangement for a country. A gold standard defines a national currency in terms of a fixed weight of gold and allows a free exchange and trade of gold. This seemingly small act of law turned out to have broad implications for almost every aspect of the domestic and global economy. Between 1880 and 1913, the years of the classical gold standard, a global fixed exchange rate system reigned. This generated low exchange rate volatility and made business more fluid and less costly for international financiers and commercial agents. During its epoch, the classical gold standard is widely seen to have contributed to the smooth equilibration of balances of payments worldwide. However, the same institution foundered in the 1920s and 1930s because of changes in the ability of governments to sacrifice monetary autonomy for external balance. The same institution that undergirded a period of remarkable globalization and economic modernization later contributed to interwar instability and the depth and length of the Great Depression of the 1930s. By the late 1930s the gold standard as a species of monetary policy was virtually extinct.

Geography. In the first half of the nineteenth century few countries had a gold-based currency. Great Britain (1821), Australia (1852), and Canada (1853) were the first movers. However, between 1870 and 1910 most nations on the planet came to adopt the gold standard. Prior to 1870 silver standards or bimetallism, which allowed for both silver and gold money, were commonly used. In 1871 a cascade of change erupted, leading Germany, Scandinavia, Holland, Belgium, Switzerland, France, Finland, and the United States to adopt gold standards by 1879. Argentina, Chile, Greece, and Italy chose gold-based regimes in the 1880s, but these experiments did not last. These countries soon reverted to fiat currency regimes, when it became impossible to trade a fixed number of domestic notes for gold specie at the legally mandated quantity. However, most of these nations adopted gold again by the first decade of the twentieth century. In the twenty years after 1890 Asian nations also linked up to the gold standard. Japan, the Straits Settlements, India, and the Philippines opted for some form of the arrangement in these years.

At the same time it is important to note that the type of regime that countries implemented typically varied. Countries had fiduciary standards (England), gold-coin standards, bullion standards (economizing on gold use, as in Holland), or gold-exchange standards (when major currencies linked to gold were held as reserves, as in India after 1892, the Philippines after 1903, and many countries during the interwar period). Nevertheless, the one factor that mattered most for determining when a country was actually on a gold standard was whether or not the domestic currency was freely and consistently convertible into a fixed quantity of gold.

Why the Gold Standard? The literature has not yet reached a verdict on whether the gold standard was the most efficient monetary regime possible for the nineteenth century. Nevertheless enough work has been done to establish which political and economic factors at the domestic and international levels drove the emergence of the classical gold standard. Researchers have identified a number of key factors that contributed to the rise of the gold standard, but no consensus exists on the principle impulses.

The reasons why other nations went onto the gold standard are often held to be similar to those that drove Great Britain onto the gold standard in 1821. Most argue that the British chose gold rather than another commodity money system because, for each nominal purchase value, less weight would have to be carried. If silver were used, carrying costs would have been higher. Because it was relatively developed, England had transactions that were on average larger than other nations, therefore England could benefit from having such a monetary system. Conveniently this also explains why England might have been the first mover. In other countries subsequent development may have generated a similar preference for gold. Additionally England's implementation coincided with the capacity to coin durable, hard-to-counterfeit token silver coins (Redish, 1990). This alleviated the need to maintain true bimetallism, since token rather than full-bodied coins could be used for smaller transactions. Prior to this token coins would have been too easy to counterfeit, and bimetallism would not have allowed concurrent use of silver and gold.

Besides these factors, other analyses have focused on the depreciation of silver vis-à-vis gold in the late nineteenth century as a prime mover of regime transformation. On the domestic side, silver's fall and the subsequent inflation would have damaged creditors' balance sheets. Internationally, exchange rate volatility against the key vehicle currency of the epoch—sterling—was a worry. As the process continued, a feedback mechanism of expectations about silver's fall operated. Nations expected silver to fall and so joined early to avoid losses from selling depreciated silver for gold. This initial jump affected silver prices, and hence a "scramble for gold" ensued (see Gallarotti, 1995).

Other research highlights transaction cost factors (see Flandreau, 1996; Eichengreen and Flandreau, 1997; and Meissner, 2001). Using a similar commodity money regime to one's trading partners could lower the transaction costs of trade. Coordination lowered exchange rate hedging costs and saved commissions on, say, the trade of silver for gold. Early joiners to the gold standard, like Scandinavia and Germany, had high and quickly rising levels of trade with Great Britain (on gold), and they cited this as one key factor in their support for a gold standard. This coordination explanation has great power because the initial shift of regimes can help explain why the rest of the world so suddenly came on to gold.

In international capital markets the gold standard may have generated credibility much as a currency board or dollarization is believed to do today (see Bordo and Rockoff, 1996). Gold convertibility served as a signal to foreign investors that countries would pursue policies compatible with convertibility and not generate unsustainable debt levels or wild outbreaks of inflation. The result was that countries could lower their borrowing costs by adopting this "Good Housekeeping Seal of Approval."

Interwar Failure versus Pre-1913 Success. Research on the interwar period has emphasized the breakdown of the gold standard more than the factors behind its slow resurrection culminating in 1926 (compare Eichengreen, 1992; and Simmons, 1994). One conventional view is that the gold standard was seen as a knee-jerk reaction by policy makers. In any case, few nations had the capability or the market's confidence to run a fiat currency system. Germany and France's episodes of hyperinflation only reinforced prior prejudices.

Much has been done in the direction of explaining why a system that worked for over forty years malfunctioned in the 1920s and 1930s. Many suspected that London's displacement by New York as a world financial center eliminated England's capacity to maintain global balance through movements in its discount rate. Other work challenges this view. Great Britain was in fact often hostage to global conditions, and during the Baring crisis of 1891 it was a borrower from other major markets.

Today the gold standard is seen through the lens of contemporary macroeconomics. A nation is given the choice of two of the following three options: democracy, monetary policy autonomy, and free capital flows. The rise of left-wing interest groups, expanded enfranchisement, and a new articulation of the way monetary policy affected unemployment, made the gold fix less credible. This fomented destabilizing capital flows. The quality and quantity of stability-enhancing cooperation had also eroded with wartime animosities and reparations difficulties.

The displacement of these permissive structures made the gold standard in its traditional form less credible. On the other hand, it became difficult to sustain a hard peg in the face of mounting political pressures to follow stabilization policies. The diverse experiences during the Great

Depression, when the gold bloc appears to have had much weaker macroeconomic performance than the "floaters," furthered the sentiment.

World War II killed any remaining hopes for a lasting system of global convertibility such as the classical gold standard. The Bretton Woods system that rose from the ashes of the interwar experience looked nothing like the hard pegs of the nineteenth century. Only the dollar was made freely convertible into gold; capital flows were largely restricted; room for maneuver in the case of persistent balance of payments disequilbria was introduced through adjustable pegs. Nevertheless the gold standard inspired the attempt to maintain stable exchange rates, no doubt because of perceptions embedded in policy makers' minds that the classical gold standard catalyzed excellent economic performance.

How the Gold Standard Operated. John Stuart Mill's pedagogic price-specie flow mechanism is often invoked as a tool to explain how the gold standard kept countries out of long-run balance of payments trouble. Mill pointed to a hypothetical case of a trade deficit. In this case gold specie would flow away from the deficit country to the surplus country to pay for excess consumption. This loss of base money causes the domestic country's price level to fall and the surplus country's prices to rise. As foreign goods became relatively more expensive, the trade balance would push back toward balance. What works in theory, however, did not always work in practice, and observers noted that price levels rarely moved in the direction predicted by such a simple model. Additional work suggested that international capital flows could help as an equilibrating force. This, like Mill, fails to explain why deficits might persist for very long. Arbitrage in securities markets as in goods markets should rule out even momentary deficits and disequilibria. Ultimately the answer partially hinges on how efficient markets in the nineteenth century were.

Other observers point to the activities of central banks. Central banks might have restored balance of payments equilibrium by manipulating domestic interest rates. A central bank in a deficit country could raise domestic interest rates to draw capital in or temper the trade balance. This would correct the deficit. Nevertheless Arthur Bloomfield noticed that central banks rarely acted according to these "rules of the game" before World War I. This empirical gap led to further research concluding that the classical gold standard was a sort of primordial target zone.

The literature now focuses on the connections among expectations, capital markets, and the credibility of central monetary authorities. In a target zone world policy makers achieve monetary autonomy (that is, do not play by the "rules") in the short-run because capital markets expect an eventual policy to maintain the peg. Michael D. Bordo and Finn Kydland (1995) dubbed the gold standard a contingent rule and pointed out that temporary abandonment of policies compatible with a hard peg in the face of visible turmoil like a war was indeed possible. Expectations of resumption of convertibility would work to reinforce stability. If an exchange rate was depreciating, authorities would be expected to take disinflationary measures in the near future. Market speculation on this led to stabilization. But it is important to realize that this explanation's cornerstone is the ultimate expectation that central banks and governments will eventually act to correct disequilbria—an expectation that was radically altered after 1917. The target zone parable neatly explains the stability of the classical gold standard and the failure to maintain such stability in the interwar period.

What Effects Did the Gold Standard Have? At the beginning of the twenty-first century few advocate a return to an orthodoxy of gold convertibility. Gold advocates hark to a day of stable price levels and high growth. But a look at the actual record of the gold standard deals a blow to contemporary goldbugs.

In terms of price stability, the gold standard simply did not achieve it. For example, between 1870 and 1896 in Great Britain, where the gold standard was continuously sustained, consumer prices fell by perhaps 20 percent, then rose by 17 percent up to 1913. Other countries on the gold standard shared similar price swings. Bordo (1993) also looked at inflation and output variability for seven countries and found no evidence that these measures were lower during the classical gold standard than after 1973, when the same countries had no nominal anchor. Commodity money regimes do not always produce price and output stability.

Prior to 1913, many financial crises rocked the globe. A major event occurred nearly every decade between 1870 and 1913. Contemporary research by Bordo and others shows, however, that financial crises were less frequent between 1880 and 1913 than between 1973 and 1998. Nevertheless recovery time from crises appears to have been slightly longer prior to 1913 than after 1973, and the depth in terms of income losses from a financial crisis might have been somewhat larger. While the evidence is not entirely conclusive yet, it appears that adherence to the gold standard inhibited rapid stabilization once problems arose.

In terms of trend growth, the classical gold standard presided over a historically unprecedented period of high productivity improvement and extreme deepening of integration in capital and goods markets. So it is plausible to suspect that the classical gold standard contributed somewhat to this and further improvements in the efficiency of capital markets. In terms of commercial integration, contemporaries argued that harmonization of all nations on a gold standard would save transaction costs of trade, such as brokers' fees or exchange rate hedging costs. Empirical evidence from J. Ernesto López-Córdoba and Christopher M. Meissner (2000) suggests that the global reduction in these frictions unequivocally and significantly contributed to nineteenth-century globalization.

In the capital markets many countries like Russia, China, Japan, and Argentina were persuaded that adoption of the gold standard would increase their connections with foreign capital markets. Bordo and Hugh Rockoff (1996) lay out the economic mechanism. Countries that adopted the gold standard had to adopt financially orthodox policies, adding credibility to the commitment and generating sound fiscal and monetary policies. The gold standard worked as a "Good Housekeeping Seal of Approval," and it lowered borrowing costs for developing countries. To the extent that increases in the capital stock led to increased gains in output per capita, the gold standard may have contributed to long-run gains in economic performance.

Lessons for the Future. The worldwide adoption and then abandonment of the gold standard reveals how nations make the trade-offs associated with the choice of monetary regime. It shows that what other nations do contributes to the formation of domestic policies, especially when these institutions decrease the transaction costs of trade and when these arrangements may significantly promote the evolution of a global economy. Moreover the success of the classical gold standard appears to have been sustained by a particular political and social constellation. The latter lesson is perhaps the most important for those wishing to draw lessons for the structure of the international monetary system today.

[*See also* Monetary Standards.]

BIBLIOGRAPHY

Bloomfield, Arthur. *Monetary Policy under the International Gold Standard*. New York, Federal Reserve Bank of New York, 1959.
Bordo, Michael D. "The Bretton Woods International Monetary System: A Historical Overview." In *A Retrospective on the Bretton Woods System: Lessons for International Monetary Reform*, edited by Michael D. Bordo and Barry Eichengreen, pp. 3–108. Chicago, 1993.
Bordo, Michael D., Barry J. Eichengreen, Daniela Klingebiel, and Maria Soledad Martinez Peria. "Is the Crisis Problem Growing More Severe?" *Economic Policy: A European Forum* 32 (April 2001), 51–75.
Bordo, Michael D., and Finn Kydland. "The Gold Standard as a Rule: An Essay in Exploration." *Explorations in Economic History* 32.4 (1995), 423–464.
Bordo, Michael D., and Hugh Rockoff. "The Gold Standard as a Good Housekeeping Seal of Approval." *Journal of Economic History* 56.2 (1996), 389–428.
Eichengreen, Barry J. *Golden Fetters: The Gold Standard and the Great Depression, 1919–1939*. Oxford, 1992.
Eichengreen, Barry J., and Marc Flandreau. "The Geography of the Gold Standard." In *Currency Convertibility: The Gold Standard and Beyond*, edited by Jorge Braga de Macedo, Barry Eichengreen, and Jaime Reis. London, 1997.
Flandreau, Marc. "The French Crime of 1873: An Essay on the Emergence of the International Gold Standard." *Journal of Economic History* 56.4 (1996), 862–897.
Gallarotti, Giulio M. *The Anatomy of an International Monetary Regime: The Classical Gold Standard, 1880–1914*. Oxford, 1995.
López-Córdoba, J. Ernesto, and Christopher M. Meissner. "Exchange-Rate Regimes and International Trade: Evidence from the Classical Gold Standard Era." Center for International and Development Economics Research (CIDER) Working Paper, C00/118, November 2000.
Redish, Angela. "The Evolution of the Gold Standard in England." *Journal of Economic History* 50 (1990), 789–806.
Meissner, Christopher M. "New World Order: Explaining the Emergence of the Classical Gold Standard." Mimeo. Cambridge, 2001.
Simmons, Beth A. *Who Adjusts: Domestic Sources of Foreign Economic Policy during the Inter-War Years*. Princeton, 1994.

CHRISTOPHER M. MEISSNER

GOMPERS, SAMUEL (1850–1924), American labor leader.

President of the American Federation of Labor (AFL) for all but one of its first thirty-seven years (1886–1924), Samuel Gompers was a leading supporter of the conservative philosophy of business unionism, which attempted to establish stable unions by focusing on the organization of skilled workers by occupation rather than all workers in an industry. Its practitioners sought stability by imposing central union control over local union affairs and imposing relatively high dues to ensure sufficient funds to finance strikes and union benefits. Also, they advocated legal reforms to improve the welfare of workers but shunned association with any specific political party and distanced themselves from socialist ideology.

Born on 26 January 1850 in a crowded cigar workers' tenement building in London's East End to Dutch Jewish immigrants, Sam Gompers immigrated with his family including his father, a cigar roller, to New York City in 1863. Following in his father's trade, Gompers helped to reorganize the Cigar Makers' Union following its near-destruction in the depression of 1873.

During the late 1870s, the largest labor organization in the United States, the Knights of Labor, called for the organization of all workers regardless of color, sex, or skill into an organization that emphasized legislation over strikes. Meeting in Pittsburgh in 1881, some 107 delegates representing trade unions formed a competing organization, the Federation of Organized Trades and Labor Unions (FOTLU). The Federation sought immediate gains for wage earners through higher wages and shorter workdays, whereas the Knights sought to improve worker conditions through self-employment and political reforms leading to the destruction of the wage system. Elected chairman of FOTLU's Organizing Committee, Gompers supported legislation to facilitate collective bargaining, including a successful effort to outlaw the tenement system of home cigar rolling in New York State. Starting in 1884, FOTLU and Gompers supported making the first Monday in September a legal holiday, Labor Day. Also in 1884, Gompers and FOTLU called on all workingmen to participate in a general strike on 1 May 1886 to establish an eight-hour working day. Approximately 350,000 workers from both the AFL and the Knights of Labor participated in this general strike.

In December 1886, FOTLU merged with a breakaway group of trade unionists from the Knights to form the AFL. Elected president of the new union, Gompers later characterized it as a loose association of independent unions "joined together for the purpose of maintaining the right to do as they think is just and proper in the matter of their own trades, without the let or hindrance of any other body of men, to insist upon the regulation of their own affairs as particular trades."

Gompers distanced the AFL from support of political upheaval, the formation of a labor party, association with Socialist labor leaders, and organizing across craft lines. Nonetheless, he stressed international labor solidarity, the organization of women, factory safety inspection, child labor laws, compulsory public schooling, and women's right to vote. Although he supported the exclusion of Chinese immigrants, Gompers initially supported the organization of Negro workers, claiming that these workers could not be blamed for breaking Federation strikes if there was no attempt to organize them. As Jim Crow segregation became legal in the 1890s, however, Gompers acquiesced to some member-union policies that excluded blacks or restricted them to racially segregated locals. With the rise of Eastern European immigration at the turn of the twentieth century, Gompers supported language tests and other restrictive immigration requirements.

Representing the AFL, in 1900 Gompers joined the National Civic Federation, an organization of large companies. An understanding was developed within the National Civic Federation that the AFL would not organize all workers in a particular shop, and, in exchange, employers would recognize certain craft unions, granting them privileges not awarded to unskilled or semiskilled workers.

The prewar years of 1906 to 1914 saw Gompers defending his labor philosophy and policies against a new competing organization, the Industrial Workers of the World (IWW). The more radical IWW sought to free wage earners from the harshness of capitalism itself, by organizing all workers, especially unskilled workers, along industrial rather than craft lines.

During World War I (1914–1918), Gompers, representing the AFL, participated in the War Labor Board, a government agency that promoted union recognition by companies in exchange for a no-strike pledge. The goal of the War Labor Board was stable wages and uninterrupted pro-

SAMUEL GOMPERS. Anonymous photograph, 1921. (National Portrait Gallery, Smithsonian Institution, Washington, D.C./Art Resource, NY)

duction for the duration of the war. Gompers participated in the War Labor Board, in part, to facilitate the spread of collective bargaining and enhance the legitimacy of trade unions. He continued to lead the AFL until his death in 1924.

Gompers's major achievement was in helping to establish a permanent national labor organization capable of outlasting economic crises and persisting within a relatively hostile political and business environment. However, his focus on organizing skilled workers left the majority of workers without representation.

BIBLIOGRAPHY

Dubofsky, Melvyn, and Foster Rhea Dulles. *Labor in America, A History*. 4th ed. Arlington Heights, Ill., 1984.

Foner, Philip S. *History of the Labor Movement in the United States*, vols. 1–3. New York, 1947–1964.

Gompers, Samuel. *Seventy Years of Life and Labor: An Autobiography*. New York, 1925. Revised, 1943.

Greene, Julie. *Pure and Simple Politics: The American Federation of Labor and Political Activism, 1881–1917*. Cambridge and New York, 1998.

Kaufman, Stuart Bruce. *Samuel Gompers and the Origins of the American Federation of Labor, 1848–1896*. Westport, Conn., 1973.

Kaufman, Stuart Bruce, Peter Albert, and Grace Palladino, eds. *The Samuel Gompers Papers*, vols. 1–8. Urbana, 1986–2000.

Laslett, John H. M. "Labor Leaders in America." In *Samuel Gompers and the Rise of American Business Unionism*. Urbana, 1987.

Mandel, Bernard. *Samuel Gompers: A Biography*. Yellow Springs, Ohio, 1963.

Reed, Louis S. *The Labor Philosophy of Samuel Gompers*. New York, 1930.

PETER PHILIPS AND CORY SINCLAIR

GOULD, JAY (1836–1892), American financier.

Jason "Jay" Gould was born in 1836 the son of a farmer in Delaware county, New York; he died in 1892 a financier and railway magnate, possessor of a fortune estimated at $125 million. He took advantage of the free-market capitalism and primitive state of corporate finance and law following the Civil War to make his fortune manipulating stocks and firms. He is perhaps the best, most imaginative market manipulator ever to have lived. One story illustrates this: in 1870, his Erie railroad and Cornelius Vanderbilt's New York Central were involved in a rate war, rapidly driving down the rate for shipping cattle from Buffalo to New York. When the New York Central price finally hit one dollar per car, Gould apparently capitulated, raising his price back to the original $125. However, unbeknownst to Vanderbilt, Gould had purchased all the available cattle west of Buffalo and was shipping them to New York on the New York Central at a dollar a car, with huge profits for himself and similar losses for Vanderbilt.

At eighteen, Gould became a freelance surveyor, making maps of Delaware County and its environs. At twenty, with five thousand dollars of capital, he entered the tanning business. Using capital from that business, he began to speculate on the New York stock market, and cornered the market for hides in 1857. He was a millionaire (on paper) by age twenty-one. By 1860, he was speculating in small railroads. With the help of James Fisk and Daniel Drew, he fought Cornelius Vanderbilt for control of the Erie railroad, winning by selling watered stock and paying the higher price for votes in the New York legislature.

Gould's most spectacular endeavor was an attempt to corner the U.S. gold market in 1869, which very nearly succeeded. It failed on Black Friday (24 September), when the U.S. treasury began selling large quantities of gold to curtail the enormous price increases. Many investors were wiped out. In 1869, he joined Russell Sage in acquiring control of the Pacific Mail Steamship Company; theirs became a long-lasting partnership. He rescued the Union Pacific Railroad from bankruptcy in the mid-1870s, and, for the first time in years, the Union Pacific paid a dividend (a rare occurrence for a Gould-controlled firm). By his near monopoly in the Midwest, he was able to control east-west freight rates, changing the face of the country. His attacks

JAY GOULD. (George Grantham Bain Collection/Prints and Photographs Division, Library of Congress)

on existing rate-setting cartels and rapid track-building activities helped open up much of the West. Forcing the merger of the competing Kansas Pacific and Union Pacific, both of which he controlled, he made a huge profit for Kansas Pacific stockholders, not least himself. By 1890, Gould owned half the trackage in the southwestern United States.

Gould was quick to see the value of the telegraph, using it to get early news on the outcomes of battles in the Civil War, with which to calculate his moves on the stock market. He never lost sight of the value of that technology, and in 1877 sought control of Western Union (WU). Refused a place on its board, he started American Union Telegraph. He built its lines parallel to WU at inflated prices, using a construction company in his control. Eventually the effect on WU was too strong, and Gould was able to gain control of it in a stock swap.

Gould left his mark on U.S. history in several ways. He is considered instrumental in changing the nature of business—said at the time to be a "wrecker of existing values like trust and honesty" although he was a pioneer in developing techniques for raising working capital through stocks and bonds. By his refusal to settle in a strike against the Texas and Pacific Railway, he destroyed the Knights of Labor, then the most powerful force in the labor movement. His ambitious track building, and responses to it by his competitors, opened up large parts of the western United States; and his violation of standing (understood) agreements regarding rates led to lower rates and increased efficiency.

Gould made a brief foray into newspapers, owning the *New York World* for three years, using it as a publicity organ to further his schemes before selling it in 1883 to Joseph Pulitzer. In the 1880s, he gained control of the elevated railways of New York which he held, along with Western Union and Union Pacific, until his death. In 1884, he suffered serious reverses and retired from speculating on the stock market, in a move that marks him as one of the few who have made a successful transition from speculator to businessman.

BIBLIOGRAPHY

Gordon, John Steele. *The Scarlet Woman of Wall Street: Jay Gould, Jim Fisk, Cornelius Vanderbilt, the Erie Railway Wars and the Birth of Wall Street.* New York, 1988.

Klein, Maury. *The Life and Legend of Jay Gould.* Baltimore, 1986.

O'Connor, Richard. *Gould's Millions.* Garden City, N.Y., 1962.

ROBIN COWAN

GOVERNMENT BORROWING

GOVERNMENT BORROWING *[This entry contains three subentries, on government borrowing before 1500, between 1500 and 1800, and after 1800.]*

Government Borrowing before 1500

Governments in western Europe resorted to borrowing in a regular and systematic way from the late twelfth and early thirteenth centuries, when state finances witnessed a progressive shift from reliance primarily on the princely domain to a system based more upon regular tax income. The availability of fiscal revenues, in fact, allowed governments to establish and maintain constant relations with major operators on the international credit market. Those who emerged as the most skilled financiers were the Italians, particularly Tuscan merchant bankers and Piedmontese moneylenders (known in northwestern Europe as "Lombards"). The role played by local bankers (in Flanders, in Artois, and in the Imperial territories) was generally secondary. Italian merchants succeeded in creating and controlling a large network of commercial relations that covered most of Europe and the Mediterranean basin. This meant that they were able to remit large amounts of money through the links among their own commercial compa-

nies, their branches, and correspondents in order to meet demand as it arose. The prominent role of Tuscans was due above all to their commercial role and their close relations with the Papal court. As managers of the collection system of the Papal tithes throughout Christian Europe, Tuscan merchants managed enormous amounts of money, which they could invest in trade and finance. It is, therefore, not surprising that in the medieval European history of credit—public as well as private—Italian merchant-bankers were the principal protagonists.

A clear example concerns the financial relations between the crown and the Italian companies in late medieval England. At first, the principal lenders to the king were the Riccardi of Lucca, followed by the Florentine Frescobaldi, and then by the Acciaiuoli, Bardi, and Peruzzi, who began furnishing loans when Edward I (r. 1272–1307) established a duty on the trade in raw wool, England's most lucrative export. The tax collection was granted, as security for the loans, to the Riccardi, who had extensive interests in the international wool trade. Anticipating the receipt of funds from Papal taxes collected in England and those provided by their own clients, they were able to make substantial loans to the crown. Receipts from their wool sales in Italy then allowed them to pay the taxes owing to the Papal treasury, be it in Rome or Avignon. But the system collapsed when the royal incapability to manage the huge debt created severe difficulties for the Tuscan companies—first at the time of the great Florentine bankruptcies of the 1340s, then in the later fifteenth century when once again loans to the crown, this time by the Medici branch in London, helped bring down that bank. Later on, local merchant financiers, mostly of London, provided loans to the crown that granted commercial and political privileges, but they were unable to match the financial resources of the Italians.

As far as France is concerned, its kings showed a lesser ability in securing lines of credit than their English adversaries. Toward the end of the thirteenth century, however, Philip IV the Fair (r. 1285–1314) did rely on sums lent by Italian financiers, and subsequently the crown resorted to other financiers, most of whom were French, for example, Jacques Coeur from 1438 to 1451. Besides merchants and occasional moneylenders, the kings of France increasingly employed forced loans imposed on towns, guilds, well-to-do-citizens, and officials as well; moreover, they sometimes also seized assets of merchants (mostly Italians). Only infrequently during the fifteenth century did they seek loans from the most important Italian banks then active (the Arnolfini, Medici, and Pazzi). Evidently, the French fiscal system, less effective than the English system (which could use as a lever its crucial export commodity, wool), made it more difficult for French kings to bind the major bankers' interests to their financial needs.

GOVERNMENT BORROWING. A session of the French Cour des Comptes (court of accounts). Miniature from *Livre de Ferre*, p. 889. France, fifteenth century. (Archives Nationales, Paris/ Giraudon/ Art Resource, NY)

The crown of Castille frequently relied on loans granted—more or less voluntarily or forcibly, according to the circumstances—by Jewish moneylenders, wealthy bourgeois, and towns. Elsewhere in central Europe, the chief financial agents for government treasuries were merchant-bankers from Flanders and northern Germany, to whom emperors and princes pledged their domain and tax revenues in return for loans. In the Italian principalities (the kingdoms of Naples and of Sicily, the duchy of Milan, the Papal states), the Tuscan merchant financiers were the most important suppliers of loans. The mechanism was the same almost everywhere: in exchange for a short-term loan, the prince obligated himself to make payments from future revenues and offered as guarantees parts of his own patrimony. It was a financial policy made up of temporary solutions, which actually impaired the future of state finances with high borrowing costs. In fact, the constant risk run by lenders of encountering defaults explains why interest rates were usually so high (well over 10 percent).

From the early thirteenth century, the towns of northern France, and then those in Flanders and the Empire, exploited some alternative methods of securing funds from the public, in particular the use of *rentes*: the sale of life or heritable (perpetual) annuities, a technique borrowed from monastic communities. Because these governments were never obligated to repay the principal (but were free to redeem them), such *rentes* were not loans, and thus not to subject to the ecclesiastical bans on usury.

In northern Italy, municipalities levied forced loans on their citizens (*prestanze prestitix*), in lieu of direct taxes, on the promise to repay the principal sometime in the future (rarely defined). Although such loans had actually commenced in the mid-twelfth century on a voluntary basis, by the later thirteenth century they had become compulsory and were levied according to a household's ability to pay. As long as governments succeeded in paying interest regularly on their debt obligations, such a system proved to be quite profitable for citizens, particularly for the wealthy. The latter thus avoided paying direct taxes on property and income, drew a relatively good return (generally about 5 percent) on their portfolio of loans, and could sell and buy obligations at market prices according to their needs. Furthermore, fiscal revenues set aside for paying interest on the loans were generally those derived from customs duties on trade and especially on staple consumption, whose burden was relatively less for the rich than for the poor. The social inequity of the system was well recognized by the "little people" (*popolo minuto*) who, on the occasion of revolts in Genoa in 1339 and in Florence in 1378, for example, criticized the system as unfair.

Between the mid-thirteenth century and the mid-fourteenth century, the debts of Venice, Genoa, and Florence were funded. That meant that obligations became perpetual and governments no longer had to repay the principal borrowed, though they remained, in the eyes of the church, true loans (*mutuum*) subject to the usury prohibitions. The funded debts (the so-called *Monti*) allowed the ruling groups to exploit the huge financial resources of citizens in order to expand militarily the boundaries of the city-state and control an ever wider economic space. The mechanism of deficit financing by the major Italian city-states worked quite well until the increasing costs of warfare put the system under relentless pressure. Between the late fourteenth century and the early fifteenth century, both increasing forced loans and severe financial difficulties forced governments to lower the return on these *prestanze*, and sometimes reneging on their obligations to pay interest as well. The consequences on both lenders—who actually became taxpayers—and the financial market were significant: squeezed by the endless requests of government, many citizens were forced to sell their bonds on the secondary market at heavy discounts in order to get money to pay for further forced loans.

The urban model of deficit financing involved a much larger portion of society than the princely way of borrowing. Kings and princes had to resort to a narrow group of financiers willing to take risks. Kings could more easily renege on their own debts, and it was not taken for granted that a ruler would agree to pay the debts of his predecessor. As far as urban debts are concerned, the close identity between ruling groups and major bondholders made the government's debt much more sound. Furthermore, a fiscal system that had become more fully evolved in the towns than in the kingdoms reassured creditors. These features continued to be important well into the early modern age, when broader financial markets emerged.

BIBLIOGRAPHY

Bonney, Richard, ed. *Economic Systems and State Finance.* Oxford, 1995.

Bonney, Richard, ed. *The Rise of the Fiscal State.* Oxford, 1999.

Day, John. *The Medieval Market Economy.* Oxford, 1987.

Fryde, Edmund B., and Fryde, M. M. "Public Credit, with Special Reference to North-Western Europe." In *The Cambridge Economic History of Europe*, vol. 3, *Economic Organisation and Policies in the Middle Ages*, pp. 430–553. Cambridge, 1963.

Hunt, Edwin S. *The Medieval Super-Companies: A Study of the Peruzzi Company of Florence.* Cambridge, 1994.

Kaeuper, Richard W. *War, Justice, and Public Order: England and France in the Later Middle Ages.* Oxford, 1988.

Mueller, Reinhold C. *The Venetian Money Market: Banks, Panics, and the Public Debt, 1200–1500.* Baltimore and London, 1997.

LUCIANO PEZZOLO

Government Borrowing: 1500–1800

Governments in the early modern period were confronted by the ever-mounting costs of the military revolution. For offensive-minded governments, the military revolution in Europe meant equipping larger armies with more artillery and muskets and then training their standing armies in the effective use of their arms in battle. For defensive-minded governments, it meant building elaborate new fortifications to protect against artillery attacks. In their search for expanded revenues to match these rising costs, the most successful governments increasingly turned to indirect taxes on a rising volume of trade or expanded their base for direct taxes on property. The frequent outbreaks of war, which always required mobilizing large sums quickly or suffering defeat, also led to various monetary and financial experiments in addition to innovations in taxation. Recoinages; changing mint ratios among gold, silver, and copper; and simple "crying up" of existing coins were among the monetary experiments even as the supply of silver from Spanish America expanded rapidly in the latter half of the sixteenth century. Monetary experiments, however, undermined the real resources available from existing taxes. Stable tax revenues were necessary if governments were to be able to raise money through large-scale borrowing during a military conflict. As military conflicts became larger in scale and longer in duration, government debts increased both in size and duration. Finding the right blend of taxes, money creation, and debt was a continuing challenge for governments in transition from medieval to modern institutions.

Medieval governments had to be content with ordinary revenues derived from the monarch or lord's domain, considered as personal property to be used for the benefit of the state. The occasional wars were then financed by extraordinary revenues, which were mainly direct taxes on property judged to be capable of generating income for the owner and usually levied as a fixed percentage of a previously assessed value. In effect these were occasional capital levies. Indirect taxes were levied on all sorts of mundane services provided by the lord and were most easily extended to include tolls on trade routes or excise taxes on goods brought to a market. Over time the base for direct taxation had often dwindled under medieval rulers, who were forced to sell off permanent tax exemptions to monasteries, town guilds, or local war lords in exchange for one-time subsidies. Increasing taxes on trade also choked the growth of the base for indirect taxes. Without credible tax backing for his or her debt, a monarch was obliged to pledge real assets to his or her creditors—silver mines in central Europe for the Austrian Habsburgs, mercury mines in Spain for Philip II, or the crown jewels in the case of Elizabeth I of England.

Modern rulers first tried to expand their tax bases. In Protestant Europe non-Catholic rulers found new revenue by secularizing Catholic church properties, as with Henry VIII in England and later Gustavus Adolphus in Sweden. Everywhere rulers tried to establish and maintain profitable monopolies, ranging from the spice trade of Portugal to the porcelain works of Saxony. In the long run success depended on regularity and frequency in collection of revenues from the monopoly. Only then could the future stream of revenues be pledged as collateral for substantial loans to the ruler. Examples from overseas trade were the annual treasure fleets of Spain from the West Indies and the regular convoys of Dutch East India ships from the East Indies. Less-successful examples were the fishing fleets of the Portuguese and Dutch and various porcelain or tapestry works because of the ease of entry by competitors.

The English Parliament set the most fruitful example under the direction of Oliver Cromwell when it made collection of the land tax a regular, annual affair, a practice it continued after the restoration of the Stuarts in 1660. Within the Habsburg Netherlands, subjected to continued extortions to support the wars of Charles V, regular excise taxes were levied by city and provincial governments that were pledged to service annuities sold to citizens and foreigners. The ability to issue large new supplies of annuities when backed by a new excise tax then helped the independent Dutch Republic rise to preeminence as a naval power in the seventeenth century. While the Dutch excise

A New Way to Pay the National Debt. King George III and Queen Charlotte stand before the treasury with moneybags under their arms, their pockets overflowing with coins (funds from the treasury to cover royal debts). William Pitt, at right, his pockets full of coins, hands the king another moneybag. The prince of Wales, later George IV, at far right, stands looking destitute; a quadriplegic sits on the ground to the left with a overturned and empty hat between his legs. Illustration by James Gilray (1756–1815). (British Cartoon Collection/Prints and Photographs Division, Library of Congress)

taxes merely mimicked the *alcabala* taxes of Spain, the Spanish taxes were pledged back to local authorities by monarchs in exchange for periodic loans to the crown. Dutch government authority over each excise tax was permanent, Spanish authority over each *alcabala* or *asiento* was sold periodically by the crown.

When the English Parliament, under the leadership of its new Dutch king William III, adopted the Dutch practice of pledging each new indirect tax to the service of its funded debt, it managed to establish for the first time in Europe a tax base almost equally balanced between direct taxes, mainly the land tax, and indirect taxes, mainly various customs duties. Under the leadership of Robert Walpole, the tax collection mechanism established for the land tax from the entire kingdom was then gradually extended to take up excise taxes collected in local markets as well. Walpole's tax initiatives were necessary to preserve the marketability of British long-term debt, issued for the first time in the form of perpetual annuities when the South Sea Company was reorganized in 1723. So successful were these annuities, bearing 5 percent annual return initially, then

reduced to 4 percent, that the Bank of England issued its own 3 percent perpetual annuity in 1726. The subsequent War of the Austrian Succession was then financed, successfully, by successive issues of 3 percent perpetual annuities backed by the permanent taxing authority of Parliament. In 1751 all the issues were consolidated into one fund, the famous Three Per Cent Consol, which became the chief form of British national debt thereafter. The ability of the British government to service a large outstanding debt, which increased sharply with each successive war during the eighteenth century, meant that it eventually became the most heavily taxed economy in Europe. But it also meant that it was able to win each of its wars with European opponents, whose absolute monarchs and local rulers resisted all such fiscal innovations as they implied loss of political power to local elites.

The French Revolution, beginning in 1789, eventually destroyed the fiscal apparatus of the ancien régime, replacing it with imitations of the British system. Tax privileges of the nobility and the church were first eliminated in France and then throughout Europe behind the triumphs of French revolutionary and Napoleonic forces. Direct taxes were then levied on all property and collected regularly, while city and guild privileges purchased from rulers in ages past were revoked summarily. The excise taxes now levied by permanent parliaments were pledged against new issues of debt, usually issued as a close imitation of the British Three Per Cent Consol. As a result the tax burdens rose from levels estimated to be less than 5 percent of national income throughout Europe to levels closer to the pre-1800 British level, around 10 percent. Similarly the levels of government debt relative to national income rose in imitation of the British example.

BIBLIOGRAPHY

Bonney, R. ed. *Economic Systems and State Finance*. Oxford, 1995.

Braddick, Michael. *The Nerves of State: Taxation and the Financing of the English State, 1558–1714*. Manchester, 1996.

Brewer, John. *Sinews of Power: War, Money, and the English State, 1688–1783*. Cambridge, Mass., 1990.

Neal, Larry. *The Rise of Financial Capitalism: International Capital Markets in the Age of Reason*. Cambridge, 1990.

O'Brien, Patrick. "The Political Economy of British Taxation, 1660–1815." *Economic History Review* 41 (February 1988), 1–32.

Tracy, James. *A Financial Revolution in the Habsburg Netherlands: Renten and Renteniers in the County of Holland, 1515–1565*. Berkeley, 1985.

LARRY NEAL

Government Borrowing after 1800

The British government's capacity to issue public debt (with which it financed its costly wars more effectively than did its enemies) has been attributed to a "financial revolution" that took place between 1688 and 1756. This consisted of the legalization of the debt and the issue and management of negotiable public debt, with bonds of low denomination, that could be placed in emerging financial markets. This capacity gave the United Kingdom financial leverage, which other rival nations lacked, that allowed it to extend its tax resources to defend its national interests. Nevertheless, the solidity of the finances of a state lay in its tax collection; without this, it would not be possible to issue debt in any great quantity. It was the capacity to collect tax, rather than to issue public debt, that was responsible for the strength of British military power. Loans are no more than taxes deferred in time because, in order to pay interest and return the loan, it is necessary to increase fiscal pressure in the future; only if the treasury is able to increase tax collection will it have "credit" to place debt in the market under good conditions. In order for a government to issue large quantities of public debt recurrently, its interest and redemption must be completely and punctually dealt with; otherwise, the treasury loses credit, the debt depreciates, and new issues have higher interest rates. It is certain that without the improvement of tax collection achieved by the British treasury from 1769 on, based on indirect taxes and an improvement in their management and collection, this financial revolution would have been impossible.

Effectively the accumulation of public debt has a limit that inevitably obliges Chancellor of the Exchequer tax reforms. The crisis of the debt faced by William Pitt when he was appointed Chancellor of the Exchequer and prime minister at the end of 1783 illustrates this since, in 1786, the interest of the national debt had already absorbed two-thirds of all tax revenues. This burden of interest and amortization worried the British authorities because, first, it left little money for war requirements; second, to continue accumulating debt would mean raising taxes considerably to accommodate this; and third, public credit, and the capacity of the treasury to get into debt, would end up deteriorating. For these reasons and, in the face of the war with France that started in 1793, Pitt had attempted to improve tax collection, fix the debt, and increase direct taxation. However, the French Revolution meant that Britain got caught up in a difficult and expensive war that required fundamental fiscal changes. The amount required for the war was unprecedented: between 1808 and 1815 the British state used 25 percent of national income, whereas before the war the state had used only 6 percent.

Inevitably, Pitt and his successors as chancellor could not, as had been the British tradition up until then, finance the war against France with national debt. Given the vast quantities required, the only strategy was to resort to taxation. Until 1798, Pitt could continue issuing debt; taxes were increased only to redeem the new debt, in accordance with his proposals for a sinking fund approved in 1786. Collaboration between the Bank of England and the treasury began to deteriorate, and difficulties in continuing to place the debt increased; only then did Pitt focus his attention on taxation. In 1797, the Bank of England's reserves diminished to such an extent that convertibility had to be abandoned, and a fiduciary system was adopted until 1821. In this situation, the banking system could lend to the government without reducing the financing of the private sector, avoiding the "crowding out effect" of private investment by more public expenditure. The chancellors of the Exchequer thought that, in any case, the accumulation of debt should be contained, to relieve the fiscal burdens of future generations and to avoid a situation whereby entrepreneurs lacked funds for investment—in which case there would be economic stagnation, and treasury income would be frozen. Additionally, those in charge of the treasury were conscious of the hyperinflation brought about in other countries by the excessive issue of "paper money," which wore away confidence in this new financial instrument, rendering it useless.

It is worth remembering the French experience after the Revolution. The chaotic situation of the treasury enforced

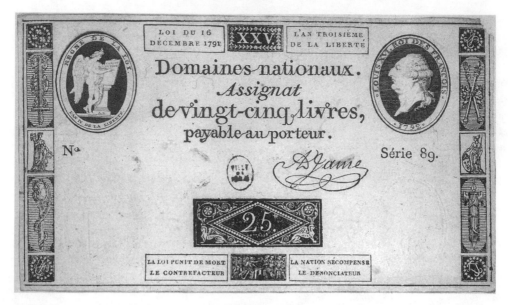

PAPER MONEY. Assignat for 25 livres, Series 89. France, late eighteeenth century. (Musée de la Ville de Paris/Musée Carnavalet, Paris/Giraudon/Art Resource, NY)

the restoration, from 1790, of some of the taxes abolished by the Revolution, including fiscal monopolies. The revolutionary finances were a true disaster; except for customs duties, kept for protectionist reasons, all the taxes had been abolished and substituted by a "single contribution" that was applied to territorial property and buildings. The main revenue of the revolutionary treasury came from the sales of "national properties," land previously expropriated from the church (disentailment). The French Treasury also collected significant sums from taxes and confiscations in countries invaded during the Napoleonic Wars. Since the treasury's income did not cover its expenditure, the fiscal deficit was monetized through the issue of large quantities of assignats. In effect, in December 1789, an issue of securities was decreed that yielded interest and would be admitted with preference in payment for sales of national property. In April 1790, the Assembly decided to legalize the 400 million assignats, converting them into paper money. In September of the same year, the maximum issue had risen to 1.2 billion. Afterward, the issue of assignats increased, and their depreciation accelerated, provoking intense inflation, which pushed the French Treasury toward bankruptcy because the real value of taxation diminished. Resulting price controls, requisition of goods, and recruitment of personnel needed by the war provoked an uprising of the French people against these measures, just as they earlier had reacted against the tax increases. "La Terreur" was the response to the rioting. Thus the issuance of paper money immediately revealed its limitations in France.

In other European countries the financial revolution took place a little later, particularly after 1800. In the Ger-

man states there was an explosion of debt between the turn of the nineteenth century and 1818 due to the massive public loans needed to finance the current expenditure of the treasury. There were several underlying causes, including: the dissolution of the empire in 1806, which meant a territorial reorganization; the Napoleonic Wars; and the high costs of loans that were either enforced or contracted for in the very short term, increasing the floating debt. The German states tried to overcome the difficulties posed by the large and costly public debt by restructuring it, which consisted basically of stripping it of its feudal characteristics in order to accommodate it in a new liberal and capitalist context.

The revolutionary approach to the public debt experimented with by the German states during the first third of the nineteenth century followed guidelines previously developed by British and Dutch financial models. These same guidelines also were applied to countries in the European Mediterranean (Italy, Portugal, Spain), which also belatedly modernized the management of their public debt. The new approach had three aspects: (1) legalization or institutionalization of public debt and reform of the formal conditions, (2) consolidation and finance with a specific purpose (with the creation of a sinking fund), and (3) new methods of commercialization, as summarized below.

In the first place, the "legalization" of public debt by liberal regimes implied a reform of legal conditions. In the *ancien régime* the debt of different political institutions could not properly be called public debt; there were very distinct kinds of debt, that issued by the monarchy, that of kingdoms, and that of councils. In the monarch's debt, as occurred with a monarch's assets connected to birthright, public elements were mixed with private ones. Kingdoms and councils issued debt autonomously, but they also took debt that the monarch endorsed. In order for these debts to become public ones, in the modern meaning of the word, the monarch's debt had to be decoupled from the monarch's estate, and the debt of the municipalities (local councils) had to be nationalized; that is, the debts had to be converted into a matter of the representative institutions of national sovereignty (Parliament) and become controlled by national government institutions. In effect, the institutionalization of the debt by liberal regimes conceded to Parliament responsibility for approving the loans and controlling debt management. Parliament established the annual restraints on the debt that the government could assume; at the same time, bureaucratic processes were established for the contracting of new loans in an effort to impede arbitrariness, favoritism, and fraud in debt management.

Second, progress was made toward unifying the debt, on the one hand, through consolidation of all the existing debts into a single security and, on the other hand, through centralization of debt administration into a single organism. In the *ancien régime* debts issued by the public authorities were abundant and of distinct character, as much because of the diverse organisms that issued them as their various characteristics. In addition, interest and amortization of the debts were satisfied by certain income and rents of particular offices of the treasury, which directly paid the bondholders. Debts situated in the office of the treasury that were more secure in the taxation of their income were of better "quality" because the payment of interest was assured to the bondholders; debts situated in offices of the treasury whose taxation was uncertain did not always earn interest. Around 1811, all the debts of the main German states were consolidated into a single bond, and autonomous organizations, called Offices of the Amortization of Public Debts, were established to manage all the state debts centrally. These amortization offices followed the principle of a sinking fund; they were legal and independent institutions, whose management, income, and accounts were separate from the administration of the budget. Their revenue came from taxes and rents handed over permanently by the state to service their burdens, without the treasury's being able to use them to finance other expenses. The sinking fund sought to reassure the debt bearers that the state would fulfill its financial obligations, and, to such an end, it reserved some income from the budget. However, given the scarce resources that these amortization offices enjoyed, this measure only served to make more evident the difficulties of debt payment by the states; some of these offices became bankrupt.

Third, new ways of placing the debt were established to accommodate it to market principles. The new commer-

cialization of the debt implied three processes, related to: (1) the characteristic of the debt, (2) the techniques of placing the debt, and (3) the structure of the moneylenders. Until the nineteenth century, personal loans predominated in Europe; the personal agreement between the moneylender and the government was registered in a promissory note bearing the moneylender's name (for example, the *asientos de Castilla*, or contract entries), in which the particular conditions for each debt were listed. As these promissory notes were hardly tradable, moneylenders demanded short-term repayment dates or floating debts (so as not to immobilize capital) and special guarantees (to protect themselves from the risk of nonpayment). These personal loans did not allow very large public debts because there were few big moneylenders and also because of the enormous concentration of risk involved in operations with the states. To avoid these problems, the increasing needs of finance obliged governors to make large-scale governmental loans. They did so by issuing a large number of securities or long-term consolidated bonds to the bearer in small nominal amounts, which were acquired in small quantities by a multitude of anonymous moneylenders. The bonds were tradable, and so could have longer expiry periods and special guarantees. The greatest advantage was that the issues of public debt reached greater volumes than ever before, owing to the mobilization of the capital of many investors. These "bonds to the bearer" provided a great benefit to the state in terms of private loans, which still had not penetrated capital markets on a large scale.

From the turn of the nineteenth century on, the techniques of placing debt also changed, thanks to the consolidation of financial intermediaries. In the *ancien régime*, debtors and creditors were in direct contact with each other because, then there were no financial markets. Afterward, issuing banks, stock markets, and other financial institutions emerged that traded public bonds. In some places, these banks placed the public debt among the public, facilitatinggovernments' access to financial markets and to stock markets, both national and international. Moreover, the structure of moneylenders to the government changed. Until the nineteenth century, the church and charitable institutions made up the bulk of the moneylenders topublic institutions. After the Napoleonic Wars, the main moneylenders to the states were individuals, followedby municipal institutions. In this regard, public debtcontributed to the consolidation of financial markets, particularly of stock markets, which also began to commercialize private securities, both shares and company bonds.

In countries of delayed industrialization, the financial revolution was not consolidated with institutionalization of the debt. On the contrary, legal changes in public debt were not accompanied by its technical management in accordance with market conditions. Therefore, modernization of techniques followed the modernization of legal and political rules concerning the debt. Debt features (characteristics) were: its size (the volume of debt and its share of gross domestic product or GDP); its structure (bonds with distinct characteristics, according to returns, amortization dates, and issuing organism); the markets in which debt would be placed (national or international); its holders (financial institutions or individuals in general); its management (mercantile or privileged conditions), and its financial burden in the public budget.

The technical modernization of public debt was achieved at the same time as economic growth and political change. The best way of explaining this is to compare the present-day (the figures refer to 1977; see Goode, 1984) characteristics of public debt in less-industrialized countries with that in industrialized countries, which can be summarized as follows:

1. State debt as a percentage of GDP tends to be larger in the developed countries (with an average of 33 percent) than in the underdeveloped ones (with an average of 27 percent).

2. Foreign debt is greater in underdeveloped countries (accounting for 52 percent of the total) than in advanced nations (making up 18 percent).

3. In poor countries, 70 percent of domestic debt is controlled by banks and financial institutions, whereas in developed countries, where financial markets are better developed, nonbanking holders of the debt predominate, accounting for about 60 percent of the domestic public debt.

4. An important part of the remaining debt issued by governments in developing countries involves enforced underwriting by "captive moneylenders," as insurance companies, pension funds, savings banks, banks, and different public bodies are obliged to invest a percentage of their liabilities in public debt bonds, computable in cash coefficients or obligatory investment, that are not tradable in the stock market afterward. These are nonvoluntary or forced loans. In this way, governments finance their budgetary deficits with interest rates that are much lower than those operating in the market; in some periods, public debts could yield negative interest owing to the high rates of inflation suffered by these countries.

5. Ministries of finance in underdeveloped countries distort financial markets to avert funds that could be loaned in the economy. They usually resort to tax allowances, total or partial, for public-debt interest when the other capital returns of private obligations are taxed. In this way, capital is attracted to the public sector at the same time that explicit costs are reduced in financing the deficit.

6. Governments of underdeveloped countries systematically have resort to floating debt (also called treasury debt or short-term debt: short-term bonds, exchequer bills, treasury bills). In this way, floating debts stop being an instrument for financing temporal gaps between taxation and office of the treasury payments, within the same budgetary framework, and become a "normal" way of financing public expenditure. This practice arises because floating debts are easier to place among subscribers than long-term debt and also because they demand fewer parliamentary transactions for their issuance.

7. Treasury ministers of less-developed countries frequently resort to irregular means of financing the budgetary deficit, such as "outstanding payment obligations," whose variations constitute a financial liability for public accounts, and for which it is not even customary to pay "interest for delays."

8. In developing countries, there is a trend to abuse the "monetization" of the public deficit, either directly by placing it in the issuing bank, which allows an increase of the monetary base, or indirectly by issuing debt that can be pawned, which the private banks subscribe to and discount afterward in the central bank. In this way banking deposits are increased. This causes inflation that reduces the real value of fixed-return bonds, including money. "Seigniorage" is a feature of treasuries in underdeveloped countries that is more difficult to be practiced in industrialized economies because there citizens have lost the "monetary illusion," and when inflation occurs, they demand higher nominal interest rates. On the other hand, financing the deficit with expansion of the monetary base means that the crowding out of private investment is less than when it is financed with the issue of public debt.

9. The importance of debt (and its financial burden) within the state budget is higher in underdeveloped countries. If it is true that the public debt/GDP ratio is greater in developed countries, the debt/public expenditure ratio tends to be superior in underdeveloped economies since the relationship of public expenditure to GDP is less in these countries. At the end of the 1970s, public expenditure in industrialized countries rose to 37.2 percent of GDP, whereas that of underdeveloped countries was 21.7 percent. In such cases, although the size of the public debt in circulation was supportable by the national economy, the weight of the financial burden of the debt could become excessive for the budgetary capacity of governments in the underdeveloped countries, as the debt/public expenditure ratio was very large. Effectively, during the end of the 1970s, in industrialized countries public debt represented 88.9 percent of public expenditure, whereas in non-industrialized countries this figure was 124.4 percent. Consequently, governments in these underdeveloped countries found it difficult to attend to the financial burdens of the public debt, a situation that could lead them to bankruptcy, repudiation, and frequent "renegotiations" with creditors. The problem was exacerbated because underdeveloped countries usually had a larger percentage of foreign debt, whose interest and amortization had to be satisfied in foreign currency.

10. A final feature of the historical evolution of public debt is the disappearance of perpetual debt and its replacement by redeemable debt, as well as the subsequent shortening of the redemption date of the debt.

When public debt in a country sheds the characteristics of an underdeveloped country, and public liabilities start to be managed the way they are in advanced nations, it can be said with certainty that the country has modernized its debt management. Then, the states finance themselves in the market without having "advantages" over private companies. This does not mean that they have to pay greater costs; as the risk of nonpayment by governments diminishes, they can place public debt in financial markets without paying a risk premium, which improves the qualification of their debts in national and international markets. To be able to issue large volumes of public debt, governments need to increase taxes to face larger financial burdens; if this were not the case, governments would simply go bankrupt. In this way, "Ricardian equivalence" is fulfilled, the concept states that it does not matter whether a government is financed by debt or taxes because any increase in debt will require tax increases in the future to pay for interest and redemption, which will be anticipated by the contributors. Historically, however, public debt has presented advantages to governments over taxes, which explain the general use of debt in all kinds of public bodies. In effect, taxpayers suffered from a fiscal illusion until well into the twentieth century, in being opposed to increases in direct taxes. Citizens are less sensitive to indirect tax increases, or fiscal monopolies, than to direct taxes, and they scarcely oppose the issue of public debt (which, being irredeemable or redeemable in the very long term, allows the transfer of the payment of public expenditure to future generations). The public also had a monetary illusion, so that the inflationary financing of the public deficit generally slipped by holders of money and fixed-return bonds. Keynes stated that the inflation tax was the most "painless" and also the most unjust. Until the great inflation of the twentieth century, the big advantage of public debt and seigniorage was that they permitted the financing of governments and easily overcame contributors' resistance, as it was not necessary to increase direct taxes. Public debt allowed, then, a leverage effect in public resources, which was especially appreciated at times when large quantities of funds were required urgently, as happened during the world wars. It is true that, as Peacock and Wiseman (1961) showed, during wartime, taxpayers underwent an "inspec-

tion effect" that led them to accept an increase in fiscal pressure; but, even so, the issue of debt and of money has been, almost always, the main way of financing war.

BIBLIOGRAPHY

Ardant, Gabriel. *Histoire de l'impôt.* Paris, 1972.

Comín, Francisco. *Historia de la hacienda pública en Europa.* Barcelona, 1996.

Goode, Richard. *Government Finance in Developing Countries.* Washington, D.C., 1984.

Middleton, R. "The Treasury in the 1930s: Political and Administrative Constraints to Acceptance of the 'New' Economics." *Oxford Economic Papers* 1 (1982), 48–77.

O'Brien, Patrick K. "The Political Economy of British Taxation, 1660–1815." *Economic History Review* 41 (1988), 1–32.

O'Brien, Patrick K. "Public Finance in the War with France, 1793–1815." In *Britain and the French Revolution, 1789–1815,* edited by H. T. Dickinson, pp. 165–188. London, 1989.

O'Brien, Patrick K., and Philip A. Hunt. "The Rise of a Fiscal State in England, 1485–1815." *Historical Research* 66.160 (1993), 129–176.

Peacock, Alan T., and Jack Wiseman. *The Growth of Public Expenditure in the United Kingdom.* Princeton, 1961.

Tedde de Lorca, P. *El Banco de San Carlos.* Madrid, 1988.

Ullmann, Hans-Peter. "The Emergence of Modern Public Debts in Bavaria and Baden between 1780 and 1820." In *Wealth and Taxation in Central Europe,* edited by P. C. Witt, pp. 63–79. New York, 1987.

White, Eugene N. "¿Fueron inflacionistas las finanzas estatales en el siglo XVIII? Una nueva interpretación de los vales reales." *Revista de Historia Económica* 3 (1987), 509–526.

White, Eugene N. "Was There a Solution to the Ancien Régime's Financial Dilemma?" *Journal of Economic History* 49 (1989), 545–568.

Witt, Peter-Christian. *Wealth and Taxation in Central Europe: The History and Sociology of Public Finance.* New York, 1987.

FRANCISCO COMÍN

GRAMSCI, ANTONIO (1891–1937), Italian Marxist theorist and Communist Party activist.

Born in Sardinia, Gramsci was educated in Turin, where he acted as ideologist of the factory council movement that occupied and ran the city's key manufacturing plants during the "red biennium" of 1919–1920. A founding member of the Italian Communist Party in 1921, he was arrested by Fascist Dictator Benito Mussolini (1883–1945) in 1926 and spent the next decade in jail. There he fell severely ill and died shortly after being released on compassionate grounds.

Gramsci's reputation as a thinker rests largely on the posthumously published *Prison Notebooks,* written during the early part of his incarceration. Here he elaborates his key concept of hegemony or ideological power. Drawing on the Italian idealist philosopher Benedetto Croce (1866–1952), Gramsci disputed the then-conventional Marxist view that revolution was determined by changes in the economic base alone. He claimed it also required mobilizing the revolutionary will among the working class to exploit favourable social and economic circumstances. After all, as he provocatively observed in an early article, the Russian Revolution had confounded Karl Marx's expectations in *Das Kapital* that communists would only come to power in developed countries. Gramsci argued that in fact revolution was far harder to organize in advanced industrial and liberal democratic societies. In such regimes, the state, in the narrow sense of the government, bureaucracy, and army, was buttressed by a broader set of institutions based in civil society, ranging from semipublic organizations such as schools and political parties to private bodies such as churches and the media. By working through civil society as well as the state, liberal democracies were able to legitimize the bourgoisie's rule by creating a popular consensus around their values and self-image. As a result, people failed to recognize the exploitative and inefficient character of the capitalist economy. Within such societies, a revolutionary party had to pursue a "war of position" by gradually winning a foothold within the various social institutions of ideological control and creating a "counter-hegemony" among the populace. Only then would a "war of manoeuvre" to overthrow the organs of the state proper be possible.

Gramsci often is regarded as having devised a third way between social democracy and Leninism, suitable for communist parties operating in the West and less authoritarian than the Marxist regimes of the former Eastern bloc. His strategy was credited with the Italian Communist Party's success during the 1950s to early 1980s. However, Gramsci's concessions to liberal democracy were tactical, and it is doubtful he saw any need for democratic politics after the revolution. Although he believed there should be mechanisms for ensuring a dialogue between the mass and the leadership of the party, and experimented with workers' control of industry in Turin, he assumed the new hegemony would be in the common interest and hence universally accepted. In his view, debates about alternative or conflicting interests and ideals arose only among the confused or the corrupt—a position, however genuinely held, likely to lead to repressive measures similar to those of other Marxist regimes.

BIBLIOGRAPHY

Adamson, Walter. *Hegemony and Revolution: A Study of Antonio Gramsci's Political and Cultural Theory*. Berkeley, 1980.

Bellamy, Richard, and Darrow Schecter. *Gramsci and the Italian State*. Manchester, U.K., 1993.

Femia, J. *Gramsci's Political Thought: Hegemony, Consciousness and the Revolutionary Process*. Oxford, 1981.

Gramsci, Antonio. *Selections from the Prison Notebooks*, edited and translated by Q. Hoare and G. N. Smith. London, 1978.

Gramsci, Antonio. *Pre-prison Writings*, edited by Richard Bellamy and translated by Virginia Cox. Cambridge, 1994.

R. P. BELLAMY

GRANADA. Encircled by rugged mountains and located at the foot of the Sierra Nevada, the city of Granada was the economic, cultural, religious, and political capital of the eponymous kingdom. For almost two and a half centuries, it was also the last outpost of Islam in the Iberian Peninsula. Its economic history was shaped by the ebb and tide of the Christian Reconquest and by the waning power of Islam on the peninsula from the early thirteenth century. Under the Umayyad caliphate, Granada was one of the five most important Andalusi cities. In 1031 CE, with the demise of the Caliphate of Córdoba, Granada became an independent kingdom and achieved great prosperity under the Almohads in the twelfth and thirteenth centuries. It served as one of the centers for a far-flung trade, connecting sub-Saharan Africa, the Maghrib, the interior regions of eastern Andalusia, the Christian kingdoms of Castile and Valencia, and the great port cities of Málaga and Almería.

Because of both the political cunning of its later rulers, the Nasrid, who continuously forged shifting alliances with their Christian overlords and with the great Maghrib rulers, and its protected location, Granada was able to withstand Christian pressures for over four centuries, until 1492. Despite being besieged by hostile forces, Granada thrived economically while it balanced hostile powers on the peninsula and across the Mediterranean.

With a large and heterogeneous population (Muslims, Jews, and Christians), Granada reached its heyday in the late fourteenth century. The boom that marked the period is best exemplified by the design and building of the Alhambra, which was not, by any means, its only important construction project. Granada's economy centered on the manufacturing of silks and other luxury textiles. As such, the city held a signal place as an exporter of high-quality and expensive cloth, sold and coveted throughout Christian Spain, other parts of the medieval world, and North Africa. Silk worms, mulberry trees (whose leaves feed the worms), and skilled artisans provided a unique combination of abundant supplies of raw materials and labor. Through a well-developed system of irrigation, Granada also served as the center for an important agricultural region. Beyond the ubiquitous olive trees (in the lower valleys) and an indispensable cereal cultivation to supply the city, the city was surrounded—so a Muslim traveler of the late fifteenth century tells us—by gardens, fig trees, and almond trees. Although a good deal of manufactured and agricultural goods went overland to Christian Córdoba and Seville, Granada's economy and lifeline were closely connected to that of its main port city, Málaga, an important commercial center on its own. Through Málaga, Granada kept active commercial exchanges with North African cities. It was also the last avenue of escape from the encircling Christians.

After the surrender of the city to Ferdinand and Isabella in 1492 and, more important, after the failed Second Alpujarras revolt (1568–1570) and the expulsion of the

Moriscos (nominal converts to Christianity), Christian settlers populated the Granadine countryside and the city itself. Lacking the skills of the original inhabitants, silk and other luxury clothing manufacturing declined. The city itself was eclipsed by the rise of Seville and the shift of the peninsula's economic center from the Mediterranean to the Atlantic.

BIBLIOGRAPHY

Arié, Rachel. *El reino nasri de Granada (1232–1492).* Madrid, 1992.

Constable, Olivia R. *Trade and Traders in Muslim Spain: The Commercial Realignment of the Iberian Peninsula, 900–1500.* Cambridge, 1994.

Ladero Quesada, Miguel Angel. *Granda: Historia de un país islámico (1232–1571).* 2d ed. Madrid, 1979.

TEOFILO F. RUIZ

GRASSLAND FARMING. Grassland farming is a system of mixed pastoral and arable husbandry in which land cycles through alternating phases of grass and arable rather than remaining permanently in one state or the other. By alternating grass with arable, nitrogen reserves accumulated when the land is under grass are made available for crops in the arable phase. A further advantage is that sown grasslands yield more forage than permanent pasture and meadow. There are two broad forms of grassland agriculture. In convertible or "up-and-down" husbandry, the alternating phases are comparatively long; in intensive mixed husbandry, the grass course is integrated into the arable rotation as an annual or biannual crop. The eighteenth-century "Norfolk" rotation of wheat, turnips, barley, and clover is an example of the latter.

The earliest form of grassland husbandry was the infield-outfield system, whereby the cultivated territory was divided between a continuously cultivated infield and a discontinuously cultivated outfield that reverted to waste for periods of up to twenty years before it was broken up and planted for a short number of years. Infield-outfield agriculture is essentially a long fallow reclaimed by natural herbage. In convertible husbandry, the phases are shorter and more balanced. The practice of putting arable periodically down to grass is doubtless ancient; the earliest documents referring to the practice, however, come from twelfth-century Flanders. Prior to the sixteenth century, land put down to grass was not seeded but simply allowed to reestablish a natural cover, which typically required several years. The most important technical innovation in grassland farming was the domestication and diffusion of quick-rooting annual grasses and forage legumes that become established in short rotations. Alfalfa, clover, and sainfoin were domesticated in western Asia during the second millennium BCE as fodder for horses and, passing into Europe via Asia Minor in 500 BCE, spread throughout the Mediterranean region. Although forage legumes were extensively planted in classical antiquity, they were abandoned in the early Middle Ages, surviving only in Muslim Spain and a few isolated districts in Italy and southern France. Their introduction to northern Europe in the sixteenth century appears to have been associated with the presence of Spanish troops operating in Italy and Flanders, although there is also contemporary evidence of seeds imported from Provence. In the seventeenth century, the crops spread to neighboring countries, and they diffused rapidly throughout northern Europe after 1775.

Because of the high opportunity cost of keeping arable land in grass rather than in grain, the spread of grassland farming typically occurred in response to rising relative prices for animal produce and fodder. The spatial distribution of artificial grasslands before the late nineteenth century indicates that the most profitable locales for this type of farming were regions that benefited from strong urban demand for meat and dairy products and fodder for horse-drawn transport services. The spread of forage legumes after 1750 made a major contribution to the growth in agricultural productivity through the extra nitrogen fixed in the soil by them. After 1880, mined and manufactured nitrates replaced legumes as the primary source of nitrogen in the soil. The crops are presently raised as high-quality fodder for cattle.

BIBLIOGRAPHY

Ambrosoli, Mauro. *The Wild and the Sown: Botany and Agriculture in Western Europe, 1350–1850.* Cambridge, 1997.

Chorley, G. P. H. "The Agricultural Revolution in Northern Europe, 1750–1880: Nitrogen, Legumes, and Crop Productivity." *Economic History Review* 34 (1981), 71–93.

Grantham, George. "The Diffusion of the 'New Husbandry' in Northern France, 1815–1840." *Journal of Economic History* 38 (June 1978), 311–337.

Kerridge, Eric. *The Agricultural Revolution.* London, 1967.

GEORGE GRANTHAM

GRAZING AND RANCH FARMING. Ranch farming describes agricultural establishments that specialize in raising livestock for the production of meat and leather. Although livestock herds were part of farming since the original development of agriculture, the raising of cattle or sheep in very large numbers did not occur until the nineteenth century, at least in European-settled areas. By the mid-nineteenth century, new frontier areas in North and South America and Australia had been settled that were conducive to raising livestock. These frontier lands on the prairies and Great Plains of the United States and Canada; the pampas of Argentina, Uruguay, and southern Brazil; and interior lands of Australia were semi-arid and therefore unsuitable for many types of crops other than grains (Alston, Libecap, Mueller, 1999). But they were covered with abundant and nutritious, native grasses on which

CATTLE RANCH. Northern Honduras, 1989. (© Mireille Vautier/Woodfin Camp and Associates, New York)

livestock could thrive. Moreover, given the amount of the landscape available for claiming, ranch units could be very large, sometimes occupying thousands of acres and taking advantage of economies of scale in herding. By 1890 ranches in the U.S. Great Plains had 15 percent of all cattle and 40 percent of all sheep in the country. By 1920 the shares had grown to 18 percent and 57 percent, respectively (Libecap, 1981a, p. 15).

With relatively expensive labor and very high land-to-labor ratios in frontier areas, production practices emerged that allowed cattle or sheep to graze with little labor input. Cattle, especially, were allowed to drift in huge herds following the available grass and water (Anderson and Hill, 1975). Labor was required only periodically, during the spring branding or marking of new calves and lambs to establish ownership, the fall roundup to separate animals for market, during cattle drives to market centers, and to control breeding. Otherwise, cattle were allowed to roam unimpeded for much of the year. Because sheep were less adaptive and resourceful, they required somewhat more attention, but they, too, grazed in large herds under the nominal watch of a few sheepherders.

Ranch farming required large amounts of grazing land per unit, and this condition affected both the nature of the ranching economy and property rights to land. In South America, very large ranches, or *estancias*, were established, often with absentee owners and a permanent labor force of cowboys or gauchos who monitored the livestock.

Somewhat similar, extremely large ranches of 20,000 acres or more also appeared in Texas, where federal land laws did not apply. In both areas there emerged a skewed distribution of landownership, wealth, and political influence that continued through the nineteenth and most of the twentieth centuries, particularly in South America. In the rest of the United States, large ranchers had to compete with small farmers or homesteaders for claims to rangeland.

At the end of the Civil War, rising cattle prices brought settlement of the Great Plains and development of huge herds of cattle. This was the period of investment by English and Scottish sources and of the great cattle drives from Texas to the central and northern plains (Osgood, 1929; Peake, 1937). The federal land laws, such as the Homestead Act, allowed private claimants 160 acres of land that could be titled after improvement and occupancy for five years. This number of acres, however, was far too limited for a viable ranch. With ranches often including five hundred to one thousand cattle or more and with the low livestock-carrying capacities in semi-arid regions, each establishment required thousands of acres of land. The 160-acre tracts that could be secured under the land laws generally included springs or other sources of water, with the remaining ranch land held informally.

Prior to 1880, there was little competition for grassland from homesteaders, and ranchers formed livestock associations to record brands, to monitor herds, and to jointly assemble livestock in large, common herds during the spring and fall roundups. Livestock associations also maintained surveillance against encroachment from homesteaders and against theft from rustlers (Dennen, 1976). Millions of acres of government land were fenced, technically illegally, to define property claims and to control the movement of livestock. Ranchers dominated the economies and politics of the Great Plains regions in a manner roughly analagous to what emerged in South America.

After 1880, however, an increase in small-farm and ranch settlement by homesteaders occasioned conflicts over property rights to land. Unlike in South America, in the United States and Canada, ranchers could not compete politically with a coalition of homesteaders, railroads, and land developers who desired much denser settlement of the frontier. The General Land Office in the United States, which administered the federal lands for private claiming, removed the fences erected by ranchers and sided with the competing claims of homesteaders. The livestock associations gradually declined in importance, and herding was increasingly confined to individual ranches. Rising wheat prices and the development of dry-farming techniques caused farming to expand to the plains, and by the turn of the century ranchers were no longer politically dominant. For example, the land laws of 1909 prevented them from obtaining liberalization to gain title to their large land claims. Their political influence also was weakened in the United States and Canada due to conflict between cattle and sheep raisers. Cattle raisers charged that sheep grazing depleted the grasslands.

Uncertain property rights to the federal range contributed to higher stocking levels and overgrazing, since continued occupancy and use was a means of establishing at least informal property rights (Libecap, 1981a, 1981b). Heavily grazed range lands were less attractive to other herders. Through 1920 homesteaders claimed the best lands for grains farming, leaving the remaining grasslands for ranches (Parr, Collier, and Klemmendson, 1928). Without the ability to title the lands they used, ranchers used a combination of privately deeded and informally occupied federal lands. The Taylor Grazing Act of 1934 formally placed the grazing lands of the United States under the regulatory mandate of the Department of the Interior, and in 1947 the Bureau of Land Management was created. Initially ranchers enjoyed grant influence over the policies of the bureau, receiving low grazing rates and comparatively secure grazing leases on federal lands. After the 1960s, however, new constituencies, such as environmentalists and urban recreation groups, gained power, gradually eclipsing the, ranchers' influence on federal land policy. Grazing permits were no longer automatically renewed, stocking limits were tightened, and grazing fees were increased. Lower per capita beef consumption and new production techniques led to the gradual decline in the ranch and grazing economy through the remaining part of the twentieth century.

[*See also* Cattle.]

BIBLIOGRAPHY

Alston, Lee J., Gary D. Libecap, and Bernardo Mueller. *Titles, Conflict and Land Use: The Development of Property Rights and Land Reform on the Brazilian Amazon Frontier*. Ann Arbor, 1999.
Anderson, Terry L., and P. J. Hill. "The Evolution of Property Rights: A Study of the American West." *Journal of Law and Economics* 18 (1995), 163–179.
Dennen, R. Taylor. "Cattlemen's Associations and Property Rights in Land in the American West." *Explorations in Economic History* 13 (1976) 423–436.
Libecap, Gary D. *Locking Up the Range: Federal Land Use Controls and Grazing*. Cambridge, 1981.
Libecap, Gary D. "Bureaucratic Opposition to the Assignment of Property Rights: Overgrazing on the Western Range." *Journal of Economic History* 41 (1981) 151–158.
Osgood, Ernest Staples. *The Day of the Cattleman*. Minneapolis, 1929.
Parr, V. V., G. W. Collier, and G. S. Klemmendson. "Ranch Organization and Methods of Livestock Production in the Southwest." *U.S. Department of Agriculture Technical Bulletin No. 68*. Washington, D.C., 1928.
Peake, Ora B. *The Colorado Range Cattle Industry*. Glendale, Colo., 1937.

GARY D. LIBECAP

GREAT BRITAIN [*This entry contains two subentries, on the economic history of Great Britain during the British Empire and during the modern period.*]

British Empire

The British Empire spanned four centuries and six continents. From the late sixteenth century to the late twentieth century, the empire provided an important element of the distinctive history of the British economy, from premodern, proto-industrial growth, through the explosion of the Industrial Revolution combined with unprecedented capital formation and overseas investment that brought world leadership and international financial hegemony, and on to the more recent world of deindustrialization and attempts to create a postindustrial, knowledge-based economy. Beyond Britain the empire also harnessed many of the economic forces and institutional structures through which large areas of Asia and Africa and the Americas were initially introduced or finally incorporated into the international economic systems of the age. Imperial networks often operated in conjunction with other elements in the creation of global connections. They always acted as part of a larger whole but often with a distinctive flavor and role.

Colonization. In the seventeenth century and the early eighteenth century, the economic activities that connected

Britain to the world beyond Europe were largely concerned with colonization and the development of plantations in the New World and with trading activities there and elsewhere to obtain luxury consumer goods to supply European markets—tea, spices, and textiles from Asia; sugar from the Caribbean; and tobacco and furs from continental North America. This "empire of adventures" was developed by private agents, many of whom held licenses from the crown to limit competition. Notably the British East India Company, which excluded all other forms of direct trade between England and Asia and looked to the state's military power to support its endeavors.

This form of imperialism was intended to strengthen England against European rivals, such as Holland, France, and Spain, and to cement its control within the British archipelago. Mercantilist calculations about the costs of such activity, notably the effects of Asian textile imports in draining silver and undermining domestic employment, led to a ban on imports of pure cotton cloth to prevent competition with the linen and silk industries. The benefits of the Atlantic trade were maximized through the Navigation Acts, which required trade between the home country and its colonies to be conducted in domestic shipping. This provided a strong motive for the Scottish parliament's decision to accept union with England in 1707. In Asia the superior power of the established Mughal and Qing Empires confined the East India Company to a few licensed trading posts, but in the Caribbean and North America agricultural land was settled using a model, first applied in Ireland, that displaced the indigenous population. The opportunities of colonization attracted those on the moral or political fringes of domestic society and economic migrants from the Celtic hinterland. In the Atlantic economy, where political and environmental conditions permitted, staple agricultural exports were produced by the slave labor of Africans transplanted to the Caribbean and the American South.

The web of economic connections that tied Britain to the rims of the Atlantic and Indian Oceans in the mid-eighteenth century were converted into large-scale territorial empire by the overspill of European warfare, especially among Britain, France, and their allies in North America and South Asia. The result was British dominance over other European powers in North America and the rise of the East India Company to the status of a formal territorial power. The process of overseas conquest that began during the Seven Years' War of 1756–1763 (the French and Indian War) rumbled on intermittently for the next few decades, culminating in the major Asian wars of the Napoleonic period (1800–1815) that left Britain the only significant European power in Asia, ruling through conquest over an extensively militarized colony. At home these events strengthened the control over the company of new forces in the military-fiscal state that were determined to secure the largest benefits for Britain from Asian trade. The American Revolution of 1776 and the transformation of Britain's North American colonies into the independent United States caused significant economic disruption to the Atlantic trades in the short-term. Subsequently the main links were reestablished, and the American merchant marine expanded to fill the gap left by the defeated maritime powers of continental Europe.

The decades of war and territorial expansion after 1750 saw the development of a distinctive "empire of enterprise" in Britain and overseas based on merchant networks, armed shipping, and a determined exploitation of connections to the state. These activities had two main foci—lumber, sugar, specie, and slaves in the Atlantic and textiles, tea, and opium in the Indian Ocean—trades that predated the British Industrial Revolution. They were concerned with satisfying consumer tastes in Europe and with capturing and expanding existing trade routes for British merchants and shipowners. Direct exports from Britain played a relatively small part in this imperial economy. There were also private profits to be made in the exercise of public power in the eighteenth-century empire, especially by the servants of the East India Company in India and its military officers and by Jamaican planters. Contemporaries often commented on the vast wealth that could be made in such exotic activities and attacked its corrupting effects on British society by giving parvenus access to land and political influence. Many historians have considered a further connection between the wealth transferred from the Caribbean and Asia after 1750 and the onset of the Industrial Revolution in Britain, but it has proved impossible to find a smoking gun that demonstrates any causal link convincingly. In general the volume of investment in British industry was much larger than any estimates of colonial transfers, while the destination of colonial wealth, where it can be traced, was largely in purchases of land or gentrified consumption. Colonial demand in the Atlantic slave plantations was important for some sectors of the early textile industry, but Indian producers dominated export markets for cotton cloth across the world until the 1790s. However, the financial and material resources that Britons could call on from overseas increased domestic economic activity.

Industrialization. The development of industrial production in Britain in the last decades of the eighteenth century began a significant change in the pattern of imperial economic activity, masked at first by the disruptions to trade caused by the Napoleonic Wars. By 1800 British cotton manufacturers could undercut Indian cloth in the British market even without the benefit of the high tariffs on Indian goods, and they achieved global dominance once political and military restrictions on international trade came to an end in 1815. The exclusive trading privileges of the East India Company were severely limited in 1813 and finally were abolished in 1833. By the 1830s imperial trade had developed into a conventional pattern of raw material supply from the periphery complementing industrial production in the core. Such trade was not confined within political boundaries. Cotton from the American South provided Lancashire with the raw material to make its world-beating products in the first half of the nineteenth century, and American and Argentinean wheat and meat and the products of Canada, Australia, and New Zealand fed the British urban population after the abolition in 1846 of the Corn Laws, removing the excise on imported grain. British industrialists now saw the world as their source of raw materials and the market for their products, while British investors expected to send their capital (at some risk) to fund potentially productive overseas enterprises. This was the "imperialism of free trade" that sought to remove local barriers to the free flow of goods and capital (by the judicious use of force if necessary) and enable all the world to participate in Britain's civilizing mission to propagate industrial production and consumption fueled by extensive capital investment.

The moral fervor that accompanied the emergence of industrial capitalism provided the justification for military action to prevent the Chinese government from molesting British traders in opium. That fervor launched campaigns that led to a ban on British participation in the slave trade in 1807 and the abolition of slavery in the British Empire in 1833, despite damage to some established interests. The "imperialism of free trade" did not depend on formal rule but preferred informal influence where possible. At the height of its imperial reach the British economy traded and invested more with other developed economies in continental Europe and North America than it did with its colonial dependencies in Asia and Africa.

The nature of the economy of the British Empire in the mid-nineteenth century can best be understood by recognizing an essential division between the colonies of settlement in temperate lands and the colonies of conquest in the tropical zones. In Canada, Australia, New Zealand, and the Cape Colony in South Africa (and outside the empire in the southern cone of Latin America), British exports of goods, capital, and labor helped develop lands where European technologies could easily be applied to local conditions. Temperate colonies were distinguished by the transplanting of European settlers, with European agricultural techniques and social organization, into "empty lands," or lands that could be emptied of their indigenous inhabitants quite easily. The expansion of the agricultural frontier in these regions provided raw materials for British industry and markets for British goods and capital. Growth

rates in such settler economies were often remarkable. By the end of the nineteenth century colonists in Australia, New Zealand, and Argentina enjoyed some of the highest per capita incomes in the world.

By contrast the acquisition and exploitation of the colonies of conquest in tropical regions, such as the Caribbean and South and Southeast Asia, were marked by social or political violence (slavery and warfare) and took place without extensive European settlement. Investment was much lower there, although India did provide a crucial market for the Lancashire cotton industry. For ecological reasons European technologies could not be transferred there easily, and exports depended on systems of production and labor relations that had no European equivalent. Colonial regimes were concerned with maintaining social stability rather than prosecuting economic development. To most contemporaries it seemed that the lack of sustained economic growth in tropical regions could best be explained by cultural factors, often linked to social Darwinist notions of racial differentiation and hierarchy. Some radical opinions in Britain and nationalist economists in India argued instead that the wealth of Britain and the poverty of India were connected by colonial mechanisms of extraction and exploitation. However, historians have found it hard to identify and quantify a debilitating drain of wealth from the colonies to the metropolis. Where economic stagnation occurred in the periphery, as in much of India under the Victorian raj, it had more to do with the weaknesses of the institutional structures of colonial regimes and their obsession with protecting local social structures, notably communitarian peasant agriculture, from the forces of international capitalism. British colonial regimes adopted the paternalist role of a night watchman state concerned with low taxation, balanced budgets, and conserving the apparent cultural distinctiveness (and therefore the inferiority) of Asian and African economies.

Internationalism. Britain ceased to be the only industrial nation in the second half of the nineteenth century. The industries of the northern industrial cities became increasingly dependent on exports to the semi-industrial economies of Asia and Latin America, but the large and successful financial services sector based in London and southeast England maintained national wealth. This division of economic activity between north and south was noted by some contemporaries and has been expanded and developed as a major explanatory tool by historians, who stress that the strength of the service sector, especially in overseas finance and investments, meant that British imperial economic policy was dominated by the interests of "gentlemanly capitalism" based around the City of London rather than the industrial capitalism of the great staple industries.

The late nineteenth century was an imperial age during which the boundaries of the British and other European empires expanded considerably, especially during the scramble for Africa that led to the division of most of the continent between the European powers between 1880 and 1900. However, as many historians have pointed out, these newly colonized territories (with the possible exception of the gold fields of Transvaal, for which the second South African War was fought in 1899–1902) were not central to the performance of the British economy. The long-established areas of imperial control and influence remained more significant for trade and investment, especially the Indian subcontinent and the colonies of settlement in Canada and Australasia plus other areas of European settlement in Latin America. All in all the British imperial economy (like the rest of western Europe) was still largely internationalized in 1913. This feature, by contrast with the much more nationalistic and competitive attitude of the 1920s and 1930s, gave the late Victorian period and the Edwardian period the retrospective aura of a golden age.

By 1914, if not before, the age of the "imperialism of free trade" was over. Increased economic difficulties and international rivalries after 1900 had led some influential commentators, both in Britain and in the major settler colonies (now widely known as dominions), to consider that closer imperial ties might solve domestic problems of economic growth and employment and might buttress support for sterling in an increasingly large and potentially unstable international financial system. The outbreak of World War I strengthened the appeal of an imperial "economics of siege" and led to close economic cooperation between Britain and its dominions and colonies. Internationalism briefly resurfaced with sterling's return to the gold standard at the prewar parity in 1925, but the problems this decision caused for British exporters and the onset of the Great Depression in 1929, which culminated in sterling leaving the gold standard again in 1931, led to the attempt to create a distinct imperial economy based on tariffs, quotas, and capital controls at the Imperial Economic Conference in Ottawa in August 1932.

The 1930s were a decade of explicit international economic rivalry, often expressed in imperial terms. Yet what the Ottawa Conference revealed was that the notion of a closed British imperial economy defied economic logic. The British economy needed larger markets for exports than the dominions could provide. They in turn were not prepared to sacrifice their domestic industries to British interests, and they also required larger markets for their exports than Britain could supply. Countries outside the empire that had received British capital investments needed access to the British market to repay their loans, while sterling could be defended more effectively by attracting European flight capital than by relying on the unstable and shrinking currency reserves of the imperial territories. In India, by far the largest economy in the dependent empire, political considerations meant the interests of British manufacturers had to be overruled in shaping economic policy. Perhaps the most serious effect of the rhetoric of British imperial collaboration of the 1930s was not economic but political. It convinced powerful outsiders, notably in the United States, Germany, Italy, and Japan, that the British Empire was the foundation of British economic power in the world and would have to be dismantled before their own ambitions of hegemony could be realized.

The imperial economics of siege surfaced again, in a much more serious form, during and after World War II, when Britain seemed to face the prospect of starvation and bankruptcy if it could not make extensive use of its imperial economic assets. In particular the problems of reconstruction after 1945 required Britain to use the dollar earnings of its West African and Southeast Asian colonies to pay for the consumer and capital goods essential to its future survival. A partially closed and tightly controlled imperial economic bloc was created around the sterling area in the late 1940s, but such short-term cooperation had to be paid for. To make the colonies work for Britain, they had to be developed, and the cost of such development fundamentally altered the political relations between the rulers and the ruled. The colonial states that had survived by isolating their subjects from the world in the name of paternalism could not change tack without a large measure of local support. Such support was not forthcoming as Britain's colonial subjects decided that political independence was their price for any future economic collaboration, and they subsequently showed little gratitude for the empire's contribution to their economic history.

Once the immediate problems of reconstruction in Britain eased in the early 1950s, economic relations with the empire were reassessed more skeptically. In the aftermath of the Suez crisis of 1956, the British government undertook an explicit cost-benefit analysis that showed that imperial commitments were a drain on Britain's resources and that preferential access to imperial markets was inhibiting the necessary modernization of the domestic economy. Decolonization followed rapidly, and empire was transmuted into commonwealth. The devaluation of sterling in 1967 fatally damaged its role as a reserve currency, and Britain's admission to the European Economic Community in 1973 completed the process of dissolving the institutional links that had bound the empire together as a distinctive economic unit. While Britain contracted its economic profile to that of a middle-ranking European power, its former colonies and dominions opened new links to the wider world through regional pacts, alliances with the superpowers, and negotiations with international agencies.

The British Empire was the largest the world has known, and the literature about it is equally wide-ranging, covering a variety of approaches and methodologies that use different conceptual tools, theoretical assumptions, and levels of empirical information. There is no simple story to be untangled nor any single lesson to be learned from the economic history of the British Empire. Instead, it represents a large laboratory in which a series of experiments to investigate the interaction between different institutions, societies, and cultures can be conducted and contested. These provide essential tools to understanding the relationship between the exercise of political, social, and cultural power and processes of economic growth and change across much of the modern and contemporary world.

BIBLIOGRAPHY

Armitage, David. *The Ideological Origins of the British Empire*. Cambridge, 2000. Contains an important analysis of political economy approaches to the imperial project in the seventeenth century within and beyond the British archipelago.

Cain, Peter, and Tony Hopkins. *British Imperialism, 1688–2000*. 2d ed. London, 2001. A wide-ranging account of the economic history of British imperialism based on a sustained analysis of the role of "gentlemanly capitalism" in the City of London.

Furber, Holden. *Rival Empires of Trade in the Orient, 1600–1800*. Minneapolis, 1975. An exposition of the vitality and variety of Asian trade in the seventeenth and eighteenth centuries and an explanation for the eventually dominant position of British merchant networks.

Gallagher, John, and Ronald Robinson. "The Imperialism of Free Trade." *Economic History Review* 6 (1953), 1–15. The starting point for many later discussions of the relationship between British imperialism and the international economic system in the nineteenth century.

Hancock, David. *Citizens of the World: London Merchants and the Integration of the British Atlantic Community, 1735–85*. Cambridge, 1995. A study of the creation of London-based merchant networks across the Atlantic world.

Hancock, W. K. *Survey of British Commonwealth Affairs*, vol. 2, *Problems of Economic Policy, 1918–1939*, pt 1. London, 1942. A convincing contemporary analysis of the impossibility of constructing a viable imperial economy in the 1930s that coined the phrase "economics of siege."

Havinden, Michael, and David Meredith. *Colonialism and Development: Britain and Its Tropical Colonies, 1850–1960*. London, 1993. A useful statistical compendium of colonial economic relationships.

Louis, William Roger, et al., eds. *The Oxford History of the British Empire*. 5 vols. Oxford, 1998. A multivolume, multiauthored compendium that provides an enormously rich quarry of information, interpretation, and analysis about all aspects of the history of the British Empire.

O'Brien, P. K. "The Costs and Benefits of British Imperialism, 1846–1914." *Past and Present* 120 (1988), 163–200. A careful and skeptical analysis of the impact of empire on the Victorian economy.

Williams, Eric. *Capitalism and Slavery*. London, 1944. The classic Marxist analysis of the economic benefits to Britain of the slave trade, setting out the "Williams thesis" that the profits of slavery fueled the Industrial Revolution and that the abolition of slavery owed more to material interest than moral fervor.

B. R. TOMLINSON

Modern Period

In the middle of the eighteenth century, Britain was a prosperous economy with income levels on a par with countries such as France and Belgium but about 20 percent below those of the European leaders, the Dutch. By 1851, after a century of sustained economic growth, Britain had become the "workshop of the world," the leading economic and political power in an increasingly global economy, in which British manufactures, carried in British ships and financed by British capital, and dominated international trade. Income levels exceeded those in the Netherlands by 20 percent and those in France and Germany by double this amount, and the structure of the British economy was uniquely "modern," with half the population living in an urban setting and almost half of all men employed in manufacturing.

However, this economic primacy was short-lived. As early as the 1880s British manufacturers lost market share to competitors based in the United States and Germany, and although Britain was still the largest exporter of manufactured goods in 1937, it was losing both its economic and its political preeminence. The cost of sustaining mass mobilization of resources during World War I (1914–1918) and even more so during World War II (1939–1945) forced a massive decumulation of overseas assets and a redirection of productive effort from exports to armaments. By 1951, when the country emerged from postwar rationing and austerity, the economy was characterized by a heavy burden of war debts and a depleted physical capital stock. Income levels were 36 percent higher than in France and 70 percent above those in war-ravaged Germany, but they were only two-thirds the level in the United States, which was now the dominant force in the international economy.

Britain's political influence was also waning. Rapid postwar decolonization unraveled the ties of empire, while in Europe, Britain remained aloof from the European Economic Community formed by the Treaty of Rome in 1957. Many commentators considered the second half of the twentieth century a period of economic decline. Productivity growth was sluggish in Britain, and Germany, France, and eventually Italy exceeded British levels of income per capita. It was also a period of substantial structural change as services replaced manufacturing as the most important sector of the economy in terms of both employment and value added. By the end of the century Britain once again had an economy not dissimilar to that of its European neighbors in structure and income levels. It was still a "big" economy in global terms and a member of the G7 group of leading industrial economies, but it was no longer the dominant economic and political power it had been for the century between the end of the war against Napoleon in 1815 and the beginning of World War I in 1914.

1760–1851. There were few indicators in the middle of the eighteenth century that Britain (a political entity forged in 1707 by the union of Scotland with England and Wales), with a population of around 7 million people, just one-third that of France and half that of Germany, would achieve economic and political success out of all proportion to its size. Over the period 1700–1760 income per capita grew slowly, at about 0.3 percent per annum, and the majority of Britons carried out their daily toil on the land or in small-scale rural-based manufacturing in ways that appeared little different from those of their forebears. The structure of life was dominated by the seasons, the pace of life by the speed at which a person and a horse could move. Innovation and development in economic activity, when it occurred at all, did so on a small scale or in a localized manner.

In 1761 Britain's first canal opened, linking the city of Manchester with nearby coal mines. It was indicative of the primitive structure of financial markets and the considerable economic and political power of the landed aristocracy that this pioneering infrastructure development was conceived and financed by the owner of the mines, the duke of Bridgewater. Three years later James Hargreaves invented a machine, the spinning jenny, that used rotating spindles to twist cotton fiber into yarn, thereby allowing one worker to spin multiple threads at the same time. But in the 1760s cotton was a small industry. It accounted for less than 2 percent of value added in British industry and coal just 4 percent, compared to over 30 percent in woolens, and 20 percent in leather goods. These traditional manufacturing sectors were characterized much more by continuity of structure and process than by innovation or change.

One aspect of British society that was changing, and changing rapidly, was its demographic structure, although this was barely perceived by contemporaries, who until the first national census in 1801 had few means by which to study the size and distribution of the population. In the second half of the seventeenth century the intrinsic growth rate of the English population was close to zero, but a sustained positive growth rate, reaching a peak of 1.75 percent per annum in 1821, led to a threefold rise in overall numbers between 1680 and 1840, by which time the British population numbered 18.5 million. This rate of population growth was far faster than in any other European country, and it was exceptional not just for its speed but also for its character.

Population growth was accompanied by rapid urbanization. London was the dominant city in England, containing half a million people in 1800, double the population it had in 1700. But in 1800 the next largest cities—Manchester with eighty-nine thousand and Liverpool with eighty-three thousand inhabitants—had expanded more than tenfold over the previous century with the growth of the manufacturing base of the Lancashire economy.

Meanwhile Norwich, England's second city in 1700 with thirty thousand inhabitants, slipped to tenth place by 1800, having added just six thousand people to its total. Scotland also experienced rapid urbanization, coming second only to England and Wales in 1850 in a ranking of European countries by degree of urbanization. Glasgow, the center of the Scottish manufacturing industry, reached over half a million people by 1870 and staked its claim as the "second city of the empire" after London.

A necessary consequence of urbanization was a steady decline in the share of the workforce residing in rural areas and working in agriculture. The total agricultural workforce remained roughly constant at 1.5 million over the entire 1700–1850 period (though with some compositional changes as adult males took jobs from female and child workers). Yet over this period output grew substantially—corn and wool by a factor of three, meat by a factor of four. By the 1840s each agricultural worker's output was capable of feeding approximately 2.7 nonagricultural workers, compared with only 1 nonagricultural worker in the 1760s.

Most other European countries struggled to achieve even half the level of agricultural labor productivity that Britain had achieved by the mid-nineteenth century. The causes of this significant and sustained rise in agricultural output and productivity remain disputed. A long-established interpretation, recently given renewed vigor by Overton (1996), emphasizes the positive effect of eighteenth-century changes in land tenure, specifically the conversion of open fields, in which each tenant farmer tilled a multitude of small, widely dispersed strips of land, into consolidated or enclosed fields. By contrast, Allen (1992) points to a process of mutually reinforcing improvements in seed quality, agricultural machinery (especially more efficient plow), animal husbandry, use of fertilizers and soil improvers, and farm management.

Whatever the cause, the rise in agricultural productivity enabled Britain to feed its growing population and avoid endemic food crises. Although Britain imported between one-fifth and one-sixth by value of all food consumed in the period 1800–1850, these imports were heavily skewed toward the high-value "luxury" supplies of tea, coffee, sugar, and spices. Most of the calories and protein consumed in Britain were produced domestically.

Despite Britain's absolute advantage in the production of agricultural goods, its rise to global economic dominance rested on the performance of the manufacturing sector. The Great Exhibition, held in London in 1851 to celebrate and promote Britain's economic and political achievements, emphasized not the progress made in raising grain yields but rather the achievements of British industry—the cotton cloth made in Lancashire, the woolen cloth from Yorkshire, and the engines and other machines manufactured in Birmingham. At this date over 60 percent of cotton output, 25 percent of woolen output, and almost 40 percent of iron output were sold abroad.

Much of this manufactured output, around two-fifths, was sold to countries in the British Empire, with the remainder divided roughly equally between Europe on the one hand and North America on the other. These empire markets had grown rapidly in economic significance since the 1770s, when they accounted for no more than 8 percent of manufactured exports. Although the net contribution of the empire to the British economy in the nineteenth century is difficult to determine (the naval and military expenditure required to expand and defend imperial possessions was considerable), it seems clear that demand from empire countries for British manufactures assisted the expansion of domestic industry.

The scale of this domestic industry was what made Britain seem so different, so modern to contemporary observers. Although many regions remained primarily agricultural, manufactured modernity had spread throughout the country in the form of the railway, which between the 1830s and 1851 developed into a network of over six thousand miles of track carrying an annual total of more than 73 million passengers (including many of the 6.2 million visitors to the Great Exhibition). The railway seemed to epitomize an economic and technological transformation that amounted to nothing less than an Industrial Revolution (a term that entered the historian's lexicon after its use by the radical historian Arnold Toynbee in the 1880s).

The development of machinery to perform tasks previously done by hand and the use of nonanimal power to drive this machinery (first waterpower and then steam engines fueled by coal, especially after James Watt's invention of the separate condenser in 1765) served not only to increase productivity but also, in stages, to transform the social relations of production. Steam-powered machinery was scarcely affected by the cycle of the seasons; mechanized production could be maintained at a steady level throughout the year. To recoup the high capital cost of investment, employers chose to operate their new machinery over extended working days, and to keep labor costs down they chose to employ many female and child workers, especially in the Lancashire cotton industry, where job tasks were often repetitive and menial.

Recent research has revealed that the physical demands placed on manual workers increased substantially in Britain between 1750 and 1830 as the average number of hours worked per year rose by something over 20 percent. Yet these extra hours were not readily translated into higher living standards. The latest consensus in a long-running historical debate on the standard of living in the industrial revolution is that real wages for manual workers in the

ENGLAND. Workers at the East Pool Mine, Cornwall, England. (The Fotomas Index, U.K.)

middle of the nineteenth century were no more than 30 percent above the level in 1780. The welfare of many people was severely compromised by the degraded environmental conditions in the rapidly expanding industrial cities. In 1841, life expectancy at birth stood at a national average of 41.7 years, but it was only 25.7 in Liverpool and 25.3 in Manchester.

Can the evidence on the slow growth of real incomes be reconciled with the idea of revolutionary transformation in the economy? Crafts's (1985) careful revisions of earlier estimates of rapid economywide growth indicate that national income per capita grew at only 0.17 percent per annum in 1760–1800 and 0.52 percent per annum in 1800–1830. Not until midcentury did growth rates touch 2 percent per annum. There was rapid growth and real structural transformation in some industrial sectors and in some parts of the country, but large parts of the economy—building, food processing, retail, and domestic service—were little touched by the productive possibilities of new technology. There was no sudden "take off" into self-sustained growth, and the famous industrial inventors were of rather less economic significance than the generations of lowly mechanics who gradually adapted new ideas to the needs of practical producers.

1851–1951. Britain's wealth relative to other European countries in 1851 was in part a consequence of early industrialization, but as noted above the economy's growth rate over the preceding century had not been particularly high. However, the economic performance of many European countries had been significantly retarded by internal and external conflicts. Revolution in France followed by Napoleon's hugely expensive wars that led to the annexation of parts of the Netherlands, Germany, Italy, and Switzerland and the invasion of Spain and Russia left the French state close to bankrupt and put a brake on economic development across a large swath of continental Europe for more than two decades.

In Britain, by contrast, sound public finance, secure property rights, and swift action to curtail minor protests from workers adversely affected by mechanization together created the conditions for long-term investment and growth. GDP grew at around 2.2 percent per annum from midcentury to 1873, and then at a more modest rate of 1.8 percent up to the eve of World War I, before returning to a rate of 2.2 percent per annum over the period 1924–1937. Britain's manufacturing sector dominated world trade and in the 1880s accounted for 43 percent of global manufactured exports—more than France, Germany, and the United States combined. Yet these impressive figures tell only part of the story. Although Britain's growth performance over this period was good relative to that achieved during the classic Industrial Revolution, it was modest relative to other industrializing countries.

For example, over the period 1899–1913 the rate of growth of GDP per man-year (that is, standardized for variations in the relative size of the workforce) in the United States, Sweden, France, Germany, Italy, and Japan exceeded that in the United Kingdom by between 0.8 and 2.0 percent per annum. Britain remained the richest European country to 1939, but GDP per capita in the United States overtook British levels before the end of the nineteenth century.

As early as the 1880s there was public discussion of (and a parliamentary enquiry into) the reasons for Britain's apparent loss of market position to overseas competitors. At the time a major complaint of British manufacturers was that their products were discriminated against in many markets because of the imposition of import tariffs by overseas governments. This, however, was not true of exports to the British Empire, which from the middle of the nineteenth century operated as a free-trade zone in which the British currency—sterling—served as a common unit of settlement.

A more recent historical critique of British economic performance in the late nineteenth century identified a lack of entrepreneurial vigor among British businesspeople as the reason for loss of market share (Wiener, 1981). This line of argument is part of a long-standing "declinist" literature that seeks the origins of Britain's relatively poor economic performance in the twentieth century in deeply rooted cultural and political practices. However, since the 1970s a number of careful quantitative studies of British manufacturing in the period 1870–1914 have revealed little evidence of entrepreneurial failure. British businesspeople did just about as well as they could in an increasingly competitive international market. The United States forged ahead in the income race on the back of an enormously favorable endowment of natural resources, and European countries advanced more quickly than Britain largely because they were catching up after a slow start in the years before 1850.

Throughout the period to 1939 the manufacturing sector was at the core of the economy, and textiles were at the core of manufacturing. In 1890 the textiles and clothing sector, which was dominated by cotton goods, accounted for over half of all employment in manufacturing and over 40 percent by value of all exports (down from over 60 percent in 1850). Metals and machinery accounted for a quarter of manufacturing workers, a share that was to rise steadily to reach almost half by 1951 as textiles went into decline after World War I. Yet in the century from 1851 to 1951 the overall share of the labor force in manufacturing barely changed, hovering around one-third of the total, while in agriculture it fell from 22 to 5 percent. Meanwhile employment in trade and transport rose from 15 to 21 percent, and in public and professional services it rose from 7 to 21 percent.

This shows that the economy, though still dominated by industry, was rapidly developing a strong service sector. Rising money wages and, from the 1870s, a decline in food prices because of cheap imports from the New World created new consumer opportunities and ushered in a retailing revolution marked by the development of department and chain stores, branded goods, and national advertising campaigns. Professional and financial services also expanded, particularly as the City of London became the undisputed center of international finance and commerce. In the period from 1850 to 1914 Britain made massive overseas investments to both empire and other countries with the result that overseas assets increased from 7 to 32 percent of total national wealth.

Not everyone benefited from this economic growth. Although the population continued to grow to reach 37 million by 1901 and almost 49 million by 1951, life expectancy at birth was stagnant at around forty-one years until the 1870s. Thereafter substantial municipal infrastructure

GREAT BRITAIN. Thousands of striking ship repair workers hold a rally in London, 1957. (*New York World-Telegram* and the *Sun* Newspaper Photograph Collection/Prints and Photographs Division, Library of Congress)

investment in water supplies and sanitation improved conditions of life in urban areas, leading to a long-run rise in life expectancy to sixty-eight years by 1951. Even so the poor living conditions of many workers induced a surge of social inquiry, including the world's first poverty survey, conducted in London in 1889, and ultimately led to a wave of welfare reforms in the early twentieth century, including old age pensions (1908) and national sickness and unemployment insurance (1911).

Both social reform and economic growth were put on hold for World War I, during which up to 60 percent of the industrial workforce was engaged in war production. But the greatest impact came later, when after a short postwar boom the "staple" export industries of textiles, shipbuilding, and coal mining suffered a devastating decline in overseas demand. This fall in demand resulted from a combination of war-induced loss of markets to overseas suppliers, a general decline in world commodity trade (exacerbated by the global economic depression from 1929), and the overvaluation of sterling as the government made moves to return to the same dollar exchange rate as had existed in 1914. The annual number of unemployed workers exceeded 1 million throughout the period 1921–1938, touching a peak of 2.8 million in 1932.

For workers in the staple industries, which were concentrated in South Wales, northern England, and southern Scotland, the unemployment rate exceeded 30 percent. But the unemployment shock of the early 1930s was less severe in Britain than in most other industrialized countries, and recovery, driven by a domestic building and consumption boom, was more rapid. A robust banking system and a swift decision by the government in 1931 to let the exchange rate fall to a more realistic level preserved internal and external financial stability. But this devaluation of sterling together with the introduction in 1932 of a general tariff, which ended an almost century-long commitment to free trade, signaled the fragility both of sterling as an international reserve currency and of the empire as an open trading bloc. Both of these were clear indicators that Britain's international economic preeminence was waning.

World War II marked a watershed for the British economy. The market mechanism was replaced by central planning as all national resources were directed toward the war effort. Strict rationing of food and consumer goods led to the share of consumption in national income falling from 79 percent in 1938 to just 52 percent in 1943. Imports declined by 30 percent, but exports fell faster and by 1943 were at only 29 percent of their 1938 volume. This led to a massive balance of payments deficit that was covered by sale of overseas assets, additional overseas borrowing, and most importantly extensive grants (lend-lease aid) from the United States. The need to repay these grants after the war was a major burden that significantly constrained the economic options faced by postwar governments (even though only 3 percent of the total was eventually repaid).

At the end of the war, with large overseas debts and minimal foreign exchange reserves, the government was forced to continue with rationing and production controls in order to restrain domestic demand and boost export earnings. A severe coal shortage in 1947 together with a failed attempt to make sterling convertible to other currencies demonstrated the internal and external weakness of the economy. Not until 1948, with the help of $2.7 million of Marshall aid, did Britain begin to turn the corner from austerity to growth.

1951–2000. The fifty years from 1951 witnessed sustained economic growth and rising incomes. By the end of the century average real incomes were between three and four times their levels at the end of World War II, and the standard of living had reached unsurpassed levels. Life expectancy at birth had risen to seventy-six years for men and eighty for women, and Britons owned more consumer durables, took more holidays, and paid for these with larger amounts of consumer credit than ever before. But this palpable economic success occurred despite a further loss of position in the international league tables.

Over the period 1950–1973 the British economy grew at an average of 2.4 percent per annum, compared with 4 percent in France and 5 percent in Germany. By the mid-1970s Britain's slow growth, high inflation, lagging labor productivity, and poor industrial relations earned it the epithet "sick man of Europe" (a Europe grudgingly acknowledged as economically more important than links with the ex-colonies when Britain belatedly joined the European Union in 1973).

However, in the last quarter of the twentieth century, when growth across the European economies was much slower, at around 2 percent per annum, Britain outperformed France and Germany and managed to stop or even marginally reverse a relative decline that had been a characteristic of British economic performance for the preceding one hundred years. The reasons for the poor economic performance until the 1970s and the good performance thereafter are not yet fully understood. For some authors the government is to blame. Government expenditure as a

proportion of national income was little more than 10 percent over the period 1851–1914, with defense and interest on the public debt (accumulated during periods of war) claiming the lion's share.

In the interwar period public expenditure accounted for around 25 percent of GDP, with social expenditure now the largest single item. But by 1951, even after the major postwar controls over production had been lifted, government expenditure accounted for 37 percent of GDP, rising to almost 46 percent in 1979, by which time the public sector, which now included a comprehensive tax-funded public welfare and health service, employed 28 percent of the working population.

Postwar governments were influenced by Keynesian ideas about macroeconomic management and were characterized by a willingness to tolerate inefficient production practices in industry in order to attain short-run export targets. According to this view, a regime change in 1979, in which a right wing (Conservative) government withdrew public support from inefficient manufacturing industry, led to improved incentives and a better competitive environment. This was achieved at the cost of more than 3 million jobs in the manufacturing sector, which declined from 29 to 17 percent of the workforce in the twenty years after 1979. Others argue that the performance of the economy in the 1950s and 1960s was in fact not too bad and that the faster growth of continental European economies was a consequence of their catch-up after wartime devastation. If there were problems in the economy, these were more likely to result from complacent management than government interference or worker militancy.

Regardless of the reasons for the pace and course of Britain's economic development in the post–World War II period, the result was that by 2000, Britain was an averagely prosperous and averagely productive member state of the European Union, with a similar economic structure—in terms of a dominant service sector—to that of its European neighbors. None of this is surprising given Britain's position as a small, densely populated island off the northwest coast of the European mainland. What is surprising is that this small country achieved, for a period of about a hundred years, from the end of the Napoleonic Wars to the beginning of World War I unrivaled domination of global manufacturing, finance, trade, and politics.

BIBLIOGRAPHY

Allen, Robert C. *Enclosure and the Yeoman*. Oxford, 1992.

Broadberry, Stephen N. *The Productivity Race*. Cambridge, 1997.

Clarke, Peter and Clive Trebilcock, eds. *Understanding Decline: Perceptions and Realities of British Economic Performance*. Cambridge, 1997.

Crafts, Nicholas F. R. *British Economic Growth during the Industrial Revolution*. Oxford, 1985.

Crafts, Nicholas F. R. *Britain's Relative Economic Decline, 1870–1999*. London, 2002.

Edgerton, David. *Science, Technology, and British Industrial "Decline," 1870-1970.* Cambridge, 1996.

Matthews, Robin. C. O., Charles. H. Feinstein and John C. Odling-Smee. *British Economic Growth, 1856–1973.* Cambridge, 1982.

Middleton, Robin. *Government versus the Market.* Cheltenham, U.K., 1996.

Overton, Mark. *Agricultural Revolution in England.* Cambridge, 1996.

Wiener, Martin. J. *English Culture and the Decline of the Industrial Spirit.* Cambridge, 1981.

PAUL JOHNSON

GREAT DEPRESSION. The Great Depression of the 1930s was the largest peacetime economic catastrophe in history. There had been hard times before, but never without war, natural disaster, or pestilence. The massive and long-lasting unemployment and hardship of the 1930s was a pathology of industrial society, caused by the malfunctioning of the economic system.

This essay first describes the magnitude and duration of the Great Depression. It then recounts the story of the Great Depression as we now understand it and compares this story with others about this massive contraction. A few thoughts on the recovery from and the legacy of the depression conclude.

Magnitude of the Great Depression. Figure 1 shows the fall in industrial production during the Great Depression in the four largest national economies. Industrial production fell the most in the United States and Germany, almost in half. By contrast, industrial production paused rather than fell in Great Britain. National income did not fall as far as did industrial production since services did not contract as much, but it did fall. (Real per-capita GNP in the United States fell by one-third, for example.) Nation-

al experiences in the depression varied greatly, but very few countries in the world escaped the economic hardship of the 1930s.

Figure 2 shows the fall in wholesale prices for the same four countries. Prices fell at the same time as production, by the same amounts or more. Unemployment grew dramatically in almost all countries. Rates for the four largest economies are shown in Table 1. Only in Great Britain were unemployment rates even approximately as high in the 1930s as in the 1920s, and that is true largely because unemployment had been so widespread in the 1920s in Great Britain. Other countries for which we have data fit the more common pattern of rising unemployment, not the British one of more stable unemployment.

Unemployment meant distress in the 1930s, most visible in Europe and North America. Diets in Europe became very monotonous despite the presence of home-grown vegetables in some areas. Families ate meat only rarely, starches were the basis of most diets, and sugar frequently was replaced by cheaper saccharine. Even this poor diet consumed almost all of family income. Families with children bought milk, most families bought coal for heat, but there was little money left over for clothes and other expenses. Shoes in particular were a problem. Families typically could not afford to replace shoes that had worn out, and so they were patched and patched again. Some families even restricted the activities of their children to save the wear and tear on their shoes.

While spending centered around food, and food became reduced to bread and coffee, movement became confined to local neighborhoods and villages. Trips to towns and town centers had been increasing during the 1920s, to go to the theater, to do Christmas shopping, or to attend

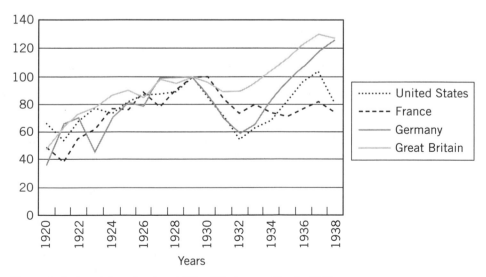

FIGURE 1. Industrial production, 1929 = 100. SOURCE: Temin, 1989

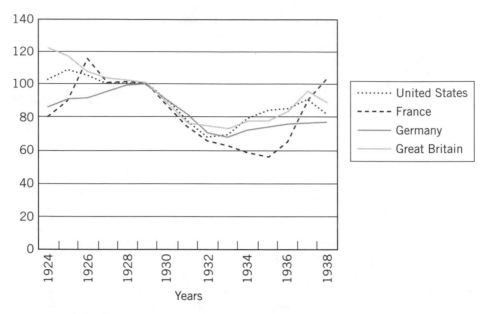

FIGURE 2. Wholesale Prices, 1929 = 100. SOURCE: Temin, 1989

school. But unemployment, the money to undertake these journeys vanished. Even tram and train fare became a burden, and people relied more heavily on their bicycles. The isolation of rural villages, reduced by the railroad and prosperity after the World War I, reappeared during the depression.

Politics, like other leisure activities, could have benefited from the increased availability of time. But this advantage was heavily outweighed by an increase of apathy that reduced all forms of recreational activity. People stopped reading newspapers; they must have stopped discussing newspaper stories and columns with their friends and neighbors. Library usage also declined. Card playing became a popular way to pass the time.

Unemployed men were exceedingly idle. They passed their time doing essentially nothing. They could not even recall much of any activity during the day when asked. They sat around the house, went for walks—walking slowly—or played cards and chess. Most men went to bed

TABLE 1. *Industrial Unemployment Rates*

COUNTRY	1921–1929	1930–1938	RATIO
France	3.8	10.2	2.7
Germany	9.2	21.8	2.4
Great Britain	12.0	15.4	1.3
United States	7.9	26.1	3.3

SOURCE: Eichengreen and Hatton, 1988.

early; there simply was no reason to stay awake. Women were far more active. They spent time cooking, mending clothes to make them last longer, and managing their budgets. The men contributed less to the running of the household than before, sometimes not even turning up on time for meals, and the women had the full responsibility. Even though women previously had a hard time completing their housework after their day jobs, they uniformly would have preferred being back at their jobs. Observing sociologists classified most European unemployed families as resigned to their condition. They were hanging on, preserving as much of their life and family as they could on their meager budgets. All their activity was dedicated to subsistence; no thought was given to the future. Some families still planned as before, but others collapsed entirely in mental and physical neglect and conflict.

Story of the Great Depression. The first question about this contraction is whether the shocks that produced the Great Depression were demand or supply shocks. The simultaneous fall in production and prices suggests strongly that the shocks were demand shocks, that the economies of the world were moving down along their upward-sloping aggregate supply curves in response to downward shifts of aggregate demand curves. The apathetic reaction to unemployment in the Great Depression confirms the hypothesis that the depression was due to a demand shock. Had it been due to a supply shock, these families would have been unemployed by choice, happy for their extra leisure. The psychological depression also put great strains on the social structure, and even the political structure in some countries. It was in environments such as these that the noxious weed of National Socialism (Nazism) could flourish.

A second question about the Great Depression is how so many countries could have had negative demand shocks at the same time. The answer is that all of these countries were adopting deflationary policies according to the dictates of the gold standard. The gold standard was characterized by the free flow of gold between individuals and countries, the maintenance of fixed values of national currencies in terms of gold and therefore each other, and the absence of an international coordinating or lending organization like the International Monetary Fund. Under these conditions, the adjustment mechanism for a deficit country was deflation rather than devaluation—that is, a change in domestic prices instead of a change in the exchange rate. Lowering prices and possibly production as well would reduce imports and increase exports, improving the balance of trade and attracting gold or foreign exchange. (This is the price-specie-flow mechanism first outlined by Hume in 1752.)

A recession began at the end of the 1920s in the United States and Germany. Both countries began to contract; that is, business activity decreased, at least partly as a result of central-bank pressure. The initial downturns appear to be independent, but the economies were connected, and it is hard to reach definite conclusions. In any case, gold-standard policies turned the downturn into the Great Depression and pulled the rest of the world down. The choice of deflation over devaluation was the most important factor determining the depth of the Great Depression. The choice was seen clearly and supported by contemporaries. Policymakers in all industrial countries insisted that the way out of depression was to cut wages and thereby the costs of production, the proper path to macroeconomic balance.

Governments and central banks could not easily deflate their economies in the aftermath of World War I, however. Workers, who had borne the burdens of international stability mutely in the past, expected and even demanded a voice in policy after their sacrifices during the war. The inability of economic policymakers to force wages down rapidly created the conditions for the Great Depression. The political strains generated by attempts to lower wages caused investors to fear for the stability of the gold standard even as policymakers struggled to maintain it. One reason the gold standard had worked well before World War I was that labor had no voice.

Another question that economists ask about the Great Depression is why the fall in demand was not absorbed entirely by falling prices. In other words, why did not prices fall more and production less than shown in Figures 1 and 2? The relative stability of wages caused production and employment to fall; falling prices and wages did not absorb the full brunt of the fall in demand. Those countries in which real wages were the highest in the mid-1930s suffered the most during the depression.

The narrative of the Great Depression begins with World War I, which altered the economic positions of countries in several ways. It brought new agricultural areas into production and redrew national boundaries, disrupting trading patterns. It transformed the capital position of nations as Great Britain sold its foreign assets and the United States loaned resources to Great Britain and France. It complicated domestic policymaking by enfranchising workers, and it poisoned the networks of international cooperation that had existed before. But while World War I and its acrimonious aftermath set the stage for the depression, they did not make it inevitable. Many adjustments were needed in the world economy, but only poor policies translated these problems into depression, into a "hard landing."

The downturn that became the Great Depression began at the end of the 1920s with contractionary policies in the United States and Germany. The United States had accumulated vast reserves of gold in the 1920s; it was in no danger of running out. The United States bore no penalty for its accumulation; it incurred no obligation to recycle its reserves. The asymmetric gold standard did not restrict the United States in the 1920s. Instead, the gold standard affected the Federal Reserve System and the U.S. administration's attitudes toward policy, and it determined the way in which actions in the United States affected other countries.

Federal Reserve policy turned contractionary at the start of 1928 to combat speculation in the New York stock market and to arrest a gold outflow started in part by previous financial ease. The gold outflow was a prominent determinant of the policy change, even though it was tiny relative to the U.S. reserves. The Federal Reserve's primary aim in 1928 and 1929 was to curb speculation on the stock exchange while not depressing the economy. It failed on both counts. Even though this policy did not impede stock-market speculation, it reduced the rate of growth of monetary aggregates and caused the price level to turn down. The monetary stringency was even tighter than it seems in terms of the aggregate stock of money, because the demand for money to effect stock-market transactions rose, leaving less for other activities.

The German economy was heavily dependent on imported capital in the 1920s. Popular history regards the capital imports as a necessary offset to Germany's outflow of war reparations payments; they were needed to solve the "transfer problem." The reality was quite different. Germany managed to avoid paying reparations by a variety of economic and political maneuvers that succeeded in

GREAT DEPRESSION. Breadline at the McCauley Water Street Mission under the Brooklyn Bridge, New York, 1930s. (Prints and Photographs Division, Library of Congress)

postponing its obligations until they could be repudiated entirely. The capital inflow therefore represented a net increase in the resources available to the German economy. The Reichsbank paradoxically worried that this capital inflow was unhealthy and acted to curtail it, sharply reducing the amount of credit available on the German market at the end of the 1920s. The capital flow from the United States to Germany ceased at the end of the 1920s, but the downturn in Germany preceded this fall and derived from German economic policies.

Great Britain, in contrast with the United States and Germany, was suffering under deflationary policies that can be traced directly to the gold standard. Having resumed gold payments at the prewar exchange rate in 1925, Great Britain was obliged to reduce domestic economic activity to sustain it. Lacking the prewar income from foreign investments, Great Britain found it hard to pay for its imports when demand was high. The Bank of England then had to raise bank rate (the Bank of England's discount rate) to attract short-term capital and retain its gold reserves. Montagu Norman, governor of the Bank of England, believed that the impact of a high bank rate was "more psychological than real" and the cost of tight money to Great Britain consequently was small. His view was tragically flawed. It subordinated care for the domestic market to maintenance of the gold standard, and it led to continuing unemployment and civil strife acute enough to produce a general strike in 1926.

At its inception, therefore, the Great Depression was transmitted internationally by a gold-standard ideology, a mentality that decreed that external balance was primary and that speculation like the booming stock market in New York was dangerous. The effect of the gold standard at this point was largely psychological, but—*pace* Norman—no less real for that. As the American, British, and German economies contracted, they depressed other economies through the mechanism of the gold standard. These countries reduced their imports as they contracted, reducing exports from other countries. They also reduced their capital exports or increased their capital imports in response to the tight credit conditions at the end of the 1920s.

The effects of fixed exchange rates can be seen in a comparison of Figures 1 and 2. Figure 1 shows the decline in industrial production in four major countries. Although they all decline, the rates differ. Figure 2 shows the decline in prices in the same four countries. The rate of deflation is strikingly similar. The fixed exchange rates of the gold standard led to uniform changes in prices even though other factors affected the change in production. This observation is extended to many more countries in Table 2. Using data from 21 countries on the gold standard, the correlation between price changes is seen to be stronger than the correlation between production changes in 1930–1932. The standard deviation of price changes is smaller than the standard deviation of changes in the industrial production index in all three years, although the standard deviation of both series rose in 1932 as some countries abandoned gold. The final row of Table 2 shows the standard deviations in 1932 for seven countries that stayed on gold in 1931. Even though data for these countries are indistinguishable from the rest of the sample for 1930 and 1931, they are far more uniform in 1932.

No country on the gold standard, however large, could escape the discipline of this harsh regime in the depression. Some countries found their prices falling as a result of the lack of demand for their products in the industrialized world. Others forced prices to fall to maintain the value of their currency. In almost all cases, deflation was accompanied by depression as declining aggregate demand moved countries down upward-sloping aggregate supply curves. Banking systems in many gold-standard countries collapsed under this deflationary pressure, further reducing economic activity. The Federal Reserve sharply raised the U.S. discount rate in October 1931 in response to a threatened outflow of gold, even though the U.S. economy was contracting rapidly and had massive gold reserves. The primary transmission channel of the Great Depression was the gold standard.

It follows that abandoning the gold standard was the only way to arrest the economic decline. Going off gold severed the connection between the balance of payments and the domestic price level. Countries could lower interest rates or expand production without precipitating a currency crisis. Changes in the exchange rate rather than in domestic prices could eliminate differences between the level of domestic and foreign demand without a painful deflation. Any single devaluation could beggar neighbors under some conditions, but universal devaluation would have increased the value of world gold reserves and allowed worldwide economic expansion.

Great Britain abandoned the gold standard in September 1931 after a speculative attack on the pound. The attack was prompted by bad budgetary news and by contagion from the German currency crisis of July 1931. The Bank of England was unwilling to raise bank rate in the face of Great Britain's domestic economic troubles, and it devalued the pound instead. Great Britain and the countries that followed Great Britain off gold were not large enough that their actions could have arrested the world decline, and they were criticized at the time for abandoning gold. But the world would have been far better off if others had followed their lead.

Even in the United States, with its vast economic resources and gold reserves, going off gold was a necessary prerequisite to economic expansion. Great Britain avoided the worst of the Great Depression, as shown in Figure 1, by going off gold in 1931. Spain avoided the depression by never being on the gold standard; Japan, by a massive devaluation in 1932. At the other extreme, the members of the gold bloc led by France endured contractions that lasted into 1935 and 1936. The single best severity predictor of the depression in different countries is the length of time they stayed on gold. The gold standard was a Midas touch that paralyzed the world economy.

Other Factors. The influence of the gold standard determined the spread and the depth of the Great Depression, but the story has other and competing dimensions. But where the literature is contentious, the apparently competing views may be elements in a more comprehensive view.

Structural imbalances. The traditional explanation for the depth and persistence of the widespread postwar difficulties is the problem of structural imbalance within and between countries. The origins of this dislocation are found in the changes in the composition of production and demand resulting from the wartime disruption of international trade, from the geopolitical effects of the Peace Treaty, and from postwar changes in technology and in patterns of demand.

Although the effects of these changes are not always clear, they may be taken to relate particularly to a misallocation of resources, which was responsible for the high rate of unemployment in Europe in the 1920s, and which also made the adjustment process longer and more costly. These structural changes affected both labor and product markets, in each of which, it is argued, there was appreciably less flexibility after 1918.

Mistakes by the Federal Reserve. A different view of the Great Depression depicts it as a U.S. contraction that was transmitted to the rest of the world. Friedman and Schwartz (1963) argued that the Federal Reserve system in the United States acted with such ineptness that it plunged the world into depression. They attributed this incompetence to the death of Benjamin Strong, president of the Fed in New York, in 1928, and they described several alternative monetary policies that they argued would have eased or even eliminated the economic contraction.

TABLE 2. *Standard Deviation of Changes in 21 Gold-Standard Countries*

YEAR	PRICES	INDUSTRIAL PRODUCTION
1930	0.037	0.081
1931	0.055	0.078
1932	0.090	0.123
1932*	0.035	0.039

SOURCE: Temin, 1993.
* Seven countries still on gold in 1932.

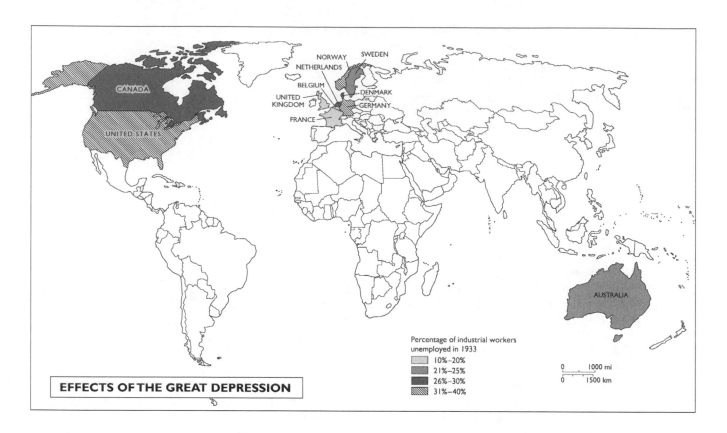

Percentage of industrial workers
unemployed in 1933

- 10%–20%
- 21%–25%
- 26%–30%
- 31%–40%

0   1000 mi
0   1500 km

EFFECTS OF THE GREAT DEPRESSION

Even their story cannot separate the United States from the rest of the world, however. The Fed raised interest rates in October 1931 to defend the dollar, as noted above, even though the economy was contracting. Friedman and Schwartz characterized this action as an inept mistake, but they acknowledged the power of the gold standard to unite the financial community behind this perverse policy. This contractionary policy in the midst of rapid economic decline was the classic central-bank reaction to a gold-standard crisis.

Lack of leadership. Another explanation, put forward by Kindleberger (1973), is the lack of central bank leadership in the operation of the restored gold standard, the proposition summed up in the phrase "no longer London, not yet Washington." The diminished financial status of Great Britain meant that London was unable to act as sole conductor of the international orchestra—or, in more modern terminology, to operate as the "hegemon"—while the United States was not yet willing to take over this role despite the enormous improvement in its international economic standing.

The ability of London to perform its traditional role as the dominant economic power was undermined further by the enhanced strength of France's relative financial position after the stabilization of the franc in 1926 and the large accumulation of gold by the Bank of France. The spe-

cific economic connotation of this lack of leadership was that no country was able and willing to stabilize the global financial environment by acting as international lender-of-last-resort.

Absence of international cooperation. Another factor put forward as the primary explanation for the problems of the interwar period is the absence of international cooperation between the United States, Great Britain, France, and Germany, and the failure of the major nations to coordinate international economic policy. Barry Eichengreen identified this behavior as a central feature of the entire period in 1992, manifest particularly in the attempt of each of the main powers to secure for itself a disproportionate share of the world's limited stocks of monetary gold. Prior to the collapse of the gold standard in 1931, their noncooperative behavior involved the imposition of tight monetary policies not only by countries in deficit, but also by those—notably the United States and France—that were in surplus. This added to the deflationary pressures on the world economy and also increased the vulnerability of the weak currencies, such as the pound and the mark, to speculative attack.

The main reason for this tendency to neutralize changes in gold and foreign exchange reserves, rather than allow them to influence internal monetary conditions, was that postwar governments were no longer willing to give unconditional support to external equilibrium and the defense of the reserves. Democratic electorates increasingly required that governments and central banks should attach greater weight to internal stability of prices and incomes. The inability of the powers to cooperate was dramatically symbolized at the World Monetary Conference in the summer of 1933, meeting in London shortly after the United States had abandoned the gold standard and allowed the dollar to depreciate. The gathering had been convened specifically to promote the coordinated stabilization of exchange rates, but in the middle of the proceedings President Roosevelt brusquely announced that he was unwilling to stabilize the dollar. This disastrous meeting starkly exposed the total lack of any common ground between countries and hastened the further disintegration of the international monetary system. With global political relations deteriorating rapidly, the decade witnessed an epidemic of competitive currency depreciation; extended resort to exchange controls, the rise of protectionism, bilateralism, import quotas, and other barriers to trade; and the development of hostile, noncooperating trade and currency blocs.

Old-fashioned political and financial ideologies. The final factor emphasized in the literature is the hold on policymakers of old-fashioned political and financial ideologies. The former are seen as responsible for the insistence on substantial reparations. This produced a new pattern of international settlements that made the smooth functioning of international payments dependent upon the capability and willingness of the United States to continue lending indefinitely to Europe. Still more important was the financial ideology reflected in the priority attached to the reintroduction of the gold standard, even where this could only be achieved by subjecting the economy to severe deflation and obstructing future trade by imposing an overvalued currency.

Under the discipline that this doctrine enjoined—or the values it projected—country after country surrendered its "monetary sovereignty" and restricted its ability to accommodate balance of payments disturbances by any means other than retrenchment. The consequences became apparent in the early 1930s when the constraints of the gold standard prevented countries from initiating policies to alleviate economic distress and even induced some countries to pursue policies that intensified the economic decline.

Recovery and Reflection. Elements of these various problems in international economic relations are evident throughout the period of the Great Depression. The dislocating effect of World War I has dominated descriptions of the preconditions for the depression in the 1920s. The lack of central-bank leadership has been invoked to account for the developments of the late 1920s. The inability of the

major nations to cooperate in coordinating international economic policy is given as a crucial factor underlying both the disintegration of the attempt to reconstruct the pre-1914 gold standard and the emergence of rival trade and currency blocs in the depths of the depression. Financial ideology and the acceptance of the gold standard were important in the propagation of financial crises, particularly the critical crises of 1931.

The world began to recover from the contraction in 1933, when the United States and Germany both abandoned the policies of the gold standard, but the Great Depression was far from over. Unemployment continued high in most countries, as indicated in Table 1. The world economy split up into competing currency and trading blocks. And domestic policies to combat the hardships of depression changed the role of government.

Unemployment continued high in most countries throughout the 1930s. Measures designed to help workers often perpetuated unemployment. The National Industrial Recovery Act of 1933 in the United States attempted to bring order to industries and income to workers by allowing industries to enforce codes of conduct that raised both prices and wages. Rising wages impeded the extension of employment, trading off the benefits to the unemployed for benefits to those working.

Unemployment policies in Great Britain were limited during the 1920s by fears that government spending would "crowd out" private investment. Once Great Britain went off gold, macroeconomic policy became the main tool to combat unemployment. Bank rate was lowered in stages from 6 percent in September 1931 to 2 percent in June 1932, and remained at that low level until the outbreak of war in August 1939. Long-term interest rates followed bank rate down after the collapse of the Labour government and the formation of a coalition dominated by the Conservatives. Cheap money for industry and for housing was the principal element in the government's policy for the remainder of the decade and the means by which it hoped to encourage economic recovery and industrial restructuring.

Monetary policy was neutral or expansive as well in Sweden, and unemployment fell after 1933. Germany under the Nazis expanded government spending and, apparently, decreased unemployment dramatically. The speed of the Nazi recovery is not known with any accuracy because faithful Nazis replaced civil servants in unemployment agencies. France and other members of the gold bloc continued to maintain contractional policies in an effort to retain convertability of their currencies into gold. Only when France devalued in 1936 could recovery begin.

But the recovery, however slow and halting, was not approaching the *status quo ante*. The world economy fragmented in the 1930s, and recovery took place within relatively isolated currency and trading blocks. The United States began the process of reducing world trade with the Hawley-Smoot Tariff Bill of 1930. Great Britain abandoned its tradition of free trade in 1932 in favor of protection for the British Commonwealth. Germany under the Nazis adopted a complex set of bilateral trading arrangements that reoriented its trade toward southeastern Europe. International trade was much reduced, and international capital flows virtually disappeared.

Countries were changed internally as well. Governments became active in the economy as they attempted to reduce unemployment or to ease the condition of the unemployed. Unions grew, helped both by legislation and by unemployment. Regulation grew as governments substituted direct controls for those of the market. And the world war that followed the Great Depression caused governments to take control even more firmly of their economies. The mixed economies and large governments that were typical of the last half of the twentieth century were the legacy of the Great Depression and its aftermath.

It is not possible to separate the effects of the depression from those of the Nazis and World War II, but it is possible to ask if the Great Depression could have been avoided. There were indeed stresses on the world economy at the end of the 1920s, and the mechanisms used in earlier times were not in good shape. The downturns in the United States and Germany would have produced a serious recession in the early 1930s in any case. But the currency crises of 1931 turned this recession into the Great Depression. If Germany and the United States had abandoned gold that fall after Great Britain chose devaluation over further contraction, the world economy would have begun to recover two years earlier and before unbearable strain had been put on economic and political institutions. Historians today debate how much freedom policymakers had in 1931. The German cabinet discussed devaluation after Great Britain left gold, but the memory of hyperinflation less than a decade before inhibited—if it did not preclude—an expansionary policy like devaluation. The United States was not under the same economic pressure as Germany, but the Federal Reserve nonetheless raised interest rates sharply in late 1931 in response to gold outflows following Great Britain's devaluation. The Fed was following the dictates of the gold standard in actions that were applauded by the local financial community. Under what circumstances would the Weimar government in Germany have been able to follow Great Britain off gold in 1931? Under what circumstances would the Fed have been able to agree with the Bank of England that the economic distress of 1931 should not be increased by the effort to preserve the gold standard?

[See also Business Cycles; Financial Panics and Crashers; and New Deal.]

BIBLIOGRAPHY

Balderston, Theo. *The Origins and Course of the German Economic Crisis*. Berlin, 1993.

Bernanke, Ben. "Nonmonetary Effects of the Financial Crisis on the Propagation of the Great Depression." *American Economic Review* 73.3 (1983), 257–276.

Bernanke, Ben. "The Macroeconomics of the Great Depression: A Comparative Approach." *Journal of Money, Credit and Banking* 27.1 (1995), 1–28.

Bernanke, Ben, and Harold James. "The Gold Standard, Deflation, and Financial Crisis in the Great Depression: An International Comparison." In *Financial Markets and Financial Crises*, edited by R. G. Hubbard, pp. 33–68. Chicago, 1991.

Borchardt, Knut. *Perspectives on Modern German Economic History and Policy*. Cambridge, 1991.

Bordo, Michael, Claudia Goldin, and Eugene N. White. *The Defining Moment: The Great Depression and the American Economy in the Twentieth Century*. Chicago, 1998.

Calomiris, Charles W. "Financial Factors in the Great Depression." *Journal of Economic Perspectives* 7.2 (1993), 61–85.

Choudhri, Ehsan U., and Levis A. Kochin. "The Exchange Rate and the International Transmission of Business Cycle Disturbances: Some Evidence from the Great Depression." *Journal of Money, Credit, and Banking* 12.4 (1980), 565–574.

Dow, Christopher. *Major Recessions: Britain and the World, 1920–1995*. Oxford, 1998.

Eichengreen, Barry. *Golden Fetters: The Gold Standard and the Great Depression*. New York, 1992.

Eichengreen, Barry, and Jeffrey Sachs. "Exchange Rates and Economic Recovery in the 1930s." *Journal of Economic History* 12.4 (1985), 925–946.

Eichengreen, Barry, and Peter Temin. "The Gold Standard and the Great Depression." *Contemporary European History* 9.2 (2000), 183–207.

Eichengreen, Barry, and Timothy J. Halton. *Inter-War Unemployment in International Perspective*. Dordrecht, 1988.

Feinstein, Charles H., Peter Temin, and Gianni Toniolo. *The European Economy between the Wars*. Oxford, 1997.

Friedman, Milton, and Anna Schwartz. *A Monetary History of the United States, 1867–1960*. Princeton, 1963.

Hamilton, James D. "The Role of the Gold Standard in Propagating the Great Depression." *Contemporary Policy Issues* 6.2 (1988), 67–89.

Hume, David. "On the Balance of Trade." In *Essays*, vol. 1. London, 1898.

James, Harold. *The German Slump: Politics and Economics, 1924–1936*. Oxford, 1986.

Kindleberger, Charles. *The World in Depression*. London, 1973.

Margo, Robert A. "Employment and Unemployment in the 1930s." *Journal of Economic Perspectives* 7.2 (1993), 41–59.

Mouré, Kenneth. *Managing the Franc Poincaré: Economic Understanding and Political Constraint in French Monetary Policy, 1928–1936*. Cambridge, 1991.

Romer, Christina D. "The Great Crash and the Onset of the Great Depression." *Quarterly Journal of Economics* 105.3 (1990) 597–624.

Romer, Christina D. "The Nation in Depression." *Journal of Economic Perspectives* 7.2 (1993), 19–39.

Temin, Peter. *Lessons from the Great Depression*. Cambridge Mass., 1989.

Temin, Peter. "Transmission of the Great Depression." *Journal of Economic Perspectives* 7.2 (1993), 87–102.

Wheelock, David C. *The Strategy and Consistency of Federal Reserve Monetary Policy, 1924–33*. Cambridge, 1991.

PETER TEMIN

GREECE [*This entry contains three subentries, on the economic history of Greece during the classical period and earlier, the Byzantine and Ottoman periods, and the modern period.*]

Classical Period and Earlier

The ancient Greeks were emphatically an agrarian people. In all periods they were dependent on their own production or acquisition of the "Mediterranean triad": grains, grapes, and olives. After 800 BCE, nearly all citizens who resided in any city owned property beyond its walls. Nearly all agricultural production was undertaken by individuals; there was little collaborative production. The state took no part in production although in the case of Athens the state frequently made policy that might shape production patterns, or found itself in the food-allocation (import) process. The climate of Greece is and was like the rest of the Mediterranean, with cool, wet winters and hot, dry summers. Unlike much of the Mediterranean, however, the microenvironments of the Greek peninsula in all of its history have suffered from extreme interannual variability in rainfall. So severe were these fluctuations that individuals and then communities were forced to learn to reciprocate with one another, yet also to learn to embrace autarchy, undoubtedly the most outstanding characteristic of the Greek polis. Yet this fierce self-sufficiency was tempered by a necessary understanding that individuals were less important than the collective, an attribute that helps one to understand many ancient Greek behaviors, especially economic ones.

The field of ancient economic history has long been one of spirited debate between primitivists and modernists, between substantivists and formalists. There are, of course, many positions on the spectrum between these extremes. In recent years the dominant, essentially substantivist school of M. I. Finley has seen its influence wane or at least become modified. His position is still the starting point for most analysis and will be the default position for much of what follows.

Finally, in what follows it should become clear that the role of women in the economic history of Greece was relatively small. Historians learn every year that the role of women in Greek communities was greater and more complex than previously thought, but there is still little change in the understanding of their role in the economy. In most city-states, including Athens, nonelite women worked outside the home, in the markets mostly. Elites stayed at home. Side by side, female slaves and family members generated textiles for use in the home and occasionally for sale outside. The elite wife seems often to have controlled the purse strings of the household and thus gained economic power within that household. The ability of women to own property (narrowly by inheritance) varied from city to city, nearly always with restrictions that encouraged transfer of property to male family members.

Bronze Age Greece (to c. 1100 BCE). Having developed on the Balkan peninsula in the shadow of the dominant culture of the Minoans, based on the island of Crete, the Greeks first achieved regional prominence shortly after 1600 BCE. Their major centers were located at Athens, Mycenae, Pylos, and Tiryns. By about 1500 BCE, the Greeks had taken over from the Minoans, and Knossos on Crete became Greek as well. The palace economies of the Minoans and the Mycenaeans, the name given to all the Greeks of the Bronze Age, were in their essentials indistinguishable from the temple economies of contemporary Asia. They were highly redistributive, highly hierarchical, and in some areas highly specialized.

In fact, the only history of the Mycenaeans that can be made is an economic one, for the documents of this civilization are restricted to inscriptions on clay tablets that articulate the movements of goods and services from peripheral areas into centers and the distributions of materials and labor out to the periphery from the centers. The documents were written in Greek, in a script called Linear B (the Minoans kept track of their affairs similarly, using Linear A to communicate in a non-Greek language). These goods and services traveled on a complex of built roads that criss-crossed southern Greece, connecting the centers to each other but also to their respective hinterlands.

The economic centers were focused on great palaces, which served simultaneously as elite residences and vast warehouses. The tablets indicate that outlying towns sent in some portion of their agricultural and pastoral production. Mineral ores and lumber also came in, often in specific ratios between or among commodities. The palaces collected these goods and in return provided services and raw materials. Hundreds of persons lived in or near the palaces; the archaeological record has not been generous with the secondary settlements. There is virtually no wealth locatable away from the central storage palaces.

A look at Pylos in southwestern Greece may reveal a coherent picture. The tablets there reflect interest in several types of information:

1. Agricultural and pastoral production. These are the tribute lists mentioned above.
2. Personnel lists. These are lists of individual and group work assignments. One tablet indicates the assignment and equipping of manpower in anticipation of a military attack, whose consequent conflagration was very likely the reason why the clay tablet has survived.
3. Land ownership and use. These tablets illustrate the enormous range of land usages. Historians are not yet close to sorting through all of this but can conclude that

there was a very wide range of usages, from ownership to leasing to usufruct.

4. Raw materials and other goods. Also collected at Pylos and subsequently dispersed were articles of furniture, but also unworked and worked bronze and precious metals, which were perhaps sent out to officers of the state who had the authority to distribute them to specialty shops. Other specialty labor appears to include perfumers, jewelers, brewers, and potters.

Contacts with foreign civilizations were numerous. The Mycenaeans were engaged in trade with the high civilizations of Egyptians to the south and Assyrians to the east; and probably were known to the Hittites of central Anatolia. They also engaged in exchange with less developed groups as far west as the Iberian peninsula, as well as up and down the Italian peninsula and the eastern Adriatic coast.

Dark Age and Archaic Period (c. 1100–479 BCE). The Bronze Age civilization of the Mycenaeans came to an end rather abruptly. As noted, the existence of Linear B records was due to the destruction by fire of the rooms in which they had just been made; this happened in the thirteenth century BCE (Knossos was destroyed slightly earlier). Lost also by 1200 BCE was Linear B itself—hence, no more record keeping. In the wake of the demise of the last of the centers around 1200 BCE, the population was subsequently reduced by as much as 80 percent over the following 150 years. The cause of the collapse of the Mycenaean world is not certain; but the stagnation that ensued from 1050 BCE on was mostly continuous and ubiquitous for the following 250 years. Large-scale redistribution was an institution of the past.

The centers were gone as political and economic magnets, and power devolved to the secondary settlements. Reciprocity replaced redistribution for the most part, and most settlements were very small and self-sufficient. There was little need any longer for the Mycenaean road system. The most successful model for the Dark Age has been the chiefdom. Lefkandi on the large island of Euboea and Kommos on central Crete are the only sites in the Aegean area that show even occasional contact with outsiders between 1050 and 850 BCE. Greeks stayed at home, and few outsiders visited.

Iron arrived at the beginning of the Dark Age, but historians cannot yet be certain if it played any role in that upheaval. It is fairly certain that iron had an important role to play in the end of the Dark Age.

Shortly after 850 BCE, the face of Greece began to change. Greeks from the island of Euboea entered into cooperative ventures with Phoenicians, which become rather elaborate by 800 BCE. In the west before 800 BCE, there were Euboeans and Phoenicians living at Pithekoussai, an island just off the coast of Naples. This was appar-

ently at first a secure spot from which to negotiate acquisition of iron from mines controlled by the indigenous Etruscans north of what would later be Rome and off the coast. Eventually, Pithekoussai became a processing center for iron and then a more diverse settlement, to be virtually abandoned after 750 BCE when these Greeks, feeling more secure, moved the focus of the operation to the mainland at Cumae. At this time, this was the westernmost limit of Greek actions overseas. (The Phoenicians, by contrast, were trading farther west, even to the Atlantic coast of Iberia.)

The eastern limit of this early Greek trading was the port of al Mina at the mouth of the Orontes river (the modern Asi) in what is now Syria. Al Mina was a port of trade, like Tyre in southeastern Anatolia (as reported by the prophet Ezekiel), where Greeks did not live, but where they came to exchange what they had in their ships for new cargoes. Historians do not even know, in fact, if they were bringing in iron or bringing it out—or, indeed, neither—but do know that they were there, again with Phoenicians. The poet Homer, composing his *Iliad* and *Odyssey* in the latter half of the eighth century BCE, tends to avoid references to trade and markets; but he nevertheless reveals that in his world there were slave markets, wine merchants, and metal movers in the Mediterranean. The poet Hesiod, composing about 700 BCE, seems to be aware either of ports of trade or of one-time markets to which he and his neighbors might bring their surplus production.

All this outside activity was going on coincident with a large population increase beginning in about 825 BCE and spiking between 780 and 720 BCE. This increase was accompanied by increased stratification; and, with the wealth from external trade, the result was pressure both to produce new political forms at home and to export extra persons by way of colonies. Writing was reinvented at this very time from a Semitic (Phoenician) source; as of 1997 CE, the earliest Greek writing known is from Gabii, 25 kilometers east of Rome, dating to at least 770 BCE perhaps earlier. Thus writing appears to have been a by-product of the Greek and Phoenician ventures stretching east to west.

At home, Greeks invented the polis, or city-state, which in most cases eventually would control the economies within which individuals and their families organized their lives and livelihoods. The *oikos* ("household") was the smallest economic as well as political unit in ancient Greece—and, of course, one half of the etymology of *oikonomia*, meaning management of the *oikos* ("economy"). Hesiod describes his *oikos* in *Works and Days*, and most scholars believe that his holding was a typical one from about 700 BCE until well into the third century if not later. It is worth dwelling on.

Hesiod's farm comprised six to ten hectares (fifteen to twenty-five acres), whereas later farms averaged about six hectares (15 acres); and it was inhabited by Hesiod and six to eleven others, some of them family, some slaves, some permanent workers, and some only temporary. There is vigorous debate over whether farms after 500 BCE were dependent on slave labor. Hesiod depended heavily on his immediate neighbors and, to some extent and reluctantly, on the nearest polis. He preferred to bring his surplus to market at places different from his own polis, which, if that were a typical situation repeated often throughout Greece, would indicate the supreme difficulty the Greek city-states must have faced in their own economic development, as the incremental advantage of town over fields apparently was very difficult to garner.

The increase in population, along with the Greek tradition of partible inheritance (property division equally among sons), led to degraded parcels for many Greeks; this in turn led to a massive colonization movement in the latter half of the eighth century BCE, as Greeks moved west to Sicily and to southern Italy. The colonization movement was initiated by the earliest Euboean Greeks, but many city-states participated. The leading colonizing state was Corinth, which by 700 BCE dominated the trade in the great sweep west to east to become the leading trading state among the Greeks through the sixth century. The seventh century BCE witnessed a second colonizing movement, this time to the north coast of the Aegean and into the shores of the Black Sea. In both Sicily and the Black Sea, this exported labor came to provide important sources of grain for Greece, and the Black Sea also provided metals, timber, and slaves. The seventh century BCE also saw the development of two major Greek ports of trade: Massalia (Marseille) was founded west of Italy in about 600 BCE by Phocaean Greeks, near the mouth of the Rhone, which was used to reach exchange opportunities with the Hallstatt and La Tene cultures in the interior; Naucratis was founded by Greeks of great ethnic variety, on the mouth of the Nile, before 610 BCE. Naucratis acted as a gateway to the wealth of Egypt, which eventually became an important source of grains for Greece and later Rome, nearly all of it traveling through Naucratis. All these commodities were moved by enormous merchantmen, a new form of ship. (Before this time the fifty-oared *pentekontor* was the dominant ship form, used for both warfare and trading.) By 600 BCE, the economic world of the Greeks extended geographically from the Rhone west of Marseilles to the shores of the Black Sea and to the coasts of the Levant and of Africa, from the Nile nearly to Tripoli.

That the land in the colonies was emphatically inalienable has led many scholars to believe that, with the advent of the polis, land became alienable for the first time, perhaps through accumulation of debt in the form of liens against property. There is no certainty about the effect of such debts everywhere, but they are known to have had an exceptionally deleterious result in Athens by the sixth century BCE, as in 594 BCE (the traditional date; some would put it twenty years later) the Athenians empowered Solon (died c. 560 BCE) to restructure political and economic relations in Athens. Solon, whose reforms were protected for ten years while he traveled abroad, instituted a *seisachtheia* ("shaking off of burdens"), which was probably most importantly the liberation of the *hektemoroi* ("sixth-parters"), who owed one-sixth of their production to large landowners. The legislation also freed those enslaved by debt and forbade enslavement for debt in the future. Further, Solon undertook certain actions, such as forbidding export of agricultural production except olive oil and promoting the cultivation of olives, that encouraged Athenians to think less in terms of self-sufficiency and more in terms of external trading. Solon divided the male population into four economic classes (which were also political divisions since more offices were available to the higher classes): *pentakosiomedimnoi* ("500-measure men," a reference to annual grain production or its equivalent), *hippeis* ("knights," at 300–500 measures per year), *zeugites* ("yoke men," by far the most numerous class, at 200–300 measures per year), and *thetes* ("laborers").

The unrest that Solon and his fellow aristocrats were attempting to avoid soon led to the ascendancy of Pisistratus (died 527 BCE) and others into tyranny from about 561 until 510 BCE, during which time Athens invested in great public works projects. Instituting a new 5 percent tax on incomes and drawing on his own family's holdings in Thrace, Pisistratus began ambitious public works projects that led to the initial monumentalization of Athens as well as the creation of new types of labor opportunities for Athenians and their dependents. In addition to construction, scholars know of at least one pottery factory, run by Nikosthenes, that appears to have responded to specific demand for particular black-figure painted pottery in northwest Italy, where the products have been found.

Classical Period (c. 479–323 BCE). After 490 BCE, the fortification of the Piraeus port southwest of Athens led to greater trading activity and an increase in tax collections there that enriched the city-state of Athens. After 483 BCE, discovery and exploitation of new lodes in the vast silver mines at Laureion, south of Athens, also fed the Athenian treasury amply. However, the most important contribution to Athens's federal cash flow was income from the Delian League, a defensive alliance against the Persians, who had invaded Greece in 490 and 480/479 BCE. By the 450s BCE, the Delian League had become an Athenian empire, and payments to the league made up probably at least 50 percent of Athenian federal income for many decades. This massive influx of cash paid both for the majority of the vast Athenian navy as well as the vast majority of the Athenian building program of the fifth century BCE, most of it on the Acropolis and undertaken by Pericles, the leading citizen of Athens from 461 BCE until his death in 429 BCE. Xenophon (c. 430–354 BCE) reported the cash outlays of the Athenian government to be about one thousand talents per year. There was no federal budget *per se*; for different councils controlled different incomes and let out contracts for different sorts of services, construction, and so on. That said, in many years during this time, the income and outlays of the Athenians may have resembled the distribution shown in Table 1.

Some words are needed about liturgies (*leitourgiai*, "works for the people"), which were not unique to Athens but are best documented there. There were two types of liturgy, the trierarchy and liturgies associated with festivals. The trierarchy involved the funding by private individuals of a ship for the navy for a year; the best known festival liturgy was the *choregia*, the payment for a chorus at one of the tragic or comedic theater competitions. Eligibility for liturgy began when personal worth reached three or four talents, and individuals were expected to provide a liturgy every two (festival) or three years (trierarchy). The cost of a trierarchy was perhaps about five thousand drachmas, or about one-quarter of the minimum qualifying wealth of a *pentakosiomedimnos*. Many citizens contributed more frequently and generously than was required, which of course brought greater prestige to their families.

From the evident determination of class divisions by agricultural production, one can see that the perception of wealth was based rather narrowly on land and its production. Other sources of a citizens's income were investments in external trade and in financial dealings, such as loans and mortgages. Internal commercial trade in most city-states and perhaps especially at Athens was undertaken by metics (resident aliens), whose status varied greatly. Metics in Athens were laborers and merchants but were subject to a tax per household and enjoyed no citizen rights or privileges. Athenians who wished to earn money to purchase property to move up a class frequently took their families to other states to earn the needed cash there as

metics since they were apparently discouraged from earning it commercially at home.

The Greeks were not the inventors of coinage. Coinage arose first in Lydia in western Anatolia about 600 BCE and spread rapidly westward into Greece. It became common at Athens by the second half of the sixth century BCE, and after the stepped-up exploitation of the mines at Laureion beginning in 483 BCE, Athenian coins became the dominant ones in circulation throughout the Greek world into the second century BCE. The Athenian "owl," the silver tetradrachm (four-drachma piece) with obverse Athena in helmet and reverse owl, was ubiquitous. There were eight *chalkoi* ("bronzers") to an obol (*obolos*, derived from *obelos*, "spit"), the smallest everyday unit; six obols made up a *drachma* ("handful"), one hundred of which made up a mina (*mna*), of which sixty equaled a talent (*talanton*).

Until recently there was a common assumption that a day's wage in Athens was perennially one drachma, regardless of the nature or the prestige of the work undertaken, and thus strong evidence of the embedded nature of the Athenian economy. However, recent scrutiny indicates that there were substantial wage fluctuations over time and within job types, coincident, usually, with price fluctuations. Workers on the Erechtheum temple on the Acropolis between 409 and 407 BCE, be they citizens, metics, or slaves, earned in most cases one drachma per day, some of them only five obols; most workers were paid by the piece. It is known that a slave's wage went to his master, but it is unclear whether some workers were forced to pay foremen for their work, thus distributing the pay less evenly. Soldiers and sailors at the same time were earning three obols per day, as were those on jury duty. Again, it is not known what other benefits soldiers and sailors may have had available in addition to their pay.

Historians tend to look at Athens as a "typical" Greek polis, but it should be emphasized that they do so because it is far and away the best documented. By contrast, Sparta, the great rival of the Athenians, is less well documented in nearly every way; but what is known indicates that Spartans were organized in a manner very different from that of the Athenians. Most Spartans did not work; they fought. There was an enormous population of state-owned slaves, who performed all agricultural work and other domestic tasks, and whose resentment on this account gave regular opportunities to citizens to hone their military prowess. Another difference from the Athenians was the Spartans' indifference to public works, which in economic terms meant many fewer public projects; and even if such projects had been executed, they would have been undertaken by slaves. There were state-owned slaves in Athens, but they were employed almost exclusively in the mines at Laureion. In 403 BCE, Athens ceded leadership after its failed war with Sparta; and over the next fifty years,

TABLE 1. *Athenian Federal "Budget," c. 430 BCE (in talents)*

INCOME		OUTGO	
Delian League	500	Military	350
Laureion mines	50	Public works	200
Taxes: customs	20+	Public distribution	250
metics	48	Government salaries	70
slave sales	38	Other	130
other	120–150		
Liturgies	194–224		
Total	1,000	**Total**	1,000

ANCIENT GREECE. Construction of a wall in the acropolis. Red figure skyphos, Penelope Painter (fifth century BCE), Athens. (Herve Lewandowski/Réunion des Musées Nationaux/Art Resource, NY)

Athens, Corinth, Sparta, and Thebes contested for Hellenic supremacy.

The fourth-century BCE evidence from Athens indicates the beginnings of banks and bankers. These institutions and players must have varied from polis to polis, and it is likely that the banking phenomenon previously was in place elsewhere; but in Athens banks appear to have made their first appearances in the fourth century. Private banks took deposits on account with and without interest, and lent money at interest, both the bank's money and the depositors'. Loans were either maritime or landed. Maritime loans produced interest not measured by time but a specific yield from the underwritten trading transaction; landed loans were secured by property-based collaterals, and generated interest that could reach 36 percent, but more routinely 12 percent (one drachma per mina per month) and sometimes as little as 10 percent per annum. Banks were largely unregulated; yet one can readily understand the plight of a metic who might act as a banker in a landed loan, but would be unable to collect the collateral upon default because metics were forbidden to own property. For those who see the Athenian economy as particularly "embedded," there was the common interest-free *eranos* loan, based on friendship. Substantivists also are interested in the debate over whether loans were routinely productive or nonproductive, and whether this distinction is relevant to one's understanding of ancient Athens.

In the fourth century BCE, one can begin to speak of economic theory. Plato (c. 429–347 BCE) in his *Republic* describes his ideal city, in which the lowest class, driven by appetite, is the money-making class. The state will fix limits on wealth; all transactions will be executed by outsiders. His grasp of the market is flimsy. By contrast, Aristotle (384–322 BCE) in his *Politics* reveals an understanding of economic development, in his discussion of barter to acquire goods at a distance and the use of surplus wealth to facilitate trade. Coined money was invented to expand the array of possible exchanges, but this led to the unfortunate idea that accumulation was *per se* a worthy goal. For Aristotle material goods were a prerequisite to the successful human life, but an excess of necessary goods was problematic.

Beginning in the 350s BCE, the rise of Macedonia under Philip II (382–336 BCE) undermined the economic well-being of the Greek cities. His son Alexander's march into Asia from Alexandria, founded in 331 BCE, also had an impact; for Athens and other cities experienced rises in prices and wages during the 320s and 310s BCE, as gold bullion flowed in from Persia. (The 310s BCE also mark the arrival in Rome of the first bankers—Greeks.)

Hellenistic Period (after 323 BCE). After Alexander died, in 323 BCE, his expansive realms eventually were divided up among his generals. The three main centers for the next 150 years were controlled by three successful dynasties: the Ptolemies in Alexandria, the Seleucids in the area from eastern Anatolia to Mesopotamia, and the Antigonids in Macedonia. There were other kingdoms, but these were the major players in the regional economy of the eastern Mediterranean and western Asia.

Of special interest here, Alexandria, the newly founded city at the western extremity of the Nile delta, was modeled after the Greek polis, perhaps especially Athens. It was developed carefully by the first two Ptolemies (I Soter, died 282 BCE; II Philadephus, died 246 BCE) and earned an international reputation for its monumental public works, including the museum, the library, and the gigantic Pharos lighthouse. As in Athens in the past, many productive industries enjoyed great success. So dominant did the city become in Egypt that the scale of redistribution in place by about 250 BCE was the largest seen in the Mediterranean since the Mycenaean citadels of the Bronze Age. Alexandria's potential domination of the eastern Mediterranean economy was made possible by its role as organizer of grain production along the Nile and its location as gateway at the delta.

In the very first decade of the city's existence, this potential was realized. When Alexander departed for Asia, he left Cleomenes, a Greek from Naucratis, in charge of the fiscal system. Taking advantage of famine and a food crisis in Greece, especially Athens, Cleomenes hoarded grain at Naucratis, using information gleaned there and at Rhodes to control the grain trade and to extract from the market optimal prices for grain from both Egypt and Sicily. When Ptolemy I returned from Asia in 323 BCE, Cleomenes had accumulated a surplus in the treasury of eight thousand talents (to be appreciated for its enormity by comparing the annual expenditures of the state of Athens one hundred years before of one thousand talents). In appropriate Athenian fashion, Cleomenes was vilified (in Pseudo-Aristotle, *Oeconomica*, and Pseudo-Demosthenes 56) for his hyperaccumulation of wealth; but one must bear in mind that the eight thousand talents were stored, safe and sound, in the treasury.

After 300 BCE, the grain and other trades moved along a great triangle of Rhodes, Alexandria, and the Levantine ports. Greece itself entered into this principal movement of goods at Rhodes directly or perhaps via Delos. Harbor fees at Rhodes reached one million drachmas annually, which sum enabled Rhodes to expand its political and economic influence to the Anatolian mainland. Rome was beginning to be a player in this arena, as demonstrated by the diplomatic mission sent to Rome by Alexandria in 273 BCE. Rhodes having refused to take sides in the Third Macedonian War, at its conclusion in 167 BCE. Rome separated Rhodes from the Anatolian properties and declared Delos a free harbor under Athenian administration, thus reducing Rhodes's annual harbor fees to 150,000 drachmas, an annual loss of over 140 talents. The previous year witnessed the defeat of the Aetolian League by Rome in the Battle of Pydna in northern Greece. Although some of Greece would not technically lose all political independence until 146 BCE, when Macedonia became a province and Greece to the south was administered through the Macedonian governor, the several events of 168/167 BCE effectively marked the end of Greek economic history. Several Greek states and leagues continued to strike coins, but by 30 BCE, when Alexandria fell to Rome, Roman coinage had taken over the eastern Mediterranean completely. Eventually to be divided into three provinces, hereafter Greece was clearly a part of Roman economic history.

One may nevertheless make remarks about that part. Rome's philhellenism translated into the support from Italy of centers of learning. Sons of Italian elites traveled to Athens to seek an education, Cicero and his son Quintus being perhaps the two most prominent examples. Tourism was always an important additional portion of the economy in all periods after 400 BCE, but perhaps especially during the Roman Empire, when wealthy Romans traveled to Greece to see both the monuments and the great athletic festivals, such as the quadrennial one at Olympia. Rome never imposed the Latin language on the Greeks, but Greece became in economic and political structural terms indistinguishable from other Roman provinces.

BIBLIOGRAPHY

Archibald, Zofia H., et al., eds. *Hellenistic Economies*. London, 2001.

Austin, M. M., and P. Vidal-Naquet. *Economic and Social History of Ancient Greece: An Introduction*. Berkeley, 1977.

Burford, Allison. *Land and Labor in the Greek World*. Baltimore, 1993.

Cartledge, Paul. *Sparta and Lakonia: A Regional History, 1330–362 B.C.* London, 1979.

Cohen, Edward E. *Athenian Banking and Society: A Banking Perspective*. Princeton, 1992.

Cullen, Tracey, ed. *Aegean Prehistory: A Review*. Boston, 2001.

Donlan, Walter. *The Aristocratic Ideal and Selected Papers*. Chicago, 1999.

Finley, Moses I. *The Ancient Economy*. 2d ed. Berkeley, 1985.

Garnsey, Peter. *Famine and Food Supply in the Greco-Roman World: Response to Risk and Crisis*. Cambridge, 1988.

Garnsey, Peter, Keith Hopkins, and C. R. Whittaker, eds. *Trade in the Ancient Economy*. Berkeley, 1983.

Goldsmith, Raymond W. *Premodern Financial Systems*. Cambridge, 1987.

Loomis, William T. *Wages, Welfare Costs, and Inflation in Classical Athens*. Ann Arbor, 1998.

Millett, Paul. *Lending and Borrowing in Ancient Athens*. Cambridge, 1991.

Möller, Astrid. *Naukratis: Trade in Archaic Greece*. Oxford, 2001.

Reden, Sitta Von. *Exchange in Ancient Greece*. London, 1995.

Saint Croix, G. E. M. de. *The Class Struggle in the Ancient Greek World from the Archaic Age to the Arab Conquest*. Ithaca, N. Y., 1979.

Snodgrass, Anthony M. *Archaic Greece: The Age of Experiment*. Berkeley, 1980.

Tandy, David W. *Warriors into Traders: The Power of the Market in Early Greece*. Berkeley, 1997.

Wood, Ellen Meiksins. *Peasant-Citizen and Slave: The Foundations of Athenian Democracy*. London, 1989.

DAVID W. TANDY

Byzantine and Ottoman Periods

In the year 400 CE the area currently known as Greece was ruled by the eastern half of the Roman Empire. The separation of the Roman Empire into east and west meant that the Greek language became predominant throughout the eastern empire, while the center of Greek culture shifted from its ancient and modern area to Constantinople. Christianity quickly spread throughout the empire, almost completely displacing the pagan religions by the sixth century.

Byzantine Empire. There was an outbreak of bubonic plague in 542, followed by large Slavic migration into northern Greece in the sixth and seventh centuries. Although the impact of the migration on the racial composition of Greece is much disputed, it appears that the incoming Slavs fairly quickly adopted the Greek language and religion, helped by an active effort at conversion by the Orthodox Church. The eighth century saw further severe outbreaks of the plague from 744 to 747, movement of the population to Constantinople, together with a withering of city life and population decline in Athens, Corinth, Thebes, and Sparta. This left the way open for further Slavic migration southward.

The centuries of the first millennium saw Greek shipping dominate the Mediterranean, but the Italian states took over in the twelfth century. Most large Greek towns had small but economically important communities of Jews, who dominated commerce and banking.

Taxation under the Byzantine administration was heavy, falling hardest on farmers. Church and military properties were often exempt, and a principle of collective responsibility for taxation was imposed, with solvent taxpayers having to make up for the nonpayment of defaulters. Tax collection was auctioned off to tax collectors, who were responsible for making up any community shortfalls from their own resources. This system naturally discouraged productivity and effort. Migration from the countryside to Constantinople and the major cities of Asia Minor left stretches of the countryside deserted. Individual farmers, who were the majority in the period leading up to the ninth century, gradually disappeared, either leaving their land or being forced by poverty into servitude on large estates. Farming was mainly for self-sufficiency rather than for trade with a town. Some village artisanship was practiced, but again it was for use within the village. Farming practices showed little or no evidence of technological advance in either implements or techniques from Roman times.

In the tenth century there was an improvement in the state of the Greek economy with the first evidence of silk manufacturing and the development of an agricultural system specializing in oil, wine, and fruits as well as goats and sheep. During Byzantine times Thessalonica was the preeminent economic center, followed by Nauplia, Corinth, Patras, Athens, and Negropont. The principal Greek export was silk. Thessalonica was also a center for jewelery manufacturing, and the plains of Thrace were an important wheat-growing area.

Population and economic growth in the Italian cities in the eleventh and twelfth centuries drove a growth in trade between them and Greece, particularly Corinth. In the twelfth century there was a shift of production away from Constantinople toward the provinces accompanied by an increase in the populations of major towns, such as Athens, Sparta, and Thebes, and a growth in the produce sold at regional fairs.

The sack of Constantinople by Crusaders in 1204 saw the beginning of western European domination over much of Greece. Small groups of Italian and French knights carved out small principalities for themselves, a phenomenon that continued up to the Ottoman conquest. Although these Latin conquerors brought Roman Catholicism to Greece, the number of practicing Catholics was small, and their cultural impact was fleeting. The level of taxation in the Latin states was noticeably less than it had been in Byzantine times. Agricultural output was generally high enough to permit export of wine, currants, wheat, silk, and cochineal.

Ottoman Empire. The Black Death struck Greece in the fourteenth century, and there was widespread fighting in the north of the country as the Ottoman Empire expanded into Europe. In the late fourteenth century and the early fifteenth century many Albanians migrated into the northern parts of Greece. At the same time the Ottomans conquered Thrace and Macedonia. After the fall of Thessalonica in 1430 and Constantinople in 1453, the Ottomans continued their expansion into the Peloponnese and the Aegean Islands, from which they took many inhabitants as slaves. Crete was the final conquest of the Ottomans in 1669.

The fall of Constantinople initiated the forced migration of many Greeks from Asia Minor to Constantinople and European Turkey. In the initial period after the Turkish invasion the Turks plundered much of the Greek Peninsula. Many towns were decimated, and the population was forced to flee to the more remote and mountainous regions. In the mountains Greeks became herders and foresters and fished the mountain streams, while Turks and Albanians immigrated and settled on the plains.

Taxation under Turkish rule was divided into two parts, regular and extraordinary. The regular taxes included a head tax on non-Muslims and a system of ad hoc land taxes, some in kind, some monetary, some of a fixed amount, some a percentage of the crop. Much more burdensome, the extraordinary taxes were imposed to cover military costs and large-scale construction projects. The burden of taxation fell most heavily on the rural population, which encouraged migration away from prime farmland to the towns, to mountainous regions, and abroad.

Education declined after the fall of the Byzantine Empire. The remaining centers of learning were the monasteries, and a few scholars lived in the main cities of Constantinople, Thessalonica, Adrianople, and Mistra. Many Greek intellectuals and students fled to Italy and were responsible for writing and disseminating books from there. Scholarship picked up in the late sixteenth century with the establishment of Greek schools and the increased publication of books.

Under Ottoman rule a considerable number of Greeks gave up the Orthodox religion for Islam and assimilated into the Turkish population. The converts tended to be the very poor, who wanted to evade the higher taxes on Christians, and the very rich, who desired to maintain positions of power and wealth under the new administration. Some conversions were genuine, while others were outward displays on the part of Greeks who practiced Orthodox Christianity in secret.

Another reason for the decline in the Greek population was the enslavement and removal of much of the population of Greece to Asia Minor, in particular to repopulate Constantinople after its sack by the Turks. There are no reliable estimates of the size of this forced relocation, but it was large relative to the size of the Greek population.

Piracy in the Aegean continued through the centuries, and pirates took both people for the slave markets of Constantinople and their property. The threat of piracy was enough to keep some islands and coastal towns deserted, although this threat tended to decrease after 1600. During the period of Ottoman rule Greeks were forbidden to carry weapons, ride horses, build or furnish churches, dress like Muslims, or build their houses higher than their Muslim neighbors. The Janissary system was also responsible for the loss of population, particularly in the earlier periods of Turkish rule. Ottoman officials selected Christian boys to be raised as Muslims and serve in the elite military corps of Janissaries.

The composition of the output of mainland Greece, principally wool, wine, cheese, skins, silk, wax, and olive oil, remained fairly constant throughout the centuries of Turkish rule. The Greek Islands, especially Crete, specialized in olive oil, wine, raisins, some cloth, and fruit.

Persecution of Jews in Europe in the fifteenth and sixteenth centuries encouraged their migration to the Ottoman Empire, where they settled in Macedonia and Thrace and tended to become bankers and traders. Skilled artisans, they brought technologies, such as printing and firearms, to the Ottoman Empire. This period saw the resurgence of Thessalonica, which became the manufacturing center of Greece, producing gunpowder and woolen cloth. The northern parts of Greece remained lawless in the sixteenth and seventeenth centuries, as Ottoman power waned and the area faced raids from Albanians and occasional military incursions from the Turks.

Demographic growth returned to Greece in the late seventeenth century and the eighteenth century. This expansion was accompanied by internal migration, as Greeks returned from the mountains and outlying areas to the cities and towns to take advantage of improved economic conditions. Although figures are unreliable, cities such as Thessalonica and Athens expanded during this era. The Peloponnese recovered from a low of a little over 100,000 people in the late seventeenth century to about a quarter of a million people in the early eighteenth century.

A brief period of Venetian rule over the Peloponnese in the late seventeenth century and early eighteenth century saw an improvement in agriculture and the inflow of colonists from other parts of Greece. The Turkish return to power in 1715 was followed by a period of placation by the Ottoman authorities, who exempted the inhabitants from taxation for a few years and encouraged settlement in the peninsula.

Although new Turkish immigrants to Greece took over much of the prime farmland, some traditional Greek farmers remained. Over the centuries Greeks successful in trade and industry increased their landholdings at the expense of Turks. Nonetheless prior to the revolution of 1821–1828, Turkish landholders owned about seven or eight times as much land as did their Greek counterparts. The Orthodox Church was granted many privileges under Ottoman rule, and rather than see land pass to Muslim landlords, many Orthodox Greeks bequeathed their land to the church. By the end of Turkish rule about one-quarter of Greece was in the hands of the church.

There was some limited self-government during this period at the village level. The commune was a legal entity recognized by the Ottoman administration. The rulers were elected by the population and had wide-ranging powers, such as the allocation of Turkish taxes to village members, responsibility for education and health, and some limited judicial power.

The Peloponnese and the southern parts of modern Greece were populated in the seventeenth and eighteenth centuries by a homogenous Greek-speaking people, in contrast to the more northern parts, where a large Turkish community remained. They lived in rural communities and were largely unmolested by Ottoman officials as long as taxes were paid on time. The Peloponnese region also had the right to appoint two representatives to Istanbul, which meant in practice that they had a fair degree of autonomy.

Books published in the Greek language became more common in the eighteenth and nineteenth centuries, and more Greeks traveled overseas to study in western Europe. In the eighteenth century trade became increasingly concentrated in the city of Thessalonica, which was both the end of land routes through the Balkans and the closest port to the trading city of Smyrna (Izmir) in Asia Minor. The city had a population of around seventy thousand at that time, the largest city in Greece, with about twenty-five thousand Jews, twenty thousand Turks and Albanians, and fewer than twenty thousand Greeks. The plains around and to the east of Thessalonica were the main grain-growing regions of Greece, and cotton and tobacco were cultivated there also. The main exports of Thessalonica were grain, wine, raisins, wool, tobacco, and cotton. The major destinations were Istanbul, southern Russia, Italy, and France. Trade fairs occurred in Macedonia several times per year and were the major purchasing points for cotton for the northern European markets of Austria and Germany.

Greek shipping increasingly took over the commercial routes of the eastern Mediterranean in the eighteenth century. Greek merchants dominated trade in the Balkan and Anatolian parts of the Ottoman Empire with trading houses situated as far away as Vienna and southern Russia. A treaty between Russia and Turkey in 1774 gave Greeks the privilege of trading under the Russian flag, which gave their fleet better protection.

Although there were sporadic, isolated uprisings against Turkish rule, they were ineffective. A major revolt in the Peloponnese in 1770 was crushed by the Turks and their Albanian allies, and recriminations lasted for ten years. This period saw another large-scale emigration of population to western Europe. Adding deaths from hostilities, the population decreased to around 100,000, although this quickly recovered in the following decades. Many young Greeks were educated in western Europe, where they came to appreciate the idea of statehood and the thoughts coming from the French Revolution. The middle class was encouraged to begin a revolution in 1821. The upper class and the Orthodox Church were indifferent or even against the idea of an independent Greece, as they were comfortable in their positions within the Ottoman Empire. Liberal-minded volunteers from western Europe enlisted with the Greek cause, and the first president was elected in 1828. At this time the country extended only a little beyond the Peloponnese Peninsula, around half the area of present-day Greece.

BIBLIOGRAPHY

Browning, Robert. *The Byzantine Empire*. New York, 1980.

Campbell, John, and Philip Sherrard. *Modern Greece*. London, 1968.

Cheetham, Nicolas. *Mediaeval Greece*. New Haven, Conn., 1981.

Clogg, Richard. *A Concise History of Greece*. Cambridge, 1992.

Diehl, Charles. *Byzantium: Greatness and Decline*. Translated by Naomi Walford. New Brunswick, N.J., 1957.

Harvey, Alan. *Economic Expansion in the Byzantine Empire 900–1200* Cambridge, 1989.

Heurtley, W. A., H. C. Darby, C. W. Crawley, and C. M. Woodhouse. *A Short History of Greece: From Early Times to 1964*. Cambridge, 1965.

Lemerle, Paul. *A History of Byzantium*. Translated by Anthony Matthew. New York, 1964.

Vakalopoulos, Apostolos E. *The Greek Nation 1453–1669*. Translated by Ian Moles and Phania Moles. New Brunswick, N.J., 1976.

Zakythenos, D. A. Translated by K. R. Johnstone. *The Making of Modern Greece: From Byzantium to Independence*. Oxford, 1976.

LYNDON MOORE

Modern Period

In the 1950s and especially in the 1960s and 1970s, debates among historians and social scientists abroad and domestically dealt with themes of belated economic development coinciding with the emergence of Greece as a new nation-state and with the nature of the modern Greek state and the orientation of the ruling class. Distortions were explained in terms of long-term structural problems of the Greek economy and society. Economic backwardness, usually demonstrated by quantitative criteria, had been determined in the development of the productive forces throughout the nineteenth century and during a large part of the twentieth century, its salient features being the predominance of the peasantry, an anemic working class, and the burgeoning of a prosperous bourgeoisie, mainly residing overseas. The internal development of the productive forces and consequent economic growth were explained in terms of, among other things, the interventionist role of the state from the late 1880s onward. Industrialization, in Greece as in many other late developers, suffered from the absence of a coherent policy and from a deep-rooted belief of those involved in policymaking that the country should rely on its primary resources and develop its trade relations. This perspective began to change only during the interwar years and especially after World War II.

Nation Building and Development. Two periods of Greek economic development are discernible, coinciding with major political changes and territorial expansion. The years 1830–1862 were formative in the life of the newly independent nation-state. During this period there was a population increase from around 600,000 in 1830 to over one million in 1861. The main economic activity was agriculture, involving the largest portion of the population. The period was dominated by the influence of the Great Powers, with domestic policies directed toward nation building through the establishment of modern political institutions. The economy remained rural, oriented toward subsistence farming, and only about 20 percent of the land appropriated by the state after independence was sold. Faster rates of development came later, coinciding with substantial territorial expansions—in the Ionian Islands in 1863 and the vast plain of Thessaly and the region of Arta in 1881—which in turn resulted in demographic increases and slow extension of the market. By 1896, the population had risen to 2,433,806, with 69 percent still living in rural areas. Of the remaining population, only about 13 percent was urban. Land distribution in 1871 consolidated small family property and strengthened the system of extensive agriculture, based on the typical Mediterranean combination of cereal, olive, and vine production. Large property owners, meanwhile, did not disappear, as rich overseas merchants acquired substantial plots of land from departing Ottomans. These landowners were to be found mainly in Thessaly, in Central Greece, and on the island of Euboea, causing political ferment until the twentieth century by fueling demands for agrarian reform. Estates were family-controlled, dedicated to extensive farming, and methods and tools remained antiquated, resulting in low production and productivity levels. The degree of monetization of the rural economy also varied; but after the 1840s, an increasing part of agriculture was dedicated to cash crops such as currants (for export and wine making), olives (for the production of oil), tobacco, and silk cocoons. Currants soon became the basis for extroversion of the whole economy, which, by the end of the century was geared to trade and shipping. Monoculture led to increased vulnerability to international demand and price fluctuations, in addition to causing crises of overproduction. A solution for the

ATHENS. View of the city, 1986. (© Robert Frerck/Woodfin Camp and Associates, New York)

population of the afflicted currants-producing areas was massive overseas emigration. From 1899 to 1924, almost 500,000 people emigrated; and for those who remained behind, integration into the political and economic patronage system reinforced the chronic overinflation of the civil service.

Twentieth-Century Development: From Extroversion to Autarchy. An agricultural policy was enforced during the interwar period, and a state rural bank was founded in 1930. Rural credit, however, was allocated mainly to cash crops, especially the currants trade, and the overall amounts of capital channeled to agriculture remained inadequate. Although rural credit contributed cumulatively to the monetization of the economy, it did not enhance capital accumulation. Links between Greek agriculture and external markets benefited, on the one hand, those entrepreneurs mediating between the producers and foreign export firms, and, on the other, the state as a recipient of revenue from duties. A vicious circle whereby exports of primary goods became a crucial source of revenue for the state reinforced the perception that Greece was predominantly a rural country. Gradually, special institutions controlling surplus produce were created, ultimately for handling many other primary products.

Faster rates of development were a function of certain preconditions achieved by the end of the nineteenth century. In the 1880s, the infrastructure was improved with the help of foreign loans despite their onerous terms and speculation, on the one hand, and an increase in military and public expenditures, on the other—which burdened the state budget, thereby leading to a default on foreign payments in 1893 and the imposition of foreign control on public finances in 1898. The period until, and especially after, World War I was marked by intense entrepreneurship in all sectors, but especially in industry, banking, and shipping. Small, labor-intensive, family-controlled industrial units proliferated when high profits from economic activities during the Balkan Wars and World War I were invested. The annexation of more new territories (Macedonia, Epirus, and the islands of the northeast Aegean in 1912–1913) and their homogenization (after 1922 and the influx of refugees from Asia Minor), gave previously local industries (e.g., shipyards and consumer goods) a national base. In agriculture, currants were replaced by tobacco, as agrarian reform further reinforced small family ownership. State intervention increased, and an institutional framework for the promotion of import-substitution industrialization and the regulation of joint-stock firms was introduced.

The influx of refugees in 1922 has been seen as the biggest tragedy in modern Greek history, but it also functioned as a blessing in disguise. Economic and cultural introversion followed the signing in 1923 of the Treaty of Lausanne for the compulsory exchange of populations between Greece and Bulgaria and Turkey, making Greece a remarkably homogeneous nation in that region. Under the aegis of the League of Nations, a series of foreign loans and newly established institutions helped the developmental effort by permitting resettlement of the refugees and the staving off of potential sociopolitical unrest. However, the lack of an articulate industrial policy and delays in promoting comprehensive housing, especially for urban refugees, and in solving debt and indemnity issues prevented systematic contributions to development. Ingenuity in devising strategies for individual and family survival had a limited effect on the structure of the national economy. Despite integration policies, cultural differences persisted, and their negative political implications became evident, as refugee votes and party affiliations shifted from the liberal to the populist or the communist party and back again, sometimes also supporting military solutions.

During this period, new industrial units and workshops proliferated in Athens, Piraeus, Thessaloniki, Volos, Patras, and several other towns around the country. A few were important units (around two thousand), belonging both to traditional (mining, cotton, food, tobacco) and "modern" (electricity, chemicals, construction material) sectors. Viable industries developed through agricultural improvement (e.g., fertilizers) and/or with the availability of abundant raw materials (oil and wine industries, can factories, and so on). The lack of a coherent state policy, caution shown by Greek banks (industrial credit developed only in the 1930s), heavy reliance on imported technology, and contradictory labor and trade policies, however, counteracted any positive effects of the availability of domestic and foreign capital resources and cheap refugee labor. Industrialization proceeded slowly and could not reverse high emigration and low productivity levels. Technological modernization was neglected, as were modern management and the specialization and social welfare of the labor force. Protectionism (import tariffs, tax exemptions, saturation laws for certain branches of industry, subsidies, and hand expropriation) enhanced short-term autarchic development but hampered modernization of the seondary sector and of the rest of the economy. A few industries grew, and some, by becoming export-oriented, survived into the post–World War II period, the most prominent examples being mining, fertilizers and chemicals, cement, and beverages. Old patterns of entrepreneurship remained strong, dominated by family control and self-financing methods, although staff education levels were impressively high in selected industries (e.g., cement, construction).

Post–World War II Modernization. After World War II development depended on the promotion of industry, including heavy industry. A coherent protective framework was devised, and monetary devaluation in 1954 helped the secondary sector along. However, there were negative side effects as well, since many industries failed to modernize. No capital-intensive sector emerged. The importance of services was recognized, and tourism was promoted. In the new conditions, new entrepreneurial groups were inclined toward short-term, often speculative ventures, as a large state sector in utilities and capital-intensive production emerged. Some multinationals were interested in investment. In the banking sector, which was diversified for the first time in the late 1920s, development had slowed, and credit policy did not respond effectively to the demands of industry. Family firms continued to dominate, as between 1941 and 1953 an impressive forty thousand new firms were founded, representing 50 percent of the total number of industrial enterprises operating in 1953. By 1951, the Greek economy had reached 1938 levels, and the industrial production index stood at 241, compared to the 1946 level of 100. In the same year, almost 95.5 percent of all industry units employed fewer than ten people, indicating that little had changed in relation to the prewar period. In contrast, the number of civil servants rose from 55,000 in 1940 to 132,000 in 1970 (an increase of 140 percent) against a demographic increase of only 19 percent. A great opportunity was missed, as from 1945 to 1952 some 50 percent of the Marshall Plan aid was channeled to military expenditures, and 25 percent was spent on consumption. Infrastructure received most of the remainder, with a minimal amount finding its way to production.

From 1958 to 1973, 85 percent of production appeared to be in the hands of larger companies (S.A.'s) but family control remained firm; only 1 percent of the total number of industrial units in the 1930s, they represented 8.1 percent in 1959–1961 and 40.5 percent by 1970–1973. Most of the older firms merged to form new ones, or were simply dissolved. Whereas in 1958 large companies (those with capital of over $100 million) comprised only 5.4 percent of total industry, in 1973 they represented 23.1 percent. The change only marginally affected the traditional structure of Greek industries, however, as it was in traditional areas that new larger firms were founded. The opportunity to benefit from a worldwide upward economic trend until 1973 was missed in the havoc created by the country's military dictatorship (1967–1973). No sooner had Greece returned to parliamentary democracy, in 1974, that an economic recession exacerbated chronic traditional imbalances. Greece ascended to full membership in the European Economic Community in 1981, and since then European funds and continuous efforts toward institutional reform have allowed increased economic integration so that today Greece is on a par with the other European Union members. The past quarter-century nevertheless has seen a growing degree of deindustrialization and consequent growth in tertiary activities, notably in tourism and shipping.

Shipping and maritime trade have had a long and impressive history. Throughout the nineteenth century, shipping extended across the eastern Mediterranean region and the Black Sea. In the twentieth century, it made the transition to steam; and after early activity centered on the Mediterranean, its focus, after World War I, shifted westward (to London and New York). After World War II, Greek vessels sailed all over the world. From only 1 percent of world capacity at the end of the nineteenth century, by 1994 the Greek merchant marine controlled 16 percent of world tonnage. The impact on Greek development has been crucial: the maritime trade has made available capital resources for investment in industry, and it has absorbed substantial portions of Greek labor, whose remittances have contributed to the maintenance of a healthy balance of payments. It also has reinforced a kind of Greek business culture marked by the continuity of family control and tight networking.

The history of tourism has yet to be written. For a long time it depended on private individual initiatives. The first signs of a state policy appeared in the 1930s, but it was not until after World War II, especially in the 1960s, that the development of mass tourism became official state policy. Since then, tourism has grown into an industry, with tourist revenue in 1997 amounting to 9.6 percent of the gross domestic product and its share in the balance of payments double that of exports.

In the last few years, developments in the rest of Europe have been mirrored in Greece. Privatization of the state sector has been high on the public-policy agenda, and considerable stress has been building as a result of high unemployment and illegal immigration. It is not certain that the new economy will lessen or absorb that tension.

BIBLIOGRAPHY

Asdrachas, S. *Helliniki koinonia kai oikonomia XVIII–XIX aiones Hypotheseis kai prosengiseis* (Greek Society and Economy XVIII–XIX Centuries, Hypotheses and Approaches). Athens, 1982.

Dertilis, G. "Les économies de la périphérie: Le cas Grec." *Annales ESC* 2 (1992), 273–291.

Dritsas, Margarita. *Viomehania kai trapezes sten Hellada tou Mesopolemou* (Industry and Banking in Interwar Greece). Athens, 1990.

Dritsas, Margarita, and T. Gourvish, eds. *European Enterprise. Strategies of Adaptation and Renewal in the Twentieth Century.* Athens, 1997.

Dritsas, Margarita, and T. Gourvish. "The Advent of the Tourist Industry in Greece during the Twentieth Century." In *Deindustrialization and Reindustrialization in Twentieth Century, Europe,* edited by F. Amatori, A. Colli, and N. Crepas. Milan, 1999.

Evelpides, Ch. *Agrotiko Programma.* Athens, 1992.

Hadziossif, C. *He gerea selene: He viomechania sten hellenike oikonomia 1830–1940* (The Waning Moon, Industry in the Greek Economy 1830–1990). Athens, 1993.

Harlaftis, Gelina. *A History of Greek-Owned Shipping.* London and New York, 1996.

Iatrides, J., ed. *Greece in the 1940s and 1950s: A Nation in Crisis.* Athens, 1984.

Kalafatis, E. *Rural Credit and Economic Transformation in N. Peloponnesus.* Athens, 1990.

Kitroeff, A. "Emigration transatlantique et stratégies familiales: La Grèce." In *Sociétés sub-européennes à travers de l'âge moderne,* edited by S. J. Woolfe. Florence, 1992.

Kostis, K. *Agrotike oikonomia kai georgike trapeza: Opsis tes hellinikes oikonomias sto mesopolemo 1919–1928* (Rural Economy and Agrarian Bank: Facets of the Greek Economy during the Interwar 1919–1928). Athens, 1987.

Koutsoumaris, G. *Financing and Development of Industry.* Athens, 1976.

Prontzas, V. *Oikonomia kai geoktesia ste Thessalia 1881–1912* (Economy and Land Property in Thessaly 1881–1912). Athens, 1992.

Svoronos, N. *Histoire de la Grèce Moderne.* Paris, 1953.

Teichova, Alice, Margarita Dritsas, and H. Lindgren, eds. *L'entreprise en Grèce et en Europe XIX–XX e siècles.* Athens, 1991.

Tsoukalas, K. *Dépendence et reproduction.* Paris, 1975.

Vergopoulos, K. *Ethinismos kai oikonomike anaptyxe* (Nationalism and Economic Development). Athens, 1981.

MARGARITA DRITSAS

GREENHOUSE AGRICULTURE. *See* Horticulture and Truck Farming.

GREEN REVOLUTION. Food scarcity has always haunted humankind. Centuries ago, few technological breakthroughs increased yields, and the food needs of growing populations had to be met by expanding the cultivated area. As the most fertile land became scarce, further expansion meant bringing lower-yielding land into cultivation. By the eighteenth century, pessimism had grown about the possibility of feeding ever-larger populations, as exemplified by the writings of Thomas Malthus (1766–1834). The task seemed even more daunting as advances in medicine and public health led to longer life expectancies and higher fertility rates.

Modern Advances. Massive public investments in modern scientific research for agriculture led to dramatic yield breakthroughs in the twentieth century. The story of English wheat is typical. It took nearly a thousand years for wheat yields to increase from 0.5 to 2 t/ha (metric tons/hectare) but only forty years to climb from 2 to 6 t/ha. Most industrial countries had achieved sustained food surpluses by the second half of the twentieth century.

These advances in plant breeding, agronomy, fertilizers, and pesticides were much slower than that to reach today's developing countries. Colonial powers had invested little in the food production systems of these countries, and populations in the colonies were growing at historic highs by the time they gained independence. By the mid-1960s, there was widespread hunger and malnutrition, especially in Asia, with growing dependence on food aid from the rich countries.

In response, the Rockefeller and Ford foundations took the lead in establishing an international agricultural research system to help transfer and adapt available scientific advances to conditions in developing countries (Tribe, 1994). The first investments were made in rice and wheat research, two of the most important food crops for the developing world. The breeding of improved varieties, combined with the expanded use of fertilizers, pesticides, and irrigation, led to dramatic yield increases in the late 1960s. This development was termed the green revolution in 1968 by USAID Administrator William S. Gaud.

Achieving higher yields required plants that were more responsive to fertilizer than traditional varieties, had shorter and stiffer straw to cope with the heavier heads of grains, and matured quickly and grew at any time of the year. The new varieties also needed to resist major pests and diseases and retain desirable cooking and consumption traits. Borrowing from rice-breeding work undertaken in China, Japan, and Taiwan, the International Rice Research Institute (IRRI) in the Philippines developed semidwarf varieties that met most of these requirements (Dalrymple, 1986a). Similar achievements were made for wheat after Norman Borlaug (later awarded a Nobel Prize for his work) crossed Japanese semidwarf varieties with Mexican wheats at what is now known as the International Center for Maize and Wheat Improvement (CIMMYT) in Mexico (Dalrymple, 1986b).

Subsequent expansion of the international agricultural research system led to the development of high-yielding varieties for a number of other major food crops important to developing countries.

Impact on Agricultural Production in Developing Countries. The adoption of the improved varieties occurred quickly, reaching about 20 percent of the wheat area and 30 percent of the rice area in developing countries by 1970. By 1990 the share of improved varieties had increased to about 70 percent for both crops. With faster-growing varieties and irrigation, farmers grew more crops on their land each year.

These changes more than doubled cereal production in Asia between 1970 and 1995, while population increased by 60 percent. Instead of widespread famine, cereal and calorie availability per person increased by nearly 30 percent, and wheat and rice became cheaper (Rosegrant and Hazell, 2000). There were also significant gains in Latin America, but the impact in sub-Saharan Africa was much more modest. Insufficient road networks, poor transport systems, limited investment in irrigation, and pricing and marketing policies that penalized farmers made the green-revolution technologies too expensive or inappropriate for much of Africa.

At the global level, these production increases led to significant reductions in world cereal prices. Evenson and Rosegrant (forthcoming) estimate that had the green revolution not occurred in the developing world, then world wheat and rice prices would have been 30 to 60 and 80 to 125 percent higher than they were in 2000.

Social Impact. The green revolution led to significant increases in farm incomes in Asia and Latin America, which boosted demand for consumer goods and farm inputs, as well as marketing services. This demand surge powerfully stimulated the rural nonfarm economy, which generated significant new income and employment of its own (Mellor, 1976; Rosegrant and Hazell, 2000). Real per capita income almost doubled in Asia between 1970 and 1995, in part as a result of the green revolution, and the absolute number of the poor fell from 1,150,000,000 in 1975 to 825,000,000 in 1995, despite a one billion increase in population (Rosegrant and Hazell, 2000). The most dramatic reductions in poverty were seen in Southeast Asia, including China, whereas it still continues to exist at high, though reduced, levels in South Asia.

The green revolution also contributed to better nutrition by raising incomes and reducing prices, permitting greater calorie consumption and a more diversified diet for the poor, among others.

Problems. A revolution of this magnitude and success was bound to create some problems. Critics have argued that large-scale farmers were the main adopters of the new technology, and small-scale farmers either were left unaffected or were made worse off because the green revolution resulted in lower crop prices, higher input prices, and efforts by larger farmers to increase rents and force tenants off the land. They also argued that the green revolution encouraged unnecessary mechanization, with a resulting reduction in rural wages and employment, particularly for women and landless laborers (see, e.g., Griffin, 1972, and ILO, 1977).

Although a number of studies conducted soon after the green-revolution technologies were released lent some support to the critics (e.g., Farmer, 1977), the conclusions often have not held up over time (see Lipton and Longhurst, 1989; Hazell and Ramasamy, 1991). Most small farmers did eventually adapt to and benefit from increased production, as well as from greater employment opportunities and higher wages in the agricultural and nonfarm sectors. The distribution of land did not worsen in most Asian countries (Rosegrant and Hazell, 1999). Large numbers of other poor people also benefited through increased employment and business earnings in the rural economy and from lower food prices (Pinstrup-Andersen and Hazell, 1985). The green revolution was not equitable everywhere, but the conditions under which it and other yield-enhancing technologies are likely to be equitable are now reasonably well-understood, and can be promoted through appropriate policy interventions.

Critics also argued that the green revolution bypassed many areas that lacked access to sufficient water. Evidence suggests that villagers in these regions did obtain important indirect benefits through increased employment, migration opportunities, and cheaper food (David and Otsuka, 1994). However, these benefits rarely prevented the widening of regional income differentials.

The green revolution has also been widely criticized for its adverse environmental impacts, including excessive and poorly used fertilizers and pesticides that pollute waterways and upset ecosystems, irrigation practices that lead to salt buildup and eventual abandonment of good farming lands, decline of groundwater levels, and loss of biodiversity. Some of these outcomes were inevitable as millions of largely illiterate farmers began to use modern inputs for the first time; but the problem was exacerbated by inadequate extension and training, an absence of effective regulation of water quality, and input pricing and subsidy policies that made modern inputs too cheap and encouraged excessive use. These problems are slowly being rectified without loss in yields, through policy reforms and better technologies and management practices (Pingali and Rosegrant, 2001).

Often ignored by the critics is the positive impact of higher yields, in saving huge areas of forest and other environmentally fragile lands that would otherwise have been needed for farming.

Overall, the green revolution was a major achievement for many of the developing countries and gave them a level of national food security that they had not experienced before. There are lingering social and environmental problems that still need to be resolved, but perhaps the biggest challenge for the future is to continue to increase yields to meet the growing food needs of developing countries. This need of especially urgent in sub-Saharan Africa, but is also a growing worry elsewhere as yield growth in many of the most productive areas has slowed considerably in recent years (Pingali and Rosegrant, 2001).

BIBLIOGRAPHY

Dalrymple, D. *Development and Spread of High-Yielding Rice Varieties in Developing Countries*. Washington, D.C., 1986a.

Dalrymple, D. *Development and Spread of High-Yielding Wheat Varieties in Developing Countries*. Washington, D.C., 1986b.

David, C., and Keijiro Otsuka, eds. *Modern Rice Technology and Income Distribution in Asia*. Boulder and London, 1994.

Evenson, R. E., and M. Rosegrant. "The Economic Consequences of Crop Genetic Improvement Programs." In *Crop Variety Improvement and Its Effect on Productivity: The Impact of International Agricultural Research*, edited by R. E. Evenson and D. Gollin, Chapter 23. Wallingford, U.K., forthcoming.

Farmer, B. H. *Green Revolution? Technology and Change in Rice Growing Areas of Tamil Nadu and Sri Lankur*. London, 1977.

Griffin, K. *The Green Revolution: An Economic Analysis*. Geneva, 1972.

Hazell, Peter B. R., and C. Ramasamy. *The Green Revolution Reconsidered: The Impact of High Yielding Rice Varieties in South India*. Baltimore, 1991.

International Labor Organization (ILO). *Poverty and Landlessness in Rural Asia*. Geneva, 1977.

Lipton, Michael, and R. Longhurst. *New Seeds and Poor People*. Baltimore, 1989.

Mellor, J. W. *The New Economics of Growth*. Ithaca, N.Y., 1976.

Pingali, Prabhu I., and Mark W. Rosegrant. "Intensive Food Systems in Asia: Can the Degradation be Reversed?" In *Tradeoffs or Synergies? Agricultural Intensification, Economic Development and the Environment*, edited by D. R. Lee and C. B. Barrett, pp. 383–398. Wallingford, U.K., 2001.

Pinstrup-Andersen, Per, and Peter B. R. Hazell. "The Impact of the Green Revolution and Prospects for the Future." *Food Reviews International* 1.1 (1985), 1–25.

Rosegrant, Mark, and P. B. R. Hazell. *Transforming the Rural Asia Economy: The Unfinished Revolution*. Oxford, 2000.

Tribe, Derek. *Feeding and Greening the World: The Role of International Agricultural Research*. Wallingford, U.K., 1994.

PETER B. R. HAZELL

GRESHAM'S LAW states simply that "bad [cheap] money drives out good [dear]." Its supposed author, Sir Thomas Gresham (1519–1579), an English adviser of Elizabeth I, merely articulated a commonplace observation about European monetary manipulations during the previous two centuries. Thus the French philosopher Nicolas Oresme, in his treatise *De Moneta* (c.1355), contended that this "law" was the inevitable consequence of coinage debasements. So did the Tower Mint's 1381 report to Parliament, in explaining that its recent coinage inactivity was due principally to continental debasements and counterfeits, while eschewing defensive debasements, advocating instead measures to ensure a "favorable balance of trade" and thus a renewed bullion influx into England.

In essence, this "law" contends that anyone possessing two coins that have the same official exchange value but differ in their precious-metal contents would rationally choose to spend only the "undervalued inferior" coin—debased, counterfeit, worn, or clipped—while selling the overvalued "better" coin (or its bullion content) to those foreign mints offering a higher relative price. The same principle holds true, *ceteris paribus*, for differences in relative bimetallic ratios between neighboring countries. For example, if country A maintains a mint ratio of 10:1 and country B one of 11:1, country A should attract silver to its mints and country B, conversely, gold.

Recently, several scholars—in particular Miskimin (1985) and Rolnick and Weber (1986)—have contended that Gresham's Law was a "fallacy": that it rarely if ever "worked." The historical evidence for medieval and early modern Europe demonstrates that, on the contrary, Gresham's Law was valid, but only under the particular circumstances of this era emanating from the techniques of hand-"hammered," die-produced coins. Because of their crudity, most honestly struck coins from any mint issue were rarely equal in size, shape, and weight; and therefore most coins circulated by "tale," at "face value," all the more so since the costs of weighing and assaying coins, with at best imperfect accuracy, were so high. As Selgin (1996) has observed, "market forces alone will favor the coin that minimizes exchange costs"; but that also meant that profits from arbitrage trade were limited by transaction costs:

in exporting the "overvalued" metal, evading bans on exporting bullion, and paying foreign mint fees.

The applicability of these principles is more obvious for silver coin transactions than those for much higher-valued gold coins, for three reasons:

1. The costs involved in weighing and assaying gold coins were relatively much lower.
2. International merchants trading with gold coins were thus more likely to treat them as bullion.
3. Gold coins were usually assigned a value in the silver-based money-of-account, one that was more likely to fluctuate in domestic transactions, while a penny or a sixpence silver coin would always be accepted at face value (i.e., would not be discounted or enhanced in value).

Nevertheless, the monetary history of late-medieval Flanders and England is instructive. The Flemish, especially when debasing their silver coins, minted chiefly silver, while the English, in generally maintaining a higher or more "pro-gold" ratio, minted chiefly gold coins, until the 1530s, when the market ratio had risen above the English mint ratio (11.16:1), thus allowing English mints to attract and coin chiefly silver. International merchants had evidently chosen which metal to spend in the two countries in accordance with their relative values.

The era of Gresham's Law in international monetary relations came to an end when modern states: (1) finally abjured coinage debasements and thus their seigniorage profits; (2) produced machine-made milled coinage; (3) effectively eliminated profits from counterfeiting; and (4) permitted a free market in precious metals (i.e., did not enforce official bimetallic ratios).

[*See also* Monetary Standards.]

BIBLIOGRAPHY

Bridrey, Émile. *La théorie de la monnaie au XIVe siècle: Nicole Oresme: étude d'histoire des doctrines et des faits économiques.* Paris, 1906.
De Roover, Raymond. *Gresham on Foreign Exchange.* Cambridge, Mass., 1949.
Gandal, Neil, and Nathan Sussman. "Asymmetric Information and Commodity Money: Tickling the Tolerance in Medieval France." *Journal of Money, Credit, and Banking* 29.4 (November 1997), 440–457.
Johnson, Charles, ed. *The* De Moneta *of Nicholas Oresme and English Mint Documents.* London, 1956.
Lane, Frederic C., and Reinhold Mueller. *Money and Banking in Medieval and Renaissance Venice,* vol. 1, *Coins and Moneys of Account.* Baltimore, 1985.
Laurent, Henri. *La loi de Gresham au moyen âge: essai sur la circulation monétaire entre la Flandre et le Brabant à la fin du 14e siècle.* Travaux de la Faculté de philosophie et lettres de l'Université de Bruxelles, vol. 5. Brussels, 1933.
Miskimin, Harry. "The Enforcement of Gresham's Law." In *Credito, banche e investimenti, secoli XIII–XX: Atti della Quarta Settimana di Studio* (Prato, 14–21 April 1972), edited by Anna Vannini Marx, Istituto internazionale di storia economica "F. Datini," pp. 147–161.
Florence, 1985. Reproduced in his *Cash, Credit, and Crisis in Europe, 1300–1600.* Variorum Reprints CS289. London, 1989.
Munro, John. *Wool, Cloth, and Gold: The Struggle for Bullion in Anglo-Burgundian Trade, 1340–1478.* Brussels and Toronto, 1973.
Munro, John. *Bullion Flows and Monetary Policies in England and the Low Countries, 1350–1500.* Variorum Collected Series CS355. Aldershot, U.K., 1992.
Pamuk, Sevket. *A Monetary History of the Ottoman Empire.* Cambridge, 2000.
Rolnick, Arthur J., and Warren E. Weber. "Gresham's Law or Gresham's Fallacy?" *Journal of Political Economy* 94.1 (February 1986), 185–199.
Rolnick, Arthur J., François R. Velde, and Warren E. Weber. "The Debasement Puzzle: An Essay on Medieval Monetary History." *Journal of Economic History* 56.4 (December 1996), 789–808.
Selgin, George. "Salvaging Gresham's Law: The Good, the Bad, and the Illegal." *Journal of Money, Credit, and Banking* 28.4 (November 1996), 637–649.
Spufford, Peter. *Money and Its Use in Medieval Europe.* Cambridge, 1988.
Watson, Andrew. "Back to Gold—and Silver." *Economic History Review* 2d ser. 20.1 (1967), 1–34.

JOHN H. MUNRO

GUANGZHOU (CANTON). Guangzhou had been a port at the mouth of the Pearl River from at least the second century BCE, but until the Southern Song dynasty (1127–1279 CE), it was primarily an imperial outpost for trade in exotics. The Southern Song government promoted a local scholarly class, and subsequent economic growth led to reclamation of the Pearl River delta. In following centuries, Guangzhou became the administrative as well as commercial center of a very prosperous region.

Arab and Southeast Asian merchants were prominent in Guangzhou until the Ming dynasty (1368–1644). As the Ming dynasty banned private overseas trade, overseas traders went to Guangzhou in the guise of tribute bearers, and private merchants who put to sea were referred to as "smugglers." By the sixteenth century, private trade exceeded the tributary trade in importance.

Guangzhou's exports consisted primarily of silk, pottery, and iron products. Some of the exports were produced in workshops located in the city, but a substantial portion came from the town of Foshan, to the west. Guangzhou also exported rice to other southern provinces, notably Fujian. By the 1550s, when the Portuguese founded their settlement at Macau, southeast of the city, Guangzhou was brought within the Nagasaki-Malacca route as a recipient of Japanese silver and an exporter of silk and pottery.

Both coastal and overseas trade were interrupted in the second half of the seventeenth century, owing to change-of-dynasty turmoil in China. The coastal evacuation policy of the newly founded Qing dynasty (1644–1911) was applied to Guangzhou from 1662 to 1684; and although some trade was pursued under the feudatories who controlled

GUANGZHOU. Narrow street lined with shops, circa 1880. (Prints and Photographs Division, Library of Congress)

the city in these years, it was severely interrupted. Guangzhou became a leader in the coastal trade again when, ever sensitive to the need to contain the Western influence, the Qing court restricted all Western merchants to that city in 1757, and required that trade be conducted through monopoly merchants known as the Co-hong. Up to the time of the First Opium War (1839–1842), the concentration of overseas trade at Guangzhou brought the city and its surroundings unprecedented prosperity. Although it was included as one of the five ports opened to foreign trade by the Treaty of Nanjing (1842), its position as a trading center on the China coast declined thereafter, primacy passing to Shanghai and Hong Kong. By the 1930s, Guangzhou had a population of 760,000, equal in size to that of Hong Kong but substantially smaller than Shanghai's three million.

Despite the relative decline of its trading position, Guangzhou remained the administrative seat of the region. In the early twentieth century, southern warlords contested for control of its taxation. In the 1920s, it became the base from which the Guomindang Party (KMT) launched its Northern Expedition to unite the country. The city became prominent again in the 1980s, when, over-

turning earlier policies, the Chinese government opened up the economy to foreign investment, and Guangzhou benefited from proximity to Hong Kong.

BIBLIOGRAPHY

Duanben, Deng, and Cheng Hao. *Gangzhou gang shi* (A History of the Port of Guangzhou). Beijing, 1985–1986.

Rhoads, Edward J. M. *China's Republican Revolution: The Case of Kwangtung, 1895–1913*. Cambridge, Mass., 1975.

Tsin, Michael Tsang-Woon. *Nation. Governance, and Modernity in China: Canton, 1900–1927*. Stanford, Calif., 1999.

Vogel, Ezra F. *One Step Ahead in China: Guangdong under Reform.* Cambridge, Mass., 1989.

DAVID FAURE

GUATEMALA. *See* Central American Countries.

GUGGENHEIM FAMILY. The Guggenheims, America's first prominent Jewish family, made their fortune in mining and smelting, secured it in financing and international mineral exploitation, and left their legacy in charitable foundations.

The family patriarch, Meyer Guggenheim (1828–1905), emigrated from Switzerland in 1847 and soon thereafter married his stepsister. They had eleven children, including eight sons, one of whom died in childhood. The seven surviving sons (Isaac, Daniel, Murry, Solomon, Benjamin, Simon, and William) went on to build the vast Guggenheim dynasty begun by their father. The family name lives on prominently through the numerous charitable foundations established by the brothers in their old age. Although several of Meyer's grandchildren participated in the family business, it largely faded in importance with the aging of the seven sons. During the decade preceding World War I, the Guggenheims were the most powerful Jewish family in the United States, second only to the Rothschilds in the world, with whom they were united when Solomon married Irene Rothschild.

When Meyer arrived in America, he was penniless; he supported his fledgling family by peddling stove polish across his adopted home state of Pennsylvania. Eventually he developed his own line of polish and soaps, and he expanded his operation into the importation of Swiss lace, building a sizable business. When Meyer invested in a Colorado copper mine, he brought his family into the industry that would become synonymous with the Guggenheim name: mining and smelting.

The Guggenheims were adept at implementing new technology, a skill that eventually led to their control of the mining industry. They learned the business from the ground up, mastered every aspect of it, and rarely allowed nonfamily members into ownership or managerial roles. Although they entered several industries that lost money early on because of conservative management and financing practices (they seldom borrowed money), they later built a vast empire, which by World War I left them in control of the world's largest smelting cartel, with the family controlling 80 percent of the world's silver and 50 percent of the world's copper output. Their far-flung mineral-exploration interests eventually led family members across the globe in search of mineral wealth and government contracts. They excelled in business and politics, with members eventually holding government offices, as U.S. senator from Colorado, ambassador to Cuba, and ambassador to Portugal.

In 1899, the American Smelting and Refining Company was formed. This smelting trust controlled all the major smelters in America except for the Guggenheims, who formed their own corporation, the Guggenheim Exploration Company, or Guggenex. Its official purpose was listed as exploring and dealing in land, mines, and mineral-resource exploration around the world. In practice, its

PEGGY GUGGENHEIM. On the terrace with the Grand Canal in the background, Venice, 5 September 1968. (Prints and Photographs Division, Library of Congress)

primary function was to secure sufficient financing for the smelting company. The corporation was so successful that within two years the Guggenheims used it to take control of the trust.

The formation of Guggenex produced the first in a series of family disagreements that ultimately led to the decline of the family empire. Internal disagreements over business decisions led to splits in the family, which, although not personal, divided the family's business interests and led to a diminution of their power.

As Meyer's seven sons aged, their dynasty declined. In 1922, they were ousted from control of the smelting trust. A year later, the family partnership was dissolved in a disagreement over what to do with the family's Chilean mines. The mines were sold, the partnership dissolved, and the family involvement in the metals industry ended. The Guggenheim interests then turned to nitrates. Although they were successful, they would never again enjoy their earlier level of control or profit, nor would they again be the envy of world industrialists. Instead, their lasting legacy would come in the form of the charitable trust funds the brothers established.

The oldest of the Guggenheim trusts is the John Simon Guggenheim Memorial Foundation, created in 1924 for academic fellowships. Other funds were endowed for hospitals, aeronautics, and dental research. The most famous Guggenheim legacy is the Guggenheim Museum in New York, established by Solomon in 1937 and later housed in a stunning building designed by Frank Lloyd Wright.

BIBLIOGRAPHY

Davis, J. H. *The Guggenheims*. New York, 1988.
Glaser-Schmidt, Elisabeth. "The Guggenheims and the Coming of the Great Depression in Chile, 1923–1934." *Business and Economic History* 20.1 (1995), 176–185.
Hoyt, Edwin P., Jr. *The Guggenheims and the American Dream*. New York, 1967.
Lomask, Milton. *Seed Money: The Guggenheim Story*. New York, 1964.
O'Brien, Thomas F. "Rich beyond the Dreams of Avarice: The Guggenheims in Chile." *Business History Review* 63.1 (1989), 122–159.
O'Connor. *The Guggenheims: The Making of an American Dynasty*. New York, 1976.

MICHAEL J. HAUPERT

GUILDS. *See* Corporatism; Craft Guilds; *and* Merchant Guilds.

GUINEA. *See* Sudan, *subentry on* Western Sudan.

GUINNESS FAMILY. The Guinness brewery and the family that controlled it for more than two hundred years occupy unique places, not only in the history of brewing, but also in the broader framework of industrialization. Beer drinking in eighteenth-century Ireland and elsewhere was largely an urban taste; the principal beverage consumption in rural areas was of grain-based alcohol—inside and outside the view of the tax collector. Success of the early Guinness brewery followed the pace of the urban, working class growth in both Ireland and Great Britain.

In 1759, Arthur Guinness purchased a small brewery at the Saint James' Gate site in Dublin. This is still the location of the main Irish brewery, although water is no longer taken from the Liffey River. Unlike the many small Irish breweries of the period, Guinness within a decade of acquiring the brewery abandoned the production of Irish ales to concentrate on the production of dark porter ale. Porter, later known as "stout," is a dark beer brewed using brown malt. Double malting produced the "Extra Stout" for bottling.

By the 1820s, Guinness had become one of the two top breweries in Ireland by sales. Its main Irish competitor was Sweetman's. The next phase of the company growth was, however, based on sales outside of Ireland. The distinctive Guinness stout followed, as a deliberate market strategy, the diaspora of the Irish to the expanding industrial centers of Britain. Such cities as Liverpool, Manchester, London, and Glasgow accounted for the growth of a substantial market for the Dublin brewery, although these were not officially exports until 1922. As the scale of the brewery grew, and with a reputation for consistency of product, Irish sales also grew; and by the 1860s, Guinness occupied the position of the preeminent Irish brewery. The increased ease and lower cost of shipping within Britain by train also contributed to its success. Expansion of the brewery site and reorganization of the production facilities enabled Guinness to increase its output almost tenfold in the third quarter of the nineteenth century. By the year of its incorporation in 1886, it produced about 1.5 million standard barrels, marking Guinness as the largest brewery in terms of sales in all of Great Britain and Ireland.

From its inception until 1886, Arthur Guinness and Company was a firm wholly owned by the Guinness family. In that year, the company incorporated and made a share offering of the company's stock. Due most likely to mishap on the part of Baring Brothers, the issuing bank, the shares were sold only in the main British cities and none were allocated for sale in Dublin. However, the Guinness family retained a large block of voting shares, which was enough to exercise effective control and day-to-day management of the firm. Thus little changed in the management structure of Guinness, and by amazing good fortune, the family produced a series of good and occasionally excellent managers.

The success of the Guinness brewery in the nineteenth century also marked the rise in the family's social status. The family acquired estates in both Ireland and England. In the early Victorian era, the family increasingly spent time in England, which was to become their principal residence later in the century. Of course, with Guinness success largely based on the sales in Great Britain, this is not surprising. The family established a variety of trusts mostly directed toward worthy Victorian aims, such as its first major project in Dublin to provide housing for the working poor. The charities of the Guinness trusts were soon found throughout Britain, and many continue their philanthropic works into the twenty-first century. Apart from their economic power as one of the richest families in late-nineteenth-century Britain, their increased participation in social events and their charitable projects drew the family into and through the ranks of the British aristocratic honors. The reigning family head, Edward Guinness, was made Baron Inveagh of County Down in 1891.

The Guinness guiding business principle remained unchanged for a remarkably long time—until the 1960s. That principle was the concentration on the production and marketing of stout rather than diversification into a range of beer types. Long-run business success derived from this specialization achieved for Guinness stout a high degree of product identification. By the early nineteenth century, Guinness had achieved what is now called "brand status." The health-giving and restorative properties of stout, and Guinness in particular, were myths much encouraged by Arthur Guinness and his successors. Product identification was further enhanced by the adoption of the registered trademark of the Brian Boru harp in the mid-1800s. Later, when the company turned to more explicit advertising, it coined one of the twentieth century's most distinctive and successful corporate slogans: "Guinness Is Good for You." First introduced in 1928, the slogan was later incorporated into the famous post–World War II advertising campaign featuring cartoons of zoo animals. These images were ubiquitous on the billboards of Ireland and Britain in the post-war years and, in a modernized form, are still part of Guinness stout advertising.

A long-standing strength of the Guinness business strategy was its relatively low average costs by industry standards. Apart from scale economies, this was achieved by the avoidance of certain capital-intensive merchandising costs (Bielenberg, 1998). It ultimately proved a weakness. Successful British and Irish breweries by the late nineteenth century distributed their beers through tied public houses—still an industry practice. Guinness did not have such a product distribution system. Instead it relied on its beer competitors (who did not produce stout) to distribute Guinness in their public houses. This marketing weakness was revealed in the 1960s when Guinness, in a break from its long-standing policy and in the face of stagnant stout sales, unsuccessfully responded to a shift in popular beer-drinking tastes toward lighter ales and lager-type beers. It introduced a new product, Harp lager, which was initially successful but ultimately proved difficult to place in the hands of the beer-consuming public.

After failing to capture any significant part of the new beer market in the 1960s, Guinness stout sales languished. The company, now without a Guinness family member at its head, acquired other companies and diversified, but not with clear strategic business goals. In the 1980s, Guinness initiated the friendly takeover of the Scottish Distillers Group, a financially ailing collection of whiskey (and gin) distilleries. Charges of irregularities, however, tainted the merger and the reputation of the Guinness firm. In May 1997, Guinness plc (public limited company) agreed to a merger with the multiproduct Grand Metropolitan Hotels company. In the process, the Guinness name disappeared as a company and it remains only as a brand in a long list of the food and beverages of the merged conglomerate, Diageo plc.

BIBLIOGRAPHY

Bielenberg, Andy. "The Irish Brewing Industry and the Rise of Guinness, 1790–1914." In *The Dynamics of the International Brewing Industry since 1800*, edited by R. G. Wilson and T. R. Gourvish, pp. 105–122. London and New York, 1998.
Dennison, S. R., and Oliver MacDonagh. *Guinness, 1886–1939: From Incorporation to the Second World War.* Cork, 1998.
Kochan, Nick, and Hugh Pym. *The Guinness Affair.* London, 1987.
Lynch, Patrick, and John Vaizey. *Guinness's Brewery in the Irish Economy, 1759–1876.* Cambridge, 1960.

DONALD G. PATERSON

GUTENBERG, JOHANNES (c. 1400–1468), German inventor.

Gutenberg is one of the most recognized names in the world. However, almost nothing is known about him. He is reputed to be "the inventor of printing," though strictly speaking he is the inventor of letterpress printing using movable type, available for the first time within the Western Hemisphere. Gutenberg is perhaps best known for what his invention produced—a cultural and social revolution.

What is actually known about Gutenberg stems almost exclusively either from court rolls or from citations mentioning him in the context of the invention of printing. He was born in Mainz. He belonged to the Patricians, who had been trying for years to defend their municipal power against the guild-corporations. In that struggle, the Patricians often left town for prolonged periods, Gutenberg among them—only he finally stayed abroad. The records mention him as a resident of Strasbourg from at least 1434 until 1444.

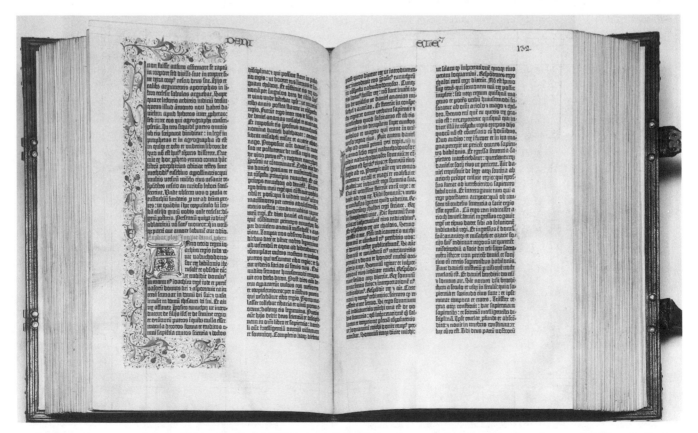

GUTENBERG BIBLE. Pages from *Bibla Latina* (Latin Bible), printed in Mainz, Germany, by Johannes Gutenberg and Johann Fust, circa 1455. (Pierpont Morgan Library, NY/Art Resource, NY)

After Gutenberg left his Alsacian "exile," he probably returned directly to Mainz. When he is mentioned in 1448, he was still living in Mainz and he possessed all that was necessary for printing as it was to be used until the last century (i.e., with movable cast-metal type and a letterpress). Contemporary documents provide convincing proof that he indeed was the inventor of printing: Gutenberg established a printing company with the calligrapher Peter Schöffer and the financier Johann Fust. One of their first productions was nothing less than the book of all books, the often so-called *Gutenberg Bible*, of which forty-nine copies still exist. It was, in its novelty and in its uniform beauty, one of the most influential works ever printed. From the beginning, Gutenberg and his companions experimented with printing techniques—color printing and even stereotyping—that were later introduced. In his final years, Gutenberg was in the service of the archbishop of Mainz. Gutenberg died on 3 February 1468. Fust and Schöffer successfully continued his work, which rapidly spread all over Europe.

The genius of Gutenberg's invention was the creation of movable letters that were of equal length and thickness but unequal width. He accomplished this by designing a mold consisting of two overlapping L-shaped parts. His knowledge of metallurgy stood him in good service here: the molds were made of an alloy of iron and copper, and the type was an alloy of tin, zinc, and lead. Movable type thus can be seen as a first successful application of the idea of interchangeable parts, since type could be reused over and over again.

Gutenberg was a rather unscrupulous businessman, and like most inventors, he was more concerned with his own interests than those of the rest of the world. Nonetheless, the importance of his invention can be described as nothing other than revolutionary. Printing reduced the cost of books so drastically that suddenly it was possible for large parts of society to gain access to knowledge, with all its consequences. The Renaissance, humanism, the Reformation, the beginning of our modern time are unthinkable without the constant creaking noise of the printing press.

[*See also* Printing Industry.]

BIBLIOGRAPHY

Eisenstein, Elizabeth L. *The Printing Revolution in Early Modern Europe*. Cambridge, 1983.

Ing, Janet. *Johann Gutenberg and his Bible*. New York, 1988.

König, Eberhard, ed. *Zur Situation der Gutenberg-Forschung*. Münster, 1995.

Ruppel, Aloys. *Johannes Gutenberg: Sein Leben und sein Werk*. Berlin, 1939, 1947; reprint, Nieuwkoop, Netherlands, 1967.

Venzke, Andreas. *Johannes Gutenberg: Der Erfinder des Buchdrucks und seine Zeit*. Munich, 2000.

Widmann, Hans, ed. *Der gegenwärtige Stand der Gutenberg-Forschung*. Stuttgart, 1972.

ANDREAS VENZKE

GUYANA. From a geographical and ecological perspective, the three Guyanas—Guyana, Suriname, and French Guyana—share some basic characteristics. Along the Wild Coast of South America, as the seashore was referred to in historical records, lies a rather narrow stretch of lowland where most of the population lives and the main cities are concentrated, including the three capital cities of Georgetown, Paramaribo, and Cayenne. In this stretch of land, the larger part of the economic activities of the three countries are concentrated.

More inland and at a somewhat higher altitude is a sandy savanna stretch, followed by highlands with pristine rainforests, which cover by far the larger part of the countries' land area, only interrupted by some mountain ranges. These forest regions are part of the much larger Guyana Shield, considered to be among the most ecologically diversified and valuable areas of the planet.

All three economies are rich in natural resources, and their population densities are very low. Exploitation of large bauxite reserves, gold mining and digging, fishing, and agricultural production, as well as some logging, are among the most important economic activities related to their natural resource endowments. Manufacturing activities are limited and mostly related to the processing of natural resources prior to their exportation.

From a political and economic perspective, however, the three Guyanas have experienced widely different development patterns during the last decades. Former British Guyana started its period of independence in 1966 and initially pursued a policy of "cooperative socialism," supported by the Soviet Union and Cuba, in which the state dominated the economy. Economic mismanagement resulted in the collapse of the nationalized bauxite and sugar markets, the key sectors of the economy. The dismal overall economic performance was reflected by long-term decline of income per capita, widespread poverty, and a massive outflow of probably 200,000 of the country's citizens. A comprehensive policy reversal occurred only in mid-1988 with the introduction of a neoliberal approach, supported by the International Monetary Fund (IMF) and the World Bank. After two decades of economic decline, a period of renewed economic growth began in the 1990s.

Suriname only became fully independent from the Dutch in 1975, after an extended period of relative autonomy that started in 1954—the so-called Period of the Statute—in which the country was allowed to run its domestic affairs, including economic policy, autonomously. To support independence both economically and politically, the former colonizer made available over 3,500 million Dutch guilders (about U.S. $1.45 billion). Never before had a process of decolonization been accompanied by such substantial financial support, particularly when one considers that the country's population at the time amounted to just 364,500 people. In the so-called golden years following the year of independence, the fortunate combination of increased nominal and real alumina and aluminium prices and record high inflows of Dutch Treaty Funds resulted in a pronounced growth of gross national product (GNP) and peaks in GNP per capita in 1978 and 1981. Never again did the Suriname economy score so high in terms of income per capita. Throughout the 1980s and 1990s, income levels showed much volatility, resulting from the boom-bust cycle in the international alumina and aluminium market, on which the country was strongly dependent for its foreign exchange revenues. Inadequate domestic policy responses to these external shocks tended to exacerbate economic instability. Human rights violations by the military government, which took power after a military coup in 1980, caused the Dutch to suspend the transfer of development aid between 1982 and 1987. The combination of the external and internal economic shocks, political instability, and the civil war of the 1980s caused average income per capita to decline during the 1980s, reaching a low point in 1987. After a brief upswing, income per capita fell back again to the 1987 level, but in subsequent years, income per capita was on the rise. As in Guyana, political turmoil and economic decline caused a massive outflow of over 110,000 citizens between 1975 and 1997.

A comparison of economic development in the Caribbean region shows that Guyana and Suriname have been at the lower extreme of the income per capita range since 1960. Between 1960 and 1998, average income per capita in Guyana increased from U.S. $676 to $825 (expressed in constant U.S. dollars of 1995), and in Suriname income levels increased from U.S. $564 to $710. At the turn of the twenty-first century, these two countries ranked lowest of all economies in the region in terms of income per capita, with the exception of Haiti. It should be noted, however, that official data do not account adequately for informal and illegal economic activities that in all likelihood may add significantly to income and welfare. Apart from the traditional activities in the informal sector, such activities include illegal logging and gold digging. Particularly in Suriname, the contribution of drug trafficking to income may have become substantial.

French Guyana has experienced a significantly different development pattern as compared to the other two Guyanas. Since 1946, it has been a French Overseas Department and consequently integrated into the French economic and political system, and, indeed, into the European Union. Moreover, it has been among the most prosperous of all countries and territories in the Caribbean region. Between 1960 and 1998, average income per capita increased from U.S. $5,370 to $13,044 (expressed in constant U.S. dollars of 1995). The establishment of the space center in Kourou (Centre Spatial Guyanais) in 1964 has contributed significantly to the diversification of the economy through direct and indirect income and spending effects, which have generated local activities in various economic sectors.

[*See also* France, *subentry on* French Empire; Great Britain, *subentry on* British Empire; *and* Low Countries, *subentry on* Dutch Empire.]

BIBLIOGRAPHY

Buddingh', H. *Geschiedenis van Suriname*. Utrecht, 1995.

Dijck, Pitou van, ed. *Suriname: The Economy—Prospects for Sustainable Development*. Kingston, Jamaica, 2001.

Dijck, Pitou van. "Structural Change and Long-Term Growth: The Suriname Experience." *Integration and Trade* 5.15 (2001), 275–299.

Hoefte, Rosemarijn, and Peter Meel, ed. *Twentieth Century Suriname: Continuities and Discontinuities in a New World Society*. Kingston, Jamaica, 2001.

PITOU VAN DIJCK

H

HABAKKUK HYPOTHESIS. Hrothgar John (Sir John) Habakkuk was professor of economic history at Oxford University from 1950 to 1967. The Habakkuk hypothesis is a proposed explanation for labor productivity differences between the United States and Great Britain that had become apparent, at least in some sectors, by the late-nineteenth century (Habakkuk, 1962, 1963).

From an economic perspective, it is natural to treat labor productivity as a function of capital per worker. Habakkuk followed this approach, but attempted to go further, exploring the mechanisms through which capital intensity came to differ across these economies. His account was primarily economic, resting on differences in factor costs and in labor supply elasticities. Where Habakkuk differed from a purely economic approach, however, was in his awareness of technological issues: he recognized that capital intensity differences involved not just more capital but also differences in the technological content and characteristics of the capital stock.

Habakkuk's argument was that the ratio of the cost of capital (machine prices and interest and depreciation rates) to the cost of labor was lower in the United States than in Britain. This was because of higher incomes in agriculture in existing farming, and higher potential incomes on new agricultural land in the United States. Not only did this raise U.S. factory wage costs, but it lowered wage differentials between skilled and unskilled labor, compared with the United Kingdom (Habakkuk, 1962, pp. 151–152). At the same time, labor supply elasticities differed: any attempt at capital-widening investment by U.S. manufacturers was therefore likely to face faster-rising marginal wage costs than in the United Kingdom. Taken together, these factors created incentives for labor-saving modes of capital investment. However, more capital-intensive techniques did not exist but had to be produced. This need led to the emergence of a different type of machine tool industry in the United States, supplying innovations adapted to the American situation, notably technologies based on interchangeable parts. Habakkuk's argument was that different economic frameworks led to different technological trajectories, and this difference underlay the productivity differences of the late nineteenth century.

Though not often cited now, the Habakkuk hypothesis has had a strong influence. Criticism of it has rested on its generality, with many questioning whether it explained specific areas of technological advance (see Saul, 1970), whether labor costs alone (in the absence of evidence of incentives, skills, and effort) are pertinent as data, and whether it is supported by empirical evidence (Mokyr, 1990). Nevertheless, the Habakkuk hypothesis remains relevant to current issues. For example, the debate on whether or not the British economy "declined" in the late-nineteenth century turns in part on whether or not entrepreneurs within it were responding to economic forces in a more or less rational way (as the Habakkuk hypothesis suggests), or whether entrepreneurial failure, or other factors, account for British performance.

[*See also* Technology.]

BIBLIOGRAPHY

Habakkuk, Hrothgar J. *American and British Technology in the Nineteenth Century.* Cambridge, 1962.

Habakkuk, Hrothgar J. "Second Thoughts on British and American Technology in the Nineteenth Century." *Business Archives and History* 3 (1963).

Mokyr, Joel. *The Lever of Riches: Technological Creativity and Economic Progress.* New York, 1990.

Saul, S. B., ed. *Technological Change: The United States and Britain in the 19th Century.* London, 1970.

KRÏSTINE BRULAND

HABER, FRITZ (1868–1934), German physicochemist.

Born on 9 December 1868 in Wrocław, Poland, Haber descended from a Jewish merchant's family. Haber studied chemistry in Berlin and Heidelberg and obtained a doctorate at the University of Berlin in 1891. From 1892 until 1894 he worked in the Chemical Institute of the University at Jena. In 1894, Haber was an assistant to Hans Bunte (1848–1925), director of the Institute of Technical Chemistry at the Technical University (Technische Hochschule) in Karlsruhe. In 1896, Haber became a lecturer and, in 1898, an assistant professor, working in the area of electrochemistry and chemical thermodynamics.

In 1906, Haber was nominated full professor and director of the Institute of Physical Chemistry in Karlsruhe. His main activity at that time was to solve the problem of fixing nitrogen from the air. Haber first worked on combining atmospheric nitrogen with oxygen in an electric arc. This process was unsatisfactory, owing to the high expenditure of energy required. Later, he examined the conditions of the reaction of nitrogen with hydrogen to synthesize ammonia. Haber and his coworkers succeeded by developing a new process in which a suitable amount of the gases continually reacted to form ammonia using a heated catalyst (uranium or osmium). The process ran under about 175 atmospheres and 550°C and the gases were recycled until a yield of 8 percent ammonia. The mixture was then separated using a cooling device.

It was the first industrially developed high-pressure process realized and was transferred to an industrial process at the Badische Anilin und Soda Fabrik (BASF) at Ludwigshafen, Germany, by Carl Bosch (1874–1940), later president of the IG Farben concern, and using cheaper catalysts (iron oxide mixtures) found by Alwin Mittasch (1869–1953).

During the decades up to the present time, the process conditions and catalysts were further developed. This may be exemplified by the change of the used reactors for a one-thousand-ton plant (from twenty-one to one), a remarkable decrease of the used compressors (from ten to one), the difference of the energy (92 to 33 gigajoules per ton (GJ/t) of ammonia), and the reduction of the catalyst stages eight to one.

For his invention and the development of this process, Haber was awarded the Nobel Prize in chemistry in 1918.

In 1911, Haber was appointed director of the newly established Kaiser-Wilhelm-Institut für Physikalische Chemie und Elektrochemie in Berlin-Dahlem. During World War I, the whole institute was involved in gas warfare, and Haber organized the development of new gas weapons and their application at the front. After the war, a project was started to find a solution to pay the German war debt by obtaining the gold in seawater. The project failed, as the amount of the gold per ton of seawater was too low.

Later, Haber with his coworkers studied new fields of research, among them reaction kinetics, atomic structure, and quantum physics. From 1921 until 1932, Haber was also actively promoting science by cofounding the Notgemeinschaft der Deutschen Wissenschaften (later Deutsche Forschungsgemeinschaft, a prominent institution for promoting science in Germany) and founding the so-called Japaninstitut for cultural exchange between Germany and Japan. He was president of the German Chemical Society and head of all German scientific and industrial chemical societies. He promoted international cooperation by overcoming the exclusion of German science from the international science organization and was one of the founders of the IUPAC (International Association of Pure and Applied Chemistry), becoming its vice-president.

In 1933, he resigned from all offices because of the defamation of the Jews by the National-Socialist regime and emigrated first to France, later to England, working at Cambridge University. Contacts with the Zionist Chaim Weizmann (1874–1952), chemist and later the first president of Israel, led to an invitation to work in what was later known as the Weizmann Institute of Science in Rehovot, Israel. Haber died on 29 January 1934 of a heart attack on the way to Israel during a meeting with relatives in Basel, Switzerland. He was buried in Hörnli/Basel.

Haber married Clara Immerwahr in 1901, who was the first woman to receive a doctorate in physical chemistry at the University of Wrocław. She committed suicide in 1915. They had one son, who died in 1946 in New York. Haber's second wife was Charlotte Nathan. They had one daughter and one son, now living in England.

BIBLIOGRAPHY

Goran, Morris. *The Story of Fritz Haber*. Norman, Okla., 1967.

Stoltzenberg, Dietrich. *Fritz Haber: Chemiker, Nobelpreisträger, Deutscher, Jude*. 2d ed. Weinheim, Germany, 1998.

Stoltzenberg, Dietrich. *Fritz Haber: Chemist, Nobel Prize Winner, German, Jew*. Translated from the German by Jenny Kien. Philadelphia, 2001.

Szöllösi-Janze, Margot. *Fritz Haber, 1868–1934, eine Biographie*. Munich, 1998.

Wille, Hermann Heinz. *Der Januskopf*. Berlin, 1970.

DIETRICH STOLTZENBERG

HABSBURG EMPIRE. *See* Austria, *subentry on* Austro-Hungarian Empire.

HACIENDA. *See* Latifundia.

HAITI. As the French colony of Saint-Domingue, Haiti was for much of the eighteenth century the world's main exporter of indigo, sugar, and coffee, one of the most materially successful slave societies. The revolution of 1789 to 1803, which ended slavery and won Haiti its independence, brought massive destruction to towns and plantations and devastated the export economy. The revolution decimated the population of African descent and expelled the French colonizers, who had almost monopolized professional, administrative, and managerial activities. The new society was characterized by extreme social cleavage. The formerly enslaved rural masses were creole-speaking, polygamous, and voodooist in religion; a large proportion was African-born. The new urban elite was mainly Catholic and French in culture, and of mixed racial descent, although it included lower-class blacks who rose through the army. After seizing the landholdings of the French, the new state made intermittent attempts, notably under King Henry Christophe (1811–1820), to revive sugar manufacture and to confine

the rural population to plantations. These attempts had to be abandoned after 1830. The ex-slaves shunned plantation labor, especially on sugar estates, and sought to construct new lives as peasant freeholders cultivating food crops and some coffee. The peasantry grew by purchasing abandoned estates piecemeal, squatting, and entering into sharecropping arrangements. Beginning in 1809, the state also periodically distributed land to soldiers. Although scholars disagree on the extent of sharecropping and peasant freehold, the predominance of smallholdings and the near absence of large estates has distinguished Haiti from other parts of Latin America. Constitutions prevented whites from owning land from 1805 to 1918.

Coffee has been Haiti's main export since independence, and taxes on coffee exports have been the main source of government revenue. Coffee production, roughly halved by the revolution, regained prerevolutionary levels in the mid-nineteenth century. A fall in world coffee prices initiated in the early 1820s by Brazilian expansion was a major blow to the country. Poor preparation of beans additionally reduced export earnings. Sugar cane cultivation produced mainly molasses and rum for domestic consumption; around 1900 Haiti was the Caribbean's major rum producer. Cotton cultivation revived in the 1860s, but the fiber was not processed locally; and timber was exported until reserves were exhausted at the start of the twentieth century. Forced to accept the decline of large-scale agriculture, the elite shifted its attention from landowning to seeking revenue from commerce, the professions, and politics. Foreign merchants, however, soon gained a dominant position in Haiti's international trade, especially as they were able to provide or negotiate loans for retailers and the government. The state became heavily indebted when it agreed in 1825 to pay $30 million (later reduced to $18 million) compensation to former colonists as the price of France's recognition of Haitian independence. The indemnity took more than fifty years to pay off. Foreign debt increased in the decades before World War I, stimulated by government corruption and compensation payments made to victimized foreign nationals. The large army also absorbed a major share of nineteenth-century budgets. Most governments have been corrupt, weak, and short-lived, and have shown little interest in the peasantry except as a source of tax revenue. Politics became a spoils system for the elite with minimal participation by other groups.

Toward the close of the nineteenth century there began a demographically driven downward economic spiral that still continues. Population pressure turned land abundance into land shortage, while traditions of equal inheritance accelerated the parcellization of landholdings. Coffee gave ground to food crops that, in largely mountainous Haiti, provoke severe soil erosion, absent any tradition of terracing. Remaining mountain forests have been cleared for cultivation and to produce charcoal for cooking, so worsening the problem. The cultivable area shrinks as the population grows. Outmigration and resultant cash remittances played an important role in the early and late twentieth century. The migration, chiefly of cane-cutters, focused on Cuba and the Dominican Republic until the 1930s. Since 1960, increasing immiseration, political repression, and instability have sent thousands of middle- and lower-class families, often illegally, to the French Caribbean, the Bahamas, and North America. Although such migration is typical of the modern West Indies, Haiti is unusual in maintaining a high fertility rate despite a sizable reduction in infant mortality. For long the poorest country in the Americas, Haiti achieved the world's lowest national level of nutrition in the 1980s.

Worsening political instability has twice led to U.S. military occupation. The occupation of 1915 to 1934 brought fiscal reform, foreign investment, infrastructural development, and a 50 percent increase in exports. Peasants in some regions lost their land to new plantations. Sisal exports flourished until the 1960s. Cotton exports peaked and then collapsed in the 1930s. The Haitian American company has met local sugar needs since 1918. Haiti's foreign debt was halved by 1930 and, under U.S. supervision, paid off in 1947. Roads, port facilities, and the telephone system began decaying after the American departure in 1934. Centralization on the capital, Port-au-Prince, and the decline of the provincial towns began during the occupation but massively increased after 1950. Since the 1940s, essential oils have become a major export. Bauxite was mined from 1953 to 1983. A struggling tourist industry was extinguished by the brutal dictatorship of François Duvalier (1957–1971) and by the AIDS crisis of the 1980s. Currency devaluation began in the early 1980s, as foreign and government debt mounted, destabilizing the rule of Jean-Claude Duvalier (1971–1986). Foreign aid increased from under $5 million per annum in 1950 to 1970 to more than $200 million after 1986. Literacy progressed slightly. Import substitution manufacturing developed in the 1960s, and light assembly industry added 60,000 jobs in the late 1970s. However, the election and overthrow in 1991 of Jean-Bertrand Aristide, the country's first democratically elected president, inspired an international embargo (1991–1994) that wrecked the assembly industries and modest gains in reforestation. The United States again intervened with a military occupation (1994–1996) to reinstate parliamentary government and to hinder drug transshipments through Haiti. At the twentieth century's close, about 70 percent of Haiti's population were still peasants, despite the tripling of Port-au-Prince's population in twenty-five years. The economy remained in crisis, and the political system fragile.

[*See also* Caribbean Region; France, *subentry on* French Empire; *and* Spain, *subentry on* Spanish Empire.]

BIBLIOGRAPHY

Barthélemy, Gérard. *Dans la splendeur d'un après-midi d'histoire*. Port-au-Prince, 1996. An argument that an egalitarian ethic causes the peasantry to resist change.

Fass, Simon. *Political Economy in Haiti: The Drama of Survival*. New Brunswick, 1988. Quirky critique of foreign aid policy, containing valuable microeconomic studies.

Heinl, Robert Debs, and Nancy Gordon Heinl. *Written in Blood: The Story of the Haitian People, 1492–1995*. 2d ed. Lanham, Md., 1996. Lurid but informative political history.

Lundahl, Mats. *Peasants and Poverty: A Study of Haiti*. New York, 1979.

Lundahl, Mats. *The Haitian Economy: Man, Land and Markets*. New York, 1983. Blames population growth and political corruption rather than international trade relations for Haiti's problems. Unlike Christian Girault, in *Le commerce du café en Haïti* (Paris, 1981), Lundahl claims commercial intermediaries do not exploit peasants in marketing their export crops.

Mathon, Alix. *Haiti, un cas*. Port-au-Prince, 1985. Defends the record of Haitian governments, emphasizing foreign-imposed constraints.

Nicholls, David. *From Dessalines to Duvalier: Race, Colour and National Independence in Haiti*. Rev. ed. New Brunswick, 1996. A political and intellectual history that argues race-consciousness has strengthened Haitian nationalism, whereas color distinctions have reinforced political divisions and weakened the country.

Rotberg, Robert I., with Christopher K. Clague. *Haiti: The Politics of Squalor*. Boston, 1971. Criticized for its psychologizing; contains a useful statistical appendix.

Trouillot, Michel-Rolph. *Haiti: State Against Nation: The Origins and Legacy of Duvalierism*. New York, 1990. Emphasizes class relations' responsibility for government deficiencies.

DAVID GEGGUS

HAMBURG, city and state in Germany, is located on the Elbe River roughly 100 kilometers (62 miles) from the river's mouth in the North Sea. The city's history began with the Carolingian castle Hammaburg, which was erected no later than CE 822. The small settlement became the seat of a bishopric in 831, which united with the archdiocese Bremen in 864. Its chief spiritual dominance was in Bremen, and therefore, transport and commerce could become the dominant factors of Hamburg's development.

After the founding of Lübeck in 1143 on the Baltic coast, some 60 kilometers (37 miles) from Hamburg, the city became the crossing point of two major trade routes. First, the east-west route from Russia and the eastern Baltic to the industrial regions in northwest Europe, which—as the backbone of Hanseatic trade—was the most important route until the second half of the fifteenth century. Second, the Elbe River, navigable up to the city of Magdeburg (today *land* Saxony-Anhalt), and its hinterland provided grain, timber, and other agrarian and forest products. The latter route became the basis for the upswing of Hamburg from the late sixteenth century.

Politically, Hamburg was subordinated to the count of Holstein. But it managed early to secure substantial autonomy and together with Lübeck was part of the Wendish quarter, the most active quarter of the Hansa. Even when in 1460 the princely rights of the counts passed to the royal house of Denmark, Hamburg was able to use its growing economic strength to play the Danish card against the imperial one. In 1618–1648, it became a free imperial city, the status for which was acknowledged by the Danish king only in 1768. Hamburg has retained its independence until today, being the second-smallest of the sixteen *Länder* of Germany.

Until the beginning of the fifteenth century (in a city of approximately 8,000 inhabitants), Hamburg's economy was founded more on services—above all, shipping—than on trade due to of Hamburg merchants. Besides shipbuilding, brewing of hopped beer emerged in the early fourteenth century and became an important export industry with its main markets in Denmark and the Netherlands. In the 1450s, Hamburg merchants developed grain trade to northwestern Europe.

Things changed dramatically as the Atlantic trade system emerged in the sixteenth century. Three factors favored Hamburg's growth. First, its favorable geographical site supplied the port with unlimited possibilities for expansion. Second, together with the Oder River, the Elbe linked Hamburg by a 750-kilometer (465-mile) waterway with the interior of Germany and central Europe, including the German Empire as well as parts of Poland and Hungary. The resources of that hinterland could easily be brought to Hamburg. In addition, the city was provided with western European and colonial goods imported by Hamburg merchants. Third, since the revolt of the Netherlands against Spain in the 1560s, the city was open to refugees from western Europe as well as to immigration by foreign merchants. Therefore, Dutch, English, Portuguese, and French merchants brought their commercial know-how, developed new trade contacts, and provided the capital necessary for trade expansion and a growing money market. Thus in 1558, the first German stock exchange was founded there, and in 1619 the Hamburg Bank was established. In addition, the Dutch stimulated Hamburg's manufacture of cloth.

Hamburg further profited by the changing trade routes that supported Leipzig and its fairs, instead of the south German cities. In the seventeenth century, the transcontinental trade favored Hamburg on both the east-northwest route (from Leipzig to Hamburg to Amsterdam) and on the south-north route (from Venice to Nuremberg, Hamburg, and Amsterdam). Due to its neutrality and supported by expensive but effective fortifications, the city prospered during the Thirty Years' War. It maintained trade connections with all belligerent powers and served as a clearing and finance center. Besides the Netherlands, Spain and Portugal were the city's most important partners.

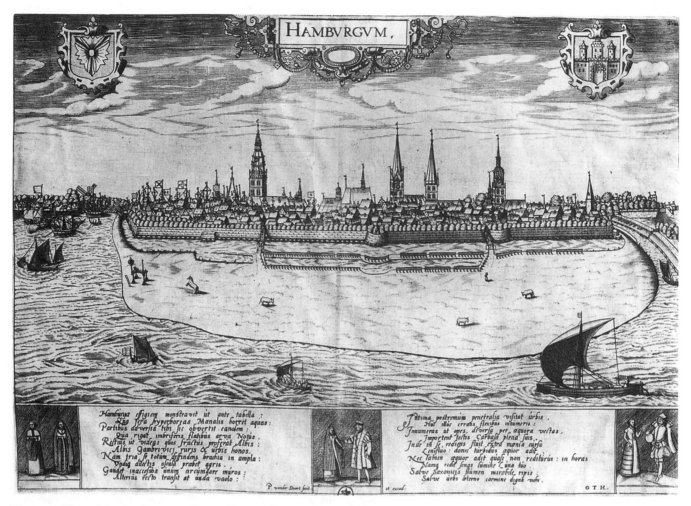

HAMBURG. View of the city. Engraving by Paullus van der Doort, sixteenth century. (Bibliothèque Nationale, Paris/Giraudon/Art Resource, NY)

Additionally, Hamburg was engaged in trade with Russia via Archangel and, by the end of the seventeenth century, with France. In this period, beer was replaced by refined sugar as the city's most important export product. By 1700, the population grew to 60,000, up from 40,000 at the start of the century.

At the end of the eighteenth century, Hamburg profited by the independence many colonies in America achieved. The way into the new trade system of the nineteenth century was opened in 1783 when Hamburg merchants took advantage of the new markets in the now independent English colonies in North America. After the deep depression caused by the seizure of the city by Napoleonic troops and by Napoleon's Continental System (blockade of Great Britain) in the 1820s, trade connections were also established with Central and South American states, which had become independent from Portugal and Spain. In the middle of the century, Hamburg had become the second-greatest trading city, in terms of volume, behind London,

and in the second half of the century, Hamburg expanded its trade to Southeast Asia and Australia as well as Africa.

Under the German Empire (founded in 1871), Hamburg received financial support to build a large free port—with fatal consequences for many harbor workers who had to move to the city's outlying districts. It was opened in 1888 and supported the settlement of industries (food industries, coffee roasters, refineries for mineral oil, and rubber and asbestos processing). Thus at the turn of the century, Hamburg (population 623,000) had become Germany's second-largest industrial city and busiest port, where 4.5 percent of the world's trade volume was loaded and unloaded. The world's largest shipping company (HAPAG) had its seat there.

Because of its strong international economic entanglement, Hamburg suffered from the British sea blockade in World War I. In 1919, when nearly all ships had to be handed over to the Allies, Hamburg's economy fell into a deep crisis. In 1937, the Greater Hamburg Ordinance (Groß

Hamburg Gesetz) incorporated the cities of Altona, Wandsbek, and Hamburg, making Hamburg Germany's largest industrial city. The city's territory was doubled, and its population grew by 40 percent to 1.7 million inhabitants.

World War II destroyed approximately 50 percent of Hamburg, but the city recovered relatively quickly. In the period of German partition (1949–1990), Hamburg handled more than half of West Germany's foreign trade. At the beginning of the twenty-first century, Hamburg's economy stands on three pillars: industry (processing and manufacturing industries, such as copper works, chemical, steel, and shipbuilding); newspaper and periodical publishing; and (Germany's second-most important center) trade (shipping cargo, rail, and airfreight) and transportation (fifteen thousand ships through the harbor each year). In 2000, Hamburg's population totaled 1,703,000 inhabitants.

BIBLIOGRAPHY

Jochmann, Werner, and Hans-Dieter Loose, eds. *Hamburg: Geschichte der Stadt und ihrer Bewohner.* 2 vols. Hamburg, 1986.

Klessmann, Eckart. *Geschichte der Stadt Hamburg.* Hamburg, 1994.

Krawehl, Otto-Ernst. *Hamburgs Schiffs- und Warenverkehr mit England und den englischen Kolonien 1814–1860: Forschungen zur internationalen Sozial- und Wirtschaftsgeschichte,* vol. 11. Cologne and Vienna, 1977.

North, Michael. "Hamburg: The Continent's Most English City." In *From the North Sea to the Baltic: Essays in Commercial, Monetary, and Agrarian History, 1500–1800,* edited by Michael North. Collected Studies Series, 548, pp. 1–13. Aldershot, U.K., 1996.

Zunckel, Julia. *Rüstungsgeschäfte im Dreißigjährigen Kkrieg: Unternehmerkräfte, Militärgüter und Marktstrategien im Handel zwischen Genua, Amsterdam, und Hamburg.* Schriften zur Wirtschafts- und Sozialgeschichte, vol. 49. Berlin, 1997.

ROLF HAMMEL-KIESOW

HANKOU is one of three cities that make up the city of Wuhan, in Hubei Province, along with Wuchang and Hanyang. The location of Hankou, in the geographic center of China where the Yangzi and Han Rivers meet, made it a prominent commercial hub as a transfer point between overland and water routes, as well as between deep-water and shallow-water vessels, owing to the different depths of the upper and lower Yangzi and the Han. The city developed during the Song dynasty (960–1279) and grew quickly because of its small interior waterways, which allowed merchants to bring boats through the area. In 1535, a dike was constructed, stretching nearly 20 miles along the northern border of the city, with a canal alongside. This served the purpose of flood control but also allowed passage and anchorage of small merchant vessels, aiding growth. By the sixteenth century, Hankou was larger than the provincial capital, with tens of thousands of households. In 1643, at the end of the Ming dynasty, Hankou was pillaged by rebel forces, but the city was able to recover quickly and achieved national prominence as a trade center during the early Qing period.

Until the mid-seventeenth century, Hankou served as a large regional market specializing in luxury goods, but as the lower Yangzi region transformed into an urban area and began to rely on grain imports, the city became a link in an integrated national commercial network. Rice from Hunan, Sichuan, and Hubei provinces passed through Hankou, enabling the city to earn huge profits through its role as an intermediary port along the trade route. The rice trade peaked in the mid-eighteenth century and declined slightly in the early nineteenth century, when the largest trades were grain, salt, tea, oils, medicinal herbs, hides and furs, and cotton. In 1853, Hankou's most important trade route, along the lower Yangzi, was sealed off during the Taiping Rebellion of 1851–1864, and rebel forces destroyed the Wuhan cities in 1854, halting trade. The government recaptured the city in the next year, but it was many years before Hankou regained its prewar economic position.

In 1861, Hankou was opened as a treaty port, one of the first Chinese cities opened to foreign trade, and concessions were granted to British, French, German, Japanese, and Russian interests. This brought the steamship to the area and enabled Hankou to enter the international tea trade, but otherwise little changed in the first few decades. By the 1890s, imperialism and the strains of the Sino-Japanese War shifted control of the Hankou trade to the West, and foreign trade tripled, aided by the railroad built in 1898. However, the influence of the West did not change the nature of Hankou's markets, since their demand was for goods such as tea, hides, tung oil, hemp, iron ore, and coal, for which markets already existed. They were unable to find markets to export goods into Hankou except for metals and opium.

After the Communist takeover, the Communist government, aided by the Soviet Union, built iron and steel mills in the 1950s, and nearby iron and coal reserves established Hankou as a metallurgical center by the late twentieth century. The iron and steel base attracted other industries producing chemicals, fertilizers, electrical equipment, glass, agricultural machinery, railroad cars, trucks, cement works, paper, distilleries, and soap. It is also the site of one of China's more important arsenals. Consumer industries produce watches, bicycles, and radios and other electronic instruments. The city still contains rice, oil, and flour mills and produces cotton and woolen fabrics and other textiles. Hankou remains the main collection and distribution point for west and southwest China, especially for tea, cotton, silk, timber, tung oil, and an assortment of manufactured goods.

BIBLIOGRAPHY

Chen, Nai-ruenn, and Walter Galenson. *The Chinese Economy under Communism.* Chicago, 1969.

Li, Cheng. *Rediscovering China: Dynamics and Dilemmas of Reform.* Lanham, Md., 1997.

Rowe, William T. *Hankow: Commerce and Society in a Chinese City, 1796–1889.* Stanford, Calif., 1984.

Rowe, William T. *Hankow: Conflict and Community in a Chinese City, 1796–1895.* Stanford, Calif., 1989.

HANSEATIC LEAGUE. The German Hanse, often called the Hanseatic League, was less a political league than a commercial organization, which made its first appearance in the mid-twelfth century and finally disappeared in the late-seventeenth century. From the later-fourteenth century on, some members tried to transform this loose organization of northern German merchants and towns into a political confederation; but they never succeeded in doing so. Nevertheless, such efforts led many nineteenth- and twentieth-century historians to portray the German Hanse as a powerful, strongly hierarchical, and well-organized league of towns.

In fact, the inadequacies of travel and communications during medieval and early modern times made it virtually impossible to create, let alone govern, such an institutionalized organization of over seventy towns spread across vast distances: in the west, from the river IJssel in the Netherlands to Lake Peipus, bordering Estonia and Russia in the northeast; and in the north, from Visby on the isle of Gotland southward to a line running from Cologne, on the Rhine, and then eastward to Erfurt, Breslau (Wrocław), and Krakau (Krakow), in Poland. Over such a large territory, close commercial contacts were made possible only through personal relations based upon families and partnerships, and, in the Baltic coastal towns, through the adoption of common or similar urban law codes, based chiefly upon those of Lübeck or Hamburg. Furthermore, most Hanse towns were in principle proprietary, and most were subordinated to the fairly substantial control of town lords. Only a few gained enough economic power to achieve even relative independence; and the most important of these was Lübeck, which became a free imperial city in 1226. During the fifteenth century, about seventy towns actively participated in Hanseatic affairs, while representing the interests of one hundred thirty smaller towns, so that the total number of so-called Hanse towns was approximately two hundred. The great majority of these towns were situated west of the Elbe river, with relatively few located in the Baltic region.

A major role of the medieval German Hanse was to serve the commercial interests of the northern German merchants in the intermediary trade from Novgorod in Russia to both Bruges in Flanders and London (and the English east-coast ports), a trade that also involved ancillary markets in Norway (principally Bergen) and those in the Rhineland and in central Germany. The chief zones, covering an area of about 500,000 square kilometers, were, from the west: the northeast Netherlands, lower Rhineland, Westphalia, Lower Saxony, the Wendish quarter (including towns in modern-day Schleswig-Holstein and Mecklenburg), Pomerania, Brandenburg, Prussia, Poland, Livonia (modern-day Latvia and Estonia), and Sweden (principally the towns of Visby and Stockholm). From the later fourteenth century on, Hanseatic trade expanded in the west to the Bay of Biscay, Spain, Portugal, and in the South, to northern Italy (chiefly Venice); and in the north, to Iceland—thus expanding the commercial zone to about six million square kilometers. Within this vast region a clear distinction has to be made about commercial functions. Only in northern Europe, and especially only in towns accessible to Hanseatic shipping, did these German trading towns gain rights, protection, and privileges common to all members of the Hanse; in contrast, in southern, Mediterranean Europe, German trade was conducted by individual merchants, who did not enjoy similar Hanseatic rights and privileges.

Obviously, even from the beginning, the commercial interests of these various Hanseatic regions differed markedly. The Rhenish towns, for example, developed a commercial economy based on the Rhineland trade and the trade with England; the Prussian towns came to depend on the grain trade between Poland and the Teutonic Order's territories in the east and the Netherlands in the west. The heart of Hanseatic commerce, therefore, somewhat paradoxically, lay in specific regional interests. Nevertheless, from about the mid-fourteenth century on, the Hanse towns together controlled four major trading kontors or "factories" (*Facktoreien*): the Steelyard in London, with its export trade in English wool and cloth; the Peterhof in Novgorod, with its trade in Russian fur and wax, and other eastern and Asian products acquired from the northern junctions of the Silk road; the Bergen kontor, with its trade in Norwegian stockfish (dried cod), whose primary markets lay in Boston (England) and Lübeck; the Bruges kontor in Flanders, by far the most important, with its staple trade in Flemish and Brabantine woolen textiles. Affiliated with these major kontors were many smaller factories under Hanseatic control.

The northern German merchants managed to gain control over northern Europe's east-west trade through a combination of certain structural economic advantages and innovations that gave them commercial superiority over any current rivals. First, with the demographic and economic growth generated during the twelfth and thirteenth centuries, the "Commercial Revolution era," the north Germans benefited from the increasing demand for both high-valued low-weight commodities and low-valued bulk goods. They opened up continental markets for Baltic and Scandinavian goods and thus became indispensable for

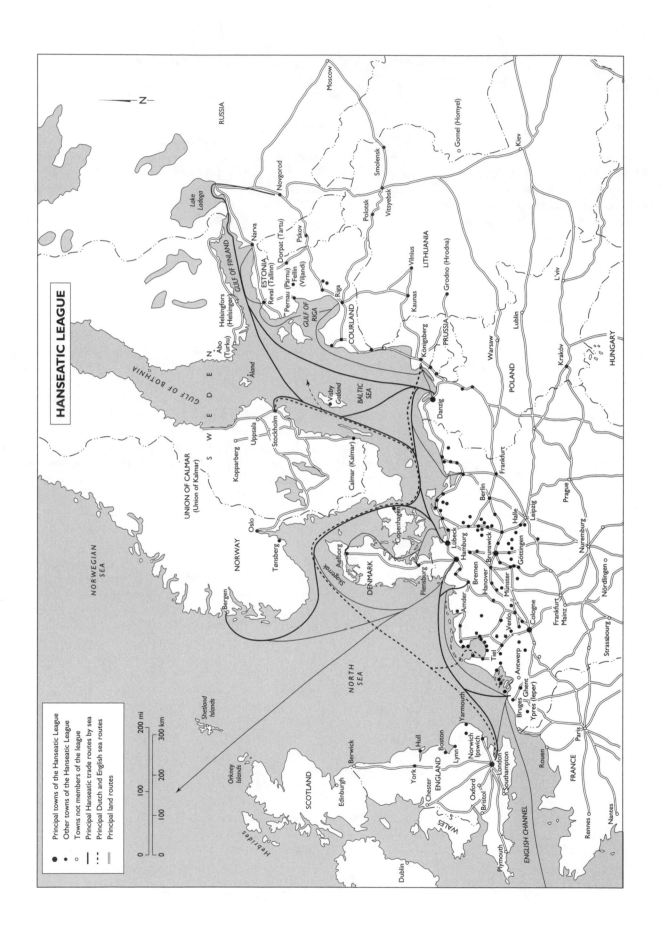

the economies of these regions. In the kontors or trading factories abroad, they managed to resolve their differences in order to use such collective bargaining powers to secure the desired legal, fiscal, and commercial privileges. Nevertheless, they never managed to monopolize this east–west trade because the indigenous merchants also managed to participate in it. Second, the north Germans also employed advances in naval technology to gain their commercial supremacy—in particular, by developing the *kogge* or cog, a capacious round ship, easily maneuverable, with ample cargo space, which allowed them lower freight rates than those of their rivals. Third, when the so-called commercial revolution changed the structure of trade, by the second half of the thirteenth century, wholesale merchants proved to be the strongest political power in town councils, especially in the coastal cities; and thus they were able to use the political powers of the towns themselves to support, to some degree, the commercial interests of just a small group of merchants. Fourth, after the breakdown of the German Empire, with the death of Emperor Frederick II Hohenstaufen, in 1250, the north German towns took advantage of the weakness of the local princes to protect their own merchants' trade by forming regional town leagues—principally to defend themselves again the depredations of pirates and robbers, and to secure adequate legal protection in the markets that they frequented. These regional town leagues became the fundamental core of the Hanse; and the evolution of the Hanseatic League may be seen as the result of such common efforts to achieve both personal and collective economic security.

Scale of Hanseatic Trade. Within this intermediary Hanseatic trade, the eastern Baltic did supply a few luxury items: Russian and Livonian furs, amber, wax, and such Far Eastern commodities as silk, spices, and incense. Of much greater importance for western Europe was the Baltic maritime commerce in high-bulk, low-valued cargoes, especially foodstuffs and industrial raw materials. During the later Middle Ages, the primary foodstuffs were salt, herring, and beer; but by the early modern era, the Baltic zone had become western Europe's primary source of imported grains, chiefly Prussian and Livonian rye and barley, as well as forest products, naval stores (flax, hemp, pitch), copper (from Sweden and Hungary), and iron (from Sweden). In return, as their most important export to the Baltic zone, Flanders and England sent woolen textiles. Because the western demand for these Baltic and eastern commodities exceeded the value of their exports, these western Europe regions developed a growing "balance-of-payments" deficit with the east, one that had to be met with shipments of silver.

The scale of this northern Hanseatic trade can be placed in proper perspective with recent estimates (Spufford, 2002) that, during the second half of the fourteenth century,

Italian trade in the Mediterranean basin was consistently about fifteen times greater in value (if not in volume). Even at the end of the fifteenth century, the net value of Venetian trade overall was many times greater than that enjoyed by Lübeck, which still remained the capital of Hanseatic east-west trade. Corresponding to these scale differences, Hanseatic commercial techniques were much less developed; indeed the distinct "backwardness" of north German banking and financial instruments may be attributed to both the small scale of Hanseatic trade and the chronic balance-of-payments deficits.

Changes in the Fourteenth Century. Nevertheless, the Hanseatic merchants continued to dominate northern Europe's east-west trade, in supplying Baltic goods to markets along the Cologne-Krakow axis, until the middle of the fourteenth century. When the Black Death, subsequent bubonic plagues, widespread debilitating warfare, and general disorder led to a severe decline in population during the second half of the fourteenth century, such decline undoubtedly manifested itself in a severe drop in the demand for these Baltic goods and thus in the eastern demand for western textiles (even if Poland did not suffer as severe a depopulation as the west). That can certainly be seen in the shrinkage in Lübeck's seaborne trade between 1368 and 1379. From that time on, the north German merchants faced a series of increasing problems. When Dutch merchant ships invaded the former Hanse preserves in the eastern Baltic, English merchants soon followed; and in England, Hanseatic privileges were now guaranteed only for the life of the reigning king. Thus the markets and the commerce of the Hanse seriously contracted during the later Middle Ages.

The formerly loose organization of towns and merchants now became more institutionalized. During the fourteenth century, all the major trading kontors were given much more organized structures; and, in connection with the 1358 blockade of Flanders, the term *dudesche hense* was chosen as a political catchword to demonstrate the power of the now more confederated towns. Thus the German Hanse is an example of a "defensive 'institution'" that developed in times of challenge "to perpetuate the dominance of these northern European cities" in northern trade (North and Thomas, 1970). This organization was, so to speak, a continuously shifting coalition of towns with roughly similar overall goals but widely differing interests. Consensus had to be reached on the assemblies of the Hanse, the Hanseatic Diets, where Hanseatic trade and common policies were governed; but they met only infrequently.

Changes in International Trade. From the fifteenth century on, two other major changes diminished the Hanseatic share of international trade. The first involved major geographic shifts in the structure of trade, which began with the revival of transcontinental overland trade from the mid-fifteenth century on and culminated with the rise of the Atlantic commercial system in the mid-sixteenth century. That first phase also led, by the end of the fifteenth century, to a major shift of commerce and finance from Bruges to Antwerp; and that shift cost the Hanse merchants the privileged position that they had earlier maintained in their western European trade via their Flemish kontor. In Antwerp they were unable to compete with the south German merchants who brought silver and copper, which the Portuguese sought as their chief commodities to conduct their newly inaugurated spice trade with the Far East. In 1508, seven years after the first spice ships arrived at Antwerp, the king of Portugal made that port the European official staple (ironically called Feitoria de Flandres) for this trade. In the 1420s, Antwerp had become the continental staple for the English cloth trade; but, subsequently, the outbreak of the Eighty Years' War (the revolt of the Netherlands against Spanish rule, which began in 1568) forced the English to desert Antwerp and thus to seek more direct access to cloth markets in north Germany and the Baltic itself. In the Baltic commerce, as early as the fifteenth century, Denmark (followed by Sweden in the 1530s) had benefited from growing trade with rivals of the Hanse, especially the Dutch, who received commercial privileges that seriously undermined the formerly quasi-monopolistic position of the German merchants. Indeed, by the 1470s, Prussia, Poland, and Livonia had become the main suppliers for the Dutch grain trade; and, by the mid-sixteenth century, Dutch ships had even won control of the Baltic, carrying trade to the west. At the beginning of the Thirty Years' War (1618–1648), they held 69 percent of the Baltic seaborne trade. In the Russian trade, the Hanseatic merchants had also lost their monopolistic position by the middle of the sixteenth century, when Russian political conquests and Swedish expansion opened new harbors for rivals of the Hanse (Narva). Furthermore, in 1553, a new trade route between Russia and western Europe was opened, via the northern Dvina and the White Sea; and, after the foundation of Archangel in 1583–1584, it took over some share of the Russian exports.

Although the Hanse share of international trade shrank dramatically during the sixteenth and seventeenth centuries, the volume and the value of trade in some Hanse towns, Hamburg, Lübeck, and Danzig (Gdansk) especially, rose in absolute terms until the 1670s. Therefore, the main reasons for the decline of the Hanse were less economic than political ones. First, it declined because it lacked any centralized power with which to withstand the power of the now-centralizing monarchies, from England to Russia. Certainly, from the mid-sixteenth century on, they were claiming absolute sovereignty over their subjects while actively supporting their indigenous merchants. Second, the increasing power of the princes in the German territories not only restricted the political independence of the Hanseatic cities, but also enabled these princes to establish interior markets within their territories, which, for most Hanseatic towns, became more important than the long-distance trade that had been concentrated on a few coastal cities (Bremen, Hamburg, Lübeck, Danzig/Gdansk). The Hanseatic Diet met for the last time in 1669.

BIBLIOGRAPHY

Dollinger, Philippe. *Die Hanse.* 5th ed. Stuttgart, 1998.

Fudge, John D. *Cargoes, Embargoes, and Emissaries: The Commercial and Political Interaction of England and the German Hanse, 1450–1510.* Toronto, Buffalo, and London, 1995.

Graßmann, Antjekathrin, ed. *Niedergang oder Übergang? Zur Spätzeit der Hanse im 16 und 17. Jahrhundert.* Cologne, Weimar, and Vienna, 1998.

Hammel-Kiesow, Rolf. *Die Hanse.* Munich, 2000.

Hammel-Kiesow, Rolf. "Lübeck and the Baltic Trade in Bulk Goods for the North Sea Region 1150–1400." In *Cogs, Cargoes and Commerce: Maritime Bulk Trade in Northern Europe, 1150–1400,* edited by Lars Berggren, Nils Hybel, and Annette Lauden, pp. 55–93. Toronto, 2002.

Jenks, Stuart. "A Capital without a State: Lübeck caput *tocius hanze* (to 1474)." *Historical Research: The Bulletin of the Institute of Historical Research* 65 (1992), 134–149.

Jenks, Stuart. *England, die Hanse und Preußen: Handel und Diplomatie 1377–1474.* 3 vols. Cologne and Vienna, 1992.

Lloyd, Terrence H. *England and the German Hanse 1157–1611: A Study of Their Trade and Commercial Diplomacy.* Cambridge, 1991.

Munro, John. "Patterns of Trade, Money, and Credit." In *Handbook of European History 1400–1600: Late Middle Ages, Renaissance and Reformation,* vol. 1, *Structures and Assertions,* edited by T. Brady, Jr., H. Oberman, and J. Tracy, pp. 147–195. Leiden, New York, and Cologne, 1994.

North, Douglas C., and Robert Paul Thomas. "An Economic Theory of the Growth of the Western World." *The Economic History Review* 23.1 (1970), 1–17.

Spufford, Peter. "Trade in Fourteenth-Century Europe." In *The New Cambridge Medieval History,* vol. 6, *c. 1300–1415,* edited by M. Jones, pp. 155–208. Cambridge, 2000.

Spufford, Peter. "The Relative Scale of Medieval Hanseatic Trade." In *Vergleichende Ansätze in der hansischen Geschichtsforschung,* edited by R. Hammel-Kiesow, pp. 125–133. Trier, 2002.

ROLF HAMMEL-KIESOW

HARD FIBERS INDUSTRY. A competitive hard fibers trade developed during the nineteenth and twentieth centuries as new fibers were introduced to manufacturers—each with its own strengths, weaknesses, and particular applications. Each new fiber jockeyed with more established rivals, and eventually the market became more segmented. Some versatile fibers had multiple applications and benefited from the growing complexity of the global market; others were confined essentially to a specific submarket. Each new fiber was first subjected to intense chemical scrutiny, followed by controlled cultivation investigations at agricultural experiment stations, before a lengthy apprenticeship in the market. In general, each hard fiber gained ascendancy in the market for the better part of a century, as each enjoyed a brief Ricardian comparative advantage. Although in some cases new uses were found or new cultivation or processing techniques were employed to postpone the inevitable denouement, bona fide development for the regions that produced these crops proved illusory. These export economies simply did not generate sufficient forward or backward linkages to prompt sustained economic growth.

History. Hemp (*Cannabis sativa*) was cultivated as early as 4000 BCE in northern China. Although it and other hard fibers had been used for multiple purposes since antiquity, it was not until the late sixteenth century that the British naval and merchant marine industry began to use large quantities to outfit ships. For the next three centuries, the shipping industry grew with the demands of commercial and industrial revolutions. Whalers, clippers, and, eventually, steamships required a seemingly endless supply of rope for rigging, cable, and towlines. The smallest schooner carried a ton of cordage; a frigate used one hundred tons. Even the advent of steamships did not curtail demand as they still required large amounts of cordage for towlines, warps, and auxiliary sails.

Cordage concerns first turned to Russian-grown hemp to satisfy the world's merchant marines and navies. Using a fermentation process called water-retting, peasants steeped the stalks in a nearby stream or pond. But the processing of water-retted hemp was so arduous that much of it did not reach Russian ports for export until two years after it was sown. Still by 1800 the United States was importing thirty-four hundred tons a year; that figure would climb to five thousand tons annually in the 1820s and 1830s. Russian hemp had disadvantages; it needed to be saturated with tar to protect it from saltwater, a procedure that not only left the rope heavier and dirtier but diminished its flexiblility in colder temperatures. Another problem was uncertainty of supply; first the Napoleonic Wars and subsequently the Crimean War left North American and western European cordage manufacturers scrambling for substitutes.

Kentucky hemp farmers tried to crack the lucrative cordage market after 1830. Utilizing slave labor on small and medium-sized farms in the Bluegrass region, they supplied ropewalks (cordage factories) in Louisiana, New England, and Kentucky with bales of dark gray fiber. Cordage concerns, however, preferred to pay more for water-retted hemp; even import duties on Russian hemp did not persuade manufacturers to purchase the American fiber. Kentucky farmers, for their part, refused to adopt the painstaking, labor-intensive harvesting techniques used in Tsarist Russia. Instead, they dew-retted their hemp as stalks were spread on the ground and left there for three or four weeks undisturbed. Dew-retting weakened the fibers and made for a darker, rougher (and cheaper) product. Although Kentucky hemp never won the confidence of the maritime trade, it helped the burgeoning Southern cotton industry by providing inexpensive baling rope and bagging. The hemp industry expanded into Missouri and Illinois, but declined after the Civil War. Some scholars contend that the hemp industry's development was arrested by farmers' reluctance to modernize; growers appeared unwilling to mechanize the crushing and breaking of stalks. The relatively small size of most hemp farms and the availability of a dependent labor force may better explain why hand brakes continued to be used on Kentucky and Missouri estates. In any case, the Civil War hurt the industry as the federal blockade of Southern ports, the embargo on cotton, the Union prohibition on the shipment of rope and bagging into the South, and the collapse of the postwar labor market all combined to weaken it.

Hemp's place was taken by Indian jute (*Corchurus capsularis* and *C. olitorius*). Although not so strong, durable, and elastic as hemp, jute was more plentiful, cheaper to produce, and easier to manufacture. It soon conquered the bagging market. Handwoven jute bags produced on looms in the Bengal Delta region (present-day Bangladesh) had been an important cottage industry as early as the sixteenth century. Inexpensive labor costs contributed to jute's popularity with fiber buyers. By the mid-nineteenth century, power-driven jute mills in Dundee, Scotland, had overtaken the Indian handloom industry. Later, Calcutta bagging manufacturers would offer serious competition to the Scottish mills. By 1910, raw jute production in East Bengal had soared to 900,000 tons a year. Although too rough for apparel, jute found a niche as a preeminent packaging material. The Dutch were the first to use the coarse fiber for coffee bags, and when the Crimean War cut supplies of Russian hemp and the U.S. Civil War caused a shortage of cotton bags, the jute industry responded. Three-quarters of manufactured jute was used as burlaps for everything from sandbags to sugar, and from fertilizers to animal feeds.

As jute and Kentucky hemp vied for control of the bagging market, Philippine-grown manila (*Musa textilis*) proved to be a more than worthy adversary for hemp in the cordage trade. A member of the banana family, manila is extracted from the plant's bark, and is naturally resistant to saltwater so that it does not have to be tarred. This clean fiber, introduced and tested by North American cordage manufacturers in 1818, is more durable and 25 percent stronger than tarred hemp, has greater flexibility and elasticity, weighs a third less, and carries a lower price tag. By 1860, manila, which was grown in the Kabikolan peninsula in southeastern Luzon, was firmly entrenched in the U.S. maritime trade, and consumption by British and other European manufacturers steadily increased. Production doubled between 1870 and 1880 alone.

The cordage industry's infatuation with manila overshadowed the introduction of a new tropical fiber. Although henequen (*Agave fourcroydes*) had been cultivated in Mexico's Yucatán peninsula since pre-Columbian times, only in the late colonial period did Spanish entrepreneurs begin to recognize its commercial potential.

Commonly, but incorrectly, known as sisal—the name of a Gulf of Mexico port from which the fiber was shipped—henequen was earmarked for low-end cordage and rigging purposes since the fiber's low tensile strength failed to sustain heavy-duty usage. Twice as strong, more rot-resistant, and smoother than the Yucatecan fiber, manila merited its higher price and remained the fiber of choice in the maritime market. Henequen quickly gained a reputation as an inferior but inexpensive substitute for manila. Blends of manila and henequen were marketed as such and priced midway between the "pure" twines. Hence, the prices of these commodities were inextricably bound. An abundance or a shortage of one commodity invariably affected the rival's price.

Expanding Markets. Demand was assured as technological advancements continued to find new industrial applications. Rope offered the most economical means of conveying power. With new factories springing up throughout North America and western Europe, manila proved ideally suited for power transmission cables and the expanding oil drilling industry. The new application of greatest consequence for henequen (and, to a lesser extent, manila) was binder twine. Labor-intensive hand binding had been supplanted in the early 1870s by mechanical wire binders attached to reapers. When bits of wire clogged the machinery and found their way into flour mills and animal feed, inventors built a mechanical twine knotter in the late 1870s that substituted biodegradable twine for wire, thus revolutionizing the farm-implement industry. Now a harvesting machine with two men to pick and shock the sheaf could reap twelve to fourteen acres of wheat a day, effectively doubling previous output with a substantial labor savings. The Deering and the McCormick harvesting machine companies quickly built their own twine binder harvesters in 1879 and 1881, respectively. Sales of mechanical grain binders soared, and, by the turn of the century, henequen and manila production grew exponentially.

When fiber prices were high, growers and merchants made bountiful profits. Local business leaders in the Philippines and Yucatán served as conduits for British and North American brokers and manufacturers, realizing sizable profits, usually in the form of commissions and kickbacks but also from the usurious loan practice that access to foreign capital allowed them. Ideally, just as foreign investors sought to carve out a durable monopoly or

corner" on the trade, local collaborators wished to enjoy exclusively the benefits of a monopoly over communication with the foreign interests controlling the market. With these limitations, it was difficult for local producers to adjust productivity and to predict prices; so local landholders were vulnerable to the repeated boom-and-bust cycles that afflicted the trade. Chronic price instability, coupled with the producers' inability to diversify, meant that these regional economies experienced severe dislocations amid sustained growth.

By 1902, the International Harvester Company, a combination of five of the largest harvesting machine companies (including McCormick and Deering), had become the world's principal buyer of raw fiber. Binder twine, manufactured in Harvester's Chicago twine plant, was an important secondary line for Harvester as farmers needed a regular supply of twine to operate their binders. Since the company made its profits by selling binding machines rather than from twine sales, Harvester and its agents sought to keep twine prices low to make its farm implements more attractive. Historians debate the leverage that Harvester enjoyed over the market, but local agents, such as Olegario Molina y Compañía in Yucatán, benefited greatly from access to foreign capital. It enabled them to acquire mortgages, purchase credits outright, and consolidate their hold on regional communications, infrastructure, and banking—all of which guaranteed control of local fiber production and generally worked to depress the price. In the short term, the boom enriched a small group of foreign investors, merchants, and local elites in Mexico and the Philippines while the great majority of producers (and tens of thousands of laborers) found themselves tied to the whims of an unforgiving market.

After World War I, henequen and manila found their comfortable niche challenged by a new fiber. Yucatecans were well acquainted with sisal (*Agave sisalana*), which was indigenous to the peninsula and had long been used by artisans to make hammocks and bagging. This true sisal reached German East Africa in the 1890s, and, by the 1920s, sisal plantations flourished in Tanganyika and Kenya. Later, Java, in the South Pacific, would commit to sisal. A formidable competitor, sisal was stronger than henequen and, unlike manila, lent itself well to defibering machines. Labor costs in these areas were even lower than in Yucatán and the Philippines. By 1927, Asian and African nations accounted for nearly half the world's hard fiber production.

The Great Depression and the invention of the combine, which did not use twine, also hurt the henequen and manila trade. Production fell drastically; henequen exports reached a low in 1940, when they were less than one-fourth the 600,000 bales exported during World War I. Although henequen would recover somewhat with the introduction of automatic baling machines, the introduction of low-cost synthetic fibers in the 1960s and 1970s would devastate natural hard fiber economies. The economic multiplier effects of these primary commodities were limited. The local economies were too small to transfer earnings to other productive enterprises. Hard fiber exports, despite the great wealth generated for some in the short run, were unable to lead to self-sustaining economic development in Mexico, the Philippines, Africa, the Bengal, or Java.

[*See also* Fiber Crops.]

BIBLIOGRAPHY

Ahmed, Rakibuddin. *The Progress of the Jute Industry and Trade (1865–1966)*. Dacca, Pakistan, 1966. An authoritative monograph on the evolution of the jute industry in the Bengal Region in present-day Bangladesh.

Crosby, Alfred W., Jr. *America, Russia, Hemp and Napoleon: American Trade with Russia and the Baltic, 1783–1812*. Columbus, Ohio, 1965. A fascinating analysis of the Russian hemp trade with vivid descriptions of the cultivation of the fiber in Russia and the evolution of the North American cordage industry at the outset of the nineteenth century.

Hopkins, James F. *A History of the Hemp Industry in Kentucky*. Lexington, Ky., 1951. A scholarly overview of the Kentucky hemp industry.

Iliffe, John. *A Modern History of Tanganyika*. Cambridge, 1979. Includes a cogent explanation of the sisal economy in northern (present-day) Tanzania under German and British colonial rule.

Joseph, Gilbert M., and Allen Wells. "Corporate Control of a Monocrop Economy: International Harvester and Yucatán's Henequen Industry during the Porfiriato." *Latin American Research Review* 17.1 (1982), 69–99. Argues that International Harvester and local agents in Yucatán collaborated to drive the price of fiber down during the first decade of the twentieth century. The article sparked a debate in a subsequent issue of the journal (18.3), as other scholars sought to explain the price drop by macroeconomic forces.

Morison, Samuel E. *The Ropemakers of Plymouth: A History of the Plymouth Cordage Company*. Boston, 1950. A company history, written by a notable U.S. historian, of one of the leading cordage manufacturers.

Owen, Norman G. *Prosperity without Progress: Manila Hemp and Material Life in the Colonial Philippines*. Berkeley, 1984. The best work on the manila industry, providing detailed analysis of land tenure, labor regimes, and marketing.

Topik, Steven. "L'état sur le marché: Approche comparative du café brésilien et du henequen mexicain." *Annales Economies, Sociétés, Civilisations* 46.2 (March–April 1991), 429–458. A fascinating comparison of the Brazilian and Mexican states' largely unsuccessful efforts to valorize the coffee and henequen industries during the first decades of the twentieth century.

Wells, Allen. *Yucatán's Gilded Age: Haciendas, Henequen and International Harvester, 1860–1915*. Albuquerque, N. Mex., 1985. A social and economic history of the henequen economy during its heyday. Includes chapters on the henequen trade, land, and labor.

ALLEN WELLS

HARRIMAN, EDWARD H. (1848–1909), railroad executive and financier.

The son of an Episcopal clergyman, E. H. Harriman was born in Hempstead, New York. Harriman left school at age fourteen to work in the Wall Street brokerage of D. C. Hays, and by age twenty was managing it. Two years later, he borrowed $3,000 from an uncle, bought a seat on the New York exchange, and opened his own brokerage.

Harriman's first involvement in railroads came shortly after his marriage to Mary Williamson Averell in 1879; he joined a consortium that purchased a bankrupt line connecting the Pennsylvania and New York Central railroads. He bought out his fellow investors in 1883, improved the line, and then set the two railroads bidding against each other for it. He made a handsome profit and learned that keeping track and rolling stock in good physical condition was of paramount importance.

After speculating in Illinois Central (IC) securities in the early 1880s, Harriman became an IC director and chairman of the finance committee. During his tenure, he pushed the board to buy up bankrupt railroads and consolidate them into the IC network. The Panic of 1893 threw 157 railroads into bankruptcy, including the Union Pacific (UP), but not the IC. For two years receivers struggled to reorganize and recapitalize the UP, partly because Harriman, who had designs on it, blocked the reorganization. In 1897 Harriman entered with a new reorganization plan and became chairman of the UP executive committee. In that position, he embarked on an extensive rebuilding program. At the same time he purchased controlling interests in the Southern Pacific and the Central Pacific. Harriman's intent was not monopoly but efficiency. By rebuilding track with fewer curves, lower grades, and better road beds, these railroads ran more powerful locomotives and cars with greater carrying capacities. Efficiency was also realized by combining the rolling stock of the formerly independent companies.

In 1901 Harriman and James J. Hill entered into a pitched battle for control of several western railroads. Hill had built the Great Northern and in 1896 acquired the Northern Pacific, which gave him a virtual monopoly of the northern route from the Great Lakes to the Pacific Ocean. Both men had designs on the Chicago, Burlington & Quincy Railroad (CBQ), as it paralleled both men's roads and would provide a Chicago terminus. Harriman formed a syndicate including the National City Bank, members of the Rockefeller family, George J. Gould (Jay's son), and Kuhn, Loeb & Company. Hill joined forces with Morgan. Both groups began buying up shares in CBQ, but Harriman quickly dropped out when it became clear he could not get a controlling interest. When Hill flatly rejected a compromise that would have given Harriman a one-third interest in the CBQ, Harriman's syndicate quietly bought shares in Hill's own Northern Pacific. It controlled a majority of the preferred shares and came within forty thousand shares of holding a majority of the common shares. Consequently, Harriman was made a director of Hill's newly organized Northern Securities Company, a holding company that consolidated the Great Northern, the Northern Pacific, and the CBQ. This holding company was immediately charged with violating the Sherman Anti-Trust Act and dissolved by order of the U.S. Supreme Court in 1904. Harriman sold out his interests, investing in a number of other important lines. Although he never held a controlling interest in any of them, his stakes were substantial enough to influence policy.

Harriman died in September 1909, not having realized his dream of building an around-the-world railroad crossing the Bering Strait. He was, however, one of the wealthiest men of his time with a fortune worth $100 million (about $25 billion in 2000 dollars). He left a legacy of several railroads with significantly improved capacity and productivity. Harriman believed that greater financial gains were had through improvement and good management than through speculative purchases and market manipulations.

BIBLIOGRAPHY

Hughes, Jonathan. *The Vital Few: The Entrepreneur and American Economic Progress*. New York, 1986.

Kennan, George. *E. H. Harriman: A Biography*. 2 vols. Boston, 1922.

Klein, Maury. *The Life and Legend of E. H. Harriman*. Chapel Hill, 2000.

Lovett, Robert A. *Forty Years After: An Appreciation of the Genius of Edward Henry Harriman (1848–1909)*. New York, 1949.

Mercer, Lloyd J. "Edward Henry Harriman." In *Encyclopedia of American Business History and Biography: Railroads in the 19th Century*, edited by Robert L. Frey, pp. 155–164. New York, 1988.

HOWARD BODENHORN

HEALTH. Health is a part of the human experience often noted only in its absence. A simple dichotomy between healthy and sick belies the range of physical capabilities that can be lost due to slight insults to bodily health and to gravely serious illness. Sources of ill health are many, and historical analysis requires assessment of each: exposure to pathogens, behavioral choices, environmental conditions, economic activities, medical interventions, and the interactions of all these. An economic perspective on health history considers the role of human choice across these risk factors amid resource constraints, but not only that. Because the problems of infectious disease spill over to third parties, responses (or nonresponses) to ill health sometimes emerge from a defective choice process that omits third-party effects. Another complication is that health and the economy affect each other. The economy can improve or harm the health of the people who constitute it, and those health differentials may have productivity differences that lead to a more or less productive economy. This essay considers primarily health as outcome with some acknowledgment of the role of health as input.

Health and the Neolithic Revolution. It is useful to classify health history into four periods: one in which humans hunted and gathered their food, followed by one of settled agriculture, then a period of trading between otherwise isolated disease pools, and finally the modern era. This is simply an organizing principle and is not meant to indicate hard and fast descriptions of all human activity then or now. The first period was one of relatively good health. The combination of a high protein diet from game and frequent abandonment of campsites solved two problems at once, finding food and disposing of excreta. Skeletal samples from burial sites as well as ethnological studies of present-day groups suggest a surprisingly high level of health among hunter-gatherers. Infectious diseases, such as tuberculosis, and nutritional diseases, such as anemia, rickets, and scurvy, seem to have been relatively rare. Life expectancy was long relative to the next era but short relative to our own time.

The transition from a nomadic existence to one of farming initiated a decline in health. The Neolithic Revolution, as it is called, occurred around 15,000 BP in the Old World and around 8000 BP in the New World. Composition of diet shifted away from game and scavenged nuts and berries toward cereal grain products lower in calories and protein per unit weight. Dental abrasions due to poorly ground grain combined with the greater sugar content in cereals led to increased rates of dental caries and abscesses, which opened the door to potentially fatal systemic infections. Infectious disease exposure increased as greater population density allowed pathogens to spread rapidly. Failure to dispose of excreta properly led to greater incidence of typhoid and hookworm. It remains a mystery why people chose to settle down in the face of what seems to have been a general decline in health as a result of doing so. Eventually life expectancy did increase, and presumably so did more general measures of health. But the process seems to have been nonlinear, and the nadir was associated with much suffering.

From Infectious to Chronic Disease. Traveling long distances to trade, migrate, and conquer militarily introduced a new set of health influences. Trade carried with it both costs and benefits. The ability of regions with poor harvests to trade with food-abundant areas improved nutritional availability for people in food-poor areas. However, costs of trade could be substantial if traders introduced infectious disease into virgin populations. Plagues that spread through trade, travel, and military expeditions appeared in classical antiquity, although their exact identities are unknown up to the bubonic plague of Justinian, 542 CE.

The Black Plague of the fourteenth century probably originated in rodent populations of central Asia and spread westward via rats that stowed away in caravans and then trading ships. Once the plague appeared in the West in 1347, the importance of the animal vectors (fleas and rats) seems to have declined as people transmitted the bacillus directly to each other in the pneumonic form of the disease. The first public health measures in Europe, such as isolation of the sick and burial regulations, date from this time.

Epidemics of infectious disease continued to beset humanity up to the present time. Perhaps the best-documented infectious disease of the nineteenth century was cholera. The bacterium *V. cholerae* is transmitted via human excreta that contaminate drinking water and food and seems to have been endemic for some time in the South Asian subcontinent. The first worldwide pandemic emerged from Bengal in 1827, dispersed across Eurasia, and appeared in North America in 1832. Western attempts to contain the disease were largely futile, but efforts to activate public health programs provided valuable lessons in organization. Decisions to engage in public health measures, such as construction of clean water and sewage systems and the levying of taxes to pay for them, were as much political as economic. Wealthy societies that could afford public health projects but lacked the political will to build them, such as Hamburg before the disastrous 1892 cholera epidemic, suffered as much as they would have had the technologies never been invented.

Mass migrations of people from isolated region to isolated region may have joined more hitherto separate disease pools than did trade of goods. The best-documented flows of migrants were those of Europeans to the New World and the Southwest Pacific, who brought with them smallpox and measles that decimated indigenous populations. Other cases of contact between seasoned and virgin populations had similar results. Medieval Europeans who struck out eastward to reclaim the Holy Land found the malarial areas of the eastern Mediterranean deadly.

In the early modern period a decisive factor in shaping the European approach to West Africa was the elevated mortality of Europeans new to the African disease environment. While Europeans fell to yellow fever and malaria, African resistance to the latter left the locals relatively healthy. This interested European and American slave traders, who believed that black African resistance to malaria would increase their productivity in tropical and near-tropical regions of the New World. Seasoning as well as adaptation must have played a role here, since later African Americans who migrated to West Africa lacked defenses against the local diseases and suffered horribly as a result.

In the present-day developed world the most common health problems are chronic illness or sudden events resulting from unseen but chronic problems rather than infectious disease. The rise of chronic illness and decline of infectious disease is often termed the epidemiologic transition after Abdel Omran's seminal paper (1971). Differential economic consequences of the epidemiologic transition followed from differential age effects of infectious and chronic diseases. Infectious diseases often struck young workers in their prime, either killing them immediately or disabling them over a longer time horizon, for example, by the exhausting effects of repeated spells of malaria or the wasting associated with pulmonary tuberculosis. By contrast, illness that predominated after the epidemiologic transition, whether a chronic problem such as arthritis or an acute event such as heart attack, commonly struck older people. Independent of secular trends in morbidity, the shift in the disease burden from younger and more productive people to the elderly probably led to increased economic growth wherever this transition occurred. At the same time health and economic growth interacted endogenously, as richer societies generally spent more on public and private health.

Intervention in Disease Processes. For as long as humans have fallen ill they have attempted to ameliorate symptoms of illness and to avoid illness in the first place. It is convenient to divide such efforts into those occurring between physician and patient (private health) and those large-scale projects designed to influence the health of many people simultaneously (public health). The form and efficacy of private health activities followed from popular theories of disease. From antiquity until perhaps a century ago most Western explanations of disease descended from classical theories of the humors, in which balance of the humors led to health and a disproportion of one or another led to ill health. As a result much medical activity consisted of attempts to regain that balance by expelling various fluids through bleeding, leeching, or dosing by emetics and purgatives.

With a few notable exceptions, such as the diphtheria antitoxin of the 1890s, private medical attention could do little for victims of disease until well into the twentieth century. The most enduring contribution of the controversial pediatrician-historian Thomas McKeown was his demonstration that private medical intervention had next to no effect on the great mortality decline in the West. Effective treatments for the most common infectious diseases were not discovered until after cause-specific mortality rates had substantially declined. Private medicine may still have improved health through teaching and demonstration. Here the physician-expert counseled the housewife-practitioner on the importance of hand washing, clean kitchens, and so on and advised government officials on clean water and sewage provision.

Whereas McKeown's work led historians to discount the importance of public health measures, in recent years the pendulum appears to be swinging back toward recognition of their efficacy. McKeown proposed that the impact of disease was primarily a function of nutrition. In turn,

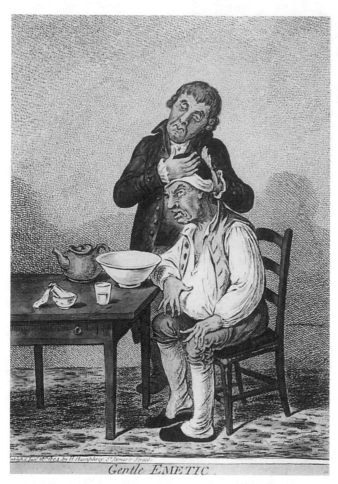

HEALTH. *The Gentle Emetic*, illustration by James Gillray (1757–1815). (Courtesy of the National Library of Medicine, Bethesda, Maryland)

because economic growth enabled greater spending on food, his policy prescriptions tended toward a laissez-faire approach that discouraged spending on public health interventions.

In an important counterattack Simon Szreter (1988) argued that, first, much of McKeown's evidentiary base had been rendered obsolete by E. A. Wrigley and R. S. Schofield's *Population History of England* (1981), second, McKeown's results may have been due to misclassification of deaths from pulmonary tuberculosis, and third, public health efforts to purify water and food supplies and to improve sewage service can explain more of the British mortality decline than nutritional changes. Here is an important question on which debate will continue at a high level of sophistication for some time to come.

As the efficacy of private medicine improved, improvement of access to medical treatment became a question of great interest to Western societies. At the beginning of the twentieth century, improvements in diagnostic if not

therapeutic technologies led many to see these services as a necessity for ordinary citizens and for workers in particular. From the Middle Ages European craftspeople had operated sickness funds through guilds and fraternal societies, and by the late nineteenth century insurance coverage through such groups became widespread in Britain. Some nations on the Continent, such as Germany, required workers to obtain sickness insurance, and others, such as France, simply encouraged it through rather weak tax incentives.

Benefits typically came bundled as sick pay plus discounted medical care. Not only did greater sickness insurance lead to a sharper decline in mortality rates, but workers who enjoyed greater access to physicians and apothecaries through insurance were more likely to recover from spells of sickness. The ability to rest without loss of pay and increased medical attention were real benefits for workers who suffered from transient conditions.

Following from the success of state-sponsored sickness insurance, two related kinds of insurance sought to improve the health of a wide range of workers. Patients who did not recover from immediate illness or injury or who suffered from chronic conditions were eventually shifted to longer-term disability insurance programs. Present-day research confirms a close relationship between disability insurance and early retirement, suggesting that it provides an incentive to leave the labor force for people who would otherwise continue to work. Here as in sickness insurance complex interactions are evident between physical pain and disease and incentives of income replacement policies. Likewise insurance against workplace injury ("workers' compensation") has become widespread in the industrialized West. In the United States such programs at the state level may actually have increased accident rates in some industries while providing relatively small net benefits after accounting for the decline in compensating wage differentials.

Measurement of Health: Mortality. This essay has discussed health in historical and policy terms while prescinding from the thorny question of defining and measuring health. To assess general health conditions of a particular society requires broad statistics that summarize the health experiences of most people in that time and place. Ideal measures would have roughly the same meaning as in the present, which suggests that simplicity is a useful characteristic. The crudest and most easily determined yet most intuitive measure of ill health is death. Crude death rates, defined as the number of deaths in a population per time period divided by the population in that time period, yield a rough overall measure of well-being. If available by age group or cohort status, they allow estimates of life tables that describe mortality or years of life to be expected after a certain age.

Historical evidence of death rates reveals cycles in health conditions over time. In Britain, Wrigley and Schofield (1981) found a steady decline in life expectancy at birth from about forty years in the late sixteenth century to perhaps thirty-four years in the mid-eighteenth century, followed by a recovery to forty-two years in the late nineteenth century. In France life expectancy rose from an abysmal twenty-five years in the mid-eighteenth century to nearly forty in the mid-nineteenth century. In the United States life expectancy at age ten cycled from about fifty years in the mid-eighteenth century to well over fifty-five years at the end of the century, declining to less than fifty years by the mid-nineteenth century before beginning its long climb upward. Asian data are too few to support close analysis of mortality, but death rates in many areas, especially Japan, seem to have resembled European and American estimates.

A finer measure is the infant mortality rate, defined as the number of deaths of all those under one year of age per one thousand live births. Infant mortality rates reflect historical health conditions closely because infants were more likely than adults to succumb to infections that stem from general environmental conditions. For example, diarrheal infections transmitted by tainted water might cause an adult discomfort but kill a baby fed contaminated gruel. Dependence upon gruels made from cereals also exposed babies to the risk of short rations after small harvests. As a result, infant mortality in the past was much higher than in the present.

For example, in early-nineteenth-century England rates were over 150 and increased along with industrialization. Workers apparently recognized that greater infant mortality meant worse living conditions in general, because labor markets where infant mortality was a problem offered higher wages to attract workers. Overall, infants accounted for a much greater share of deaths than of population, and they benefited disproportionately from public health programs to purify water and provide sewage. Because infant mortality declined dramatically (today in the United States it stands at about a twentieth of the rate a century ago), it is important to note that much of the concurrent increase in life expectancy at birth was due to that decline in infant mortality, which in turn stemmed from water and sewage provision.

Measurement of Health: Nonlethal Conditions. Ill health usually stops short of death. Measuring that ill health proceeds indirectly because there are so many ways to be sick. One method examines insurance records, as James Riley has done with English friendly societies in *Sick, Not Dead* (1997). The unit of measurement is a missed day of work, for which the society's sick fund paid a claim. Fund requirements that a physician determine the validity of the claim limit the confounding effects of cultural ideas of the degree of sickness that would justify staying home. Riley found that sick days per worker year generally increased during the late nineteenth century and early twentieth century which he linked to better management of illness by medical personnel. Particularly as a short-term measure of sickness, absenteeism is a promising variable for further study of sickness in the past.

Other measures reflect longer-term states of health. Various measurements of body size have been found to correlate with other measures of health. These include height as measured any time between early childhood and young adulthood and weight as measured from birth to any age. While an individual's height is strongly determined by that of his or her parents, average height of a large sample can be a valuable measure of "net" nutrition. The body takes incoming nutrition, in quantity (calories) and quality (protein, vitamins), and metabolizes it to maintain itself, fight disease, and provide energy for work. The remainder, during the years before early adulthood, is given over to growth, which can be influenced by either nutrition or disease or both in tandem. Lack of proper nutrition can magnify the wasting effects of some diseases, such as tuberculosis.

Evidence of decreasing heights of successive cohorts during industrialization emerging from Europe and North America indicates a decline in nutritional intake or an increase in disease burden or work intensity. These possibilities are the subjects of much debate reminiscent of the McKeown controversies, in which participants again place differing emphases on nutrition, infectious disease, and the interactions between the two. Robert Fogel noted in his Nobel Prize lecture the severely stunted heights of late-eighteenth-century Europeans. If scholarly assumptions about diets are accurate, he estimated, the poorest one-fifth of the population simply would not have had the strength to work. John Komlos has advanced a Malthusian explanation of height trends in which population growth pushed against food production possibilities just prior to industrialization. A role for infectious disease, such as tuberculosis, in causing height deficits appears in the evidence, but so far height data has shed more light on net nutritional differences by sex and class than on long-term consequences of disease conditions. Skepticism remains among historians about relationships between height and mortality.

Analysis of weight measurements further illustrates connections between health and important demographic and economic decisions. Nonlinear relationships have been demonstrated between weight for height and mortality risk, fertility, and retirement. In each case people of average size enjoyed better health, were less likely to die soon, were more likely to have children, and were more likely to continue working. Weight at birth reflects the health of both mother and child, which is especially important since historical data of women are scarce. The mother's health and nutrition in the final trimester of pregnancy largely determines birth weight, which in turn predicts the child's developmental prospects. Most historical birth weight records of the nineteenth and twentieth centuries originated in hospitals for the poor and suggest that maternal health was dependent upon economic conditions.

If birth weight represents an initial condition for a child's health, breast-feeding was a critical determinant of the path his or her development would take. This simple and seemingly natural act was fraught with meaning in many cultures, so that the incidence of breast-feeding varied tremendously with the mother's wealth, marital status, religion, and geographical region. Some societies saw breast milk as a means of transmitting a life force, analogous to semen in men, and developed an ideology that promoted the practice through the mother or a wet nurse.

Others found the act too intimate to be performed in public, or indeed, at all. In many cases, paradoxically, it was precisely the lack of animal milk among the poor and landless that led them to breast-feed their babies while the more prosperous bottle fed theirs. Where systematic statistics from the past are available, breast-feeding has consistently been associated with lower infant mortality rates, even after controlling for other economic and social factors.

Another marker of female health is age at menarche. The age at which a girl begins to menstruate is dependent upon the same general health conditions as height: nutrition, disease, and workload. In general the healthier a girl is, the sooner she begins to menstruate. The few available records indicate more or less continuous improvement in girls' health; that is, the age at menarche in the West has declined from about age sixteen in the early nineteenth century to about age thirteen today.

Health and Well-Being in the Past and Present. Assessment of the economic history of human health should emphasize the positive course of developments while acknowledging temporary reversals. It begins with the great increase in longevity and notes the decline in the West of the spectacular infectious diseases, such as tuberculosis and cholera, and indeed the near extinction of polio (again in the West) and smallpox. Data on stature and infant mortality suggest that the early stages of industrialization were times of worsening health. Study of the decline and subsequent recovery in health status over the last two centuries may increase our understanding of policies that might improve public health.

By no means have the greatest questions of infectious disease answered, in an era in which worldwide prevalence of HIV infection runs to some 40 million people, of malaria some ten times that, and of tuberculosis infection perhaps a third of all people in the world. Precisely because today's health conditions in more prosperous lands are so different from the past while far less has changed in the disease environment of poor countries, historical study of health and disease is particularly enlightening, both in the way things have been in the past and the way they could be in the future.

BIBLIOGRAPHY

Ackerknecht, Erwin H. *Malaria in the Upper Mississippi Valley, 1760–1900* (1945). Reprint, New York, 1977. Illustrates the role played by disease in the settlement of low-lying Midwest areas.

Baten, Jörg, and John E. Murray. "Heights of Men and Women in Nineteenth-Century Bavaria." *Explorations in Economic History* 37.4 (2000), 351–369.

Bynum, W. F. *Science and the Practice of Medicine in the Nineteenth Century.* Cambridge, 1994. Discusses the transition from harmful to helpful medical practices; especially good in distinguishing between diagnostic and therapeutic advances.

Cohen, Mark Nathan. *Health and the Rise of Civilization.* New Haven, 1989. Good introduction to the historical context of physical anthropology.

Curtin, Philip D. *Death by Migration: Europe's Encounter with the Tropical World in the Nineteenth Century.* Cambridge, 1989. A comparative study of mortality of Europeans at home and in African, Asian, and American colonies.

Crosby, Alfred W. *Ecological Imperialism: The Biological Expansion of Europe, 900–1900.* Cambridge, 1986. Describes the introduction of Europeans and the plants, animals, and diseases that came along with them into the extra-European world.

Dubos, René, and Jean Dubos. *The White Plague: Tuberculosis, Man, and Society* (1952). Reprint, New Brunswick, N.J., 1987. A landmark in the social history of medicine; not as systematic as later analyses but unsurpassed in breadth of coverage.

Evans, Richard J. *Death in Hamburg: Safety and Politics in the Cholera Years, 1830–1910.* Oxford, 1987. Brilliant examination of political failure to protect the public health with disastrous consequences.

Fildes, Valerie. *Breasts, Bottles, and Babies: A History of Infant Feeding.* Edinburgh, 1986.

Fishback, Price V., and Shawn Everett Kantor. *A Prelude to the Welfare State: The Origins of Workers' Compensation.* Chicago, 2000. Analyzes the interactions of politics, markets, and workplace injuries in late-nineteenth-century and early-twentieth-century America.

Fogel, Robert. "Economic Growth, Population Theory, and Physiology. *American Economic Review* 84.3 (1994), 369–395.

Kiple, Kenneth F., ed. *The Cambridge World History of Human Disease.* Cambridge, 1993. As thorough a reference as could be imagined. Encyclopedic in coverage of infectious diseases.

Komlos, John. *Nutrition and Economic Development in the Eighteenth-Century Habsburg Monarchy: An Anthropometric History.* Princeton, 1989. Notable for hypotheses on Malthusian interactions of politics, agriculture, and health and the broader impact of industrialization on health.

Lee, James Z., and Wang Feng. *One-Quarter of Humanity: Malthusian Mythology and Chinese Realities.* Cambridge, Mass., 1999. Not a history of Chinese demography but an assessment of Malthus's speculations on same. Especially good on role of female infanticide.

Livi-Bacci, Massimo. *Population and Nutrition: An Essay on European Demographic History.* Cambridge, 1991. Interpretive essay that supplies copious amounts of quantitative evidence.

Mansson, S. Ryan. "Food for Thought." *Historical Methods* 27.3 (1994), 101–125.

McKeown, Thomas. *The Modern Rise of Population*. London, 1976. Clear and forceful. Some arguments have been superceded, but it remains a touchstone of health history.

McNeill, William H. *Plagues and Peoples*. New York, 1976. Vast in scope, learned in presentation, a pioneering work in the history of human-pathogen interactions.

Mokyr, Joel, and Rebecca Stein. "Science, Health, and Household Technology." In *The Economics of New Goods*, edited by T. F. Bresnahan and R. J. Gordon. Chicago, 1997.

Omran, Abdel. "The Epidemiologic Transition." *Milbank Memorial Fund Quarterly* 29 (1971), 509–538.

Parsons, Donald O. "Decline in Male Labor Force Participation." *Journal of Political Economy* 88.1 (1980), 117–134.

Preston, Samuel H., and Michael R. Haines. *Fatal Years: Child Mortality in Late Nineteenth-Century America*. Princeton, 1991. Exploits early-twentieth-century census data to examine causes of infant mortality. Rigorous and thorough, a model of quantitative history.

Riley, James C. *Sick, Not Dead: The Health of British Workingmen during the Mortality Decline*. Baltimore, 1997. Finds increasing incidence and duration of illness during the mortality decline, which the author attributes to rest and access to medical attention.

Rosenberg, Charles E. *The Cholera Years: The United States in 1832, 1849, and 1866*. Chicago, 1987. How the United States reacted to cholera and how those reactions changed over time frames this view into early public health efforts.

Spree, Reinhard. *Health and Social Class in Imperial Germany: A Social History of Mortality, Morbidity, and Inequality*. Oxford, 1988. Translation of *Soziale Ungleichheit vor Krankheit und Tod: zur Sozialgeschichte des Gesundheitsbereichs im Deutschen Kaiserreich*. Göttingen, 1981. A complete social history of medicine and health in industrializing Germany.

Steckel, Richard H., and Jerome C. Rose, eds. *The Backbone of History: Health and Nutrition in the Western Hemisphere*. Cambridge, 2002. A collection of essays by historians and anthropologists that links the pre-Columbian skeletal record to modern bone and written records.

Szreter, Simon. "The Importance of Social Intervention in Britain's Mortality Decline." *Social History of Medicine* 1.1 (1988), 1–37.

Ward, W. Peter. *Birth Weight and Economic Growth: Women's Living Standards in the Industrializing West*. Chicago, 1993. Analysis of birth weights to infer the well-being of relatively poor women.

Williamson, Jeffrey G. "Urban Disamenities, Dark Satanic Mills, and the British Standard of Living Debate." *Journal of Economic History* 41.1 (1981), 75–83.

Winegarden, C. R., and John E. Murray. "Contributions of Early Health Insurance to Mortality Decline in Pre–World War I Europe." *Explorations in Economic History* 35.4 (1998), 431–446.

Wrigley, E. A., and R. S. Schofield. *Population History of England*. Cambridge, 1981.

JOHN E. MURRAY

HEALTH INDUSTRY *[This entry contains five subentries, a historical overview, and discussions of technological change, the pharmaceutical industry, medical practitioners, and hospitals.]*

Historical Overview

Health was transformed in the twentieth century; for the first time across the globe most people lived to be old, whereas earlier most died in infancy or childhood. Most people survived long enough to become acquainted with their grandchildren, and long enough to suffer the protracted and often intractable diseases of old age. Before that health was dominated by popular concern about communicable diseases, particularly epidemics of such diseases as smallpox and tuberculosis, especially threatening to the young. Such diseases were partially controlled by new medicines, public health measures, and changes in personal behavior. The late twentieth century was characterized by chronic degenerative diseases, especially heart and circulatory diseases and cancers, for which treatments have been mostly palliative and cures mostly promised for the future. If the first transformation of health has been rising life expectancy, and the second transformation a transition from a profile of mostly communicable to mostly degenerative diseases, the third transformation has been the expansion of the health sector. What formerly accounted for a small share of economic activity, certainly less than 2 percent even with an expansive definition, grew everywhere, but especially in rich countries, led by the United States.

It would seem unarguable that higher spending on health must have driven the achievements that took the form of longer lives, the conquest of many communicable diseases, and high expectations about an impending conquest of degenerative diseases. The great puzzle of the health industry lies in the assessment of its effects, and the relationship between a rising supply of health services and spending on health, on the one hand, and health experience, on the other. There is little question that economic growth has given people money to spend on goods and services not previously considered essential; the health industry is one beneficiary. Likewise, it is beyond dispute that people have been spending more money on things that may improve their health, even if the decisions about spending have not usually been driven directly by ambitions for health. People have bought better housing, piped water, and sewage disposal for their houses, more and better foods, and better education for their children; and they have also engaged doctors and other health providers, bought over-the-counter medications and prescription drugs, and, through their taxes, paid for public investments in water treatment, the training of health practitioners, and much else. Still, it is extraordinarily difficult to find direct relationships between spending on health and changes in health status, whether in individual countries across time or across a group of countries at the same time.

Many questions arise, all part of a modern puzzle: Why are the relationships between spending on health and health outcomes in morbidity and mortality so difficult to penetrate? More especially, why have so many poor and middle-income countries been able to achieve much the same thing as the rich countries in life expectancy and

HEALTH INDUSTRY. French hospital, fifteenth century. (Archives de l'Assistance Publique, Paris/ Giraudon/Art Resource, NY)

the transition from communicable diseases, mostly of the young, to degenerative diseases, mostly of the old? How can it be that Costa Rica, Cuba, and Jamaica by the 1990s had life expectancies at birth virtually the same as the United States had, without having become rich, without having a costly health care industry, and without spending such a large share of their domestic products on health services?

Early History. For most of the history of the health industry people expected health practitioners to take steps that would restore their health and allow them, once better, to maintain their health; but they did not expect a cure or a longer life. Medical historians distinguish between traditional medicine and modern medicine. Traditional medicine provided health care across the ages. In the hierarchy of practitioners that had emerged in the West by the eighteenth century, the leaders were university-trained physicians who had studied the theory of health and who understood Galenic ideas about why individuals become sick and Hippocratic ideas about why groups of people fall victim to epidemics. The physicians were few; they treated the rich and sometimes also, because of social welfare provisions, the very poor; they understood diseases not as singular effects with singular causes but as effects capable of changing form and of having quite varied causes. They listened to the sick or read their letters, consulted their own grasp of theory, made a diagnosis, and suggested a treatment.

For the bulk of the population, who could not afford physicians or did not think that physicians provided a certain range of treatments, health services came from general practitioners, who trained mostly in an apprentice system, learning from older practitioners; apothecaries, who dispensed medicaments, more often of their own devising than on the order of a physician; respected members of the community, such as wise women and medically attuned clergymen, who suggested treatments; bonesetters; midwives; leeches, who bled patients in a Western medical system in which bleeding was expected to recapture a balance in bodily humors; shamans, high priests who performed magical cures; and even blacksmiths, who extracted teeth. At each rung on this ladder, practitioners proclaimed their own value and blackguarded rivals. Those at the top called their inferiors charlatans or quacks or something worse, without having to demonstrate the greater efficacy of the treatments they themselves provided. The health industry was wildly disorganized. Yet its members already, by the Renaissance, knew how to promote their services and the medications they sold. Medicines and medical services were elements of the consumer revolution of the early-modern era. Still, people spent only meager sums on health.

This medical mélange acquired some greater order in the mid-nineteenth century when physicians, the better trained of the general practitioners, and apothecaries all persuaded public authorities to license practitioners who met certain standards. In the Western world the chief technique previously used to control the quantity and the quality of practitioners had been the guild formed by surgeons, who claimed the right to set broken bones and to treat exterior wounds or lesions, or by apothecaries. Licensing was a far more effective tactic, which gradually separated physicians, surgeon-general practitioners, and apothecaries from other practitioners in the legal practice of medicine and in the public mind. Others who practiced traditional medicine were pushed into the informal economy, where they continued to treat people.

Development of Efficacious Treatments. It is entirely a coincidence that medicine began to acquire a capacity to treat some diseases effectively in the 1800s. By 1800, historians had distinguished a few effective treatments, among them the care provided by a trained midwife, which had already dramatically reduced maternal mortality in several countries; quinine, a drug that, when given in appropriate doses, could limit the ill effects of certain fevers; digitalis, a drug used as a heart stimulant; the doctor's advice to rest and convalesce when sick; and the spectacularly effective vaccination against smallpox, introduced in 1797. By 1900, there were a few more effective treatments, including a diphtheria antitoxin and Salvarsan for treating syphilis. Yet even into the 1920s, the health industry was characterized far more by the diseases and injuries that it could not relieve or cure than those it could. That began to change with the introduction of insulin in 1921, sulfa drugs in the mid-1930s, antibiotics in the 1940s, a growing number of vaccinations in the 1950s and afterward, and new diagnostic techniques and surgical procedures using replacement parts. Armed with these advances, biomedicine acquired a capacity to prevent disease, to abbreviate the course of many diseases and injuries, and to cure disease more often than without treatments and faster than allowed by the course of nature. These things gave doctors and, to a lesser degree, apothecaries, dentists, and even veterinarians, a valid claim to respect and higher incomes. Meanwhile, licensing provided a way to limit the flow of people into medicine, thus allowing higher fees. Also doctors began to treat more people, no longer visiting patients in their own homes but requiring patients to come to a clinic or doctor's office. In these ways conditions were created to turn medicine into a profession.

The period from the 1850s to the 1950s saw other important changes in the conceptualization of disease and its origins and in the health industry. Hospitals, which formerly relieved the poor, infirm, and old as well as treating the sick, began to specialize in diseases and injuries and to isolate patients with communicable maladies. They began also to expand in number, to serve as centers for training new health workers, and to become the centerpiece of costly medicine. Formal practitioners gained their higher rank only at the cost of considerable social and economic tension. In a "battle of the clubs," or struggle to control the medical market, repeated in country after country in the 1890s and thereafter, working people, accustomed to inexpensive medical services provided on terms they set, fought and lost a struggle against medical practitioners cooperating with one another to raise fees. Medicine began also to deploy more and more effective technology and practice. The postmortem examination, first widely performed in the early nineteenth century, revealed the signs of disease, allowing medical people to shift to a theory of specific diseases with specific causes. Germ theory, developed by Louis Pasteur and Robert Koch, identified causal agents. The X-ray, discovered in 1895, initiated a long period of improvement in diagnostic techniques, whose broad effect has been to reveal the signs of disease by noninvasive means.

Between the 1850s and the 1950s, three theories emerged about the origins of disease, all pointing toward certain specific ways of preventing disease. The oldest of these, filth theory, attributed disease to air and water contaminated with disease matter, and led to water filtration, sewage treatment, swamp drainage, and other steps to protect people from environmental toxins. Second, social welfare theorists investigated whether the conditions of life, specifically poverty, poor housing, an absence of sunlight, dankness, and other circumstances especially common in crowded urban neighborhoods, could cause or promote disease. Finding such links, social welfare theorists promoted steps to reduce poverty, including public investments in housing, health education, and other means of removing the poverty-disease link. Third, germ theorists attributed disease to microorganisms and focused on how to reduce exposure to germs by such means as washing hands, and on discovering natural substances or chemicals toxic to germs but safe for humans. All three theories engaged medicine in a broader world where social and scientific research mattered, and where health was recognized as a global issue. A country could not attempt to solve its health problems without considering its exposure to outside diseases and its access to outside treatments. The new doctors of this era were public health doctors, epidemiologists, and laboratory scientists, none of whom treated patients, but all of whom meant to improve the health of the populace. Besides teaching hospitals, the new institutions were international organizations, such as the Rockefeller Foundation and the Health Organization of the League of Nations, which sought to improve survival by improving health.

Expansion. Within countries, the health industry and the health sector began a relentless expansion. In 1960, in 1996 dollars, U.S. health spending totaled $125 billion, by

1980, it totaled not quite $450 billion, and by 2000 it had reached $1.3 trillion, about 14 percent of the U.S. domestic product. In current dollars, Americans spent an average of $4,657 per person on health in 2000, a sum greater than the per capita income of more than two-thirds of the world's people. Other rich countries lagged behind the United States in health spending and the scale of the health industry, but in nearly all of them the health sector was growing. The World Bank, charged with the task of promoting the economic development of poor countries, engaged ever more extensively in health policy and health research. At the aggregate level, no one could show how higher spending would reduce morbidity or mortality; but at the individual level, few would forsake the chance to do whatever they could afford to regain health or to defer the moment of death. This was the dilemma the health industry had created.

[*See also* Diseases; Epidemics; *and* Insurance, *subentry on* Health and Accident Insurance.]

BIBLIOGRAPHY

Callahan, Daniel. *False Hopes: Why America's Quest for Perfect Health Is a Recipe for Failure*. New York, 1998.

Kiple, Kenneth F., ed. *The Cambridge World History of Human Disease*. Cambridge, 1993.

McMichael, Tony. *Human Frontiers, Environments and Disease: Past Patterns, Uncertain Futures*. Cambridge, 2001.

Porter, Roy. *The Greatest Benefit to Mankind: A Medical History of Humanity*. New York, 1997.

Riley, James C. *Rising Life Expectancy: A Global History*. Cambridge, 2001.

Risse, Guenter B. *Mending Bodies, Saving Souls: A History of Hospitals*. Oxford, 1999.

Schwartz, William B. *Life Without Disease: The Pursuit of Medical Utopia*. Berkeley, 1998.

Wang, Jia, Dean T. Jamison, Eduard Bos, Alexander Preker, and John Peabody. *Measuring Country Performance on Health: Selected Indicators for 115 Countries*. Washington, D.C., 1999.

Wear, Andrew Wear, ed. *Medicine in Society: Historical Essays*. Cambridge, 1992.

Wilkinson, Lise, and Anne Hardy. *Prevention and Cure: The London School of Hygiene & Tropical Medicine: A 20th Century Quest for Global Public Health*. London, 2001.

JAMES C. RILEY

Technological Change

People have practiced medicine since time immemorial, using a variety of tools and materials; but except in the later twentieth century, treatments have depended to a great extent on placebo effects for successful outcomes. In the twenty-first century, a wide range of mental and physical disorders are amenable to treatment, and the international market for medical technologies is worth trillions of dollars. The economic aspects of this transformation in medicine have received relatively little attention from historians with respect to either the industrial production and distribution of drugs and medical instruments or their impact on longevity, efficiency, and productivity, their social impact, or their contribution to the rising cost of modern welfare systems. Certain important developments may be singled out for their national and global economic significance.

Preventive Technologies.   Beyond such material infrastructures as sewers and clean water supplies, the technology of disease prevention rests on immunization against infectious diseases caused by bacteria and viruses. The first such specific technology used against a particular disease was inoculation against smallpox, a highly unpleasant, fatal, and infectious viral disease. Long practiced in China and the Near East, the technique was introduced into Europe by Lady Mary Wortley Montagu, wife of the British ambassador to Turkey, in 1721. It was hazardous because it involved the deliberate infection of individuals with, intendedly, mild smallpox, but it became widely used. In 1796, an English country doctor, Edward Jenner, introduced vaccination, which utilized cowpox, a similar but harmless virus, to confer immunity against smallpox. During the nineteenth century, vaccination became widely available, often through state intervention, and was effective in greatly reducing morbidity and mortality from smallpox in Europe. This was the agent by which eradication of the disease eventually was achieved, in 1977.

The immunological principles behind the success of vaccination were unraveled by French scientist Louis Pasteur in the 1870s and 1880s. In 1876, a German physician, Robert Koch, identified the specific cause of anthrax; and as the causal organisms of other diseases began to be identified, scientists began to experiment with other types of immunization. By the early 1900s, several new treatments and immunizations had become available against anthrax (1880), rabies (1885), diphtheria (1894), tetanus (1900), cholera (1892), and typhoid (1896). Typhoid immunization is thought to have played an important part in reducing sickness and death during World War I. By the 1930s, many countries were using immunization against diphtheria and tuberculosis. Vaccines against whooping cough, measles, rubella, and mumps followed after World War II, although the timing and the extent of their adoption varied considerably between different countries. Of special note was the development in the mid-1950s of vaccines against poliomyelitis. Polio's ability to cripple as well as kill made it the object of the World Health Organization's second global disease eradication campaign after the successful elimination of smallpox. In recent decades, Western governments have placed increasing emphasis on the availability of immunizations against influenza as a means of reducing sickness in workforces, serious illness among the elderly, and crisis pressure on health services.

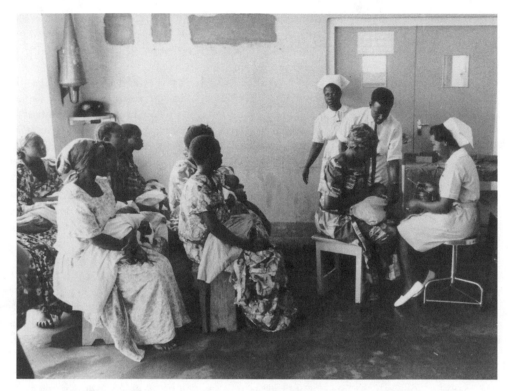

VACCINATIONS. Group of Ugandan mothers having their babies vaccinated against smallpox during an eradication campaign, circa 1975. (Jean Mohr/Courtesy of the National Library of Medicine, Bethesda, Maryland)

The economic impact of the various immunizations is incalculable. The infectious diseases involved not only were major killers but often had long-term side-effects for survivors, such as blindness, deafness, and heart or lung impairment. Effective immunization is a relatively inexpensive form of prevention, and infectious disease remains a threat to human populations. In the 1990s, epidemic diphtheria reappeared in the former Soviet Union, following the abandonment of immunization programs; and many Western countries experienced an unexpected upsurge in tuberculosis infection after preventive structures were dismantled as having achieved their ends.

Curative Technologies. Effective curative therapies began to emerge in the eighteenth century, but were often misused or misapplied because their properties were not fully understood. Among the earliest was quinine, useful in controlling malarial infection. Although it was first introduced into Europe around 1650, the medical properties of quinine were properly evaluated in 1711 when Italian physician Francesco Torti demonstrated that it was effective only in treating malaria and not other types of fever. Similarly, the value of digitalis in the treatment of heart disease, described by English physician William Withering in 1785, remained poorly understood for many years thereafter. Nineteenth-century developments in chemistry

led to the isolation of the effective principles of these and other drugs, which stimulated their commercial production. From the 1860s on, drugs shared in the general decline in the price of raw materials entering world markets; the cost of quinine acetate, for example, fell from one pound per ounce in 1833 to two shillings by 1897. Into the 1880s, however, the number of effective drugs available to medical practitioners was limited to quinine, digitalis, mercury, arsenic, and the opiates.

The bacteriological revolution of the 1880s was relatively slow in yielding therapeutic dividends. Antitoxin serum for the treatment of diphtheria became available in 1894, and was quickly taken up by drug companies such as the British firm Burroughs Wellcome. Scientific interest in the power of chemical dyes to stain bacteria led German bacteriologist Paul Ehrlich to develop the concept of a "magic bullet" (modern chemotherapy)—chemical agents that would target and destroy disease organisms without damaging their human host. The first such successful product, the antisyphilitic drug Salvarsan, was launched in 1910; the second, the sulfonamide Prontosil, did not appear until 1935. The sulfonamides were, however, effective against a range of devastating infections, including puerperal fever and various pneumonias, and marked a highly significant therapeutic breakthrough, although they were soon overshadowed by the excitement generated by the antibiotics. The first antibiotic, penicillin, was developed as a therapeutic agent during World War II and reached civilian markets in 1945, the research necessary for its commercial production having been undertaken by U.S. drug companies. The years after 1945 saw an explosion in the introduction of more or less effective therapeutic substances as researchers and pharmaceutical companies vied with each other to discover new products. A further spur to research was the discovery that certain groups of bacteria, notably *Staphylococcus aureus* (which can cause serious wound infections), were capable of developing resistance to specific antibiotics, including penicillin.

Also overshadowed by penicillin, but as significant in commercial and therapeutic terms, was the discovery of the natural hormone cortisone, basis of the steroid group of drugs, by workers at the Mayo Clinic in Rochester, Minnesota, in the 1940s. Experimental use soon demonstrated the efficacy of steroids in the treatment of a wide range of acute and chronic conditions, significantly extending the range of effective preparations available to medical practitioners. Unlike the antibiotics, which are useful only in bacterial infections, the steroids can be used to treat more than eighty different conditions as diverse as meningitis and allergy.

Although the pace of drug discovery slowed in the mid-1970s, significant new drugs continued to be introduced, with researchers increasingly looking to the natural world for substances with therapeutic properties. The medical and economic benefits of modern drug therapy have to a great extent been unequally distributed in global terms, with wealthy Western populations helped the most.

Although substantive gains in drug therapy were made only after 1935, the practice of surgery saw steady improvement in competence and safety after 1850. Previously undertaken only in emergencies or for intolerable conditions, surgery had by 1914 become a much more routine, if increasingly expensive, procedure. Several important technical developments contributed to this transformation. Anesthesia was introduced in the late 1840s, although its administration remained hazardous for many decades until the discovery of barbiturate preparations in the 1920s. Asepsis and antisepsis began to be developed by surgeons circa 1860. The Scottish surgeon Joseph Lister is famous for the introduction of a carbolic acid–based antiseptic technique although his methods were cumbersome, expensive, and imprecise. Hospitals increasingly used them in combination with basic hygiene and sterilization (asepsis). Meanwhile, the invention of the artery clamp (1865) permitted surgeons to work in relatively dry operating sites. By 1900, the modern surgical environment of a dedicated theater and the wearing of disposable gloves, caps, and gowns had become commonplace, and the

number and the type of operations performed had risen dramatically. Hernia, for example, a major cause of pauperism in nineteenth-century Britain, was increasingly treated surgically after 1870.

Although postoperative death rates plummeted in the nineteenth century, surgical shock remained a problem. Blood transfusion had been repeatedly attempted with very uncertain results until the Austrian scientist Karl Landsteiner elucidated the significance of blood groups in 1901. Organizational factors delayed the routine use of transfusion in surgical practice until World War II although experimental blood banks were introduced in the United States in the 1930s. After 1945, and again after 1970, the world blood products industry grew rapidly; by the early 1980s, the U.S. industry alone was valued at $150 million per annum.

In the last decades of the twentieth century, surgery became big business in developed countries in terms of both patient numbers and institutional and technological costs. The focus of intervention changed radically, away from emergency treatment and toward an ideal of planned, preventive action.

The practice of dentistry witnessed a similar transformation, from emergency practice to an ethos of prevention and maintenance. The dental profession emerged in eighteenth-century France, essentially through the provision of artificial teeth and corrective fixtures; and around 1950, artificial teeth were the mainstay of the dentist's business. Landmarks were achieved with the development of porcelain paste teeth in 1792 and the introduction of vulcanized rubber for denture bases in the 1890s. However, as late as 1946, dental fitness in Britain was estimated at 1 percent of the civilian population; at a cost of ten guineas a set, dentures were beyond the reach of most. The provision of free dentures under the National Health Service after 1948 saw rapidly escalating costs. In 1950–1951 alone, 65.6 million artificial teeth were supplied; high cost was the main consideration behind the introduction of charges for dentures (as for eyeglasses) in 1951. Mass-produced acrylic teeth became available after 1945; and the introduction of the air turbine, which enabled diamond burrs to cut through tooth enamel, transformed the repair of decayed teeth and contributed significantly to the development of preventive dentistry after 1950.

Palliative Technologies. Palliative technologies ease or control a medical problem and cover a wide spectrum of interventions, from simple painkillers to complex machinery. Drugs such as opium, which was the basis of a flourishing patent-medicine industry by the eighteenth century, were used for centuries to dull pain until they were medically discredited in the nineteenth century because of their addictive properties. Effective, less potent, and nonaddictive replacements gradually emerged, notably aspirin, which was first produced commercially in 1899 and commanded worldwide markets by 1950.

The twentieth century brought new forms of palliative medicine, with extensive economic consequences. The first was insulin, a preparation used in treating diabetes, an invariably fatal condition that had been increasing in Western countries since the 1890s. An extract of calf pancreas, insulin initially was concocted by Canadian researchers Frederick Banting, Charles Best, and their co-workers, but was developed as a successful therapeutic agent by the pharmaceutical firm Eli Lilly. Techniques of producing synthetic and human insulin have since been developed. With one in a hundred persons in the West suffering from diabetes by 2000, insulin became an economically significant therapy in terms of both production and the prevention of premature disability and death.

A great expansion in palliative therapy occurred after 1945, partly because of extraordinary developments in the pharmaceutical industry; but the complex economic impacts of these technologies remain to be explored. Significant innovations include drugs effective against brain disorders beginning with chlorpromazine (c. 1955) and including Valium (1963), the most successful psychotropic drug of all time until its replacement by Prozac (1989). New immunosuppresive drugs, used in combination with steroids, permitted the emergence of organ-transplant surgery, which by the 1980s had become in many respects a routine type of operation. By 2000, many thousands of successful kidney, liver, heart, and heart/lung transplants had been achieved in Europe, the United States, and elsewhere. Useful and active lives were restored to many severely ill patients, but at the cost of surgery and of dependence on immunosuppressive drugs for the remainder of their lives. Treatments for hypertension, developed in the mid-1960s, resulted in screening programs to discover "hidden hypertensives," who were subsequently treated at enormous, and probably unnecessary, expense. More than a third of U.S. citizens aged thirty-five to seventy-four were taking medication for hypertension by 1996, at an annual cost of over $6 billion. Other important palliative technologies include mechanical aids, notably ventilators (the pioneering device being the Drinkwater Tank Respirator of 1928), now the central technology of intensive care units; kidney dialysis machines, which came into use in the mid-1960s; implantable cardiac pacemakers (1960); and artificial joints (deriving from the artificial hip successfully developed by British orthopedic surgeon John Charnley around 1962).

Obstetrics. Childbirth and the intricacies of the female reproductive system remained largely beyond the scope of medical intervention until the twentieth century. The first significant development in this field came in the eighteenth century, with the introduction of obstetric forceps. More frequent medical intervention in childbirth almost certainly had deleterious effects in increasing rates of postpartum infection, especially puerperal fever, with invariably fatal results. Estimated maternal death rates in the West ranged from twenty to sixty per ten thousand births in 1925, with puerperal fever the leading cause of maternal death. The introduction of the sulfonamide drugs (c. 1936) all but ended this scourge within a few years, making childbirth far safer. Anesthetics had been used to ease the pains of labor since their introduction in the late 1840s, but were by no means routinely available, even for hospital births, before 1945.

After 1945, issues surrounding the management of fertility became increasingly important. The oral contraceptive pill was developed by American endocrinologist Gregory Pincus in the mid-1950s and approved for clinical use in the United States in 1960 and in Britain the following year. Intrauterine devices became available at about the same time "the pill" became the contraceptive of choice for many Western women. By 1975, some 2.25 million British women were using the pill, despite associated health scares. Although pharmaceutical companies could rely on vast markets for these means of controlling female fertility, researchers in the medical world turned their attention to the problem of infertility. The first "test-tube baby," the result of in vitro fertilization, was born in Britain in 1978. Forty thousand such pregnancies followed in the next two decades. With the extension and refinement of such techniques, including acceptance of the principles of surrogate motherhood and the use of donor eggs, the treatment of infertility had become a minor medical industry by the 1990s.

Diagnostic Technologies. For most of human history, healers have relied on their own senses and patients' own account of their diseases, in the diagnosis of medical conditions. From the early nineteenth century on, however, a range of increasingly sophisticated mechanical aids began to be incorporated into the business of diagnosing and monitoring disease processes. The first important such instrument was the stethoscope, developed by French chest physician Rene Laennec in 1816, which enabled the physician to listen to sounds of the heart and the lungs, including the fetal heart. Other similar technologies followed, including the opthalmoscope (1851) and the laryngoscope (1857), which enabled physicians to increase their familiarity with conditions inside the living body. The thermometer, probably invented by Galileo between 1593 and 1597, has a somewhat checkered history until 1868, when German physician Carl Wunderlich published a seminal work on its use. Although all these technologies took time to filter into everyday practice, their use had become widely established by the twentieth century.

Another important device that acquired a crucial medical role in the nineteenth century was the microscope. Although it had been known since circa 1620, optical defects had limited the instrument's usefulness until the discovery of aplanatic foci in the 1820s enabled satisfactory objectives to be made for the first time. These microscopes were fundamental to developments in both medical research and diagnosis, and remain essential to these activities in the twenty-first century. As knowledge of disease processes accumulated during the nineteenth century, the microscope became one of the basic tools of the diagnostic process, whether in detecting the causal bacteria of diseases such as diphtheria and tuberculosis, or in the study of diseased body tissue. By 1900, modernizing hospitals throughout Europe and the United States had acquired diagnostic laboratories as a central component of their expertise.

The market for medical instruments received a notable boost with the 1895 discovery of X-rays by German physicist Wilhelm Roentgen. X-ray pictures soon became widely popular, but the medical community was quick to exploit the scientific possibilities of the new technology. A flourishing medical X-ray industry was rapidly established, based in part among the many long-established small-instrument makers. Another innovation, which took longer to achieve medical and manufacturing success, was the electocardiogram (ECG), first constructed by Dutch physiologist Willem Einthoven in 1903. Before 1914, production was on a very small scale, but the ECG became an integral part of medical diagnostic technology and remains so in the twenty-first century.

Unrelated developments in military and naval technology during and after World War II yielded unexpected medical benefits with the emergence of a new generation of diagnostic technologies after 1945. The most significant of these innovations were in diagnostic imaging, where capabilities far beyond the static, local pictures produced by the X-ray eventually were developed. Commercial potential played a central role in the development of the most successful of these technologies, which were evolved from echo-ranging and radar devices, generally through a collaboration between medical researchers and commercial firms. Diagnostic ultrasound (c. 1962), computed axial tomography (CAT scanner, c. 1972), and magnetic resonance imaging (c. 1984), which made the whole human body transparent, were products of such collaboration. The development of the latest generation of imaging technologies was closely related to that of the modern computer, without which their functions could not have been generated.

[See also Diseases and Epidemics.]

BIBLIOGRAPHY

Berridge, Virginia, and Grifiths Edwards. *Opium and the People: Opiate Use in Nineteenth-Century England.* London, 1987.

Blume, Stuart. *Insight and Industry: On the Dynamics of Technological Change in Medicine.* Cambridge, Mass., and London, 1992.

Cartwright, Frederick D. *The Development of Modern Surgery.* London, 1967.

Cooter, Roger, and John Pickstone, eds. *Medicine in the Twentieth Century.* Amsterdam, 2000.

Drake, Alvin W., and Stan N. Finkelstien. *The American Blood Supply.* Cambridge, Mass., 1982.

Fenner, F., D. A. Henderson, I. Arira, Z. Jezek, and I. D. Ladniyi. *Smallpox and Its Eradication.* Geneva, 1988.

Le Fanu, James. *The Rise and Fall of Modern Medicine.* London, 1998.

Loudon, Irvine. *Death in Childbirth.* Oxford, 1992.

Mercer, Alex. *Disease, Mortality and Population.* Leicester, 1990.

Parish, H. J. *A History of Immunisation.* Edinburgh, 1965.

Reiser, Stanley J. *Medicine and the Reign of Technology.* Cambridge, 1978.

Rivett, Geoffrey. *From Cradle to Grave: Fifty Years of the National Health Service.* London, 1998.

Watkins, Elizabeth. *On the Pill: A Social History of Oral Contraception 1950–1970.* Baltimore and London, 1998.

Weatherall, Miles. *In Search of a Cure.* Oxford, 1990

ANNE HARDY

Pharmaceutical Industry

Pharmaceuticals are products of the chemical industry, intended for use as prescription drugs or as over-the-counter (OTC) medications. The pharmaceutical industry generally pays wages above average, so there have been relatively few labor disputes on pay or on work conditions. In developed countries, pharmaceuticals account for about 10 percent of the chemical industry. The pharmaceutical sector provides a great variety of products, and drug companies have become huge enterprises. Basic products are widely used, although local markets, controlled by governments, are extremely segmented. About 80 percent is directed at human treatment, with 20 percent for treatment of animals. If some companies concentrate on animal health, most major firms have only a veterinary division. Since the 1960s, the market for pharmaceuticals has grown much faster than most others. World consumption, per capita, doubled from the 1970s to the 1990s.

Medications and the healing arts are as old as human need, but the pharmaceutical industry is fairly young, with industrial manufacturing starting in the late 1800s. The growth of the sector was closely linked to the use of man-made chemicals and chemical agents in the treatment of disease. Science-based applications really began with the drug Salvarsan, used against syphilis, and developed in 1909 by P. Ehrlich and J. Hata, not as a byproduct but as a specific medicine. That step initiated a revolution in medication as well as in industry. Biotechnology in the twenty-first century may have a similar effect on the industry as chemotherapy had during the twentieth. The pharmaceutical industry today offers three categories of drugs: in-patent (prescribed specifics), out-of-patent (generics), and over-the-counter (OTC). The first two are to be prescribed by physicians and are termed *ethical drugs*. Despite of the dynamic development of the sector, the majority, as well as the most sophisticated medications, are manufactured in only a few industrialized countries. About fifty multinational firms produce two-thirds of world output. About 75 percent of pharmaceuticals are bought in developed states. In 1990, production by the largest enterprise, Merck (U.S.), exceeded the pharmaceutical production of the whole of Latin America.

The pharmaceutical industry has preserved old, established macroeconomic patterns. According to the 1992 survey of the United Nations Industrial Development Organization (UNIDO), a "sophisticated industry with a significant research basis" is to be found only in the United States, Japan, and eight European countries (Belgium, France, Germany, Italy, the Netherlands, Sweden, Switzerland, and the United Kingdom). A group of seventeen states with "innovative capabilities" consisted of Argentina, Australia, China, Russia, and other European countries; a group had only "reproductive capabilities" (e.g., Indonesia, Hong Kong, South Africa); a final group was without any such industry (e.g., Iceland, Vanuatu, and the African countries of Botswana and Rwanda).

Legal Framework. Within the pharmaceutical industry, besides patent law (for filing the production of invented chemical recipes developed in research facilities), there are usually two important fields of legal regulation: for approval of new medicines and for prices. Approval regulation is quite old, and in many cases the legislation dates back to the 1870s. Price regulation became important in the 1980s. Official or governmental approval of medications was important for the growth of the industry. It was intended to remove all quacks and establish responsibility and reliability. The consumer's trust, not only to a personally known pharmacist but to an anonymous producer institution, was the precondition for the industrial manufacture of drugs. Institutions for testing and approval were set up with cooperation between the industry and the state. After 1945, the time needed for approval was increased, mainly because drug recipes (and their side effects) became more complicated. The process today takes several years, and since all countries have their own procedures, it is also costly. There are tendencies to ease that process within the European Union (EU), if one member-state has approved the drug. Still, it is a major but necessary obstacle in launching a new product. Many countries have also fixed prices for drugs. The original purpose was to protect indigenous industry—following a concept of "national treatment"—and to make medicine available to all. Socialist countries controlled the industry entirely, as do many developing states. Other countries paid subsidies for research and development, supplied venture capital, and

constructed nontariff barriers against imports. Such opportunities tempted firms to set up branches and caused one of the worst reputations for bribery of all industries.

Outside the Soviet Union before World War II, consumers had to pay for medications, to a large extent, themselves. More generous solutions during the boom years, or in the many new socialist states, often made drug treatment available for free. Since the 1980s, there are not enough national funds to meet the growing demand for free medications. Therefore, interventions of various kinds were set up in most countries, and the result was a growth of competition. Since markets today are considered global, the possibility for developing countries to have their own pharmaceutical industry was reduced (with the exception of the People's Republic of China, because of its vast market, its tradition of government intervention, and the international interest in Chinese herbal medicines).

Patent law and its construction was considered crucial for the development of the industry. Today most countries protect both the pharmaceutical product and the process of development. Historically, patent law, in covering only the process, helped the German industry by giving incentive to develop new processes; British and French law, in covering the product, slowed down research and development. For the same reason, most of today's developing countries protect only the process.

Foundations of the Industry. Some companies can be traced for several centuries, among which are E. Merck (1668) and Allen & Hanburys (1715). Many of today's major firms were founded in the late 1800s; others were set up in the 1920s and 1930s. In the United States, a few firms were started, among them were Bristol-Myers, Eli Lilly, and Squibb. In Europe, many firms were originally founded as pharmacies; then, by extending production, they became industries (e.g., Schering). Others expanded from their main business in coal-tar dyes. Before World War I, pharmaceuticals and organic dyes were very similar, in some cases identical, which meant that dyestufffirms (e.g., Sandoz of Switzerland; Hoechst or Bayer of Germany) could diversify. Development of firms from traditional medicine (herbs, etc.) was then limited. In the United States, Johnson & Johnson started with antiseptic equipment. In Japan, all the major firms (Takeda, Sankyo, or Yamanouchi) started from trade; in Europe, that was the exception, with Nycomed of Norway one such. In special cases, an expropriation of foreign investment caused the start of a new enterprise; thus Merck and Schering-Plough, both offspring of the still existing but much smaller German firms E. Merck and Schering, are the most prominent. In the United States, Merck severed its ties to the German parent firm only after World War I (before 1917, when the United States entered the war, Merck was supplied by a German trade submarine). In contrast, such expropriations during the 1970s in some developing countries had little positive effects. Another group of firms, including Organon of the Netherlands, was started by scientists who wanted to apply their knowledge commercially. Focusing on biotechnics, this last pattern is still widespread today, together with another reason, marketing (see below).

Strategy and Structure of Enterprises. From their beginnings, two types of firms competed: those that concentrated on pharmaceuticals (Roche, Eli Lilly, Roussel, or Boehringer Ingelheim) and those that were diversified chemical companies (ICI, Rhone-Poulenc, DuPont, Bayer, Hoechst, Pfizer, Ciba-Geigy, or Sandoz). The concept of the specialist producers was to focus on their core competitiveness, while the drug division of the diversified firms was only a fraction of overall business; however, the drug divisions claimed to enjoy considerable synergies within their firms.

The three drug categories (in-patent, generics, OTC) corresponded with three different markets. Whereas in-patent medicine yielded high profit margins, and thus stimulated research and development, generics became competitive with high competition but low profit margins. OTC drugs were usually characterized by high advertising budgets and low research expenditure. Research-oriented companies used to concentrate on the patented category; however, since the 1980s, they have increasingly tried to capture the other categories as well, putting second-rank firms under great economic pressure. For reasons of demography and distribution of wealth, the generics and OTCs grew faster than the in-patent pharmaceuticals. The largest research-oriented companies soon paid more attention to that market segment, even buying up firms that had concentrated in it. Their interest made generic-oriented firms invest in more research and development.

Advantages through various types of cooperation were realized among some otherwise competing firms. In 1906 and 1907, a few German pharmaceutical firms (Merck, Knoll, Boehringer, Gehe, and Riedel) remained independent but pooled their profits. During the 1930s, Organon (Dutch), Schering (German), and Ciba (Swiss) formed a cartel for hormones. In 1989, Johnson & Johnson founded a joint-venture with Merck, called Consumer Pharmaceuticals Company. From 1997 to 1999, Bayer invested U.S. $1 billion in joint research with U.S. biotech firms. These are but examples that represent many others. The most widespread form of cooperation was licensing and cross-licensing (where for payment, a firm leased another's property for marketing purposes in one, several, or even all markets). It was extremely widespread for many reasons: ease of marketing; to overcome tariff or nontariff barriers; for strategic alliances, and more. The pharmaceutical industry, characteristically and throughout time, had companies that competed fiercely in several fields while they instantly cooperated in others.

Until the 1950s, large and small firms established themselves in the industrialized countries. National leaders emerged but exceptional size was limited to a few. American Home Products became a sizable U.S. firm, while in Europe giant mergers occurred (IG Farben, ICI). The small and the medium-size firms grew, too, but generally stayed small to medium. Before 1914, drug-exporting nations were Britain, Germany, Switzerland, and France; after World War I, U.S. firms entered the export market, especially to Latin America. The biggest importers were originally Germany, Japan, the Soviet Union, and the United States. Both patterns remained until the 1990s. After World War II ended in 1945, the U.S. industry was the world leader, yet German firms were surprisingly fast in reentering the world market, bolstered by U.S. redevelopment aid and the Marshall Plan. From the 1950s to the 1980s, pharmaceutical firms concentrated on internal growth. With the emerging mass consumption in Europe and U.S.–aided postwar Japan, and with the growth of the welfare state, profits in pharmaceuticals were strong—health-insurance institutions were poised to pay. Historically, it was an exceptionally good time for the sector, although that was not then understood by most firms. Despite a relatively easy market, there was little change in corporate structure—few new firms entered or left the market and the number of mergers or acquisitions was not significant.

From the mid-1980s the favorable environment changed, caused by internal and external forces. Since the 1990s, the industry has been in constant merger mode, with some splittings and reallocations. The internal reasons include the increasing costs of innovation, the declining payback, the rising unpredictability in timing new products, and the loss of income from a decreasing level of patent protection. The main external reasons include deregulation, the adoption of U.S. patterns of behavior by European firms (concern for shareholder value; leveraged financing though the capital market, instead of using traditional bank loans), and heavy criticism by customers about high prices. The industry reacted with a wave of contraction that featured two main strategies: alliances and acquisitions. Nearly all major firms took part in alliances, in most cases with co-marketing strategies: in 1987, for example, SmithKline and DuPont on the drug Tagamet; Upjohn and Sankyo on an oral form of cephalosporin; Schering and Sandoz on spirapril. About four hundred such cooperations have been counted annually since the end of the 1980s. While co-marketing alliances are limited in scope and time, mergers are intended to last. From 1980 to 1990, there were 783 mergers of sizable firms, in which France had 150 and the United States had 113. They were not only made to consolidate a firm's national marketshare but for transnational purposes. The United Kingdom, Germany, and France were active in buying U.S. companies. In most cases, these mergers involved a major and a minor partner. Then the first wave of exceptionally large firms merged: SmithKline merged with Beecham, Glaxo with Wellcome, Bristol-Myers with Squibb. The trend reached Europe during the late 1990s; Ciba-Geigy (which had merged in 1970) integrated with Sandoz, leaving only two major Swiss firms; Hoechst merged with Rhone-Poulenc, by far the largest cross-border merger (Germany and France). In these two cases, old established names disappeared and new ones were founded (Novartis, Aventis). Concentration will continue. To a large extent, such mergers and acquisitions have put an end to the diversified type of firms; Ciba-Geigy and Hoechst split off their nonpharmaceutical businesses before they merged. Today, only a few distinguished diversified firms remain, such as Bayer, DuPont, ICI, and Johnson & Johnson.

Although corporate mergers were many, they did not change world distribution, since they took place in the so-called Triad only (United States, European Union, and Japan). Within the Triad, Japanese firms were special; their conditions were favorable. After the United States, Japan became the second largest market for medicinals, so the companies enjoyed a protected market. At the same time, Japanese companies were guided by government policy; they turned out to be extremely conservative, relatively small, and slow growing. They took foreign licenses for their products and invested very little in research. While the five large export nations (Germany, the United States, Switzerland, France, and the United Kingdom) each had a share of world exports of between 10 and 15 percent, Japan had less than 3 percent. That started to change when, in the early 1990s, Japan's government started a more liberal policy. Immediately, non-Japanese firms captured more than 20 percent of the market, but Japanese firms started to invest in research and development and to look for outside cooperation and investment. The largest Japanese drug companies are still smaller than the U.S. and European giants of the early twenty-first century.

Research and Development. A key characteristic of successful firms in the in-patent sector of the industry was investment in research. They established laboratories not for monitoring quality but for chemical research. The German and Swiss firms did that first, around the turn of the twentieth century, and they branched out from similar research in dyestuffs, which established German-Swiss supremacy in the world market before 1914. In addition, they cooperated with and used the work of researchers based at universities—and both sources have been employed since. The unaffiliated research laboratory was instituted in the United States and soon became an enterprise for innovation; the rest of the process of development, diversification, and testing was taken on by the pharmaceutical companies. Since the 1980s, a few such laboratories were established in Europe and Japan. The U.S. biotechnology industry has grown from the 1990s onward, and nearly all major international firms have signed research contracts with such U.S. enterprises. Also in the 1990s, international firms established their own research centers, including some in developing countries. Most such centers had the assignment of adapting pharmaceuticals to the respective national market. A few went beyond that and took part in integrated research with the host company or its research division. High rates of capital investment in research are budgeted by firms such as Roche or Boehringer Ingelheim (about 20 percent of annual income). Johnson & Johnson and Ciba-Geigy invest about 15 percent; Warner Lambert and SmithKline invest about 10 percent.

Firms patent not only the drugs they develop for sale but all the related chemical combinations and processes, to prevent competitors from offering a slightly modified drug or process and, by so doing, saving enormous costs. A major problem for research-oriented firms is that ten years usually pass between the registration of a patent and the start of sales—because the drug is not in final form when patented and the approval tests take years. In the majority of cases, the time it takes for firms to recoup invested capital for a new drug is some 30 to 35 percent of the patent-cover period.

Marketing. The pharmaceutical industry is known to be ethical, and it enjoys a relatively positive reputation. For the most part, people trust the drugs they consume and respect the company that manufactured them, which is a special asset to the industry. Some firms, such as Beiersdorf, kept their drug division mainly because they expect the positive spillover to their other health-care or cosmetic products. Another characteristic is that consumers do not choose the products. Only OTC drugs are chosen and paid directly by consumers. In contrast, ethical drugs—the largest market share—are prescribed by physicians and often paid by the state, by private insurance, or by welfare institutions. Until the 1980s, these rarely interfered, but marketing has had to bow to their cost-cutting demands. Nearly all sales go to independent wholesale firms and hospitals. Early in its history (1897), Merck tried to establish its own pharmacy in New York but closed after two years, because of the resistance to its products by independent pharmacies, which feared for their own futures. Most firms of the industry never tried to link themselves to retail trade.

Although there was extremely little direct selling, there was a great commitment to advertising. The pharmaceutical industry has advertised almost as much as tobacco or drink companies. The reason was an attempt at establishing

PHARMACY. Germany, eighteenth century. (Private Collection/Art Resource, NY)

identifiable brands and trademarks that could stabilize sales. The prolongation of the product cycle of a drug, through marketing, can extend returns on investment. Aspirin, about one hundred years old, is a good example; much of the marketing efforts were originally directed at physicians who, by prescription, chose it as trustees for the consumers.

The industry still has marketing operations in which sales people sell to physicians, to emphasize the ethical side of the business; salespeople advise on the new drugs, they hand out useful lists or materials on medications, and they give out free samples. Such marketing has become important, owing to the growth of the generic and OTC sectors, as well as to the rising number of drugs available. Since the 1990s in the United States, magazine and television advertisements for such ethical drugs ask consumers to request them from their physicians by trade names. The firm's trademark has also become increasingly important, since it represents the seal of quality for all its products. This was the reason why, in 1995, Bayer paid U.S. $1 billion to reacquire its trademark—the Bayer-cross—in

North America (which had been sequestered as a German firm during World War I). Bayer also renamed its U.S. subsidiary, Miles, as Bayer.

A special type of cooperation was found in pharmaceutical marketing. In many countries, transnational firms gave the marketing of parts or all of their products to local firms, because these were considered best adapted to local markets, and they often enjoyed government protection. Such firms usually adapted or repackaged the product. The majority of pharmaceutical firms worldwide are of this type.

BIBLIOGRAPHY

Agrawal, Madhu. *Global Competitiveness in the Pharmaceutical Industry: The Effect of National Regulatory, Economic and Market Forces*. New York, 1999.

Ballance, Robert, Janos Pogany, and Helmut Forstner. *The World's Pharmaceutical Industries: An International Perspective on Innovation, Competition and Politics*. Prepared for the United Nations Industrial Development Organization. Aldershot, U.K., 1992.

Boussel, Patrice, Henry Bonnemain, and Frank J. Bove. *The History of the Pharmaceutical Industry*. Paris, 1982.

Corley, T. A. B. *The British Pharmaceutical Industry since 1851*. Discussion Papers in Economies and Management: Series A, 404. Reading, U.K., 1999.

Club de Bruxelles, ed. *Public Health and the Pharmaceutical Industry in Europe*. Brussels, 1994.

Drake, Donald, and Marian Uhlman. *Making Medicine, Making Money*. Kansas City, 1993.

Helms, Robert B., ed. *Competitive Strategies in the Pharmaceutical Industry*. Washington, D.C., 1996.

Hounshell, David, and John Kenley Smith, Jr. *Science and Corporate Strategy. DuPont R&D, 1892–1980*. Cambridge, 1988.

Liebenau, Jonathan. *Medical Science and the Medical Industry: The Formation of the American Pharmaceutical Industry*. Basingstoke, U.K., 1987.

Matravest, Catherine. "Market Structure, R&D, and Advertising in the Pharmaceutical Industry." *The Journal of Industrial Economics* 47 (1999), 169–194.

Spivey, Richard N., et al. *International Pharmaceutical Services: The Drug Industry and Pharmacy Practice in Twenty-Three Major Countries of the World*. New York, 1996.

Swann, John P. *Academic Scientists and the Pharmaceutical Industry: Cooperative Research in Twentieth-Century America*. Baltimore, 1988.

Wimmer, Wolfgang. "Wir haben fast immer etwas neues." In *Gesundheitswesen und Pharma-Industrie in Deutschland, 1880–1935*. Berlin, 1993.

HARM G. SCHRÖTER

Medical Practitioners

Medical practice was of considerable economic importance in major population centers throughout the West and elsewhere, notably in China and the Indian subcontinent. This article concentrates on medical practice as an economic activity in Europe since the Middle Ages and the United States.

Medical Practice, Medical History, and Economic History. The economic history of medicine, particularly of medical practice, has suffered from neglect. It has been a peripheral concern of most medical historians. Medical economics, which has developed rapidly as an academic field since about 1960, tends to concentrate on macroanalyses of health care systems, though medical practice and practitioners have also received some attention, driven in part by the practical interests of physicians. But few medical economists have shown much inclination for historical scholarship.

One reason for the lack of attention is the sheer difficulty of the task for the earlier periods, for which sources are sparse and often unreliable. Another reason may be that some of the historic features of medical practice, even in more recent times, do not fit easily into a broad narrative of economic development in the West. These features include:

- the importance of self-treatment and medical care in the household;
- the generally small scale of medical practice considered as a business, more like a shop than a factory and characterized by one-on-one encounters between a self-employed practitioner and a client;
- the persistence of corporatism, in which state-sanctioned occupational bodies exercised control over transactions in the marketplace;
- the continuing role of the state in licensing and regulating medical practice, even as state intervention in the economy was declining in many other areas.

Historic Characteristics of Medicine as an Economic Activity. These characteristics can provide a convenient starting point for the present discussion. Because medical knowledge was widely disseminated, individuals offering medical services had to compete both with domestic healing and with many other would-be practitioners. Even after the creation of medical faculties at late-medieval universities, when learned physicians claimed to be uniquely qualified providers of theory-based advice, medical practitioners of all stripes continued to sell medicines with supposed therapeutic virtues. They often made agreements in which payment was contingent on a successful cure; in a sense they were marketing health itself.

The small scale of medical enterprise fostered competition; only a modest capital outlay was required to set up as an unlicensed practitioner. Scale, together with the limited size of the market outside major urban centers, also affected the division of labor. In principle, following the traditional tripartite structure of the health occupations in medieval and early modern Europe, physicians offered advice and dispensed prescriptions, which apothecaries filled; surgeons, trained by apprenticeship, performed procedures,

such as bloodletting, at the direction of a physician; midwives were subordinated to the surgeons, whom they were supposed to summon in difficult cases. But many individuals worked as independent general practitioners, blurring the theoretical division of labor and undermining the supervisory authority of the physicians. There were also surgical experts, such as lithotomists, who cut for bladder stones, but they were essentially highly skilled craftspeople who lacked a grounding in medical theory and, in most cases, formal recognition. Because the pool of patients in any one place was limited, many were forced to travel, following the well-worn path of the itinerant quacks who moved from town to town hawking their nostrums in the public square. Into the early nineteenth century specialization, like itinerancy, was considered the mark of a quack.

The organized medical occupations have also shared with other modern professions certain corporatist features, inherited from the guilds of the Old Regime. The thrust of many of these practices and principles, from fee schedules to limits or bans on advertising, was anticompetitive. The most economically significant was market closure, depicted in modern times less as a privilege pertaining to guild membership and more as a form of consumer protection. In the medical field, the argument ran, it was too difficult for consumers to make an informed judgment among providers in an unregulated marketplace. The possible consequences of buyer error—loss of health, even death—were too grave to allow the free-market principle of caveat emptor ("let the buyer beware") to prevail. The modern professional ideologies that emerged in the nineteenth century also retained the ethos that had set the learned professions apart both from the "mechanical arts," which did not involve the higher faculties of the mind, and from the pursuit of profit based on the work of others or of machines. The physician's fee was an "honorarium," a token of esteem and appreciation, rather than a salary. Professional etiquette, it has been argued, derived from noble codes of honor.

This at least was the ideal. As the remainder of this article shows, the historic development of medical practice cannot be separated from larger economic trends. But political and cultural factors loomed larger than for many other economic activities.

Age of the Guilds. In late antiquity household healing predominated; in the absence of medical degrees or qualifications, many different kinds of practitioners offered their services to those willing to pay. With the growth of the Church as the center of learning in the Latin West, monks and clerics often doubled as medical practitioners. The universities founded in the twelfth and thirteenth centuries, during the same period that saw the development of urban merchant and craft guilds, were communities of scholars with the power to confer degrees. Surgeons and apothecaries formed companies on the standard guild model; medical faculties, supplemented by colleges of physicians in towns that lacked a faculty, performed many of the same functions for their members, setting standards and regulating practice. This model was at its strongest in western continental Europe and was weaker in the less-urbanized east. Guilds declined in Britain over the early modern period and did not take root in Britain's American colonies.

Urbanization also correlated roughly with the density of practitioners, high in the Mediterranean region and low in eastern Europe. Limited effective demand resulted in small patient loads by modern standards and limited revenues; clients often paid in kind. All but the most successful medical practitioners commonly sought to augment their earnings by pursuing a second occupation. Contracts to provide medical services to a town or monastery and government appointments were eagerly sought after as steady sources of income. Practitioners visited patients in their homes or, in the case of itinerant empirics, held consultations in the public square or a rented room at an inn; the most prominent also consulted by correspondence. Especially in the countryside, practitioners charged for a visit by the distance traveled; the indirect price for a consultation remained a substantial part of medical fees well into the nineteenth century.

Medicine was one of the sectors of economic activity most affected by what has been called the consumer revolution of the eighteenth century, in which the demand generated by rising disposable incomes, together with new techniques of production and marketing, resulted in a proliferation of goods and services for mass consumption. Whether this can be called the commodification or commercialization of medicine, as some historians have suggested, is debatable, since the key changes occurred in the drug trade, and medical practitioners had in any case long been active in the marketplace. But many medical practitioners, some of them legally authorized, seized the opportunity to expand their revenue base by selling proprietary remedies, blurring the line between "profession" and "quackery." Eighteenth-century medicines were among the first nationally marketed brand-name products, the forerunners of the specialties produced by the large-scale pharmaceutical industry that emerged in the nineteenth century. The pharmacy, largely a retail outlet for mass-produced medications, gradually supplanted the shop where the apothecary compounded medicines according to the formulary or a physician's prescription.

The early modern period also saw an increasing role for the state in public health, starting with the health boards of Renaissance Italy, in the provision of medical assistance, and in the regulation of medical practice. Town and district physicians were common in the states of Germany and Italy; medical boards in Prussia, Spain, and elsewhere licensed practitioners and supervised their activities.

Nineteenth Century. In the 1790s the French Revolution abolished the old guilds and faculties. Regulation of medical practice was restored in 1803, but the right to practice now depended on a license issued by the state, following an examination, rather than membership in a privileged corporation. The guild model subsequently declined elsewhere in Europe, though government controls on many aspects of medical practice remained. In the liberal model that the nineteenth-century profession took as its ideal, the relationship between physician and patient was based on a direct contract freely entered into by autonomous economic actors. In the heyday of liberalism in the middle decades of the century, even professional monopoly came under question; it was lifted in the United States in the Jacksonian era, in Britain in 1858, and in the German Empire in 1871.

The number of practitioners rose rapidly in the nineteenth century, leading to complaints of overcrowding. Purchasing the practice of a retired or deceased physician increased, though some questioned whether it was consistent with liberal principles of free choice. Productivity rose, helped by the increasing number of patients who were willing to come to the physician's office and, starting at the century's end, by the use of the motor car for visiting those who were not.

Three key changes transformed traditional medical practice over the nineteenth century: a restructuring of the profession, the rise of the hospital as a medical center, and the development of new forms of third-party payment. Medicine and surgery were fused as professions; the latter was now a specialty of the former and required the same fundamental training. New specialties appeared on the same basis. Second-order practitioners below the rank of medical doctor persisted, however, in central and eastern Europe and in France, where between 1803 and 1892 it was possible to obtain a diploma as a "health officer" after a simpler, more practical, and less-expensive training than that doctors received. At the same time new auxiliary medical occupations appeared, notably the medically trained nurse, following the example of Florence Nightingale. During the same period the medical profession itself was opened to women. The first female physician, Elizabeth Blackwell, received her degree in the United States in 1849; European medical faculties opened their doors to women in the last three decades of the century. The restructured occupation created associations that, unlike the old guilds, were open to all practitioners. The British Medical Association was founded in 1832, the American Medical Association in 1847, and the General Association of French Physicians in 1858. Some professional organizations worked actively to protect their members' economic

PHYSICIANS. Physician and attendant with heliotrop, from an Arabic translation of *De Materia Medica* by Dioscorides, Baghdad, 1224. (Freer Gallery of Art, Smithsonian Institution, Washington, D.C.: Purchase, F1938.1)

interests; they included the late-nineteenth-century French groups known as *syndicats*, the same term applied to labor unions.

Hospitals, which under the Old Regime had served mainly as shelters for the homeless, the disabled, and the chronically ill, developed in the nineteenth century into fully medicalized institutions devoted to surgical operations, the treatment of acute diseases, and the practical training of physicians. It was in this setting that the scale and division of labor in medical work first approached those of modern industry, though the health "factory" in this period was nearly always a public institution or charitable organization rather than a profit-making enterprise. Hospital appointments brought income as well as prestige; hospital privileges came to confer a greater advantage on licensed physicians than their legal monopoly, which unqualified practitioners routinely defied.

Even in the Old Regime, individual patients had not always purchased medical services directly from providers. But the nineteenth century saw the development of new forms of third-party payment and on a new scale: voluntary organizations known variously as friendly societies,

benefit societies, and mutual aid societies; employers practicing "welfare capitalism," especially in the railroad industry; and the national sickness insurance program launched in Germany by Otto von Bismarck in 1883 and emulated elsewhere over the next several decades (notably the National Health Insurance plan adopted in Britain in 1911). Physicians signed contracts to treat employees or club members for a fixed annual payment. State insurance funds, supported by employer and employee contributions, offered capitation or fee-for-service schemes or a choice between the two. British general practitioners largely accepted capitation; the French profession overwhelmingly preferred fee-for-service. The overall reaction of the profession was mixed. Insurance schemes increased the effective demand for medical services and could raise physicians' incomes. On the other hand, there was a cost to be paid in professional autonomy, and some rank-and-file practitioners complained that the bargaining power of the major third payers drove down fees and actually reduced practitioners' revenues.

Twentieth Century. Two divergent trends marked the development of medical practice in the twentieth century, both of which tended to curtail the physician's autonomy as an economic actor: in Europe the development of state-sponsored health care programs; in the United States the growth of private health insurance and of large-scale medical organizations, from group practices to for-profit health care corporations running both hospitals and health maintenance organizations (HMOs), which provided services for a fixed annual charge.

During the interwar period western Europe followed the German model of social insurance, in which self-employed practitioners entered into contracts with the plan administrators. The Soviet Union offered an alternative model of socialized medicine, in which medical personnel worked as employees of the state. Although they retained some autonomy in making medical decisions, they had virtually none as economic actors. After World War II the British National Health Service (1948) nationalized the hospitals and used general tax revenues to pay for the system; this was "socialized medicine" but with doctors who were still independent agents. In France postwar social security legislation extended insurance to a much larger part of the population, though universal coverage was not finally secured until 1999. In the United States, in contrast, drives for national health insurance failed in the early part of the century and after World War II, when the schemes were denounced as socialized medicine or even communism. The Medicaid and Medicare amendments to the Social Security Act of 1965 targeted the unemployed and the elderly, while it was left to employer-based insurance programs to address the needs of the working population. The entitlement programs in the United States and elsewhere offered new revenue streams to physicians and hospitals, but rapidly rising costs led the government to impose fee schedules and other cost-control measures.

The United States led the way in the development of private-sector health insurance (generally offered through employers), group practice, and health care companies. The HMOs that proliferated starting in the 1980s promised to contain escalating costs but also to provide a healthy return to investors; they profoundly changed both physicians' and patients' experience of health care. The former found themselves under increasing pressure to maximize productivity by seeing more patients and to reduce costs by limiting treatments. These trends can be seen as part of a broader movement in the United States to extend market principles to sectors, such as health care, in which they hitherto had not fully applied. In Europe more providers worked in the public sector and fewer in private group practices, and legislation impeded the growth of a health care industry on the American model. In France, for example, only a minority of physicians belonged to a group practice, and the creation of each new partnership required the authorization of the national Order of Physicians.

Twenty-First Century. By the beginning of the twenty-first century there were signs that the pattern of American exceptionalism had begun to erode. The "marketization" of the health care sector proceeded apace in Latin America, after the World Bank and the International Monetary Fund decided in 1993 that the "structural adjustments" required as a condition for new loans would include privatizing health care institutions and social security programs. The trend in Europe was more modest but nonetheless clear. In the United Kingdom the 1990 National Health Service and Community Care Act, inspired by the American model, sought to create an internal market. "Purchasers," including government authorities and some general practitioners, would receive a budget with which they would buy the services of providers on a competitive basis. In France, under legislation implemented in 1994, physicians could henceforth incorporate and receive either a salary or dividends in lieu of traditional fees. In the United States supporters of marketization pushed to extend managed care principles to Medicare, facing rapidly rising costs as the baby boom generation entered the system. At the same time public dissatisfaction with the limits of private insurance increased pressures to develop a national model that would meet the needs of the uninsured and underinsured without making the federal government the single payer for all health care services. The outcome remained uncertain at the time of the writing of this article. What was clear was that, over the space of half a century, the practice of medicine as an economic activity had been radically transformed. Pockets of the old model remained,

in "boutique practices" for wealthy patients who paid their own way. But the work of the new-style professional was increasingly shaped by the new buyers of his or her services, the government, and capitalist enterprise. Cost-containment measures were driving down the incomes of providers; bureaucratic guidelines constrained their decisions on patient care.

BIBLIOGRAPHY

Brockliss, Laurence, and Colin Jones. *The Medical World of Early Modern France.* Oxford, 1997. Ambitious synthesis with stimulating discussion of medical entrepreneurship in the eighteenth century.

Digby, Anne. *Making a Medical Living: Doctors and Patients in the English Market for Medicine, 1720–1911.* Cambridge, 1994. The fullest historical study on a national scale of the economics of medical practice.

Fissell, Mary E. *Patients, Power and the Poor in Eighteenth-Century Bristol.* Paperback repr. Cambridge, 2002. Includes a chapter on the medical marketplace.

Krause, Elliott A. *Death of the Guilds: Professions, States, and the Advance of Capitalism, 1930 to the Present.* New Haven, 1996. Historical sociology of the professions, including medicine.

Lindemann, Mary. *Health and Healing in Eighteenth-Century Germany.* Baltimore, 1996. Detailed information on the lives of medical practitioners in the state of Braunschweig-Wolfenbüttel.

Lindemann, Mary. *Medicine and Society in Early Modern Europe.* Cambridge, 1999. Considers a wide variety of medical practitioners.

Loudon, Irvine. *Medical Care and the General Practitioner, 1750–1850.* Oxford, 1989. Includes three chapters on income and practice.

Pomata, Gianna. *Contracting a Cure: Patients, Healers, and the Law in Early Modern Bologna.* Baltimore, 1998. Economic, legal, and moral dimensions of the healer-patient relationship.

Porter, Roy. *The Greatest Benefit to Mankind: A Medical History of Humanity.* New York, 1998. The best one-volume history of medicine; limited attention to economic issues but useful for background on medical ideas and practice.

Porter, Roy. *Quacks: Fakers and Charlatans in English Medicine.* Stroud, U.K., and Charleston, S.C., 2000. Quacks (and doctors) as entrepreneurs in the period of the eighteenth-century consumer revolution.

Ramsey, Matthew. *Professional and Popular Medicine in France, 1770–1830: The Social World of Medical Practice.* Paperback repr. Cambridge, 2002. Considers a wide variety of medical practitioners with attention to the economic aspects of their activities.

Siraisi, Nancy G. *Medieval and Early Renaissance Medicine: An Introduction to Knowledge and Practice.* Chicago, 1990. The best survey of medieval and early modern medicine and its classical antecedents.

Starr, Paul. *The Social Transformation of American Medicine: The Rise of a Sovereign Profession and the Making of a Vast Industry.* New York, 1982. Strong discussions of economic aspects of medical practice and the development of the American health care industry.

MATTHEW RAMSEY

Hospitals

Hospitals since the Middle Ages have been characterized by a transition from church to lay control. Once sparsely distributed, hospitals began to be erected in most towns and became progressively more central to health care as well as medical education. Over the last hundred years hospital treatments have developed, albeit unevenly, with scientific and technological innovations. Their administration has become more bureaucratic, while their finances have continued to escalate and grow more complex. Although hospitals have become the centerpieces of health-care systems globally, most historical works on hospitals have concentrated on hospitals in Europe and North America, and a number are studies of single institutions.

Middle Ages. In Europe the hospital took one of two main forms. First, there were the religious institutions, usually attached to a priory and under the supervision of a bishop through a prior. Most were located near monasteries and routes of pilgrimage and offered shelter or "hospitality" to pilgrims and travelers, separating pilgrims and paupers from distinguished guests. Second, there were those located in villages and towns, generally created using alms collected by cathedrals and episcopal seats in response to illness and poverty in the community. The common denominator of patients was poverty, not illness. At the heart of the medieval and early modern hospital regime lay the idea of charity, predicated upon the relationship between Christ and the pauper. Medicine and morality were closely tied, the arrangement of beds, often in rows, dictated by the location of an alter rather than modern considerations of cross-infection. In many cases early hospital architecture had an overwhelming effect, far outstripping any practical purposes, such as ventilation. Large Renaissance hospitals and civic hospitals administered by guilds and town corporations developed alongside medieval monasteries and even adopted a cruciform construction. The original religious nature of many institutions was kept alive in hospital names, such as Hôtel-Dieu in Paris or St. Bartholomew's in London. With secularization the conviction grew that health facilities ensured stability and prosperity. Some trading communities including Venice, Pisa, Genoa, Regensberg, Lübeck, and Novgorod, invested in hospitals.

Near the end of the Middle Ages many European towns and villages supported local hospices, leprosaria, or "hospitals." In 1266 in France, under Louis VIII, over 2,000 *léproseries*, typically comprising a chapel, huts, and an enclosed garden, were enumerated, while England had 130. A number of the nineteen thousand leprosaria established across Europe became plague hospitals in the fourteenth century, and many remained hospitals after the decline of epidemics. Additional pesthouses were built in Dubrovnik (1377), Venice (1423 and 1468), Milan (1488), and Nuremberg (1498), the latter becoming a model for other German hospitals.

Early Modern. The Reformation brought about the secularization of many hospitals, while others were dissolved or reformed under new constitutions by monarchs and municipalities. In England in 1534, under Henry VIII, the dissolution of the monasteries and priories resulted in the closure of almost all the country's medieval hospitals. Three were restored to the city of London to be administered and supported locally and served a population of 200,000. In contrast, the Reformation caused far less disruption to hospitals in Catholic countries. Those run by confraternities in Italy, for example, flourished and remained the envy of Europe, the hospital in Florence outshining all others, though inmates in other cities numbered in the thousands. From the eleventh century to the fourteenth century crusading and nonmilitary brotherhoods helped greatly expand hospital facilities. Besides establishing hospitals in Italy and France, the Order of St. John of God, a sixteenth-century Spanish confraternity, founded some two hundred hospitals throughout the Americas. Similarly the missionary movement in more recent centuries introduced Western hospitals worldwide.

During this period the growth in hospital numbers was greatest in Europe. Much like the Holy Roman Emperor Sigismund's plan of 1439 to provide free medical attendance in every town, in France, the Edict of Moulin (1566) recognized the responsibility of each community to care for its poor and sick. In most other continental states during this period central governments expressed greater concern for the sick and indigent. In the name of efficiency, the authorities of the French crown directed three major initiatives in the seventeenth century to shut down local hospitals and centralize services in its cities through the establishment of general hospitals, or *hôpitaux-généraux*. An edict of 1656 under Cardinal Mazarin (1602–1661) created the Hôpital-Général de Paris, while another in 1662 ordered all major cities of the kingdom to set up similar institutions. With hospital inmates numbering 100,000 in 1700 and the creation of 100 *hôpitaux-généraux*, this period in French history has been described by Michel Foucault as "the great confinement," though recent work suggests this to be an exaggeration (see Jones, 1989). Despite attempts to centralize and rationalize local institutions, many older hospitals remained because of local opposition.

In the late sixteenth century and early seventeenth century voluntary charity triumphed over community obligation, most notably in England, owing to the resurgent and revitalized church as well as the initiative of the Tudor state, which provided the framework for endowed charity law. While this potentially made many hospitals vulnerable to the growth of religious indifference, before receiving treatment most patients were to be found worthy or "deserving" of care and then were lodged like the poor. To the public and especially to benefactors, magnificent hospital constructions suggested excess funds and little economy. Convinced that luxury was rarely allied with utility, Johann Peter Frank (1745–1821), the former district medical officer of Baden who expounded the concept of medical police, suggested a hospital's site should be its only ornamental luxury. Though an important part of founding hospitals, charity retained its ulterior motives. Practices of charity remained enmeshed within a matrix of moral obligation, religious dutifulness, and social exigency and expectation. According to those most critical of medical charities, such as Bernard Mandeville (1670–1733), pride and vanity built more hospitals than all the virtues together. By failing to target recipients properly, charities became luxuries. Unlike on the Continent, the uncoordinated nature of charitable initiatives in England led to the creation of many hospitals in commercial districts, while other areas were deprived of similar provisions. In 1700 there were two hospitals in London, five in the rest of the country.

Modern. The destruction of Paris's Hôtel-Dieu by fire in 1772 led to a famous debate on the values and forms of hospital care. Jacques Tenon (1724–1816), a surgeon, anatomist, and member of the French Academy of Sciences who was familiar with the English literature on hospital construction, visited dozens of English hospitals and became impressed with the Royal Naval Hospital at Plymouth, the pavilion plan and location of which permitted thorough ventilation. Although the revolution and its aftermath long delayed the implementation of Tenon's observations, his plans culminated in the construction of the Hôpital Riboisière between 1846 and 1854. Equally influential was the sixteen-hundred-bed Allgemeine Krankenhaus built in Vienna in 1784 by order of Joseph II. While representing the absolutist leader's commitment to centralized administration and rationalized function, it demonstrated a growing conviction that hospitals were primarily for sick people. With separate medical and surgical sections and eighty-six teaching beds, it became the model for hospital construction in Habsburg lands. Imitations were built at Prague (1789), Laibach and Brünn (1786), Olmütz (1787), Linz (1788), and Lemberg (1789). Hospitals in Zagreb (1804) and Trieste (1833–1841) were also based on the Vienna model.

Despite a general proliferation of hospitals, Paris was unique among cities in the number of hospitals devoted to sick care at this time. A 1788 report stated that thirty-five thousand inmates, or 5 percent of the city's population, inhabited its hospitals. Mirroring rationalization in factory production, administrators attempted to transform the hospitals into "machines" for investigating disease and teaching vast numbers of students, many from outside France, in clinical medicine. In general medicine's professional bodies throughout Europe and North America began to promote bedside teaching. Nationalized in 1794, France's hospitals further streamlined operations to reduce cost, though ultimately inflation led the revolutionary

government to promote home care instead. Having considered returning hospitals to local parishes, the Directory retained control of hospitals and placed them under the newly created Ministry of the Interior and in the hands of private contractors. Charitable donations were again sought as eagerly as a new generation of practitioners sought hospital posts. Highlighting their importance to national health, Napoleon in 1811 decreed a hospital be built in every department. His invasion of Egypt in 1798 similarly encouraged Western medicine outside Europe.

In England the sale of hospital subscriptions remained the main source of hospital funding in the late eighteenth century and early nineteenth century. For a small annual fee, usually a pound, benefactors received tickets, which were distributed to the sick and deserving poor. The position of governor was reserved for more substantial donors, who brought their administrative skills to hospital management. Paid staff included nurses or servants, a matron, and an apothecary, usually assisted by a porter, while medical practitioners volunteered their services. The entire institution was usually managed by a secretary, who was person of many skills. Often playing marginal administrative roles, women were active as fundraisers and hospital visitors, regularly inquiring into the management of hospitals and receiving complaints from patients and staff. Most materials were purchased through a system of competitive tendering, though some hospitals established their own breweries, bakeries, and laundries. Surviving into the twentieth century, this model emerged throughout the British Empire, and many colonial hospitals, such as that at Wellington (1847), were created using imperial funds.

Hospital expenditure in these years can be divided into four general categories: hospital expenses (including building, furniture, insurance, and rents), wages and salaries, drugs and spirits, and general house expenses (food, stationary, and legal services). The lack of any uniform system of hospital accounting, however, makes comparisons of institutions problematic. Though subscriptions remained central to hospital finance into the nineteenth century, casual benefactions at social events, church collections, and personal donations began to defray more than the usual amount of expenditure, as did capital assets. Patients occasionally made minor contributions to expenses, at times providing food, sheets, and caution money, a deposit intended to cover the cost of burial should treatment be less successful than annual reports suggested. Though built to control disease, hospitals have been described by historians as centers for disease communication. Their greatest critics refer to them as gateways to death, leading some to suggest that temporary sheds were healthier alternatives. Instead, the two-story, well-ventilated, pavilion plan was championed by hospital reformers, including Florence Nightingale (1820–1910),

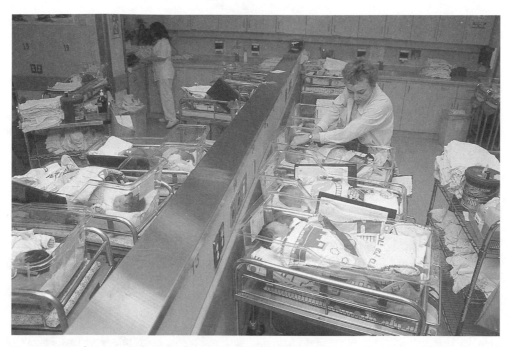

HOSPITALS. Pediatric ward at Hadassah-Ein Kerem Medical Center, Jerusalem, 2002. (© Dani Porges/Woodfin Camp and Associates, New York)

and remained an influential design into the first decades of the twentieth century. Along with other proposals, including the removal of hospitals from urban to rural areas, improvements in hospital organization came primarily with better training for nurses. Many Catholic sisterhoods, including the Daughters of Charity and the Sisters of Mercy, provided systematic training. Among Protestants, the lead was taken by Theodore Fliedner (1800–1864), whose two-hundred-bed hospital (acquired in 1842) at Kaiserswerth inspired similar training institutions worldwide. Nightingale trained there before undergoing instruction with the Daughters of Charity in Paris.

Hospitals were established in most European provincial centers by 1800, and two general hospitals were constructed in the American colonies at Philadelphia (1751) and New York (1773). Also emerging in these years was the specialist institution. Unlike general hospitals, these were often founded by medical practitioners, who worked to further their careers and plant specialisms, beginning with lunatic asylums, venereal, and lying-in hospitals in the eighteenth century. Those specializing in particular diseases were frequently dismissed as quack enterprises. By the early nineteenth century orthopedic, eye, women's, and children's institutions appeared, the last founded in Paris (1802), Berlin (1830), St. Petersburg (1834), Vienna (1837), and Liverpool (1851). In 1860 London alone claimed at least sixty-six specialist hospitals. Many of those served as models for American institutions, like Mount Sinai Hospital (1852), which were distinct in catering to

particular immigrant groups. In addition by 1875 there existed 148 smaller rural cottage hospitals in England, and numbers doubled over the following twenty years.

Clerical power and the workings of the charitable imperative kept medical power in check within hospitals throughout much of the modern period. Most institutions were governed by lay administrators and were domestic in their layout, despite growing esteem for the medical profession. Hospital facilities noticeably improved from the 1860s, often in step with the latest technological and scientific developments and generally offering treatments beyond the scope of general practitioner or informal care. Germ theory replaced earlier ideas of the causes of disease, such as social situation and morality, while hospital staff saw themselves as providers of medical treatment, not moral or social reformers. As financial considerations shortened patients' hospital stays, the abilities of institutions to morally reform inmates also declined. As clinical knowledge of doctors developed, most assumed greater control of hospital administration. Innovations in medicine also greatly increased expenditure, and teaching hospitals incurred the heaviest costs because of their particular need for comprehensive and up-to-date facilities. In total England and Wales supported 904 hospitals (or 65,000 beds) in 1860.

Much like medical science, hospital finance was also beginning to grow more complex in these years. While the introduction of congregational collections has been traced to the eighteenth century, workplace collections were similarly arranged and are said to have democratized benevolence, though such schemes had greater impact outside London. Similar hospitals supported by working-class subscriptions in North America were known as "penny hospitals." In some cases businesses and workers, especially in mining, built their own hospitals. More often hospitals invested in commercial enterprises. By 1891 investments at London hospitals represented 43.7 percent of income, but subscriptions rarely amounted to more than 10 percent of receipts by 1900. Though growing more popular, direct charges were limited to some London, specialist, and cottage hospitals and produced only 4 percent of England's voluntary hospitals' £3 million ordinary income in 1911. State funding was generally limited to grants covering the costs of military patients, venereal disease wards, tuberculosis care, and maternity and child welfare until the establishment of the National Health Service in 1948.

Payments by patients were more common in North America. By 1836, half of those individuals treated at the Massachusetts General Hospital (1811) were paying patients, who generally stayed a third less time in the hospital than charity patients. As in Europe patients were segregated by sex as well as race. Nationally hospital numbers increased from a couple in 1800 to almost 200 in 1870—hospital admissions stood at 146,500 in 1873—and hospital numbers rapidly climbed to more than 5,000 in 1915. New York alone had twenty-one hospitals in 1870 and more than forty-six by 1910. In most urbanized regions competition for the patronage of leading families grew intense, and hospitals had to devise new fund-raising methods. Both large and small institutions, many still run on domestic lines, received comparable stipends from local governments. Many hospitals had few options but to charge their patients. By 1900 the percentage of paying patients reached 27, up from 14 percent in 1892, rising quickly to 43 percent in 1902 and 52 percent in 1910. As in Europe technological realities and the promise of medical breakthroughs were turning hospitals into capital-intensive entities, with patient costs increasing in the first decades of the twentieth century. With 7,000 hospitals, or 400,000 beds, in the United States by the 1920s, hospitals absorbed two-thirds of all health-care resources. Subsequent changes signaled a move to more corporate forms of health-care organization. By the 1930s hospitals represented a $3 billion investment and constituted the largest American industry after iron and steel. Of American hospitals, 70 percent were private, compared to 12 percent in Europe. The hospital's image clearly changed from charity to a commercialized medical service. Said to reflect North American individualism, hospital wards were smaller in the United States than in the rest of the world. Accordingly hospital staffs were ten times larger than in Europe.

Much like the English philanthropist and prison reformer John Howard (1726–1790), who inspected and condemned Europe's hospitals in 1780, twentieth-century critics continued to regard hospitals as hotbeds of infection, while feminists lambasted the evils of "patriarchal medicine" as evidenced in the hospitalization of normal births. Despite disparaging evaluations and a reversal in the number of hospital beds since the 1960s, many more patients passed through twentieth-century hospitals. Much like the ailing public, the medical profession itself had been hospitalized in increasing numbers, and ever larger proportions of physicians were being socialized and educated in hospitals. Captives of high technology and worst-case justifications, hospitals and the health industry more generally struggled to reduce costs. In European nations renewed centralization of health services after World War II intended to reduce the costs associated with health care. In North America private insurance was seen as the best solution for all parties. In most countries a balance between the private and public systems continues to be negotiated, while hospitals worldwide account for the bulk of health budgets.

BIBLIOGRAPHY

Abel-Smith, Brian. *The Hospitals*. London, 1964.

Borsay, Anne. *Medicine and Charity in Georgian Bath: A Social History of the General Infirmary, c. 1739–1830*. Aldershot, U.K., 1999.

Cherry, Stephen. *Medical Services and the Hospitals in Britain, 1860–1939*. Cambridge, 1996.

Foucault, Michel. *The Birth of the Clinic*. Translated by A. M. Sheridan Smith. New York, 1975.

Gorsky, Martin. *Don't Look Back? Voluntary and Charitable Finance of Hospitals in Britain, Past and Present*. London, 2001.

Granshaw, Lindsay, and Roy Porter, eds. *The Hospital in History*. London, 1989.

Hickey, Daniel. *Local Hospitals in Ancien Régime France: Rationalization, Resistance, Renewal, 1530–1789*. Montreal, 1997.

Jones, Colin. *The Charitable Imperative: Hospitals and Nursing in Ancien Régime and Rvolutionary France*. London, 1989.

Rawcliffe, Carole. *Medicine for the Soul: The Life, Death and Resurrection of an English Medieval Hospital*. Stroud, England, 1999.

Risse, Guenter B. *Mending Bodies, Saving Souls: A History of Hospitals*. Oxford, 1999.

Rosenberg, Charles. *The Care of Strangers: The Rise of America's Hospital System*. Baltimore, 1987.

Stevenson, Christine. *Medicine and Magnificence: British Hospital and Asylum Architecture, 1660–1815*. New Haven, 2000.

Thompson, John D., and Grace Goldin. *The Hospital: A Social and Architectural History*. New Haven, 1975.

Waddington, Kier. *Charity and the London Hospitals, 1850–1898*. Rochester, N.Y., 2000.

JONATHAN REINARZ

HECKSCHER, ELI F. (1879–1952), Swedish economist.

Heckscher obtained in 1904 a licentiate degree at Uppsala University, with a major in history and with minors in economics and political science. He then had a five-year sojourn in the Institute of Social Science under Cassel at Stockholm University, during which period he also earned a doctoral degree at Uppsala University, studying the importance of the railroads in the economic development of Sweden. During the remainder of his career, Heckscher was tied to the Stockholm School of Economics. Here he held, from 1909 to 1929, the chair in economics and statistics and, from 1929 to 1949, in affiliation with Stockholm University, a personal research chair in economic history.

Among historians as well as economists, Heckscher's name is above all tied to his interpretation of mercantilism. But the former group would count his pioneering work on the economic history of Sweden as an achievement of even higher distinction, and the latter group might well point to his contribution to the theory of foreign trade as his main accomplishment.

Heckscher wrote extensively on economic theory in the early part of his career but did not consider this to be his main area of accomplishment. However, one of these contributions has turned out to be a seminal work for the modern neoclassical theory of foreign trade, the so-called Heckscher-Ohlin theory. In a paper written in 1919, spelling out the impact of foreign trade on the distribution of income, Heckscher clarified the role of the factor endowment of a country as a determinant of the structure of its foreign trade, while also stating the so-called factor-price equalization effect, the core theorem of neoclassical trade theory.

Heckscher considered his work on the economic history of Sweden as his major achievement. This contribution stands as the path-breaking work on which later Swedish economic historians have had to build, both in filling out what was missing in his account and in following up on its time coverage. But above all, Heckscher defined their target by offering a synthesis to challenge. Although much in the Heckscher overview has now been revised or superseded, his magnificent presentation is still engaging—posing Sweden's past as the roots of and holding it to the comparative light of the present in which Heckscher was writing.

Heckscher's work on mercantilism is not only his most recognized but also his most controversial contribution. Heckscher argued that the principles of economic policy in the seventeenth and eighteenth centuries were based on an empirically weak but logically somewhat coherent conception of the workings of the economic system, a view that could be upheld partly because economic policy actions were never efficient enough to be proven wrong. Generally, Heckscher's thesis that mercantilist thinking may be seen as a phase in the history of economic theory has fared better than his thesis that the economic policies of the era can be adequately subsumed under the abstract label of mercantilism. However, economists adopting the so-called public choice view of economic policies seem to have judged Heckscher's interpretation of economic policymaking in the period more benignly than historians.

It may be argued that the main present-day importance of Heckscher is a methodological one on account of his early plea for theory in economic history. Although it is somewhat problematical to view Heckscher as a precursor of the so-called New Economic History, his tenets on the task and method of historical reconstruction so far have not gained the attention they deserve.

Heckscher was resourceful and influential in shaping the institutional base of economics in Sweden, but he played an even greater role as the founder of the field of economic history as an autonomous Swedish academic discipline, separate from both economics and history. During his lifetime, however, these entrepreneurial activities were overshadowed not only by his scholarly contributions but also by his brilliant performance as an academic teacher and by his participation in the economic policy debate. He often excelled as a sharp critic as well as a forceful constructive voice on various concrete issues of public concern. He also earned a reputation for his fearless stand for high ethical principles on the ideological front, where he, with rhetorical skill, defended the tradition of economic liberalism.

BIBLIOGRAPHY

WORKS BY HECKSCHER

Till belysning af järnvägarnas betydelse för Sveriges ekonomiska utveckling. Stockholm, 1907. Illumination of the importance of the railroads for Sweden's Economic Development.

The Continental System: An Economic Interpretation. Oxford and New York, 1922.

"A Plea for Theory in Economic History." *Economic Journal, Historical Supplement* 4 (1929), 525–534. Also in *Enterprise and Secular Change, Readings in Economic History,* edited by F. C. Lane and J. C. Riemersma, pp. 421–430. Homewood, Ill., 1953.

"The Aspects of Economic History." In *Economic Essays in Honour of Gustav Cassel,* pp. 705–720. London, 1933.

Sveriges ekonomiska historia från Gustav Vasa, vols. I: 1–2, *Före Frihetstiden* (The Economic History of Sweden from Gustav Vasa, vols. I: 1–2, Before the Age of Liberty). Stockholm, 1935–1936.

"Quantitative Measurements in Economic History." *Quarterly Journal of Economics* 53 (1939), 167–193.

Sveriges ekonomiska historia från Gustav Vasa, vols. II: 1–2, *Det moderna Sveriges grundläggning* (The Economic History of Sweden from Gustav Vasa, vols. II: 1–2, The Founding of Modern Sweden). Stockholm, 1949.

An Economic History of Sweden. Translated by Göran Ohlin. Cambridge, Mass., 1954. This publication offers Heckscher's revision of his *Svenskt arbete och liv från Medeltiden till nutiden* (Swedish Labor and Life from the Middle Ages Until the Present) published in Stockholm in 1941.

Mercantilism 2d ed., rev., edited by E. F. Söderlund. Translated by M. Shapiro. 2 vols. London and New York, 1955. This second edition is a slightly revised version of the first English edition of 1935 and includes Heckscher's response to various reviews of the first edition and also a translation of his criticism of Keynes's views on mercantilism that Heckscher's treatise had provoked. The first English edition of 1935 was reprinted in 1994 with an introduction by L. Magnusson. The first Swedish edition appeared as *Merkantilismen* published in Stockholm in 1931.

"The Effect of Foreign Trade on the Distribution of Income." In *Heckscher-Ohlin Trade Theory*, translated, edited, and introduced by Harry Flam and M. J. Flanders, pp. 41–69. Cambridge, Mass., and London, 1991.

WORKS ABOUT HECKSCHER

Carlson, Benny. *The State as Monster: Gustav Cassel and Eli Heckscher on the Role and Growth of the State.* Lanham, New York, and London, 1994.

Coleman, Donald C., ed. *Revisions in Mercantilism.* London, 1969.

Ekelund, Robert B., and Robert D. Tollison. *Mercantilism as a Rent-Seeking Society: Economic Regulation in Historical Perspective.* College Station, Texas, 1981.

Ekonomisk-historiska Institutet. *Eli F Heckschers bibliografi, 1897–1949.* Stockholm, 1950.

Henriksson, Rolf G. H. "Eli F. Heckscher: The Economic Historian as Economist." In *The History of Swedish Economic Thought*, edited by Ba Sandelin, pp. 141–167. London and New York, 1990.

Henriksson, Rolf G. H. "Nationalekonomiska Föreningen." *Royal Economic Society Newsletter* 113 April 2001, 11–15.

Montgomery, Arthur. "Eli F. Heckscher. " In *Architects and Craftsmen in History: Festschrift für Abbot Payson Usher*, edited by J. T. Lambie, pp. 119–156. Tübingen, 1956.

ROLF G. H. HENRIKSSON

HEDGES AND FENCES. Hedges and fences have served as a principal means of defining property rights to agricultural land in Europe, North and South America, and Australia. Hedges have been used more in Europe than elsewhere because of higher precipitation levels, which facilitate their growth, smaller-scale farms requiring shorter distances for enclosure, the relatively cheap labor needed to plant and maintain the hedges, the high costs of the timber and wooden planks used prior to the development of wire fencing, and, finally, the relatively few roaming livestock that could invade planted crops. By contrast, in Australia and the Americas, farms typically have been larger, with wood cheaper and labor more costly, and with livestock, especially cattle and hogs, often allowed to forage unattended for long periods of time.

With enclosure of the common fields in England and elsewhere in Europe in the seventeenth and eighteenth centuries, scattered small holdings were consolidated into more compact and larger tracts for growing grain or raising sheep, demarcated by ditches or hedges. Hedges served to visibly define property boundaries, and when thick enough they could block the entry and exit of livestock (Ashton, 1955; Bradley, 1918). In eastern North America, wooden plank fences were constructed both to mark the outer limits of farms and to protect fields of crops that could be damaged by foraging livestock. As long as open-range conditions dominated, farmers were responsible for fencing their fields to ensure that cattle or hogs did not destroy their crops. Until liability rules were changed in the late nineteenth century, if farmers did not build such fences and cattle invaded a field, the farmers had no recourse against the livestock owners. Fences had to be built according to the standards specified in the legal code. Even with such fences, if trespass took place, the farmer still had to meet the burden of proof before compensation could be obtained from the livestock owner. With growing population densities and changes in relative agricultural prices, legislation was enacted in eastern states to close the open range and shift liability rules for trespass (Kantor, 1991).

In the western parts of North America, farms and ranches were larger, and, particularly in the Great Plains, wood was too scarce to be an effective fencing material. Where property rights to land were legally well defined and secure, as they were in the upper Midwest, and where livestock was confined to restricted areas, the outer boundaries of farms did not have to be fenced. Fencing was necessary only to enclose fields where livestock would graze. Wire fencing with wood end posts was the most common arrangement. In the more arid western regions where cattle grazed on the open range and where property rights to land were contested in the last half of the nineteenth century between ranchers and homesteaders, fencing served both to define property claims and to constrain livestock. Especially after the introduction of barbed wire, fences were used by livestock associations to restrict the drift of cattle herds and to block entry by homesteaders (Anderson and Hill, 1975). Grazing lands often were on the public domain and vulnerable to legal entry by homestead claimants. The fences constructed by livestock associations and by individual ranchers were illegal, but they enclosed millions of acres of grassland as part of western grazing practices. Conflicts between ranchers and homesteaders after 1880, however, led to the removal of many of the fences by the Department of the Interior at the behest of homesteaders (Libecap, 1981). Barbed wire represented a major technological innovation in fencing for the low-cost control of livestock, and it continued to be used. By the twentieth century it was the primary fencing material for ranchers throughout North and South America.

BIBLIOGRAPHY

Anderson, Terry L., and P. J. Hill. "The Evolution of Property Rights: A Study of the American West." *Journal of Law and Economics* 18 (1975), 163–179.

Ashton, Thomas S. *An Economic History of England: The Eighteenth Century.* London, 1955.

Bradley, Harriett. *The Enclosures in England: An Economic Reconstruction.* New York, 1918.

Kantor, Shawn Everett. "Razorbacks, Ticky Cows, and the Closing of the Georgia Open Range: The Dynamics of Institutional Change Uncovered." *Journal of Economic History* 51.4 (1991), 861–885.

Libecap, Gary D. *Locking Up the Range: Federal Land Use Controls and Grazing.* Cambridge, Mass., 1981.

GARY D. LIBECAP

HILL, JAMES J. (1838–1916), American railroad magnate.

Hill, known as "the Empire Builder," was born 16 September 1838, in Wellington, Ontario, Canada. At eighteen he moved to Saint Paul, Minnesota (although he did not become a U.S. citizen until 1880), and for the next sixty years he lived and worked in Saint Paul, ruling a kingdom of railroads, steamships, farms, and iron mines. He died there on 29 May 1916.

Hill spent his early years in the Mississippi steamboat trade. This experience convinced him that transportation would play a key role in the development of the American economy. In particular, he recognized the need for low-cost transportation to and from the farms of northwestern Minnesota and eastern North Dakota and, more importantly, for links from this rich agricultural region to the rest of the American economy by means of a transcontinental railroad.

Hill began implementing these ideas in 1878 when he (and three partners) acquired a bankrupt railroad, which they promptly renamed the Saint Paul, Minneapolis, and Manitoba Railway Company. By the end of 1879, "the Manitoba" connected the Twin Cities with the Red River Valley and ran north to meet the newly chartered Canadian Pacific Railway.

Hill hoped that he could join with the Canadian Pacific to realize his dream of a transcontinental railroad from Saint Paul to the Pacific. By 1883, he concluded that cooperation with the Canadian Pacific was impossible, and he explored other options. Hill ultimately decided that the best course was to build a new transcontinental route along his own preferred route, south of the Canadian Pacific and north of the Northern Pacific, from Grand Forks due west to the Pacific. In the mid-1880s, Hill began the project by extending the Manitoba west to the rich mining districts of western Montana. He then built the renamed Great Northern Railway westward from Montana and eastward from Seattle, Washington, completing the project in 1893.

In 1900 and 1901, Hill purchased the Northern Pacific and the Chicago, Burlington, and Quincy Railroad. These roads gave Hill control of two transcontinental routes from Chicago to the West Coast. The Burlington was the critical purchase, since it connected the Northern Pacific and Great Northern systems with Chicago. This threatened the interests of the E. H. Harriman and the Union Pacific Railroad. In retaliation, Harriman tried to gain control of the Northern Pacific by purchasing shares on the open market. This ignited a fierce battle on Wall Street, with Hill and Harriman each offering higher and higher prices for Northern Pacific stock and setting off a panic in the New York markets.

J. P. Morgan, worried that this competition would threaten the stability of the entire New York financial

JAMES J. HILL. Portrait by Adolph Mueller-Ury. (National Portrait Gallery, Smithsonian Institution, Washington, D.C./Art Resource, NY)

market, negotiated a compromise in 1902. The warring parties would jointly own the Great Northern, the Northern Pacific, and the Burlington through a huge new entity, the Northern Securities Company.

Soon after the company was formed, the Justice Department sued Northern Securities for antitrust violations. The Supreme Court ruled in March 1904 that Northern Securities had violated the Sherman Antitrust Act and ordered all of the railroads returned to their original owners. Hill thus retained ownership of the Great Northern, the Northern Pacific, and the Burlington, but the Court forbade their merger into one company. Hill continued to manage the roads and reap the monetary rewards of ownership until his death, but he never again tried to create an integrated rail network from Chicago to the Pacific.

The focus of this article is on the role James J. Hill played in the development of American railways. The vital contributions he made to the development of Great Lakes shipping, iron mining, agriculture, and the lumber industry are described in the sources listed in the bibliography.

BIBLIOGRAPHY

PRIMARY SOURCE MATERIAL
The complete papers of James J. Hill are available at the James J. Hill Reference Library, Saint Paul, Minnesota. The archives of the Great Northern and the Northern Pacific Railroads are available at the Minnesota Historical Society in Saint Paul, Minnesota.

BOOKS ABOUT JAMES J. HILL
Malone, Michael P. *James J. Hill: Empire Builder of the Northwest*. Norman, Okla., 1996. This is a short, three-hundred-page biography that provides an excellent introduction to and overview of Hill's life and work. It is an important contribution to the literature on Hill because Malone integrates labor history and regional history to provide a balanced portrait of Hill's impact (for good and bad) on individuals and communities of the Northwest.

Martin, Albro. *James J. Hill and the Opening of the Northwest*. New York, 1976. This is the definitive biography of Hill. The book passes lightly over Hill's paternalistic attitudes toward and treatment of railroad workers and generally takes Hill's point of view in such disputes as the Northern Securities case, despite evidence that contradicts Hill's positions. Despite these problems, the book is filled with information and insight that is available in no other source save the Hill papers themselves. The book was recently reissued by the Minnesota Historical Society with an extremely useful introduction by Thomas W. White, Curator of the Hill Papers. If possible, get this edition in order to balance Martin's views with White's.

Pyle, Joseph G. *The Life of James J. Hill*. 2 vols. New York, 1916–1917. In the mid-1890s, Hill bought the *Saint Paul Globe* and brought Pyle to Saint Paul to edit the paper. In 1905, Hill liquidated the paper but kept Pyle on the payroll as his "personal editor" (Martin, 1976, p. 591). Pyle used the opportunity to interview Hill about his life and to utilize the records of the Great Northern and its ancestor companies to compile Hill's biography. Pyle is obsequious at times, but the book contains marvelous details about Hill's early years in Saint Paul and provides a bird's-eye view of Hill's actions during the fight with the Union Pacific and the Northern Securities case.

BOOKS ABOUT THE GREAT NORTHERN RAILWAY
Hidy, Ralph W., Muriel E. Hidy, and Roy V. Scott, with Don L. Hofsommer. *The Great Northern Railway: A History*. Boston, 1988. This book provides an excellent description and analysis of both the construction and operation of the Manitoba and the Great Northern from the 1850s through 1970, when the Great Northern, Northern Pacific, and the Burlington merged to form the Burlington Northern. The book is based on a more detailed and documented manuscript, which is available "in major historical research libraries" (p. xi), including the Hill Library.

LOUIS D. JOHNSTON

HOMESTEADING. The settlement process for public lands has long been a source of controversy for most developing countries; that is, should the government sell the public lands at prices that would maximize public revenues, or should these public lands be offered at low rates that would induce rapid settlement? Homesteading, the practice of offering free public lands to those who would settle on the land and improve it, was not unknown in North America before the nineteenth century. Richard C. Overton (1944) notes that the principle of homesteading was part of the colonial policy of the French and Spanish as well as the "head right" system of the English.

The Spanish *encomienda* system and the French *seigneuries* system were both attempts by the monarch to expand settlement in the New World through the granting of land in exchange for settlement while maintaining the trappings of a feudal system. The *encomienda* system offered land and the right to demand the labor of Indians (serfs) in exchange for settlement. To keep people in America, a *seignor* was granted land along waterways that could be rented to peasants. The head right system entailed granting land to residents of America who brought in new settlers. (See Faulkner, 1924, pp. 38–53.) In each case, these methods resulted from efforts of the Crown to establish settlement.

Between 1842 and 1854, the United States offered 160 to 640 acres free to those who would settle and defend remote areas of Florida, Oregon, Washington, and New Mexico. The United States used homesteading repeatedly to establish settlement of lands where federal ownership was either contested or questionable. According to Douglas W. Allen (1991), homesteading, which entailed the loss of revenue from land sales, resulted in lower government expense than attempting to maintain claims to the land through a military presence until the land sold.

By the 1850s, the United States had acquired a large expanse of Western land that was sparsely settled. The Preemption Act in 1841 (repealed in 1891) allowed squatters, who had occupied lands before these lands were surveyed and offered for sale, the option of purchasing up to forty acres at the minimum government price before speculators could purchase the land at market prices. This act encouraged settlers to occupy the Western lands ahead of the surveyors because it reduced the risk of their eventually being forced off the land by buyers who could afford the market price. It was a means of compensating the squatters for incurring the risks associated with settling land before a military presence was well established.

Between 1841 and the beginning of the Civil War, Southern congressmen repeatedly blocked bills that would have allowed homesteading of Western lands because they feared total Northern domination of the settlement of those lands. In 1862, in the absence of Southern congressmen, the Homestead Act was passed by Congress and signed into law by President Lincoln. This act offered to any person who was head of a family and over twenty-one years of age 160 acres of surveyed public land after five years of continuous residence and payment of a registration fee ($26 to $34). Available land was that covered under the Preemption Act (for $1.25 per acre) and the eighty-acre lots within the lateral limits of railway grants. After six months, the homesteader was allowed to purchase the land at $1.25 per acre. Bining and Cochran (1964) indicate that the Homestead Act was not so great a democratic measure as many argued because it generally applied to lands west of the 100th meridian, the Great Plains to the Pacific, whereas the area east of this, which was better suited to small farms, was either already settled or in the hands of speculators. Stanley Lebergott (1984) notes that ten million people lived west of the Mississippi River by 1860, an indication that land that may have been especially well suited to small farming was already settled.

Much of the better public land was set aside for the establishment of agricultural schools or technical colleges (by the Morrill Land Grant Act of 1862) or given to railroad companies as an inducement to build railroads in the West. Both the states and the railroads sold these lands at market prices although railroads often reduced prices if people would settle on and improve land near the railroad within a short time. Lebergott (1984) points out that in the first ten years after passage of the Homestead Act, ten times more acres were sold for cash than were homesteaded. Although the rate of growth declined, cash sales continued to occur more than three times as often as acreage was homesteaded for the next two decades. Settlers realized that the farther they were from water or rail transportation, the lower the return was from the sale of farm produce. Thus, many paid three or four times the minimum public land price in order to have access to transportation.

Richard C. Overton (1944) notes that out of the approximately 1.4 billion acres in the original twenty-nine public land states, over one billion remained unclaimed or unappropriated in 1862, whereas by 1905, less than 500 million acres remained unclaimed. Nearly as much land went to the railroads, 110 million acres, as was claimed by homesteading, 136 million acres. Approximately 1.5 million original homestead entries were filed in the forty years after the Homestead Act was passed, and slightly fewer than half of these were patented by the original filer. As settlement spread westward, Gates (1963) notes that many of the homesteads were aggregated into larger landholdings because the total number of farms that existed was soon much smaller than the number of homesteads patented. Aggregation was necessary because the minimum efficient size for a farm was much larger than 160 acres. Moreover, the minimum efficient size increased as one moved westward across the plains and prairie states.

In 1891 the Preemption Act and the Timber Culture Act were repealed, and safeguards were enacted to prevent fraud under the Desert Land Act and the Homestead Act. Previously, it had been possible for speculators to acquire large tracts of land by hiring people to occupy land for the minimum period (six months) necessary to purchase it at $1.25 per acre. The land could be sold to the speculator as soon as the original homesteader had purchased it—even though homesteaders were required to state that a company had not hired them, and that they were going to continue occupying the land after purchase.

As over half of the land settled during this period was sold initially for cash payment, was the Homestead Act a success? The answer depends on what the purpose of the act was. Douglas W. Allen (1991) maintains that the purpose of U.S. land policy, and the Homestead Act in particular, was to rush settlers to the areas of the country where federal claims or property rights were uncertain. When Allen compares the land policies of Canada and Australia with those of the United States, his argument seems reasonable. According to Allen, although very similar to that of the United States, the Canadian system added the possibility of reserving a neighboring quarter of land to be purchased with money. (Land near railroads was not exempted because the railroads were already built.) Allen indicates that the Philippines passed a homestead act in 1903 for much the same reason as Canada: to preempt the occupation of the land by outsiders. Australia, on the other hand, has never had a homestead policy. Allen's argument is consistent with the view of economic historians who point out that the lands open for homesteading in the United States were those far away from the railroads and the main economic centers. Thus, the federal government's objective may be interpreted as that of following the least-cost method of establishing claim to the land over which the government wished to maintain ownership and control, especially when various parties were contesting the government's claims.

BIBLIOGRAPHY

Allen, Douglas W. "Homesteading and Property Rights: Or, 'How the West was Really Won.'" *Journal of Law and Economics* 34 (April 1991), 1–23. An excellent analysis of the underlying rationale for the Homestead Act.

Bining, Arthur Cecil, and Thomas C. Cochran. *The Rise of American Economic Life*. 4th ed. New York, 1964. A general discussion of the Homestead Act and other land policies.

Faulkner, Harold Underwood. *American Economic History*. New York, 1924. An earlier view of settlement programs as well as the Homestead Act and its success.

Gates, Paul W. "The Homestead Law in an Incongruous Land System."*American Historical Review* 41 (July 1936), 652–681. An examination of the inconsistency of the Homestead Law with existing land policy.

Gates, Paul W. "The Homestead Act: Free Land Policy in Operation, 1862–1935." In *Land Use Policy and Problems in the United States*, edited by Howard W. Ottoson, pp. 28–46. Lincoln, Nebr., 1963. A reexamination of many of the topics covered in his 1936 paper with additional data and analysis.

Gates, Paul W. *History of Public Land Law Development*. Washington, D.C., 1968. A thorough discussion of public land policy in the United States.

Lebergott, Stanley. *The Americans: An Economic Record*. New York, 1984. A short analysis of the resulting settlement pattern, which points out that public land policies that offer land at below-market prices have all been subject to graft and corruption.

Overton, Richard C. "Westward Expansion since the Homestead Act." In *The Growth of the American Economy: An Introduction to the Economic History of the United States*, edited by Harold F. Williamson, pp. 342–378. New York, 1944. A good overview of the effects of land policy in the United States.

U.S. Department of Interior, Bureau of Land. *Management Public Lands Bibliography*. Washington, D.C., 1962. An extensive collection of bibliographic sources related to public land policy in the United States.

WILLIAM K. HUTCHINSON

HONDURAS. *See* Central American Countries.

HONG KONG. When Hong Kong was ceded to Britian in 1842 after China's defeat in the Opium War, Lord Palmerston, the British foreign secretary, dismissed it as "a barren island with hardly a house upon it." The story of the rapid development of Hong Kong since 1842 from a "barren island" to a modern metropolis is well known. What is less known is that Hong Kong had a history of two thousand years of trade and salt production before the arrival of the British.

Around 110 BCE, the Han army was stationed in Hong Kong to administer the state salt monopoly. In the Tang (618–907 CE) and Song (960–1279 CE) dynasties, China's trade with Southeast Asia, India, and Arabia thrived. Hong Kong's Tuen Mun area at the eastern entrance of the Pearl River estuary was the first port of call for ships bound for Guangzhou, China's historic port at the tip of the estuary. Today, Hong Kong still has placed container terminals and its new airport on its western side near the historic Tuen Mun area, the part of Hong Kong closest to the Pearl River estuary.

As Hong Kong was a natural crossroads of trade, it prospered when China pursued an open policy, but declined after the Song dynasty when China turned inward. Hong Kong became a haven for pirates.

British Occupation (1841) to Pearl Harbor (1941). Hong Kong was declared a free port with British occupation in mid-1841. The advent of steamships dictated that the deep seaport of Hong Kong would replace the river ports of Macau and Guangzhou as *the* trading center of South China.

Besides geography, British rule was an important asset, as private property was protected, and Hong Kong was insulated from the political and social disturbances in China. China ceded Hong Kong to Britain in three stages: (1) the Treaty of Nanjing (1842) ceded Hong Kong Island; (2) the Convention of Beijing (1860) ceded Kowloon Peninsula; and (3) the Convention of 1898, leased the New Territories to Britain until 1997.

Growth was rapid after the 1860 Beijing Convention, because of sociopolitical instability in China as well as prosperity in Hong Kong. By 1880, China–Hong Kong trade accounted for 37 percent of China's imports and 21 percent of its exports; and by 1890, these shares had risen to 55 percent and 37 percent. These data excluded rampant smuggling by junks from Hong Kong, an offshore port beyond Chinese jurisdiction, to ports along China's coast to evade China's customs. The opening of the Kowloon Canton Railway in 1910 further strengthened the position of Hong Kong as an entrepôt.

Hong Kong's economy suffered greatly from World War I. Although its postwar recovery was rapid, reaching a peak in the late 1920s, the entrepôt trade declined again with the Great Depression, starting in 1929, and Japan's invasion of China in 1937 aggravated the decline.

Owing to war and social instability in China, Hong Kong's population continued to rise, from 300,000 in 1898 to over 800,000 in 1931. The Japanese invasion of China led to a doubling of the population to 1.6 million on the eve of the 1941 war in the Pacific. Hong Kong's industries started to develop as immigrants brought in labor, capital, and skills, and its exports were facilitated by the Commonwealth Preference established in 1932. However, Hong Kong's trade could not surpass the peak of the late 1920s.

Postwar Industrialization (1945–1979). Hong Kong's trade rapidly passed pre–World War II levels in the postwar years. However, the outbreak of the Cold War in East Asia soon strangled Hong Kong's entrepôt trade. After China's entry into the Korean War in 1951, the United Nations embargoed sales of strategic materials to China, and the United States banned all imports from China. Moreover, Beijing redirected to the Soviet bloc most of China's trade, which was state-to-state trade bypassing Hong Kong. In 1950, China–Hong Kong trade accounted for 38 percent of China's imports and 25 percent of China's exports. In 1955, the corresponding figures were only 2 percent and 11 percent. All that was left of the entrepôt trade was a small percentage of China's exports via Hong Kong to Southeast Asia. The rest of China's exports to Hong Kong were foodstuffs consumed locally.

The population of Hong Kong reached two million in 1950 because of refugees fleeing the Chinese civil war or Chinese Communism. Just as Hong Kong's entrepôt trade was strangled by the Cold War, refugee capital and labor from China, especially from Shanghai, transformed Hong Kong into the world's first successful example of export-oriented industrialization. Refugees made better industrial workers than regular migrants because the refugees had their backs to the wall and could not go home. Since the Cold War sealed the border to free migration, Hong Kong was spared the many problems of rural migration and return migration, namely, unemployment, high labor turnover, poor sanitation, and contagious diseases.

HONG KONG. City scene, with Bank of China building in the background, 1993 (© Frank Fournier/Woodfin Camp and Associates, New York)

The establishment of the General Agreement on Tariffs and Trade (GATT) in 1948 heralded an era of uninterrupted expansion of world trade and provided a favorable environment for export-oriented industrialization. However, most developing economies were nationalistic and pursued strategies of import substitution. Hong Kong could not aspire to be independent because it is geographically and culturally part of China. Since it was the only developing economy to specialize according to its comparative advantages in the 1950s, its export effort was very successful. In 1965, tiny Hong Kong supplied half of the world's exports of light manufactures (other than food and industrial raw materials) from the less developed countries (LDCs). Given Hong Kong's dependence on trade, it has been a staunch supporter of free trade and liberal economic policies. Hong Kong's liberalism has won the praise of Milton Friedman and other admirers of the free market.

Hong Kong's dazzling success in exporting textiles and clothing soon led to trade conflicts with developed economies, culminating in 1974 in establishment of the Multi-Fibre Arrangement (MFA). To circumvent the MFA, Hong Kong's textile manufacturers started to invest in LDCs not yet under restriction. Hong Kong firms became multinational at an early stage. Today, Hong Kong still has the biggest multinationals among newly industrializing economies (NIEs).

Reintegration after China's Opening (1979–1997). The success of export-oriented industrialization led to full employment and rising wages. The opening of China in 1979 presented a golden opportunity to Hong Kong manufacturing firms, which relocated to China in droves. With cheap labor, they expanded production, helping Guangdong to become China's number one province in exports since 1986 and in gross domestic product (GDP) since 1989. The industrial base in Guangdong depended on Hong Kong for logistical support, and Hong Kong became the service hub of Guangdong as well as China. In East Asia, the Hong Kong–Guangdong economic nexus was the first and most successful example of subregional economic integration (integration among geographically contiguous but politically separated border areas).

The success of Guangdong strengthened reformers in Beijing. Deng Xiaoping toured Guangdong in 1992 to give fresh impetus to China's reform drive, stalled by the 1989 Tiananmen incident. Hong Kong's response to Deng's tour was immediate: its contracted foreign direct investment (FDI) in China quintupled in 1992. Hong Kong's investment diversified from manufacturing to services, and spread northward from Guangdong to every corner of China.

Hong Kong's investment in China was very large. From 1979 to 2000, Hong Kong accounted for half of the cumulative FDI in China. From 1993 to 2000, largely because of the size of Hong Kong's investment there, China was the second largest recipient of FDI in the world after the United States. From 1993 to 1996, Hong Kong was the world's fourth largest source of FDI. Hong Kong is China's gateway to the world.

Challenge since 1997 Reversion. Beijing has largely honored its promise of noninterference in Hong Kong under the formula of "One Country, Two Systems" since the 1997 reversion; but Hong Kong has suffered severely from the shocks of the Asian financial crisis of 1997–1998, as well as the 2001 slowdown of the U.S. economy, aggravated by the terrorist attacks of 11 September.

Besides external shocks, the rapid economic development of China has narrowed the gap in skills between Hong Kong and the mainland. If Hong Kong is to continue to function as the gateway to China, it must maintain its lead in skills and preserve its uniqueness among Chinese cities in the rule of law and freedom of information flow.

Only time can tell whether Hong Kong can surmount these challenges. However, in the short 160 years since 1842, Hong Kong has repeatedly made economic history.

[*See also* China *and* Great Britain, *subentry on* British Empire.]

BIBLIOGRAPHY

Mok, Victor. "The Process of Development of a Modern Trading System." In *Hong Kong History: New Perspectives*, edited by Gangwu Wang, pp. 281–324, Hong Kong, 1997.

Sung, Yun-Wing. *Hong Kong and South China: The Economic Synergy.* Hong Kong, 1998.

YUN-WING SUNG

HORSES. The internal combustion engine did not finally supplant animal power in Western society until well into the twentieth century, and in some parts of the world it still has not done so. In Europe, horses (and, in places, asses and mules) and oxen were the animals used, and individual choice depended upon a number of factors. Horses were more expensive to keep, were of little value when their working lives were over, and were less effective on heavy soils. Oxen were slower and less powerful. In the Netherlands, horses largely had replaced oxen by the end of the Middle Ages, whereas in England this only happened in the nineteenth century. Where both animals were employed, oxen were more likely to pull the plow and horses the harrow and cart. Many peasant farmers only kept horses because of their greater flexibility. From medieval times, the strongest draft horses were bred in northern Europe, especially in the Low Countries. Although professional carrier services existed in early modern Europe, farmers, operating at slack times of the year, acted as haulers, too. Goods were carried by cart and by packhorse. The latter offered certain advantages, as they were faster, were more flexible in numbers, and coped better with rough ground. In nineteenth-century Spain, with its inadequate road system and few navigable waterways, packhorses and mules predominated. In wartime, armies required horses for their artillery and baggage trains.

Horsemanship was an essential attribute of a gentleman, but mere ownership of a horse to ride was a mark of status. Most people chose mounts by functional criteria, but the upper classes valued them equally as a fashion accessory and therefore paid greater attention to peripherals, such as color, conformation, pace, and breed. In the Middle Ages, it was possible to travel by conveyance, but this was no more comfortable than riding on horseback. From the fifteenth century, sprung coaches, originating in Hungary, helped a little. Richly furnished and pulled by a matching set of fine horses, they too were designed for ostentatious display. The population at large soon adopted the fashion, and public (hackney) carriages caused congestion in London in the early seventeenth century. By the early nineteenth century, a network of stagecoach routes had been established throughout Europe. At the same time, mail coaches took over from traditional postal systems employing riders and relays of horses.

The upper classes in particular used horses for sport and recreation, in the tilt yard, on the hunting or polo field, on the racecourse, or in the dressage (manège) ring. Federico Grisone first taught the manège in early-sixteenth-century Naples, but his influence soon spread far and wide. The Spanish Riding School at Vienna was established in the 1560s. In the High Middle Ages, horse racing, already established among the Arabs, was revived in the West. In England, the first public meetings took place in the sixteenth century, and thereafter the sport flourished under royal and aristocratic patronage. Interest led to the importation of suitable horses, primarily Arabs, Barbs, and Turcomans. In the eighteenth century, the English thoroughbred emerged.

In the Middle Ages, warhorses (destriers), especially those from Spain, fetched the highest prices. European rulers imported large numbers of Andalusian stallions, improved by infusions of Barb and Eastern blood, for their cavalry and to stand at stud. This type of horse reached its apogee in the "Great Horse" of the early sixteenth century, ideally a Neapolitan courser. In contrast, Near and Middle Eastern cavalries mainly comprised lighter and more nimble horses. Europeans followed suit. Commanders, such as Gustavus Adolphus of Sweden, adopted cavalry tactics that emphasized speed and maneuverability over weight and strength. Of the European horses, the Spanish *ginete* was valued for its courage and agility. Many mounts had Turcoman, Arab, or Barb blood. As cavalry tactics developed, schooling became more important.

Horses played a central role in the social and economic lives of many societies both in the East and in the West, and the business they generated was considerable. Many Western farmers bred horses on a small scale and, where conditions were favorable, became specialists. In the East, herdspeople maintained considerable stocks. The upper classes owned the largest and most valuable studs. In the fourteenth century, Edward III paid £150 for an English destrier, and in Egypt the Mamluk sultan El Nacer laid out far more for purebred Arabs. At Mantua, the Gonzagas possessed a celebrated stud, drawing on horses from all over Europe and the Mediterranean littoral.

The horse trade was a profitable and wide-ranging one. Apart from the local traffic in ordinary, all-purpose stock, long-distance commercial links also existed. From the Middle Ages onward, horses were exported from noted breeding areas, such as Spain, Germany, Italy, and the Low Countries. Farther afield there was a thriving market in India for horses from the Persian Gulf. In the seventeenth

HORSE MARKET. Illumination from *Insegna degli anziani*, Italian, seventeenth century. (Archivio di Stato, Bologna, Italy/Alinari/Art Resource)

century, traffic in Eastern horses developed through ports in the Levant, especially from Aleppo. To the west, Spain and subsequently other colonial powers sent large numbers of horses to the Americas. By the eighteenth century, the North American colonists were selling droves of horses in the West Indies. From about 1850, European breeders benefited from the growing North American demand for pedigree draft horses, initially British shires and Clydesdales but later French Percherons and Belgian Brabançons. By 1900, the Americans were exporting crossbred draft horses back to Europe. They also developed their own breeds of saddle horse, including the Appaloosa, the Morgan, and the quarter horse.

In the West, fairs for centuries acted as nodal points in the trade, and a handful, including Antwerp, Cologne, Geneva, and Leipzig, acquired international reputations. The East had its horse-trading centers too. In the Persian Gulf, Aden was a major entrepôt for horses, and in India, Delhi had a thriving horse market. In Europe, fairs began to decline in the eighteenth century as more informal means of doing business evolved, but some did retain their vitality. In England, dealers at Howden (Yorkshire) in 1834 came from Russia, Prussia, Germany, France, and Spain seeking thoroughbreds, hunters, carriage horses, and broodmares. For the domestic market, many were sold as cavalry remounts. Leading dealers both in the West and in the East traded on a grand scale, as they had from medieval times.

[*See also* Draft and Pack Animals.]

BIBLIOGRAPHY

Chivers, Keith. *The Shire Horse.* London, 1976.
Clutton-Brock, Juliet. *Horse Power.* London, 1992.
Edwards, Peter. *The Horse Trade of Tudor and Stuart England.* Cambridge, 1988.
Hyland, Ann. *The Warhorse, 1250–1600.* Sutton, U.K., 1998.
Hyland, Ann. *The Horse in the Middle Ages.* Sutton, U.K., 1999.
Thompson, Francis M. L., ed. *Horses in European Economic History: A Preliminary Canter.* Reading, U.K., 1983.

PETER EDWARDS

HORTICULTURE AND TRUCK FARMING. Although horticulture dates back to the Garden of Eden or earlier, it is of growing importance today. Horticulture is traditionally associated with the garden, from *ager* in Latin, whereas agriculture is linked with the field, from *agro* in Greek, a related distinction defines agriculture as cultivation with a plow and horticulture as cultivation without one. Under modern conditions such technical distinctions are blurred, leading to a definition of horticulture embracing the production of foods such as fruits and nuts (pomology), vegetables (olericulture and truck farming), and ornamental plants such as flowers (floriculture), nursery plants, and turf grass.

These activities differ from the core cereal-producing agricultural activities in three ways. First, they tend to be more labor intensive and resistant to mechanization, at least in harvest operations. As an example, in U.S. farming on the eve of World War II (1939), cultivating an acre of

HORTICULTURE. Greenhouse and nursery, Bridgeton, New Jersey, 1942. (Prints and Photographs Division, Library of Congress)

wheat required about 9 man hours, whereas an acre of lemons required 286 hours and grapes 185 hours. Second, they are characterized by higher income elasticity of demand (and therefore are less subject to Engal's law of relative decline). Third, the quality dimensions (freshness, size, freedom from pest damage, absence of bruising, and so forth) matter more than for relatively homogeneous commodities, such as grains, therefore suppliers have a greater incentive to create brand names based on a reputation for careful processing.

These characteristics have generated a distinctive locational pattern for horticultural production. Production tends to be centered in the vicinity of large cities, which have a concentration of high-demand consumers for these perishable products, and in small geographical regions with climatic and soil conditions especially suited to the production of specific crops. The fuller development of such specialized production centers distant from the centers of consumption required the elaboration of transportation systems and processing techniques. Reduced transport costs and increased speed have encouraged horticulturalists to spread production between the northern and southern hemispheres and over the globe to supply the core markets with fruit, vegetables, and cut flowers year-round.

The historical development of horticulture has been crucially intertwined with the process of biological globalization, the spread of plants domesticated in one area to favorable environments around the world. Among the important examples of this process are the diffusion of the stone fruits (peaches, plums, and cherries) from their origin in China to Europe by Roman times and the citrus fruits from southeastern Asia to Europe in Roman times and again in the Middle Ages. This was a two-way street, as the pome fruits (apples and pears) traveled from their origin in southwestern Asia to China by the fourth century BCE. Undoubtedly the most important example of biological globalization was the great Columbian exchange following 1492. Among the horticultural crops transferred from the New World to the Old were maize, peppers, tomatoes, and pineapples. Included in the counterflow were the pome, stone, and citrus fruits as well as bananas and coconuts.

The introduction of a new plant can have a surprisingly profound effect on the receiving population. This is true even of ornamentals. The tulip, imported into western Europe from Turkey in the 1550s, seems to have brought such color and flair into the lives of the sober Dutch that it induced the famed tulip mania of 1634–1637. Hyacinth set off a similar craze in 1734. The seventeenth and eighteenth centuries were of course the period when gardening became fashionable among Europe's elite. Versailles became a showcase for the majesty of the Louis XIV, and the classic "English garden" took root. Reflecting changes in tastes, the English shifted from formal, symmetric designs to a more naturalistic look at the end of the eighteenth century. Gardening took a parallel course in North America under the influence of Thomas Jefferson's Monticello. The nineteenth century witnessed the emergence of the prototypical American landscaping form, the lawn. Following the introduction of Bermuda grass from Africa and the facilitating inventions of the push mower (1830) and the lawn sprinkler (1871), the little piece of green spread widely across the United States to become the symbol of great American middle-class.

In a sense the middle-class suburbanite was re-creating the American farm with its house situated in the middle of its own land. From the beginning of settlement, American farmers too sought to re-create familiar settings by introducing the fruit trees and plants of Europe. In this process of biological globalization the pome and stone fruits became the trees of choice on American farms. Every schoolchild learns of the exploits of "Johnny Appleseed" (John Chapman, 1774–1849), who disseminated apples in the Ohio River valley in the early nineteenth century. But more fundamental contributions to American horticulture were made by Andrew Jackson Downing (1815–1852), Liberty Hyde Bailey (1858–1954), and Luther Burbank (1849–1926).

By 1900 a thriving fruit and vegetable industry had developed in the United States. Leading the way was apple production. Areas of traditional specialization included New York's Ontario shore and Hudson River valley, Virginia's Shenandoah Valley, western Michigan, the Ozarks, and the Missouri River valley. The Pacific Northwest rapidly became the leading supplier. The cultivation of peaches, the second leading fruit crop, was centered in Georgia and on the eastern shores of the Great Lakes but increasingly shifted to the central valley of California. Indeed the "Golden State" emerged as the nation's number one producer of grapes, citrus, and a wide range of specialty crops.

Commercial horticulture also underwent change in Europe during the late nineteenth century and the early twentieth century. Apples were the most common fruit grown across northwestern Europe, with centers of production in Kent, Herefordshire, and the southwestern peninsula in England; Normandy in France; Rhenish Prussia and Baden-Württemberg in Germany; and the northwest coast in Spain. Peaches were less important, with production concentrated in the Rhone Valley of France. Select areas of France and Germany had produced wine since Roman times, and Bordeaux, Burgundy, and Champagne have lent their names to top-quality wines. But viticulture was actually much more common along the shores of the Mediterranean, including southern France, eastern Spain, and most of Italy. With the outbreak of the phylloxera disease

in France (from 1864 on), grape and currant production expanded in Algeria, Greece, and western Turkey. Olives were grown almost universally across the Mediterranean, with Andalusia, southern Italy, and southeastern Tunis serving as the leading commercial centers.

For most other crops small regions in one or two countries typically accounted for a majority of the marketed production. As examples, almost all lemons and oranges came from a few pockets in Sicily and southern Italy; fresh grapes came from Almería, Spain; currants came from western Peloponnesus and the Ionian islands in Greece; figs came from Smyrna, Turkey; almonds came from Provence in France, Bari and Sicily in Italy, and Andalusia and Majorca in Spain; and raisins came from Valencia and Málaga in Spain and Smyrna in Turkey. Such crops frequently accounted for a significant fraction of local export earnings. Over the nineteenth century the organization of fruit and nut production across the Mediterranean world evolved from a structure characterized by a poorly tended mix of trees (or vines) interspersed among other crops or planted along roads to a highly specialized, capital-intensive monoculture linked by improved transportation systems to the rapidly expanding urban centers of the Atlantic world.

The prosperity promised by this export-led development path was cut short by the spread of Mediterranean production to suitable new lands around the globe. In particular between 1880 and 1920 California became a major competitor in citrus, raisins, prunes, and almonds; Florida specialized in oranges, and South Africa, Australia, and Brazil emerged as important players in world horticultural markets. The new producers typically used more advanced production techniques and marketed higher-quality products. As traditional Mediterranean growers lost the U.S. market and eventually faced stiff competition in their home markets, prices and incomes lagged. In many regions outright crisis brought episodes of social unrest and massive migration from the agricultural sector. Over the same period tropical products, such as bananas, coconuts, and pineapples, also entered the fruit markets of Europe and North America on a large scale. Such fruits were characterized by plantation-production techniques and soon fell under the control of large multinational processors, such as United Fruit and Dole.

A similar process of biological globalization of horticultural production continues. With reductions in transportation costs and the spread of knowledge about modern cultural and marketing techniques, farmers in the Southern Hemisphere have begun growing increasing quantities of deciduous fruits and cut flowers for the markets of Europe, Japan, and North America. These producers can take advantage of the difference in seasons, and they also face lower labor costs and in some cases looser environmental restrictions on the use of pesticides. A countervailing recent movement has arisen to favor local, organically grown horticultural products, as reflected in the increasing popularity of farmers' markets and "natural" foods. With the diffusion of techniques to develop genetically modified crops, the organic movement is likely to gain strength over the coming years.

BIBLIOGRAPHY

Finch, V. C., and Baker, O. E. *Geography of the World's Agriculture.* Washington, D.C., 1917.

Halfacre, R. Gordon, and John A. Barden. *Horticulture.* New York, 1979.

Jenkins, Virginia Scott. *The Lawn: A History of an American Obsession.* Washington, D.C., 1994.

Morilla Critz, José, Alan L. Olmstead, and Paul W. Rhode. "'Horn of Plenty': The Globalization of Mediterranean Horticulture and the Economic Development of Southern Europe, 1880–1930." *Journal of Economic History* 59.2 (1999), 316–352.

Sauer, Jonathan D. *Historical Geography of Crop Plants: A Select Roster.* Boca Raton, Fla., 1993.

PAUL W. RHODE

HOSPITALITY INDUSTRY. The hospitality industry has received insufficient attention from economic historians, who have been interested in production rather than consumption, in concentrated large-scale industrial plants rather than landscapes of scattered small businesses, and in the organized labor of full-time male breadwinners rather than ill-paid, underunionized, footloose hospitality workers, who often have been female and frequently part-time. The statistics of hospitality, too, are notoriously "soft," providing a deterrent for would-be quantifiers. As Pope points out in the British context, however, basic employment statistics do indicate the importance of an industry whose workforce grew by nearly 60 percent, despite the interwar depression, between 1924 and 1938, reaching nearly half a million in the latter year. It employed far more workers than, for example, iron and steel, shipbuilding, and cotton, and in 1938 it employed over 100,000 more than the obvious key growth sector of aircraft, motor vehicle, and cycle construction and repair. Its importance has continued to increase as tourism, especially, has become a leading sector in global economic growth, to such an extent that the bias of the historiography toward these smaller but more concentrated industries looks like a collective professional misjudgment.

The concept of hospitality on an industrial scale is of recent origin and contains elements of inherent contradiction. Hospitality has enduring uncommercial connotations, as a virtue founded in gift relationships, noblesse oblige, religious obligations, charity, family, and friendship, which cut across the profit-maximizing exploitation of supplying food, drink, shelter, and associated services competitively in the marketplace. This realization can inform, and

embarass, the prescribed forms of provider/customer expectations and interaction even in the most assembly-line type of contemporary hospitality outlets, with the most transient and ephemeral of customer contact—even if management instructions to staff to present a friendly face are not always carried out convincingly in practice by hard-pressed workers. A consciousness that there should somehow be more to commercial hospitality than a simple series of market transactions continues to haunt the most hard-nosed of suppliers. The ghosts of monastic hospitality, or of the expected largesse of the lady of the manor in early modern England, or even the classical legends about the fate of those who abuse the host/guest relationship continue to haunt many providers of budget accommodations and accountancy-led fast-food outlets.

Questions about the timing and the pervasiveness of the advent of a hospitality industry that deserves the label are closely related to these moral ambiguities. Inns and alehouses as enterprises employing servants and seeking profit from the supply of accommodations and services to travelers and locals have a long pedigree; they were being regulated by English local authorities from at least the twelfth century, and they grew rapidly in number and—in strategic locations and at the top end of the market—in scale during the sixteenth and seventeenth centuries. Specialized restaurants, catering to urban markets among the leisured and those whose workplaces were at a distance from their homes, were mainly a product of the later-nineteenth century, with some earlier antecedents. The first chains seeking to sustain a corporate identity through themed decor, uniformed staff, standard menus, and quality control began to develop at about the same time; and here, in a small but highly visible minority of premises and locations (such as the Lyons Corner Houses or the Aerated Bread Company's cafes in English cities), there began to be a level of organization and division of labor that marked a transition from, in effect, craft-based domestic hospitality services to something "industrial."

It was not until the 1960s and the 1970s, however, that the full panoply of management techniques, as derived from the adoption of mass-production methods used in manufacturing, began to be applied in earnest across a broad swathe of the hospitality trades in a transformative way, taking advantage of the growing purchasing power of working-class as well as middle-class consumers across the Western world, and at the same time identifying new sources of cheap labor among women and young people who were anxious to augment family incomes or to attain a measure of individual spending power of their own, especially while in school or college. The restaurant business, in particular, was inherently labor-intensive, and until the postwar decades the labor of the preparation staff, dishwashers, and even waiters had been cheap and

HOSPITALITY INDUSTRY. Illustration of a French inn (c. 1400) from *Histoire des Hôtelleries*, by Francisque-Michel Fournier and Édouard Fournier, Paris, 1859. (Prints and Photographs Division, Library of Congress)

available enough at the lower end of the market to limit the attractiveness of innovations in machinery and organization. Chefs were craftsmen, and below them, in the larger establishments, stretched elaborate hierarchies of workers according to wages, seniority, and security. Franchises and chains offered well-established avenues to business growth; but even the preparation of food, which was in effect a manufacturing process, had not traditionally lent itself to concentration. Franchising itself might almost be regarded as a "proto-industrial" form of the hospitality industry, in which scattered producers worked for a central organization, nominally as independent small businesses but actually leasing the plant from the franchising company, and generating income for it, in a way that resembled to wage-labor while entailing self-exploitation through long hours and the pressing into service of family members who had limited choice in the matter. The gamut of services that represented the rest of a notional hospitality industry was even more resistant to the conventional industrialization process, especially as this was a set of activities in which the customer came to the provider and sought on-the-spot service under conditions where waiting time was an important factor in satisfaction.

The most important postwar changes came at the popular end of the restaurant market, which was greatly expanded through a combination of fast food, with most of the preparation stages completed centrally in advance, and a strictly controlled assembly-line division of labor, supported by intensive advertising. Wartime innovations in freezing, dehydration, and packaging were adopted alongside conveyor and cleaning technologies, making routine restaurant jobs less unattractive; and the adaptation of management theories from manufacturing to services created strong drives toward task definition and simplification, technological substitution, and the standardization of products and services. These trends developed rapidly from the mid-1950s onward, building on more dilute and diffuse antecedents, and were spearheaded during the 1960s and 1970s by the rise of the great fast-food chains, of which McDonald's became the flagship and the symbol. Ritzer (1998), indeed, built on that firm's reputation to argue for its wider influence in the "McDonaldization" of society as a whole, as its prioritization of predictability, calculability, profit-maximizing efficiency, and technological substitution was extended into field after field, seemingly undermining alternative values involving choice, variety, tradition, and genuine, as opposed to ersatz, commodified human warmth. This latter analysis certainly would be endorsed by advocates of the "traditional" diet in, for example, Italy; and it is a reminder that from the beginning the fast-food restaurant version of commercial hospitality competed with domestic cooking and hospitality (providing birthday parties at Burger King, for example), as well as with older-style restaurants and

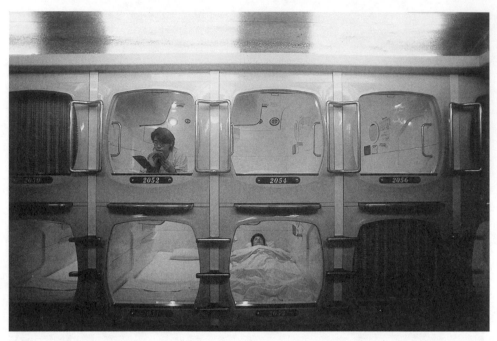

INNS AND HOTELS. Green Plaza Shinjuku, Tokyo, 1988. Japan's largest "capsule" hotel, Green Plaza can accommodate 660 guests. (© Mike Yamashita/Woodfin Camp and Associates, New York)

diners. However, such reactions also would need to acknowledge not only the extensive survival of smaller enterprises that have found their own niches in an expanding market, but also the ways in which the big companies have had to expand their menus and consider their strategies for making customers and workers as content as possible. A recognizable hospitality industry thus was emerging during the second half of the twentieth century, fueled by the rise of the automobile and associated changing travel patterns as well as the separation of home from workplace in the city and the growth of spending power among the working class as well as the middle class; but an older sector of small, family-run businesses survived alongside it, and not only at the top of the market.

Despite the hyperbole of advertisers on the one hand and critics on the other, the industrial revolution in hospitality has been less than complete even in the United States, where most of it began; and this applies to a greater extent outside the popular restaurant sector. Even here, one can point to the development in Britain of that classic foodstuff of the industrial working class, fish and chips, through the multiplication of small independent family-run corner-shop enterprises—conceived more often as part of a survival strategy than as a quest for riches—which drew on working-class values and worked with the grain of popular culture during a period of impressive expansion from the 1870s to the 1930s. Even under pressure from postwar competition, this trade proved resistant to franchising and other forms of innovation while accepting

new developments in affordable production technology. The case of Harry Ramsden's, with its successful franchising and stock-market entry in the 1990s, was an eccentric exception. Two of the great competitors of fish and chips in the British popular restaurant and take-out markets, Indian and Chinese restaurants, similarly proliferated from the 1960s onward, through the multiplication of small-scale, family-run enterprises relying on self-exploitation and the thoroughgoing use of family labor. Chains were more evident at the popular end of the Italian restaurant market, which also expanded rapidly in Britain over a similar period; but here, too, the small family business proved resilient. Despite more recent attempts at up-market franchising, as in the Pierre Victoire chain, the widespread desire for a distinctive, special dining-out experience, in which only the overall quality is predictable, has sustained autonomy and independence at the upper levels of the restaurant industry, leaving a craft or an artisan model still much in evidence, and giving full play to the notion of the celebrity chef as artiste. The Cambridge (England) of the year 2000 may have been represented as a "city of a thousand Cafe Flos, Garfunkels, All Bar Ones, Cafe Rouges, etc."; but the same restaurant critic also remarked on the quality and character of its independent up-market eating places. (Matthew Fort, *Guardian Weekend* 26 [2000], p. 45). This remains a widespread paradox.

The beverage and hotel trades show similar patterns, suggesting limits to the potential expansion of an industrial approach to hospitality. The alehouse and its successors in England, offering food, drink, and sometimes basic accommodations to locals and sometimes to impecunious travelers, were family-run enterprises from the twelfth century to the twentieth. Campaigns in the sixteenth and seventeenth centuries to reduce the number of uncontrollable cottage alehouses ran up against their role in providing an acceptable form of poor relief for otherwise unsupported widows; and when a combination of licensing intervention and market forces had reduced their importance considerably by the early-nineteenth century, a whole new landscape of small drinking outlets was opened out by the free-trade legislation of 1830, which allowed any householder to set up as a beerhouse keeper on payment of an annual licensing fee of two guineas (£2.10) to the central government. This gave the imperative to free trade in almost everything a higher priority than magistrates' fears of sedition and trade-union activity based on unsupervised beerhouses. The extension of hospitality to the provision of sexual services was a common theme among critics of the new arrangements, but it was not until legislation in 1869 and 1872 that the magistrates' authority was reasserted. Wherever the sale of alcoholic drinks was central to the hospitality trade, tensions and conflicts over the proper amount and nature of government intervention, as guardian of morality and order, cut across and influenced the more straightforward economic trends. This remained a strong cross-cultural theme in the twentieth century, reaching a climax in the Prohibition era in the United States, with the attendant rise of black-market economies and associated criminal groups.

The switch from home brewing to specialist breweries with controlled houses (operated by tenants and increasingly by managers) has been a long-running theme in the British drink trade, having accelerated in the twentieth century and especially since World War II, with brewery mergers and incorporation into conglomerates more interested in real estate than manufacturing. The imposition of corporate identities, standard menus, and regular style makeovers, in the interests of profit maximization through comparing financial outcomes and standardizing experiences for the consumer, has compromised more personal and idiosyncratic versions of hospitality, which survive in the free trade, where small boutique breweries retain their firmest foothold. The preservation of the pub as site of a personalized, "authentic" kind of hospitality was one of the subsidiary concerns of the Campaign for Real Ale from the mid-1970s onward, perhaps the most successful of consumer pressure groups; but it is in the British licensed trade that the dominance of big firms and corporate identities has perhaps gone furthest across the board, franchised hamburger restaurants and related fast-food outlets aside.

Significantly, Britain's biggest interwar hotel chain, Trust Houses Ltd., grew out of a concern to reform the pub by diversifying its activities and extending the social range of its customers. By 1919 its seventy-one hotels (and eighty-four other licensed premises) allowed it to claim the status of largest hotel chain in Europe although it was a long way behind American pioneers such as Statler and Biltmore. Until the second half of the twentieth century such chains were exceptional. The high-profile hotels were family-run (with the D'Oyly Carte Savoy, the Ritz, and the Berkeley chain in London's West End at the top of the ladder), and the eccentricities of a Fothergill at Thame or a Laughton at Scarborough were the stuff of alluring anecdote. At the lower end of the market, the family business was absolutely dominant. Blackpool, the pioneer working-class seaside resort, counted over five thousand holiday lodging-houses in the 1921 census, most employing family labor with a few seasonal servants; and this pattern was enduringly replicated elsewhere right across the British tourist industry. Large hotels were unusual (and, across the provinces, the first to suffer as the higher levels of the market were peeled away from the 1960s onward). This dominant pattern of small businesses has proved hard to research, in the absence of extensive surveys or available business records; and this difficulty (as with fish and chip shops and other small restaurant outlets) helps to explain historians' neglect. The same undoubtedly applies in other countries: in Spain, for example, the backbone of the accommodations trades, as they expanded from the late nineteenth century onward, was the small family business; and the concentration of academic attention on international tour operating companies as accommodations providers since the 1960s has diverted attention from persisting local inputs and the continuing role of the family-run hotel and pension.

This is not to argue that work on the great chains and franchises (Hilton, Holiday Inn, Kentucky Fried Chicken, and so on) is to be eschewed: the attraction for business historians is easy to see, and the tentacles of such enterprises play their own role in molding tastes and changing values and expectations around the globe; but to focus solely on these "successes" (on assumptions about "success" that are being effectively challenged by environmental campaigners, among others) is to neglect the cumulative importance of layer upon layer of smaller firms and family businesses. Moreover, alternatives with a social rather than a profit-maximizing agenda need to be brought into the mainstream of historical analysis—organizations such as the Youth Hostels Association and the Holiday Fellowship in Britain, for example, with their own chains of low-cost accommodations and their agenda of improving access to the countryside and "communion with nature" with an earnest educational and moral purpose, growing out of the anticonsumerist "outdoor movement" of the late nineteenth and early twentieth centuries. Here, as elsewhere, economic history is incomprehensible without the values providers and consumers bring to their transactions. The enduring preference of Manchester's Holts brewery chain for simple old-fashioned pubs and traditional beers at low prices offers a successful illustration from the commercial world.

All these examples demonstrate some of the contradictions that run through the hospitality industry. Its tendency to employ footloose, low-wage labor, under circumstances that often make gratuities vital to economic survival and provoke debate about the morality of such a system (which the Spanish Second Republic, for example, tried to suppress in the early 1930s), might be thought to be at odds with the ideals of hospitality to which it has sought to lay claim. The industry generally has been hostile to trade-union organization, which, in turn, has been difficult to sustain. It also has resisted the imposition of tighter regulation of, for example, fire precautions and food hygiene, while being increasingly interested in a rationalist approach to portion control. Under these circumstances workers have often had recourse to a range of scams, sometimes winked at by management, that have involved raising wages by cheating customers. This has been a particularly common outcome in settings with a rapid throughput of customers and no expectation of building the relationships of mutual trust and loyalty between provider and customer that might be thought to be the essence of hospitality. It is no wonder that domestic hospitality (exchanging meals, spending holidays with friends) has been resilient in the face of growing pressures to commodify. This subject merits further investigation.

BIBLIOGRAPHY

Alfino, Mark, John S. Caputo, and Robin Wynard, eds. *McDonaldization Revisited*. Westport, Conn., 1998.

Clark, Peter. *The English Alehouse: A Social History, 1200–1830*. Leicester, 1993.

Gabriel, Yiannis. *Working Lives in Catering*. London, 1988.

Girouard, Mark. *Victorian Pubs*. New Haven, 1984.

Jakle, John, and Keith Sculle. *Fast Food: Roadside Restaurants in the Automobile Age*. Baltimore, 2000.

Lashley, Conard, and Alison J. Morrison, eds. *In Search of Hospitality*. London, 2000.

Pope, Rex. "A Consumer Service in Inter-war Britain: The Hotel Trade, 1924–38." *Business History Review* 74 (2000), 657–682.

Rappaport, Erika D. *Shopping for Pleasure: Women in the Making of London's West End*. Princeton, 2000.

Reiter, Ester. *Making Fast Food*. Montreal, 1991.

Ritzer, George. *The McDonaldization Thesis: Explorations and Extensions*. New York, 1998.

Shaw, Gareth, and Allan Williams, eds. *The Rise and Fall of British Coastal Resorts*. London, 1997.

Taylor, Harvey. *A Claim on the Countryside*. Edinburgh, 1997.

Walton, John K. *The Blackpool Landlady: A Social History*. Manchester, 1978.

Walton, John K. *Fish and Chips and the British Working Class, 1870–1940*. Leicester, 1992.

Ward, Colin, and Dennis Hardy. *Goodnight Campers!* London, 1986.

JOHN K. WALTON

HOUSEHOLD. The members of a household include all persons, whether or not they are related to each other, who share a clearly defined living space. Households may also have other attributes. Members of the household (or some of them) may pool their incomes, share a meal at least once a day, or even earn their livelihood from working together to exploit assets that are rented, leased, or owned by the household such as a farm or workshop. By participating in these activities, other ties among members of the household can develop, such as respect for the authority of the household head and a desire to preserve the privacy of the physical space occupied by the household. The household also serves as the locus for the socialization of the young and may afford shelter to members of the local community (primarily relatives but in some cases also nonrelatives such as foster children and the childless elderly) whose own resources leave them unable to provide for their own needs. In addition, some elements of the religious and judicial functions of the household have survived from medieval times.

Nevertheless, households are not autonomous economic and social units, since members of different households, whether related or not, may agree to cooperate in a wide range of tasks. Nor are the resources of the household shared out equitably among its various members, even though some redistribution of income between higher and lower (or nonearners) is achieved by pooling their incomes. The extent of inequality, however, is difficult to gauge and must have varied considerably, reflecting in part the earning capacities of the members and their contribution to the well-being of the household. For example, in the United States the share of household expenditure devoted to the needs of one child has been estimated at about 38 percent of that of one adult in the mid-twentieth century. For European populations in the nineteenth and early twentieth century, the few budgets that detail the consumption of food by each member of the household have been used to suggest that a married woman received only two-thirds of the share of household resources consumed by her husband.

Classification of Households. Households can be classified in terms of size and on the basis of the age, gender, and relationships of the members. The categorization scheme most widely used in historical studies was initially developed by Peter Laslett in *Household and Family in Past Time* (Cambridge, 1972) and identifies different types of households on the basis of kinship composition. In this classification, simple or nuclear family households consisting of married couples with or without coresident children (of any age) or widowers or widows with children are distinguished from more complex households that contain one or more relatives in addition to the core family group (married couple or parent-child). Complex households are then further described as multiple or extended according to whether they contain two or more core family groups. Two other types of households complete the classification scheme: solitaries, if individuals live alone or only with servants and lodgers; and "no-family households," if they live with relatives or nonrelatives but with none of them constituting a core family, for example, coresident siblings. There are, however, a number of weaknesses with this way of classifying households. First, the exclusive focus on kinship implicitly minimizes the role of other members of the household, such as servants. Second, the categorization of more complex households as either extended or multiple fails to distinguish stem-family households, in which one child (usually a son) marries and remains within the parental household, from other multiple households that contain two or more married sons. Other analyses are therefore required to indicate, for example, the variations in the numbers of children and servants in the household or the presence of lodgers and inmates, which would show the difficulties some sections of the population were experiencing in forming full households.

These analyses have revealed evidence of considerable variation in household forms across both space and time but fail to confirm the existence of distinct familial regions within Europe. Nor is there evidence of a linear trend toward the establishment of less complex households. It had been argued that industrialization in the nineteenth century encouraged the fragmentation of complex households as industrialists required a mobile labor force or, conversely, that small, simple family households facilitated the advancement of industrialization. However, as Table 1 makes clear, instances of fewer complex households in successive time periods were almost matched by instances when there were more complex households later on (40 against 32). A trend toward more complex households is even evident after 1900 in certain populations, although increasing complexity of household structures was most in evidence in the nineteenth century.

It is also apparent that the pace of change could at times be considerable: a doubling of the proportion of complex households in some instances and a halving of the proportion in others, all within fifty years. However, as a rule household forms evolved much more slowly. Just a 1 to 2 percent change in the percentage of households recorded as complex in the thirty years between successive enumerations was typical for populations from England, France, Switzerland, Italy, and Finland, and close to three-quarters

of all populations experienced a change of under 10 percent in the proportion of complex households between successive enumerations. This can be contrasted with the much faster pace of change in the composition of the household that occurred across western Europe since the end of World War II. Data are not available to provide a direct comparison, but the speed of change in recent times in household forms can be appreciated from the fact that in all west European countries (apart from France and Ireland) and in all Nordic countries, there were over 10 percent more one-person households in the early 1980s than in the immediate postwar period.

Changes in Households. To account for the degree of change and to explain the spatial variations at a point in time, scholars have identified a broad range of economic, cultural, and demographic factors. Economic forces have probably commanded the greatest deal of attention in the attempts to explain historical family structures. In contrast, contemporary household structures, particularly the so-called new forms such as nonmarital cohabitation and "living apart together" as well as the increased numbers of lone parents and persons living alone, are seen as the result of personal choice on the part of those concerned—in other words, as cultural preference, with the economic wherewithal to live in the desired way as a prerequisite.

The capacity of economic forces to shape family and household patterns is self-evident and can take a multitude of forms. For example, environmental factors, particularly the varying labor requirements of different mountain communities, have been used to explain variations in the demographic and family patterns of Northern Italy. The significance of the local labor market has also been stressed in studies of Austrian, Swedish, and French societies. More generally, economic factors appear to underpin the marriage and household patterns of northwest Europe. According to this scenario, marriage and the formation of a new household were postponed until a suitable farm became available, sufficient savings had been accumulated, or an appropriate skill gained on the labor market. In eastern Europe, on the other hand, a combination of political and economic circumstances caused the formation of complex households. In societies where land was a key resource, a shortage of land—whether as a result of population growth or landlord restrictions on land use—could bring about the formation of more complex households. However, greater security of tenure could encourage this as well.

In the twentieth century, higher personal incomes and changed tastes encouraged more people to live alone. Economic factors in conjunction with personal tastes have also influenced the number of households containing nonrelatives. The incidence of boarding and lodging has declined as it has become easier to form independent

TABLE 1. *Evolution of European household forms, 1750–1950 (percentage of all complex households)*

EUROPEAN REGION AND COUNTRY	LOCALITY	DATES	C. 1750	C. 1800	C. 1850	C. 1900	C. 1950
WESTERN EUROPE							
England	Forthampton	1752, 1851	7	—	17	—	—
	West Wycombe	1760, 1851	15	—	14		
	Bampton	1787, 1851	13	—	20	—	—
	Binfield	1801, 1851	—	8	16	—	—
	Littleover	1811, 1851	—	14	21	—	—
	Mickelover	1811, 1851	—	16	23	—	—
	Corfe Castle	1790, 1851	—	12	14	—	—
	Ardleigh	1796, 1851	—	11	16	—	—
	Barkway + Reed	1801, 1851	—	14	20	—	—
France	Saint Jean Trolimon	1851, 1901, 1946	—	—	20	19	14
	Esparros	1846, 1881	—	—	37	22	—
	Vescovato*	1770, 1818, 1846, 1906, 1968, 1770,	24	4	7	26	19
	Loreto*	1818, 1846, 1906, 1968	34	7	23	32	26
	Porri*	1770, 1818, 1846, 1906, 1968	23	16	24	70	57
Germany	Belm[†]	1772, 1858	24	—	36	—	—
Switzerland	Törbel	1850, 1880	—	—	26	27	—
NORDIC COUNTRIES							
Iceland	Hruni[†]	1801, 1845, 1901, 1930	—	62	34	30	43
	Gardar[†]	1801, 1845, 1901, 1930	—	21	9	22	17
Norway	Rendalen	1762, 1801	35	28	—	—	—
Sweden	Tillinge	1790, 1890, 1825,	—	15	—	8	—
	Hållnäs	1851, 1901	—	34	38	30	—
	Tynderö	1860, 1900	—	—	15	5	—
	Hasslö	1823, 1850, 1881	—	1	3	0	—
	Dala	1810, 1850	—	16	11	—	—
Finland	Finström	1760, 1840	69	—	34	—	—
	Iniö	1770, 1809, 1859, 1895	42	36	26	13	—
	Kumlinge + Brandö	1740, 1809, 1859, 1895	56	48	49	42	—
	Korpo + Houtskär	1770, 1809, 1859, 1895	41	32	23	21	—
SOUTHERN EUROPE							
Portugal	Lanheses	1850, 1899	—	—	27	27	—
Spain	La Ñora	1850, 1901	—	—	10	3	—
	Cuenca	1750, 1780, 1817, 1860, 1876, 1900, 1940	4	6	5	5	7
	Lograño	1752, 1797	12	7	—	—	—
	Santa Maria del Monte	1752, 1956	6	—	—	—	26

TABLE 1. *Continued.*

EUROPEAN REGION AND COUNTRY	LOCALITY	DATES	C. 1750	C. 1800	C. 1850	C. 1900	C. 1950
Italy	Alagna	1749, 1788, 1848, 1879, 1935	33	37	28	29	14
	Rongio	1748, 1843	28	—	36	—	—
	San Bonnino	1748, 1843	38	—	35	—	—
	Gniva	1846, 1894	—	—	35	44	—
	Oseacco	1846, 1894	—	—	47	52	—
	Corniglio	1736, 1803, 1850	33	36	34	—	—
	S Giovanni al Natisone	1850, 1900	—	—	44	46	—
	Parma	1765, 1851	15	—	14	—	—
	San Nicrendo	1740, 1778	32	26	—	—	—
	Luccera Cattedrale	1755, 1814, 1838	18	22	24	—	
	Turi	1781, 1855	—	11	16	—	—
	Procida	1764, 1794, 1856	18	14	8	—	—
Greece	Syrrako	1898, 1929	—	—	—	41	35
CENTRAL AND EASTERN EUROPE							
Austria	Metnitz	1757, 1796	31	25	—	—	—
Estonia	Sangaste	1816, 1850	—	26	48	—	—
	Türi	1816, 1850	—	31	56	—	—
	Anseküla	1816, 1850	—	40	66	—	—
Lithuania	Linden	1797, 1858	—	77	48	—	—
Croatia	Cernik	1803, 1854	—	71	45	—	—
Russia	Mishino	1814, 1850	—	85	79	—	—

*Indicates no family households of coresident unmarried siblings.
†Percentage of households with relatives.

households. The disappearance of the domestic servant during the first half of the twentieth century has also been attributed to economic forces as other opportunities in the labor market increased. However, at the same time, in part perhaps as a consequence of the appearance of new employment opportunities, there was a decline in the status of domestic service. There is no doubt that the impact on middle-class households of the disappearance of the domestic servant was eased by the burgeoning market in household appliances, but the nature and strength of the causal relationship remains far from clear. Short-term crises may also alter living arrangements. Households in England, for example, appear to have been at their most complex during the temporary housing crisis that accompanied World War I and World War II.

Other research, however, has identified limitations on the impact of economic factors on the household. First, it is surprising that there was so little change in household forms right through the nineteenth century, despite the fast pace of economic change. It is also important to note that over the centuries the proportion of the population in England and Wales that formed part of a core family group (couple, married, or nonmarried with or without unmarried children, or a lone parent and unmarried child) actually increased. The notion that the nineteenth century also saw a change from the family economy to the family wage economy has also been challenged. Theories of the family economy maintain that the family was the unit of production and consumption and the household the locus of work and residence. Family members were thus retained in the household to meet its labor requirements, while those whose labor was not needed left to work elsewhere. On the other hand, one of the main features of the family wage economy is the absence of any limit on the number of wage earners that a wage-earning family could use and, hence, no limit on the number of children who could live in the parental home.

A number of factors, however, appear to have been overlooked. First, the effect on the household of the family wage economy ignores the power of employers to determine not only what labor should be employed but where that labor should reside. Indeed, it is now known that the number of unmarried children in English households actually fell between the late eighteenth century and 1851. Second, the concept of the family economy seems to exclude the possibility of any household member working for wages. In practice, there was a much greater diversity, and a fresh concept developed to describe it: the adaptive family economy. In the adaptive family economy, some members of the household worked for wages, permanently or intermittently, while others served the market and/ or the subsistence needs of their household by laboring in the household economy in an attempt to maximize its economic well-being. From a re-analysis of the family budgets collected by Le Play and others, it is shown that even in the second half of the nineteenth century, the wives of craftsmen, peasants, and laborers continued to work at least intermittently in the labor market while they had young children at home.

The role of demographic factors as determinants of family patterns is also evident. High mortality in historical populations limited the opportunities for parents to coreside with their adult children. Higher life expectancy for women than for men (in most populations) meant that greater proportions of women were at risk of living alone. Long-term changes to the levels of fertility, nuptiality, and mortality have also promoted change in household patterns. For example, reductions in mortality at older ages during the course of the twentieth century have increased the number of persons at risk of living on their own, while the fall in maternal mortality has reduced the number of widowed lone fathers. The concentration of childbearing into the first years of marriage has also meant that more couples now experience the "empty-nest" phase of the family life cycle.

Much more difficult to identify with any degree of precision are the norms and expectations influencing residential choices. Most interpretations of historical household structures, however, even while according preeminence to economic factors, have awarded at least a minor role to cultural forces. In the extreme east and west of Austria, such forces, for example, modified the impact of ecotypes on household patterns. In coastal areas of northern Sweden, cultural factors, including the assistance of a strong regional church, helped shape the family patterns of landed peasants within the context established by demographic and economic factors. Cultural influences are also embedded in the ways in which property is transferred between generations and in whether the family acts virtually alone in the care of the elderly or shared this responsibility with the community. In the twentieth century, the number of households headed by lone mothers in Europe and North America is influenced by the practice of the courts in normally granting the mother the custody and care of underaged children after a divorce.

Admittedly, there have been some dissenting voices who have argued that there was a natural preference in historical populations for the formation of simple, noncomplex households either because of the resemblance between the simple family and the basic biological unit or because of a "natural" preference for every adult not part of a couple to maximize his or her individual autonomy. These accounts effectively award the impact of culture as the prime determinant of a presumably universal family system. Other, mostly economic, factors (but also including well-established behavioral patterns) feature only in the role of constraints, which prevent individuals from following what would otherwise be their natural inclinations to live separately from other adults. This is to assume a major disjunction between the real (but largely unexpressed) preferences for particular types of living arrangements and the households that are actually formed. The natural preferences of populations are thus completely subverted by economic and other constraints.

Others have predicated a more harmonious relationship between economic and demographic realities and the familial system in which choices are framed, taking account of the options available. Such arguments have been advanced to explain both the evolution of family patterns in a specific microregion in Croatia after the defeat of the Ottomans, the long-term persistence of simple family households in the Spanish province of Cuenca, and, more generally, to explain the rarity of large complex households in western and northern Europe. The significant factors shaping family patterns in northeast Croatia were the timing of resettlement, the amount of land available, and the family patterns of the first settlers. These factors acted in combination to establish preferences for particular types of households. In a similar vein, it has been argued that in Cuenca relative early and universal marriage, neolocal household formation, and property transfers through inheritance ceased to be demographic, social, and legal acts and became normative cultural behavior. Finally, the presence of large proportions of simple and stem-family households in western and central Europe has been explained by the combined influences of the Catholic Church and a tighter control over access to land, following the deterioration of the land-labor ratio in the early Middle Ages. The argument, therefore, is that this particular household system was the joint creation of economic circumstances and a specific institutional structure (which was itself embedded in a number of cultural values). These forces then shaped the cultural preferences of various European populations, which kept the system in place thereafter.

Thus, the focus of much of the research on the history of household forms has been on charting how households responded to economic, demographic, and cultural change. Much less attention has been given to how households themselves may have constrained change or promoted change of a particular type. However, it has also been argued that certain household structures were better adapted than others to enable individuals to survive demographic and economic crises and ideological transformations. For example, it has been claimed that state welfare systems were more necessary and thus developed earlier in societies in which simple family households predominated. It has also been noted that formal rules of inheritance were not necessarily or, indeed, usually followed blindly. Instead, families selected versions of those inheritance rules and practices that best suited the needs of their current household and safeguarded the long-term future of their members, including, in some instances, the interests of children who had already left the parental household.

The allocation of tasks and division of resources between members of the household were subject to negotiations. Such negotiations, however, are poorly documented in the historical record, while the theories that have been advanced to explain the process of income allocation have little to say about how resources have been distributed between husband and wife or between parents and children. Nevertheless, a reasonable presumption would be that the positions of the wife and children will be strengthened, the greater their opportunities to enter the labor market outside the household. Conventionally prescribed work roles on the basis of gender and age within, as well as outside, the household would have the same effect, as it would then be more difficult for households to substitute female labor with male and young for old (or vice versa). When these pressures become too acute, whether as a result of expanding opportunities in the labor market, low and irregular male earnings, or the equalization of gender roles, couples may hesitate to form households, and existing households may fragment.

[*See also* Children; Family Structures and Kinship; *and* Marriage.]

BIBLIOGRAPHY

Becker, Gary S. *A Treatise on the Family*. Cambridge, Mass., 1981.
Folbre, Nancy. *Who Pays for the Kids?* London, 1994.
Fontaine, Laurence, and Jürgen Schlumbohm, eds. *Household Strategies for Survival, 1600–2000: Fission, Faction, and Cooperation*. Cambridge, 2000.
Hajnal, John. "Two Kinds of Pre-Industrial Household Formation System." In *Family Forms in Historic Europe*, edited by Richard Wall, Jean Robin, and Peter Laslett, pp. 65–104. Cambridge, 1983.
Janssens, Angelique. *Family and Social Change: The Household as a Process in an Industrializing Community*. Cambridge, 1993.
Janssens, Angelique, ed. *The Rise and Decline of the Male Breadwinner Family?* International Review of Social History, Supplement 5. Cambridge, 1998.
Laslett, Peter. "The Character of Familial History, Its Limitations and the Conditions for its Proper Pursuit." *Journal of Family History* 12.1–3 (1987), 263–284.
Lazear, Edward P., and Robert T. Michael. *Allocation of Income within the Household*. Chicago, 1988.
Saito, Osamu. "Marriage, Family Labour, and the Stem-Family Household: Traditional Japan in a Comparative Perspective." *Continuity and Change* 15.1 (2000), 17–45.
Smith, Daniel Scott. "American Family and Demographic Patterns and the North West European Model." *Continuity and Change* 8.3 (1993), 389–415.
Smith, Richard, ed. *Land, Kinship, and Life-Cycle*. Cambridge, 1984.
Tilly, Louise A., and Joan W. Scott. *Women, Work, and Family*. New York, 1978.
Wall, Richard. "Work, Welfare, and the Family: An Illustration of the Adaptive Family Economy." In *The World We Have Gained: Histories of Population and Social Structure*, edited by Lloyd Bonfield, Richard M. Smith, and Keith Wrightson, pp. 251–294. Oxford, 1986.
Wall, Richard. "The Transformation of the European Family across the Centuries." In *Family History Revisited: Comparative Perspectives*, edited by Richard Wall, Tamara K. Hareven, and Josef Ehmer, pp. 217–241. Newark, N.J., 2001.
Wall, Richard, Jean Robin, and Peter Laslett, eds. *Family Forms in Historic Europe*. Cambridge, 1983.

RICHARD WALL

HOUSING, INVESTMENT IN. Until the 1960s, the number of dwellings started or built was often used as a proxy to estimate investment in housing (in constant prices). Thereafter, the concept was increasingly defined within a national accounting framework, which led to the development of more precise estimation procedures.

In accordance with international agreements, gross domestic capital formation in dwellings includes all expenses relating to the construction or complete reconstruction of houses and flats. The building of emergency dwellings is left out of consideration because of the temporal nature of the constructions. Neither the purchase price of building land nor the expenses involved in maintenance and repair are included in capital formation, as they do not raise the capacity for production of housing services. The installation costs for electricity and water supply and for other items of equipment that are an integral part of the completed house or flat are considered as part of investment in dwellings.

Structural alterations, including the conversion of nonresidential buildings (e.g., warehouses) into dwellings, are counted as capital formation since they increase the production capacity of housing services. In principle, all transaction costs involved in the transfer of building land and existing dwellings, such as fees for architects, registration, and notarization must be taken into account. In practice, it is usually difficult to produce a reliable long-term series of transaction costs, so they are often ignored.

In the 1950s and early 1960s, the analysis of long swings in nineteenth and early-twentieth-century housing construction attracted a lot of attention from American and British researchers. They observed that residential building cycles were characterized by a much longer periodicity and a considerably wider variation in amplitude than ordinary business fluctuations. During building booms, residential construction not only rose in the general upswing but also continued to expand after the cyclical downturn of the economy as a whole had taken place. When the building boom finally came to an end, the slump was deep and persisted for many years.

In Great Britain, researchers identified residential construction cycles of about twenty years, with peaks in the mid-1870s and around 1900. In the United States, house-building cycles were found with an almost similar periodicity. The American peaks and troughs, however, showed an approximately opposite timing compared to the British experience. The inverse character of the fluctuations on both sides of the Atlantic was, of course, not exact, but it was remarkable enough for economic historians to start looking for a causal connection. The context of an emerging Atlantic economy in the course of the nineteenth century provided the background for scholars such as Brinley Thomas to put forward a challenging hypothesis.

When economic conditions were favorable in the United States, the country attracted a flood of immigrants and capital from Great Britain. Massive emigration reduced the demand for housing in the British Isles, thereby exerting downward pressure on rents. At the same time, high capital exports pushed up domestic interest rates. Emigration also diminished the supply of labor available for building purposes in Great Britain, with adverse consequences on construction costs. As a result, investors' profit margins in residential building activities were squeezed between crumbling rents and increasing costs. Conversely, periods of recession or economic stagnation in the United States slowed down the flows of foreign investment and immigration. Demand for houses in Great Britain rose, rents soared, and more labor and financial resources became available to the construction industry. With all variables pointing in the right direction, a new residential building boom in the British Isles could take off.

The Atlantic economy explanation of the building cycle soon provoked much criticism. Researchers such as H. J. Habakkuk, S. B. Saul, and J. Parry Lewis stressed that the thesis was based too much on *a priori* reasoning and, therefore, lacked solid empirical verification. More detailed investigations pointed out, for instance, that the fluctuations in emigration were simply too small to influence substantially the growth rate of households in Great Britain. So, the role of one of the key explanatory factors in the "Atlantic model" was put in jeopardy. Because of these and other qualifications, the conviction grew that the inverse character of British and American building fluctuations mainly reflected accidental factors. Could domestic forces explain the British building cycle?

New research emphasized that the second half of the nineteenth century was characterized by a growing stability of real household incomes in periods of a general economic slump. Financial stability also increased at the moment that more diversified institutional sources of capital became available for residential construction purposes (e.g., early property companies). These elements enabled building booms to continue even when a general downswing of the economy had set in. In the late nineteenth century, the increasing share of suburban building in total residential construction also favored the emergence of long swings. Once minimum transport facilities and public utilities had been constructed, the developed area provided ample opportunities for prolonged building activity. By the mid-1960s, the thesis that domestic factors largely determined residential construction in nineteenth-century Great Britain was well established.

Research in continental European countries suggests two distinct patterns of residential construction in the latter half of the nineteenth century. A first group of countries, including Belgium and Sweden, showed building fluctuations similar to the British experience. The second group (e.g., Finland, the Netherlands) was characterized by several short-term cycles culminating in a sharp upward trend from about 1890. France belonged to neither of the two groups, which comes as no surprise, taking into consideration France's peculiar demographic development during the nineteenth and the first half of the twentieth century.

Until 1914, there was a broad consensus that the private market should meet housing demand. So, public intervention usually remained restricted to local authorities issuing general codes on building, sanitation, and overcrowding. World War I, however, brought housing construction to a standstill almost everywhere. Even the neutral countries were affected as interest rates went up sharply and building materials became scarce on an international scale. As a result, a severe housing shortage emerged in Europe, and central governments were forced to intervene in the real estate market.

Most countries imposed rent restrictions to keep housing costs under control, and many forms of state assistance were developed to stimulate construction activity. Belgium, for instance, established immediately after the war a state housing bank, which directly channeled funds into working-class housing projects. Other schemes were designed to promote the private sector, either through subsidies for private building (Great Britain), through tax incentives designed to promote homeownership, or through public financial institutions providing cheap mortgage credit. Few European countries pursued these policies on a large scale for more than a couple of years. The huge financial costs related to the programs obviously played a decisive role, but another factor was the fundamental belief among many politicians that the private market should finally meet housing demand.

Despite a partial withdrawal of the public sector in the second half of the 1920s, total residential investment continued to expand in many European countries. The outbreak of the Great Depression caused a short-lived decline in the early 1930s, but afterward building activity resumed swiftly. In several instances, rent controls were lifted or scaled down, which increased the profitability of housing investment. Low interest rates and falling construction costs also pushed private building activity forward.

An important exception to this general picture was the United States. After a strong housing boom in the mid-1920s building activity collapsed. The subsequent recovery proceeded slowly, which was partly due to severe dislocations in the American mortgage credit market. To remedy these problems, the government provided mortgage insurance through the Federal Housing Administration. Other measures included the reduction of the periodic payments made by mortgage borrowers by lowering interest rates and lengthening contract terms.

After World War II, state intervention in residential construction increased dramatically in most European countries. A broad array of instruments was put in place, including direct housing provision by the state, (in)direct financial support for rented housing, and the promotion of homeownership. The importance of every instrument, however, varied considerably from country to country and through time. Moreover, from the 1950s to the 1970s, many governments used the building industry to shape their Keynesian-inspired macroeconomic stabilization policies. During general economic recessions, for instance, subsidies to residential construction were increased and mortgage rates were lowered. By stimulating housebuilding activity, governments hoped to revive the economy as a whole. These policies proved costly and not always effective. In many instances, the destitute remained literally in the cold. During the austerity policies of the 1980s and 1990s, involvement of the public sector in total housing investment declined again but remained substantial in many European countries.

[*See also* Public Housing and Housing Policies.]

BIBLIOGRAPHY

Buyst, Erik. *An Economic History of Residential Building in Belgium between 1890 and 1961.* Brussels, 1992.

Grebler, Leo, David M. Blank, and Louis Winnick. *Capital Formation in Residential Real Estate: Trends and Prospects.* Princeton, 1956.

Pooley, Colin G., ed. *Housing Strategies in Europe, 1880–1930.* Leicester, 1992.

Powell, Christoper G. *An Economic History of the British Building Industry, 1815–1979.* London, 1980.

Richardson, Harry W., and Derek H. Aldcroft. *Building in the British Economy between the Wars.* London, 1968.

ERIK BUYST

HUGHES, JONATHAN (1928–1992), economic historian.

Jonathan Hughes was a member of the famous group of Purdue wunderkinder in economic history in the late 1950s and 1960s that included Hughes's collaborators, Lance Davis, Nathan Rosenberg, Duncan McDougall, and economic theorist Stanley Reiter. After a brief stint at the New York Federal Reserve Bank from 1955 to 1956, Hughes went to Purdue, where he stayed until 1966. Hughes spent the remainder of his career at Northwestern University, where he served until his death in 1992. He was one of the founders of the cliometric movement in economic history, which brought modern econometric tools to the study of economic history.

Hughes was born in Wenatchee, Washington, in 1928 and graduated from Utah State Agricultural College in 1950. After two years at the University of Washington, he was named a Rhodes Scholar. He received his doctor of philosophy degree at Oxford in 1955 under the direction of Professor Hrothgar J. (later Sir John) Habakkuk.

Hughes's doctoral thesis at Oxford was revised and published as *Fluctuations in Trade, Industry, and Finance*. It remains the definitive history of British industrial activity during the 1850s. Although he began his career as a macroeconomist and financial markets specialist, Hughes's contributions were remarkably diverse. His other major works include his biographical compendium of America's great entrepreneurs (*The Vital Few: The Entrepreneur and American Economic Progress*), a general treatment of industrialization (*Industrialization and Economic History*), and an investigation into the causes and effects of the growth of government in the United States (*The Governmental Habit*). Other books and essays explore topics as diverse as the growth of British steam shipping, the origins of American colonial law and regulation (*Social Control in the Colonial Economy*), the politics of World War II internment camps for Japanese Americans, the roots of the American system of land settlement, and exchange rate movements during the nineteenth century. Hughes is also the author of one of the most successful textbooks on American economic history; he was planning the fourth edition with a coauthor prior to his death.

Hughes was known for choosing topics and research approaches that were off the beaten path and that combined empiricist and humanist perspectives in novel ways. In *The Vital Few*, Hughes sought to "trick" readers (his word) into learning American economic history through the medium of biography. That work and others also sought to emphasize the critical role of particular people and circumstances in economic history. *The Governmental Habit*, first published in 1977, was a path-breaking work exploring the history of the political economy of regulation, written at a time when most economists had, in Hughes's view, a too naive and ahistorical understanding of government, which Hughes sought to change. He wrote in the preface to the revised 1991 edition about the intellectual atmosphere of economics in the 1970s: "Everyone knew that government regulation was a good thing. . . . My answer to my distinguished colleagues was simply: That is not how it is. Read the book. We have a history, and it really isn't what you seem to think. The world did not begin in 1933, and neither did our American habit of superimposing the decisions of regulators upon those derived from free-market contracting. We have politicized the economy in favor of special interests since colonial times: it is the All American way."

Hughes's many contributions were commemorated by his colleagues in his festschrift, *The Vital One*.

BIBLIOGRAPHY

Hughes, Jonathan R. T. *Fluctuations in Trade Industry, and Finance: A Study of British Economic Development, 1850–1860*. New York, 1960.

Hughes, Jonathan R. T. *The Vital Few: The Entrepreneur and American Economic Progress*. New York, 1965; exp. ed., New York, 1986.

Hughes, Jonathan R. T. *Industrialization and Economic History*. New York, 1970.

Hughes, Jonathan R. T. *Social Control in the Colonial Economy: Theses and Conjectures*. Charlottesville, Va., 1976.

Hughes, Jonathan R. T. *The Governmental Habit: Economic Controls from Colonial Times to the Present*. New York, 1977; rev. ed., Princeton, 1991.

Hughes, Jonathan R. T. *American Economic History*. Glenview, Ill., 1983. Currently with Louis P. Cain in its 6th ed., Boston, 2003.

Mokyr, Joel, ed. *The Vital One: Essays in Honor of Jonathan Hughes*. Greenwich, Conn., 1991.

CHARLES W. CALOMIRIS